READING the
MIDDLE AGES

READING THE MIDDLE AGES

SOURCES FROM EUROPE, BYZANTIUM, AND THE ISLAMIC WORLD

EDITED BY BARBARA H. ROSENWEIN · SECOND EDITION

UNIVERSITY OF TORONTO PRESS

LIBRARY AND ARCHIVES CANADA CATALOGUING IN PUBLICATION

Reading the Middle Ages : sources from Europe, Byzantium, and the Islamic world / edited by Barbara H. Rosenwein.—Second edition.

Includes bibliographical references and index.
Issued in print and electronic formats.
ISBN 978-1-4426-0821-4 (bound).—ISBN978-1-4426-0602-9 (pbk.).—
ISBN 978-1-4426-0603-6 (pdf).—ISBN 978-1-4426-0604-3 (html)

1. Middle Ages—Sources. I. Rosenwein, Barbara H., editor of compilation

D113.R38 2013   909.07   C2013-905490-1
                                                  C2013-905491-X

We welcome comments and suggestions regarding any aspect of our publications—please feel free to contact us at news@utphighereducation.com or visit our Internet site at www.utppublishing.com.

North America
5201 Dufferin Street
North York, Ontario, Canada, M3H 5T8

2250 Military Road
Tonawanda, New York, USA, 14150

ORDERS PHONE: 1–800–565–9523
ORDERS FAX: 1–800–221–9985
ORDERS E-MAIL: utpbooks@utpress.utoronto.ca

UK, Ireland, and continental Europe
NBN International
Estover Road, Plymouth, PL6 7PY, UK
ORDERS PHONE: 44 (0) 1752 202301
ORDERS FAX: 44 (0) 1752 202333
ORDERS E-MAIL: enquiries@nbninternational.com

Every effort has been made to contact copyright holders; in the event of an error or omission, please notify the publisher.

The University of Toronto Press acknowledges the financial support for its publishing activities of the Government of Canada through the Canada Book Fund.

Printed in Canada

For Amy

GREENLAND

Eriksfjord

Reykjavik

ICELAND

ATLANTIC
OCEAN

NORTH
SEA

KJØLEN MOUNTAINS

BALTIC SEA

Reval

Novgorod

Riga

Vilnius

Gdansk

Gniezno

Odra

Niemen

Kiev

Dnieper

Dniester

York

Worcester   Lincoln   Bishop's Lynn

Hereford

Clarendon   Thames   London

Runnymede   Canterbury

Hastings

Bremen   Lübeck

Hamburg

Magdeburg

Wienhausen

Elbe

Merseburg

Lower
Silesia

Legnica

Upper
Silesia

Prague

Arras

Cambrai   Aachen

Cologne

Bayeux   Rouen   Thionville

Bec   Mainz

Reims   Frankfurt

Paris   Seine   Verdun   Metz   Trier   Worms

Angers   Loire   Troyes   Strasbourg

Tours   Orleans   Rhine

Bourges   Dijon

Poitiers   Berne

Cluny   ALPS

Limoges   Lyon   Vienna

Rhone   Milan

Avignon   Genoa   Venice

Marseille   Po   Ravenna

Pistoia   Florence

Lucca   Siena

Tiber   Assisi

Rome

Salerno

ADRIATIC SEA

Danube

Garonne   PYRENEES

Oporto   Douro

Lisbon   Tagus   Toledo

Córdoba

Seville

Tangiers

Tlemcen

MEDITERRANEAN SEA

Carthage

AEGEAN SEA

Thessalonica   Constantinople

Nicaea

Tarnow

BLAC[K]

Alexandria

Cairo

Nile

IMPORTANT PLACES
MENTIONED
IN THE SOURCES

Yet research continues, and it continues to be fruitful, because historians are not passive instruments, and because they read the same old documents with fresh eyes and with new questions in mind.

—Georges Duby, *History Continues*

Contents

IV POLITICAL COMMUNITIES REORDERED (*c.*900–*c.*1050)

VII   DISCORDANT HARMONIES (*c.1250–c.1350*)

VIII CATASTROPHE AND CREATIVITY (*c.1350–c.1500*)

Preface

The major difference between *Reading the Middle Ages* and other medieval history source books is its systematic incorporation of Islamic and Byzantine materials alongside Western readings. This second edition also includes new materials from East Central Europe. The idea is for students and teachers continually to make comparisons and contrasts within and across cultures. I have sometimes provided questions that I hope will aid this process, and Professor Bruce Venarde (University of Pittsburgh) has posed still other questions on the website for *Reading the Middle Ages* (www.utphistorymatters.com). Although this book may be used independently or alongside any textbook, it is particularly designed to complement the fourth edition of *A Short History of the Middle Ages*. The chapters have the same titles and chronological scope; the readings here should help expand, deepen, sharpen, and modify the knowledge gained there.

The sources in *Reading the Middle Ages* are varied; there are, for example, records of sales, biographies, hagiographies, poems, and histories.[1] There is also a new section on visual sources, "Containing the Holy." Some teachers may wish to assign all the readings in each chapter; others may wish to concentrate on only a few texts from each chapter. It is also easy to organize readings thematically by region: the index groups together all the sources pertaining to Italy, Spain, France, and so on.

The introduction to the first text in this book includes a discussion of how to read a primary source. The same project is repeated in chapter 4, this time with a very different sort of document. It should become clear to users of this book that the kinds of questions one brings to all documents are initially the same, but the answers lead down very different paths that suggest their own new questions and approaches. Each reader's curiosity, personality, and interests become part of the process; this, even more than the discovery of hitherto unknown sources, is the foundation of new historical thought.

This is the place for me to acknowledge—with pleasure and enormous gratitude—the many debts that I have incurred in the preparation of this book. All those who contributed

---

[1] To make the texts translated from the Greek, Slavic languages, and Arabic more accessible, I have left out diacritical marks and non-Latin letters. Users of this book should, however, keep in mind that Arabic terms such as *sura* and names such as al-Bukhari should more properly be spelled *sūra* and al-Bukhārī, Slavic names such as Boleslaw are more correctly written Bolesław, and Greek terms such as *lorikion* and *komes* are more accurately *lōrikion* and *komēs*.

translations for this second edition deserve special thanks: Kristina Markman, Maureen Miller, Thomas F. X. Noble, William L. North, Frances Freeman Paden, William D. Paden, Carole Straw, and Bruce Venarde.

For advice, I thank Sheila S. Blair, Jonathan M. Bloom, Paul Cobb, Florin Curta, Zouhair Ghazzal, Monica Greene, Edin Hajdarpasic, Christine Meek, Maureen Miller, Faith Wallis, and Hiltrud Westermann-Angerhausen.

For special help, I thank The Emeryk Hutten-Czapski Museum, Jarosław Bodzek, Edyta Głogowska; Loyola's librarians Elizabeth Andrew, Jennifer Jacobs, and Linda Lotten; and the University of Toronto Press people with whom I worked: Martin Boyne, Judith Earnshaw, Natalie Fingerhut, Beate Schwirtlich, and Daiva Villa.

I offer special thanks to Riccardo Cristiani, whose thoughtful and careful reading of the entire manuscript led to numerous corrections and clarifications. His index for this book provides the user with numerous reference tools, such as dates for all persons and titles of all readings and their dates. He also helped coordinate all names, places, and facts in this book with those in *A Short History*. I thank Bruce Venarde for his creative questions, posted on the web site for this book. Elina Gertsman, Piotr Górecki, and Kiril Petkov provided indispensible counsel. Finally I thank my family, and with this book I thank in particular its newest and very dear member, Amy Rosenwein. May she enjoy reading medieval sources almost as much as she loves playing the violin!

Abbreviations and Symbols

AH	Anno Hijra = year 1 of the Islamic calendar, equivalent to 622 CE
b.	before a date = born
b.	before a name = son of (*ibn, ben*)
BCE	before common era. Interchangeable with BC. See CE below.
BEF.	On timelines = before
beg.	beginning
bt.	daughter of (*bint*)
c.	century (used after an ordinal number, e.g. 6th c. means "sixth century")
c.	circa (used before a date to indicate that it is approximate)
CE	common era. Interchangeable with AD. Both reflect Western dating practices, which begin "our" era with the birth of Christ. In *Reading the Middle Ages*, all dates are CE unless otherwise specified or some confusion might arise.
d.	date of death
d.	dinar = *denarius*, penny
Douay	The standard English version of the Vulgate (Latin) version of the Bible. Ordinarily the books are the same as in the AV version (see above). The chief differences are that (1) the Douay version accepts some books considered apocryphal in the AV; and (2) the Psalm numbers sometimes differ. The Douay numbers follow the psalm numbering in the Greek Bible, whereas the AV and other Protestant Bibles follow the numbering of the Hebrew text.
e.g.	*exempli gratia* = for example
ff.	folios (or pages) following; this means that the reference is to a particular page and those that follow
fl.	*floruit* (used—when birth and death dates are not known—to mean that a person "flourished" or was active at the time of the date)
ibid.	in the same place, referring to the reference in the preceding note
i.e.	that is (from the Latin *id est*)
£	pound (from the first letter of the Latin word *libra*)
MS	manuscript
pl.	plural

r.	ruled
s.	shilling = *solidus*, sous
sing.	singular
...	Ellipses, indicating that words or passages of the original have been left out.
[]	Brackets, indicating words or passages that are not in the original but have been added by the editor to aid in the understanding of a passage.

A date such as Boethius (d. 524/526) means that the exact date of his death is not known or disputed, but it is, at least, within the date range of 524 to 526.

Abbreviations for the Authorized Version of the Bible

In *Reading the Middle Ages*, references to the Bible are to the Authorized Version (AV). (Psalms are cited in both AV and Douay versions.) The standard abbreviations for the books of the AV are set out below. The Revised Standard Version of the Bible, which is perhaps the best translation in English, derives from the AV, which is based on the King James Version.

Old Testament

Genesis	Gen.
Exodus	Exod.
Leviticus	Lev.
Numbers	Num.
Deuteronomy	Deut.
Josue	Josue
Judges	Judges
Ruth	Ruth
1 Samuel	1 Sam.
2 Samuel	2 Sam.
1 Kings	1 Kings
2 Kings	2 Kings
1 Chronicles	1 Chron.
2 Chronicles	2 Chron.
Ezra	Ezra
Nehemiah	Neh.
Esther	Esther
Job	Job
Psalms	Ps.
Proverbs	Prov.
Ecclesiastes	Eccles.

Song of Solomon (This is also often called the Song of Songs)	Song of Sol.
Isaiah	Isa.
Jeremiah	Jer.
Lamentations	Lam.
Ezekiel	Ezek.
Daniel	Dan.
Hosea	Hos.
Joel	Joel
Amos	Amos
Obadiah	Obad.
Jonah	Jon.
Micah	Mic.
Nahum	Nah.
Habakkuk	Hab.
Zephaniah	Zeph.
Haggai	Hag.
Zechariah	Zech.
Malachi	Mal.

Apocrypha

1 Esdras	1 Esd.
2 Esdras	2 Esd.
Tobit	Tob.
Judith	Jth.
The Rest of Esther	Rest of Esther
The Wisdom of Solomon	Wisd. of Sol.
Ecclesiasticus	Ecclus.
Baruch	Bar.
The Song of the Three Holy Children	Song of Three Children
Susanna	Sus.
Bel and the Dragon	Bel and Dragon
Prayer of Manasses	Pr. of Man.
1 Maccabees	1 Macc.
2 Maccabees	2 Macc.

New Testament

Matthew	Matt.
Mark	Mark
Luke	Luke
John	John
Acts of the Apostles	Acts
Romans	Rom.
1 Corinthians	1 Cor.
2 Corinthians	2 Cor.
Galatians	Gal.
Ephesians	Eph.

Philippians	Phil.
Colossians	Col.
1 Thessalonians	1 Thess.
2 Thessalonians	2 Thess.
1 Timothy	1 Tim.
2 Timothy	2 Tim.
Titus	Titus
Philemon	Philem.
Hebrews	Heb.
James	James
1 Peter	1 Pet.
2 Peter	2 Pet.
1 John	1 John
2 John	2 John
3 John	3 John
Jude	Jude
Revelation	Rev.

To test your knowledge and gain deeper understanding of the chapters, please go to www.utphistorymatters.com for Study Questions.

Psalter Page (2nd quarter, 9th cent.).

In this sumptuous manuscript dedicated to King Louis the German (r.843–876) the artist (a monk at the monastery of Saint Omer, today in northern France) drew on the decorative, abstract traditions of the British Isles to form the letters BEATUS VIR (Blessed is the man), the first words of the first psalm.

(Image courtesy of bpk, Berlin / Staatsbibliothek zu Berlin / Art Resource, NY)

I

Prelude: The Roman World Transformed (c.300–c.600)

A CHRISTIANIZED EMPIRE

1.1 Toleration or favoritism? *Edict of Milan* (313). Original in Latin.

No edict (an order issued to governors throughout the empire) was issued at Milan. But Emperors Constantine (r.306–337) and Licinius (r.308–324) met there in 313 and agreed to the provisions of what would be promulgated a few months later—the so-called *Edict of Milan*. It gave notice that Constantine and Licinius agreed to tolerate Christianity along with other religions and that they determined to restore the properties that the Church had lost under Emperor Diocletian (r.284–305). The current owners of the property might be compensated from the emperors' private funds if they applied to their "vicar," an imperial administrator with regional authority.

The *Edict of Milan* is the first source in this collection. Let us use it to begin a discussion of how to read primary sources. Each primary source calls for its own methodology and approach; there is no one way to handle all of them. Moreover, as the epigraph of this book points out, readers should bring their own special insights to old sources. Nevertheless, it is usually helpful to begin by asking a standard series of questions.

Who wrote it, and for what audience was it written? Normally this is fairly easy to answer, but often it is not. In this case, it seems that Emperors Constantine and Licinius conceived of the statement, though civil servants in an imperial writing office drafted and published it. The immediate recipients were provincial governors, each referred to as "your Excellency" in this document; they were expected to publish—that is, publicize—the contents to the public.

When was it written? Your editor has given the date 313, which is the year in which the document was issued. At this stage in your historical work, you need not worry about how this date was arrived at. It is more important for you to consider the circumstances and historical events in the context of which this date takes on meaning. In this instance, you should be thinking that the date is pertinent to the history of the Roman Empire; that it comes directly after Constantine won a major battle at the Milvian Bridge in 312; that he attributed his victory to a sign from the Christian God; that immediately thereafter he took over administration of the western portion of the Roman Empire and soon (in 313) allied with Licinius; and that a few months later Licinius became ruler of the eastern half of the Empire. Therefore you should expect the document to have to do with both imperial authority and religion, which is precisely what you will discover when you read it.

Where was it written? In this case "Milan" is not the right answer. In fact the *Edict* was issued by Licinius at Nicomedia (today Izmit), in the eastern half of the Empire. But sometimes you will not know so specific an answer, and you must work with what information you have.

Why was it written? Often you will find a provisional answer to this question right in the text of the primary source. Ostensibly the *Edict* was written, as it says, "to give both to Christians and to all others free facility to follow the religion which each may desire." But you should go beyond this obvious answer to ask what other motives might have been at work, what sorts of negotiations may have been involved in its writing, and who benefited.

What is it? In this case, you know that it is *called* an *Edict* but is something a bit different. You might choose to call it an "imperial ordinance," an "official document," or even a "policy statement."

What does it say? This is the most important question of all. To answer it, you need to analyze the document for its various provisions, taking care to understand them fully and seeking further information (if necessary) about its vocabulary.

What are the implications of what it says? This requires you to ask many questions about matters that lie behind the text. Important questions to ask are: *What does the document reveal about such institutions as family, power, social classes and groups, religion, and education and literacy in the world that produced it? What are its underlying assumptions about gender; about human nature, agency, and goals; about the nature of the divine? Does the source apply to men and women in the same way?*

How reliable is it? If the document is authentic—if it really is what it purports to be—then at the very least you can know that it was issued by its writer(s). In this case, you can be sure that Constantine and Licinius did indeed want the *Edict of Milan* promulgated. You may wish to speculate about how much of it was Constantine's idea and how much Licinius's by considering what else you know about their religious convictions and political motives. The document certainly tells you about the ideals and intentions that they wanted the world to believe they had. But it alone cannot tell you whether the provisions were carried out. To know that, you need other documents and evidence about the nature of Roman imperial power at the time. One document that may help here is the *Creed* declared by the Council of Nicaea (p. 13 below), since Constantine presided over that council.

Are there complicating factors? Medieval texts were all handwritten, and they were "published"—in the sense of being made public and distributed—in relatively small numbers. In many cases we do not have them in their original state. The *Edict of Milan* was issued in multiple handwritten copies in Latin. However, none of these has survived. We know its contents because it was incorporated into the writings of two Christian apologists:[1] Lactantius's *On the Deaths of the Persecutors* (written perhaps in 318) and Eusebius's *History of the Church* (the first edition of which was published at some time between 303 and 312). Eusebius's text of the *Edict*, which he translated and presented in Greek, is not entirely the same as the one given by Lactantius. Scholars think that the one in Lactantius is the original, and that is the one printed here. But you should not be content with that. You should instead ask yourself at least two questions about these intermediary sources: *What motives might lead a later source to reproduce a text? What new meanings does the original source take on when it is embedded in a larger document with its own agenda?* You might also consider the fact that the *Edict* was not considered important enough to be drawn upon by the legal experts who compiled *The Theodosian Code* (438; see below, p. 4) or the later *Codex Justinianus* (529).

You should ask these questions of every source you read. Soon you will see how different the answers are for each document, for every one of them poses special challenges. If you like, look ahead to p. 167 to see this point clearly demonstrated in connection with a very different source, al-Tabari, *The Defeat of the Zanj Revolt*.

[Source: *Church and State Through the Centuries: A Collection of Historic Documents with Commentaries*, trans. and ed. Sidney Z. Ehler and John B. Morrall (Westminster, MD: Newman Press, 1954), pp. 5–6.]

We, Constantine and Licinius the Emperors, having met in concord at Milan and having set in order everything which pertains to the common good and public security, are of the opinion that among the various things which we perceived would profit men, or which should be set in order first, was to be found the cultivation of religion; we should therefore give both to Christians and to all others free facility to follow the religion which each may desire, so that by this means whatever divinity is enthroned in heaven may be gracious and favorable to us and to all who have been placed under our authority. Therefore we are of the opinion that the following decision is in accordance with sound and true reasoning: that no one who has given his mental assent to the Christian persuasion or to any other which he feels to be suitable to him should be compelled to deny his conviction, so that the Supreme Godhead ("Summa Divinitas"), whose worship we freely observe, can assist us in all things with his usual favor and benevolence. Wherefore it is necessary for your Excellency to know that it is our pleasure that all restrictions which were previously put forward in official pronouncements concerning the sect of the Christians should be removed, and that each one of them who freely and sincerely carries out the purpose of observing the Christian religion may endeavor to practice its precepts without any fear or danger. We believed that these points should be fully brought to your attention, so that you might know that we have given free and absolute permission to practice their religion to the Christians. Now that you perceive what we have granted to them,

---

[1] An "apologist" is someone who justifies or argues in favor of a doctrine or ideology.

your Excellency must also learn that for the sake of peace in our time a similar public and free right to practice their religion or cult is granted to others, so that every person may have free opportunity to worship according to his own wish. This has been done by us to avoid any appearance of disfavor to any one religion. We have decided furthermore to decree the following in respect of the Christians: if those places at which they were accustomed in former times to hold their meetings (concerning which a definite procedure was laid down for your guidance in previous communications) have been at any previous time acquired from our treasury or from any other person, let the persons concerned be willing and swift to restore them to the Christians without financial recompense and without trying to ask a price. Let those who have received such property as a gift restore whatever they have acquired to the Christians in similar manner; if those who have bought such property or received it as a gift seek some recompense from our benevolence, let them apply to the vicar, by whom their cases will be referred to our clemency. You are to consider it your duty that all these things shall be handed over to the Christian body immediately and without delay by your intervention. And since the aforesaid Christians are known to have possessed not only those places at which they are accustomed to assemble, but others also pertaining to the law of their body, that is of the churches, not of private individuals, you are to order in accordance with the law which we have described above the return of all those possessions to the aforesaid Christians, that is to their bodies and assemblies without any further hesitation or argument. Our previous statement is to be borne in mind that those who restore this property without price may, as we have said, expect some compensation from our benevolence.

You ought to bring into play your very effective intervention in all these matters concerning the aforesaid Christian body so that there may be a swift fulfillment of our Edict, in which the interests of public quiet have been consulted by our clemency. Let all this be done, so that as we stated above, the divine favor, of which we have experienced so many instances, may continue with us to bless our successors through all time with public wellbeing. In order that the character of this our perpetual benevolence can reach the knowledge of all, it will be well for you to circulate everywhere, and to bring to the awareness of all, these points which have been written to you as above, so that the enactment of this our benevolence may not be hidden.

1.2 Law: *The Theodosian Code* (438). Original in Latin.

The Theodosian Code, a massive compilation of imperial edicts and letters issued in 438 under Roman Emperor Theodosius II (r.408–450), was meant to serve as an authoritative standard for determining legal cases throughout the Empire. Covering topics as diverse as legal procedure, marriage, the army, and the Church, the *Code* was immediately adopted by Roman judicial authorities and was later influential on the laws drawn up in the barbarian successor states. The *Code* divided its topics into "Books," which were further subdivided into "Titles." Under each Title were arranged excerpts from pertinent imperial legislation. These were followed, when the compilers thought necessary, by legal interpretations. The passages below concern two issues: marriage (and divorce) and asylum. The first demonstrates the *Code*'s attempt to control social and moral behavior. The topic of asylum reveals that emperors not only came to recognize the holiness of the altar but also bowed to bishops' desire to allow even criminals the opportunity to do penance.

[Source: *The Theodosian Code and Novels and the Sirmondian Constitutions*, trans. Clyde Pharr (Princeton, NJ: Princeton University Press, 1952), pp. 76–77, 264–66 (slightly modified).]

Book 3, Title 14: Marriages with Foreigners

1. EMPERORS VALENTINIAN AND VALENS AUGUSTUSES TO THEODOSIUS, MASTER OF THE HORSE. [368–373]

No provincial, of whatever rank or class he may be, shall marry a barbarian wife, nor shall a provincial woman be united with any foreigner. But if there should be any alliances between provincials and foreigners through such marriages and if anything should be disclosed as suspect or criminal among them, it shall be expiated by capital punishment.

Interpretation: No Roman shall presume to have a barbarian wife of any nation whatever, nor shall any Roman woman be united in marriage with a barbarian. But if they should do this, they shall know that they are subject to capital punishment.

Title 16: Notices of Divorce

1. EMPEROR CONSTANTINE AUGUSTUS TO ABLAVIUS, PRAETORIAN PREFECT. [331]

It is Our[1] pleasure that no woman, on account of her own depraved desires, shall be permitted to send a notice of divorce to her husband on trumped up grounds, as, for instance, that he is a drunkard or a gambler or a philanderer, nor indeed shall a husband be permitted to divorce his wife on every sort of pretext. But when a woman sends a notice of divorce, the following criminal charges only shall be investigated, that is, if she should prove that her husband is a homicide, a sorcerer, or a destroyer of tombs, so that the wife may thus earn commendation and at length recover her entire dowry. For if she should send a notice of divorce to her husband on grounds other than these three criminal charges, she must leave everything, even to her last hairpin, in her husband's home, and as punishment for her supreme self confidence, she shall be deported to an island. In the case of a man also, if he should send a notice of divorce, inquiry shall be made as to the following three criminal charges, namely, if he wishes to divorce her as an adulteress, a sorceress, or a procuress.[2] For if he should cast off a wife who is inno-cent of these crimes, he must restore her entire dowry, and he shall not marry another woman. But if he should do this, his former wife shall be given the right to enter and seize his home by force and to transfer to herself the entire dowry of his later wife in recompense for the outrage inflicted upon her.

Interpretation: The right to send notice of divorce is extended to a wife or husband for certain approved reasons and causes; for they are forbidden to dissolve a marriage for a trivial charge. If perchance a woman should say that her husband is either a drunkard or given to licentiousness, she shall not send him notice of divorce on that account. But if perchance she should prove that he is either a homicide, a sorcerer, or a violator of tombs, the husband who is convicted of these crimes appears to be justly divorced, without any fault of the woman; and she may recover her dowry and depart. If the woman should not be able to prove such crimes, she shall be subjected to the following punishment: namely, that she shall forfeit both the dowry which she had given or which had been given on her behalf and the gift[3] which she received, and she shall also be liable to exile by relegation.[4] But if a man should cast off his wife, he also is not permitted to divorce her for a trivial quarrel, as often happens, unless perhaps he should be able to prove that she is guilty of certain crimes, that is, if he is able to prove that she is an adulteress, a sorceress, or a procuress. But if he cannot prove this, he shall restore her dowry to the woman, and he shall not presume to take another wife. But if perchance he should attempt to do so, the woman who was cast off, though innocent, shall have the right to vindicate [claim] for herself her husband's home and all his substance. It is recognized that this is ordained in order that if a woman should be unjustly divorced, she is ordered to acquire the dowry of the second wife also.

2. EMPERORS HONORIUS, THEODOSIUS, AND CONSTANTIUS AUGUSTUSES TO PALLADIUS, PRAETORIAN PREFECT. [421]

If a woman should serve notice of divorce upon her husband and separate from him and if she should prove no grounds for divorce, the gifts shall be annulled which she had received when betrothed. She shall also be deprived

---

[1] This is the "imperial 'we'"—the emperor refers to himself, as representative of the state, in the plural.

[2] I.e., a madam or prostitute.

[3] The betrothal and prenuptial gifts.

[4] There were two forms of punishment by exile: in the harshest, the exile lost all civil rights. In exile by relegation, he or she retained these rights.

of her dowry, and she shall be sentenced to the punishment of deportation. We deny her not only the right to a union with a subsequent husband, but even the right of postliminium.[1] But if a woman who has revolted against her marriage should prove merely flaws of character and ordinary faults, she shall lose her dowry and restore to her husband all gifts, and never at all shall she be associated in marriage with any man. In order that she may not defile her unmarried state with wanton debauchery, We grant to the repudiated husband the right to bring an accusation.[2]

1. It remains to say that if a woman who withdraws[3] should prove serious grounds and a conscience involved in great crimes, she shall obtain possession of her dowry and shall also retain the betrothal bounty, and she shall regain the right to marry after a period of five years from the day of the divorce. For then it will appear that she has done this from loathing of her own husband rather than from a desire for another husband.[4]

2(1). Certainly if the husband should be the first to give notice of divorce and if he should charge his wife with a grave crime, he shall prosecute the accused woman in accordance with the law, and when he has obtained his revenge, he shall both get possession of her dowry and recover his bounty [gifts] to her, and he shall acquire the unrestricted right to marry another woman immediately. 3. If it is a fault of character and not of criminality, the husband shall recover his gifts but relinquish the dowry, and he shall have the right to marry another woman after a period of two years. 4. But if the husband should wish to dissolve the marriage because of a mere disagreement and should charge the repudiated woman with no vices or sins, he shall lose both his gifts and the dowry and be compelled to live in perpetual celibacy; he shall suffer punishment for his insolent divorce in the sadness of solitude; and the woman shall be granted the right to marry after the termination of a year. Moreover, We order to be preserved the guarantees of the ancient law in regard to the retentions from dowries, on account of children.

Interpretation: If a woman should be the first to serve a notice of divorce upon her husband and should not prove the statutory grounds for divorce, she shall forfeit the betrothal bounty, and she shall not recover that which she gave her husband as dowry. In addition, she shall also be sent into exile by relegation, and she shall not have the right to marry or to return to her own.[5] Indeed, if she should prove slight faults in her husband, for which she appears to seek a divorce, she shall forfeit her dowry and shall restore the betrothal gifts, and she shall not have the right to marry another man. If, however, after divorcing her husband, she should become involved in adultery, her husband shall have the right to prosecute her even after the divorce. But if a woman who has separated from her husband should prove that he is guilty of grave and definite crimes, she shall both recover her dowry and vindicate that which her husband bestowed upon her as a betrothal bounty, and she shall have the unrestricted right of marriage after five years.

Indeed, if the husband should be the first to serve notice of divorce, he shall secure his revenge on grounds approved by law, he shall vindicate the dowry of his repudiated wife, shall recover his betrothal gifts, and shall have the right to marry another woman immediately if he wishes. If indeed there were no definite crimes, but, as often happens, the husband is displeased with the frivolity of his wife's character, he shall recover his gifts and shall restore to her immediately anything which he has received from her, and after a period of two years he shall have the right to marry another wife. But if no defect of character should be proved but merely mental discord, the innocent woman who is rejected by her husband shall both vindicate the gifts made to her by the man and shall recover her dowry. But he shall remain alone forever and shall not presume to associate himself in marriage with another woman. The woman, however, is permitted to proceed to another marriage after a year if she should so wish. But for the sake of their common children, if there should be any, the Emperor orders those rules to be observed which have been established in the law concerning retentions according to the number of children, which law Paulus sets forth in his *Book of Responses* under the title, *A Wife's Property*.[6] ...

---

[1] The right to return home and resume her former life.

[2] On grounds of immorality.

[3] From her marriage.

[4] The husband of another woman?

[5] That is, she shall not have the right of postliminium—to return home and resume her normal life.

[6] The juridical writings of Julius Paulus (*fl. c.*200) were considered authoritative.

Book 9, Title 44: *Those Persons Who Flee for Sanctuary to the Statues of the Emperors*

1. EMPERORS VALENTINIAN, THEODOSIUS, AND ARCADIUS AUGUSTUSES TO CYNEGIUS, PRAETORIAN PREFECT. [386]

We suffer those persons who have taken refuge at the statues of the Emperors, either for the purpose of avoiding danger or of creating ill will, neither to be taken away by anyone before the tenth day nor to go away of their own accord; provided that, if they had definite reasons for which they had to flee to the statues of the Emperors, they shall be protected by law and the statutes. But if they should be revealed to have wished to create ill will against their enemies by their own artifices, an avenging sentence shall be pronounced against them.

Title 45: *Those Persons Who Flee for Sanctuary to the Churches*

1. EMPERORS THEODOSIUS, ARCADIUS, AND HONORIUS AUGUSTUSES TO ROMULUS, COUNT OF THE SACRED IMPERIAL LARGESSES. [392]

If public debtors[1] should suppose that they may take refuge in the churches, they shall either be dragged out of their hiding places at once, or payment of their debts shall be exacted of the bishops who are proved to have harbored them. Your Eminent Authority shall know, therefore, that no debtor hereafter shall be defended by clerics, or else the debts shall be paid by the clerics for a debtor who they suppose ought to be defended.

2. EMPERORS ARCADIUS AND HONORIUS AUGUSTUSES TO ARCHELAUS, AUGUSTAL PREFECT. [397]

If Jews should be harassed by some criminal charge or by debts and should pretend that they wish to be joined to the Christian law,[2] in order that they may be able to avoid criminal charges or the burden of debts by taking refuge in the churches, they shall be driven away, and they shall not be received until they have paid all their debts or have been cleared of criminal charges by proof of their innocence.

3. THE SAME AUGUSTUSES TO EUTYCHIANUS, PRAETORIAN PREFECT. [398]

If, in the future, any slave, maidservant, decurion,[3] public debtor, procurator,[4] collector of purple dye fish, or anyone, finally, who is involved in public or private accounts should take refuge in a church, and if he should be either ordained a cleric or defended in any way by clerics and if he should not be returned to his former condition immediately by the issuance of a summons, decurions, indeed, and all others who are called by a customary function to the duty that they owe shall be recalled to their former lot by the energy and wisdom of the judges, as if by forcible seizure. We no longer permit such persons to have the benefit of the law which did not forbid decurions to be clerics after surrender of their patrimonies had ensued. But also those persons who are called stewards, that is, those who customarily manage ecclesiastical accounts shall be compelled without any delay to the repayment of a public or private debt to which it appears that those persons are obligated whom clerics received to be defended and did not suppose should be produced immediately.

4. EMPERORS THEODOSIUS AND VALENTINIAN AUGUSTUSES TO ANTIOCHUS, PRAETORIAN PREFECT. [431]

The temples of the Most High God shall be open to those persons who are afraid. Not only do We sanction that the altars and the surrounding oratory of the temple, which encloses the church with a barrier of four walls on the inside, shall be set aside for the protection of those persons who take refuge, but also the space up to the outside doors of the church, which people desiring to pray enter first, We order to be an altar of safety for those who seek Sanctuary. Thus if there should be any intervening space within the circumference of the walls of the temple which We have marked off[5] and within the outer doors of the church behind the public grounds, whether it be in the cells or in the houses, gardens, baths, courtyards, or colonnades, such space shall protect the fugitives just as the interior of the temple does. No one shall attempt to lay sacrilegious hands on them to drag them out, lest a person who dares to do this, when he sees his own peril, may himself also take refuge and seek aid. Moreover, We

---

1. Most of the public debtors were delinquent taxpayers.
2. I.e., become Christians.
3. A decurion was a member of a provincial city senate.
4. In this case, probably an imperial procurator—a fiscal agent or administrator—is meant.
5. By the boundary of walls mentioned above.

grant this extent of space for this purpose, namely, that it may not be permitted that any fugitive remain or eat or sleep or spend the night in the very temple of God or on the sacrosanct altars. The clerics themselves shall forbid this for the sake of reverence for religion, and those who seek sanctuary shall observe it for the sake of piety.

1. We also command that those persons who seek sanctuary shall not have within the churches any arms at all, in the form of any weapon, either of iron or of any other kind. For weapons are barred not only from the temples and divine altars of the Most High God, but also from the cells, houses, gardens, baths, courtyards, and colonnades.

2. Hereafter if any persons should flee without arms to the most holy temple of God or to its sacrosanct altar, either anywhere else in the world or in this fair City, they shall be prevented by the clerics themselves, without any injury to such persons, from sleeping or from taking any food at all within the temple or at the altar. The clerics shall designate spaces within the ecclesiastical enclosures which shall be sufficient for their protection and shall explain that capital punishment has been decreed if anyone should attempt to enter forcibly and seize them. If the fugitive should not agree to these restrictions and should not obey them, reverence for religion must be preferred to humanity, and reckless lawlessness must be driven from these holy places to those that We have mentioned.

3. We warn beforehand those persons who dare to enter the temples with arms that they shall not do this. Then if they should be equipped with weapons in any place in the church, either near the enclosure of the temple or around it or outside it, We command that they be notified immediately and very severely by the clerics alone, under the authority of the bishop, to lay aside their arms, and they shall be given the assurance that they are defended by the name of religion better than by the protection of arms. But if, warned by the voice of the Church and by the declarations of so many and so important persons, the refugees should be unwilling to relinquish their weapons, then the case of Our Clemency and of the bishops is cleared in the sight of God; armed men shall be sent in, if the case so demands, and the refugees shall know that they will be dragged forth, dragged away, and subjected to all kinds of misfortunes. But no armed persons shall be dragged out from the churches without consulting the bishop or without Our order or the order of the judges either in this fair City or anywhere else, lest, if many persons should be generally permitted to do this, confusion may arise.

Interpretation: Churches and places dedicated to God shall so protect accused persons who flee to them, driven by fear, that no one shall presume to bring force and violence to holy places in order to seize accused persons. But We command that whatever space belongs to the church, either in the colonnades, or in the halls, in the houses, or in the courtyards adjacent to the church shall be guarded just as the inner parts of the temple, so that the compulsion of fear may not constrain accused persons to remain around the altars or to defile places to which reverence is due. Certainly, if they should take refuge in holy places, they shall lay aside at once whatever arms they have brought with them, and they shall not suppose that they are defended by the protection of arms more than by reverence for holy places. But if they should be unwilling to lay aside their arms, and if they should not have confidence in the priest or the clerics, they shall know that they will be dragged out by the force of armed men. But if anyone should attempt for any reason to drag out from a holy place any accused person at all, the offender shall know that he will be condemned to capital punishment.

5. THE SAME AUGUSTUSES TO HIERIUS, PRAETORIAN PREFECT. [432]

We believe that a sanction should be promulgated, which shall be valid forever, concerning those persons who take refuge at the altars of holy religion, to the effect that if the slave of any person, relying only on reverence for the place, should seek refuge in the church or at the altars without any weapon, he shall be sent away after not more than one day in such place; furthermore, notice shall be given by the clerics whom it concerns to his master or to the person for fear of whom the slave appears to have avoided imminent punishment. The master shall grant pardon for his wrongs, and, with no remnants of anger remaining in his heart, in honor of the place and in respect for Him to whose aid the slave has fled, he shall take the slave away.

But if, armed and suspected of this by no one, the slave should rush in suddenly, then he shall be dragged out immediately, or at least notice shall be given at once to his master or to the person from whom such frantic fear has driven the slave, and the opportunity to drag him out at once shall not be denied. But if, relying upon arms and driven by madness, he should conceive the intention of resisting, his master shall be granted the right to drag him out and take him away by whatever means he can effect it. If it should happen that the slave should be killed in the struggle and battle, the master shall incur no blame, nor shall there be an occasion for anyone to originate a criminal action, if a person is killed who has changed from a servile status to the legal condition of a public enemy and a homicide.

If these regulations, so usefully constituted, should be perverted either by negligence or connivance, or in any other manner by those persons who are placed in charge of such matters in accordance with the duties of their office, just punishment will not be lacking, and, under the decision of an episcopal trial, they shall be removed from that place which they could not protect, they shall be cast back into the rank of plebeians,[1] and they shall receive the force of judicial severity.

1.3 Plague: Gregory the Great, *Letter to Bishop Dominic of Carthage* (600). Original in Latin.

The Plague of Justinian lasted from 541 to *c.*750. Named after the emperor under whom it first appeared, the plague spread across the Mediterranean and beyond, from the Middle East to Europe. Pope Gregory the Great (590–604) was well known for spearheading a drive to convert English to Christianity (see Bede, below, p. 94), for his commentaries on the Book of Job and other exegetical works, and for his "biography" (in fact the second book of his *Dialogues* on the holy men of Italy) of Saint Benedict of Nursia (for whose Rule see below, p. 17). He was also a devoted pastor who wrote a *Pastoral Rule* that served as a handbook for priests throughout the Middle Ages. In his letter to Dominic, who held the important position of bishop of Carthage, Gregory set forth in brief many of the ideas about the purposes of tribulation in this world that earlier had been elaborated in detail by Augustine (see the *City of God*, below p. 14). To counter the plague at Rome, Gregory organized penitential processions there at the beginning of his papacy and probably again *c.* 602; these fulfilled the "good deeds and tears of penitence" that he mentioned in his letter to Dominic. He also wanted bishops like himself and Dominic to restrain the members of their churches from "wicked deeds." Gregory did not concern himself with disposing of thousands of dead bodies, but at Constantinople Emperor Justinian ordered a court official to pay high wages to pit diggers and corpse bearers to handle the burials.

[Source: *Gregorii Magni Registrum epistularum libri VIII-XIV* 10.20, ed. Dag Norberg, Corpus Christianorum, Series Latina 140A (Turnhout: Brepols, 1982), pp. 850–51. Translated by Carole Straw.]

Gregory to Dominic, Bishop of Carthage

We already know how great a plague has invaded Africa;[2] and since neither is Italy free from the stroke of the sword, the groans of our grief are doubled. But amidst these evils and other innumerable calamities, dearest brother,[3] our heart would fail in tribulation without hope unless the Lord's voice had forearmed our frailty. For long ago, the trumpet of the gospel warned faithful listeners of the impending end of the world: pestilence, war and many other things would happen, which up to now, as you know, we only feared. But since we suffer these things that were foreknown, surely we ought not to be struck down by them as if they were from the unknown. For often even the

---

[1] This was the lowest class in Roman society. Plebeians had few rights and were subject to taxes and compulsory services.

[2] Gregory is using the "royal we" here; he means himself.

[3] Why would Gregory invoke the metaphor of brotherhood with Dominic even though they were not blood brothers?

kind of death is a consolation, considering other ways of dying. How many maimings and cruelties have we seen for which only death was the remedy, when life was torture? When the choice of a death was offered David, did he not decide that his people should die at the hand of God, rejecting famine and the sword?[1] Gather from this how much grace there is in those who die from a divine blow, when they die in the way that was offered as a gift to the holy prophet. And so let us give thanks in every adversity to our Creator and, trusting in his mercy, patiently endure everything since we suffer quite less than we deserve. Moreover, since we are scourged in earthly life that we may by no means be left without the consolation of eternal life, so the more we know the nearness of the judge to come announced in these signs, the more we should safeguard our accounts—which we must render to his examination—with the zeal of good deeds and tears of penitence, so that, through his benevolent grace, such great blows do not become the beginning of damnation, but the blessing of purification. But since the nature of our weakness is that we are unable not to grieve for those dying, let this teaching of your fraternity be a comfort to those in tribulation. Let it sink in that the goods promised them will endure, so that, strengthened by the most certain hope, they learn not to grieve for the loss of earthly things, in comparison to the gift awaiting them. Let your tongue (so we believe) compel them more and more away from the commission of wicked works, let it set forth in full the reward of the good and the punishment of evil so that those who love good the less should at least thoroughly fear wrong doing and restrain themselves from what must be punished. For those subjected to the scourge to commit crimes against the Punisher[2] worthy of the scourge is to be extremely proud, and it is to inflame his wrath to sharper fury; and it is the first order of madness not to want someone to cease justly his evil deeds, and to wish unjustly that God would check his vengeance. But since we need divine assistance in these things, let us, beloved brother, with joined prayers beseech the clemency of almighty God that he both may grant that we present these things worthily and also goad the hearts of the people mercifully to do these things, so that as we govern our actions wholesomely in fear of God, we may merit both to be rescued from the evils assailing us and also to come to heavenly joys, led by his grace, without which we can do nothing.

HERESY AND ORTHODOXY

1.4 Heretics: *A Donatist Sermon* (*c.*318). Original in Latin.

Emperor Constantine's (r.306–337) recognition and favoring of the Christian church ironically brought numerous tensions within Christianity to the fore. No longer united against a common foe, Christians formed splinter groups that maintained a particular interpretation of doctrine or demanded a certain standard of behavior. In North Africa, the key issue after Constantine's conversion was how to deal with those who had handed over their Bibles, church furnishings, and other emblems of their faith to escape persecution and death during Diocletian's persecutions. The Donatists scorned the *traditores* (from the Latin verb *tradere*: to hand over), and, when Constantine ended the persecutions, they refused to allow such people to pick up their Christian lives again as if nothing had happened. In particular, they denied the pastoral rights of priests and bishops who had been *traditores*, and they were equally wary of anyone even *ordained* by men so compromised. In 311, when Caecilian—whom the Donatists suspected of collaborating with the persecutors—was ordained bishop of Carthage, the Donatists insisted on

---

[1] In 2 Sam. 24, David orders a census to count the number of fighting men in Israel and Judah. Then he repents. God gives him three ways to die: seven years' famine, three months' flight from the enemy in hot pursuit, or three days of pestilence. Afraid of falling into human hands, David chooses death at God's hand, namely by pestilence. Many die, but he does not.

[2] I.e., God.

their own bishop, Majorinus. An appeal by the Catholics to resolve the crisis provoked Constantine to send troops. The Donatists interpreted the resulting bloodshed as a new persecution of Christians, strengthening their resolve. In this sermon, given a few years later to commemorate the event, the preacher hoped to fire his listeners to remain—or join—with the Donatists. He saw the "Catholics" and the emperor as inspired by the Devil, and he made fun of their epithet "heretic" for what he understood to be the true "Church of Christ."

[Source: *Donatist Martyr Stories: The Church in Conflict in Roman North Africa*, trans. Maureen A. Tilley, Translated Texts for Historians, 24 (Liverpool: Liverpool University Press, 1996), pp. 54–57 (notes modified).]

The Lord himself does not wish the death of the one who is perishing but rather that that person should return and live.[1] He was ready to receive the confession of those who were sorry. Knowing this, when the contriver [i.e., the Devil, working largely through his creature, Constantine] came face to face with times of peace, by worldly seduction, he revived those minds he had overcome in battle by fear of torture.[2] He took away their humility, the only way to tame the anger of an indignant God, and he substituted pride, which he knew for certain would gravely offend God. He promoted the idea that the lapsed, the deserters of heavenly sacraments, could illicitly hold ecclesiastical office again.[3]

As much as he recently took pleasure in their weakness of faith, so now he rejoices in this fraud. He is even more secure when they are called "bishops" or "Christians," than when they fell to ruin in their denial of the Christian name. He has these nominal enemies while he remains secure in deception. As we have already said, this is how he holds onto those he deceives by this false use of the Name. Not only does he delight these miserable men with vainglory but he also ensnares the greedy by royal friendship and earthly gifts.

Nevertheless, this rapacious robber was frustrated that he did not control everyone by this ruse. So the enemy of salvation concocted a more subtle conceit to violate the purity of faith. "Christ," he said, "is the lover of unity. Therefore, let there be unity." Those people who were already fawning on him and were deserted by God came to be called "Catholics." By prejudice in favor of the name, those who refused to communicate with them were called "heretics." He sent funds so that he might weaken their faith or provide an occasion for avarice through the publication of the law.[4] But when the course of justice holds firm and inflexible in the face of these seductive temptations, judges are ordered to intervene; the secular powers are forced to use coercion. Homes are encircled with battle standards; at the same time, threats of proscriptions[5] are launched against the rich. Sacraments are profaned; crowds are bedecked with idolatry; holy assemblies are transformed into splendid banquets.

O most faithful brothers and sisters, it is a crime even to publish what was said and done among the banquets of lascivious youths where despicable women were present.

How swiftly and completely did the situation change! The basilica, shameful to say, was turned into a fast-food restaurant. What grief to see such a crime in the house of the Lord, this place accustomed to pious prayers, now profaned by impure deeds and illegitimate incantations! Now I ask you, what person in whatever desperate condition would allow this to be done in their own home? No one would consent except the sort of person who

---

[1] See Ezek. 33: 11.

[2] Those who were wavering, about to abjure their alliance with the *traditores*, were deterred from repenting of their association with them by the prospect of being persecuted for being Donatists.

[3] Donatists did not allow Catholic leaders who joined the Donatist fold to continue to preside over their congregations. They were admitted to the Donatist church as members of the laity. Catholics, on the other hand, recognized pastoral necessity and political prudence in cases where an entire Donatist congregation went over to the Catholic side under the leadership of its priest or bishop. Donatists treated schismatic Donatists returning to their church on a case-by-case basis.

[4] The author is again referring to imperial gifts.

[5] Confiscations of property.

would actually do it. Who denies that such deeds have the children of the Devil as their authors? Who calls the authors of the actions Christians, except the person who wishes to excuse the Devil himself or to disavow Christ the Lord? What diligence by the Serpent! So many evils let loose! How many hatched so that its family might assume the divine Name and hide itself from that Name, the Name it disgraces by its deeds! O the strength of the divine patience so worthy of praise, bearing up while the villainy of evil is spreading! Divine patience puts up with having the deeds of the crafty enemy imputed to itself or to its Name. Let no one think that something trivial happens when so many schisms and heresies arise. Satan's disguise surely dishonors God and Christ through his wicked ministry and adulterous work.

But lest we wander too far from the main point, let us omit their defilement of holy virgins. I repress any mention of their slaughter of the priests of God. I keep silent about their assaults, their pillaging, their booty. This way even they may know that we deliberately select few things from among many and we expose it quickly and modestly, seeing that we are eager not to exact vengeance on our enemies but to free the souls of these miserable people from the jaws of the ravenous wolf, indeed from the very mouth of the Dragon.[1]

Therefore, the one who corrupts holy discipline could violate the chastity of faith under the by-word of unity, i.e., by compelling unity with himself, not with God. Neither the rulers of this world nor those of darkness arrange things to happen in such a way that what is ordered might reveal the person giving the order. What glorious examples, how many glorious examples of "the Church of God" or "the Church of Christ" issue among them? What signs of Christian confession? What exiles, public tokens of true faith and perfect devotion, might there be? By these deeds truth obviously could not lie hidden unless someone in defiance of conscience determined to place their hope in deceit just as the prophet said.[2]

Let us proceed to the final events. They erupted in open threats and unmistakable fury once their subter-fuges failed and their snares wore out. At that time you could have seen bands of soldiers serving the Furies of the traditors. They were brought together to perform a crime, but they were thinking only of pay. They stood around with most attentive curiosity lest mercenary cruelty be allowed to do something too gently. The cruel mercenaries asserted that attention to so improper a spectacle was not so much defense of a perverse claim, as the exaction of blood according to some contract.

Although the people of God might have anticipated the coming slaughter and known about it from the arrangements being made, they did not flee out of fear of an imminent death. On the contrary, they flew undaunted to the house of prayer with a desire to suffer. There faith grazed on the sacred readings, and prescribed fasts fed them with continual prayers. When these souls are delivered into the hands of the iniquitous, by their prayers they are actually commended into the hands of God.[3] Behold, in imitation of the Lord's passion, this cohort of soldiers marshaled by latter-day Pharisees sets forth from their camps to the death of Christians. Against innocent hands stretched out to the Lord, their right hands are armed with cudgels.[4] But it may be said that those who are not slaughtered by the sword are less martyrs for having been beaten to death in this impious massacre.[5]

The sword of the tribune had not yet pierced though the honored throat of the holy bishop of Siciliba, but it pricked him and the rage of the devil revealed who his agents were. In the same way the patience of the glorious bishop revealed the Church of Christ. No one else appears as servant of Christ the Lord as much as someone who suffered the same things as the Lord. It says: "No servant is greater than his master; if they persecute me, they will persecute you."[6] This is why these blind "servants of God" who are loved by the world show how the Lord himself was "loved" by the world. If the world does not love even those who are its own, it is necessary for it to hate those whom the Lord Jesus chose from out of the world. It says: "If you were from the world, the world would love what is its own; but because you are not from

---

[1] Matt. 7: 15; see Ezek. 22: 27.

[2] See Jer. 7: 4 and 13: 25.

[3] See Luke 23: 46.

[4] See Matt. 26: 47.

[5] This alludes to the belief that the only true martyrs were those who had actually shed blood. Thus a person beaten to death without the breaking of the skin would be considered less than a martyr. The author obviously repudiates this differentiation among those dying for their faith.

[6] John 15: 20.

the world, since I have chosen you from out of the world, for that reason does the world hate you."[1]

Finally, bloodshed marked the end of this hatred. Now the soldiers endorsed the contract and the covenant of crime in no other way than by the seal of blood. Everyone kept their eyes shut tight while each age group and sex was killed, cut down in the midst of the basilica. It is this very basilica, I say, between whose walls so many bodies were cut down and buried. Here, in the inscriptions, memory preserves the name of the persecution as Caecilianist[2] until the end of time, lest after his episcopate the parricide deceive others who were not privy to the things done in his name.

1.5 Orthodoxy's declaration: *The Nicene Creed* (325). Original in Greek.

A dispute between Bishop Alexander of Alexandria and Arius, an Alexandrian priest, concerning the relationship between the Father and the Son (Jesus Christ) within the Godhead had such far-flung repercussions that Emperor Constantine (r.306–337) called the Council of Nicaea (325), the first "ecumenical" (universal) council, to adjudicate the matter. We do not know precisely what Arius taught, but he clearly subordinated the Son to the Father. The Council declared that the Son was of the "same substance" (*homousios*) as the Father and thus not subordinate, a formulation that Arius could not accept. Although Arius was excommunicated, some of his supporters remained in high positions. When Constantius II (r.337–361) came to the imperial throne, he favored the position that the Orthodox called "Arian" and supported Ulfila, whose missionary work among the Goths led to their adoption of "Arianism." Although—or perhaps because—the Goths were allowed into the empire in 376, the Council of Constantinople, held in 381, affirmed the ban on Arianism, in effect branding as heretics the Goths and other barbarian tribes who adopted the Arian positions.

[Source: John N.D. Kelly, *Early Christian Doctrines*, 2nd ed. (New York: Harper and Row, 1958), p. 232.]

We believe in one God, the Father almighty, maker of all things, visible and invisible;

And in one Lord Jesus Christ, the Son of God, begotten from the Father, only-begotten, that is, from the substance of the Father, God from God, light from light, true God from true God, begotten not made, of one substance [*homousios*] with the Father, through Whom all things came into being, things in heaven and things on earth, Who because of us men and because of our salvation came down and became incarnate, becoming man, suffered and rose again on the third day, ascended to the heavens, and will come to judge the living and the dead;

And in the Holy Spirit. But as for those who say, There was when He was not, and, Before being born He was not, and that He came into existence out of nothing, or who assert that the Son of God is from a different hypostasis or substance, or is created, or is subject to alteration or change—these the Catholic Church anathematizes.[3]

---

[1] John 15: 19.

[2] A reference to Caecilian, appointed bishop of Carthage against Donatist wishes.

[3] I.e., excommunicates.

PATRISTIC THOUGHT

1.6 Relating this world to the next: Augustine, *The City of God* (413–426). Original in Latin.

As a young man, St. Augustine (354–430) wanted to be an orator and teacher—that is, a rhetorician—but his restless quest for life's meaning led him to make a dramatic conversion, chronicled in his *Confessions*. Later, as bishop of Hippo in North Africa (395–430), he became the most influential churchman of his day and for centuries to come. Counted among the Church Fathers, Augustine formulated many of the key themes of Western Christianity until at least the twelfth century. Perhaps the most enduring of his works was *The City of God*, which, by postulating two cities—the City of God and the City of Man—permitted Augustine to explore the mingling of the sacred with the secular realms, the uses of adversity in the world, the vision of Heaven as a place of total peace, and the idea that the life of man on earth is a pilgrimage—a holy trek—from home (the here-and-now) to a longed-for place of succor (the City of God). In spite of these universal and timeless themes, the book was written in response to a very specific historical event: the sack of Rome by the Visigoths under King Alaric in 410.

[Source: Augustine, *Concerning the City of God against the Pagans*, trans. Henry Bettenson (New York: Penguin, 1972), pp. 5–7, 13–17, 858–59, 881, 891–92.]

Book 1

PREFACE. THE PURPOSE AND ARGUMENT OF THIS WORK

Here, my dear Marcellinus,[1] is the fulfilment of my promise, a book in which I have taken upon myself the task of defending the glorious City of God against those who prefer their own gods to the Founder of that City. I treat of it both as it exists in this world of time, a stranger among the ungodly, living by faith,[2] and as it stands in the security of its everlasting seat. This security it now awaits in steadfast patience, until "justice returns to judgment,"[3] but it is to attain it hereafter in virtue of its ascendancy over its enemies, when the final victory is won and peace established. The task is long and arduous; but God is our helper.[4]

I know how great is the effort needed to convince the proud of the power and excellence of humility, an excellence which makes it soar above all the summits of this world, which sway in their temporal instability, overtopping them all with an eminence not arrogated by human pride, but granted by divine grace. For the King and Founder of this City which is our subject has revealed in the Scripture of his people this statement of the divine

---

[1] Marcellinus (d.413) was an intimate disciple of St. Augustine sent by the Emperor Honorius to preside over the council summoned at Carthage to settle the dispute between Catholics and Donatists. Marcellinus was anxious to convert Volusianus (d.437), proconsul of Africa. Volusianus showed interest, but among his objections to Christianity was the charge that it had undermined the Roman Empire. Marcellinus wrote to ask for help from St. Augustine (who had already corresponded with Volusianus), and this led eventually to the writing of *The City of God*.

[2] See Hab. 2: 4; Rom. 1: 17; Gal. 3: 11; Hebr. 10: 38.

[3] Ps. 94: 15; Douay Ps. 93: 15.

[4] See Ps. 118: 7; Douay Ps. 117: 7.

Law, "God resists the proud, but he gives grace to the humble."[1] This is God's prerogative; but man's arrogant spirit in its swelling pride has claimed it as its own, and delights to hear this verse quoted in its own praise: "To spare the conquered, and beat down the proud."[2]

Therefore I cannot refrain from speaking about the city of this world, a city which aims at dominion, which holds nations in enslavement, but is itself dominated by that very lust of domination. I must consider this city as far as the scheme of this work demands and as occasion serves.

1. THE ENEMIES OF CHRISTIANITY WERE SPARED BY THE BARBARIANS AT THE SACK OF ROME, OUT OF RESPECT FOR CHRIST

From this world's city there arise enemies against whom the City of God has to be defended, though many of these correct their godless errors and become useful citizens of that City. But many are inflamed with hate against it and feel no gratitude for the benefits offered by its Redeemer. The benefits are unmistakable; those enemies would not today be able to utter a word against the City if, when fleeing from the sword of their enemy, they had not found, in the City's holy places, the safety on which they now congratulate themselves.[3] The barbarians spared them for Christ's sake; and now these Romans assail Christ's name. The sacred places of the martyrs and the basilicas of the apostles bear witness to this, for in the sack of Rome they afforded shelter to fugitives, both Christian and pagan. The bloodthirsty enemy raged thus far, but here the frenzy of butchery was checked; to these refuges the merciful among the enemy conveyed those whom they had spared outside, to save them from encountering foes who had no such pity. Even men who elsewhere raged with all the savagery an enemy can show, arrived at places where practices generally allowed by laws of war were forbidden and their monstrous passion for violence was brought to a sudden halt; their lust for taking captives was subdued.

In this way many escaped who now complain of this Christian era, and hold Christ responsible for the disasters which their city endured. But they do not make Christ responsible for the benefits they received out of respect for Christ, to which they owed their lives. They attribute their deliverance to their own destiny; whereas if they had any right judgment they ought rather to attribute the harsh cruelty they suffered at the hands of their enemies to the providence of God. For God's providence constantly uses war to correct and chasten the corrupt morals of mankind, as it also uses such afflictions to train men in a righteous and laudable way of life, removing to a better state those whose life is approved, or else keeping them in this world for further service.

Moreover, they should give credit to this Christian era for the fact that these savage barbarians showed mercy beyond the custom of war—whether they so acted in general in honor of the name of Christ, or in places specially dedicated to Christ's name, buildings of such size and capacity as to give mercy a wider range. For this clemency our detractors ought rather to give thanks to God; they should have recourse to his name in all sincerity so as to escape the penalty of everlasting fire, seeing that so many of them assumed his name dishonestly, to escape the penalty of immediate destruction. Among those whom you see insulting Christ's servants with such wanton insolence there are very many who came unscathed through that terrible time of massacre only by passing themselves off as Christ's servants. And now with ungrateful pride and impious madness they oppose his name in the perversity of their hearts, so that they may incur the punishment of eternal darkness; but then they took refuge in that name, though with deceitful lips, so that they might continue to enjoy this transitory light....

8. BLESSINGS AND DISASTERS OFTEN SHARED BY GOOD AND BAD

No doubt this question will be asked, "Why does the divine mercy extend even to the godless and ungrateful?" The only explanation is that it is the mercy of one "who makes his sun rise on the good and on the bad, and sends rain alike on the righteous and the unrighteous."[4] Some of the wicked are brought to penitence by considering these facts, and amend their impiety, while others, in the words of the Apostle, "despise the riches of God's goodness and forbearance, in the hardness and

---

[1] 1 Peter 5: 5.

[2] Virgil, *Aeneid* 6. 853.

[3] This refers to Alaric's clemency toward those who took sanctuary in Christian shrines, and especially in the basilicas of St. Peter and St. Paul.

[4] Matt. 5: 45.

impenitence of their hearts, and lay up for themselves a store of wrath in the day of God's anger and of the revelation of the just judgment of God, who will repay every man according to his actions."[1] Yet the patience of God still invites the wicked to penitence, just as God's chastisement trains the good in patient endurance. God's mercy embraces the good for their cherishing, just as his severity chastens the wicked for their punishment. God, in his providence, decided to prepare future blessings for the righteous, which the unrighteous will not enjoy, and sorrows for the ungodly, with which the good will not be tormented. But he has willed that these temporal goods and temporal evils should befall good and bad alike, so that the good things should not be too eagerly coveted, when it is seen that the wicked also enjoy them, and that the evils should not be discreditably shunned, when it is apparent that the good are often afflicted with them.

The most important question is this: What use is made of the things thought to be blessings, and of the things reputed evil? The good man is not exalted by this world's goods; nor is he overwhelmed by this world's ills. The bad man is punished by misfortune of this kind just because he is corrupted by good fortune....

Book 19

5. SOCIAL LIFE; ITS VALUE AND ITS DANGERS

The philosophies hold the view that the life of the wise man should be social; and in this we support them much more heartily. For here we are, with the nineteenth book in hand on the subject of the City of God; and how could that City have made its first start, how could it have advanced along its course, how could it attain its appointed goal, if the life of the saints were not social? And yet, who would be capable of listing the number and the gravity of the ills which abound in human society amid the distresses of our mortal condition? Who would be competent to assess them? Our philosophers should listen to a character in one of their own comedies, voicing a sentiment with which all mankind agrees:

I married a wife; and misery I found! Children were born; and they increased my cares.[2]

Again, think of the disorders of love, as listed in another quotation from Terence:

Wrongs and suspicions, enmities and war— Then, peace again.[3]

Have they not everywhere filled up the story of human experience? Are they not of frequent occurrence, even in the honorable love of friends? The story of mankind is full of them at every point; for in that story we are aware of wrongs, suspicions, enmities and war—undoubted evils, these. And even peace is a doubtful good, since we do not know the hearts of those with whom we wish to maintain peace, and even if we could know them today, we should not know what they might be like tomorrow. In fact, who are, in general, more friendly, or at any rate ought to be, than those within the walls of the same home? And yet, is anyone perfectly serene in that situation, when such grievous ills have so often arisen from the secret treachery of people within those walls? And the bitterness of these ills matches the sweetness of the peace that was reckoned genuine, when it was in fact only a very clever pretense.

This explains why some words of Cicero come so close to our hearts that we cannot but sigh when we read:

No treachery is more insidious than that which is hidden under a pretense of loyalty, or under the name of kinship. For against an open adversary you could be on your guard and thus easily avoid him; but this hidden evil, within the house and family, not only arises before you are aware but even overwhelms you before you can catch sight of it and investigate it.[4]

Hence also that inspired utterance, "A man's enemies are those of his own household,"[5] is heard with deep sorrow of heart. For even if anyone is strong enough to bear these ills with equanimity, or watchful enough to guard with foresight and discretion against the contrivances

---

[1] Rom. 2: 4–6; "the Apostle" refers always to St. Paul in the works of the early Fathers of the Church.

[2] Terence, *Adelphi* 5.4.13–14.

[3] Terence, *Eunuchus* 1.1.14–15.

[4] Cicero, *Actio in Verrem* 2.1.13.

[5] Matt. 10: 36.

of pretended friendship, nevertheless he cannot but feel grievous anguish, if he himself is a good man, at the wickedness of the traitors, when by experience he knows their utter viciousness, whether they were always evil and their goodness was a sham, or whether they suffered a change from good-nature to the malice that they now display. If, then, safety is not to be found in the home, the common refuge from the evils that befall mankind, what shall we say of the city? The larger the city, the more is its forum filled with civil lawsuits and criminal trials, even if that city be at peace, free from the alarms or—what is more frequent—the bloodshed, of sedition and civil war. It is true that cities are at times exempt from those occurrences; they are never free from the danger of them....

20. THE FELLOW-CITIZENS OF THE SAINTS ARE IN THIS LIFE MADE HAPPY BY HOPE

We see, then, that the Supreme Good, of the City of God is everlasting and perfect peace, which is not the peace through which men pass in their mortality, in their journey from birth, to death, but that peace in which they remain in their immortal state, experiencing no adversity at all. In view of this, can anyone deny that this is the supremely blessed life, or that the present life on earth, however full it may be of the greatest possible blessings of soul and body and of external circumstances, is, in comparison, most miserable? For all that, if anyone accepts the present life in such a spirit that he uses it with the end in view of that other life on which he has set his heart with all his ardor and for which he hopes with all his confidence, such a man may without absurdity be called happy even now, though rather by future hope than in present reality. Present reality without that hope is, to be sure, a false happiness, in fact, an utter misery. For the present does not bring into play the true goods of the mind; since no wisdom is true wisdom if it does not direct its attention, in all its prudent decisions, its resolute actions, its self-control and its just dealings with others, towards that ultimate state in which God will be all in all,[1] in the assurance of eternity and the perfection of peace....

26....."Blessed is the people, whose God is the Lord."[2] It follows that a people alienated from that God must be wretched. Yet even such a people loves a peace of its own, which is not to be rejected; but it will not possess it in the end, because it does not make good use of it before the end. Meanwhile, however, it is important for us also that this people should possess this peace in this life, since so long as the two cities are intermingled we also make use of the peace of Babylon—although the People of God is by faith set free from Babylon, so that in the meantime they are only pilgrims in the midst of her. That is why the Apostle instructs the Church to pray for kings of that city and those in high positions, adding these words: "that we may lead a quiet and peaceful life with all devotion and love."[3] And when the prophet Jeremiah predicted to the ancient People of God the coming captivity, and bade them, by God's inspiration, to go obediently to Babylon, serving God even by their patient endurance, he added his own advice that prayers should be offered for Babylon, "because in her peace is your peace"[4]—meaning, of course, the temporal peace of the meantime, which is shared by good and bad alike.

1.7 Monasticism: *The Benedictine Rule* (*c.*530–*c.*560). Original in Latin.

St. Benedict (d.*c.*550–*c.*560), founder of several monasteries near Rome, wrote the most famous *Rule* for monks. In large measure it is an organized and institutionalized presentation of biblical directives, especially those inspired by the gospels. The key virtue of the monk in Benedict's *Rule* is obedience. The key duty is the Work of God, the hours of daily chant—known as the offices[5]—centered on the Psalter, all 150 psalms of which the monks

---

[1] 1 Cor. 15: 28.

[2] Ps. 144: 15; Douay Ps. 143: 15.

[3] 1 Tim. 2: 2.

[4] Jer. 29: 7.

[5] These are Vigils (the Night Office), Lauds, Prime, Terce, Sext, None, Vespers, and Compline.

were to complete each week. Within a half-century or so, Benedict's *Rule* had been incorporated alongside others in many Western monasteries. In the ninth century, it was adopted as the official norm for the monasteries of the Carolingian Empire. Compare its notions of human virtue and life on earth with those expressed in Augustine's *City of God*, p. 14 above.

[Source: *The Rule of St. Benedict*, ed. and trans. Bruce L. Venarde (Cambridge, MA: Harvard University Press, 2011), pp. 3, 7, 11, 13, 15, 17, 19, 21, 23, 29, 31, 33, 35, 37, 45, 47, 57, 59, 61, 79, 85, 87, 89, 97, 123, 125, 139, 141, 143, 161, 163, 177, 179, 187, 189, 191, 193, 229 (notes modified).]

In the name of our Lord Jesus Christ, here begins the prologue of the Rule by the great father Saint Benedict

Listen carefully, my son, to the teachings of a master and incline the ear of your heart. Gladly accept and effectively fulfill the admonition of a loving father so that through the work of obedience you may return to him from whom you had withdrawn through the sloth of disobedience. To you, therefore, my word is now directed—to whoever, renouncing his own will in order to fight for the Lord Christ, the true king, takes up the brilliant and mighty weapons of obedience....

Therefore our hearts and bodies must be prepared to fight for holy obedience to his instructions and what is not possible in us by nature let us ask God to order the aid of his grace to supply us. And if, fleeing the punishments of hell, we desire to attain eternal life, while there is still time and we are in this body and there is time to carry out all these things by the light of this life, we must hurry and do now what would profit us for eternity.

Thus we must found a school for the Lord's service.[1] In its design we hope we will establish nothing harsh, nothing oppressive. But if, according to the dictates of fairness, there emerges something a little severe in the interest of amending sins or preserving love, do not at once be frightened by fear and flee the path of salvation, which can only be narrow at the start. Instead, by progress in monastic life and faith, with hearts expanded in love's indescribable sweetness, we run along the path of God's commands so that, never turning away from his instruction and persevering in his doctrine in the mon-

astery until death, through patience we may share the sufferings of Christ and also deserve to be sharers in his kingdom. Amen.

Here begins the text of the Rule. It is called that because it rules the conduct of those who obey it.

Chapter 1
The Kinds of Monks

It is clear there are four kinds of monks. First are the cenobites, those in a monastery serving under a rule and an abbot. The second kind are anchorites, that is, hermits, those no longer fresh in the fervor of monastic life but long tested in a monastery, who have learned, by now schooled with the help of many, to fight against the Devil. Well trained among a band of brothers for single combat in the desert, by now confident even without another's encouragement, they are ready with God's help, to fight the vices of body and mind with hand and arm alone. The third, a very vile kind, are the sarabaites, tested by no rule nor instructed by experience, like gold in the furnace; but softened like lead, still keeping faith with worldly ways, they are known to lie to God by having tonsures.[2] They go around in pairs or threes or, of course, singly with no shepherd, shut in their own sheepfolds, not the Lord's, and the pleasure of their desires is their law, since they call holy whatever they have thought or chosen and they deem forbidden what they have not wished to do. The fourth kind of monks are those called gyrovagues,[3] who spend their whole lives lodging in different regions and

---

[1] In the Latin of this period, "school" could mean not only a place where instruction was received, but also the group receiving instruction, as well as, more generally, a vocational corporation (such as a guild) of people devoted to a common craft or service. A similar usage can be seen in the English "school of painters" or "school of porpoises."

[2] The tonsure is a haircut, reminiscent of male-pattern baldness, characteristic of monks. Interestingly, Benedict does not mention it elsewhere in the *Rule*.

[3] A combination word from the Greek for "circle" and the Latin for "to wander," reminiscent of the English idiom "to go around in circles."

different monasteries three or four days at a time, always wandering and never stable, serving their own wills and the lure of gluttony worse than sarabaites in every way. It is better to keep silent than to discuss the utterly wretched monastic ways of all these people. Therefore, leaving them aside, with God's help let us proceed to specifications for a very strong kind of monk, the cenobites.

Chapter 2
What Sort of Man the Abbot Should Be

An abbot who is worthy to lead a monastery should always remember what he is called and fulfill the name of "superior" in his deeds. For he is believed to act in the place of Christ in the monastery when he is called by Christ's title, as the apostle says: "You have received the spirit of the adoption of sons, in which we cry out 'Abba, Father.'"[1] Therefore, the abbot must not teach or establish or decree anything that is outside the Lord's commandments, but instead, his decrees and his teaching should sprinkle the yeast of divine justice in the minds of his disciples. The abbot must always be mindful that there will have to be a trial in God's fearsome court concerning two matters: his teaching and his disciples' obedience. And an abbot should know that whatever use the father of the household finds lacking in the sheep will be blamed on the shepherd. It will be equally the case that if all assiduous diligence is applied to a shepherd's unsettled and disobedient flock and every effort to cure its unhealthiness is applied, let their shepherd, acquitted in the Lord's judgment, say to the Lord, with the prophet, "I did not hide your justice in my heart and I spoke your truth and your salvation,[2] yet they scornfully rejected me."[3] And then in the end the punishment for disobedient sheep in his care will be death itself prevailing over them....

Chapter 3
Summoning the Brothers for Counsel

Whenever there is important business to do in the monastery, the abbot should call the whole community together and tell the brothers what it is about, After hearing the brothers' counsel, he should mull things over and do what he judges most beneficial. We said that all should be called to counsel because often the Lord reveals what is best to a junior brother.[4] Thus the brothers should give advice with all humble deference and not presume to defend their views too insistently, and instead let the decision depend on the abbot's judgment so that all may comply with what he has deemed most salutary. But just as it is fitting for disciples to obey their master, so too is it seemly for him to arrange everything justly and prudently.

Everybody therefore, should follow the Rule as a master in all things and nobody should rashly deviate from it. Nobody in the monastery should follow his own heart's will, nor presume to argue with the abbot insolently or outside the monastery.[5] Anyone who so presumes should be subject to the discipline of the Rule.[6] However, the abbot himself should do everything in fear of God and in observance of the Rule, knowing beyond all doubt that he will have to render an account concerning all his decisions to God, the most just judge.

If minor business concerning monastic interests is to be done, let the abbot take only the advice of the senior monks, as it is written: "Do everything with counsel and you will not regret it later."[7]

Chapter 4
The Tools of Good Works

First of all, "to love the Lord God with your whole heart, whole soul, and whole strength," then "your neighbor

---

1. Rom. 8: 15.
2. Ps. 40: 11; Douay Ps. 39: 11.
3. Ezek. 20: 27.
4. Junior could mean "younger" or "lesser in rank."
5. The meaning here is obscure; as it stands, it means that respectful disagreement with the abbot is permitted only within the cloister but never outside. Some manuscripts read "inside or out," which would restrict much more severely the brothers' opportunities to question the abbot's decision.
6. This discipline is described in chapters 23–30. It mainly involved "excommunication," that is, an internal shunning and restriction of privileges in the community.
7. Ecclus. 32: 24.

as yourself."[1] Then "not to kill, commit adultery, steal, covet, or give false testimony; honor all men,"[2] and never do to another what you do not want done to yourself.[3] "Renounce yourself to follow Christ. Punish your body,"[4] do not embrace pleasure, love fasting. Give relief to the poor, clothe the naked, visit the sick, bury the dead. Help those in trouble, comfort those in mourning. Make yourself a stranger to the ways of the world, put nothing above the love of Christ.

Do not give in to anger, or waste time holding a grudge. Keep no deceit in your heart, nor give false peace, nor abandon charity. Do not swear oaths, lest by chance you perjure yourself, speak truth with heart and tongue. "Do not return evil for evil."[5] Do no injury, but even bear patiently those done to you. "Love your enemies."[6] Do not curse in return those who curse you, but bless them instead. "Endure persecution for the sake of justice. Do not be proud, nor overly fond of wine,"[7] nor a glutton, a sluggard, "slothful," a grumbler, or a detractor....

Look: these are the tools of the spiritual craft. When we have used them day and night without ceasing and given them back on the Day of Judgment, we will receive in return the reward God himself promised: "What the eye has not seen nor the ear heard, God has prepared for those who love him."[8] The workshops where we should industriously carry all this out are the cloisters of the monastery and stability in the community....

Chapter 7
Humility

Divine Scripture calls out to us, brothers, saying, "Everyone who exalts himself will be humbled, and he who humbles himself will be exalted."[9] When it says these words, it shows us that all exaltation is a kind of pride, which the prophet shows he guards against, saying, "Lord, my heart is not exalted, nor my eyes lifted up, nor did I move among great affairs or marvels that are beyond me." But what "if I did not understand humbly if I exalted my soul, would you refuse me in my soul like a weaned child on his mother's lap?"[10] So, brothers, if we want to reach the summit of the greatest humility and arrive quickly at that heavenly exaltation toward which we ascend through humility in this present life, as we ascend through our deeds we must raise the ladder that appeared to Jacob in his dream, on which ascending and descending angels were shown to him. We understand without a doubt that this descent and ascent can be nothing other than to descend by exaltation and ascend by humility. That raised ladder is our life in the world, which, in humble hearts, should be hoisted by the Lord to heaven. For we say that the sides of the ladder are our body and soul, in which our divine calling has placed the various rungs of humility and discipline we must climb.

The first step of humility, therefore, is that, placing the fear of God before his eyes at all times, one should altogether shun forgetfulness and always remember everything God commanded so that he always turns over in his mind both how hell burns those who scorn God for their sins and the eternal life prepared for those who fear God. Guarding himself at all times from sins and vices, those of thought, the tongue, the hands, the feet, and of his own will, but also the desires of the flesh, let him consider that he is always observed by God from heaven at all times and that his actions everywhere are seen by the divine gaze and reported by angels at all times....

Chapter 8
Divine Offices at Night

In wintertime, that is, from the first of November until Easter, reason dictates that monks should rise at the eighth hour of the night, so that after resting a little past

---

1   Matt. 22: 37, 39; Mark 12: 30–31; Luke 10: 27.
2   Rom. 13: 9; 1 Pet. 2: 17.
3   Tab. 4: 16.
4   Matt. 16: 24; Luke 9: 23; 1 Cor. 9: 27.
5   1 Thess. 5: 15.
6   Matt. 5: 44; Luke 6: 27.
7   Matt. 5: 10; Titus 1: 7.
8   1 Cor. 2: 9.
9   Luke 18: 14.
10   Ps. 131: 1–2, Douay Ps. 130: 1–2.

midnight, they should rise with digestion complete.[1] The time remaining after Vigils should be for study of the Psalter and readings by brothers who need it. From Easter to the abovementioned first of November, the schedule should be regulated so that, Vigils complete, there is a very brief break during which the brothers may go out for the necessities of nature, then Matins follows immediately, at first light.

Chapter 9
How Many Psalms Should Be Said[2] at the Night Offices

During wintertime as defined above, first this verse is to be said three times: "Lord, you will open my lips, and my mouth will proclaim your praise."[3] To that should be added Psalm 3 and the Gloria.[4] After that, Psalm 94 with an antiphon,[5] or at least chanted. Then an Ambrosian hymn[6] should follow, and then six psalms with antiphons. That done, after the verse is said, the abbot should give a blessing, and with everyone sitting down on benches, three readings should be recited in turn by brothers from the books on the lectern, and three responsories[7] should be chanted in between the readings. Two responsories should be said without the Gloria, but after the third reading, the chanter should say the Gloria. When the chanter begins it, all should rise from their seats at once out of honor and reverence for the Holy Trinity. Books of divine authority should be read at Vigils, from both the Old and New Testaments, and also commentaries on them written by well-known orthodox Catholic Fathers.

After these three readings with their responsories, there should follow the remaining six psalms, sung with an Alleluia. After those, there should follow a reading from the apostle, recited by heart, the verse, and the supplication of the litany that is, the Kyrie Eleison.[8] And Vigils should be concluded in this way....

Chapter 16
How Divine Works Should Be Done During the Day

As the prophet says, "I praised you seven times a day."[9] This sacred number seven will be completed by us if we fulfill the duties of our service at Matins, Prime, Terce, Sext, None, Vespers, and Compline, because he said concerning these daytime hours, "I praised you seven times a day."[10] Concerning nighttime Vigils, the same prophet says, "I rose in the middle of the night to confess your name."[11] Therefore at these times we should praise our creator "for the judgments of his justice,"[12] that is, at Matins, Prime, Terce, Sext, None, Vespers, Compline, and at night we should rise to profess his name....

Chapter 18
The Order in Which Psalms Should Be Said

... We urge this in particular: if this distribution of the psalms happens to displease someone, he should arrange it otherwise if he thinks it better, although in any case he must ensure that the entire Psalter is sung every week, the

---

[1] "Midnight" probably means "in the middle of the night," a time that varies according to the season.

[2] Benedict used verbs meaning "say," "sing," and "chant psalms" somewhat haphazardly, but it is likely that the psalms were sung rather than spoken. Certainly that was soon the case in most monasteries.

[3] Ps. 51: 17; Douay Ps. 50: 17. The "verses" that Benedict refers to are brief excerpts from scripture.

[4] That is, this short hymn of praise or doxology:

   Glory to the Father, the Son, and the Holy Spirit
   As it was in the beginning, is now, and will always be, forever. Amen.

[5] Here, "antiphon" probably means that Psalm 94 was to be sung interspersed with the repetition of a short phrase from scripture.

[6] I.e., a hymn by Saint Ambrose of Milan (d.397).

[7] Short, sung responses from scripture.

[8] Greek for "Lord, have mercy."

[9] Ps. 119: 164; Douay Ps. 118: 164.

[10] Ps. 119: 164; Douay Ps. 118: 164.

[11] Ps. 119: 62; Douay Ps. 118: 62.

[12] Ps. 119: 164; Douay Ps. 118: 164.

full complement of 150 psalms, and it is taken up again from the beginning, at Sunday Vigils. For those monks who sing less than the entire Psalter with the customary canticles in the course of a week show themselves lazy in the service of devotion, since what—as we read—our Holy Fathers energetically completed in a single day we, more lukewarm as we are, ought to manage in an entire week....

Chapter 22
How Monks Should Sleep

Each one should sleep in his own bed. They should get bedding suited to their monastic life according to their abbot's determination.[1] If possible, all monks should sleep in one place; if their number does not allow that, they should rest in tens or twenties with senior monks to take care of them. A candle should burn in that room continually until morning. They should sleep clothed, girded with belts or cords, so they do not have their knives at their sides when they sleep, lest by chance they wound another sleeper when dreaming and so that the monks are always ready and, arising immediately at the signal, may hasten to be the first to do the work of God, yet with all seriousness and modesty. Younger brothers should not have beds next to one another, but be interspersed among seniors. Rising for the work of God, they should gently encourage one another, to counter the excuses of the sleepy....

Chapter 33
Whether Monks Should Have Any Private Property

This vice in particular should be torn out at the roots in the monastery: no one should presume to give or receive anything without the abbot's permission, or have any private property, nothing at all, no book or tablets or stylus, but absolutely nothing, since the brothers my not have either their bodies or their wills under their own

control. They should look to the father of the monastery for everything they need and not be allowed to have anything that the abbot has not given or permitted. "All things should be common to all," as it is written, "lest somebody say something is his,"[2] or presume it is. If anyone is caught indulging in this most wicked vice, let him be warned once, then a second time; if he does not amend, let him undergo correction.

Chapter 34
Whether Everyone Should Accept Necessities in Equal Measure

As it is written, "There was allotment to individuals according to their need."[3] By which I do not say that there should be favoritism,[4] God forbid, but consideration of weaknesses, so that he who needs less should thank God and not be upset, but he who needs more should be humbled by his weakness, not puffed up because of the mercy shown him, and in this way all members will be at peace. Most of all, the evil of grumbling should not show itself for any reason or in any word or sign whatsoever; anyone caught at it should be subjected to very severe discipline....

Chapter 39
The Measure of Food

For the daily meal, whether at the sixth or ninth hour, we believe that two cooked dishes for every table will suffice, taking into account individual weaknesses, so that he who cannot eat one may eat the other. Therefore, two cooked dishes should be enough for all the brothers, and if fruit or fresh vegetables are available, they may be added as a third course. A generous pound of bread should suffice for the day, whether there is one meal or both dinner[5] and supper.[6] If the brothers are to have supper, a third of the pound should be set aside by the cellarer for distribution at supper.

---

[1] The meaning here is uncertain: does the abbot hand out bedding appropriate to the level of communal asceticism, or does he treat each individual differently?

[2] Acts 4: 32.

[3] Acts 4: 35.

[4] See Rom. 2: 11.

[5] That is, the midday meal.

[6] The evening meal.

If the workload happens to be increased, the abbot will have the choice and the power to increase the portion somewhat, if it is expedient, but above all excess is to be avoided so that indigestion never steals up on a monk, because nothing is so inappropriate to every Christian as excess, our Lord says: "See to it that your hearts are not weighed down by overindulgence."[1] Younger boys should not be served the same amount, but less than their elders, frugality being maintained in all things. They should all abstain entirely from the consumption of the meat of quadrupeds, except the gravely ill.

Chapter 40
The Measure of Drink

"Everyone has his own gift from the Lord, one this, another that,"[2] and therefore it is with some uneasiness that we fix the portion of others' sustenance. Nevertheless, contemplating the frailty of the weak, we think that one *hemina*[3] of wine each per day is enough. Those to whom God gives the endurance to abstain should know that they will have their own reward. But if circumstances of the place or work or summer heat demand more, let it be up to the judgment of the superior, who must always take care lest excess or drunkenness creep in. Although we read that wine is not for monks at all, but since in our times monks cannot be persuaded of this, let us at least agree that we should not drink to excess but sparingly "because wine makes even the wise lose their way."[4] If the circumstances of the place are such that not even the aforementioned measure can be obtained, but much less or none at all, those who live there should bless God and not grumble. We caution this, above all: brothers should refrain from grumbling.

Chapter 41
At What Times the Brothers Should Eat

From holy Easter until Pentecost, the brothers should dine at the sixth hour and have supper in the evening.[5] From Pentecost through the summer, if the monks do not have work in the fields and excessive heat does not bother them, they should fast until the ninth hour on Wednesday and Friday. On other days they should dine at the sixth hour, and keep dinner at the sixth hour regularly if they have work in the fields or the summer heat is too great, according to the abbot's decision. The abbot must regulate and arrange everything so that souls are saved and what the brothers do they do without justifiable grumbling.

From the ides of September until the beginning of Lent, they should always eat at the ninth hour. But in Lent until Easter they should eat in the evening; Vespers should be done so that the monks do not need lamplight to eat, but everything should be finished in daylight. Both supper and dinner hours should always be adjusted so that everything may be done in daylight....

Chapter 48
Daily Manual Labor

Idleness is the enemy of the soul. Therefore, the brothers should be occupied at set times in manual labor, and again at other set times in divine reading. Therefore we think that the times for each should be established according to this arrangement, that is: from Easter until the [first] of October, brothers leaving Prime in the morning should work until almost the fourth hour at whatever is necessary; from the fourth hour until almost the sixth they should be free for reading. Rising from the table after Sext, they should rest in their beds in complete silence, and those who want to read to themselves should do so as not to disturb others; and None should be done a little early, at the middle of the eighth hour, and again they should work at whatever is needed until Vespers. They should not be upset if the circumstances of the place or poverty demand they do their own harvesting of produce, because then they are truly monks if they live by the work of their hands, like our Fathers and the apostles. Yet all tasks should be done in moderation out of consideration for the weak.

From the [first] of October until the beginning of Lent, they should be free for reading until the end of the

---

[1] Luke 21: 34.

[2] 1 Cor. 7: 7.

[3] The equivalent modern measure is unknown. Estimates generally range from a pint to a quart.

[4] Ecclus. 19: 2.

[5] That is, the traditional Mediterranean pattern in which the largest meal is in the middle of the day.

second hour; Terce should be done at the second hour, and then all should work at the tasks assigned to them until None. At the first signal for None, each should set aside his work and be ready when the second signal sounds. After the meal, they should be free for their reading or psalms....

Chapter 54
If a Monk Should Receive Letters or Anything Else

In no way should it be allowed for a monk to receive letters, gifts, or keepsakes, not from his relatives, any other person, or another monk, nor should he give them, without the abbot's permission. But if something has been sent to him by his relatives, he should not presume to receive it unless the abbot is informed beforehand. But if the abbot orders it to be received, it should be in his power to command to whom it should be given and the brother to whom it happened to have been sent should not be upset, lest "the Devil be given an opportunity."[1] Let anyone who presumes to do otherwise be subject to the discipline of the Rule.

Chapter 55
The Brothers' Clothing and Shoes

Clothing should be given to the brothers according to the nature and the climate of the place where they live, since more is required in colder regions, less in warmer ones. This consideration is the abbot's concern. However, we believe that in milder places, a cowl and a tunic for each monk will suffice—a woolen cowl in winter, a light or worn one in the summer—a scapular for work[2] and footwear: leggings and boots. Monks should not object to the color or coarseness of any of these items, but have what is available in the region where they live and can be purchased cheaply....

Chapter 58
The Discipline of Receiving Brothers

Easy entry to the religious life should not be granted to a newcomer, but as the apostle says, "Test the spirits to see if they are from God."[3] Therefore, if one comes knocking, perseveres, and, after four or five days, seems to suffer patiently ill-treatment directed at him and the difficulty of entry and persists in his request, let entry be granted him and let him stay in the guest quarters for a few days. After that, he should be in the novices' quarters, where they study, eat, and sleep. A senior monk should be assigned to them, someone suited to win souls, in order to watch over them very carefully.

The concern should be whether he truly seeks God, if he is attentive to the work of God, to obedience, and to reprimands. All the difficult and harsh things involved in the approach to God should be made clear to him. If he promises perseverance in his stability, after two months this Rule should be read to him straight through and let this be said to him: "This is the law under which you want to serve. If you can observe it, enter, but if you cannot, you are free to go." If he still stays, he should then be led into the abovementioned novices' quarters and have his patience thoroughly tested again. After six months, the Rule should be read to him so he knows what he is getting into. And if he still stays, after four months the same Rule should be read to him again. And if, after deliberating within himself, he promises to take care in all things and carry out every task given him, then let him be received into the community, knowing that it is stated in the law of the Rule that from that day forward it is not permitted to him to leave the monastery, nor shake his neck from the yoke of the Rule that he was free to reject or accept after such exacting deliberation.

Moreover, the one to be received should give assurances in the oratory, before everyone, concerning his stability, religious life and ways, and obedience. Before God and his saints, let him know that if ever he does otherwise, he will be damned by the one he mocks. He should make a petition concerning this promise of his in the name of the saints whose relics[4] are there and of the abbot who is present....

---

[1] 1 Tim. 5: 14.

[2] It is not clear exactly what this garment was. A plausible explanation is that it was an overshirt, smock, or apron-like garment meant to keep other clothes from getting dirty or torn during manual labor.

[3] 1 John 4: 1.

[4] Bones or other remnants of a saint.

If he has any property, he should either distribute it to the poor beforehand or, having made a solemn donation, give it to the monastery, keeping none of it whatsoever for himself, since indeed he knows that from that day forward, he will not even have control over his own body. Right there in the oratory, let him be stripped of the clothes in which he is dressed and put on the monastery's clothes. Let the clothing he removed be put in the wardrobe for safekeeping, so that if ever he gives in to the Devil's urging that he should leave the monastery, God forbid, then let him be thrown out, stripped of the monastery's clothes. However, he should not get back the petition that the abbot took from the altar, which should be kept in the monastery.

Chapter 59
Sons of Nobles and the Poor Who Are Offered

If it happens that a nobleman offers his son to the monastery, if the boy is young, his relatives should make the petition we discussed above, and they should tie together the petition and the boy's hand in an altar cloth, with the oblation,[1] and offer him that way. Concerning his property, they should either promise under oath in this same petition that they will never give him anything themselves, nor through a third party nor by any means, nor offer him the opportunity to own anything. Of course, if they do not want to do that and desire to offer something to the monastery for their own reward, let them make a donation to the monastery of the property they wish to give, keeping usufruct[2] themselves if they so desire. In this way everything is closed off, so that the boy cannot harbor any hope by which, God forbid, he could be deceived and ruined, which we have learned through experience.

Let poorer people do likewise. Those who have no property at all should simply draw up the petition and offer their son before witnesses, with the oblation....

Chapter 73
Not Every Practice of Justice Is Set Out in This Rule

We have sketched this Rule so that those of us practicing it in monasteries may show that we have some honor in our ways and the rudiments of monastic life. But for one who hastens toward perfection in monastic life, there are the teachings of the Holy Fathers, observance of which should direct a man to the peak of perfection. For which page, which word of the divine authority of the Old and New Testament is not the most righteous guide for human life? And which book by the Holy Catholic Fathers does not resound with how we may arrive at our creator by a straight path? As for the *Conferences*, *Institutes*, and *Lives of the Fathers*, as well as the Rule of our holy father Basil,[3] what else are they but tools of virtue for good and obedient monks? For us, lazy, wicked, and neglectful, they cause a blush of shame.

Therefore, whoever you are, hastening toward your heavenly home, with Christ's help carry out this little Rule sketched as a beginning, and then at last you will reach those greater heights of learning and virtues we mentioned above, with God's protection. Amen.

---

[1] Apparently this means at the offering of the bread and wine during the Mass, an oblique indication of the circumstances of profession. Here as elsewhere, Benedict assumes his readers know a great deal already.

[2] Meaning that the gift is in trust; the donors receive any profit or return during their lifetimes, and then the property is transferred to the monastery.

[3] The *Conferences* and *Institutes* refer to the works of John Cassian (d.c.435), who spent the first part of his life as a monk in Bethlehem, Egypt, and Constantinople. Later he founded two monasteries, one for men and the other for women, at Marseille. The *Lives of the Fathers* is probably a reference to Athanasius, *Life of St. Antony* (see below, p. 27), along with other monastic biographies. The Rule of Basil was a collection of precepts written by Basil (d.379) in Greek for Byzantine monks, but it was available to Western monks through a Latin translation made by Rufinus of Aquileia in 397.

SAINTLY MODELS

1.8 The virginal life: Jerome, *Letter* 24 *(To Marcella)* (384). Original in Latin.

St. Jerome (*c.*347–419/420) was born in the Roman province of Dalmatia, near present-day Ljubljana. As a youth he went to Rome to study rhetoric and philosophy, and there, increasingly ashamed of his reckless student ways, he converted to Christianity. He subsequently lived in Trier, Aquileia, Antioch, and again in Rome; he spent the last decades of his life in a hermit's cell near Bethlehem. His most famous work is his translation of the entire Bible into Latin: the Old Testament from the original Hebrew and the New Testament from the original Greek. This so-called Vulgate Bible, completed around 405, was the standard in the Christian West for the next millennium. Jerome also wrote biblical commentaries, history, theological tracts, and more than a hundred letters. *Letter* 24 dates to his second period in Rome, during which time he was surrounded by a circle of elite women, including Marcella, a well-educated and wealthy widow who had already begun a life of Christian asceticism before Jerome arrived. The letter describes the way of life of the virgin Asella, Marcella's sister (although Jerome never says so explicitly). As a girl, Asella exchanged a gold necklace for a humble dark garment. She lived in a tiny cell and devoted herself to prayer and self-denial amidst the hustle and bustle of Rome, probably on a patch of family property. Jerome offers no specific rationale for why virginity is the ideal state for a Christian woman. What can you gather on this subject from the contents of the letter?

[Source: *Sancti Eusebii Hieronymi Epistulae pars 1: Epistulae I-LXX*, 2nd ed., ed. Isidorus Hilberg, Corpus Scriptorum Ecclesiasticorum Latinorum 54 (Vienna: Verlag der Österreichischen Akademie der Wissenschaften, 1996), pp. 214–17. Translated and introduced by Bruce L. Venarde.]

To Marcella, concerning the life of Asella.

1. Nobody should find fault that I praise or carp at certain people in my letters, since in exposing the wicked there is a reproach to others and zeal for virtue is spurred by preaching the best deeds of good people. The day before yesterday we had spoken concerning a certain Lea of blessed memory; immediately it pricked my conscience and came to mind that it is not fitting for me, having spoken of the second order of chastity,[1] to keep silent concerning a virgin. Therefore I must briefly sketch the life of our Asella, to whom I ask you not read this letter, since she finds praise of herself burdensome. I ask instead that you deem it worthy to read to young women who, instructing themselves by her example, may think that her way of life is the standard of perfection.

2. I pass over the fact that before she was born, she was blessed in her mother's womb. She was presented to her father, in his sleep, as a virgin in a bowl of gleaming glass more pure than any mirror; still wrapped in infants' clothing, scarcely ten years old, she was consecrated with the honor of future blessedness.[2] May everything that was before her work be attributed to grace,[3] although God, knowing the future in advance, blessed Jeremiah in the womb and made

---

[1] I.e., Lea, however holy, was a chaste widow, not a virgin, and thus she belonged to the "second order" of chastity. She was a wealthy Roman widow who gave up her privileges for a life of asceticism and prayer, directing a community of Christian virgins.

[2] This means that she vowed herself virginity at age ten. The reference to swaddling clothes, the material in which Mary wrapped the infant Jesus, is poetic license that stresses Asella's innocence.

[3] That is, before her "adult" work starting at age twelve, mentioned at the end of the paragraph.

John [the Baptist] leap in his mother's womb and before the creation of the world set [Saint] Paul apart to preach his son [Christ] [see Jer 1: 5, Luke 1: 41, and Eph 1: 5]. I now come to the things that she, by the sweat of her brow, chose, took up, held onto, began, and completed after her twelfth year.

3. Shut up in one narrow cell, she enjoyed the expanse of paradise. Likewise, the soil of the earth was her place of prayer and peace. Fasting was her pleasure and hunger her refreshment. When the human condition, rather than the desire to eat, drew her to food she stirred up hunger more than she suppressed it on a diet of bread, salt, and cold water. And since I nearly forgot what I should have said in the beginning, when she first took up her plan for living, she sold a gold necklace that is commonly called a *murenula* (because, the metal being made supple in little bars, a flexible sort of chain is woven together)[1] without her parents' knowledge. She put on a dark garment that she was unable to obtain from her mother; dressed in a pious portent of her undertaking, she quickly vowed herself to the Lord, so that all her kind would know that they would not be able to force anything out of one who had already condemned the world by means of her clothing.[2]

4. But, as I began to say, she always behaved with such restraint and guarded herself in the retreat of her room to the point that she never set foot in public, nor conversed with men. What is even more astonishing, she loved her virgin sister rather than seeing her.[3] She worked with her hands, knowing what is written: he who does not work does not eat [see 2 Thess. 3: 10]. In prayer and psalm-singing she spoke to her bridegroom. She hastened nearly unseen to martyrs' shrines, and although she took joy in her plan, she was all the more greatly pleased that nobody recognized her. Not only fasting all year, eating every two or three days, in Lent she stretched out her sails to the fullest, nearly joining week to week in abstinence with a cheerful face. And because what is perhaps impossible for men to believe is possible with God's help, living this way she reached her fiftieth year, without stomach pain and free from bowel torments. The dry ground on which she lay did not harm her body, nor was her skin, roughened by sackcloth, subject to stench or abrasion. Sound in body and sounder still in mind, she thought her solitude a delight and found a monk's retreat in a busy city.

5. I have learned these few things from you, who know them better. Your eyes have also seen the hardness of camels' knees—the result of frequent prayer—on her holy little body. I offer what I can know. Nothing is more delightful than her seriousness or more serious than her delightfulness; nothing is sadder than her laugh or sweeter than her sadness. The paleness of her face, although it demonstrates continence, does not smack of ostentation. Her speech is silent and her silence speaks; her walk is neither fast nor slow; her bearing likewise. She gives no thought to neatness and her unstylish clothing is style without style. She has earned, by the quality of her life alone, that in a city of ostentation, lewdness, and pleasures, in which it is a misery to be humble, the good acclaim her and the wicked do not dare to disparage her. Let widows and virgins imitate her, married women cherish her, evil women fear her, and priests admire her.

1.9 The eremetical life: Athanasius, *Life of St. Antony of Egypt* (357). Original in Greek.

Athanasius, bishop of Alexandria (d.373), a ferocious upholder of the Nicene—and therefore anti-Arian—view of the Trinity, saw Saint Antony (or Anthony, d.*c.*356) as the living embodiment of his notion of salvation through Christ. His *Life of St. Antony*, which was translated into Latin in the later fourth century, was the first of what would become an enormously popular genre in the Middle Ages: the saint's biography, or hagiography. The

---

[1] *Murenula* is a diminutive for *murena*, the moray eel. The necklace, made of many tiny pieces of metal joined together, has the supple character of an eel in motion.

[2] It is a commonplace in writing about holy people that families resisted the desires of individuals to "leave the world." Asella's mother did not, it seems, want to offer her virgin daughter something that was, in the Roman world, a mourning costume.

[3] This is almost certainly a reference to Marcella, the addressee of this letter, who would have stayed in the family home before her marriage. Although Asella did sometimes leave her cell, as noted below, apparently her only destinations were Christian shrines.

virtues that Athanasius ascribed to Antony—seriousness of vocation even in childhood; resistance to all the temptations of the Devil; application to prayer, vigils, and fasts—were copied in nearly every subsequent saint's Life. This was not mechanical imitation, for Antony's Life was meant to be not just the story of one person but also the model for all Christians. At the same time, Antony's vocation as a solitary—a monk—became the ideal that even many Christians active in the hurly-burly of worldly life admired and strove to imitate. In what ways might the *Life of St. Antony* have influenced Augustine's ideas in the *City of God*, above, p. 14?

[Source: Athanasius of Alexandria, *Life of St. Antony of Egypt*, trans. David Brakke, in *Medieval Hagiography: An Anthology*, ed. Thomas Head (New York: Garland, 2000), pp. 7–14 (notes modified).]

LETTER OF ATHANASIUS, ARCHBISHOP OF ALEXANDRIA, TO THE MONKS IN FOREIGN PLACES CONCERNING THE LIFE OF THE BLESSED ANTONY THE GREAT
(Preface.) It is a good competition that you have begun with the monks in Egypt by seeking either to equal or surpass them in your discipline in virtue.[1] For at last there are monasteries among you as well, and the reputation of the [Egyptian] monks is the basis of their organization: therefore, this plan [of yours] deserves praise; may God bring it to completion through your prayers.

Inasmuch as you have asked me about the blessed Antony's way of life and want to learn about how he began the discipline, who he was before this, what the end of his life was like, and if the things that have been said about him are true, so that you might guide yourselves by imitation of him, I have received your charge with great enthusiasm. Indeed, for me as well it is of great profit just to remember Antony, and I know that once you have heard about him, in addition to admiring the man, you too will want to imitate his determination, since monks have in Antony's lifestyle a sufficient pattern for their discipline.

Therefore, do not disbelieve what you have heard from those who have brought reports of him; rather, think that you have heard only a little from them, for even they scarcely can have completely related such great matters. And since I too, urged by you, am telling you what I can by letter, I am sending only a few of the things that I have remembered about him. You for your part should not stop questioning those persons who sail from here, for it is likely that after each person tells what he knows, the account concerning him will still hardly do him justice. Therefore, when I received your letter, I decided to send for certain monks, particularly those who had spent the most time with him, in the hope that I could learn more and send you the fullest possible account. But since the sailing season was coming to an end and the letter carrier was ready to go, I hurried to write to your piety what I know—for I saw him often—and what I was able to learn from the man who followed Antony no short period of time and who poured water on his hand.[2] I have in every place kept my mind on the truth, so that no one, having heard too much, would disbelieve it, or, having learned less than necessary, would look down on the man.

(1.) Antony was an Egyptian by birth, and his parents were well-born and possessed considerable wealth. Since they were Christians, he was raised in a Christian manner. As a child, he lived with his parents and was familiar with nothing other than them and their house. When he grew to become a boy and became older, he did not put up with learning letters because he wanted to be removed even from the companionship of children. It was his complete desire, as it is written, to live in his house as an unformed person.[3] He would go to church with his parents. As a boy, he was not lazy, nor did he become rude as he got older. Rather, he was

---

[1] Athanasius presents his biography in the form of a letter to monks in places outside Egypt, most likely in areas of the western Mediterranean, such as North Africa and southern Europe. Many of the sentences in this opening section appear complicated and obscure to us because we do not know the exact situation in which Athanasius writes and because such a style is typical of prefaces to ancient works, in which the writer hopes to impress his readers with his rhetorical skill.

[2] See 2 Kings 3: 11.

[3] See Gen. 25: 27.

obedient to his parents, and by paying attention to the readings,[1] he preserved in himself what was beneficial in them. Although as a boy he lived in moderate wealth, he did not trouble his parents for diverse and expensive foods, nor did he seek such pleasures. He was happy merely with whatever he found and asked for nothing more.

(2.) After the death of his parents, he was left alone with one small sister; he was about eighteen or twenty, and it was his responsibility to care for the house and his sister. Not six months after his parents' death, he was going to church as usual, and he was thinking to himself and considering all this: how the apostles abandoned everything and followed the Savior;[2] how the people in Acts [of the Apostles] sold their possessions and brought the proceeds and laid them at the feet of the apostles for distribution to the needy;[3] and how such a great hope was stored up for these people in heaven.[4] Considering these things, he entered the church, and it happened that just then the Gospel was being read, and he heard the Lord saying to the rich man, "If you wish to be perfect, go, sell all your possessions, and give the proceeds to the poor, and come, follow me, and you will have treasure in heaven."[5] And Antony, as if the remembrance of the saints had been placed in him by God and as if the readings had been made on his account, left the church immediately and gave to the villagers the possessions he had received from his ancestors—three hundred *arourae* of fertile and very beautiful land—so that they would no longer trouble him and his sister.[6] He sold all their other movable possessions, collecting a sizable sum of money, and gave it to the poor, although he kept a little for his sister's sake.

(3.) But when he again entered the church and heard in the Gospel the Lord saying, "Do not worry about tomorrow,"[7] he could not stay: he went out and gave even that [little money remaining] to the common people. When he had delivered his sister to known and faithful virgins in order to be brought up for virginity, he at last devoted himself to the discipline outside the house, attending to himself and guiding himself with patience. For there were not yet so many monasteries in Egypt, and no monk knew the great desert; rather, each of those who wanted to attend to himself practiced the discipline alone, not far from his own village. Now, at this time there was an old man in the neighboring village who had practiced the solitary life from his youth: when Antony saw him, he imitated him in virtue.[8] At first he too began by remaining in the places around the village; then if he heard of some zealous one somewhere, like the wise bee, he went and sought that person, and he did not return to his own place until he had seen the man and had received from him, so to speak, travel supplies for the road to virtue.

And so, spending time there at first, he strengthened his intention never to return to the things of his parents nor to remember his relatives, but he directed all his desire and all his zeal toward the effort required by the discipline. Therefore, he worked with his hands, since he had heard, "Let not the idle one eat,"[9] and he spent some of the money on bread and some for the needy. He prayed continuously since he knew that it is necessary to pray in secret without ceasing.[10] For indeed he so devoted himself to the reading that nothing of what is written fell from him to the ground,[11] but he retained everything, so that his memory replaced books for him.

(4.) Conducting himself in this way, then, Antony was loved by everyone. He sincerely submitted to the zealous ones whom he visited, and he learned thoroughly the advantage in zeal and discipline that each one possessed in comparison to himself. He contemplated the graciousness of one and the devotion to prayers of another; he

---

[1] See 1 Tim. 4: 13.

[2] See Matt. 4: 20; 19: 27.

[3] See Acts 4: 35–37.

[4] See Col. 1: 5.

[5] Matt. 19: 21.

[6] Three hundred *arourae* may have been around two hundred acres; thus, Antony is portrayed as very wealthy by the standards of third-century Egypt.

[7] Matt. 6: 34.

[8] See Gal. 4: 18.

[9] See 2 Thess. 3: 10.

[10] See Matt. 6: 6; 1 Thess. 5: 17.

[11] See 1 Sam. 3: 19.

observed one's lack of anger and another's love of people; he attended to the one who kept vigils and the other who loved to study; he admired one for his perseverance and another for his fasting and sleeping on the ground; he watched closely the gentle nature of one and the patience of another; but in all he noticed piety toward Christ and love for one another. And when he had been filled in this way, he returned to his own place of discipline, and then he gathered into himself the virtues of each and strove to display them all in himself. Indeed, he was not contentious with those of his own age, except only that he should not appear to be second to them in the better things. And he did this in such a way that he did not hurt anyone's feelings; rather, they rejoiced in him. And so when the people of the village and the lovers of virtue with whom he associated saw that he was this kind of person, they all called him "Beloved of God"; some welcomed him as a son, others as a brother.

(5.) But the devil, who hates and envies the good, could not bear to see such resolution in a young man, but set out to do against Antony the kinds of things he usually does. First he tried to dissuade him from the discipline by suggesting the memory of possessions, the care of his sister, the intimacy of family, love of money, love of glory, the varied pleasure of food, and the other indulgences of life—and finally the difficulty of virtue and the great effort that it requires. He introduced the weakness of the body and the long duration of time. In short, he raised up a dust cloud of thoughts in Antony's mind, desiring thereby to separate him from his upright intention.

But the enemy saw that he himself was weak in the face of Antony's resolve and saw instead that he was defeated by the other's stubbornness, overthrown by his faith, and falling due to Antony's constant prayers. Then he took confidence in the weapons of the belly's navel[1] and, boasting in these—for they are his primary means of trapping the young—he advanced against the youth, troubling him at night and harassing him by day so that those who watched could sense the struggle that was going on between the two. The one would suggest dirty thoughts, and the other would turn them back with prayers; the one would titillate, and the other, as if seeming to blush, would fortify his body with faith and fasts.

And the miserable devil dared at night to dress up like a woman and imitate one in every way merely to deceive Antony. But Antony, by thinking about Christ and the excellence one ought to possess because of him, and by considering the soul's rational faculty, extinguished the ember of the other's deception.

Once again the enemy suggested the ease of pleasure. But Antony, like someone fittingly angry or grieved, thought about the threat of fire and the torment of the worm, and by setting these thoughts against [those of the enemy], he passed through these things unharmed. All this was a source of shame for the enemy, for he who had considered himself to be like God[2] was now being mocked by a youth, and he who boasted over flesh and blood was being overthrown by a human being who wore flesh. For working with Antony was the Lord, the one who for our sake took flesh and gave to the body the victory over the devil, so that each of those who truly struggle says, "Not I, but the grace of God that is with me."[3]

(6.) At last, when the dragon could not defeat Antony in this way but instead saw himself thrust out of his heart, he gnashed his teeth, as it is written.[4] As if he were beside himself, he finally appeared to Antony in his form just as he is in his mind, as a black boy. And as though he had fallen down, he no longer attacked Antony with thoughts—for the crafty one had been tossed down—but finally he used a human voice and said, "Many people I have deceived, and most I have defeated, but now coming against you and your efforts as I have against others, I have been weakened." Antony asked, "Who are you who say such things to me?" Immediately he answered with a pitiful voice, "It is I who am fornication's lover. It is I who have been entrusted with its ambushes and its titillations against the youth, and I am called the spirit of fornication. How many persons who desired to be prudent I have deceived! How many persons who professed to be so I have persuaded to change by titillating them! It is I on whose account even the prophet blames those who have fallen, saying, "You have been deceived by the spirit of fornication."[5] For it was through me that they were tripped up. It is I who so often troubled you and who as often was overthrown by you." But Antony gave thanks

---

[1] See Job 40: 16.

[2] See Isa. 14: 14; Ezek. 28: 2.

[3] 1 Cor. 15: 10.

[4] See Ps. 35: 16; 37: 12; 112: 10; Douay Ps. 34: 16; 36: 12; 111: 10.

[5] Hos. 4: 12.

to the Lord and took courage in him, and he said to him, "You are very despicable then, for you are black in your mind and as weak as a boy. From now on I will have no anxiety about you, 'for the Lord is my helper, and I will look down on my enemies.'"[1] When he heard this, the black one immediately fled, cowering before these words and afraid even to approach the man.[2]

(7.) This was Antony's first struggle against the devil, or rather this was the achievement in Antony of the Savior, "who condemned sin in the flesh so that the righteousness of the Law might be fulfilled in us, who walk not according to the flesh, but according to the spirit."[3] But Antony did not, because the demon had fallen, now become negligent and take no thought of himself, nor did the enemy, because he had been defeated, stop lying in ambush. For the enemy went around again like a lion, looking for some opportunity against him.[4] But Antony, since he had learned from the Scriptures that the wiles of the enemy are numerous,[5] practiced the discipline intensely, figuring that, even if the enemy had been unable to deceive his heart through bodily pleasure, he would attempt to trap him by another method. For the demon is a lover of sin.

Therefore, Antony more and more punished his body and enslaved it,[6] so that, even though he had triumphed in some ways, he would not be overcome in others; he resolved, then, to accustom himself to more severe training measures. Many people were amazed, but he himself endured the labor with ease, for his soul's intention, which had lasted for a long time, created in him a good habit so that, when he received even slight encouragement from others, he would show great enthusiasm for the task. He would keep vigil to such an extent that often he spent the entire night without sleep, and when he did this not once but many times, people were amazed. He ate once a day after sunset, but there were times when he went two days and often four days without eating. His food was bread and salt; his drink, only water. Indeed, it is superfluous even to speak about meat and wine, for nothing of the sort was ever found among the other zealous ones. For sleeping he was content with a rush mat, but mostly he lay upon the bare ground. He would not anoint himself with oil, saying that young men ought to pursue the discipline with zeal and should not seek what would pamper the body, rather that they should accustom the body to labors and consider the Apostle's statement, "Whenever I am weak, then I am strong."[7] For at that time he used to say that the soul's intellect grows strong when the body's pleasures are made weak.

He had this truly wonderful thought: that one should not measure progress in virtue or withdrawal made for this purpose by the length of time, but by the desire and intention. Therefore, he himself did not keep track of the time that had gone by; rather, every day, as if he were just starting the discipline, he would make his effort toward advancement greater, constantly saying to himself Paul's statement, "forgetting what lies behind and straining forward to what lies ahead,"[8] and remembering also the voice of the prophet Elijah, saying, "The Lord lives, before whom I stand today."[9] He observed that in saying "today" he was not measuring the time that had gone by, but, as if he were always making a new start, he was zealous every day to show himself to God to be such that one should appear to God: pure in heart and ready to obey his will and nothing else. He would say to himself, "The ascetic ought always to observe his own life in the conduct of the great Elijah as if in a mirror."

(8.) Having constrained himself in this way, Antony departed to the tombs, which happened to lie far outside the village. He commanded one of his acquaintances

---

[1] Ps. 118: 7; Douay 117: 7.

[2] The symbolism of this scene is on two levels. First, the appearance of the devil as a boy reflects the homoerotic interest in male adolescents pervasive in the ancient world and condemned by Christian leaders such as Athanasius. Second, the devil's black skin illustrates the prejudice based on skin color present in late antique Egypt, which was a multiethnic society. Most Alexandrians such as Athanasius were descendants of the Greeks who founded the city in the fourth century BCE and so were of lighter skin color than those of more sub-Saharan African descent.

[3] Rom. 8: 3–4.

[4] See 1 Pet. 5: 8.

[5] See Eph. 6: 11.

[6] See 1 Cor. 9: 27.

[7] 2 Cor. 12: 10.

[8] Phil. 3: 13.

[9] See 1 Kings 17: 1; 18: 15.

to bring him bread every several days, and he himself entered one of the tombs; when the other had shut the door, he remained inside by himself. Then, when the enemy could not bear this but was afraid that in a short time Antony would fill the desert with the discipline, he came one night with a crowd of demons and so cut Antony with wounds that he lay on the ground speechless from the tortures. For he used to maintain that the pains were so severe that he would say that blows inflicted by human beings could not have inflicted such torture. But by God's Providence—for the Lord does not neglect those who hope in him—his acquaintance came the next day to bring him the bread. When he opened the door and saw Antony lying on the ground as if dead, he lifted him up, carried him to the village church, and laid him on the ground. Many of his relatives and the villagers sat around Antony as if beside a corpse. But around midnight Antony came to himself and got up; when he saw everyone asleep and only his acquaintance keeping watch, he motioned with his head for him to approach and then asked him to pick him up again and carry him to the tombs without waking anybody.

(9.) And so he was carried back by the man, and as usual, the door was shut, and he was once again inside by himself. He was unable to stand because of the blows from the demons, and so he prayed lying down.[1] After the prayer, he said with a loud voice, "Here I am: Antony! I do not flee from your blows. For even if you do more, nothing shall separate me from the love of Christ."[2] Then he sang, "Though an army encamp against me, my heart shall not fear."[3] This is what the ascetic thought and said.

But the enemy, who hates the good, was amazed that he dared to return after such blows. He called together his dogs and burst out, "See that we have not stopped this one with the spirit of fornication or with blows; rather, he bravely comes against us. Let us attack him in some other way." It is easy for the devil to change forms for his evil purposes, and so at night they raised such a tumult that it seemed as though that entire place was being shaken by an earthquake. The demons, as if they had shattered the four walls of the dwelling, seemed to enter through them, transformed into the appearance of beasts and serpents. And the place was immediately filled with the appearances of lions, bears, leopards, bulls, snakes, asps, scorpions, and wolves, and each of them was moving according to his own form. The lion was roaring, wishing to attack; the bull seemed to butt with his horns; the serpent writhed but did not approach; and the wolf rushed forward but was restrained. Altogether the ragings of their apparitions and the sounds of their voices were completely terrifying. Antony, whipped and tortured by them, felt even more severe bodily pain; but his soul was not trembling, and he remained vigilant. He groaned because of his body's pain, but he was sober in his thinking, and as if to mock them, he said, "If you had had the power, it would have been enough for one of you to come alone. But since the Lord has made you weak, you are trying to frighten me by your number. But it is a proof of your weakness that you imitate the shapes of irrational beings." And again he took courage and said, "If you are able and have received authority against me, don't delay, but attack! But if you cannot, why are you harassing me in vain? For faith in our Lord is our seal and wall for safety." And so after many attempts, they gnashed their teeth against him because they were making fools of themselves rather than of him.

(10.) Meanwhile the Lord had not forgotten Antony's struggle, but came to him in assistance. Thus, Antony looked up and saw the roof as if it were being opened[4] and a certain ray of light coming down to him. The demons suddenly vanished; his body's pain immediately stopped; and the building was once again intact. When Antony perceived the assistance, got his breath back, and was relieved of his pains, he asked the vision that appeared to him, "Where were you? Why didn't you appear at the beginning and make my pains stop?" And a voice came to him, "Antony, I was here, but I waited to see your struggle. Because you endured and were not beaten, I will always be your help, and I will make you famous everywhere." When he heard this, he got up and prayed, and he became so strong that he felt that he had more strength in his body than he had had before. At this time he was around thirty-five years old.

(11.) The next day Antony went out even more enthusiastic about the piety, and when he came to that old man [whom he had imitated earlier], he asked him to live with him in the desert. But when this man declined due to his

---

[1] It was contemporary custom to pray standing with one's arms extended.

[2] See Rom. 8: 35–39.

[3] Ps. 26: 3; Douay Ps. 25: 3.

[4] See Acts 7: 55–56.

age and because there was not yet such a custom, immediately he himself set out for the mountain. Yet again the enemy, when he saw his zeal and wanted to impede it, cast in his way an apparition of a large silver disk. But Antony recognized the trick performed by the hater of good; he stood and said to the disk, because he saw the devil in it: "How did a disk end up in the desert? This path is not well-trod, nor is there any trace of people having traveled through here. If it had fallen, it would have been missed thanks to its size; rather, the one who lost it would have turned back, searched, and found it since the place is a desert. This is the devil's work. You will not impede my intention in this way, devil! Indeed, let this go with you into destruction."[1] When Antony had said this, it vanished like smoke from before a fire.[2]

(12.) Next, as he went along, he again saw this time not an apparition, but real gold scattered in the path. He himself has not said nor do we know whether it was the enemy who showed this to him or whether it was some better power who was training the athlete and showing the devil that he truly did not care about money at all, but what appeared really was gold. Antony marveled at the amount, but as if stepping over fire, he passed by it so as not to turn back; rather, he ran so fast that the place became hidden and forgotten.

Having intensified his resolve more and more, he hurried to the mountain. On the other side of the river he found a deserted fort, abandoned for so long that it was full of serpents; he situated himself there and lived in it. The reptiles, as if someone were chasing them, immediately withdrew, but he barricaded the door, and since he had stored up enough bread for six months—the people of the Thebaid[3] do this, and their bread often stays fresh for a year—and since he had a water supply inside, he descended as if into a shrine, and he remained alone inside the monastic retreat, neither going out himself nor seeing anyone who came. And so in this way he devoted himself to the discipline for a long time, receiving only bread let down from above the house twice each year.

(13.) Those of his acquaintances who came, since he would not allow them to enter, often used to spend days and nights outside, and they would hear what sounded like crowds making a commotion, clamoring, raising up

pitiful voices and crying out, "Leave our places! What have you to do with the desert? You cannot endure our attack!" At first those outside thought that there were certain people fighting with him and that these people had gone in to him by ladders. But when they stooped and peeped through a hole and saw no one, then they reckoned that they were demons; they became frightened and called for Antony. He heard them, although he did not give a thought to the demons: coming near to the door, he exhorted the people to withdraw and not to be afraid, for he said, "In this way the demons create apparitions against the cowards. Therefore, seal yourselves [with the sign of the cross] and depart with courage, and let these [demons] make fools of themselves." And so they went away fortified with the sign of the cross, but he stayed behind and was in no way harmed by the demons, nor did he grow weary of fighting them. Indeed, the assistance of the visions that came to his intellect and the weakness of the enemies gave him much rest from his labors and made his intention even greater. For his acquaintances would always come, expecting to find him dead, but instead would hear him singing, "Let God rise up, and let his enemies be scattered; and let those who hate him flee before him. As smoke disappears, let them disappear; as wax melts before fire, let the wicked perish before God."[4] And again: "All nations surrounded me; in the name of the Lord I repelled them."[5]

(14.) For nearly twenty years he continued to discipline himself in this way, not going out himself and being seen by others only rarely. After this, when many eagerly desired to imitate his discipline, and others of his acquaintances came and were pulling down and wrenching out the door by force, Antony emerged, as if from some shrine, initiated into the mysteries and filled with God. Now for the first time he appeared outside the fort to those who had come to him. And they, when they saw him, were amazed to see that his body had its same condition: it was neither fat as if from lack of exercise nor withered as if from fasting and fighting demons, but it was such as they had known it before his withdrawal. The disposition of his soul was pure again, for it was neither contracted from distress, nor dissipated from pleasure, nor constrained by levity or dejection. Indeed, when he

---

[1] See Acts 8: 20.

[2] See Ps. 68: 2; Douay Ps. 67: 2.

[3] The Egyptian province to which Antony had retreated.

[4] Ps. 68: 1–2; Douay Ps. 67: 1–2.

[5] Ps. 118: 10; Douay Ps. 117: 10.

saw the crowd, he was not disturbed, nor did he rejoice to be greeted by so many people. Rather, he was wholly balanced, as if he were being navigated by the Word and existing in his natural state.

Therefore, through Antony the Lord healed many of the suffering bodies of those present, and others he cleansed of demons. He gave Antony grace in speaking, and thus he comforted many who were grieved and reconciled into friendship others who were quarreling,

exhorting everyone to prefer nothing in the world to the love for Christ. While he discussed and recalled the good things to come and the love for humanity that has come to us from God, "who did not withhold his own son, but gave him up for all of us."[1] he persuaded many to choose the solitary life. And so at last there came to be monasteries even in the mountains, and the desert was made a city of monks, who left their homes and enrolled in the heavenly commonwealth.[2]

1.10 The active life: Sulpicius Severus, *The Life of St. Martin of Tours* (397). Original in Latin.

Sulpicius Severus (*c.360–c.420*), a well-to-do and well-educated man of Aquitaine (southern Gaul), became a monk later in life. He met St. Martin (d.397) in 393 or 394 and, impressed by the holy man, wrote his *Life* shortly afterwards. It was a great success: St. Martin soon became the subject of a number of supplementary accounts—letters concerning his death; descriptions of his miracles—and was adopted as the patron saint of the Merovingian kings. Unlike St. Antony, Martin was a bishop, and thus Sulpicius needed to find a way to combine the model of the ascetic monk with that of the active life of a man in the world. Compare the virtues and lifestyles of Antony and Martin. What message did Martin's *Life* have for warriors? What ideals of behavior did it offer to bishops?

[Source: *Medieval Saints: A Reader*, ed. Mary-Ann Stouck (Toronto: University of Toronto Press, 1999), pp. 139–42, 144–49 (slightly modified).]

Martin, then, was born at Sabaria in Pannonia [modern Hungary], but was brought up at Ticinum [Pavia], which is situated in Italy. In terms of worldly dignity, his parents were not of the lowest rank, but they were pagans. His father was at first simply a soldier, but afterwards a military tribune. He himself took up a military career while a youth and was enrolled in the imperial guard, first under king Constantine,[3] and then under the Caesar Julian.[4] This, however, was not done of his own free will, for, almost from the earliest years of his holy childhood, this distinguished boy aspired rather to the service of God. For when he was ten years old, against the wish of his parents, he fled to a church and begged to

become a catechumen [to begin instruction in Christianity]. Soon afterwards, in a wonderful manner he became completely devoted to the work of God, and when he was twelve years old, he longed for a life in the desert [to become a hermit]; and he would have made the necessary vows if his youthfulness had not been an obstacle. His mind, however, was always intent upon hermitages or the Church, and already meditated in his boyish years on what he later fulfilled as a religious. But since an edict was issued by the rulers of the state that the sons of veterans should be enrolled for military service, his father (who grudged his pious behavior) delivered him up when he was fifteen years old, and he was arrested and put

---

[1] Rom. 8: 32.

[2] See Phil. 3: 20; Heb. 12: 23. Compare with Augustine's idea of the City of God, above, p. 14.

[3] Constantine I (r.306–337).

[4] Julian was at this time Caesar in Gaul. Later, when emperor (r.361–363), he was known as "the Apostate."

in chains and was bound by the military oath. He was content with only one servant as his attendant, and then, reversing roles, the master waited on the servant to such a degree that, for the most part, it was he who pulled off his [servant's] boots and he who cleaned them with his own hand; and while they took their meals together, it was he who more often served them. For nearly three years before his baptism, he was a professional soldier, but he kept completely free from those vices in which that class of men become too frequently involved. He showed great kindness towards his fellow-soldiers, and wonderful affection, and his patience and humility surpassed what seemed possible to human nature. There is no need to praise the self-denial which he displayed: it was so great that, even at that date, he was regarded not so much as being a soldier as a monk. By all these qualities he had so endeared himself to the whole body of his comrades that they held him in extraordinary affection. Although not yet regenerated in Christ, by his good works he acted the part of a candidate for baptism.[1] This he did, for instance, by aiding those who were in trouble, by giving help to the wretched, by supporting the needy, by clothing the naked, while he reserved nothing for himself from his military pay except what was necessary for his daily sustenance. Even then, far from being a senseless hearer of the Gospel, he took no thought for the morrow.[2]

So it happened one day when he had nothing except his weapons and his simple military dress, in the middle of a winter which had been very bitter and more severe than usual, so that the extreme cold had caused the death of many, he chanced to meet at the gate of the city of Amiens a poor naked man. He [the beggar] was entreating the passers-by to have pity on him, but all passed the wretched man without notice, when Martin, that man full of God, recognized that the beggar to whom others showed no pity was reserved for him. But what should he do? He had nothing except the cloak in which he was dressed, for he had already parted with the rest of his garments for similar purposes. Taking, therefore, his sword, which he was wearing, he divided his cloak in half, and gave one part to the beggar, and clothed himself again with what was left. At this, some of the bystanders laughed, because he was now an unsightly object in his mutilated clothing. Many, however, who were of sounder understanding, regretted deeply that they themselves had

done nothing similar. They especially felt this because, possessing more than Martin, they could have clothed the poor man without reducing themselves to nakedness.

The following night while he slept Martin had a vision of Christ wearing the part of his cloak with which he had clothed the beggar. He was told to regard the Lord with the greatest care, and to recognize [the Lord's] robe as his own. Before long, he heard Jesus saying in a clear voice to the multitude of angels standing round, "Martin, who is still only a catechumen, clothed me with this robe." Truly the Lord remembered his own words, which he had spoken [while on earth]: "Inasmuch as ye have done these things to one of the least of these, ye have done them unto me,"[3] when he declared that he himself had been clothed in that beggar; and he confirmed the testimony he bore to such a good deed by condescending to show himself in that very garment which the beggar had received.

After this vision the sainted man was not puffed up with vainglory, but he acknowledged the goodness of God in his own action, and as he was now twenty years old he rushed off to receive baptism. However, he did not immediately retire from military service, but gave into the entreaties of his tribune, whom he served as one of his private staff. For the tribune promised that, after his term of office had expired, he too would retire from the world. Martin was held back by this expectation, and continued to act the part of a soldier (although only in name) for nearly two years after he had received baptism.

In the meantime, the barbarians were invading the two divisions of Gaul, and the Caesar [Julian] brought an army together at the city of Worms, and began to distribute a donative [bonus] to the soldiers. As the custom was, they were called forward, one by one, until it came to Martin's turn. Then, indeed, thinking it a good time to ask for his discharge—for he did not think it would be proper for him to receive a donative if he did not intend to continue as a soldier—he said to Caesar, "Until now I have served you as a soldier: permit me now to be a soldier for God. Let the man who is to fight for you receive your donative; I am a soldier of Christ: it is not lawful for me to fight." Then the tyrant began to rage at what he said, declaring that [Martin] was withdrawing from military service from fear of the battle which was to take place the next day, and not from any religious motive. But Martin, full of courage, and all the more

---

[1] In this era, infant baptism was unusual; most Christians were baptized in adulthood.

[2] Matt. 6: 34.

[3] Matt. 25: 40.

resolute in the face of this attempt at intimidation, said, "If this is attributed to cowardice and not to faith, tomorrow I will confront the battle-line unarmed, and in the name of the Lord Jesus, protected by the sign of the cross and not by shield or helmet, I will advance unharmed into the ranks of the enemy." Then he was ordered to be thrown back into prison, so that he might keep his promise by exposing himself unarmed to the barbarians. But the next day, the enemy sent ambassadors to negotiate peace, surrendering themselves and everything they possessed. From these circumstances, who can doubt that this victory was indeed due to the saintly man? For it was granted him that he should not be sent unarmed into battle. And although the good Lord could have preserved his own soldier even from the swords and spears of the enemy, yet he removed all necessity for fighting so that [Martin's] blessed eyes might not have to witness the death of others. For Christ could not have granted any victory on behalf of his own soldier other than subduing the enemy without bloodshed or the death of anyone.

After leaving military service, [Martin] sought out blessed Hilary [d.c.367], bishop of the city of Poitiers whose proven faith in the things of God was highly regarded, and he stayed with him for some time.... [Later, Martin left Hilary in order to return home to convert his parents. Hilary, meanwhile, was exiled and lived for a time in Italy. When he was allowed to return to Poitiers, Martin joined him there.]

After he [Martin] had been most joyfully welcomed by him [Hilary], he established for himself a monastery not far from the town [at Ligugé]. At this time he was joined by a certain catechumen who wished to have instruction in the teachings of the most holy man. Only a few days later, however, the catechumen fell suddenly ill, suffering from a high fever. It so happened that Martin was then away from home. He was absent for three days, and on his return he found the lifeless body; and death had been so sudden, that he had left this world without receiving baptism. The body had been laid out in public, and the grieving brethren were visiting it as their sad duty required, when Martin hurried up, weeping and lamenting. But with his soul completely filled with the Holy Spirit, he ordered the others to leave the cell in which the body was lying; and bolting the door, he stretched himself at full length on the dead limbs of the departed brother. After he had stayed lying there for some time in prayer, and had

become aware through the Spirit that the power of God was present, he rose up for a short time, and fixing his gaze on the dead man's face he waited with confidence for the result of his prayer and the mercy of the Lord. And after scarcely two hours had passed he saw the dead man begin to move all his limbs little by little, and his eyes trembling and blinking as he recovered his sight. Then indeed he raised a loud voice to the Lord and gave thanks, filling the cell with cries. Hearing the noise, those who had been standing at the door immediately rushed inside. And truly a marvelous spectacle met them, for they beheld the man alive whom they had left for dead.

Thus restored to life, he immediately received baptism and lived for many years afterwards; and he was the first one among us to give both substantial proof of Martin's virtues and to testify to them. He often related that, when he left the body, he was brought before the tribunal of the Judge [God], and had a dismal sentence pronounced on him which relegated him to the dark places among the crowd of common men.[1] Then, however, he added, it was suggested by two angels of the Judge that he was the man for whom Martin was praying; and so the same angels were ordered to lead him back and to give him to Martin, and restore him to his former life. From this time forward, the name of the blessed man became famous, so that he was treated as if he were already a saint by everyone, and was also held to be powerful and a true apostle....

At about the same time, Martin was sought after to be bishop of the church at Tours,[2] but when he could not easily be persuaded to leave his monastery, a certain Rusticius, one of the citizens, pretended that his wife was ill, and by throwing himself down at [Martin's] knees, prevailed on him to leave. A crowd of citizens had previously been posted along the road on which he traveled, and in this way he was escorted to the city as if under guard. In an amazing manner, an incredible number of people not only from that town but also from the neighboring cities had assembled to give their votes. They all had only the same wish, the same desire, the same opinion: that Martin was most worthy of being bishop, and that the Church would be happy with such a priest.

A few impious persons, however, including some of the bishops who had been summoned to appoint the prelate, resisted, asserting strongly that Martin's person was contemptible, that he was unworthy of being a bishop, that he was despicable in appearance, his cloth-

---

[1] This is a very early reference to Limbo, the eternal home of the souls of the unbaptized.

[2] In 371.

ing was shabby and his hair disgusting. This madness of theirs was ridiculed by people of sounder judgment, since even while they attempted to slander him they were proclaiming his extraordinary merits. And in truth, they were not allowed to do anything other than what the people wished for, in accordance with Divine will....

And now it is beyond my power to describe completely what Martin was like after he became bishop, and how he distinguished himself. For with the utmost constancy he remained the same as he had been before. There was the same humility in his heart and the same simplicity of clothing. Filled with both authority and courtesy, he kept up the position of a bishop properly, yet in such a way as not to abandon the life and virtues of a monk. For some time he lived in a cell adjacent to the church; but afterwards, when he could not tolerate the disturbance caused by the numbers of visitors, he established a monastery for himself about two miles outside the city.

This spot [Marmoutier] was so hidden and remote that he no longer had to wish for the solitude of a hermit. For on one side it was surrounded by the steep rock of a high mountain, while the rest of the land had been enclosed in a gentle curve of the Loire river; there was only one means of access, and that was very narrow. Here, then, he inhabited a cell built of wood, and a great number of the brothers were housed in the same fashion, but most of them had made themselves shelters by hollowing caves out of the overhanging rock. There were about eighty disciples who were instructed by the example of their holy master. There, no one possessed anything of his own; everything was held in common. No one was allowed either to buy or to sell anything, as is the custom among many monks. No art was practiced there, except that of the scribes, and even this was assigned to the younger brothers while the elder spent their time in prayer. It was rare for any of them to leave his cell, except to gather at the place of prayer. After a period of fasting was over, they all ate their meals together. No one used wine, except when illness compelled them to do so. Most of them wore garments of camel's hair; softer clothing was considered a serious fault there. This must be considered all the more remarkable, because many of them were considered to be of high rank, brought up in a very different fashion, and yet they had forced themselves to accept humility and patience; and we have seen many of these afterwards made bishops. For what city or church would not want a priest from the monastery of Martin?[1]

But let me go on to describe the other virtues that Martin displayed as a bishop....

While Martin was going on a journey he met the body of a pagan that was being carried to the tomb with superstitious funeral rites. Seeing from a distance a crowd approaching, and not knowing what it was about, he stood still for a little while. For there was nearly half a mile between him and the crowd, so that it was difficult to make out what he was seeing. Nevertheless, because he saw it was a group of peasants, when the linen cloths covering the body were blown about by the wind, he believed that some profane sacrificial rites were being performed. For it was the custom among the peasants of Gaul in their wretched madness to carry about through the fields the images of demons covered with a white veil.

Therefore he raised the sign of the cross against them and commanded the crowd not to move from the place where they were and to put down what they were carrying. At this, wonderful to relate, you might have seen the wretched creatures first become as rigid as rocks. Next, when they tried with a great effort to move forward, but were not able to take a step farther, they began to whirl themselves about in the most ridiculous fashion until they were defeated and had to put down the dead body. They were thunderstruck and looked at each other, silently wondering what had happened to them. But when the saintly man discovered that the peasants were simply performing funeral rites, and not sacrifices, with raised hand he gave them back the power of leaving and of lifting up the body. Thus when he wished, he made them stand still, and when he pleased, he let them go.

On another occasion, in a certain village he demolished a very ancient temple, and set about cutting down a pine-tree that stood close to the temple. The chief priest of that place and a crowd of other pagans began to oppose him. And although these people had, at the Lord's command, been quiet while the temple was being destroyed, they could not endure the cutting-down of the tree. Martin carefully impressed upon them that there was nothing sacred in the trunk of a tree, and urged them instead to honor God whom he himself served; the tree had to be cut down because it was dedicated to a demon.

Then one of them who was bolder than the others said, "If you have any trust in your God, whom you say you worship, we ourselves will cut down this tree, and you stand in its path; for if, as you say, your Lord is with you, you will not be hurt." Then Martin, courageously

---

[1] Compare the standards at Marmoutier with those described in *The Benedictine Rule* (above, p. 17).

trusting in the Lord, promised to do so. Upon this, all that crowd of pagans agreed to the condition; for they held the loss of their tree a small matter, so long as they got the enemy of their religion buried under its fall. Since that pine-tree was leaning to one side, so that there could be no question as to which way it would fall when it was cut, Martin was bound to the spot where the tree would certainly fall, as the pagans had stipulated.

Then they began to cut down their own tree, with great delight and rejoicing. A wondering crowd stood some distance away. Little by little the pine-tree began to shake, and, on the point of falling, threatened its own ruin. The monks at a distance grew pale and, terrified by the approaching danger, they lost all hope and faith, expecting only Martin's death. But he, trusting in the Lord, waited courageously, even as the falling pine made a cracking noise, even as it was falling and as it rushed down upon him: simply lifting his hand against it, he held up the sign of salvation. Then, indeed—you would

have thought it driven back like a spinning top—it swept round to the opposite side, so that it almost crushed the peasants, who had stood in what seemed to be a safe spot.

Then a shout went up to heaven: the pagans were amazed by the miracle while the monks wept for joy, and the name of Christ was proclaimed by them all together. And as it is well known, on that day salvation came to that region. For there was hardly one of that huge crowd of pagans who did not long for the laying-on of hands [to become a catechumen] and, abandoning their impious errors, they believed in the Lord Jesus. Certainly, before Martin's time, very few, indeed hardly any in those regions had received the name of Christ. Through his virtues and example that name has prevailed to such an extent that now there is no region that is not filled either with crowded churches or monasteries. For wherever he destroyed pagan temples, there immediately he used to build either churches or monasteries.

1.11 St. Radegund as ascetic: Venantius Fortunatus, *The Life of St. Radegund* (before c.600). Original in Latin.

Venantius Fortunatus (*c.*535–*c.*605?) was born and educated in Italy, where he trained in the late classical rhetorical tradition. He came to Gaul when he was about thirty years old to earn his living by writing poetry for wealthy Merovingian aristocrats, both lay and clerical. A few years later he settled at Poitiers, where he became a priest and a close associate of Queen Radegund (d.587). She had originally been a member of the royal house of Thuringia, a kingdom bordering on Frankish territory. When King Clothar I (r.511–561) invaded Thuringia, Radegund became one of his prizes of war and, eventually, his wife. But following the execution of her brother, probably with Clothar's connivance, Radegund founded—and retired to—a monastery (as medieval nunneries are often called, just like their male counterparts) at Poitiers, known as Holy Cross. Toward the end of his life, around 600, Fortunatus became the bishop of Poitiers. In his *Life* of Radegund, Fortunatus was concerned above all to praise her piety, charity, and asceticism. As we shall see, her community wanted other aspects of her work recognized, and so shortly after Fortunatus wrote his hagiography, another was written by a nun at Holy Cross. How might you compare the virtues of Fortunatus's St. Radegund with those of Athanasius's St. Antony (p. 27 above)? What ideals of queenship does Fortunatus's portrait suggest?

[Source: *Sainted Women of the Dark Ages*, ed. and trans. Jo Ann McNamara and John E. Halborg, with E. Gordon Whatley (Durham, NC: Duke University Press, 1992), pp. 70–81 (slightly modified).]

1. Our Redeemer is so richly and abundantly generous that He wins mighty victories through the female sex and, despite their frail physique, He confers glory and greatness on women through strength of mind. By faith, Christ makes them strong who were born weak so that, when those who appeared to be imbeciles are crowned with their merits by Him who made them, they garner praise for their Creator who hid heavenly treasure in earthen vessels. For Christ the king dwells with his riches in their bowels. Mortifying themselves in the world, despising earthly consort, purified of worldly contamination, trusting not in the transitory, dwelling not in error but seeking to live with God, they are united with the Redeemer's glory in Paradise. One of that company is she whose earthly life we are attempting to present to the public, though in homely style, so that the glorious memory that she, who lives with Christ, has left us will be celebrated in this world. So ends the Prologue.

Here begins the Life.

2. The most blessed Radegund was of the highest earthly rank, born from the seed of the kings of the barbarian nation of Thuringia. Her grandfather was King Bassin, her paternal uncle, Hermanfred and her father, King Bertechar. But she surpassed her lofty origin by even loftier deeds. She had lived with her noble family only a little while when the victorious Franks devastated the region with barbaric turmoil and, like the Israelites, she departed and migrated from her homeland. The royal girl became part of the plunder of these conquerors and they began to quarrel over their captive. If the contest had not ended with an agreement for her disposition, the kings would have taken up arms against one another. Falling to the lot of the illustrious King Clothar,[1] she was taken to Athies in Vermandois, a royal villa, and her upbringing was entrusted to guardians. The maiden was taught letters and other things suitable to her sex, and she would often converse with other children there about her desire to be a martyr if the chance came in her time. Thus, even as an adolescent, she displayed the merits of a mature person. She obtained part of what she sought, for, though the church was flourishing in peace, she endured persecution from her own household. While but a small child, she herself brought the scraps left at table to the gathered children, washing the head of each one, seating them on little chairs and offering water for their hands, and she mingled with the infants herself. She would also carry out what she had planned beforehand with Samuel, a little cleric. Following his lead, carrying a wooden cross they had made, singing psalms, the children would troop into the oratory as somber as adults. Radegund herself would polish the pavement with her dress and, collecting the drifting dust around the altar in a napkin, reverently placed it outside the door rather than sweep it away. When the aforementioned king, having provided the expenses, wished to bring her to Vitry, she escaped by night from Athies through Beralcha[2] with a few companions. When he settled with her that she should be made his queen at Soissons,[3] she avoided the trappings of royalty, so she would not grow great in the world but in Him to Whom she was devoted and she remained unchanged by earthly glory.

3. Therefore, though married to a terrestrial prince, she was not separated from the celestial one and, the more secular power was bestowed upon her, the more humbly she bent her will—more than befitted her royal status. Always subject to God following priestly admonitions, she was more Christ's partner than her husband's companion. We will only attempt to publicize a few of the many things she did during this period of her life. Fearing she would lose status with God as she advanced in worldly rank at the side of a prince, she gave herself energetically to almsgiving. Whenever she received part of the tribute, she gave away a tithe[4] of all that came to her before accepting any for herself. She dispensed what was left to monasteries, sending the gifts to those she could not reach on foot. There was no hermit who could hide from her munificence. So she paid out what she received lest the burden weigh her down. The voice of the needy was not raised in vain for she never turned a deaf ear. Often she gave clothes, believing that the limbs of Christ concealed themselves under the garments of the poor and that whatever she did not give to paupers was truly lost.

4. Turning her mind to further works of mercy, she built a house at Athies where beds were elegantly made up for needy women gathered there. She would wash them herself in warm baths, tending to the putrescence

---

[1] Clothar I (r.511–561) was the third son of Clovis and shared his kingdom with Childebert until the latter's death in 558.

[2] Not identified.

[3] Soissons was the capital of Clothar's kingdom.

[4] I.e., ten per cent.

of their diseases. She washed the heads of men, acting like a servant. And before she washed them, she would mix a potion with her own hands to revive those who were weak from sweating. Thus the devout lady, queen by birth and marriage, mistress of the palace, served the poor as a handmaid. Secretly, lest anyone notice, at royal banquets, she fed most deliciously on beans or lentils from the dish of legumes placed before her, in the manner of the three boys.[1] And if the singing of the hours started while she was still eating, she would make her excuses to the king and withdraw from the company to do her duty to God. As she went out, she sang psalms to the Lord and carefully checked what food had been provided to refresh the paupers at the door.

5. At night, when she lay with her prince, she would ask leave to rise and leave the chamber to relieve nature. Then she would prostrate herself in prayer under a hair shirt[2] by the privy so long that the cold pierced her through and through and only her spirit was warm. Her whole flesh prematurely dead, indifferent to her body's torment, she kept her mind intent on Paradise and counted her suffering trivial, if only she might avoid becoming cheap in Christ's eyes. Re-entering the chamber thereafter, she could scarcely get warm either by the hearth or in her bed. Because of this, people said that the King had yoked himself to a *monacha* rather than a queen.[3] Her goodness provoked him to harsher irritation but she either soothed him to the best of her ability or bore her husband's outbursts modestly.

6. Indeed, it will suffice to know how she bore herself during the days of Quadragesima [Lent], a singular penitent in her royal robes. When the time for fasting drew near, she would notify a *monacha* named Pia, who, according to their holy arrangement, would send a haircloth sealed carefully in linen to Radegund. Draping it over her body through the whole of Quadragesima,[4] the holy woman wore that sweet burden under her royal garment. When the season was over, she returned the haircloth similarly sealed. Who could believe how she would pour out her heart in prayers when the king was away? How she would cling to the feet of Christ as though He were present with her and satiate her long hunger with tears as though she was gorging on delicacies! She had contempt for the food of the belly, for Christ was her only nourishment and all her hunger was for Christ.

7. With what piety did she care solicitously for the candles made with her own hands that burned all night long in oratories and holy places? When the king asked after her at table during the late hours, he was told that she was delayed, busy about God's affairs. This caused strife with her husband and later on the prince compensated her with gifts for the wrong he did her with his tongue.

8. If she received a report that any of God's servants was on his way to see her, either of his own accord or by invitation, she felt full of celestial joy. Hastening out in the night time with a few intimates, through snow, mud or dust, she herself would wash the feet of the venerable man with water she had heated beforehand and offer the servant of God something to drink in a bowl. There was no resisting her. On the following day, committing the care of the household to her trusted servants, she would occupy herself wholly with the just man's words and his teachings concerning salvation. The business of achieving celestial life fixed her attention throughout the day. And if a bishop should come, she rejoiced to see him, gave him gifts, and was sad to have to let him go home.

9. And how prudently she sought to devote everything possible to her salvation. If the girls attending her when she dressed praised a new veil of coarse linen ornamented with gold and gems in the barbarian fashion as particularly beautiful, she would judge herself unworthy to be draped in such fabric. Divesting herself of the dress immediately, she would send it to some holy place in the neighborhood where it could be laid as a cloth on the Lord's altar.

10. And if the king, according to custom, condemned a guilty criminal to death, wasn't the most holy queen near dead with torment lest the culprit perish by the sword? How she would rush about among his trusty men, ministers, and nobles, whose blandishments might soothe the prince's temper until the king's anger ceased and the voice of salvation flowed where the sentence of death had issued before!

11. Even while she remained in her worldly palace, the blessed acts which busied her so pleased Divine Clemency that the Lord's generosity worked miracles through her. Once at her villa in Péronne, while that holiest of women was strolling in the garden after her meal, some sequestered criminals loudly cried to her from the prison for help. She asked who it might be. The servants lied that

---

[1] See Dan. 1: 12, where Daniel and three other boys at court eat plain food, yet thrive.

[2] A hair shirt was a coarse and rough garment, worn by ascetics next to their skin as part of their penitential practices.

[3] *Monacha* (pl. *monachae*): female monk.

[4] Lent.

a crowd of beggars was seeking alms. Believing that, she sent to relieve their needs. Meanwhile the fettered prisoners were silenced by a judge. But as night was falling and she was saying her prayers, the chains broke and the freed prisoners ran from the prison to the holy woman. When they witnessed this, those who had lied to the holy one realized that they were the real culprits, while the erstwhile convicts were freed from their bonds.

12. If Divinity fosters it, misfortune often leads to salvation. Thus her innocent brother was killed so that she might come to live in religion. She left the king and went straight to holy [Bishop] Médard at Noyon. She earnestly begged that she might change her garments and be consecrated to God. But mindful of the words of the Apostle: "Art thou bound unto a wife? Seek not to be loosed,"[1] he hesitated to garb the Queen in the robe of a *monacha*. For even then, nobles were harassing the holy man and attempting to drag him brutally through the basilica from the altar to keep him from veiling the king's spouse lest the priest imagine he could take away the king's official queen as though she were only a prostitute. That holiest of women knew this and, sizing up the situation, entered the sacristy, put on a monastic garb and proceeded straight to the altar, saying to the blessed Médard: "If you shrink from consecrating me, and fear man more than God, Pastor, He will require His sheep's soul from your hand." He was thunderstruck by that argument and, laying his hand on her, he consecrated her as a deaconess.[2]

13. Soon she divested herself of the noble costume that she was wont to wear as queen when she walked in procession on the day of a festival with her train of attendants. She laid it on the altar and piled the table of Divine Glory with purple, gems, ornaments and like gifts to honor Him. She gave a heavy girdle of costly gold for the relief of the poor. Similarly, arriving at the cell of St. Jumer one day on which the happy queen decorated herself [with finery] composed of what I would call by the barbarian term "stapio"—blouses, tunics, hair coverings, buckles, all made of gold and some with circlets of gems—she put them on the holy altar for future benefits. Again, proceeding to the venerable Dato's cell one day, spectacularly adorned, as she should have been in the world with whatever she could put on, having rewarded the abbot, she gave the whole from her woman's wealth to the community. Likewise going on to the retreat of holy Gundulf, later Bishop of Metz, she exerted herself just as energetically to enrich his monastery.

14. From there her fortunate sails approached Tours. Can any eloquence express how zealous and munificent she showed herself there? How she conducted herself around the courts, shrines, and basilica of Saint Martin, weeping unchecked tears, prostrating herself at each threshold! After mass was said, she heaped the holy altar with the clothing and bright ornaments with which she used to adorn herself in the palace. And when the handmaid of the Lord went from there to the neighborhood of Candes whence the glorious Martin, Christ's senator and confidant, migrated from this world, she gave him no less again, ever profiting in the Lord's grace.

15. From there, in decorous manner, she approached the villa of Saix near the aforesaid town in the territory of Poitiers, her journey ever prospering. Who could recount the countless remarkable things she did there or grasp the special quality of each one? At table she secretly chewed rye or barley bread, which she had hidden under a cake to escape notice. For from the time she was veiled, consecrated by Saint Médard, even in illness, she ate nothing but legumes and green vegetables: not fruit nor fish nor eggs. And she drank no drink but honeyed water or perry[3] and would touch no undiluted wine nor any decoction of mead[4] or fermented beer.

16. Then, emulating Saint Germanus' custom, she secretly had a millstone brought to her. Throughout the whole of Quadragesima, she ground fresh flour with her own hands. She continuously distributed each offering to local religious communities, in the amount needed for the meal taken every four days. With that holy woman, acts of mercy were no fewer than the crowds who pressed her; as there was no shortage of those who asked, so was there no shortage in what she gave so that, wonderfully, they could all be satisfied. Where did the exile get such wealth? Whence came the pilgrim's riches?

17. How much did she spend daily on relief? Only she who bore it to the beggars ever knew. For beyond the daily meal, which she fed to her enrolled paupers twice

---

[1] 1 Cor. 7: 27.

[2] There is no reason to suppose that a deaconess was bound to celibacy; conceivably, Médard had found an ingenious solution to his particular dilemma in consecrating a woman who was still married to the king.

[3] Fermented pear juice.

[4] A drink made from fermented honey and water.

a week, on Thursday and Saturday, she prepared a bath. Girding herself with a cloth, she washed the heads of the needy, scrubbing away whatever she found there. Not shrinking from scuff, scabs, lice or pus, she plucked off the worms and scrubbed away the putrid flesh. Then she herself combed the hair on every head she had washed. As in the gospel, she applied oil to their ulcerous sores that had opened when the skin softened or that scratching had irritated, reducing the spread of infection. When women descended into the tub, she washed their limbs with soap from head to foot. When they came out, if she noticed that anyone's clothes were shoddy with age, she would take them away and give them new ones. Thus she spruced up all who came to the feast in rags. When they were gathered around the table and the dinner service laid out, she brought water and napkins for each of them and cleaned the mouth and hands of the invalids herself. Then three trays laden with delicacies would be carried in. Standing like a good hostess before the diners, she cut up the bread and meat and served everyone while fasting herself. Moreover, she never ceased to offer food to the blind and weak with a spoon. In this, two women aided her but she alone served them, busy as a new Martha until the "brothers" were drunk and happily satisfied with their meal.[1] Then, leaving the place to wash her hands, she was completely gratified with her well-served feast. And if anyone protested, she ordered that they sit still until they wished to get up.

18. Summer and winter, on Sundays, she followed a praiseworthy rule. She would provide an undiluted drink of sweet wine to the assembled paupers. First she doled it out herself and then, while she hurried off to Mass, she assigned a maid to serve everyone who remained. Her devotions completed, she would meet the priests invited to her table, for it was her royal custom not to let them return home without a gift.

19. Doesn't this make one shudder, this thing she did so sweetly? When lepers arrived and, sounding a warning,[2] came forward, she directed her assistant to inquire with pious concern whence they came or how many there were. Having learned that, she had a table laid with dishes, spoons, little knives, cups and goblets, and wine and she went in herself secretly that none might see her. Seizing some of the leprous women in her embrace, her heart full of love, she kissed their faces. Then, while they were

seated at table, she washed their faces and hands with warm water and treated their sores with fresh ointments and fed each one. When they were leaving, she offered small gifts of gold and clothing. To this there was scarcely a single witness, but the attendant presumed to chide her softly: "Most holy lady, when you have embraced lepers, who will kiss you?" Pleasantly, she answered: "Really, if you won't kiss me, it's no concern of mine."

20. With God's help, she shone forth in diverse miracles. For example, if anyone was in desperate straits because of pus from a wound, an attendant would bring a vine leaf to the saint speaking with her about what was to be done with it. As soon as the saint made the sign of the cross over it, the attendant would take it to the desperate one, placing it on the wound which would soon be healed. Similarly an invalid or someone with a fever might come and say that he had learned in a dream that to be healed he should hasten to the holy woman and present one of her attendants with a candle. After it had burned through the night his disease would be killed while the invalid was healed. How often when she heard of someone lying bedridden would she sally forth like a pilgrim bearing fruit or something sweet and warm to restore their strength? How quickly would an invalid who had eaten nothing for ten days take food when she served it herself and thus receive both food and health together? And she ordered these things herself lest anyone tell tales.

21. Weren't there such great gatherings of people on the day that the saint determined to seclude herself that those who could not be contained in the streets climbed up to fill the roofs? Anyone who spoke of all the most holy woman had fervently accomplished in fasting, services, humility, charity, suffering and torment, proclaimed her both confessor and martyr. Truly every day except for the most venerable day of the Lord, was a fast day for that most holy woman. Her meal of lentils or green vegetables was virtually a fast in itself for she took no fowl or fish or fruit or eggs to eat. Her bread was made from rye or barley, which she concealed under the pudding lest anyone notice what she ate. And to drink she had water and honey or perry and only a little of that was poured out for her, however thirsty she was.

22. The first time she enclosed herself in her cell throughout Quadragesima, she ate no bread, except on Sundays, but only roots of herbs or mallow greens

---

[1] See Luke 10: 40. Martha is customarily presented as the model of the active religious life for women, whereas her sister Mary symbolizes the contemplative life.

[2] Lepers wore bells to signal their approach.

without a drop of oil or salt for dressing. In fact, during the entire fast, she consumed only two *sestaria* [pints] of water. Consequently, she suffered so much from thirst that she could barely chant the psalms through her desiccated throat. She kept her vigils in a shift of haircloth instead of linen, incessantly chanting the offices. A bed of ashes served her for a couch, which she covered with a haircloth. In this manner, rest itself wearied her but even this was not enough to endure.

23. While all the *monachae* were deep in sleep, she would collect their shoes, restoring them cleaned and oiled to each. On other Quadragesimas, she was more relaxed, eating on Thursday and again on Sundays. The rest of the time when health permitted, except for Easter and other high holy days, she led an austere life in sackcloth and ashes, rising early to be singing psalms when the others awoke. For no monasterial offices pleased her unless she observed them first. She punished herself if anyone else did a good deed before she did. When it was her turn to sweep the pavements around the monastery, she even scoured the nooks and crannies, bundling away whatever nasty things were there, never too disgusted to carry off what others shuddered to look upon. She did not shrink from cleaning the privies but cleaned and carried off the stinking dung. For she believed that she would be diminished if these vile services did not ennoble her. She carried firewood in her arms. She blew on the hearth and stirred the fire with tongs and did not flinch if she hurt herself. She would care for the infirm beyond her assigned week, cooking their food, washing their faces, and bringing them warm water, going the rounds of those she was caring for and returning fasting to her cell.

24. How can anyone describe her excited fervor as she ran into the kitchen, doing her week of chores? None of the *monachae* but she would carry as much wood as was needed in a bundle from the back gate.[1] She drew water from the well and poured it into basins. She scrubbed vegetables and legumes and revived the hearth by blowing so that she might cook the food. While it was busy boiling, she took the vessels from the hearth, washing and laying out the dishes. When the meal was finished, she rinsed the small vessels and scrubbed the kitchen till it shone, free of every speck of dirt. Then she carried out all the sweepings and the nastiest rubbish. Further, she never flagged in supporting the sick and even before she took up the Rule of Arles[2] did her weekly tour of service preparing plenty of warm water for them all. Humbly washing and kissing their feet, the holy one prostrated herself and begged them all to forgive her for any negligence she might have committed.

25. But I shudder to speak of the pain she inflicted on herself over and above all these labors. Once, throughout Quadragesima, she bound her neck and arms with three broad iron circlets. Inserting three chains in them, she fettered her whole body so tightly that her delicate flesh, swelling up, enclosed the hard iron. After the fast was ended, when she wished to remove the chains locked under her skin, she could not—for the flesh was cut by the circlet through her back and breast over the iron of the chains, so that the flow of blood nearly drained her little body to the last drop.

26. On another occasion, she ordered a brass plate made, shaped in the sign of Christ. She heated it up in her cell and pressed it upon her body most deeply in two spots so that her flesh was roasted through. Thus, with her spirit flaming, she caused her very limbs to burn. One Quadragesima, she devised a still more terrible agony to torture herself in addition to the severe hunger and burning thirst of her fast. She forced her tender limbs, already suppurating and scraped raw by the hard bristles of a haircloth, to carry a water basin full of burning coals. Then, isolated from the rest, though her limbs were quivering, her soul was steeled for the pain. She drew it to herself, so that she might be a martyr though it was not an age of persecution. To cool her fervent soul, she thought to burn her body. She imposed the glowing brass and her burning limbs hissed. Her skin was consumed and a deep furrow remained where the brand had touched her. Silently, she concealed the holes, but the putrefying blood betrayed the pain that her voice did not reveal. Thus did a woman willingly suffer such bitterness for the sweetness of Christ! And in time, miracles told the story that she herself would have kept hidden.

[Fortunatus continues with accounts of Radegund's miracles.]

---

[1] Presumably left there by the monks attached to a small service community nearby.

[2] This was the strict Rule for nuns written by Caesarius of Arles (d.542).

1.12 St. Radegund as relic collector: Baudonivia, *The Life of St. Radegund* (*c*.600). Original in Latin.

We know nothing about Baudonivia beyond what she tells us in the preface to her *Life* of Radegund. She was a nun at Holy Cross who, around 600, was asked by her abbess and other members of her community to supplement the *Life* written by Fortunatus. As she says, they thought that Fortunatus had not recounted enough of Radegund's miracles. They also must have wanted more discussion of Radegund's interest in relics, since Baudonivia spends much time on this topic. We should not take literally her profession of intellectual inadequacy; this was a *topos*—a commonplace, or customary practice—of ancient and medieval writings, meant to make the reader sympathetic to the author. How would you characterize the different ideals of sainthood presented in Baudonivia's and Fortunatus's two *Lives*, and how might you account for those differences?

[Source: *Sainted Women of the Dark Ages*, ed. and trans. Jo Ann McNamara and John E. Halborg, with E. Gordon Whatley (Durham, NC: Duke University Press, 1992), pp. 86–87, 94–99 (slightly modified).]

To the holy ladies adorned with the grace of virtuous living, Abbess Dedimia[1] and all Holy Radegund's congregation, from Baudonivia, humblest of all.

I can as easily touch heaven with my fingers as perform the task you have imposed upon me—namely to write something about the life of the holy Lady Radegund, whom you knew best. This task should be assigned to those who have fountains of eloquence within them. For whatever such people are commissioned to write is laid out generously in flowing song. On the contrary, people who are narrow of understanding and lack the full fluency of eloquence to relieve their own sterility and aridity—let alone refresh others—not only have no wish to speak out on their own but become terrified when they are commanded to do so. For in myself, I know that I am weak-minded and have but few intelligent things to say. For good as it is for the learned to speak, it is best for the unlearned to keep silence. For the former know how to produce something great from very little while the latter cannot even make a little from a great deal. Therefore what the learned seek eagerly terrifies the unlearned. I am the smallest of the small ones she nourished familiarly from the cradle as her own child at her feet! So that I may, in obedience to your most gracious wishes, compose, not the full story but a partial account in writing of her famous works, and so that I may offer a public

celebration of her glorious life to the ears of her flock, in devout though unworthy language, I pray that you will aid me with your prayers, for I am more devoted than learned. In this book, we will not repeat what the apostolic Bishop Fortunatus[2] recorded of her blessed life but speak of what he omitted in his fear of prolixity, as he explained in his book when he said: "But let this small sample of the blessed one's miracles suffice, lest their very abundance arouse contempt. And even this should in no way be reckoned a small amount, since from these few tales we may recognize in the miracles the greatness with which she lived." Therefore, inspired by the Divine Power whom Radegund strove to please in this world and with Whom she reigns in the next, we will attempt to relate, in rustic rather than refined language, what she did here and to publish a few of her many miracles....

13. While Radegund was still at the villa of Saix, her faithful and devoted mind intent on Christ, she determined, with great devotion, to collect relics of all the saints. At her request, a venerable priest named Magnus brought her relics of Lord Andrew and many others which she placed above the altar. When, at night, she lay prostrate in prayer keeping vigil on her couch, a little sleep came over her while the Lord declared her wish granted, saying: "Know thou, blessed woman, that not only the relics brought by Magnus the priest are here,

---

[1] The abbess was the female counterpart of the abbot in a women's monastery.

[2] See above, p. 38.

but all those you gathered together in the villa of Athies are assembled here." When she opened her eyes she saw that a most resplendent man had told her these things and she rejoiced and blessed the Lord.

14. After she had entered into the monastery, she assembled a great multitude of the saints through her most faithful prayers, as the East bears witness and North, South and West acknowledge. For from all sides, she managed to obtain those precious gems which Paradise has and Heaven hoards and as many came freely to her as gifts as came in response to her pleas. In their company, she gave herself up to chanting hymns and psalms continuously in ceaseless meditation. At last, news came to her that the holy limbs of Lord Mammas the Martyr[1] rested at Jerusalem. She drank the information in greedily and thirstily; as the dropsical[2] only increase their thirst by drawing more water, so she, though refreshed by God's dew, was burning up.[3] She sent the venerable priest, Reoval, who was then a secular[4] and still abides in the flesh with us, to the patriarch of Jerusalem to ask Blessed Mammas for a token. The man of God received him benignly and, seeking the will of God, announced his request to the people. Three days later, after celebrating Mass, he approached the blessed martyr's sepulchre with all his people and, full of faith, proclaimed in a loud voice: "I ask you, Confessor and Martyr of Christ, that if the blessed Radegund is truly a handmaid of the Lord, you will make it known to all the nations by your power; permit that faithful soul to receive the relic she asks from you." At the end of the prayer, everyone responded, "Amen." Continually declaring his faith in the Blessed One, he went to the holy sepulchre and touched the limbs in such a way that the most blessed saint might indicate what he would give in response to the Lady Radegund's request. He touched each finger of the right hand and, when he came to the little finger, it came away from the hand it belonged to with a gentle pull. Thus the blessed queen's desire was satisfied and her wish granted. With

fitting honors, the apostolic man sent the finger to the blessed Radegund and from Jerusalem even to Poitiers God's praises resounded in her honor. Can you imagine the ardent spirit, the faithful devotion with which she threw herself into abstinence while awaiting the prize, the mighty relic? And then on receiving the heavenly gift, her joy was ecstatic. She devoted herself and all her flock to psalmody, with vigils and fasts for an entire week, blessing the Lord that she had deserved to receive such a reward. For God does not deny the faithful what they ask of Him. Frequently she would say sweetly, in a sort of veiled figure of speech that none could understand: "Anyone who has the care of souls must be sore afraid of universal praise."[5] But no matter how much she wanted to avoid it, the Giver of Virtue labored more and more to display her faith to everyone. Thus, whenever the infirm invoked her, they would be healed of whatever illnesses imprisoned them....

16... What Helena did in oriental lands, Radegund the blessed did in Gaul![6] Since she wished to do nothing without counsel while she lived in the world, she sent letters to the most excellent King Sigibert who held this land in his power asking that, for the welfare of the whole fatherland and the stability of his kingdom, he would permit her to ask the emperor for wood from the Lord's cross.[7] Most graciously, he consented to the blessed queen's petition. She who had made herself a pauper for God, full of devotion and inflamed with desire, sent no gifts to the emperor. Instead she sent her messengers bearing nothing but prayers and the support of the saints whom she invoked incessantly. She got what she had prayed for: that she might glory in having the blessed wood of the Lord's cross enshrined in gold and gems and many of the relics of the saints that had been kept in the east living in that one place. At the saint's petition, the emperor sent legates with gospels ornamented in gold and gems. And the wood where once hung the salvation of the world came with a congregation of saints to the city

---

[1] A fourth-century martyr particularly venerated in the Eastern Church.

[2] I.e., those affected by dropsy, or edema, in which fluids accumulate in the tissues.

[3] See Horace, *Carmina* 2.2.13.

[4] The "secular" clergy—priests and bishops—were "in the world," as opposed to the "religious"—the monks.

[5] Baudonivia takes every opportunity to emphasize Radegund's pastoral and quasi-priestly activities. Priests were responsible for the "care of souls."

[6] Saint Helena, the mother of Constantine, to whom the discovery of the True Cross was attributed, was much admired as a model of medieval queenship.

[7] In the partition of Clothar I's lands among his sons, Tours and Poitiers had come to Sigibert (r.561–575). The Byzantine emperor was Justin II, and the date of the mission was 568–569.

of Poitiers. The bishop of that place should have wished to welcome it devoutly with all the people but the Enemy of humankind, to subject the blessed Radegund to trials and tribulations, worked through his satellites to make the people reject the world's ransom and refuse to receive it in the city. So one and another played the role of the Jews, which is not part of our story.[1] But they would see; the Lord knows His own. Her spirit blazing in a fighting mood, she sent again to the benevolent king to say that they did not wish to receive Salvation itself into the city. Until her messengers could return from the lord king, she entrusted the Lord's cross and the tokens of the saints for shelter in a male monastery that the king had founded at Tours for his own salvation, amidst the chanting of priests.

Thus envy inflicted no less injury on the holy cross than on the Lord Himself, who endured every malicious act patiently when He was summoned time and again by the minions of judges and governors so that the people He created might not perish. She cast herself into agonies of fasts and vigils, lamenting and wailing with her whole flock every day until at last the Lord respected his handmaid's humility and moved the heart of the king to do judgment and justice in the midst of the people. Thus the devout king sent word by his trusted man, the famous Count Justin, to the apostolic Bishop, Lord Eufronius of the city of Tours, to deposit the Lord's most glorious cross and the relics of the saints with due honors in the Lady Radegund's monastery. So it was done. The blessed woman exulted in joy with all her cell when Heaven conferred this gift and perfect present on the congregation which she had gathered for God's service, for she had felt in her soul that they might have all too little after her passing. Thus, though she would always be able to help them when she was in glory with the King of Heaven, this best provider, this good shepherdess, would not leave her sheep in disarray. She bequeathed a heavenly gift, the ransom of the world from Christ's relics, which she had searched out from faraway places for the honor of the place and the salvation of the people in her monastery.[2] Thus, with the aid of God's might and heaven's power, the blind receive light for their eyes, the ears of the deaf open, the tongues of the mute resume their office, the lame walk, and demons are put to flight in that place. What more? Anyone who comes in faith, whatever the infirmity that binds them, goes away healed by the virtue of the Holy Cross. Who could attempt to tell the greatness and richness of the gift the blessed woman conferred on this city? For this, all who live by faith do bless her name. And she solemnly called God to witness when she commended her monastery to the most excellent lord king and his most serene lady Queen Brunhild, all of whom she loved with dear affection, and to the sacrosanct churches and their bishops.

BARBARIAN KINGDOMS

1.13 Gothic Italy as Rome's heir: Cassiodorus, *Variae (State Papers)* (*c*.507–536). Original in Latin.

Theodoric and his successor kings of the Ostrogoths saw themselves as continuators of Roman traditions. Depending on classically educated men such as Cassiodorus (d.583) to work for them as writers and publicists, they issued edicts, gave orders, and negotiated with other rulers. The documents here were among the papers that Cassiodorus compiled into his twelve-book *Variae* (or *State Papers*) *c*.537, when the Ostrogothic king Witigis was at war with Emperor Justinian (r.527–565). In 2.27 (i.e., *Variae* book 2, document no. 27), Theodoric demonstrates his adherence to Roman law: even though he considers Jews "destitute of God's grace," he grants them the right, as enshrined in the laws of Theodosius (see above, p. 4), to maintain their synagogues. In 2.40 he responds to the request of Frankish King Clovis (r.481/482–511) to send a lyre-player, a symbol

---

[1] This is most likely another attempt to parallel Radegund with Helena, whose efforts to find and glorify the True Cross were said to have been resisted by the Jews of Jerusalem.

[2] Thereafter the monastery was named Holy Cross.

of classical refinement and rulership, by writing to Boethius (d.524/526). Trained in the classics like Cassiodorus, Boethius had just written a book on music theory. Writing in Theodoric's name, Cassiodorus borrows some of Boethius's ideas, thereby both flattering Boethius and burnishing the king's reputation for learning. In 3.1, Theodoric presents himself as a peaceful elder statesman mediating between the Visigothic King Alaric and the Frankish King Clovis. His aims were frustrated, however, as Clovis soon attacked the Visigoths and defeated them at the Battle of Vouillé (507). In 10.31, a much later text, Cassiodorus writes in the name of King Witigis, who overthrew Theodahad, the last king of Theodoric's line, and tried unsuccessfully to counter Justinian's conquest of Italy. Note how Witigis claimed the mantle of Theodoric.

[Source: *The* Variae *of Magnus Aurelius Cassiodorus Senator*, trans. S.J.B. Barnish (Liverpool: Liverpool University Press, 1992), pp. 34–35, 38–39, 45–46, 142–43 (notes modified).]

2.27 *King Theodoric to All Jews Living at Genoa (507–12)*

As it is my desire, when petitioned, to give a lawful consent, so I do not like the laws to be cheated through my favors, especially in that area where I believe reverence for God to be concerned. You, then, who are destitute of His grace, should not seem insolent in your pride.

Therefore, by this authority, I decree that you add only a roof to the ancient walls of your synagogue, granting permission to your requests just so far as the imperial decrees allow.[1] It is unlawful for you to add any ornament, or to stray into an enlargement of the building. And you must realize that you will in no way escape the penalty of the ancient ordinance if you do not refrain from illegalities. Indeed, I give you permission to roof or strengthen the walls themselves only if you are not affected by the thirty year limitation.[2] Why do you wish for what you ought to shun? I grant leave, indeed; but, to my praise, I condemn the prayers of erring men. I cannot command your faith, for no one is forced to believe against his will....

2.40 *King Theodoric to the Patrician Boethius (506)*

Although the king of the Franks, tempted by the fame of my banquets, has earnestly requested a lyre-player from

me, I have promised to fulfill his wishes for this reason only, that I know you to be skilled in musical knowledge. To choose a trained man is a task for you, who have succeeded in attaining the heights of that same discipline.

For what is more glorious than music, which modulates the heavenly system with its sonorous sweetness, and binds together with its virtue the concord of nature which is scattered everywhere? For any variation there may be in the whole does not depart from the pattern of harmony. Through [music] we think with efficiency, we speak with elegance, we move with grace. Whenever, by the natural law of its discipline, it reaches our ears, it commands song. The artist changes men's hearts as they listen; and, when this artful pleasure issues from the secret place of nature as the queen of the senses, in all the glory of its tones, our remaining thoughts take to flight, and it expels all else, that it may delight itself simply in being heard. Harmful melancholy he turns to pleasure; he weakens swelling rage; he makes bloodthirsty cruelty kindly, arouses sleepy sloth from its torpor, restores to the sleepless their wholesome rest, recalls lust-corrupted chastity to its moral resolve, and heals boredom of spirit which is always the enemy of good thoughts. Dangerous hatreds he turns to helpful goodwill, and, in a blessed kind of healing, drives out the passions of the heart by means of sweetest pleasures....

Among men all this is achieved by means of five *toni* [scales or modes], each of which is called by the name of

---

[1] This refers to a new law (a "Novel") by Emperor Theodosius II that prohibited Jews from building new synagogues but granted them the right to strengthen those already standing if they threatened to collapse.

[2] This probably means "if no one, for thirty years, has legally challenged the right of your synagogue to exist on that site, and in that form." Theodoric considered property arrangements in place before his conquest of Italy (489–493) to be valid.

the region where it was discovered.[1] Indeed, the divine compassion distributed this favor locally, even while it assuredly made its whole creation something to be praised. The Dorian *tonus* bestows wise self-restraint and establishes chastity; the Phrygian arouses strife, and inflames the will to anger; the Aeolian calms the storms of the soul, and gives sleep to those who are already at peace; the Iastian [Ionian] sharpens the wits of the dull, and, as a worker of good, gratifies the longing for heavenly things among those who are burdened by earthly desire. The Lydian was discovered as a remedy for excessive cares and weariness of the spirit: it restores it by relaxation, and refreshes it by pleasure....

3.1 *King Theodoric to Alaric, King of the Visigoths (507)*

Although the countless numbers of your clan gives you confidence in your strength, although you recall that the power of Attila yielded to Visigothic might,[2] nevertheless, the hearts of a warlike people grow soft during a long peace. Therefore, beware of suddenly putting on the hazard men who have assuredly had no experience in war for many years. Battle terrifies those who are unused to it, and they will have no confidence in a sudden clash, unless experience gives it in advance. Do not let some blind resentment carry you away. Self-restraint is fore-sighted, and a preserver of tribes; rage, though, often precipitates a crisis; and only when justice can no longer find a place with one's opponent, is it then useful to appeal to arms.

Wait, therefore, until I send my envoys to the Frankish king [Clovis], so that the judgment of friends may terminate your dispute. For I wish nothing to arise between two of my marriage kinsmen that may, perhaps, cause one of them to be the loser.[3] There has been no slaughter of your clansmen to inflame you; no occupied province is deeply incensing you; the quarrel is still trivial, a matter of words. You will very easily settle it if you do not enrage yourself by war. Though you are my relative, let me set against you the notable tribes allied to me, and justice

too, which strengthens kings and quickly puts to flight those minds which it finds are so armed against it. And so, giving first the honor of my greeting, I have seen fit to send you X and Y[4] as my envoys. They will convey my instructions, as requisite, and, with your approval, will hasten on to my brother Gundobad and the other kings, lest you should be harassed by the incitements of those who maliciously rejoice in another's war. May Providence prevent that wickedness from overcoming you. I judge your enemy to be our common trouble. For he who strives against you will find in me his due opponent....

10.31 *King Witigis to All the Goths (536)*

Although every promotion must be ascribed to the gift of God, nor is anything a blessing unless we know that He bestowed it, nonetheless, the case of royal office must be especially ascribed to the judgment of Heaven. For God Himself has certainly ordained the man to whom He assigns the obedience of His people.

Hence I thank my originator most humbly, and announce that my kinsmen the Goths, placing me on a shield among the swords of battle, in the ancestral way, have conferred on me the kingly office by God's gift. Thus arms bestow an honor based on a reputation won in war. For you must know that I was chosen not in privy chambers, but in the wide and open fields; I was not sought among the subtle debates of sycophants, but as the trumpets blared, so that the Gothic race of Mars, roused by such a din, and longing for their native courage, might find themselves a martial king.[5] For could brave men, nourished among the turmoil of war, long endure a prince so untried that they were anxious for his fame, although they trusted in their own courage?[6] For inevitably, the reputation of a whole people corresponds to the ruler which that race has earned. Now as you may have heard, I was summoned by the perils of my kindred, and came prepared to endure the common fortune with you all; but who were looking for an experienced king did not suffer me to be [only] their general. Therefore,

---

[1] Tones were a way to categorize melodic practices, and theorists differed on their number.

[2] The Visigoths, fighting as part of the Roman army, won a battle over Attila's Huns in 451.

[3] Theodoric's wife was the sister of Clovis, while Alaric's wife was Theodoric's daughter.

[4] The letters were drafted for specific situations but also for use as models for future correspondence. Here we have the form of the model.

[5] Mars was the war god of the pre-Christian Romans.

[6] The prince referred to here was Theodahad.

give your assent first to the judgment of divine favor, then to the judgment of the Goths, since, by voting for me unanimously, all of you make me king.

Put aside now your fear of punishment, discard suspicions that you will suffer loss: you need fear no harsh treatment under my rule. I who have waged war many times know how to love the brave. Moreover, I am the witness to each of your warriors. There is no need for another to recount your deeds to me: I am a partner in your toils, and know them all. Gothic arms will never be broken by any change in my promises to you: all that

I do will look to the benefit of our race; I will not have private attachments; I promise to pursue what will honor the royal name. Finally, I promise that my rule will, in all things, be such as the Goths should possess following the glorious Theodoric. He was a man peculiarly and nobly formed for the cares of kingship, so that every prince is rightly considered excellent only in so far as he is known to love his policies. Hence, he who can imitate his deeds should be thought of as his kinsman. And therefore you should take thought for the general good of our realm, with, by God's help, an easy mind as to its internal affairs.

1.14 Gothic Spain converts: *The Third Council of Toledo* (589). Original in Latin.

In 589, 63 bishops and other clerics, abbots, and nobles met at Toledo in Spain at the request of King Reccared (r.586–601). They were there to "restore ecclesiastical discipline" by converting the kingdom from the Arian form of Christianity to the Catholic. In 587, Reccared had announced his own conversion, and even before that, in 580, an Arian council at Toledo had accepted part (though not all) of the Catholic Creed on the Trinity, agreeing that the Father and Son were equal and co-eternal, but not the Holy Spirit. The Third Council of Toledo added Catholic teaching on the Holy Spirit and instituted all the canons (laws) of the Catholic Church. Since opposition to the conversion of 589 seems to have been very weak, it is likely that most Visigoths were happy to accept Catholicism, which brought them into agreement with the large Hispano-Roman population in Spain.

[Source: *Medieval Iberia: Readings from Christian, Muslim, and Jewish Sources*, ed. Olivia Remie Constable with the assistance of Damian Zurro, 2nd ed. (Philadelphia: University of Pennsylvania Press, 2012), pp. 12–20. Translated by David Nirenberg.]

In the name of our Lord Jesus Christ, in the fourth year of the reign of the most glorious, most pious and most faithful to God Lord Reccared, king, on the eighth day of the Ides of May, era 627 [589],[1] this sacred council was celebrated in the royal city of Toledo, by the bishops of all Spain and of the Gauls who are inscribed below.

This most glorious prince having commanded, because of the sincerity of his faith, that all the prelates of his kingdom should convene in one [council] in order that they might exult in the Lord, both for his conversion

and for the renewal of the Gothic people, and that they should at the same time give thanks to the divine dignity for such an extraordinary gift, this same most blessed prince addressed the venerable council saying: "I do not believe that you are unaware of the fact, most reverend bishops, that I have summoned you into our serene presence for the restoration of ecclesiastical discipline. And because throughout past times the threatening heresy [of Arianism] did not allow a synod [council] of all the Catholic Church to be convened, God, whom it pleased

---

[1] In the Spanish system of dating, used until the fourteenth century, the year 1 began in what is today 38 BCE. The calculation of the day of the month, however, followed the ancient Roman dating system: the eighth day of the Ides of May was the seventh day counting backwards from May 15, so May 8.

to eliminate the said heresy through us, admonished us to repair the institutions of the customs of the church...."

Upon [hearing] this, the entire council, giving thanks to God and acclaiming the most religious prince, decreed in that instant a fast of three days. And all the bishops of God having come together again on the eighth day of the Ides of May, after the preliminary oration [prayer], each of the bishops was again seated in his proper place, when behold, among them appeared the most serene prince, having joined himself to the oration of the bishops of God, and filled thereafter with divine inspiration, he began to address [the bishops] saying: "We do not believe that your holinesses are unaware of how long a time Spain labored under the error of the Arians, and how, not long after our father's death, when it was known that we had associated ourselves with your holy Catholic faith, there [arose] everywhere a great and eternal rejoicing. And therefore, venerable fathers, we decided to unite you [in order] to celebrate this council, so that you yourselves may give eternal thanks to the Lord for the peoples newly come to Christ. The rest of the agenda that we present before your priestliness concerning our faith and hope which we profess, we have written down in this book. Read it, therefore, among yourselves. And [then] approved by the judgment of council and decorated with this testimony of faith, our glory shall shine throughout all times to come."

The... book the king offered was received, therefore, by all the bishops of God, and [it] being read in a clear voice by the clerk, the following was heard: Although the omnipotent God has, for the benefit of the populace, given us charge of the kingdom, and has delivered the governance of not a few peoples into our royal stewardship, nevertheless we remember that we too are of mortal condition, and that we cannot merit the happiness of future blessedness unless we esteem the cult of the true faith, and, at least, please our creator with the creed of which he is worthy. For which reason, the higher we are extolled above our subjects by royal dignity, the more we should provide for those things that pertain to God, both to increase our faith, and to take thought for the people God has entrusted to us....

Therefore, most holy fathers, these most noble peoples, who have been brought near to the Lord by our diligence, I offer to the eternal God through your hands, as a holy and propitiating sacrifice. Truly it shall be for me an unfad-ing crown and a delight in the reward of the just if these peoples, who because of our dexterity have rushed to the unity of the church, remain rooted and firm within it. And truly, just as it was [entrusted] to our care by the divine will to bring these peoples to the unity of the Church of Christ, it is your duty to instruct them in the dogmas of the Catholics so that, instructed in the full knowledge of the truth, they [shall] know [how] stolidly to reject the errors of the pernicious heresy, and to keep to the path of the true faith through love, embracing the communion of the Catholic Church with an ever more ardent desire....

To these my true confessions I added the sacred decrees of the abovementioned councils, and I signed them, with God [as my] witness, in all innocence of heart....

I, Reccared, king, faithful to this holy and true creed, which is believed by the Catholic Church throughout the world, holding it in my heart, affirming it with my mouth, signed it with my right hand, [under] God's protection.

I, Bado, glorious queen, signed with my hand and with all my heart this creed, which I believed and professed.

Then the entire council broke into acclamations, praising God and applauding the prince....

Here begin the decrees that, in the name of God, were established by the third holy synod in the city of Toledo.

1. THAT THE STATUTES OF THE COUNCILS AND THE DECREES OF THE ROMAN PONTIFFS BE MAINTAINED

After the condemnation of the Arian heresy and the exposition of the holy Catholic faith, the holy council decreed the following: that since in some Spanish churches, whether because of heresy or paganism, canonical discipline was passed over, license for transgression abounded, and the option of discipline was denied, so that any excess of heresy found favor and an abundance of evil made lukewarm the strictness of discipline, [because of these things,] the mercy of Christ having restored peace to the church, [we order that] all that which the authority of the ancient canons[1] prohibited, let it also be restricted by the revived discipline, and let that be performed which [the canons said] ought to be performed....

2. THAT IN ALL THE CHURCHES THE CREED[2] SHOULD BE RECITED ON SUNDAY ...

---

[1] Canons were the laws determined by Church councils.

[2] See the *Nicene Creed* (above, p. 13), to which was added the "filioque," which said that Holy Spirit proceeded from the Father and the Son.

4. THAT IT IS PERMITTED THE BISHOP TO CONVERT A CHURCH IN HIS PARISH INTO A MONASTERY...

5. THAT BISHOPS AND DEACONS SHOULD LIVE CHASTELY WITH THEIR WIVES

It has come to the attention of the holy council that the bishops, presbyters, and deacons who are coming out of heresy [i.e., Arians] copulate with their wives out of carnal desire. So that this shall not be done in the future, we decree what prior canons had already determined: that they are not allowed to live in libidinous union, but rather with the conjugal bond remaining between them they should mutually help each other, without living in the same room. Or if [his] virtue is strong enough, let him make his wife live in some other house, as good witness to [his] chastity, not only before God, but also before men. But if any should choose to live obscenely with his wife after this accord, let him be a lector.[1] [And concerning any of] those who have always been subjected to ecclesiastical canons [i.e., Catholics], if against ancient command they have had consort in their cells with women who could provoke a suspicion of infamy, let them be punished canonically, the women being sold [into slavery] by the bishop, their price being distributed to the poor....

9. THAT THE CHURCHES OF THE ARIANS SHALL BELONG TO THE CATHOLIC BISHOPS IN WHOSE DIOCESES THEY ARE LOCATED...

10. THAT NO ONE COMMIT VIOLENCE AGAINST THE CHASTITY OF A WIDOW, AND THAT NO ONE MARRY A WOMAN AGAINST HER WILL

In the interests of chastity (the increase of which the council should most avidly incite) and with the agreement of our most glorious lord king Reccared, this holy council affirms that widows who wish to maintain their chastity may not be forced with any violence into a second marriage. And if before taking a vow of chastity they wish to be married, let them marry him who of their own free will they wish to have as husband. The same should be maintained concerning virgins, [for] they should not be forced to take a husband against their parents' will or their own. If anyone impedes the desire of a widow or virgin to remain chaste, let him be held a stranger from holy communion and the thresholds of the church.

11. THAT PENITENTS DO PENANCE

[We are] aware of the fact that in some churches of Spain men do penitence for their sins, not in accordance with the canons, but in a disgusting way: as often as they wish to sin, they ask the presbyter to be reconciled. Therefore, in order to eliminate such an execrable presumption, the council decrees that penitence be given in accordance with the form of the ancient canons, that is: that he who repents should first be separated from communion, and he should avail himself often of the laying on of hands, along with the other penitents. Once his time of satisfaction is finished, he should be restored to communion as the bishop sees fit. But those who return to their old vice, whether during the time of penitence or afterwards, shall be condemned in accordance with the severity of the ancient canons....

14. CONCERNING THE JEWS

At the suggestion of the council, our most glorious lord has commanded [that the following] be inserted in the canons: It is not permitted for Jews to have Christian women as wives or concubines, nor to purchase slaves for their personal use. And if children are born of such a union, they should be taken to the baptismal font. They may not be assigned any public business by virtue of which they [might] have power to punish Christians. And if any Christians have been stained by them, [or] by Jewish ritual, or been circumcised, let them return to liberty and the Christian religion without paying the price [of their freedom]....

16. THAT BISHOPS ALONG WITH JUDGES DESTROY THE IDOLS, AND THAT LORDS FORBID THEIR SERVANTS IDOLATRY

Because the sacrilege of idolatry is taking root in nearly all of Spain and Gaul, the holy synod, with the consent of the glorious prince, commands the following: that each bishop in his respective area, along with the judge of that region, should diligently search out the aforesaid sacrilege, and should nor refrain from exterminating that which they find, and should correct those who participate in such error with any punishment available, save that which endangers life....

17. THAT THE BISHOPS AND THE JUDGES CORRECT WITH BITTER DISCIPLINE THOSE WHO MURDER THEIR OWN CHILDREN

Among the many complaints which have come to the ears of the holy council, there has been denounced to it a

---

[1] A demotion to minor orders.

crime so great, that the ears of the present bishops cannot bear it, and this is that in some parts of Spain, parents kill their own children, [because they are] eager to fornicate, and know nothing of piety. Those to whom it is troublesome to have many children should first refrain from fornication. [For once] they have contracted marriage under the pretext of procreation, they make themselves guilty of parricide and fornication, who, by murdering their own children, reveal that they were married not for procreation but for libidinous union. Our most glorious lord king Reccared, having taken account of such evil, his glory has deigned to instruct the judges of those regions to inquire diligently concerning such a horrible crime, in conjunction with the bishops, and to forbid it with all severity. Therefore this sacred council sorrowfully urges the bishops of [those] regions that together with the judges they diligently inquire [about this crime], and forbid it with the most severe penalties, excepting death....

19. THAT THE CHURCH AND ALL ITS GOODS ARE UNDER THE ADMINISTRATION OF THE BISHOP

Many people, against that which is established in the canons, request the consecration of churches which have been built [by them] in such a way that the endowment they gave it not fall under the administration of the bishop, which thing was displeasing in the past and is forbidden in the future. Rather everything is [now] under the administration and power of the bishop, in accordance with the ancient edicts....

22. THAT THE BODIES OF [DECEASED] RELIGIOUS BE PROCESSED [TO BURIAL] AMID THE CHANTING OF PSALMS

The bodies of all religious who, called by God, depart from this life, should be carried to the grave amid psalms and the voices of the chanters only, but we absolutely forbid burial songs, which are commonly sung for the dead, and the accompaniment [of the corpse] by the family and dependents of the deceased beating their breast. It suffices that, in the hope of the resurrection

of the Christians, there be accorded to bodily remains the tribute of divine canticles.[1] For the Apostle forbids us to mourn the dead, saying: "I do not wish you to sadden yourselves about those who are asleep, as do those who have no hope."[2] And the Lord did not mourn the dead Lazarus, but rather shed tears for his resurrection to the hardships of this world. Therefore if the bishop is able, he should not hesitate to forbid all Christians to do this. Clerics, too, should not act in any other way, for it is fitting that throughout the world deceased Christians should be buried thus.

23. THAT DANCES BE PROHIBITED ON THE BIRTHDAYS OF THE SAINTS

That unreligious custom which the vulgar people practice on the feast days of the saints must be completely destroyed. That is, that the people who ought to attend to the divine offices instead dedicate themselves to unseemly songs and dances, injuring not only themselves, but also interfering with the offices of the religious. The holy council commends [this] to the care of the bishops and judges: that this custom may be banished from all of Spain.

HERE BEGINS THE EDICT OF THE KING IN CONFIRMATION OF THE COUNCIL

... We decree that all these ecclesiastical rules which we have summarized briefly above [should be] maintained with eternal stability as is amply explained in the canons. If any cleric or layperson does not wish to obey these decrees, [let them be punished as follows]: If they are a bishop, presbyter, deacon, or cleric, let them be subject to excommunication by the entire council. If they are laypeople of substance in their region, let them give [as a fine] half of their possessions to the fisc,[3] and if they are people of inferior status in their region, let them lose [all] their possessions and be sent into exile.

I, Flavius Reccared, have signed as confirmation these decrees that we established with the holy synod.

[There follow the signatures of the bishops, etc.]

---

[1] This probably refers to any of the poetry of the Old Testament, including the psalms.
[2] 1 Thess. 4: 12.
[3] The fisc was the property or treasury of the state, in this case the king.

1.15 Merovingian Gaul's bishop-historian: Gregory of Tours, *History* (576–594). Original in Latin.

Bishop of Tours from 573 until his death *c.*594, Gregory began his *History* with the Creation itself but soon turned to Gaul and to his own day, which he chronicled in the Augustinian spirit (see *The City of God*, p. 14 above), with both good and bad people and events intermingled. As the successor of St. Martin as bishop of Tours (see *The Life of St. Martin*, above p. 34), Gregory was responsible for the well-being of his flock. But his authority was checked and balanced by that of dukes, counts, and kings. In the excerpt below, in which the former count of Tours, Leudast (d.582), accuses Gregory of slandering Chilperic's Queen Fredegund (d.597), the role of Merovingian kings in Church affairs and the importance of bishops in royal policy are illuminated. Gregory's trial before King Chilperic at Berny-Rivière was a very dangerous moment for the bishop, who might well have been exiled or even executed for treason. Why, then, was he let off with a token sentence?

[Source: *Gregory of Tours: The Merovingians*, trans. and ed. Alexander Callander Murray (Toronto: University of Toronto Press, 2005), pp. 112–20 (slightly modified).]

Book 5

47. [King] Chilperic [r.561–584] heard all about the harm that Leudast [count of Tours] was doing to the churches of Tours and the entire population, and so the king sent Ansovald there. He came on the festival of Saint Martin, and as the choice of count was granted to me on behalf of the people, Eunomius was raised to the comital office.

Leudast, seeing himself set aside, went to Chilperic.

"Most dutiful king," he said, "up to now I have guarded the city of Tours. But now that I have been removed from office, look how it will be guarded. You should know that Bishop Gregory is preparing to surrender it to the son of Sigibert."

"Not at all," said the king on hearing this, "you bring this up only because you have been removed."

"The bishop speaks of even greater matters that concern you," said Leudast; "for he says that your queen [Fredegund] is committing adultery with Bishop Bertram."

At that point the king became angry. He punched and kicked Leudast, ordering him thrown into prison, loaded with chains.

48. Although this book should come to an end, I would like to tell something of Leudast's career. It seems best to begin with his birth, his homeland, and his character.

Gracina is the name of an island off Poitou, where Leudast was born to Leuchadius, a slave of a vinedresser

of the fisc [i.e., royal estates]. From there Leudast was summoned to service and assigned to the royal kitchen. But as his eyes were poor when he was young, and the bitter smoke did not agree with them, he was removed from the pestle and promoted to the baker's basket. Although he pretended to be happy among the fermented dough, he soon ran away and abandoned his service. And when he had been brought back two or three times and could not be prevented from attempting to escape, he was punished by having one of his ears clipped. Then since there was no way for him to conceal the mark imprinted on his body, he fled to Queen Marcovefa, whom King Charibert [r.561–567] loved very much and had admitted to his bed in the place of her sister. She received him willingly, promoted him, and appointed him keeper of her best horses. On this account, now overcome with self-importance and full of arrogance, he canvassed for the office of count of the stables. When he got it, he looked down his nose at everyone, holding them of no account. He was swollen with conceit and undone by the pleasures of the senses; he burned with greed and, as a favorite of his patroness, went here and there on her affairs. After her death, being well-provided with plunder, he tried to maintain with King Charibert his former position by giving gifts.

After this, due to the sinfulness of the people, he was sent as count to Tours, and there the prestige of the high office allowed him to be even more arrogant. He showed himself to be a greedy plunderer, a loud-mouthed brawler, and a filthy adulterer. By sowing dissension and bringing false charges, he there amassed no small fortune.

After Charibert's death, when the city became part of Sigibert's share,[1] he went over to Chilperic, and everything that he had unjustly amassed was seized by the adherents of Sigibert. Then king Chilperic, through his son Theudebert, overran Tours. Since by this time I had arrived in Tours, Theudebert strongly recommended to me that Leudast should hold the office of count, which he had held before. Leudast acted very humbly toward me and was subservient, repeatedly swearing on the tomb of the holy bishop Martin that he would never act unreasonably and that he would be loyal to me in matters affecting my own person as well as in all the needs of the church. For he was afraid that King Sigibert would bring the city back under his authority, as later happened. On Sigibert's death, Chilperic succeeded to his rule and Leudast again became count. When Merovech came to Tours,[2] he plundered all Leudast's property. During the two years that Sigibert held Tours, Leudast took refuge among the Bretons.

When he assumed the office of count, as we have said, his capriciousness reached the point of his entering the bishop's house wearing body armor and mail, with a bow case slung from a belt, a lance in his hand and a helmet on his head, a man safe from no one because he was the enemy of everyone. If he presided over a trial along with leading members of the clergy and laity and saw someone pursuing justice, he would now immediately go into a rage and belch forth abuse on the citizens; he used to order priests dragged away in fetters and soldiers beaten with staves, and he showed such cruelty as to beggar description.

When Merovech, who had plundered his property, went away, Leudast came forward with false charges against me, claiming that Merovech had followed my advice in taking away his property. But after the injury had been done, he again repeated his oath and offered a covering from the tomb of the blessed Martin as a pledge that he would never be my enemy.

49. But as it is a long story to follow step by step Leudast's perjuries and other crimes, let me come to his attempt to overthrow me by unjust and execrable cal-

umnies and the divine vengeance wreaked upon him, fulfilling the saying, "Everyone who overthrows shall be overthrown,"[3] and again, "Whoever digs a pit shall fall therein."[4]

After the many wrongs Leudast inflicted on me and mine, and after the many seizures of ecclesiastical property, he joined forces with the priest Riculf, a man as twisted as himself, and blurted out the charge that I had accused Queen Fredegund of a criminal act;[5] he claimed that, should my archdeacon Plato or my friend Galien be put to torture, they would certainly convict me of having spoken in this way. It was then, as I have said above, that the king had become angry and, after punching and kicking him and loading him with chains, had him thrown into prison.

Now Leudast said that he had the support of the cleric Riculf, on whose testimony he made these charges. This Riculf was a subdeacon, just as unstable as Leudast. The year before, he had plotted with Leudast on this matter and looked for grounds for going over to him due to my anger. At last he found them and went to him. After preparing all their tricks for four months and having laid their traps, Riculf then came back to me with Leudast and begged me to take him back without penalty. I did it, I confess, and publicly received a secret enemy into my household.

On Leudast's departure, Riculf threw himself at my feet.

"Unless you help me quickly, I am lost," he said. "At the instigation of Leudast, I have said what I should not have said. Send me now to another kingdom; if you do not, I shall be arrested by the king's men and suffer tortures that will kill me."

"If you have said anything that does not correspond to the truth, your words shall be on your own head," I said. "I will not send you to another kingdom in case I fall under suspicion of the king."

After this Leudast came forward as Riculf's accuser, claiming that he had heard the previously mentioned testimony from Riculf the subdeacon. Riculf was bound and put under guard, while Leudast in turn was released. Riculf claimed that Galien and the archdeacon Plato were present on the very day the bishop had uttered his charge.

---

[1] King Sigibert I (r.561–575).

[2] Merovech (d.578) was a rebellious son of King Chilperic.

[3] See Jer. 9: 14.

[4] See Prov. 26: 27.

[5] Note there are two clerics called Riculf to be distinguished in the narrative that follows: the priest Riculf, and the subdeacon Riculf.

The priest Riculf, who by this time had been promised the episcopal office by Leudast, was so carried away with himself that his pride was the equal to that of Simon Magus.[1] On the sixth day after Easter [April 26], he who had taken an oath to me three or more times on the tomb of Saint Martin spewed out such abuse that he could scarcely keep his hands off me, confident, of course, in the trap that he had laid.

On the next day, that is, the Sabbath after Easter, Leudast came to the city of Tours pretending to have some business to attend to. He arrested Plato the archdeacon and Galien, tied them up, and ordered them taken to the queen, loaded with chains and stripped of their robes. I heard of this while in my quarters in the bishop's house and, saddened and disturbed, I entered the oratory and took up the Psalms of David so that some consoling verse might be revealed when I opened them. This is what was found: "He led them away in hope and they were not afraid, and the sea covered their enemies."[2]

Meanwhile, as they began crossing the river on a ferry whose deck rested on two skiffs, the boat that was supporting Leudast sank, and if he had not escaped by swimming, he might have perished with his comrades. As for the other boat, which was connected to the first and carried the bound prisoners, it was kept above water by God's help.

Then the prisoners were taken to the king and charges that carried a death sentence were immediately laid against them. But the king, on reflection, freed them from their bonds and kept them under guard, unharmed and unshackled.

At Tours, in the meantime, Duke Berulf and Count Eunomius concocted a tale that King Guntram [r.561–592] wanted to take the city, and for that reason, to prevent anything going wrong, they said, the city must be provided with a guard. They pretended to set watches at the gates to protect the city, but they were really guarding me. They also sent people to advise me to take valuables from the church and make off secretly to Clermont. But I would not take their advice.

Next the king summoned the bishops of his kingdom and ordered the case carefully investigated.

When the cleric Riculf was repeatedly being examined in secret and, as he often did, was uttering many lies against me and my associates, Modestus, a certain carpenter, said to him, "Unlucky man, who so stubbornly has these designs against his bishop, it would be better for you to be quiet, beg pardon from the bishop, and procure his favor."

At this Riculf began to shout out in a loud voice, "Look at this man who bids me be silent and not pursue the truth. He is an enemy of the queen and will not allow the reasons for the charge against her to be investigated."

These words were immediately reported to the queen. Modestus was arrested, tortured, whipped, put in chains, and kept under guard. He was bound to a post by chains between two guards, but in the middle of the night, when the guards fell asleep, he prayed for the Lord to be so kind as to exert his power on behalf of a wretched man and to let an innocent prisoner in bonds be freed by the visitation of the bishops Martin and Médard.[3] The bonds were broken, the post shattered, the door opened, and soon he entered the basilica of Saint Médard [in Soissons], where I was keeping vigils.

The bishops then assembled at the villa of Berny and were ordered to meet in one building. Next the king arrived and took his seat, after greeting everyone and receiving their blessing. At that point Bertram, bishop of Bordeaux, against whom, along with the queen, this charge had been brought, explained the case and addressed me, saying that the charge [of adultery] had been brought against him and the queen by me. I denied in truth having uttered these things, saying, I heard others say them, but I had not devised them.

Outside the building there was a lot of talk among people, who said, "Why are these charges made against a bishop of God? Why does the king prosecute such charges? How could a bishop have said such things, even about a slave. Lord God, help your servant."

The king said, "The charge against my wife dishonors me. If therefore it is your judgment that witnesses should be presented against the bishop, here they are. But if it seems that this should not be done, and that the matter should be left to the honor of the bishop, speak up. I will gladly pay heed to your command."

All were amazed at the king's wisdom and forbearance.

At that point, when all the bishops said, "The testimony of an inferior cannot be admitted against a bishop," the case came down to this, that I should say three masses

---

[1]   Simon Magus figures in Acts 8: 9–24, where he is a magician who thinks that the power of the Holy Spirit exercised by the apostles is a type of magic that he can buy.

[2]   See Ps. 78: 53; Douay Ps. 77: 53.

[3]   Bishop Martin was St. Martin (see above, p. 34); Médard (d.c.545) was bishop of Vermandois; his body lay at the church at Soissons.

at three altars and clear myself of the alleged charges by taking an oath. And though these conditions were contrary to the canons, still they were fulfilled for the sake of the king. Also I cannot be silent about the fact that Queen Rigunth,[1] out of sympathy for my suffering, fasted with all her household until a slave reported that I had fulfilled all that had been required of me.

Then the bishops returned to the king.

"All that was imposed upon the bishop has been carried out," they said. "What remains to be done now, king, if not the excommunication of you and Bertram, the accuser of a brother?"

"Oh no," said the king, "I only reported what I had heard."

They asked who had said this, and he answered that he had heard these things from Leudast. He had already fled owing to the weakness of his plan or his resolution. All the bishops then decided that this sower of discord, traducer of the queen, and accuser of a bishop, should be shut out of all churches, because he had withdrawn from the hearing. To the bishops who were not present, they sent a letter to this effect, bearing their signatures. After this, each of them returned to his own see.

When Leudast heard, he took refuge in the church of Saint Peter in Paris. But on hearing the royal edict prohibiting anyone in Chilperic's kingdom from receiving him, and especially since the son whom he had left at home had died, he came to Tours in secret and carried away his more valuable possessions to Bourges. The king's retainers pursued him, but he escaped by flight. They captured his wife, and she was sent into exile in the district of Tournai.

The subdeacon Riculf was sentenced to death. I managed to obtain his life but I could not free him from torture. Nothing, not even metal, could have endured such beating as was given this wretch. With his hands tied behind his back, he was suspended from a tree from the third hour of the day; at the ninth hour, he was taken down, wracked on pulleys, beaten with staves, rods, and doubled thongs, and not by one or two assailants, but by as many as could reach his wretched limbs. Only at the critical point in the torture did he then reveal the truth and make known the secrets of the plot. This was the explanation he gave for the charge being made against the queen: when she was driven from power, Clovis would

obtain the kingdom, once his brothers and father had been killed;[2] Leudast would get a ducal office. As for the priest Riculf, who had been a friend of Clovis from the times of the blessed Bishop Eufronius, he would win appointment to the bishopric of Tours. The subdeacon Riculf was promised the archdiaconate.

I returned to Tours by God's grace and found the church thrown into turmoil by the priest Riculf. Now this man had been picked out from among the poor under bishop Eufronius and appointed archdeacon. Later he was raised to the priesthood and withdrew to his own property. He was always self-important, arrogant, and impudent. For example, while I was still with the king, he brazenly entered the bishop's house as if he were already bishop, inventoried the church silver, and brought the rest of the property under his control. He enriched the more important clergy with gifts, granted vineyards, and parceled out meadows; to the lesser clergy, he administered beatings and many blows, even raising his own hand against them.

"Acknowledge your master," he said. "He has gained victory over his enemies, and it is by his devices that Tours has been purged of that crew from Clermont."[3]

The wretched man did not know that, with the exception of five bishops, all the others who have held the bishopric of Tours were descendants of my ancestors. He was accustomed to repeating to his intimates the proverb that no one can expect to trick a wise man without using perjury.

Upon my return, when he continued to hold me in disdain and did not come to greet me as did the other citizens, but rather threatened to kill me, I ordered him taken away to a monastery on the advice of the bishops of my province. While he was closely confined, representatives of bishop Felix [of Nantes], who had supported the charge against me, intervened. The abbot was taken in by their perjuries; Riculf slipped away and went to Bishop Felix, who received him warmly, though he should have cursed him.

Leudast meanwhile went to Bourges, taking with him all the treasure that he had plundered from the poor. Not long after, forces from Bourges under their count attacked him and carried off all his gold and silver and whatever else he had brought with him, leaving him nothing but what he had on his person; and they would have taken

---

[1] Rigunth (d.585) was the daughter of King Chilperic and Queen Fredegund.

[2] This Clovis (d.580) was the son of King Chilperic and his first wife, Audovera.

[3] Gregory of Tours's father's family was closely associated with Clermont, and Gregory spent much of his childhood there.

his very life if he had not fled. He regained his strength and in turn led some men from Tours in an attack against his plunderers; killing one of them, he recovered some of his property and returned to the territory of Tours. Duke Berulf heard about this and sent his own retainers outfitted for war to seize him. Leudast realized that he would now be captured, and so he abandoned his property and fled to the church of Saint Hilary in Poitiers.[1] Duke Berulf meanwhile sent the property that he seized to the king.

Leudast would leave the basilica and attack the houses of various people, taking plunder without trying to disguise the fact. He was also repeatedly caught in adultery in the holy confines of the very porch of the basilica. For these reasons, the queen, disturbed that a place consecrated to God was being defiled in such a fashion, ordered him to be expelled from the holy basilica. On being expelled, he went again to his supporters in Bourges, begging them to hide him.

50. I should have mentioned my conversation with the blessed Bishop Salvius earlier, but, as it slipped my mind, I do not consider it unwarranted if it is written later.[2]

When I had said farewell to the king after the council that I mentioned [at Berny], and was anxious to return home, I did not want to go without taking leave of Salvius with a kiss. I looked for him and found him in the courtyard of the domain of Berny. I told him that I was about to return home.

We had moved off a little and were speaking of one thing and another when he said to me, "Do you see what I see upon this roof?"

"Why, I see the roof-covering that the king lately had installed," said I.

"Don't you see anything else?"

"I see nothing else." I suspected that he was making some kind of a joke.

"Tell me what more do you see?" I added.

Drawing a deep breath, he said, "I see the sword of divine wrath unsheathed and hanging over this house."

Indeed, the bishop's words were not wrong; for twenty days later died the two sons of the king, whose deaths I have already described.[3]

---

[1] How does the description of this particular case of asylum in the Merovingian Kingdom fit with the provisions in *The Theodosian Code*, above, p. 4?

[2] Salvius was bishop of Albi 571–584.

[3] In an earlier chapter, Gregory had described the deaths of the two sons of King Chilperic.

TIMELINE FOR CHAPTER ONE

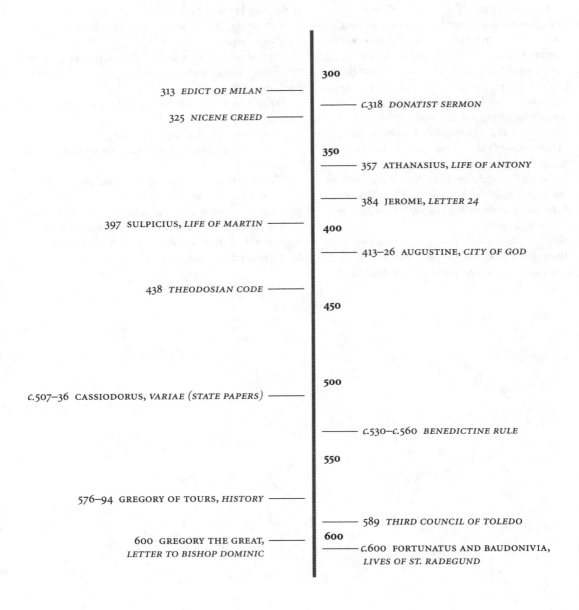

300

313 *EDICT OF MILAN* ——————

—————— *c.*318 *DONATIST SERMON*

325 *NICENE CREED* ——————

350

—————— 357 ATHANASIUS, *LIFE OF ANTONY*

—————— 384 JEROME, *LETTER 24*

397 SULPICIUS, *LIFE OF MARTIN* ——————

400

—————— 413–26 AUGUSTINE, *CITY OF GOD*

438 *THEODOSIAN CODE* ——————

450

500

*c.*507–36 CASSIODORUS, *VARIAE (STATE PAPERS)* ——————

—————— *c.*530–*c.*560 *BENEDICTINE RULE*

550

576–94 GREGORY OF TOURS, *HISTORY* ——————

—————— 589 *THIRD COUNCIL OF TOLEDO*

600 GREGORY THE GREAT, —————— 600
LETTER TO BISHOP DOMINIC

—————— *c.*600 FORTUNATUS AND BAUDONIVIA,
LIVES OF ST. RADEGUND

*To test your knowledge and gain deeper understanding of this chapter,
please go to www.utphistorymatters.com for Study Questions.*

The Emergence of Sibling Cultures (c.600–c.750)

2.1 Byzantine village life and the education of a saint: *The Life of St. Theodore of Sykeon* (7th c.). Original in Greek.

One of St. Paul's letters was written to the Galatians, a Celtic people that settled in north-central Anatolia. By the seventh century, they were thoroughly Christianized, as the anonymous *Life of St. Theodore* makes clear. Although the story is set in the time of Justinian, it probably best reflects the period of its writing, just before the Arab invasions of Anatolia. What evidence do you find that villagers were aware of the imperial court? How many local churches can you count? What sort of schooling was normal in a village?

[Source: *Three Byzantine Saints: Contemporary Biographies translated from the Greek*, trans. Elizabeth Dawes and Norman H. Baynes (Crestwood, NY: St. Vladimir's Seminary Press, 1977), pp. 88–96 (notes modified).]

(3) In the country of Galatia[1] there is a village called Sykeon under the jurisdiction of the town of Anastasioupolis which belongs to the province of Galatia Prima, namely that of Ancyra. Sykeon lies twelve miles distant from Anastasioupolis.

The public highway of the imperial post ran through this village, and on the road stood an inn kept by a very beautiful girl, Mary, and her mother, Elpidia, and a sister Despoinia. And these women lived in the inn and followed the profession of courtesans.

At that time when Justinian of pious memory was Emperor [r.527–565] certain imperial decrees were being dispatched from the capital, and thus it chanced that a certain well-known man, Cosmas by name, who had become popular in the Hippodrome in the corps of those who performed acrobatic feats on camels, was appointed to carry out the Emperor's orders.

On this man's journey to the East he stayed for some time in the inn, and seeing Mary and how fair she was, he desired her and took her to his bed. From this union

---
[1] Galatia was an Anatolian province of Byzantium.

she conceived and saw in a dream a very large and brilliant star descending from heaven into her womb. She awoke all trembling with fear and related the vision she had seen in the night to Cosmas, the imperial messenger, and he said to her, "Take good care of yourself, dear, for perchance God will watch over you and give you a son who will be deemed worthy to become a bishop." With these words he left her in the morning and went on his way rejoicing.

(4) Next the woman visited a holy father who could foresee the future who lived six miles off near the village of Balgatia, and related to him what she had seen in her dream. The old man said to her, "I tell you of a truth that the son who shall be born of you will become a great man, not as men hold greatness, but he will be well-pleasing to God. For a brilliant star is held to signify the glory of a king by those who are expert in interpreting visions; but with you it must not be read thus. For it is the brilliant adornment of virtues and graces which God has sent down upon the babe in your womb that you saw in the likeness of a brilliant star; for thus He is wont to consecrate His worthy servants in the womb before they are born." When Theodosius, who had been appointed bishop of the town of Anastasioupolis, heard of her vision, he, too, by God's inspiration gave to her the same interpretation.

(5) When her full time was accomplished, Mary bore the servant of God; and after some days had passed, she carried him, as is the custom among Christians, to the Holy Church of the Orthodox and showed him to the priests who baptized him in the name of the Holy Trinity and named him "Theodore," thus showing by this name that he would be the "gift of God." When the child was about six years old, his mother wanted him to enter the Emperor's service in the capital, so she made ready for him a gold belt and expensive clothes and everything else necessary, and then she prepared herself for the journey. On the night when she intended to start, God's holy martyr, St. George, appeared to her and said, "What is this plan, lady, which you have made for the boy? Do not labor in vain, for the King in heaven has need of him."[1] And in the morning she arose and related her vision and wept saying, "Assuredly death has drawn near to my boy." After this she abandoned her journey. She wore herself away with increasing care of her son, and when he was eight years old she gave him to a teacher to be taught his letters. By the grace of God he was quicker at learning than all the other boys and made great progress.

He was beloved by all and in his daily life became known to all for his virtues; for when he played with the others he always beat them, but no oath or blasphemy nor any unfitting word ever escaped his lips, nor did he allow the others to use one. And whenever any dispute arose in their games, he at once withdrew and through his actions put an end to it.

(6) Now there lived in the house a God-fearing man called Stephen who used to make skillfully prepared dishes. The women by this time had become quite respectable, for they had abandoned their profession as prostitutes and followed the path of sobriety and godliness. They now relied upon the goodness of the fare when they entertained the many governors and officers who came to the inn, and they congratulated Stephen who had made the food so tasty. Whenever he received any money, either from the women or their guests, he spent it on the churches where he prayed regularly morning and evening. During Lent, although he prepared all the food for the women, he fasted till the evening partaking of nothing except perhaps a little boiled wheat and water.

The women loved him and looked upon him as a father because he was such a true lover of Christ. The boy noticing this abstinence was moved by divine love and desired to copy Stephen's mode of life, according to the words of the apostle who said, "Remember them that have the rule over you who spake unto you the word of God; and consider the issue of their life and imitate their faith… For it is good that the heart be established by grace; not by meats wherein they that occupied themselves were not profited."[2] "For meat commends us not to God."[3]

His mother and the other women, unconscious of his heart's desire, compelled him to eat with them when he returned home from school at the dinner hour; so when school was over he no longer came home for dinner but spent the whole day in the school fasting and in the evening he would come back and go off with the pious man, Stephen, to the holy churches and there pray and partake of the body and blood of Christ. Returning home he would share with Stephen his boiled wheat

---

[1] St. George (d.303) was martyred in Palestine. He had possibly been a soldier. In any event, he soon became a patron saint of the Byzantine army.

[2] Heb. 13: 7, 9.

[3] 1 Cor. 8: 8.

and water. However much the women and even Stephen himself urged him, he could not be persuaded to do as they wished. Then his mother asked the schoolmaster to send him home at the dinner-hour as she wished to persuade him to eat at least a little vegetable food, because he was getting run down from want of food and from eating only so late in the day. The schoolmaster accordingly sent him away with the other boys, but Theodore did according to the song of David which says: "In the Lord I have trusted; how shall ye say to my soul, Flee as a bird to your mountain?"[1]

(7) When he came out of school he went up the rocky hill which lay near the village. Here there was a shrine dedicated to the martyr St. George. The Saint would guide him to the spot appearing visibly before his eyes in the form of a young man. Entering the shrine, Theodore would sit down and busy himself with the study of the Holy Scriptures, and after midday he went back to the school and returned home in the evening. When his mother inquired why he had not appeared at dinner time, he tricked her saying either that he had not been able to say his lesson and was therefore kept in, or that he had a pain in his stomach and therefore had no appetite. So she again sent word to the master to send him home with the others, and he replied that since he had received her message he always did send him away with the others. Then she found out that he went up to the shrine and so she sent some of her servants to fetch him, and they brought him down to her. She threatened him and told him to come straight home from school to her, but he continued to act as he had been accustomed to do. His mother was very troubled about him, but in spite of all her threats and advice she was quite unable to make him change his fixed purpose, or to break the rules of abstinence which he had prescribed for himself.

(8) When he was about twelve years old an epidemic of bubonic plague fell upon the village and it attacked him along with the others so that he came near to dying. They took him to the shrine of St. John the Baptist near the village and laid him at the entrance to the sanctuary, and above him where the cross was set there hung an icon of our Savior Jesus Christ. As he was suffering great pain from the plague suddenly drops of dew fell upon him from the icon and immediately by the grace of God, freed from his suffering, he recovered and returned to his home....

(10) The boy had made very good progress in learning to read when one day he went into the church of the holy martyr Gemellus,[2] which was near his home, and spent the night there. And he saw himself as though he were in the presence of a king surrounded by a strong bodyguard and a woman clad in purple at his side, and he heard the king say, "Fight the good fight, Theodore, that you may receive full pay in the heavenly army, and on earth I will give you glory and honor in the sight of men." When he had heard this voice, he awoke.

He was twelve years old when his heart was stirred by the message given to him by the King, Christ, in this vision, and in his zeal to follow the path leading to those better things which pertain to salvation he began to shut himself up in one of the cellars of his home from Epiphany to Palm Sunday, and during two weeks in Lent, the first and the middle one, he spoke to no one at all but offered prayers to God alone, and practiced abstinence as he had done before.

(11) Now when the devil, the enemy of truth, saw that Theodore was industriously acquiring the spiritual weapons of virtue against him, he determined to destroy him. Accordingly one day he assumed the appearance of one of Theodore's schoolfellows, Gerontius by name, and took him and led him up to the cliffs of a place called Tzidrama, and, setting him on a lofty crag of the cliffs there, put the temptation to him which was put to our Savior, and said, "If you are willing, master Theodore, to display your powers of conquest, display them here and jump down from this cliff." But Theodore looked at the height which was really great and said to Gerontius, "It is high and I am afraid." The devil said to him, "In the eyes of all the boys you are considered braver than I, and you outshine me, but in this matter I am no coward and will throw myself down." The boy answered him, "Don't do it! You may lame yourself, or even be killed." As the other asserted he could do the feat without any danger, Theodore finally said to him, "If you will, then I will too." So the devil standing with him on the rock jumped down, and alighting on his feet shouted up to the boy Theodore, saying, "See, I have done it! If you dare, come down too, that I may see your bravery: if you can, as in all else, distinguish yourself in this test too." While the boy stood debating within himself full of fear at this utterly useless ordeal, and staggered at the boldness of the supposed Gerontius, who had never previously been

---

[1] Ps. 11: 1; Douay Ps. 10: 1.

[2] St. Gemellus (d.362) was martyred under Emperor Julian (r.361–363) in Galatia.

so bold, George, the martyr of Christ, suddenly appeared and taking Theodore by the hand, led him away from the place, saying, "Come, follow me, and do not listen to the tempting of him who is seeking your soul; for he is not Gerontius but the enemy of our race." And so saying the holy martyr brought him to his oratory.

(12) One day when Theodore was staying in the chapel of St. George his mother and his mother's mother came up to him and with much coaxing tried to force him to come down home saying that they expected the visit of some important friends. But the boy could not be persuaded by them to go down, for he fulfilled literally the words of holy scripture which says, "The friendship of this world is enmity with God, and whoever would be a friend of the world makes himself an enemy of God,"[1] and "No one can serve God and Mammon."[2] He also regarded the wealth of the world as nought, and wishing to get rid of it, he unbuckled his gold belt, took off his necklace and the bracelet from his wrist and threw them down in front of the women saying, "You suspect that these things may get lost and it is because of them you trouble me. Take them then and begone! for I will not leave this place." And the women took them and went, as they could not persuade him. For all his thoughts were towards the Lord Whom he imitated and in Whose footsteps he followed; he fled from his parents and ran to God; he gave up wealth and houses in order to be rewarded a hundredfold and inherit eternal life,[3] as the Lord who has promised this says: "He that wishes to come after me, let him deny himself and take up his cross and follow me!"[4]

For the boy nobly mortified his body, keeping it under and wearing it down, as though it were some alien thing which warred against his soul; and on his forehead he bore the Cross; and just as Peter and James and John and the rest of the apostles "left all and followed Jesus"[5] so this boy likewise believed in the witness of the Scriptures and sought earnestly to mold his life thereon.

(13) Further, he wanted to imitate David in his holy hymn-writing and accordingly began to learn the Psalter.[6] With difficulty and much labor he learnt as far as the sixteenth psalm, but he could not manage to get the seventeenth psalm by heart. He was studying it in the chapel of the holy martyr Christopher[7] (which was near the village) and as he could not learn it, he threw himself on his face and besought God to make him quick of learning in his study of the psalms. And the merciful God, Who said, "Ask and it shall be given you,"[8] granted him his request. For as the boy got up from the ground and turned to the icon of our Savior in prayer, he felt a sweetness more pleasant than honey poured into his mouth. He recognized the grace of God, partook of the sweetness and gave thanks to Christ, and from that hour on he memorized the Psalter easily and quickly, and had learnt the whole of it by heart in a few days.

And he would wander about to all the churches, "with psalms and hymns and spiritual songs singing and praising the Lord," and wherever a commemorative service in honor of a saint was being held, he attended it with joy. Similarly, on the occasion of the all-night service for the holy martyr Heuretus[9] held in the town of Iopolis, fifteen miles away, he left at the hour of supper and ran fasting to this service and after praying and partaking of the divine mysteries of Christ, he returned and reached his home at midnight. For he was an exceedingly swift runner, so much so that several times for a wager he ran a race of three miles with horses and outstripped them.

---

[1] James 4: 4.

[2] Luke 16: 13.

[3] Luke 18: 29.

[4] Matt. 16: 24.

[5] Luke 5: 11.

[6] The book of the 150 psalms.

[7] Nothing is known about St. Christopher, possibly a third-century martyr, except that he died in Anatolia and that a cult grew up around him from a very early period.

[8] Matt. 7: 7.

[9] St. Heuretus cannot be identified.

2.2 The argument for icons: John of Damascus, *On Holy Images* (730s or early 750s). Original in Greek.

Once Emperor Leo III adopted a policy against icons, later dubbed "iconoclasm," a spirited debate about holy images began. An early defender was John of Damascus (*c.*675–749), who became a major spokesman for the iconophile (icon-loving) or iconodule (icon-serving) position. John was born at Damascus when it was under Umayyad rule; his father, although Christian, was employed by the caliph, and John succeeded him in the same position. Eventually he became a monk at Mar Saba, near Jerusalem, where he spent the rest of his life practicing the ascetic life while studying, writing, and preaching. His book *The Fount of Knowledge* was a foundational text for Greek Orthodox theology.

[Source: *St. John Damascene on Holy Images*, trans. Mary H. Allies (London: Thomas Baker, 1898), pp. 1, 4–6, 8–17 (slightly modified).]

With the ever-present conviction of my own unworthiness, I ought to have kept silent and confessed my shortcomings before God, but all things are good at the right time. I see the Church which God founded on the Apostles and Prophets, its corner-stone being Christ His Son, tossed on an angry sea, beaten by rushing waves, shaken and troubled by the assaults of evil spirits. I see rents in the seamless robe of Christ, which impious men have sought to part asunder, and His body cut into pieces, that is, the word of God and the ancient tradition of the Church. Therefore I have judged it unreasonable to keep silent and to hold my tongue.…

I believe in one God, the source of all things, without beginning, uncreated, immortal, everlasting, incomprehensible, bodiless, invisible, uncircumscribed [i.e., in no one place], without form. I believe in one supersubstantial being, one divine Godhead in three entities, the Father, the Son, and the Holy Ghost, and I adore Him alone with the worship of latreia.[1] I adore one God, one Godhead but three Persons, God the Father, God the Son made flesh, and God the Holy Ghost, one God. I do not adore creation more than the Creator, but I adore the creature created as I am, adopting creation freely and spontaneously that He might elevate our nature and make us partakers of His divine nature. Together with my Lord and King I worship Him clothed in the flesh, not as if it were a garment or He constituted a fourth person of the Trinity—God for-

bid. That flesh is divine, and endures after its assumption. Human nature was not lost in the Godhead, but just as the Word made flesh remained the Word, so flesh became the Word remaining flesh, becoming, rather, one with the Word through union. Therefore I venture to draw an image of the invisible God, not as invisible, but as having become visible for our sakes through flesh and blood. I do not draw an image of the immortal Godhead. I paint the visible flesh of God, for if it is impossible to represent a spirit, how much more God who gives breath to the spirit.

Now adversaries say: God's commands to Moses the law-giver were, "Thou shalt adore the Lord thy God, and thou shalt worship him alone, and thou shalt not make to thyself a graven thing that is in heaven above, or in the earth beneath."[2] They err truly, not knowing the Scriptures, for the letter kills whilst the spirit quickens—not finding in the letter the hidden meaning.…

These injunctions were given to the Jews on account of their proneness to idolatry. Now we, on the contrary, are no longer in toddler harnesses. Speaking theologically, it is given to us to avoid superstitious error, to be with God in the knowledge of the truth, to worship God alone, to enjoy the fullness of His knowledge. We have passed the stage of infancy and reached the perfection of manhood. We receive our habit of mind from God and know what may be imaged and what may not. The Scripture says, "You have not seen the likeness of Him."[3]

---

[1] Latreia is the worship due to God alone.

[2] See Exod. 20: 4–5.

[3] Exod. 33: 20.

What wisdom in the lawgiver! How depict the invisible? How picture the inconceivable? How give expression to the limitless, the immeasurable, the invisible? How give a form to immensity? How paint immortality? How localize mystery? It is clear that when you contemplate God, who is a pure spirit, becoming man for your sake, you will be able to clothe Him with the human form. When the Invisible One becomes visible to flesh, you may then draw a likeness of His form. When He who is a pure spirit, without form or limit, immeasurable in the boundlessness of His own nature, existing as God, takes upon Himself the form of a servant in substance and in stature, and a body of flesh, then you may draw His likeness, and show it to anyone willing to contemplate it. Depict His ineffable condescension, His virginal birth, His baptism in the Jordan, His transfiguration on Tabor, His all-powerful sufferings, His death and miracles, the proofs of His Godhead, the deeds which He worked in the flesh through divine power, His saving Cross, His Sepulcher, and resurrection, and ascent into heaven. Give to it all the endurance of engraving and color. Have no fear or anxiety; worship is not all of the same kind. Abraham worshiped the sons of Hamor, impious men in ignorance of God, when he bought the double cave for a tomb.[1] Jacob worshiped his brother Esau and the Pharaoh, the Egyptian, but on the point of his staff.[2] He worshiped, he did not adore. Joshua and Daniel worshiped an angel of God; they did not adore him.[3] The worship of latreia is one thing, and the worship that is given to merit another. Now, as we are talking of images and worship, let us analyze the exact meaning of each. An image is a likeness of the original with a certain difference, for it is not an exact reproduction of the original. Thus, the Son is the living, substantial, unchangeable Image of the invisible God, bearing in Himself the whole Father, being in all things equal to Him, differing only in being begotten by the Father, who is the Begetter; the Son is begotten. The Father does not proceed from the Son, but the Son from the Father. It is through the Son, though not after Him, that He is what He is, the Father who generates. In

God, too, there are representations and images of His future acts—that is to say, His counsel from all eternity, which is ever unchangeable. That which is divine is immutable; there is no change in Him, nor shadow of change.[4] Blessed Denis [i.e., Pseudo-Dionysius][5] who has made divine things in God's presence his study, says that these representations and images are marked out beforehand. In His counsels, God has noted and settled all that He would do, the unchanging future events before they came to pass. In the same way, a man who wished to build a house, would first make and think out a plan. Again, visible things are images of invisible and intangible things, on which they throw a faint light. Holy Scripture clothes in figure God and the angels, and the same holy man [Blessed Denis] explains why. When sensible things sufficiently render what is beyond sense, and give a form to what is intangible, a medium would be reckoned imperfect according to our standard, if it did not fully represent material vision, or if it required effort of mind. If, therefore, Holy Scripture, providing for our need, ever putting before us what is intangible, clothes it in flesh, does it not make an image of what is thus invested with our nature, and brought to the level of our desires, yet invisible? A certain conception through the senses thus takes place in the brain, which was not there before, and is transmitted to the judicial faculty, and added to the mental store. Gregory, who is so eloquent about God, says that the mind that is set upon getting beyond corporeal things is incapable of doing it.[6] For the invisible things of God since the creation of the world are made visible through images.[7] We see images in creation which remind us faintly of God, as when, for instance, we speak of the holy and adorable Trinity, imaged by the sun, or light, or burning rays, or by a running fountain, or a full river, or by the mind, speech, or the spirit within us, or by a rose tree, or a sprouting flower, or a sweet fragrance.

Again, an image is expressive of something in the future, mystically shadowing forth what is to happen. For instance, the ark represents the image of Our Lady,

---

[1] See Gen. 23: 7; Acts 7: 16.

[2] See Gen. 33: 3, and 47: 7, 10.

[3] See Jos. 5: 14–15.

[4] See James 1: 17.

[5] Today scholars call the man whom John referred to as Denis "Pseudo-Dionysius." He was a mystical theologian of the late fifth or early sixth century.

[6] This may be a reference to Gregory of Nyssa (d.c.394).

[7] See Rom. 1: 20.

Mother of God, as does the staff and the earthen jar. The serpent brings before us Him who vanquished on the Cross the bite of the original serpent; the sea, water, and the cloud [signify] the grace of baptism.[1]

Again, things which have taken place are expressed by images for the remembrance either of a wonder, or an honor, or dishonor, or good or evil, to help those who look upon it later on, so that we may avoid evils and imitate goodness. It is of two kinds, the written image in books, as when God had the law inscribed on tablets, and when He enjoined that the lives of holy men should be recorded and sensible memorials be preserved in remembrance; as, for instance, the earthen jar and the staff in the ark.[2] So now we preserve in writing the images and the good deeds of the past. Either, therefore, take away images altogether and be out of harmony with God who made these regulations, or receive them with the language and in the manner that befits them. In speaking of the manner let us go into the question of worship.

Worship is the symbol of veneration and of honor. Let us understand that there are different degrees of worship. First of all the worship of latreia, which we show to God, who alone by nature is worthy of worship. Then, for the sake of God who is worshipful by nature, we honor His saints and servants, as Josue and Daniel worshiped an angel, and David His holy places, when he says, "Let us go to the place where His feet have stood."[3] Again, in His tabernacles, as when all the people of Israel adored in the tent, and standing round the temple in Jerusalem, fixing their gaze upon it from all sides, and worshiping from that day to this; or in the rulers established by Him, as Jacob rendered homage to Esau, his elder brother, and to Pharaoh, the divinely established ruler....

Of old, God the incorporeal and uncircumscribed was never depicted. Now, however, when God is seen clothed in flesh and conversing with men, I make an image of the God whom I see. I do not worship matter, I worship the God of matter, who became matter for my sake, and deigned to inhabit matter, who worked out my salvation through matter. I will not cease from honoring that matter which works my salvation. I venerate it, though not as God. How could God be born out of lifeless things? And if God's body is God by union, it is immutable. The nature of God remains the same as before, the flesh created in time is quickened by a logical and reasoning soul. I honor all matter besides and venerate it. Through it, filled, as it were, with a divine power and grace, my salvation has come to me. Was not the thrice happy and thrice blessed wood of the Cross matter? Was not the sacred and holy mountain of Calvary matter? What of the life-giving rock, the Holy Sepulcher, the source of our resurrection: was it not matter? Is not the most holy book of the Gospels matter? Is not the blessed table matter that gives us the Bread of Life? Are not gold and silver matter out of which crosses and altar-plate and chalices are made? And before all these things, is not the body and blood of our Lord matter? Either do away with the veneration and worship due to all these things, or submit to the tradition of the Church in the worship of images, honoring God and His friends, and following in this the grace of the Holy Spirit. Do not despise matter, for it is not despicable. Nothing is that which God has made. This is the Manichean heresy.[4] That alone is despicable which does not come from God but is our own invention, the spontaneous choice of will to disregard the natural law—that is to say, sin.

2.3 The iconoclastic argument: *The Synod of* 754. Original in Greek.

The Byzantine Emperor Leo III (r.717–741) may have launched the period of iconoclasm, but he treated icons as an abuse, not a heresy. His son, Constantine V (r.741–775), took the next step, calling a church council in 754 to declare the veneration of icons a violation of "the fundamental doctrine of our salvation." The synod, whose proceedings survive

---

[1] See 1 Cor. 10: 1.

[2] See Exod. 34: 28 and Heb. 9: 4.

[3] Ps. 132: 7; Douay Ps. 131: 7.

[4] The Manicheans thought that the world consisted of two entities: evil (matter) and good (spirit).

only because they were included in the account of the later iconodule (pro-icon) synod of 787, compared "unlawful art" to the great heresies of Nestorius and Arius, who challenged the orthodox view concerning the nature of the persons of the Trinity. No representation of Christ, the bishops argued, could accurately portray the correct union of His two natures, man and God. The synod included no patriarch or papal representative, but it did involve over 300 bishops—a very large number. What evidence in this document shows that the synod constituted a major triumph for the emperor? How might you argue that iconoclasm was more popular in its day than later iconodule propaganda might suggest?

[Source: *A Select Library of Nicene and Post-Nicene Fathers of the Christian Church*, 2nd ser., ed. Philip Schaff and Henry Wace, vol. 14: *The Seven Ecumenical Councils* (Grand Rapids, MI: Wm. B. Eerdmans, 1971), pp. 543–45 (slightly modified).]

The holy and Ecumenical synod, which by the grace of God and most pious command of the God-beloved and orthodox Emperors, Constantine and Leo[1] now assembled in the imperial residence city, in the temple of the holy and inviolate Mother of God and Virgin Mary, surnamed in Blachernai[2] have decreed as follows.

Satan misguided men, so that they worshiped the creature instead of the Creator. The Mosaic law and the prophets co-operated to undo this ruin; but in order to save mankind thoroughly, God sent his own Son, who turned us away from error and the worshiping of idols and taught us the worshiping of God in spirit and in truth. As messengers of his saving doctrine, he left us his Apostles and disciples, and these adorned the Church, his Bride, with his glorious doctrines. This ornament of the Church the holy Fathers and the six Ecumenical Councils have preserved inviolate. But the before-mentioned demiurgos of wickedness [i.e., Satan] could not endure the sight of this adornment and gradually brought back idolatry under the appearance of Christianity. As then Christ armed his Apostles against the ancient idolatry with the power of the Holy Spirit and sent them out into all the world, so has he awakened against the new idolatry his servants our faithful Emperors and endowed them with the same wisdom of the Holy Spirit. Impelled by the Holy Spirit they could no longer be witnesses of the Church being laid waste by the deception of demons and summoned the sanctified assembly of the God-beloved

bishops, that they might institute at a synod a scriptural examination into the deceitful coloring of the pictures which draws down the spirit of man from the lofty adoration of God to the low and material adoration of the creature, and that they, under divine guidance, might express their view on the subject.

Our holy synod therefore assembled, and we, its 338 members, follow the older synodal decrees and accept and proclaim joyfully the dogmas handed down, principally those of the six holy Ecumenical Synods. In the first place the holy and ecumenical great synod assembled at Nicaea, etc.[3]

After we had carefully examined their decrees under the guidance of the Holy Spirit, we found that the unlawful art of painting living creatures blasphemed the fundamental doctrine of our salvation—namely, the Incarnation of Christ—and contradicted the six holy synods. These condemned Nestorius because he divided the one Son and Word of God into two sons, and on the other side, Arius, Dioscorus, Eutyches, and Severus, because they maintained a mingling of the two natures of the one Christ.[4]

Wherefore we thought it right to make clear with all accuracy in our present definition the error of such as make and venerate these, for it is the unanimous doctrine of all the holy Fathers and of the six Ecumenical Synods that no one may imagine any kind of separation or mingling in opposition to the unsearchable, unspeakable, and

---

[1] Constantine V (r.741–775); his son Leo was only four years old at the time; he eventually ruled as Leo IV (r.775–780).

[2] A church at Constantinople, the shrine of the Virgin at the west end of the Theodosian walls.

[3] A shorthand way to refer to the other synods.

[4] Nestorius, Arius, Dioscorus, Eutyches, and Severus represent the heresiarchs (the originators of the heresies) of early Christianity. Each had a different view of the nature of the persons of the Trinity.

incomprehensible union of the two natures in the one hypostasis or person. What avails, then, the folly of the painter, who from sinful love of gain depicts that which should not be depicted—that is, with his polluted hands he tries to fashion that which should only be believed in the heart and confessed with the mouth? He makes an image and calls it Christ. The name *Christ* signifies *God and man*. Consequently it is an image of God and man, and consequently he has in his foolish mind, in his representation of the created flesh, depicted the Godhead which cannot be represented and thus mingled what should not be mingled. Thus he is guilty of a double blasphemy—the one in making an image of the Godhead and the other in mingling the Godhead and manhood. Those fall into the same blasphemy who venerate the image, and the same woe rests upon both, because they err with Arius, Dioscorus, and Eutyches, and with the heresy of the Acephali.[1] When, however, they are blamed for undertaking to depict the divine nature of Christ, which should not be depicted, they take refuge in the excuse: We represent only the flesh of Christ which we have seen and handled. But that is a Nestorian error.[2] For it should be considered that that flesh was also the flesh of God the Word, without any separation, perfectly assumed by the divine nature and made wholly divine. How could it now be separated and represented apart? So is it with the human soul of Christ which mediates between the Godhead of the Son and the dullness of the flesh. As the human flesh is at the same time flesh of God the Word, so is the human soul also soul of God the Word, and both at the same time, the soul being deified as well as the body, and the Godhead remained undivided even in the separation of the soul from the body in his voluntary passion. For where the soul of Christ is, there is also his Godhead; and where the body of Christ is, there too is his Godhead. If then in his passion the divinity remained inseparable from these, how do the fools venture to separate the flesh from the Godhead and represent it by itself as the image of a mere man? They fall into the abyss of impiety since they separate the flesh from the Godhead, ascribe to it a subsistence of its own, a personality of its own, which they depict, and thus introduce a fourth person into the Trinity. Moreover, they represent as not being made divine that which has been made divine by

being assumed by the Godhead. Whoever, then, makes an image of Christ either depicts the Godhead which cannot be depicted and mingles it with the manhood (like the Monophysites),[3] or he represents the body of Christ as not made divine and separate and as a person apart, like the Nestorians.

The only admissible figure of the humanity of Christ, however, is bread and wine in the holy Supper. This and no other form, this and no other type, has he chosen to represent his incarnation. Bread he ordered to be brought, but not a representation of the human form, so that idolatry might not arise. And as the body of Christ is made divine, so also this figure of the body of Christ, the bread, is made divine by the descent of the Holy Spirit; it becomes the divine body of Christ by the mediation of the priest who, separating the oblation [offering] from that which is common, sanctifies it.

The evil custom of assigning names to the images does not come down from Christ and the Apostles and the holy Fathers; nor have these left behind them any prayer by which an image should be hallowed or made anything else than ordinary matter.

If, however, some say we might be right in regard to the images of Christ on account of the mysterious union of the two natures, but it is not right for us to forbid also the images of the altogether spotless and ever-glorious Mother of God, or of the prophets, apostles, and martyrs, who were mere men and did not consist of two natures; we may reply, first of all: If those fall away, there is no longer need of these. But we will also consider what may be said against these in particular. Christianity has rejected the *whole* of heathenism, and so not merely heathen sacrifices, but also the heathen worship of images. The Saints live on eternally with God, although they have died. If anyone thinks to call them back again to life by a dead art, discovered by the heathen, he makes himself guilty of blasphemy. Who dares attempt with heathenish art to paint the Mother of God, who is exalted above all heavens and the Saints? It is not permitted to Christians, who have the hope of the resurrection, to imitate the customs of demon-worshipers and to insult the Saints, who shine in so great glory, by common dead matter....

Supported by the Holy Scriptures and the Fathers, we declare unanimously, in the name of the Holy Trinity, that

---

[1] The Acephali was another name for the followers of Eutyches.

[2] The "error of Nestorius" was to stress the independence of the two natures—divine and human—of Christ.

[3] The Monophysites, like the followers of Eutyches, rejected both the Orthodox assertion of the hypostatic (or "underlying") union of the "two natures" of Christ and the Nestorian assertion of a union that was not hypostatic but rather accidental.

there shall be rejected and removed and cursed out of the Christian Church every likeness which is made out of any material and color whatever by the evil art of painters.

Whoever in future dares to make such a thing, or to venerate it, or set it up in a church, or in a private house, or possesses it in secret, shall, if bishop, presbyter, or deacon, be deposed; if monk or layman, be anathematized[1] and become liable to be tried by the secular laws as an adversary of God and an enemy of the doctrines handed down by the Fathers. At the same time we ordain that no incumbent of a church shall venture, under pretext of destroying the error in regard to images, to lay his hands on the holy vessels in order to have them altered because they are adorned with figures. The same is provided in regard to the vestments of churches, cloths, and all that is dedicated to divine service. If, however, the incumbent of a church wishes to have such church vessels and vestments altered, he must do this only with the assent of the holy Ecumenical patriarch and at the bidding of our pious Emperors. So also no prince or secular official shall rob the churches, as some have done in former times, under the pretext of destroying images. All this we ordain, believing that we speak as does the Apostle, for we also believe that we have the spirit of Christ; and as our predecessors who believed the same thing spoke what they had synodically defined, so we believe and therefore do we speak and set forth a definition of what has seemed good to us following and in accordance with the definitions of our Fathers.

(1) If anyone shall not confess, according to the tradition of the Apostles and Fathers, in the Father, the Son and the Holy Ghost one godhead, nature and substance, will and operation, virtue and dominion, kingdom and power in three subsistences, that is in their most glorious Persons, let him be anathema.[2]

(2) If anyone does not confess that one of the Trinity was made flesh, let him be anathema.

(3) If anyone does not confess that the holy Virgin is truly the Mother of God, etc.

(4) If anyone does not confess one Christ both God and man, etc.

(5) If anyone does not confess that the flesh of the Lord is life-giving because it is the flesh of the Word of God, etc.

(6) If anyone does not confess two natures in Christ, etc.

(7) If anyone does not confess that Christ is seated with God the Father in body and soul, and so will come to judge, and that he will remain God forever without any grossness, etc.

(8) If anyone ventures to represent the divine image of the Word after the Incarnation with material colors, let him be anathema!

(9) If anyone ventures to represent in human figures by means of material colors by reason of the incarnation, the substance or person of the Word, which cannot be depicted, and does not rather confess that even after the Incarnation he [i.e., the Word] cannot be depicted, let him be anathema!

(10) If anyone ventures to represent the hypostatic union of the two natures in a picture and calls it Christ and thus falsely represents a union of the two natures, etc.

(11) If anyone separates the flesh united with the person of the Word from it and endeavors to represent it separately in a picture, etc.

(12) If anyone separates the one Christ into two persons and endeavors to represent Him who was born of the Virgin separately and thus accepts only a relative union of the natures, etc.

(13) If anyone represents in a picture the flesh deified by its union with the Word, and thus separates it from the Godhead, etc.

(14) If anyone endeavors to represent by material colors God the Word as a mere man, who, although bearing the form of God, yet has assumed the form of a servant in his own person, and thus endeavors to separate him from his inseparable Godhead so that he thereby introduces a quaternity into the Holy Trinity, etc.

(15) If anyone shall not confess the holy ever-virgin Mary, truly and properly the Mother of God, to be higher than every creature whether visible or invisible and does not with sincere faith seek her intercessions as of one having confidence in her access to our God, since she bore him, etc.

(16) If anyone shall endeavor to represent the forms of the Saints in lifeless pictures with material colors which are of no value (for this notion is vain and introduced by the devil) and does not rather represent their virtues as living images in himself, etc.

(17) If anyone denies the profit of the invocation of Saints, etc.

(18) If anyone denies the resurrection of the dead and the judgment and the condign [appropriate] retribution to everyone, endless torment and endless bliss, etc.

---

[1] I.e., excommunicated from the Church.

[2] I.e., excommunicated from the Church.

(19) If anyone does not accept this our Holy and Ecumenical Seventh Synod, let him be anathema from the Father and the Son and the Holy Ghost and from the seven holy Ecumenical Synods!

[At this point the making or teaching of any other faith is prohibited, and the penalties for disobedience are enumerated.]

The divine Kings Constantine and Leo said: Let the holy and ecumenical synod say, if with the consent of all the most holy bishops the definition just read has been set forth.

The holy synod cried out: Thus we all believe, we all are of the same mind. We have all with one voice and voluntarily subscribed. This is the faith of the Apostles. Many years to the Emperors! They are the light of orthodoxy! Many years to the orthodox Emperors! God preserve your Empire! You have now more firmly proclaimed the inseparability of the two natures of Christ! You have banished all idolatry! You have destroyed the heresies of Germanus [of Constantinople], George and Mansur.[1] Anathema to Germanus, the double-minded, and worshiper of wood! Anathema to George, his associate, to the falsifier of the doctrine of the Fathers! Anathema to Mansur, who has an evil name and Saracen[2] opinions! To the betrayer of Christ and the enemy of the Empire, to the teacher of impiety, the perverter of Scripture, Mansur, anathema! The Trinity has deposed these three!

2.4 Vilifying the iconoclasts: *The Chronicle of Theophanes Confessor* (before 818). Original in Greek.

The bitter feelings of the iconodules were given free expression in the *Chronicle* of Theophanes Confessor (*c.*760–817/818), which was in fact written by two men, Theophanes and a high church official named George Syncellus (d. after 810). Both lived during the turbulent period in which iconoclasm was first the norm, then condemned (in 787), and later revived (815–843). It is very likely that the *Chronicle* was written in secret, finished before Theophanes' death, and "published" only after 843. The passage here represents the iconodule take on the Synod of 754.

[Source: *The Chronicle of Theophanes Confessor: Byzantine and Near Eastern History, AD* 284–813, trans. Cyril Mango and Roger Scott (Oxford: Clarendon Press, 1997), pp. 591–92.]

In this year [754] Anastasius, who had held in unholy fashion the episcopal throne of Constantinople, died a spiritual as well as a bodily death of a dreadful disease of the guts after vomiting dung through his mouth, a just punishment for his daring deeds against God and his teacher. In the same year the impious Constantine [V (r.741–775)] convened in the palace of Hiereia an illegal assembly of 338 bishops against the holy and venerable icons under the leadership of Theodosius of Ephesus, son of Apsimarus, and of Pastillas of Perge. These men by themselves decreed whatever came into their heads, though none of the universal sees was represented, namely those of Rome, Alexandria, Antioch, and Jerusalem. Starting on February 10th, they went on until August 8th of the same 7th indiction.[3] On the latter day the enemies of the Theotokos[4] having come to Blachernai [Palace], Constantine ascended the ambo [pulpit] holding the monk Constantine, former bishop of

---

[1] Germanus I (r.715-730) was the Patriarch of Constantinople. He opposed iconoclasm and was sent into exile. Mansur ("Victorious") was the Arabic surname of John of Damascus, whose iconodule arguments may be read above on p. 63.

[2] I.e., Arab.

[3] I.e., 754.

[4] Theotokos means Mother of God in Greek.

Syllaion, and, after reciting a prayer, said in a loud voice, "Long live Constantine, the ecumenical patriarch!" On the 27th of the same month the emperor went up to the Forum together with the unholy bishop Constantine and the other bishops and they proclaimed their misguided heresy in front of all the people after anathematizing the most holy Germanus, George of Cyprus, and John Damascene [i.e., John of Damascus] of the Golden Stream, son of Mansur, holy men and venerable teachers.

....

THE FORMATION OF THE ISLAMIC WORLD

2.5 Pre-Islamic Arabic poetry: Al-Aʿsha, *Bid Hurayra Farewell* (before 625). Original in Arabic.

Al-Aʿsha (which means the "Near-Blind") was a member of the Bakr tribe—thus related to the caliph Abu-Bakr (r.632–634)—and well known for his satires and songs of wine and women. Like other pre-Islamic poetry, his was written down between the 7th and 11th centuries, and the written version probably, like a piece of jazz, reflects both the original idea and the riffs of subsequent poetry reciters. *Bid Hurayra Farewell* is a parody of a traditional Arabic ode. Like the others, it may be divided into three parts: a departure, a journey, and the poet's boast. (In the translation below these parts are labeled by your editor.) But here the departed beloved is overdrawn—"full at the bodice, at the waist sash nil"—and her delicacy over-emphasized—"she braces herself or she'd be thrown back flat." In place of the "journey" is a lover's lament that borders on the ridiculous—"I fell for her by chance. She fell for another who fell for another…"—and then a depiction of a storm mingled with thoughts about inebriation. "Foretell!" the poet says, and instead of recounting the places that he visits in his "journey," he prophesies where the rain will fall. Then the poet begins the journey, sometimes "barefoot," at other times "wearing boots," combining the normally separate adventures of the shoeless brigand and the well-shod warrior, the accounts of both veiled in a drunken stupor. Then suddenly the poet is serious: "How many a land, like the flat back of a shield… /Have I cut through." Finally comes the boast "To Yazid of the Bani Shayban," and the poet recalls battles and challenges his enemies to new ones.

[Source: *Desert Tracings: Six Classic Arabian Odes by ʿAlquama, Shanfara, Labid, ʿAntara, Al-Aʿsha, and Dhu al-Rumma*, trans. Michael A. Sells (Middletown, CT: Wesleyan University Press, 1989), pp. 60–66.]

[The Departure]

Bid Hurayra farewell.
The riders are departing.
Can you, man that you are,
bear bidding farewell?
    Brow aglow, hair flowing,   5

a gleam from the side teeth as she smiles,
    she walks gently as a gazelle,
    tender-hoofed in wet soil,
As if her walk
from the tent of a neighbor   10
were the gliding of a cloud
neither slow nor hurried.

You hear her anklets whisper
as she turns away
   like cassia[1] rustling   15
supplicant in the breeze.
She's not one of those
whose neighbors hate to see her face.
You won't find her,
ear to their secrets, listening.   20
   She braces herself
or she'd be thrown back flat,
     when rising to visit a neighbor,
by languor.
She entertains her companion awhile,   25
then slackens,
lower back and buttocks
quivering,
   Full at the bodice,
at the waist sash nil,   30
     a belle, seeming as she comes near
to divide in two.
How sweet a bedmate
on a cloudy afternoon,
not for some unbathed rude   35
to lay and take some pleasure,
   Wide-hipped, delicate,
elbows soft, walk tender,
     as if a thorn were caught
in the arch of her sandal.   40
As she rises
a fragrance of musk trails,
her sleeve-cuffs with the scent
of rose jasmine brimming over.
   No meadow of the meadows   45
of the roughland plateau,
     luxuriant and green, blessed
by dark-trailing big-dropped clouds,
Where the sun is teased
by a blossom in full flower,   50
drenched in color,
mantled deep in rushes and greens,
   Is ever more fragrant,
more redolent
     than she, or more beautiful   55
when evening shadows fall.

———————

[The Journey]

Hurayra said
when I came to pay her call
woe to you, woe,
you woesome male!   60
   I fell for her by chance.
  She fell for another
    who fell for another
    other than her,
For him a girl was falling   65
he didn't desire,
while a cousin on her father's side
was weakening for her, and dying.
   Then for me there fell another,
   not to my liking,   70
    love in love on love,
   beside itself, entangled, mad,
Each of us afflicted,
raving to this friend or that,
approaching, backing off,   75
ensnared, ensnaring.
   Hurayra shut us off,
   not speaking,
    ignorance on the part of Umm Khulayd
of the bond she tied.   80
Didn't she see a man,
night-blind, wounded
by intimations of death shades
and by time, the demented, the undoing?

———————

   Have you seen it blocking the horizon? 85
I passed the night in watch,
   lightning kindled along its edges,
  flickering,
With a dark trail behind it,
its middle full and moving,   90
girded and held together
by buckets of rain.
   No play diverts me
from foretelling the rain's direction,
    no pleasure from a cup of wine, 95
  no languor.
I told them at Durna,
the drinkers, already sodden:

———————

[1] A cinnamon tree.

Foretell! But how
can a wine-faced drinker heed? 100
    Lightning lit up the slopes
where the rain would fall,
    in Khabiyya, a blackening cloud
against the horizon.
They said let it pour 105
on Leopard Streak and Camel Belly,
on Horse Trappings, Tired Man,
and Legland,
    Flowing over the Edgelands,
    then Boar with its tracts 110
    of rock and sand,
until the hills and mountains burst,
Until the grouse meadows
and the tree-hedged
soft-curved dunes 115
take all they can bear,
    A gushing, quenching draught
for abodes long since desolate,
    off the track
shunned by horse and camel mare. 120

———————

You may well find me barefoot,
not a scrap of shoe leather to my name.
Wearing boots or shoeless,
that's the way I am.
    I might well steal upon 125
some master of his house
    and catch him unawares. Wary once,
now he finds no haven.
I might one day lead the reins
of youthful passion, 130
and it might follow,
a hot-blooded love-talker at my side.
    Many's the time I have set out at dawn
to the wine shop,
    followed by a bob-skewing, quick-witted, 135
path-wise fast-hander,
In a crowd of men like Indian swords
who know that everyone,
barefoot or bootshod,
will perish. 140
    I rivaled them down for the snip of basil,
head on elbow, reclining,

and for a tangy wine
from a porous, moistened jug of clay.
They don't come to 145
while there is any of it left,
except to call for more
after a third round or after a second,
    The glass-bearer
    busying here and there, 150
    shirt bottom tucked up,
    alert, agile.
How many a song—you'd think it sung
to a Persian harp—
when a singing girl in a nightslip 155
sings it,
    How many a gowned lady,
    trailing silk,
    how many a girl
with a leather wine flask at her side, 160
Have I spent my time enjoying,
enduring trial
by amorous talk
and length of pleasure.
    How many a land 165
    like the flat back of a shield,
    wild, where jinn[1] are overheard
in the corners, rustling,
That no one dares enter,
riding upon the burning heat, 170
except one who, in what he undertakes,
is unhurried,
    Have I cut through
on a well-worn, rock-ribbed,
    easy-gaited mare, elbows well apart 175
when you show her.

———————

[The Boast]

To Yazid of the Bani Shayban
bear this word:
Abu Thubayt,
stop gnawing at your heart! 180
    Stop carving at the grain
    of our ancient name
    that nothing can harm

---

[1]   Jinn are half-spirit creatures.

as long as burdened camels groan,
Like a mountain goat   185
butting against a rock
to split it, the rock unharmed,
the horns weakening.
      I know you well
when the battle signal calls us,   190
      when war blazes
with arms, night raids, and plunder.
You inflame Mas'ud's kin
and his brothers against us,
sowing destruction when we meet,   195
then drawing away.
      Don't sit alone
when you've stoked the fire!
      You'll implore refuge one day
from its burning, praying.   200
There were among the people of Kahf,
when they fought, and the Jashiriyya,
those who were quick,
those who would take their time.
      You claimed we wouldn't fight you.   205
We are—tribe of ours!—
      for the likes of you,
the killers,
Until the chief of the tribe
lies fallen, head on arm,   210
protected by child-bereft women's
flailing hands,
      Struck down by an Indian sword
well aimed toward its target,

or a supple, well-tempered spear   215
      from Khatt.
We might well spear the chieftain
in the hollow of his thigh,
and a champion might perish
on our spear tips, unavenged.   220
      End it!
      Nothing curbs the overbearing
      like a gaping wound
      unstaunched by oil and gauze.
By the life of the one   225
to whom stamping camels
and long-horned cattle of every kind
are led in offering,
      Kill a chief
who never stood in your way   230
      and we'll kill one of yours
      like him, one to our choosing.
Try us. You won't find us
after the battle
from the tribe's blood-right   235
turning away.
      Under the noon sun,
      the day of the Bowbend,
      around Futayma, we were the riders,
      not shirking, not giving way.   240
They called for a mounted attack.
We said we can do that.
They prepared to fight on foot.
We're a tribe that fights unmounted.

2.6 The sacred text: *Qur'an Suras* 1, 53:1–18, 81, 87, 96, 98 (*c.*610–622). Original in Arabic.

Muhammad (*c.*570–632), born in Mecca, orphaned, raised by an uncle, married to Khadija, heard (*c.*610) what he understood to be revelations from God. He recited them (Qur'an means "recitation"), scribes wrote them down, and they became the foundation of a new religion, Islam. The whole process of recording and arranging the Qur'an did not end until after Muhammad's death. The resulting book begins with a prayer (the *fatihah*, or "Opening"), followed by chapters (suras) that gradually diminish in length. While different from the odes of the pre-Islamic period (see *Bid Hurayra Farewell*, above, p. 70), the verses of the Qur'an are poetry, and they often take up the traditional themes: remembrance of the beloved (who is now God), the journey (turned into a spiritual quest), and the boast (a celebration of God's generosity and justice). The earliest suras generally are found toward the end of the book. Muhammad's first vision is described in Sura 53, "The Star"; his first auditory revelation was probably "Recite in the name of your lord who created…," which is found in Sura 96. Other suras come from the period after Muhammad made the *hijra*, or emigration, to Medina (622; the year 1 in the Islamic calendar). Most of those presented here are from Muhammad's earliest Meccan period. Note that there is relatively little punctuation (mirroring the Arabic); this is the translator's way of suggesting the open and multiple meanings of the verses.

[Source: *Approaching the Qur'an: The Early Revelations*, trans. Michael Sells (Ashland, OR: White Cloud Press, 1999), pp. 42, 44, 48, 50, 72, 96, 104, 106.]

1: *The Opening*

In the name of God
    the Compassionate the Caring
Praise be to God
    lord sustainer of the worlds
the Compassionate the Caring
master of the day of reckoning
To you we turn to worship   5
    and to you we turn in time of need
Guide us along the road straight
the road of those to whom you are giving
    not those with anger upon them
    not those who have lost the way

53: 1–18 *The Star*

In the Name of God the Compassionate the Caring
    By the star as it falls
    Your companion[1] has not lost his way nor is he
        deluded
    He does not speak out of desire
    This is a revelation
    taught him by one of great power   5
    and strength that stretched out over
    while on the highest horizon—
    then drew near and came down
    two bows' lengths or nearer
    He revealed to his servant what he revealed   10
    The heart did not lie in what it saw
    Will you then dispute with him his vision?

He saw it descending another time
    at the lote tree of the furthest limit
    There was the garden of sanctuary   15
    when something came down over the
        lote tree, enfolding
    His gaze did not turn aside nor go too far
    He had seen the signs of his lord, great signs

81: *The Overturning*

In the Name of God the Compassionate the Caring
    When the sun is overturned
    When the stars fall away
    When the mountains are moved
    When the ten-month pregnant camels
        are abandoned
    When the beasts of the wild are herded together   5
    When the seas are boiled over
    When the souls are coupled
    When the girl-child buried alive
    is asked what she did to deserve murder
    When the pages are folded out   10
    When the sky is flayed open
    When Jahim[2] is set ablaze
    When the garden is brought near
    Then a soul will know what it has prepared
    I swear by the stars that slide,   15
    stars streaming, stars that sweep along the sky
    By the night as it slips away
    By the morning when the fragrant air breathes
    This is the word of a messenger ennobled,
    empowered, ordained before the lord of the throne,   20

---

[1] "Your companion" is ordinarily interpreted as referring to Muhammad.

[2] A term for the Day of Reckoning.

holding sway there, keeping trust
Your friend[1] has not gone mad
He saw him on the horizon clear
He does not hoard for himself the unseen
This is not the word of a satan   25
   struck with stones

Where are you going?
This is a reminder to all beings
For those who wish to walk straight
Your only will is the will of God   30
   lord of all beings

87: The Most High

In the Name of God the Compassionate the Caring
   Holy be the name of your lord most high
   Who created then gave form
   Who determined then gave guidance
   Who made the meadow pasture grow
   then turned it to a darkened flood-swept remnant 5

   We will make you recite. You will not forget
      except what the will of God allows
   He knows what is declared
      and what lies hidden
   He will ease you to the life of ease
   So remind them if reminder will succeed[2]
   Those who know awe will be brought to remember 10
   He who is hard in wrong will turn away
   He will be put to the fire
   neither dying in it nor living
   He who makes himself pure will flourish
   who remembers the name of his lord and   15
      performs the prayer

   But no. They prefer the lower life
   Better is the life ultimate, the life that endures
   As is set down in the scrolls of the ancients
   the scrolls of Ibrahim and Musa[3]

96: The Embryo

In the Name of God the Compassionate the Caring
   Recite in the name of your lord who created—
   From an embryo created the human
   Recite your lord is all-giving
   who taught by the pen
   Taught the human what he did not know before 5

   The human being is a tyrant
   He thinks his possessions make him secure
   To your lord is the return of every thing

   Did you see the one who stopped a servant
   from performing his prayer?   10
   Did you see if he was rightly guided
   or commanded mindfulness?
   Did you see him call lie and turn away?
   Did he not know God could see?

   But no. If he does not change   15
      we will seize him by the forelock
   the lying, wrongful forelock
   Let him call out his gang
   We will call out the Zabaniya[4]
   Do not follow him
      Touch your head to the earth in prayer
      Come near

98: The Testament[5]

In the Name of God the Compassionate the Caring
   Those who denied the faith—
      from the peoples of the book
      or the idolators—
      could not stop calling it a lie   5
      until they received the testament

   A messenger of God
      reciting pages that are pure

---

[1] "Your friend" refers to Muhammad.

[2] Muhammad is to "remind" people about God and justice. There is no notion of "original sin" in Islam, but people "forget" the purpose of human life and the Day of Reckoning.

[3] Ibrahim is Abraham in the Bible; Musa is Moses.

[4] The Zabaniya are probably a species of *jinn*, half-spirit creatures.

[5] This sura is from a later period in Muhammad's career, after he experienced the rejection of not only polytheists but also the "peoples of the book"—Christians and Jews—he had expected to join him.

Of scriptures that are sure

Those who were given the book   10
    were not divided one against the other
    until they received the testament

And all they were commanded
    was to worship God sincerely
    affirm oneness, perform the prayer   15
    and give a share of what they have
    That is the religion of the sure

Those who deny the faith—
    from the peoples of the book
    or the idolators—
    are in Jahannam's fire,[1]   20

eternal there
    They are the worst of creation

Those who keep the faith
    and perform the prayer   25
    they are the best of creation

As recompense for them with their lord—
    gardens of Eden
    waters flowing underground
    eternal there forever   30
    God be pleased in them
    and they in God

That is for those who hold their lord in awe

2.7 Umayyad diplomacy: *The Treaty of Tudmir* (713). Original in Arabic.

Although the Islamic conquests seemed to take place with lightning speed, they were at times piecemeal and even non-violent. Five years after Islamic forces entered Spain in 711, almost the entire peninsula was under the rule of the caliph. Yet documents such as the *Treaty of Tudmir* (713) suggest that in some cases the take-over was peaceful, accomplished via agreements with local rulers. In this case 'Abd al-'Aziz (d.716), son of Musa (the governor of much of North Africa and a leader in the conquest of Spain), came to an agreement with Theodemir, the local Visigothic commander of the region of Murcia (in the southeast corner of Spain). The Murcians were not to aid any enemies of the Muslims, and they had to pay a modest tax in money and kind. In return, they were offered local autonomy and permission to practice their Christian religion. The Arabic for Theodemir was Tudmir, which for years afterwards was the Arabic name for the region of Murcia.

[Source: *Medieval Iberia: Readings from Christian, Muslim, and Jewish Sources*, ed. Olivia Remie Constable (Philadelphia: University of Pennsylvania Press, 1997), pp. 37–38. Translated by Olivia Remie Constable.]

In the name of God, the merciful and the compassionate.

This is a document [granted] by 'Abd al-'Aziz ibn Musa ibn Nusair to Tudmir, son of Ghabdush, establishing a treaty of peace and the promise and protection of God and his Prophet (may God bless him and grant him peace). We ['Abd al-'Aziz] will not set special conditions for him or for any among his men, nor harass him, nor remove him from power. His followers will not be killed or taken prisoner, nor will they be separated from their women and children. They will not be coerced in matters of religion, their churches will not be burned, nor will sacred objects be taken from the realm, [so long as] he [Tudmir] remains sincere and fulfills the [following]

---

[1]   The fire of eternal punishment.

conditions that we have set for him. He has reached a settlement concerning seven towns: Orihuela, Valentilla, Alicante, Mula, Bigastro, Ello, and Lorca. He will not give shelter to fugitives, nor to our enemies, nor encourage any protected person to fear us, nor conceal news of our enemies. He and [each of] his men shall [also] pay one dinar every year, together with four measures of wheat, four measures of barley, four liquid measures of concentrated fruit juice, four liquid measures of vinegar, four of honey, and four of olive oil. Slaves must each pay half of this amount.

[Names of four witnesses follow, and the document is dated from the Muslim month of Rajab, in the year 94 of the *hijra* (April 713).]

2.8 Taxation: *A Tax Demand in Egypt* (710). Original in Arabic and Greek.

The Umayyads generally adopted the administrative apparatus and offices of the regions that they conquered, and often they used the indigenous elite to carry out administrative duties. In Egypt, from which we have many papyri attesting to the fiscal system, the Arab governor of Egypt in the early eighth century was Qurra ibn Sharik (r.709–715). In the letter below, he is writing to Basil, *pagarch*—or provincial governor—of Aphrodite, located in the Thebaid just south of Asyut in Upper (i.e., southern) Egypt. Basil was neither Arab nor Muslim but rather a Christian local magnate who cooperated with his Islamic overlords. Qurra's letter shows that Basil was in charge of collecting the *jizya*, a poll tax imposed on non-Muslims. Qurra intended to use the revenue to pay his army.

[Source: *Islam from the Prophet Muhammad to the Capture of Constantinople*, ed. and trans. Bernard Lewis, vol. 2: *Religion and Society* (New York: Oxford University Press, 1987), p. 130 (slightly modified).]

In the name of God, the Merciful and the Compassionate.

From Qurra ibn Sharik to Basil, *pagarch* of Aphrodite. I praise God, other than Whom there is no God.

As follows: You know how much time has passed, and you still delay the *jizya*, and now the time has come for the pay of the troops and the families and for the departure of the armies on campaign, please God. When this my letter reaches you, take whatever *jizya* is due from your lands, and send whatever you collect, batch by batch. Let me not learn that you have delayed what you have gathered, and let it not be held back, for the people of your land have already completed their sowing. God is their helper in what is due from them to the Commander of the Faithful. Therefore, let there be no deficiency in your affair and no delay or holding back of what you have. Had the money been in my possession, I would have given the troops their pay, please God. Write and inform me what has accumulated with you, of what you have collected of the *jizya*, and how you have done this. Peace be upon those who follow the right guidance.[1]

Written by Jarir in the month of Rabi' I of the year 91 [January–February 710].

---

[1] A form of greeting used when addressing non-Muslims.

2.9 Praising the Caliph: Al-Akhtal, *The Tribe Has Departed* (c.692). Original in Arabic.

When Caliph 'Abd al-Malik (r.685–705) suppressed a major rebellion and established his rule, he needed a way to legitimize his authority and assert its roots in Arabic tradition. This he did largely by patronizing poets, for poetry was both highly valued and adaptive to a variety of purposes. In Syria, where the Umayyads established their capital, most of the population was Christian, but that did not prevent the Christian al-Akhtal (c.640-c.710) from becoming one of the caliph's most important poetic eulogists. In *The Tribe Has Departed*, al-Akhtal drew on traditional forms. The poem begins, as had many pre-Islamic poems (see al-A'sha, above p. 70), with the departure of women. The usual "journey" section (the parts are labeled here by your editor) takes up only one line. The "boast" section includes a declaration of victory; words of praise for the caliph and the Banu Umayyah, the caliph's clan; the poet's boast proper; and denigration of opposing clans.

[Source: Suzanne Pinckney Stetkevych, *The Poetics of Islamic Legitimacy: Myth, Gender, and Ceremony in the Classical Arabic Ode* (Bloomington: Indiana University Press, 2002), pp. 89–94, 96–97 (notes added).]

[The Departure]

1. Those that dwelt with you have left in haste,
     departing at evening or at dawn,
   Alarmed and driven out by fate's caprice,
     they head for distant lands.

2. And I, on the day fate took them off,
     was like one drunk
   On wine from Hims or Gadara
     that sends shivers down the spine,

3. Poured generously from a brimming wine-jar
     lined with pitch and dark with age,
   Its clay seal broken
     off its mouth,

4. A wine so strong it strikes
     the vital organs of the reveler,
   His heart, hungover, can barely
     sober up[1]

5. I was like that, or like a man
     whose limbs are racked with pain,
   Or like a man whose heart is struck
     by charms and amulets,

6. Out of longing for them and yearning
     on the day I sent my glance after them
   As they journeyed in small bands
     on Kawkab Hill's two slopes.[2] . . .

[The Journey]

17. They alighted in the evening,
     and we turned aside our noble-bred camels:
   For the man in need, the time had come
     to journey

[The Boast]

18. To a man whose gifts do not elude us,
     whom God has made victorious,
   So let him in his victory
     long delight!

19. He who wades into the deep of battle,
     auspicious his augury,
   The Caliph of God
     through whom men pray for rain

---

1   By invoking the inebriating power of wine, al-Akhtal here pays tribute to al-A'sha (above, p. 70), who was known for celebrating wine's heady effects.

2   Kawkab Hill is southwest of Damascus.

20. When his soul whispers its intention to him
  he resolutely sends it forth,
His courage and his caution
  like two keen blades.

21. In him the common weal resides,
  and after his assurance
No peril can seduce him
  from his pledge.

22. Not even the Euphrates when its tributaries
  pour seething into it
And sweep the giant swallow-wort from its two banks
  into the middle of its rushing stream,

23. And the summer winds churn it
  until its waves
Form agitated puddles
  on the prows of ships,

24. Racing in a vast and mighty torrent
  from the mountains of Byzance[1]
Whose foothills shield them from it
  and divert its course,

25. Is ever more generous than he is
  to the supplicant
Or more dazzling
  to the beholder's eye.

26. They did not desist from their treachery and cunning
  against you
Until, unknowingly, they portioned out
  the maysir players' flesh.[2] ...

29. Like a crouching lion, poised to pounce,
  his chest low to the ground,
For a battle in which there is
  prey for him,

30. [The caliph] advances with an army
  two hundred thousand strong,

The likes of which no man or jinn[3]
  has ever seen.

31. He comes to bridges which he builds
  and then destroys,
He brands his steeds with battle scars,
  above him fly banners and battle dust,

32. Until at al-Taff
  they wreaked carnage,
And at al-Thawiyyah
  where no bowstring twanged.[4]

33. The tribesmen saw clearly
  the error of their ways,
And he straightened out the smirk
  upon their faces....

44. O Banu Umayyah, your munificence
  is like a widespread rain;
It is perfect,
  unsullied by reproach.

45. O Banu Umayyah, it was I
  who defended you
From the men of a tribe
  that sheltered and aided [the Prophet].

46. I silenced the Banu Najjar's endless braying
  against you
With poems that reached the ears
  of every chieftain of Ma'add,

47. Until they submitted,
  smarting from my words—
For words can often pierce
  where sword points fail.

48. O Banu Umayyah, I offer you
  sound counsel:
Don't let Zufar dwell secure
  among you,[5]

---

[1] Byzantium.

[2] Maysir means gambling; pre-Islamic maysir players would gamble for the parts of a sacrificed animal. Here the enemies of the caliph are likened to maysir players, but the flesh they gamble for and cut apart is their own.

[3] Jinn are half-spirit creatures.

[4] Al-Taff is where an enemy leader was slain, while al-Thawiyyah was the burial site of another enemy leader.

[5] Zufar was initially an enemy of Caliph al-Malik, but by the time of this poem, he rivaled al-Akhtar and his clan, the Banu Taghlib, for the caliph's favors.

49. But take him as an enemy:
    for what you see of him
And what lies hid within
    is all corruption.

50. For in the end you'll meet
    with ancient rancor
That, like mange,[1] lies latent for a while
    only to spread the more.

51. Through us you were victorious,
    O Commander of the Faithful,
When the news reached you
    within al-Ghutah [of Damascus],

52. They identified for you the head
    of Ibn al-Hubab,

Its nose bridge now marked
    by the sword.

53. Ears deaf, never will he
    hear a voice;
Nor will he talk till stones
    begin to speak.[2] ...

78. And remember the Banu Ghudanah
    like herds of young slit-eared goats,
Runty ones, for whom
    corrals are built,

79. That pee on their forelegs
    when they're hot,
And shiver with cold
    when wet with rain.[3] ...

THE IMPOVERISHED BUT INVENTIVE WEST

2.10 A world explained by words: Isidore of Seville, *Etymologies* (*c.*615-*c.*630)

Isidore, bishop of Seville (*c.*560–636), gathered together much of the lore of the ancient world in his *Etymologies*, which attempted not only to explain the derivation of words but also, through their linguistic roots (which were often mistaken), to get at the nature and essence of things. A huge manuscript, divided by one of Isidore's younger colleagues into twenty books, the *Etymologies* began with the subjects of the liberal arts (grammar, rhetoric, dialectic, mathematics, music, astronomy); moved on to human institutions like law and medicine; continued with God and angels; and then considered human beings, animals, the cosmos, clothing, and tools (among other things). The section printed here, on the ages of human beings, followed a consideration of the parts of the human body and preceded a section on portents. The *Etymologies* was a major reference work for subsequent generations of medieval scholars and poets.

[Source: Stephen A. Barney, W.J. Lewis, J.A. Beach, and Oliver Berghof, with the collaboration of Muriel Hall, *The* Etymologies *of Isidore of Seville* (Cambridge: Cambridge University Press, 2006), pp. 241–43 (slightly modified).]

---

[1] Mange is a skin disease.

[2] Al-Akhtar here boasts that his clan defeated and beheaded al-Hubab, the leader of an enemy clan, while the caliph himself relaxed in the park of al-Ghutah.

[3] For a society that values camels above all other animals, it is a great slur to liken the Ghudanah to runty goats.

On the Ages of Human Beings

There are six stages in a lifetime: infancy, childhood, adolescence, youth, maturity, and old age. The first age, the infancy (*infantia*) of a newborn child, lasts seven years. The second age is childhood (*pueritia*), that is, a pure (*purus*) age, during which a child is not yet suited for procreating; it lasts until the fourteenth year. The third age, adolescence (*adolescentia*), is mature (*adultus* is the past participle of *adolescere*) enough for procreating and lasts until the twenty-eighth year. The fourth age, youth (*iuventus*), is the strongest of all ages, ending in the fiftieth year. The fifth is the age of an elder person (*senior*), that is, maturity (*gravitas*), which is the decline from youth into old age; it is not yet old age, but no longer youth.… This age begins in the fiftieth and ends in the seventieth year. The sixth age is old age (*senectus*), which has no time limit in years; rather, however much life is left after the previous five ages is allotted to old age. *Senium*, however, is the last part of old age, so called because it is the end of the sixth (cf. *seni*, "six") age.

Into these six intervals, therefore, the philosophers have divided human life—ages in which life is changed, runs its course, and reaches the final point of death. Let us therefore proceed briefly through the aforementioned stages in a lifetime, demonstrating their etymologies with regard to the terms used for a human being.

A human being of the first age is called an infant (*infans*); it is called an infant, because it does not yet know how to speak (*in-*, "not"; *fari*, present participle of *fans*, "speaking"), that is, it cannot talk. Not yet having its full complement of teeth, it has less ability to articulate words. A boy (*puer*) is so called from purity (*puritas*), because he is pure and still retains, without the hint of a beard, the bloom of the cheeks. They are ephebes (*ephebus*), so called after Phoebus, gentle youths, not yet [grown] men. The word child (*puer*), however, is used in three ways: in reference to birth, as in Isaiah, "A child (*puer*) is born to us."[1] To indicate age, as in "an eight-year-old," "a ten-year-old"—whence the following expression.

Now he took a child's (*puerilis*) yoke on his tender neck.[2]

And finally, in reference to obedience and purity of faith, as in the words of the Lord to the prophet: "You are my child (*puer*), do not be afraid," spoken when Jeremiah had already left behind the years of childhood a long time before.[3]

Puella is "little girl" (*parvula*), as if the term were "chick" (*pulla*). Hence we use the term "wards" (*pupillus*), not because of the legal status of wards, but because of their youthful age. A ward, named like the pupil (*pupillus*) of the eye, is one bereft of parents. Those truly called *pupilli*, however, are children whose parents died before giving them a name. Other "bereft ones" (*orbus*) are called orphans (*orphanus*), the same as are those called *pupilli*; for *orphanus* is a Greek word and *pupillus* a Latin word. Thus in the psalm, where it is said, "Thou wilt be a helper to the orphan (*pupillus*)," the Greek has the word *orphanos*.[4]

Those who have reached puberty (*puberes*) are so called from *pubes*, that is, the private parts, for this is the first time that this area grows hair. There are those who calculate puberty from age, that is, they take someone who has completed his fourteenth year to have reached puberty, even though he may begin to show the signs of puberty very late; however, it is most certain that he who shows the outward signs of puberty and can already procreate has reached puberty. *Puerpera* are those who give birth at a youthful (*puerilis*) age. Whence Horace says

The young woman in labor (*puerpera*) is praised
for her firstborn.[5]

And they are called *puerperae* either because they are burdened with their "first birth" (*primus partus*), or else because they first "give birth to children" (*pueros parere*). An adolescent (*adolescens*) is so called because he is "old enough" to procreate, or by derivation from "growing" (*crescere*) and "being strengthened" (*augere*). A youth (*iuvenis*) is so called because he begins to be able to help (*iuvare*), just as we name the young bullocks (*iuvencus*) among oxen, when they have separated from the calves. A youth is at the peak of his development and ready to give assistance—for a person's "helping" is his contributing

---

[1]   See Isa. 9:6.

[2]   From an anonymous poetic fragment in Latin.

[3]   See Jer. 1: 6–8.

[4]   Ps. 10: 14; Douay Ps. 9: 14. If you check these versions in Latin, you will see that many of them use *orphanus*, but Isidore's version used the word *pupillus* instead.

[5]   Horace (65–8 BCE) was a Roman poet. The quotation comes from his *Odes* 4.5.23.

some work. As in human beings the thirtieth year is the time of full maturity, so in cattle and beasts of burden the third year is the strongest.

A man (*vir*) is so called, because in him resides greater power (*vis*) than in a woman—hence also "strength" (*virtus*) received its name—or else because he deals with a woman by force (*vis*). But the word woman (*mulier*) comes from softness (*mollities*), as if *mollier* (compare *mollior*, "softer"), after a letter has been cut and a letter changed, is now called *mulier*. These two are differentiated by the respective strength and weakness of their bodies. But strength is greater in a man, lesser in a woman, so that she will submit to the power of the man; evidently this is so lest, if women were to resist, lust should drive men to seek out something else or throw themselves upon the male sex. As I was saying, woman (*mulier*) is named for her feminine sex, not for a corruption of her innocence,[1] and this is according to the word of Sacred Scripture, for Eve was called woman as soon as she was made from the side of her man, when she had not yet had any contact with a man, as is said in the Bible: "And he formed her into a woman (*mulier*)."[2]

The term "virgin" (*virgo*) comes from "a greener (*viridior*) age," just like the words "sprout" (*virga*) and "calf" (*vitula*). Otherwise it is derived from lack of corruption, as if the word were formed from "heroic maiden" (*virago*), because she has no knowledge of female desire. A "heroic maiden" is so called because she "acts like a man" (*vir* + *agere*, "to act"), that is, she engages in the activities of men and is full of male vigor. The ancients would call strong women by that name. However, a virgin cannot be correctly called a heroic maiden unless she performs a man's task. But if a woman does manly deeds, then she is correctly called a heroic maiden, like an Amazon.

She who is nowadays called a woman (*femina*) in ancient times was called *vira*; just as "female slave" (*serva*) was derived from "male slave" (*servus*) and "female servant" (*famula*) from "male servant" (*famulus*), so also woman (*vira*) from man (*vir*). Some people believe that the word for "virgin" (*virgo*) is from *vira*. The word "woman" (*femina*) is derived from the parts of the thighs (*femur*, plural *femora* or *femina*) where the appearance of the sex distinguishes her from a man. Others believe that through a Greek etymology *femina* is derived from "fiery force," because she desires more vehemently, for females are said to be more libidinous than males, both in human beings and in animals. Whence among the ancients excessive love was called feminine (*femineus*) love.

The "elder" (*senior*) is still fairly vigorous. In the sixth book Ovid speaks of the elder, who is

Between the youth and the old man (*senex*).[3]

And Terence

By the privilege I enjoyed when I was younger (*adulescentior*).[4]

...

The term "old man" (*senex*), however, some believe to be derived from decay of the senses (*sensus*), because from that time on they act foolishly due to old age. Physiologists maintain that human beings are stupid due to colder blood, wise due to warm blood. Hence also old people, in whom blood has turned cold, and children, in whom it has not yet warmed up, are less wise. This is the reason why infancy and old age resemble one another: old people dote because they are too old, while children have no insight into their actions due to playfulness and childishness....

Old age brings with it much that is good and much that is bad. Much that is good, because it frees us from despotic masters, imposes moderation on desires, breaks the drive of lust, augments wisdom, and imparts riper counsel. Much that is bad, however, because of the weakness and unpopularity it brings, for

Diseases and sorrowful old age creep up.[5]

Indeed, there are two things whereby the forces of the body are diminished: old age and disease.

Death (*mors*) is so called, because it is bitter (*amarus*), or by derivation from Mars, who is the author of death; [or else, death is derived from the bite (*morsus*) of the first human, because when he bit the fruit of the forbid-

---

[1] The word *mollities*, softness, could also connote sexual licentiousness.

[2] See Gen. 2: 22.

[3] Ovid (43 BCE–17 CE) was a Roman poet. The quotation comes from his *Metamorphoses* 12.464.

[4] Terence (*c.*195–159? BCE) was a Roman comic playwright. The quotation comes from his *The Mother-in-Law* 11.

[5] Virgil (70–19 BCE) was a Roman poet. The quotation comes from his *Georgics* 3.67.

den tree, he incurred death].[1] There are three kinds of death: heartrending, premature, and natural death. That of children is heartrending, that of young people premature, that of old people merited, that is, natural. However, it is uncertain from which part of speech *mortuus* ("dead, a dead person") is inflected. Indeed, as Caesar says, because it is the perfect participle of *morior* ("die")

it ought to end in *-tus*—that is, it ought to have one *u* only, not two. Where the letter *u* is doubled, it is inflected substantively, not as a participle, as in *fatuus* ("foolish") and *arduus* ("difficult"). This makes sense in this way: just as what *mortuus* means cannot be "declined" by any behavior of ours (i.e. we cannot avoid death), so the term itself cannot be "declined" grammatically.

2.11 A modern martyr in Francia: *The Passion of Leudegar* (680s). Original in Latin.

The martyrs of the pre-Constantinian Church were replaced by heroic ascetics such as St. Antony (see his *Life* above, p. 27) and St. Martin (see his *Life* above, p. 34). Hagiographers of late-seventh-century Merovingian Francia (as we may now call Gaul) created a new generation of martyrs, portraying men and women embroiled in the violent political life of the period as saints. Leudegar (Saint-Léger in French) was one of these. Brother of Gaerin, the count of Paris, and appointed to the bishopric of Autun (an important see in Burgundy that Leudegar held *c*.662–*c*.677?) by Queen Balthild, regent for her son Clothar III (r.657–673), Leudegar was an important man at court. But he had a falling out with Ebroin, mayor of the palace, who eventually had him executed in *c*.678. His *Passion*, which means "suffering" or "martyrdom," was written soon thereafter by an anonymous author who dedicated the work to Hermenar, Leudegar's successor at Autun and originally his rival. The cult of Leudegar was evidently becoming so strong that Hermenar needed to try to claim it, and he appears in the *Passion* as a sympathetic figure. How have the roles and virtues of the bishop changed from the time of St. Martin to that of Leudegar? How might you explain the reasons for these changes?

[Source: From *Roman to Merovingian Gaul: A Reader*, ed. and trans. Alexander Callander Murray (Toronto: University of Toronto Press, 2000), pp. 509–18, 524–26 (slightly modified).]

[1] Glorious and renowned Leudegar, bishop of the city Autun, has been created a new martyr in Christian times. Just as he was nobly born according to earthly descent, so, accompanied by divine grace and growing in manly strength from an early age, he stood out prominently ahead of others no matter what the office or order in life to which he was promoted. His uncle Dido, bishop of Poitiers,[2] who was provided with a notable abundance of prudence and wealth beyond that of his neighbors, took great pains to raise him; and so, thoroughly polished in

all respects by the file of instruction in the various studies that the powerful of the world are accustomed to undertake, Leudegar was chosen to assume the burden of the archdiaconate of the same city.

His courage and wisdom became so conspicuous that he appeared to have no equal among his predecessors. Especially because he was not unacquainted with the penalties of the temporal law, he was a terrifying judge of secular matters. And since he was filled with the doctrines of the church canons, he emerged as a distinguished

---

[1] The words in brackets are found in some, but not all, of the manuscripts of the *Etymologies*.

[2] Bishop Dido of Poitiers died in 669.

teacher of clerics. He was also spirited in the punishment of offenders and never tried to be lenient with excesses of the flesh. He was vigilant, keenly concerned with the duties of church personnel, energetic in keeping accounts, prudent in giving advice, and glowing with eloquence.

[2] Meanwhile it became necessary to ordain him bishop of the city of Autun. For lately a dispute between two candidates for the episcopal office of that city had erupted and had reached the point of bloodshed. When one of the candidates lay dead on the spot and the other had been exiled for committing the crime, Balthild, who with her son Clothar [III] was in charge of the palace of the Franks, at that point, inspired, I believe, by divine counsel, sent this energetic man to that city to be its bishop. The church which, as if widowed, had already been left to the uncertainties of the world for almost two years, would now be protected by his direction and strength and defended against those who were attacking it.

How much more should be said? All the enemies of the church and the town, as well as those who endlessly disputed among themselves with hateful acts and killings, were so afraid on his arrival that they did not want to hear the outrage that had taken place recalled. Those whom his preaching could not persuade to accept peace, the terror of justice forced to do so.

Now that he was in office by God's will, he lavished such concern on giving alms to the poor that it would take too long to recount it in detail. But if we are silent, his works are a witness: the station for poor relief that he established stands at the doors of the church; the beauty of the precious objects which glow with the flash of gold in the service of the church; and also the decorations of the baptistery made with marvelous workmanship. The tomb of Saint Symphorian and the translation of his body reveals to those who remain silent the extent to which he was devoted to the love of the martyrs.[1] Moreover the pavement and the golden awning of the church, the construction of a new atrium, the repair of the town walls, the restoration of buildings and his reconstruction of whatever had deteriorated through great age, suggest as visible reminders to onlookers the extent of his energy.

Let these few special examples among many suffice. We turn in our account to the time the champion of Christ first took up the fight against the devil....

[4] In those days Ebroin was, as we say, mayor of the palace. He ran the palace at that time under King Clothar [III, r.657–673], for the queen whom we mentioned above was now living in the monastery which she had previously prepared for herself.[2] Moreover, envious men came to Ebroin and roused his anger against Leudegar the man of God, and whereas they found no charge to lay that was true, they made up a false one that, while everyone obeyed Ebroin's commands, only Bishop Leudegar defied his orders.

The aforesaid Ebroin was so inflamed by the torch of gain and so captive to the desire for money that only those who brought more money had their cause judged to be just by him. As some out of fear, and others to purchase justice, lavished immense sums of gold and silver on him, for this reason the hearts of certain people were roused against him, distressed at being robbed but especially because he not only trafficked in plunder but even shed the innocent blood of many nobles for a minor offense. And so Ebroin continued to be suspicious of Bishop Leudegar; for Ebroin could not conquer him by words, and Leudegar, unlike others, did not pay court to him with flattery. Ebroin recognized that Leudegar always remained firm in the face of all his threats.

At the time, Ebroin had issued a tyrant's edict that no one should presume to come to the palace from Burgundy without receiving his authorization.[3] Out of fear, all the leading men were now suspicious that he was contemplating adding to his crime by condemning certain people to lose their heads or by inflicting losses of property on them.

[5] While the matter remained unresolved, King Clothar, called by God, passed away [673]. But although Ebroin ought to have called the magnates together and, as is customary, solemnly raised to the kingship the king's brother, Theuderic [III, r.673, 675–690/691] by name, he was puffed up with pride and decided not to call them from this time onwards. They became more afraid because as long as he kept control of the king, whom

---

[1] Symphorian was martyred at Autun c.180. A monastery was dedicated to him there while, as we see here, his tomb was in the cathedral church. The "translation of his body" refers to the ritual in which his body was moved from one place to another.

[2] Queen Balthild was "eased" out of court and went to live at Chelles, a monastery for women that she had founded and endowed.

[3] Autun was in Burgundy, so this edict was directed at Leudegar and his flock.

he should have raised up in public for the glory of the homeland, he would be able fearlessly to inflict evil on anyone he desired in the king's name. A host of nobles were hastening to meet the new king when Ebroin sent a command for them to give up their journey. They took counsel among themselves, abandoned the king, and all sought out Childeric [II, d.675], the king's younger brother who had been allotted the kingship in Austrasia. Whoever did not want to accept this decision either escaped by flight or agreed against his will under threat of death by burning.

[6] When, out of fear of the tyrant Ebroin, they had all brought Childeric into the kingdom of Neustria as well as that of Burgundy, the tyrant recognized that it was his own villainy that brought this about and took refuge at the altar of the church; his treasure was at once broken into many pieces and what the wicked man had gathered together wrongly for so long was immediately well dispersed. They did not kill him because certain bishops stepped in between them, and especially because the bishop Leudegar intervened; but they sent him to the monastery of Luxeuil in exile so that, through penance, he might escape the consequences of the crimes he had committed. But since the eyes of his heart were blinded by the dust of earthly desire, spiritual wisdom did not prevail in his spiteful soul.

Childeric ordered his brother, against whom he had been asked to come, brought into his presence so he could speak with him. That is when certain leaders in the kingdom who wanted to dissuade Childeric from bloodshed through flattery had the audacity to order the hair of their lord cut and took pains to deliver him before his brother in this condition.[1] But when Theuderic was asked by his brother what he wished done to him, he declared only that he was awaiting the swift judgment of God because he had been unjustly degraded from his position as king. Then orders were given that Theuderic live in the monastery of the holy martyr Dionysius;[2] and he was kept safe there until such time as he grew back the hair they cut off. And the God of heaven, whom he had declared as his judge, happily allowed him to reign afterwards.

[7] Meanwhile everyone asked King Childeric to issue throughout the three kingdoms he had acquired[3] edicts to the following effect. Judges must, as in antiquity, preserve the law and custom of each of the homelands. Officials (*rectores*) must not pass from one province into another. And one person must not be allowed to usurp power in the fashion of Ebroin and then, like him, hold his peers in disdain; as long as it was recognized that advancement to the top offices would take place by turns, no one would dare set himself before another. Although the king granted the requests freely, he was corrupted by foolish, almost heathen, counselors—for the superficiality of youth got the better of him—and immediately opposed what he had authorized with the advice of wise men.

[8] The king kept holy Leudegar constantly by his side in the palace because he had seen that the bishop outshone everyone in wisdom. For this reason the envy of evil men revived and grew. Again they looked for grounds for making accusations against him, so that whatever the king did, whatever just or unjust decision he made, they accused Leudegar of doing it. Had the king complied with Leudegar's advice, he would have acted with divine authority. But by now the sentence laid down by heaven had overtaken him, so that his heart could not comprehend the teachings of justice; instead he deserved that a swift sentence carry out the judgment that Theuderic declared he was awaiting from God.

When the man of God saw the envy of the devil heat up once more against him, following the apostle, he took up the armor of faith, the helmet of salvation, and the sword of the Spirit, which is the word of God, and went into single combat with the ancient enemy. And since priestly integrity knows not how to fear the threats of a king, Leudegar censured him for suddenly altering the customs of the kingdoms after he had ordered them to be preserved; and likewise, it is said, he told him that the queen [Bilichild], his wife, was the daughter of his uncle [Sigibert III]; and, if he did not emend these deeds as well as other transgressions, he should know truly that divine vengeance would immediately be at hand.

Indeed, at first the king began to listen willingly, but the advice of his followers got the better of him. At the

---

[1] "The audacity to order the hair of their lord cut" means that they tonsured him—the sign of the monk. He could not reign until his hair grew back.

[2] This was Saint-Denis, near Paris.

[3] I.e., Austrasia, Neustria, and Burgundy—the whole of the Frankish Kingdom. Childeric had become king of Austrasia in 662; now, 673–675, he ruled over all of them.

same time as he should have been using Leudegar's words to reform himself, the king began to look for pretexts for bringing about the bishop's death. This was on the advice of those who wanted to overturn justice and, disorderly themselves, were in favor of the king acting in an immature fashion, as well as of those who enticed the king into breaking his own decree. All of them, and others like them living amidst the desires of the world, feared their works would be destroyed by the man of God, for by now they knew that he marched a straight course along the path of justice. The old world, weighed down by vices, could not withstand the manly power of the heavenly citizen.

[9] There was in those days a certain nobleman called Hector, who had taken up the fasces of office over the patriciate of Marseille.[1] He was endowed beyond others with nobility of birth and worldly wisdom, being descended from a famous lineage. He had come to see King Childeric about a certain legal case and hoped to gain what he was seeking through the intercession of the man of God. The holy man of God had welcomed Hector to his city and provided him with lodging, waiting for the time when he could recommend Hector to the king and speak on his behalf, as Hector had requested. For Leudegar had asked Childeric to come to the church of his city[2] during the celebration of Easter. The envious ones found this the pretext by which they might fill the king's heart to the full with the vileness they had lately been pouring into it. They brought the then mayor of the palace, who was called Wulfoald, into their subterfuge and made up a lying story that Leudegar and Hector had joined together to overthrow royal authority and usurp for themselves the reins of power.

[10] There was also at the time in the monastery of Saint Symphorian a certain man in the garb of a religious by the name of Marcolinus, a recluse in body but not in mind and, as was publicly revealed afterwards, rather too eager to seek human praise and honors through the false appearance of religion. Of his way of life I think it better to be silent than to speak, especially since it was revealed to everyone. The king, therefore, mistook this fellow for

a prophet of God in all matters because Marcolinus flattered his desire to be favored above all else with accusations against the man of God.

And so on the night when the holy vigils of Easter were celebrated in the city, the king, by now suspicious, refused to come there, but with a few flatterers sought the advice of the aforesaid hypocrite; and since the king bore ill feelings towards the servant of God, he had no qualms about receiving the Easter sacrifice at the right time where he was.

But afterwards, shamefully drunk on wine, he entered the church while others, fasting, were awaiting the holy services. He looked for Leudegar, shouting out his name, trying to put him to flight; all the while he terrified those who now relayed messages, threatening to strike them with the sword. Frequently calling for Leudegar, the king learned that he was in the baptistery, and when he entered it, stood amazed at the brightness of the light and the aroma of the chrism that was used by those conducting baptisms there to give blessings. But although Leudegar answered the shouting by saying, "I am here,"[3] the king completely failed to see him. He crossed the baptistery and took up quarters in the bishop's mansion of the church, which had been made ready.

The other bishops who were celebrating the vigils with the man of God returned to their quarters. But when Leudegar finished the holy office, showing no sign of fear, he approached the angry king and gently asked him why he had not come before the vigils and why he stayed so angry through the celebrations of such a holy night. Disturbed, the king could only answer the ineffable wisdom of Leudegar by saying that he had suspicions about him concerning a certain matter.

[11] Leudegar the man of God saw that the king had not changed his mind. The king, at the urging of his followers, would inflict death on him and Hector, just as he had resolved; or Hector, with no place to turn, would rise up against the despised king, just as the king's men feared. Leudegar was not concerned for his own life but for those who had come to him for protection, and looking for safety, chose for the time being to find refuge in flight rather than offer a pretext for the church to be

---

[1]   The patriciate of Marseille was the major governmental authority in the city. "Fasces of office": rods bound together with an ax were carried before ancient Roman magistrates, and although this had for centuries ceased to be the case, it remained a literary image of authority.

[2]   I.e., Autun.

[3]   See 1 Sam. 3: 4.

bloodied by his martyrdom or to be ravaged during the celebrations of Christ's resurrection, or for those who had turned to him to lose their lives without any consideration. For surely there is no one who thinks that he was afraid even of martyrdom.

In fact, when earlier he got word of his own destruction through a monk by the name of Berthar on the day of the Lord's supper, the next day, that of the passion of the Lord, he went to the king's palace, and, bursting in uninvited, tried to offer his blood to Christ on the very day that Christ poured forth his own blood for the salvation of the world. On the same day the king even tried to strike him with his own hand, but, because of the respect due the day, was prevented from doing so by the wise advice of certain magnates. One must believe without doubt that he was saved at that moment by heaven so that the furnace of lengthy persecution would purify any impurity he might have acquired from living a human life, which cannot be led without fault. And placed like pure gold in the crown of his own king, he would afterward shine like gleaming jewels by the power of miracle.

Those who were waiting to exploit this opportunity thereupon mounted a swift pursuit of him. Hector was killed on the spot; and since he manfully tried to defend himself, as was God's will, it took large numbers to overcome him and some of those accompanying him. And it is believed to be not impossible that indulgence can be obtained from God through the merits of the holy martyr for those souls who along with him tried innocently to ward off the storm of persecution.

[12] As soon as Leudegar, the servant of God, had been taken into custody by certain of his pursuers, they immediately sent word to Childeric that the deed was done; he who had successfully arrested Leudegar thought that he would enjoy the utmost favor of the king. On the advice of the magnates and bishops, orders were given for Leudegar to be taken to the monastery of Luxeuil until such time as they could deliberate together as to what to do with a man of such rank.

In the meantime, Childeric inquired of all the chief officials of the palace together what judgment they would determine for this saint of God, and they answered unanimously that, if the king granted him his life, he should order Leudegar to remain in perpetual exile in Luxeuil. The king immediately authorized the judgment decreed against him. Some bishops and priests, for their part,

agreed to it to free Leudegar for the moment from the anger of the king.

For, led astray by the advice of the wicked, the king had given orders for him to be taken from Luxeuil and placed at the disposal of his accusers as an object of mockery for them to have killed as they wished, as formerly Herod had intended the Jews to do to Peter.[1] Now there was present a venerable abbot of the church of Saint Symphorian by the name of Hermenar—it was to him that the king assigned the city at the request of the people after the death of the man of God—and he repeatedly threw himself at the feet of the king begging him over and over again to allow Leudegar to remain in Luxeuil and not to have him led into the waiting arms of cruel men whose anger the devil had inflamed against him. Because of entreaties of this kind, Leudegar was at that time at last saved from death. But some were of the false belief that Hermenar often visited the lodging of the king to be first among Leudegar's accusers and thereby more readily get permission to hold the bishopric. At length the truth emerged, and because the eye of the flesh does not see spiritual love, the deeds of that man afterwards bore witness, for as long as Leudegar was still alive he tended to his needs with devout charity as best he could.

[13] In those days Ebroin was still lodged as an exile in Luxeuil, tonsured and in a monk's garb, pretending to act with the peaceable intention that as long as both he and Leudegar were serving the same but separate sentences of exile they would lead their lives in harmony.

In the meantime, after these events had taken place, divine vengeance did not refrain long from imposing its judgment on Childeric. For his loose behavior among the palace magnates grew worse. Then one of them, who found this more troubling than the others, gave him his death wound as he was hunting in safety in the forest.

[14] But before that happened, while a certain two dukes to whom the orders had been given to remove Leudegar from Luxeuil were waiting to do that, one of their servants agreed to put Leudegar to the sword if he saw him outside Luxeuil. When the time came to do it, an unbearable trembling so engulfed the man's heart that he not only said in a public confession that he was contemplating such a momentous deed but also told why. Trembling, he threw himself at Leudegar's feet begging to be forgiven by him for this wickedness.

---

[1] See Acts 12: 3–4.

[15] As soon as Childeric's death was suddenly announced, certain of those who had been sentenced to exile at his command returned without fear, like poisonous snakes after wintertime that come forth from their caves in the spring. Their wild rage caused a huge disturbance in the homeland, so that it was openly believed that the approach of the Antichrist was at hand.[1] As for those who should have been in charge of the regions, they rose against each other, and those who should have kept the bonds of peace together began to provoke each other with hateful deeds. And as long as the king was not established on top, each one did what seemed right according to his own desires, without fear of punishment. Indeed we recognized at that time that the anger of God became manifest, so that even a star that the astrologers call a comet was seen in the sky [August 676]: on its rising, they say, the land is thrown into confusion by famine, by the succession of kings, and by disturbance among the nations, and destruction by the sword is imminent. It is certain that all these events plainly happened after that. But as it is written that the foolish cannot be corrected by words, much less by portents, they returned from exile with evil intent. They made the claim that whatever they had suffered for their crimes was the fault of Leudegar's supporters.

[16] In these days the man of God was held in custody by the aforementioned dukes for safety's sake and had by now recently been taken by them from Luxeuil. At that very moment divine grace had granted its servant a venerable honor whereby those same dukes, their wives, all their servants and their households, and also the common people in those districts, were joined together in such love of him that, if the need had arisen, they would not have hesitated to sacrifice themselves on his behalf. When those who were holding the servant of God in their custody informed the other authorities round about that they could see that divine grace was upon the servant of God, they now came together in pious Christian love to support him. Reaching an agreement among themselves, they affirmed that, as long as the disorderly confusion that had arisen prevailed in those districts, holy Leudegar would be protected with their help should anyone try to do harm to him before they had also raised Theuderic to the kingship.

In those days Ebroin also came forth from Luxeuil, like Julian [the Apostate] who pretended to live the life of a monk.[2] And since he was immediately mobbed by a swarm of friends as well as servants, the aforesaid exiles, who were seeking to serve him—and an evil service it was, tacked together from their own claim of injustice—made him leader. This way they could use Ebroin's help and advice to take vengeance on the man of God all together. Ebroin himself raised his venomous head, and like a viper restoring its poison, he pretended to be a follower of Theuderic, hurrying to his side for that reason as quickly as possible.

[17] As the man of God was traveling quickly along the same road with his above-mentioned allies, it happened that, when they were less than a day's journey from the city of Autun, Ebroin, forgetting the pledge of friendship he had once made and at the urging of his associates, would have seized him at that point, had he not been prevented by the advice of Genesius, metropolitan of Lyon, or been frightened by the strong band accompanying Leudegar. Again Ebroin feigned friendship, and joining forces they reached the city together.

The church rejoiced at the restored presence of its shepherd, the streets were strewn with fresh boughs, the deacons prepared candles, the clergy celebrated with singing, the whole city rejoiced at the advent of its bishop after the storm of persecution. And not undeservedly was the display of praise offered to him, for in the presence of God he rushed toward the crown of martyrdom, and there, as part of the advent of their pastor, they made ready pleasures for his enemies.

The next day Leudegar and Ebroin moved on together so that they might arrive at a meeting with Theuderic united.

[18] The journey begun, they went to meet the king, but in the meantime, almost in the middle of the trip, the tyrant Ebroin abandoned their company and pressed straight on to his own people, tossing aside his clerical status and returning to his wife behind the holy veil [i.e., she was now a nun] "as a dog returns to its vomit."[3] He who could not serve in the camp of Christ took up the weapons of the world with his enemies. And whereas he had now abandoned faith and God, he showed himself an open enemy of his earthly lord.

---

[1]   The false Christ who was expected to rule as an antagonist to Christ before the Second Coming—and triumph—of Christ himself.

[2]   Emperor Julian (r.361–363), called "the Apostate," was vilified by Christians. He was never a monk.

[3]   Prov. 26: 11.

Now Theuderic had already recovered the kingdom and was staying safely at the time at the villa of Nogent-les-Vierges when Ebroin attacked swiftly with Austrasians. Who can recount fully the plundering that then took place of the royal treasury and of the vessels of the church that previous Catholic princes had devoutly conferred on the Lord's sanctuary out of Christian love, and who can recount the killing of Theuderic's mayor of the palace?

[19] The reason Ebroin committed this evil was that he was furnished with advice by diabolical and envious men. Their complaint was that they had been brought down by the punishment they deserved. Since they saw that the whole realm had faithfully taken Theuderic's side, that he was now established in the kingship, and that Leudegar the servant of God was living in his own city with the king's favor, envious, they began to be tormented by spite again. For as long as the just were standing tall, the wicked would be unable to make a comeback. Under the influence of the devil, who stripped them of faith, and now blinded, they could devise no truthful strategy for bringing about the ruin of the man of God; and so they resorted to greater destruction by inventing a lie: with this they introduced into the kingdom great evil and devastating slaughter in persecuting many people....

[Ebroin and his faction controlled the kingdom in the name of a "certain young lad," Clovis, who was said to be the son of Clothar III and rightful king. They now carried through the plan to get rid of Leudegar by bringing him to trial at the palace.]

[33] ... When Leudegar had been brought forward into the midst of the assembly [of bishops], they tried to get from him a confession that he had been privy to the killing of Childeric. Then realizing that again conflict threatened him because of a diabolical fiction, Leudegar said that, just as he did not absolve himself from human wrongdoing, so too he had never advised this deed, but declared that God knew this rather than man. They interrogated him for some time but could not get anything else out of him. So they tore apart his tunic from top to bottom, and the impious tyrant gave orders for him to be handed over to a certain Chrodobert, who was count of the palace at the time, and for his life in this world to be taken from him by a stroke of the sword.

The martyr of God found joy in all his suffering, for he could sense the approach of the martyr's crown that was due to him as a reward from God. Now Chrodobert took him to his own residence. And he obtained such a

heavenly blessing on his arrival that, when all those living there saw this plainly, they abandoned their own sins by confessing and eagerly took refuge in the healing medicine of penance. God had adorned his servant with this gift so that whenever he was handed over as an exile to be treated badly, those who received him, on the contrary, all paid him the reverence due from servants.

[34] At last arrived the day of death on which his persecution came to an end. At that time the results of a judicial decision were issued by the palace that Leudegar must live no longer. The impious Ebroin, fearing that faithful Christians would pay Leudegar the respect of a martyr, gave orders for a well to be found deep in the woods and his mutilated corpse to be sunk in it so that, once the mouth of the well was filled in with earth and stones, people would not know where he was buried.

Meanwhile Leudegar, by his preaching to Chrodobert, had already begun to some extent to bring about the latter's conversion. Because Chrodobert could not bear to look at the death of the man of God, he charged two of his servants to carry out the orders he had been given. When this news reached his house, his wife began to weep in bitter distress because such a cruel and shameful act had become the duty of her husband.

[35] When the man of God saw that his end was now at hand, he began to comfort the weeping woman, saying, "Please do not weep over my passing. No demand for vengeance will ever be made against you for my death, but rather a blessing will be given by God from heaven if you devoutly bury my body in its grave."

And when he had spoken these words, he said goodbye at the urging of the servants and was taken to the woods for them to carry out the sentence of the order.

Now they had previously found a well where they could hide his body as they had been told; but they never found it again. While looking for the well, they wandered hopelessly about and on this account put off killing him. In the meantime the martyr of God was allowed to prostrate himself in prayer and to entrust his passing to God. To both of his killers, who were looming over him, he began to predict the future through the spirit of prophecy. One of them, sparked by the ancient enemy, was quite anxious to carry out the deed. But the other, who was a gentle man, tremblingly begged him not to take vengeance on Leudegar.

Leudegar addressed the two of them.

"You, who follow orders against your will," he said, "confess your previous sins immediately to a priest and by doing penance you shall also escape the consequences of this deed."

To the other he said, "And as for you, if you do not do the same, you shall have to be delivered up immediately to God for swift vengeance."

Again, prostrating himself in prayer, he confidently entrusted his soul to Christ the lord. And getting up, he extended his neck and bade the executioner do what he had been ordered to do. And when the man we mentioned above suddenly cut off his head, a chorus of angels, rejoicing, conducted the spirit of the blessed martyr to heaven to be presented to the Lord so he might reign in heaven with all the saints. There in joyful company of the saints is our lord Jesus Christ, who with the Father and holy Spirit lives and reigns through the course of the ages.

2.12 The settlement of disputes: *Judgment of Childebert III* (709 or 710). Original in Latin.

In the Merovingian period, as today, most disputes were probably settled out of court. Nevertheless, some did lead to formal action in assemblies or meetings. Normally a document was drawn up, called a *placitum*, reporting on the proceedings and the outcome. These were kept by the institution that won the case. In the judgment below, King Childebert (r.694–711) presided over an assembly at which Abbot Dalfinus of the monastery of Saint-Denis (near Paris) litigated against Grimoald, mayor of the palace. Dalfinus claimed for his monastery all the tolls collected from merchants at the annual fair held at Saint-Denis. While most such disputes were real, this one seems to have been "fictive"—a way for the abbot of Saint-Denis to get public reaffirmation of rights that had long been granted to his monastery. As in real cases, the proceedings included the testimony of witnesses and the production of written documents, in this case "the directives" of former kings who had issued such grants to Saint-Denis against the interest of the "fisc"—the king's own treasury. What factors might lead you to argue that the fair at Saint-Denis generated a lot of income? What might lead you to conclude the opposite—that these revenues were negligible? What might be the uses of a fictive dispute for the abbot—or even for the mayor of the palace?

[Source: *From Roman to Merovingian Gaul: A Reader*, ed. and trans. Alexander Callander Murray (Toronto: University of Toronto Press, 2000), pp. 585–87.]

Childebert [III], king of the Franks, to those of illustrious rank.

Representatives of the venerable Dalfinus, abbot of the basilica of our own special patron Saint Dionysius [i.e., Saint-Denis], wherein lies the precious body of this lord, came before us and our leading men in our palace at Montmacq. They claimed in opposition to the representatives of the illustrious Grimoald, mayor of our palace, that over a long period of time our grandfather the late Clovis [II], and after him our uncle Childeric [II] and our father Theuderic [III], as well as our brother Clothar [III, IV, Clovis III?] had issued directives granting to that basilica of Saint Dionysius the entire toll collected from all merchants, whether of Saxon or other nationality, who attend the fair held on the holy feast of Lord Dionysius [9 October]; as a consequence of the grant, they said, the fisc was precluded at that time [of Clovis II] and later from exacting or collecting on its own behalf tolls from those merchants either there, at the fair, or within the district of Paris or within the city of Paris; the basilica of Saint Dionysius, they said, had been granted and awarded this right in its entirety for all time.

They then produced the directives of the aforesaid

princes to that effect for the court to read. Those directives were deposited and examined, and it was determined that such a grant in its entirety had been made to that house of God by those princes.

Then the representatives of Dalfinus said that the representatives of Grimoald, mayor of our palace as well as count of the district of Paris, collected half the toll from them, removing its benefits from the basilica.

The representatives of the mayor of our palace Grimoald replied on the contrary that for a long time it had been customary for the house of Saint Dionysius to receive one half the toll and the count the other on behalf of the fisc.

The representatives of Saint Dionysius contended in reply that Gaerin,[1] the late count of Paris, introduced this custom by force and at times collected half the toll from them; but those representatives informed the palace of this and, they said, always renewed their royal directives without diminution of the grant.

Again an examination was undertaken of numerous people and of the directives that the aforesaid princes had granted originally and had subsequently confirmed without diminution of the grant.

And so, with Grimoald's agreement and that of many other loyal followers of the king, a determination was made and judgment given that the representatives of Grimoald were on behalf of our fisc to invest that toll in its entirety once again upon the agents of the abbot by means of a pledge. And so they did.

Whereas it is known that the suit has been brought forward and settled, investigated and adjudicated, in just such a fashion as the illustrious count of our palace Rigofred has reported, it is our command, now that the previous directives granted to the monastery have been examined, that for all time the aforesaid monastery of Saint Dionysius, wherein that most precious lord's body rests, and abbot Dalfinus and his successors have successfully sued for and laid claim to that entire toll collected at the feast of Saint Dionysius, both that which arises on the lands of the basilica and later in Paris.

In earlier times, the market was moved on account of a catastrophe from the site of Saint Dionysius and was established in the city of Paris between the basilicas of Saints Martin and Laurence. The abbey received directives from the aforesaid princes to the effect that the aforesaid basilica of Saint Dionysius should get the toll in its entirety either there or wherever it set up to conduct business and commerce on the occasion of that feast. In view of these circumstances, if it happens that on account of some catastrophe or interruption the fair should be moved somewhere else, let that aforesaid toll, because of our devotion to that holy place, in present and future times, remain granted to and bestowed upon that house of God to offset the cost of lighting. And between our fisc and the representatives of Saint Dionysius, may all dispute and contention be laid to rest.

Actulius has been ordered to certify this.

Given, under auspicious signs, in December, on the thirteenth day, in the sixteenth year of our reign at Montmacq.

2.13 Reforming the Continental church: *Letters to Boniface* (723–726). Original in Latin.

Born in Wessex, England, Boniface (672/675–754) entered a monastery at the age of seven, where he received an excellent education. In 716 he undertook the first of his missionary efforts, going to Frisia, where he followed in the footsteps of earlier English evangelists. In 717 he traveled to Rome—where he changed his name from the Anglo-Saxon "Wynfrith" to the Latinate "Boniface"—and received a commission from Pope Gregory II (715–731) to evangelize the people living east of the Rhine—in Bavaria and Thuringia. In fact, these regions had already been Christianized, and Boniface spent most of his time reforming churches already established rather than preaching the Word to pagans. In all of his work he was avidly supported by Charles Martel (d.741), the powerful mayor of the palace in Francia (as we may now call Gaul). After Charles's death, Boniface focused on reforming the Frankish church itself, which he did through a series of church councils

---

[1] Leudegar's brother; see above, p. 83.

that he called between 742 and 744. A year later he became archbishop of Mainz, but not long thereafter he returned to Frisia, which had not yet been Christianized, and there suffered a martyr's death in 754. The letters below come from Boniface's earliest period in Germany. In the first, Charles Martel offers him protection. In the second, Gregory II commends him to the Thuringians, whose Christianization he does not recognize. In the third, the pope instructs Boniface on particular matters of Christian practice. Why did Gregory II support Boniface's work? In what ways did the model of Pope Gregory the Great's missionary work in England (see the letters in Bede, p. 94) inspire Gregory II? What might explain Charles Martel's support of Boniface?

[Source: *The Letters of Saint Boniface*, trans. Ephraim Emerton (New York: W.W. Norton, 1940), pp. 47, 52–56.]

[CHARLES MARTEL COMMENDS BONIFACE TO ALL FRANKISH OFFICIALS, 723]

To the holy and apostolic bishops, our fathers in Christ, and to the dukes, counts, vicars, palace officials, all our lower agents, our circuit judges [missi] and all who are our friends, the noble Charles, mayor of the palace, your well-wisher, sends greeting.

Be it known to you that the apostolic man in Christ, Father Boniface, a man of apostolic character and a bishop, came to us with the request that we should take him under our guardianship and protection. Know that we have acquiesced with pleasure and, hence, have granted his petition before witnesses and commanded that this written order signed by our own hand be given him, that wheresoever he may choose to go, he is to be left in peace and protected as a man under our guardianship and protection to the end that he may render and receive justice. If he shall be in any need or distress which cannot be remedied according to law, let him and those dependent upon him come in peace and safety before our presence, so that no person may hinder or do him injury, but that he may rest at all times in peace and safety under our guardianship and protection.

And that this may the more surely be given credit, I have signed it with my own hand and sealed it with our ring.

[POPE GREGORY II COMMENDS BONIFACE TO THE THURINGIANS, DECEMBER 724]

Gregory, servant of the servants of God, to all the people of the Thuringians.

The Lord Jesus Christ, Son of God and very God, descended from Heaven, was made man, deigned to suffer and be crucified for us, was buried, rose from the dead on the third day, and ascended into Heaven. To His holy Apostles and disciples He said: "Go forth and teach all peoples, baptizing them in the name of the Father, the Son, and the Holy Spirit (Matt. 28:19)"; and He promised those who believed in Him eternal life.

We, therefore, desiring that you may rejoice with us forever where there is no ending, neither sorrow nor any bitterness, but eternal glory, have sent to you our most holy brother, Bishop Boniface, that he may baptize you and teach you the doctrine of Christ and lead you out of error into the way of safety, that you may win salvation and life eternal. But do you be obedient unto him in all things, honor him as your father, and incline your hearts to his instruction, for we have sent him to you, not for any temporal gain, but for the profit of your souls. Therefore love God and receive baptism in his name, for the Lord our God has prepared for those who love him things which the eye of man hath not seen, and which have never entered into the heart of man. Depart from evil doing, and do what is right. Worship not idols, neither sacrifice offerings of flesh to them, for God does not accept such things, but observe and do as our brother Boniface shall direct, and you and your children shall be in safety forever.

Build also a house where this your father and bishop may live and churches where you may offer up your prayers, that God may forgive your sins and grant you eternal life.

[REPLIES OF POPE GREGORY II TO QUESTIONS OF BONIFACE, NOVEMBER 22, 726]

Gregory, servant of the servants of God, to his most reverend and holy brother and fellow bishop Boniface.

Your messenger, the pious priest Denuald, has brought us the welcome news that you are well and prospering, with the help of God, in the service for which you were sent. He also brought a letter from you showing that the field of the Lord which had been lying fallow, bristling with the thorns of unbelief, has received the plowshare of your instruction, plowing in the seed of the word, and is bringing forth an abundant harvest of true belief.

In this same letter you inserted several paragraphs of inquiries as to the faith and teaching of this Holy and Apostolic Roman Church. And this was well done; for the blessed apostle Peter stands as the fountainhead of the apostolate and the episcopate. And to you who consult us about ecclesiastical matters we show what decision you have to take according to the teaching of apostolic tradition, and we do this not as if by our own personal authority, but by the grace of Him who opens the mouth of the dumb and makes eloquent the tongues of infants.

You ask first within what degrees of relationship marriage may take place. We reply: strictly speaking, in so far as the parties know themselves to be related they ought not to be joined together. But since moderation is better than strictness of discipline, especially toward so uncivilized a people, they may contract marriage after the fourth degree.

As to your question, what a man is to do if his wife is unable, on account of disease, to fulfill her wifely duty: it would be well if he could remain in a state of continence. But, since this is a matter of great difficulty, it is better for him who cannot refrain to take a wife. He may not, however, withdraw his support from the one who was prevented by disease, provided she be not involved in any grievous fault.

In regard to a priest or any cleric accused by the people: unless the evidence of the witnesses to the charge against him is positive, let him take oath before the assembly, calling as witness of his innocence Him to whom all things are plain and open; and so let him keep his proper standing.

In the case of one confirmed by a bishop, a repetition of this rite is prohibited.

In the celebration of the Mass, the form is to be observed which our Lord Jesus Christ used with his disciples. He took the cup and gave it to them, saying: "This cup is the new testament in my blood; this do ye as oft as ye take it." Wherefore it is not fitting that two or three cups should be placed on the altar when the ceremony of the Mass is performed.

As to sacrificial foods: You ask whether, if a believer makes the life-giving sign of the cross above them, it is permitted to eat them or not. A sufficient answer is given in the words of the blessed apostle Paul: "If any man say unto you, This is offered in sacrifice unto idols, eat not for his sake who showed it, and for conscience' sake."[1]

You ask further, if a father or mother shall have placed a young son or daughter in a cloister under the discipline of a rule, whether it is lawful for the child after reaching the years of discretion to leave the cloister and enter into marriage. This we absolutely forbid, since it is an impious thing that the restraints of desire should be relaxed for children offered to God by their parents.

You mention also that some have been baptized by adulterous and unworthy priests without being questioned whether they believe, as it is in the ritual. In such cases you are to follow the ancient custom of the Church. He who has been baptized in the name of the Father, Son, and Holy Spirit may on no account be baptized again; for he has received the gift of His grace not in the name of the one who baptizes, but in the name of the Trinity. Let the word of the Apostle be observed: "One God, one faith, one baptism."[2] We require you to convey spiritual instruction to such persons with especial zeal.

As to young children taken from their parents and not knowing whether they have been baptized or not, reason requires you to baptize them, unless there be someone who can give evidence in the case.

Lepers, if they are believing Christians, may receive the body and blood of the Lord, but they may not take food together with persons in health.

You ask whether, in the case of a contagious disease or plague in a church or monastery, those who are not yet attacked may escape danger by flight. We declare this to be the height of folly; for no one can escape from the hand of God.

Finally, your letter states that certain priests and bishops are so involved in vices of many sorts that their lives are a blot upon the priesthood and you ask whether it is lawful for you to eat with or to speak with them, supposing them not to be heretics. We answer, that you by apostolic authority are to admonish and persuade them and so bring them back to the purity of church discipline. If they obey, you will save their souls and win reward for yourself. You are not to avoid conversation or eating at the same table with them. It often happens that those who are slow in coming to a perception of the truth under strict discipline may be led into the paths of righteousness by the influence of their table companions and by gentle admonition. You ought also to follow this same rule in dealing with those chieftains who are helpful to you.

This, my dear brother, is all that need be said with the authority of the Apostolic See. For the rest we implore the mercy of God, that He who has sent you into that region in our stead and with apostolic authority and has caused the light of truth to shine into that dark forest by means of your words may mercifully grant the increase, so that

---

[1] 1 Cor. 10: 28.

[2] Eph. 4: 5.

you may reap the reward of your labors and we may find remission for our sins.

God keep you in safety, most reverend brother.

Given on the tenth day before the Kalends of December, in the tenth year of our most pious and august Lord Leo, by God crowned emperor, in the tenth year of his consulship and the seventh of the Emperor Constantine his son, in the tenth indiction.[1]

2.14 Creating a Roman Christian identity for England: Bede, *The Ecclesiastical History of the English People* (731). Original in Latin.

A child of the cloister—he entered the monastery of Wearmouth-Jarrow in the north of England at the age of seven—Bede (673–735) was among the best-educated men of his day in the Roman, papal tradition and the expertise in Latin that went with it. Because his monastery was extraordinarily well stocked with books—brought back from the Continent (mainly Rome) by Wearmouth and Jarrow's founder, Benedict Biscop—Bede was able to consult a wide range of sources for his numerous writings. These included biblical commentaries, the lives of saints, liturgical works, sermons, scientific texts (his *Computation of Time* was particularly important for calculating the date of Easter and other movable feasts), and histories, including a *History of the Abbots of Wearmouth and Jarrow* and *The Ecclesiastical History*. Although Christianity came to England in a variety of ways, Bede emphasized the Roman contribution. How did Bede's writings enhance the reputation of Gregory the Great?

[Source: Bede, *The Ecclesiastical History of the English People*, ed. Judith McClure and Roger Collins (Oxford: Oxford University Press, 1994), pp. 37–41, 55–59, 65–71, 152–59, 370–75, 397 (slightly modified).]

Book 1

CHAPTER 23

In the year of our Lord 582 Maurice,[2] the fifty-fourth from Augustus, became emperor; he ruled for twenty-one years. In the tenth year of his reign, Gregory,[3] a man eminent in learning and in affairs, was elected pontiff of the apostolic see of Rome; he ruled for thirteen years, six months, and ten days. In the fourteenth year[4] of this emperor and about 150 years after the coming of the Angles to Britain, Gregory, prompted by divine inspiration, sent a servant of God named Augustine[5] and several more God-fearing monks with him to preach the word of God to the English race. In obedience to the pope's commands, they undertook this task and had already gone a little way on their journey when they were paralyzed with terror. They began to contemplate returning home rather than going to a barbarous, fierce, and unbelieving nation whose language they did not even understand. They all agreed that this was the safer course; so forthwith they

---

[1] The letter is thus dated by the reign of Byzantine Emperor Leo III (r.717–741) and his son Constantine, for whom see *The Synod of 754* (above, p. 65) and the *Chronicle of Theophanes* (above, p. 69).

[2] Emperor Maurice Tiberius (r.582–602).

[3] Pope Gregory the Great (590–604).

[4] August 595 to August 596.

[5] Augustine—who should not be confused with St. Augustine (d.430), the bishop of Hippo—had been prior (just below the abbot in administrative status) of the monastery that Gregory founded on his own family property on the Caelian Hill in Rome.

sent home Augustine whom Gregory had intended to have consecrated as their bishop if they were received by the English. Augustine was to beg St. Gregory humbly for permission to give up so dangerous, wearisome, and uncertain a journey. Gregory, however, sent them an encouraging letter in which he persuaded them to persevere with the task of preaching the Word and trust in the help of God. The letter was in these terms:

Gregory, servant of the servants of God, to the servants of our Lord.

My dearly beloved sons, it would have been better not to have undertaken a noble task than to turn back deliberately from what you have begun: so it is right that you should carry out with all diligence this good work which you have begun with the help of the Lord. Therefore do not let the toilsome journey nor the tongues of evil speakers deter you. But carry out the task you have begun under the guidance of God with all constancy and fervor. Be sure that, however great your task may be, the glory of your eternal reward will be still greater. When Augustine your prior returns, now, by our appointment, your abbot, humbly obey him in all things, knowing that whatever you do under his direction will be in all respects profitable to your souls. May Almighty God protect you by His grace and grant that I may see the fruit of your labors in our heavenly home. Though I cannot labor with you, yet because I should have been glad indeed to do so, I hope to share in the joy of your reward. May God keep you safe, my dearly loved sons.

Given on July 23, in the fourteenth year of the reign of our most religious emperor Maurice Tiberius, and the thirteenth year after his consulship, and the fourteenth indiction.[1] [July 23, 596]

CHAPTER 24

The venerable pontiff at the same time also sent a letter to Etherius of Arles,[2] asking him to receive Augustine kindly on his return to Britain. This is the text:

To his most reverend and holy brother and fellow bishop Etherius, Gregory, servant of the servants of God.

Although religious men stand in need of no recommendation with those bishops who have that love which is pleasing to God, yet because a suitable occasion for writing presents itself, we think fit to send this letter to you our brother, informing you that we have directed thither the bearer of this document, Augustine, the servant of God, of whose zeal we are assured, together with other servants of God devoted to winning souls with the Lord's help. It is essential that your holiness should assist him with episcopal zeal and hasten to provide him with what he needs. And in order that you may be the more prompt with your help, we have specially enjoined him to tell you of his mission. We are sure that when you know this you will be prepared with all zeal to afford him your help for the Lord's sake as the occasion requires. We also commend to your charity the priest Candidus,[3] a son of both of us, whom we have sent to take charge of a small patrimony of our church. God keep you safe, most reverend brother.

Given on July 23, in the fourteenth year of the reign of our most religious emperor, Maurice Tiberius, and the thirteenth year after his consulship and the fourteenth indiction. [July 23, 596]

CHAPTER 25

So Augustine, strengthened by the encouragement of St. Gregory, in company with the servants of Christ, returned to the work of preaching the word, and came to Britain. At that time Ethelbert, king of Kent [d.616], was a very powerful monarch. The lands over which he ruled stretched as far as the great river Humber, which divides the northern from the southern Angles. Over against the eastern districts of Kent there is a large island called Thanet which, in English reckoning, is 600 hides[4] in extent. It is divided from the mainland by the river Wantsum, which is about three furlongs wide,[5] can be

---

[1] "Indiction" was a regular cycle of fifteen years, used initially for tax-assessment purposes, but which remained a conventional way of dating documents in the late Roman Empire.

[2] Etherius was actually bishop of Lyon (r.586–602), not of Arles. Bede adopts the term "archbishop" used in the Anglo-Saxon Church, but the Frankish equivalents were called metropolitan bishops. Similar letters were sent to the bishops of Marseille, Arles, and Tours to secure assistance and safe passage for the mission.

[3] Candidus was being sent as Rector of the papal Patrimony, to take charge of the running of the estates owned by the Roman Church in southern Gaul.

[4] The "hide" was theoretically the amount of land that supported one family, its extent varying from place to place.

[5] A furlong is one-eighth of a mile.

crossed in two places only, and joins the sea at either end. Here Augustine, the servant of the Lord, landed with his companions, who are said to have been nearly forty in number. They had acquired interpreters from the Frankish race according to the command of Pope St. Gregory. Augustine sent to Ethelbert to say that he had come from Rome bearing the best of news, namely the sure and certain promise of eternal joys in heaven and an endless kingdom with the living and true God to those who received it. On hearing this the king ordered them to remain on the island where they had landed and be provided with all things necessary until he had decided what to do about them. Some knowledge about the Christian religion had already reached him because he had a Christian wife of the Frankish royal family whose name was Bertha.[1] He had received her from her parents on condition that she should be allowed to practice her faith and religion unhindered, with a bishop named Liudhard whom they had provided for her to support her faith.

Some days afterwards the king came to the island and, sitting in the open air, commanded Augustine and his comrades to come there to talk with him. He took care that they should not meet in any building, for he held the traditional superstition that, if they practiced any magic art, they might deceive him and get the better of him as soon as he entered. But they came endowed with divine not devilish power and bearing as their standard a silver cross and the image of our Lord and Savior painted on a panel.[2] They chanted litanies and uttered prayers to the Lord for their own eternal salvation and the salvation of those for whom and to whom they had come. At the king's command they sat down and preached the word of life to himself and all his officials and companions there present. Then he said to them: "The words and the promises you bring are fair enough, but because they are new to us and doubtful, I cannot consent to accept them and forsake those beliefs which I and the whole people of the Angles have held so long. But as you have come on a long pilgrimage and are anxious, I perceive, to share with us things which you believe to be true and good, we do not wish to do you harm; on the contrary, we will

receive you hospitably and provide what is necessary for your support; nor do we forbid you to win all you can to your faith and religion by your preaching." So he gave them a dwelling in the city of Canterbury, which was the chief city of all his dominions; and, in accordance with his promise, he granted them provisions and did not refuse them freedom to preach. It is related that as they approached the city in accordance with their custom carrying the holy cross and the image of our great King and Lord, Jesus Christ, they sang this litany in unison: "We beseech Thee, O Lord, in Thy great mercy, that Thy wrath and anger may be turned away from this city and from Thy holy house, for we have sinned. Alleluia."

CHAPTER 26

As soon as they had entered the dwelling-place allotted to them, they began to imitate the way of life of the apostles and of the primitive church. They were constantly engaged in prayers, in vigils and fasts; they preached the word of life to as many as they could; they despised all worldly things as foreign to them; they accepted only the necessaries of life from those whom they taught; in all things they practiced what they preached and kept themselves prepared to endure adversities, even to the point of dying for the truths they proclaimed. To put it briefly, some, marveling at their simple and innocent way of life and the sweetness of their heavenly doctrine, believed and were baptized. There was nearby, on the east of the city, a church built in ancient times in honor of St. Martin,[3] while the Romans were still in Britain, in which the queen who, as has been said, was a Christian, used to pray. In this church they first began to meet to chant the psalms, to pray, to say mass, to preach, and to baptize, until, when the king had been converted to the faith, they received greater liberty to preach everywhere and to build or restore churches.

At last the king, as well as others, believed and was baptized, being attracted by the pure life of the saints and by their most precious promises, whose truth they confirmed by performing many miracles. Every day more and more began to flock to hear the Word, to forsake

---

[1] Bertha was the daughter of the Merovingian king Charibert I (r.561–567), whose short-lived realm had been centered on Paris. As Bede points out, she was a Catholic Christian who brought her own bishop, Liudhard, with her.

[2] How might Bede's emphasis on this image be an indirect critique of Byzantine iconoclasm? Bede was writing at the very beginning of that movement.

[3] The western section of the chancel (the space around the altar) of the extant church of St. Martin in Canterbury is thought to have formed part of the church of Queen Bertha. This reference, like that to Liudhard, hints at the survival of Christian worship in post-Roman lowland Britain prior to the arrival of Augustine.

their heathen worship, and, through faith, to join the unity of Christ's holy Church. It is related that the king, although he rejoiced at their conversion and their faith, compelled no one to accept Christianity; though nonetheless he showed greater affection for believers since they were his fellow citizens in the kingdom of heaven. But he had learned from his teachers and guides in the way of salvation that the service of Christ was voluntary and ought not to be compulsory. It was not long before he granted his teachers a place to settle in, suitable to their rank, in Canterbury, his chief city, and gave them possessions of various kinds for their needs....

CHAPTER 29

Since Bishop Augustine had advised him that the harvest was great and the workers were few, Pope Gregory sent more colleagues and ministers of the word together with his messengers. First and foremost among these were Mellitus, Justus, Paulinus, and Rufinianus; and he sent with them all such things as were generally necessary for the worship and ministry of the Church, such as sacred vessels, altar cloths and church ornaments, vestments for priests and clerks, relics of the holy apostles and martyrs, and very many manuscripts. He also sent a letter in which he announced that he had dispatched the pallium[1] to him and at the same time directed how he should organize the bishops in Britain. Here is the text of this letter:

To the most reverend and holy brother Augustine, our fellow-bishop, Gregory, servant of the servants of God.

While it is certain that untold rewards in the eternal kingdom are laid up for those who labor for Almighty God, nevertheless it is necessary that we should bestow rewards and honors upon them so that they may be encouraged by this recognition to toil more abundantly in their spiritual work. And because the new church of the English has been brought into the grace of Almighty God through the bounty of the Lord and by your labors, we grant to you the use of the pallium in the church but only for the performance of the solemn rites of the mass, so that you may ordain twelve bishops in various places who are to be subject to your jurisdiction. However, the bishop of London[2] shall, for the future, always be consecrated by

his own synod and receive the honor of the pallium from that holy and apostolic see which, by the guidance of God, I serve. We wish to send as bishop to the city of York one whom you yourself shall decide to consecrate. But if this city together with the neighboring localities should receive the Word of the Lord, he [the bishop of York] is also to consecrate twelve bishops and enjoy the honorable rank of a metropolitan. For it is our intention, God willing, if we live, to give him the pallium too. Nevertheless, brother, we wish him to be subject to your authority. But after your death, he should preside over the bishops he has consecrated, being in no way subject to the authority of the bishop of London. There is, however, to be this distinction in honor, in future, between the bishops of London and York, that he who was first consecrated is to be reckoned senior. But let them agree to do whatever has to be done, taking counsel together and acting out of zeal for Christ. Let them judge rightly and with one mind and so carry out their decisions without disagreement.

You, brother, are to have under your subjection those bishops whom you have consecrated as well as those who shall be consecrated by the bishop of York, and not those only but also all the bishops of Britain, under the guidance of our Lord God, Jesus Christ, so that they may see from the words and actions of your Holiness what true faith and good living are like and so, fulfilling their office in faith and righteousness, may attain to the heavenly kingdom when it shall please the Lord. May God keep you safe, most reverend brother.

Given June 22 in the nineteenth year of the reign of our most religious emperor Maurice Tiberius, the eighteenth year after his consulship and in the fourth indiction. [June 22, 601]

CHAPTER 30

When these messengers had departed, St. Gregory sent after them a letter which is worth recording, in which he plainly showed his eager interest in the salvation of our race. This is what he wrote:

To my most beloved son, Abbot Mellitus, Gregory, servant of the servants of God.

---

[1] The "pallium" was a thin band of white wool worn by the popes in the performance of the liturgy, the use of which could be conferred on approved metropolitan bishops. It was regularly given to the archbishops of Canterbury.

[2] Gregory, relying on the former Roman administrative structures, assumed that London (actually in the kingdom of the East Saxons) would be the seat of the new archbishopric; contemporary political realities had already led to Canterbury's taking this role instead.

Since the departure of our companions and yourself I have felt much anxiety because we have not happened to hear how your journey has prospered. However, when Almighty God has brought you to our most reverend brother Bishop Augustine, tell him what I have decided after long deliberation about the English people, namely that the idol temples of that race should by no means be destroyed, but only the idols in them. Take holy water and sprinkle it in these shrines, build altars and place relics in them. For if the shrines are well built, it is essential that they should be changed from the worship of devils to the service of the true God. When the people see that their shrines are not destroyed they will be able to banish error from their hearts and be more ready to come to the places they are familiar with, but now recognizing and worshiping the true God. And because they are in the habit of slaughtering many cattle as sacrifices to devils, some solemnity ought to be given them in exchange for this. So on the day of the dedication or the festivals of the holy martyrs, whose relics are deposited there, let them make themselves huts from the branches of trees around the churches which have been converted out of shrines, and let them celebrate the solemnity with religious feasts. Do not let them sacrifice animals to the devil, but let them slaughter animals for their own food to the praise of God, and let them give thanks to the Giver of all things for His bountiful provision. Thus while some outward rejoicings are preserved, they will be able more easily to share in inward rejoicings. It is doubtless impossible to cut out everything at once from their stubborn minds, just as the man who is attempting to climb to the highest place, rises by steps and degrees and not by leaps. Thus the Lord made Himself known to the Israelites in Egypt, yet he preserved in his own worship the forms of sacrifice which they were accustomed to offer to the devil and commanded them to kill animals when sacrificing to him. So with changed hearts they were to put away one part of the sacrifice and retain the other; even though they were the same animals as they were in the habit of offering, yet since the people were offering them to the true God and not to idols, they were not the same sacrifices. These things then, dearly beloved, you must say to our brother so that in his present position he may carefully consider how he should order all things. May God keep you in safety, most beloved son.

Given July 18 in the nineteenth year of the reign of our most religious emperor Maurice Tiberius, and in the eighteenth year after his consulship and in the fourth indiction. [July 18, 601]

CHAPTER 31

At the same time Pope Gregory heard that Augustine had been performing miracles and sent him a letter on the subject, in which he exhorts Augustine not to incur the danger of being elated by their great number:

I know, most beloved brother, that Almighty God out of love for you has worked great miracles through you for the race which it was his will to have among the chosen. It is therefore necessary that you should rejoice with trembling over this heavenly gift and fear as you rejoice. You will rejoice because the souls of the English are drawn by outward miracles to inward grace: but you will fear lest among these signs which are performed, the weak mind may be raised up by self-esteem and so the very cause by which it is raised to outward honor may lead through vainglory to its inward fall. We ought to remember that when the disciples were returning from their preaching full of joy, they said to their heavenly Master, "Lord, even the devils are subject to us through thy name (Luke 10: 17)." And forthwith they received the reply, "In this rejoice not, but rather rejoice that your names are written in heaven (Luke 10: 20)." They had set their minds on personal and temporal joys when they rejoiced over their own miracles, but they are recalled from private to common joys and from temporal to eternal joys by his words, "Rejoice in this that your names are written in heaven." For not all the elect work miracles, but nevertheless all their names are written in heaven. Therefore those who are true disciples ought not to rejoice except in that good thing which they have in common with all the elect and which they will enjoy for ever. So it remains, most dear brother, that amidst those outward deeds which you perform through the Lord's power you should always judge your inner self carefully and carefully note within yourself what you are and how great is the grace shown to that people for whose conversion you have received the gift of working miracles. And if you remember that you have at any time sinned against your Creator either in word or deed, always call this to mind in order that the memory of your guilt may suppress the vainglory which arises in your heart. And whatever power of working miracles you have received or shall receive, consider that these gifts have been conferred not on you, but on those for whose salvation they have been granted you.

CHAPTER 32

Pope Gregory at the same time also sent a letter to King Ethelbert as well as numerous gifts of every kind. He was anxious to glorify the king with temporal honors, while at the same time he rejoiced to think that Ethelbert had attained to the knowledge of heavenly glory by Gregory's own labor and industry....

Book 2

CHAPTER 1

About this time, in the year of our Lord 605,[1] Pope St. Gregory, who had reigned in great glory over the apostolic Roman see for thirteen years, six months, and ten days, died and was taken up to reign for ever in the kingdom of heaven. Well indeed may we, the English nation converted by his efforts from the power of Satan to the faith of Christ, give a somewhat full account of him in this *History*. We can and should by rights call him our apostle, for though he held the most important see in the whole world and was head of Churches which had long been converted to the true faith, yet he made our nation, till then enslaved to idols, into a Church of Christ, so that we may use the apostle's words about him, "If he is not an apostle to others yet at least he is to us, for we are the seal of his apostleship in the Lord (see 1 Cor. 9: 2)."

He was of Roman race, his father's name being Gordianus. He traced his descent from ancestors who were not only noble but also devout. Felix,[2] for example, who was once bishop of the apostolic see and a man of great reputation both in Christ and in the Church, was his forefather. That ancestral tradition of religion he followed with the same religious devotion as his parents and kinsmen, while the noble position which was accounted his, according to the standards of the world, was by God's grace entirely sacrificed to winning glory and honor of a higher kind. He promptly renounced his secular habit and entered a monastery,[3] in which he proceeded to live with such grace and perfection—as he used afterwards to declare with tears—that his soul was then above all transitory things, and he soared beyond all things subject to change. He used to think nothing but thoughts of heaven so that, even though still imprisoned in the body, he was able to pass in contemplation beyond the barriers of the flesh. He loved death, which in the eyes of almost everybody is a punishment, because he held it to be the entrance to life and the reward of his labors.

He used to relate all this, not boasting over his progress towards moral perfection, but rather bewailing the loss which he seemed to have incurred as the result of his pastoral cares. Once, for instance, when he was talking privately with his deacon Peter and enumerating the former virtues of his soul, he added mournfully that now on account of his pastoral cares he had to trouble himself with the business of men of this world, and after the enjoyment of peace so lovely, he was soiled by the dust of earthly activities. After dissipating his strength on outward things by descending to the affairs of all and sundry, even when he sought the things of the spirit, he inevitably returned to them impaired. "I realize," he said, "what I endure and what I have lost; and when my mind turns to what I have lost, then what I endure becomes so much the more burdensome."

The holy man said all this in a spirit of great humility. We need not believe, however, that he had lost any of his monastic perfection by reason of his pastoral cares. It would appear that he profited more by his efforts over the conversion of many than he had done from the quiet retirement of his earlier way of life. This was largely because, while fulfilling his pontifical duties, he turned his own house into a monastery; and when he was first taken from the monastery and was ordained to the ministry of the altar, having been sent to Constantinople as delegate of the apostolic see, he never ceased from his heavenly manner of life, though he had to live in an earthly palace. He even used some of the brothers from his monastery who had followed him out of brotherly love to the royal city [Constantinople] to protect him in his observance of the Rule. Thus, as he himself writes, through their unremitting example he could bind himself, as it were by an anchor cable, to the calm shores of prayer, while he was being tossed about on the ceaseless tide of secular affairs. So his mind, shaken by worldly business, could be strengthened by the encouragement derived from daily reading and contemplation in their company. By their fellowship he was thus not only defended against worldly assaults, but was also encouraged more and more to the activities of the heavenly life.

They urged him to unfold by spiritual interpretation the Book of Job, a work which is shrouded in great obscurity. Nor could he refuse the task imposed on him

---

[1] Gregory died on 12 March 604; otherwise Bede is right about the length of his pontificate. But Bede's facts and dates are not always accurate.

[2] Felix IV was pope 526–530.

[3] Gregory turned his own family home on the Caelian Hill in Rome into the monastery of St. Andrew.

by his loving brethren, seeing that it was likely to be of great use to many. So in thirty-five books[1] of exposition he taught in a marvelous manner the literal meaning of the book, its bearing on the mysteries of Christ and the Church, and the sense in which it applies to each of the faithful. He began this work while he was delegate in the royal city and finished it after he was made pope at Rome. While he was still in the royal city, helped by the grace of the catholic truth, he crushed at its birth a new heresy which arose there concerning our state at the resurrection. Eutychius, the bishop of the city, taught that our body in its resurrection glory, would be impalpable and more subtle than wind or air.[2] When Gregory heard this he proved both by sound reasoning and by the example of our Lord's resurrection that this dogma was contrary in every particular to the orthodox belief. For the catholic faith maintains that our body, while it is indeed exalted by the glory of immortality and made subtle by the effectual working of the spirit, is palpable by the reality of its nature as was our Lord's body, concerning which he said to his disciples, when it had been raised from the dead, "Touch me and see, for a spirit has not flesh and bones as you see me have (Luke 24: 39–40)." The venerable father Gregory strove so earnestly in his declaration of the faith against this newborn heresy and, with the help of the most religious emperor Tiberius Constantine,[3] suppressed it with such resolution, that no one has since been found to resuscitate it.

He composed another remarkable book called the *Pastoral Care*, in which he set forth in the clearest manner what sort of persons should be chosen to rule the Church and how these rulers ought to live; with how much discrimination they should instruct different types of listeners; and how earnestly they ought each day to reflect on their own frailty. He composed forty *Homilies on the Gospel*, which he divided into two volumes of equal size, and made four books of *Dialogues* in which, at the request of Peter his deacon, he collected the virtues of the most famous saints he knew or could learn of in Italy as an example of life to posterity; as in his expository works he taught what virtues men

ought to strive after, so, by describing the miracles of the saints, he showed how glorious those virtues are. He also showed in twenty-two homilies how much inner light is to be found within the most obscure sections of the prophet Ezekiel, namely the first part and the last. There is also a useful Synodal book which he composed in collaboration with the bishops of Italy, dealing with some of the Church's vital problems, together with familiar letters to certain individuals, not to mention the book of answers to the questions of St. Augustine, the first bishop of the English race, which I have described above and of which the whole is included in this *History*. It is all the more wonderful that he was able to produce so many books and of such length, since almost continually throughout his early manhood he had been, to use his own words, tortured with frequent pains in the bowels, and every moment of the day he was exhausted by a weakness of the internal organs, and his breathing was affected by a low but unremitting fever. Yet always amid these troubles, when he carefully reflected on the testimony of the scriptures that, "He scourges every son whom he receives,"[4] the more severely he was oppressed by present evils, the more surely he was refreshed by eternal hope.

This much may be said of his immortal spirit, which could not be quenched by so much bodily pain. Other popes applied themselves to the task of building churches and adorning them with gold and silver, but he devoted himself entirely to winning souls. Whatever money he had he took diligent care to distribute and give to the poor, so that "his righteousness might endure for ever and his horn be exalted with honor,"[5] so that the words of the blessed Job might truly be said of him: "When the ear heard me, then it blessed me and when the eye saw me it gave witness to me because I delivered the poor that cried and the fatherless also that had none to help him. The blessing of him that was ready to perish came upon me and I consoled the widow's heart. I put on righteousness and I clothed myself with my judgment as with a robe and a diadem. I was eyes to the blind and feet was I to the lame. I was a father to the poor and the cause which I knew not,

---

[1] This was the *Moralia in Job*.

[2] Eutychius was the Patriarch of Constantinople 552–565.

[3] Tiberius Constantine became Caesar and regent in 574, when Justin II (r.565–578) became insane; he was sole emperor from 578 to 582.

[4] Heb. 12: 6.

[5] Ps. 112: 9; Douay Ps. 111: 9.

I diligently searched out. I broke the jaws of the wicked and plucked the spoil out of his teeth."[1] And again a little further on he says, "If I have withheld their desire from the poor or have caused the eyes of the widow to fail; if I have eaten my morsel myself alone and the fatherless has not eaten thereof; for from my youth my compassion grew up with me and from my mother's womb it came forth with me."[2]

To his works of piety and justice this also belongs: that he snatched our race from the teeth of the ancient foe and made them partakers of everlasting freedom by sending us preachers. Rejoicing in their faith and commending them with worthy praise he says in his commentary on the blessed Job: "Lo, the mouth of Britain, which once only knew how to gnash its barbarous teeth, has long since learned to sing the praises of God with the alleluia of the Hebrews. See how the proud Ocean has become a servant, lying low now before the feet of the saints, and those barbarous motions, which earthly princes could not subdue with the sword, are now, through the fear of God, repressed with a simple word from the lips of priests; and he who, as an unbeliever, did not flinch before troops of warriors, now, as a believer, fears the words of the humble. For having received the heavenly Word and being enlightened by miracles as well, he is filled with the grace and the knowledge of God. He is restrained by the fear of God so that he dreads to do evil and with all his heart he longs to attain to everlasting grace." In these words St. Gregory also declares that St. Augustine and his companions led the English race to the knowledge of the truth, not only by preaching the Word but also by showing heavenly signs.

Among other things, Pope St. Gregory arranged that masses should be celebrated in the churches of the apostles St. Peter and St. Paul over their bodies. And in the celebration of the mass, he added three quite perfect petitions, "Dispose our days in peace, and command that we be saved from eternal damnation, and that we be numbered among the flock of thine elect."

He ruled the Church during the days of the Emperors Maurice and Phocas.[3] He departed this life in the second year of Phocas and passed to the true life in heaven. His body was buried in the church of St. Peter the Apostle, before the sanctuary, on 12 March; and in that body he will one day rise again in glory together with the other pastors of the Church. His epitaph written on his tomb runs as follows:

> Earth, take this corpse—'tis dust of thine own
>   dust:
> When God shall give new life, restore thy trust.
> Star-bound his soul: for Death's writ does not run
> Where grave's but gateway to life new-begun.
> A great high-priest this sepulcher inherits,
> Who lives for ever by uncounted merits;
> Hunger with meat, winter with clothes he ended,
> Souls with sound learning from the foe defended;
> Whate'er he taught, himself fulfilled in act—
> Mystic his words, but his example fact.
> Anglia to Christ at piety's dictation
> He turned, won thousands from an unknown
>   nation.
> Thus that great shepherd labored, thus he wrought;
> To increase his Master's flock was all his thought.
> Take thy reward in triumph and in joy,
> Who in God's council sits eternally!

We must not fail to relate the story about St. Gregory which has come down to us as a tradition of our forefathers. It explains the reason why he showed such earnest solicitude for the salvation of our race. It is said that one day, soon after some merchants had arrived in Rome, a quantity of merchandise was exposed for sale in the market place. Crowds came to buy and Gregory too among them. As well as other merchandise he saw some boys put up for sale, with fair complexions, handsome faces, and lovely hair. On seeing them he asked, so it is said, from what region or land they had been brought. He was told that they came from the island of Britain, whose inhabitants were like that in appearance. He asked again whether those islanders were Christians or still entangled in the errors of heathenism. He was told that they were heathen. Then with a deep-drawn sigh he said, "Alas that the author of darkness should have men so bright of face in his grip, and that minds devoid of inward grace should bear so graceful an outward form." Again he asked for the name of the race. He was told that they were called *Angli*. "Good," he said, "they have the

---

[1]   Job 29: 11–17.

[2]   Job 31: 16–18.

[3]   Emperor Maurice (r.582–602) was overthrown in a military revolt led by Phocas (r.602–610).

face of angels [*angeli* in Latin], and such men should be fellow heirs of the angels in heaven." "What is the name," he asked, "of the kingdom from which they have been brought?" He was told that the men of the kingdom were called *Deiri*. "*Deiri*," he replied. "*De ira!* [=From anger!] good! snatched from the wrath of Christ and called to his mercy. And what is the name of the king of the land?" He was told that it was Ælle;[1] and playing on the name, he said, "Alleluia! the praise of God the Creator must be sung in those parts." So he went to the bishop of Rome and of the apostolic see, for he himself had not yet been made pope, and asked him to send some ministers of the word to the race of the Angles in Britain to convert them to Christ. He added that he himself was prepared to carry out the task with the help of the Lord provided that the pope was willing. But he was unable to perform this mission, because although the pope was willing to grant his request, the citizens of Rome could not permit him to go so far away from the city. Soon after he had become pope, he fulfilled the task which he had long desired. It is true that he sent other preachers, but he himself helped their preaching to bear fruit by his encouragement and prayers. I have thought it proper to insert this story into this Church *History*, based as it is on the tradition that we have received from our ancestors....

Book 3

CHAPTER 25

Meanwhile, after Bishop Aidan's death,[2] Finan succeeded him as bishop,[3] having been consecrated and sent over by the Irish. He constructed a church on the island of Lindisfarne suitable for an episcopal see, building it after the Irish method, not of stone but of hewn oak, thatching it with reeds; later on the most reverend Archbishop Theodore[4] consecrated it in honor of the blessed apostle Peter. It was Eadberht,[5] who was bishop of Lindisfarne, who removed the reed thatch and had the whole of it, both roof and walls, covered with sheets of lead.

In those days there arose a great and active controversy about the keeping of Easter. Those who had come from Kent or Gaul declared that the Irish observance of Easter Sunday was contrary to the custom of the universal church. One most violent defender of the true Easter was Ronan[6] who, though Irish by race, had learned the true rules of the church in Gaul or Italy. In disputing with Finan he put many right or at least encouraged them to make a more strict inquiry into the truth; but he could by no means put Finan right. On the contrary, as he was a man of fierce temper, Ronan made him the more bitter by his reproofs and turned him into an open adversary of the truth. James, once the deacon of the venerable Archbishop Paulinus, as we have already said,[7] kept the true and catholic Easter with all those whom he could instruct in the better way. Queen Eanfleda[8] and her people also observed it as she had seen it done in Kent, having with her a Kentish priest named Romanus who followed the Catholic observance. Hence it is said that in these days it sometimes happened that Easter was celebrated twice in the same year, so that the king had finished the fast and was keeping Easter Sunday, while the queen and her people were still in Lent and observing Palm Sunday. This difference in the observance of Easter was patiently tolerated by all while Aidan was alive, because they had clearly understood that although he could not keep Easter otherwise than according to the manner of those who had sent him, he nevertheless labored diligently to practice the works of faith, piety, and love, which is the mark of all the saints. He was therefore deservedly loved by all, including those who had other views about Easter. Not only was he respected by the ordinary people but also by bishops, such as Honorius of Kent and Felix of East Anglia.

---

1   Ælle was king of the Deirans (in England) 559–588.

2   Aidan (d.651) was the bishop of Lindisfarne (in northern England). He had come from Ireland to teach the Christian faith at the request of Oswald, king of Northumbria (d.642).

3   Finan (d.661).

4   Theodore was archbishop of Canterbury 668–690.

5   Eadberht was bishop of Lindisfarne 688–698.

6   Nothing else is known of Ronan. The church in the south of Ireland had by this time largely adopted Continental practices with respect to the dating of Easter.

7   Paulinus (d.644) was bishop of York and Rochester.

8   Eanfleda (d.c.704) was the daughter of Edwin, king of Deira, and Ethelburg Tata, daughter of Ethelbert and Bertha of Kent. She married Oswiu, king of Bernicia (r.642–670).

When Finan, Aidan's successor, was dead and Colman,[1] who had also been sent from Ireland, had become bishop, a still more serious controversy arose concerning the observance of Easter as well as about other matters of ecclesiastical discipline. This dispute naturally troubled the minds and hearts of many people who feared that, though they had received the name of Christian, they might have done so in vain. All this came to the ears of the rulers [of Northumbria] themselves, Oswiu [d.670] and his son Alhfrith. Oswiu, who had been educated and baptized by the Irish and was well versed in their language, considered that nothing was better than what they had taught. But Alhfrith had as his instructor in the Christian faith one Wilfrid, a most learned man who had once been to Rome to study church doctrine and had spent much time at Lyon with Dalfinus,[2] archbishop of Gaul, having received there his ecclesiastical tonsure in the form of a crown. So Alhfrith rightly preferred his teaching to all the traditions of the Irish and had therefore given him a monastery of forty hides in the place called Ripon. He had presented the site, a short time before, to those who followed Irish ways, but because, when given the choice, they preferred to renounce the site rather than change their customs, he gave it to one who was worthy of the place both by his doctrine and his way of life. At that time there had come to the kingdom of Northumbria Agilbert, bishop of the West Saxons, whom we have mentioned before, a friend of Alhfrith and of Abbot Wilfrid; he stayed some time with them and, at the request of Alhfrith, he ordained Wilfrid priest in his own monastery. Agilbert had with him a priest called Agatho.

When this question of Easter and of the tonsure and other ecclesiastical matters was raised, it was decided to hold a council [in 664] to settle the dispute at a monastery called *Streanæshealh* (Whitby), a name which means the bay of the lighthouse; at this time Hild, a woman devoted to God, was abbess.[3] There came to the council the two kings, both father and son, Bishop Colman with his Irish clergy, and Agilbert with the priests Agatho and Wilfrid. James and Romanus were on their side while the Abbess Hild and her followers were on the side of the Irish; among these also was the venerable Bishop Cedd, who, as has been mentioned, had been consecrated long before by the Irish and who acted as a most careful interpreter for both parties at the council.

First King Oswiu began by declaring that it was fitting that those who served one God should observe one rule of life and not differ in the celebration of the heavenly sacraments, seeing that they all hoped for one kingdom in heaven; they ought therefore to inquire as to which was the truer tradition and then all follow it together. He then ordered his bishop Colman to say first what were the customs which he followed and whence they originated. Colman thereupon said, "The method of keeping Easter which I observe, I received from my superiors who sent me here as bishop; it was in this way that all our fathers, men beloved of God, are known to have celebrated it. Nor should this method seem contemptible and blameworthy seeing that the blessed evangelist John, the disciple whom the Lord specially loved, is said to have celebrated it thus, together with all the churches over which he presided." When he had said all this and more to the same effect, the king ordered Agilbert to expound the method he observed, its origin, and the authority he had for following it. Agilbert answered, "I request that my disciple, the priest Wilfrid, may speak on my behalf, for we are both in agreement with the other followers of our church tradition who are here present; and he can explain our views in the English tongue better and more clearly than I can through an interpreter." Then Wilfrid, receiving instructions from the king to speak, began thus: "The Easter we keep is the same as we have seen universally celebrated in Rome, where the apostles St. Peter and St. Paul lived, taught, suffered, and were buried. We also found it in use everywhere in Italy and Gaul when we traveled through those countries for the purpose of study and prayer. We learned that it was observed at one and the same time in Africa, Asia, Egypt, Greece, and throughout the whole world, wherever the Church of Christ is scattered, amid various nations and languages. The only exceptions are these men and their accomplices in obstinacy, I mean the Picts and the Britons, who in these, the two remotest islands of the Ocean, and only in some parts of them, foolishly attempt to fight against the whole world."

Colman answered, "I wonder that you are willing to call our efforts foolish, seeing that we follow the example of that apostle who was reckoned worthy to recline on

---

[1]   Colman was bishop of Lindisfarne 661–664.

[2]   Bede confused Dalfinus, who was the prefect (secular ruler) of Lyon, with his brother Aunemundus, the bishop of Lyon (*c*.650–658). Wilfrid (d.709), bishop of York and Hexham, was the chief proponent of the Roman date for Easter.

[3]   Under Hild, Whitby was a double monastery with both men and women (in separate quarters). Hild presided over both.

the breast of the Lord; for all the world acknowledges his great wisdom." Wilfrid replied, "Far be it from me to charge John with foolishness: he literally observed the decrees of the Mosaic law when the Church was still Jewish in many respects, at a time when the apostles were unable to bring to a sudden end the entire observance of that law which God ordained in the same way as, for instance, they made it compulsory on all new converts to abandon their idols which are of devilish origin. They feared, of course, that they might make a stumbling-block for the Jewish proselytes dispersed among the Gentiles. This was the reason why Paul circumcised Timothy, why he offered sacrifices in the temple, and why he shaved his head at Corinth in company with Aquila and Priscilla; all this was of no use except to avoid scandalizing the Jews. Hence James said to Paul, 'Thou seest, brother, how many thousands there are among the Jews of them which have believed; and they are all zealous for the law (Acts 21: 20).' But in these days when the light of the Gospel is spreading throughout the world, it is not necessary, it is not even lawful for believers to be circumcised or to offer God sacrifices of flesh and blood. So John, in accordance with the custom of the law, began the celebration of Easter Day in the evening of the fourteenth day of the first month, regardless of whether it fell on the sabbath or any other day. But when Peter preached at Rome, remembering that the Lord rose from the dead and brought to the world the hope of the resurrection on the first day of the week, he realized that Easter ought to be kept as follows: he always waited for the rising of the moon on the evening of the fourteenth day of the first month in accordance with the custom and precepts of the law, just as John did, but when it had risen, if the Lord's Day, which was then called the first day of the week, followed in the morning, he proceeded to celebrate Easter as we are accustomed to do at the present time. But if the Lord's Day was due, not on the morning following the fourteenth day of the moon but on the sixteenth or seventeenth or any other day until the twenty-first, he waited for it, and began the holy Easter ceremonies the night before, that is, on the Saturday evening; so it came about that Easter Sunday was kept only between the fifteenth day of the moon and the twenty-first. So this evangelical and apostolic tradition does not abolish the law but rather fulfils it, by ordering the observance of Easter from the evening of the fourteenth day of the moon in the first month up to the twenty-first of the moon in the same month. All the successors of St. John in Asia since his death and also the whole church throughout the world have followed this observance. That this is the true Easter and that this alone must be celebrated by the faithful was not newly decreed but confirmed afresh by the Council of Nicaea as the history of the Church informs us.[1] So it is plain, Colman, that you neither follow the example of John, as you think, nor of Peter, whose tradition you knowingly contradict; and so, in your observance of Easter, you neither follow the law nor the gospel. For John who kept Easter according to the decrees of the Mosaic law, took no heed of the Sunday; you do not do this, for you celebrate Easter only on a Sunday. Peter celebrated Easter Sunday between the fifteenth and the twenty-first day of the moon; you, on the other hand, celebrate Easter Sunday between the fourteenth and the twentieth day of the moon. Thus you very often begin Easter on the evening of the thirteenth day of the moon, which is never mentioned in the law. This was not the day—it was the fourteenth, in which the Lord, the author and giver of the Gospel, ate the old passover in the evening and instituted the sacraments of the new testament to be celebrated by the church in remembrance of his passion. Besides, in your celebration of Easter you utterly exclude the twenty-first day, which the law of Moses specially ordered to be observed. So, as I have said, in your celebration of the greatest of the festivals you agree neither with John nor Peter, neither with the law nor the Gospel."

Colman replied, "Did Anatolius, a man who was holy and highly spoken of in the history of the Church to which you appeal, judge contrary to the law and the Gospel when he wrote that Easter should be celebrated between the fourteenth and the twentieth day of the moon? Or must we believe that our most reverend father Columba and his successors,[2] men beloved of God, who celebrated Easter in the same way, judged and acted contrary to the holy scriptures, seeing that there were many of them to whose holiness the heavenly signs and the miracles they performed bore witness? And as I have no

---

[1] This is a reference to the account of the First Council of Nicaea of 325 in Rufinus' translation and in the continuation in Eusebius' *History of the Church*.

[2] Columba (d.597) was an Irish monk who left his homeland to found the monastery of Iona (in Scotland), which he used as a base for missionary work. Though he was highly praised in the Irish world, Wilfrid seems to have known very little about him—or, at least, he is presented as knowing little by Bede.

doubt that they were saints, I shall never cease to follow their way of life, their customs, and their teaching."

Wilfrid replied, "It is true that Anatolius was a most holy and learned man, worthy of all praise; but what have you to do with him since you do not observe his precepts? He followed a correct rule in celebrating Easter, basing it on a cycle of nineteen years, of which you are either unaware or, if you do know of it, you despise it, even though it is observed by the whole Church of Christ. He assigned the fourteenth day of the moon to Easter Sunday, reckoning after the Egyptian manner that the fifteenth day of the moon began on the evening of the fourteenth. So also he assigned the twentieth day to Easter Sunday, reckoning that after evening it was the twenty-first day. But it appears that you are ignorant of this distinction, in that you sometimes clearly keep Easter Day before full moon, that is on the thirteenth day of the moon. So far as your father Columba and his followers are concerned, whose holiness you claim to imitate and whose rule and precepts (confirmed by heavenly signs) you claim to follow, I might perhaps point out that at the judgment, many will say to the Lord that they prophesied in His name and cast out devils and did many wonderful works, but the Lord will answer that He never knew them. Far be it from me to say this about your fathers, for it is much fairer to believe good rather than evil about unknown people. So I will not deny that those who in their rude simplicity loved God with pious intent, were indeed servants of God and beloved by Him. Nor do I think that this observance of Easter did much harm to them while no one had come to show them a more perfect rule to follow. In fact I am sure that if anyone knowing the Catholic rule had come to them they would have followed it, as they are known to have followed all the laws of God as soon as they had learned of them.

But, once having heard the decrees of the apostolic see or rather of the universal Church, if you refuse to follow them, confirmed as they are by the holy Scriptures, then without doubt you are committing sin. For though your fathers were holy men, do you think that a handful of people in one corner of the remotest of islands is to be preferred to the universal Church of Christ which is spread throughout the world? And even if that Columba of yours—yes, and ours too, if he belonged to Christ—was a holy man of mighty works, is he to be preferred to the most blessed chief of the apostles, to whom the Lord said, 'Thou art Peter and upon this rock I will build my Church and the gates of hell shall not prevail against it, and I will give unto thee the keys of the kingdom of heaven.'"?[1]

When Wilfrid had ended, the king said, "Is it true, Colman, that the Lord said these words to Peter?" Colman answered, "It is true, O King." Then the king went on, "Have you anything to show that an equal authority was given to your Columba?" Colman answered, "Nothing." Again the king said, "Do you both agree, without any dispute, that these words were addressed primarily to Peter and that the Lord gave him the keys of the kingdom of heaven?" They both answered, "Yes." Thereupon the king concluded, "Then, I tell you, since he is the doorkeeper I will not contradict him, but I intend to obey his commands in everything to the best of my knowledge and ability. Otherwise, when I come to the gates of the kingdom of heaven, there may be no one to open them, because the one who on your own showing holds the keys has turned his back on me." When the king had spoken, all who were seated there or standing by, both high and low, signified their assent, gave up their imperfect rules, and readily accepted in their place those which they recognized to be better.

---

[1] Matt. 16: 18.

TIMELINE FOR CHAPTER TWO

600

c.610–22 *QUR'AN SURAS* ———

——— c.615– c.630 ISIDORE, *ETYMOLOGIES*

BEF. 625 AL-A'SHA, *BID HURAYRA FAREWELL* ———

650

——— 7TH C. *LIFE OF ST. THEODORE OF SYKEON*

680S *PASSION OF LEUDEGAR* ———

——— c.692 AL-AKHTAL, *THE TRIBE HAS DEPARTED*

700

709/710 *JUDGMENT OF CHILDEBERT III* ———

——— 710 *TAX DEMAND IN EGYPT*

713 *TREATY OF TUDMIR* ———

——— 723–26 *LETTERS TO BONIFACE*

——— 730S/EARLY 750S JOHN OF DAMASCUS, *ON HOLY IMAGES*

731 BEDE, *ECCLESIASTICAL HISTORY* ———

750

754 *ICONOCLASTIC SYNOD* ———

800

BEF. 818 *CHRONICLE OF THEOPHANES* ——— *CONFESSOR*

To test your knowledge and gain deeper understanding of this chapter, please go to www.utphistorymatters.com for Study Questions.

III

Creating New Identities (c.750–c.900)

THE MATERIAL BASIS OF SOCIETY

3.1 Manors in the West: *Polyptyque of the Church of Saint Mary of Marseille* (814–815). Original in Latin.

In the very year that Charlemagne died (814), an enterprising official began to make an inventory of 13 of the estates (*villae*; sing. *villa*) held by the cathedral of Marseille—Saint Mary, the seat of the bishop—and the monastery of Saint-Vincent of Marseille. Since the properties of Saint-Vincent were administered by the bishop of Marseille, there tended to be some overlap. The resulting register, called a *polyptyque*, provides a partial snapshot of some peasant households and the products and taxes that they owed. Each villa consisted of tenements, or small landholdings. In this polyptyque they are called *colonicae* (sing. *colonica*); in other regions they were called *mansi* (sing. *mansus*).

The entries (which are labeled A, B, and so on) follow a predictable pattern. First the villa is named, and then there are entries for each holding (*colonica*). First comes the holding's location, followed by the name and status of the male tenant (*colonus, mancipium*), the name of his wife and children, the age of the children (if under 14 or 15) or indication that the child is grown (here translated as "adult"). Sometimes the entry indicates which of the children are in school (precious evidence of village schooling in the period) and which are in holy orders, that is, ordained as priests, deacons, and so on. The adult children's husbands and wives are sometimes named, and sometimes we learn whether they were "foreigners"—that is, from outside the village. Dues are mentioned occasionally, but sometimes not. How does this document compare with a modern census? What evidence does it provide for the size and composition of peasant households in early-ninth-century Provence? In the welter of names, can you discover any family naming patterns?

[Source: *Carolingian Civilization: A Reader*, ed. Paul Edward Dutton, 2nd ed. (Toronto: University of Toronto Press, 2004), pp. 214–18 (slightly modified).]

B: *Description of the Dependents of Saint Mary of Marseille from the Villa Domado of that Third Part, Made in the Time of the lord bishop Waldus [r.814–818], from the seventh indiction [814]*

1. Holding [colonica] at Nemphas. Martinus, colonus. Wife Dominica. Bertemarus, an adult son. Desideria, an adult daughter. It pays the tax: 1 pig, 1 suckling [pig]; 2 fattened hens; 10 chickens; 40 eggs. Savarildis, an adult woman. Olisirga, a daughter 10 years old. Rica, a daughter 9 years old.
2. Holding of a colonus in vineyards. Ingoaldus, a dependent [mancipium]. Wife Unuldis. Martinus, a son; wife Magna. Onoria, a daughter, with a foreign husband. Deda, a daughter. Danobertus, an adult son. Ingolbertus, an adult son. Arubertus, an adult son.
3. Holding at Code: 1 lot without tenant.
4. Holding at Ruinolas: 1 lot without tenant.
5. In total these make 4 holdings.
6. Holding at Ursiniangas: 1 lot without tenant.

F. *Description of the Dependents of Saint Mary of Marseille from the Villa of Betorrida,[1] Made in the Time of the lord bishop Waldus, from the seventh indiction*

1. Holding in Cenazello. Dructaldus, tenant (*accola*); with his foreign wife. Dructomus, a son. Dutberta, an adult daughter. Drueterigus, a son at school. Sinderaldus, a son at school. Joannis. For pasturage: 1 denarius.[2]
2. Holding in Albiosco. Teodorus, colonus. Wife Eugenia. Marius, a deacon. Teobaldus, an adult son. Teodericus, a cleric. Ing… dus, a son 7 years old. Teodesia, a daughter 7 years old. For pasturage: 1 denarius.
3. Therein a holding: 1 lot without tenant. 2 denarii.[3]
4. Holding in Asaler. Candidus, colonus. Wife Dominica. Celsus, a son: information required. Mariberta, an adult daughter. Regitrudis, an adult daughter. Gennarius, a son, shepherd. Saviniana, a daughter: information required. It pays in tax: 1 pig, 1 sucking [pig]; 2 fattened hens; 10 chickens; 40 eggs; for pasturage: 1 castrated ram; in tribute: 1 denarius.
5. Holding without tenant in Nonticlo, which Bertarius,

priest, holds in benefice. It pays tax and tribute similarly: [plus] a castrated ram.
6. Holding in the same place: 1 lot without tenant. Paulus and Valeriana, with their infants: information required. It pays tax and tribute similarly; for pasturage: 1 castrated ram.
7. Holding in Albiosco: information required.
8. Holding in Curia. Calumniosus, colonus, with a foreign wife. It pays tax: 1 denarius and similarly in tribute. Saumo, with his infants: information required.
9. Holding in the same place. Colonus Martinus. Wife Primovera. Felicis, an adult son. Deidonus, an adult son. Leobertga, an adult daughter. Martina, a daughter 6 years old. An infant at the breast. It pays tax and tribute similarly; for pasturage: 1 denarius.
10. Holding [in] Cusanulas, which Nectardus holds in benefice. It pays tax and tribute similarly.
11. Holding in Carmillo Sancto Promacio, held by the priest of the local church. It pays for pasturage: 1 denarius.
12. Holding in Cumbis: 1 lot without tenant, which Dructebertus has. For pasturage: 2 denarii.
13. Holding in Massimana. Donaldus, dependent. Wife Dominica. Domnildis, daughter. Bertarius, an adult son. Bertulfus, an adult son. Bertelaicus, an adult son. Saisa, an adult daughter. It pays for pasturage: 2 denarii.
14. Holding in Asinarius: 1 lot without tenant. For pasturage: 1 castrated ram.
15. Holding in Terciago, which Martinus holds in benefice. For pasturage: 2 denarii.
16. Holdings in Cenazellis: 2 lots without tenants. For pasturage: 1 castrated ram.
17. Holding in Tullo: 1 lot without tenant. For pasturage: 1 castrated ram. Vuarmetrudis, with her infants: information required.
18. Holding in Galiana. Cannidus, colonus. Wife Inguildis. An infant at the breast. Domecianus, a cleric. Laurada, a daughter 8 years old. It pays tax and tribute similarly. For pasturage: 2 denarii.
19. Holding in Cleo. Aquilo, an equitarius [a serf performing messenger duty on horseback]. Wife Vumiberga. Candidus, a son 6 years old. An infant at the breast. For pasturage: 1 denarius.
20. Holding in Gencianicus. Ursius, cleric. The dependent Lubus, son, with foreign wife, who ought to

---

[1] Today Bezaudun, near Grasse.
[2] A denarius (pl. denarii) was a silver penny.
[3] Presumably this means that it pays 2 denarii when occupied by a tenant.

manage that holding.... Gencuonca, an adult daughter. Teodo, an adult son.

21. Holding in Nidis: 1 lot without tenant. Bernarius, cotidianus [owing daily service to the lord]. Wife Dominica. Magnildis, daughter: information required. Dominico, son. Bernardus, son. Teodranus, son: information required. In tribute: 1 denarius. Montigla, a female [serf], with foreign husband. Cenazello, son: information required.

22. Holding in Vencione. Ildebertus, a dependent. Wife Luborfolia. It pays tax: 2 denarii.

23. Holding in Cumbis: 1 lot without tenant. It pays for pasturage: 2 denarii.

24. Holding in Tasseriolas: 1 lot without tenant. For pasturage: 1 denarius.

25. Holding in Massimiana Sancto Promacio: belonging to the office of the local priest. Donobertus, Babilda: information required.

26. Holding in Camarjas, which Bertaldus, priest, holds.

27. We have a holding in Sugnone, a third part of that small village, and there are 10 holdings [there].

28. Holding in Camarja: 1 lot without tenant. 29. We have in Salo a third part of that small village, and there are three holdings without tenants.

30. Holding in Puncianicus: 1 lot without tenant.

31. Holding in Campellis: 1 lot without tenant.

32. Holding in Rosolanis: 1 lot without tenant.

33. Holding in Speluca: 1 lot without tenant.

34. Vualdebertus, Guirbertus, Ragnebertus: information required.

35. In total that makes 49 holdings.

3.2 Byzantine guilds: *The Book of the Prefect* (886–912). Original in Greek.

Constantinople teemed with merchants, craftsmen, and notaries (the ancient version of lawyers). Organized into collective professional organizations—guilds—the people who plied these trades were regulated by the chief official of the city, the Prefect. *The Book of the Prefect*, an imperial edict issued by Emperor Leo VI (r.886–912), shows how tightly the economy of the capital was controlled—or supposed to be controlled—by the state. What evidence does this document provide for arguing that the early-tenth-century economy of Constantinople was well organized and vibrant? What evidence does it offer for the contrary argument: that the economy of the capital was stifled by rules and regulations?

[Source: Arthur E.R. Boak, "Notes and Documents: The Book of the Prefect," *Journal of Economic and Business History* 1 (1929): 600–602, 604–6 (slightly modified).]

Preface

God, after having created all things that are and given order and harmony to the universe, with his own finger engraved the Law on the tables and published it openly so that men, being well directed thereby, should not shamelessly trample upon one another and the stronger should not do violence to the weaker but that all things should be apportioned with just measure. Therefore it has seemed good for Our Serenity also to lay down the following ordinances based on the statutes in order that the human race may be governed fittingly and no person may injure his fellow.

I. The Notaries

1. Whoever wishes to be appointed a notary must be elected by a vote and decision both of the *primicerius*[1] and the notaries acting with him to ensure that he has a

---

[1] The chief of the guild of the notaries.

knowledge and understanding of the laws, that he excels in handwriting, that he is not garrulous or insolent, and that he does not lead a corrupt life, but on the contrary is serious in his habits, guileless in his thoughts, eloquent, intelligent, a polished reader, and accurate in his diction, to guard against his being easily led to give a false meaning in places to what he writes or to insert deceptive clauses. And if at any time a notary is found to be doing something contrary to the law and the authorized written regulations, those who have acted as his witnesses shall be responsible.

2. The candidate must know by heart the forty titles of the *Manual of Law*[1] and must also know the sixty books of the Basilika.[2] He shall also have received a general education so that he may not make mistakes in formulating his documents and be guilty of errors in his reading. He shall also have abundant time to give proof of his ability both mental and physical. Let him prepare a handwritten document in a meeting of the guild, so that he may not later commit unforeseen errors; but if he should then be detected in any, let him be expelled from the order.

3. The election of the candidate shall be carried out as follows. After the hearing of the witnesses and the examination he shall present himself wearing a cloak before the most glorious Prefect of the City accompanied by the guild of the notaries and the *primicerius*. These shall swear before God and by the safety of the emperors that he is being enrolled in the order not through any favor, influence, family connection, or friendship, but by reason of his good conduct, knowledge, ability, and general fitness. After the oaths have been taken, by means of a sign the Prefect in office shall elect him in the prefectural bureau, and he shall be enrolled in the guild and numbered among the notaries. Then he shall go to the church nearest his residence, while all the notaries wear their cloaks, and doffing his cloak and donning a white surplice shall be consecrated by a prayer of the priest. He shall be escorted on his way by all the notaries clad in their cloaks, while the *primicerius* himself holds a censer[3] and directs the fumes towards the newly elect, who carries the Bible openly before him. This signifies that his ways shall be made straight as the incense ascending before the face of God. In this glorious fashion he shall proceed to the seat to which he has been allotted and then return home

with the same pomp, there to feast and rejoice with his associates.

4. Any notary who intends to absent himself from a royal procession or ceremony in the hippodrome or a meeting or assembly summoned by the most glorious Prefect or from any other gathering of this sort shall pay four *keratia*[4] to the officers of the Prefect and an equal sum to the members of the guild. But if he shows a clear and reasonable ground for his absence, which is not for his own profit, he shall be excused from the penalty if the *primicerius* approves.

5. If a notary has been summoned by the *primicerius* for a necessary purpose and has failed to come once, twice, or thrice, he shall pay on the first occasion two *keratia*, on the second, four, and on the third, six. But if he does this out of bravado and a spirit of contempt, he shall be punished by whipping at the Prefect's order.

6. If a notary should be summoned to draw up a contract, and afterwards another should be called in, let them both do the work and share the fee equally. But if one should come uninvited, let him not only be chased out without pay but also be punished by whipping. And if one of the two should leave voluntarily while the work is being completed, he shall not receive any part of the fee.

7. If a notary who is called in to draw up a contract wishes to leave for some adequate reason and calls in another, the one thus summoned shall receive two thirds of the fee, while the one first called in shall get a third.

8. If a notary has been called in and has completed the agreement, and then another has been summoned and has both completed the agreement and finished the work, the latter shall receive the whole fee if he is ignorant that it had previously been completed by the other. But if he came with knowledge of this, he shall receive one third, while the former received two thirds. And if two have been called in together, the junior shall yield to his senior in rank, but they shall share the fee equally.

9. If a notary approaches the seat of another and the latter does not greet him respectfully, or if one seats himself at table without regard to precedence, or if one is convicted of having verbally abused another, the guilty one shall in each case pay six *keratia*. But if one also lays violent hands upon another, he shall be punished by the Prefect....

---

[1] A brief compilation of laws in forty titles published by Basil I between 870 and 878.

[2] The great codification of Byzantine Law begun under Basil I and completed and published by Leo VI (r.886–912).

[3] A vessel for burning incense.

[4] The Byzantine coins mentioned in the Edict are the following: the *nomisma* (pl. *nomismata*), a gold coin; the *miliarision* (pl. *miliarisia*), a silver coin equal to 1/12 of a *nomisma*; the *keration* (pl. *keratia*) also of silver, equal to 1/12 of a *miliarision* or 1/24 of a *nomisma*; the copper *follis* or *obol* worth about 1/12 of a *keration*.

II. The Jewelers

1. We ordain that the jewelers may, if any one invites them, buy the things that pertain to them, such as gold, silver, pearls, or precious stones; but not bronze and woven linens or any other materials which others should purchase rather than they. However, they are not hereby prevented from buying anything they wish for private use.

2. They must not depreciate or increase the price of things for sale to the detriment of the vendors, but shall appraise them at their just value. If anyone acts deceitfully in this, he shall forfeit the appraised value of the things to the vendor.

3. Following the old custom, on the regular market days the jewelers shall take their seats in their shops along with their statores or attendants in charge of their sales tables. Their money is to be counted out in *miliarisia* so that if anyone tries to sell some jewelers' ware they may purchase it.

4. If a jeweler discovers a woman offering for sale objects of gold or silver, or pearls, or precious stones, he shall inform the Prefect of these things to prevent their being exported to foreign peoples.

5. If anyone adulterates uncoined metal and manufactures things for sale from it, he shall have his hand cut off.

6. If any foreigner sells gold or silver in a worked or unworked state, he is to be questioned as to its origin and to be reported to the chief of the guild, in order that stolen goods may be detected.

7. If any jeweler is found to have bought a sacred object, whether damaged or intact, without having shown it to the Prefect, both he and the seller shall suffer confiscation.

8. We command that no goldsmith, whether slave or free, shall purchase for his work more than a single pound of unminted gold, be it unwrought or wrought.

9. And if one does take from somebody more than a pound of uncoined gold for his work, and does not declare it at once to the chief of the goldsmiths, if he is a slave he shall be confiscated by the state, but if a freeman he shall be whipped and subjected to a fine of a pound of gold.

10. A slave who is going to be set up in a jeweler's shop shall be sponsored by his own master if the latter is a man of means. But a freeman shall be vouched for by five persons, who shall assume the same risk as he whom they have nominated.

11. We order that no goldsmith shall have the right to work gold or silver in his home, but only in the shops on the Mese.[1] Also that no one shall be nominated as a goldsmith without the knowledge of the Prefect.

12. The jewelers shall not undertake any work of evaluation without the knowledge of the Prefect, nor shall they when making appraisals stir up strife with one another. If they are caught doing any of these things, they shall be whipped; shorn;[2] and removed from the roll of their guild.

IV. The Silk-Garment Merchants[3]

1. The silk-garment merchants shall buy silk garments but not any other merchandise except something for their personal needs which they may not sell to others. They shall not give foreigners any of the prohibited articles, such as red or purple silk goods of large size, so that these may not be transported to strange peoples. Whoever violates these regulations shall be flogged and suffer confiscation of goods.

2. Silk-garment merchants, whether slaves or free persons, when purchasing garments valued at ten *nomismata* from persons of any sort whatsoever, even from princes or silk weavers, shall declare this to the Prefect so that he may know where they are to be sold. Those who fail to do so are liable to the aforesaid punishment.

3. Whoever fails to declare to the Prefect cloaks or robes of a blue color or purple two-thirds red, shall be liable to punishment.

4. Whoever fails to show to the Prefect goods that are to be exported to foreign peoples so that they may receive his seal, shall suffer punishment.

5. Whoever is to be enrolled in the craft of the silk-garment merchants shall first be declared by five persons of the same guild in the presence of the Prefect to be worthy to be in this trade. He shall then be entered on the roll, shall open a shop, and engage in trade. He shall also pay to the corporation six *nomismata*.

6. Whoever wishes to become the owner of a silk garment shop, shall pay ten *nomismata*. He must also have the approval of the Prefect.

7. One who is both a silk-garment merchant and a silk weaver shall be allowed to choose one of these trades but must give up the other. If he dares to practice both, he

---

1   The Middle Street, the main industrial and commercial thoroughfare of Constantinople.

2   That is, their hair and beard cut off.

3   *Vestiopratai*: dealers in manufactured articles of clothing and the like, as opposed to raw or spun silk.

shall come under the punishment mentioned above [i.e., flogging and confiscation of goods].

8. Strangers who reside in the inns of the city must be carefully prevented from purchasing either prohibited articles of clothing or those woven in a single piece, except something for personal use and that prepared in the imperial city. Upon their departure they shall declare such articles to the Prefect so that he may know the goods that they have bought. Whoever helps them to conceal such

things shall be flogged and suffer confiscation of goods.

9. Any silk-garment merchant who secretly or openly seeks to raise the rental of another, shall be flogged, shorn, and suffer confiscation of goods....

[Further sections include regulations for dealers in raw silk, silk weavers, linen merchants, perfume dealers, candle makers, grocers, leather cutters, butchers (except pork), pork dealers, fishmongers, bakers, tavern keepers, and contractors (such as joiners, plasterers, locksmiths, and painters).]

Map 3.1: Major European Slave Exports (700–900).

Coin hoard evidence suggests that Islamic—and, to a lesser extent, Byzantine—money came into Europe in considerable abundance during the period 700–900. What did the Europeans provide in return? Swords is one answer; slaves is another, as this map demonstrates. It shows where European slaves were captured and the places to which they were transported. Some remained in Europe (as *A Contract of Sale*, below, p. 113 attests); many others were traded to the Islamic world. Note the convergence of many routes at Córdoba. As you read through the other documents in this book, take note of how often slaves are mentioned. How differently were they treated from free men and women?

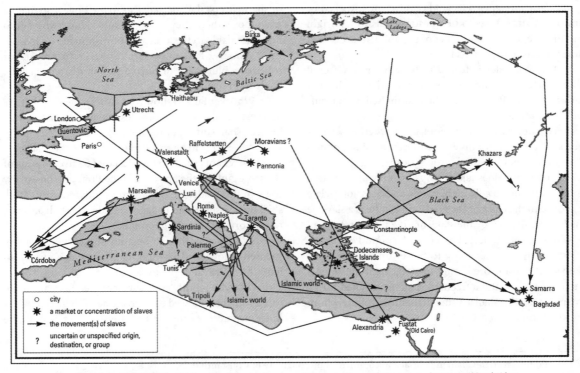

[Based on Michael McCormick, *Origins of the European Economy: Communications and Commerce* a.d. 300–900 (Cambridge: Cambridge University Press, 2001), p. 562, Map 25.1, modified by, and with many thanks to, Michael McCormick.]

3.3 The sale of a slave in Italy: *A Contract of Sale* (725). Original in Latin.

This is an absolutely ordinary record of a sale, much like many others drawn up at the same time in the Lombard kingdom of Italy for land and animals. In this case, however, the item sold was a boy. What does this transaction add to the information presented in the map of Major European Slave Exports on p. 112?

[Source: *Medieval Trade in the Mediterranean World*, trans. and ed. Robert S. Lopez and Irving W. Raymond (New York: Columbia University Press, 2001), pp. 45–46 (notes modified).]

Milan, June 6, 725

In the thirteenth year of the reign of our lord, most excellent man, King Liutprand,[1] on the eighth day before the Ides of June, eighth indiction; good fortune. I, Faustino, notary by royal authority, wrote this document of sale, invited by Ermedruda, honorable woman, daughter of Lorenzo, acting jointly with consent and will of that parent of hers, and being the seller. And she acknowledges that she has received, as indeed she at the present time is receiving from Totone, most distinguished man, 12 new gold solidi [coins] as the full price for a boy of the Gallic people named Satrelano, or by whatever other name the boy may be called. And she declared that it[2] had come to her from her father's patrimony. And she, acting jointly with her aforesaid father, promises from this day to protect that boy against all men on behalf of the buyer. And if the boy is injured or taken away and they [Ermedruda and Lorenzo] are in any way unable to protect it against all men, they shall return the solidi in the double to the buyer, [including all] improvements in the object.[3] Done in Milan, in the day, reign, and in the eighth indiction mentioned above.

The sign[4] of the hand of Ermedruda, honorable woman, seller, who declared that she sold the aforesaid Frankish boy of her own good will with the consent of her parent; and she asked this sale to be made.

The sign of the hand of Lorenzo, honorable man, her father, consenting to this sale.

The sign of the hand of Theoperto, honorable man, maker of cuirasses, son of the late Giovannace, relative of the same seller, in whose presence she proclaimed that she was under no constraint, giving consent.

The sign of the hand of Ratchis, honorable man, Frank, witness.

Antonino, devout man, invited by Ermedruda, honorable woman, and by her father giving his consent, undersigned as a witness to this record of sale.

I, the above Faustino, writer of this [record] of sale, after delivery gave [this record].

---

[1] Liutprand, King of the Lombards 712–744, ruled over much of northern Italy.

[2] A slave in Lombard as well as in Roman law was not considered as a person but as a thing (*res*); hence the document uses the neuter pronoun when referring to the boy.

[3] Again, the boy is considered as a thing. He may learn some skill and hence become more valuable.

[4] Ermedruda could not write her name, but she indicated her assent to the terms of the contract with a cross or other sign, recorded by the notary as her "sign." He himself supplied her name.

THE ABBASID RECONFIGURATION

3.4 An early view of the Prophet: Muhammad ibn Ishaq, *Life of Muhammad* (754–767). Original in Arabic.

Writing under the patronage of the Abbasid Caliph al-Mansur, Ibn Ishaq (*c.*704–767), who was born in Medina, wrote the first extant life of Muhammad. It was soon attacked for including spurious poetry and for lacking sufficient *isnad*—the chains of named sources that were, by the end of the eighth century, considered essential to prove the authenticity of any narrative about the Prophet (hadith). (For hadith considered authoritative, see al-Bukhari, *On Fasting*, below, p. 117). Ibn Ishaq was also accused of Shi'ite sympathies. It is thus not surprising that his original work is lost. The version that we have today is an edition by Ibn Hisham (d.833), a scholar who, though somewhat critical of the original, also considered it of great value. Throughout, Ibn Ishaq calls Muhammad "the apostle of God" and emphasizes how fully he fulfilled the Christian and Jewish prophecies. In what ways were the mission, virtues, and lifestyle of Muhammad in Ibn Ishaq's account similar to—and different from—those of saints in Christian hagiography, such as the *Life of St. Antony*, above, p. 27?

[Source: *The Life of Muhammad: A Translation of Ishaq's* Sirat Rasul Allah, trans. and ed. Alfred Guillaume (London: Oxford University Press, 1955), pp. 81–83, 104–7 (slightly modified).]

The apostle of God grew up, God protecting him and keeping him from the vileness of heathenism because he wished to honor him with apostleship, until he grew up to be the finest of his people in manliness, the best in character, most noble in lineage, the best neighbor, the most kind, truthful, reliable, the furthest removed from filthiness and corrupt morals through loftiness and nobility, so that he was known among his people as "The trustworthy" because of the good qualities which God had implanted in him. The apostle, so I was told, used to tell how God protected him in his childhood during the period of heathenism, saying, "I found myself among the boys of Quraysh[1] carrying stones such as boys play with; we had all uncovered ourselves, each taking his shirt and putting it round his neck as he carried the stones. I was going to and fro in the same way, when an unseen figure slapped me most painfully saying, 'Put your shirt on'; so I took it and fastened it on me and then began to carry the stones upon my neck wearing my shirt alone among my fellows."…

The Apostle of God Marries Khadija

Khadija was a merchant woman of dignity and wealth. She used to hire men to carry merchandise outside the country on a profit-sharing basis, for Quraysh were a people given to commerce. Now when she heard about the prophet's truthfulness, trustworthiness, and honorable character, she sent for him and proposed that he should take her goods to Syria and trade with them, while she would pay him more than she paid others. He was to take a lad of hers called Maysara.

The apostle of God accepted the proposal, and the two set forth until they came to Syria. The apostle stopped in the shade of a tree near a monk's cell, when the monk came up to Maysara and asked who the man was who was resting beneath the tree. He told him that he was of Quraysh, the people who held the sanctuary; and the monk exclaimed: "None but a prophet ever sat beneath this tree."

Then the prophet sold the goods he had brought and bought what he wanted to buy and began the return jour-

---

[1]   The tribe at Mecca to which Muhammad also belonged.

ney to Mecca. The story goes that at the height of noon, when the heat was intense as he rode his beast, Maysara saw two angels shading the apostle from the sun's rays. When he brought Khadija her property she sold it and it amounted to double or thereabouts. Maysara for his part told her about the two angels who shaded him and of the monk's words. Now Khadija was a determined, noble, and intelligent woman possessing the properties with which God willed to honor her. So when Maysara told her these things, she sent to the apostle of God and—so the story goes—said: "O son of my uncle I like you because of our relationship and your high reputation among your people, your trustworthiness and good character and truthfulness." Then she proposed marriage. Now Khadija at that time was the best born woman in Quraysh, of the greatest dignity and, too, the richest. All her people were eager to get possession of her wealth if it were possible.

Khadija was the daughter of Khuwaylid b. Asad b. 'Abdu'l-'Uzza b. Qusayy b. Kilab b. Murra b. Ka'b b. Lu'ayy b. Ghalib b. Fihr.[1] Her mother was Fatima bt. Za'ida b. al-Asamm b. Rawaha b. Hajar b. 'Abd b. Malis b. 'Amir b. Lu'ayy b. Ghalib b. Fihr. Her mother was Hala bt. 'Abd Manaf b. al-Harith b. 'Amr b. Munqidh b. 'Amr b. Ma'is b. 'Amir b. Lu'ayy b. Ghalib b. Fihr. Hala's mother was Qilaba bt. Su'ayd b. Sa'd b. Sahm b. 'Amr b. Husays b. Ka'b b. Lu'ayy b. Ghalib b. Fihr.

The apostle of God told his uncles of Khadija's proposal, and his uncle Hamza b. 'Abdu'l-Muttalib went with him to Khuwaylid b. Asad and asked for her hand and he married her.

She was the mother of all the apostle's children except Ibrahim, namely al-Qasim (whereby he was known as Abu'l-Qasim); al-Tahir, al-Tayyib, Zaynab, Ruqayya, Umm Kulthum, and Fatima.

Al-Qasim, al-Tayyib, and al-Tahir died in paganism. All his daughters lived into Islam, embraced it, and migrated with him to Medina.

Khadija had told Waraqa b. Naufal b. Asad b. 'Abdu'l-'Uzza, who was her cousin and a Christian who had studied the scriptures and was a scholar, what her slave Maysara had told her that the monk had said and how he had seen the two angels shading him. He said, "If this is true, Khadija, then truly Muhammad is the prophet of this people. I knew that a prophet of this people was to be expected. His

time has come," or words to that effect. Waraqa was finding the time of waiting wearisome and used to say "How long?" Some lines of his on the theme are:

I persevered and was persistent in remembering
An anxiety which often evoked tears. And
Confirmatory evidence kept coming from Khadija.
Long have I had to wait, O Khadija,
In the vale of Mecca in spite of my hope
That I might see the outcome of thy words.
I could not bear that the words of the monk
You told me of should prove false
That Muhammad should rule over us
Overcoming those who would oppose him.
And that a glorious light should appear in the land
To preserve men from disorders.
His enemies shall meet disaster
And his friends shall be victorious.
Would that I might be there then to see,
For I should be the first of his supporters,
Joining in that which Quraysh hate
However loud they shout in that Mecca of theirs.
I hope to ascend through him whom they all dislike
To the Lord of the Throne though they are cast down.
Is it folly not to disbelieve in Him
Who chose him Who raised the starry heights?
If they and I live, things will be done
Which will throw the unbelievers into confusion.
And if I die, 'tis but the fate of mortals
To suffer death and dissolution....

The Prophet's Mission

When Muhammad the apostle of God reached the age of forty, God sent him in compassion to mankind, "as an evangelist to all men."[2] Now God had made a covenant with every prophet whom he had sent before him that he should believe in him, testify to his truth, and help him against his adversaries. He required His prophets to transmit that to everyone who believed in them, and they carried out their obligations in that respect. God said to Muhammad, "When God made a covenant with the prophets, [He said], 'This is the scripture and wisdom which I have given you; afterwards an apostle will come

---

1   The abbreviation b. means "ibn," son of, while bt. means "bint," daughter of. Through this string of names, the author is authenticating Khadija's lineage. Compare Matt. 1: 1–11.

2   Sura 34: 27.

confirming what you know that you may believe in him and help him.' He said, 'Do you accept this and take up my burden?' i.e., the burden of my agreement which I have laid upon you. They said, 'We accept it.' He answered, 'Then bear witness and I am a witness with you.'"[1] Thus God made a covenant with all the prophets that they should testify to his truth and help him against his adversaries, and they transmitted that obligation to those who believed in them among the two monotheistic religions.

Al-Zuhri related from 'Urwa b. Zybayr that 'A'isha[2] told him that when Allah [God] desired to honor Muhammad and have mercy on His servants by means of him, the first sign of prophethood granted to the apostle was true visions, resembling the brightness of daybreak, which were shown to him in his sleep. And Allah, she said, made him love solitude so that he liked nothing better than to be alone.

'Abdu'l-Malik b. 'Ubaydullah b. Abu Sufyan b. al-'Ala' b. Jariya the Thaqafite, who had a retentive memory, related to me from a certain scholar that the apostle at the time when Allah willed to bestow His grace upon him and endow him with prophethood would go forth for his affair and journey far afield until he reached the glens of Mecca and the beds of its valleys where no house was in sight; and there was no stone or tree that he passed that didn't say, "Peace unto thee, O apostle of Allah." And the apostle would turn to his right and left and look behind him and he would see nothing but trees and stones. Thus he stayed seeing and hearing so long as it pleased Allah that he should stay. Then Gabriel came to him with the gift of God's grace while he was on Hira'[3] in the month of Ramadan.

Wahb b. Kaisan, a client of the family of al-Zubayr, told me: I heard 'Abdullah b. al-Zubayr say to 'Ubayd b. 'Umayr b. Qatada the Laythite, "O 'Ubayd tell us how began the prophethood which was first bestowed on the apostle when Gabriel came to him." And 'Ubayd in my presence related to 'Abdullah and those with him as follows: The apostle would pray in seclusion on Hira' every year for a month to practice *tahannuth* as was the custom of Quraysh in heathen days. *Tahannuth* is religious devotion. Abu Talib said:

By Thaur and him who made Thabir firm in its place
And by those going up to ascend Hira' and coming down.[4]

Wahb b. Kaisan told me that 'Ubayd said to him: Every year during that month the apostle would pray in seclusion and give food to the poor that came to him. And when he completed the month and returned from his seclusion, first of all before entering his house he would go to the Ka'ba[5] and walk round it seven times or as often as it pleased God; then he would go back to his house until, in the year when God sent him, in the month of Ramadan in which God willed concerning him what He willed of His grace, the apostle set forth to Hira' as was his custom, and his family with him. When it was the night on which God honored him with his mission and showed mercy on His servants thereby, Gabriel brought him the command of God. "He came to me," said the apostle of God, "while I was asleep, with a coverlet of brocade whereon was some writing, and said, 'Read!' I said, 'What shall I read?' He pressed me with it so tightly that I thought it was death; then he let me go and said, 'Read!' I said, 'What shall I read?' He pressed me with it again so that I thought it was death; then he let me go and said 'Read!' I said, 'What shall I read?' He pressed me with it the third time so that I thought it was death and said 'Read!' I said, 'What then shall I read?'—and this I said only to deliver myself from him, lest he should do the same to me again. He said:

Read in the name of thy Lord who created,
Who created man of blood coagulated.
Read! Thy Lord is the most beneficent,
Who taught by the pen,
Taught that which they knew not unto men.[6]

So I read it, and he departed from me. And I awoke from my sleep, and it was as though these words were written on my heart. When I was midway on the mountain, I heard a voice from heaven saying, 'O Muhammad! thou art the apostle of God and I am Gabriel.' I raised my head towards heaven to see (who was speaking), and lo, [there was] Gabriel in the form of a man with feet astride the

---

[1] Sura 3: 75.
[2] One of Muhammad's wives.
[3] A nearby mountain.
[4] Thaur and Thabir are mountains near Mecca.
[5] This was Mecca's holy site. At this time, before Mecca became Muslim, it was filled with images of many gods.
[6] Sura 96: 1–5. For a different translation, see "The Embryo" above, p. 75.

horizon, saying, 'O Muhammad! thou art the apostle of God and I am Gabriel.' I stood gazing at him, moving neither forward nor backward; then I began to turn my face away from him, but towards whatever region of the sky I looked, I saw him as before. And I continued standing there, neither advancing nor turning back, until Khadija sent her messengers in search of me and they gained the high ground above Mecca and returned to her while I was standing in the same place; then he parted from me and I from him, returning to my family. And I came to Khadija and sat by her thigh and drew close to her. She said, 'O Abu'l-Qasim,[1] where have you been? By God, I sent my messengers in search of you, and they reached the high ground above Mecca and returned to me.' Then I told her of what I had seen; and she said, 'Rejoice, O son of my uncle, and be of good heart. Truly, by Him in whose hand is Khadija's soul, I have hope that you will be the prophet of this people.'" Then she rose and gathered her garments about her and set forth to her cousin Waraqa b. Naufal b. Asad b. 'Abdu'l-'Uzza b. Qusayy, who had become a Christian and read the scriptures and learned from those that follow the Torah and the Gospel. And when she related to him what the apostle of God told her he had seen and heard, Waraqa cried, "Holy! Holy! Truly, by Him in whose hand is Waraqa's soul, if you have spoken the truth to me, O Khadija, then the greatest Namus [i.e., Gabriel], who came to Moses in the past, has come to him [Muhammed], and lo, he is the prophet of this people. Bid him be of good heart." So Khadija returned to the apostle of God and told him what Waraqa had said. And when the apostle of God had finished his period of seclusion and returned [to Mecca], in the first place he performed the circumambulation of the Ka'ba, as was his custom. While he was doing it, Waraqa met him and said, "O son of my brother, tell me what you have seen and heard." The apostle told him, and Waraqa said, "Surely, by Him in whose hand is Waraqa's soul, you are the prophet of this people. Unto you has come the greatest Namus, who came unto Moses. You will be called a liar, and they will use you spitefully and cast you out and fight against you. Truly, if I live to see that day, I will help God in such ways as He knows." Then he brought his head near to him and kissed his forehead; and the apostle went to his own house.

Isma'il b. Abu Hakim, a freedman[2] of the family of al-Zubayr, told me on Khadija's authority that she said to the apostle of God, "O son of my uncle, are you able to tell me about your visitor, when he comes to you?" He replied that he could, and she asked him to tell her when he came. So when Gabriel came to him, as he was wont, the apostle said to Khadija, "This is Gabriel who has just come to me." "Get up, O son of my uncle," she said, "and sit by my left thigh." The apostle did so, and she said, "Can you see him?" "Yes," he said. She said, "Then turn round and sit on my right thigh." He did so, and she said, "Can you see him?" When he said that he could she asked him to move and sit in her lap. When he had done this she again asked if he could see him, and when he said yes, she disclosed her form and cast aside her veil while the apostle was sitting in her lap. Then she said, "Can you see him?" And he replied, "No." She said, "O son of my uncle, rejoice and be of good heart, by God he is an angel and not a satan."

I told 'Abdullah b. Hasan this story and he said, "I heard my mother Fatima, daughter of Husayn, talking about this tradition from Khadija, but as I heard it she made the apostle of God come inside her shift, and thereupon Gabriel departed, and she said to the apostle of God, 'This truly is an angel and not a satan.'"

3.5 Hadith: Al-Bukhari, *On Fasting* (9th c.). Original in Arabic.

The hadith are the traditions about the prophet handed down by authoritative transmission. There are two parts to every hadith: the first consists of the chain of oral transmitters (*isnad*), with the most recent one listed first; the second part consists of the text of the tradition, which is always about the Prophet, his family, and his close associates.

---

[1] Abu'l-Qasim means "Father of Qasim," and Muhammad was so called because Qasim was the name of his first-born son. It was Muhammad's "name of honor."

[2] I.e., a former slave who has been freed.

(Shi'ite hadith also include traditions about the imams—those few leaders who possessed the "Muhammadan light.") Numerous questions occurred to Muslims after the time of Muhammad; they attempted to answer them by recourse to "what the Prophet would do in such-and-such situation," for that was the guide to "right behavior" (*sunna*). By the early Abbasid period, numerous, sometimes conflicting, answers to these questions were circulating. Al-Bukhari (810–870) and other scholars who followed him attempted in their collections (though not entirely successfully) to include only the "authentic" hadith. The *isnad*—which should be unbroken and come from reliable sources close to Muhammad—were an important element in their winnowing process. The section below, on fasting, illustrates their attempt to account for every possible situation.

[Source: *A Reader on Islam: Passages from Standard Arabic Writings Illustrative of the Beliefs and Practices of Muslims*, ed. Arthur Jeffery ('S-Gravenhage: Mouton & Co., 1962), pp. 88–90, 92–94, 98–101.]

1. ON THE NECESSITY OF THE FAST OF RAMADAN, AND ON THE VERSE (II, 183/179): "O YOU WHO HAVE BELIEVED, FASTING IS PRESCRIBED FOR YOU, JUST AS IT WAS PRESCRIBED FOR THOSE WHO WERE BEFORE YOU. MAYBE YOU WILL SHOW PIETY."

Qutaiba related to us, saying: Isma'il b. Ja'far related to us from[1] Abu Suhail, from his father, from Talha b. 'Ubaidallah, that a nomad Arab came to the Apostle of Allah—on whom be Allah's blessing and peace—with dishevelled head, saying: "O Apostle of Allah, inform me of what Allah has laid on me as incumbent duty in the matter of saying prayers." He answered: "The five prayer-services, unless you would voluntarily add thereto." Then [the Arab] said: "O Apostle of Allah, inform me of what Allah has laid on me as incumbent duty in the matter of fasting." He answered: "The month of Ramadan, unless you would voluntarily add thereto." Said [the Arab]: "Inform me of what Allah has laid on me as incumbent duty in that matter of alms [i.e. charity]." So the Apostle of Allah informed him of the legal prescriptions of Islam [with regard to alms]. Said he: "By Him who has honored you with the truth, I will not voluntarily add anything, but neither will I come short of what Allah has prescribed as incumbent duties for me." Then the Apostle of Allah—upon whom be Allah's blessing and peace—said: "He will be one of the fortunate ones, if he means that." Or [according to another version, he said]: "He will be brought into Paradise, if he means that."

Musaddad related to us, saying: Isma'il related to us from Ayyub, from Nafi', from Ibn 'Umar, who said: "The Prophet—upon whom be Allah's blessing and peace—fasted 'Ashura'[2] and bade it be kept as a fast, but when Ramadan was made an incumbent duty [on the Muslims], it was abandoned. 'Abdallah[3] used not to fast therein save when it happened to coincide with his [voluntary] fasts."

Qutaiba b. Sa'id said: al-Laith has related to us from Yazid b. Abi Habib, that 'Irak b. Malik related to him that 'Urwa informed him from 'A'isha[4] that the Quraysh[5] used to fast the Day of "Ashura" in the pre-Islamic days, and then the Apostle of Allah—upon whom be Allah's blessing and peace—bade it be kept as a fast, [which it was] till Ramadan was made an incumbent duty. Said the Apostle of Allah—upon whom be Allah's blessing and peace—: "If anyone so wishes, let him still keep it as a fast, but if anyone so wishes, let him eat thereon."

---

[1] The particle *'an* used in these *isnad*s really means "on the authority of," but as the transmission of the Tradition was "from" one authority to another, it is translated throughout by "from" for brevity's sake. The b. in names means "son of."

[2] A fast said to have been observed by the Jews and some of the Arabs in the pre-Islamic days as commemoration of their deliverance from their enemies.

[3] Probably the companion of the Prophet 'Abdallah ibn 'Abbas.

[4] The Prophet's youngest wife, who is quoted as the source for a vast number of Traditions.

[5] The ruling Arab tribe in Mecca in the days of the Prophet.

2. ON THE MERITS OF THE FAST.

'Abdallah b. Maslama related to us from Malik, from Abu'z-Zinad, from al-A'raj, from Abu Huraira,[1] that the Apostle of Allah—upon whom be Allah's blessing and peace—said: "Fasting is a protective covering [from the fires of Hell], so let there be no unseemly speech, no foolish acting [during it]. If a man is attacked or vilified [during it], let him say twice: 'I am fasting;' for by Him in whose hand is my soul, the odor from the mouth of him who fasts is sweeter to Allah than the perfume of musk. [Allah says to Himself]: 'He is giving up his food and his drink and his body lusts for My sake when he is fasting unto Me, so I shall reward him, and for each good deed [that he does] grant him the merit of ten.'"

3. ON FASTING AS AN EXPIATION.

'Ali b. 'Abdallah related to us, saying: Sufyan related to us, saying: several have related to us from Abu Wa'il, from Hudhaifa, who said: "Umar once asked: 'Who is there who has memorized a Tradition from the Prophet—upon whom be Allah's blessing and peace—about discord?' Hudhaifa answered: 'I heard him say that discord arises for a man from [three sources: from] his family, from his property, and from his neighbor; but prayer, fasting and gifts of charity may be its expiation.' Said ['Umar]: 'I am not asking about this [general matter of discord arising among men], but about that [which will come at the Last Days] billowing like the billows of the sea.' 'Facing that,' said [Hudhaifa], 'there is a gate shut.' 'Will it be opened,' asked ['Umar], 'or broken down?' 'It will be broken down,' answered [Hudhaifa]. 'Then,' said he, 'it is not likely to be shut again until the Day of Resurrection.'" We said to Masruq: "Ask him if 'Umar knew who the 'Gate' would be?"[2] So he asked him, and he answered: "Yes, [he knew that] just as he knew that night is before morning."…

8. ON HIM WHO DOES NOT GIVE UP SAYING FALSE WORDS AND DOING FALSE DEEDS DURING RAMADAN.

Adam b. Abi Iyas related to us, saying: Ibn Abi Dhi'b related to us, saying: Sa'id al-Maqburi related to us from his father, from Abu Huraira, who said: Said the Prophet—upon whom be Allah's blessing and peace—: "If one does not give up saying false words and doing false deeds in Ramadan, his giving up eating and drinking means nothing to Allah."

9. ON WHETHER, IF ONE IS REVILED, HE SHOULD SAY: "I AM FASTING."

Ibrahim b. Musa related to us, saying: Hisham b. Yusuf informed us from Ibn Juraij, who said: 'Ata' informed me from Abu Salih az-Zayyat, that he heard Abu Huraira say: The Apostle of Allah—upon whom be Allah's blessing and peace—said: "Allah, mighty and majestic is He, has said: 'Every deed of a child of Adam is his [and will be recorded and rewarded in due measure] save fasting, which is Mine, and which I will reward [in My own measure].' Fasting is a protective covering, so when the day comes for anyone of you to fast, let there be no unseemly speech, no clamoring. If anyone reviles such a person, or attacks him, let him say: 'I am fasting.' By Him in whose hand is my soul, the odor from the mouth of him who fasts is sweeter to Allah than the perfume of musk. He who fasts has two occasions of rejoicing. He will have joy when he breaks his fast, and when he meets his Lord he will have joy because of his fasting."

10. ON FASTING [AS A HELP] FOR ONE WHO FEARS [THE TEMPTATIONS OF ONE WHO REMAINS] CELIBATE.

'Ubdan related to us from Abu Hamza, from al-A'mash, from Ibrahim, from 'Alqama, [who said]: While I was walking with 'Abdallah he said: "I was once with the Prophet—upon whom be Allah's blessing and peace—when he said: 'Let him who is able to marry take a wife, for it is the best way of averting lascivious glances and of providing chaste enjoyment, but let him who is not able [to marry] fast, for it will be a remover [of unseemly passions] for him.'"

11. ON THE SAYING OF THE PROPHET—UPON WHOM BE ALLAH'S BLESSING AND PEACE—: "WHEN YOU SEE THE NEW MOON, FAST, AND WHEN YOU SEE IT, BREAK YOUR FAST."

Sila quoted from 'Ammar: "Whosoever fasts on a doubtful

---

[1] Abu Huraira was a highly celebrated "Companion" of the Prophet. Thousands of hadith named him as the final transmitter in the isnad.

[2] The technical word in this Tradition is *fitna*, "dissension," "discord," and in Muslim accounts of the events of the Last Days preceding the great Day of Judgment there are innumerable stories about the dissensions that will arise among the people. The "gate" (*bab*) is the individual who will usher in any particular dissension.

day is disobeying Abu'l-Qasim,[1]—upon whom be Allah's blessing and peace.

'Abdallah b. Maslama related to us from Malik, from Nafi', from 'Abdallah b. 'Umar, that the Apostle of Allah—upon whom be Allah's blessing and peace—mentioned Ramadan, and said: "Do not fast until you see the new moon, and do not break the fast until you see it, and if it is cloudy make a computation for it."

'Abdallah b. Maslama related to us, saying: Malik related to us from 'Abdallah b. Dinar, from 'Abdallah b. 'Umar, that the Apostle of Allah—upon whom be Allah's blessing and peace—said: "The month is twenty-nine nights, so do not fast till you see it (i.e., the new moon), and if it is cloudy then compute the number to thirty."

Abu'l-Walid related to us, saying: Shu'ba related to us from Jabala b. Suhaim, who said: "I heard Ibn 'Umar say that the Prophet—upon whom be Allah's blessing and peace—said: 'The month is so-and-so,' and he tucked in [his] thumb the third time."

Adam related to us, saying: Shu'ba related to us, saying: Muhammad b. Ziyad related to us, saying: I heard Abu Huraira say that the Prophet—upon whom be Allah's blessing and peace—said:—or maybe he said: Abu'l-Qasim, upon whom be, etc. said:—"Fast when it (i.e., the moon) becomes seeable, and break your fast when it becomes seeable, and if it is cloudy then complete the number of Sha'ban,[2] [i.e.,] thirty."

Abu 'Asim related to us from Ibn Juraij, from Yahya b. 'Abdallah b. Saifi, from 'Ikrima b. 'Abd al-Rahman from Umm Salama, that the Prophet—upon whom be Allah's blessing and peace—took an oath to abstain from his women for a month. When twentynine days had elapsed be came in the morning—or maybe it was in the evening—[to 'A'isha]. Someone objected, "But you swore that you would not enter for a month," and he replied: "A month has twentynine days."

'Abd al-'Aziz b. 'Abdallah related to us, saying: Sulaiman b. Bilal related to us from Humaid, from Anas, who said: "The Apostle of Allah—upon whom be Allah's blessing and peace—took an oath to abstain from his women. As his foot was injured he stayed in an upper chamber for twenty-nine nights. Then he came down, but they said: 'O Apostle of Allah, you took an oath for a month', whereat he said: 'The month is twenty-nine [days].'"

12. ON HOW THE TWO MONTHS OF FESTIVAL MAY NOT BE CURTAILED.

Musaddad has related to us, saying: Mu'tamir related to us, saying: I heard Ishaq b. Suwaid [quoting] from 'Abd al-Rahman b. Abi Bakra, from his father, from the Prophet—upon whom be Allah's blessing and peace—[or according to another *isnad*], Musaddad related to me, saying: Mu'tamir related to us from Khalid al-Hadhdha', who said: 'Abd al-Rahman b. Abi Bakra related to me from his father, from the Prophet—upon whom be Allah's blessing and peace—who said: "There are two months which may not be curtailed, the two months of festival, Ramadan and Dhu'l-Hijja."[3] Said Abu 'Abdallah: "Ishaq said: 'Twenty-nine complete days.' Ahmed b. Jundub said: 'If Ramadan is curtailed, complete Dhu'l-Hijja, and if Dhu'l-Hijja is curtailed, complete Ramadan.' Abu'l-Hasan said: 'Ishaq b. Rahuwaih used to say, 'Let neither be curtailed in [their] meritoriousness, whether it is twenty-nine or thirty [days].'"…

22. ON THE FASTER WHO AWAKES IN THE MORNING IN A STATE OF SEXUAL POLLUTION.

'Abdallah b. Maslama related to us from Malik, from Sumayy, a client of Abu Bakr b. 'Abd al-Rahman b. al-Harith b. Hisham b. al-Mughira, that he heard Abu Bakr b. 'Abd al-Rahman say: "I was with my father when we entered to 'A'isha and Umm Salama," [or as another *isnad* has it], Abu'l-Yaman related to us, saying: Shu'aib informed us from al-Zuhri, who said: Abu Bakr b. 'Abd al-Rahman b. al-Harith b. Hisham informed me that his father 'Abd al-Rahman informed Marwan that 'A'isha and Umm Salama had both informed him, that the Apostle of Allah—upon whom be Allah's blessing and peace—would be overtaken by the dawn while he was still in a state of pollution from [sexual contact with] his wives, but he would bathe and then fast. Marwan said to 'Abd al-Rahman b. al-Harith: "I swear by Allah you shall surely [go and] disturb Abu Huraira by that [information]." Marwan was at that time [Governor] over Medina. Said Abu Bakr: "'Abd al-

---

[1] Abu'l-Qasim means "Father of Qasim," and Muhammad was so called because Qasim was the name of his first-born son. It was Muhammad's "name of honor."

[2] Sha'ban is the month that precedes the fasting month of Ramadan.

[3] Ramadan, the month of fasting, is the ninth month in the Islamic calendar, and Dhu'l-Hijja is the twelfth month, the month during which the annual pilgrimage to Mecca—the *hajj*—takes place.

Rahman, however, disliked [the idea of doing] that, so it was decided among us that we would gather together at Dhu'l-Hulaifa, where Abu Huraira had some land. Then 'Abd al-Rahman said to Abu Huraira: 'I am about to mention to you a matter that I should never have mentioned to you had not Marwan sworn that I should.' Then he mentioned what 'A'isha and Umm Salama had said. Said [Abu Huraira]: 'That is so. Al-Fadl b. 'Abbas related [it] to me, and no one would know better than him.'" Said Hammam and Ibn 'Abdallah b. 'Umar [quoting] from Abu Huraira: "The Prophet—upon whom be Allah's blessing and peace—used to order [in such a case that] the fast be broken," but the first [version] has the better *isnad*.

23. ON THE [RESTRICTIONS OF] SEX RELATIONS FOR ONE WHO IS FASTING.

'A'isha said: "It is her vulva which is forbidden to him."

Sulaiman b. Harb related to us from Shu'ba, from al-Hakam, from Ibrahim, from al-Aswad, from 'A'isha, who said: "The Prophet—upon whom be Allah's blessing and peace—used to kiss and handle [his wives] while he was fasting, but he had more control over his *irb* than any of you." [As to this word *irb*], Ibn 'Abbas said that [the derivative from it] *ma'arib* means "need," and Tawus used to use the phrase "one who possesses no *irba*" for a defective who has no need of women. Jabir b. Zaid said: "If one looks [at a woman] and has an emission let him go on with his fast."

24. ON THE [LEGITIMACY OF] KISSING FOR ONE WHO IS FASTING.

Muhammad b. al-Muthanna related to us, saying: Yahya related to us from Hisham, who said: My father informed me from 'A'isha—with whom may Allah be pleased—from the Prophet—upon whom be Allah's blessing and peace—[or by another *isnad*], 'Abdallah b. Maslama related to us from Malik, from Hisham, from his father, from 'A'isha—with whom may Allah be pleased—who said: "There were times when the Apostle of Allah—upon whom be Allah's blessing and peace—would kiss certain of his wives while he was fasting." Then she laughed.

Musaddad related to us, saying: Yahya related to us from Hisham b. Abi 'Abdallah, who said: Yahya b. Abi Kathir related to us from Abu Salama, from Zainab daughter of Umm Salama, from her mother,[1] who said: "While I was with the Prophet—upon whom be Allah's

blessing and peace—in bed, my menses started, so I slipped out and put on my menstrual clothes. He asked: 'What is the matter with you? has your period come on?' 'Yes,' I replied, and I entered the bed with him again." Now she and the Apostle of Allah—upon whom be Allah's blessing and peace—used both to bathe at the same [water] vessel, and he used to kiss her when he was fasting.

25. ON THE BATHING OF ONE WHO IS FASTING.

Ibn 'Umar soiled his garment with urine but put it on him while he was fasting. Ash-Sha'bi entered the [public] baths while he was fasting. Ibn Abbas said: "There is no harm in tasting [what is in] the cooking pot [while fasting] or [any other] thing." Al-Hasan said: "There is no harm in the faster gargling or cooling himself off" (i.e., provided he does not drink the water). Ibn Mas'ud said: "When the day comes around for any one of you to fast he may, as he rises in the morning, use oil and comb." Anas said: "I had a copper wash-basin in which I used to plunge even while I was fasting, and Ibn 'Umar used to brush his teeth at the beginning and at the end of the day [while he was fasting]." Ibn Sirin said: "There is no harm in the use of the tooth-brush if it is fresh." The objection was raised: "But it has taste," and [he replied]: "and so does the water have taste when you gargle with it, [yet that is not considered to be breaking the fast]. Anas, al-Hasan and Ibrahim also saw no harm in the faster making use of kohl [for the eyes].

Ahmad b. Salih related to us, saying: Ibn Wahb related to us, saying: Yunus related to us, from Ibn Shihab, from 'Urwa and Abu Bakr, who said: 'A'isha—with whom may Allah be pleased—said: "The dawn used to overtake the Prophet in Ramadan when he was polluted—and not from an [erotic] dream—but he would bathe and [then commence the] fast."

Isma'il related to us, saying: Malik related to me from Sumayy, a client of Abu Bakr b. 'Abd al-Rahman b. al-Harith b. Hisham b. al-Mughira, that he heard Abu Bakr b. 'Abd al-Rahman say: "I was with my father and went along with him till we entered to 'A'isha—with whom may Allah be pleased—who said: 'I bear witness of the Apostle of Allah—upon whom be Allah's blessing and peace—that he used to wake up in the morning polluted [by sperm] from intercourse, not from dreaming, and then he would fast [that day].' Then we entered to Umm Salama, who said the same thing."

---

[1] Her mother was one of the Prophet's wives.

26. ON THE FASTER WHO EATS AND DRINKS FROM FORGETFULNESS.

'Ata' said: "If one snuffs up water and some of it enters the throat so that one is not able to reject it, no harm is done [thereby to one's fast]." Also al-Hasan said: "If a fly should get into one's throat, that is nothing," and al-Hasan and Mujahid both said: "If one should have sexual intercourse forgetfully, that is nothing."

'Abdan related to us [saying], Yazid b. Zurai' informed us, saying, Hisham related to us, saying: Ibn Sirin related to us from Abu Huraira, from the Prophet—upon whom be blessing and peace—that he said: "If anyone forgets and eats or drinks, let him complete his fast, for it was Allah who caused him thus to eat or drink."

27. ON THE FRESH AND THE DRY TOOTHBRUSH FOR HIM WHO IS FASTING.

It is reported from 'Amir b. Rabi'a, who said: "I have seen the Prophet—upon whom be Allah's blessing and peace—using the toothbrush while he was fasting more times than I can reckon or count." 'A'isha said, quoting the Prophet—upon whom be Allah's blessing and peace—: "The toothbrush is a purifier for the mouth and a thing well-pleasing to the Lord." 'Ata' and Qatada said: "One may swallow one's saliva [without thereby breaking one's fast]." Abu Huraira said, quoting the Prophet—upon whom be Allah's blessing and peace—: "Were it not that I might be causing distress to my community I should bid them use the toothbrush at every ablution." The like of this Tradition is transmitted from Jabir and Zaid b. Khalid from the Prophet—upon whom be Allah's blessing and peace—who [in this matter] did not particularize the one fasting from anyone else.

'Abdan related to us, saying: 'Abdallah informed us, saying: Ma'mar informed us, saying: al-Zuhri related to us from 'Ata' b. Yazid, from Humran, who said: "I saw 'Uthman [i.e., the third Caliph] performing ablutions. He poured [the water out] over his hands three times. Then he gargled and snuffed up [the water]. Then he washed his face three times. Then he washed his right arm up to the elbow three times. Then he washed his left arm up to the elbow three times. Then he rubbed his head [with his moist hands]. Then he washed his right foot three times. Then he washed his left foot three times. Then he said: 'I have seen the Apostle of Allah—upon whom be Allah's blessing and peace—performing ablution just like this ablution of mine, after which he [i.e., the Prophet] said: Whosoever performs [his] ablutions as I have done here, and prays a two-bow prayer, not allowing anything to distract him during them, will have all his past sins forgiven him.'"

3.6 The "New Poetry": Abu Nuwas, *Turning the Tables* (*c.*800). Original in Arabic.

Umayyad poetry (see above p. 78) added eulogies of the caliphs and the rhythms of the Qur'an to the forms of pre-Islamic poetry. Abbasid poetry was even more experimental, playing with traditional structures and vocabularies and adding poems of the hunt, satire, and obscenity to the traditional genres of wine songs, laments, elegies, and love poems. Abu Nuwas (d.813/815) was an exceptionally versatile poet who lived a relatively short and irreverent life. He was a lover of beardless boys yet also taken with a slave girl; a boon companion of al-Amin, heir to the caliphate, yet imprisoned by al-Amin and his father at least twice; an impious pilgrim to Mecca, yet well-versed in the Qur'an and hadith (see above, p. 117). In *Turning the Tables,* he portrays a servant who turns his masters into sex slaves during the night. But the tables are turned once again as the poem ends, with a longing lament that suggests real love.

[Source: Philip F. Kennedy, *Abu Nuwas: A Genius of Poetry* (Oxford: One World, 2005), pp. 40–42 (note added).]

Turning the Tables

Young men assembled,
   Sterling coins at the count
      To whom chance time delivered me
"Sunday is close," they said; so I ambled to the promised
   location
   And was the first to arrive   5
Dressed like a preacher, in full-covering robes
   Kept fast by a plaited cord.
When they had purchased what they wanted,
   Eager to slake their desire,
I approached and offered: "I'll carry this stuff;   10
   I have the necessary saddle bags:
My ropes are sturdy, and I am brisk and dependable."
"Take it," they said, "You seem to be what you claim
   And we'll reward you according to your efforts."
So I advanced in their company   15
   And was told to climb with them [to the spot we were
      making for];
There vessels were unveiled for them (like wives exposed
   for the first time)
   While a bird warbled in a melancholy strain.
I skipped up to the glasses, and polished them,
   Leaving them like dazzling snow;   20
My dexterity impressed the beardless young men
   (Though with my skill I intended no good for them);
I served them without respite wine mixed with water
   —It was as warming and bright as kindled fire—
Until I noticed their heads incline,
   Bent and crooked with drunkenness   25

And their tongues tied and heavy,
   They now either slept or reclined;
I got up trembling to have sex with them
   (All those who creep stealthily tremble [at the
   thought]!);
Their trouser-bands stymied my pleasure [at first]   30
   But then, with subtle art, I untied them
To reveal each man's quivering backside
   Oscillating supply like a green bough.
O for this night which I spent enraptured
   In continual enjoyment and excess,   35
Making from this to that man,
   Screwing whomever I could find in the house
Until the first one awoke and got up
   Feeling bruised at the thighs;
Then I rose with fear to wake up the others,   40
   Saying: "Do you feel the same thing as me?
Is this sweat we've all been stained with?"
   They said: "It looks more like butter."
And when I saw them now alert
   I went off to relieve myself;   45
And when the *majlis*[1] came to life anew
   I joined them, as the cups passed briskly around,
Draped in the finest colored robes,
   All spanking new;
I was asked: "Who are you?" And replied: "Your
   servant;   50
   From whom you need fear no rude behavior."
Then I sang a love song, captured by the mood:
   "O would that Salma discharged her vows."

AL-ANDALUS

3.7 The minority—that is, Christian—view: *Chronicle of Albelda* (*c.*883). Original in Latin.

The *Chronicle of Albelda* is generally considered to be the earliest of the surviving histories from Asturias, one of the small Christian kingdoms in the very north of the Spanish Peninsula. Most of it apparently dates from 881, with an additional section that we know was completed in November 883. Its author(s) and place of composition are unknown, but given that the work promoted the legitimacy of the Asturian monarchy we can safely assume its author was connected in some way to the Asturian court.

---

[1] The assembly, the group.

The *Chronicle of Albelda* has come down to us as part of a broader historical mélange containing geographical information, genealogies, lists of bishops, and curious prophetic materials. The chronicle proper begins with a summary of the reigns of Roman rulers from Romulus to Tiberius II (r.698–705), followed by a similar outline of the reigns of the Visigothic kings. It ends with entries describing Pelayo and his descendants, the rulers of Asturias. We begin here with the entry for Ordoño I.

[Source: *Medieval Iberia: Readings from Christian, Muslim, and Jewish Sources*, ed. Olivia Remie Constable (Philadelphia: University of Pennsylvania Press, 1997), pp. 67, 70–74. Translated and introduced by Kenneth B. Wolf.]

[Ordoño I: 850–866]

Ordoño, the son of Ramiro, ruled for seventeen years. He increased the kingdom of the Christians with the help of God. He populated León and Astorga as well as Tuy and Amaya and he garrisoned many other fortresses. Many times he emerged victorious over the Saracens.[1] He took the city of Talamanca in battle and he permitted its king, Mozeror, whom he captured there, to go freely to Peña Santa with his wife, Balkaiz. He likewise stormed the strong city of Albelda. He ambushed its exceedingly powerful king Musa[2] at Mt. Laturce and weakened [Musa's] army with the sword. Musa himself was wounded with a lance, but was saved by a certain friend—who was known to have been one of our [men]—and was carried to a safe place by this friend on horseback. In Ordoño's time, the Northmen came again to the shores of Galicia, where they were killed by a count named Peter. The Moors,[3] coming in their ships, were also defeated on the coasts of Galicia. Such gentleness of soul and mercy [was attributed] to this prince, being so pious to everyone, that he was worthy of being called a father to his people. He died a peaceful death in Oviedo on the sixth day before the Kalends of June [May 27], in the era 904 [866].

[Alfonso III: 866–910]

Alfonso, the son of Ordoño, assumed the kingship in his eighteenth year. In the first flower of his adolescence—in the first year of his kingship and the eighteenth since his birth—he was deprived of his rule as the result of a rebellion by the apostate count of Galicia, Fruela. The king left for Castile. After a short time, this same rebel and unfortunate king, Fruela, was killed by those faithful to our prince [Alfonso] in Oviedo, and the glorious young man was brought back from Castile. He rejoiced, ruling happily from the throne of his father. From the outset of his reign he always enjoyed victory over his enemies. Twice he humiliated and overcame the fierceness of the Basques with his army. During his reign, in a year long past, the Ishmaelite host advanced toward León under the command of Almundar, son of King Abd al-Rahman [II][4] and brother of King Muhammad [I][5] of Córdoba. No sooner had Almundar arrived than he was impeded [from achieving his goal], for after losing many of his soldiers there, the rest of the army left in flight. Another army approached Bierzo at that time and was completely annihilated. This happened in many regions controlled by the enemy. [Alfonso] took the fortress Deza and then acquired Atienza peacefully. He depopulated Coimbra, which was held by the enemy, and afterward peopled it with Galicians. He subjected many more fortresses to his rule. In his time the church grew and his

---

[1] *Saraceni* is the most common Latin designation for "Arabs." It is somewhat misleading in the context of Spanish history since the bulk of the original invading force was made up not of Arabs but of Berbers from Morocco.

[2] Musa ibn Musa, one of the leaders of the Banu Qasi, a clan of *muwallads* (converts to Islam) that controlled much of the Ebro region in the ninth century.

[3] Berbers.

[4] Emir of Córdoba (r.822–852). The "Ishmaelite host" refers to the Islamic army.

[5] Emir of Córdoba (r.852–886).

kingdom increased in size. The cities of Braga, Oporto, Orense, Eminio, Viseo, and Lamego were populated with Christians. By means of yet another victory, he depopulated and destroyed Coria, Idanha, and the rest of the territory of Lusitania[1] all the way to Mérida and the sea, consuming it with the sword as well as hunger. Shortly before that, in the era 915 [877], Abuhalit, the consul of Spain and counselor to King Muhammad, was captured in battle in the territory of Galicia and was taken to our king in Oviedo. Afterward he redeemed himself, handing over his two brothers, his son, and his nephew [to be held as hostages], until he paid the king 100,000 gold *solidi*. During that same time in the era 916 [878], Almundar, son of King Muhammad,[2] came from Córdoba to Astorga and León with the general Ibn Ganim and an army of Saracens. One contingent of the enemy forces, following opposite the army—a force of 13,000 from Toledo, Talamanca, Guadalajara and other fortresses—was destroyed by our prince in Polvorosa at the river Orbigo. The [king] knew that Almundar wanted to press on to the fortress of Sublancio because of what happened in Polvorosa. Once Almundar learned that our king was waiting with his entire army to do battle with him in the fortress of Sublancio, he fearfully fled before the light of dawn. At the instigation of Abuhalit, there was a three-year truce between the two kings. Afterward our king, waging war against the Saracens, mobilized his army and entered [Muslim] Spain, in the era 919 [881]. After plundering the castle of Nefza, Alfonso pressed on through the province of Lusitania and, after crossing the Tagus River, advanced to the territory of Mérida. Ten miles outside of Mérida, he crossed the Guadiana River and came to Mt. Oxiferio, which no one before him had ever tried to approach.[3] There he triumphed over enemies with a glorious victory: for more than 15,000 others are known to have been killed at the same mountain. Thus our prince returned to his royal throne in victory. All of the churches of the Lord were restored by this prince and a city was built in Oviedo with a royal palace. He was brilliant in his knowledge and placid in his appearance, dress, and stature. The Lord always inclined [Alfonso's] soul to rule his people piously. After his long rule, he passed from his earthly kingdom to his heavenly one. Amen.

[Continuation]

While this king [Alfonso] was ruling, in the era 920 [882], the above-mentioned Almundar, son of King Muhammad, set out from Córdoba to Zaragoza, accompanied by the general Abuhalit and an army from [Muslim] Spain numbering 80,000. [This was because] Ismail ibn Musa[4] of Zaragoza had become an enemy of the Cordobans. When the army arrived at Zaragoza, it fought there for twenty-two days but won no victory. From there it advanced to Tudela and attacked a fortress held by Fortun ibn Musa,[5] but accomplished nothing. Then Ababdella—also known as Muhammad ibn Lope,[6] who had always been, like his father, a friend to us—made peace with the Cordobans and sent the strongest of his [men] to their army out of envy for his uncles to whom the king [Alfonso] had entrusted his son Ordoño to be reared. Thus the army of the Chaldeans,[7] entering the confines of our kingdom, first attacked the fortress at Cellorigo but accomplished nothing except to lose many of their own men. Vigila Jimenez was the count in Alava at that time. This same army, coming to the frontier of Castile, attacked the fortress called Poncorbo for three days, but won no victory and lost many of its own [men] to the avenging sword. Diego, son of Roderic, was the count in Castile [at that time]. Munio, son of Nuño, left the fortress of Castrojeriz deserted on account of the

---

[1] The old Roman province that corresponds more or less with modern-day Portugal but that also included the cities of Mérida and Salamanca.

[2] It is not clear whether this is a different Almundar from the brother (of the same name) of Muhammad mentioned above, or simply an error on the part of the chronicler.

[3] The success of this long-distance raid in particular seems to have been regarded by the chronicler (and presumably his royal patrons) as a sign that the days of Muslim rule in Spain were numbered. Hence the flurry of self-promoting historical literature produced in Asturias in the 880s.

[4] Son of Musa ibn Musa (a member of the Banu Qasi).

[5] Another son of Musa ibn Musa.

[6] A grandson of Musa ibn Musa.

[7] Yet another synonym for Saracens, this one emphasizing the biblical role of the "scourge" that Christians often invoked when trying to make sense out of their defeat at the hands of Muslims.

advance of the Saracens, because it was not yet heavily fortified. Our king, formidably garrisoned in the city of León with his army, waited for the enemy forces so that he might fight them in the suburbs of the city. But when the [Saracen] forces learned that our king was eagerly and daily anticipating their approach to the city, they, on the advice of Abuhalit, who had spied the king's men [in the city], crossed the river Esla fifteen miles from the city and burned a number of garrisoned fortresses. From the plains of Alcoba, [Abuhalit] sent envoys to the Orbigo River to meet our king, asking for the release of his son Abulkazim, whom the king had been holding [as a hostage] up to that time. So Abuhalit sent [as a hostage], for the sake of peace, the son of Ismail ibn Musa, who had been sent to his father from Córdoba, along with Fortun ibn Alazela, whom they had captured by trickery in Tudela. And so, entreating [King Alfonso] and giving him many gifts, [Abuhalit] received his son and made his way across the river Orbigo to Cea. Then he returned to Córdoba. They arrived in Córdoba, whence they had set out the previous March, in September. Later our king handed over the [hostages] from the Banu Qasi—whom he had received from Abuhalit in exchange for his son— to their friends without ransom. The above-mentioned Ababdella, the son of Lope, turned in hate against his uncles and cousins on account of his friendship with the Cordobans, and the question of war arose between them. That winter, on account of the insolence of Ababdella, his uncle Ismail ibn Musa and his cousin Ismail ibn Fortun moved their armies about seven miles wanting to do battle against Ababdella. Ababdella waited for them in rough terrain. Both Ismails, with light escorts, came to the same rugged mountain where they knew

him to be, and ascended it with a few men and servants. Ababdella rushed toward them at full speed and, as they broke into flight, Ismail ibn Fortun fell from his horse and was immediately captured. Likewise Ismail ibn Musa was captured as he tried to seize his nephew. Many of the nobles of the Banu Qasi were also captured. The rest of the army, which had been waiting in the plain, escaped in flight. Having won a victory, Ababdella transported those whom he had captured, bound in chains, to his fortress called Viguera. From there he proceeded to Zaragoza, and took it in the name of peace without resorting to the sword, thus subjecting it to his authority. He sent messengers to Córdoba at once, acting as if he had done all of this for the sake of the king, so as to appear faithful in all things. But when the Cordoban king requested the city of Zaragoza itself along with the others that Ababdella had captured, and Ababdella would by no means consent to do this, the Cordobans were moved to anger. As a result, [Ababdella and his kinsmen] were reconciled. He released his uncle and received the fortress of Valtierra from him. Likewise Ababdella released his cousin and on account of this received Tudela and the fortress of St. Stephan from him. Ababdella retained (and still holds) Zaragoza, which he had taken before. During this same period, Ababdella sustained many raids and attacks from the counts of Castile and Alava, Diego and Vigila. When he saw that he was hard pressed by them, he immediately sent legates to our king [Alfonso] for the sake of peace and indeed he still sends them, but as yet he has not received any firm peace from the prince. Still he remains friendly toward us and wants to remain that way even if our king does not consent [to a formal peace].

3.8 An Islamic Andalusian voice: Ibn 'Abd Rabbihi, *I Have Never Seen* (before 940). Original in Arabic.

Arabic poetry in al-Andalus, as in the rest of the Arabic world, became newly experimental and free when the Umayyad caliphate fell. Having lost regular contact with the eastern half of the Islamic world, Andalusian poets abandoned the imagery of the desert, concentrating on urban life and metaphors of leisure and opulence. Ibn 'Abd Rabbihi (860–940) was a Córdoban poet of great renown, and his poetry is exemplary for its simplicity. Compare it with Abu Nuwas, *Turning the Tables*, above p. 122.

[Source: *Poems of Arab Andalusia*, trans. Cola Franzen from the Spanish versions of Emilio Garcia Gómez (San Francisco: City Lights Books, 1989), pp. 3–4.]

White Skin

I have never seen
nor heard of such a thing

her modesty turns
pearl into carnelian.

Her face is so clear
that when you gaze
on its perfections

you see your own face
reflected.

....

3.9 A Jewish poet in al-Andalus: Dunash ben Labrat, *There Came a Voice* (mid-10th c.). Original in Hebrew.

Born in Fez (today Morocco), Dunash ben Labrat (*fl.* mid-10th c.) became a rabbi in Spain (perhaps at Córdoba). He was one of many scholars and writers to flourish under the patronage of Hasdai ibn Shaprut, the first Jew to be an important figure at the Islamic Spanish court. Under these favorable conditions, ben Labrat and others debated Hebrew grammar, compiled Hebrew dictionaries, and created a new, secular form of Hebrew poetry. Mastering the traditions of Arabic poetic meter and rhyme, ben Labrat took up many of the same themes as the Arabic poets while invoking a very specific Jewish identity.

[Source: *Wine, Women, & Death: Medieval Hebrew Poems on the Good Life*, trans. and ed. Raymond P. Scheindlin (Oxford: Oxford University Press, 1986), pp. 41–42.]

There came a voice: "Awake!
Drink wine at morning's break.
'Mid rose and camphor make
A feast of all your hours,

'Mid pomegranate trees   5
And low anemones,
Where vines extend their leaves
And the palm tree skyward towers,

Where lilting singers hum
To the throbbing of the drum,   10
Where gentle viols thrum
To the plash of fountains' showers.

On every lofty tree
The fruit hangs gracefully.
And all the birds in glee   15
Sing among the bowers.

The cooing of the dove
Sounds like a song of love.

Her mate calls from above—
Those trilling, fluting fowls.   20

We'll drink on garden beds
With roses round our heads.
To banish woes and dreads
We'll frolic and carouse.

Dainty food we'll eat.   25
We'll drink our liquor neat,
Like giants at their meat,
With appetite aroused.

When morning's first rays shine
I'll slaughter of the kine   30
Some fatlings; we shall dine
On rams and calves and cows.

Scented with rich perfumes,
Amid thick incense plumes,
Let us await our dooms,   35
Spending in joy our hours."

I chided him: "Be still!
How can you drink your fill
When lost is Zion hill[1]
To the uncircumcised.   40

You've spoken like a fool!
Sloth you've made your rule.
In God's last judgment you'll
For folly be chastised.

The Torah, God's delight   45
Is little in your sight,
While wrecked is Zion's height,
By foxes vandalized.

How can we be carefree
Or raise our cups in glee,   50
When by all men are we
Rejected and despised?"

THE WESTERN CHURCH AND EMPIRE

3.10 The pope and the Carolingians: Pope Stephen II, *Letters to King Pippin III* (755–756). Original in Latin.

The letters from Pope Stephen II (752–757) to King Pippin III (r.752–768) are crucial sources for the commencement and early years of the Franco-papal alliance, the emergence of the Papal States, the development of papal administration in and around Rome, and the political history of central Italy in the eighth century. Contained in the so-called *Codex Carolinus* (or "Charlemagne's Book"), these letters form part of a collection of 99 letters sent by a series of popes to the Carolingian mayors of the palace and kings from 739 to about 791. The *Codex* survives in a single late-ninth-century manuscript prepared on the order of Archbishop Willibert of Cologne, but not all of the papal letters survive in the *Codex*. The excerpt here represents only some of the letters that Pope Stephen sent to Pippin. Why did he put great emphasis on the role of Saint Peter? What, exactly, did he want from the Carolingians? Why did he represent himself as "shedding tears and beating our breast"? Do you think such rhetoric was effective? Why?

[Source: *Codex Carolinus, Epistolae* 6–10, ed. Wilhelm Gundlach, Monumenta Germaniae Historica, Epistolae 3, Epistolae Merovingici et Karolini Aevi 1 (Berlin: Weidmann, 1892), pp. 488–503. Translated and introduced by Thomas F. X. Noble.]

1 (6): Stephen II to Pippin III (755)

Pope Stephen to the most excellent lords and sons, Pippin, king and our spiritual co-father,[2] and Charles and Carloman, likewise kings and all of them Patricians of the Romans.[3]

So long as your realm's reputation for sincere faith in blessed Peter will shine brilliantly among other peoples because of your sincere faith in the blessed Peter, prince of the apostles, it is crucial to pay particular attention that, even as all Christians declare that you are more glorious than

---

[1] A reference to the land of Israel, "lost" to the Jews of the Diaspora.

[2] Stephen anointed Pippin's sons Charles and Carloman as kings of the Franks and thus entered a spiritual relationship that made Stephen and Pippin "co-fathers" of the two boys. Compaternity was normally associated with baptismal sponsorship.

[3] "Patrician" was a Roman honorific title that conferred no specific rights. In principle, only the Roman (i.e Byzantine) emperor could confer this title, but the popes began conferring it on the Carolingians.

other peoples in the service of blessed Peter, you should in the same way please the almighty Lord, "who gives salvation to kings,"[1] more perfectly in the defense of his holy church, so that you might have as a helper in all things the faith which you cherish for that same prince of the apostles.

Indeed, we had hoped, most exceptional sons, to delay a while longer amplifying our discourse, but because our heart is terribly worn down by sadness and our spirit grieves because of the many trials borne upon us by the wicked King Aistulf of the Lombards, so we have turned away from the wordiness of many speeches and we have been keen to bring one thing, because it is necessary, to the attention of your most excellent Christianity.

Our spiritual co-father, protected by God, and you, our sweetest sons, for the benefit of your souls, just as our merciful God has deigned to bestow victories upon you from heaven, you have been diligent to demand, as far as you could, the rights of blessed Peter, and through a charter of donation your goodness has confirmed that restitution should be made.[2] Now, however, just as we previously instructed your Christianity about the malice of this same wicked king, behold how his deceit and wicked perversity and perjury have been proclaimed recently. Indeed, the devil, the ancient enemy of the human race, has invaded his wicked heart and what was affirmed by the bond of an oath he has been seen to render worthless, and he has not suffered to return one hand's-breadth of land to blessed Peter and to his holy church, the Republic of the Romans.[3] Indeed, since that day when we [the pope and Pippin] parted from one another, he has attempted to afflict us and to hold the holy church of God in great disgrace to such an extent that the tongues of men cannot describe it, since the very stones themselves, if it may be said, cry out with great lamentation at our tribulation.[4] And he has been seen to afflict us to such a degree that our weakness has been renewed in us once again. For I deeply lament, most excellent sons, that not hearing the words of our unhappiness, you, deceiving yourselves and mocking, have chosen to believe falsehood [spread by Aistulf] rather than truth. Whence even without having

achieved the justice of blessed Peter we have returned to our own flock and to the people committed to us.

Finally, all Christians used to believe so firmly that blessed Peter, the prince of the apostles, would now have received his justice through your most potent right arm, since through the intercession of his prince of the apostles the Lord God and Savior Jesus Christ has displayed such a great and resplendent miracle in your most blessed times and has deigned to bestow such an immense victory upon you for the defense of his holy church. But nevertheless, good sons, trusting that same wicked king in what he promised through the bond of an oath, by your own will you have confirmed by a charter of donation that the cities and localities of blessed Peter and of the republic of the holy church of God ought to be restored. But he, having forgotten the Christian faith and the God who ordered him to be born, has been seen to have rendered empty what was confirmed by an oath. Wherefore "his iniquity falls upon his own head";[5] indeed, the trap that he has dug has been revealed, and he is caught in it for his mendacity and perjury.

I implore you most excellent and God-protected sons, through the Lord our God and his holy, glorious and ever virgin mother Mary, our lady, and all the powers of heaven, and through blessed Peter the prince of the apostles, who anointed you as kings, that you grieve for the holy church of God, and that according to that donation which you ordered to be offered to your very protector, our lord, the blessed Peter, you eagerly restore and hand over everything to the holy church of God, and that by no means would you now trust the seductive words or lying illusion of that most wicked king, or his representatives. Behold, his mendacity is indeed manifest such that it ought not by any means to have any further capacity to attract belief but rather, his wicked spirit and wicked will being known, his treachery is uncovered. Indeed, what you once promised blessed Peter, and what was confirmed through a donation in your own hand, for the good of your soul, hasten to restore and hand over to blessed Peter. Finally, the blessed apostle Paul says "It is better not to make a vow than, having made a vow, not to fulfill it."[6]

---

[1] Ps. 144: 10; Douay Ps. 143: 10

[2] Stephen refers to the so-called "Quierzy Document" (754), which spelled out the lands that Pippin would make Aistulf restore to the pope.

[3] Historically only the Roman Empire could be designated this way; the pope is calling the lands assigned to him by Pippin the "Republic" of the Romans.

[4] See Luke 19: 40.

[5] Ps. 7: 17; Douay Ps. 6: 17.

[6] Actually, not Paul but Eccles. 5: 4.

For truly we commend to your heart all the causes of the holy church of God, and you will render account to God and to blessed Peter on the day of the fearful judgment for exactly how you struggled in the cause of that same prince of the apostles and for the restoration his cities and localities. For ultimately this good work has been reserved for you already for a long period of time now, so that through you the holy church might be exalted, and the prince of the apostles might obtain his justice. None of your ancestors merited such a magnificent gift, but God chose and foreknew you before all time, just as is written "Those whom he foreknew and predestined, those he also called; and those whom he called, he also justified."[1] You have been called. Attend with all haste to effect the justice of this very prince of the apostles because it is written "Faith is justified by works."[2]

Concerning all our tribulations, which we have suffered or are yet suffering, with God's help, let our son Fulrad,[3] your counselor, and his associates inform you. And so act then in the cause of blessed Peter so that in this life you may be victorious with the Lord's favor and, in the future life, through the intercession of that very same prince of the apostles, blessed Peter, you may possess eternal joys.

Farewell, most excellent sons.

3 (8) Stephen II to Pippin (c.Feb. 24, 756)

Pope Stephen to his most excellent lord son and spiritual co-father Pippin, king of the Franks and patrician of the Romans.

We believe that the very creation of the whole universe would declare by what great, mournful, and extremely bitter sadness we are on every side surrounded, and by what great anxiety and difficulty we are hemmed in, and what great tears our streaming eyes pour forth as unceasing evils increase. Who, seeing these tribulations, would not mourn? Who, hearing of the calamities weighing upon us, would not wail? Wherefore we speak in the words of a certain good and modest woman, Susannah: "Difficulties lie upon our every side and we do not know what to do."[4] O, most excellent and Christian sons, just as

the almighty creator of all things, the Lord, in former times had sent the prophet Habakkuk, carried thence suddenly by an angel to revive and console the distinguished prophet Daniel who was concealed in the lion's den, so also now, if I may say so, if only his most merciful patience had made your God-preserved excellence present here even for the space of a single hour so that you might behold the miserable and mournful hardships and tribulations which we are suffering helplessly at the hands of the Lombard people and their wicked king! Behold, the days of hardship have come upon us. Days of weeping and bitterness, the day of anxiety and groans of grief are at hand, for what we feared is happening, and what we dreaded is coming to pass. And so, attacked, afflicted, and overwhelmed and surrounded on every side by their most wicked king and their Lombard people, shedding tears and beating our breast we say, calling upon the Lord with the prophet "Help us, Lord of our salvation, and for the honor of your name, deliver us."[5] And again "Take up arms and a shield and rise up in our assistance; Lord, condemn those who are harming us and defeat those who are attacking us."[6] Indeed, though we seem often to bring our tribulations to the attention of your goodness, now however we have taken care to relate the perils of the evils that we have suffered from that same shameless king and his Lombard people, since the magnitude of the danger compels us.

We believe, most Christian and excellent son, and spiritual co-father, that everything is already known to your nobility: How the peace treaty has been overthrown by the wicked King Aistulf and his people; and how we have been able to obtain nothing in the way that he agreed to and which was confirmed through the bond of an oath; and even that no gain has come to us but instead after the desolation of our whole region even more murders have been perpetrated by that same people. And now may you recognize what we are saying with great tears and sorrow in our heart, most excellent son and spiritual co-father. On the very first of January the entire army of that same King Aistulf of the Lombards mustered from the area of Tuscany against this Roman city and camped right at the gate of Saint Peter, and the gate of Saint Pancras, and the gate of Portuensis. Indeed Aistulf himself joined with other troops from a different area and pitched his tents at

---

[1] A paraphrase of Rom. 8: 29–30.

[2] James 2: 24.

[3] Abbot of Saint-Denis and key adviser to Pippin and later to his son Charlemagne.

[4] Dan. 13: 22.

[5] Ps. 78: 9; Douay Ps. 77: 9 (slightly paraphrased).

[6] See Ps. 34: 2; Douay Ps. 33: 2.

the Salarian gate and at other gates too and he sent to us, saying "Open the Salarian Gate to me that I might enter the city, and hand over to me your pontifical office, and I might have mercy on you.[1] Otherwise, overturning the walls, I shall kill you with a single sword and we shall see who can rescue you from my hands." And indeed all the Beneventans as a whole mustering against this Roman city have taken up a position at the gate of blessed John the Baptist, at the gate of blessed Paul the apostle, and at the rest of the gates of this Roman city.

To be sure, they have laid waste with fire and sword all the estates far and wide outside the city and, burning up all the houses, they have razed them almost to their foundations. They have set fire to the churches of God, and, casting the most holy images of the saints into the fire, they have destroyed them with their swords. And as for the holy gifts, that is the body of our Lord Jesus Christ, they have put them in their foul vessels that they call bags, and stuffed with abundant food of flesh, they eat those same gifts.[2] Carrying off the veils or all the ornaments of the churches of God, which it is too cruel to have to relate, they have used them for their own purposes. Beating the monks, the servants of God who live in monasteries for the sake of the divine office,[3] with immense blows, they have mutilated quite a few. They have dragged away and polluted with great cruelty the nuns and recluses who, for the love of God, handed themselves over to be cloistered from infancy or the age of puberty, and they seem in that same contamination even to have killed some of them. They have put to the torch all the *Domuscultae*[4] of blessed Peter or, as is reported, they have utterly destroyed by fire the houses of all the Romans outside the city, stolen all the flocks, cut the vines almost to the roots, and completely destroyed the crops by grinding them down. Neither to the house of our holy church nor to anyone living in this Roman city has there remained any hope of surviving because, as it is reported, they have destroyed everything with fire and sword and have killed many. And they have also slain the abundant family[5] of blessed Peter and of all the Romans, both men and women, and they have led away many others as captives. These same

wicked Lombards have killed the innocent little children whom they have snatched from their mothers' breasts as well as the mothers themselves, whom they have polluted by force. Indeed they have committed such evils in this Roman province as certainly not even the pagan peoples ever before perpetrated so that, as one could say, even the very stones, seeing our losses, cry out with us.[6]

Besieging this suffering Roman city and surrounding it on every side for five and fifty days, they have waged the fiercest battles against us at the walls of this Roman city incessantly, day and night, and they do not stop attacking us with the aim of subjecting all the people to his power— may God prevent it!—so that wicked king Aistulf may kill them with a single sword. For in such a way, mocking us with great fury, they were proclaiming: "Behold, you are surrounded by us and you will not escape our hands. Let the Franks come now and save you from our hands."

Now they have seized the city of Narni, which your Christianity conceded to us, and they have taken certain cities of ours. Afflicted in such a way, we have barely been able, through great cleverness and by using a sea route, to send our envoys and our present letter, which we have written with great tears, to your excellent Christianity. We even—we speak with the truth bearing us out—would express through each and every letter tears mixed with blood; and if only the Lord would grant it to us, at the moment when you read our mournful exhortation a tear filled with blood might flow in your presence through every letter of this message.

Whence, most excellent son and spiritual co-father, I ask you, and as though appearing in your very presence bowed down upon the ground and prostrating myself at your feet, with the divine mysteries, I adjure you before the living and true God and blessed Peter his prince of the apostles, that you come to our assistance with all possible haste and the greatest speed, lest we perish, for after God, it is in your hands that we have placed all our souls, those of all the Romans. Do not abandon us; so also may the Lord not abandon you in all your works and deeds. Do not spurn us; so also may the Lords not spurn you when you call upon his power. Do not withdraw your aid

---

[1] The Latin is tortured here but it seems that Aistulf was asking Stephen to resign.

[2] This is a reference to the consecrated bread of the altar, the Eucharist.

[3] Monks gathered several times each day to pray the *Opus Divinum,* the Divine Office.

[4] Beginning with Pope Zachary (741–752) the papacy began reorganizing some of its scattered rural estates into large-scale farms called *Domuscultae.*

[5] *Familia* means household more than a small group of related people. The word here relates to the peasants who worked the lands of the Roman Church.

[6] See Luke 19: 40.

from us, most Christian son and spiritual co-father; so also may the Lord not withdraw his aid and protection from you and your people when you have marched out to fight against your enemies. Come to our assistance and help us with great speed, most Christian one: Thus may you receive support from almighty God who anointed you into kingship above all the masses of the peoples through the disposition of blessed Peter. Hasten, hasten, son, hasten to help us before the enemy's sword reaches our heart; I plead with you, lest we perish, lest the peoples who are in all the earth have occasion to say "What has become of the trust of the Romans which they used to place, after God, in the kings and people of the Franks?" Do not suffer us to perish and do not hold back or delay to relieve us or cut us off from your support; thus may you not be a stranger from the kingdom of God and be cut off by force from your dearest wife, the most excellent queen and our spiritual co-mother. Do not permit us to be worried and endangered any further and to continue in mourning and weeping, fine excellent son and spiritual co-father; in the same way, may sorrow not come upon you over your and my sweetest sons, the lords Charles and Carloman, most outstanding kings and patricians. Do not shut your ear from hearing us and do not turn your face from us lest we be disappointed in our petitions and we be imperiled to the very extremity. In the same way, may the Lord not shut his ear from hearing your prayers and may he not turn his face from you on that day of judgment to come when, with the blessed Peter and with the rest of his apostles, he shall sit to judge through fire every order, both sexes, and every human and worldly power and—God forbid it!—may he not say to you "I do not know you because you have not helped to defend the church of God and you scarcely took any care to rescue his special people in their time of danger."

Hear me, son, hear me and come to our assistance. Behold, the time for saving us has arrived. Save us, before we perish, most Christian king. For what could be better, or finer, or more outstanding than to save those who are in grave danger and caught in dire straits? For it is written: "He who saves is like he who builds up."[1] On this point indeed the eminent prophet Isaiah said: "Relieve the oppressed."[2] For all peoples who are located all around you and have sought protection from your people of the Franks, most mighty through the power of God, have been made safe, and if you do not hesitate to bestow assistance upon all peoples and they are made safe by you, you ought much more to have freed the holy church of God and his people from the attack of their enemies. O how much confidence there was in our heart when we were worthy to behold your honeyed countenance and we were bound and connected in a bond of love that we would remain in great peace and comfort! But while we were expecting to see the light from you, darkness burst forth[3] and our new situation became worse than the former one. Consider, son, consider and reflect deeply, I adjure you through the living God, how our soul and the souls of all the Roman people, committed to you by God, depend, after God and his prince of the apostles, upon your God-protected excellence and the people of the Franks, for as has already been related, we have committed our souls into your keeping. And if it should happen that we perish—let it not be so and may divine mercy prevent it—weigh carefully, I beseech you, and in every way consider upon whose soul the sin shall lie. Believe with all certainty, most Christian one, that if some perilous disaster shall befall us—may it not happen—you, of all people, protected by God, and most beloved to us, will be destined to give account before the tribunal of God with all your officials because, as has been related, we have, through the precept of God and of blessed Peter, committed the holy church of God and our people of the republic of the Romans for protection to no one else but only to your most beloved excellence and to your sweetest sons and to the whole people of the Franks.

Behold, we have made known all our sorrows and anxieties and difficulties to your God-protected goodness. As for you, most excellent son and spiritual co-father, act, and after God, free those who are fleeing to you so that, bearing good fruit, on the day of future judgment you shall be worthy to say "My lord, blessed Peter, prince of the apostles, behold I, your unworthy servant, having run the race, having kept faith with you, having defended the church of God commended to you by heavenly mercy, I freed it from the hands of its persecutors and, standing unblemished before you, I offer you the sons whom you committed to me for the purpose of rescuing them from the hands of enemies, standing here now unharmed and safe." Then, both holding the helm of the kingdom in this present life and also reigning with Christ in the world to come, you would deserve to obtain the joys of heavenly rewards, hearing without doubt that longed-for fatherly

---

[1] Although reminiscent of passages in Psalms and Proverbs, this quotation cannot be identified.

[2] Isa. 1: 17.

[3] See Job 30: 26.

voice of the one who says "Come, blessed of my father, and receive the kingdom that has been prepared for you from the beginning of the world."[1]

May heavenly grace keep your Excellency safe and sound.

4 (9) Pope Stephen II to Pippin, Charles, and Carloman (c.Feb. 24, 756)

To the most excellent lords Pippin, Charles, and Carloman, three kings and our patricians of the Romans, and also to all the bishops, abbots, priests and monks, and to the glorious dukes, counts, and to the entire army of the kingdom and provinces of the Franks, Pope Stephen and all the bishops, priests, deacons, and dukes, soldiers, counts, tribunes, and the whole people and army[2] of the Romans, all placed in affliction.

[The rest of this letter repeats the previous one almost verbatim. What is different is the address to all the officials of the Frankish world and the letter's dispatch from all the religious and secular officials of Rome.]

5 (10) Pope Stephen II writes in the name of Saint Peter to Pippin, Charles, and Carloman (c.Feb. 24, 756)

Peter, called to be an apostle by Jesus Christ the son of the living God who, reigning before all time with the Father in the unity of the Holy Spirit, in the last days became incarnate and was made a man for the salvation of us all and redeemed us by his precious blood through the will of the Father's glory, just as he ordained through his holy prophets in the holy scriptures; and through me the entire catholic and apostolic Roman church of God, the head of all the churches of God, founded by the blood of our very redeemer upon a solid rock, and Stephen, prelate of that same nourishing church: May Grace, peace, and strength for rescuing from the hands of its persecutors that same holy church of God and its Roman people committed to me, be bestowed fully upon you by our Lord God, most excellent men, Pippin, Charles, and

Carloman, all three kings, and also upon the most holy bishops, abbots, priests and all the religious monks, as well as upon the dukes, counts, and all the rest of the armies and people living in Francia.

I, Peter the Apostle, when I was called by Christ, the son of the living God, by the will of divine clemency, was foreordained as the teacher of the whole world by his power, as that very same Lord our God confirmed: "Go, teach all nations, baptizing them in the name of the Father and of the Son and of the Holy Spirit";[3] and again "Receive the Holy Spirit; whose sins you shall remit, they are remitted for them."[4] And commending his sheep in particular to me, his meager servant yet called as an apostle, he said: "Feed my sheep, feed my lambs." And again "You are Peter and upon this rock I shall build my church, and the gates of Hell will not prevail against it, and I shall give you the keys of the kingdom of heaven; whatever you will have bound on earth will also be bound in heaven and whatever you will have loosed on earth will also be loosed in heaven."[5] Wherefore, let all those who, hearing my teaching, fulfill it, believe with certainty that in this world their sins are forgiven by the precept of God and they shall proceed clean and without blemish into that life. Thus, because the inspiration of the Holy Spirit has shone forth in your gleaming hearts and you have been made lovers of his unique and holy Trinity by receiving the word through the preaching of the gospel, your hope of future reward is held bound up in this holy Roman church of God that has been committed to us.

Therefore, I, Peter, the apostle of God, who regard you as adopted sons, appealing to the love of all, I implore you to defend from the hands of its enemies this Roman city and the people committed to me by God, and also to rescue the house where I lie at rest according to the flesh from the defilement of the nations, and bearing witness I warn you to liberate the church of God commended to me by the divine power of God because they are suffering immense afflictions and oppressions from the awful nation of the Lombards. May you by no means believe otherwise, most beloved, but instead trust in it as a certainty: Through my very own self, just as if I were standing alive in the flesh before you, we constrain and bind with mighty adjurations through this exhortation

---

[1] Matt. 25: 34.

[2] The presence of these military figures may be surprising, but the popes seem to have retained something of the military establishment of the formerly Byzantine Duchy of Rome. They were neither numerous nor effective, as these letters make clear.

[3] Matt. 28: 19.

[4] John 20: 22–23.

[5] Matt. 16: 18–19.

because, according to the promise which we received from that same Lord God, our redeemer, we consider all you peoples of the Franks to be a special people among all the nations. So I bear witness and I warn you as if through a mysterious vision and with firm obligation I adjure you, most Christian kings Pippin, Charles, and Carloman, and also all the archbishops, bishops, abbots, priests, and all the religious monks, and all the officials, and the dukes, counts, and the whole people of the kingdom of the Franks, and believe, all of you, just as firmly that the words of the exhortation are addressing you as you would if I, Peter, the apostle of God, were standing before you alive in the flesh in person, because, even if I am not there in the flesh, I am not absent from you spiritually, for it is written: "He who receives a prophet in the name of a prophet, receives the prophet's reward."[1]

And also our mistress, the mother of God, the ever-virgin Mary, bears witness, warns, and commands you, along with us, adjuring by great obligations, likewise also thrones and dominions, and all the troops of the heavenly host, not to mention the martyrs and confessors of Christ, and everyone wholly pleasing to God. And these, urging and imploring along with us, testify to how much you grieve for this Roman city committed to us by the Lord God, and for the Lord's flocks dwelling within it, and also for the holy church of God commended to me by the Lord. So, defend and free it, with great haste, from the hands of the persecuting Lombards, lest—may it never be!—my body which suffered torments for the sake of the Lord Jesus Christ, and my house, where by God's command it lies at rest, be contaminated by them and lest my special people be further maimed or they be butchered by that very people of the Lombards who stand guilty of such a great crime of treachery and are proven to be transgressors of the divine scriptures. Offer therefore to my Roman people, committed to me by God in this life, your own brothers, protection with all your strength, with the Lord assisting you, so that I, Peter, called to be an apostle of God, may extend in turn patronage to you in this life and on the day of future judgment, so that in the kingdom of God the most shining and distinguished tents may be prepared for you and that I, giving my word, may bestow upon you in turn the rewards of eternal recompense and the endless joys of paradise, provided that you will have defended my Roman city and my special people, your brothers, the Romans, with great swiftness, from the hands of the wicked Lombards.

Hasten, hasten, I urge and protest by the living and true God, hasten and assist, before the living font whence you were nourished and reborn dries up; before that little spark that remains from the most blazing flame, from which you have known your light, is extinguished; before your spiritual mother, the holy church of God, in which you hope to receive eternal life, is humiliated, overwhelmed, and is violated and contaminated by the impious. I witness before you, my most beloved adoptive sons, through the grace of the Holy Spirit, I bear witness and I greatly urge and admonish before God the terrible creator of all, I, the apostle of God, Peter, and together with me the holy, catholic, and apostolic church of God, which the Lord committed to me: Do not suffer this Roman city to perish in which the Lord laid my body and which he commended to me and established as the foundation of the faith.

Free it and its Roman people, your brothers, and in no way permit it to be invaded by the people of the Lombards; thus may your provinces and possessions not be invaded by peoples of whom you know nothing. Let me not be cut off from my Roman people; thus may you not be foreign and cut off from the kingdom of God and eternal life. In whatever you have demanded of me, I shall come to your aid, that is to say, I shall also bestow my patronage. Come to the aid of my Roman people, your brothers, and struggle more perfectly and achieve final success in freeing them. For no one receives the crown except he who has genuinely struggled. And you, struggle bravely for the liberation of the holy church of God lest you perish for eternity. I adjure you, I adjure you, most beloved, as I have already said, by the living God, and I stand true witness: Do not in the slightest permit this my Roman city and the people living in it to be mutilated any further by the people of the Lombards; thus may your bodies and souls not be slashed and tormented in the eternal and inextinguishable fire of Tartarus with the devil and his stinking angels. And let not the sheep of the Lord's flock, committed to me by God, that is the Roman people, be further scattered; may the Lord not scatter and drive you out just as the Israelite people has been scattered.

For it has been declared that your people of the Franks is devoted to me, to the apostle of God, Peter, beyond all peoples who are under heaven; thus I have commended to you through the hand of my vicar the church, which the Lord handed to me, so that you might free it from the hands of its enemies. Believe most confidently that I, the servant of God, called to be an apostle, have lent my aid in all your needs when you have called on me, and I have bestowed victory upon you, through the power of

---

[1] Matt. 10: 41.

God, over your enemies, and in the future I shall bestow no less, believe me, if you make haste with great dispatch to free this my Roman city. Remember this as well: How I also caused the enemies of the holy church of God to be struck down by you when they threatened battle against you who were few in number against them. Therefore, struggle; fulfill this warning of mine quickly, that you may more perfectly deserve to obtain my help through the grace that has been given to me by Christ, our Lord God.

Behold, dearest sons, for in preaching I have warned you. If you shall have obeyed quickly it will lead to great reward for you and assisted by my intercession you will overcome your enemies in the present life and you will endure to a great age, and you will have the goods of the earth at your disposal and beyond doubt you will enjoy eternal life. If not, however, which we do not believe, you will have made some delay or excuse for making no haste to fulfill this our exhortation to defend this Roman city of mine and the people living in it and the holy apostolic church of God committed to me by the Lord, and likewise his prelate, then know this: That by the authority of the holy and unique Trinity, through the grace of the apostolic office, a grace that has been given to me by the Lord Christ, we disinherit you from the kingdom of God and from eternal life for your transgression of our exhortation.

But may our God and Lord Jesus Christ who, redeeming us by his precious blood, has led us to the light of truth and established us as preachers and teachers for the whole world, grant it to you to judge these things wisely, and to understand and to make arrangements concerning them exceedingly quickly so that you may more swiftly hasten to rescue this Roman city and its people and the holy church of God committed to me by the Lord and, with my intercession intervening on your behalf, may he keep you safe and victorious with the mercy he shows to those who are faithful to his power, and in the world to come may he make you worthy many times over of the gifts of his reward with his saints and chosen ones.

Farewell.[1]

3.11 Charlemagne as Roman emperor: Einhard, *Life of Charlemagne* (825–826?). Original in Latin.

Born to an elite Frankish family, Einhard (*c.*770–840) received a good education in biblical studies and Latin classics at the monastery of Fulda, which was founded in 744 by Saint Sturm, a disciple of Boniface, a religious reformer closely tied to the early Carolingians (see above, p. 91). Einhard was probably in his early twenties when he started to serve at the court of Charlemagne (r.768–814). There he was known by the other courtiers as "little Nard" – probably to rhyme with the "hard" of his name and to stress his tiny stature – and also as "Bezaleel," Moses' wonderful craftsman (see Exod. 31: 1–5). But Einhard's expertise extended beyond the arts to elegant writing. This allowed him to serve as an ambassador and administrator under Charlemagne and also, for a time, under Charlemagne's heir, Louis the Pious (r.814–840). He did not produce any major writings while living at court, but later, after retiring with his wife, Emma, to the estates that he received for his service to the king, he began to write books. He was so taken with classical Latin models that his *Life of Charlemagne* was, to some degree, patterned on *The Lives of the Caesars*, portraits of the first Roman emperors written by the Roman writer and imperial official Suetonius (69–after 122).

[Source: *Charlemagne's Courtier: The Complete Einhard*, ed. and trans. Paul Edward Dutton (Toronto: University of Toronto Press, 1998), pp. 15–39 (notes added).]

---

[1] Soon after this letter Pippin mustered his army, marched into Italy, defeated Aistulf, and drew up the Second Peace of Pavia, better known as the "Donation of Pippin."

[Preface]

After I decided to describe the life and character, and many of the accomplishments, of my lord and foster father, Charles, that most outstanding and deservedly famous king, and seeing how immense this work was, I have expressed it in as concise a form as I could manage. But I have attempted not to omit any of the facts that have come to my attention, and [yet I also seek] not to irritate those who are excessively critical by supplying a long-winded account of everything new [I have learned]. Perhaps, in this way, it will be possible to avoid angering with a new book [even] those who criticize the old master-pieces composed by the most learned and eloquent of men.

And yet I am quite sure that there are many people devoted to contemplation and learning who do not believe that the circumstances of the present age should be neglected or that virtually everything that happens these days is not worth remembering and should be condemned to utter silence and oblivion. Some people are so seduced by their love of the distant past, that they would rather insert the famous deeds of other peoples in their various compositions, than deny posterity any mention of their own names by writing nothing. Still, I did not see why I should refuse to take up a composition of this sort, since I was aware that no one could write about these things more truthfully than me, since I myself was present and personally witnessed them, as they say, with my own eyes. I was, moreover, not sure that these things would be recorded by anyone else.

I thought it would be better to write these things down [that is, his personal observations], along with other widely known details, for the sake of posterity, than to allow the splendid life of this most excellent king, the greatest of all the men in his time, and his remarkable deeds, which people now alive can scarcely equal, to be swallowed up by the shadows of forgetfulness.

There is still another reason, an understandable one, I believe, which even by itself might explain why I felt compelled to write this account; namely, the foster care [Charlemagne] bestowed on me and the constant friend-ship [I had] with him and his children after I began living at his court. Through his friendship he so won me over to him and I owed him so much both in life and death, that I might both seem and be fairly criticized as ungrateful if I forgot the many kindnesses he conferred upon me. Could I keep silent about the splendid and exceedingly brilliant deeds of a man who had been so kind to me and could I allow his life to remain without record and proper praise, as if he had never lived? But to write and account [for such a life] what was required was [an almost] Ciceronian eloquence,[1] not my feeble talent, which is poor and small, indeed almost non-existent.

Thus [I present] to you this book containing an account of the most splendid and greatest of all men. There is nothing in it that you should admire but his accomplishments, except perhaps that I, a German with little training in the language of Rome, should have imagined that I could write something correct and even elegant in Latin. Indeed, it might seem [to you] that my headlong impudence is very great and that I have will-fully spurned the advice of Cicero [himself], since in the first book of his *Tusculan* [*Disputations*], when speaking of Latin authors, he had said: "for people to set their thoughts down in writing when they cannot organize them, make them clear, or charm their readers with any style is a complete waste of time and energy."[2] Indeed, this opinion of the famous orator might have stopped me from writing [this book, at all], if I had not decided in advance that it was better to risk the criticisms of people and to endanger my own small reputation by writing [this book], than to neglect the memory of so great a man and [instead] say myself.

[The Life of Charlemagne]

1. The family of the Merovingians, from which the Franks used to make their kings, is thought to have lasted down to King Childeric [III], whom Pope Stephen [II] ordered deposed. His [long] hair was shorn and he was forced into a monastery. Although it might seem that the [Merovin-gian] family ended with him, it had in fact been without any vitality for a long time and [had] demonstrated that there was nothing of any worth in it except the empty name of 'king'. For both the [real] riches and power of the kingdom were in the possession of the prefects of the palace, who were called the mayors of the palace [*maiores domus*], and to them fell the highest command. Noth-ing was left for the king [to do] except sit on his throne

---

1   In fact Cicero (106–43 BCE), a Roman orator and writer whose Latin style was (and continues to be) greatly admired, was a major influence on Einhard. Note his reference to Cicero's *Tusculan Disputations* in the next paragraph.

2   Cicero, *Tusculan Disputations*, 1.3.6.

with his hair long and his beard uncut, satisfied [to hold] the name of king only and pretending to rule. [Thus] he listened to representatives who came from various lands and, as they departed, he seemed to give them decisions of his own, which he had [in fact] been taught or rather ordered [to pronounce]. Except for the empty name of 'king' and a meager living allowance, which the prefect of the court extended to him as it suited him, he possessed nothing else of his own but one estate with a very small income. On that estate, he had a house and servants who ministered to his needs and obeyed him, but there were few of them. He traveled about on a cart that was pulled by yoked oxen and led, as happens in the countryside, by a herdsman to wherever he needed to go.[1] In this way he used to go to the palace and so also to the public assembly of his people, which was held annually for the good of the kingdom, and in this manner he also returned home. But it was the prefect of the court [the mayor of the palace] who took care of everything, either at home or abroad, that needed to be done and arranged for the administration of the kingdom.

2. When Childeric was deposed, Pepin [III, the Short], the father of King Charles, held the office [of mayor of the palace], as if by hereditary right. For his father Charles [Martel] had brilliantly discharged the same civil office, which had been laid down for him by his father Pepin [II, of Herstal]. This Charles overthrew those oppressors who claimed personal control over all of Francia and he so completely defeated the Saracens,[2] who were attempting to occupy Gaul, in two great battles—the first in Aquitaine near the city of Poitiers [in 732] and the second near Narbonne on the River Berre [in 737]—that he forced them to fall back into Spain. For the most part, the people [that is, the Frankish nobles] only granted the office [of mayor of the palace] to those men who stood out above others because of the nobility of their birth and the magnitude of their wealth.

For a few years Pepin, the father of King Charles, had held, as if under that [Merovingian] king, the office [of mayor of the palace], which was left to him and his brother Carloman by his grandfather and father. He shared that office with his brother in splendid harmony. [Then in 747] Carloman walked away from the oppressive

chore of governing an earthly kingdom. It is not clear why he did this, but it seems that he was driven by a desire to lead a contemplative life. [Hence] he went to Rome in search of a quiet life and there changed his way [of dress and life] completely and was made a monk. With the brothers who joined him there, he enjoyed for a few years the quiet life he so desired in the monastery [he] built on Mount Soracte near the church of St-Sylvester. But since many nobles from Francia frequently visited Rome in order to fulfill their solemn vows and did not wish to miss [seeing] the man who had once been their lord, they interrupted the peaceful life he so loved by constantly paying their respects and so forced him to move. For when he realized that this parade [of visitors] was interfering with his commitment [to the monastic life], he left Mount [Soracte] and retreated to the monastery of St. Benedict located on Monte Cassino in the province of Samnium. There he spent what was left of his earthly life [until 755] in religious contemplation.[3]

3. Moreover, Pepin, who had been mayor of the palace, was established as king [in 751] by the decision of the Roman pope [Zacharias] and he ruled the Franks by himself for fifteen years or more. When the Aquitainian war, which Pepin waged against Waifar, the duke of Aquitaine, for nine straight years, was over, he died of edema in Paris [in 768]. He was survived by two sons, Charles and Carloman, and upon them, by divine will, fell the succession of the kingdom. Indeed, the Franks at a general assembly solemnly established both of them as their kings, but on the condition, agreed to in advance, that they should divide up the entire territory of the kingdom equally. Charles was to take up and govern that part [of the kingdom] which their father Pepin had held and Carloman that part which their uncle Carloman had [once] governed. Both of them agreed to these conditions and each of them received the portion of the kingdom allotted to him by the plan. That peaceful agreement of theirs held fast, but with the greatest strain, since many on Carloman's side sought to drive the brothers apart. Some went so far as to plot to turn them [against each other] in war. But the outcome of things proved that the threat [of war] was more suspected than real in this case, and when Carloman died [in 771] his wife and sons, along with some of

---

[1] Although Einhard presents the Merovingians as ridiculous, in fact the cart as well as their right to wear long hair and beard had been signs of their royal and religious status.

[2] Muslims.

[3] For the Rule that St. Benedict wrote for this monastery, see above, p. 17.

his chief nobles, took refuge in Italy. For no reason at all, she spurned her husband's brother and placed herself and her children under the protection of Desiderius, the king of the Lombards. In fact, Carloman had died [naturally] from disease after ruling the kingdom for two years with his brother. After his death, Charles was established as king by the agreement of all the Franks.

4. I believe it would be improper [for me] to write about Charles's birth and infancy, or even his childhood, since nothing [about those periods of his life] was ever written down and there is no one still alive who claims to have knowledge of these things. Thus, leaving aside the unknown periods [of his life], I have decided to pass straight to the deeds, habits, and other aspects of his life that should be set forth and explained. Nevertheless, so that I might not skip anything either necessary or worth knowing, I shall first describe his deeds inside and outside [the kingdom], then his habits and interests, and finally his administration of the kingdom and his death.

5. Of all the wars he waged, [Charles] began first [in 769] with the one against Aquitaine, which his father had started, but left unfinished, because he thought that it could be quickly brought to a successful conclusion. His brother [Carloman] was [still] alive at the time and [Charles] even asked for his help. And despite the fact that his brother misled him [by not delivering] the promised help, he pursued the campaign with great energy. He refused to back away from a war already in progress or to leave a job undone, until he had by sheer determination and persistence completely achieved the goal he had set for himself. For he forced Hunold, who had tried to take possession of Aquitaine after Waifar's death and to revive a war that was almost over, to give up Aquitaine and seek [refuge in] Gascony. But [Charles], unwilling to allow him to settle there, crossed the River Garonne and through messengers commanded Lupus, the duke of the Gascons, to hand over the fugitive. If he did not do this quickly, [Charles] would demand his surrender by waging war. Lupus not only gave way to wiser counsel and returned Hunold, but he even entrusted himself and the territory he governed to [Charles's] power.

6. With things settled in Aquitaine and the war over, and since the co-ruler [of Francia, his brother Carloman] was now also dead, [Charles] took up war against the Lombards [in 773]. Hadrian [I], the bishop of the city of Rome, [had] asked and appealed to him to do this. Indeed, his father had previously taken up this war at the

request of Pope Stephen [II], [but] with great trouble, since some of the chief Franks, whom he regularly consulted, were so opposed to his plan that they openly stated that they would abandon the king and return home. Despite that [threat], [Pepin] took up the war against King Haistulf and quickly finished it at that time. But, although [Charles] and his father seem to have had a similar or, rather, identical reason for taking up this war, all agree that the [actual] fighting and conclusion [of the two conflicts] were different. For in fact, after laying siege to King Haistulf for a short time [in 756] in Pavia, Pepin forced him to surrender hostages, to restore the cities and fortified places seized from the Romans, and to swear that he would not try to regain the things he had returned. But Charles after he had begun the war did not stop until he had, by means of a long siege [in 774], worn King Desiderius down and had accepted his complete surrender. He forced [Desiderius's] son Adalgis, on whom the hopes of all [the Lombards] seemed to rest, to depart not only from the kingdom, but also from Italy. [Charles] restored everything that had been seized from the Romans. He also overcame Rotgaud, the duke of Friuli, who was plotting new [uprisings in 776], and brought all Italy under his control. He set up his own son Pepin as the king of this conquered land.

I would relate here how difficult it was for one to enter Italy across the Alps and what a struggle it was for the Franks to overcome unmarked mountain ridges, upthrust rocks, and rugged terrain, were it not my intention in this book to record the manner of his life, rather than the details of the wars which he waged. Nevertheless, the end result of this war [against the Lombards] was that Italy was conquered, King Desiderius was sent into permanent exile, his son Adalgis was driven out of Italy, and the properties stolen by the Lombard kings were returned to Hadrian, the head of the Roman church.

7. At the conclusion of this campaign, the Saxon war, which had seemed merely postponed, was begun again. No war taken up by the Frankish people was ever longer, harder, or more dreadful [than this one], because the Saxons, like virtually all the peoples inhabiting Germany, were naturally fierce, worshiped demons, and were opposed to our religion. Indeed, they did not deem it shameful to violate and contravene either human or divine laws. There were underlying causes that threatened daily to disturb the peace, particularly since our borders and theirs ran together almost everywhere in open land except for a few places where huge forests or mountain ridges came between our respective lands and

established a clear boundary. Murder, theft, and arson constantly occurred along this border. The Franks were so infuriated by these [incidents], that they believed they could no longer respond [incident for incident], but that it was worth declaring open war on the Saxons.

Thus, a war was taken up against them, which was waged with great vehemence by both sides for thirty-three straight years [772–804]. But the damage done to the Saxons was greater than that suffered by the Franks. In fact, the war could have been brought to a close sooner, if the faithlessness of the Saxons had [but] allowed it. It is almost impossible to say how many times they were beaten and pledged their obedience to the king. They promised [on those occasions] to follow his orders, to hand over the hostages demanded without delay, and to welcome the representatives sent to them by the king. At different times, they were so broken and subdued that they even promised to give up their worship of demons and freely submit themselves to Christianity. But though they were on occasion inclined to do this, they were always so quick to break their promises, that it is not possible to judge which of the two ways [of acting] can be said to have come more naturally to them. In fact, since the start of the war with the Saxons there was hardly a single year in which they did not reverse themselves in this way. But the king's greatness [of spirit] and steadfast determination—both in bad times and good—could not be conquered by their fickleness or worn down by the task he had set himself. Those perpetrating anything of this sort were never allowed to go unpunished. He took vengeance on them for their treachery and exacted suitable compensation either by leading the army [against them] himself or by sending it under [the charge of] his counts. Finally, when all those who were in the habit of resisting had been crushed and brought back under his control, he removed ten thousand men who had been living with their wives and children along both sides of the Elbe river and he dispersed them here and there throughout Gaul and Germany in various [small] groups. Thus, that war which had lasted for so many years ended on the terms laid down by the king and accepted by the Saxons, namely that they would reject the worship of demons, abandon their ancestral [pagan] rites, take up the Christian faith and the sacraments of religion, and unite with the Franks in order to form a single people....

9. While he was vigorously pursuing the Saxon war, almost without a break, and after he had placed garrisons at selected points along the border, [Charles] marched into Spain [in 778] with as large a force as he could [mount]. His army passed through the Pyrenees and [Charles] received the surrender of all the towns and fortified places he encountered. He was returning [to Francia] with his army safe and intact, but high in the Pyrenees on that return trip he briefly experienced the treachery of the Basques. That place is so thoroughly covered with thick forest that it is the perfect spot for an ambush. [Charles's] army was forced by the narrow terrain to proceed in a long line and [it was at that spot], high on the mountain, that the Basques set their ambush. They fell upon the last part of the baggage train and drove the men of the rear guard, who were protecting the troops in front, down into the valley below. In the skirmish that followed, they slaughtered every last one of those men. Once they had looted the baggage train, the Basques, under the cover of darkness, since night was then coming on, quickly dispersed in every direction. The Basques had the advantage in this skirmish because of the lightness of their weapons and the nature of the terrain, whereas the Franks were disadvantaged by the heaviness of their arms and the unevenness of the land. Eggihard, the overseer of the king's table, Anselm, the count of the palace, and Roland, the lord of the Breton March, along with many others died in that skirmish.[1] But this deed could not be avenged at that time, because the enemy had so dispersed after the attack that there was no indication as to where they could be found.

10. [Charles] also conquered the Bretons, who live along the sea in the westernmost part of Gaul. Since they were not subject to him, he sent a force against them [in 786]. The Bretons were forced to surrender hostages and to promise that they would follow his orders....

11. Then the Bavarian war suddenly broke out, but it was brought to a quick end. That war was a product of the pride and foolishness of Duke Tassilo. His wife, who urged him to it, was the daughter of King Desiderius and she thought that she could take revenge for [Charles's] expulsion of her father [from the kingdom of Lombardy] through her husband. Thus, after Tassilo had struck a deal with the Huns,[2] who lived to the east of the Bavarians, he

---

[1] This battle of Roncevaux formed the core of the later epic poem, *The Song of Roland*.

[2] There were no longer any Huns; it was the name Einhard sometimes used for the Avars, a group from Central Asia who had taken the place of the Huns in East Central Europe.

attempted not only to disobey the king, but to provoke him to war. The king in his fury could not abide [the duke's] defiance, which seemed outrageous [to him], and so he gathered troops from all over [Francia] and prepared to invade Bavaria. He himself led that great force [in 787] to the River Lech, which separates the Bavarians from the Alemannians. Before entering the province [of Bavaria], he set up camp on the bank of the river [Lech] and sent representatives to learn the duke's intentions. But Tassilo [now] realized that holding out would benefit neither himself nor his people and so he humbly surrendered to the king. He submitted the hostages demanded, among whom was his own son Theodo, and he also swore with an oath that he would not [in the future] listen to anyone who advised him to rebel against the king's authority. And so this war, which [had] seemed likely to be the greatest conflict of all, was brought to the quickest end. But a little later [that was in 788] Tassilo was summoned before the king and not allowed to leave. The province, which he had [once] held, was not given to another duke to rule, but to [a series of] counts.

12. After [Tassilo's] insurrection had been settled in this way, [the king] declared war against the Slavs, whom we normally refer to as the Wilzi, but who are properly called the Welatabi in their own language. In that war the Saxons fought as auxiliaries alongside the other peoples who were ordered to march in the king's army, but the obedience [of the Saxons] was insincere and lacking in complete commitment. That war came about because [the Slavs] were constantly harassing and attacking the Abodrites, who had once allied themselves with the Franks. [The Slavs] were not inclined [in this matter] to listen to the [king's] commands.

A certain gulf [the Baltic Sea] with an unknown length and a width no more than a hundred miles wide and in many places [much] narrower runs from the western ocean towards the east. Many peoples live around this sea. In fact, the Danes and Swedes, whom we call Northmen, live along the northern shore [of the Baltic] and on all the islands located there. The Slavs, Estonians, and other peoples live along the southern shore [of the Baltic]. The Welatabi were the most prominent of these peoples and it was against them that the king now took up war. He beat them so [badly] and brought them under his control in the one and only campaign he personally waged [against them], that from that point on they never thought of refusing to obey his commands.

13. Aside from the war against the Saxons, the greatest of all the wars waged by [Charles] was the one against the Avars or Huns, which came next [in 791]. He managed that war with greater attention and preparation than his other wars. Even then, he still led one campaign himself into Pannonia, a province then occupied by the Avars. He turned the other campaigns over to his son Pepin, to the governors of the provinces, and to the counts and even their representatives. These men very vigorously conducted this war and finally brought it to a close in its eighth year [it actually ended in 803]. How many battles occurred in that war and how much blood was spilled is indicated by the utter depopulation of Pannonia and the desertion of the khan's palace; in fact, there is hardly a trace [now] that people once lived there. All the nobility of the Huns died out in this war and all their glory vanished. All the wealth and treasure they had collected over many years was seized. No one can recall any war against the Franks that left them richer or better stocked with resources. Until then they had seemed almost impoverished. So much gold and silver was found in the [khan's] palace and so many precious objects were taken in this war, that it might be fairly said that the Franks had justly seized from the Huns what the Huns had unjustly seized from other peoples. Only two Frankish leaders died in that war: Eric, the duke of Friuli, who was ambushed by the people of Tersatto, a seaside city in Liburnia and Gerold, the governor of Bavaria....

14. Charles's final war was the one taken up against the Northmen who are called Danes. First they had operated as pirates, but then they raided the coasts of Gaul and Germany with larger fleets. Their king, Godefrid, was so filled with vain ambition, that he vowed to take control of all Germany. Indeed, he already thought of Frisia and Saxony as his own provinces and had [first] brought the Abodrites, who were his neighbors, under his power and [then] made them pay tribute to him. He even bragged that he would soon come to Aachen, where king [Charles] held court, with a vast army. Some stock was put in his boast, although it was idle, for it was believed that he was about to start something like this, but was suddenly stopped by death. For he was murdered by one of his own attendants and, thus, both his life and the war he had begun came to a sudden end [at the same time].

15. These [then] were the wars that that mighty king waged with great skill and success in many lands over the forty-seven years he reigned. In those wars he so splendidly added to the Frankish kingdom, which he had received

in great and strong condition from his father Pepin, that he nearly doubled its size....

16. He also increased the glory of his kingdom by winning over kings and peoples through friendly means. In this way he so completely won over Alfonso [II], the king of Galicia and Asturias, that when he sent letters or emissaries to Charles, he ordered that in Charles's presence he was only to be referred to as his subject. By his generosity he had so impressed the Irish kings with his goodwill, that they publicly declared that he was certainly their lord and they were his subjects and servants. Some letters they sent to [Charles] still survive and testify to this sort of feeling toward him.

He had such friendly relations with Harun-al-Raschid, the king of the Persians,[1] who held almost all the east except India, that [Harun] counted the favor of his friendship as more valuable than that of all the kings and rulers in the world and thought that only [Charles] was worthy of receiving his honor and generosity. Indeed, when [Charles's] representatives, whom he had sent loaded with gifts for the most Holy Sepulcher of our Lord and Savior [in Jerusalem] and for the place of his resurrection, came before [Harun] and informed him of their lord's wishes, he not only allowed them to complete their mission, but even handed over that sacred and salvific place, so that it might be considered as under Charles's control.[2] [Harun] sent his own representatives back with [Charles's] and he sent magnificent gifts for him, among which were robes, spices, and other riches of the east. A few years before this he had sent an elephant, the only one he then possessed, to Charles who had asked him [for such an animal].

The emperors of Constantinople, Nicephorus [I], Michael [I], and Leo [V], who were also voluntarily seeking friendship and an alliance with Charles, sent many representatives to him. But when he took up the title of emperor, [it seemed] to them that he might want to seize their empire. Thus, [Charles] struck a very strong treaty [with them], so that no [potential] source of trouble of any sort might remain between them. For the Romans and Greeks were always suspicious of Frankish power; hence that Greek proverb which still circulates: "Have a Frank as a friend, never as a neighbor."

17. Despite being so committed to increasing the size of the kingdom and to subduing foreign peoples and being so constantly preoccupied with business of this kind, [Charles] still took up many projects in different places to improve and beautify the kingdom. He achieved some of them, but not all. Probably the most outstanding of these [projects] are the church of the Holy Mother of God in Aachen, which is a remarkable edifice, and the bridge spanning the Rhine River at Mainz, which was half a mile long, the width of the river at that point. But that bridge burned down the year before Charles died. Although he thought of rebuilding it, this time in stone rather than wood, his sudden death prevented that. He also began [to build two] splendid palaces, one not far from the city of Mainz, on the [royal] estate of Ingelheim, and the other at Nijmegen on the River Waal, which passes along the south side of the island of the Batavians. Even then, if he learned that sacred churches had fallen into ruin because of their age anywhere in his kingdom, he ordered the bishops and priests responsible for them to repair them and charged his representatives with insuring that his orders had been followed.

He [also] constructed a fleet for use against the Northmen. Ships were built for this purpose near the rivers that flow from Gaul and Germany into the North Sea. Since the Northmen were constantly raiding and ravaging the coasts of Gaul and Germany, fortifications and guards were set up at all the ports and at the mouth of every river that seemed large enough to accommodate ships. With such fortifications he stopped the enemy from being able to come and go [freely]. He took the same [precautions] in the south, along the coasts of the province of Narbonne and Septimania and along the whole coast of Italy up to Rome, where the Moors[3] had recently taken to plundering. Through these measures, Italy suffered no great harm from the Moors while [Charles] lived, nor did Gaul and Germany suffer from the Northmen. The Moors did, however, through betrayal capture and pillage Civitavécchia, a city of Etruria, and the Northmen raided some islands in Frisia not far from the German coastline.

18. It is widely recognized that, in these ways, [Charles] protected, increased the size of, and beautified his kingdom. Now I should begin at this point to speak of the

---

[1] Harun (r.786–809) was the caliph at Baghdad.

[2] One of Charlemagne's ambassadors had obtained the keys of the Holy Sepulcher from the Patriarch of Jerusalem in 799. Harun had nothing to do with this, and Jerusalem was never under Charlemagne's control.

[3] Muslims.

character of his mind, his supreme steadfastness in good times and bad, and those other things that belong to his spiritual and domestic life.

After the death of his father [in 768], when he was sharing the kingdom with his brother [Carloman], he endured the pettiness and jealousy of his brother with such great patience, that it seemed remarkable to all that he could not be provoked to anger by him. Then [in 770], at the urging of his mother [Bertrada], he married a daughter of Desiderius, the king of the Lombards, but for some unknown reason he sent her away after a year and took Hildegard [758–783], a Swabian woman of distinct nobility. She bore him three sons, namely Charles, Pepin, and Louis, and the same number of daughters, Rotrude, Bertha, and Gisela. He had three other daughters, Theoderada, Hiltrude, and Rothaide, two by his wife Fastrada, who was an eastern Frank (that is to say, German), and a third by some concubine, whose name now escapes me. When Fastrada died [in 794], [Charles] married Liutgard, an Alemannian woman, who bore no children. After her death [in 800], he took four concubines: Madelgard, who gave birth to a daughter by the name of Ruothilde; Gersvinda, a Saxon, by whom a daughter by the name of Adaltrude was born; Regina, who bore Drogo and Hugh; and Adallinda who gave him Theoderic.

[Charles's] mother, Bertrada, also spent her old age in great honor with him. He treated her with the greatest respect, to the point that there was never any trouble between them, except over the divorce of King Desiderius's daughter, whom he had married at her urging. She died [in 783], not long after Hildegard's death, but [had lived long enough] to have seen three grandsons and the same number of granddaughters in her son's house. [Charles] saw to it that she was buried with great honor in St-Denis, the same church where his father lay.

He had only one sister, whose name was Gisela. She had devoted herself to the religious life from the time she was a girl. As he had with his mother, he treated her with the greatest affection. She died a few years before him [in 810] in the monastery [that is, the convent of Chelles where she was abbess] in which she had spent her life.

19. [Charles] believed that his children, both his daughters and his sons, should be educated, first in the liberal arts, which he himself had studied. Then, he saw to it that when the boys had reached the right age they were trained to ride in the Frankish fashion, to fight, and to hunt. But he ordered his daughters to learn how to work with wool, how to spin and weave it, so that they might not grow dull from inactivity and [instead might] learn to value work and virtuous activity.

Out of all these children he lost only two sons and one daughter before he himself died: Charles, his eldest son [who died in 811], Pepin, whom he had set up as king of Italy [died in 810], and Rotrude, his eldest daughter, who [in 781] was engaged to Constantine, emperor of the Greeks [she died in 810]. Pepin left behind only one surviving son, Bernard [who died in 818], but five daughters: Adelhaid, Atula, Gundrada, Berthaid, and Theoderada. The king displayed a special token of affection toward his [grandchildren], since when his son [Pepin] died he saw to it that his grandson [Bernard] succeeded his father [as king of Italy] and he arranged for his granddaughters to be raised alongside his own daughters. Despite the surpassing greatness [of his spirit], he was deeply disturbed by the deaths of his sons and daughter, and his affection [toward his children], which was just as strong [a part of his character], drove him to tears.

When he was informed of the death of Hadrian, the Roman pontiff [d.795], he cried so much that it was as if he had lost a brother or a deeply loved son, for he had thought of him as a special friend. [Charles] was, by nature, a good friend, for he easily made friends and firmly held on to them. Indeed, he treated with the greatest respect those he had bound closely to himself in a relationship of this sort.

He was so attentive to raising his sons and daughters, that when he was home he always ate his meals with them and when he traveled he always took them with him, his sons riding beside him, while his daughters followed behind. A special rearguard of his men was appointed to watch over them. Although his daughters were extremely beautiful women and were deeply loved by him, it is strange to have to report that he never wanted to give any of them away in marriage to anyone, whether it be to a Frankish noble or to a foreigner. Instead he kept them close beside him at home until his death, saying that he could not stand to be parted from their company. Although he was otherwise happy, this situation [that is, the affairs of his daughters] caused him no end of trouble. But he always acted as if there was no suspicion of any sexual scandal on their part or that any such rumor had already spread far and wide.

20. Earlier I chose not to mention with the others [Charles's] son Pepin [the Hunchback] who was born to him by a concubine [named Himiltrude]. He was hand-

some in appearance, but hunchbacked. When his father had taken up the war against the Huns [in 792] and was wintering in Bavaria, [Pepin] pretended to be sick and entered into a conspiracy against his father with certain leading Franks who had enticed him with the false promise of a kingdom [of his own]. After the plot was uncovered and the conspirators were condemned, [Pepin] was tonsured and allowed to pursue the religious life he had always wanted in the monastery of Prüm [where he died in 811].

Another powerful conspiracy against Charles had arisen even earlier [in 785–786] in Germany, but all its perpetrators [led by Hardrad] were sent into exile; some blinded, others unharmed. Only three conspirators lost their lives, since to avoid arrest they had drawn their swords to defend themselves and had even killed some men [in the process]. They were cut down themselves, because there was [simply] no other way to subdue them. But it is [widely] believed that the cruelty of Queen Fastrada was the cause and source of these conspiracies, since in both cases these men conspired against the king because it looked as if [Charles] had savagely departed from his usual kind and gentle ways by consenting to the cruel ways of his wife. Otherwise, [Charles] passed his whole life with the highest love and esteem of everyone, both at home and abroad, and not the least charge of cruelty or unfairness was ever brought against him by anyone....

22. [Charles] had a large and powerful body. He was tall [at slightly over six feet or 1.83 meters], but not disproportionately so, since it is known that his height was seven times the length of his own foot. The crown of his head was round, his eyes were noticeably large and full of life, his nose was a little longer than average, his hair was grey and handsome, and his face was attractive and cheerful. Hence, his physical presence was [always] commanding and dignified, whether he was sitting or standing. Although his neck seemed short and thick and his stomach seemed to stick out, the symmetry of the other parts [of his body] hid these [flaws]. [When he walked] his pace was strong and the entire bearing of his body powerful. Indeed, his voice was distinct, but not as [strong as might have been] expected given his size. His health was good until four years before he died, when he suffered from constant fevers. Toward the very end [of his life] he also became lame in one foot. Even then he trusted his own judgment more than the advice of his physicians, whom he almost loathed, since they urged

him to stop eating roast meat, which he liked, and to start eating boiled meat [which he did not].

He kept busy by riding and hunting frequently, which came naturally to him. Indeed, there is hardly a people on earth who can rival the Franks in this skill. [Charles] also liked the steam produced by natural hot springs and the exercise that came from swimming frequently. He was so good at swimming that no one was considered better than him. For this reason [that is, the existence of the hot springs], he built his palace in Aachen and lived there permanently during the final years of his life until he died. He invited not only his sons to the baths, but also his nobles and friends. Sometimes he invited such a crowd of courtiers and bodyguards, that there might be more than a hundred people bathing together.

23. He normally wore the customary attire of the Franks. [Closest] to his body he put on a linen shirt and underwear, then a silk-fringed tunic and stockings. He wrapped his lower legs with cloth coverings and put shoes on his feet. In winter he covered his shoulders and chest with a vest made of otter or ermine skin, above which he wore a blue cloak. He was always armed with a sword, whose handle and belt were made of gold or silver. On occasion he bore a jeweled sword, but only on special feast days or if the representatives of foreign peoples had come [to see him]. He rejected foreign clothes, however gorgeous they might be, and never agreed to be dressed in them, except once in Rome when Pope Hadrian had requested it and, on another occasion, when his successor Leo had begged him to wear a long tunic, chlamys [a Greek mantle], and shoes designed in the Roman [that is to say, Greek] fashion. On high feast days he normally walked in the procession dressed in clothes weaved with gold, bejeweled shoes, in a cloak fastened by a golden clasp, and also wearing a golden, gem-encrusted crown. But on other days his attire differed little from people's usual attire.

24. [Charles] was moderate when it came to both food and drink, but he was even more moderate in the case of drink, since he deeply detested [seeing] anyone inebriated, especially himself or his men. But he was not able to abstain from food, and often complained that fasting was bad for his health. He seldom put on [large] banquets, but when he did it was for a great number of people on special feast days. His dinner each day was served in four courses only, not including the roast, which his hunters used to carry in on a spit. He preferred [roast meat] over all other food. While eating, he was entertained or

listened to someone read out the histories and deeds of the ancients. He was fond of the books of Saint Augustine, particularly the one called the *City of God*.[1]

He was so restrained in his consumption of wine and other drinks, that he seldom drank more than three times during a meal. After his midday meal in the summertime, he would eat some fruit and take a single drink. Then, after he had removed his clothes and shoes, just as he did at night, he would lie down for two or three hours. While sleeping at night, he would not only wake four or five times, but would even get up. [In the morning] while putting on his shoes and dressing, he not only saw friends, but if the count of the palace informed him that there was some unresolved dispute that could not be sorted our without his judgment, he would order him to bring the disputing parties before him at once. Then, as if he were sitting in court, he heard the nature of the dispute and rendered his opinion. He not only looked after cases such as this at that time, but also matters of any sort that needed to be handled that day or to be assigned to one of his officials.

25. [Charles] was a gifted and ready speaker, able to express clearly whatever he wished to say. Not being content with knowing only his own native tongue [German], he also made an effort to learn foreign languages. Among those, he learned Latin so well, that he spoke it as well as he did his own native language, but he was able to understand Greek better than he could speak it. Indeed, he was such a fluent speaker, that [at times] he actually seemed verbose.

He avidly pursued the liberal arts and greatly honored those teachers whom he deeply respected. To learn grammar, he followed [the teaching of] Peter of Pisa, an aged deacon. For the other disciplines, he took as his teacher Alcuin of Britain, also known as Albinus, who was a deacon as well, but from the [Anglo-]Saxon people. He was the most learned man in the entire world. [Charles] invested a great deal of time and effort studying rhetoric, dialectic, and particularly astronomy with him. He learned the art of calculation [arithmetic] and with deep purpose and great curiosity investigated the movement of the stars. He also attempted to [learn how to] write and, for this reason, used to place wax-tablets and notebooks under the pillows on his bed, so that, if he had any free time, he might accustom his hand to forming letters. But his effort came too late in life and achieved little success.

26. With great piety and devotion [Charles] followed the Christian religion, in which he had been reared from infancy. For this reason he constructed a church of stunning beauty at Aachen and adorned it with gold and silver, with lamps, grillwork, and doors made of solid bronze. When he could not obtain the columns and marble for this building from any place else, he took the trouble to have them brought from Rome and Ravenna. As long as his health allowed him to, [Charles] regularly went to church both morning and evening, and also to the night reading and to the morning Mass. He was particularly concerned that everything done in the church should be done with the greatest dignity and he frequently warned the sacristans that nothing foul or unclean should be brought into the church or left there. He made sure that his church was supplied with such an abundance of sacred vessels made of gold and silver and with such a great number of clerical vestments, that, indeed, in the celebration of the Mass not even those looking after the doors, who hold the lowest of all ecclesiastical orders, found it necessary to serve in their normal clothes. He very carefully corrected the way in which the lessons were read and the psalms sung, for he was quite skilled at both. But he himself never read publicly and would only sing quietly with the rest of the congregation.

27. [Charles] was so deeply committed to assisting the poor spontaneously with charity, which the Greeks call alms, that he not only made the effort to give alms in his own land and kingdom, but even overseas in Syria, Egypt, and Africa. When he learned that the Christians in Jerusalem, Alexandria, and Carthage were living in poverty, he was moved by their impoverished condition and used to send money. It was chiefly for this reason that he struck up friendships with kings overseas, so that the poor Christians living under their rule might receive some relief and assistance.

He loved the church of St. Peter the Apostle in Rome more than all other sacred and venerable places and showered its altars with a great wealth of gold, silver, and even gems. He [also] sent a vast number of gifts to the popes. During his whole reign he regarded nothing as more important than to restore through his material help and labor the ancient glory of the city of Rome. Not only did he protect and defend the church of St. Peter, but with his own money he even embellished and enriched it above all other churches. Despite holding it in

---

1 See the excerpt from this book above, p. 14.

such high regard, he only traveled there four times during the twenty-seven years he reigned [in 774, 785, 787, and 800–801] to fulfill his vows and pray.

28. The reasons for his last visit [to Rome] were not just those [that is, his religious vows and for prayer], but rather because residents of Rome had attacked Pope Leo [III]. They had inflicted many injuries on him, including ripping out his eyes and cutting off his tongue.[1] This [attack] forced him to appeal to the loyalty of the king [in 799 at Paderborn]. Thus, [Charles] traveled to Rome to restore the state of the church, which was extremely disrupted, and he spent the whole winter there [until April 801]. It was at that time that he received the title of emperor and augustus, which at first he disliked so much that he stated that, if he had known in advance of the pope's plan, he would not have entered the church that day, even though it was a great feast day [Christmas 800]. But he bore the animosity that the assumption of this title caused with great patience, for the Roman [that is, Greek] emperors were angry over it. He overcame their opposition through the greatness of his spirit, which was without doubt far greater than theirs, and by often sending representatives to them and by calling them his brothers in his letters.

29. After assuming the imperial title, [Charles] realized that there were many deficiencies in the laws of his own people, for the Franks have two sets of laws that differ tremendously at a number of points. He decided, therefore, to fill in what was lacking, to reconcile the disagreements, and also to set right what was bad and wrongly expressed. He did nothing more about this than to add a few items to these laws, but even those were left in an imperfect state. But he did direct that the unwritten laws of all the peoples under his control should be gathered up and written down.

[Charles] also [ordered] that the very old Germanic poems, in which the deeds and wars of ancient kings were sung, should be written down and preserved for posterity. He began [as well] a grammar of his native language. He even gave [German] names to the months, since before then the Franks were used to referring to them by a mix of Latin and Germanic names. He also assigned individual names to the twelve winds, since until then scarcely more than four of them had been named....

30. At the very end of his life, when he was already weighed down by poor health and old age, [Charles] summoned his son Louis [the Pious], the king of Aquitaine and the only one of Hildegard's sons still alive, to come to him. When all the leading Franks from the entire kingdom had solemnly assembled and had given their opinion, he established Louis as the co-ruler of the entire kingdom and the heir to the imperial title. Then [on 11 September 813] he placed a crown upon his [son's] head and ordered that he should [henceforth] be addressed as emperor and augustus. This decision of his was widely approved by all who were present, for it seemed to have been divinely inspired in him for the general good of the kingdom. This act [the elevation of Louis] enhanced his powerful reputation and filled foreign peoples with great fear.

[Charles] then sent his son back to Aquitaine and, despite being slowed down by old age, went hunting, as was his usual habit. But he did nor travel far from the palace at Aachen and passed what was left of the autumn hunting. He returned to Aachen around the beginning of November [813]. While spending the winter there, he was overcome by a strong fever and took to his bed in January. He immediately decided to abstain from food, as he usually did when he had a fever, because he thought that he could overcome the sickness by fasting or, at least, relieve [its symptoms]. But on top of the fever he developed a pain in his side, which the Greeks call pleurisy. Still he continued his fast and sustained his body with nothing more than an occasional drink. On the seventh day after taking to his bed, he died after receiving Holy Communion. It was nine o'clock in the morning on 28 January [814]. He died in the seventy-second year of his life and in the forty-seventh year of his reign.

31. His body was washed and looked after in a solemn manner and was [then] carried into the church and interred while everyone there wept. At first there had been some uncertainty about where he should be laid to rest, since when he was alive he had specified nothing about it. Finally everyone agreed that the most honorable place for him to be entombed was, in fact, in the very cathedral that he himself had built out of his own resources in Aachen, for the love of God and our Lord Jesus Christ and to honor his mother, the holy and eternal Virgin. He was buried in that church on the same day on which he died and a gilded arch with an image and

---

[1] The attack attempted to mutilate the pope, but it did not succeed.

inscription was erected above his tomb. That inscription ran as follows:

> UNDER THIS TOMB LIES THE BODY OF CHARLES, THE GREAT AND CATHOLIC EMPEROR, WHO GLORIOUSLY INCREASED THE KINGDOM OF THE FRANKS AND REIGNED WITH GREAT SUCCESS FOR FORTY-SEVEN YEARS. HE DIED IN HIS SEVENTIES, IN THE SEVENTH INDICTION, ON THE TWENTY-EIGHTH DAY OF JANUARY, IN THE YEAR OF THE LORD 814.

32. There were so many signs of his approaching death, that not only other people, but even he himself knew that the end was near. For three straight years near the end of his life there were frequent eclipses of the sun and moon and a dark mark was seen on [the face of] the sun for a space of seven days. The arcade that he had erected with great effort between the church and palace fell to the ground in unexpected ruin on the day of the Ascension of our Lord. Similarly, the bridge over the Rhine River at Mainz, which he built, had taken ten years to complete. Though it was built out of wood with such great labor and remarkable skill that it seemed that it might last forever, it accidentally caught on fire and burned down in three hours [in May 813]. In fact, not a single piece of the bridge's wood survived, except some that was below water.

He himself, when he was waging his last campaign [in 810] in Saxony against Godefrid, the king of the Danes, was leaving camp before dawn one morning, when he saw a brilliant meteor suddenly fall from the sky. It cut across the open sky from right to left. As everyone pondered what this sign meant, the horse on which [Charles] was sitting suddenly fell down headfirst and threw him to the ground with such a bang that the clasp holding his cloak snapped and his sword belt was ripped off. The attendants who were present rushed to his side and lifted him up without his weapons or mantle. Even the javelin that he had been grasping tightly in his hand had fallen and now lay twenty feet or more distant from him.

Added to these events, the palace at Aachen frequently shook [from earthquakes] and the [wooden] ceilings of the buildings in which he lived constantly creaked. The church in which he was later entombed was hit by lightning and the golden apple that stood at the peak of the roof was struck by lightning and landed on top of the bishop's house next door. In that same church an inscrip-

tion written in red letters that ran between the upper and lower arches along the inside of the building [the inner octagon] gave the name of the builder of the church. In the last line of that inscription [the words] KAROLVS PRINCEPS[1] were to be read. But it was observed by some people that in the very year he died, a few months before his death, the letter that formed PRINCEPS became so faint that they were almost invisible. Yet Charles either rejected all these things or acted as if none of them had anything to do with him.

33. [Charles had] decided to draw up a will, so that he might make his daughters and illegitimate children heirs to some part of his estate. But the will was left too late and could not be completed. Nevertheless, three years before he died, he divided up his precious possessions, money, clothes, and other moveable goods in the presence of his friends and officials. He called on them to insure that, with their support, the division he had made would remain fixed and in force after his death. He described in a charter what he wanted done with the goods he had [so] divided. The terms and text of this [division of properties] are such:

In the name of the Lord God Almighty—the Father, Son, and Holy Spirit—[this] inventory and division [of goods] was made by the most glorious and pious Lord Charles, emperor and augustus, in the eight hundred and eleventh year from the Incarnation of our Lord Jesus Christ [that is, 810], in the forty-third year of his reign in Francia and thirty-sixth in Italy, [and] in the eleventh year of his empire, and in the fourth Indiction.

With pious and prudent reflection he decided to make this inventory and division of his precious possessions and the wealth that was located in his treasury on that day and with God's support he accomplished it. In this division he particularly wanted to insure that not only the gift of alms, which Christians solemnly provide for from their own resources, would be looked after on his behalf out of his own wealth and in an orderly and reasonable manner, but also that his heirs should be in no doubt as to what would come to them and so that they might plainly know and divide without legal strife or dispute those things among themselves in an appropriate partition [of goods].

Therefore, with this intention and purpose in mind, he first divided all the wealth and moveable goods (that is, all the gold, silver, precious stones, and royal vestments), that were found in the treasury on that day, into three lots. Then he subdivided two of those [three] lots into twenty-one parts, but kept the other lot whole. He divided those two lots into twenty-one parts because

---

[1] I.e., Prince Charles.

there are twenty-one metropolitan cities in his kingdom. In the name of charity his heirs and friends should pass one of those [twenty-one] parts to each metropolitan city. The archbishop then presiding over that church should receive the part given to his church and divide it among his suffragans [i.e. his bishops] in this way: one third should remain with his own church, two thirds should be divided among the suffragans [of his diocese]. Each of these divisions, which was made from the first two lots according to the recognized existence of the twenty-one metropolitan cites, has been separated off from the others and lies individually stored in its own repository under the name of the city to which it should be carried. The names of the metropolitan cities to which these alms or gifts should be given are: Rome, Ravenna, Milan, Cividale del Friuli [Aquiliea], Grado, Cologne, Mainz, Salzburg, Trier, Sens, Besançon, Lyons, Rouen, Rheims, Arles, Vienne, Moutiers-en-Tarantaise, Embrun, Bordeaux, Tours, and Bourges.

He wished the third lot to be kept intact so that, while the [other] two lots had been stored under seal in the [twenty-one] parts described, this third lot might serve his own daily needs as if it were property which he was under no obligation to part with or see alienated from his direct possession. This [arrangement] should hold for as long as he lived or he deemed the use [of the property] necessary for his well-being. But after his death or voluntary withdrawal from the world [into a monastery], this [third] lot should be divided into four parts and one of them should be added to the already [allotted] twenty-one parts. Another [the second] part should be taken up and divided by his sons and daughters, and by the sons and daughters of his sons in a fair and reasonable partition [of goods]. The third part, in keeping with Christian practice, should be set aside for the poor. The fourth part should, in like charitable fashion, be set aside to support the male and female servants of the palace itself. It was his wish to add to the third lot of his complete wealth, which also consists of gold and silver, everything else that was found in his treasury and wardrobe on the day [of his death]: namely, all the vessels and utensils of bronze, iron, and other metals, along with the arms, garments, and other moveable goods, both precious and ordinary, used for various things, such as curtains, bedspreads, tapestries, woolen goods, leather articles, and saddles. [He hoped] in this way that the size of the parts of the third lot would increase and that the distribution of charity would reach more people.

He arranged that his chapel, that is to say its church property, both that which he himself had provided and gathered together, and that which had come by way of family inheritance, should remain whole and not be divided up in any way. If, however, any vessels, books, or other objects should be found in the chapel which he had not indisputably given to the chapel, these could be purchased and retained by anyone who wished to have them after a fair price was determined. He similarly stipulated that the books that he had collected in great number in his personal library could be sold for a fair price to people who wished to own them and that the money [so raised] should be distributed among the poor.

Among his other possessions and riches, it is known that there are three silver tables and a gold one of great size and weight. He arranged and ordered that one of the silver tables, a square-shaped one containing an outline of the city of Constantinople, was to be sent to Rome to the church of St. Peter the Apostle along with the other gifts assigned to the saint. Another [silver table], this one having a round shape and bearing a likeness of the city of Rome, was to be transported to the episcopal seat of Ravenna. The third [silver table], which far surpasses the others in the beauty of its workmanship and its weight, contains a delicate and fine line drawing of the whole universe set within three linked circles. He stipulated that it and the gold table, which is referred to as the fourth, should be used to increase the third lot among his heirs and to increase the share of charity to be distributed from it.

[Charles] made and established this disposition and arrangement [of his goods] in the presence of the bishops, abbots, and counts who were able to be present at that time. Their names are inscribed here. The bishops [were] Hildebald [archbishop of Cologne], Richolf [archbishop of Mainz], Arn [archbishop of Salzburg], Wolfar [archbishop of Rheims], Bernoin [archbishop of Clermont], Leidrad [archbishop of Lyons], John [archbishop of Arles], Theodulf [bishop of Orléans], Jesse [bishop of Amiens], Heito [bishop of Basel], [and] Waltgaud [bishop of Liège]. The abbots [were] Fridugis [of St-Martin of Tours], Adalung [of Lorsch], Angilbert [of St-Riquier], Irmino [of St-Germain-des-Prés]. The counts were Wala, Meginher, Otulf, Stephen, Unruoc, Burchard, Meginhard, Hatto, Rihwin, Edo, Ercangar, Gerold, Bero, Hildigern, Hroccolf.

After examining this same charter his son Louis, who succeeded by divine right, saw to it that [this division of properties] was fulfilled as quickly and faithfully as possible after his [father's] death.

3.12 Modeling the state on Old Testament Israel: *The Admonitio Generalis* (789). Original in Latin.

Eleven years before he was crowned emperor, King Charlemagne drew up a set of general instructions, *The Admonitio Generalis*, for the great men of his realm, both lay and ecclesiastical, "to lead the people of God to the pastures of eternal life." He took as his model the biblical King Josiah, who discovered a copy of "the book of the law," realized how badly his people deviated from what was written therein, and immediately took steps to reform his kingdom (see 2 Kings 22–23). In effect, the many laws set forth by *The Admonitio Generalis*, only some of which are excerpted here, were Charlemagne's attempts to govern his kingdom according to the laws of God.

[Source: *Christianity through the Thirteenth Century*, ed. Marshall W. Baldwin (New York: Harper and Row, 1970), pp. 115–19.]

Our Lord Jesus Christ ruling forever.

I, Charles by the grace of God and the gift of His mercy, king and ruler of the kingdom of the Franks, devout defender and humble supporter of holy church, give greetings of lasting peace and beatitude to all grades of the ecclesiastical order and to all ranks of the secular power, in Christ our Lord, eternal God. Reflecting with dutiful and calm consideration, along with our priests and councilors, on the abundant mercy of Christ the King toward us and our people, we have considered how necessary it is not only with our whole heart and voice to offer thanks for His goodness unceasingly, but also to persist in the continuous exercise of good works in His praise so that He who has given our kingdom such honors may deign to preserve and protect us and our kingdom forever. Accordingly it has pleased us to solicit your efforts, O pastors of the churches of Christ and leaders of His flock and distinguished luminaries of the world, to strive to lead the people of God to the pastures of eternal life by watchful care and urgent advice and stir yourselves to bring back the wandering sheep within the walls of ecclesiastical constancy on the shoulders of good example or exhortation, lest the wolf, plotting against anyone who transgresses the canonical laws or evades the fatherly traditions of the ecumenical councils—which God forbid!—find him and devour him. Thus they must be admonished, urged, and even forced by the great zeal of piety, to restrain themselves within the bonds of paternal sanctions with staunch faith and unrelenting constancy. Therefore, we have sent our missi who by the authority of our name are to correct along with you what should be corrected. And we append herewith certain chapters from canonical ordinances which seem to us to be particularly necessary.

Let no one judge this admonition to piety, by which we endeavor to correct errors, remove superfluous matter, and condense those things which are right, to be presumptuous. I entreat him rather to accept it with a benevolent spirit of charity. For we read in the book of Kings how the holy Josiah, traveling around the kingdom bestowed on him by God, correcting and admonishing, labored to recall it to the worship of the true God: not that I hold myself equal to his holiness, but because the examples of the saints are always to be followed by us, and we must bring together whomsoever we can to a devotion to the good life in the praise and glory of our Lord Jesus Christ....

Chapter 70, to the Clergy

Bishops should carefully see to it that throughout their dioceses (*parochiae*) the priests observe their Catholic faith and baptism and understand well the prayers of the mass; and that the psalms are chanted properly according to the divisions of the verses and that they understand the Lord's Prayer and preach that it is to be understood by all, so that each person may know what he is asking of God; and that the "Glory be to the Father" be sung with all dignity by everyone and that the priest himself with the holy angels and all the people of God with one voice intone the "Holy, Holy, Holy." And it should in every way be made clear to priests and deacons that they should not bear arms but trust in the protection of God rather than in arms.

Chapter 71, Something to the Priest, Something to People

It is likewise our will to urge your reverences that each throughout his diocese see that the church of God is held in His honor and the altars venerated with suitable dignity, and that the house of God is not used as a pathway for dogs and that the vessels consecrated to God are kept with great care or used with honor; and that secular or mundane affairs are not transacted in churches because the house of God must be a house of prayer and not a den of thieves;[1] and that the people when they come to the solemnities of the mass are attentive and do not leave before the completion of the priest's blessing.

Chapter 72, to the Clergy

And we also demand of your holiness that the ministers of the altar of God shall adorn their ministry by good manners, and likewise the other orders who observe a rule and the congregations of monks. We implore them to lead a just and fitting life, just as God himself commanded in the Gospel. "Let your light so shine before men that they may see your good works and glorify your Father which is in heaven,"[2] so that by their example many may be led to serve God; and let them join and associate to themselves not only children of servile condition, but also sons of free men. And let schools be established in which boys may learn to read. Correct carefully the Psalms, the signs in writing (notas), the songs, the calendar, the grammar in each monastery or bishopric, and the catholic books; because often some desire to pray to God properly, but they pray badly because of the incorrect books. And do not permit your boys to corrupt them in reading or writing. If there is need of writing the Gospel, Psalter, and Missal, let men of mature age do the writing with all diligence.

Chapter 73, to the Clergy

We have likewise taken pains to ask that all, wherever they are, who have bound themselves by the vow of a monastic life live in every way regularly in a monastic manner according to that vow. For it is written, "Render your vows to the Lord God";[3] and again, "it is better not to vow than not to fulfill."[4] And let those coming to monasteries according to the regular manner be first tested in the examination room and so accepted. And let those who come to the monastery from the secular life not be sent immediately on monastic tasks outside before they are well educated within. And monks are not to seek worldly pleasures. Likewise, those who are admitted to that clerical state which we call the canonical life, we desire that they live such a life canonically and in every way according to its rule; and the bishop should govern their life as the abbot does the monks.

Chapter 74, to All

Let all have equal and correct weights and just and equal measures, whether in the towns or in the monasteries, whether in giving in them or in receiving, as we have the command in the law of the Lord,[5] and likewise in Solomon, when the Lord says, "[Different] weight and [different] measure, my soul abhors."[6] …

Chapter 80, to All the Clergy

Let them teach fully the Roman chant and let the office be followed according to the direction of the nocturnal or gradual as our father Pepin, of blessed memory, ordered done when he suppressed the Gallican use for the sake of unity with the apostolic see and the peaceful harmony of the holy church of God.[7]

---

[1] See Matt. 21: 13.

[2] Matt. 5: 16.

[3] Deut. 23: 21.

[4] Eccles. 5: 4.

[5] See Lev. 19: 35–36.

[6] Prov. 20: 10.

[7] The "Gallican use" refers to the words and melodies used in Church liturgy in Francia under the Merovingians. Although Charlemagne here attributes the suppression of this liturgy to his father, Pippin III (d.768), in fact it was Charlemagne himself who was most instrumental in reforming the chants used in his kingdom along Roman models.

Chapter 81, to All

And we also decree, according to what the Lord ordained in the law,[1] that there be no servile work on Sundays, as my father, of good memory, ordered in the edicts of his synods, that is: that men do no farm work, either in plowing fields or in tending vineyards, in sowing grain or planting hedges, in clearing in the woods or in cutting trees, in working with stone or in building houses, or in working in the garden; nor are they to gather for games or go hunting. Three tasks with wagons may be performed on Sunday, the arms' cart or the food wagon, or if it is necessary to bear someone's body to the grave.

Likewise, women are not to work with cloth nor cut out clothes, nor sew or embroider; nor is it permissible to comb wool or crush flax or wash clothes in public, or shear sheep, to the end that the honor and quiet of the Lord's day be kept. But let people come together from all places to the church for the solemnities of the mass and praise God on that day for all the good things He has done for us.

Chapter 82, to All

And you are to see to it, O chosen and venerable pastors and rulers of the church of God, that the priests whom you send through your dioceses (*parochiae*) for ruling and preaching in the churches to the people serving God, that they rightly and justly preach; and you are not to allow any of them to invent and preach to the people new and unlawful things according to their own judgment and not according to Holy Scripture. And you too are to preach those things which are just and right and lead to eternal life, and instruct others that they are to preach these same things.

3.13 Ideals of family and fidelity: Dhuoda, *Handbook for Her Son* (841–843). Original in Latin.

A precious document for the values of the Carolingian laity—or, more precisely, for aristocratic lay women of the time—Dhuoda's *Handbook for Her Son* was written in the time of crisis just before the Treaty of Verdun (843). Her husband, Bernard, count of the Spanish March (Septimania), had once been an important courtier under Louis the Pious, but, accused of adultery with the queen, he was expelled from the court by Louis's sons. Her son William, to whom she wrote, was being held hostage at the court of Charles the Bald, partly to guarantee his father's "good behavior" and partly to ensure William's own advancement at court. Dhuoda herself was in the south of the Frankish kingdom, attempting, as she put it, "to defend the interests of my lord and master, Bernard." She had just given birth to another son, whom Bernard had "brought to him in Aquitaine." In her *Handbook*, motherhood, politics, and religion mingle as she tries to define a righteous and honorable rule of conduct for this life and the next. Just as Carolingian court scholars wrote "Mirrors of Princes" for kings to model themselves upon (see Einhard, p. 135 above), so Dhuoda wrote a "mirror" for her son in which he could "contemplate the health" of his soul, measuring it against the mirror's standard. We have no idea how William responded to Dhuoda's advice. Bernard was executed by the king shortly after she wrote, and William was executed in 850. Dhuoda may have died before she knew about these sad events; she was certainly contemplating death as she wrote her *Handbook*'s near-final section (Book 10). Compare the sources of conduct and the ideals of behavior that Dhuoda presents to William with those in *The Benedictine Rule* (p. 17 above). What evidence can you find

---

[1] See Exod. 20: 8–10.

in Dhuoda's writings to suggest that the Carolingian laity was influenced by the norms of monasticism? What evidence is there for other—and divergent—ideals, and where might they have come from? What does Dhuoda's writing suggest about the nature of lay aristocratic education in the Carolingian empire?

[Source: *Handbook for William: A Carolingian Woman's Counsel for Her Son*, trans. Carol Neel (Washington, DC: Catholic University of America Press, 1991), pp. 1, 5–6, 21–23, 95–100, and corresponding notes (notes slightly modified).]

The little book before you branches out in three directions. Read it through and, by the end, you will understand what I mean. I would like it to be called three things at once, as befits its contents—rule, model, and handbook.[1] These terms all mirror each other. The rule comes from me, the model is for you, and the handbook is as much from me as for you—composed by me, received by you....

Here Begins the Prologue.

Things that are obvious to many people often escape me. Those who are like me lack understanding and have dim insight, but I am even less capable than they.[2] Yet always there is he at my side who "opened the mouths of the dumb, and made the tongues of infants eloquent."[3] I, Dhuoda, despite my weakness of mind, unworthy as I am among worthy women—I am still your mother, my son William, and it is to you that I now address the words of my handbook. From time to time children are fascinated by dice more than all the other games that they enjoy. And sometimes women are absorbed in examining their faces in mirrors, in order then to cover their blemishes and be more beautiful for the worldly intention of pleasing their husbands. I hope that you may bring the same care, burdened though you may be by the world's pressures, to reading this little book addressed to you by

me. For my sake, attend to it—according to my jest—as children do to their dice or women to their mirrors.

Even if you eventually have many more books, read this little work of mine often. May you, with God's help, be able to understand it to your own profit. You will find in it all you may wish to know in compact form. You will find in it a mirror in which you can without hesitation contemplate the health of your soul, so that you may be pleasing not only in this world, but to him who formed you out of dust.[4] What is essential, my son William, is that you show yourself to be such a man on both levels that you are both effective in this world and pleasing to God in every way.

My great concern, my son William, is to offer you helpful words. My burning, watchful heart especially desires that you may have in this little volume what I have longed to be written down for you, about how you were born through God's grace. I shall best begin there.

Preface.

In the eleventh year of the imperial rule of our lord Louis, who then reigned by Christ's favor—on the twenty-ninth of June 824—I was given in marriage at the palace of Aachen to my lord Bernard, your father, to be his legitimate wife.[5] It was still in that reign, in its thirteenth year on the twenty-ninth of November,[6] that with God's help,

---

[1] Dhuoda begins by describing her own work as threefold, reflecting the trinity of the one Christian God—Father, Son, and Holy Spirit. In doing so, she affirms her adherence to this central element in Catholic doctrine.

[2] See 2 Cor. 11: 23.

[3] Wisd. of Sol. 10: 21.

[4] See Gen. 1: 7.

[5] The marriage of Bernard and Dhuoda at the Carolingian capital, Aachen, suggests that they were children of families of great importance.

[6] The year was 826.

as I believe, you were born into this world, my firstborn and much-desired son.

Afterward, as the wretchedness of this world grew and worsened, in the midst of the many struggles and disruptions in the kingdom, that emperor followed the path common to all men. For in the twenty-eighth year of his reign, he paid the debt of his earthly existence before his time.[1] In the year after his death, your brother was born on the twenty-second of March in the city of Uzès.[2] This child, born after you, was the second to come forth from my body by God's mercy. He was still tiny and had not yet received the grace of baptism when Bernard, my lord and the father of you both, had the baby brought to him in Aquitaine in the company of Elefantus, bishop of Uzès, and others of his retainers.

Now I have been away from you for a long time, for my lord [Bernard] constrains me to remain in this city. Nonetheless I applaud his success. But, moved by longing for both of you, I have undertaken to have this little book—a work on the scale of my small understanding—copied down and sent to you. Although I am besieged by many troubles, may this one thing be God's will, if it please him—that I might see you again with my own eyes. I would think it certain that I would, if God were to grant me some virtue. But since salvation is far from me, sinful woman that I am,[3] I only wish it, and my heart grows weak in this desire.[4]

As for you, I have heard that your father, Bernard, has given you as a hostage to the lord king Charles.[5] I hope that you acquit yourself of this worthy duty with perfect good will. Meanwhile, as Scripture says, "Seek ye therefore the kingdom of God … and all these things shall be added unto you,"[6] that is all that is necessary for the enjoyment of your soul and your body.

So the preface comes to an end.

[In Book One, Dhuoda expounds on William's primary task: to love God. In Book Two, she discusses the Trinity, the trinity of virtues (faith, hope, and charity), and the importance of prayer.]

Book Three

1. ON THE REVERENCE YOU SHOULD SHOW YOUR FATHER THROUGHOUT YOUR LIFE.

Now I must do my best to guide you in how you should fear, love, and be faithful to your lord and father, Bernard, in all things, both when you are with him and when you are apart from him. In this, Solomon is your teacher and your wisest authority. He chastises you, my son, and says to you in warning, "For God hath made the father" who flourishes in his children "honorable."[7] And likewise: "He that honoreth his father shall have joy in his own children"[8] and "shall enjoy a long life. He that obeyeth the father shall be a comfort to his mother."[9] "As one that layeth up good things,"[10] so is he who honors his father. "He that feareth the Lord, honoreth his parents."[11] "So honor thy father," my son, and pray for him devotedly, "that thou mayest be longlived upon the land,"[12] with a full term of earthly existence. "Remember that thou hadst not been born" but through him.[13] In every matter be obedient to your father's interest and heed his judgment.[14] If by God's help you come to this, "support the old age of thy father and grieve him

---

[1] Louis the Pious died in 840, in his late sixties, so Dhuoda's comment is polite.

[2] The year was 841. It is possible, given the long period between the births of Dhuoda's two sons, that she saw little of her husband in the interim. Bernard was heavily involved in politics and warfare across the Frankish dominions throughout their marriage.

[3] See Ps. 119: 155; Douay Ps.118: 155.

[4] See Job 30: 16.

[5] William had been entrusted to Charles the Bald after the battle of Fontenoy in 841.

[6] Matt. 6: 33.

[7] Ecclus. 3: 3. Dhuoda here assumes a traditional attribution of this Old Testament book to David's son Solomon.

[8] Ecclus. 3: 6.

[9] Ecclus. 3: 7.

[10] Ecclus. 3: 5.

[11] Ecclus. 3: 8.

[12] Exod. 20: 12.

[13] Ecclus. 7: 30.

[14] See Ecclus. 3: 2.

not in his life."[1] "Despise him not when thou art in thy strength."[2]

May you never do this last, and may the earth cover my body before such a thing might happen. But I do not believe that it will. I mention it not because I fear it but rather so that you may avoid it so completely that such a crime never comes to your mind, as I have heard that it indeed has done among many who are not like you.[3] Do not forget the dangers that befell Elias's sons, who disobediently scorned the commands of their father and for this met with a bitter death.[4] Nor should I fail to mention the tree of Absalom, who rebelled against his father and whom a base death brought to a sudden fall. Hung from an oak and pierced by lances, he ended his earthly life in the flower of his youth, with a groan of anguish. Lacking as he did an earthly kingdom, he never reached that highest of kingdoms promised to him.[5]

What of the many more who behave as he did? Their path is perilous. May those who perpetrate such evil suffer accordingly. It is not I who condemn them, but Scripture that promises their condemnation, threatening them terribly and saying, "Cursed is he that honoreth not his father."[6] And again, "He who curseth his father, dying let him die"[7] basely and uselessly. If such is the punishment for harsh, evil words alone, what do you think will happen to those who inflict real injury upon their parents and insult the dignity of their fathers? We hear of many in our times who, thinking their present circumstances unjust, consider such crimes without taking into account the past. On them and on those like them fall hatred, jealousy, disaster, and calamity, and "nourishment to their envy."[8] They lose rather than keep those goods of others that they seek, and they are scarcely able even to keep their own property. I say these things not because I have seen them happen, but because I have read about such matters in books. I have heard of them in the past, you hear about them yourself, and I am hearing them even now. Consider what will happen in the future to those who treat others in this fashion. But God has the power to bring even these people—if there are such—to lament their evil ways and, in their conversion, to do penance and be worthy of salvation. May anyone who behaves so ill stay away from you, and may God give him understanding.

Everyone, whoever he may be, should consider this, my son: if the time comes that God finds him worthy to give him children of his own, he will not wish them to be rebellious or proud or full of greed, but humble and quiet and full of obedience, so that he rejoices to see them. He who was a son before, small and obedient to his father, may then be fortunate in his own fatherhood. May he who thinks on these things in the hope that they will happen consider too what I have said above. Then "all his limbs" will work "in concert, peacefully."[9]

Hear me as I direct you, my son William, and "listen carefully," follow the "instructions... of a father."[10] Heed the words of the holy Fathers, and "bind them in thy heart"[11] by frequent reading so that "years of life may be multiplied to thee"[12] as you grow continually in goodness. For "they that wait upon"[13] God, blessing him, obeying the Fathers and complying freely with their precepts— such men "shall inherit the land."[14] If you listen to what I say above and if you put it into worthy practice, not only will you have success here on this earth, but also you will be found worthy to possess with the saints what the Psalmist describes: "I believe to see the good things

---

[1] Ecclus. 3: 14.

[2] Ecclus. 3: 15.

[3] Dhuoda here clearly refers to the conflict among Louis the Pious and his sons.

[4] 1 Sam. 4: 11.

[5] See 2 Sam 18: 15.

[6] Deut. 27: 16.

[7] Lev. 20: 9.

[8] Gen. 37: 8.

[9] See *The Benedictine Rule*, chap. 34 above, p. 22: "all the members will be at peace." See as well 1 Cor. 12: 12–30.

[10] Here Dhuoda recalls the opening words of *The Benedictine Rule*. See above, p. 18.

[11] Prov. 16: 21.

[12] Prov. 4: 10.

[13] Ps. 37: 9; Douay Ps. 36: 9.

[14] Ibid.

of the Lord in the land of the living."[1] So that this other land may be your inheritance, my son, I pray that he who lives eternally may deign to prepare you to dwell there.

2. ON THE SAME TOPIC, ON REVERENCE FOR YOUR FATHER.

In the human understanding of things, royal and imperial appearance and power seem preeminent in the world, and the custom of men is to account those men's actions and their names ahead of all others, as though these things were worthy of veneration and as though worldly power were the highest honor. This attitude is testified in the words of him who said, "whether it be to the king as excelling, or to the governors."[2] But despite all this, my wish is as follows, my son. In the smallness of my understanding—but also according to God's will—I caution you to render first to him whose son you are special, faithful, steadfast loyalty as long as you shall live. For it is a fixed and unchangeable truth that no one, unless his rank comes to him from his father, can have access to another person at the height of power.

So I urge you again, most beloved son William, that first of all you love God as I have written above. Then love, fear, and cherish your father. Keep in mind that your worldly estate proceeds from his. Recognize that from the most ancient times, men who have loved their fathers and have been truthfully obedient to them have been found worthy to receive God's benediction from those fathers' hands....

[Dhuoda continues Book Three by citing examples of good sons in the bible and then turning to how William should act toward Charles the Bald and the magnates at court. In Books Four through Nine, Dhuoda takes up in turn the moral life; sin, punishment, and God's justice; the beatitudes; the two deaths of man (of body and spirit); prayer; and biblical and numerical metaphors.]

Book Ten

1. ON THE AGE YOU HAVE ATTAINED.

1 You have now reached four times four years.
   If my second son too were of this age,
   I would have another copy of this little book made
      for him.

2 And if in twice as many years and half again
   I were to see your image,
   I would write to you of more difficult things, and in
      more words.

3 But because the time of my parting hastens,
   And the suffering of pains everywhere wears my
      body down,
   I have in haste gathered this book for your benefit
      and your brother's.

4 Knowing that I cannot reach that time I have
      mentioned,
   I urge you to taste this as if it were the food of your
      mouth,
   Like a sweetened drink mixed with grain.

5 For the time at which I came to your father,
   Or when you were born of us into this earthly
      world—
   All this is known to us according to the dates of the
      months.

6 From the first line of this little book
   To its last syllable, know that
   All this is written for your salvation.

7 To find what is included here,
   Read the chapter headings
   So that you may easily take up what follows.

8 All the verses here—above and below, with all the
      rest—
   I have dictated for the good of your spirit and your
      body.
   I never cease directing you to read them aloud and
      keep them in your heart.

2. ON THE VERSES I HAVE BEGUN WITH THE LETTERS OF YOUR NAME.[3]

1 So that you may flourish and be strong, best of
      children,
   Do not hesitate to read the things I have spoken,
   Written down, and addressed to you.
      There you will easily find what is pleasing for you.

---

[1] Ps. 27: 13; Douay Ps. 26: 13.

[2] 1 Pet. 2: 13–14.

[3] The first letters of the following stanzas spell VERSI AD VVILHELMUM F[ILIUM], or "verses to William, my son." These verses form a synopsis of the preceding text.

2 God's word is living.[1] Seek it out.
   Diligently study its sacred learning.
   For your mind will be filled with great joy
       Throughout all time.

3 May that great and strong king, the good, bright
       Lord,
   Deign to nurture your mind through all that befalls
       you,
   My young son. May he protect you and defend you
       In every hour.

4 May you be humble of mind and chaste
   Of body, ready to do good service,
   So that you can readily accommodate yourself to all,
       Both great and small.

5 Foremost, fear and love the Lord God
   With all your mind and heart, and all your strength,
   And then honor your father
       In every way.[2]

6 As for that bountiful descendant of a line,
   Scion of his race and lineage,
   Him who shines in his great deeds—
       Never hesitate to serve him constantly.[3]

7 Love the great magnates; esteem
   Those who are first in the court, and act as the equal
       of those of low degree.
   Join yourself to those of good will, and take care
       Not to yield to the proud and the evil.

8 Always hold in honor the rightly constituted ministers
       of the divine rites,
   Those who are worthy of the prelate's status.
   With simple sincerity, commend yourself always with
       outstretched hands
       To those who keep the altars.

9 Help widows and orphans often,
   And be generous to pilgrims with food and drink,
   Prepare lodgings for them, and extend your hand
       with
       Clothing for the naked.

10 Be a strong and fair judge in legal matters,
    Never take a bribe from anyone,
    Nor oppress anyone. For he who has been your
        benefactor
        Will repay you.

11 Generous in gift giving, always watchful and
        prudent,
    Agreeable to all, with a winning manner,
    Profoundly joyful—such a countenance
        Will always be yours.

12 There is one who weighs out, who gives out in one
        direction or another.
    He returns for the merits of all what their deeds
        deserve,
    Granting the greatest reward, the stars of heaven,[4]
        For words and works.

13 And so, my noble son, seek diligently.
    Take care to hasten to receive
    Such great rewards, and turn away your eyes
        From the fires of blackened wood.

14 Although you count to your flourishing youth
    Only four times four years' growth,
    Your tender limbs grow older
        As you travel your course.

15 It seems very far from me,
    Wishing as I do to see the shape of your face—
    If strength were given me, still my merits
        Are not enough to win it.

16 May you live for him who made you
    With a clear mind, and join the worthy company of
        his servants,
    So that you may rise again in joy
        After your course is ended.

17 Although my mind is wrapped in shadows,
    Nevertheless I urge this, that you constantly read
    The pages of this little book written out above,
        And that you fix them in your mind.

---

[1] See Heb. 4: 12.
[2] See Mark 12: 33.
[3] Dhuoda here refers to Charles the Bald.
[4] Compare Rev. 2: 28.

18 With God's help these verses end,
  Now that eight years have twice gone by,
  At the beginning of December, feast of St. Andrew,
    The season of the coming of the Word.

  The verses end.

3. A POSTSCRIPT ON PUBLIC LIFE.

Here the words of this little book conclude. I have dictated them with an eager mind and have had them copied down for your benefit, as a model for you.

For I wish and urge that, when with God's help you have grown to manhood, you may arrange your household well, in appropriate order. As is written of another man who lived in this fashion, a man "like the most tender little worm of the wood,"[1] perform all the duties of your public life with loyalty, in a well-ordered fashion.

As for whether I survive to that time when I may see this with my own eyes, I am uncertain—uncertain in my own merits, uncertain in my strength, battered as I am among the waves in my frail toil. Although such is what I am, all things are possible for the Almighty. It is not in man's power to do his own will; rather whatever men accomplish is according to God's will. In the words of Scripture, "it is not of him that willeth, nor of him that runneth, but of God that showeth mercy."[2] Now, trusting in him, I say nothing else but "as it shall be the will of God in heaven so it be done."[3] Amen.

4. RETURNING TO MYSELF, I GRIEVE.

The sweetness of my great love for you and my desire for your beauty have made me all but forget my own situation. I wish now, "the doors being shut,"[4] to return to my own self. But because I am not worthy to be numbered among those who are mentioned above,[5] I still ask that you—among the innumerable people who may do so—pray without ceasing for the remedy of my soul on account of your special feeling for me, which can be measured.

You know how much, because of my continual illnesses and other circumstances, I have suffered all these things and others like them in my fragile body—according to the saying of a certain man, "in perils from my own nation, in perils from the Gentiles"[6]—because of my pitiful merits. With God's help and because of your father, Bernard, I have at last confidently escaped these dangers, but my mind still turns back to that rescue. In the past I have often been lax in the praise of God, and instead of doing what I should in the seven hours of the divine office, I have been slothful seven times seven ways.[7] That is why, with a humble heart and with all my strength, I pray that I may take my pleasure in continually beseeching God for my sins and my transgressions. May he deign to raise even me into heaven, shattered and heavy though I am.

And since you see me as I live in the world, strive with watchful heart—not only in vigils and prayer but also in alms to the poor—that I may be found worthy, once I am liberated from the flesh and from the bonds of my sins, to be freely received by the good Lord who judges us.

Your frequent prayer and that of others is necessary to me now. It will be more and more so in time to come if, as I believe, my moment is upon me. In my great fear and grief about what the future may bring me, my mind casts about in every direction. And I am unsure how, on the basis of my merits, I may be able to be set free in the end. Why? Because I have sinned in thought and in speech. Ill words themselves lead to evil deeds. Nevertheless I will not despair of the mercy of God. I do not despair now and I will never despair. I leave no other such as you to survive me, noble boy, to struggle on my behalf as you do and as many may do for me because of you, so that I may finally come to salvation.

I acknowledge that, to defend the interests of my lord and master Bernard, and so that my service to him might not weaken in the March and elsewhere[8]—so that he not abandon you and me, as some men do—I know that I have gone greatly into debt. To respond to great necessities, I have frequently borrowed great sums, not only from Christians but also from Jews. To the extent that I have been able, I have repaid them. To the extent that I

---

[1] 2 Sam 23: 8.

[2] Rom. 9: 16.

[3] 1 Macc. 3: 60.

[4] John 20: 26.

[5] Dhuoda may mean William's deceased ancestors, for whom he should pray; or she may mean the great men of the past.

[6] 2 Cor. 11: 26.

[7] See Gen. 7: 2.

[8] Dhuoda refers to her support for Bernard's position as count of the Spanish March.

can in the future, I will always do so. But if there is still something to pay after I die, I ask and I beg you to take care in seeking out my creditors. When you find them, make sure that everything is paid off either from my own resources, if any remain, or from your assets—what you have now or what you eventually acquire through just means, with God's help.

What more shall I say? As for your little brother, I have above directed you time and again concerning what you should do for him. What I ask now is that he too, if he reaches the age of manhood, deign to pray for me. I direct both of you, as if you were together here before me, to have the offering of the sacrifice and the presentation of the host made often on my behalf.

Then, when my redeemer commands that I depart this world, he will see fit to prepare refreshment for me. And if this transpires through your prayers and the worthy prayers of others, he who is called God will bring me into heaven in the company of his saints.

This handbook ends here. Amen. Thanks be to God....

[The book does not end, however. Dhuoda continues with the names of the dead in William's family; an epitaph that Dhuoda writes for her tombstone; and the psalms that William should recite on important occasions and how they should be said "with the heart's concentration."]

5. NAMES OF THE DEAD.

Here, briefly, are the names of those persons whom I failed to mention above. They are William, Cunigund, Gerberge, Witburgis, Theoderic, Gotzhelm, Guarnarius, Rothlindis.[1]

Other members of your lineage still flourish in this world with God's help. It is entirely at the will of him who made them to summon them too. Son, what should you do in regard to them but say with the Psalmist, "we that live bless the Lord: from this time now and for ever"?[2]

When a member of your family passes on, this does not befall except through God's power. When the Lord so commands, as in the case of your uncle the lord Aribert, you who survive must effect that his name be written down among the others, and you must pray for him.

6. I ASK THAT YOU WRITE THIS EPITAPH ON MY GRAVE.[3]

When I too have reached the end of my days, see to it that my name as well be written down among the names of those dead persons. What I wish and what I yearn for with all my might, as though it were happening now, is that you order the following verses to be cut in the stone of the place where I am buried, on the slab that hides my body. Then those who see this epitaph on my burial place may pour out worthy prayers to God for my unworthy self.

And as for any other who may someday read the handbook you now peruse, may he too ponder the words that follow here so that he may commend me to God's salvation as if I were buried beneath these words.

Find here, reader, the verses of my epitaph:[4]

† D † M †[5]

Formed of earth, in this tomb
Lies the earthly body of Dhuoda.
    Great king, receive her.

The surrounding earth has received in its depths
The flimsy filth of which she was made.
    Kind king, grant her favor.

The darkness of the tomb, bathed with her sorrow,
Is all that remains to her.
    You, king, absolve her failings.

You, man or woman, old or young, who walk back and forth
In this place, I ask you, say this:
    Holy one, great one, release her chains.

Bound in the dark tomb by bitter death,
Closed in, she has finished life in earth's filth.
    You, king, spare her sins.

---

1. The names here seem to refer to members of Bernard's family, not Dhuoda's, and thus contribute to the mother's emphasis on William's obligation to his patrilineage. Dhuoda surely does not wish her son to ignore his spiritual duty toward the other side of his family, however, for she argues that prayer on her behalf is among his primary responsibilities.
2. Ps. 115: 18; Douay Ps. 113: 18.
3. Other Carolingian authors, such as Alcuin, likewise composed their own epitaphs.
4. Dhuoda here offers another acrostic. The initial letters of the following verses spell dhuodane, perhaps an alternate Latin spelling of her name or an adjectival form.
5. Dhuoda abbreviates *dis manibus*, "to the Manes," the spirits of the dead.

So that the dark serpent
Not carry away her soul, say in prayer:
    Merciful God, come to her aid.

Let no one walk away without reading this.
I beseech all that they pray, saying:
    Give her peace, gentle father,

And, merciful one, command that she at least be
    enriched
With your saints by your perpetual light.
    Let her receive your amen after her death.

$$\alpha \dagger \omega^{1}$$

[In the final book, Eleven, Dhuoda copies a work by Alcuin on how to read and use the psalms.]

EXPANDING CHRISTIANITY

3.14 The Slavic conversion: Constantine/Cyril, *Prologue to the Gospel* (863–867). Original in Old Church Slavonic.

In 863 the brothers Constantine and Methodius were sent to Moravia at the behest of the Byzantine Patriarch Photius and at the invitation of the Moravian ruler Ratislav. They stayed about four years, translating the Scriptures into the Slavic dialect they had learned in Macedonia, which was not the language of Moravia but was nevertheless comprehensible to the people living there. Today this language is called Old Church Slavonic. In the prologue to his translation of the Gospels, Constantine speaks of the importance of literacy: "The soul lacking letters / Grows dead in human beings."

[Source: Roman Jakobson, "St. Constantine's Prologue to the Gospel," *St. Vladimir's Seminary Quarterly* 7 (1963): 16–19.]

I am the Prologue to the Holy Gospels:
As the prophets prophesied of old—
"Christ comes to gather the nations and tongues,
Since He is the light of the world"[2]—
So it has come to pass in this seventh millennium.   5
Since they have said, "The blind shall see,
The deaf shall hear the Word of the Book,
For it is proper that God be known."[3]
Therefore hearken, all ye Slavs!
For this gift is given by God,   10
The gift on God's right hand,
The incorruptible gift to souls,
To those souls that will accept it.
Matthew, Mark, Luke, and John
Teach all the people, saying: 15
"If you see and love the beauty of your souls,
And hence are striving
To dispel the darkness of sin,
And to repel the corruptness of this world,
Thus to win paradise life   20
And to escape the flaming fire,
Then hear now with your own mind,
Since you have learned to hear, Slavic people,
Hear the Word, for it came from God,

---

1   Dhuoda uses the Greek letters alpha and omega to invoke Christ. See Rev. 1: 8.

2   See Isa. 66: 8 and John 8: 12.

3   See Isa. 29: 18.

The Word nourishing human souls, 25
The Word strengthening heart and mind,
The Word preparing all to know God."
As without light there can be no joy—
For while the eye sees all of God's creation,
Still what is seen without light lacks beauty— 30
So it is with every soul lacking letters,
Ignorant of God's law,
The sacred law of the Scriptures,
The law that reveals God's paradise.
For what ear not hearing 35
The sound of thunder, can fear God?
Or how can nostrils which smell no flower
Sense the Divine miracle?
And the mouth which tastes no sweetness
Makes man like stone; 40
Even more, the soul lacking letters
Grows dead in human beings.
Thus, considering all this, brethren,
We speak fitting counsel
Which will divide men 45
From brutish existence and desire,
So that you will not have intellect without intelligence,
Hearing the Word in a foreign tongue,
As if you heard only the voice of a copper bell.
Therefore St. Paul has taught: 50
"In offering my prayer to God,
I had rather speak five words
That all the brethren will understand
Than ten thousand words which are incomprehensible."[1]
What man will not understand this? 55
Who will not apply the wise parable,
Interpreting to us the true message?
As corruption threatens the flesh,
Decaying and rotting everything worse than pus
If there is no fit nourishment, 60
So each soul no longer lives
Deprived of Divine Life,
Hearing not the Divine Word.
Let another very wise parable
Be told, ye men that love each other 65
And wish to grow toward God!
Who does not know this true doctrine?

As the seed falls on the field,
So it is upon human hearts
Craving the divine shower of letters 70
That the fruit of God may increase.
What man can tell all the parables
Denouncing nations without their own books
And who do not preach in an intelligible tongue?
Even one potent in all tongues 75
Lacks power to tell their impotence.
Let me add my own parable
Condensing much sense into few words:
Naked indeed are all nations without their own books
Who being without arms cannot fight 80
The Adversary of our souls
And are ripe for the dungeon of eternal torments.
Therefore, ye nations whose love is not for the Enemy
And who truly mean to fight him:
Open eagerly the doors of your intelligence— 85
You who have now taken up the sturdy arms
That are forged through the Lord's Books,
And who mightily crush the head of the Enemy.
Whoever accepts these letters,
To him Christ speaks wisdom, 90
Feeds and strengthens your souls,
And so do the Apostles with all the Prophets.
Whoever speak their words
Will be fit to slay the Foe,
Bringing God good victory, 95
Escaping the suppurant corruption of flesh—
Flesh that lives as in a sleep;
These will not fall but hold fast,
And come forth before God as men of valor,
Standing on the right hand of God's throne, 100
When He judges the nations with fire,
And rejoicing throughout the ages with the angels,
Eternally praising God the merciful,
Always with songs from the holy books,
Singing to God who loves man: 105
To Him befits all glory,
To the Son of God, honor and praise forever,
With the Father and the Holy Ghost,
Unto the ages of ages, from all creatures!

---

[1] See 1 Cor. 14: 19.

3.15 The Bulgarian Khan in Byzantine guise: *Seal of Boris-Michael* (864–889).

The Bulgars established themselves in Bulgaria in the 670s, as Byzantine control over the region south of the Danube weakened. The Bulgar khans (khan means "supreme ruler") and nobles subjected both Slavs and Greek-speaking Byzantines to their rule; they employed the Greek speakers in administering their new state. Influenced by Byzantine practices, these administrators affixed seals to official documents sent out in the name of the seal's owner. The seals were made of lead, a common metal. They were locally stamped and decorated with monograms or inscriptions or even human heads. Lead was used not only because it was malleable, but also to indicate the low-level, routine, and administrative, nature of the correspondence involved. Use of the inferior metal also acknowledged the lower status of the Bulgarian ruler within the Byzantine political hierarchy. Only the Byzantine emperor had the right to use gold seals, while notables with the highest titles were allowed, in exceptional circumstances, to use silver. Lower-ranking rulers who recognized the superior position of the emperors used lead.

When Khan Boris converted to the Christian religion and adopted the name Michael and the title of "prince" (see below, p. 161) he had seals made to advertise his new faith. On the seal shown here, the "obverse"—or "heads," as in "heads or tails"—side of the seal has a circle with the inscription, "Christ help your servant Michael ruler of Bulgaria." Inside the circle is the head of a long-haired and bearded Christ with a cross nimbus (halo) behind him. His right hand gives a sign of blessing, while his left hand holds the gospels. On the "reverse"—or tails—side is, again, a circle with an inscription, this time reading: "Mother of God help your servant Michael ruler of Bulgaria." Inside the circle is the head of Mary, mother of God, wearing a *maphorion* (a mantel with a hood), her hands upraised in prayer. Note that, influenced by Byzantine notions of rulership, the seal presents Boris-Michael as a territorial ruler (over "Bulgaria") rather than ruler of the Bulgar people (the "Bulgarians").

See Plate 11, p. 247, for a color reproduction of the seal.

(Kiril Petkov, ed. and trans., *The Voices of Medieval Bulgaria, Seventh-Fifteenth Century: The Records of a Bygone Culture* [Leiden: Brill, 2008], p. 33. Images courtesy of Dr. Ivan Jordanov.)

3.16 The Bulgarians adopt Christianity: Pope Nicholas I, *Letter to Answer the Bulgarians' Questions* (866). Original in Latin.

Christians mingled with Bulgars in the Bulgar state, and more arrived gradually in the course of the ninth century via Greek captives and deserters. In *c*.864 Boris converted to the Byzantine form of Christianity, taking the baptismal name of Michael, after Emperor Michael III (r.842–867). (See one of his seals in Plate 11, pictured on p. 247 in Reading through Looking.) But Boris-Michael did not intend to be subservient to the emperor. Thus in 866, seeking to reconcile Bulgar practices with Christian, he turned to Pope Nicholas I to clarify various points of the faith and how they should apply to the Bulgarians. His original questions have been lost, but the pope's advice suggests what they were.

[Source: Nicholas I, *Epistola* 99, in *Epistolae* 6, ed Ernest Perels, Monumenta Germaniae Historica (Berlin, 1925), pp. 568–600. Translated by William L. North.]

Not much needs to be said in response to your inquiries nor have we considered it necessary to pause long over each question, since we, with God's aid, are going to send to your country and to your glorious king,[1] our beloved son, not only the books of divine law but also suitable messengers of ours[2] who will instruct you concerning the details insofar as time and reason dictate; to them, as well, we have committed books that we thought they would need.

Chapter I.

Now then, at the very beginning of your questions, you state in excellent and praiseworthy fashion that your kind seeks the Christian law. If we tried to explain this law fully, countless books would have to be written. But in order to show briefly in what things it chiefly consists, you should know that the law of Christians consists in faith and good works....

Chapter IV.

We do not think we need to explain to you, who are rough and in some ways children in the faith, how many times

or days in the course of a year one should abstain from meat. For the time being, on the days of fasting when one should especially supplicate the Lord through abstinence and the lamentation of penance, one should completely abstain from meat. For, although it is fitting to pray and abstain at all times, one should nevertheless be even more of a slave to abstinence during times of fasting. This is to say that he who recalls that he has committed illicit deeds, should abstain on these days even from licit things in accordance with the sacred decretals, namely during Lent, which is before Easter, on the fast before Pentecost, at the fast before the assumption of the holy mother of God and the ever virgin Mary, our Lady, as well as on the fast before the feast of the birth of our Lord Jesus Christ: these are the fasts which the holy Roman church received in antiquity and maintains. But on the sixth day of every week, and on all the vigils of famous feasts one should cease from eating meat and should apply oneself to fasting....

Chapter VII.

You further inquire, whether a clean or unclean person is allowed to kiss or carry the cross of the Lord when he holds it. [We answer] that for the person who is clean, it is completely permissible; for what is indicated in a kiss if

---

[1] Boris-Michael. Note that the pope bestows the title of king on him.
[2] Paul, bishop of Populonia, and Formosus, bishop of Porto.

not the love with which someone burns for these things? And in carrying it, what else is expressed if not the mortification or fellow-suffering of the flesh? Indeed, the Lord also ordered him to carry this cross, but in his mind; but when it is performed with the body, one is more easily reminded that it should also be performed in the mind....

Chapter IX.

You ask whether you should partake of the body and blood of the Lord every day during greater Lent.[1] We humbly pray to omnipotent God and exhort you all most vehemently that you do so, but not if your mind is disposed towards sin, or if your conscience—because it is unrepentant or unreconciled perhaps—accuses your mind of criminal sins; or if one of you is not reconciled to a brother through his own fault....

Chapter X.

You wish to know if anyone is permitted to perform any labor on Saturday or Sunday. Concerning this matter the oft-remembered holy Pope Gregory said, while addressing the Romans: "It has come to my attention that certain men of a perverse spirit have sowed some depraved things among you which are contrary to the holy faith, so that they forbid anything to be done on Saturday. What else should I call such people except preachers of the Antichrist, who shall, when he comes, make Saturday and Sunday be kept free from any work?... But on Sundays one should cease from earthly labor and devote oneself to prayers in every way, in order that whatever act of negligence has been committed during the other six days, may be expiated with prayers throughout the day of the Lord's resurrection.[2]

Chapter XI.

You ask whether you should cease from earthly work on the feast days of these apostles, martyrs, confessors, and virgins. Yes, [you should cease from work] on the feasts of the blessed virgin Mary, of the twelve apostles, of the evangelists and of their precursor, the lord John, of St. Stephen the Protomartyr as well as on the birthdays of those saints whose celebrated memory and feast day shall be held among you by God's favor. You should know clearly, that worldly work should cease on feast days in order for Christians to attend church more easily; to engage in psalms, hymns, and spiritual songs; to spend time in prayer; to offer oblations; to share in the remembrance of the saints; to rise to imitate them; to concentrate on divine scriptures, and to distribute alms to the needy....

Chapter XII.

Because you ask whether it is permitted to carry out judgment on the feasts of the saints, and whether the person, if he deserves it, should be sentenced to death on this same day, you should know that on those feasts when, as we have shown, one should cease from all worldly labor, we think that one should abstain all the more from secular affairs and especially from executions...

Chapter XIII.

Among your questions and inquiries, you said that you are requesting secular laws.[3] Regarding this matter, we would willingly have sent the volumes that we thought you might need at present, if we had learned that one among you could interpret them for the rest; if we have given some books concerning secular law to our messengers, we do not want them to be left [with you] when they return, lest by chance someone interpret them for you in a perverse way or violate them with some falsehood....

Chapter XVII.

Now then, you have told us about how you received the Christian religion by divine clemency and made your

---

[1] The forty days preceding Easter.

[2] Here Nicholas is thinking of Gregory the Great, Letter 13.1 to the citizens of Rome.

[3] Note the close association that newly converted kings made between becoming Christian and gaining secular laws: see, for example, King Stephen's *Laws* for Hungary (below, p. 205). But the Bulgarians, who (as Nicholas implies) were more familiar with Greek than with Latin, did not write a written law code until the ninth century. It was based on an eighth-century Byzantine code that in turn depended on the law codes sponsored by Justinian.

entire people be baptized, and how these people, after they had been baptized, fiercely rose up against you with one spirit, claiming that you had not given them a good law and wishing to kill you and establish another king. [You then recounted] how you, prepared to oppose them with the help of divine power, conquered them from the greatest to the least and held them captives in your hands, and how all the leaders and magnates along with every one of their children were slaughtered by the sword, though the mediocre and lesser persons suffered no evil. Now you desire to know whether you have contracted any sin on account of those who were deprived of their lives. Clearly what did not escape sin nor could have happened without your fault was that a child who was not privy to their parents' plot nor is shown to have born arms against you, was slaughtered along with the guilty, even though he was innocent.... You also should have acted with greater mildness concerning the parents who were captured, that is, [you should have] spared their lives out of love for the God Who delivered them into your hands. For thus you might be able to say to God without hesitation in the Lord's Prayer: "Forgive us our debts, as we forgive our debtors."[1] But you also could have saved those who died while fighting, but you did not permit them to live nor did you wish to save them, and in this you clearly did not act on good advice; for it is written: "There shall be judgment without mercy for the person who does not exercise mercy."[2] ... But because you erred more because of your zeal for the Christian religion and your ignorance than because of any other vice, with subsequent penance seek mercy and indulgence for these sins through the grace of Christ....

Chapter XXVI.

With regard to those who have slaughtered their kinsman, that is, someone related by blood such as a brother, cousin, or nephew, the venerable laws [of the Bulgarians] should be properly enforced. But if they have fled to a church, they should be saved from the laws of death but they should also submit without hesitation to the penance which the bishop or priest of the place has decided. "I do not want the death of the sinner," says the Lord, "but rather wish that he be converted and live."[3] ...

Chapter XXXIII.

When you used to go into battle, you indicated that you carried the tail of a horse as your military emblem, and you ask what you should carry now in its place. What else, of course, but the sign of the cross? ...

Chapter XXXIV.

You also asked, if, when a messenger arrives, you should set off immediately in order to get to the fighting or whether there are any days when it is not fitting to go forth into battle. On this matter we answer: there is no day which should be kept completely free from beginning or carrying out any kind of business, except (if too great a necessity does not compel you) the most celebrated days mentioned above, which are venerated by all Christians. But this is not because it is forbidden to do such things on these days. For our hope should be placed not in days nor determined by days, but all salvation should be expected absolutely from the true and living God alone. Rather it is because on these days, if the necessity is not unavoidable, one should spend time in prayer and the mysteries of so great a festival should be attended more zealously than usual....

Chapter XXXV.

You say that when you went forth into battle, you used to watch the days and hours and perform incantations, games, songs and some auguries, and you wish to be instructed on what you should do now. Regarding this matter, we would of course instruct you, if we did not think that you have been divinely instructed on this matter; for atop the divine foundation, we cannot build anything. Therefore, when you decide to go forth into battle, do not fail to do what you yourselves have recalled, i.e. go to the churches, carry out prayers, forgive sinners, be present at the solemnities of the Mass, offer oblations, make a confession of your sins to the priests, receive the reconciliation and communion, open the jails, loose the fetters and grant liberty to servants and especially to those who are broken and weak and captives, and distribute alms to the needy,

---

[1] Matt. 6: 12.

[2] James 2: 3.

[3] Ezek. 33: 11.

so that you may fulfill what the Apostle admonishes when he says: "Do everything, whether it be in word or deed, do it all in the name of the Lord Jesus."[1] For the things that you mentioned, that is, the observations of days and hours, the incantations, the games, iniquitous songs, and auguries are the pomp and workings of the devil, which you already renounced, thank God, in baptism and you cast off all these things completely along with the old man and his actions, when you put on the new....

Chapter XLI.

With regard to those who refuse to receive the good of Christianity but instead sacrifice to and bow down before idols, we can write nothing more to you than that you win them over to the correct faith with warnings, exhortations, and reason rather than with force. For they have knowledge but it is in vain: although they are people with capable intellects, they adore the products of their own hands and senseless elements, or to speak more truly, they bend their necks and sacrifice to demons....

Chapter XLVII.

You ask whether it is permitted to play games during Lent. Christians are not permitted to do this not only during Lent but also at any other time. But you are weak and are not yet strong enough to climb to the mountain to receive the highest commandments of God but instead have been placed in the flatlands like the former children of Israel, so that you may at least receive some of the simpler, lesser commandments. Therefore, because we cannot yet to convince you to refrain from games at all times, you should at least abstain from games, from the vain conversation and scurrility that do not befit the occasion, and idle chatter during the time of Lent and fasting when you should be spending more time and be more intent on prayer, abstinence, and every kind of penance....

Chapter XLIX.

Furthermore, you ask whether you are permitted to show your wives gold, silver, cattle, horses, etc. as dowry just

as [you did] before. Because it is no sin and the laws do not forbid it, we, too, do not forbid this from occurring; and not only this, but also whatever else you did before baptism, you are now clearly permitted to do....

Chapter LI.

You ask if you are permitted to have two wives at the same time; if this is not permitted, you know what the person in this situation should do at this point. Neither the origin of the human condition nor any Christian law allows a man to have two wives at once. For God, Who made the human being, made one male and one female at the very beginning. Of course, he could have given him two wives, if he wished but he did not want to do so....

Chapter LVII.

You claim that the Greeks forbid eunuchs to kill your animals, so that they assert that anyone who has eaten [meat] from animals killed by them has committed a grave sin. This sounds truly strange and silly to us. But because we have not heard the reasoning of the people who say these things, we cannot decide anything definitive concerning their assertion, since it is not yet fully known....

Chapter LXIV.

The number of days after a woman gives birth to a child that a man should abstain from [having intercourse] with her is proclaimed not by the products of our own wit but by the words of the Roman Pope and apostle of the English nation, Gregory [the Great] of blessed memory. Among other things, he says when he writes to Bishop Augustine, whom he had sent to [the Anglo-Saxons]: "A woman's husband should not come to lie with her until the infants to whom she has given birth, have been weaned...."[2]

Chapter XCV.

You ask what we think should be done about those who flee to a church because of certain crimes. Now then,

---

[1] Col. 3: 17.

[2] Gregory the Great, in a set of letters transmitted by Bede (see above, p. 94).

although the sacred canons require that the decrees of the worldly laws be upheld and these laws appear to be without mercy towards certain persons, we who do not accept the spirit of this world nevertheless say that if someone flees to a church, he should not be removed unless he wishes [to come out] voluntarily.[1] For if long ago robbers and those guilty of various crimes fled to the Temple of Romulus for asylum and received protection from harm, so much more should those who flee to the Temple of Christ receive remission for their sins and be restored to their original state of complete safety, once the suspect has offered an oath on his own behalf.

[Closing]

... We have given these responses to your questions and proposals, insofar as the Lord has given them to us. It is not as much as we could say but rather as much as we thought could satisfy you for the time being. But when, by God's concession, you shall possess a bishop through the ministry of our prelacy, he shall teach you everything that pertains to his office. And if there are things that he does not understand, he shall receive them again from the authority of the apostolic see. May God, who has worked the greatest salvation among you, bring this to completion, make it solid, and give it stability and strength to the end [of time]. Amen.

---

[1] Compare with the provisions on asylum in *The Theodosian Code* (above, p. 4).

TIMELINE FOR CHAPTER THREE

700

725 SALE OF A SLAVE IN ITALY ———

754–67 ISHAQ, *LIFE OF MUHAMMAD* ——— 750

——— 755–56 STEPHEN II, *LETTERS TO KING PIPPIN III*

——— 789 *ADMONITIO GENERALIS*

*c.*800 ABU NUWAS, *TURNING THE TABLES* ——— 800

——— 9TH C. AL-BUKHARI, *ON FASTING*

814–15 POLYPTYQUE OF THE CHURCH ———
OF SAINT MARY OF MARSEILLE

——— 825–26? EINHARD, *LIFE OF CHARLEMAGNE*

841–43 DHUODA, *HANDBOOK* ——— 850

863–67 CONSTANTINE/CYRIL, ———
PROLOGUE TO THE GOSPEL

——— 864–89 *SEAL OF BORIS-MICHAEL*

866 NICHOLAS I, *LETTER TO* ———
ANSWER THE BULGARIANS' QUESTIONS

——— *c.*883 *CHRONICLE OF ALBELDA*

700–900 MAJOR EUROPEAN ——— 900
SLAVE EXPORTS (MAP)

——— 886–912 *BOOK OF THE PREFECT*

BEF. 940 IBN 'ABD RABBIHI, *I HAVE NEVER SEEN* ———

950

MID-10TH C. DUNASH BEN LABRAT, ———
THERE CAME A VOICE

---

*To test your knowledge and gain deeper understanding of this chapter,
please go to www.utphistorymatters.com for Study Questions.*

IV

Political Communities Reordered (c.900–c.1050)

REGIONALISM: ITS ADVANTAGES AND ITS DISCONTENTS

4.1 Fragmentation in the Islamic world: Al-Tabari, *The Defeat of the Zanj Revolt* (*c*.915). Original in Arabic.

Al-Tabari (839–923) was born in Amul, on the southern shore of the Caspian Sea. His education took him to Baghdad, Basra, and Egypt before he returned to Baghdad (*c*.870) to write and teach. He was a prolific author, producing works on jurisprudence, the Qur'an, and history. His universal history, from which the excerpt below comes, began with Creation and continued to 915. He modestly called this extremely long work *The Short Work on the History of Messengers, Kings, and Caliphs.* The section printed here covers the last part of the reign of Caliph al-Mu'tamid (r.870–892), a period through which al-Tabari himself lived. Key to the events of this period was the revolt of the Zanj, black slaves who were put to work removing the salt from the marshes formed by the Tigris and Euphrates rivers. Led by 'Ali b. Muhammad, whom al-Tabari calls "the abominable" and "the traitor," the Zanj pillaged the cities around Basra and incited some local groups to challenge the caliph's authority. In response, al-Mu'tamid called on his brother al-Muwaffaq Abu Ahmad and Abu Ahmad's son Abu al-Abbas (later Caliph al-Mu'tadid) to wage war against the Zanj. The passage here begins in 880 with a victory by Abu al-Abbas. Although ruthlessly killing all the captives in this instance, father and son also offered amnesty and "robes of honor" to those who deserted the Zanj cause, severely dividing and weakening the opposition. They ultimately won the war against the Zanj in 883, but al-Tabari hints of other local defections from the caliphate, presaging its eventual decline.

Let us use this document to discuss once again how to read a primary source. Al-Tabari's account of the Zanj revolt is very different from the *Edict of Milan* on p. 1. Nevertheless, it should be subjected to the same series of questions. The answers lead to new questions that work just for al-Tabari (and perhaps for a small cluster of similar documents as well), in the same way as the answers to the questions about the *Edict of Milan* led to questions largely pertinent to it alone.

Who wrote it, and for what audience was it written? In this case, the answer is quite simple: the author was al-Tabari, and you know a bit about his career from the introductory note above. You can easily guess that his audience was meant to be his students and other educated readers in the Islamic world.

When was it written? Your editor has given you the date *c.*915. At this point in your studies, you need not worry much about how this date was arrived at. It is more important to consider the circumstances and historical events in the context of which a date such as 915 takes on meaning. Here you should be considering how, even as the caliphate was weakening, the Islamic world was open to wandering students and supported scholarly work.

Where was it written? The answer is, no doubt, Baghdad. But you should not be content with that. You should consider its significance at the time. Was it still the capital of the Islamic world? If not, why do you suppose al-Tabari settled there?

Why was it written? Al-Tabari begins this voluminous history with an extended passage in praise of God. He then says that he intends to begin with the Creation of the world and to continue by chronicling all the kings, messengers, and caliphs that he has heard about. But the first topic that he addresses in some detail is philosophical: "What is Time?" Thus, although al-Tabari does not say precisely why he wrote, he clearly wished to produce both a comprehensive chronicle about the powerful men in the world and a reflective work on the nature of history itself. But you should go beyond this answer to ask what other motives might have been at work. For example, might al-Tabari have thought that there were moral, practical, and religious—even doctrinal—lessons to be learned from history? Might he have been interested in legitimizing the Abbasids or other caliphs?

What is it? Clearly it is a history; the word is in the title. But what sort of history? Al-Tabari was careful to document many of his facts by citing the chain of sources (*isnad*) that attested to them. This technique was important in Islamic religious studies (see above, p. 114) and legal studies as well. Al-Tabari's work thus assimilates history with the scholarly traditions of other disciplines. Moreover his history might be called "universal," given its huge time frame. On the other hand, it is not a history of everything but rather of certain key figures.

What does it say? This is the most important question of all. To answer it, you need to analyze the text (or, here, the excerpt) carefully, taking care to understand what the author is describing and seeking further information (if necessary) about the institutions that he takes for granted.

What are the implications of what it says? This requires you to ask many questions about matters that lie behind the text. Important questions to ask are: *What does the document reveal about such institutions as family, power, social classes and groups, religion,* *and education and literacy in the world that produced it? What are its underlying assumptions about gender; about human nature, agency, and goals; about the nature of the divine?*

How reliable is it? Certainly al-Tabari's citations of his sources suggest that he was interested in reliability. On the other hand, you may ask if al-Tabari included everything that he knew, or if he had a certain "slant" on the events.

Are there complicating factors? In the Middle Ages authors often dictated their thoughts and then reworked them over time. Al-Tabari apparently finished lecturing on his *History* in about 915, but he continued to rework it. After his death, the work was copied numerous times—by hand. Paper was prevalent in the Islamic world, and it was cheaper and more abundant than parchment, which the West and the Byzantine Empire relied on. Nevertheless today we have no complete manuscript of al-Tabari's history, and scholars have had to reconstruct the full text from the various parts that are extant.

If you compare the questions and answers here with those introducing the *Edict of Milan*, you should be convinced that reading primary sources is both complex and fascinating.

[Source: *The History of al-Tabari*, vol. 37: *The ʿAbbasid Recovery*, trans. Philip M. Fields, annotated by Jacob Lassner (Albany: State University of New York Press, 1987), pp. 24–27, 65–66, 132–36.]

Abu Ahmad remained in al-Firk for several days to permit his troops, and any others who wanted to proceed with him, to join on. He had prepared the barges, galleys, ferries and boats. Then, on Tuesday, the second of Rabiʿ I [October 11, 880], he and his clients, pages, cavalry and infantry reportedly left al-Firk, bound for Rumiyat al-Madaʿin. From there they journeyed on, stopping at al-Sib, Dayr al-ʿAqul, Jarjaraya, Qunna, Jabbul, al-Silh and a place one *farsakh* [about four miles] from Wasit.[1] He remained at the latter for one day and one night and was met by his son Abu al-ʿAbbas and a squadron of cavalry including his leading officers and men. Abu Ahmad inquired about the state of his men, and getting from his son a picture of their gallantry and devotion in fighting, he ordered that robes of honor be bestowed upon them and Abu al-ʿAbbas. Thereupon, the son returned to his camp at al-ʿUmr where he remained throughout the day. In the early morning of the next day, Abu Ahmad took to the water where he was met by his son, Abu al-ʿAbbas, and all his troops in military formation, as fully equipped as they would be when confronting the traitor's forces. Abu Ahmad sailed on until he reached his camp on the waterway called Shirzad, where he stopped. On Thursday, the twenty-eighth of Rabiʿ I [November 6, 880], he departed

from there and stopped at the canal called Nahr Sindad, opposite the village called ʿAb-dallah. He instructed his son Abu al-ʿAbbas to halt on the eastern side of the Tigris, opposite the mouth of the Barduda, and put him in charge of the vanguard. Then he allotted the soldiers' allowances and paid them. Following that, he instructed his son to advance in front of him with the equipment that he had in his possession, toward the mouth of the Bar Musawir Canal.

Abu al-ʿAbbas set out with the best of his officers and troops, including Zirak al-Turki, the commander of his vanguard, and Nusayr Abu Hamzah, the commander of the barges and galleys. After this it was Abu Ahmad who set out with his selected cavalry and infantry, leaving the bulk of his army and many of his horsemen and foot soldiers behind in his place of encampment.

His son Abu al-ʿAbbas met him with a show of captives, heads and bodies of slain enemies from among the troops of al-Shaʿrani. For, on that same day, before the arrival of his father Abu Ahmad, Abu al-ʿAbbas had been attacked by al-Shaʿrani who came upon the former's camp. Abu al-ʿAbbas dealt him a severe blow, killing a great many of his men and taking captives. Abu Ahmad ordered that the captives be beheaded, which was

---

[1] The places mentioned in this document are in or near Iraq.

done. Then Abu Ahmad descended to the mouth of the Bar Musawir, where he stayed for two days. From there, on Tuesday, the eighth of Rabi' II [November 17, 880], he departed from Suq al-Khamis with all his men and equipment bound for the city which the leader of the Zanj had named al-Mani'ah bi-Suq al-Khamis. He proceeded with his ships along the Bar Musawir while the cavalry marched before him along the eastern side of the waterway until they reached the waterway called Baratiq, which led to Madinat al-Sha'rani. Abu Ahmad preferred to begin fighting against Musa al-Sha'rani before he fought Sulayman b. Jami' because he feared that al-Sha'rani, who was to his rear, might attack and thus divert him from the adversary in front of him. That is why he set out against al-Sha'rani. He ordered the cavalry to cross the canal and proceed along both banks of the Baratiq. Abu Ahmad also instructed his son Abu al-'Abbas to advance with a flotilla of barges and galleys, and he himself followed with barges along with the bulk of his army.

When Sulayman, his Zanj troops and others noticed the cavalry and infantry proceeding on both banks of the canal and the ships advancing along the waterway—this was after Abu al-'Abbas had met them and engaged them in a skirmish—they fled and scattered. The troops of Abu al-'Abbas climbed the walls killing those who opposed them. When the Zanj and their supporters scattered, Abu al-'Abbas and his forces entered the city, killed a great many of its people, took many prisoners and laid hold of whatever was there. Al-Sha'rani and the others who escaped with him fled; they were pursued by Abu Ahmad's men up to the marshes where many drowned. The rest saved themselves by fleeing into the thickets.

Thereupon, Abu Ahmad instructed his troops to return to their camp before sunset of that Tuesday, and he withdrew. About five thousand Muslim women and some Zanj women, who were taken in Suq al-Khamis, were saved. Abu Ahmad gave instructions to take care of all the women, to transfer them to Wasit and return them to their families.

Abu Ahmad spent that night opposite the Baratiq Canal and in the early morning of the next day, he entered the city and gave the people permission to take all the Zanj possessions there. Everything in the city was seized. Abu Ahmad ordered the walls razed, the trenches filled, and the remaining ships burned. He left for his camp at Bar Musawir with booty taken in the districts and villages previously possessed by al-Sha'rani and his

men; this included crops of wheat, barley and rice. He ordered that the crops be sold and the money realized from the sale be spent to pay his mawla's pages,[1] the troops of his regular army, and other people of his camp.

Sulayman al-Sha'rani escaped with his two brothers and others, but he lost his children and possessions. Upon reaching al-Madhar he reported to the traitor [that is, the leader of the Zanj] what had befallen him and that he had taken refuge in al-Madhar.

According to Muhammad b. al-Hasan—Muhammad b. Hisham, known as Abu Wathilah al-Kirmani: I was in the presence of the traitor—he was having a discussion—when the letter from Sulayman al-Sha'rani arrived with the news of the battle and his flight to al-Madhar. As soon as he had the letter unsealed and his eye fell on the passage describing the defeat, his bowel muscles loosened and he got up to relieve himself, then he returned. As his Assembly came to order, he took the letter and began reading it again, and when he reached the passage which had disturbed him the first time, he left once more. This repeated itself several times. There remained no doubt that the calamity was great, and I refrained from asking him questions. After some time had elapsed, I ventured to say, "Isn't this the letter from Sulayman b. Musa?" He replied, "Yes, and a piece of heartbreaking news, too. Indeed, those who fell upon him dealt him a crushing blow 'that will not spare nor leave unburned.' He has written this letter from al-Madhar, and he has barely saved his own skin."

I deemed this news momentous and only God knows what a joy filled my heart, but I concealed it and refrained from rejoicing at the prospect of the approaching relief. However, the traitor regained self-control in face of vicissitude, and showed firmness. He wrote to Sulayman b. Jami', cautioning him against al-Sha'rani's fate and instructing him to be vigilant and watchful concerning what might lie before him....

On Tuesday, the first day of al-Muharram [August 12, 881], Ja'far b. al-Ibrahim, who was known as al-Sajjan, sought safe-conduct from Abu Ahmad al-Muwaffaq. It is mentioned that the reason for this was Abu Ahmad's battle at the end of Dhu al-Hijjah 267 [July 3–31, 881], to which we have referred above, as well as the flight of Rayhan b. Salih al-Maghribi and his men from the camp of the deviate, and their linking up with Abu Ahmad. The abominable one became completely discouraged at this; al-Sajjan was, reportedly, one of his trustworthy associates.

---

[1] A mawla could mean either master or servant. Here it undoubtedly refers to a servant or dependent.

Abu Ahmad conferred on this al-Sajjan robes of honor, various gifts, as well as a military allotment, and a place of lodging. Al-Sajjan was assigned to Abu al-'Abbas, who was ordered to transport him in a barge to a position in front of the abominable one's fortress so his [former] compatriots could see him. Al-Sajjan addressed them and told them that they were misled by the abominable one; he informed them what he had experienced because of the latter's lies and immoral behavior. The same day that al-Sajjan was placed in front of the abominable one's camp, a great many Zanj officers and others sought guarantees of safety; all of them were treated kindly. One after another the enemy sought safety and abandoned the abominable one.

After that battle which I have mentioned as having taken place on the last day of Dhu al-Hijjah of the year 267 [July 31, 881], Abu Ahmad did not cross over to fight the abominable one, thus giving his troops a respite until the month of Rabi' II [November 9–December 7, 881].

In this year, 'Amr b. al-Layth went to Fars to fight Muhammad b. al-Layth, his own governor in this province. 'Amr routed Muhammad b. al-Layth and auctioned off the spoils of his camp; the latter escaped with a small group of his men. 'Amr entered Istakhr, which was looted by his troops, and then sent a force to chase after Muhammad b. al-Layth. They seized him, and then delivered him to 'Amr as a prisoner. Thereupon, 'Amr went to Shiraz where he remained....

Now [August, 883] Abu Ahmad was sure of victory, for he saw its signs, and all the people rejoiced at what God had granted—namely, the rout of the profligate and his men. They rejoiced as well at God's having made it possible to expel the enemy from their city, and seize everything in it, and distribute what had been taken as booty—that is the money, treasures and weapons. Finally there was the rescue of all the captives held by the rebels. But Abu Ahmad was angry at his men because they disobeyed orders and abandoned the positions in which he had placed them. He ordered that the commanders of his mawlas and pages and the leading men among them be gathered together. When they were assembled for him, he scolded them for what they had done, judging them weak and castigating them in harsh language. Then they made excuses; they supposed that he had returned, and they had not known about his advance against the profligate, nor about his having pressed so far into the rebel's camp. Had they known this, they would have rushed toward him. They did not leave their places until they had taken a solemn oath and covenant that, when sent against the abominable one, none of them would

withdraw before God had delivered him into their hands; and should they fail, they would not budge from their positions until God had passed judgment between them and him. They requested of al-Muwaffaq that, after they had left al-Muwaffaqiyyah to fight, he order the ships transporting them to return and, thus, eliminate any temptation to those who might seek to leave the battle against the profligate.

Abu Ahmad accepted their apologies for their wrong-doing and again took them into his favor. Then he ordered them to prepare for crossing and to forewarn their troops just as they themselves had been forewarned. Abu Ahmad spent Tuesday, Wednesday, Thursday and Friday preparing whatever he would need. When this was completed, he sent word to his entourage and the officers of his pages and mawlas, instructing them as to their tasks when crossing [into combat]. Friday evening he sent word to Abu al-'Abbas and the officers of his pages and mawlas to set out for places which he, that is, Abu Ahmad, had specified.

Al-Muwaffaq instructed Abu al-'Abbas and his troops to set a course for a place known as 'Askar Rayhan, which lay between the canal known as Nahr al-Sufyani and the spot where the rebel sought refuge. He and his army were to follow the route along the canal known as Nahr al-Mughirah, so that they would exit where the canal intersects the Abu al-Khasib and reach 'Askar Rayhan from this direction. He forwarded instructions to an officer of his black pages to reach the Nahr al-Amir and cross at its center. At the same time, he ordered the rest of his officers and pages to pass the night on the eastern side of the Tigris, opposite the profligate's camp, and be prepared to attack him in the early morning.

During Friday night, al-Muwaffaq made the rounds among the officers and men in his barge. He divided amongst them key positions and locations which he had arranged for them in the profligate's camp. According to the assigned plan, they were to march towards these places in the morning. Early Saturday morning, on the second of Safar, 270 [August 11, 883], al-Muwaffaq reached the Abu al-Khasib Canal in his barge. He remained there until all his men had crossed [the water-way] and disembarked from their vessels, and the cavalry and infantry had assumed their positions. Then, after giving instructions for the vessels and ferries to return to the eastern side, he gave the troops the go-ahead to march against the profligate. He himself preceded them until he reached the spot where he estimated the profligates would make a stand in an attempt to repel the government army. Meanwhile, on Monday, after the army had withdrawn, the traitor and his men returned to the city and stayed there, hoping to prolong their defense and repel the attack.

Al-Muwaffaq found that the fastest of his cavalry and infantry among the pages had preceded the main force of the army and had attacked the rebel and his companions, dislodging them from their positions. The enemy force fled and dispersed without paying attention to one another, and the government army pursued them, killing and capturing whomever they managed to catch. The profligate, with a group of his fighting men, was cut off from [the rest] of his officers and troops— among them was al-Muhallabi. Ankalay, the rebel's son, had abandoned him, as had Sulayman b. Jami'. Moving against each of the contingents which we have named was a large force of al-Muwaffaq's mawlas, and cavalry and infantry drawn from his pages. Abu al-'Abbas's troops, assigned by al-Muwaffaq to the place known as 'Askar Rayhan, met the rebel's fleeing men and put them to the sword. The officer assigned to the Amir Canal also arrived there, and having blocked the rebels' path he attacked them. Encountering Sulayman b. Jami', he took the fight to him, killing many of his men and seizing Sulayman. He made Sulayman a captive and delivered him to al-Muwaffaq without conditions. The people were glad to learn of Sulayman's capture, and there were many cries of "God is Great!" and great clamor. They felt certain of victory, since Sulayman was known to be the most able of the rebel's companions. After him, Ibrahim b. Ja'far al-Hamdani, one of the field commanders of the rebel's army, was taken captive; then Nadir al-Aswad, the one known as al-Haffar, one of the earliest companions of the rebel, was captured.

Upon al-Muwaffaq's order, precautionary measures were taken, and the captives were transferred in barges to Abu al-'Abbas.

Following this, those Zanj who had separated from the main body, together with the profligate, assaulted the government force, dislodging them from their positions and causing them to lose the initiative. Al-Muwaffaq noticed the loss of initiative, but he pressed on with the search for the abominable one, advancing quickly in the Abu al-Khasib Canal. This bolstered his mawlas and pages, who hastened to pursue (the enemy) with him. As al-Muwaffaq reached the Abu al-Khasib Canal, a herald arrived with the good news of the rebel's death; before long another herald arrived carrying a hand, and claimed that this was the hand of the rebel. This seemed to lend

credence to the report of the rebel's demise. Finally a page from Lu'lu"s troops arrived, galloping on a horse and carrying the head of the abominable one. Al-Muwaffaq had the head brought closer, and then showed it to a group of former enemy officers who were in his presence. They identified it, and al-Muwaffaq prostrated himself in adoration to God for both the hardships and bounties He had conferred upon him. Abu al-'Abbas, the mawlas and the officers of al-Muwaffaq's pages then prostrated themselves, offering much thanks to God, and praising and exalting Him. Al-Muwaffaq ordered the head of the rebel raised on a spear and displayed in front of him. The people saw it and thus knew that the news of the rebel's death was true. At this, they raised their voices in praise to God.

It is reported that al-Muwaffaq's troops surrounded the abominable one after all his field commanders had abandoned him save al-Muhallabi; the latter now turned away from him and fled, thus betraying the rebel. The rebel then set off for the canal known as Nahr al-Amir and plunged into the water, seeking safety. Even before that, Ankalay, the son of the abominable one, had split off from his father and fled in the direction of the canal known as Nahr al-Dinari, where he entrenched himself in the swampy terrain.

Al-Muwaffaq retired, with the head of the abominable one displayed on a spear mounted in front of him on a barge. The vessel moved along the Abu al-Khasib Canal, with the people on both sides of the waterway observing it. When he reached the Tigris, he took his course along the river and gave the order to return the vessels, with which he had crossed to the western side of the Tigris at daylight, to the eastern side of the river. They were returned to ferry the troops [back] across the river.

Then al-Muwaffaq continued his trip, with the abominable one's head on the spear before him, while Sulayman b. Jami' and al-Hamdani were mounted for display. When he arrived at his fortress in al-Muwaffaqiyyah, he ordered Abu al-'Abbas to sail the barge, keeping the rebel's head and Sulayman b. Jami' and al-Hamdani in place, and to take his course to the Jatta Canal where the camp of al-Muwaffaq began. He was to do this so that all the people of the camp could have a look at them. Abu al-'Abbas did this, and then returned to his father, Abu Ahmad, whereupon the latter imprisoned Sulayman b. Jami' and al-Hamdani and ordered that the rebel's head be properly prepared and cleaned.

4.2 The powerful in the Byzantine countryside: Romanus I Lecapenus, *Novel* (934). Original in Greek.

In Byzantine legal terms, a "novel" is a "new law." Emperor Romanus I Lecapenus (r.920–944) issued one such law on behalf of the poor in the countryside in 934. Newly powerful provincial landowners, collectively known as *dynatoi*, were taking advantage of a recent famine to buy up whole villages, enhancing both their economic and social positions. Romanus tried to set back the clock—he wanted the land to stay in the hands of the original peasant families or at least in the hands of their village neighbors. He insisted that the powerful "return [the land] without refund to the owners." What reasons can you give for Romanus's opposition to the powerful?

[Source: *The Land Legislation of the Macedonian Emperors*, trans. and ed. Eric McGeer (Toronto: Pontifical Institute of Mediaeval Studies, 2000), pp. 53–56, 59–60 (notes modified).]

Novel of the Lord Emperor Romanus the Elder

PROLOGUE

To dispose the soul in imitation of the Creator is the desire and ardent endeavor of those for whom it is a great and blessed thing to regard and to call themselves the work of the all-creating hand. As for those by whom this has not been accounted great and holy, they have the task of denying the Creation and the reckoning of Judgment, and, as with persons wholly content with life on earth and who choose to live their lives upon the earth alone, the display of their choice has been left in their wake.[1] Hence the great confusion of affairs, hence the great tide of injustices, hence the great and widespread oppression of the poor, and the great sighing of the needy, for whose sake the Lord rose from the dead. For He says, "For the oppression of the poor, for the sighing of the needy, now will I arise, saith the Lord."[2] If God, our Creator and Savior, Who made us emperor, rises in retribution, how will the poor man, who awaits only the eyes of the emperor for intercession, be neglected and altogether forgotten by us? Therefore, not only upon examination of the actions taken against them in the recent past or attempts to make amends, but also administering a common and lasting remedy to the matter, we have issued the present law to avenge them, having prepared this as a purgative and a cleansing of the predilection of greed. We have considered it advantageous

that now no longer will anyone be deprived of his own properties, nor will a poor man suffer oppression, and that this advantage is beneficial to the common good, acceptable to God, profitable to the treasury, and useful to the state. Careful attention to this subject, for the sake of which decrees and judgments restraining the wickedness of the will and curtailing the reach of the grasping hand have streamed down to all the officials under our authority, has not been long neglected, nor has [our concern] arisen inappropriately. But since evil is versatile and multifarious, and all evils—not least greed, if indeed not even more so—contrive to evade the grip of laws and edicts and to regard the inescapable eye of divine justice as of no account, these measures, ejecting and excising the crafty workings of the will of the evildoers, have as a result now warranted more secure and rigorous codification.

1.1. We ordain therefore that those living in every land and district, where after God our rule extends, are to keep the domicile which has come down to them free and undisturbed. If time continues to preserve this arrangement, let the subsequent acquisition by the offspring or relatives through testamentary disposition, or the intention of the owner's preference, be fulfilled. If, though, given the course of human life and the ebb and flow of time, the pressure of necessity or even the prompting of the will alone, be it as it may, the owner embarks on the alienation

---

[1] The general sense seems to be this: people who see themselves as part of God's Creation try to act in accordance with God's ways, while people who do not venerate the Creation will have to reckon with the Last Judgment; such people have left ample evidence behind them of their choice to ignore divine justice and to lead their lives in pursuit of earthly, not eternal, rewards.

[2] Ps. 12: 5; Douay Ps. 11: 6.

of his own lands either in part or in whole, the purchase must first be set before the inhabitants of the same or adjacent fields or villages. We do not introduce this legislation out of animosity or malice towards the powerful; but we issue these rulings out of benevolence and protection for the poor and for public welfare. Whereas those persons who have received authority from God, those risen above the many in honor and wealth, should consider the care of the poor an important task, these powerful persons who regard the poor as prey are vexed because they do not acquire these things more quickly. Even if such impious conduct is not true of all, let adherence to the law be common to all, lest the tare [weeds] brought in with the wheat escape notice.[1]

1.2. As a result, no longer shall any one of the illustrious *magistroi*[2] or *patrikioi*,[3] nor any of the persons honored with offices, governorships, or civil or military dignities, nor anyone at all enumerated in the Senate,[4] nor officials or ex-officials of the themes nor metropolitans most devoted to God, archbishops, bishops, *higoumenoi* [abbots], ecclesiastical officials, or supervisors and heads of pious or imperial houses,[5] whether as a private individual or in the name of an imperial or ecclesiastical property, dare either on their own or through an intermediary to intrude into a village or hamlet for the sake of a sale, gift, or inheritance—either whole or partial—or on any other pretext whatsoever. As this sort of acquisition has been ruled invalid, the acquired properties, along with the improvements since added, are to return without refund to the owners or, if they or their relatives are no longer alive, to the inhabitants of the villages or hamlets. For the domination of these persons has increased the great hardship of the poor, bringing upheavals, persecutions, coercion, and other concomitant afflictions and difficulties through the multitude of their servants, hirelings or other attendants and followers, and, to those able to see it, will cause no little harm to the commonwealth unless the present legislation puts an end to it first. For the settlement[6] of the population demonstrates the great benefit of its function—the contribution of taxes and the fulfillment of military obligations—which will be completely lost should the common

people disappear. Those concerned with the stability of the state must eliminate the cause of disturbance, expel what is harmful, and support the common good.

2.1. Let time hereafter maintain these measures for the common benefit and settled order of our subjects; but it is necessary to apply the approved remedy not only to the future, but also to the past. For many people seized upon the indigence of the poor—which time bringer of all things brought, or rather, which the multitude of our sins, driving out divine charity, caused—as the opportunity for business instead of charity, compassion, or kindness; and when they saw the poor oppressed by famine, they bought up the possessions of the unfortunate poor at a very low price, some with silver, some with gold, and others with grain or other forms of payment. Harsher than the duress at hand, in those times which followed they were like a pestilential attack of disease to the miserable inhabitants of the villages, having entered like gangrene into the body of the villages and causing total destruction....

EPILOGUE It is our desire that these regulations remain in force for the safety of our subjects for whose sake great and constant care is our concern. For if we have expended so much care for those under our authority, so as to spare nothing that contributes to freedom, on account of which lands, towns, and cities have, with the help of God, come into our hands from the enemy, some as the result of war, while others have passed over to us by the example [of the conquered towns] or through fear of capture and were taken before the trumpet's call to battle; and if we have striven, with the help of God, to provide our subjects with such great freedom from enemy attack, setting this as the goal of our prayers and exertions, how will we, after accomplishing so much against the onslaught of external enemies, not rid ourselves of our own enemies within, enemies of the natural order, of the Creation, and of justice, by reviling and repressing insatiety [endless desire], by excising the greedy disposition, and by liberating our subjects from the yoke of the tyrannical, oppressive hand and mind with the righteous intention to free them with the cutting sword of the present legislation? Let each of

---

[1] Echoing the parable of the wheat and the tares related in Matt. 13: 24–30; 36–43.

[2] Those holding the highest possible dignity conferred on non-imperial family members.

[3] Those who hold a high dignity conferred on governors of themes (military districts) or military leaders.

[4] The Byzantine Senate was an advisory body whose members were high civil officials and dignitaries.

[5] Philanthropic foundations administered by crown officials.

[6] The Greek word for "settlement" also embraces the notions of stability and prosperity among the rural populace.

those to whom judicial authority has fallen see to it that these provisions remain in force in perpetuity [forever], for the service of God and for the common benefit and advantage of our empire received from Him.

In the Month of September of the eighth indiction in the year 6443 from the creation of the world, Romanus, Constantine, Stephanus, and Constantine, emperors of the Byzantines and faithful to God.

4.3 Donating to Cluny: Cluny's *Foundation Charter* (910) and various charters of donation (10th–11th c.). Originals in Latin.

William, Duke of Aquitaine (875–918), and his wife Ingelberga, anxious to ensure their eternal salvation, founded the monastery of Cluny on family property in the region of Mâcon (Burgundy, France). Soon the monastery gained an astonishing reputation for piety, and the prayers of its monks were praised for sending souls to heaven. Local donors, ranging from small peasants to rich aristocrats, gave land to Cluny in order to associate themselves with the monks' redemptive work. The donations were recorded in charters. The charters below consist, first, of the original donation, made by William and Ingelberga, and then of a group of charters drawn up for one family, later known as the Grossi. The family relationships were as follows:

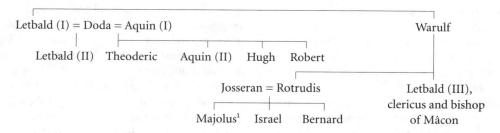

What reasons did people give for donating to the monastery of Cluny? What roles did women have in supporting the monastery? How do these charters show the conflicting tugs of family ties and charitable desires?

[Source: Patrick J. Geary, ed., *Readings in Medieval History*, 4th ed. (Toronto: University of Toronto Press, 2010), pp. 315–22 (slightly modified).]

[The Foundation Charter of Cluny: Charter # 112 (September 11, 910)]

To all right thinkers it is clear that the providence of God has so provided for certain rich men that, by means of their transitory possessions, if they use them well, they may be able to merit everlasting rewards. As to which thing, indeed, the divine word, showing it to be possible and altogether advising it, says: "The riches of a man are the redemption of his soul."[2] I, William, count and

---

[1] The Majolus of this family was *not* the same person as the Majolus who was abbot of Cluny 954–994.

[2] See Prov. 13: 8.

duke by the grace of God, diligently pondering this, and desiring to provide for my own salvation while I am still able, have considered it advisable—nay, most necessary, that from the temporal goods which have been conferred upon me I should give some little portion for the gain of my soul. I do this, indeed, in order that I who have thus increased in wealth may not, perchance, at the last be accused of having spent all in caring for my body, but rather may rejoice, when fate at last shall snatch all things away, in having reserved something for myself. Which end, indeed, seems attainable by no more suitable means than that, following the precept of Christ: "I will make his poor my friends"[1] and making the act not a temporary but a lasting one, I should support at my own expense a congregation of monks. And this is my trust, this my hope, indeed, that although I myself am unable to despise all things, nevertheless, by receiving despisers of the world, whom I believe to be righteous, I may receive the reward of the righteous. Therefore be it known to all who live in the unity of the faith and who await the mercy of Christ, and to those who shall succeed them and who shall continue to exist until the end of the world, that, for the love of God and of our Savior Jesus Christ, I hand over from my own rule to the holy apostles, Peter, namely, and Paul, the possessions over which I hold sway, the villa[2] of Cluny, namely, with the court and demesne *mansus*,[3] and the chapel in honor of St. Mary the mother of God and of St. Peter the prince of the apostles, together with all the things pertaining to it, the villas, indeed, the chapels, the serfs of both sexes, the vines, the fields, the meadows, the woods, the waters and their outlets, the mills, the incomes and revenues, what is cultivated and what is not, all in their entirety. Which things are situated in or about the county of Mâcon, each one surrounded by its own bounds. I give, moreover, all these things to the aforesaid apostles—I, William, and my wife Ingelberga—first for the love of God; then for the soul of my lord king Odo;[4] of my father and my mother; for myself and my wife—for the salvation,

namely, of our souls and bodies;—and not least for that of Ava who left me these things in her will;[5] for the souls also of our brothers and sisters and nephews, and of all our relatives of both sexes; for our faithful ones who adhere to our service; for the advancement, also, and integrity of the catholic religion. Finally, since all of us Christians are held together by one bond of love and faith, let this donation be for all,—for the orthodox, namely, of past, present or future times.

I give these things, moreover, with this understanding, that at Cluny a regular monastery shall be constructed in honor of the holy apostles Peter and Paul, and that there the monks shall congregate and live according to the rule of St. Benedict,[6] and that they shall possess, hold, have and order these same things unto all time, provided that the venerable house of prayer which is there shall be faithfully filled with vows and supplications, and that celestial converse shall be sought and striven after with all desire and with the deepest ardor; and also that there shall be diligently directed to God prayers, beseechings and exhortations both for me and for all, according to the order in which mention has been made of them above. And let the monks themselves, together with all the aforesaid possessions, be under the power and dominion of the abbot Berno, who, as long as he shall live, shall preside over them according to the Rule and consistent with his knowledge and ability. But after his death, those same monks shall have power and permission to elect any one of their order whom they please as abbot and rector, following the will of God and the rule promulgated by St. Benedict,—in such a way that neither by the intervention of our own or of any other power may they be impeded from making a purely canonical election. Every five years, moreover, the aforesaid monks shall pay to the church of the apostles at Rome ten *solidi*[7] to supply them with lights; and they shall have the protection of those same apostles and the defense of the Roman pontiff; and those monks may,

---

[1] Luke 16: 9.

[2] In this instance, the word *villa* means an estate, which included an enclosed area (the "court"), land, waste, meadow and various other appurtenances. In many of the other charters of Cluny, however, the word *villa* refers to a small district in which many landowners held land.

[3] A *mansus* (pl. *mansi*) was a farming unit. A "demesne *mansus*" was an outsize farming unit belonging to the lord (in this case William, and soon the monastery of Cluny), which included the *mansi* of dependent peasants.

[4] Odo, related to the later Capetians, was king of the west Franks 888–898.

[5] Ava was a sister of the donor.

[6] For *The Benedictine Rule* see above, p. 17.

[7] A *solidus* was a coin, in this case silver.

with their whole heart and soul, according to their ability and knowledge, build up the aforesaid place. We will, further, that in our times and in those of our successors, according as the opportunities and possibilities of that place shall allow, daily, works of mercy towards the poor, the needy, strangers, and pilgrims will be performed with the greatest zeal. It has pleased us also to insert in this document that, from this day, those same monks there congregated shall be subject neither to our yoke, nor to that of our relatives, nor to the sway of any earthly power. And, through God and all his saints, and by the awful day of judgment, I warn and abjure that no one of the secular princes, no count, no bishop whatever, not the pontiff of the aforesaid Roman see, shall invade the property of these servants of God, or alienate it, or diminish it, or exchange it, or give it as a benefice to any one, or constitute any prelate over them against their will. And that such unhallowed act may be more strictly prohibited to all rash and wicked men, I subjoin the following, giving force to the warning. I adjure you, oh holy apostles and glorious princes of the world, Peter and Paul, and you, oh supreme pontiff of the apostolic see, that, through the canonical and apostolic authority which you have received from God, you remove from participation in the holy church and in eternal life, the robbers and invaders and alienators of these possessions which I do give to you with joyful heart and ready will; and be protectors and defenders of the aforementioned place of Cluny and of the servants of God abiding there, and of all these possessions—on account of the clemency and mercy of the most holy Redeemer. If any one—which Heaven forbid, and which, through the mercy of the God and the protection of the apostles I do not think will happen—whether he be a neighbor or a stranger, no matter what his condition or power, should, through any kind of wild attempt to do any act of violence contrary to this deed of gift which we have ordered to be drawn up for the love of almighty God and for reverence of the chief apostles Peter and Paul; first, indeed, let him incur the wrath of almighty God, and let God remove him from the land of the living and wipe out his name from the book of life, and let his portion be with those who said to the Lord God: Depart from us; and, with Dathan

and Abiron whom the earth, opening its jaws, swallowed up, and hell absorbed while still alive, let him incur everlasting damnation.[1] And being made a companion of Judas let him be kept thrust down there with eternal tortures, and, lest it seem to human eyes that he pass through the present world with impunity, let him experience in his own body, indeed, the torments of future damnation, sharing the double disaster with Heliodorus and Antiochus, of whom one being coerced with sharp blows and scarcely escaped alive; and the other, struck down by the divine will, his members putrefying and swarming with worms, perished most miserably.[2] And let him be a partaker with other sacrilegious persons who presume to plunder the treasure of the house of God; and let him, unless he come to his senses, have as enemy and as the one who will refuse him entrance into the blessed paradise, the key-bearer of the whole hierarchy of the church,[3] and, joined with the latter, St. Paul; both of whom, if he had wished, he might have had as most holy mediators for him. But as far as the worldly law is concerned, he shall be required, the judicial power compelling him, to pay a hundred pounds of gold to those whom he has harmed; and his attempted attack, being frustrated, shall have no effect at all. But the validity of this deed of gift, endowed with all authority, shall always remain inviolate and unshaken, together with the stipulation subjoined. Done publicly in the city of Bourges. I, William, commanded this act to be made and drawn up, and confirmed it with my own hand.

[Here follow the names of Ingelberga and 42 other people, mainly bishops, nobles, and members of William's family.]

[Charters of the Grossi Family: Charter # 802 (March, 951)]

To all who consider the matter reasonably, it is clear that the dispensation of God is so designed that if riches are used well, these transitory things can be transformed into eternal rewards. The Divine word showed that this was possible, saying "Wealth for a man is the redemption of

---

[1] For Dathan and Abiron, Hebrews who challenged Moses in the desert and were swiftly swallowed up by the earth, see Num. 16: 12–15, 25–34.

[2] Judas is the betrayer of Christ. In 2 Macc. 3: 7–27, Heliodorus, minister of King Seleusis of Syria, is sent to plunder the Temple at Jerusalem but is beaten up by mysterious persons sent by divine will. In 2 Macc. 9: 7–9, King Antiochus of Syria falls from a chariot and suffers horribly thereafter.

[3] The "key-bearer of the whole hierarchy of the church" is Saint Peter.

his soul," and again, "Give alms and all things will be clean unto you."[1]

We, that is, I, Doda, a woman, and my son Letbald [II], carefully considering this fact, think it necessary that we share some of the things that were conferred on us, Christ granting, for the benefit of our souls. We do this to make Christ's poor our friends, in accordance with Christ's precept and so that He may receive us, in the end, in the eternal tabernacle.

Therefore, let it be known to all the faithful that we—Doda and my son Letbald—give some of our possessions, with the consent of lord Aquin [I], my husband, for love of God and his holy Apostles, Peter and Paul,[2] to the monastery of Cluny, to support the brothers [i.e., monks] there who ceaselessly serve God and His apostles. [We give] an allod[3] that is located in the *pagus*[4] of Mâcon, called Nouville.[5] The serfs [*servi*] that live there are: Sicbradus and his wife, Robert, Eldefred and his wife and children, Roman and his wife and children, Raynard and his wife and children, Teutbert and his wife and children, Dominic and his wife and children, Nadalis with her children, John with his wife and children, Benedict with his wife and children, Maynard with his wife and children, another Benedict with his wife and children, and a woman too…[6] with her children.

And we give [land in] another *villa*[7] called Colonge and the serfs living there: Teotgrim and his wife and children, Benedict and his wife and children, Martin and his children, Adalgerius and his wife and children, [and] Sicbradus.

And [we give] a *mansus*[8] in Culey and the serfs there: Andrald and his wife and children, Eurald and his wife and children. And [we give] whatever we have at Chazeux along with the serf Landrad who lives there. We also give a little harbor on the Aar river and the serfs living there: Agrimbald and Gerald with their wives and children.

In addition, we give an allod in the *pagus* of Autun, in the *villa* called Beaumont and the serfs living there, John,

Symphorian, Adalard and their wives and children, in order that [the monks] may, for the love of Christ, receive our nephew, Adalgysus, into their society.[9]

[We give] all the things named above with everything that borders on them: vineyards, fields, buildings, serfs of every sex and age, ingress and egress, with all mobile and immobile property already acquired or to be acquired, wholly and completely. We give all this to God omnipotent and His apostles for the salvation of our souls and for the soul of Letbald [I], the father of my son, and for the salvation of Aquin [I], my husband, and of all our relatives and finally for all the faithful in Christ, living and dead.

Moreover, I, the aforesaid Letbald, uncinch the belt of war, cut off the hair of my head and beard for divine love, and with the help of God prepare to receive the monastic habit in the monastery [of Cluny]. Therefore, the property that ought to come to me by paternal inheritance I now give [to Cluny] because of the generosity of my mother and brothers. [I do so] in such a way that while [my mother and brothers] live, they hold and possess it. I give a *mansus* in Fragnes, along with the serf Ermenfred and his wife and children, to [my brother] Theoderic, *clericus*,[10] and after his death let it revert to [Cluny]. And I give another *mansus* at Verzé with the serf Girbald and his wife and children to my brother Hugo. In the *pagus* of Autun I give to [my brother] Aquin [II] the allod that is called Dompierre-les-Ormes, and the serf Benedict and his wife and their son and daughter. [I give Aquin also] another allod in Vaux, and the serfs Teutbald and his wife and children and Adalgarius. [I give all this] on condition that, if these brothers of mine [Hugh and Aquin], who are laymen, die without legitimate offspring, all these properties will go to the monastery as general alms.

If anyone (which we do not believe will happen) either we ourselves (let it not happen!) or any other person, should be tempted to bring a claim in bad faith against

---

[1] Prov. 13: 8 and Luke 11: 41.

[2] As William's foundation charter stipulated, Cluny had been handed over to the apostles Saints Peter and Paul.

[3] An allod in this region was land that was owned outright, in contrast to land held in fief, for example.

[4] A *pagus* was a Roman administrative subdivision.

[5] Almost all the places mentioned in these charters are within about ten miles of the monastery of Cluny.

[6] Effaced in the manuscript.

[7] Here the word *villa* refers to a district.

[8] The reference here is no doubt to a demesne *mansus*.

[9] Possibly Adalgysus is to become a monk; but it is more likely that he is to become a special "friend" of the monastery for whom prayers will be said.

[10] I.e., a priest.

this charter of donation, let him first incur the wrath of God, and let him suffer the fate of Dathan and Abiron and of Judas, the traitor of the Lord. And unless he repents, let him have the apostles [Peter and Paul] bar him from the celestial kingdom. Moreover, in accordance with earthly law, let him be forced to pay ten pounds. But let this donation be made firm by us, with the stipulation added. S[ignum][1] of Doda and her son Letbald, who asked that it be done and confirmed. S. of Aquin, who consents. S. of Hugo. S. of Evrard. S. of Walo. S. of Warembert. S. of Maingaud. S. of Giboin. S. of Leotald. S. of Widald. S. of Hemard. S. of Raimbald. Dated in the month of March in the 15th year of the reign of King Louis.[2] I, brother Andreas, *levite*,[3] undersign at the place for the secretary.

[Charter # 1460 (November 12, 978–November 11, 979)][4]

I, Majolus, humble abbot [of Cluny] by the will of God, and the whole congregation of brothers of the monastery of Cluny. We have decided to grant something from the property of our church to a certain cleric, named Letbald [III] for use during his lifetime, and we have done so, fulfilling his request.

The properties that we grant him are located in the *pagus* of Mâcon, in the *ager*[5] of Grevilly, in a *villa* called Collonge: *mansi*, vineyards, land, meadows, woods, water, and serfs of both sexes and whatever else we have in that place, which came to us from Raculf.[6] And we grant two *mansi* at Boye and whatever we have there. And in Massy, one *mansus*. And in "Ayrodia" [not identified], in a place called Rocca, we give *mansi* with vineyards, land, woods, water, and serfs of every sex and age; and we grant all the property of Chassigny [a place near Lugny that has disappeared]: vineyards, land, meadows, woods, water,

mills and serfs and slaves. And at "Bussiacus" [near Saint-Huruge], similarly [we grant] *mansi*, vineyards, lands, meadows, and woods. And at "Ponciacus" [not id.] [we give] *mansi*, vineyards, and land. Just as Raculf gave these things to us in his testament, so we grant them to [Letbald] on the condition that he hold them while he lives and after his death these things pass to Cluny. And let him pay 12 dinars every year to mark his taking possession.

We also grant to him other property that came from lord Letbald [I], his uncle: a *mansus* at La Verzé and another at Bassy and another at Les Légères, and again another in Fragnes and another in Chazeux. And again a *mansus* in the *pagus* of Autun, at Dompierre-les-Ormes and another in Vaux and the serfs and slaves of both sexes that belong to those *mansi*. Let him hold and possess these properties as listed in this *precaria*[7] for as long as he lives. And when his mortality prevails— something no man can avoid—let this property fall to [Cluny] completely and without delay. [Meanwhile] let him pay 12 dinars every year, on the feast day of Apostles Peter and Paul.

I have confirmed this decree with my own hand and have ordered the brethren to corroborate it, so that it will have force throughout his lifetime. S. of lord Majolus, abbot. S. of Balduin, monk. S. of Vivian. S. of John. S. of Arnulf. S. of Costantinus. S. of Tedbald. S. of Joslen. S. of Grimald. S. of Hugo. S. of Rothard. S. of Ingelbald. S. of Achedeus. S. of Vuitbert. S. of Ingelman. Dated by the hand of Rothard, in the 25th year of the reign of King Lothar.

[Charter # 1577 (Nov. 12, 981–Nov. 11, 982)]

To this holy place, accessible to our prayers [et cetera].[8] I, Rotrudis, and [my husband] Josseran, and my sons, all of us give to God and his holy Apostles, Peter and Paul

---

[1] Usually laypeople did not sign charters; rather they made a mark or sign (their *signum*) that was indicated by the scribe in front of their name. The S refers to this sign.

[2] This was King Louis D'Outremer (r.936–954), one of the last of the Carolingians.

[3] A *levite* was a deacon.

[4] This charter has this range of dates because the scribe dated it in the 25th year of the reign of King Lothar, the son of King Louis, whose rule began on November 12, 954.

[5] The *pagus* of Mâcon was divided into subdivisions called *agri* (sing. *ager*). There were perhaps ten or more *villae* in each *ager*.

[6] Raculf was probably a member of the Grossi family.

[7] This document is a "precarial" donation. A *precaria* was a conditional grant of land *by* a monastery to someone outside of the monastery for his or her lifetime.

[8] This charter began with a formula considered so commonplace that it did not need to be fully written out.

and at the place Cluny, half of a church[1] that is located in the *pagus* of Mâcon, named in honor of St. Peter, with everything that belongs to it, wholly and completely, and [property in] the *villa* that is called Curtil-sous-Buffières. There [we give] a field and a meadow that go together and have the name *ad Salas*. This land borders at the east on a *via publica*[2] and a manmade wall; at the south on a meadow; at the west on a *via publica*, and similarly at the north. [I make this gift] for the salvation of the soul of my husband Josseran, and [for the soul of my son] Bernard. Done at Cluny. Witnesses: Rotrudis, Josseran, Bernard, Israel, Erleus, Hugo, Odo, Raimbert, Umbert. Ingelbald wrote this in the 28th year of the reign of King Lothar.

I will pay a tax of 12 dinars on the feast day of the Prince of the Apostles [i.e., St. Peter]. After my death, let [the property] go to Cluny without delay.

But if anyone wants to bring any bad-faith claim against this donation, let him first incur the wrath of the Omnipotent and all His saints; and unless he returns to his senses, let him be thrust into Hell with the devil. As in the past, let this donation remain firm and stable, with the stipulation added. Done publicly at Cluny. S. of Majolus, who asks that it be done and confirmed. S. of Bernard, S. of Israel, S. of Arleius, S. of Bernard, S. of Hubert. Aldebard, *levita*, wrote this in the 4th year of the reign of Hugh [Capet].

[Charter # 1845 (990–991)]

By the clemency of the Savior a remedy was conceded to the faithful: that they could realize eternal returns on His gifts if they distributed them justly. Wherefore, I, Majolus,[3] in the name of God, give to God and his holy apostles Peter and Paul and at the place Cluny some of my property which is located in the county of Lyon, in the *villa* "Mons" [not id.]. It consists of a demesne *mansus* with a serf named Durannus and his wife, named Aldegard, and their children, and whatever belongs or appears to belong to this *mansus*, namely fields, vineyards, meadows, woods, pasturelands, water and water courses, that is already acquired or will be acquired, whole and complete. I make this donation first for my soul and for my burial [in Cluny's cemetery] and for the soul of my father Josseran and of my mother Rotrudis and of my brothers, and for the souls of my *parentes*[4] and for the salvation of all the departed faithful, so that all may profit in common. [I give it] on the condition that I may hold and possess it while I live, and that every year

[Charter # 2508 (994–1030?)][5]

Notice of a quitclaim[6] that took place at Cluny in the presence of lord Rainald, venerable prior at that place; and of other monks who were there, namely Walter, Aymo, Amizon, Warner, Lanfred, Locerius, Giso; and of noblemen: Witbert, Robert, Ildinus, Gislebert, Bernard, and Hugo. In the first place, let all, present and future, know that a long and very protracted quarrel between the monks of Cluny and Majolus[7] finally, by God's mercy, came to this end result: first that he [Majolus] quit his claim to the land which Oddo and Teza [Oddo's] daughter[8] destined for us and handed over by charter: the woods in *Grandi Monte* with its borders [as follows]: on the east [it borders on] its own inheritance [namely] passing between mountains and through wasteland and across the castle of Teodoric; on the south [it borders on] *terra francorum*;[9] on the west and north [it borders on] land of St. Peter. [Majolus] draws up this notice at this time so that he may reunite himself with the favor of St. Peter and the brothers, and so that he may persevere in future

---

[1] Churches could be given in whole or in part—since the revenues could be divided—and with or without their tithes (which often belonged not to the holder of the church but to the local bishop).

[2] In this region, a *via publica* was a dirt road. There was a very extensive network of roads in the area around Cluny left over from the Roman period.

[3] Not the Cluniac abbot but rather a member of the Grossi family.

[4] The *parentes* were much broader than the nuclear family but perhaps not quite as large as a clan.

[5] The scribe did not give a date. But we know that Rainald was prior at Cluny beginning in 994 and that Majolus died *c.*1030. These give us, respectively, the *terminus post quem* [time after which] and the *terminus ante quem* [the time before which] the document must have been drawn up.

[6] That is, this gives notice that a claim has been dropped ("quit").

[7] The donor from the Grossi family.

[8] Oddo and Teza were probably relatives of Majolus.

[9] This probably refers to land of free peasants.

as a faithful servant in the service of St. Peter. S. Hugo, S. Witbert, S. Robert, S. Ildinus, S. Gislebert, S. Bernard.

[Charter # 2946 (1018–1030?)¹]

In the name of the incarnate Word. I, Raimodis, formerly the wife of the lord Wichard, now dead, and now joined in matrimony to lord Ansedeus, my husband; with the consent and good will [of Ansedeus], I give or rather give again some land which is called Chazeux to St. Peter and Cluny. [I give it] for the soul of my husband Wichard. This land once belonged to St. Peter and Cluny. But the abbot and monks gave it as a precarial gift to lord Letbald [III], a certain cleric who afterwards became bishop

of Mâcon. Letbald, acting wrongly, alienated [the land] from St. Peter and gave it to Gauzeran to make amends for killing Gauzeran's relative, Berengar.

Therefore I give it again to St. Peter for the soul of my husband Wichard, and for Gauzeran, Wichard's father. I also give a slave named Adalgarda and her children, and [I give] the whole inheritance for the soul of my husband Wichard, and of my daughter Wiceline, and for my own soul.

If anyone wants to bring false claim against this donation, let him not prevail, but let him pay a pound of gold into the public treasury. S. of Raimodis, who asked that this charter be done and confirmed. S. of Ansedeus. S. of another Ansedeus. S. of Achard. S. of Walter. S. of Costabulus. S. of Ugo.

4.4 Love and complaints in Angoulême: *Agreement between Count William of the Aquitanians and Hugh IV of Lusignan* (1028). Original in Latin.

This document of a series of disputes and their eventual settlement is written from the point of view of Hugh, who was the castellan (the lord of a castle and its garrison) of Lusignan, although he here calls himself Chiliarch—"leader of one thousand." The events described may be dated between about 1022 and 1028. The chief protagonists of Hugh's drama are Hugh himself and William, whom he calls "count of the Aquitainians" but who was, more importantly, count of Poitou (he ruled from *c.*995–1030). The center of his county was Poitiers, which included Lusignan (about 15 miles southwest of Poitiers) and many of the other locations mentioned in this document. Other characters who appear are mainly laymen, laywomen, and a few bishops. The *Agreement* presents an admittedly one-sided picture of the activities of the French aristocracy in the early eleventh century. As you read this document, consider what it meant to be the "man" of a lord. In what ways were legal and quasi-legal proceedings essential institutions in the Poitou? What were the meanings of "love," "anger," and "sorrow" in early eleventh-century Poitou? Try writing an account of the agreements between Hugh and the count from the *count's* point of view.

[Source: Jane Martindale, "Conventum inter Guillelmum Aquitanorum comitem et Hugonem Chiliarchum," in *Status, Authority and Regional Power: Aquitaine and France, 9th to 12th Centuries* (Aldershot: Variorum, 1997), Paper VIIb, pp. 541–52. Translated by Thomas Greene and Barbara H. Rosenwein from the Latin text, in consultation with translations by George Beech, "Hugh of Lusignan: Agreement between Lord and Vassal," in *Readings in Medieval History*, ed. Patrick J. Geary, 4th ed. (Toronto: University of Toronto Press, 2010), pp. 377–81; Martindale, "Conventum," pp. 542a–552; and Paul Hyams and others, "Agreement between Duke William V of Aquitaine and Hugh IV of Lusignan" at http://www.fordham.edu/halsall/source/agreement.asp]

¹ This date, which is quite uncertain, is suggested on the basis of other charters that tell us at what date Raimodis, the donor in this charter, became a widow.

William, called count of the Aquitainians, had an agreement with Hugh the Chiliarch that when Viscount Boso died, William would give Boso's honor in commendation to Hugh.[1] Bishop Roho saw and heard this and kissed the arm of the count.[2] But Viscount Savary seized from Hugh land which Hugh held from Count William.[3] When the viscount died the count promised Hugh that he would make no agreement or accord with Ralph, the brother of the dead viscount, until the land had been restored. He said this in the presence of all, but afterwards he secretly gave the land to Ralph. For that land itself, or for a larger one, or for other things, Hugh had an agreement with Viscount Ralph that he would accept Ralph's daughter as his wife. When the count heard this he was greatly angered and he went humbly to Hugh and said to him, "Don't marry Ralph's daughter. I will give to you whatever you ask of me, and you will be my friend before all others except my son." Hugh did what the count ordered, and out of love and fidelity for the count he secretly rejected the woman.

At that time it happened that Joscelin of Parthenay castle died.[4] The count said that he would give Joscelin's honor and wife to Hugh, and if Hugh refused to accept them, he would no longer have confidence in him. Hugh did not entreat or request this from the count, either for himself or for anyone else. Thinking it over, he said to the count, "I will do all that you have ordered." The count, however, after holding a public meeting with Count Fulk,[5] promised to give Fulk something from his own benefices, and Fulk promised that he would give Hugh what belonged to him. At the meeting, the count called for Viscount Ralph and said to him: "Hugh will not keep the agreement he has with you because I forbid him to. But Fulk and I have an agreement that we will give to Hugh the honor and wife of Joscelin. We do this to mess up your life, because you are not faithful to me." When he heard this Ralph was very hurt and he said to the count, "For God's sake do not do that." So the count said, "Pledge

to me that you will not give Hugh your daughter, nor keep your agreement with him, and in turn I will arrange that he not possess the honor and wife of Joscelin." And they so acted that Hugh got neither the one nor the other. Ralph went to Count William, who was at Montreuil castle, sending a message to Hugh that they should talk together. That was done. And Ralph said to Hugh, "I tell you this in confidence so that you will not give me away. Pledge to me that you will help me against Count William, and I will keep your agreement for you and will aid you against all men." But Hugh refused all of this out of his love for Count William. Hugh and Ralph parted unhappily. Then Ralph began to prosecute a public dispute with Count William, while Hugh, out of love for the count, started one with Ralph. And Hugh suffered great harm.

When Ralph died, Hugh asked the count to restore to him the land which Ralph had seized from him. Moreover the count said to Hugh, "I will not make an agreement with Viscount Josfred, the nephew of Ralph, nor with the men of Thouars castle, until I return your land." Yet none of this was done, and the count went and made an agreement with Viscount Josfred and with the men of Thouars castle. He never made an agreement with Hugh, and Hugh did not get his land. And because of the misdeeds which Hugh committed on the count's behalf, Josfred got into a dispute with Hugh, and he burned Mouzeuil castle and captured Hugh's horsemen and cut off their hands and did many other things. The count did not help Hugh at all nor did he broker a good agreement between Josfred and Hugh, but Hugh even now has lost his land, and for the sake of the count he has lost still other land that he was holding peacefully. And when Hugh saw that he was not going to get his land he took forty-three of the best horsemen of Thouars. He could have had peace and his land and justice for the wrongdoing; and if he had been willing to accept a ransom he could have had 40,000 solidi.[6]

When the count heard this he should have been glad, but he was sad and sent for Hugh, saying to him, "Give

---

[1] Boso (d. by 1033) was viscount of Chatellerault, 20 miles northeast of Poitiers. An "honor" referred to property.

[2] Roho was bishop of Angoulême (r.1020–1036). Formal agreements were often concluded by a kiss of peace; sometimes witnesses participated in this gesture of concord and, as here, the kiss might function as well as a sign of deference.

[3] Savary was viscount of Thouars.

[4] The "castles" that this document refers to were not luxurious chateaux but rather strongholds or fortresses. Some of them were thrown up haphazardly and minimally fortified; others were built more solidly and sometimes included a stone tower. Armed garrisons of horsemen guarded the castles and were important players—as victims, hostages, and guarantors—in the disputes and negotiations between regional lords. Included in the notion of the castle was the surrounding district that it dominated.

[5] Fulk was count of Anjou (r.987–1040).

[6] A solidus (pl. solidi) is here a silver coin.

me back the men." Hugh answered him, "Why do you ask these things of me, Lord? I am a loser only because of my loyalty to you." Then the count said, "I do not ask this of you to hurt you, but in fact because you are mine to do my will. And as all will know by our agreement, I will take over those men on condition that I make a settlement with you that your lands will be secured and the wrongdoing compensated, or I will return the men to you. Do this without doubting my credibility and good faith, and if anything should turn out badly for you, you can be sure that I will hand them over to you." Hugh put his trust in God and the count and handed the men over to the count according to this agreement. Later on Hugh got neither the men nor justice, and he lost his land.

The count of the Poitevins[1] and Bishop Gilbert[2] had an agreement among themselves with Joscelin, Hugh's uncle.[3] It was about the castle at Vivonne, and it said that after the death of Bishop Gilbert it was to be Joscelin's castle. During his lifetime, the bishop made the men of that castle commend themselves to Joscelin, and he gave Joscelin the tower. And after the death of both men, the count made an agreement between Hugh and Bishop Isembert[4] that Hugh would get half of the castle and half of the demesne and two shares of the vassals' fiefs.[5] Then the count made Hugh commend himself to Bishop Isembert—but now he has taken the better estate from them.

A certain official named Aimery seized the castle called Civray from Bernard, his lord, but this castle was rightly Hugh's, as it had been his father's. Because of his anger at Aimery, Count William urged Hugh to become the man[6] of Bernard for the part of the castle that had belonged to his father, so that together they might wage a dispute with Aimery. But it seemed wrong to Hugh that he become Bernard's man, and he did not want to do it. The count persisted in this admonition for a year, and the more he got angry, the more he urged Hugh to become the man of Bernard. After a year passed, the count came to Hugh as if in anger and said to him, "Why don't you make an agreement with Bernard? You owe so much to me that if I should tell you to make a peasant into a lord

you should do it. Do what I say, and if it should turn out badly for you, come and see me about it." Hugh believed him and became the man of Bernard for the fourth part of Civray castle. But Bernard made the count a guarantor to Hugh, as well as four hostages. The count said to Hugh, "Commend those hostages to me under such conditions that if Bernard does not faithfully keep your agreements, I will turn them over to your custody and I will faithfully aid you." How strongly the count promised this to Hugh he himself knows very well. Hugh trusted in his lord and began a fierce dispute on account of Civray castle and suffered great losses in men and many other things. The count started to build a castle, which he called Couhé, but he did not finish it for Hugh. Instead, he talked it over with Aimery, abandoned the castle, and in no way aided Hugh.

Afterwards the count grew even more unhappy with Aimery on account of the castle called Chizé, which Aimery had seized, and Hugh and the count joined together in a dispute against Aimery. The count besieged the castle called Mallevault because of the injuries that Aimery had done to him and captured it, and Hugh aided him as best he could. Before Hugh left the count, the count promised him—just as a lord ought rightly to promise to his man—that he would make no agreement or alliance with Aimery without Hugh, and that Mallevault would not be rebuilt without his advice. But the count did make an agreement with Aimery and allowed him to rebuild Mallevault without the advice of Hugh. As long as Aimery lived, none of the property mentioned above came to Hugh.

After the death of Aimery a great dispute began between his son Aimery and Hugh. At the same time Hugh went to the count and said to him, "Things are going badly for me now, my Lord, because I have none of the property that you acquired for me." The count answered him, "I am going to hold a public hearing with them so that if they act well, good; if not, I will turn over to you the castle which I started." And the castle was constructed on the advice of Bernard, who thus far had helped Hugh in the dispute. When they saw the heavy

---

[1] That is, Count William.

[2] Gilbert was bishop of Poitiers (r.975–1023/1024).

[3] This is presumably a different Joscelin from the one of Parthenay.

[4] Isembert was Gilbert's successor as bishop of Poitiers.

[5] It was possible to have "half a castle" because what was at stake were the revenues due the castle, not the stronghold itself. The "demesne" was land belonging to the fortress directly; other land pertaining to it was granted out in fief.

[6] The word used here is *homo*, which may be translated as "man" or "vassal," depending on your view of the relations among these aristocrats and the implications of these words.

demands Hugh was making on them, the men of Civray were not able to hold out, and they made an agreement with Bernard and returned the castle to him. He received it without the advice of Hugh. Now both Bernard and Aimery were in dispute with Hugh, and he was alone against them. Coming to the count, Hugh said to him, "Lord, I am doing very badly because the lord whom I got upon your advice has just taken away my property. I beg and urge you by the faith which a lord owes to aid his man: either let me have a proper public hearing or my property, just as you pledged to me; or return to me the hostages which I commended to you; and above all help me as you pledged to me." The count, however, neither aided him, nor made an agreement with him, nor returned the hostages but released them and gave them back to Bernard. And after that the dispute between Bernard and Aimery and Hugh increased.

And since Hugh saw that the count aided him in no way, he went to seek the advice of Gerald, the bishop of Limoges. Gerald and Hugh went together into La Marche against Bernard and built a castle. But the count, who ought to have aided Hugh, seized the castle from him and burned it. And the count and his son ordered all their men not to help Hugh unless they wished to die. Then Bernard accepted the council of his men that they should do harm to Hugh on the advice of the count, and they appointed a deadline fifteen days away. During those fifteen days the count arranged a truce between Bernard and Hugh. Three days into the truce the count took Hugh along with his army to Apremont castle, and a meeting was held in his castle. From there the count went to Blaye, where he was to have a meeting with Count Sancho, and he told Hugh that he should come along. And Hugh responded, "Lord, why do you ask me to go with you? You yourself know how short the truce is which I have with Bernard, and he himself is threatening to do me harm." The count said to him: "Do not fear that they will do anything to you as long as you are with me." And the count took Hugh with him by force and against Hugh's will.

While they were staying at the meeting place, Hugh's men heard that Bernard was coming against him; they sent a message to Hugh to come. Then Hugh said to the count, "Bernard is attacking me." And the count said, "Don't be afraid that they will dare attack you; and, besides, you need them to attack so that I can destroy them and aid you." In that same hour the count sent orders through his men, and he told Hugh to go on ahead, and he followed him. When Hugh reached Lusignan, Bernard was at Confolens castle. He had captured the suburb and the outskirts and burned everything; he had taken spoils, captured men, and done plenty of other evil deeds. A messenger ran up to Hugh and said to him, "Bernard has your wife besieged in the old castle which survived the fire." Hugh came to the count and said to him: "My lord, help me now, because my wife is now being besieged." But the count gave him no aid or advice at all. And Bernard turned back, and he and his men did so much harm to Hugh and his men that 50,000 *solidi* would not have paid for it. And Hugh suffered this damage during the truce that the count offered to him at Blaye.

Not long after this Hugh went to Gençay castle and burned it and seized the men and women and took everything with him. Hastening to the count, he said to him, "Lord, give me permission to build the castle which I burned." And the count said to him, "You are the man of Fulk, how can you build the castle? Fulk will demand it of you, and you will not be strong enough to keep it from him." Hugh said, "Lord, when I became Fulk's man I told him that his men were seizing what was my right and that if I was able to regain possession of them, I would do it, but I would only hold it in his fealty, which is what I want to do. And Fulk said to me, 'If you take anything from them, don't take from me.'" When the count heard that Fulk and Hugh had such an agreement, he was pleased. And the count said to Hugh: "Build the castle under such an agreement that if I am able to negotiate with Count Fulk about my price and yours, one part will be mine and the other yours."

And Hugh built the castle. Then Fulk asked the count for it. The count responded to him, "Ask Hugh for it." And Fulk did that. Hugh answered him, "When I became your man, I said to you that if I would be strong enough to take castles from my enemies, I should take them and hold them in your fealty, and I wanted to do that because the castle which you are demanding belonged to my relatives, and I have a better right to it than those who were holding it." But Fulk said, "You who are mine, how can you hold against my will something I didn't give to you?" And Hugh sought advice from the count. The count told him, "If he is willing to give you guarantees that your enemies will not have the castle, then you cannot keep it. If not, keep it, because he will not be able to accuse you of anything." Hugh asked that Fulk give hostages to him, and Fulk gave him nothing, but said, "I will make my demands known to the count and give hostages to him and he will give you some of his own." Then the meeting turned angry. Fulk demanded Hugh's castle from the count. Hugh said, "I will not give it up without assurances." The count said to him, "I will give an assurance, and he has told me what sort to give." Hugh said, "Take what you want from Count Fulk and give me what I'm asking for. Give me the man who has custody of the tower at Melle, so that if Aimery should get the castle without my advice, and harm should befall me, that man will turn the tower over to me." The count said to him, "I will not do this, because I cannot." Hugh said, "If you don't want to do this with Melle, make the same agreement with regard to Chizé." But the count didn't to do either.

It seemed to Hugh and his men that the count was treating him badly. And they parted in anger. Then Hugh sent all kinds of necessities into the castle and intended to hold it against all comers if they would not give him assurances. The count came out of the city,[1] asked Hugh to come to him, and commanded through Count William of Angoulême that he submit himself to the mercy of the count, because the count could not change the fact that he had to aid Fulk; and he was afraid to lose either Fulk or Hugh. Then Hugh committed himself to the trust and friendship of the count his lord, and he did this out of love for him because he was assured that he would not suffer harm at Fulk's hands. And the count said: "Let Hugh do this for me and I will keep the faith with him that a lord ought to keep with his man. If he suffers harm, he will know that I have betrayed him, and he will never trust me again." And Hugh said, "My lord has spoken similarly to me about many things by which he has deceived me." And not a single one of Hugh's men would advise him to trust the count. But the count reminded Hugh of all the good things which he had done for him, and Hugh, holding back the count by his love and entreaties—that is by their common oath—said to the count, "I will put all my trust in you, but watch out that you do not do me wrong, for if you do, I will not be faithful to you nor will I serve you, nor will I render fidelity to you. But, on account of the fact that I will be separated from you and you are not able to give me guarantees, I want you to give me my fief as a pledge that then I will no longer serve you, and release me from the oath which I have made to you." The count answered, "Gladly."

Hugh returned the castle to the count, against the wishes of his men, on condition that Aimery would not have it without Hugh's advice and that Hugh would suffer no harm. On account of hearing those lies, Hugh accepted his fief as a pledge, and the count gave it to him on condi-

tion that if he should suffer harm because of the agreement about Gençay, Hugh would never again serve him. And the count released him from his oaths, so that he would no longer do anything for the count on account of them, but not out of ill will. [But] the count handed over Gençay without the advice of Hugh and got money and some demesne land. It went very badly for Hugh, with men killed, houses burned, booty taken, land seized and many other things which in truth cannot be enumerated. When this had ended the count gave Hugh a respite and promised that he would give him a benefice either of something that was his by right or something that would be pleasing to him. But when this period passed the count did nothing for Hugh. He sent an order to him: "Don't wait, because I am not going to do anything for you. Even if the whole world were mine I would not give you as much as a finger could lift with regard to this matter."

When Hugh heard this he went to the court of the count and made the case for his rights, but it did him no good. This saddened Hugh, and in the hearing of all he renounced his fealty[2] to the count, except what he owed for the city [of Poitiers] and his own person. Before either Hugh or his men did any harm, the men of the count seized a benefice from Hugh's men in the name of war. When Hugh saw this he went to Chizé castle, which had been his uncle's but which Peter[3] was holding unjustly, and from which much harm was being done to Hugh. He seized the tower and threw out Peter's men. Hugh did this because he thought he had the right—because it had belonged to his father or others of his relatives—which he was losing. When the count heard of this he was greatly saddened and sent an order to Hugh that he turn over the tower that he had taken away from Peter. Hugh demanded that the count return the honor of his father and the other things which belonged to his relatives and to which he had right, and he would surrender the tower and all the things that he had taken within it, and in addition the entire honor which had belonged to Joscelin[4] and which the count had given him. The count thought this over and they arranged for a hearing. And the count said to Hugh, "I will not give you those honors which you ask of me, but I will give you that honor which was your uncle's—the castle, the tower and the entire honor—on

---

[1] Presumably Poitiers.

[2] The Latin word here is *defidavit*, which means defied. The root of the word is "faith"; a man declares his faith (*fides*=fidelity) to his lord, but if he formally renounces that fealty, as here, he "defies"—"de-fealties"—him.

[3] Peter has not been identified.

[4] This Joscelin was Hugh's uncle.

condition that you no longer demand of me that honor which was your father's, or others of your relatives, nor anything which you claim as your right."

When he heard this Hugh greatly mistrusted the count, because through evil trickery in the past the count had deceived Hugh in many things. He said to the count, "I don't dare do this, because I fear that you will threaten me with harm, as you have done with regard to many other things." The count said to Hugh, "I will give such assurances to you that you will no longer distrust me." Hugh said to him, "What kind of assurances?" The count said, "I will produce a serf who will undergo an ordeal for you so that you will not doubt that the agreement which we make among ourselves will be good and firm. And with regard to all the affairs of the past, no harm will ever again be done to you, but the agreement will be kept firmly without any evil trickery." When Hugh heard what the count was saying in this way, he said, "You are my lord. I will not take a guarantee from you, but I will simply rely on the mercy of the Lord and yourself." The count said to Hugh, "Give up all those claims that you have demanded from me in the past and swear fidelity to me and my son, and I will give you your uncle's honor or something else of equal value in exchange for it." And Hugh said, "Lord, I beg you by God and this blessed crucifix which is made in the figure of Christ that you do not make me do this if in future you and your son intend to threaten me with evil trickery." The count said, "My son and I will do this in faith and without evil trickery." Hugh said, "And when I have sworn fidelity to you, you will ask me for Chizé castle, and if I should not turn it over to you, you will say that it is not right that I deny you the castle which I hold from you; but if I should turn it over to you, you and your son will take it away from me because you will have given me no guarantee except the mercy of God and yourself." The count said, "We will not do that, but if we should demand it of you, don't turn it over to us."

They received Hugh as their man in faith and trust under the terms of the agreement as it was finally pronounced: that the count and his son should bear faith to Hugh without evil trickery. And they made Hugh give up everything that he claimed from the past. And he swore fidelity to them, and they gave him the honor of his uncle Joscelin, just as Joscelin held it one year before he died.

Here end the agreements between the count and Hugh.

4.5 The Peace of God at Bourges: Andrew of Fleury, *The Miracles of St. Benedict* (1040–1043). Original in Latin.

The Peace of God was a movement initiated by bishops, and eventually declared by kings as well, to protect unarmed people (including clerics) and property (including church property) from armed predators. At church synods, laypeople and churchmen alike met to proclaim the Peace. Those who fought (the *bellatores* or *milites*: the knights) swore oaths not to violate the Peace. In the late 1030s, at one such synod, Aimon, the archbishop of Bourges from 1030 to 1070, organized a militia consisting of clergy, peasants, and a few nobles that succeeded in forcing most of the nobility of the region to take the oath. The militia even enforced the Peace by going to war against breakers of the oath. But it ran into opposition from one holdout, Odo, lord of Déols, who defeated it soundly. Andrew, a monk at the monastery of Fleury, recounted the incident in the course of his work on the *Miracles of St. Benedict*, written 1040–1043. He praised the militia's initial promise but berated it for its "ambition" and confidence in its own power rather than God's. From this document, consider what might have been the interest of common people in the Peace of God. How might the sorts of disputes described in the *Agreement between Count William and Hugh* (above, p. 181) have contributed to the Peace of God movement?

[Source: *The Peace of God: Social Violence and Religious Response in France around the Year* 1000, ed. Thomas Head and Richard Landes (Ithaca, NY: Cornell University Press, 1992), pp. 339–42.]

5.1 In the 1038th year after the incarnation of the Lord, on the eighth day of August, in the middle of the day, the sun was darkened and hid the rays of its splendors for a space of almost two hours. Again the following morning it remained under the same appearance for the entire day and unremittingly gave off bloody flames.

5.2. At this very same time, Archbishop Aimon of Bourges wished to impose peace in his diocese through the swearing of an oath. After he had summoned the fellow bishops of his province and had sought advice from these suffragans, he bound all men of fifteen years of age and over by the following law: that they would come forth with one heart as opponents of any violation of the oath they had sworn, that they would in no way withdraw secretly from the pact even if they should lose their property, and that, what is more, if necessity should demand it, they would go after those who had repudiated the oath with arms. Nor were ministers of the sacraments excepted, but they often took banners from the sanctuary of the Lord and attacked the violators of the sworn peace with the rest of the crowd of laypeople. In this way they many times routed the faithless and brought their castles down to the ground. With the help of God they so terrified the rebels that, as the coming of the faithful was proclaimed far and wide by rumor among the populace, the rebels scattered. Leaving the gates of their towns open, they sought safety in flight, harried by divinely inspired terror. You would have seen [the faithful] raging against the multitude of those who ignore God, as if they were some other people of Israel. Presently they trampled [the rebels] underfoot so that they forced them to return to the laws of the pact which they had ignored.

We thought it fitting to insert in writing that which was agreed to in the pact which the archbishop himself, along with various fellow bishops, promised under oath in the following way: "I Aimon, by the gift of God archbishop of Bourges, promise with my whole heart and mouth to God and to his saints that I shall discharge with my whole spirit and without any guile or dissimulation everything that follows. That is, I will wholeheartedly attack those who steal ecclesiastical property, those who provoke pillage, those who oppress monks, nuns, and clerics, and those who fight against holy mother church, until they repent. I will not be beguiled by the enticement of gifts, or moved by any reason of bonds of kinship or neighborliness, or in any way deviate from the path

of righteousness. I promise to move with all my troops against those who dare in any manner to transgress the decrees and not to cease in any way until the purpose of the traitor has been overcome."

He swore this over the relics of Stephen, the first martyr for Christ, and urged the other [bishops] to do likewise. Obeying with one heart, his fellow bishops made among everyone age fifteen or older (as we already said) in their separate dioceses subscribe [the pact] with the same promise. Fear and trembling then struck the hearts of the unfaithful so that they feared the multitude of the unarmed peasantry as if it were a battle line of armored men. Their hearts fell so that, forgetting their status as knights and abandoning their fortified places, they fled from the humble peasants as from the cohorts of very powerful kings. The prayer of David fitted the situation most aptly: "For thou dost deliver a humble people, but the haughty eyes thou dost bring down, for who is God but the Lord?"[1] ... Odo of Déols remained alone among the whole multitude [of rebels], reserved by the judgment of God for the punishment of evil doers.

5.3. When by the will of God they had, trusting in the help of divine strength, established peace in every direction, ambition (the root and aid of all evil) began to seep along the stalks of such good works. They forgot that God is the strength and rampart of his people and ascribed the power of God to their apostate power.... Thus the aforementioned bishop was touched by the sting of mammon[2] and raged around and around in blind ambition. Unmindful of his episcopal dignity, he attacked Beneciacum, the castle of one Stephen, along with a multitude of the people of Bourges. He reproached Stephen for the fault of having ignored the peace, he tried to burn the castle with flames and ordered it to be leveled to the ground, as if he were exacting the vengeance of God upon it. They burned the castle, which was hemmed in on all sides by the siege, with more than one thousand four hundred people of both sexes inside. Stephen alone of that great number escaped, although his brothers, wife, and sons were all consumed by the fire, and he placed the laurel wreath of his great victory on their wretched heads. The inhabitants of that region for a radius of fourteen miles had fled to this castle and, since they feared the theft of their possessions, they had brought them along. The cruel victors were hardly moved by the laments of

---

[1] Ps. 18: 27, 31; Douay, Ps. 17: 28, 32.

[2] The false god personifying riches and avarice.

the dying, they did not take pity on women beating their breasts; the crowd of infants clinging to their mothers' breasts did not touch any vein of mercy.... And so the just bore responsibility for the crime of the iniquitous and the just perished in place of the impious. Having been granted this great triumph, the people returned to their homes dancing with a pitiable joy. Stephen was placed under guard in a prison in Bourges.

5.4. Almighty God wished to avenge the blood of his servants and, not long after this, set the aforesaid bishop against Odo, the sole rebel. The bishop sought to force Odo to join in the pact common to all, but he would not delay in making an armed attack. Discovering that Odo's spirit remained inflexible, as was God's will, Aimon began—while the blood of the innocents was not yet dry—to collect allies together from all sides, including a large contingent of God's ministers. Confiding in lesser things, he directed his battleline against the enemy. When both armies stood almost at grips, a sound was made heavenward [indicating that Aimon's forces should] retreat, since they no longer had the Lord with them as a leader. When they made no sign of following this advice, an enormous globe of flashing light fell in their midst. Thus it came to pass, as it is said, "Flash forth the lightning and scatter them, send out the arrows and rout them!"[1] Then the people perceived that they were much inferior to their adversaries, since those exceeded in number the sands of the sea. They decided that some foot soldiers should be mounted on various animals and mixed into the cohorts of mounted warriors [*milites*] so that they would be judged mounted warriors by their opponents, more because of the appearance of their being mounted than because of the setting of their weapons. Without delay up to two thousand of the plebeian rabble were mounted on asses and arrayed as knights among the order of knights. But these men were terrified and they took flight along the banks of the Cher. They were killed in such numbers that they blocked the river in such a way that they made a bridge out of the bodies of the dying over which their enemies proceeded. More fell by their own swords than by those of their pursuers.... The number of the dying could not be comprehended: in one valley seven hundred clerics fell. Thus the most tempered judgment of God made those people—who had refused obedience to any requests for mercy, and had not been moved by the smell of their brothers' being burned, and had rejoiced more than was just to have their hands in an unfortunate victory—lost their lives along with that victory.

4.6 A castellan's revenues and properties in Catalonia: *Charter of Guillem Guifred* (1041–1075). Original in Latin.

Some time between 1041 and 1075 Bishop Guillem Guifred had a memorandum drawn up of the dues, properties, and services that were owed him as one of the lords of Sanahuja, a castle in Catalonia (today Spain). Although other castellans, such as Hugh of Lusignan (see p. 181), could not claim precisely the same mix that Guillem commanded, this list provides a good example of the sort of resources that holders of fortifications might count on. Compare it with the revenues that the bishop of Marseille could command in the Carolingian period, as evidenced by the *Polyptyque of the Church of Saint Mary of Marseille*, above, p. 107.

[Source: Pierre Bonnassie, "The Banal Seigneury and the 'Reconditioning' of the Free Peasantry," in *Debating the Middle Ages: Issues and Readings*, ed. Lester K. Little and Barbara H. Rosenwein (Oxford: Basil Blackwell, 1988), pp. 114–15.]

---

[1] Ps.144: 6; Douay Ps. 143: 6.

This is a brief reminder of what the bishop ought to have in his castellany of Sanahuja, by use and by right.

In the first place, half of the revenue of the courts without deceit. From the market, half of what comes to the lords, by justice and by right, that is to say of the fines, with the exception of rights on the udders of the cows, which belong to the castle. Of the oven, half. Of rights on minting, half.

And the bishop agrees with the lords of Sanahuja that they should bring before him the men [of the castellany], and that he should levy on them, every year, the *queste* [a tax] of bread and meat. The bailiff of the lord should go with the bailiff of the bishop to the cellars of Sanahuja, and they should judge the barrels together for levying the *compra* [a tax] of the bishop. And that the bailiffs of the lords should assess the service of those who owe army service with donkeys and other equipment, that it should be estimated under oath, and when it has been estimated, the revenue should be shared by the lord and the *castlà* [the head of the garrison that guards the castle], and the *castlà* should give the bishop his part....

In the houses of Sanahuja, the bishop has the use of the wood, cabbages, chard, cheese, ewes, except in the houses of the priests, the *cabalers* [horsemen] and the bailiffs of the lords; and all this he may use in all the other houses of Sanahuja.... And the peasants of Sanahuja who work with a team should give the bishop a *sextarius* [a unit of measure] of oats and a sheaf, those who share a team with several others should give a *hemina* [another unit of measure] of oats, and a sheaf.

And if an animal enters into the bishop's *dominicatura* [demesne—the land belonging to the lord] in Sanahuja, and is retaken there, his master should buy him back for as many pennies as the animal has feet. And the bishop's woods enjoy a franchise [a privilege] such that no man may hunt within a stone's throw of it... and a man of Sanahuja who catches a rabbit in the woods must give an ox, a pig, and nine pairs of live rabbits to the bishop in reparation.

And all the men of Sanahuja must work for the bishop on the construction of his houses and owe him transport services on the back of their beasts, with the exception of priests, *cabalers*, the lords' bailiffs, and merchants.

And no lord may award any franchise at Sanahuja without the consent of the bishop.

And the men of Sanahuja must carry the bishop's bulls and messages at his command, to any place he may desire....

And in all the mills in the territory of Sanahuja already constructed, or those to be constructed, the bishop should have the quarter [of the revenues?], and in all the use of *destre mugar* [free use of the mill for his grain], under compulsion....

This was enacted by Guillem Guifred, bishop.

BYZANTINE EXPANSION

4.7 Military life: Constantine VII Porphyrogenitus, *Military Advice to His Son* (950–958). Original in Greek.

Emperor Constantine VII Porphyrogenitus (r.913–959) was a major force behind the revival of art and learning at Byzantium known as the Macedonian Renaissance. Likely the author of a famous book on the ceremonies of the court, he also wrote other treatises including the shorter work on military expeditions excerpted here, intended for his son but never finished. Here, as in his book on ceremonies, he concentrated on the formal aspects of the job: the requisitioning of materiel, the opportunities for gift-giving, the triumphal return, and the officials involved in all of these events. What would Dhuoda (p. 150 above) say about Constantine's advice to his son? What would Constantine say about Dhuoda's?

[Source: *Constantine Porphyrogenitus: Three Treatises on Imperial Military Expeditions*, ed. and trans. John F. Haldon (Vienna: Österreichischen Akademien der Wissenschaften, 1997), pp. 95, 97, 99, 101, 107, 109, 123, 141, 143, 145 (slightly modified).]

Constantine, Emperor of the Romans in Christ the Eternal King, Son of Leo the Most Wise Emperor of Blessed Memory, Descendant of Basil the Most Courageous and Most Brave Emperor, to Romanus, God-Crowned Emperor, His Son

What Should Be Observed When the Great and High Emperor of the Romans Goes on Campaign

Listen, son, to the words of your father, Solomon exhorts you. For you will hear about duties from many, but you will not reap the lessons of virtue by nature alone unless you hear the best things from your father. For when you have accepted his words as genuinely truthful, you will have what amounts to a paternal legacy, always promoting your salvation. For the words of others, spoken for favors, often lack truth; whereas those from a father's heart, being honest, bestow upon their sons perpetual advantage. Listen, therefore, son, to your father, whose advice it is not good to ignore; for if ignorance is bad, it is clear that a knowledge of practical matters is good, and most especially of those things touching upon the affairs of the state, to which much care has been devoted. For what could be more important than courage in warfare and the ancient discipline of our forefathers, the order of things to which they held formerly in imperial wartime expeditions? ...

When the great and high emperor is about to go on an expedition and to mobilize arms and troops against the enemy, he orders first of all that a *lorikion*[1] and a sword and shield should be hung up on the Chalke, outside the gates.[2] From this, the preparation of an imperial expedition is made clear to all, and from this moment each officer and soldier begins to prepare his weapons and such things as are necessary and required of a soldier. Then, after this has taken place, he orders the *logothetes* of the herds that a fair distribution and rationing (of baggage animals) from the *mitata*[3] of Asia and Phrygia, and according to the strength and capacity of each *mitaton*, should be carried out in the fear of God and in all truth and piety. For each of the above-mentioned *mitata* has a specific number of animals

due from it according to its status, which is set down clearly for all: from Asia and Phrygia 200 mules at 15 *nomismata*, 200 pack-horses at 12 *nomismata*, in total 5,424 *nomismata*, which is 76 lbs. gold.[4]

ON THE CUSTOMARY DUES OF THE OFFICERS OF THE IMPERIAL STABLES, BOTH IN THE CITY AND IN THE PROVINCIAL STABLES:

From the *komes* of the stable, 4 mules and 4 pack-horses; from the *chartoularios* and the *epeiktes* 4 mules and 4 pack-horses; from the provincial *chartoularios* 2 mules and 2 pack-horses; from the commissariat 1 mule and 1 pack-horse; from the 4 *komites* 1 mule.[5] Altogether from the officers, 322 *nomismata*, which is 4 lbs. 26 *nomismata*. In sum, 80 lbs. 26 *nomismata*.

The *logothetes* of the herds brings the 200 mules and likewise the 200 pack-horses down to Malagina, and the *komes* of the stable and the inner *chartoularios* of the stable select five-, six- and seven-year old animals, with no blemishes on their flanks. These 400 are then branded with the imperial seal on both sides of the forequarters. The same requisition and branding takes place furthermore in the following year. All the packhorses are castrated and thus become geldings, and serve as a supplement for the expedition's needs. The *logothetes* brings the 200 pack-animals fully harnessed, with felt coverings over their saddle-cloths, carrying ropes for the loads, equipped with leggings, horseshoes and with their halters. ...

FROM THE METROPOLITANS AND ARCHBISHOPS:

Fifty-two fully-harnessed mules from the metropolitans; 52 mules from the fifty-two archbishops. These 104 fully harnessed mules, with their loads, are also to be shoed. The *komes* of the stable, together with the *chartoularios* of the inner stable takes them, and brands them with the rest of the baggage train, in all 104 mules. And the grand total from both sources, the *mitata* of the *logothetes* of the herds, and the (animals provided as) gifts, 585 mules.

---

[1] A *lorikion* was a suit of mail. Special clothing was often displayed to signal a special event.

[2] The Chalke was the bronze gate of the imperial palace in Constantinople.

[3] *Logothetes* was a bureaucrat of high position. The *logothetes* of the herds was the man in charge of the farms (*mitata* [sing: *mitaton*]) that supplied horses and pack animals for military expeditions.

[4] *Nomismata* were Byzantine gold coins.

[5] The *komes* (pl. *komites*), or "count," of the stable was the chief officer of the imperial stable, who purchased the animals from the *mitata* at a set price. The *chartoularios* and *epeiktes* were the titles of other officials of the stable. The "inner chartoularios," referred to in the next paragraph, is, by contrast with the "provincial chartoularios," in charge of the office in the capital.

FROM THE PIOUS MONASTERIES:

One hundred complementary horses, led before the emperor to left and right. They should be castrated and gelded; but they are not branded, since when the emperor orders a gift to be made, it is from among these that animals are presented wherever he commands. Likewise from the animals brought as gifts to the emperor during the course of the expedition. The *komes* of the stable, along with the *chartoularios* of the stable takes 3 lbs. of gold from the *eidikon* for expenses.[1]...

FOR THE PERSONAL IMPERIAL VESTIARION AND FOR THOSE SECONDED BY THE BEDCHAMBER FOR THE BAGGAGE OF THE SAME IMPERIAL VESTIARION, 30 PACK-ANIMALS:[2]

All the imperial clothing and the remaining regalia in vessels encased in purple leather and burnished iron chains and straps likewise burnished, so that they can be carried by the pack-animals; eight silver coolers with covers, for scented wine, rose-water, and water: of these, one small cooler for white wine, two large ones for rosewater, and four large ones for water. Two silver pails for water; various water-skins, large and small; four other coolers, large, of burnished copper, like earthenware pots, for water; two burnished copper pails; and sacred vessels for the chapel, which the *minsourator* transports.[3]

Books: the liturgy of the Church, military manuals, books on mechanics, including siege machinery and the production of missiles and other information relevant to the enterprise, that is to say, to wars and sieges; historical books, especially those of Polyainos and Syrianos;[4] an oneirocritical book;[5] a book of chances and occurrences; a book dealing with good and bad weather and storms, rain and lightning and thunder and the vehemence of the winds; and in addition to these a treatise on thunder and a treatise on earthquakes, and other books, such as those to which sailors are wont to refer. Note that such a book was researched and compiled from many books by myself, Constantine emperor of the Romans in Christ the eternal King.

Tufted rugs for reclining, so that guests may rest;... theriac, serapium juice, other antidotes, both mixed and unmixed, for those who have been poisoned; receptacles with all kinds of oils and remedies; and diverse salves and unguents and ointments and other medical substances, herbs and whatever else is necessary for the curing of men and beasts. Small silver pails and sprinklers with covers for the emperor, and others of polished bronze for officers and distinguished refugees; thick and thin double-bordered cushions for the emperor to recline upon; two chairs for the cortège [procession], chairs for the chamberpot, of metal gilded with beaten gold, with covers, and with other covers above concealing the space for the latrine; and for the distinguished refugees two other, similar, seats, bound in silver; imperial chalices for the guests invited to dine with the emperor; two imperial swords, one ceremonial, one for the campaign; one sabre; ointments, various perfumes: incense, mastic, frankincense, sachar, saffron, musk, amber, bitter aloes, moist and dry, pure ground cinnamon of first and second quality, cinnamon wood, and other perfumes. Silken sheets, rough linen blankets, linen towels, sheets, "western" patchwork covers, "western" towels.

FROM THE UNTAILORED CLOTHS DISPATCHED TO FOREIGNERS AS GIFTS:

Skaramaggia of different colors and patterns:[6] all-white, all-yellow and all-blue *skaramaggia;* tunics of high value, produced in the imperial workshops; undergarments of middling value produced in the imperial workshops; undergarments of lower value produced in the imperial workshops; undergarments of lower value of varying colors and patterns produced in the imperial workshops; off-white coats, two-tone silk garments of white and violet; triple-warped striped garments of violet, of purple and a selection of different hues. Note that all these are carried in containers encased in purple leather and burnished chains, with straps similarly burnished....

Once the emperor has passed into the *themata*, he is welcomed by each *thema*, when the *thema* is drawn up in

---

[1] The *eidikon* was an imperial office for fiscal matters.

[2] The *vestiarion*, also part of fiscal administration, was in charge of cloth production as well as metals and bullion.

[3] The *minsourator* was responsible for the imperial tent.

[4] Polyainos (*fl.* 2nd c. CE) wrote a book on military strategy for the Roman emperors that was highly prized later at Constantinople. Syrianos was a later (perhaps 9th c.) writer on the same topic.

[5] I.e., a book that interprets dreams.

[6] *Skaramaggia* were silk tunics decorated with embroidery. They might be worn or used as altar cloths or banners.

parade order, of course.[1] When the emperor approaches, the *strategos* and the *protonotarios* of the *thema* and the *tourmarchai* and the *drouggarokomites* and the *merarches* and the *komes* of the tent and the *chartoularios* and the *domestikos* of the *thema* dismount from their horses while the emperor is still some distance from reaching them, and form a reception party.[2] And when the emperor passes through, all the aforementioned fall to the ground, paying homage to the emperor; but the soldiers all remain mounted. After the *strategoi* and the officers referred to have paid homage to the emperor, the latter makes a short detour from the road, saying to them: "Well met!" Then he asks them: "How are you, my children? How are your wives, my daughters-in-law, and the children?" And they reply that "In the life of your Majesty, so we, your servants, are well." And again, the emperor responds: "Thanks be to Holy God who keeps us in health." When all have acclaimed the emperor, he commands the *strategos* and all the above-mentioned officers to mount up, and to leave with their army for their own ordained position....

THE VICTORIOUS RETURN OF THE CHRIST-LOVING EMPEROR BASIL [I] FROM CAMPAIGN IN THE REGIONS OF TEPHRIKE AND GERMANIKEIA[3]

When the emperor returned victorious from the war against Tephrike and Germanikeia, he passed via Hiereia to the Hebdomon, where citizens of every age met him, with crowns prepared from flowers and roses.[4] Likewise the whole senate then in the City received him there also, and the emperor greeted them verbally. And when he had entered and prayed in the Church of the Baptist in the Hebdomon, and lit candles, he went out; and donning a triple-bordered *skaramaggion*, and riding together with his son Constantine, they came to the Church of the

All-Holy Virgin of the Abramites, with the whole senate going ahead with the people of the City, and with processional banners. Dismounting from their horses, they entered the Church of the Virgin; and having prayed and lit candles, they sat for a short time.

In the meantime, the Eparch of the City had prepared the City in advance, garlanding the route from the Golden Gate as far as the Chalke with laurel and rosemary and myrtle and roses and other flowers, also with a variety of *skaramaggia* and silk hangings and candelabra; he similarly strewed the ground, which was completely covered in flowers.[5]...

On the meadow outside the Golden Gate, tents were set up, and they brought over the noble and important Hagarene prisoners[6] together with the best of the booty of war, banners, and weapons. When it had been deposited in the tents, this was divided up and paraded triumphally along the Mese from the Golden Gate to the Chalke of the palace, for the central, great Golden Gate was then opened.

After the booty had been paraded, the emperors rose and, changing out of their *skaramaggia*, the autocrat and great emperor donned a gold-embroidered breastplate-tunic covered in pearls set in a criss-cross pattern, and with perfect pearls along the hems; girding himself also with a belted sword, bearing upon his head a Caesar's diadem.... His son Constantine wore a gold *klibanion*[7] and a belted sword, golden greaves, and in his hand a gilded spear decorated with pearls. On his head he wore a low turban with a circlet of white embroidered with gold, having on the forehead a likeness of a gold-embroidered crown. Both rode mounted on white horses equipped with gem-encrusted caparisons. While mounted, they received the demarchs and the two factions, wearing deme tunics and segmented diadems on their heads, with other garlands made from roses and flowers around their necks,

---

[1] The *themata* (sing. *thema*) are the themes.

[2] The *strategos* (pl. *strategoi*) and the *protonotarios* were the chief military officers of the theme, while the other officials named here were their subordinates.

[3] The emperor that Constantine is referring to here is Basil I the Macedonian (r.867–886). The "regions of Tephrike and Germanikeia" were in southeastern Anatolia.

[4] The Hebdomon palace complex was outside the walls of Constantinople on the Sea of Marmara, by the route to the Golden Gate.

[5] The Mese, the main boulevard from the Golden Gate, led to the Chalke. The Eparch of Constantinople was in effect the "mayor" of the city.

[6] The "Hagarene prisoners" were the Muslims who were captured in the wars.

[7] A *klibanion* was sleeveless body armor, in this case of gold, covering the chest to the waist. At this point in the procession, the emperor and his son were still outside the Golden Gate.

carrying kerchiefs in their hands.[1] The demarchs wore their triumphal mantles, and their officials tunics and ordinary mantles. The acclamations were to begin with as follows: "Glory to God, who returns our own Lords to us victorious! Glory to God, who exalts you, autocrats of the Romans! Glory to you, All-Holy Trinity, that we see our own Lords victorious! Welcome as conquerors, most courageous Lords!" Then other acclamations in praise of victory were made, and processional military hymns were sung, as the two factions processed before (the emperor).

When they had come from the Church of the Abramites to the Golden Gate, as we said, which was open to them, they stood before the entry to it, and were similarly acclaimed. They received then the Eparch of the City and the emperor's representative who, falling to the ground, paid homage, and presented to the emperor a golden crown, after the old custom, along with other crowns of laurel, as symbols of victory. And they then received from the emperor coin to the value and above of the golden crown. When the demes had completed their acclamations, the emperors went in procession through the great Golden Gate.

4.8 Imperial rule: Michael Psellus, *Portrait of Basil II* (*c*.1063). Original in Greek.

Michael Psellus (1018–1078), probably born and certainly educated in Constantinople, served at the courts of many of the emperors and empresses of the second half of the eleventh century. Among his many writings was the *Chronographia*, a book containing the biographies of the very Byzantine emperors and empresses whom he had known personally. Its first subject, however, was Basil II the Bulgar-Slayer, whose rule (976–1025) just barely overlapped Psellus's birth and early childhood. In his account, Psellus suggested that Basil's military successes and autocratic attitude went hand in hand. How might you put this document together with Constantine [VII]'s description of the military activities of the emperor, in the treatise above, p. 189 to help explain Byzantium's extraordinary expansion in the early eleventh century?

[Source: *Fourteen Byzantine Rulers: The* Chronographia *of Michael Psellus*, trans. Edgar R.A. Sewter (New York: Penguin Books, 1966), pp. 28–30, 43–48.]

Once invested with supreme power over the Romans, Basil was unwilling to share his designs with anyone else; he refused advice on the conduct of public affairs. On the other hand, having had no previous experience of military matters or of good civil administration, he discovered that to rely on his own unaided judgment was impossible. He was compelled to turn for help to the *parakoimomenus* (Lord Chamberlain).[2] This man, called Basil, happened at that time to be the most remarkable person in the Roman Empire, outstanding in intellect, bodily stature, and regal appearance. Although he was born of the same father as the father of Basil and Constantine [VIII], on his mother's side he came of different stock. In early infancy he had suffered castration—a natural precaution against a concubine's offspring, for as a eunuch he could never hope to usurp the throne from a legitimate heir. Actually he was resigned to his fate and was genuinely attached to the Imperial house—after all, it was his own family. He was particularly devoted to his nephew Basil, embracing the young man in the most affectionate manner and watching over his progress like some kindly foster-parent. One should not be surprised,

---

[1] The demarchs were the leaders of the Blues and the Greens, the two traditional hippodrome factions—the chariot-racing teams and their supporters (the demes)—at Constantinople.

[2] Son of Emperor Romanus I Lecapenus (r.920–944), he was promoted by Emperor Nicephorus II Phocas (r.963–969).

then, that Basil placed on this man's shoulders the burden of Empire. The older man's serious nature, too, had its influence on the emperor's character. The *parakoimomenus*, in fact, was like an athlete competing at the games while Basil watched him as a spectator—not a spectator present merely to cheer on the victor, but rather one who trained himself in the running and took part in the contests himself, following in the other's footsteps and imitating his style. So the *parakoimomenus* had the whole world at his feet. It was to him that the civilian population looked, to him that the army turned, and he was responsible, indeed solely responsible, for the administration of public finance and the direction of government. In this task he was constantly assisted by the emperor both in word and in deed, for Basil not only backed up his minister's measures, but confirmed them in writing.

To most men of our generation who saw the Emperor Basil he seemed austere and abrupt in manner, an irascible person who did not quickly change his mind, sober in his daily habits and averse to all effeminacy, but if I am to believe the historians of that period who wrote about him, he was not at all like that when his reign began. A change took place in his character after he acceded to the throne, and instead of leading his former dissolute, voluptuous sort of life, he became a man of great energy. The complete metamorphosis was brought about by the pressure of events. His character stiffened, so to speak. Feebleness gave way to strength and the old slackness disappeared before a new fixity of purpose. In his early days he used to feast quite openly and frequently indulged in the pleasures of love; his main concern was with his banqueting and a life spent in the gay, indolent atmosphere of the court. The combination of youth and unlimited power gave him opportunities for self-indulgence, and he enjoyed them to the full. The change in his mode of living dates from the attempted revolutions of the notorious Sclerus[1] and of Phocas.[2] Sclerus twice raised the standard of revolt, and there were other aspirants to the throne, with two parties in opposition to the emperor. From that time onward, Basil's carefree existence was forgotten and he wholeheartedly applied himself to serious objects. Once the first blow had been struck against those members of his family who had seized power, he set himself resolutely to compass their utter destruction.

[Psellus discusses the rebellion of Phocas, the two rebellions of Sclerus, and downfall of the eunuch Basil, the Lord Chamberlain. He then turns to Basil II's reconciliation with Sclerus.]

As soon as he saw Sclerus enter, Basil rose and they embraced one another. Then they held converse, the one excusing his revolt and explaining the reason why he had plotted and carried it out, the other quietly accepting the apology and attributing to bad luck what had occurred. When they shared a common drinking-bowl, the emperor first put to his own lips the cup offered to Sclerus and took a moderate sip of its contents before handing it back to his guest. Thus he relieved him of any suspicion of poison, and at the same time proved the sanctity of their agreement. After this Basil questioned him, as a man accustomed to command, about his Empire. How could it be preserved free from dissension? Sclerus had an answer to this, although it was not the sort of advice one would expect from a general; in fact, it sounded more like a diabolical plot. "Cut down the governors who become over-proud," he said. "Let no generals on campaign have too many resources. Exhaust them with unjust exactions, to keep them busied with their own affairs. Admit no woman to the imperial councils. Be accessible to no one. Share with few your most intimate plans."

On this note their conversation came to an end. Sclerus went off to the country estate which had been apportioned him, and soon afterwards he died. We will leave him and return to the emperor. In his dealings with his subjects, Basil behaved with extraordinary circumspection. It is perfectly true that the great reputation he built up as a ruler was founded rather on terror than on loyalty, for as he grew older and became more experienced, he relied less on the judgment of men wiser than himself. He alone introduced new measures, he alone disposed his military forces. As for the civil administration, he governed, not in accordance with the written laws, but following the unwritten dictates of his own intuition, which was most excellently equipped by nature for the purpose. Consequently he paid no attention to men of learning; on the contrary, he affected utter scorn—towards the learned folk, I mean. It seems to me a wonderful thing, therefore, that while the emperor so

---

[1]   Bardas Sclerus had been brother-in-law of Emperor John I Tzimisces (r.969–976), who had married his sister Maria. He had expected to succeed John, for he had been promised the throne by the emperor on his deathbed.

[2]   The Phocas family came from Cappadocia and for several generations had enjoyed high repute as soldiers. Bardas Phocas's uncle was Emperor Nicephorus.

despised literary culture, no small crop of orators and philosophers sprang up in those times. One solution of the paradox, I fancy, is this: the men of those days did not devote themselves to the study of letters for any ulterior purpose—they cultivated literature for its own sake and as an end in itself, whereas the majority nowadays do not approach the subject of education in this spirit, but consider personal profit to be the first reason for study. Perhaps I should add that though gain is the object of their zeal for literature, if they do not immediately achieve this goal, then they desist from their studies at once. Shame on them!

However, we must return to the emperor. Having purged the Empire of the barbarians, he dealt with his own subjects and completely subjugated them too—I think "subjugate" is the right word to describe it. He decided to abandon his former policy, and after the great families had been humiliated and put on an equal footing with the rest, Basil found himself playing the game of power-politics with considerable success. He surrounded himself with favorites who were neither remarkable for brilliance of intellect, nor of noble lineage, nor too learned. To them were entrusted the imperial rescripts,[1] and with them he was accustomed to share the secrets of State. However, since at that time the emperor's comments on memoranda or requests for favors were never varied, but only plain, straightforward statements (for Basil, whether writing or speaking, avoided all elegance of composition), he used to dictate to his secretaries just as the words came to his tongue, stringing them all together, one after the other. There was no subtlety, nothing superfluous in his speech.

By humbling the pride or jealousy of his people, Basil made his own road to power an easy one. He was careful, moreover, to close the exit-doors on the monies contributed to the treasury. So a huge sum was built up, partly by the exercise of strict economy, partly by fresh additions from abroad. Actually the sum accumulated in the imperial treasury reached the grand total of 200,000 talents. As for the rest of his gains, it would indeed be hard to find words adequately to describe them. All the treasures amassed in Iberia and Arabia, all the riches found among the Celts or contained in the land of the Scyths[2]—in brief, all the wealth of the barbarians who surround our borders—all were gathered together in one place and deposited in the emperor's coffers. In addition to this, he carried off to his treasure-chambers, and sequestrated there, all the money of those who rebelled against him and were afterwards subdued. And since the vaults of the buildings made for this purpose were not big enough, he had spiral galleries dug underground, after the Egyptian style, and there he kept safe a considerable proportion of his treasures. He himself took no pleasure in any of it; quite the reverse, indeed, for the majority of the precious stones, both the white ones (which we call pearls) and the colored brilliants, far from being inlaid in diadems or collars, were hidden away in his underground vaults. Meanwhile Basil took part in his processions and gave audience to his governors clad merely in a robe of purple, not the very bright purple, but simply purple of a dark hue, with a handful of gems as a mark of distinction. As he spent the greater part of his reign serving as a soldier on guard at our frontiers and keeping the barbarian marauders at bay, not only did he draw nothing from his reserves of wealth, but even multiplied his riches many times over.

On his expedition against the barbarians, Basil did not follow the customary procedure of other emperors, setting out at the middle of spring and returning home at the end of summer. For him the time to return was when the task in hand was accomplished. He endured the rigors of winter and the heat of summer with equal indifference. He disciplined himself against thirst. In fact, all his natural desires were kept under stern control, and the man was as hard as steel. He had an accurate knowledge of the details of army life, and by that I do not mean the general acquaintance with the composition of his army, the relative functions of individual units in the whole body, or the various groupings and deployments suited to the different formations. His experience of army matters went further than that: the duties of the *protostates*, the duties of the *hemilochites*,[3] the tasks proper to the rank immediately junior to them—all these were no mysteries to Basil, and the knowledge stood him in good stead in his wars. Accordingly, jobs appropriate to these ranks were not devolved on others, and the emperor, being personally conversant with the character and combat duties of each individual, knowing to what each man was fitted either by temperament or by training, used him in this capacity and made him serve there.

---

[1] Laws written in response to particular cases.

[2] Iberia was an eastern theme of the Byzantine empire. The "riches of the Celts" refers to the riches of western states. The Slavs were called "Scyths" by classicizing authors such as Psellus.

[3] Military ranks, junior officers.

Moreover, he knew the various formations suited to his men. Some he had read of in books, others he devised himself during the operations of war, the result of his own intuition. He professed to conduct his wars and draw up the troops in line of battle, himself planning each campaign, but he preferred not to engage in combat personally. A sudden retreat might otherwise prove embarrassing. Consequently, for the most part he kept his troops immobile. He would construct machines of war and skirmish at a distance, while the maneuvering was left to the light-armed soldiers. Once he had made contact with the enemy, a regular military liaison was established between the different formations of the Roman army. The whole force was drawn up like a solid tower, headquarters being in touch with the cavalry squadrons, who were themselves kept in communication with the light infantry, and these again with the various units of heavy-armed foot [soldiers]. When all was ready, strict orders were given that no soldier should advance in front of the line or break rank under any circumstances. If these orders were disobeyed, and if some of the most valiant or daring soldiers did ride out well in front of the rest, even in cases where they engaged the enemy successfully, they could expect no medals or rewards of valor when they returned. On the contrary, Basil promptly discharged them from the army, and they were punished on the same level as common criminals. The decisive factor in the achievement of victory was, in his opinion, the massing of troops in one coherent body, and for this reason alone he believed the Roman armies to be invin-cible. The careful inspections he made before battle used to aggravate the soldiers and they abused him openly, but the emperor met their scorn with common sense. He would listen quietly, and then with a gay smile point out that if he neglected these precautions, their battles would go on for ever.

Basil's character was twofold, for he readily adapted himself no less to the crises of war than to the calm of peace. Really, if the truth be told, he was more of a villain in wartime, more of an emperor in time of peace. Outbursts of wrath he controlled, and like the proverbial "fire under the ashes" kept anger hidden in his heart, but, if his orders were disobeyed in war, on returning to his palace he would kindle his wrath and reveal it. Terrible then was the vengeance he took on the miscreant. Generally he persisted in his opinions, but there were occasions when he did change his mind. In many cases, too, he traced crimes back to their original causes, and the final links in the chain were exonerated. So most defaulters obtained forgiveness, either through his sympathetic understanding, or because he showed some other interest in their affairs. He was slow to adopt any course of action, but never would he willingly alter the decision once it was taken. Consequently his attitude to friends was unvaried, unless perchance he was compelled by necessity to revise his estimate of them. Similarly, where he had burst out in anger against someone, he did not quickly moderate his indignation. Whatever estimate he formed, indeed, was to him an irrevocable and divinely-inspired judgment.

SCHOLARSHIP ACROSS THE ISLAMIC WORLD

4.9 Education: Al-Qabisi, *A Treatise Detailing the Circumstances of Students and the Rules Governing Teachers and Students* (before 1012). Original in Arabic.

Abu al-Hasan Ali ibn Khalaf al-Qabisi (935–1012) was an important leader of one school of Islamic legal thought, the Maliki, named after its founder, Malik ibn Anas (d.796). After studying with scholars at Mecca and Cairo, al-Qabisi settled in Tunisia. Among his many writings were collections of hadith (traditions about the Prophet: see above, p. 117) and commentaries on the Qur'an. Above all, al-Qabisi was interested in law, and his treatise on students, parents, and teachers, some of which is presented here, formed part of his legal corpus. Teachers were under contract to parents and students, so al-Qabisi was concerned to clarify their obligations and to justify payments for instruction. (In the thirteenth century, western scholastics would take up similar issues.) The treatise was written in the form of a response to "an urgent questioner"; the views of al-Qabisi and other authorities were given in the third person in chains of transmission in the same way that the hadith were transmitted by *isnad*. In al-Qabisi's view, it was the obligation of parents and guardians to teach their children (usually by sending them to a teacher), and if they could not be responsible, it was up to the state to educate the young. However, al-Qabisi limited the kinds of education girls should have.

[Source: *Classical Foundations of Islamic Education Thought*, ed. Bradley J. Cook with Fathi H. Malkawi (Provo, UT: Brigham Young University Press, 2010), pp. 45–51, 54. Translated by Michael Fishbein. (Notes modified.)]

In the name of God, the Merciful, the Compassionate; God Bless Muhammad.

25. Abu al-Hasan [al-Qabisi] said: What I have told you about the merit a father can be expected to acquire from teaching his child the Qur'an should serve to encourage the father to teach his young child who, being unable to help or harm himself and unable to distinguish for himself what to take up and what to turn away, has only his father as a refuge, whose duty it is to provide his means of support....

27. Muslims throughout their history have diligently taught their children the Qur'an and provided them with teachers. This is something that no father refrains from doing for his child if he has the means to do so, unless he is following his soul's avarice. The latter is no excuse for him, for God, who is praised, has said: "Souls are very prone to avarice."[1] And, "whosoever is guarded against the avarice of his own soul—they are the prosperers."[2] Not one father would leave off doing this, deeming its omission trivial and insignificant, except a coarse father with no desire for good....

28. A child's religious status, as long as he is a minor, is the status of his father. Will the father then leave his minor child, not teaching him religion, when his teaching him the Qur'an will make his knowledge of religion firm? Has he not heard the words of the Messenger of God, on whom be peace? "Every infant is born in a state of nature; then his parents make him a Jew or a Christian. It is just as camels are brought forth as beasts intact. Do you discern any that are mutilated?"[3]...

29. If the children of unbelievers experience harm from their parents, it behooves the children of believers to benefit religiously from their parents. The first generations of believers had no need to trouble themselves arguing about this; they made do with the desire that had been placed in their hearts; they acted according to it, and they left it as customary practice that each generation passed on from the previous one. No father was ever reproved regarding this, nor did any father ever turn out to have omitted to do so from desire or from negligence. That is no attribute of a believing Muslim! Had it ever become evident that someone had omitted to teach his child the Qur'an out of negligence, his condition would have been deemed one of ignorance, ugliness, and deficiency, beneath that of people of contentment and satisfaction. Sometimes, however, lack of means causes parents to lag behind in this matter; then their behavior is excusable—depending on how sound their excuse turns out to be.

30. If the child has property, his father or his guardian (if his father has died) should not leave him. Let him enter the primary school and engage the teacher to teach him the Qur'an from his wealth, as is due. If the orphan has no guardian, the ruler[4] of the Muslims should oversee his affairs and proceed with his instruction as the father or guardian would have proceeded. If the child

---

[1] Qur'an 4: 128.

[2] Qur'an 64: 16.

[3] After they were born, the ears of camels were notched (and thus mutilated) to brand them.

[4] The word used here was *hakim*, which could refer to a leader of any sort, from the ruler of a country to a judge to a community official.

is in a town where there is no ruler, oversight would be exercised for him in a matter such as this if the town's righteous people came together to oversee the interests of the town's people, for overseeing this orphan is one of those interests.

31. If the orphan has no property, his mother or next of kin should be encouraged to take charge of teaching him the Qur'an. If someone else volunteers to bear the burden for them, that person shall have his reward. If the orphan has no kin to care for him, any Muslim who cares for him shall have his reward. If the teacher, reckoning on a heavenly reward, teaches him solely for God's sake, bearing it patiently, his reward for it, God willing, shall be doubled, especially since it is his craft from which he supports himself....

32. As for teaching a female the Qur'an and learning, it is good and of benefit to her. However, her being taught letter-writing or poetry is a cause for fear. She should be taught only things that can be expected to be good for her and protect her from temptation. It would be safer for her to be spared learning to write. When the Prophet (may God bless him and grant him peace) permitted women to attend the festival, he commanded them to bring out adolescent girls and those who normally are secluded behind a curtain.[1] At the same time he commanded menstruating women to avoid the place where people pray. He said, "Let women be present where there is blessing and at the prayers of Muslims." On this basis it is acceptable to teach them good things that are safe for them; as for things from which harm to them can be feared, it is preferable that such things be kept away from them, and this is the duty of their guardian. Understand what I have explained to you. Seek guidance from God, and He will guide: He is a sufficient guide and helper for you.

33. Know that God, who is mighty and exalted, has imposed certain duties on believing women, just as He has imposed certain duties on believing men. This may be inferred from God's words: "It is not for any believer, man or woman, when God and His Messenger have decreed a matter, to have the choice in the affair."[2] And, "The believers, the men and the women."[3] In more than one verse of His Book He has joined men and women together in being well rewarded. For example, "God has promised the believers, men and women, gardens underneath which rivers flow, forever therein to dwell, and goodly dwelling-places in the Gardens of Eden; and greater God's good pleasure, that is the mighty triumph."[4] And He commanded the wives of His Prophet (on whom be peace) to remember what they had heard from the Prophet: "And remember that which is recited in your houses of the signs of God and the Wisdom."[5] How should they not be taught the good and what helps to its attainment? But whoever is in charge of them should turn from them anything of which one should beware on their behalf, since he is their protector and responsible for them....

37. Know that there was not one of the religious leaders[6] of the Muslims in the first days of this community but who gave thought to what would be of benefit to Muslims in all their affairs, private and public. We have never heard that any of them appointed teachers to teach people's children in elementary schools[7] during their childhood or gave such teachers a share from the public treasury, as they did for anyone they charged to serve the Muslims either by judging between them in lawsuits, calling them to prayer in the mosque, or anything else that they established to protect Muslims and guard their affairs. They could not have neglected the business of teachers for young children. However—and God only knows—they thought it was a matter that concerned each individual personally, inasmuch as what a person taught his child was part of his own welfare that was of special concern to him. They therefore left it as one of the tasks of fathers, something that it was not fitting for someone else to do for them if they were able to do it themselves. Since the religious leaders of the Muslims had made no provision for the matter and it was one that Muslims had to carry out for their children and without which they would not feel at ease, they got themselves a teacher for their children, someone to devote himself to them on a regular basis and to care for them as he would care for his own young children. Since

---

[1] An "adolescent girl" (*awatiq*) had begun puberty and was kept behind the curtain in the tent of her family, but she was not yet married.

[2] Qur'an 33: 36.

[3] Qur'an 9: 71.

[4] Qur'an 9: 72.

[5] Qur'an 33: 34.

[6] The word used here was *a'immah*, the plural of *imam*, a religious scholar and especially the founder of a legal school.

[7] The word used here was *katatib*, the plural of *kuttab*, a school in which students learned to read the Qur'an.

it was unlikely that anyone could be found to volunteer for the Muslims, teach their children for them, devote himself entirely to them, and give up seeking his own livelihood and his profitable activities and other needs, it was appropriate for Muslims to hire someone to take care of teaching their children on a constant basis, to the exclusion of any other business. Such a teacher would relieve the children's parents of the burden of educating them; he would make them understand how to live upright lives, and he would increase their understanding of the good and turn them away from evil.

38. This is an occupation that few people volunteer to perform free of charge. If one had waited for people to volunteer to teach young children the Qur'an, many children would have been neglected and many people would not have learned the Qur'an. This would necessarily have led to loss of the Qur'an from people's hearts. It would have caused Muslim children to be confirmed in ignorance.

39. Yet there is no good reason to cause a shortage where there is no scarcity, and no injunction to abstain [from being paid to teach the Qur'an] has been confirmed as coming from the Messenger of God (may God bless him and grant him peace).

40. Al-Harith ibn Miskin,[1] in a report dated to the year [789–90], said: "Ibn Wahb gave us the following report: 'I heard Malik say, "None of the scholars I have known saw anything wrong with paying teachers—teachers of the Qur'an school."'"[2]

41. The following is also attributed to Ibn Wahb in his *Muwatta* from 'Abd al-Jabbar ibn 'Umar: "No one I asked in Medina sees anything wrong in teachers teaching for pay."…

53. The aforementioned people disagreed only about paying the teacher to teach something other than the Qur'an and writing. They did not disagree about subjects meant to reinforce the Qur'an, such as writing and penmanship.

54. Ibn Sahnun[3] mentioned: "It is fitting for the teacher to teach his students [the correct reading of] the case-endings of [the words of] the Qur'an—it is his duty to do so—and vocalization, spelling, good handwriting, good reading, when to pause [in recitation], and how to articulate clearly; it is his duty to do so. It is his duty to teach them the good reading that has become well-known, namely the reading of Nafi',[4] but there is no harm in his having them read according to another [authority] if [the reading] is not considered disagreeable. There is no harm in his teaching them homilies, if they desire.

55. "He should teach them good manners, for it his duty toward God to give good advice, protect them, and care for them. The teacher should command them to perform the ritual prayer when they are seven years old and beat them for [omitting to pray] when they are ten. That is what Malik said.…"

56. [Malik also said:] "Let him take care to teach them supplications,[5] that they may make their humble petitions to God; and let him teach them God's greatness and majesty, that they may magnify Him for it. If the people suffer from drought and the imam leads them in prayers for rain, I would have the teacher bring the children out [those of them who know how to pray], and let them beseech God with supplications and make their humble petitions to Him, for I have been told that when the people to whom Jonah was sent (may God's blessing be upon our Prophet and upon him) saw the chastisement with their own eyes, they brought out their children and entreated God by means of them, and the chastisement was lifted. He should teach them arithmetic, but it is not his duty unless it has been stipulated for him; and likewise poetry, obscure words, Arabic language, and the whole of grammar—in these matters he acts voluntarily. There is no harm in his teaching them poetry—words and reports of the [ancient] Arabs that contain nothing indecent—but it is not incumbent upon him." According to Sahnun there is nothing wrong if the person who teaches Qur'an and writing teaches all this, whether voluntarily or by stipulation. However, as for paying the teacher to teach these things with no intent to teach the Qur'an and writing, Sahnun, as mentioned previously, rejects it based on Malik's saying that he did not like payment for the teaching of poetry.

---

[1] Al-Harith ibn Miskin was an earlier scholar of the Maliki school.

[2] Because ibn Wahb (743–812) here transmitted the words of Malik ibn Anas, founder of the Maliki school, this passage and others like it linked al-Qabisi himself to the founder.

[3] Ibn Sahnun (817–870) was an earlier scholar of the Maliki school and a student of ibn Wahb. Al-Qabisi was much influenced by ibn Sahnun's writings on education and quoted him extensively.

[4] The Maliki school considered the reading of Nafi', i.e., the Qur'anic text cited as correct by Nafi' of Medina, to be best.

[5] That is, prayers on various occasions that were not part of the five obligatory times of ritual prayers.

57. Ibn Habib, on the other hand, said: "There is nothing wrong with paying a teacher to teach poetry, grammar, letter-writing, the Days of the Arabs, and similar things, such as the knowledge of famous men and of chivalrous knights: there is nothing wrong with paying for the teaching of all this. I, however, am opposed to the teaching, learning, or recitation by an adult or child of any poetry containing accounts of unbridled violence, obscenity, or foul satire."

4.10 Political theory: Al-Farabi, *The Perfect State* (*c.*940–942). Original in Arabic.

Abu Nasr al-Farabi (872–950) was born in Turkestan, spent most of his adulthood in Baghdad, where he made a very modest living as a philosopher and writer, and joined the court of the emir of Aleppo in Syria toward the end of his life. His *Perfect State* engaged a long tradition of Greek thought on a great variety of spiritual, biological, and social topics; al-Farabi wanted to show their importance for a Muslim audience. His work thus began with God, angels, the heavens, the "bodies below the heavens," and so on, leading to the chapters below, which deal with human societies and their different degrees of excellence. How does al-Farabi's view of the "excellent and ignorant cities" compare with Augustine's notion of the "cities of God and Man" in *The City of God*, above, p. 14?

[Source: *Al-Farabi on the Perfect State*, ed. and trans. Richard Walzer (Oxford: Clarendon Press, 1985), pp. 231, 235, 239, 241, 253, 255, 257, 259.]

Chapter 15
Perfect Associations and Perfect Ruler; Faulty Associations

...§3. The most excellent good and the utmost perfection is, in the first instance, attained in a city, not in a society which is less complete than it. But since good in its real sense is such as to be attainable through choice and will and evils are also due to will and choice only, a city may be established to enable its people to cooperate in attaining some aims that are evil. Hence felicity is not attainable in every city. The city, then, in which people aim through association at cooperating for the things by which felicity in its real and true sense can be attained, is the excellent city, and the society in which there is a cooperation to acquire felicity is the excellent society; and the nation in which all of its cities cooperate for those things through which felicity is attained is the excellent nation. In the same way, the excellent universal state will arise only when all the nations in it cooperate for the purpose of reaching felicity.

§4. The excellent city resembles the perfect and healthy body, all of whose limbs cooperate to make the life of the animal perfect and to preserve it in this state. Now the limbs and organs of the body are different and their natural endowments and faculties are unequal in excellence, there being among them one ruling organ, namely the heart, and organs which are close in rank to that ruling organ, each having been given by nature a faculty by which it performs its proper function in conformity with the natural aim. So, too, the parts of the city are by nature provided with endowments unequal in excellence which enable them to do one thing and not another. But they are not parts of the city by their inborn nature alone but rather by the voluntary habits which they acquire such as the arts and their likes; to the natural faculties which exist in the organs and limbs of the body correspond the voluntary habits and dispositions in the parts of the city.

§5. The ruling organ in the body is by nature the most perfect and most complete of the organs in itself and in its specific qualification, and it also has the best of everything of which another organ has a share as well; beneath it, in turn, are other organs which rule over organs inferior to them, their rule being lower in rank than the rule of the first and indeed subordinate to the rule of the first; they rule and are ruled. In the same way, the ruler of the city is the most perfect part of the city in his specific qualification and has the best of everything which anybody else shares with him; beneath him are people who are ruled by him and rule others.

The heart comes to be first and becomes then the cause of the existence of the other organs and limbs of the body, and the cause of the existence of their faculties in them and of their arrangement in the ranks proper to them, and when one of its organs is out of order, it is the heart which provides the means to remove that disorder. In the same way the ruler of this city must come to be in the first instance, and will subsequently be the cause of the rise of the city and its parts and the cause of the presence of the voluntary habits of its parts and of their arrangement in the ranks proper to them; and when one part is out of order he provides it with the means to remove its disorder.

The parts of the body close to the ruling organ perform of the natural functions, in agreement—by nature—with the aim of the ruler, the most noble ones; the organs beneath them perform those functions which are less noble, and eventually the organs are reached which perform the meanest functions. In the same way the parts of the city which are close in authority to the ruler of the city perform the most noble voluntary actions, and those below them less noble actions, until eventually the parts are reached which perform the most ignoble actions. The inferiority of such actions is sometimes due to the inferiority of their matter, although they may be extremely useful—like the action of the bladder and the action of the lower intestine in the body; sometimes it is due to their being of little use; at other times it is due to their being very easy to perform. This applies equally to the city and equally to every whole which is composed by nature of well ordered coherent parts: they have a ruler whose relation to the other parts is like the one just described.

§6. This applies also to all existents.[1] For the relation of the First Cause to the other existents is like the relation of the king of the excellent city to its other parts.[2] For the ranks of the immaterial existents are close to the First [Cause]. Beneath them are the heavenly bodies, and beneath the heavenly bodies the material bodies. All these existents act in conformity with the First Cause, follow it, take it as their guide and imitate it; but each existent

does that according to its capacity, choosing its aim precisely on the strength of its established rank in the universe: that is to say the last follows the aim of that which is slightly above it in rank, equally the second existent, in turn, follows what is above itself in rank, and in the same way the third existent has an aim which is above it. Eventually existents are reached which are linked with the First Cause without any intermediary whatsoever. In accordance with this order of rank all the existents permanently follow the aim of the First Cause. Those which are from the very outset provided with all the essentials of their existence are made to imitate the First [Cause] and its aim from their very outset, and hence enjoy eternal bliss and hold the highest ranks; but those which are not provided from the outset with all the essentials of their existence, are provided with a faculty by which they move towards the expected attainment of those essentials and will then be able to follow the aim of the First [Cause]. The excellent city ought to be arranged in the same way: all its parts ought to imitate in their actions the aim of their first ruler according to their rank.

§7. The ruler of the excellent city cannot just be any man, because rulership requires two conditions: (a) he should be predisposed for it by his inborn nature, (b) he should have acquired the attitude and habit of will for rulership which will develop in a man whose inborn nature is predisposed for it. Nor is every art suitable for rulership, most of the arts, indeed, are rather suited for service within the city, just as most men are by their very nature born to serve. Some of the arts rule certain [other] arts while serving others at the same time, whereas there are other arts which, not ruling anything at all, only serve. Therefore the art of ruling the excellent city cannot just be any chance art, nor due to any chance habit whatever. For just as the first ruler in a genus cannot be ruled by anything in that genus—for instance the ruler of the limbs cannot be ruled by any other limb, and this holds good for any ruler of any composite whole—so the art of the ruler in the excellent city of necessity cannot be a serving art at all and cannot be ruled by any other art, but his art must be an art towards the aim of which all the other arts tend, and for which they strive in all the actions of the excellent city....

[Al-Farabi now explores the qualities of the ruler of the excellent city: his Passive Intellect (the only sort of

---

1 I.e., that which exists, whether thing, action, or quality.

2 The First Cause is God. The term "First Cause" is found in Aristotle's *Physics*, book 8, and his *Metaphysics*, book 12. However, the hierarchy of Being that al-Farabi describes here is neo-Platonic.

intellect that human beings have) learns all the intelligibles—all that can be understood by the intellect alone—from the Active Intellect, which is God.]

§15. In opposition to the excellent city are the "ignorant" city, the wicked city, the city which has deliberately changed its character and the city which has missed the right path through faulty judgment. In opposition to it are also the individuals who make up the common people in the various cities.

§16. The "ignorant" city is the city whose inhabitants do not know true felicity, the thought of it never having occurred to them. Even if they were rightly guided to it they would either not understand it or not believe in it. The only good things they recognize are some of those which are superficially thought of as good among the things which are considered to be the aims in life such as bodily health, wealth, enjoyment of pleasures, freedom to follow one's desires, and being held in honor and esteem. According to the citizens of the ignorant city each of these is a kind of felicity, and the greatest and perfect felicity is the sum total of all of them. Things contrary to these goods are misery such as deficiency of the body, poverty, no enjoyment of pleasures, no freedom to follow one's desires, and not being held in honor.

§17. The ignorant city is divided into a number of cities. One of them is the city of necessity, that is the city whose people strive for no more food, drink, clothes, housing and sexual intercourse than is necessary for sustaining their bodies, and they cooperate to attain this. Another is the city of meanness; the aim of its people is to cooperate in the acquisition of wealth and riches, not in order to enjoy something else which can be got through wealth, but because they regard wealth as the sole aim in life. Another is the city of depravity and baseness; the aim of its people is the enjoyment of the pleasure connected with food and drink and sexual intercourse, and in general of the pleasures of the senses and of the imagination, and to give preference to entertainment and idle play in every form and in every way. Another is the city of honor; the aim of its people is to cooperate to attain honor and distinction and fame among the nations, to be extolled

and treated with respect by word and deed, and to attain glory and splendor either in the eyes of other people or among themselves, each according to the extent of his love of such distinction or according to the amount of it which he is able to reach. Another is the city of power; the aim of its people is to prevail over others and to prevent others from prevailing over them, their only purpose in life being the enjoyment which they get from power. Another is the "democratic" city: the aim of its people is to be free, each of them doing what he wishes without restraining his passions in the least.

§18. There are as many kings of ignorant cities as there are cities of this kind, each of them governing the city over which he has authority so that he can indulge in his passion and design.

We have herewith enumerated the designs which may be set up as aims for ignorant cities.

§19. The wicked city is a city whose views are those of the excellent city; it knows felicity, God Almighty, the existents of the second order, the Active Intellect and everything which as such is to be known and believed in by the people of the excellent city; but the actions of its people are the actions of the people of the ignorant cities.

The city which has deliberately changed is a city whose views and actions were previously the views and actions of the people of the excellent city, but they have been changed and different views have taken their place, and its actions have turned into different actions.

The city which misses the right path [the "erring" city] is the city which aims at felicity after this life, and holds about God Almighty, the existents of the second order, and the Active Intellect pernicious and useless beliefs, even if they are taken as symbols and representations of true felicity. Its first ruler was a man who falsely pretended to be receiving "revelation"; he produced this wrong impression through falsifications, cheating and deceptions.

§20. The kings of these cities are contrary to the kings of the excellent cities: their ways of governing are contrary to the excellent ways of governing. The same applies to all the other people who live in these cities.

4.11 Logic: Ibn Sina (Avicenna), *Treatise on Logic* (1020s or 1030s). Original in Persian.

The study of logic as a discipline was the original achievement of the ancient Greek philosopher Aristotle (384–322 BCE). His treatises on the topic, later grouped together under the title *Organon*, dealt with what would remain the classic issues of the topic: the relationship of words to reality, the valid forms by which we may derive new truths from what is already known, and the criteria by which we may make and judge inferences. Aristotelian logic was a topic of keen interest in the pre-Christian world and remained important even into the Christian era, with the commentaries of Boethius (d. 524/526). After that, its study continued in the Islamic world, beginning in the ninth century and gaining real momentum in the tenth. The Muslim Persian scholar Ibn Sina (980–1037), known as Avicenna in the West, was one of the most important scholars in this tradition. He was able to draw on translations of Aristotle, made from the original Greek mainly by Christians living in Muslim societies. In the excerpt below he talks about the importance of logic for attaining a particularly high-grade form of knowledge that he calls "science," and he argues that such knowledge is concerned with universals such as "human being" rather than with singulars such as "Mohammed" or "Zid." For Ibn Sina, logic—and philosophy more generally—was essential for understanding Islam itself. Compare the conception and role of logic in the text of al-Farabi above, p. 200, with Ibn Sina's view.

[Source: *Avicenna's Treatise on Logic*, ed. and trans. Farhang Zabeeh (The Hague: Martinus Nijhoff, 1971), pp. 13–17 (slightly modified).]

The Purpose and Use of Logic

There are two kinds of cognition: One is called intuitive or perceptive or apprehensive. For example, if someone says, "Man," or "Fairy," or "Angel," or the like, you will understand, conceive, and grasp what he means by the expression. The other kind of cognition is judgment. As for example, when you acknowledge that angels exist or human beings are under surveillance and the like.

Cognition can again be analyzed into two kinds. One is the kind that may be known through Intellect; it is known necessarily by reasoning through itself. For example, there are the intuitive cognitions of the whatness of the soul, and judgments about what is grasped by intuitive cognition, such as, the soul is eternal.

The other kind of cognition is one that is known by intuition. Judgments about these intuitions, however, are made, not by Intellect, or by reason but by the First Principle.[1] For example, it is known that if two things are equal to the same thing then those things are equal to each other. Then there is the kind of cognition known by the senses, such as, the knowledge that the sun is bright. Also, there is the knowledge that is received from authority such as those received from sages and prophets. And the kind that is obtained from the general opinion and those we are brought by it, for example, that it is wrong to lie and injustice ought not to be done. And still other kinds—which may be named later.

Whatever is known by Intellect, whether it is simple intuitive cognition, or judgment about intuitive cognition, or cognitive judgment, should be based on something which is known prior to the thing.

An example of an intuitive or perceptual cognition is this: If we don't know what "man" means, and someone tells us that man is an animal who talks, we first have to know the meaning of "animal" and "talking," and we must have intuitive cognition of these things before we can learn something we didn't know before about man.

---

[1] The First Principle, as defined by Aristotle, was that which was self-evident.

An example of a judgment acquired by Intellect is this: If we don't know the meaning of "the world was created," and someone tells us that the world possesses color, and whatever possesses color is created; then, and only then, can we know what we didn't know before about the world.

Thus, whatever is not known but desired to be known, can be known through what is known before. But it is not the case that whatever is known can be a ground for knowing what is unknown. Because for everything that is unknown there is a proper class of known things that can be used for knowing the unknown.

There is a method by which one can discover the unknown from what is known. It is the science of logic. Through it one may know how to obtain the unknown from the known. This science is also concerned with the different kinds of valid, invalid, and near valid inferences.

The science of logic is the science of scales. Other sciences are practical, they can give direction in life. The salvation of men lies in their purity of soul. This purity of soul is attainable by contemplating the pure form and avoiding this-worldly inclinations. And the way to these two is through science. And no science which cannot be examined by the balance of logic is certain and exact. Thus, without the acquisition of logic, nothing can be truly called science. Therefore, there is no way except learning the science of logic. It is characteristic of the ancient sciences that the student, at the beginning of his study, is unable to see the use or application of the sciences. This is so, because only after a thorough study of the whole body of science will the real value of his endeavor become apparent. Thus I pray that the reader of this book will not grow impatient in reading things which do not appear of use upon first sight.

The Beginning of the Science of Logic, and a Discussion of What is Called Simple Expressions and Simple Meanings

It should be known that there are two kinds of expressions: One is simple, the other compound.[1] A simple expression is one which has no part signifying a part of the meaning of the expression, e.g., "Zid," "Mohammed," "Man," and "Wise." A compound expression is one which has some part of it denoting some part of the meaning of the expression, such as when you say, "Human beings are

wise," or "The wise people." An inquiry into the nature of compound expressions first requires a discussion of the nature of simple expressions.

A Discussion of Simple and Compound Expressions

Every simple expression is either universal or individual. A universal expression is one whose meaning applies to many entities. For example, "man" signifies the same meaning when applied to Zid, Omar and Mohammed. However, even if a universal expression applies to only one entity it can be used in such a way as to indicate many entities, since it is possible to imagine, by understanding the meaning of that term, many other entities. For example, by knowing the meaning of "sun" and "moon," you can imagine many suns and moons.

An individual expression is one which signifies a single entity. It is such that it cannot be imagined that the same expression could be applied to many entities. When you say "Zid," "Zid" signifies only Zid. If you call some other entities "Zid" you are giving the term another meaning. The business of the scientist is not to deal with individual expressions and their meanings, but to investigate the nature of universals. No doubt, each universal has many particular instances.

A Discussion of Essential and Accidental Universals

The universal contains its particulars either (a) essentially or (b) accidentally. The Essential Universal and its Particulars are apprehended if, at least, three conditions are fulfilled:

(1) The particular has meaning. Thus, if you know the meaning of "animal," "man," "number," and "number four," you cannot help knowing the meaning of the expressions, "man is an animal" and "four is a number." But if you add "exists" or "is white" to the word "animal" and "number," you will not understand the meaning of the resulting expressions "man exists," "number four exists," or "man is not white" or "man is white."

(2) The existence of the Essential Universal is prerequisite for the existence of its Particular. For example, there should first be animal in order that animal be man,

---

[1] The topic of simple and complex expression and universal or individual or common name and proper name corresponds to Aristotle's statements in the *Categories*.

and first there should be number in order that number be four, and first there should be human being in order that human being be Zid.

(3) Nothing gives meaning to a particular; rather its meaning is derived from its essence. For example, nothing makes human being animal, and nothing makes four number, except its essence. For if it were otherwise, if the essence of a thing did not exist, there could be a man which is not animal, and there could be four, but no number; but this is impossible.

To further elaborate what has been said, take the saying "something may make some other thing." Its meaning is this: a thing can not be in its essence another thing, but only could be that other thing by means of something else which is accidental to it. If it is impossible for a thing to be what another thing is, nothing could make it that thing. That thing which makes man, man, makes animal, animal. But it does not make man, animal, since man in itself is animal, and four in itself is number. But this relation does not exist between whiteness and man. Hence, there should be something which makes man, white.

Thus, when every meaning has the above three characteristics it is essential. Whatever does not have all these characteristics is accidental. Accidental qualities are those which can never arise from the essence of a thing, not even by imagination. Therefore, they are unlike kinds of deduction that are made in the case of number thousand which is an even number or in the case of a triangle, the sum total of whose angles is equal to two right angles. An example of an accidental quality is laughter, an attribute of men. This problem will be discussed later on.

And I should have mentioned also that a human being has two characteristics: essential and accidental. His essential characteristic may be exemplified by his ability to speak, because this property is the essence of his soul. An accidental quality of his is laughter, because it is the character of man, on seeing or hearing a strange and unfamiliar thing, (unless hindered by instinct or habit), to perchance laugh. But before there be wonder and laughter there must be a soul for a man, in order that this soul be united with a body and man becomes a man. First, there should be a soul in order that there be a man; not first, there should be laughter in order that there be a soul. Thus, the characteristic which comes first is essential, and whatever does not come from a man is not essential, but accidental. When you say, "Zid is seated," "Zid slept," "Zid is old," and "Zid is young," these characteristics, without doubt, are accidental, no matter what their temporal sequence be.

....

KINGDOMS IN EAST CENTRAL EUROPE

4.12 Hungary as heir of Rome: King Stephen, *Laws* (1000–1038). Original in Latin.

The Bulgarians entered a largely Byzantine orbit when they settled in the region just south of the Danube. By contrast, the Magyars (called Hungarians in the rest of Europe), entered a region contested by both the Byzantines and the Germans. When they arrived in the Pannonian plains (north of the Danube), they contributed to the dismantling of the formerly powerful Moravian empire, which had kept its independence from Germany, in part by converting to Christianity under the aegis of the Byzantines (it was for the Moravians that Cyril and Methodius—see above, p. 158—first made their translations). The Hungarians, by contrast, eventually allied themselves with Germany and with the Catholicism that its emperor represented. Thus Hungarian prince Géza (r.972–997) converted under the auspices of German churchmen and invited German priests to spread the religion, using Christianity to enforce his rule. His son Stephen (r.997–1038), married to the sister of Duke Henry IV of Bavaria (who later became Emperor Henry II), defeated his chief rival for rule with the help of German warriors, and around the year 1000, with the approval of Emperor Otto III, received a royal crown and a blessing from Pope Sylvester II. As king, Stephen adopted many of the institutions of the post-Roman successor states, including written laws. Those excerpted below are from the oldest of the laws that he promulgated. The code was clearly concerned above all with moral and religious issues and should be compared with Charlemagne's *Admonitio generalis* (above, p. 148) and the near-contemporary Anglo-Saxon legislation of King Æthelred (below, p. 222).

[Source: *The Laws of the Medieval Kingdom of Hungary*, vol 1: 1000–1301, trans. and ed. János M. Bak, György Bónis, and James Ross Sweeney (Bakersfield, CA: Charles Schlacks, Jr. Publisher, 1989), pp. 1, 3–8, 80–83 (slightly modified).]

Preface to the Royal Law

The work of the royal office subject to the rule of divine mercy is by custom greater and more complete when nourished in the Catholic faith than any other office. Since every people use their own law, we, governing our monarchy by the will of God and emulating both ancient and modern caesars, and after reflecting upon the law, decree for our people too the way they should lead an upright and blameless life. Just as they are enriched by divine laws, so may they similarly be strengthened by secular ones, in order that as the good shall be made many by these divine laws so shall the criminals incur punishment. Thus we set out below in the following sentences what we have decreed....

6. ROYAL CONCESSIONS OF FREE DISPOSITION OF GOODS.

We, by our royal authority have decreed that anyone shall be free to divide his property, to assign it to his wife, his sons and daughters, his relatives, or to the church;[1] and no one should dare to change this after his death.

7. THE PRESERVATION OF ROYAL GOODS.

It is our will that just as we have given others the opportunity to master their own possessions, so equally the goods, warriors,[2] bondmen,[3] and whatever else belongs to our royal dignity should remain permanent, and no one should plunder or remove them, nor should anyone dare to obtain any advantage from them.

8. THE OBSERVANCE OF THE LORD'S DAY.

If a priest or *ispán* [local lord], or any faithful person find anyone working on Sunday with oxen, the ox shall be confiscated and given to the men of the castle to be eaten;[4] if a horse is used, however, it shall be confiscated, but the owner, if he wishes, may redeem it with an ox which should be eaten as has been said. If anyone uses other equipment, this tool and his clothing shall be taken, and he may redeem them, if he wishes, with a flogging.

9. MORE ON THE SAME.

Priests and *ispánok* shall enjoin village reeves[5] to command everyone both great and small, men and women, with the exception of those who guard the fire, to gather on Sundays in the church. If someone remains at home through their negligence let them be beaten and shorn.

---

[1] The king seems to have wanted to transform the undivided property of clans into the personal property of freemen and nobles, as was the case in western European societies of the time. But he was not successful.

[2] The Latin word used here was *milites* (sing. *miles*), the same word for "fighters" or "warriors" that was used in the Peace Movement. In the *Laws of Hungary* the *milites* seem to have been armed servants of the king and magnates.

[3] The Latin word used here was *servi*, (sing. *servus*), which could mean either "slave" or "serf." Since the meaning here is not clear, the neutral term "bondmen" is used.

[4] The "men of the castle" (*cives* in Latin) were dependent men attached to the castles of the royal *ispánok* (the plural of *ispán*) for their defense and maintenance, much like the garrisons that guarded the castles in the document about Hugh of Lusignan and his lord (above, p. 181).

[5] In this period the reeves (*villici* in Latin) were free peasants in charge of enforcing some laws.

10. THE OBSERVANCE OF EMBER DAYS.[1]

If someone breaks the fast known to all on the Ember day, he shall fast in prison for a week.

11. THE OBSERVANCE OF FRIDAY.

If someone eats meat on Friday, a day observed by all Christianity, he shall fast incarcerated during the day for a week.

12. THOSE WHO DIE WITHOUT CONFESSION.

If someone has such a hardened heart—God forbid it to any Christian—that he does not want to confess his faults according to the counsel of a priest, he shall lie without any divine service and alms like an infidel. If his relatives and neighbors fail to summon the priest, and therefore he should die unconfessed, prayers and alms should be offered, but his relatives shall wash away their negligence by fasting in accordance with the judgment of the priests. Those who die a sudden death shall be buried with all ecclesiastical honor, for divine judgment is hidden from us and unknown.

13. THE OBSERVANCES OF CHRISTIANITY.

If someone neglects a Christian observance and takes pleasure in the stupidity of his negligence, he shall be judged by the bishops according to the nature of the offense and the discipline of the canons.[2] If he rebelliously objects to suffer the punishment with equanimity, he shall be subject to the same judgment seven times over. If, after all this, he continues to resist and remains obdurate, he shall be handed over for royal judgment, namely to the defender of Christianity.[3]

14. ON HOMICIDE.

If someone driven by anger and arrogance, willfully commits a homicide, he should know that according to the decrees of our [royal] council he is obliged to pay one hundred ten gold *pensae*,[4] from which fifty will go to the royal treasury, another fifty will be given to relatives, and ten will be paid to arbiters and mediators. The killer himself shall fast according to the rules of the canons.

MORE ON THE SAME.

If someone kills a person by chance, he shall pay twelve *pensae* and fast as the canons command.

THE KILLING OF SLAVES.

If someone's slave kills another's slave, the payment shall be a slave for a slave, or he may be redeemed and do penance as has been said.

MORE ON THE SAME.

If a freeman kills the slave of another, he shall replace him with another slave or pay his price, and fast according to the canons.

15. THOSE WHO KILL THEIR WIVES.

If an *ispán* with a hardened heart and a disregard for his soul—may such remain far from the hearts of the faithful—defiles himself by killing his wife, he shall make his peace with fifty steers[5] to the kindred of the woman, according to the decree of the royal council, and fast according to the commands of the canons. And if a warrior or a man of wealth commits the same crime he shall pay according to that same council ten steers and fast, as has been said. And if a commoner has committed the same crime, he shall make his peace with five steers to the kindred and fast.

16. DRAWING THE SWORD.

In order that peace should remain firm and unsullied among the greater and the lesser of whatever station, we forbid anyone to draw the sword with the aim of injury. If anyone in his audacity should put this prohibition to the test, let him be killed by the same sword.

17. ON PERJURY.

If a powerful man of stained faith and defiled heart be found guilty of breaking his oath by perjury, he shall atone for the perjury with the loss of his hand; or he may redeem it with fifty steers. If a commoner commits perjury, he shall be punished with the loss of his hand or may redeem it by twelve steers and fast, as the canons command.

---

[1] The observance of three days' fast during the weeks following Ash Wednesday, Pentecost, the Exaltation of the Holy Cross, and the feast of St. Lucy was widespread in the Carolingian realm and, as we see here, adopted in Hungary.

[2] This chapter in fact authorizes the introduction of canon (church) law into Hungary.

[3] The "defender of Christianity" was Stephen himself.

[4] The *pensa auri* was a coin equivalent to the contemporary Byzantine gold *solidus*.

[5] Steers were valued at one gold *pensa* each; hence fifty oxen, that is fifty *pensa*, here reflect the cost of legal compensation for the death of a woman by a man of the *ispán* class.

18. ON MANUMISSION.

If anyone, prompted by mercy, should set his male and female slaves free in front of witnesses, we decree that no one out of ill will shall reduce them to servitude after his death. If, however, he promised them freedom but died intestate, his widow and sons shall have the power to bear witness to this same manumission and to render *agape*[1] for the redemption of the husband's soul, if they wish.

19. GATHERING AT CHURCH AND THOSE WHO MUTTER OR CHATTER DURING MASS.

If some persons, upon coming to church to hear the divine service mutter among themselves and disturb others by relating idle tales during the celebration of mass and by being inattentive to Holy Scripture with its ecclesiastical nourishment, they shall be expelled from the church in disgrace if they are older, and if they are younger and common folk they shall be bound in the narthex of the church[2] in view of everyone and punished by whipping and by the shearing off of their hair.

20. INADMISSIBILITY OF ACCUSATIONS AND TESTIMONY OF BONDMEN OR BONDWOMEN AGAINST THEIR MASTERS OR MISTRESSES.

In order that the people of this kingdom may be far removed and remain free from the affronts and accusations of bondmen and bondwomen, it is wholly forbidden by decree of the royal council that any servile person be accepted in accusation or testimony against their masters or mistresses in any criminal case.

21. THOSE WHO PROCURE LIBERTY FOR BONDMEN OF OTHERS.

If anyone thoughtlessly brings the bondman of another, without the knowledge of his master, before the king or before persons of higher birth and dignity in order to procure for him the benefits of liberty after he has been released from the yoke of servitude, he should know that if he is rich, he shall pay fifty steers of which forty are owed to the king and ten to the master of the bondman, but if he is poor and of low rank, he shall pay twelve steers of which ten are due to the king and two to the master of the bondman.

22. THOSE WHO ENSLAVE FREEMEN.

Because it is worthy of God and best for men that everyone should conduct his life in the vigor of liberty, it is established by royal decree that henceforth no *ispán* or warrior should dare to reduce a freeman to servitude. If, however, compelled by his own rashness he should presume to do this, he should know that he shall pay from his own possessions the same composition, which shall be properly divided between the king and the *ispánok*, as in the other decree above.

SIMILARLY ON THE SAME.

But if someone who was once held in servitude lives freely after having submitted to a judicial procedure[3] held to consider his liberty, he shall be content with enjoying his freedom, and the man who held him in servitude shall pay nothing.

23. THOSE WHO TAKE THE WARRIORS OF ANOTHER FOR THEMSELVES.

We wish that each lord have his own warriors and no one shall try to persuade a warrior to leave his longtime lord and come to him, since this is the origin of quarrels.

24. THOSE WHO TAKE GUESTS OF ANOTHER FOR THEMSELVES.[4]

If someone receives a guest with benevolence and decently provides him with support, the guest shall not leave his protector as long as he receives support according to their agreement, nor should he transfer his service to any other.

25. THOSE WHO ARE BEATEN WHILE LOOKING FOR THEIR OWN.

If a warrior or a bondman flees to another and he whose warrior or man has run away sends his agent to bring him back, and that agent is beaten and whipped by anyone,

---

[1] The *agape* was a memorial meal shared by the manumitted (those released from slavery) or an offering made in memory of the dead.

[2] The entrance hall or porch.

[3] The "judicial procedure" refers to the ordeal by hot iron: the subject (in this case a person claiming to be free) must carry a hot iron for a few paces, and then put it down. His hand is bandaged. After three days the wound is inspected. If "clean," he is judged to have told the truth (or, in criminal cases, he is judged not guilty); if discolored or infected, he is judged to have lied.

[4] The "guests" were foreigners, most of whom were Western clerics and knights.

we decree in agreement with our magnates that he who gave the beating shall pay ten steers.

26. WIDOWS AND ORPHANS.

We also wish widows and orphans to be partakers of our law in the sense that if a widow, left with her sons and daughters, promises to support them and to remain with them as long as she lives, she shall have the right from us to do so, and no one should force her to marry. If she has a change of heart and wants to marry and leave the orphans, she shall have nothing from the goods of the orphans except her own clothing.[1]

MORE ABOUT WIDOWS.

If a widow without a child promises to remain unmarried in her widowhood, she shall have the right to all her goods and may do with them what she wishes. But after her death her goods shall go to the kin of her husband, if she has any, and if not, the king is the heir.

27. THE ABDUCTION OF GIRLS.

If any warrior debased by lewdness abducts a girl to be his wife without the consent of her parents, we decree that the girl should be returned to her parents, even if he raped her, and the abductor shall pay ten steers for the abduction, although he may afterwards have made peace with the girl's parents. If a poor man who is a commoner should attempt this, he shall compensate for the abduction with five steers.

28. THOSE WHO FORNICATE WITH BONDWOMEN OF ANOTHER.

In order that freemen preserve their liberty undefiled, we wish to warn them. Any transgressor who fornicates with a bondwoman of another, should know that he has committed a crime, and he is to be whipped for the first offense. If he fornicates with her a second time, he should be whipped and shorn; but if he does it a third time, he shall become a slave together with the woman, or he may redeem himself. If, however, the bondwoman should conceive by him and not be able to bear but dies in childbirth, he shall make compensation for her with another bondwoman.

THE FORNICATION OF BONDMEN.

If a bondman of one master fornicates with the bond-woman of another, he should be whipped and shorn, and if the woman should conceive by him and dies in childbirth, the man shall be sold and half of his price shall be given to the master of the bondwoman, the other half shall be kept by the master of the bondman.

29. THOSE WHO DESIRE BONDWOMEN AS WIVES.

In order that no one who is recognized to be a freeman should dare commit this offense, we set forth what has been decreed in this royal council as a source of terror and caution so that if any freeman should choose to marry a bondwoman of another with her master's consent, he shall lose the enjoyment of his liberty and become a slave forever.

30. THOSE WHO FLEE THEIR WIVES BY LEAVING THE COUNTRY.

In order that people of both sexes may remain and flourish under fixed law and free from injury, we establish in this royal decree that if anyone in his impudence should flee the country out of loathing for his wife, she shall possess everything which her husband rightfully possessed, so long as she is willing to wait for her husband, and no one shall force her into another marriage. If she voluntarily wishes to marry, she may take her own clothing leaving behind other goods, and marry again. If her husband, hearing this, should return, he is not allowed to replace her with anyone else, except with the permission of the bishop.

31. THEFT COMMITTED BY WOMEN.

Because it is terrible and loathsome to all to find men committing theft, and even more so for women, it is ordained by the royal council, that if a married woman commits theft, she shall be redeemed by her husband, and if she commits the same offense a second time, she shall be redeemed again; but if she does it a third time, she shall be sold.

32. ARSON OF HOUSES.

If anyone sets a building belonging to another on fire out of enmity, we order that he replace the building and whatever household furnishings were destroyed by the fire, and also pay sixteen steers which are worth forty *solidi*.[2]

---

[1] Here women apparently did not have a right to their dower—the gift that a husband gave his new wife—after the death of their husbands, though in later laws that right was recognized.

[2] In this particular case, Bavarian silver *solidi* are meant, of which 25 were equal to a Byzantine gold *solidus*.

33. ON WITCHES.

If a witch is found, she shall be led, in accordance with the law of judgment into the church and handed over to the priest for fasting and instruction in the faith. After the fast she may return home. If she is discovered in the same crime a second time, she shall fast and after the fast she shall be branded with the keys of the church in the form of a cross on her bosom, forehead, and between the shoulders. If she is discovered on a third occasion, she shall be handed over to the judge [of the secular court].

34. ON SORCERERS.

So that the creatures of God may remain far from all injury caused by evil ones and may not be exposed to any harm from them—unless it be by the will of God who may even increase it—we establish by decree of the council a most terrible warning to magicians and sorcerers that no person should dare to subvert the mind of any man or to kill him by means of sorcery and magic. Yet in the future if a man or a woman dare to do this he or she shall be handed over to the person hurt by sorcery or to his kindred, to be judged according to their will.

If, however, they are found practicing divination as they do in ashes or similar things, they shall be corrected with whips by the bishop.

35. THE INVASION OF HOUSES.

We wish that peace and unanimity prevail between great and small according to the Apostle: Be ye all of one accord, etc.,[1] and let no one dare attack another. For if there be any *ispán* so contumacious that after the decree of this common council he should seek out another at home in order to destroy him and his goods, and if the lord of the house is there and fights with him and is killed, the *ispán* shall be punished according to the law about drawing the sword.[2] If, however, the *ispán* shall fall, he shall lie without compensation. If he did not go in person but sent his warriors, he shall pay compensation for the invasion with one hundred steers. If, moreover, a warrior invades the courtyard and house of another warrior, he shall pay compensation for the invasion with ten steers. If a commoner invades the huts of those of similar station, he shall pay for the invasion with five steers.

4.13 Coming to terms with Catholic Poland: Thietmar of Merseburg, *Chronicle* (1013–1018). Original in Latin.

Poland, like Hungary, became a state in the wake of Moravia's collapse. Mieszko I (r.c.960–992) was the first leader to unite a region that was (roughly speaking) between the Oder and Vistula rivers. Baptized in 966, he expanded his realm by taking advantage of Bohemian and German rivalries. In 990 or 991 he placed his duchy under the direct protection of the pope. Mieszko's son and successor, Boleslaw the Brave (r.992–1025), maintained good relations with Emperor Otto III (r.996–1002) and helped him destabilize Bohemia. Thus he welcomed the exiled bishop of Prague, Saint Adalbert. Two years later he retrieved the relics of Adalbert, who had been martyred on a mission to convert the Prussians. When Otto III came on pilgrimage to see those relics at Gniezno, Poland's capital city, Boleslaw orchestrated a synod that raised Gniezno to an archbishopric. The major sources for this early history come not from Poland, however, but from Germany. An example is the *Chronicle* of Thietmar of Merseburg (975–1018). Thietmar came from a prominent Saxon family. Educated in the classics and Christian texts at Magdeburg, Thietmar was (like Ruotger and Bruno, see below, p. 216) a product of the Ottonian Renaissance, groomed to serve the king as well as to preside in a high

---

[1]   See Phil. 2: 2–4.

[2]   See chapter 16 of this same law code, above.

church office. In 1009, he became bishop of Merseburg, a key bishopric created by the Ottonians to strengthen the empire's control over its eastern border. Thietmar was well aware of events in Poland; he rather admired Mieszko, but he vilified Boleslaw even while recording Boleslaw's acts of piety. Why might a bishop near the eastern edge of Germany be wary of a contemporary Polish ruler?

[Source: *Ottonian Germany: The Chronicon of Thietmar of Merseburg*, trans. David A. Warner (Manchester: Manchester University Press, 2001), pp. 171–72, 191–93, 361–63 (notes modified).]

4.28 In the beginning of the summer, Adalbert, bishop of the Bohemians, arrived.[1] He had received the name Woyciech at his baptism, the other name, at his confirmation, from the archbishop of Magdeburg. He was educated in letters, in that same city.... As he was unable to separate his flock from the ancient error of wickedness through godly teaching, he excommunicated them all and came to Rome to justify himself before the pope. For a long time, with the pope's permission, he lived an exemplary life according to the strict rule of Abbot Boniface.[2] With the same pope's permission, he later tried to subdue the Prussians, their thoughts still estranged from Christ, with the bridle of holy preaching. On 23 April, pierced by a spear and beheaded, he alone received the best martyrdom, without a groan. This occurred just as he himself had seen it in a dream and had predicted to all the brothers, saying: "I thought I saw myself celebrating mass and communicating alone." Seeing that he had now died, the authors of this wicked crime increased both their wickedness and the vengeance of God by throwing the blessed body in the water. His head, however, they scornfully transfixed with a stake. They returned home in great joy. After learning of this, Boleslaw, Mieszko's son, immediately purchased both the martyr's celebrated body and his head. In Rome, after the emperor [Otto III] had been informed, he humbly offered praises to God because, during his lifetime, he had taken such a servant for himself through the palm of martyrdom....

4.55 I cannot place in its correct order everything that ought to be treated within the context of this book. In what follows, therefore, I will not be embarrassed to add a few recollections. Indeed, I rejoice in the change of pace much as the traveller who, because of its difficulty or perhaps from ignorance, leaves the course of the more direct road and sets out on some winding secondary path. Hence, I will relate the remaining deeds of Mieszko [I], the celebrated duke of the Poles, who has already been treated in some detail in the previous books. He took a noble wife from the region of Bohemia, the sister of Boleslaw the Elder. Her life corresponded to her name—she was called Dobrawa in Slavic, which, in German, means 'the good'. For this one, faithful to Christ, and realizing that her husband was mired in various heathen errors, turned her humble spirit to the task of binding him to the faith as well. She tried in every way to conciliate him, not because of the threefold appetite of this evil world but rather for the sake of the admirable and, to all the faithful, desirable fruit of future salvation.[3]

4.56 She sinned willingly for a while, that she might later be good for a long time. For during Lent, which closely followed her marriage, though she intended to offer an acceptable tithe to God by abstaining from meat and through the affliction of her body, her husband asked and tried to coax her into giving up her plan. She consented, thinking that he might therefore be more willing to listen to her on some other occasion. Some say that she only ate meat during a single Lenten period, others say three. Now, O reader, you have heard her sin, now also consider the attractive fruit of her pious will. She labored for the sake of her husband's conversion and was heard by the Creator in

---

[1] Adalbert (956–997), of Bohemian noble birth, was (like Thietmar) educated at Magdeburg (Germany) and became bishop of Prague in 983. He was martyred in 997.

[2] That is, Adalbert spent time at the monastery of Santi Bonifacio e Alessio in Rome. That Boniface was a martyr saint of the early church.

[3] For the "three-fold" appetites, see 1 John 2: 16.

his kindness; and through his infinite goodness that most zealous persecutor came to his senses. After being admonished frequently by his beloved wife, he vomited out the poison of his unbelief and, in holy baptism, wiped away the stain of his birth. Immediately, members of his hitherto reluctant people followed their beloved head and lord and, after accepting the marriage garments, were numbered among the wards of Christ. Jordan, their first bishop, labored much with them, while he diligently invited them by word and deed to the cultivation of the heavenly vineyard. Then the couple rightly rejoiced, namely the man and the noble woman, and all who were subject to them rejoiced at their marriage in Christ. After this, the good mother gave birth to a son who was very different from her and the misfortune of many mothers. She named him Boleslaw [the Brave], after her brother. He first revealed his innate evil to her and then raged against his own flesh and blood, as I will reveal in the following.

4.57 But when his mother died [977], his father married Margrave Dietrich's daughter, a nun at the convent called Calbe, without the approval of the church. Oda was her name and great was her presumption. She rejected her celestial spouse in favor of a man of war, which displeased all the pastors of the church but most of all her own bishop, the venerable Hildeward.[1] But the welfare of the land, and the need to strengthen the peace, kept this from leading to a break; rather it provided a healthy and continuous incentive for reconciliation. For she increased the service of Christ in every way: many captives were returned to their homeland, prisoners were released from their chains, and the prisons of those who had been accused were opened. I hope that God will forgive her the magnitude of her sin, since such love of pious deeds was revealed in her. We read, however, that he who does not entirely abandon the evil he has begun, will try in vain to placate the Lord. She bore her husband three sons: Mieszko, Swentepulk and [...]. She passed her life there, highly honored, until her husband's death. She was beloved among those with whom she lived and useful to those from whom she had come.

4.58 But on 25 May, in the year of the Incarnation 992, in the tenth year of Otto III's kingship,[2] the aforementioned duke [Mieszko], now old and feverish, went from this place of exile to his homeland,[3] leaving his kingdom to be divided among many claimants. Yet, with fox-like cunning, his son Boleslaw unified it once more in the hands of one ruler, after he had expelled his stepmother and brothers, and had their familiars Odilien and Przibiwoj blinded. That he might be able to rule alone, he ignored both human and divine law. He married the daughter of Margrave Rikdag, but later sent her away and took a Hungarian woman as his wife. She bore him a son, named Bezprym, but he also sent her away. His third wife was Emnilde, a daughter of the venerable lord, Dobromir. Faithful to Christ, she formed her husband's unstable character completely for the better and strove unceasingly to wash away both of her sins through the generous dispersal of alms and abstinence. She bore two sons, Mieszko and another one whom the father named after his beloved lord.[4] She also produced three daughters of whom one was an abbess, the second married Count Herman, and the third the son of King Vladimir. I will say more about them later....

8.1 In the year 1018 of the Incarnation, in the second indiction, in the sixteenth year of Lord Henry's reign, and his fourth as emperor, the same Henry celebrated the Circumcision and Epiphany of the Lord in Frankfurt, with great solemnity.[5] On 25 January, Ezzelin the Lombard was granted his liberty. He had been held in custody for four years. Afterwards, on 30 January, Bishops Gero and Arnulf, the counts Herman and Dietrich, and the emperor's chancellor Frederick agreed to a sworn peace at the burg Bautzen. The agreement was made at the emperor's order and in response to Boleslaw's constant supplications. This was not as it should have been, however. Rather, it was the best that could be accomplished under the circumstances. In the company of a select group of hostages, the aforesaid lords returned. After four days, Oda, Margrave Ekkehard's daughter, whom Boleslaw had long desired, was escorted to Zützen by Otto, the duke's son.[6] When they arrived, they were greeted by a large

---

[1] A nun was supposed to be married to Christ and thus could not take another husband.

[2] In fact, the ninth year.

[3] I.e., he died.

[4] Referring to Otto III.

[5] Thietmar here refers to Emperor Henry II (r.1014–1024), the successor of Otto III.

[6] This Oda was Boleslaw's fourth wife.

crowd of men and women, and by many burning lamps, since it was night-time. Contrary to the authority of the canons, Oda married the duke after Septuagesima.[1] Until now, she has lived outside the law of matrimony and thus in a manner worthy only of a marriage such as this one.

8.2 In her husband's kingdom, the customs are many and varied. They are also harsh, but occasionally quite praiseworthy. The populace must be fed like cattle and punished as one would a stubborn ass. Without severe punishment, the prince cannot put them to any useful purpose. If anyone in this land should presume to abuse a foreign matron and thereby commit fornication, the act is immediately avenged through the following punishment. The guilty party is led on to the market bridge, and his scrotum is affixed to it with a nail. Then, after a sharp knife has been placed next to him, he is given the harsh choice between death or castration. Furthermore, anyone found to have eaten meat after Septuagesima is severely punished, by having his teeth knocked out. The law of God, newly introduced in these regions, gains more strength from such acts of force than from any fast imposed by the bishops. There are also other customs, by far inferior to these, which please neither God nor the inhabitants, and are useful only as a means to inspire terror. To some extent, I have alluded to these above. I think that it is unnecessary for me to say any more about this man whose name and manner of life, if it please Almighty God, might better have remained concealed from us. That his father and he were joined to us, through marriage and great familiarity, has produced results so damaging that any good preceding them is far outweighed, and so it will remain in the future. During false periods of peace, Boleslaw may temporarily regard us with affection. Nevertheless, through all kinds of secret plots, he constantly attempts to sow dissension, diminish our inborn freedom, and, if time and place permit, rise up and destroy us.

8.3 In the days of his father,[2] when he still embraced heathenism, every woman followed her husband on to the funeral pyre, after first being decapitated. If a woman was found to be a prostitute, moreover, she suffered a particularly wretched and shameful penalty. The skin around her genitals was cut off and this 'foreskin', if we may call it that, was hung on the door so that anyone who entered would see it and be more concerned and prudent in the future. The law of the Lord declares that such a woman should be stoned, and the rules of our ancestors would require her beheading.[3] Nowadays, the freedom to sin dominates everywhere and to a degree that is not right or normal. And so it is not just a large number of frustrated girls who engage in adultery, having been driven by the desire of the flesh to harmful lust, but even some married women and, indeed, with their husbands still living. As if this were not enough, such women then have their husbands murdered by the adulterer, inspiring the deed through furtive hints. After this, having given a wicked example to others, they receive their lovers quite openly and sin at will. They repudiate their legal lord in a most horrible fashion and prefer his retainer, as if the latter were sweet Abro or mild Jason.[4] Nowadays, because a harsh penalty is not imposed, I fear that many will find this new custom more and more acceptable. O you priests of the Lord, forcefully rise up and let nothing stop you! Take a sharp ploughshare and extirpate this newly sprouted weed, down to the roots! You also, lay people, do not give aid to such as these! May those joined in Christ live innocently and, after these supplanters have been rooted out, forever groan in shame. Unless these sinners return to their senses, may our helper, Christ, destroy them with a powerful breath from his holy mouth and scatter them with the great splendor of his second coming.[5]

---

[1] Septuagesima was supposed to inaugurate a period of fasting before Easter and was therefore not an appropriate time to celebrate a marriage.

[2] I.e., in the days of Mieszko I.

[3] For the "law of the Lord," see John 8: 5.

[4] Abro was a rich ancient Greek proverbially known for high living; Jason was the mythological leader of the Argonauts.

[5] For the image of the Lord slaying sinners with his breath, see 2 Thess. 2: 8.

4.14 Poland's self-image: *Boleslaw's Coin* (992–1000).

Although we have few written sources from tenth-century Poland, we do have material sources, including this coin, which was issued by Boleslaw the Brave (r.992–1025) either right after 992, when he ousted his half brothers and ascended to rulership, or around the year 1000, when Emperor Otto III met Boleslaw at Gniezno and the city was established as a archbishopric. In the emperor's eyes, Boleslaw was subservient to Germany. But Boleslaw clearly had other ideas about himself. His coin shows him in profile, like a Roman emperor (obverse). He wears a helmet with earflaps, cultivating a martial image. On the other side of the coin (reverse) is a cross, proclaiming his Christian religion, and the Latin inscription reads "Gnezdun civitas" (City of Gniezno), elevating the status of his chief city to a Christian center (whether or not the coin was struck after Gniezno was declared an archbishopric by Otto).

See Plate 12, p. 248, for a color reproduction of the coin.

(From the collection of the National Museum in Kraków)

4.15 Kievan Rus': *The Russian Primary Chronicle* (*c.*1113, incorporating earlier materials). Original in Russian.

The Russian Primary Chronicle is one of the earliest sources that we have for Russian history. Composed *c.*1113 by an anonymous monk of the Crypt Monastery near Kiev, it was clearly tied to the history of the princes of Kiev. In the excerpt below, Kievan Prince Yaroslav the Wise (r.1019–1054) is portrayed as following the model of the Christian ruler, especially the Byzantine emperor, even to the point of naming the church that he founded "St. Sophia," after the church built by Justinian at Constantinople. The passage says that Yaroslav not only patronized monks but had the learned among them copy books to be distributed in turn to new monasteries. Russian dates, which counted the years from the time of the Creation, followed the Byzantine dating system. In parentheses are the corresponding dates CE. Consider other ways in which Rus' was the child of Byzantium. In what ways was it rather more like Poland and Hungary, even though its Christianity did not come from Rome?

[Source: *The Russian Primary Chronicle: Laurentian Text*, trans. and ed. Samuel Hazzard Cross and Olgerd P. Sherbowitz-Wetzor (Cambridge, MA: Medieval Academy of America, 1953), pp. 136–38 (slightly modified).]

6544 (1036) Thereafter Yaroslav assumed the entire sovereignty, and was the sole ruler in the land of Rus'. Yaroslav went to Novgorod, where he set up his son Vladimir as prince, and appointed Zhidyata bishop.[1] At this time, a son was born to Yaroslav, and he named him Vyacheslav. While Yaroslav was still at Novgorod, news came to him that the Pechenegs were besieging Kiev.[2] He then collected a large army of Varangians[3] and Slavs, returned to Kiev, and entered his city. The Pechenegs were innumerable. Yaroslav made a sally from the city and marshaled his forces, placing the Varangians in the center, the men of Kiev on the right flank, and the men of Novgorod on the left. When they had taken position before the city, the Pechenegs advanced, and they met on the spot where the metropolitan church of St. Sophia now stands. At that time, as a matter of fact, there were fields outside the city. The combat was fierce, but toward evening Yaroslav with difficulty won the upper hand. The Pechenegs fled in various directions, but as they did not know in what quarter to flee, they were drowned, some in the Setoml',[4] some in other streams, while the remnant of them disappeared from that day to this. In the same year, Yaroslav imprisoned his brother Sudislav in Pskov because he had been slanderously accused.

6545 (1037). Yaroslav built the great citadel at Kiev, near which stands the Golden Gate. He founded also the metropolitan Church of St. Sophia, the Church of the Annunciation over the Golden Gate, and also the Monastery of St. George and the convent of St. Irene. During his reign, the Christian faith was fruitful and multiplied, while the number of monks increased, and new monasteries came into being. Yaroslav loved religious establishments and was devoted to priests, especially to monks. He applied himself to books, and read them continually day and night. He assembled many scribes, and translated from Greek into Slavic. He wrote and collected many books through which true believers are instructed and enjoy religious education. For as one man plows the land, and another sows, and still others reap and eat food in abundance, so did this prince. His father Vladimir[5] plowed and harrowed the soil when he enlightened Rus' through baptism, while this prince sowed the hearts of the faithful with the written word, and we in turn reap the harvest by receiving the teaching of books. For great is the profit from book-learning.

Through the medium of books, we are shown and taught the way of repentance, for we gain wisdom and continence from the written word. Books are like rivers that water the whole earth; they are the springs of wisdom. For books have an immeasurable depth; by them we are consoled in sorrow. They are the bridle of self-restraint. For great is wisdom. As Solomon said in its praise, "I (wisdom) have inculcated counsel; I have summoned reason and prudence. The fear of the Lord is the beginning of wisdom. Mine are counsel, wisdom, constancy, and strength. Through me kings rule, and the mighty decree justice. Through me are princes magnified and the oppressors possess the earth. I love them that love me, and they who seek me shall find grace."[6] If you seek wisdom attentively in books, you obtain great profit for your spirit. He who reads books often converses with God or with holy men. If one possesses the words of the prophets, the teachings of the evangelists and the apostles, and the lives of the holy fathers, his soul will derive great profit therefrom. Thus Yaroslav, as we have said, was a lover of books, and as he wrote many, he deposited them in the Church of Saint Sophia which he himself had founded. He adorned it with gold and silver and churchly vessels, and in it the usual hymns are raised to God at the customary seasons. He founded other churches in the cities and districts, appointing priests and paying them out of his personal fortune. He bade them teach the people, since that is the duty which God has prescribed them, and to go often into the churches. Priests and Christian laymen thus increased in number. Yaroslav rejoiced to see the multitude of his churches and of his Christian subjects, but the devil was afflicted, since he was now conquered by this new Christian nation.

---

[1] The first bishop of Novgorod died in 1030 after designating his successor. Yaroslav, however, insisted on Luka Zhidyata, who presided over the see from 1036 to 1055.

[2] The Pechenegs were a Turkic nomadic people who in the tenth century occupied the region between the Don and the Danube but, squeezed by other nomadic groups and the expanding Byzantines and Rus, raided into Rus' only to be repulsed by Yaroslav.

[3] The Varangians were the Scandinavian settlers of Rus'.

[4] The Setoml' was a small stream in Kiev.

[5] Saint Vladimir I (r.c.980–1015) converted to Christianity under the influence of Byzantine Emperor Basil II, took the baptismal name of Basil, and married Basil's sister.

[6] Prov. 8: 12, 13, 14–17.

6546 (1038). Yaroslav attacked the Yatvingians.[1]

6547 (1039). The Church of the Blessed Virgin, which had been founded by Vladimir, Yaroslav's father, was consecrated by the Metropolitan Theopemptos.

6548 (1040). Yaroslav attacked Lithuania.

6549 (1041). Yaroslav attacked the Mazovians by boat.

NORTHERN EUROPE

4.16 An Ottonian courtier-bishop: Ruotger, *Life of Bruno, Archbishop of Cologne* (late 960s). Original in Latin.

Bruno (925–965) was the youngest of the three sons of King Henry I of Saxony (r.919–936). Destined from an early age for the church, Bruno first studied in Utrecht, a city in the present-day Netherlands. In the tenth century Utrecht was part of Lotharingia, a turbulent territory that Henry occupied the year Bruno was born. In his teens, Bruno was summoned by his brother, Henry's successor Otto I (r.936–973), to be a member of the royal court. The court had no fixed capital; rather, the king and his entourage were constantly on the move. In effect, the king ruled on horseback! Bruno continued and extended his studies as he met learned people across his brother's realm. At age 28, he became archbishop of Cologne, in Lotharingia, and a few months later Otto made him duke of Lotharingia, the highest civilian authority there, amidst a rebellion against Otto. Bruno served his brother as general and chief administrator of Lotharingia while he served the church as archbishop of Cologne, pastor, and reformer, until his death at the age of 40.

By contrast, little is known about Bruno's biographer Ruotger. He was a monk in Cologne; from comments in the *Life of Bruno*, it is clear that he knew Bruno personally. Certainly Ruotger was staggeringly learned, likely a member of Bruno's intellectual circle, and perhaps his student. Besides more than twenty biblical citations or echoes, the excerpts of the *Life of Bruno* below include allusions to eight pagan Roman authors, nine Latin Christian authors, mentions of the pagan Roman orator and statesman Cicero (106–43 BCE) and Christian Latin poet Prudentius (348–after 405), and a paraphrase of the Roman historian Sallust (86–35/34 BCE). Highly conscientious, Ruotger produced a reliable account of a prince who was unique: at one and the same time a courtier, a warrior, and an archbishop.

[Source: *Ruotgers Lebensbeschreibung des Erzbischofs Bruno von Köln* (*Ruotgeri Vita Brunonis Archiepiscopi Coloniensis*), ed. Irene Ott, Monumenta Germaniae Historica, Scriptores rerum Germanicarum, Nova series, 10 (Cologne: Böhlau-Verlag, 1958), pp. 3–4, 5–7, 11, 20–21, 23–24, 31–32, 33–34, 38–39, 55. Translated and introduced by Bruce L. Venarde.]

---

[1] The Yatvingians were a Lithuanian people. Attacks on them and on Lithuania and the Mazovians (below) were evidently designed both to protect Rus's northwest flank and to keep open access to eastern Poland, on which Yaroslav made claim.

2. … He was born in the time when his father, the glorious king Henry, was very zealously rebuilding what had been destroyed after he had quelled the ferocity of the barbarians and subdued the menace of civil strife.[1] Now at last Henry ruled a willing people with the reins of justice and, now at last, amidst a most secure and long-awaited peace. Thus the time of Bruno's birth already heralded, as it were, the future signs of his good will. For since he always approached every good thing very vigorously, he very carefully sought out the gift of peace as the nourishment and adornment of other virtues, because he knew it would benefit all good things. In tranquil times, virtues can be nourished and strengthened. Then in any disturbance, they will not allow a man to be weakened in the force of his power.…

4. When he was about four years old, the noble progeny of kings was sent to Utrecht and to the venerable Bishop Baldric (who still survives) to be steeped in study of the liberal arts.[2] There, while he progressed as befits a boy of good character, with excellent discipline and according to a wise nature, at long last, as if by a considerable siege on the hateful tyranny of the Normans,[3] churches and other buildings of which scarcely ruins had survived were restored on this occasion.

Thus he passed through no stage of his life without benefit to the holy Church of God. Through him, although he did not know it yet, the Christian populace, freed from its enemies, rejoiced in the praise of God. When he had learned the first rudiments of grammar—as we often heard from him as he meditated on the glory of the almighty God—next he began to read the poet Prudentius as taught by his master.[4] Because Prudentius is catholic in faith and purpose, outstanding in eloquence and truth, and most elegant in the variety of his meters and his books, such sweetness was so immediately pleasing to the taste of Bruno's heart that he drank in with greater eagerness than can be described not only knowledge of the external words but also the marrow of inner meaning and its purest nectar, if I may put it that way.

After that there was nearly no type of liberal study in Greek or Latin that escaped the vitality of his genius. Never, which is unusual, did great riches or the abundance of clamoring crowds or the approach of any other bother turn his spirit from this noble leisure. Perpetual meditation and tireless eagerness for mental exercise testified to the purity of his heart, since already nearly all disposition of this sort became habit, as it is written: "A boy is known from his inclinations, if his behavior is pure and righteous" [Prov. 20: 11]. It reached the point that just as he did not allow the fire of his soul to be put out by the idleness and frivolity of others nor be corrupted by empty and unnecessary conversation, he bore it very sorrowfully if the books he was studying or any that were in his sight were carelessly handled or creased or treated in any way with too little attention. Indeed, he considered that nothing that pertained to him should be neglected since indeed, as Solomon says, "He who neglects the small things dies little by little" [Eccles. 19: 1].

5. After his father, Henry, who had founded and pacified his realm to the last detail, went the way of all flesh, his first-born son Otto, blessed by the Lord and anointed with the oil of happiness, with the full will and consent of his chief men began to reign in the 188th lustrum and the 63rd cycle of the indiction since the birth of our lord Jesus Christ.[5] Otto was a man on whom the spirit of God had conferred a gift of singular truthfulness and faithfulness. If I promised that I would catalogue his virtues, I would take too much on myself and be tolerated little, for praise and glory owed him exceed whatever eloquence Cicero himself might offer. Otto honorably called his brother Bruno, dedicated to God, still a youth but as if an equal, from the schools to his court, a place fitting for such a bright mirror where whatever was unseemly in almost the whole world showed itself more

---

[1] The "barbarians" are the Vikings, who had frequently raided Utrecht and its vicinity. A less partisan description of civil strife would emphasize the struggles King Henry had in establishing full authority in Lotharingia.

[2] Bishop Baldric of Utrecht, a relative of Bruno's mother, lived for several years after the composition of Ruotger's account; he was bishop from 918 to 975! Utrecht was a center of learning.

[3] I.e., the Vikings (Norsemen).

[4] The Spanish poet Prudentius was a highly placed imperial official who withdrew to the ascetic life in his 40s. It was during this period that he wrote the Christian epics for which he was best known, including the *Psychomachia*, an allegory of the duels between personified virtues and vices.

[5] Ruotger's dating method, which derived from ancient Rome, refers only to a range of years. The precise date is July 2, 936.

FOUR: POLITICAL COMMUNITIES REORDERED (C.900–C.1050)

clearly through studies.[1] From all of Otto's borders came everything that seemed important. Likewise, all harassed by any accusation sought this sole refuge [Otto's court]. For there presided a model of wisdom, piety, and justice beyond human memory. Returning from the court, those who just before had seemed to themselves very learned, blushingly approached the rudiments of the liberal arts as if saying, "Now I begin." When nothing stirred on the left side of the breast, he thereafter modestly abstained from that high tribunal, so to speak.[2] The Lord filled this his vessel with the spirit of wisdom and thoughtfulness. It did not suffice to him to gather what he had ready at hand in the treasury of his own heart; he additionally considered foreign puzzles, and whatever philosophic matter he thought remote from earthly understanding he drew forth from wherever it came. He unveiled the seven liberal arts long forgotten. Whatever historians, orators, poets, and philosophers trumpeted was the great new thing he examined with great diligence along with teachers of whatever language it was in, and there where a master excelled in genius, he humbly offered himself as a student....

11. Then Wicfrid,[3] shepherd of the holy church of Cologne, for a long time quite feeble, yet faithful to the majesty of the kingdom and fatherland, at last returning his exhausted body to earth, was joined with heavenly spirits. The people, deprived of a shepherd, in grief chose for consolation, neither ambivalently nor wavering among candidates, the one solely hoped for: Lord Bruno, a splendid and most experienced man, following the counsel of great men and the whole clergy.[4] Youthful in body, he was mature in habits, humble and gentle despite the greatest nobility, at the height of his wisdom, which had taught him not to think himself wiser than is fitting to think, but wise in measure. Sparing of himself in his royal affluence, he was a rich man to his friends....

20. The emperor, disturbed about this event,[5] so sudden and unforeseen, and grieving more for the misery of its citizens than his own loss, lifted the siege of Mainz, having finally gotten the treaty he wanted. Turning from his camp toward the east along with those he knew to be loyal, Otto decided quickly to make a plan for the region he was leaving [i.e., Lotharingia] and made his brother [Bruno] the guardian and supervisor in the west, an archduke, so to speak, in such dangerous times. He gave him these orders. [The king said to Bruno,] "How much I rejoice, my dearest brother, that we have always understood matters as one and the same, and that it cannot be said we ever had different desires in any matter. It is the thing that greatly comforts me most of all in bitter times: I see royal priesthood, by the grace of almighty God, come into our kingdom. Both priestly religion and royal power are mighty in you, in that you know how to give everyone his due, which is justice, and you are able to withstand the dread and deceit of enemies, which is power and justice. For a long time now you have investigated the very mother of the liberal arts and truly its virtue, philosophy, which has trained you in modesty and greatness of spirit...."

23. Some people ignorant of divine will may object: why did a bishop assume public office and the dangers of war when he had undertaken only the care of souls? If they understand any sane matter, the result itself will easily satisfy them, when they see a great and very unaccustomed (especially in their homelands) gift of peace spread far and wide through this guardian and teacher of a faithful people, lest in this matter those objecting further stumble around in darkness where there is no light. Nor was governing this world new or unusual for rectors of the holy Church, previous examples of which, if someone needs them, are at hand. But we, moving on to other things, leave it to the judgment of each what he wants to say concerning this pious man, in the knowledge that nobody of sound mind would strive to blacken the

---

1   The summons was in 939 or 940, when Bruno was a teenager. Otto's itinerant court allowed Bruno to travel widely during the next dozen or so years. The unseemliness here apparently refers to poor Latin, since the rest of the paragraph focuses on Bruno's intellectual pursuits, as teacher and learner, while a member of his brother's entourage.

2   The right side of the breast is the seat of wisdom; here Ruotger is paraphrasing the Latin poet Juvenal. The meaning appears to be that if a line of study did not seem fruitful for him, he left it to others.

3   Archbishop of Cologne (924–953).

4   Bruno became archbishop of Cologne in 953.

5   Bruno was elected amidst a rebellion against Otto I led by his son Liudolf and Duke Conrad (duke since 944 and also Otto's son-in-law), as described in chapters 18 and 19, omitted here. Chapter 20 picks up with Otto besieging rebels in Mainz. Although Otto did not take the title of emperor until 962, Ruotger calls him such retrospectively.

most evident blessing with the curse of reproach. Everything that Bruno did was honorable and useful for our republic.[1] In his deeds he by no means had as object that by gaining favor, news of his actions should fly through the mouths of men, but rather he lived this way: he regulated all his works before men so that they would be a horror to the worst and a reward for the best. He made it clear to all that in the episcopate he sought a good work, in which he could not easily be censured by the hostile and jealous, but that it worked even more to his credit that he displeased such people. Therefore, engaged in this wonderful occupation, the ever watchful manager of the highest head of the household and chief priest, bearing in his hands a burning lamp, namely an example of good work, he led some willing and dragged others unwilling to the ways of God....

31. Bruno gathered from everywhere the bodies of the saints and relics and other kinds of monuments in order to increase protection for his people and by means of this glory spread the glory of the Lord among peoples near and far. He arranged places and service for them very copiously, at great expense and in great sumptuousness, concerning each of which many things could be said if my promised brevity would allow it. These are signs of invincible faith, through which he sought not what was his but what was Jesus Christ's. Everyone knows with what care, fervor, and joy he brought the staff and chain of St. Peter to Cologne, the former from Metz and the latter from Rome. In honor of St. Peter, he wondrously expanded his most honorable house, which he changed from beautiful to very beautiful.[2]...

33. Meanwhile, in many places in the parishes of his diocese, this faithful and wise servant of the Lord built churches, monasteries and other buildings suited for the service of his one lord God and in honor of God's saints. Certain other structures already founded he enlarged and others long ruined he restored. With the foreseeing skill of his nature, he placed in each one those who would serve almighty God by the rule of canonical life, and in so doing generously provided for them, lest anything be

lacking to carry out this way of life.[3] The memorials of his work and most salutary zeal, lasting as the air, remain fixed in place where he put them, so that for the praise and glory of Jesus Christ the memory of such a great man never suffer a time of obscurity. He poured out the same effort for foreign people; in the kingdom entrusted to his wisdom he provided sometimes by example, sometimes through his works, sometimes through qualities in other people and in repeated exhortation.[4] He did not allow any of his people to be occupied in vain or be inactive in lazy leisure, specifying, as he often said, that a lazy beast ought to be blocked from the trough and that according to the apostle [Paul], he who does not work does not eat [see 2 Thess. 3: 10]. All the good things he did, taught, and loved cannot be written out one by one. So much material would remain for those attending to it that they would quickly leave off in exhaustion before finishing what they had undertaken. In preaching the word of God and in the subtlety of his debates concerning the truth of the scriptures, we can marvel at such and so great a man, but we cannot sum him up....

37. The merciful shepherd Bruno, champion of truth, sower of the gospel, with the greatest care sought out zealous and diligent men who would keep watch over the republic, in loyalty and strength, each in his own place. He took great care that neither advice nor resources would be lacking to them. At Bruno's most beneficial urgings, all the princes and regional chiefs and others who had to do with the interests of the kingdom agreed to treaties in full faith for the common good of the property of all people. He considered them among the highest men and his intimates, and especially won over his brother the emperor to them, thinking—not foolishly—about a maxim of a wise man: "A good man gets slower when you ignore him, but a bad one is made more wicked." He cherished above all with great honor Archbishop Henry of Trier, a man of great merit and the highest integrity, who succeeded the great prelate Ruotbert, who died during a serious epidemic at Cologne when the emperor, too, was there; and also William of Mainz, an archbishop of most brilliant and agreeable excellence,

---

[1] Ruotger does not distinguish between kingdom and republic, which in the Roman tradition he knew so well meant simply "public sphere."

[2] That is, the cathedral of Cologne, which was dedicated to St. Peter. The chain was from Peter's imprisonment in Rome before his execution.

[3] The canonical rule was that of Saint Benedict, from which this sentence quotes to underline the connection.

[4] Bruno's rebuilding, reforming, and evangelizing efforts, then, went beyond his diocese and into other parts of Lotharingia.

Bruno's nephew and successor to Frederick: both of them outstanding men, both wholly trained in the Lord's law, both closely connected in friendship, the one through blood relation to the emperor, the other for his integrity.[1] Bruno often turned for advice to these two very illustrious men, so wise and religious and learned in all the good arts, lest he alone chance to stray anywhere off the path of truth, as is the way in human affairs. We saw them together with him not only in reading, counsel, and debate, but even in the line of battle, caring for good not only before God but before men. For there was in the western parts of Lotharingia a nearly untamable barbarism, which seemed a race of the church, begrudging the salvation of others no less than their own, scornful of gentle paternal admonition, nearly without fear of power.[2] Had they been allowed their own judgment, they would have seemed evil to their own and the worst thing for themselves. Bruno before all things practiced a forethoughtful way of governing, so that according to the nature of times and places, he pondered the rule of our very wise emperor in the elevation of shepherds for the peace and harmony of the Lord's flock.[3] He preferred those who understood several matters fully: a shepherd's duty, the vice of hirelings, the taking up of ministry, and what should be done or hoped for in this service. Some, like richly dyed curtains, would adorn the interiors of the Lord's house and others, like hair shirts, would guard against the violence of external storms....

49. [A lament for the now deceased Bruno]

Hearts, pour out prayers, send forth tearful words
Behold the father of his fatherland shut up in stone.
Royal stock to be remembered in all lands,
Bruno the peacemaker, a good and pious man.
Archbishop whose seat was famed Cologne,
He seemed dear to all good people everywhere.
His long-lasting light struck out against foul darkness.
The envious tongue falls silent; only true praise
   satisfies.
This world was not worthy of so rare a gift:
Taken from this world's shortcomings, he now rejoices
   in the company of the Lord.
On the ides of October in his twelfth year as bishop[4]
He gave up this life, hope his loving companion.

4.17 Literacy: King Alfred, *Prefaces* to Gregory the Great's *Pastoral Care* (c.890). Original in Old English.

Alfred the Great (r.871–899), the king of Wessex, energetically beat back Viking invaders, promulgated a code of law that drew from all the others in England—thus establishing a "common" law—and undertook a program to translate major works of Latin into the vernacular, Anglo-Saxon (also known as Old English), so that everyone could understand them. The text below presents Alfred's twin prefaces to his translation of Gregory the Great's *Pastoral Care* (590), a handbook for bishops.

[Source: *Alfred the Great: Asser's* Life of King Alfred *and Other Contemporary Sources*, trans. Simon Keynes and Michael Lapidge (New York: Penguin Books, 1983), pp. 124–27, 294–96 (slightly modified).]

---

[1] Cologne, Trier, and Mainz were the seats of the three archbishops of Lorraine. Ruotbert was Bruno and Otto's uncle, and William was the natural son of Otto and thus Bruno's nephew. Frederick was archbishop of Mainz from 937 to 954, not unstintingly loyal to Otto, which explains why Otto's son succeeded him.

[2] That is, they were nominally Christians but so savage and destructive to themselves and others as to be Christians in name only.

[3] This sentence refers to Bruno's consultation with Otto about the appointment of bishops in the cities of western Lorraine.

[4] I.e., October 15, 965.

Prose Preface

King Alfred sends words of greeting lovingly and amicably to [...].[1]

And I would have it known that very often it has come to my mind what men of learning there were formerly throughout England, both in religious and secular orders; and how there were happy times then throughout England; and how the kings, who had authority over this people, obeyed God and his messengers; and how they not only maintained their peace, morality and authority at home but also extended their territory outside; and how they succeeded both in warfare and in wisdom; and also how eager were the religious orders both in teaching and in learning as well as in all the holy services which it was their duty to perform for God; and how people from abroad sought wisdom and instruction in this country; and how nowadays, if we wished to acquire these things, we would have to seek them outside.[2] Learning had declined so thoroughly in England that there were very few men on this side of the Humber who could understand their divine services in English, or even translate a single letter from Latin into English: and I suppose that there were not many beyond the Humber either. There were so few of them that I cannot recollect even a single one south of the Thames when I succeeded to the kingdom. Thanks be to God Almighty that we now have any supply of teachers at all! Therefore I beseech you to do as I believe you are willing to do: as often as you can, free yourself from worldly affairs so that you may apply that wisdom which God gave you wherever you can. Remember what punishments befell us in this world when we ourselves did not cherish learning nor transmit it to other men.[3] We were Christians in name alone, and very few of us possessed Christian virtues.

When I reflected on all this, I recollected how—before everything was ransacked and burned—the churches throughout England stood filled with treasures and books. Similarly, there was a great multitude of those serving God. And they derived very little benefit from those books, because they could understand nothing of them, since they were not written in their own language.[4] It is as if they had said: "Our ancestors, who formerly maintained these places, loved wisdom, and through it they obtained wealth and passed it on to us. Here one can still see their track, but we cannot follow it." Therefore we have now lost the wealth as well as the wisdom, because we did not wish to set our minds to the track.

When I reflected on all this, I wondered exceedingly why the good, wise men who were formerly found throughout England and had thoroughly studied all those books, did not wish to translate any part of them into their own language. But I immediately answered myself, and said: "They did not think that men would ever become so careless and that learning would decay like this; they refrained from doing it through this resolve, namely they wished that the more languages we knew, the greater would be the wisdom in this land." Then I recalled how the Law was first composed in the Hebrew language, and thereafter, when the Greeks learned it, they translated it all into their own language, and all other books as well. And so too the Romans, after they had mastered them, translated them all through learned interpreters into their own language. Similarly all the other Christian peoples turned some part of them into their own language.[5] Therefore it seems better to me—if it seems so to you—that we too should turn into the language that we can all understand certain books which are the most necessary for all men to know, and accomplish this, as with God's help we may very easily do provided we have

---

[1] It is probable that in Alfred's original, no name was given at this point, but that the name of the bishop to whom a particular copy was to be sent would be added as the copy was being made. If each bishop in Alfred's kingdom of Wessex were to receive a copy, at least ten would have been needed; and we may assume that other important monastic centers would have been sent copies as well.

[2] Alfred is here alluding to his own activities in the 880s, when it was necessary to seek learned men from outside the kingdom of Wessex—from Mercia (to the north), Francia (across the English Channel), and Wales (to the west).

[3] This is presumably a reference to the Viking invasions of the central decades of the ninth century; in common with many Christian authors before and after him, Alfred regarded the invasion of hostile peoples as a form of divine punishment for decadence and decay.

[4] The books were written in Latin.

[5] There is no certainty about what translations Alfred is referring to here. The Bible was translated into Gothic by Ulfila in the fourth century, but Alfred is unlikely to have known of this work. It is more likely that he knew of one of the translations made in Germany during the ninth century: a prose translation of the gospel story in East Franconian made at the monastery of Fulda *c.*830; a metrical version of the same gospel story in Old Saxon made during the decade 830–840, known as the *Heliand*; and a metrical version of the gospels in Rhenish Franconian made by the monk Otfrid of Weissenburg sometime between 863 and 871.

peace enough, so that all the free-born young men now in England who have the means to apply themselves to it, may be set to learning (as long as they are not useful for some other employment) until the time that they can read English writings properly. Thereafter one may instruct in Latin those whom one wishes to teach further and wishes to advance to holy orders.

When I recalled how knowledge of Latin had previously decayed throughout England, and yet many could still read things written in English, I then began, amidst the various and multifarious afflictions of this kingdom, to translate into English the book which in Latin is called *Pastoralis*, in English "Shepherd-book,"[1] sometimes word for word, sometimes sense for sense, as I learnt it from Plegmund my archbishop, and from Asser my bishop, and from Grimbald my mass-priest and from John my mass-priest. After I had mastered it, I translated it into English as best I understood it and as I could most meaningfully render it; I intend to send a copy to each bishopric in my kingdom; and in each copy there will be an *Æstel* worth fifty mancuses.[2] And in God's name I command that no one shall take that *Æstel* from the book, nor the book from the church. It is not known how long

there shall be such learned bishops as, thanks be to God, there are now nearly everywhere. Therefore I would wish that they [the book and the *Æstel*] always remain in place, unless the bishop wishes to have the book with him, or it is on loan somewhere, or someone is copying it.

Verse Preface

Augustine brought this work from the south over the salt sea to the island-dwellers, exactly as the Lord's champion, the pope of Rome, had previously set it out. The wise Gregory was well versed in many doctrines through his mind's intelligence, his hoard of ingenuity. Accordingly, he won over most of mankind to the guardian of the heavens, this greatest of Romans, most gifted of men, most celebrated for his glorious deeds.

King Alfred subsequently translated every word of me into English and sent me south and north to his scribes;[3] he commanded them to produce more such copies from the exemplar, so that he could send them to his bishops, because some of them who least knew Latin had need thereof.

4.18 Law: King Æthelred, *Law Code* (1008). Original in Old English.

Written law codes were, among other things, a way for early medieval kings to signal that their realms were part of the "Roman" tradition. That is why *The Theodosian Code* (see above, p. 4) was of enduring importance. Although these codes were drawn up to seem timeless, they were very much products of local conditions and circumstances. Æthelred the Unready's reign was beset by Viking invasions and internal feuds. The nickname "Unready" came from the Anglo-Saxon word *unræd*, meaning "no-counsel." But Æthelred's code says that it was issued with the approval of his "ecclesiastical and lay councilors." In fact, one of those councilors was the most distinguished churchman of his age, Archbishop Wulfstan of York (r.1002–1023), whose handwriting may be detected in several of the entries in the manuscripts of this code. What evidence can you find in this code of military crisis? How does it compare with the roughly contemporary law code of King Stephen of Hungary (above, p. 205)?

[Source: *English Historical Documents*, Vol. 1: *c.* 300–1042, ed. Dorothy Whitelock, 2nd ed. (London: Routledge, 1979), pp. 442–46 (slightly modified).]

---

[1] Today in English it is ordinarily known as *Pastoral Care*.

[2] An *æstel* was a "book-mark." A mancus (pl. mancuses) was a coin or a unit of value equal to 30 pennies.

[3] In Old English poetry, it is a common convention to have the book speak in the first person.

PROLOGUE. This is the ordinance which the king of the English and both ecclesiastical and lay councilors have approved and decreed.

1. First, namely, that we all shall love and honor one God and zealously hold one Christian faith and entirely cast off every heathen practice; and we all have confirmed both with word and with pledge that we will hold one Christian faith under the rule of one king.

1.1. And it is the decree of our lord and his councilors that just practices be established and all illegal practices abolished, and that every man is to be permitted the benefit of law;

1.2. and that peace and friendship are to be rightly maintained in both religious and secular concerns within this country.

2. And it is the decree of our lord and his councilors that no Christian and innocent men are to be sold out of the country, and especially not among the heathen people, but care is earnestly to be taken that those souls be not destroyed which God bought with his own life.

3. And it is the decree of our lord and his councilors that Christian men are not to be condemned to death for all too small offences.

3.1. But otherwise life-sparing punishments are to be devised for the benefit of the people, and God's handiwork and his own purchase which he paid for so dearly is not to be destroyed for small offences.

4. And it is the decree of our lord and his councilors that men of every order are each to submit willingly to that duty which befits them both in religious and secular concerns.

4.1 And especially God's servants—bishops and abbots, monks and nuns, priests and women dedicated to God— are to submit to their duty and to live according to their rule and to intercede zealously for all Christian people.

5. And it is the decree of our lord and his councilors that every monk who is out of his monastery and not heeding his rule, is to do what behooves him: return readily into the monastery with all humility, and cease from evil-doing and atone very zealously for what he has done amiss; let him consider the word and pledge which he gave to God.

6. And that monk who has no monastery is to come to the bishop of the diocese, and pledge himself to God and men that from that time on he will at least observe three things, namely his chastity, and monastic garb, and serve his Lord as well as ever he can.

6.1. And if he keeps that, he is then entitled to the greater respect, no matter where he dwell.

7. And canons,[1] where there is property such that they can have a refectory and dormitory, are to hold their minster [church] with right observance and with chastity, as their rule directs; otherwise it is right that he who will not do that shall forfeit the property.

8. And we pray and instruct all mass-priests to protect themselves from God's anger.

9. They know full well that they may not rightly have sexual intercourse with a woman.

9.1. And whoever will abstain from this and preserve chastity, may he have God's mercy and in addition as a secular dignity, that he shall be entitled to a thegn's wergild and a thegn's rights, in life as well as in the grave.[2]

9.2. And he who will not do what belongs to his order, may his dignity be diminished both in religious and secular concerns.

10. And also every Christian man is zealously to avoid illegal intercourse, and duly keep the laws of the Church.[3]

10.1. And every church is to be under the protection of God and of the king and of all Christian people.

10.2. And no man henceforth is to bring a church under subjection, nor illegally to traffic with a church,[4] nor to expel a minister of the church without the bishop's consent.

11. And God's dues are to be readily paid every year.

11.1. Namely, plough-alms 15 days after Easter, and the tithe of young animals by Pentecost, and of the fruits

---

[1] Canons here refer to priests who live together in common.

[2] The wergild was the price of compensation, which varied with the status of the victim. Thegns were noblemen, and they had the high wergild of 1200 shillings.

[3] This provision involves not marrying within six degrees of relationship, or with the widow of so near a kinsman, or a close relative of a previous wife, or a nun, or anyone related by spiritual affinity, or a deserted woman.

[4] This refers to buying a church office or bartering a church.

of the earth by All Saints' day, and "Rome money" by St. Peter's day and light-dues three times a year.[1]

12. And it is best that payment for the soul be always paid at the open grave.

12.1. And if any body is buried elsewhere, outside the proper parish, the payment for the soul is nevertheless to be paid to the minster to which it belonged.

12.2. And all God's dues are to be furthered zealously, as is needful.

12.3. And festivals and fasts are to be properly observed.

13. The Sunday festival is to be diligently observed, as befits it.

13.1. And one is readily to abstain from markets and public meetings on the holy day.

14. And all the festivals of St. Mary are to be diligently observed, first with a fast and afterwards with a festival.

14.1. And at the festival of every Apostle there is to be fasting and festivity, except that we enjoin no fast for the festival of St. Philip and St. James, because of the Easter festival.

15. Otherwise other festivals and fasts are to be kept diligently just as those kept them who kept them best.

16. And the councilors have decreed that St. Edward's festival is to be celebrated over all England on March 18th.[2]

17. And there is to be a fast every Friday, except when it is a feast day.

18. And ordeals and oaths are forbidden on feast days and the legal Ember days, and from the Advent of the Lord until the octave of Epiphany, and from Septuagesima [Lent] until 15 days after Easter.

19. And at these holy seasons, as it is right, there is to be peace and unity among all Christian men, and every suit is to be laid aside.

20. And if anyone owes another a debt or compensation concerning secular matters, he is to pay it readily before or after [these seasons].

21. And every widow who conducts herself rightly is to be under the protection of God and the king.

21.1. And each [widow] is to remain unmarried for twelve months; she is afterwards to choose what she herself will.

22. And every Christian man is to do what is needful for him, heed zealously his Christian duties, form the habit of frequent confession, and freely confess his sins and willingly atone for them as he is directed.

22.1. And everyone is to prepare himself often and frequently for going to communion;

22.2. and to order words and deeds rightly and keep carefully oath and pledge.

23. And every injustice is to be zealously cast out from this country, as far as it can be done.

24. And deceitful deeds and hateful abuses are to be strictly shunned, namely, false weights and wrong measures, and lying witnesses and shameful frauds,

25. and horrible perjuries and devilish deeds of murder and manslaughter, of stealing and spoliation, of avarice and greed, of over-eating and over-drinking, of deceits and various breaches of law, of injuries to the clergy and of breaches of the marriage law, and of evil deeds of many kinds.

26. But God's law henceforth is to be eagerly loved by word and deed; then God will at once become gracious to this nation.

26.1. And people are to be zealous about the improvement of the peace, and about the improvement of the coinage everywhere in the country, and about the repair of boroughs in every province and also about military service,[3] according to what is decreed, whenever it is necessary,

27. and about the supplying of ships, as zealously as possible, so that each may be equipped immediately after Easter every year.

28. And if anyone deserts without leave from an army that the king himself is with, it is to be at the peril of his life and all his property.

28.1. And he who otherwise deserts from the army is to forfeit 120 shillings.

29. And if any excommunicated man—unless it be a suppliant for protection—remain anywhere in the king's

---

[1] "Rome money" refers to Peter's Pence, dues sent to Rome to support the papacy. "Light-dues" were revenues to pay for church candles.

[2] St. Edward was the martyred King Edward (r.975–978), the brother of Æthelred.

[3] Boroughs, or burhs, were fortifications.

neighborhood before he has submitted readily to ecclesiastical penance, it is to be at the peril of his life and all his possessions.

30. And if anyone plots against the king's life, he is to forfeit his life; and if he wishes to clear himself, he is to do it by [an oath of the value of] the king's wergild or by the three-fold ordeal in [the area under] English law.[1]

31. And if anyone commit obstruction or open resistance anywhere against the law of Christ or the king, he is to pay either wergild or fine or *lahslit*,[2] ever in proportion to the deed.
  31.1. And if he illegally offers resistance with assault, and so brings it about that he is killed, no wergild is to be paid to any of his friends.

32. And ever henceforth the abuses are to cease which hitherto have been too common far and wide.

33. And every abuse is to be zealously suppressed.
  33.1. For [only] as a result of suppressing wrong and loving righteousness will there be improvement at all in the country in religious and secular concerns.

34. We must all love and honor one God and entirely cast out every heathen practice.

35. And let us loyally support one royal lord, and all together defend our lives and our land, as well as ever we can, and pray Almighty God from our inmost heart for his help.

4.19 Christianity comes to Denmark: *The Jelling Monument* (960s).

The Jelling Monument is a large boulder with writing and carvings on it. It is important for understanding how Christianity became incorporated into the networks of power and prestige in Scandinavia.

Powerful people with great resources had long lived in Jelling, close to what is today Vejle, on the Jutland peninsula. During the Bronze age, before 500 BCE, they built an earthen mound, and, just south of the mound, they lined up several large standing stones to suggest the outline of a ship.

In 958 the Viking King Gorm died at Jelling. His son Harald Bluetooth buried his father in the old mound, adding more soil to make it taller. He also constructed another mound a short distance to the south, in the process destroying the "ship." The construction of mounds was a newly resuscitated custom in the tenth century. It was a self-conscious appeal to old traditions in the face of Christian customs spreading from Denmark's southern neighbors, the Germans. Accompanying Gorm in his tomb were a horse, riding gear, an elegant silver cup, a chest, a small wooden cross, and other artifacts. A powerful man or woman was not to arrive in the afterlife without suitable equipment. This was entirely the opposite of Christian customs, which by the tenth century prohibited burying goods with bodies: the Christian afterlife was supposed to be immaterial.

Harald took over his father Gorm's kingdom. Then, in the 960s, he became a Christian. The reminders in Jelling of his pagan past, including his father, became an embarrassment, so Harald built a large wooden church close to the northern mound. He dug up the

---

[1] In the "three-fold" ordeal, the hot iron weighed three times more than its usual weight. For the ordeal, see above, p. 208, n. 3.
[2] *Lahslit* meant "breach of the law"; it was the term given in the Danelaw (the law in the eastern region of England heavily settled by the Danes) to a fine varying with the rank of the offender, 10 half-marks for the king's thegn, 6 half-marks for other landowners, 12 ores (there were 8 ores to the mark) for the ordinary freeman.

body of his father and moved him to an honored place in the middle of the church, thus posthumously Christianizing Gorm. The centerpiece of the new Christian compound was a piece of art, a large granite boulder situated exactly at the midpoint between the two mounds—the "Jelling Monument." Harald had the boulder inscribed on three sides with large pictures and a text in runic characters, a special alphabet. When they were new, the pictures and the text would have been painted in bright colors. The stone proudly proclaimed that this was a Christian site. One side depicts a great rampant animal (a dragon? a lion?) entwined by a snake. Another side (see photo) portrays Christ crucified. Remarkably, the cross itself is lacking. Instead, interlacing bands surround Christ.

The inscription reads: "King Harald had this monument made in memory of his father Gorm and in memory of his mother Thyre; that Harald who won for himself all of Denmark and Norway and made the Danes Christian." The last words are visible on the photo under the figure of Christ.

Thousands of runestones still dot the landscape of Scandinavia, most put up in the eleventh century, when most of the population had converted to Christianity. The text of these runestones was usually along the lines of the formula of Jelling: "X had this stone made/raised in memory of Y, his/her mother/father/brother/companion-at-arms." Many stones added "God save his (or her) soul," and others had crosses.

These inscriptions may appear to be selfless acts of remembrance of loved ones, but they served at least as much to remind all who passed of the power and wealth of the sponsor of the inscription, the person who was able to afford such a great monument. Certainly Harald did not hide behind any false humility; he forthrightly included his name twice to drive the point home. Harald, no one else, was the powerful conqueror and the religious benefactor of those he conquered. In this he appeared both as a traditional warlord and as a good Christian ruler.

The Jelling compound was part of Harald's efforts to consolidate his power, which also included the construction of forts all over his kingdom. It did not help. His son Svein Forkbeard rebelled against him in 986 or 987. Harald had to go into exile, where he soon died. The tomb that he had reserved for himself in the church next to his father Gorm is still empty. Taking this monument together with Bede's account of the Christianization of England, above, p. 94, consider how the new religion was—and was not—compatible with pre-Christian forms of kingship. Why, do you suppose, interlace was used in place of the cross?

See Plate 13, p. 249, for a color reproduction of *The Jelling Monument.*

(Caption by Anders Winroth. Image courtesy of the Nationalmuseet, Denmark)

TIMELINE FOR CHAPTER FOUR

850

c.890 KING ALFRED, *PREFACES* ———

900

——— 910 CLUNY'S *FOUNDATION CHARTER*

c.915 AL-TABARI, *THE DEFEAT OF THE ZANJ* ———

——— 934 ROMANUS I LECAPENUS, *NOVEL*

——— c.940–42 AL-FARABI, *THE PERFECT STATE*

950–58 CONSTANTINE VII, *MILITARY ADVICE* ——— **950**

——— 960S *JELLING MONUMENT*

LATE 960S RUOTGER, *LIFE OF BRUNO*

——— 992–1000 *BOLESLAW'S COIN*

1000–38 STEPHEN, *LAWS* ——— **1000**

BEF. 1012 AL-QABISI, *TREATISE* ——— ——— 1008 ÆTHELRED, *LAW CODE*

1013–18 THIETMAR, *CHRONICLE* ——— ——— 1020S OR 1030S IBN SINA (AVICENNA),

1028 *AGREEMENT OF WILLIAM AND HUGH* ——— *TREATISE ON LOGIC*

1040–43 ANDREW OF FLEURY, ——— ——— 1041–75 *CHARTER OF GUILLEM GUIFRED*
MIRACLES OF BENEDICT **1050**

c.1063 PSELLUS, *PORTRAIT OF BASIL II* ———

1100

c.1113 *RUSSIAN PRIMARY CHRONICLE* ———

> *To test your knowledge and gain deeper understanding of this chapter,*
> *please go to www.utphistorymatters.com for Study Questions.*

Containing the Holy

The theme "containing the holy" applies to all three of the major religions of the Western Middle Ages: Islam, Judaism, and Christianity in both its Greek Orthodox and Catholic traditions. Each object included in this insert should be treated in much the same way as a written primary source. A procedure for using them fruitfully might include:

1. Reading the caption for each plate.
2. Looking carefully at each object and considering what ideas (and even feelings) it evokes in you.
3. Asking (and trying to answer) the following general questions:
    a. When and where was the object made? See if you can find written sources in *Reading the Middle Ages* from the same region and/or time period. Read up on the object's larger context in *Short History of the Middle Ages* and/or other texts.
    b. Who made the object? In many cases you will not know the exact identity of the creator, but you will know (or at least you will be able to speculate about) the status (monk, craftsman, mosaicist) of both the person who made the object and the person or corporation (very often a nobleman or noblewoman, a ruler, or a person affiliated with the church) who paid for it or asked that it be made.
    c. For what purpose(s) was the object made? Consider the possible audiences that saw the object and how they might have understood and used it.
    d. What does the object say about the nature of holiness? Can holiness indeed be "contained," according to that object? Does the object imply a "theory" of the holy that can be teased out and analyzed?
    e. Does the container itself just "contain" the holy? To what extent is the container itself holy?
4. Asking specific questions (and seeking answers) that apply just to the particular object you are analyzing.

PLATE 1

Dome of the Rock (692)

While Caliph 'Abd al-Malik's forces were defeating a rival caliph, *c.*692, he ordered and paid for the building of a shrine in Jerusalem known as the Dome of the Rock. Its site had once held the Jewish Temple, destroyed by the Romans in 70 CE. Some Christian and Jewish traditions held that the rock within the edifice had been the place where the Messiah would appear at the end of time. Islamic *hadith* reported that after the creation, God had left earth and ascended to heaven from that very place.

Still other traditions, today largely accepted in the Islamic world, held that Muhammad ascended to heaven from the rock. The building itself is in the style of a centrally planned Christian *martyrium*—a church built over the tomb of a saint. Octagonal, its exterior walls (see the exterior view in Plate 1A) were originally covered with mosaics (replaced by tiles in the Ottoman period), while its dome was made of wood and gilded. The interior (see the interior view in Plate 1B) is still covered with mosa-

ics reflecting the original program of the founder. These appear for the most part above two arcades of piers and columns. The imagery on the interior arcade spandrels (the triangular space between the arch curves) reuses and reinterprets traditional forms: vegetation and other decorative elements are combined with representations of Persian and Byzantine crowns, jewels, and breastplates. Across the entire circumference of the shrine are quotations from the Qur'an. Typical is this one: "O People of the Book, do not exaggerate in your religion, and say only the truth about God. The messiah, Jesus, son of Mary, was only a messenger of God, and His word, which He committed to Mary, and a spirit from Him. So believe in God and His messengers, and do not say 'three.'" What sorts of claims were being made by the caliph via the Dome and its decoration?

PLATE 2

Icon with Saint Demetrios (2nd half 10th c.)

Icons are images believed to be holy. In the second half of the tenth century, when this one was probably carved, some icons were painted on panels, while others were composed of mosaics. Still others were represented in stained glass or, as here, made of ivory. (Personal icons, which were small, might be made of gold or silver, embellished with gems, and decorated with cloisonné enamel.) Demetrios, the patron saint of Thessalonica and popular elsewhere as well, was a late-third-century martyr. A church was built in his honor at the end of the fifth century, the earliest collection of miracle stories about him was composed at the beginning of the seventh century, and stories about his life and death began to be written in the ninth century. Above all, he was known as the protector of his city. In this relatively large (7 ¼ x 4 ¾ x ⅜ in.) plaque, he is dressed in the splendid armor of a high imperial military officer. He holds a spear (broken today) and a shield. Slung diagonally over his shoulder is the scabbard for his sword. The inscription on either side of his head says "Saint Demetrios." Although carved in relief (i.e., not in the round), the relief is so deep that Demetrios appears almost three-dimensional. The icon was probably originally nailed (you can see the four holes at the corners) alongside images of other saints. Later the area between the saint's feet was carved out to allow the plaque to be clamped to a pole during processions on the saint's feast day. Why did the artist show Demetrios so large that his halo required carving out the frame of the icon? What sort of power do you suppose this icon had on and for its devotees? How does the icon present a warrior as a holy man? What was happening to Byzantium in the tenth century that might help explain this imagery?

PLATE 3
Reliquary Locket (10th–11th c.)

This pendant, made of silver, gold, and niello (the black areas), was produced at Constantinople in the 10th or 11th century. On one side is a scene of the nativity, with the Christ Child (watched over by an ox and ass) in the space above the reclining Virgin. Saint Joseph sits by the foot of her bed. Below is a scene showing the Magi bearing gifts to the Child. The other side of the pendant shows a cross; the symbols on the two ends of the arms are ambiguous. The inscription on the rim says: "Secure deliverance and aversion from all evil," while the edge of the lid shows that the saints invoked were the twin doctors Cosmas and Damian, third-century martyrs renowned by this time throughout the Christian world for their ability to cure and heal and their refusal to take money for their work. The cavity in the locket held a relic, probably to ward off illnesses. What does this locket suggest about the importance of relics even in post-iconoclastic Byzantium? What other forms did reliquaries take—in both the East and the West—apart from lockets? (For some ideas, see below, Plates 7, 8, and 10.) What sorts of powers did relics have? What made them holy?

234

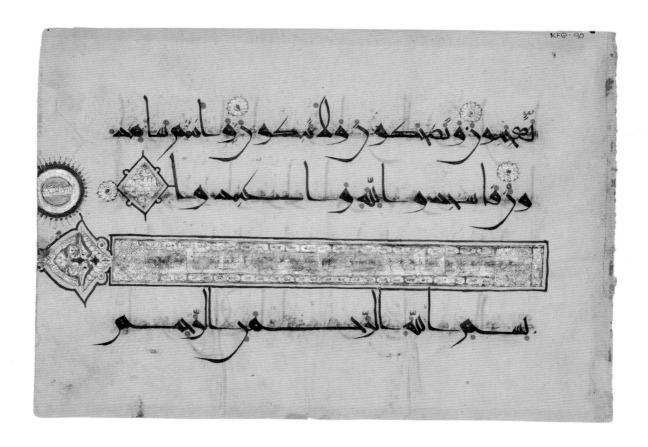

PLATE 4

Page from a Qur'an (993)

Each Qur'an not only contains the word of God but is itself a holy object. The script used to write it, therefore, had to be special: this is why the art of calligraphy was so highly valued in the Islamic world. Precious materials, too, were used in the making of the Qur'an: parchment at first and later paper, the formula for which was learned from Chinese prisoners of war captured during the Umayyad conquest of Transoxiana. The design of the page was also important. The large (about 9 ½ × 13 ¼ in.) page shown here is from a Qur'an manuscript copied in 993 in Isfahan (Iran). It was written on paper in the so-called "New Style" of script, making it quite untraditional. But it also drew on highly traditional elements. The very fact that the page is wider than it is long from top to bottom is a throwback to an early Qur'an format. The band of gold across the page is also traditional. The

writing on that band announces the number of the sura (chapter) to come, its familiar name, and the number of verses that it contains. The band's decorative "handle" at one end (on your left) is a motif ultimately derived from one kind of Roman tablet. The small gold rosettes (in the lines above the band) mark the end of each verse. Diacritical marks (in colors) hark back to an older way to indicate vowels and consonants. Given all this, and considering the sacred nature of the text of the Qur'an and of the container of the text itself, what variants were nevertheless possible? Compare the "holiness" of a Qur'an with that of a Christian reliquary. Usually the Qur'an was learned by heart and chanted, so why would Muslims want to have one as costly and beautiful as this is?

PLATE 5
A Holy Vestment (late 10th–early 11th c.)

The outermost vestment worn by a Christian priest during the Mass was the chasuble. Although the poncholike garment developed from a humble late-Roman cape (called a *paenula*), by the Carolingian era the priestly chasuble was often highly ornamented and made of precious fabrics. This splendid example (Plate 5A) is made of a patterned golden silk produced in Byzantine Anatolia (perhaps Syria) in the late tenth or early eleventh century. The heavy weave, called samite, is in a complex repeat pattern with ovals enclosing palm-fronds linked by floral motifs (for these details, see Plate 5B). This vestment is one of

two surviving "holy Willigis chasubles" associated with Willigis, Archbishop of Mainz (r.975–1011): this one was preserved in the castle chapel at Aschaffenburg, where the archbishop had supported a school to train clerics. The other is from the church Willigis founded in honor of Saint Stephen in 990 in the city of Mainz (where Willigis was buried). Willigis served as chancellor to Emperor Otto I, whose son and heir Otto II raised him to the see of Mainz and made him arch-chancellor. Otto II's Byzantine bride, Theophanu, supported Willigis in the building of several churches, including Saint Stephen's, and she is

PLATE 5B

the most likely source for the beautiful Byzantine silk of this chasuble. The empress's generosity was repaid during the crisis provoked by the death of Otto II in 983: Archbishop Willigis orchestrated the election of her son Otto III, consecrated him as king at Aachen on Christmas day, and then negotiated the three-year-old monarch's release and return to his regent mother after he was seized by the usurper Henry the Quarrelsome. Although never officially canonized, Willigis's date of death, February 23, was commemorated as a feast at Mainz, and the woven golden bands decorating the chasuble, which date from the thirteenth to the fifteenth centuries, attest to the continued

use of this "holy Willigis chasuble" by the clergy of Mainz. Why might this garment be called "holy"? What does it tell us about how objects become holy? In what ways is it similar to or different from the holiness of the Reliquary Locket (Plate 3)? Try to imagine the feelings of priests who donned the Holy Willigis Chasuble long after Willigis had died. In light of your readings of the clergy in action (see below, p. 262), what various possible motives—and qualms— might these priests have had?

(Caption by Maureen C. Miller. Images by permission of the Bayerisches Nationalmuseum)

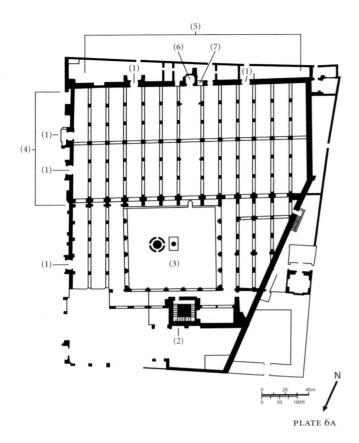

PLATE 6A

PLATE 6B

PLATE 6

Tlemcen, Great Mosque (1236)

The congregational mosque in Tlemcen, Algeria, rebuilt in 1136 by the Almoravids, provides a nice example of the general layout of a mosque. Most mosques are rectangular in plan, but an adjacent fortress forced the builders at Tlemcen to make a diagonal adjustment when they extended the mosque in 1236. This mosque, like most others, has several entrances (see the plan in Plate 6A) labeled (1), a minaret (2) added in 1236, adjacent to an internal courtyard with a fountain for ablutions (3). The prayer hall (4) is characterized by evenly placed piers that hold up the arcades and the roof. The focus of the mosque, and of all who pray within it, is the *qibla* wall (5), which points in the direction of Mecca. The *mihrab* (6) is a niche set off by a lobed horseshoe arch. A dome marks the space before the *mihrab* and the place of the *minbar* (7), a stepped pulpit that is brought out for the Friday noon sermon.

Plate 6B shows the dome, which was made of stucco and decorated with pierced arabesque patterns.

Plate 6C shows the *mihrab*, normally in the center of the *qibla* and the holiest spot of all. It is symbolic, perhaps, of the place where the Prophet Muhammad once stood when leading prayers in his house/mosque at Medina. In some ways, the *mihrab* is analogous to the ark in a Jewish synagogue (see Plate 9) or the altar in a medieval church.

What does the organization of space in the mosque communicate about the holy? How does this organization compare to the plan of a Christian church (see, for example, Plate 7)? How does it compare with the layout of a synagogue (see Plate 9)?

(Images courtesy of Jonathan Bloom and Sheila Blair)

PLATE 6C

PLATE 7

The Church as Reliquary: Sainte-Chapelle (1248)

Completed in 1248, the Sainte-Chapelle (Holy Chapel) in Paris was built to house many of the sacred objects of Christ's Passion—the Crown of Thorns, pieces of the True Cross, and so on—that had once been part of the Byzantine emperor's relic collection. These had once been kept in the Pharos (lighthouse) Chapel—an architectural reliquary that held both relics and reliquaries—within the imperial palace. After the conquest of Constantinople by the crusaders of the Fourth Crusade (1202–1204), the weak rulers of the Latin Empire, needing money, sold the relics to Western rulers, including French King Louis IX (r.1226–1270). Between 1239 and 1241 Louis amassed 22 of these relics. He brought them to Paris with great fanfare. To house them fittingly, he commissioned Sainte-Chapelle right within the royal palace (mimicking in this way the Pharos Chapel). The architect was probably Thomas de Cormont, who had worked on the cathedral at Amiens. Sainte-Chapelle had two stories: a relatively somber first floor for the members of the court, and an upper story, glowing with the bright colors of its stained glass wall-to-ceiling windows, for the royal family. Every consecrated church is in a sense a reliquary (and all altars contain a relic), but the Sainte-Chapelle was built to *look* like a reliquary. Within it was another, smaller reliquary, the Grande Châsse (destroyed during the French Revolution). Kept behind the altar of the upper story, it held the precious objects of the Passion. (Some, like the Crown of Thorns, were also broken up into smaller pieces, put into smaller reliquaries, and sent off as gifts to other notables.) The instruments of the Passion were now in Paris, and pilgrims flocked to see them. How might the acquisition of these relics and the building of the Sainte-Chapelle have influenced the urban space around it and the status of the city of Paris? What messages did the Sainte-Chapelle communicate about the kings of France and their power?

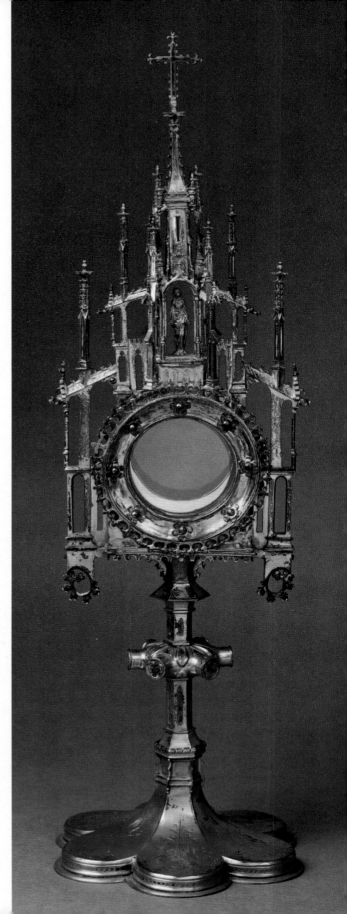

PLATE 8

Monstrance (*c.*1430)

The word "monstrance" comes from a Latin word meaning "to show." In the later Middle Ages, priests wanted to "show"—and their flocks wanted to "see"—the central mystery of the Christian religion: the host. Bread turned into the body of the crucified Christ took on new importance in a society that was intensely focused on Christ's life and death and that found salvation in the act of Holy Communion. The monstrance was designed to hold and show the host. This particular example, made in Cologne (Germany) *c.*1430 of silver gilt, is, at about 20 inches in height, relatively small. In the precise center, measuring top to bottom, is a crystal cylinder for the host itself; the rest exists to honor and frame Christ's body. Around the cylinder, a golden circle decorated with flowers is itself framed—as if it were a Gothic church—by delicate buttresses that rise up to a central tower topped by a crucifix. (The tiny figure of the Virgin within the tower is a much later addition.) The whole is meant to echo the Heavenly Jerusalem, which Rev. 21: 11, 18–19 describes as lighted "like to a precious stone... even as crystal," while "the city itself [was] of pure gold.... And the foundations of the wall of the city were adorned with all manner of precious stones." In the Cologne monstrance the six-part base is engraved with images of saints and the Virgin and Child alongside a petition for prayers on behalf of the monstrance's donor and his family. Why would a donor want his monstrance to look like a church? How was the host like (and unlike) a relic?

242

PLATE 9

Synagogue and Ark (1435)

This full-page illumination is in a manuscript made at Mantua, Italy, in 1435. Not a holy object itself, the illumination represents what is very hard to find today: the interior of a medieval synagogue. Unlike churches, which persisted (though often much changed) into the modern period, most medieval synagogues were destroyed over time. Yet the synagogue was a container of holiness. Symbolically, it replaced the Temple at Jerusalem (whose most recent incarnation was destroyed by the Romans in 70 CE). Within the synagogue was the Torah ark (here on the right), which replaced the Temple's Inner Holy of Holies. The Torah scroll—consisting of the first five books of the Hebrew Bible and itself a holy object—is about to be replaced in the ark after the reading for the day. (The reader and his lectern are in the middle of the room.) The faithful, even the women, are clothed in special prayer shawls. On the four corners of the page are the animals invoked by Judah ben Tema (a 2nd-c. CE Talmudic scholar) ("Be strong as a leopard, swift as the eagle, fleet as the gazelle, and brave as the lion"). Compare the architecture of this synagogue and its ark with the architecture of Sainte-Chapelle and its Grande Châsse (see Plate 7) and with the mosque and its *mihrab* at Tlemcen (see Plate 6C). What commonalities and what differences do you see?

PLATE 10
The Wienhausen Sepulcher (15th c.)

In the later Middle Ages, numerous churches in Europe wanted to have replicas of the Holy Sepulcher, Christ's tomb in Jerusalem. As "props" for liturgical dramas, these sepulchers played an especially important role in Easter celebrations. In 1448, the abbess Katherina von Hoya consecrated an elaborately decorated sepulcher (Plate 10A) for her convent at Wienhausen, in northern Germany. For the body, the nuns used a thirteenth-century wooden effigy of Christ, his side wound gaping open and blood dripping down his hands and spurting out holes in the soles of his feet. The tomb was generally opened only for the Easter rituals, so that the nuns could see scenes of the infancy of Christ (here sheltering Christ's left side) and Christ's passion (the lid that hangs down on Christ's right.) Small doors at Christ's head and feet (Plate 10B) were opened during the course of the celebrations to allow the whole of

PLATE 10B

PLATE 10C

Christ's bleeding body to be eventually revealed. A hole in his head and the wounds on the soles of his feet once held relics, while the Good Friday host was tucked into his side wound. On Easter Sunday, the nuns removed the effigy of the dead Christ and substituted an image of the resurrected Christ (Plate 10C). Thus the sepulcher served as a site not only for holy objects but also for the re-enactment of the holiest of Christian rites: Christ's resurrection and with it the promise of the salvation of all Christians. What transformations in Christian "containers of the holy" do you see taking place over time? Compare the meanings of the Wienhausen tomb with those of the Grande Châsse of Sainte-Chapelle (Plate 7), the *mihrab* of the mosque at Tlemcen (Plate 6C), and the ark of the Torah (Plate 9). How do their various decorative programs compare? What might explain the differences?

(Images courtesy of the Kloster Wienhausen/Lüneburger Klosterarchive and Elina Gertsman)

Reading through Looking

The plates in this section are meant to complement some of the readings; they represent another way to understand the topic at hand. For example, Plate 14, a portion of *The Bayeux Tapestry,* should be considered alongside the texts from William of Jumièges, "Florence of Worcester," and the *Domesday Book* in order to explore the many ways in which the Norman Conquest of England was understood and portrayed.

OBVERSE

REVERSE

PLATE 11
Seal of Boris-Michael (864–889)

When the Bulgarian Khan Boris converted to the Christian religion in *c*.864, he had seals such as this made to advertise his link to that faith. On its obverse (or "heads") side, an image of Christ is encircled by the inscription: "Christ help your servant Michael ruler of Bulgaria."

(Images courtesy of Dr. Ivan Jordanov)

OBVERSE

REVERSE

PLATE 12
Boleslaw's Coin (992–1000)

Boleslaw the Brave of Poland (r.992–1225) issued coins that celebrated his rulership. On the obverse ("heads") side he is shown in profile, like a Roman emperor; on the reverse ("tails"), a cross is surrounded by an inscription referring to his chief city, Gniezno.

(From the collection of the National Museum in Kraków)

PLATE 13
The Jelling Monument (960s)

In the 960s, when Danish King Harald Bluetooth converted to Christianity, he "Christianized" his father's burial place by building a church on the site and marking the spot with this granite monument depicting the crucified Christ.

(Courtesy of the Nationalmuseet, Denmark)

PLATE 14
The Bayeux Tapestry (end of the 11th c.)

This detail from a long embroidery commissioned by a supporter of Duke William of Normandy depicts a crucial moment in the Duke's conquest of England. It shows his chief competitor to English kingship swearing fealty to him.

(Detail of the Bayeux Tapestry—11th Century. With special permission from the City of Bayeux)

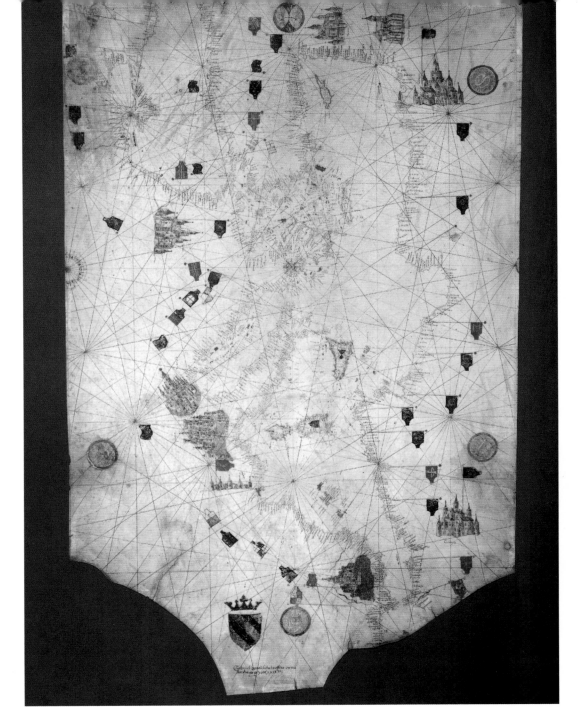

PLATE 15

Gabriel de Valseca, *Portolan Map* (1447)

Unlike many earlier maps, which were meant to symbolize the world rather than to be practical guides for travelers, portolan maps such as this one showed coastlines with considerable precision, allowing sailors to skirt headlands where they might run aground and find estuaries that supplied fresh water.

(By permission of the Bibliothèque nationale de France)

V

The Expansion of Europe (c.1050–c.1150)

COMMERCIAL TAKE OFF

5.1 Cultivating new lands: *Frederick of Hamburg's Agreement with Colonists from Holland* (1106). Original in Latin.

The commercial revolution took place in both town and countryside. In the countryside it depended on the enterprise of peasants and the support of people in power. In this charter the archbishop of Hamburg-Bremen, Frederick (r.1105–1123), granted swamp land in his diocese to colonists from Holland willing to undertake the backbreaking, collective work of drainage. (They were used to this sort of work; much of Holland itself was swampland.) The bishop required payments in return, not only for the produce of the land but also for the right of the colonists to hear their own court cases. His call to settlers was part of a wider movement. Hamburg-Bremen was on the Slavic frontier. Bringing Christians to settle it was one way that German leaders meant to subdue the polytheistic natives. For a contemporary account of a later phase of this development, see Helmold, *Chronicle of the Slavs*, below, p. 303.

[Source: *Ausgewählte Urkunden zur Erläuterung der Verfassungsgeschichte Deutschlands im Mittelalter*, ed. Wilhelm Altmann and Ernst Bernheim, 5th ed. (Berlin: Weidmannsche Buchhandlung, 1920), pp. 161–62, no. 80. Translated by Barbara H. Rosenwein.]

[1] In the name of the holy and individual Trinity, Frederick, bishop of the church of Hamburg by grace of God, [gives] to all the faithful in Christ, present and future, perpetual benediction. We wish to notify all of a certain agreement that certain people living on this side of the Rhine, who are called Hollanders, made with us.

[2] The aforementioned men came to Our Majesty resolutely asking us to concede to them territory for them

to cultivate. This land is situated in our bishopric and has hitherto been uncultivated, marshy, and useless to our locals. And so, having taken counsel with our vassals (*fideles*) and thinking it would be beneficial for us and our successors not to refuse their petition, we gave [our] assent.

[3] Moreover, the agreement of their petition was that they give to us a single denar [a silver coin] each year for every manse of this land.[1] We have thought it necessary to write down here the dimensions of a manse, lest there be a dispute later on among the people: a manse is 720 royal rods long and 30 wide, including the streams which flow through the land, which we grant in similar manner.

[4] Finally, they promised to give us a tithe according to our decree, that is, the eleventh part of the fruit of the earth, the tenth of the lambs, similarly of pigs, similarly of goats, the same of geese, and also they will give in the same way a tenth of the amount of honey and flax. They will render a dinar for each foal on the feast of St. Martin [November 11], and an obol [a coin worth less than a dinar] for each calf.

[5] They promised that they would obey us always in all matters pertaining to ecclesiastical law according to the decrees of the holy fathers, canon law, and the customs of the church of Utrecht [the home diocese of the colonists].

[6] With regard to judgments and court hearings involving secular law, they affirm that they will pay 2 marks [a gold or silver coin worth a substantial amount] each year for every 100 manses so that they may try all disputes themselves, lest they suffer from the prejudice of foreign [judges]. If they are unable to settle the more serious hearings or judgments, they shall refer them to the tribunal of the bishop. If they bring him with them to decide the case, for however long he remains [with them] they shall provide for him at their own expense in this manner: they shall keep two thirds of the court fees and give the last third to the bishop.

[7] We have allowed them to construct churches on said territory wherever it seems appropriate to them. We have offered to each church, for the express use of the priests serving God there, a tithe from our tithes of those parish churches. They confirm that the parishioners of each church will give no less than one manse to each church as an endowment for the use of the priest.

[8] The names of the men who came together to make and confirm this agreement are: Heinricus, the priest, to whom we have granted the aforesaid churches for life, and other laymen: Helikinus, Arnoldus, Hiko, Fordoltus, and Referic. To them and their heirs after them we concede the said land according to the secular laws and abovementioned agreement.

[9] The affirmation of this agreement was made in the year of our Lord's incarnation 1106, in the sixth indiction, in the reign of Lord Henry IV, Emperor Augustus of the Romans. To confirm this document with our affirmation, it pleases us that the charter be affixed with the impression of our seal. If anyone says anything against it, let him be anathema.

[10] In confirmation of this document, I, Bishop Wernherus was present and signed. I, Bishop Marquardus. I, Bishop Hasoko. I, Bishop Hujo. I, Adelbero. I, Thieto was present and signed. I, Gerungus, *advocatus* [a lay protector of a church] was present and witnessed. I, Hericus, was present. I, Thidericus. I, Willo, was present. I, Erpo, was present and witnessed. I, Adelbertus. I, Gerwardus. I, Ermbertus. I, Reinwardus. I, Ecelinus.

5.2 Ibn 'Abdun, *Regulations for the Market at Seville* (early 12th c.). Original in Arabic.

Muslim Spain was urbanized before most other Western regions and, as the document here demonstrates, its economic life was integrated into its notions of religion and morality. Ibn 'Abdun may well have been a market inspector—a *muhtasib*—responsible not only for making sure that products sold were up to a certain standard and that prices were legitimate but also for regulating relations between Christians, Muslims, and Jews

---

[1] A manse (*mansus*) was a farming unit: it often included a house, waste, meadow, a garden, and, of course, land for crops. Here its dimensions are standardized and declared because the land is considered "virgin" and ready to be parceled out at will.

and enforcing Muslim rules regarding sexuality and purity. Compare these regulations to those in the Byzantine *Book of the Prefect*, above, p. 109, from an earlier period, and to the later ordinances at Pistoia in response to the plague, below p. 448. What are the similarities, what are the differences, and what do these comparisons reveal about economic life in the different periods and cultures?

[Source: Bernard Lewis, ed. and trans., *Islam: From the Prophet Muhammad to the Capture of Constantinople*, vol. 2: *Religion and Society* (New York: Oxford University Press, 1987), pp. 157–65.]

Shopkeepers must be forbidden to reserve regular places for themselves in the forecourt of the great mosque or elsewhere, for this amounts to a usurpation of property rights and always gives rise to quarrels and trouble among them. Instead, whoever comes first should take his place.

The *muhtasib* [market inspector] must arrange the crafts in order, putting like with like in fixed places. This is the best and most orderly way.

There must be no sellers of olive oil around the mosque, nor of dirty products, nor of anything from which an irremovable stain can be feared.

Rabbits and poultry should not be allowed around the mosque, but should have a fixed place. Partridges and slaughtered barnyard birds should only be sold with the crop plucked, so that the bad and rotten can be distinguished from the good ones. Rabbits should only be sold skinned, so that the bad ones may be seen. If they are left lying in their skins, they go bad.

Egg sellers must have bowls of water in front of them, so that bad eggs may be recognized.

Truffles should not be sold around the mosque, for this is a delicacy of the dissolute.[1]

Bread should only be sold by weight. Both the baking and the crumbs must be supervised, as it is often "dressed up." By this I mean that they take a small quantity of good dough and use it to "dress up" the front of the bread which is made with bad flour.…

The cheese which comes from al-Madāin[2] should not be sold, for it is the foul residue of the curds, of no value. If people saw how it is made, no one would ever eat it. Cheese should only be sold in small leather bottles, which can be washed and cleaned every day. That which is in bowls cannot be secured from worms and mold.

Mixed meats should not be sold on one stall, nor should fat and lean meat be sold on one stall. Tripe should only be sold dry on boards, for water both spoils it and increases its weight. The entrails of sheep must be taken out, so that they should not be sold with the meat and at the same price, which would be a fraud. The heads of sheep should not be skinned, except for the young. The guts must always be removed from the bodies of animals, except lambs, and should not be left there, for this too would be an occasion for fraud.

No slaughtering should take place in the market, except in the closed slaughterhouses, and the blood and refuse should be taken outside the market. Animals should be slaughtered only with a long knife. All slaughtering knives should be of this kind. No animal which is good for field work may be slaughtered, and a trustworthy and incorruptible commissioner should go to the slaughterhouse every day to make sure of this; the only exception is an animal with a defect. Nor should a female still capable of producing young be slaughtered. No animal should be sold in the market which has been brought already slaughtered, until its owner establishes that it is not stolen.…

Women should be forbidden to do their washing in the gardens, for these are dens for fornication.

Grapes in large quantities should not be sold to anyone of whom it is known that he would press them to make wine. This is a matter for supervision.

Fruit must not be sold before it is ripe for this is bad, except only for grapes, which are good for pregnant women and for the sick.…

The seller of grapes should have baskets and nets in which to arrange them, as this is the best protection for them.

Cakes should be properly baked and should only be made wide, as thin ones are good only for the sick.

If someone assays gold or silver coins for a person,

---

1 Apparently a common view. A Spanish Arabic proverb includes the large consumption of truffles among the signs by which the dissolute may be recognized.

2 A term applied to the fertile islands in the lower Guadalquivir, below Seville.

and later it emerges that there is base metal in them, the assayer must make good, for he deceived and betrayed the owner of the coins, who placed his trust in him. Swindlers when detected must be denounced in all crafts, but above all in assaying coin, for in this case the swindler can only be a person who is expert in matters of coin.

Women should not sit by the river bank in the summer if men appear there.

No barber may remain alone with a woman in his booth. He should work in the open market in a place where he can be seen and observed.

The cupper.[1] He should only let blood into a special jar with graduation marks, so that he can see how much blood he has let. He should not let blood at his discretion, for this can lead to sickness and death.

The water wheel. Most of the holes for the spindles should be wedged, as this is best for its working.

No one may be allowed to claim knowledge of a matter in which he is not competent, especially in the craft of medicine, for this can lead to loss of life....

Only a skilled physician should sell potions and electuaries and mix drugs. These things should not be bought from the grocer or the apothecary whose only concern is to take money without knowledge; they spoil the prescriptions and kill the sick, for they mix medicines which are unknown and of contrary effect....

Only good and trustworthy men, known as such among people, may be allowed to have dealings with women in buying and in selling. The tradespeople must watch over this carefully. The women who weave brocades must be banned from the market, for they are nothing but harlots.

On festival days men and women shall not walk on the same path when they go to cross the river....

The basins in the public baths should be covered. If they are left uncovered, they cannot be protected from pollution, yet this is a place of purity. The bath attendant, the masseur, and the barber should not walk about in the baths without a loincloth or drawers.

A Muslim must not massage a Jew or a Christian nor throw away his refuse nor clean his latrines. The Jew and the Christian are better fitted for such trades, since they are the trades of those who are vile. A Muslim should not attend to the animal of a Jew or of a Christian, nor serve him as a muleteer, nor hold his stirrup. If any Muslim is known to do this, he should be denounced.

Muslim women shall be prevented from entering their abominable churches for the priests are evil-doers, fornicators, and sodomites. Frankish[2] women must be forbidden to enter the church except on days of religious services or festivals, for it is their habit to eat and drink and fornicate with the priests, among whom there is not one who has not two or more women with whom he sleeps. This has become a custom among them, for they have permitted what is forbidden and forbidden what is permitted. The priests should be ordered to marry, as they do in the eastern lands. If they wanted to, they would....

A Jew must not slaughter meat for a Muslim. The Jews should be ordered to arrange their own butcher's stalls.

A garment belonging to a sick man,[3] a Jew, or a Christian must not be sold without indicating its origin; likewise, the garment of a debauchee. Dough must not be taken from a sick man for baking his bread. Neither eggs nor chickens nor milk not any other foodstuff should be bought from him. They should only buy and sell among themselves.

The sewer men must be forbidden to dig holes in the streets, as this harms them and causes injury to people, except when they are cleaning the entire street.

Itinerant fortune-tellers must be forbidden to go from house to house, as they are thieves and fornicators.

A drunkard must not be flogged until he is sober again.

Prostitutes must be forbidden to stand bareheaded outside the houses. Decent women must not bedeck themselves to resemble them. They must be stopped from coquetry and party making among themselves, even if they have been permitted to do this [by their husbands]. Dancing girls must be forbidden to bare their heads.

No contractor,[4] policeman, Jew, or Christian may be allowed to dress in the costume of people of position, of a jurist, or of a worthy man. They must on the contrary be abhorred and shunned and should not be greeted with the formula, "Peace be with you," for the devil has gained mastery over them and has made them forget the name

---

[1] Muslims practiced "wet" bloodletting. A cup was applied to the skin to create a mild suction, and then the swollen area was cut with the proper tools. A second application of the cup drew out the blood.

[2] That is, Christians from outside Spain and from those parts of Spain not under Muslim rule.

[3] Probably lepers are meant.

[4] I.e., tax farmer.

of God. They are the devil's party, "and indeed the devil's party are the losers."[1] They must have a distinguishing sign by which they are recognized to their shame.

Catamites[2] must be driven out of the city and punished wherever any one of them is found. They should not be allowed to move around among the Muslims nor to participate in festivities, for they are debauchees accursed by God and man alike.

When fruit or other foodstuffs are found in the possession of thieves, they should be distributed in prisons and given to the poor. If the owner comes to claim his goods and is recognized, they should be returned to him.

5.3 The role of royal patronage: Henry I, *Privileges for the Citizens of London* (1130–1133). Original in Latin.

Towns were permanent commercial centers, and their citizens often demanded and received special privileges that gave them considerable autonomy. In this charter, Henry I, king of England (r.1100–1135), grants privileges to the citizens of London c.1130, basing them on grants handed out by previous kings. The Londoners have the right to the "farm" or revenues of their own borough, Middlesex, holding it, as a vassal might hold a fief, of the king and his heirs. The citizens are also allowed to have their own courts and freedom from various duties and tolls (called "customs" here). The reference to "sokes" in this text means "jurisdictions," which, among other things, were sources of revenues. Compare the freedoms granted by King Henry to those granted by Bishop Frederick in his *Agreement with Colonists*, p. 253 above.

[Source: *English Historical Documents*, vol. 2: 1042–1189, ed. David C. Douglas and George W. Greenaway, 2nd ed. (London: Routledge, 1981), pp. 1012–13 (slightly modified).]

Henry, by the grace of God, king of the English, to the archbishop of Canterbury, and to the bishops and abbots, and earls and barons and justices and sheriffs, and to all his liegemen, both French and English, of the whole of England, greeting. Know that I have granted to my citizens of London that they shall hold Middlesex at "farm" for 300 pounds "by tale" for themselves and their heirs from me and my heirs, so that the citizens shall appoint as sheriff from themselves whomsoever they may choose, and shall appoint from among themselves as justice whomsoever they choose to look after the pleas of my crown and the pleadings which arise in connection with them. No other shall be justice over the men of London.

And the citizens shall not plead outside the walls of the city in respect of any plea; and they shall be quit of scot and of Danegeld and the murder-fine.[3] Nor shall any of them be compelled to offer trial by battle.[4] And if any one of the citizens shall be impleaded [sued] in respect of the pleas of the crown, let him prove himself to be a man of London by an oath which shall be judged in the city. Let no one be billeted within the walls of the city, either of my household, or by the force of anyone else. And let all the men of London and their property be quit and free from toll and passage and lestage and from all other customs throughout all England and at the seaports. And let the churches and barons and citizens

---

[1] Qur'an 57: 22.

[2] A young man who has sexual relationships with men.

[3] The "murder-fine" (*murdrum*) penalized an entire community for the death of any Norman. It dated from the period after the Norman Conquest, when feelings ran high against the invaders. The Londoners are here exempt from paying this.

[4] This was a duel to determine which party was in the right; the tradesmen of London preferred other forms of trial.

hold and have well and in peace their sokes, with all their customs, so that those who dwell in these sokes shall pay no customs except to him who possesses the soke, or to the steward whom he has placed there. And a man of London shall not be fined at mercy[1] except according to his "were,"[2] that is to say, up to 100 shillings: this applies to an offence which can be punished by a fine. And there shall no longer be "miskenning"[3] in the hustings court, nor in the folk-moot,[4] nor in other pleas within the city. And the hustings court shall sit once a week, to wit, on Monday. I will cause my citizens to have their lands and pledges and debts within the city and outside it. And in respect of the lands about which they make claim to me, I will do them right according to the law of the city. And if anyone has taken toll or custom from the citizens of London, then the citizens of London may take from the borough or village where toll or custom has been levied as much as the man of London gave for toll, and more also may be taken for a penalty. And let all debtors to the citizens of London discharge their debts, or prove in London that they do not owe them; and if they refuse either to pay or to come and make such proof, then the citizens to whom the debts are due may take pledges within the city either from the borough or from the village or from the county in which the debtor lives. And the citizens shall have their hunting chases, as well and fully as had their predecessors, namely, in Chiltern and Middlesex and Surrey. Witness: the bishop of Winchester; Robert, son of Richer; Hugh Bigot; Alfred of Totnes; William of Aubigny; Hubert the king's chamberlain; William of Montfiquet; Hagulf "de Tani"; John Belet; Robert, son of Siward. Given at Westminster.

CHURCH REFORM

5.4 The royal view: Henry IV, *Letter to Gregory VII* (1075). Original in Latin.

The movement for church reform was initially supported by both popes and emperors. But as the issue of church leadership came to the fore, the two powers inevitably clashed. When, in 1075, King Henry IV (r.1056–1106) "invested"—put into office—his episcopal candidate at Milan, Pope Gregory VII (1073–1085) complained. Henry reacted vigorously. He met with his bishops at Worms, and the assembly denounced Gregory (called by his old name, Hildebrand) as a usurper of the papal throne. The letter below, which was circulated within Germany, charges Gregory with throwing the church into chaos and calls upon him to resign. A milder version was sent to the pope himself.

[Source: *Imperial Lives and Letters*, ed. Robert L. Benson; trans. Theodor E. Mommsen and Karl F. Morrison (New York: Columbia University Press, 2000), pp. 150–51.]

Henry, King not by usurpation, but by the pious ordination of God,[5] to Hildebrand, now not Pope, but false monk:

You have deserved such a salutation as this because of the confusion you have wrought; for you left untouched no order of the Church which you could make a sharer

---

[1] I.e., fined at discretion, and to an unlimited amount.

[2] The "were" was the wergild, the price a murderer had to pay as compensation to the kin of his victim. In this case, the price of 100 shillings is slightly higher than the "were" of a commoner but lower than that of a thegn.

[3] A "miskenning" was a verbal error in reciting the formal oaths protesting innocence; this entailed the loss of the case.

[4] The "hustings court" and the "folk-moot" were both judicial assemblies, but the folk-moot was slightly larger.

[5] Rom. 13: 2.

of confusion instead of honor, of malediction instead of benediction.

For to discuss a few outstanding points among many: Not only have you dared to touch the rectors of the holy Church—the archbishops, the bishops, and the priests, anointed of the Lord as they are[1]—but you have trodden them under foot like slaves who know not what their lord may do.[2] In crushing them you have gained for yourself acclaim from the mouth of the rabble. You have judged that all these know nothing, while you alone know everything. In any case, you have sedulously used this knowledge not for edification, but for destruction,[3] so greatly that we may believe Saint Gregory, whose name you have arrogated to yourself, rightly made this prophesy of you when he said: "From the abundance of his subjects, the mind of the prelate is often exalted, and he thinks that he has more knowledge than anyone else, since he sees that he has more power than anyone else."[4]

And we, indeed, bore with all these abuses, since we were eager to preserve the honor of the Apostolic See. But you construed our humility as fear, and so you were emboldened to rise up even against the royal power itself, granted to us by God. You dared to threaten to take the kingship away from us—as though we had received the kingship from you, as though kingship and empire were in your hand and not in the hand of God.

Our Lord, Jesus Christ, has called us to kingship, but has not called you to the priesthood. For you have risen by these steps: namely, by cunning, which the monastic profession abhors, to money; by money to favor; by favor to the sword. By the sword you have come to the throne of peace, and from the throne of peace you have destroyed the peace. You have armed subjects against their prelates; you who have not been called by God have taught that our bishops who have been called by God are to be spurned; you have usurped for laymen the bishops' ministry over priests, with the result that these laymen depose and condemn the very men whom the laymen themselves received as teachers from the hand of God, through the imposition of the hands of bishops.

You have also touched me, one who, though unworthy, has been anointed to kingship among the anointed. This wrong you have done to me, although as the tradition of the holy Fathers has taught, I am to be judged by God alone and am not to be deposed for any crime unless—may it never happen—I should deviate from the Faith. For the prudence of the holy bishops entrusted the judgment and the deposition even of Julian the Apostate not to themselves, but to God alone. The true pope Saint Peter also exclaims, "Fear God, honor the king."[5] You, however, since you do not fear God, dishonor me, ordained of Him.

Wherefore, when Saint Paul gave no quarter to an angel from heaven if the angel should preach heterodoxy,[6] he did not except you who are now teaching heterodoxy throughout the earth. For he says, "If anyone, either I or an angel from heaven, preach any other gospel unto you than that which we have preached unto you, let him be accursed."[7] Descend, therefore, condemned by this anathema and by the common judgment of all our bishops and of ourself. Relinquish the Apostolic See which you have arrogated. Let another mount the throne of Saint Peter, another who will not cloak violence with religion but who will teach the pure doctrine of Saint Peter.

I, Henry, King by the grace of God, together with all our bishops, say to you: Descend! Descend!

---

[1] Ps. 105: 15; Douay Ps. 104: 15; 2 Sam. 1: 14.

[2] See John 15: 15.

[3] See 2 Cor. 10: 8, 13: 10.

[4] Gregory I, *Pastoral Care* 2. 6.

[5] 1 Pet. 2: 17.

[6] That is, doctrine that diverges from correct belief.

[7] Gal. 1: 18.

5.5 The papal view: Gregory VII, *Letter to Hermann of Metz* (1076). Original in Latin.

Soon after receiving Henry's letter, the pope met with *his* bishops and excommunicated Henry. Many of Henry's supporters abandoned the king, and Bishop Hermann of Metz, one of a handful of bishops at Worms who had opposed the condemnation of Gregory, was important in fomenting the resulting war. Yet Hermann needed arguments to back up the actions of the pope and convince others to separate themselves from the excommunicated king. Gregory supplied some reasons in this letter, downgrading the dignity of kingship and maintaining that the act of excommunicating kings had a long and illustrious history.

[Source: Herbert E.J. Cowdrey, *The Register of Pope Gregory VII, 1073–1085: An English Translation* (Oxford: Oxford University Press, 2002), pp. 208–11 (notes modified).]

Gregory, bishop, servant of the servants of God, to Hermann, bishop of Metz, greeting and apostolic blessing.

By your questioning you are seeking many things of me who am exceedingly busy, and you send a messenger who presses me too much at his own pleasure. Accordingly, if I do not reply sufficiently, I ask you to bear it with patience.

Therefore how I am in my bodily health, or how the Romans and the Normans[1] who are proving themselves to be with regard to me, the bearer of this letter may tell you. But as regards the other matters about which you have questioned me, would that blessed Peter[2] might answer through me, for he is often honored or suffers injury in me, his servant such as I am.

Now, who the excommunicated bishops, priests, or laymen are there is no need that you should inquire of me, for undoubtedly they are those who are known to have held communion with the excommunicated King Henry, if it is right that he should be called king. For they do not scruple to set human favor or fear before the precept of the eternal King, nor do they fear by their support to drive their king towards the wrath of Almighty God.

He, however, by communicating with his own courtiers who were excommunicated for the simoniac heresy[3] has not feared to incur excommunication, and has not been ashamed to draw others to be excommunicated by communicating with him. Concerning such men, what else is there that we might think except what we have learnt in the Psalms: "The fool has said in his heart, 'There is no God,'" and again, "All have together been made unprofitable" in their intentions?[4]

Now, as for those who say, "it is not right that the king should be excommunicated," although in view of their great folly we have no need so much as to answer them, yet lest we seem to pass impatiently over their foolishness we direct them to the words or deeds of the holy fathers, in order that we may call them back to sound teaching. Let them, therefore, read what blessed Peter commanded to the Christian people at the ordination of St. Clement about him whom they knew not to have the favor of the pontiff.[5] Let them learn why the Apostle says, "Ready to avenge every act of disobedience,"[6] and of whom he says, "With such a man not even to take food."[7] Let them ponder why Pope Zacharias deposed the king of the Franks

---

[1] When Gregory spoke of the Romans, he meant the people—and above all the nobles—of Rome. By the Normans he meant the rulers of Southern Italy, with whom the papacy had been allied since 1059.

[2] This refers to St. Peter, whose "servant" but also spokesman Gregory considered himself.

[3] Gregory called the purchasing of church offices "simony" or the "simoniac heresy" after Simon Magus, who in Acts 8: 18–24 offered money to Peter and John if they would give him the power to confer the Holy Spirit.

[4] Ps. 14: 1–3; Douay Ps. 13: 1–3.

[5] *Epistola Clementis prior*, chap. 18.

[6] 2 Cor. 10: 6.

[7] 1 Cor. 5: 11.

and absolved all the Frankish people from the bond of the oath that they had taken to him.[1] Let them also learn in the Register of blessed Gregory that in privileges that he drew up for certain churches he not only excommunicated kings and dukes who contravened his words but also adjudged that they should forfeit their office.[2] Nor let them overlook that blessed Ambrose not only excommunicated Theodosius—not only a king but indeed an emperor in habitual conduct and power, but even debarred him from remaining in church in the place of the priests.[3]

But perhaps these men wish to have it thought that, when God three times committed his church to blessed Peter saying, "Feed my sheep,"[4] he made an exception of kings. Why do they not take notice, or rather shamefacedly confess, that, when God gave principally to blessed Peter the power of binding and loosing in heaven and upon earth,[5] he excepted nobody and withheld nothing from his power. For when a man denies that he can be bound by the chain of the church, it remains that he must deny that he can be loosed by its power; and whoever brazenly denies this altogether separates himself from Christ. And if the holy apostolic see, deciding through the pre-eminent power that is divinely conferred upon it, settles spiritual matters, why not also secular matters? In truth, as for the kings and princes of this world who place their own honor and temporal gains before the righteousness of God, and who by neglecting his honor seek their own, whose members they are or to whom they cleave your charity is not in ignorance. For just as those who set God before their own entire will and obey his command rather than men[6] are members of Christ,[7] so also those of whom we have been speaking above are members of Antichrist. If, then, spiritual men are judged when it is necessary, why are not secular ones the more under constraint concerning their wicked deeds?

But perhaps they think that the royal dignity excels the episcopal. From their origins they can gather how greatly they each differ from the other. For human pride has instituted the former; divine mercy has instituted the latter. The former ceaselessly snatches at vain glory; the latter always aspires to the heavenly life. And let them learn what the blessed Pope Anastasius wrote to the Emperor Anastasius about these dignities,[8] and how blessed Ambrose distinguished between these dignities in his pastoral letter: "The episcopal honor and excellence," he said, "if you compare them with the splendor of kings and the diadem of emperors, leave them much more inferior than if you compare the metal of lead with the splendor of gold."[9] Being not unaware of these things, the Emperor Constantine the Great chose not the principal but the least place to sit amongst the bishops; for he knew that "God resists the proud, but he gives favor to the humble."[10]

Meanwhile, brother, we are letting you know that, having received letters from certain of our brother bishops and dukes, by the authority of the apostolic see we have given licence to these bishops to absolve those excommunicated by us who are not afraid to keep themselves from communion with the king. As regards the king himself, [Henry IV] we have absolutely forbidden that anyone should venture to absolve him until his assured penitence and sincere satisfaction shall have been reported to us by trustworthy witnesses, so that we may at the same time ascertain how, if divine mercy shall look upon him, we may absolve him to the honor of God and to his own salvation. For it is not hidden from us that there are some of you who, seizing any pretext that might seem to come from us, would be led astray by fear or human favor and presume to absolve him if we were not to forbid, and to add wound to wound in place of medicine. If any who are bishops in truth should forbid them, they would conclude that they were not defending righteousness but pursuing enmities.

---

[1] In 751, Pope Zacharias (741–752) sanctioned the deposition of Childeric III (r.743–c.751), the last of the Merovingian kings.

[2] This refers to the letters of Pope Gregory the Great (590–604).

[3] The reference is to St. Ambrose's measures against the Emperor Theodosius I (r.379–395) after the emperor responded to a revolt at Thessalonica by massacring its inhabitants.

[4] John 21: 15–17.

[5] See Matt. 16: 19. The power of binding and loosing, as interpreted by the papacy, was the priestly power to impose penance and to administer absolution.

[6] See Acts 5: 29.

[7] See 1 Cor. 6: 15.

[8] This refers to a letter from Pope Anastasius II (496–498) to the Emperor Anastasius I (r.491–518).

[9] We now know that the work in question was not written by St. Ambrose.

[10] James 4: 6. The reference is to Emperor Constantine I (r.306–337) at the Council of Nicaea (325).

Now, as for the ordination and consecration of bishops who venture to communicate with the excommunicated king, as blessed Gregory testifies, before God they become an execration.[1] For when they proudly resist to obey the apostolic see, as Samuel is witness, they fall into the crime of idolatry.[2] For if he is said to be of God who is stirred up by the zeal of divine love to destroy vices, he assuredly denies that he is of God who refuses, so far as he is able, to reprove the life of carnal men. And if he is accursed who withholds his sword from blood,[3] that is, the word of preaching from the slaying of carnal life, how much more is he accursed who from fear or favor drives the soul of his brother to eternal perdition [damnation]? In sum, that the accursed and excommunicated can bless and bestow upon anyone the divine grace that they do not fear to deny by their own works, can be discovered in no ruling of the holy fathers.

Meantime, we order you to have a word with the venerable archbishop of Trier,[4] our brother that is, who is to forbid the bishop of Toul[5] from intruding into the affairs of the abbess of the monastery of Remiremont,[6]

and who, in concert with you, is to annul whatever he has decided against her. Now, as regards Matilda,[7] the daughter of us both and the faithful handmaid of blessed Peter, what you wish, I wish. But in what state of life she should continue under God's direction, I do not yet grasp for certain. But of Godfrey her late husband,[8] you may know for a certainty that I, although a sinner, frequently make memorial before God; for neither his enmity nor any vain consideration holds me back and, moved by your own brotherly love and Matilda's pleading, I long for his salvation.

May Almighty God, by the intercession of the queen of heaven, Mary ever-virgin, and by the authority of the blessed apostles Peter and Paul which is granted by him to them, absolve from all sins both you and all our brothers in whatever order who are defending the Christian religion and the dignity of the apostolic see; and, giving to you the increase of faith, hope, and charity, may he make you strong in the defense of his law, so that you may deserve to attain to eternal salvation. Given at Tivoli on August 25th, in the fourteenth indiction.

THE CLERGY IN ACTION

5.6 *Vesting Prayers* (*c.*1000?). Original in Latin.

Even before the Gregorian reform, clerics themselves developed devotions to prepare spiritually for their sacramental duties. One practice used the special garments that the priest wore to celebrate the Mass to help him cultivate purity and virtue, prescribing prayers to be said as each liturgical vestment was put on. These vesting prayers developed into a pre-Mass ritual performed in the sacristy: the clerics participating in the liturgy chanted a few psalms to put them in the proper frame of mind and then recited prayers as they donned their vestments. This clerical devotion emerged in response to ninth-century Carolingian reforms (as the manuscript excerpted below, dated to the late tenth century or the beginning of the eleventh, demonstrates), but was more widely disseminated through the eleventh-century Gregorian movement. Vesting prayers proved

---

[1] This is a reference to a letter of Gregory the Great.

[2] See 1 Sam. 15: 23.

[3] See Jer. 48: 10.

[4] Bishop Udo.

[5] Bishop Pibo.

[6] Gisela.

[7] Matilda was countess of Tuscany and a staunch supporter of Gregory.

[8] Godfrey, duke of Lorraine, was killed on February 26, 1076.

incredibly popular with clerics and were required until the Second Vatican Council in 1965 made them optional. Brief prayers such as these were sometimes recorded before the text or *ordo* of the Mass, but they were also copied into margins and on blank spaces at the beginning and ends of liturgical manuscripts. Often, as in the example below, variant prayers are given so that clerics could choose versions that spoke to them.

[Source: Biblioteca Apostolica Vaticana, Ottoboniensis Latinus 6, fol. 9v. Translated and introduced by Maureen C. Miller.]

Here begins the rite *(ordo)* for a bishop or priest to prepare himself to say Mass.

First, chant the psalms "Quam dilecta," "Benedixisti," "Inclina," and "Credidi."[1] Then recite the "Kyrie eleison" and the Lord's Prayer.[2] Then pray,

Let your mercy, O God, be upon us
You will turn, O God, and bring us to life
Show us, O Lord, your mercy
And enter not into judgment with your servant
Hear, O Lord, my prayer.[3]

To the amice:[4] Rend, O Lord, my garment and wrap me in joy. To the same: Protect my shoulders, O Lord, with the grace of the Holy Spirit and gird my spirit, all sins having been removed, [so that I might] sacrifice to you, O God, [who] lives and reigns forever.

To the alb:[5] Clothe me, O Lord, in the vestment of salvation and gird me with the breastplate of fortitude. To the same: Gird me, O Lord, with the armor of faith, so that having been shielded from the arrows of iniq-

uity, I might have the strength to preserve righteousness and justice. To the same: Omnipresent and eternal God, I humbly beseech you in order that having cast off the deception of all evasions and put on this white garment, I might be worthy to follow you into the realm of true joy.

To the cincture:[6] Equip me, O Lord, with a watchfulness for my soul, lest my mind be warped by a prideful spirit. To the same: Gird me, O Lord, with virtue and make my soul immaculate. To the same: Fasten most powerfully upon my thigh, O Lord, your sword, so that I may be able manfully to vanquish your enemies with the steadfast hope of eternal truth.

To the stole:[7] Place the stole of justice around my neck, O Lord, and purify my soul of all sinful corruption; break the chain of my sins, so that having taken up the yoke of your service, I might be worthy to attend you with fear and reverence.

To the chasuble:[8] Robe me, O Lord, with the ornament of humility, love, and peace so that having been completely fortified with virtues I might be able to withstand sins and enemies of mind and body, through you, Jesus Christ.

---

[1] Psalms 84, 85, 86, and 116; Douay 83, 84, 85, and 115, here identified by their opening word or words in the Latin in which they would have been chanted.

[2] The "Kyrie eleison" is a brief Greek prayer incorporated into the Latin Mass during the early Middle Ages. Meaning "Lord have mercy," the phrase appears in the Greek translation of the Old Testament (the Septuagint) and in the New Testament. The Lord's Prayer is thus called because the gospels of Matthew (6: 9–15) and Luke (11: 2–4) describe Jesus teaching it to his disciples. It is also known by its opening phrase as the Our Father (in Latin, *Pater noster*).

[3] All of these are lines from the Psalms: 33: 22, 85: 7-8, 143: 2, 143: 1; Douay 32: 22, 84: 7–8; 142: 2; 142: 1.

[4] The amice, the first vestment to be put on, was a rectangular piece of linen or cotton with ties extending from the long ends of one side. It was draped over the shoulders with the ties crossing the chest, crossing again in back, and then tied in front. It likely served to protect the neckline of other vestments from grime (the amice being more easily washable).

[5] A white line or cotton long-sleeved tunic that was the base garment worn for the Mass and other ceremonies.

[6] A belt worn over the alb and used to adjust its length by pulling fabric up over the belt.

[7] A sort of liturgical scarf worn by deacons and priests, but especially associated with priestly status. Usually eight to ten feet long and two to three inches wide, the stole was put on over the alb, resting on the neck with both ends falling down straight over the front of the body.

[8] See Plate 5, p. 236, in Containing the Holy.

5.7 *The Star of Clerics* (*c.*1200?). Original in Latin.

Church reformers in the eleventh century demanded that priests be celibate, obtain their offices without payment, and generally be more devout and better prepared than before to minister to their flocks. In response to these demands, many new educational aids were produced to help bishops to train priests and clerics to study. The *Stella clericorum* was one of the most popular, surviving in over 450 manuscript copies. Although the earliest-known manuscript dates from the late thirteenth or early fourteenth century, internal evidence indicates that this anonymously authored miscellany of admonitions was a product of innovations *c.*1200 in theology and clerical spirituality. The entire text is brief—26 small manuscript pages, and about the same today in its published form—and its content unoriginal, but it offered pithy summaries and memorable adages to help priests meet the pastoral expectations of the post-Gregorian church.

[Source: *Stella clericorum*, ed. Eric H. Reiter (Toronto: Pontifical Institute of Medieval Studies, 1997), pp. 22–24. Translated and introduced by Maureen C. Miller.]

[5.] Every pastor or priest should cultivate three things, namely: knowledge, eloquence, and a good [manner of] life. He ought to have knowledge and understanding of divine books, through which he may first learn about himself and then others. He who does not know himself, knows nothing. This excellent maxim is found among worldly philosophers: as they say, "know yourself." Moreover, Augustine in his book on the Holy Trinity preferred knowledge of his own infirmity to knowledge of the heavens or of earthly or infernal places.[1] Whence also Bernard [said]: "O Lord, let me know you, understand myself, [and] love you."[2]

He ought also to have discreet eloquence so that he may preach to others those things that he knows and understands, lest he "hide his lord's money,"[3] and lest he be a mute dog[4] in God's house (that is, in church).

Whence Isaiah: "Cry, cease not, lift up your voice like a trumpet and show my people their wicked doings,"[5] and Cicero: "It is better that I speak at length and prudently than someone without eloquence keenly hold forth."[6]

Therefore, let a priest have knowledge with eloquence. Whence Gregory: "The ignorance of a priest is neither forgiven nor excused."[7] Daniel [too wrote]: "But they who are learned shall shine as the brightness of the firmament" (that is, the sun) "and those that instruct many to justice are like stars for all eternity."[8] Whence another: "Doubly honored are priests, first by the dignity of their office [and] second by doctrine, especially those who faithfully labor in the Gospel because the order of faithful preachers is distinguished."[9]

Let a priest have a good [manner of] life so that what he preaches with his mouth he may fulfill in his works.

---

[1] This expression is actually not from the esteemed fourth-century Bishop of Hippo and Father of the Church, but from a work (*De spiritu et anima liber unus*, 50) that circulated under his name during the Middle Ages.

[2] The author probably is intending to quote the twelfth-century Cistercian abbot Bernard of Clairvaux, but this sentence is not found in his works.

[3] Matt. 25: 18.

[4] Isa. 56: 10.

[5] Isa. 58: 1.

[6] Citation not found.

[7] Pope Gregory the Great (590–604), as quoted in the important collection and textbook of ecclesiastical law, Gratian's *Decretum* D.38 c.3.

[8] Dan. 12: 3.

[9] 1 Tim. 5: 17.

Luke: "Jesus began to do and to teach."[1] Jerome: "Does not the one who speaks or preaches well but lives perversely not condemn himself with his own mouth?"[2] Origen: He who does not instruct others [through his manner of life] cannot himself teach it.[3] Gregory: "Let the preacher glory not in the splendor of words but in works of virtue."[4] Jerome: "The helping hand of the learned reaches out to the fallen and shows the way of truth to the erring."[5] Gregory: "The good teacher is the one who humbly serves learning and through discipline does not fall into pride."[6] Chrysostom: "Is holy strength evident? You shall be strict regarding your own life, and merciful regarding the sins of others. Let men hear you commanding small things, and doing burdensome things."[7] Gregory: "He whose life is despised finds his preaching condemned."[8] ...

[13] Accordingly, O you prelates and priests, the souls of your subordinates, having been committed to you[r care], weigh upon you. He is called priest (*presbiter*), as it were, "one showing the way" (*prebens iter*) for the flock committed to him, through his word and the example of his life, and even by offering temporal help—although he seeks not so much the gain of temporal things as the profit of souls from whom the Son of God endured death.

5.8 *A Visitation Record* (1268). Original in Latin.

Reformers not only disseminated "best practices" for the clergy, but they also made more rigorous and systematic efforts to enforce these standards. An important tool was the visitation of parishes. Church councils from the fifth century set out the requirement that bishops, or their delegates, visit the churches of their dioceses to inspect their physical condition, their equipment (the books and ceremonial objects essential to delivering pastoral care), their ministers, and more generally the spiritual and moral condition of both clergy and laity. Sporadic prescriptive and documentary sources reveal episcopal attempts to carry out visitations from the ninth through the twelfth centuries, but it is only in the thirteenth century that we begin to get detailed records produced by visitations. Usually the checklist or questionnaire that the prelate carried into the field does not survive, but the notes taken down by the scribe or notary accompanying the visitor reveal ecclesiastical concerns and the standards being enforced. Translated below are the records of a visitation of the churches in the deanery (an ecclesiastical district within a large diocese) of Demouville in the Norman see of Bayeux. It was conducted in 1268 by Henri de Vézelay, then archdeacon of Bayeux, on behalf of his bishop. Henri went on to have a brilliant career in royal administration, serving as chancellor and advisor to French kings Louis IX (Saint Louis, r.1226–1270) and his son Philip III the Bold (r.1270–1285).

[Source: L. Delisle, "Visites pastorales de maître Henri de Vezelai, archidiacre d'Hiémois en 1267 et 1268," *Bibliothèque de l'École des Chartes* 54 (1893): 465–67. Translated and introduced by Maureen C. Miller.]

---

[1] Acts 1: 1.

[2] In fact not Jerome but Pseudo-Isidore of Seville, *Commandments of Divine Scripture and of the Fathers* (*Testimonia divinae scripturae <et patrum>*), 6.3.

[3] Citation not found.

[4] Gregory the Great, in his commentary on the first book of Kings (*In librum I Regum*), 6.16.

[5] Jerome (*c.*347–419/420) in his commentary on the book of Jonah at Jon. 4: 10–11.

[6] Isidore, bishop of Seville (d.636), *Three Books of Sentences*, 3.41.1.

[7] Pseudo-Chrysostom, *Opus imperfectum* 43, quoted in Gratian's *Decretum* C.26 q.7 c.12.

[8] Gregory the Great, *Forty Gospel Homilies* 12.1, quoted in Gratian's *Decretum* C.3 q.7 c.2.

1268, ON THE MONDAY BEFORE THE FEAST
OF BLESSED MICHAEL [24 SEPTEMBER 1268],
DEANERY OF DEMOUVILLE.

At Robehomme the *chrismatorium*[1] should be restored and a Gradual and Psalter[2] ought to be bought. The spider cloth[3] above the altar ought to be removed, the blessed altar renewed and repaired, and thus we ordered the people of the place and their treasurers to do this. Garinus Hayche, a married man, is defamed[4] of Johanna, the unmarried daughter of William Viel.

TUESDAY [25 SEPTEMBER 1268]

At Bavent a few things are lacking in the church and its ornaments. A lantern ought to be bought for doing the viaticum.[5] Henry Hemet, a cleric, is defamed of Maltide, daughter of the deceased Noel and he has a child by her. Henry Prestrel is defamed of the wife of Hormont, she whom he had abjured, and he threw out his own wife. Master Gelscuel of Bigarz, a cleric, keeps his own concubine at home.

At Petiville the church gate is falling down and very dangerous. Neither the tabernacle where the body of the Lord [is kept] nor the font are secured due to the negligence of the priest.

At Varaville the Missal[6] is old and unreadable.

At Sallenelles we did not enter the church because the priest was absent and the key to the church could not be found.

At Amfreville the priest was absent, however we visited the church and came upon the chalice in a bag without any other cloth [protecting it]. The church was uncovered[7] through the negligence of the priest. Neither the receptacle where the body of the Lord is kept nor the [baptismal] font was secured. The vestments are very dirty and horrible. Finally, the priest arrived and everything was shown [to us] by him. He was ordered on pain of suspension to get a key for the receptacle for the body of Christ by the following Monday and to correct other things.

At Colombelles the church is being re-roofed; books are lacking.

At Giberville nothing is lacking in the church's ornaments, [but] the church is uncovered. The two chaplains frequent taverns. Thomas Diaconus, a cleric, is denounced for usury and for keeping a kitchen maid. William Synemande, an excommunicate, has been excommunicated several times for a long time. The cleric Aliotus keeps a kitchen maid. Regnaudus Basile, a cleric, is defamed of Petronilla, the widow of the deceased Martin son of Philip.

At Demouville nothing is lacking in the church or its ornaments. The cleric Henry, brother of the dean, is defamed of the widow Florencia. Herbert Boet has a child by Matilda. The cleric Richard Boti still has Marieta. Richard Carsanoz is defamed of Juliana, wife of Selle Guerart and took her to his native land.[8] The cleric Robert Biquet has Matilda and has a child with her. Men don't keep feast days.

THURSDAY [27 SEPTEMBER 1268]

At Banneville-la-Campagne the ornaments, corporals,[9] and

---

1. A *chrismatorium* is a vessel for storing chrism, a mixture of olive oil and balsam consecrated by the bishop that is used in the administration of several sacraments.

2. The Gradual was a book containing the chants to be sung by the choir at Mass. It takes its name from the step (*gradus*) on which the cantor stood to lead the responsorial psalms intoned after the reading of the Epistle and before the Gospel. The Psalter was a book of the psalms used to recite the cycle of daily prayer known as the Divine Office, a devotion increasingly enjoined on priests from the twelfth century. It was also used to teach reading.

3. A cloth protecting the altar from spiders and other potential sources of contamination.

4. The visitor's inquiries allowed parishioners to comment on the conduct and morals of their pastor, but they also brought their own behavior under scrutiny. The passive verb *diffamatur* (here translated "defamed"), from *diffamo*, to accuse or slander, indicates that someone made an accusation of immoral, usually sexual, conduct.

5. The viaticum was the Eucharist administered to those on the verge of death. The term originally denoted traveling provisions and in Christian usage conveyed the idea that the Eucharist would aid believers on the journey into eternal life. The concern registered here seems to be that if the clergy were summoned in the middle of the night to administer the viaticum, they would have a lamp to light their way in carrying the sacrament.

6. The Missal is the liturgical book containing all the texts (prayers, readings) need for saying Mass.

7. *Ecclesia discooperta* likely comments on the state of the building's roofing.

8. The text uses *patria*—fatherland, country—suggesting that Richard was not from Normandy.

9. A corporal is a piece of linen upon which the chalice and paten are placed on the altar.

vestments are dirty. The Breviary[1] is old and unreadable.

At Guillerville the church is poor. The ornaments are good enough.

At Émiéville [the church] lacks a key for the font and chrismatorium; the cemetery is not enclosed. These things ought to be corrected within three years. A Psalter and Manual[2] are also lacking. The person assigned to the church does not want to live here so the bishop holds the church. Robert Hardiz still has Luceta au Tabour, whom he is unable to have as his wife because of their consanguinity.

At Manneville the chrismatorium lacks a key through the priest's negligence. He also owes the church treasury three *sextaria* [of grain].

At Cagni all that was lacking in the church has been corrected.

At Vimont the person assigned to the church is still defamed of Petronilla, his blood relative whom he had abjured, and she goes about with him. We ordered a person to remove his straw from the church.

THE CRUSADES AND RECONQUISTA

5.9 Martyrs in the Rhineland: Rabbi Eliezer b. Nathan ("Raban"), *O God, Insolent Men* (early to mid-12th c.). Original in Hebrew.

In the spring of 1096, irregular crusader armies passed through the Rhine valley. They were responding to Pope Urban II's call to regain the Holy Land from the Muslim "infidels" who ruled it, but they also decided to attack the "infidels in their midst"—the Jews. Confronting their persecutors with a new and unprecedented religious fervor, the Jews actively sought martyrdom rather than submit to the enemy's demand that they convert. Indeed, not only did hundreds of Jews meet their death at the hands of the crusaders, but many preferred to kill themselves and their children rather than be defiled by the crusaders' swords. These suicide-martyrdoms became a rallying image for northern European Jews over the next century. Three short chronicles dramatized the resistance and martyrdom of the Rhineland Jews in 1096. In addition, dozens of liturgical poems—including *O God, Insolent Men* by Rabbi Eliezer b. Nathan (*c*.1090–1170), known as the "Raban"—described the martyrdoms of 1096 and those of subsequent persecutions.

Poems such as Rabbi Eliezer's, excerpted here, were written as hymns and often performed in commemorative liturgies that were rich in symbolic display. The texts were written for a highly literate audience, men deeply immersed in the study of Jewish texts and trained to recognize the shorthand allusions to them in the verses. *O God, Insolent Men* taps all the motifs of the new genre of Hebrew martyrological verse: it is polemical, including a number of insulting comments about Christianity; it is eschatological, interpreting historical catastrophe as a prelude to messianic redemption and overlaying

---

[1] The Breviary is a liturgical book containing all the texts (psalms, antiphons, hymns, lessons) needed to recite the Divine Office. It appears to date from the eleventh century, and Pope Gregory VII is often credited with this abridged and simplified form of the hours suited to the active lives of secular clerics. Since it could replace several books—the Psalter, Antiphonary, Lectionary—the Breviary was well suited to rural churches.

[2] A Manual is a book containing ceremonial directions for performing various liturgies or services.

images of violence with biblical images of revelation and covenant; and it offers consolation, particularly in its call for vengeance. Formally, the poem is an alphabetic acrostic; it is extremely controlled, as if to reassure its listeners that order prevails over seeming chaos.

[Source: Abraham Habermann, *Sefer gezerot ashkenaz vetzarfat* (Jerusalem: 1945, repr. 1971), pp. 84–87. Introduced and translated by Susan L. Einbinder.]

O God, insolent men have risen against me[1]
They have sorely afflicted us from our youth[2]
They have devoured and destroyed us in their wrath against us[3]
Saying, let us take [their] inheritance for ourselves.[4]
...

Their hearts were turned to plotting evil and trouble.[5]
They went to seek pollution far away:[6]
The crucified one, buried and placed in a deep pit
in the depths of hell.[7]   20

And the insolent ones, alien idolators, plotted.
They stubbornly sought deceit and treachery[8]

And put their hand to leaving the House of Jacob in ruins,[9]
Saying, God will not see.

"O abandoned ones, why do you hope for relief and healing?[10]   25
Your King has abandoned you to the nations to be devoured
Do this and live: worship the icon!"[11]
Remember this, O Lord, how the enemy scoffs![12]

"Heaven forbid," cried the innocent ones.
"It would be shameful to abandon Him," they   30
proclaimed from the bare heights.[13]

---

1   Ps. 86: 14. The Douay version will not be cited for R. Eliezer's text. R. stands for Rabbi in the notes here.

2   Ps. 124: 3; Ps. 129: 1–2.

3   The first half of the verse echoes Jer. 10: 25, which begins with the vengeful "pour out thy wrath upon the nations," echoed in Psalm 79 (evoked below). The end of Raban's verse is from Ps. 124: 3.

4   Ps. 83: 12.

5   Isa. 59: 7 (see also Isa. 55: 7 and Mic. 2: 1); 1 Sam. 25: 31.

6   The tone is contemptuous. The speaker inverts the crusaders' mission, in its sense of a pilgrimage to the site of Jesus' life and death, to a journey toward impurity. By Jewish law, contact with a corpse, or with anything that has come into contact with a corpse or other unclean thing, is a source of pollution (See Lev. 11 and 21). Thus the crusaders, by returning to the site of Jesus' crucifixion, seek their own contamination.

7   This verse cannot be translated literally. It is clipped from Prov. 30: 16, where it is already corrupt and caused the commentators great trouble. The great northern French commentator, R. Solomon b. Isaac ("Rashi," d.1105), referred to an exegetical tradition according to which the expression refers to Sheol, or Gehenna, i.e., hell. R. Eliezer would have known this tradition.

8   See Num. 25: 18; Ps. 78: 57.

9   See Isa. 24: 12.

10   See Jer. 33: 6.

11   The polemical literature of medieval Jews often represented Christians as worshiping "icons" or "idols." As with the case of biblical critiques of the use of idols, the writers probably understood that the image was not the actual object of worship but a representation of something immaterial. However, it served their purposes to emphasize the stupidity of those who would worship pieces of wood and stone. Here, too, R. Eliezer puts in the Christian speech the type of argument Jews must have actually heard: God's covenant with the Jews had been superseded by a new covenant with the Christians, and the flourishing of Christendom, like the abasement of the Jews, proved this.

12   Ps. 74: 18.

13   Perhaps an allusion to Jer. 3: 21, "a voice on the bare heights is heard, the weeping and pleading of Israel's sons...."

"We live by His favor, and his anger is but a moment to the weak,[1]
The Lord is merciful and compassionate and long-suffering."[2]

When the impure ones heard this, they were filled with poison.
They slaughtered them, they wrung their necks. No household was spared.[3]

They piled together infants and women, young and old.[4]
The prideful ones concealed [their] trap for me, and spread their snares.[5]

Together, with a full heart, the remnant came forth willingly.[6]
They went out to perform their worship and fulfilled it energetically.

Their lips moved as they made their peace with Heaven:[7]
"There is a God who judges the earth."[8]   40

Brides and grooms behaved identically[9]
As one they were determined to sanctify You, O Awesome and Dreadful One.
Our eyes failed [watching] them day after day[10]
For we are killed for You every day.[11]

Tender children said sweetly to their mothers,   45
"Make us whole offerings! We are desired in Heaven."
Weep for all this, weep, O daughters of Israel.
Teach your daughters mourning; let each woman teach her companion laments.[12]

Youths like saplings pleaded with their fathers:
"Hurry! Hasten to do our Maker's Will!   50
The One God is our portion and destiny
Our days are over, our end has come."[13]

---

[1] Rearranging the language of the Hebrew version of Ps. 30: 5 ("his anger is but for a moment, [but] his favor is for a lifetime"). The Hebrew word for "weak" may echo a passage in the Talmud, B.Hullin 3b, where it refers to a weakness in the hands before the slaughter of sacrificial animals.

[2] A common tribute to God: see, e.g., Exod. 34: 6.

[3] Literally, the verse says "according to the number of persons, they were counted," which is an allusion to Exod. 12: 4. The cryptic formulation makes sense when its biblical context is recalled. In Exod. 12, God orders the enslaved Israelites to slaughter a lamb per household and mark their doorposts with its blood. If "a household is too small for a lamb," two neighboring households may combine their number ("according to the number of persons") and so "make the count" for the lamb. By analogy, the medieval Jews are slaughtered "per household," meaning that no household is spared.

[4] References to the mingled blood of male and female, young and old, etc., are a common motif in 1096 poetry, including this example. The demographic variety of the martyrs is equalized in death. In the next century, this equality will disappear in the literature to emphasize the martyrdom of elite, scholarly, men.

[5] See Ps. 140: 5; Prov. 29: 5.

[6] See 1 Chron. 29: 9, but evoking also Exod. 35: 21, 29. Notice how this section switches its allusions to Exodus and its tale of collective revelation and covenant. Thus the martyrological lament becomes a polemical response to the dreadful possibility voiced in Exod. 25–28. God has not abandoned the Jews but is with them and renewing his covenant precisely at this moment of suffering.

[7] Alternatively, it is possible to read this line as "they reconciled themselves in vigor" or, possibly, "they reconciled themselves in fear."

[8] Ps. 58: 11.

[9] Literally, brides and grooms "did not divide their twin-ness." The verse alludes to the allegorical readings of the Song of Songs, interpreted as the "twinned" marriage of Israel and God.

[10] Ps. 69: 3, 119: 82.

[11] Or, all day long. See Ps. 44: 22.

[12] See Jer. 9: 20. A number of Hebrew martyrological poems include a call to women to make lament, perhaps an allusion to professional keeners or to the prominence of women among public mourners.

[13] See Lam. 4: 18.

"Bound on Mt. Moriah, [Isaac's] father tied him
so he would not kick and ruin his slaughter.[1]
In our love for God, we will be slaughtered without   55
    being tied
Our souls will rejoice in the Lord and be glad for His
    salvation."[2]

The fathers were glad when they heard these pleasing
    words.
They hastened to lay hands upon the pure lambs[3]
They trilled: "God is One!" They cried out in
    consolation:[4]

"My witness is in Heaven, my witness is above!"[5]   60
They took their stations and slaughtered them while
    weeping
Free-will offerings as if on God's altars
Mothers swooned, naked, upon their children[6]
For this I weep.[7]
...

Their blood spatters on [God's] purple robe[8]
In exchange for silver, I bring gold.[9]

---

[1] This legend would be familiar to most medieval Jews. The ancient rabbis determined by adding and subtracting their way through the first chapters of Genesis that Isaac must have been a grown man (37!) at the time Abraham was ordered to "offer him up" in Gen. 22. How could it be that he would not have resisted? The rabbis concluded that Isaac knew very well what Abraham intended, and asked his father to tie him down tightly so as not to mar the sacrifice (comparing himself to the ritual offerings of the Temple cult). Here, R. Eliezer claims that the Jewish children slaughtered by their fathers also undertook to die willingly; moreover, their courage and piety exceeded that of the biblical Isaac because they did not flinch or require restraint. The idea of the exemplary piety of the Ashkenaz (German) communities and in particular of their martyrs is found throughout this poetry. It is a hallmark of the Ashkenazic "self-image," and undoubtedly contributed to the resistance of the communities to conversion.

[2] See Ps. 35: 9.

[3] Again, comparing the young victims to the sacrificial lambs of the Temple cult.

[4] Deut. 6: 4. This is the "battle-cry" of the Jewish martyr. According to tradition, these were the last words of the famous first-century Jewish martyr, R. Akiba, who was executed by the Romans. The stories of the so-called "Ten Martyrs" of the Roman period were well known to medieval Jews and recited annually on Yom Kippur (the Day of Atonement). Two versions of the "Ten Martyrs" were current, one in the Babylonian Talmud, Avodah Zara 18ab, and one in the long poem known as "Eleh ezkerah" ("These I shall remember").

[5] See Job 16: 19.

[6] They have been stripped by the crusaders. See Mic. 1: 11, but also the description in Ezek. 16 of God as a lover who finds Israel naked and covered in blood, pledges his love for her, and makes his covenant with her. Like the allusion to the paschal lambs in v.34, this passage would be associated with the Jewish holiday of Passover, as it is included in the Haggadah—the service book for that holiday. For medieval Jews, however, the Passover liturgy and imagery were messianic, i.e., they enacted a dramatic, sacred, narrative in which God's intervention in history and redemption of his people was an event to be anticipated as much as recalled.

[7] Lam. 1: 16.

[8] R. Eliezer alludes here to an ancient legend, which underwent a powerful revival in medieval martyrological laments. According to rabbinic legend, God would not step into history to avenge the deaths of the innocent until his coat was sufficiently saturated with their blood (hence, the "purple" coat). In the writings of the 1096 survivors and their followers, this ancient legend came to justify the suicide-martyrdoms of medieval Ashkenaz: if God's coat was not yet saturated with the blood of the martyrs, the innocent Jews who killed themselves and their families were adding to it, hoping to prod God into action. This motif is eschatological as well as a call for vengeance.

[9] Here again, as in the preceding line, R. Eliezer is "speaking in shorthand" for a complex theological argument. It was possible that Jewish communities would interpret their persecution as a deserved punishment for wrongdoing. Many did, but not in Ashkenaz (Germany). On the contrary, the rabbis would argue, the Jewish communities of Ashkenaz and their holy martyrs were exemplars of piety. Precisely because of their unimpeachable goodness, God had waited to exact from them the cost of earlier transgressions, most notably the biblical sale of Joseph by his brothers for twenty pieces of silver. In exchange for this "silver," therefore, the Rhineland Jews offer the "gold" of their own meritorious lives.

For these the Almighty's pious ones, no ransom has been set.[1]

I will avenge their blood, and I will not clear the guilty.[2]

[So] cry and call out to Your Creator always

Demand the blood of Your servants from those who shed it[3]

Give them, O Lord, what their evil deeds deserve.[4]

Give them broken hearts, let Your curse be upon them.[5]

95

100

5.10 A Westerner in the Holy Land: Stephen of Blois, *Letter to His Wife* (March 1098). Original in Latin.

The crusaders had moderate success in their war against the Muslims. During the long siege of Antioch, which began in October 1097 and was not over until July 1098, one of the crusade leaders, Count Stephen of Blois (d.1102), dictated a letter to his wife, Adela. Full of love, bravado, false claims (e.g., that he was the leader of the "whole expedition"), and pious sentiments, the letter betrays little sign that Stephen was about to desert the army and return home. The letter is a good illustration of what a crusader was supposed to think about the enterprise, whether he did or not.

[Source: *The Crusades: A Reader*, ed. S.J. Allen and Emilie Amt (Toronto: University of Toronto Press, 2003), pp. 63–66, revised from *Translations and Reprints from the Original Sources of European History*, ed. Dana C. Munro, Ser. 1, Vol. 1 (Philadelphia: University of Pennsylvania Department of History, 1895), no. 4, pp. 5–8.]

Count Stephen to Adela, his sweetest and most amiable wife, to his dear children, and to all his vassals of all ranks—his greeting and blessing.

You may be very sure, dearest, that the messenger whom I sent to give you pleasure, left me before Antioch safe and unharmed, and through God's grace in the greatest prosperity. And already at that time, together with all the chosen army of Christ, endowed with great valor by him, we had been continuously advancing for twenty-three weeks toward the home of our Lord Jesus. You may know for certain, my beloved, that of gold, silver and many other kind of riches I now have twice as much as your love had assigned to me when I left you. For all our princes, with the common consent of the whole army, against my own wishes, have made me up to the present time the leader, chief and director of their whole expedition.

You have certainly heard that after the capture of the city of Nicaea we fought a great battle with the perfidious Turks and by God's aid conquered them. Next we

---

[1] It is critical that the survivors believe that repentance and prayer can atone for sin. In the case of the holy martyrs, however, there was no "ransom" (this word can also be translated as "redemption," as in the redemption of slaves) because their exemplary piety had pre-determined that their lives would pay for the sins of earlier generations.

[2] Joel 3: 21.

[3] Echoing the call for vengeance in Ps. 79: 10, "Let the avenging of the outpoured blood of thy servants be known among the nations...." This psalm, too, is a familiar element of the Passover liturgy.

[4] Ps. 28: 4.

[5] See Lam. 3: 65, which the Revised Standard Version of the Bible translates as "dullness of heart." Rashi notes this as a secondary meaning, and perhaps then the sense would be numbness, rather than broken-ness, of heart. His first gloss is "broken-hearted."

FIVE: THE EXPANSION OF EUROPE (C.1050–C.1150)

conquered for the Lord all Romania[1] and afterwards Cappadocia. And we learned that there was a certain Turkish prince Assam, dwelling in Cappadocia; thither we directed our course. All his castles we conquered by force and compelled him to flee to a certain very strong castle situated on a high rock. We also gave the land of that Assam to one of our chiefs and in order that he might conquer the above-mentioned Assam, we left there with him many soldiers of Christ. Thence, continually following the wicked Turks, we drove them through the midst of Armenia, as far as the great river Euphrates. Having left all their baggage and beasts of burden on the bank, they fled across the river into Arabia.

The bolder of the Turkish soldiers, indeed, entering Syria, hastened by forced marches night and day, in order to be able to enter the royal city of Antioch before our approach. The whole army of God, learning this, gave due praise and thanks to the omnipotent Lord. Hastening with great joy to the aforesaid chief city of Antioch, we besieged it and very often had many conflicts there with the Turks; and seven times with the citizens of Antioch and with the innumerable troops coming to its aid, whom we rushed to meet, we fought with the fiercest courage, under the leadership of Christ. And in all these seven battles, by the aid of the Lord God, we conquered and most assuredly killed an innumerable host of them. In those battles, indeed, and in very many attacks made upon the city, many of our brethren and followers were killed and their souls were borne to the joys of paradise.

We found the city of Antioch very extensive, fortified with incredible strength and almost impregnable. In addition, more than 5,000 bold Turkish soldiers had entered the city, not counting the Saracens, Publicans, Arabs, Turcopolitans, Syrians, Armenians and other different races of whom an infinite multitude had gathered together there. In fighting against these enemies of God and of our own we have, by God's grace, endured many sufferings and innumerable evils up to the present time.

Many also have already exhausted all their resources in this very holy passion. Very many of our Franks, indeed, would have met a temporal death from starvation, if the clemency of God and our money had not succored them. Before the above-mentioned city of Antioch indeed, throughout the whole winter we suffered for our Lord Christ from excessive cold and enormous torrents of rain. What some say about the impossibility of bearing the heat of the sun throughout Syria is untrue, for the winter there is very similar to our winter in the west.

When truly Caspian,[2] the emir of Antioch—that is, prince and lord—perceived that he was hard pressed by us, he sent his son Sensodolo[3] by name, to the prince who holds Jerusalem, and to the prince of Calep, Rodoam[4] and to Docap prince of Damascus.[5] He also sent into Arabia for Bolianuth[6] and to Carathania for Hamelnuth.[7] These five emirs with 12,000 picked Turkish horsemen suddenly came to aid the inhabitants of Antioch. We, indeed, ignorant of all this, had sent many of our soldiers away to the cities and fortresses. For there are 165 cities and fortresses throughout Syria which are in our power. But a little before they reached the city, we attacked them at three leagues' distance with 700 soldiers, on a certain plain near the "Iron Bridge."[8] God, however, fought for us, his faithful, against them. For on that day, fighting in the strength that God gives, we conquered them and killed an innumerable multitude—God continually fighting for us—and we also carried back to the army more than two hundred of their heads, in order that the people might rejoice on that account. The emperor of Babylon also sent Saracen messengers to our army with letters, and through these he established peace and concord with us.[9]

I love to tell you, dearest, what happened to us during Lent. Our princes had caused a fortress to be built before a certain gate which was between our camp and the sea. For the Turks, daily issuing from this gate, killed some of our men on their way to the sea. The city of Antioch is about five leagues' distance from the sea. For this rea-

---

1 "Romania" here refers to the Byzantine Empire; at the time Stephen was writing, much of Anatolia had been taken by the Seljuk Turks.

2 This was Yaghi Siyan, appointed emir in 1087.

3 Shams ad-Daulah.

4 This was Ridwan of Aleppo.

5 Docap was Duqaq, Seljuk ruler of Damascus (r.1095–1104).

6 This was Kerbogha, the Turkish governor of Mosul (d.1102).

7 Carathania refers to Khorasan, today in Iran.

8 The "Iron Bridge" crossed the Orontes River, about 7 miles north of Antioch.

9 A reference to an offer of neutrality by the Fatimid caliph of Egypt, who was Shi'a, and thus hostile to the Sunni Turks.

son they sent the excellent Bohemond[1] and Raymond, count of St. Gilles,[2] to the sea with only sixty horsemen, in order that they might bring mariners to aid in this work. When, however, they were returning to us with those mariners, the Turks collected an army, fell suddenly upon our two leaders and forced them to a perilous flight. In that unexpected flight we lost more than 500 of our footsoldiers—to the glory of God. Of our horsemen, however, we lost only two, for certain.

On that same day truly, in order to receive our brethren with joy, and ignorant of their misfortunes, we went out to meet them. When, however, we approached the above-mentioned gate of the city, a mob of horsemen and footsoldiers from Antioch, elated by the victory which they had won, rushed upon us in the same manner. Seeing these, our leaders sent to the camp of the Christians to order all to be ready to follow us into battle. In the meantime our men gathered together and the scattered leaders, namely, Bohemond and Raymond, with the remainder of their army came up and narrated the great misfortune which they had suffered.

Our men, full of fury at these most evil tidings, prepared to die for Christ and, deeply grieved for their brethren, rushed upon the sacrilegious Turks. They, the enemies of God and of us, hastily fled before us and attempted to enter their city. But by God's grace the affair turned out very differently; for, when they wanted to cross a bridge built over the great river Moscholum,[3] we followed them as closely as possible, killed many before they reached the bridge, forced many into the river, all of whom were killed, and we also slew many upon the bridge and very many at the narrow entrance to the gate. I am telling you the truth, my beloved, and you may be very certain that in this battle we killed thirty emirs, that is princes, and, three hundred other Turkish nobles, not counting the remaining Turks and pagans. Indeed, the number of Turks and Saracens killed is reckoned at 1,230, but of ours we did not lose a single man.

While on the following day (Easter) my chaplain Alexander was writing this letter in great haste, a party of our men, lying in wait for the Turks, fought a successful battle with them and killed sixty horsemen, whose heads they brought to the army.

These which I write to you are only a few things, dearest, of the many which we have done, and because I am not able to tell you, dearest, what is in my mind, I charge you to do right, to carefully watch over your land, to do your duty as you ought to your children and your vassals. You will certainly see me just as soon as I can possibly return to you. Farewell.

5.11 The Muslim reaction: Ibn al-Athir, *The First Crusade* (13th c.). Original in Arabic.

From the Muslim point of view, the conquests "for the Lord" that Stephen of Blois spoke about were, to the contrary, entirely ungodly. In the writings of Ibn al-Athir (1160–1233), the key events of the First Crusade—the siege and conquest of Antioch, the capture of Jerusalem—are told with some dispassion, for al-Athir, while drawing on earlier sources, was writing over a century after the events. His inclusion of a poem by al-Abiwardi shows that, just as a new Hebrew literature of martyrdom emerged after the massacre of the Jews, so too an Arabic literature of lamentation accompanied the Muslim experience of the First Crusade. How would you compare his account of the siege of Antioch with that of Stephen of Blois in his letter home, above, p. 271? How would you compare the sentiments in the poem of al-Abiwardi here with those of Raban in his poem above, p. 267?

[Source: *Arab Historians of the Crusades*, ed. and trans. (from Arabic) Francesco Gabrieli, trans. (from Italian) E.J. Costello (Berkeley: University of California Press, 1969), pp. 3–12 (slightly modified).]

---

[1] Bohemond of Taranto (d.1111), leader of the Norman contingent.

[2] Raymond of St. Gilles (d.1105) was the count of Toulouse and an important crusade leader.

[3] The Orontes River; this was another battle at the Iron Bridge.

The Franks Seize Antioch

The power of the Franks first became apparent when in the year 478 [1085][1] they invaded the territories of Islam and took Toledo and other parts of Andalusia, as was mentioned earlier. Then in 484 [1091] they attacked and conquered the island of Sicily[2] and turned their attention to the African coast. Certain of their conquests there were won back again but they had other successes, as you will see.

In 490 [1097] the Franks attacked Syria. This is how it all began: Baldwin, their King,[3] a kinsman of Roger the Frank who had conquered Sicily,[4] assembled a great army and sent word to Roger saying: "I have assembled a great army and now I am on my way to you, to use your bases for my conquest of the African coast. Thus you and I shall become neighbors."

Roger called together his companions and consulted them about these proposals. "This will be a fine thing both for them and for us!" they declared, "for by this means these lands will be converted to the Faith!" At this Roger raised one leg and farted loudly, and swore that it was of more use than their advice. "Why?" "Because if this army comes here it will need quantities of provisions and fleets of ships to transport it to Africa, as well as reinforcements from my own troops. Then, if the Franks succeed in conquering this territory they will take it over and will need provisioning from Sicily. This will cost me my annual profit from the harvest. If they fail they will return here and be an embarrassment to me here in my own domain. As well as all this Tamim[5] will say that I have broken faith with him and violated our treaty, and friendly relations and communications between us will be disrupted. As far as we are concerned, Africa is always there. When we are strong enough we will take it."

He summoned Baldwin's messenger and said to him: "If you have decided to make war on the Muslims your best course will be to free Jerusalem from their rule and thereby win great honor. I am bound by certain promises and treaties of allegiance with the rulers of Africa." So the Franks made ready and set out to attack Syria.

Another story is that the Fatimids of Egypt were afraid when they saw the Seljuks extending their empire through Syria as far as Gaza, until they reached the Egyptian border and Atsiz[6] invaded Egypt itself. They therefore sent to invite the Franks to invade Syria and so protect Egypt from the Muslims.[7] But God knows best.

When the Franks decided to attack Syria they marched east to Constantinople, so that they could cross the straits and advance into Muslim territory by the easier, land route. When they reached Constantinople, the Emperor of the East refused them permission to pass through his domains.[8] He said: "Unless you first promise me Antioch, I shall not allow you to cross into the Muslim empire." His real intention was to incite them to attack the Muslims, for he was convinced that the Turks, whose invincible control over Asia Minor he had observed, would exterminate every one of them. They accepted his conditions and in 490 [1097] they crossed the Bosphorus at Constantinople. Iconium and the rest of the area into which they now advanced belonged to Qilij Arslan ibn Sulaiman ibn Qutlumísh, who barred their way with his troops. They broke through in rajab 490 [July 1097], crossed Cilicia, and finally reached Antioch, which they besieged.

When Yaghi Siyan, the ruler of Antioch, heard of their approach, he was not sure how the Christian people of the city would react, so he made the Muslims go outside the city on their own to dig trenches and the next day sent the Christians out alone to continue the task. When they were ready to return home at the end of the day he refused to allow them. "Antioch is yours," he said, "but you will have to leave it to me until I see what happens between us and the Franks." "Who will protect our children and our wives?" they said. "I shall look after them for you." So they resigned themselves to their fate, and

---

[1] The first date is the Islamic one, the *anno Hejirae* (AH), named after the *hijra* or emigration of Muhammad to Medina; the second date is CE. The year 1 AH is equal to 622 CE.

[2] This date clearly refers to the end of the Norman conquest of Sicily.

[3] No "King Baldwin" led the First Crusade, but several Baldwins were involved in it, and later one of them, Baldwin of Boulogne (d.1118), was crowned King of Jerusalem.

[4] Roger Guiscard (d.1101).

[5] Tamim was the Zirid emir of Tunisia.

[6] Atsiz ibn Uwaq, a Seljuk general.

[7] The Fatimid rulers of Egypt were Shi'ite Muslims.

[8] The "Emperor of the East" refers to Byzantine Emperor Alexius (d.1118).

lived in the Frankish camp for nine months, while the city was under siege.

Yaghi Siyan showed unparalleled courage and wisdom, strength and judgment. If all the Franks who died had survived they would have overrun all the lands of Islam. He protected the families of the Christians in Antioch and would not allow a hair of their heads to be touched.

After the siege had been going on for a long time the Franks made a deal with one of the men who were responsible for the towers. He was a breast-plate maker called Ruzbih whom they bribed with a fortune in money and lands. He worked in the tower that stood over the riverbed, where the river flowed out of the city into the valley. The Franks sealed their pact with the breast-plate maker, God damn him! and made their way to the water-gate. They opened it and entered the city. Another gang of them climbed the tower with ropes. At dawn, when more than 500 of them were in the city and the defenders were worn out after the night watch, they sounded their trumpets. Yaghi Siyan woke up and asked what the noise meant. He was told that trumpets had sounded from the citadel and that it must have been taken. In fact the sound came not from the citadel but from the tower. Panic seized Yaghi Siyan and he opened the city gates and fled in terror, with an escort of thirty pages. His army commander arrived, but when he discovered on enquiry that Yaghi Siyan had fled, he made his escape by another gate. This was of great help to the Franks, for if he had stood firm for an hour, they would have been wiped out. They entered the city by the gates and sacked it, slaughtering all the Muslims they found there. This happened in jumada I [491; April/May 1098].[1] As for Yaghi Siyan, when the sun rose he recovered his self control and realized that his flight had taken him several *farsakh*[2] from the city. He asked his companions where he was, and on hearing that he was four *farsakh* from Antioch he repented of having rushed to safety instead of staying to fight to the death. He began to groan and weep for his desertion of his household and children. Overcome by the violence of his grief he fell fainting from his horse. His companions tried to lift him back into the saddle, but they could not get him to sit up, and so left him for

dead while they escaped. He was at his last gasp when an Armenian shepherd came past, killed him, cut off his head and took it to the Franks at Antioch.

The Franks had written to the rulers of Aleppo and Damascus to say that they had no interest in any cities but those that had once belonged to Byzantium. This was a piece of deceit calculated to dissuade these rulers from going to the help of Antioch.

The Muslim Attack on the Franks, and Its Results

When Qawam ad-Daula Kerbuqa[3] heard that the Franks had taken Antioch he mustered his army and advanced into Syria, where he camped at Marj Dabiq. All the Turkish and Arab forces in Syria rallied to him except for the army from Aleppo. Among his supporters were Duqaq ibn Tutush,[4] the Ata-beg Tughtikin, Janah ad-Daula of Hims, Arslan Tash of Sanjar, Sulaiman ibn Artuq and other less important emirs. When the Franks heard of this they were alarmed and afraid, for their troops were weak and short of food. The Muslims advanced and came face to face with the Franks in front of Antioch. Kerbuqa, thinking that the present crisis would force the Muslims to remain loyal to him, alienated them by his pride and ill-treatment of them. They plotted in secret anger to betray him and desert him in the heat of battle.

After taking Antioch the Franks camped there for twelve days without food. The wealthy ate their horses and the poor ate carrion and leaves from the trees. Their leaders, faced with this situation, wrote to Kerbuqa to ask for safe-conduct through his territory but he refused, saying "You will have to fight your way out." Among the Frankish leaders were Baldwin, Saint-Gilles, Godfrey of Bouillon, the future Count of Edessa, and their leader Bohemond of Antioch. There was also a holy man who had great influence over them, a man of low cunning, who proclaimed that the Messiah had a lance buried in the Qusyan, a great building in Antioch:[5] "And if you find it you will be victorious and if you fail you will surely die." Before saying this he had buried a lance in a certain spot and concealed all trace of it. He exhorted them to fast and

---

[1] June 3rd, according to European sources.

[2] One *farsakh* is about four miles.

[3] This was Kerbogha, the Turkish governor of Mosul (d.1102).

[4] Duqaq was Seljuk ruler of Damascus 1095–1104.

[5] This is a reference to the church of St. Peter in Antioch.

repent for three days, and on the fourth day he led them all to the spot with their soldiers and workmen, who dug everywhere and found the lance as he had told them.[1] Whereupon he cried "Rejoice! For victory is secure." So on the fifth day they left the city in groups of five or six. The Muslims said to Kerbuqa: "You should go up to the city and kill them one by one as they come out; it is easy to pick them off now that they have split up." He replied: "No, wait until they have all come out and then we will kill them." He would not allow them to attack the enemy, and when some Muslims killed a group of Franks, he went himself to forbid such behaviour and prevent its recurrence. When all the Franks had come out and not one was left in Antioch, they began to attack strongly, and the Muslims turned and fled. This was Kerbuqa's fault, first because he had treated the Muslims with such contempt and scorn, and second because he had prevented their killing the Franks. The Muslims were completely routed without striking a single blow or firing a single arrow. The last to flee were Suqman ibn Artuq and Janah ad-Daula, who had been sent to set an ambush. Kerbuqa escaped with them. When the Franks saw this they were afraid that a trap was being set for them, for there had not even been any fighting to flee from, so they dared not follow them. The only Muslims to stand firm were a detachment of warriors from the Holy Land, who fought to acquire merit in God's eyes and to seek martyrdom. The Franks killed them by the thousand and stripped their camp of food and possessions, equipment, horses and arms, with which they re-equipped themselves.

The Franks Take Ma'arrat an-Nu'man

After dealing this blow to the Muslims the Franks marched on Ma'arrat an-Nu'man and besieged it. The inhabitants valiantly defended their city. When the Franks realized the fierce determination and devotion of the defenders they built a wooden tower as high as the city wall and fought from the top of it, but failed to do the Muslims any serious harm. One night a few Muslims were seized with panic and in their demoralized state thought that if they barricaded themselves into one of the town's largest buildings they would be in a better position to defend themselves, so they climbed down from the wall and abandoned the position they were defending. Others saw them and followed their example, leaving another stretch of wall undefended, and gradually, as one group followed another, the whole wall was left unprotected and the Franks scaled it with ladders. Their appearance in the city terrified the Muslims, who shut themselves up in their houses. For three days the slaughter never stopped; the Franks killed more than 100,000 men and took innumerable prisoners. After taking the town the Franks spent six weeks shut up there, then sent an expedition to 'Arqa, which they besieged for four months. Although they breached the wall in many places they failed to storm it. Munqidh, the ruler of Shaizar, made a treaty with them about 'Arqa and they left it to pass on to Hims. Here too the ruler Janah ad-Daula made a treaty with them, and they advanced to Acre by way of an-Nawaqir. However they did not succeed in taking Acre.

The Franks Conquer Jerusalem

Taj ad-Daula Tutush was the Lord of Jerusalem but had given it as a fief to the emir Suqman ibn Artuq the Turcoman. When the Franks defeated the Turks at Antioch the massacre demoralized them, and the Egyptians, who saw that the Turkish armies were being weakened by desertion, besieged Jerusalem under the command of al-Afdal ibn Badr al-Jamali. Inside the city were Artuq's sons, Suqman and Ilghazi, their cousin Sunij and their nephew Yaquti. The Egyptians brought more than forty siege engines to attack Jerusalem and broke down the walls at several points. The inhabitants put up a defence, and the siege and fighting went on for more than six weeks. In the end the Egyptians forced the city to capitulate, in sha'ban 489 [August 1096].[2] Suqman, Ilghazi and their friends were well treated by al-Afdal, who gave them large gifts of money and let them go free. They made for Damascus and then crossed the Euphrates. Suqman settled in Edessa and Ilghazi went on into Iraq. The Egyptian governor of Jerusalem was a certain Iftikhar ad-Daula, who was still there at the time of which we are speaking.[3]

After their vain attempt to take Acre by siege, the Franks moved on to Jerusalem and besieged it for more

---

[1] The finding of the Sacred Lance at the instigation of Peter Bartholomew was a major turning point for the crusade armies. Western sources do not accuse Peter of burying it.

[2] In fact, the Fatimids took Jerusalem in August 1098.

[3] The crusaders' attack on Jerusalem began in June 1099.

than six weeks. They built two towers, one of which, near Sion, the Muslims burnt down, killing everyone inside it. It had scarcely ceased to burn before a messenger arrived to ask for help and to bring the news that the other side of the city had fallen. In fact Jerusalem was taken from the north on the morning of Friday 22 sha'ban 492 [15 July 1099]. The population was put to the sword by the Franks, who pillaged the area for a week. A band of Muslims barricaded themselves into the Oratory of David[1] and fought on for several days. They were granted their lives in return for surrendering. The Franks honored their word, and the group left by night for Ascalon. In the Masjid al-Aqsa the Franks slaughtered more than 70,000 people, among them a large number of Imams and Muslim scholars, devout and ascetic men who had left their homelands to live lives of pious seclusion in the Holy Place. The Franks stripped the Dome of the Rock[2] of more than forty silver candelabra, each of them weighing 3,600 drams, and a great silver lamp weighing forty-four Syrian pounds, as well as a hundred and fifty smaller silver candelabra and more than twenty gold ones, and a great deal more booty. Refugees from Syria reached Baghdad in ramadan, among them the qadi Abu Sa'd al-Harawi. They told the Caliph's ministers a story that wrung their hearts and brought tears to their eyes. On Friday they went to the Cathedral Mosque and begged for help, weeping so that their hearers wept with them as they described the sufferings of the Muslims in that Holy City: the men killed, the women and children taken prisoner, the homes pillaged. Because of the terrible hardships they had suffered, they were allowed to break the fast....

It was the discord between the Muslim princes, as we shall describe, that enabled the Franks to overrun the country. Abu l-Muzaffar al-Abiwardi[3] composed several poems on this subject, in one of which he says:

We have mingled blood with flowing tears, and there
    is no room left in us for pity.

To shed tears is a man's worst weapon when the
    swords stir up the embers of war.
Sons of Islam, behind you are battles in which heads
    rolled at your feet.
Dare you slumber in the blessed shade of safety,
    where life is as soft as an orchard flower?
How can the eye sleep between the lids at a time of
    disasters that would waken any sleeper?   5
While your Syrian brothers can only sleep on the
    backs of their chargers, or in vultures' bellies!
Must the foreigners feed on our ignominy, while you
    trail behind you the train of a pleasant life, like
    men whose world is at peace?
When blood has been spilt, when sweet girls must for
    shame hide their lovely faces in their hands!
When the white swords' points are red with blood,
    and the iron of the brown lances is stained with
    gore!
At the sound of sword hammering on lance young
    children's hair turns white.   10
This is war, and the man who shuns the whirlpool to
    save his life shall grind his teeth in penitence.
This is war, and the infidel's sword is naked in his
    hand, ready to be sheathed again in men's necks
    and skulls.
This is war, and he who lies in the tomb at Medina
    seems to raise his voice and cry: "O sons of
    Hashim![4]
I see my people slow to raise the lance against the
    enemy: I see the Faith resting on feeble pillars.
For fear of death the Muslims are evading the fire of
    battle, refusing to believe that death will surely
    strike them."   15
Must the Arab champions then suffer with resignation,
    while the gallant Persians shut their eyes to
    their dishonor?

---

[1] Known as the Tower of David in European sources, it was in the citadel at Jerusalem (and is not to be confused with the small sanctuary of the same name in the Temple precinct).

[2] The rock from which, Muslims believe, Muhammad ascended into heaven. Over it was built the "Dome of the Rock," the chief Islamic monument in Jerusalem. See Plate 1, p. 230.

[3] An Iraqi poet, writing after the fall of Jerusalem.

[4] The image here is of the Prophet who, from the tomb, raises his voice to rebuke his descendants (the sons of Hashim), that is, the unworthy caliphs whose opposition to the crusades is only half-hearted.

5.12 The crusade in Spain and Portugal: *The Conquest of Lisbon* (1147–1148). Original in Latin.

Many European Catholics considered the *Reconquista* of the Iberian Peninsula another theater of the crusade. In fact, one group of crusaders left for the Second Crusade by way of the North Sea and England. They arrived in Spain in 1147 and were immediately put to work conquering the Muslims at Lisbon. The anonymous author of *The Conquest of Lisbon*, evidently an Anglo-French priest with high connections in both England and Spain, personally participated in the siege. In the excerpt below he records a speech given by Peter, bishop of Oporto, who rallied the army to undertake the assault. Peter's rhetoric was precisely that of the popes and other preachers who had inspired armies for the First and now Second Crusades. The siege was, Peter said, a sacrifice, a pious pilgrimage, and a righteous use of force against robbers and murderers. Although the warriors were on their way to Jerusalem, they could do no better than pause to do God's good work in Spain first. In this text the term "Moors" refers to the first Islamic invaders of Spain, who had by 1147 been settled there for about 400 years, while the "Moabites" are the Almoravids, more recent arrivals from the Maghreb. The passage below begins as the crusaders' ships pulled into the port of Oporto on their way to the Holy Land. What justifications does Peter give for the attack on Lisbon? Compare the ways Peter and Rabbi Eliezer (in the poem above, p. 267) use passages from the Bible to make their points.

[Source: *De expugnatione Lyxbonensi: The Conquest of Lisbon*, trans. Charles Wendell David (New York: Columbia University Press, 2001), pp. 69, 71, 73, 77, 79, 81.]

Early next morning we all gathered from all the ships before the bishop on a hilltop in the cathedral church-yard, for our numbers were so great that the church would not hold us. When silence had been proclaimed of all, the bishop delivered a sermon in Latin, so that it might be made known to everyone in his own language through interpreters. Thus it begins:

"'Blessed is the nation whose God is the Lord, and the people whom he hath chosen for his own inheritance.'[1] And assuredly are they blessed on whom God has by some inestimable privilege conferred both understanding and riches: understanding, in order that they should know the ways of discipline; and riches, in order that they should be able to accomplish that which they piously desire. And truly fortunate is your country which rears such sons, and in such numbers, and unites them in such a unanimous association in the bosom of the mother church. And deservedly is the truth of that highest beatitude accomplished in you, in which it is said, 'Blessed are they that have not seen me and yet have believed.'[2]

"Christ, the mediator between God and men, when he came in person into the world, found very few who were followers of this way and of pure religion; hence, when a certain young man who said that he had fulfilled and kept the law asked him how he could be perfect, he answered, 'Go and sell all,' etc. Weigh carefully what follows: 'He was sad, for he had great possessions.'[3] Oh how great is the righteousness and mercy of our Creator! Oh how great the blindness and the hardness of the human mind! The young man spoke with Truth and about truth, and the voice of Truth was in his ears, and yet, since the hardness of his callous mind was not soft-

---

[1] Ps. 33: 12; Douay Ps. 32: 12.

[2] John 20: 29.

[3] Compare Matt. 19: 16–22; Mark 10: 17–22; Luke 18: 18–23.

ened by the word of Truth, it is not to be wondered at if, when his mind had been emptied of the joy of sincerity, sadness entered in. And what shall we say to all this? How many there are among you here who are richer in possessions than this young man! How many who are higher in the rank of honors! How many who are more fortunate in a prolific stock and a numerous offspring! Yet it is a fact that they have exchanged all their honors and dignities for a blessed pilgrimage in order to obtain from God an eternal reward. The alluring affection of wives, the tender kisses of sucking infants at the breast, the even more delightful pledges of grown-up children, the much desired consolation of relatives and friends— all these they have left behind to follow Christ, retaining only the sweet but torturing memory of their native land. Oh, marvelous are the works of the Savior! Without the urging of any preacher, with the zeal of the law of God in their hearts, led by the impulse of the [Holy] Spirit, they have left all and come hither to us, the sons of the primitive church, through so many perils of lands and seas and bearing the expenses of a long journey. They are the most recent proof of the mysterious power of the cross. Oh, how great is the joy of all those who present a more cheerful face to hardships and pain than we do, we who, alas, are vegetating here in slothful idleness. Verily, 'this is the Lord's doing, and it is marvelous in our eyes.'[1] Verily, dear brothers, you have gone forth without the camp bearing the reproach of the cross;[2] you are seeking God while he may be found,[3] in order that you may lay hold on him. For it seems not strange that men should go unto God, since for the sake of man God also came among men. Even now unto you at the ends of the earth hath the seed of the word of God been borne, for 'a sower went out to sow his seed.' 'The seed is the word of God.'[4] The word of God is God. If it ascend the throne of your mind, your mind is accordingly good, but not without it. These divine seeds have been sown in your bodies, and, if you receive them as good husbandmen, they must needs produce fruit like unto its source and the counterpart of that from which it sprang; but, if you prove bad husbandmen, the result can only be that sterile and swampy ground will destroy the seeds, and afterwards it

will bring forth trash instead of fruit. And may the good God 'increase the fruits of your righteousness.'[5]

"Verily, dear sons, reborn of a new baptism of repentance, you have put on Christ once more, you have received again the garment of innocence to keep it stainless. Take care lest you wander away again after your own lusts....

"We believe it has already become well enough known in the countries from which you come that through the presence of the Moors and Moabites divine vengeance has smitten all Spain with the edge of the sword,[6] and that but few Christians, resident in but a few cities, have been left in it, [and these] under the yoke of a grievous servitude. But these matters, of which a knowledge was brought to you by fame only, now most certainly lie open to your view more clear than day. Alas, that in all Galicia and the kingdom of Aragon and in Numantia, of the numberless cities, castles, villages, and shrines of the saints there should now remain hardly anything to be seen but the signs of ruin and marks of the destruction which has been wrought! Even this city of ours which you see, once among the populous, now reduced to the semblance of an insignificant village, has within our memory repeatedly been despoiled by the Moors. Indeed, but seven years ago it was so oppressed by them that from the church of the blessed Virgin Mary, which according to my poor talents by God's grace I serve, they carried away the insignia, the vestments, the vessels, and all the ecclesiastical ornaments, after they had slain the clergy or made them captive. And from among the citizens and from the surrounding territory as far as the church of St. James the Apostle, they bore away with them into their own country almost innumerable captives, though not without bloodshed on the part of our nobles; and everything that remained they destroyed with fire and sword. Indeed, what does the coast of Spain offer to your view but a kind of memorial of its desolation and the marks of its ruin? How many cities and churches have you discovered to be in ruins upon it, either through your own observation or through information given you by the inhabitants? To you the mother church, as it were with her arms cut off and her face disfigured, appeals for help;

---

[1]   Ps. 118: 23; Douay Ps. 117: 23.

[2]   See Heb. 13: 13.

[3]   See Isa. 55: 6.

[4]   Luke 8: 5, 11.

[5]   2 Cor. 9: 10.

[6]   Compare 2 Kings 10: 25.

she seeks vengeance at your hands for the blood of her sons. She calls to you, verily, she cries aloud. 'Execute vengeance upon the heathen and punishments upon the people.'[1] Therefore, be not seduced by the desire to press on with the journey which you have begun; for the praiseworthy thing is not to have been to Jerusalem, but to have lived a good life while on the way; for you cannot arrive there except through the performance of His works. Verily, it is through good work that anyone deserves to come to a glorious end. Therefore, as worthy rivals [strive together] to raise up the fallen and prostrate church of Spain; reclothe her soiled and disfigured form with the garments of joy and gladness. As worthy sons, look not on the shame of a father nor say to a mother, 'It is a gift by whatsoever thou mightest be profited by me.'[2] Weigh not lightly your duty to your fellow men; for, as St. Ambrose says, 'He who does not ward off an injury from his comrades and brothers, if he can, is as much at fault as he who does the injury.'[3]

"Now, as worthy sons of the mother church, repel force and injury; for in law it happens that whatever anyone does in self-defense he is held to have done lawfully. Brothers, you have laid aside the arms [of violence] by which the property of others is laid waste—concerning which it is said, 'He that strikes with the sword shall perish with the sword,'[4] that is, he who, without the command or consent of any higher or legitimate power, takes up arms against the life of his brothers—but now by God's inspiration you are bearing the arms [of righteousness] by means of which murderers and robbers are condemned, thefts are prevented, acts of adultery are punished, the impious perish from the earth, and parricides are not permitted to live nor sons to act unfilially. Therefore, brothers, take courage with these arms, courage, that is to say, either to defend the fatherland in war against barbarians or to ward off enemies at home, or to defend comrades from robbers; for such courage is full of righteousness. Indeed, such works of vengeance are duties which righteous men perform with a good conscience."

THE NORMAN CONQUEST OF ENGLAND

5.13 The pro-Norman position: William of Jumièges, *The Deeds of the Dukes of the Normans* (*c.*1070). Original in Latin.

Celebrating Duke William of Normandy's victory at Hastings (1066) and justifying his anointment as king of England was William, a monk of Jumièges, a monastery near Rouen founded and supported by the Norman ducal family. William's account was enormously popular, surviving in many manuscripts and inspiring numerous other chroniclers, so that his became the predominant voice in depicting the events of 1066. In the passage below, Duke Harold is the man who was crowned king of England after the death of Edward the Confessor. William of Jumièges portrays this as a usurpation.

[Source: *The Norman Conquest*, ed. and trans. R. Allen Brown (London: Edward Arnold, 1984), pp. 13–15 (slightly modified).]

---

[1] Ps. 149: 7.
[2] Matt. 15: 5.
[3] Ambrose, *De officiis* 1.36.
[4] See Matt. 26: 52.

23 Edward, king of the English,[1] by Divine disposition lacking an heir, had formerly sent Robert [of Jumièges] archbishop of Canterbury to the duke[2] to nominate him as the heir to the kingdom which God had given him. Furthermore he afterward sent to the duke Harold,[3] the greatest of all the earls of his dominions in riches, honor and power, that he should swear fealty to him[4] concerning Edward's crown and confirm it with Christian oaths. Harold, hastening to fulfill this mission, crossed the narrow seas and landed in Ponthieu, where he fell into the hands of Guy, count of Abbeville, who at once took him and his companions prisoner. When the duke heard of this he sent envoys and angrily caused them to be released. Harold remained with the duke for some time, and swore fealty concerning the kingdom with many oaths, before being sent back to the king laden with gifts.

At length king Edward, having completed the term of his fortunate life, departed this world in the year of Our Lord 1066. Whereupon Harold immediately usurped his kingdom, perjured in the fealty which he had sworn to the duke. The duke at once sent envoys to him, exhorting him to withdraw from this madness and keep the faith which he had sworn. But he not only would not listen but caused the whole English people also to be faithless to the duke. Then there appeared in the heavens a comet[5] which, with three long rays, lit up a great part of the southern hemisphere for 15 nights together, foretelling, as many said, a change in a kingdom.

24 Duke William therefore, who himself by right should have been crowned with the royal diadem, seeing Harold daily grow in strength, quickly caused a fleet of 3,000 vessels to be built and anchored at St. Valery (sur-Somme) in Ponthieu, loaded both with splendid horses and the finest warriors, with hauberks[6] and with helmets. Thence with a following wind, sails spread aloft, he crossed the sea and landed at Pevensey, where he at once raised a strongly entrenched castle. Leaving a force of warriors in that, he hastened on to Hastings where he quickly raised another. Harold, hastening to take him by surprise,

raised an immense army of English and, riding through the night, appeared at the place of battle in the morning.

25 The duke however, in case of night attack, ordered his army to stand to arms from dusk to dawn. At daybreak he marshalled the squadrons of his warriors in three divisions and fearlessly advanced against the dread foe. He engaged the enemy at the third hour (9 a.m.) and the carnage continued until nightfall. Harold himself fell in the first shock of battle,[7] pierced with lethal wounds. The English, learning that their king had met his death, despairing of their lives, with night approaching, turned about and sought safety in flight.

26 The victorious duke returned to the battlefield from the pursuit and slaughter of his enemies in the middle of the night. Early next morning, the loot having been collected up from the fallen foe and the corpses of his own cherished men buried, he began his march towards London. It is said that in this battle many thousands of English lost their lives, Christ in them exacting retribution for the violent and unlawful death meted out to Alfred, brother of king Edward [the Confessor]. At length the fortunate war-leader, who was no less protected by good counsel, leaving the highroad, turned away from the city at Wallingford, where he crossed the river and ordered camp to be pitched. Moving on from there he came to London, where an advance-party of warriors on entering the city found a large force of rebels determined to make a vigorous resistance. At once engaging them, the warriors inflicted much sorrow upon London by the death of many of her sons and citizens. At length the Londoners, seeing that they could resist no longer, gave hostages and submitted themselves and all they had to their noble conqueror and hereditary lord. And thus his triumph duly completed in spite of so many perils, our illustrious duke, to whom our inadequate words do not begin to do justice, on Christmas Day, was chosen king by all the magnates both Norman and English, anointed with holy oil by the bishops of the kingdom and crowned with the royal diadem, in the year of Our Lord 1066.

---

[1]   Edward the Confessor, king 1042–1066.

[2]   I.e., Duke William of Normandy. Throughout this document he is the man known as the "duke."

[3]   Harold, son of the powerful Earl Godwine of Wessex, and thus known as Harold Godwineson.

[4]   I.e., Duke William.

[5]   This was, in fact, Halley's comet, which, in its orbit around the sun, passes near the earth about once every 76 years.

[6]   A hauberk is a long tunic made out of chain mail.

[7]   This is unlikely; Harold seems to have fallen at the end of the battle, not at the start.

5.14 The native position: "Florence of Worcester," *Chronicle of Chronicles* (early 12th c.). Original in Latin.

Not everyone agreed that William ruled "by right." Members of the Anglo-Saxon lay and ecclesiastical aristocracy bitterly resented their displacement by William's followers. Monks, too, were unhappy, as William imposed a new regime on English monastic life closely modeled on the elaborate round of collective prayer at Cluny. Submerged opposition may be seen in the *Chronicle of Chronicles*, produced in the early twelfth century by a monk at Worcester who was for a long time thought to be "Florence" but is now thought to have been a different monk, named John. The source is still generally known as "Florence of Worcester." In the passage below the author gives the Anglo-Saxon view of William (whom he calls "count" of Normandy) and the events of 1066. Note that Wulfstan, bishop of Worcester (d.1095), is mentioned in the text as among the few Anglo-Saxon prelates to swear fealty to William. At the same time, Wulfstan was almost certainly the person who commissioned "Florence of Worcester" to write. After analyzing the accounts of "Florence of Worcester" and William of Jumièges (p. 280, above), consider whose side you are on and explain why.

[Source: *English Historical Documents*, vol. 2: 1042–1189, ed. David C. Douglas and George W. Greenaway, 2nd ed. (London: Routledge, 1981), pp. 225–28 (slightly modified).]

1066 On Thursday the vigil of our Lord's Epiphany, in the Fourth Indiction, the pride of the English, the pacific king, Edward, son of King Æthelred, died at London, having reigned over the English twenty-three years six months and seven days. The next day he was buried in kingly style amid the bitter lamentations of all present. After his burial the under-king, Harold, son of Earl Godwine, whom the king had nominated as his successor, was chosen king by the chief magnates of all England; and on the same day Harold was crowned with great ceremony by Aldred, archbishop of York. On taking the helm of the kingdom Harold immediately began to abolish unjust laws and to make good ones; to patronize churches and monasteries; to pay particular reverence to bishops, abbots, monks and clerks; and to show himself pious, humble and affable to all good men. But he treated malefactors with great severity, and gave general orders to his earls, ealdormen, sheriffs and thegns to imprison all thieves, robbers and disturbers of the kingdom. He labored in his own person by sea and by land for the protection of his realm. On April 24th in this year a comet was seen not only in England but, it is said, all over the world, and it shone for seven days with an exceeding brightness. Shortly afterwards Earl Tosti[1] returned from Flanders and landed in the Isle of Wight. After making the islanders pay tribute he departed and went pillaging along the sea-coast until he came to Sandwich. As soon as King Harold who was then at London heard this, he assembled a large fleet and a contingent of horsemen, and prepared himself to go to Sandwich. Tosti, learning of this, took some of the shipmen of that place (whether willing or unwilling) and set his course towards Lindsey, where he burnt many villages and put many men to death. Thereupon Edwin, earl of the Mercians, and Morcar, earl of the Northumbrians, hastened up with an army and expelled them from that part of the country. Afterwards he went to Malcolm, king of Scots, and remained with him during the whole of the summer. Meanwhile, King Harold arrived at Sandwich and waited there for his fleet. When it was assembled, he crossed over with it to the Isle of Wight, and, inasmuch as William, count of the Normans, was preparing to invade England with an army, he watched all the summer and autumn for his coming. In addition he distributed a land

---

[1] Earl Tosti was King Harold's brother. He sided with the Norwegian claimant to the English throne, Harald Hardraada, and the two were killed at the battle of Stamford Bridge on September 25, 1066.

force at suitable points along the sea coast. But about the feast of the Nativity of St. Mary[1] provisions fell short so that the naval and land forces returned home. After this Harald Hardraada, king of the Norwegians and brother of St. Olaf, the king, suddenly arrived at the mouth of the river Tyne with a powerful fleet of more than five hundred large ships. Earl Tosti, according to previous arrangement, joined him with his fleet. Hastening, they entered the Humber and, sailing up the Ouse against the stream, landed at Riccall. On hearing this, King Harold marched with speed towards Northumbria. But before his arrival the two brother earls, Edwin and Morcar, at the head of a large army fought a battle with the Norwegians on the northern bank of the river Ouse near York on Wednesday[2] which was the vigil of the feast of St. Matthew the Apostle. They fought so bravely at the onset that many of the enemy were overthrown; but after a long contest the English were unable to withstand the attacks of the Norwegians and fled with great loss. More were drowned in the river than slain on the field.[3] The Norwegians remained masters of the place of carnage, and having taken one hundred and fifty hostages from York and left there the same number of their own men as hostages they went to their ships. Five days after this, namely on Monday, September 25th, as Harold, king of the English, was coming to York with many thousand well-armed fighting men, he fell in with the Norwegians at a place called Stamford Bridge. He slew King Harald and Earl Tosti with the greater part of their army and gained a complete victory. Nevertheless the battle was stoutly contested. Harold, king of the English, permitted Olaf, the son of the Norwegian king, and Paul, earl of Orkney, who had been sent off with a portion of the army to guard the ships, to return home unmolested with twenty ships and the survivors, but only after they had sworn oaths of submission and had given hostages. In the midst of these things, and when the king might have thought that all his enemies were subdued, it was told him that William, count of the Normans, had arrived with a countless host of horsemen, slingers, archers and footsoldiers, and had brought with him also

powerful help from all parts of Gaul. It was reported that he had landed at Pevensey. Thereupon the king at once, and in great haste, marched with his army to London. Although he well knew that some of the bravest Englishmen had fallen in the two former battles, and that one-half of his army had not yet arrived, he did not hesitate to advance with all speed into Sussex against his enemies. On Saturday, October 22nd,[4] before a third of his army was in order for fighting, he joined battle with them nine miles from Hastings, where his foes had erected a castle. But inasmuch as the English were drawn up in a narrow place, many retired from the ranks, and very few remained true to him. Nevertheless from the third hour of the day until dusk he bravely withstood the enemy, and fought so valiantly and stubbornly in his own defense that the enemy's forces could make hardly any impression. At last, after great slaughter on both sides, about twilight the king, alas, fell. There were slain also Earl Gyrth, and his brother, Earl Leofwine, and nearly all the magnates of England. Then Count William returned with his men to Hastings. Harold reigned nine months and as many days. On hearing of his death earls Edwin and Morcar, who had withdrawn themselves from the conflict, went to London and sent their sister, Queen Edith,[5] to Chester. But Aldred, archbishop of York, and the said earls, with the citizens of London and the shipmen planned to elevate to the throne Prince Edgar, nephew of Edmund Ironside, and promised they would renew the contest under his command.[6] But while many were preparing to go to the fight, the earls withdrew their assistance and returned home with their army. Meanwhile Count William was laying waste Sussex, Kent, Hampshire, Surrey, Middlesex and Hertfordshire, burning villages and slaying their inhabitants until he came to Berkhamsted. There Archbishop Aldred, Wulfstan, bishop of Worcester, Walter, bishop of Hereford, Prince Edgar, the earls Edwin and Morcar, the chief men of London, and many others came to him, and giving hostages they surrendered and swore fealty to him. So he entered into a pact with them, but none the less permitted his men to burn villages and keep on pillaging. But

---

[1] September 8, 1066.

[2] September 20, 1066.

[3] This was the battle of Fulford.

[4] This is an error; the battle of Hastings was fought on St. Calixtus's day, Saturday, October 14, 1066.

[5] She had married King Harold.

[6] Edmund Ironside was a son of King Æthelred II the Unready of England. For Æthelred, see the introduction to his *Law Code* above, p. 222.

when Christmas day drew near, he went to London with his whole army in order that he might be made king. And because Stigand, the primate of all England, was accused by the pope of having obtained the *pallium* in an uncanonical manner, William was anointed king by Aldred, archbishop of York.[1] This was done on Christmas day with great ceremony. Before this (since the archbishop made it

a condition), the king had sworn at the altar of St. Peter the Apostle,[2] and in the presence of the clergy and people, that he would defend the holy churches of God and their ministers, that he would rule justly and with kingly care the whole people placed under him, that he would make and keep right law, and that he would utterly prohibit all spoliation and unrighteous judgments.

5.15 The Conquest depicted: *The Bayeux Tapestry* (end of the 11th c.).

Not a tapestry at all but rather an embroidery, this long (230 feet) and narrow (20 inches) piece of linen tells in uninterrupted pictures, comic-strip style, the story told by William of Jumièges (above, p. 280). It covers Harold's early fealty to Duke William, his usurpation of the crown, and his defeat at the Battle of Hastings. Borders at top and bottom add picturesque details to the pictures, while embroidered labels in Latin identify important people and briefly explain the action. Probably commissioned by Odo of Bayeux, Duke William's half brother and a key figure in the story, the Tapestry is a work of propaganda. The portion shown here depicts Harold taking an oath before William. On the left is Duke William, sitting in authority upon a throne. Behind him are two Norman witnesses. Each of Harold's hands touches a reliquary as he swears an oath recognizing his dependency on William. To his right, pointing a finger at him, is an English witness. Harold's going back on his oath—his perjury—justifies the invasion of England. Might William's conquest have been a dress rehearsal for the First Crusade? What does the visual evidence suggest?

See Plate 14, p. 250, for a color reproduction of *The Bayeux Tapestry*.

(Detail of the Bayeux Tapestry—11th Century. With special permission from the City of Bayeux)

---

[1] A "pallium" was a thin band of white wool worn by the popes in the performance of the liturgy, the use of which could be conferred on approved metropolitan bishops. It was regularly given to the archbishops of Canterbury.

[2] This was Westminster Abbey.

5.16 Exploiting the Conquest: *Domesday Book* (1087). Original in Latin.

In 1086 William ordered a survey of England's counties (or shires) that came to be called "Domesday." Completed in 1087, *Domesday* consists of two books. The first and longer is a well-digested and abbreviated account of the commissioners' reports for all except three counties. The second contains less reworked reports for the remaining counties. The excerpt below, from the first volume, is part of the survey of Huntingdonshire. The excerpt begins with the landholders—the king and his tenants-in-chief—in the shire. There follows an itemization of the properties of each of these landholders along with the geld, or tax, they yielded in the "time of King Edward" (= *tempore Regis Edwardi*, abbreviated TRE). For example, in the time of Edward, the lands at Cotton were assessed at 2 hides when a geld was collected. "There is land for 3 ploughs" was a way to express the acreage: "1 plough" was the theoretical amount of land that could be ploughed each year by a team of 8 oxen. The "demesne" was the lord's share of the land. The villans (sometimes spelled villains or villeins) were fairly well-off peasants, at least in comparison with bordars, who represented the poorest peasants. The whole manor at Cotton was worth 40 shillings, both in 1066 and in 1086, when the royal commissioners were asking their questions. While the tenant-in-chief holding Cotton was the bishop of Lincoln, he gave it to Tursin to "hold," probably in return for knight's service. Compare this document with the *Polyptyque of the Church of Saint Mary of Marseille*, above, p. 107, with regard to their purposes and the things they inventory. Did any women "hold" land?

[Source: *Domesday Book: A Complete Translation*, ed. Ann Williams and G.H. Martin (New York: Penguin, 2002), pp. 551–53 (slightly modified).]

Huntingdonshire

Here Are Entered the Holders of Lands in Huntingdonshire

I KING WILLIAM
II The Bishop of Lincoln
III The Bishop of Coutances
IIII The Abbey of Ely
V The Abbey of Crowland
VI The Abbey of Ramsey
VII The Abbey of Thorney
VIII The Abbey of Peterborough
IX Count Eustace
X The Count of Eu
XI Earl Hugh
XII Walter Giffard
XIII William de Warenne

XIIII Hugh de Bolbec
XV Eudo fitzHubert
XVI Swein of Essex
XVII Roger d'Ivry
XVIII Ernulf de Hesdin
XIX Eustace the sheriff
XX Countess Judith
XXI Gilbert de Ghent
XXII Aubrey de Vere
XXIII William fitzAnsculf
XXIIII Ranulph, Ilger's brother
XXV Robert Fafiton
XXVI William Engaine
XXVII Ralph fitzOsmund
XXVIII Rohais, Richard's wife
XXIX The king's thegns

I. The Land of the King

HURSTINGSTONE HUNDRED[1]

IN HARTFORD King EDWARD had 15 hides of land to the geld. [There is] land for 17 ploughs. Ranulph, Ilger's brother, has custody of it now. There are now 4 ploughs in demesne; and 30 villans and 3 bordars have 8 ploughs. There is a priest and 2 churches, and 2 mills [rendering] £4, and 40 acres of meadow, [and] woodland pasture 1 league long and half a league broad. TRE worth £24; now £15.

NORMANCROSS HUNDRED

In BOTOLPH BRIDGE [in Peterborough] King Edward had 5 hides to the geld. [There is] land for 8 ploughs. There the king now has 1 plough in demesne; and 15 villans having 5 ploughs. There is a priest and a church, and 60 acres of meadow, and 12 acres of woodland pasture in Northamptonshire. TRE worth 100s;[2] now £8 Ranulph has custody of it. In this manor of the king and in other manors the sluice of the Abbot of Thorney has flooded 300 acres of meadow.

In STILTON the king's sokemen [dependents, rather freer than villans] of Normancross [Hundred] have 3 virgates of land to the geld. [There is] land for 2 ploughs, and 5 oxen ploughing.

In ORTON WATERVILLE [in Peterborough] the king has soke [jurisdictional rights, which brought in revenue] over 3½ hides of land in the land of the Abbot of Peterborough which was Godwine's.

TOSELAND HUNDRED

In GREAT GRANSDEN Earl Ælfgar had 8 hides of land to the geld. [There is] land for 15 ploughs. There are now 7 ploughs in demesne; and 24 villans and 8 bordars having 8 ploughs. There is a priest and a church, and 50 acres of meadow and 12 acres of scrubland. From the pasture come 5s4d [5 shillings, 4 pennies]. TRE worth £40; now £30. Ranulph has custody of it.

LEIGHTONSTONE HUNDRED

In ALCONBURY and Great Gidding, a BEREWICK,[3] there were 10 hides to the geld. [There is] land for 20 ploughs. There are now 5 ploughs belonging to the hall, on 2 hides of this land; and 35 villans have 13 ploughs there, and 8

acres of meadow. TRE worth £12; now the same. Ranulph, Ilger's brother, has custody of it.

In KEYSTON King Edward had 4 hides of land to the geld. [There is] land for 12 ploughs. There are now 2 ploughs in demesne; and 24 villans and 8 bordars have 10 ploughs, and [there are] 86 acres of meadow. [There is] woodland, pasture in places, 5 furlongs long and 1½ furlongs broad. TRE, as now, worth £10. Ranulph, Ilger's brother, has custody of it.

In BRAMPTON King Edward had 15 hides to the geld. [There is] land for 15 ploughs. There are now 3 ploughs, and 36 villans and 2 bordars have 14 ploughs. There is a church and a priest and 100 acres of meadow, woodland pasture half a league long and 2 furlongs broad, and 2 mills rendering 100s. TRE, as now, worth £20. Ranulph, Ilger's brother, has custody of it.

In GRAFHAM are 5 hides to the geld. [There is] land for 8 ploughs. The soke [is] in "Leightonstone" Hundred. There 7 sokeman and 17 villans now have 6 ploughs, and 6 acres of meadow. [There is] woodland pasture 1 league long and broad. TRE worth £5: now 10s less.

In GODMANCHESTER King Edward had 14 hides to the geld. [There is] land for 57 ploughs. There are 2 ploughs now in the king's demesne, on 2 hides of this land; and 80 villans and 16 bordars have 24 ploughs. There is a priest and a church, and 3 mills [rendering] 100s, and 160 acres of meadow and 50 acres of woodland pasture. From the pasture 20s. From the meadows 70s. TRE worth £40: now the same, by tale [counting rather than weighing].

II. The Land of the Bishop of Lincoln

TOSELAND HUNDRED

In COTTON the Bishop of Lincoln had 2 hides to the geld. [There is] land for 3 ploughs. There are now 2 ploughs in demesne; and 3 villans having 2 oxen, and [there are] 20 acres of meadow. TRE, as now, worth 40s. Turstin holds it of the bishop.

In GREAT STAUGHTON the Bishop of Lincoln had 6 hides to the geld. [There is] land for 15 ploughs. There are now 2½ ploughs in demesne: and 16 villans and 4 bordars having 8 ploughs. There is a priest and a church, and 24

---

[1] In Anglo-Saxon England the shires (i.e., counties) were divided into hundreds for administrative and other purposes.

[2] "100s" means 100 shillings, or *solidi*.

[3] Berewick = an outlying estate.

acres of meadow and 100 acres of woodland pasture. TRE, as now, worth £10. Eustace holds it of the bishop. The Abbot of Ramsey claims this manor against the bishop.

In DIDDINGTON the Bishop of Lincoln had 2½ hides to the geld. [There is] land for 2 ploughs. There are now 2 ploughs in demesne; and 5 villans having 2 ploughs. There is a church, and 18 acres of meadow, [and] woodland pasture half a league long and a half broad. TRE worth 60s; now 70s. William holds it of the bishop.

In BUCKDEN the Bishop of Lincoln had 20 hides to the geld. [There is] land for 20 ploughs. There are now 5 ploughs in demesne; and 37 villans and 20 bordars having 14 ploughs. There is a church and a priest and 1 mill [rendering] 30s, and 84 acres of meadow, [and] woodland pasture 1 league long and 1 league broad. TRE worth £20; now £16.10s.

NORMANCROSS HUNDRED

In DENTON Godric had 5 hides to the geld. [There is] land for 2 ploughs. There is now 1 plough in demesne; and 10 villans and 2 bordars have 5 ploughs. There is a church and a priest, and 24 acres of meadow and 24 acres of scrubland. TRE worth 100s; now £4. Turstin holds it of the bishop.

In ORTON WATERVILLE [in Peterborough] Leofric had 3 hides and 1 virgate of land to the geld. [There is] land for 2 ploughs and 1 ox. There is now 1 plough in demesne, and 2 villans, and 9 acres of meadow. TRE worth 20s; now 10s. John holds it of the bishop. The king claims the soke of this land.

In STILTON Tovi had 2 hides to the geld. [There is] land for 2 ploughs and 7 oxen. There is now 1 plough in demesne; and 6 villans with 3 ploughs, and 16 acres of meadow and 5 acres of scrubland. TRE, as now, worth 40s. John holds it of the bishop. This land was given to Bishop Wulfwine TRE.

LEIGHTONSTONE HUNDRED

In LEIGHTON BROMSWOLD Thorkil the Dane had 15 hides to the geld. [There is] land for 17 ploughs. There are now 6 ploughs in demesne; and 33 villans and 3 bordars having 10 ploughs, and 1 mill [rendering] 3s. 3 knights hold 3 hides, less 1 virgate, of this land. There they have 3 ploughs, and 3 villans with half a plough. There are 30 acres of meadow and 10 acres of scrubland. TRE, as now, the bishop's demesne was worth £20; the land of the knights, 60s. Earl Waltheof gave this manor in alms to ST. MARY of Lincoln.

In PERTENHALL Alwine had 1 virgate of land to the geld. [There is] land for half a plough. This land is situated

in Bedfordshire but renders geld and service in Huntingdonshire. The king's servants claim this [land] for his use. TRE, as now, worth 5s. William holds it of Bishop Remigius and ploughs it there with his own demesne.

III. *The Land of the Bishop of Coutances*

In HARGRAVE [Northants] Sæmær had 1 virgate of land to the geld. [There is] land for 2 oxen. The SOKE [is] in Leightonstone [Hundred]. The same man himself holds it now of the Bishop of Coutances, and ploughs there with 2 oxen, and has 2 acres of meadow. TRE worth 5s; now the same.

IIII. *The Land of the Abbey of Ely*

[HURSTINGSTONE HUNDRED]

In COLNE the Abbot of Ely had 6 hides to the geld. [There is] land for 6 ploughs, and in demesne [he had] land for 2 ploughs apart from the 6 hides. There are now 2 ploughs in demesne; and 13 villans and 5 bordars having 5 ploughs; and 10 acres of meadow. [There is] woodland pasture a league long and a half broad, and as much marsh. TRE worth £6; now 100s.

In BLUNTISHAM the Abbot of Ely had 6½ hides to the geld. [There is] land for 8 ploughs and, apart from these hides, [he had] land for 2 ploughs in demesne. There are now 2 ploughs in demesne; and 10 villans and 3 bordars with 3 ploughs. There is a priest and a church, and 20 acres of meadow, [and] woodland pasture 1 league long and 4 furlongs broad. TRE, as now, worth 100s.

In SOMERSHAM the Abbot of Ely had 8 hides to the geld. [There is] land for 12 ploughs and, apart from these hides, [he had] land for 2 ploughs in demesne. There are now 2 ploughs in demesne; and 32 villans and 9 bordars having 9 ploughs. There are 3 fishponds [rendering] 8s. and 20 acres of meadow, [and] woodland pasture 1 league long and 7 furlongs broad. TRE worth £7; now £8.

In SPALDWICK the Abbot of Ely had 15 hides to the geld. [There is] land for 15 ploughs. There are now 4 ploughs in demesne, on 5 hides of this land; and 50 villans and 10 bordars having 25 ploughs. There is 1 mill [rendering] 2s, and 160 acres of meadow and 60 acres of woodland pasture. TRE worth £16; now £22.

In Little Catworth, a BEREWICK of Spaldwick, [there are] 4 hides to the geld. [There is] land for 4 ploughs. There 7 villans have 2 ploughs now.

THE TWELFTH-CENTURY RENAISSANCE

5.17 Logic: Peter Abelard, *Glosses on Porphyry* (c.1100). Original in Latin.

While Avicenna (see above, p. 203) could draw directly on the works of Aristotle, only a small sample of those writings was available in the West when the philosopher Peter Abelard (1079–1142) was fired up to use logic as a tool to arrive at truth. Abelard could draw on only a few of Aristotle's works on logic. He had, in addition, a treatise that the Greek neo-Platonist Porphyry (d.c.305) had written as an introduction to Aristotle's *Categories*; it had been commented on and translated into Latin by the late Roman philosopher Boethius (d.524/526). Like Avicenna, whose writings at the time were, however, unknown in the West, Abelard was interested in using and developing logic. He concentrated particularly on understanding the kind of reality possessed by "universals"—the "genera and species" that Aristotle spoke of in his writings on logic. Confronting William of Champeaux (d.1121), a scholar of Abelard's day who believed that universals existed outside the mind as common entities, Abelard formulated a set of arguments against this possibility. In his view, every real being outside the mind was entirely singular and in no way common. So-called universals, he concluded, were nothing more than names. They were common not because they possessed any kind of common being but simply because they could be predicated of many different subjects. We can say, for example, that Peter is human; Paul is human; Mary is human; and so on for countless others. As 'human' is thus predicable of many, it is accordingly a universal. In the selection below, we see some of Abelard's arguments against William's view, which has come to be known as realism. These arguments were apparently so successful that, much to Abelard's delight, they forced William to modify his position.

[Source: *Basic Issues in Medieval Philosophy*, ed. Richard N. Bosley and Martin Tweedale (Peterborough, ON: Broadview Press, 1997), pp. 382–83. Introduced by Blake Dutton.]

It remains now to object to those who say that each individual in that it agrees with others is universal and who allow that the same items are predicated of many, not in that many are essentially them, but because many agree with them. But if to be predicated of many is the same as agreeing with many, how is it that we say an individual is predicated of only one, since there is nothing which agrees with only one thing? Also how does being predicated of many constitute a difference between universal and singular, since Socrates agrees with many in exactly the same way as a human being agrees with many? Certainly a human being insofar as he is a human being and Socrates insofar as he is a human being agrees with others. But neither a human being insofar as he is Socrates nor Socrates insofar as he is Socrates agrees with others.

Therefore, whatever a human being has Socrates also has, and in the same way.

Besides, since human being which is in Socrates and Socrates himself are conceded to be completely the same things, there is no difference of the latter from the former. For no thing is diverse from itself at one and the same time, because whatever it has in itself it has and in entirely the same way. Thus Socrates while white and literate is not in virtue of these diverse from himself, although he has diverse things in himself, for he has both these and in entirely the same way. He is not in one way of himself literate and another way white, just as it is not one thing which of itself is white and another literate.

Also when they say that Socrates and Plato agree in human being, how is that to be understood when it is agreed that all humans differ from each other both in matter and in form? For if Socrates agrees with Plato in the thing which is human being, but no thing is human being other than Socrates himself or some other human being, he will have to agree with Plato either in himself or in someone else. But in himself he is diverse from Plato and likewise in another since he is not the other.

There are those who understand agreeing in human being negatively as if it were said: Socrates does not differ from Plato in human being. But we could also say that he does not differ from Plato in stone since neither is a stone. Then we note no greater agreement between them in human being than in stone, unless perhaps there is an earlier proposition, as though we said: They are human being because they do not differ in human being. But this cannot be since it is altogether false that they do not differ in human being. For if Socrates does not differ

from Plato in the thing which is human being, neither does he in himself. For if he differs in himself from Plato, since he is the thing which is human being, certainly he will differ from Plato in the thing which is human being.

Now that we have given the arguments why things either individually or collectively cannot be called universal, i.e. said to be predicated of many, it remains to ascribe universality to utterances alone. So just as grammarians call some nouns common and others proper, so dialecticians call some simple expressions universal, some particular, i.e. singular. A word is universal when it is apt to be predicated of many individually on account of its establishment, like the noun "human being" which is conjoinable to particular names of humans in virtue of the nature of the subject things to which it is applied. A singular word is one which is predicable of only one, like "Socrates," since it is taken to be a name of only one.

5.18 Medical science: Constantine the African's translation of Johannitius's *Isagoge* (before 1098). Original in Latin.

We know very little about Constantine the African except that he came to Salerno before 1077 and died at the monastery of Monte Cassino (near Rome) between 1085 and 1098—and that his writings initiated a wholesale revival of medical learning in the West! Among his works, excerpted here, was a translation of the *Masa'il fi-tibb* ("Questions about Medicine") by the Nestorian Christian Hunayn ibn Ishaq, who lived in Baghdad in the ninth century. That, in turn, had been a distillation of Galen's *Art of Medicine*, an important medical textbook of the ancient world. Constantine Latinized Hunayn into "Johannitius" and used the Greek word *Isagoge* ("Introduction") in place of Hunayn's Arabic title. The work soon joined other medical texts in translation—some from Hippocrates, the ancient Greek doctor, and others from more recent Byzantine writings—to form the *Articella*, the standard textbook for learning "Greek" medicine in the West. Even after the *Articella* was superseded by other medical texts, the *Isagoge* remained important in medical education, especially at Salerno.

[Source: *Medieval Medicine: A Reader*, ed. Faith Wallis (Toronto: University of Toronto Press, 2010), pp. 140–48 (notes added from glossary). Translated by Faith Wallis.]

1. Medicine is divided into two parts, namely, theory and practice. And of these, theory is further divided into three, that is to say, the consideration of things that are natural, and of things that are non-natural (whence comes knowledge of health, disease, and the neutral

state), and when these natural things depart from the course of nature—that is, when the four humors increase beyond the course of nature; and from what cause and symptoms disease may arise.

[The Naturals[1]]

2. **Natural things.** There are seven natural things: the elements, the mixtures [of qualities], the humors,[2] the members [of the body], the powers,[3] the faculties, and the spirits.[4] Some people add to these four others: namely, the ages of life, the colors, the shapes, and the distinction between male and female.

3. **The four elements.** There are four elements: fire, air, water, and earth. Fire is hot and dry; air is hot and moist; water is cold and moist; earth is cold and dry.

4. **The mixtures [of qualities].** There are nine mixtures [of qualities]. Eight are unequal and one equal. Of the unequal, four are simple: namely, hot, cold, moist, and dry. And from these come four composite [mixtures], namely, hot and moist; hot and dry; cold and moist; cold and dry. [A mixture is] equal when the body is brought to a state where it is sound and intact through a balance [of all four qualities].

5. **The humors.** There are four compound [humors]: blood, phlegm, red bile, and black bile. Blood is hot and moist, phlegm is cold and moist, red bile is hot and dry, black bile is cold and dry.

6. **Phlegm.** There are five varieties of phlegm. There is the salty phlegm, hotter and drier than the other kinds, and tinged with red bile. There is the sweet phlegm, associated with warmth and moisture, and tinged with blood. There is the acrid phlegm, associated with cold and dryness, and tinged with black bile. There is the glassy phlegm, caused by great coldness and coagulation, such as occurs in old people who are destitute of natural warmth. And there is

one which is cold and moist; it has no savor, but retains its characteristic coldness and moisture.

7. **Red bile.** Red bile exists in five kinds. There is red bile which is naturally and substantially clear, and it originates in the liver. There is another which is lemon-colored; it originates from the watery humor phlegm and from red bile, and therefore it is less hot. There is a bile which is like egg yolk, which originates from the mixture of coagulated phlegm and clear red bile, and which is less hot. 8. A fourth kind of bile is green, like *prasius* [*a light green semi-precious stone*] and it generally originates in the stomach; and there is another bile that is green like verdigris and it burns like a poison. It comes from too much adustion[5] and it possesses its own innate heat and innate harmful quality.

9. **Black bile.** Black bile comes in two kinds. One kind is natural—the dregs of the blood and its perturbation, so to speak. It is known from its black color when it flows out of the body from below [through the bowel] or above [from the mouth], and this kind is truly cold and dry. The other kind is unnatural and its origin is from the adustion of the choleric mixture, and so it is rightly called black (that is, black bile). It is hotter and lighter than the abovementioned kind, having in itself a vigorous action and a quality which is extremely deadly and pernicious.

10. **Kinds of members.** There are four kinds of members. Some of them are principal—the foundations and material, so to speak. These are four: the brain, the heart, the liver, and the testicles. Other members serve the aforesaid principal members, such as the nerves, which minister to the brain, and the arteries which minister to the heart, and the veins, which minister to the liver, and the sper-

---

[1] In Arabic-Galenic physiology, the term "naturals" or "things natural" referred to the unalterable "givens" of the physical world and the human body: the elements, complexions, humors, organs, etc.

[2] Depending on the context, the humors were either a) a moisture or fluid of some kind, or b) one of the four bodily fluids deemed to constitute the physiological basis of human life. The classic humors were blood, red bile (also called yellow bile or choler), phlegm, and black bile (or melancholy).

[3] The powers were the natural principles within the body that organized and executed the three major functions of life. Natural powers were nutrition, growth, and reproduction. Spiritual or vital powers were respiration, heat, and emotion. Animal powers were sensation, voluntary motion, and cognition. The powers were manifestations of the spirits.

[4] The spirits were the life forces that organized the principal functions of the body. The natural spirit, whose seat was the liver, controlled nutrition, growth, and reproduction. The vital (or spiritual) spirit, located in the heart, controlled respiration, vital heat, and, to some degree, motion and emotion. The animal spirit, which resided in the brain, governed sensation, voluntary motion, and (in humans) reason.

[5] Adustion is the burning or scorching of a humor caused by excessive heat.

matic vessels, which convey sperm to the testicles. Some members have their own inherent power that governs these members and comprises their quality—for example bones, all the cartilages or the membranes that are between the skin and the flesh, the muscles, fat, and flesh. 11. There are other [members] that originate from their own innate power and derive vigor from the fundamental [members], for example, the stomach, kidneys, intestines, and all the muscles. By their own proper power, these members seek out food and transform it, and they perform their actions according to nature. They also have other inherent powers that derive from the fundamental principal [members]; sensation, life, and voluntary motion come from these.

12. **The powers.** The powers are divided into three. There is the natural power, the spiritual power, and the animal power. One natural power ministers, and another is ministered to. Sometimes it generates, at another time it nourishes, and at another time it feeds. But the power that ministers sometimes seeks out, retains, digests, and expels the things that minister to the feeding power, just as the feeding power ministers to the nourishing power. 13. The other two serve the generating power, one by altering food, the other by re-fashioning it. These differ from one another in that the first power alters, and it serves the generating power through the activity of refashioning. But the operations of the re-fashioning power are five: assimilation, hollowing out, perforating, roughening, and smoothing.

14. **Spiritual power.** From the spiritual power, two others proceed: one is operative and the other is operated upon. The operative power is that which dilates the heart and arteries and then contracts them. From the one which is operated upon come anger, indignation, triumph, domination, astuteness, and anxiety.

15. **Animal power** [*the power of* **animus** *or* *mind*]. Animal power encompasses three things. One animal power arranges, discriminates, and assembles; a second one moves with voluntary motions; the third is called "sensing." From the ordering, discriminating, and assembling power come these things: imagination in the front part

of the head, cognition or reasoning in the brain, and memory in the occipital region. The [second animal] power moves with voluntary motion. And the sensing power consists in sight, hearing, taste, smell, and touch.

16. **Faculties.** Faculties are of two kinds. There are faculties of which each accomplishes on its own what pertains to it, such as appetite for food [which works] by means of heat and dryness; digestion [which works] by means of heat and moisture; retention [which works] by means of cold and dryness; expulsion [which works] by cold and moisture. There are also composite faculties which are composed of two [faculties]: such are desire and expulsion.

17. **Spirit.** The spirits are three. First, the natural spirit takes its origin from the liver; second, the vital spirit, [originating] from the heart; third, the animal spirit, from the brain. Of these three the first is diffused throughout the whole body in the veins which have no pulse; the second is transmitted by the arteries; and the third by the nerves. These are considered in the seventh division of the seven natural things, that is, the spirit.

18. **The ages [of life].**[1] There are four ages; namely, youth, prime of life, maturity, and old age. Adolescence is of a hot and moist complexion;[2] in adolescence the body increases and grows up to the twenty-fifth or thirtieth year. The prime of life follows, which is hot and dry, preserving the body in a perfect state, with no diminution of its powers, and it ends at age thirty-five or forty. After this comes maturity, which is cold and dry, in which the body begins to decline and decrease, although its power is not abated, and it lasts to the fiftieth or sixtieth year. After this comes old age, abounding in phlegmatic humor, cold and wet, in which it is apparent that there is a decline of power, and it ends with the end of life.

22. **The tunics of the eye.** The eye has seven coats and three humors. The first coat is called the retina, the second the secundine, the third the sclera, the fourth the web [*choroid*], the fifth the uveal, the sixth the cornea, and the seventh the conjunctiva. The first humor is the vitreous, the second the crystalline, and the third the albugineous.

---

[1]   Compare these ages, derived from Galen, with those given by Isidore of Seville, above, p. 80.

[2]   Complexion referred to the blending of qualities or humors natural to an individual. It is more or less equivalent to temperament. The term survives today to denote the quality of the skin because pre-modern physicians made an initial determination of the patient's complexion from examining the face.

23. **The colors of the eyes.** The colors of the eyes are four: black, whitish, varied, and grey. Black color is due to a defect of the visual spirit,[1] because it is clouded, or from a lack of crystalline humor, or because most of the crystalline humor remains on the inside [of the eye], or from abundance of the humor that is like the white of an egg [*the albugineous humor*], or because it is perturbed, or from the high quality of the uveal humor. 24. Whitish [color] comes from seven things which are the opposite of those just mentioned, namely from an abundance or clarity of the visual spirit, the magnitude and prominence of the crystalline humor, a reduction in the quantity and clarity of the albugineous humor, and a deficiency in the quality of the uveal humor. Varicolored and grey come about when the circumstances which result in black and white converge. Variable color signifies by its variety that the visual spirit is more abundant and brighter; grey color signifies by its greyness that the visual humor is less abundant, and somewhat darkened.

25. **The qualities of the body.** The qualities of the body are five in number; namely, obesity; thinness; emaciation, atrophy, and the mean state. Fatness of flesh arises from lack of heat and overabundance of moisture; thinness arises from heat and intense dryness. Emaciation arises from cold and intense dryness; atrophy from cold and intense moisture. And a mean state arises from a mean proportion of the humors. These are the shapes of the body.

26. **The difference between male and female.** The male differs from the female because he is hotter and dryer; she, on the contrary, is colder and more moist.

[The Non-naturals[2]]

27. **Changes of air.** Changes of the air come about in five different ways; from the seasons, from the rising and setting of the stars, from the winds, from the lands, and from the vapors that arise from them.

28. **The four seasons of the year.** The seasons of the year are four: spring, which is hot and moist; summer, which is hot and dry; autumn, which is cold and dry; winter, which is cold and moist. The nature of the air is changed by the stars, for when the sun approaches a star or a star the sun, the air becomes hotter. But when they separate the coldness of the air is increased.

29. **The winds.** There are four winds: the east wind, the west wind, the north wind, and the south wind. Of the latter two, the nature of the first [that is, the north wind] is cold and dry and of the second [the south wind] is hot and moist. The two others are of an equal nature, for the east wind is hot and dry and the west wind is cold and moist. The south wind is slightly hotter and moister and the north wind colder and dryer.

32. **Exercise.** Exercise produces change in the body. When it is moderate, it causes a moderate amount of heat; when it is increased, it warms it to a greater degree and afterwards cools it down.

33. **Rest.** Rest produces change in the body; if excessive, it increases cold and moisture.

34. **Baths.** Baths are either of fresh water or of water which is not fresh. A fresh-water bath softens the body, a hot bath warms it, a cold bath cools it. But a fresh-water bath dries out the body, while baths of salt or bitter or sulphurous waters heat and dry the body, and alum or alkaline baths cool and dry it.

35. **Kinds of foods.** Foods are of two kinds. Good food generates good humor and bad food generates an evil humor. That which produces a good humor is that which generates good blood; namely, that which is in a balanced state as regards mixture [of qualities] and operation, such as clean bread [with bran removed] and the flesh of yearling lamb or kid. Bad food brings about the contrary state, for example old bread, or bread with bran in it, or the flesh of old rams or goats. Foods producing good or evil humors are of two kinds, heavy or light. Pork and beef are heavy; chicken or fish are light. And of the latter, the flesh of the middle-sized and more active kinds is better than that of the fatter and scaly varieties.

---

[1]   The visual spirit was, according to one school of thought, a subtle ray emitted by the eye that contacted the object of sight and connected the mind to it.

[2]   The non-naturals referred to environmental and behavioral factors affecting health or disease. These were variable (including air, food and drink, sleep and wakefulness, rest and motion, retention and elimination, and emotional states), and they exerted an influence on the naturals.

36. Some kinds of vegetables produce an evil humor of red bile; for instance, nasturtium, mustard, and garlic. Lentils, cabbage, and the meat of old goat's flesh or beef produce black bile. Suckling pig, lamb, purslane,[1] and mountain spinach beget phlegm. Moreover, heavy foods produce phlegm and black bile, and light food produces red bile; in either case, this is bad.

37. **Kinds of drink.** Drinks are of three kinds. First, there is drink which is nothing but a drink: for example, water. Secondly, there is drink which is both drink and food, such as wine. Thirdly, there is drink which is both of these, and this is the potion [medicine] which is given to counteract the harm from a disease, such as melicrate [*honey and water*], mead, or spiced tonic. Food is useful because it restores the integrity of the body in its proper order. Drink is useful because it distributes food throughout the body. But that kind of drink which we called "potion" is useful because it changes the nature of the body into itself.[2]

[The Contra-naturals[3]]

42. **Fever.** Fever is unnatural heat, exceeding the normal course of nature, proceeding from the heart into the arteries; and it inflicts harm by its effect. There are three kinds: the first is in the spirit, and it is called "ephemeral"; the second arises from humors which putrefy, and it is called "putrid"; and the third damages the members of the body, and this one is called "hectic." Of these, the ephemeral variety arises from incidental causes, and putrid [fever] also, [which arises] from things that are putrefied. 43. Some of these are simple and not combined with others, and these are four. The first is that which arises from the putrid state of the blood, scorching both the interior and exterior of the body; for instance, a continued fever. The second is that which arises from the putrid state of red bile; for instance, tertian fever. The third arises from the putrid state of phlegm; for instance, quotidian fever. And the fourth arises from the putrid state of black bile; this attacks the sick man after an interval of two days, and this is called quartan [fever].[4]

46. **What produces health.** If each of the natural things in the human body preserves its proper nature, health is maintained. If any should lose its proper nature, this will make either for illness or the neutral state. There are three classes of illness: similar, universal, and official. 47. A [similar disease] is one affecting the similar members[5] and they have a similar name when the type of suffering is the same, for example, an *aching* head. An [official disease] befalls official members[6] such as the feet, hands, tongue, or teeth. This takes its name from the infirmity incident to them, for instance podagra [in the foot] or chiragra [in the hand]. And finally there is a universal disease, which is linked to the other two, for example dislocation of the members.

---

1 A succulent plant sometimes cooked as a vegetable or put into salads.

2 That is, the potion transforms the body to conform to the nature of the potion itself.

3 The contra-naturals were all the diseases and trauma that threatened the natural body.

4 Continuous fevers never broke; tertian fevers peaked every third day; quotidian fevers peaked every day; quartan fevers peaked every fourth day.

5 Similar diseases were diseases of bad mixtures of humors or qualities, while similar members referred to homogenous parts. Here Constantine gives the example of aches; they were caused by bad mixtures and could affect similar members—i.e., the head or other body parts—indifferently.

6 An official disease was not of bad mixture but of bad conformation, such as a deformity. Official members were parts of the body with particular, "official," functions, such as the feet, which have the function of walking. Podagra (today called gout of the foot) and chiragra (today known as gout of the hand) were seen as diseases of bad conformation.

5.19 The healing power of stones: Marbode of Rennes, *The Book of Stones* (? late 11th c.). Original in Latin.

Marbode of Rennes (*c*.1035–1123), a native of western France, studied at the cathedral school (the predecessor institution to the university that emerged in the twelfth century) in Angers and later became its director. In 1096, he was elected bishop of Rennes, a city about 80 miles to the northwest of Angers. Marbode was a distinguished author of poetry and prose, writing everything from erotic poetry to biographies of saints. His interest in stones derives from three traditions: scientific writings of the pre-medieval Mediterranean world, books on magic, and Christian commentaries explaining the symbolic meaning of the various stones that appear in the Bible. Framed as a practical guide, the *Liber lapidum* ("The Book of Stones"), excerpted below, is a self-conscious display of erudition. Written in verse and drawing in particular on medical writings, the *Liber* described the properties and powers of sixty different stones. It offered a guide to the medicinal uses of minerals that supplemented similar sorts of writings on plants. The poem was very popular in the Middle Ages, quickly translated into a number of languages, including Hebrew, from the twelfth century forward. However, its purpose is hard to figure out: a prologue claims that the mysteries the poem reveals should be shared with at most three friends but proceeds to claim it will help physicians in general. The entry on green stone begins to catalog its twelve varieties and then gives up in boredom after four or five. Some lines are very difficult to interpret. Other texts are frequently cited, but only vaguely: "it is said…" or "we read…." Some of Marbode's other poetry is openly sarcastic and satirical. Is this poem a scholarly send-up? If so, what exactly is Marbode mocking? In what ways might the *Liber* be considered among the early writings of the twelfth-century Renaissance? Does it seem to reflect some knowledge of the translation into Latin of medical texts by Constantine the African (above, p. 289)?

[Source: John M. Riddle *Marbode of Rennes' De lapidibus: Considered as a Medical Treatise with Text, Commentary, and C. W. King's Translation, Together with Text and Translation of Marbode's Minor Works on Stones*, Sudhoffs Archiv, Zeitschrift für Wissenschaftsgeschichte, Beihefte; Heft 20 (Wiesbaden: Franz Steiner, 1977), pp. 45, 49, 50, 51. Translated by Bruce L. Venarde.]

Green Stone (de smaragdo)[1]

Smaragdus triumphs over every green thing in its
   greenness;[2]
Its types are said to be twelve: twice five plus two.

These include Scythian, Bactrian, and Nile.[3]
There are furthermore those kinds said to appear in veins
   of copper
whose foul nature the metal makes known in its failings.[4]
        5

---

[1] *Smaragdus* eventually came to mean "emerald" exclusively, but in Marbode's time and for many centuries before, it could refer to any number of green stones, including green marble and alabaster.

[2] A possible reference to texts concerning the medicinal uses of plants, which Marbode identifies as effective, but less so than gems, in the prologue to the *Liber lapidum*.

[3] That is, from what are now, roughly, Ukraine, Afghanistan, and Egypt.

[4] This seems to mean that any so-called *smaragdus* associated with the relatively common copper gathered in mines is tainted, an unsurprising association given that copper is quite liable to oxidation that turns it green.

There are also those from Chalcedon,[1] — it is annoying
    to enumerate the others.
Greatest honor and gift belongs to the Scythian stones.
Sarmatians[2] seize it with the help of guardian griffons.[3]
Those whose sight pierces the stone have greater
    reputation,
as do those whose nearby air is touched with its green
    tint of light.   10
Neither sun nor bright light nor shadows change it.
Its surface is flat or its form concave, in the way
that still water copies the face of one looking at it.
Word has it that Nero made this use of mirrors
when he watched the gladiatorial shows.[4]   15
The best structure for these stones is a flat surface.
This stone is said to be useful to those who search out its
    hidden qualities
Because they want to know things in advance, to see into
    the future.
It increases the power of anyone who carries it reverently,
granting the power of persuasion in any sort of matter
    (*causa*).[5]   20
Hung around the neck, *smaragdus* wards off frightful
    fever
and in the same way cures epilepsy.
It improves weakened vision with its gentle greenness —
and is thought able to ward off storms.
It is also said to calm lustful urges.   25
It is refined in its greenness, and its color is perfected
when it is bathed in wine and anointed with green olive
    oil.

Chrysolite (de chrysolito)[6]

Chrysolite flashes with gold and glitters like fire.
It is like the sea, suggesting a certain greenness.
Set in gold, it is said to be an amulet.
It is a strong protection against night frights.
If it is pierced and strung on donkey's hairs,   5
it scares away demons and is thought to upset them.
Thus pierced, it is fit to be worn on the left bicep.
We read that Ethiopians send us this stone.

Beryl (de berillo)[7]

A six-faceted shape makes beryls outstanding.
If not it is made weak, and seems to be pale.
People want its outstanding specimens to be like olive oil
or watery blue; knowledgeable age approves of them.[8]
This stone comes to us from India.   5
It is said to support conjugal love
and to glorify someone who carries it
and to burn the right hand of one who clutches it.
Water in which this stone lies heals weak eyes
and a drink of it relieves belching and labored
    breathing.   10
They say it cures all liver complaints.
The masters have it that there are nine kinds.

Topaz (de topazio)[9]

An island of the same name produces topaz,[10]
precious to the same degree it is rare.

---

[1] Probably a reference to a town in Asia Minor, now Turkey, but green stones with this name are most likely to have come from the south Asian subcontinent.

[2] Likely a reference to peoples of western Scythia (to the north and east of the Black Sea).

[3] The griffon is a legendary creature with the body of a lion and the head and wings of an eagle.

[4] Nero was the infamously self-absorbed and ineffective emperor of Rome, 54–68, also the first to persecute Christians in his empire. This is an especially interesting reference since Nero is said to have demanded thinly cut green stones to guard his eyes against the harsh light of the gladiatorial games; that is, Nero perhaps demanded a distant ancestor of modern sunglasses twelve centuries or so before corrective lenses as we know them appeared in Europe.

[5] The Latin word (*causa*) can refer to legal cases, and that is surely one of its meanings here; in all his writings, Marbode often chose Latin words with what had, by his time, multiple meanings.

[6] The exact identity of this stone is uncertain. It is probably what is now referred to as olivine or peridot.

[7] Here, a simple reference: this is the gem known in our times as beryl.

[8] The meaning of this phrase is somewhat obscure. "Knowledgeable age" seems to refer to the wisdom of elders.

[9] Marbode describes two types, the first of which is probably our modern topaz.

[10] This is an island in the Red Sea, known to the Greeks as Topazion and today as Zabargad or St. John's Island.

It is said to have only two varieties.
The one has a color more like pure gold,
the other is clearer and finer.   5
This same stone is said to help with hemorrhoids

and what is more wondrous, it is thought to feel the
     moon.[1]
It is further claimed to calm raging waves,
and the land of the Arabs, very rich in gems, produces it.

CLUNIACS AND CISTERCIANS

5.20 The Cistercian view: Saint Bernard, *Apologia* (1125). Original in Latin.

An apologia is a defense, not an apology. This one emerged from the growing tension between the competing claims of holiness of the Cistercians and the traditional Bene-dictines, the "black monks," particularly Cluny. Bernard's *Apologia*, written in the guise of a letter to William of Saint-Thierry, the reform-minded abbot of a Cluniac-style house, is modeled on classical rhetorical practice: first you belittle your own side and then you turn to demolish your opponent. The passage below begins at the end of Ber-nard's criticism of his own order, the Cistercians, which, he says, ought not to be overly proud of its own style of life. Then he turns to "certain monks of yours"—he means the black monks in general and the Cluniacs in particular—offering a bit of "friendly" advice. What follows is a scathing satire on what Bernard took to be the excess, luxury, and laxity of the Cluniacs.

[Source: *The Cistercian World: Monastic Writings of the Twelfth Century*, trans. and ed. Pauline Matarasso (New York: Penguin Press, 1993), pp. 47–51, 55–58 (notes modified).]

15 If this is to be a letter, it is time I finished it. I have taken up the pen and rebuked as vigorously as I could those monks of ours whom you, Father, complained of as having criticized your Order,[2] and have cleared myself at the same time, as it behoved me, of any unfounded suspicion on this count. However, I feel bound to add a few remarks. Because I give our own men no quarter, I might seem to condone the behavior of certain monks of yours—conduct which I know you disapprove of, and which all good monks must necessarily avoid. I refer to abuses that, if they exist in the Order, God forbid should ever be a part of it. Certainly no order can contain an element of disorder, for disorder and order are incompat-ible. So long, therefore, as I attack in the men I censure not the Order they belong to but their vices, I shall be seen as arguing for the Order and not against it. In doing this I have no fear of offending those who love the Order. On the contrary they will surely thank me for hunting down what they themselves detest. Any who might be dis-pleased would prove by their refusal to condemn the vices that corrupt it that they did not have the Order's good at heart. To them I make the Gregorian rejoinder: better that scandal erupt than that the truth be abandoned.[3]

---

[1] This may mean that topaz cured or warded off lunacy, i.e., mental afflictions.

[2] Throughout the following passage Bernard plays on the meaning of "order," which can refer to the general and abstract notion of order; the monks of the Benedictine Order—that is, those who adhere to the *Benedictine Rule*—and finally, the monks of the Order of Cluny—that is, those who were juridically under the abbot of Cluny, whether at Cluny or not, or, more loosely, those who belonged to a "Cluniac-style" monastery.

[3] Gregory the Great, *Homilies on Ezechiel* 1.7.5.

Against Superfluity

VIII, 16 It is said, and quite rightly, that the Cluniac way of life was instituted by holy Fathers; anxious that more might find salvation through it, they tempered the Rule to the weak without weakening the Rule. Far be it from me to believe that they recommended or allowed such an array of vanities or superfluities as I see in many religious houses. I wonder indeed how such intemperance in food and drink, in clothing and bedding, in horses and buildings can implant itself among monks. And it is the houses that pursue this course with thoroughgoing zeal, with full-blown lavishness, that are reputed the most pious and the most observant. They go so far as to count frugality avarice, and sobriety austerity, while silence is reputed gloom. Conversely, slackness is called discretion, extravagance liberality, chattering becomes affability, guffawing cheerfulness, soft clothing and rich caparisons are the requirements of simple decency, luxurious bedding is a matter of hygiene, and lavishing these things on one another goes by the name of charity. By such charity is charity destroyed, and this discretion mocks the very word. It is a cruel mercy that kills the soul while cherishing the body. And what sort of charity is it that cares for the flesh and neglects the spirit? What kind of discretion that gives all to the body and nothing to the soul? What kind of mercy that restores the servant and destroys the mistress? Let no one who has shown that sort of mercy hope to obtain the mercy promised in the Gospel by him who is the truth: "Blessed are the merciful, for they shall receive mercy."[1] On the contrary, he can expect the sure and certain punishment which holy Job invoked with the full force of prophecy on those whom I call "cruelly kind": "Let him be no longer remembered, but let him be broken like a sterile tree." The cause—and a sufficient cause for that most proper retribution—follows at once: "He feeds the barren, childless woman and does no good to the widow."[2]

17 Such kindness is obviously disordered and irrational. It is that of the barren and unfruitful flesh, which the Lord tells us profits nothing[3] and Paul says will not inherit the kingdom of God.[4] Intent on satisfying our every whim it pays no heed to the Sage's wise and warning words: "Have mercy on your own soul and you will please God."[5] That is indeed true mercy, and must perforce win mercy, since one pleases God by exercising it. Conversely it is, as I said, not kindness but cruelty, not love but malevolence, not discretion but confusion to feed the barren woman and do no good to the widow—in other words, to pander to the desires of the profitless flesh while giving the soul no help in cultivating the virtues. For the soul is indeed bereaved in this life of her heavenly Bridegroom.[6] Yet she never ceases to conceive by the Holy Spirit and bring forth immortal offspring, which, provided they are nurtured with diligent care, will rightfully be heirs to an incorruptible and heavenly inheritance.[7]

18 Nowadays, however, these abuses are so widespread and so generally accepted that almost everyone acquiesces in them without incurring censure or even blame, though motives differ. Some use material things with such detachment as to incur little or no guilt. Others are moved by simple-mindedness, by charity or by constraint. The first, who do as they are bidden in all simplicity, would be ready to act differently if the bidding were different. The second kind, afraid of dissension in the community, are led, not by their own pleasure, but by their desire to keep the peace. Lastly there are those who are unable to stand out against a hostile majority that vociferously defends such practices as pertaining to the Order and moves swiftly and forcibly to block whatever judicious restrictions or changes the former try to bring in.

IX, 19 Who would have dreamed, in the far beginnings of the monastic order, that monks would have slid into such slackness? What a way we have come from the monks who lived in Anthony's day![8] When one of them paid on occasion a brotherly call on another, both were so avid for the spiritual nourishment they gained from the encounter that they forgot their physical hunger

---

[1] Matt. 5: 7.

[2] Job 24: 20–21.

[3] John 6: 64.

[4] 1 Cor. 15: 50.

[5] Ecclus. 30: 24; the "Sage" is the author of Ecclesiasticus, Jesus son of Sirach.

[6] The "heavenly Bridegroom" is Christ.

[7] See 1 Pet. 1: 4.

[8] A reference to St. Antony, for whose life see above, p. 27.

and would commonly pass the whole day with empty stomachs but with minds replete. And this was the right order of precedence—to give priority to what is nobler in man's make-up; this was real discretion—making greater provision for the more important part; this indeed true charity—to tend with loving care the souls for love of whom Christ died.

As for us, when we come together, to use the Apostle's words, it is not to eat the Lord's supper.[1] There is none who asks for heavenly bread and none who offers it. Never a word about Scripture or salvation. Flippancy, laughter and words on the wind are all we hear. At table our ears are as full of gossip as our mouths of festive fare, and all intent on the former we quite forget to restrain our appetite.

On Meals

20 Meanwhile course after course is brought in. To offset the lack of meat—the only abstinence—the laden fish dishes are doubled. The first selection may have been more than enough for you, but you have only to start on the second to think you have never tasted fish before. Such are the skill and art with which the cooks prepare it all that one can down four or five courses without the first spoiling one's enjoyment of the last, or fullness blunting the appetite. Tickle the palate with unaccustomed seasonings and the familiar start to pall, but exotic relishes will restore it even to its preprandial sharpness; and since variety takes away the sense of surfeit, one is not aware that one's stomach is overburdened. Foodstuffs in their pure and unadulterated state have no appeal, so we mix ingredients pell-mell, scorning the natural nutriments God gave us, and use outlandish savors to stimulate our appetite. That way we can eat far more than we need and still enjoy it.

To give but one example: who could itemize all the ways in which eggs are maltreated? Or describe the pains that are taken to toss them and turn them, soften and harden them, botch them and scotch them, and, finally serve them up fried, baked and stuffed by turns, in conjunction with other foods or on their own? What is the purpose of all this unless it be to titillate a jaded palate? Attention is also lavished on the outward appearance of a dish, which must please the eye as much as it grati-

fies the taste buds, for though a belching stomach may announce that it has had enough, curiosity is never sated. Poor stomach! the eyes feast on color, the palate on flavor, yet the wretched stomach, indifferent to both but forced to accept the lot, is more often oppressed than refreshed as a result.

On Drink

21 What can I say about the drinking of water when even watering one's wine is inadmissible? Naturally all of us, as monks, suffer from a weak stomach, which is why we pay good heed to Paul's advice to use a little wine.[2] It is just that the word *little* gets overlooked, I can't think why. And if only we were content with drinking it plain, albeit undiluted. There are things it is embarrassing to say, though it should be more embarrassing still to do them. If hearing about them brings a blush, it will cost you none to put them right. The fact is that three or four times during the same meal you might see a half-filled cup brought in, so that different wines may be not drunk or drained so much as carried to the nose and lips. The expert palate is quick to discriminate between them and pick out the most potent. And what of the monasteries—and there are said to be some—which regularly serve spiced and honeyed wine in the refectory on major feasts? We are surely not going to say that this is done to nurse weak stomachs? The only reason for it that I can see is to allow deeper drinking, or keener pleasure. But once the wine is flowing through the veins and the whole head is throbbing with it, what else can they do when they get up from table but go and sleep it off? And if you force a monk to get up for vigils before he has digested, you will set him groaning rather than intoning. Having got to bed, it's not the sin of drunkenness they regret if questioned, but not being able to face their food....

On Mounting One's High Horse

Leaving the rest aside, what evidence is there of humility when one solitary abbot travels with a parade of horse-flesh and a retinue of lay-servants that would do honor to two bishops? I swear I have seen an abbot with sixty horses and more in his train. If you saw them passing, you

---

[1] 1 Cor. 11: 20.

[2] 1 Tim. 5: 35.

would take them for lords with dominion over castles and counties, not for fathers of monks and shepherds of souls. Moreover, napery, cups, dishes and candlesticks have to be taken along, together with packs stuffed full, not with ordinary bedding, but with ornate quilts. A man cannot go a dozen miles from home without transporting all his household goods, as though he were going on campaign or crossing the desert where the basic necessities were unobtainable. Surely water for washing one's hands and wine for drinking can be poured from the same jug? Do you think that your lamp will fail to burn and shine[1] unless it stands in your very own candlestick, and a gold or silver one at that? Can you really not sleep except on a chequered blanket and under an imported coverlet? And is a single servant not capable of loading the packhorse, serving the food and making up the bed? And lastly, if we must travel with these retinues of men and beasts, can we not mitigate the evil by taking the necessary provisions instead of battening on[2] our hosts?

On the Place of Pictures, Sculpture, Gold and Silver in Monasteries

XII, 28 But these are minor points. I am coming to the major abuses, so common nowadays as to seem of lesser moment. I pass over the vertiginous height of churches, their extravagant length, their inordinate width and costly finishings. As for the elaborate images that catch the eye and check the devotion of those at prayer within, they put me more in mind of the Jewish rite of old. But let this be: it is all done for the glory of God. But as a monk I ask my fellow monks the question a pagan poet put to pagans: "Tell me, O priests, why is there gold in the holy place?"[3] "Tell me, O poor men," say I—for it is the meaning, not the measure that concerns me—"tell me, O poor men, if poor you are, what is gold doing in the holy place?" It is one thing for bishops but quite another for monks. Bishops are under an obligation both to the wise and the foolish. Where people remain impervious to a purely spiritual stimulus, they use material ornamentation to inspire devotion. But we who have separated ourselves

from the mass, who have relinquished for Christ's sake all the world's beauty and all that it holds precious, we who, to win Christ, count as dung[4] every delight of sight and sound, of smell and taste and touch, whose devotion do we seek to excite with this appeal to the senses? What are we angling for, I should like to know: the admiration of fools, or the offerings of the simple? Or have we perhaps, through mixing with the Gentiles, learned their ways and taken to worshipping their idols?

To put it plainly: suppose that all this is the work of cupidity,[5] which is a form of idol-worship; suppose that the real objective is not yield but takings. You want me to explain? It's an amazing process: the art of scattering money about that it may breed. You spend to gain, and what you pour out returns as a floodtide. A costly and dazzling show of vanities disposes to giving rather than to praying. Thus riches elicit riches, and money brings money in its train, because for some unknown reason the richer a place is seen to be the more freely the offerings pour in. When eyes open wide at gold-cased relics, purses do the same. A beautiful image of a saint is on show: the brighter the colors the holier he or she will be considered. Those who hasten to kiss the image are invited to leave a gift, and wonder more at the beauty than at the holiness they should be venerating.

Instead of crowns one sees in churches nowadays great jewelled wheels bearing a circle of lamps, themselves as good as outshone by the inset gems. Massive tree-like structures, exquisitely wrought, replace the simple candlestick. Here too the precious stones glimmer as brightly as the flames above.

What is this show of splendor intended to produce? Tears of contrition or gasps of admiration? O vanity of vanities,[6] but above all insanity! The walls of the church are ablaze with light and color, while the poor of the Church go hungry. The Church revets its stones in gold and leaves its children naked. The money for feeding the destitute goes to feast the eyes of the rich. The curious find plenty to relish and the starving nothing to eat. As for reverence, what respect do we show for the images of the saints that pattern the floor we tread beneath our feet? People often spit on angels' faces, and their tramp-

---

[1] See John 5: 35.

[2] Thriving at someone else's expense.

[3] Persius, *Satires* 2.69.

[4] See Phil. 3: 8.

[5] I.e., greed.

[6] Eccles. 1: 2.

ing feet pummel the features of the saints. If we care little for the sacred, why not save at least the lovely colors? Why decorate what is soon to be defaced? Why paint what is bound to be trodden on? What good are beautiful pictures where they receive a constant coating of grime? And lastly, what possible bearing can this have on the life of monks, who are poor men and spiritual? And yet perhaps the poet's well-known line can be countered by the Prophet's words: "Lord, I have loved the beauty of your house and the place where your glory dwells."[1] Very well, we will tolerate such doings in our churches on the grounds that they harm only the foolish and the grasping and not the simple-hearted and devout.

29 But what can justify that array of grotesques in the cloister where the brothers do their reading, a fantastic conglomeration of beauty misbegotten and ugliness transmogrified? What place have obscene monkeys, savage lions, unnatural centaurs, manticores, striped tigers, battling knights or hunters sounding their horns? You can see a head with many bodies and a multi-bodied head. Here is a quadruped with a dragon's tail, there an animal's head stuck on a fish. That beast combines the forehand of a horse with the rear half of a goat, this one has the horns in front and the horse's quarters aft. With such a bewildering array of shapes and forms on show, one would sooner read the sculptures than the books, and spend the whole day gawking at this wonderland rather than meditating on the law of God. Ah, Lord! if the folly of it all does not shame us, surely the expense might stick in our throats?

30 This is a rich vein, and there is plenty more to be quarried, but I am prevented from carrying on by my own demanding duties and your imminent departure, Brother Oger.[2] Since I cannot persuade you to stay, and you do not want to leave without this latest little book, I am falling in with your wishes: I am letting you go and shortening my discourse, particularly since a few words spoken in a spirit of conciliation do more good than many that are a cause of scandal. And would to heaven that these few lines do not occasion scandal! I am well aware that in rooting out vices I shall have offended those involved. However, God willing, those I fear I may have exasperated may end up grateful for my strictures if they desist from their evil ways—that is to say, if the rigorists stop carping and the lax prune back their excesses, and if both sides act in conscience according to their own beliefs, without judging the others who hold different views. Those who are able to live austerer lives should neither despise nor copy those who cannot. As for the latter, they should not be led by admiration for their stricter brethren to imitate them injudiciously: just as there is a danger of apostasy when those who have taken a more exacting vow slip into easier ways, not everyone can safely scale the heights.

5.21 The Cluniac view: Peter the Venerable, *Miracles* (mid-1130s–mid-1150s). Original in Latin.

Peter the Venerable (1092/1094–1156) was born into a well-to-do land-owning family. When he became abbot of Cluny in 1122, he inherited a troubled institution, weakened by a revolt against a former abbot and struggling to find a way to deal with hundreds of monasteries that, in one way or another, were dependent on Cluny. After he read Bernard's *Apology*, Peter responded to it in a long letter, rebutting each point. But he also answered the Cistercian critique by regulating the Cluniac lifestyle in his *Statutes* and by praising Cluny in his *Miracles*. Written over the course of the last twenty years of his life, the *Miracles*, which contained mainly stories having to do with Cluny, had

---

[1] Ps. 26: 8; Douay Ps. 25: 8.

[2] Oger was Bernard's friend and a canon at Mont-Saint-Éloi, in the very north of France. The idea that Oger was a sort of messenger, on the point of taking the letter to William of Saint-Thierry, is a literary conceit. In fact, Bernard revised and polished the *Apologia* over the course of many months.

one major purpose: to praise Cluniac monks. For Peter, Cluny was the embodiment of Christian virtue on earth, the "refuge" of sinners, and the model of monastic life. In the passage below he prefaces a discussion of miraculous visions of the dead with thoughts about Cluny's particular excellence. How did his emphasis on Cluny's function as the "asylum of all Christians" implicitly belittle the Cistercians?

[Source: Peter the Venerable, *De miraculis* 1.9, ed. Denise Bouthillier (Turnhout: Brepols, 1988), pp. 35–36. Translated by Barbara H. Rosenwein.]

The monastery of Cluny is the best known in just about the entire world for its religion, the severity of its discipline, the number of its monks, and its complete observance of the monastic rule. It is the individual and collective place of refuge for sinners by means of which much harm has been inflicted on Hell and a great many profits have been gained by the Heavenly Kingdom. There [at Cluny] innumerable multitudes of men, casting off the heavy burdens of the world from their shoulders, have submitted their necks to the sweet yoke of Christ.[1] There the men of every profession, dignity, and order have changed secular arrogance and luxury into the humble and poor life of monks. There the venerable fathers of these churches [i.e., bishops], fleeing the burdens of church affairs, have chosen to live more safely and more quietly and to obey rather than to command. There the unending and turbulent struggle against spiritual evils offers daily palms of victory to the soldiers of Christ. For the inhabitants of this place, who subject their flesh to the spirit by a continuous effort, the Apostle speaks truly: "To live is Christ, and to die is gain."[2]

By the balm of spiritual virtues that is diffused from this place, the whole house of the world has been filled with the odor of ointment,[3] while the ardor of monastic religion, which at one time had grown cold, grew warm again by the example and zeal of these men. Gaul, Germany, and even Britain across the sea bear witness to this; Spain, Italy, and all of Europe acknowledge it. All of them are full of monasteries either newly founded by them or restored from their earlier decline. There [at these Cluniac houses] colleges of monks, like the celestial troops that surround God in their proper orders, with other armies of holy power, apply themselves day and night to divine praises, so that the saying of the prophet may be understood to also be about them: "Blessed are they that dwell in thy house, O Lord: they shall praise thee for ever and ever."[4] But why do I list other parts of the world, since Cluny's fame has reached from our westernmost regions all the way to the East and has not been hidden from even a corner of the Christian world? For Cluny is the vineyard, and its monks are the branches which, truly clinging to the vine, Christ, and pruned by the Father, the gardener, bear much fruit according to the words of the Evangelist.[5] We read about this vineyard in the Psalms: "It stretched forth its branches unto the sea, and its boughs unto the river."[6] Although this was said about the synagogue of the Jews brought out of Egypt, and above all about the present Church, nevertheless nothing prevents us from understanding it also about this Cluniac Church, which is not the least member of the Universal Church.

---

[1] See Matt. 11: 28–30.

[2] Phil.1: 21.

[3] See John 12: 3.

[4] Ps. 84: 4; Douay Ps. 83: 5.

[5] See John 15: 1–17.

[6] Ps. 80: 11; Douay Ps. 79: 12.

TIMELINE FOR CHAPTER FIVE

*C.*1000? *VESTING PRAYERS* ———	**1000**
	1050
*C.*1070 WILLIAM OF JUMIÈGES, *DEEDS OF THE DUKES* ———	——— 1075 HENRY IV, *LETTER TO GREGORY VII*
1076 GREGORY VII, *LETTER TO HERMANN OF METZ* ———	——— 1087 *DOMESDAY BOOK*
? LATE 11TH C. MARBODE OF RENNES, *BOOK OF STONES* ———	——— BEF. 1098 CONSTANTINE'S TRANSLATION OF *ISAGOGE*
1098 STEPHEN OF BLOIS, *LETTER TO HIS WIFE* ———	
END OF 11TH C. *BAYEUX TAPESTRY* ———	**1100**
1106 FREDERICK'S *AGREEMENT WITH COLONISTS* ———	——— *C.*1100 ABELARD, *GLOSSES ON PORPHYRY*
EARLY 12TH C. IBN 'ABDUN, *REGULATIONS* ———	——— EARLY 12TH C. "FLORENCE OF WORCESTER," *CHRONICLE OF CHRONICLES*
1100–50 RABBI ELIEZER, *O GOD, INSOLENT MEN* ———	
1125 ST. BERNARD, *APOLOGIA* ———	——— 1130–33 HENRY I, *LONDON PRIVILEGES*
1130S–1150S PETER THE VENERABLE, *MIRACLES* ———	——— 1147–48 *CONQUEST OF LISBON*
	1150
*C.*1200? *STAR OF CLERICS* ———	**1200**
	——— 13TH C. IBN AL-ATHIR, *FIRST CRUSADE*
	1250
1268 *VISITATION RECORD* ———	
	1300

To test your knowledge and gain deeper understanding of this chapter, please go to www.utphistorymatters.com for Study Questions.

Institutionalizing Aspirations (c.1150–c.1250)

THE CRUSADES CONTINUE

6.1 The Northern Crusades: Helmold, *The Chronicle of the Slavs* (1167–1168). Original in Latin.

Helmold (*c.*1125–after 1177?) was a priest at Bosau, a small town about 25 miles north of Lübeck. Equipped with an adequate education and the zeal to praise the Church by writing about the conversion of the Slavs, he became a major chronicler of the Northern Crusades. The excerpt here begins with his account—some of it prejudiced—of the religious practices of the Slavs. This helped to justify the deflection of part of the Second Crusade to the north.

[Source: Helmold, Priest of Bosau, *The Chronicle of the Slavs*, trans. Francis Joseph Tschan (New York: Columbia University Press, 1935), pp. 158–60, 168–69, 180–81 (notes modified).]

52. *The Rites of the Slavs*

After the death of Cnut, surnamed Laward, the king of the Abodrites, there succeeded to his place Pribislav and Niclot.[1] They divided the principate into two parts so that one governed the country of the Wagiri and the Polabi, the other, that of the Abodrites.[2] These two men were truculent beasts, intensely hostile to the Christians. In those days a variety of idolatrous cults and superstitious aberrations grew strong again throughout all Slavia.[3]

---

1   Here the term "Abodrites," which were strictly speaking one Slavic group, refers to the Slavs as a whole. The "king of the Abodrites" was the man given the title by the emperor in Germany; Cnut Laward, whose father had been king of Denmark, gained it in *c.*1128 and ruled for four years. Pribislav and Niclot were native Slavs, heirs of an earlier ruling dynasty.

2   The Abodrites, Wagiri, and Polabi were various Slavic groups. The Lutici, mentioned below, was another.

3   By Cnut's time, the Slavs in the region had been both evangelized and ruled by Christians, but the Slavs revolted politically and religiously from time to time, as here, upon Cnut's death.

Besides the groves and the household gods in which the country and towns abound, the first and foremost deities are Prove, the god of the land of Oldenburg; Siva, the goddess of the Polabi; Redigast, the god of the land of the Abodrites.[1] To these gods are dedicated priests, sacrificial libations, and a variety of religious rites. When the priest declares, according to the decision of the lot, what solemnities are to be celebrated in honor of the gods, the men, women, and children come together and offer to their deities sacrifices of oxen and sheep, often, also, of Christians with whose blood they say their gods are delighted. After the victim is felled, the priest drinks of its blood in order to render himself more potent in the receiving of oracles. For it is the opinion of many that demons are very easily conjured with blood. After the sacrifices have been consummated according to custom, the populace turns to feasting and entertainment.

The Slavs, too, have a strange delusion. At their feasts and carousals they pass about a bowl over which they utter words, I should not say of consecration but of execration, in the name of the gods—of the good one, as well as of the bad one—professing that all propitious fortune is arranged by the good god, adverse, by the bad god. Hence, also, in their language they call the bad god Diabol, or Zcerneboch, that is, the black god. Among the multiform divinities of the Slavs, however, Svantowit, the god of the land of the Rugiani, stands out as the most distinguished: he is so much more effective in his oracular responses that out of regard for him they think of the others as demigods. On this account they also are accustomed every year to select by lot a Christian whom they sacrifice in his especial honor. To his shrine are sent fixed sums from all the provinces of the Slavs toward defraying the cost of sacrifices. The people are, moreover, actuated by an extraordinary regard for the service of the fane [temple], for they neither lightly indulge in oaths nor suffer the vicinity of the temple to be desecrated even in the face of an enemy. Besides, there has been inborn in the Slavic race a cruelty that knows no satiety, a restlessness that harries the countries lying about them by land and sea. It is hard to tell how many kinds of death they have inflicted on the followers of Christ. They have even torn out the bowels of some and wound them about a stake and have affixed others to crosses in ridicule of the sign of our redemption. It is said that they crucify their most infamous criminals. Those, too, whom they hold for ransom they afflict with such tortures and fetter so tightly that one who does not know their ways would hardly believe....

57. The Building of the City of Lübeck

Matters having been arranged in this manner, Adolph began to rebuild the fortress at Segeberg and girded it with a wall.[2] As the land was without inhabitants, he sent messengers into all parts, namely, to Flanders and Holland, to Utrecht, Westphalia, and Frisia, proclaiming that whosoever were in straits for lack of fields should come with their families and receive a very good land—a spacious land, rich in crops, abounding in fish and flesh and exceeding good pasturage. To the Holzatians and Sturmarians[3] he said:

> Have you not subjugated the land of the Slavs
> and bought it with the blood of your brothers
> and fathers? Why, then, are you the last to enter
> into possession of it? Be the first to go over into
> a delectable land and inhabit it and partake of
> its delights, for the best of it is due you who have
> wrested it from the hands of the enemy.

An innumerable multitude of different peoples rose up at this call and they came with their families and their goods into the land of Wagria to Count Adolph that they might possess the country that he had promised them. First of all the Holzatians received abodes in the safest places to the west in the region of Segeberg along the River Trave, also the Bornhöved open and everything extending from the River Schwale as far as Agrimesov[4]

---

[1] These are Helmold's names, but perhaps "Prove" corresponds to the Slavic diety Perun, the god of weather and fertility.

[2] Adolph II, count of Holstein (r.1131–1164) was granted some Slavic territory by Emperor Lothar; these are the "arrangements" that Helmold refers to.

[3] These were Christian natives of Saxony, and thus neighbors of the Slavs. For an earlier precedent to this sort of colonization, see *Frederick of Hamburg's Agreement with Colonists from Holland*, above, p. 253.

[4] Today Grimmelsberg near Tensebeck, east of Bornhöved.

and the Plöner-See. The Westphalians settled in the region of Dargune, the Hollanders around Eutin, and the Frisians around Süssel. The country about Plön, however, was still uninhabited. Oldenburg and Lütjenburg and the rest of the lands bordering on the sea he gave to the Slavs to live in, and they became tributary to him.

Count Adolph came later to a place called Bucu and found there the wall of an abandoned fortress which Cruto, the tyrant of God, had built, and a very large island, encircled by two rivers. The Trave flows by on one side, the Wakenitz on the other. Each of these streams has swampy and pathless banks. On the side, however, on which the land road runs there is a little hill surmounted by the wall of the fort. When, therefore, the circumspect man saw the advantages of the site and beheld the noble harbor, he began to build there a city. He called it Lübeck, because it was not far from the old port and city that Prince Henry had at one time constructed.[1] He sent messengers to Niclot, prince of the Abodrites, to make friends with him, and by means of gifts drew to himself all men of consequence, to the end that they would all strive to accommodate themselves to him and to bring peace upon his land. Thus the deserted places of the land of Wagria began to be occupied and the number of its inhabitants was multiplied. Vicelin, the priest, too, on the invitation as well as with the assistance of the count, got back the properties about the fortress of Segeberg which the emperor Lothar had in times past given him for the construction of a monastery and for the support of servants of God....

[Helmold turns to the activities of crusade armies: the first went through Hungary to Greece; the second fought the battle of Lisbon (see above, p. 278); a third was directed against the Slavs.]

65. *The Siege of Demmin*

In the meantime the news spread through all Saxony and Westphalia that the Slavs had broken forth and had been the first to engage in war. All that army, signed with the sign of the cross,[2] hastened to descend upon the land of the Slavs and to punish their iniquity. They divided the army and invested two fortresses, Dobin and Demmin, and they "made many engines of war against" them.[3] There came also an army of Danes, and it joined those who were investing Dobin, and the siege waxed. One day, however, those who were shut up noticed that the army of the Danes acted dilatorily—for they are pugnacious at home, unwarlike abroad. Making a sudden sally, they slew many of the Danes and laid them as a thickness for the ground. The Danes, also, could not be aided on account of intervening water. Moved to anger by this, the army pressed the siege more obstinately. The vassals of our duke and of the margrave Albert, however, said to one another: "Is not the land we are devastating our land, and the people we are fighting our people? Why are we, then, found to be our own enemies and the destroyers of our own incomes? Does not this loss fall back on our lords?"

From that day, then, uncertainty of purpose began to seize the army and repeated truces to lighten the investment. As often as the Slavs were beaten in an engagement, the army was held back from pursuing the fugitives and from seizing the stronghold. Finally, when our men were weary, an agreement was made to the effect that the Slavs were to embrace Christianity and to release the Danes whom they held in captivity. Many of them, therefore, falsely received baptism, and they released from captivity all the Danes that were old or not serviceable, retaining the others whom more robust years fitted for work. Thus, that grand expedition broke up with slight gain. The Slavs immediately afterward became worse: they neither respected their baptism nor kept their hands from ravaging the Danes....

---

[1] Prince Henry was a Slavic ruler.

[2] I.e., wearing the symbols of the crusaders.

[3] 1 Macc. 11: 20.

6.2 The Fourth Crusade: Nicetas Choniates, *O City of Byzantium* (*c.*1215). Original in Greek.

Innocent III (1198–1216) called a new crusade in the first year of his reign. But the Fourth Crusade that resulted was deflected from its course; its chief "triumph" was the conquest of Constantinople. Nicetas Choniates (*c.*1150–*c.*1217), an official at the imperial court, wrote a long lament about the event. The excerpt below begins on February 2, 1204, when the crusaders' armies went on a foraging expedition to Philea, on the Black Sea, and on their return encountered the imperial troops.

[Source: *O City of Byzantium, Annals of Niketas Choniates*, trans. Harry J. Magoulias (Detroit: Wayne State University Press, 1984), pp. 312–17 (slightly modified).]

When Baldwin, count of Flanders, ravaged the lands around Philea and collected tribute thence, the emperor marched against him.[1] As the Romans[2] were moving out and the enemy troops returning from their battle array, they met in close combat. The Romans were paralyzed by fear and took to impetuous flight; the emperor, left all alone, very nearly perished, and the icon of the Mother of God, which the Roman emperors reckon as their fellow general, was taken by the enemy.

Not only were these events dreadful, but those that followed were much worse than expected and most calamitous. In the larger ships frightful scaling ladders were once again fabricated and all manner of siege engines were constructed. Banners were flown on top, and huge rewards were offered those who would ascend to give battle.

A measure of the horrors was about to begin, others were already under way, and still others were to follow; the deliberations on amity were disregarded, wholly ignored. Certain wicked Telchines[3] frequently confounded the negotiations. The doge of Venice, Enrico Dandolo, electing to discuss peace terms with the emperor, boarded a trireme and put in at Kosmidion. As soon as the emperor arrived there on horseback, they exchanged views on the peace, paying no heed to anyone else. The demands made by the doge and the remaining chiefs were for the immediate payment of five thousand pounds of gold and certain other conditions which were both galling and unacceptable to those who have tasted freedom and are accustomed to give, not take, commands.[4] These demands were deemed to be heavy Laconian lashes[5] to those for whom the danger of captivity was imminent and universal destruction had erupted, while the doge loudly again declared what had been stated earlier, that the conditions were quite tolerable and not at all burdensome. As the conditions for peace were being negotiated, Latin cavalry forces, suddenly appearing from above, gave free rein to their horses and charged the emperor, who wheeled his horse around, barely escaping the danger, while some of his companions were taken captive. Their inordinate hatred for us and our excessive disagreement with them allowed for no humane feeling between us.

Thereupon [April 8, 1204], the enemy's largest ships, carrying the scaling ladders that had been readied and as many of the siege engines as had been prepared, moved out from the shore, and, like the tilting beam of a scale's

---

[1] Count Baldwin of Flanders (1172–*c.*1205) became the first Latin Emperor at Constantinople in 1204. It was in fact his brother who led the expedition to Philea. The emperor, who had just been crowned, was Alexius V Ducas Murtzuphlus.

[2] I.e., the Byzantines.

[3] The Telchines were spiteful sorcerers with webbed fingers and feet.

[4] The crusaders, and particularly Doge Enrico Dandolo (r.1192–1205), had negotiated with Alexius IV Angelus (r.1203–1204), the rival emperor, to help him and his father, Isaac II Angelus (r.1185–1195, 1203–1204), regain the imperial throne at Constantinople in return for various favors, including nearly 200,000 marks of silver. The crusaders were here asking for about half of that from Murtzuphlus.

[5] A reference to practices at Sparta as recorded in Xenophon, *Republica Lacedaemoniorum* 2.2.

balance, they sailed over to the walls to take up positions at sufficient intervals from one another. They occupied the region extending in a line from the Monastery of Evergetes to the palace in Blachernai, which had been set on fire, the buildings within razed to the ground, thus stripping it of every pleasant spectacle. Observing these maneuvers, Ducas[1] prepared to resist the enemy. He issued instructions for the imperial pavilion to be set up on the hill of the Pantepoptes monastery whence the warships were visible and the actions of those on board were in full view.

As dawn broke on the ninth day of the month of April in the seventh indiction of the year 6712 [April 9, 1204], the warships and dromons[2] approached the walls, and certain courageous warriors climbed the scaling ladders and discharged all manner of missiles against the towers' defenders. All through the day, a battle fraught with groans was waged. The Romans had the upper hand: both the ships carrying the scaling ladders and the dromons transporting the horses were repulsed from the walls they had attacked without success, and many were killed by the stones thrown from the City's engines.

The enemy ceased all hostilities through the next day and the day after, which was the Lord's day [Sunday, April 10–11, 1204]; on the third day, the twelfth day of the month of April, Monday of the sixth week of the Great Lent, they again sailed towards the City and put in along the shore. By midday our forces prevailed, even though the fighting was more intense and furious than on the preceding Friday. Since it was necessary for the queen of cities to put on the slave's yoke, God allowed our jaws to be constrained with bit and curb[3] because all of us, both priest and people, had turned away from him like a stiff-necked and unbridled horse. Two men on one of the scaling ladders nearest the Petria Gate, which was raised with great difficulty opposite the emperor, trusting themselves to fortune, were the first from among their comrades to leap down onto the tower facing them. When they drove off in alarm the Roman auxiliaries on watch, they waved their hands from above as a sign of joy and courage to embolden their countrymen. While they were jumping onto the tower, a knight by the name of Peter entered through the gate situated there. He was deemed most capable of driving in rout all the battalions,[4] for he was nearly nine fathoms tall[5] and wore on his head a helmet fashioned in the shape of a towered city. The noblemen about the emperor and the rest of the troops were unable to gaze upon the front of the helm of a single knight so terrible in form and spectacular in size and took to their customary flight as the efficacious medicine of salvation. Thus, by uniting and fusing into one craven soul, the cowardly thousands, who had the advantage of a high hill, were chased by one man from the fortifications they were meant to defend. When they reached the Golden Gate of the Land walls, they pulled down the new-built wall there, ran forth, and dispersed, deservedly taking the road to perdition and utter destruction. The enemy, now that there was no one to raise a hand against them, ran everywhere and drew the sword against every age and sex. Each did not join with the next man to form a coherent battle array, but all poured out and scattered, since everyone was terrified of them.

That evening the enemy set fire to the eastern sections of the City not far from the Monastery of Evergetes; from there the flames spread to those areas that slope down to the sea and terminate in the vicinity of the Droungarios Gate. After despoiling the emperor's pavilion and taking the palace in Blachernai by assault without difficulty, they set up their general headquarters at the Pantepoptes monastery. The emperor went hither and yon through the City's narrow streets, attempting to rally and mobilize the populace who wandered aimlessly about. Neither were they convinced by his exhortations nor did they yield to his blandishments, but the fiercely shaken aegis filled all with despair.[6]

To continue with the remaining portions of my narrative, the day waned and night came on, and each and every citizen busied himself with removing and burying his possessions. Some chose to leave the City, and whoever was able hastened to save himself.

When Ducas saw that he was gaining nothing,[7] he was fearful lest he be apprehended and put into the jaws of

---

[1] The emperor.

[2] A sailing galley.

[3] See Ps. 32: 9; Douay Ps. 31: 9.

[4] The imagery is from Homer, *Iliad* 5.93–96. This was Peter of Amiens, who led a party of ten knights and sixty sergeants.

[5] The image is from Homer, *Odyssey* 11.312.

[6] See Homer, *Iliad* 15.229–30. The aegis was the shield or breastplate of Zeus and Athena.

[7] See Matt. 27: 24.

the Latins as their dinner or dessert, and he entered the Great Palace. He put on board a small fishing boat the Empress Euphrosyne, Emperor Alexius's wife, and her daughters, one of whom he loved passionately [Eudocia] (for he had frequently engaged in sexual intercourse from the first appearance of hair on his cheek, and he was a proven lecher in bed, having put away two wedded wives[1]) and sailed away from the City [night of April 12–13, 1204], having reigned two months and sixteen days.

When the emperor had fled in this manner, a pair of youths sober and most skillful in matters of warfare, these being Ducas[2] and Lascaris,[3] bearing the same name as the first emperor of our faith [Constantine], contested the captaincy of a tempest-tossed ship, for they viewed the great and celebrated Roman empire as Fortune's prize, depending upon the chance move of a chessman. They entered the Great Church,[4] evenly matched, competing against each other and being compared one with the other, neither one having more or less to offer than the other, and they were deemed equal in the balance because there was no one to examine them and pass judgment.

Receiving the supreme office by lot, Lascaris refused the imperial insignia; escorted by the patriarch to the Milion, he continuously exhorted the assembled populace, cajoling them to put up a resistance. He pressed those who lift from the shoulder and brandish the deadly iron ax, sending them off to the imminent struggle, reminding them that they should not fear destruction any less than the Romans should the Roman empire fall to another nation: no longer would they be paid the ample wages of mercenaries or receive the far-famed gifts of honor of the imperial guard, and their pay in the future would be counted at a hair's worth.[5] Thus did Lascaris, but not a single person from the populace responded to his blandishments. The ax-bearers agreed to fight for wages, deceitfully and cunningly exploiting the height of the danger for monetary gain, and when the Latin battalions clad in full armor made their appearance, they took flight to save themselves [early morning of April 13, 1204].

The enemy, who had expected otherwise, found no one openly venturing into battle or taking up arms to resist; they saw that the way was open before them and everything there for the taking. The narrow streets were clear and the crossroads unobstructed, safe from attack, and advantageous to the enemy. The populace, moved by the hope of propitiating them, had turned out to greet them with crosses and venerable icons of Christ as was customary during festivals of solemn processions. But their disposition was not at all affected by what they saw, nor did their lips break into the slightest smile, nor did the unexpected spectacle transform their grim and frenzied glance and fury into a semblance of cheerfulness. Instead, they plundered with impunity and stripped their victims shamelessly, beginning with their carts. Not only did they rob them of their substance but also the articles consecrated to God; the rest fortified themselves all around with defensive weapons as their horses were roused at the sound of the war trumpet.

What then should I recount first and what last of those things dared at that time by these murderous men? O, the shameful dashing to earth of the venerable icons and the flinging of the relics of the saints, who had suffered for Christ's sake, into defiled places! How horrible it was to see the Divine Body and Blood of Christ poured out and thrown to the ground! These forerunners of Antichrist, chief agents and harbingers of his anticipated ungodly deeds, seized as plunder the precious chalices and patens; some they smashed, taking possession of the ornaments embellishing them, and they set the remaining vessels on their tables to serve as bread dishes and wine goblets. Just as happened long ago, Christ was now disrobed and mocked, his garments were parted, and lots were cast for them by this race; and although his side was not pierced by the lance, yet once more streams of Divine Blood poured to the earth.[6]

The report of the impious acts perpetrated in the Great Church are unwelcome to the ears. The table of sacrifice,[7] fashioned from every kind of precious material and fused by fire into one whole—blended together into a perfection of one multicolored thing of beauty, truly extraordinary and admired by all nations—was broken into pieces and divided among the despoilers, as was the

---

1   See Homer, *Iliad* 1.114.

2   This Constantine Ducas was probably the son of John Angelus Ducas, the uncle of Isaac II and Alexius III.

3   Constantine Lascaris was the brother of the future emperor of Nicaea, Theodore I Lascaris (r.1205–1222).

4   The Great Church was Hagia Sophia, built by Justinian.

5   Homer, *Iliad* 9.378.

6   See John 19: 1–4, 23–24, 34.

7   I.e., the altar.

lot of all the sacred church treasures, countless in number and unsurpassed in beauty. They found it fitting to bring out as so much booty the all-hallowed vessels and furnishings which had been wrought with incomparable elegance and craftsmanship from rare materials. In addition, in order to remove the pure silver which overlay the railing of the bema,[1] the wondrous pulpit and the gates, as well as that which covered a great many other adornments, all of which were plated with gold, they led to the very sanctuary of the temple itself mules and asses with packsaddles; some of these, unable to keep their feet on the smoothly polished marble floors, slipped and were pierced by knives so that the excrement from the bowels and the spilled blood defiled the sacred floor. Moreover, a certain silly woman laden with sins, an attendant of the Erinyes, the handmaid of demons, the workshop of unspeakable spells and reprehensible charms, waxing wanton against Christ, sat upon the synthronon and intoned a song, and then whirled about and kicked up her heels in dance.[2]

It was not that these crimes were committed in this fashion while others were not, or that some acts were more heinous than others, but that the most wicked and impious deeds were perpetrated by all with one accord. Did these madmen, raging thus against the sacred, spare pious matrons and girls of marriageable age or those maidens who, having chosen a life of chastity, were consecrated to God? Above all, it was a difficult and arduous task to mollify the barbarians with entreaties and to dispose them kindly towards us, as they were highly irascible and bilious and unwilling to listen to anything. Everything incited their anger, and they were thought fools and became a laughingstock. He who spoke freely and openly was rebuked, and often the dagger would be drawn against him who expressed a small difference of opinion or who hesitated to carry out their wishes.

The whole head was in pain.[3] There were lamentations and cries of woe and weeping in the narrow ways, wailing at the crossroads, moaning in the temples, outcries of men, screams of women, the taking of captives, and the dragging about, tearing in pieces, and raping of bodies

heretofore sound and whole. They who were bashful of their sex were led about naked, they who were venerable in their old age uttered plaintive cries, and the wealthy were despoiled of their riches. Thus it was in the squares, thus it was on the corners, thus it was in the temples, thus it was in the hiding places; for there was no place that could escape detection or that could offer asylum to those who came streaming in.

O Christ our Emperor, what tribulation and distress of men at that time! The roaring of the sea, the darkening and dimming of the sun, the turning of the moon into blood, the displacement of the stars—did they not foretell in this way the last evils?[4] Indeed, we have seen the abomination of desolation stand in the holy place,[5] rounding off meretricious and petty speeches and other things which were moving definitely, if not altogether, contrariwise to those things deemed by Christians as holy and ennobling the word of faith.

Such then, to make a long story short, were the outrageous crimes committed by the Western armies against the inheritance of Christ. Without showing any feelings of humanity whatsoever, they exacted from all their money and chattel, dwellings and clothing, leaving to them nothing of all their goods. Thus behaved the brazen neck, the haughty spirit, the high brow, the ever-shaved and youthful cheek, the bloodthirsty right hand, the wrathful nostril, the disdainful eye, the insatiable jaw, the hateful heart, the piercing and running speech practically dancing over the lips. More to blame were the learned and wise among men, they who were faithful to their oaths, who loved the truth and hated evil, who were both more pious and just and scrupulous in keeping the commandments of Christ than we "Greeks."[6] Even more culpable were those who had raised the cross to their shoulders, who had time and again sworn by it and the sayings of the Lord to cross over Christian lands without bloodletting, neither turning aside to the right nor inclining to the left, and to take up arms against the Saracens and to stain red their swords in their blood; they who had sacked Jerusalem, and had taken an oath not to marry or to have sexual intercourse with women as long as they carried the cross on their

---

[1] In the Greek Church the area in which the altar is placed is called the bema, or sanctuary.

[2] The Erinyes were the Furies of mythology. The synthronon were the thrones of the bishop and the clergy behind the altar in the sanctuary. The words "waxing wanton against Christ" echoes 1 Tim. 5: 11.

[3] See Isa. 1: 5.

[4] See Matt. 24: 29; Mark 13: 24; Luke 21: 25; Rev. 6: 12.

[5] Matt. 24: 15.

[6] This sentence is meant to be sarcastic, as is shown by the use of the term *Graikoi*, the Latin term of derision for the Byzantines.

shoulders, and who were consecrated to God and commissioned to follow in his footsteps.

In truth, they were exposed as frauds. Seeking to avenge the Holy Sepulcher, they raged openly against Christ and sinned by overturning the Cross with the cross they bore on their backs, not even shuddering to trample on it for the sake of a little gold and silver. By grasping pearls, they rejected Christ, the pearl of great price, scattering among the most accursed of brutes the All-Hallowed One.[1] The sons of Ismael did not behave in this way, for when the Latins overpowered Sion the Latins showed no compassion or kindness to their race. Neither did the Ismaelites neigh after Latin women,[2] nor did they turn the cenotaph[3] of Christ into a common burial place of the fallen, nor did they transform the entranceway of the life-bringing tomb into a passageway leading down into Hades, nor did they replace the Resurrection with the Fall. Rather, they allowed everyone to depart in exchange for the payment of a few gold coins; they took only the ransom money and left to the people all their possessions, even though these numbered more than the grains of sand.[4] Thus the enemies of Christ dealt magnanimously with the Latin infidels, inflicting upon them neither sword, nor fire, nor hunger, nor persecution, nor nakedness, nor bruises, nor constraints. How differently, as we have briefly recounted, the Latins treated us who love Christ and are their fellow believers, guiltless of any wrong against them.

O City, City, eye of all cities, universal boast, supramundane wonder, wet nurse of churches, leader of the faith, guide of Orthodoxy, beloved topic of orations, the abode of every good thing! O City, that hast drunk at the hand of the Lord the cup of his fury![5] O City, consumed by a fire far more drastic than the fire which of old fell upon the Pentapolis![6] "What shall I testify to thee? What shall I compare to thee? The cup of thy destruction is magnified," says Jeremias, who was given to tears as he lamented over ancient Sion.[7] What malevolent powers have desired to have you and taken you to be sifted?[8] What jealous and relentless avenging demons have made a riotous assault upon you in wild revel? If these implacable and crazed suitors neither fashioned a bridal chamber for thee, nor lit a nuptial torch for thee, did they not, however, ignite the coals of destruction?

....

GROUNDING JUSTICE IN ROYAL LAW

6.3 English common law: *The Assize of Clarendon* (1166). Original in Latin.

The Assize of Clarendon reflected the decisions of a meeting at Clarendon in which King Henry II (r.1154–1189) and his leading men determined to reform the English legal system. Building on administrative institutions already in place, they fortified and regularized them, so that royal law would pervade every county and hundred (English local districts). The Assize provided for a regular system of itinerant (traveling) judges with important police powers. Encroaching on older methods of keeping law and order, it called for the widespread use of sworn inquests to bring criminal cases to the attention of royal justices.

---

[1] See Matt. 13: 45 and 7: 6.

[2] See Jer. 5: 8. The "sons of Ismael" refers to the Muslims.

[3] I.e., tomb.

[4] This passage refers to the Muslim retaking of Jerusalem in 1187.

[5] See Isa. 51: 17.

[6] See Wisd. of Sol. 10: 6 and Gen. 19: 24; the Pentapolis refers to the five cities that united to defeat King Chedorlaomer (Gen. 14: 1)—Sodom, Gomorrah, Segor, Adama, and Seboim—only one of which was not destroyed by God.

[7] See Lam. 2: 13.

[8] See Luke 22: 31.

[Source: *English Historical Documents*, vol. 2: 1042–1189, ed. David C. Douglas and George W. Greenaway, 2nd ed. (London and New York: Routledge, 1981), pp. 440–43 (notes modified).]

Here begins the assize of Clarendon made by King Henry II with the assent of the archbishops, bishops, abbots, earls and barons of all England.

1. In the first place the aforesaid King Henry, on the advice of all his barons, for the preservation of peace, and for the maintenance of justice, has decreed that inquiry shall be made throughout the several counties and throughout the several hundreds[1] through twelve of the more lawful men of the hundred and through four of the more lawful men of each vill upon oath that they will speak the truth, whether there be in their hundred or vill any man accused or notoriously suspect of being a robber or murderer or thief, or any who is a receiver of robbers or murderers or thieves, since the lord king has been king.[2] And let the justices inquire into this among themselves and the sheriffs among themselves.[3]

2. And let anyone, who shall be found, on the oath of the aforesaid, accused or notoriously suspect of having been a robber or murderer or thief, or a receiver of them, since the lord king has been king, be taken and put to the ordeal of water,[4] and let him swear that he has not been a robber or murderer or thief, or receiver of them, since the lord king has been king, to the value of 5 shillings, so far as he knows.

3. And if the lord of the man, who has been arrested, or his steward or his vassals shall claim him by pledge within the third day following his capture, let him be released on bail with his chattels[5] until he himself shall stand his trial.

4. And when a robber or murderer or thief or receiver of them has been arrested through the aforesaid oath, if the justices are not about to come speedily enough into the county where they have been taken, let the sheriffs send word to the nearest justice by some well-informed person that they have arrested such men, and the justices shall send back word to the sheriffs informing them where they desire the men to be brought before them; and let the sheriffs bring them before the justices. And together with them let the sheriffs bring from the hundred and the vill, where they have been arrested, two lawful men to bear the record of the county and of the hundred as to why they have been taken, and there before the justice let them stand trial.

5. And in the case of those who have been arrested through the aforesaid oath of this assize, let no man have court or justice or chattels save the lord king in his court in the presence of his justices; and the lord king shall have all their chattels.[6] But in the case of those who have been arrested otherwise than by this oath let it be as is customary and due.

6. And let the sheriffs, who have arrested them, bring them before the justice without any other summons than that they have from him. And when robbers or murderers or thieves, or receivers of them, who have been arrested through the oath or otherwise, are handed over to the sheriffs, let them receive them immediately and without delay.

7. And in the several counties where there are no gaols,[7] let such be made in a borough or some castle of the king at the king's expense and from his wood, if one shall be near, or from some neighboring wood at the oversight of the king's servants, to the end that in them the sheriffs may be able to guard those who shall

---

[1] The inquiries were to be made by the visitation of itinerant justices, also called "justices in eyre."

[2] These "lawful men" on oath are the ancestors of the modern jury. The "vill"—or village—was smaller than the "hundred," hence the jury was smaller. The jury—technically termed a jury of presentment—was asked to "speak the truth" about criminals or suspected criminals in the locality. Here Henry was regularizing an institution (the frankpledge) already in place.

[3] I.e., the sheriff was left with certain powers of criminal jurisdiction beyond the powers of the justices.

[4] Ordeals were meant to show guilt or innocence through "tests," the outcome of which was determined by God's judgment. In the case of the ordeal of water, the accused was immersed in a pool or stream. If the accused immediately rose to the surface, he or she was guilty; if the accused sank, he or she was innocent.

[5] I.e., movable property.

[6] "Court or justice or chattels" refers to the fees generated by the case. By this provision the king claimed the sole rights to the profits of jurisdiction in this new procedure. But, as the next sentence makes clear, profits arising from arrests according to the older system were to be distributed in the old way.

[7] I.e., jails.

be arrested by the officials accustomed to do this, or by their servants.

8. Moreover, the lord king wills that all shall come to the county courts to take this oath, so that none shall remain behind on account of any franchise which he has, or any court or soke,[1] which he may have, but that they shall come to take this oath.

9. And let there be no one within his castle or without, nor even in the honor of Wallingford, who shall forbid the sheriffs to enter into his court or his land to take the view of frankpledge and to see that all are under pledges; and let them be sent before the sheriffs under free pledge.[2]

10. And in cities or boroughs let no one hold men or receive them into his house or on his land or in his soke, whom he will not take in hand to produce before the justice, should they be required; or else let them be in frankpledge.

11. And let there be none in a city or a borough or a castle or without it, nor even in the honor of Wallingford, who shall forbid the sheriffs to enter into their land or their soke to arrest those who have been accused or are notoriously suspect of being robbers or murderers or thieves or receivers of them, or outlaws, or persons charged concerning the forest;[3] but the king commands that they shall aid the sheriffs to capture them.

12. And if anyone shall be taken in possession of the spoils of robbery or theft, if he be of evil repute and bears an evil testimony from the public and has no warrant, let him have no law.[4] And if he has not been notoriously suspect on account of the goods in his possession, let him go to the ordeal of water.

13. And if anyone shall confess to robbery or murder or theft, or to harboring those who have committed them, in the presence of the lawful men or in the hundred court, and afterwards he wish to deny it, let him not have his law.[5]

14. Moreover, the lord king wills that those who shall be tried by the law and absolved by the law, if they have been of ill repute and openly and disgracefully spoken of by the testimony of many and that of the lawful men, shall abjure the king's lands, so that within eight days they shall cross the sea, unless the wind detains them; and with the first wind they shall have afterwards they shall cross the sea, and they shall not return to England again except by the mercy of the lord king; and both now, and if they return, let them be outlawed; and on their return let them be seized as outlaws.[6]

15. And the lord king forbids that any vagabond, that is, a wanderer or unknown person, shall be given shelter anywhere except in a borough, and even there he shall not be given shelter longer than one night, unless he become sick there, or his horse, so that he can show an evident excuse.

16. And if he shall remain there longer than one night, let him be arrested and held until his lord shall come to give surety for him, or until he himself shall procure safe pledges; and let him likewise be arrested who gave him shelter.[7]

17. And if any sheriff shall send word to another sheriff that men have fled from his county into another county, on account of robbery or murder or theft or the harboring of them, or on account of outlawry or of a charge concerning the king's forest, let him (the second sheriff) arrest them; and even if he knows of himself or through others that such men have fled into his county, let him arrest them and guard them until he has taken safe pledges for them.

18. And let all the sheriffs cause a record to be made of all fugitives who have fled from their counties; and let them do this before the county courts and carry the names of those written therein before the justices, when next they come to them, so that these men may be sought

---

[1] Franchises, courts, and sokes were private jurisdictions, often granted by privilege or charter. This clause was aimed at limiting the powers of private courts.

[2] This clause overrode guarantees of privilege—often granted by kings—against the entry of public officials into private jurisdictions. The frankpledge was a group of men pledged not to commit any offenses and to produce any of their number who did so. (Another name for this group was a "tithing.") Most ordinary freemen were part of one. The "view of frankpledge" was customarily taken twice a year by the sheriff to verify membership in the frankpledge and to hear of any of its members' criminal activities.

[3] The king claimed special jurisdiction over forests.

[4] I.e., criminals taken red-handed and without "warrant" (or surety)—namely, a person to guarantee their court appearance—were to be punished without trial.

[5] I.e., the case was not to be tried after the accused had pleaded guilty to the offense. In all these clauses the particular importance attached both to the past record of the accused and to local opinion concerning him should be noted.

[6] This is a new feature in criminal law administration: even those who have been acquitted on a particular indictment are not regarded as free and lawful persons if their past record is shady, and they are to suffer exile.

[7] Sureties and "safe pledges" are all ways to insure that the person will appear in court if allowed to go free.

throughout England, and their chattels may be seized for the needs of the king.

19. And the lord king wills that from the time the sheriffs shall receive the summons of the itinerant justices to present themselves before them, together with the men of the county, they shall assemble them and make inquiry for all who have newly come into their counties since this assize; and they shall send them away under pledge to attend before the justices, or they shall keep them in custody until the justices come to them, and then they shall present them before the justices.

20. Moreover, the lord king forbids monks or canons or any religious house to receive any men of the lower orders as a monk or a canon or a brother, until it be known of what reputation he is, unless he shall be sick unto death.

21. Moreover, the lord king forbids anyone in all England to receive in his land or his soke or in a house under him any one of that sect of renegades who were branded and excommunicated at Oxford.[1] And if anyone shall so receive them, he himself shall be at the mercy of the lord king, and the house in which they have dwelt shall be carried outside the village and burnt. And each sheriff shall swear an oath that he will observe this, and shall cause all his officers to swear this, and also the stewards of the barons and all knights and freeholders of the counties.

22. And the lord king wills that this assize shall be kept in his realm so long as it shall please him.

6.4 English litigation on the ground: *The Costs of Richard of Anstey's Lawsuit* (1158–1163). Original in Latin.

The complexity and expense of litigating in twelfth-century England is well illustrated by the account of Richard of Anstey's suit to recover lands bequeathed to him by his uncle, William "de Secqueville." The lands were being held by Mabel "de Francheville," William's daughter by a second marriage. That marriage had been condemned as "null and void" by the papacy, a verdict that was pronounced in an ecclesiastical court in London. Richard's claim to the land was based on that decision. Nevertheless, as the following account makes clear, he had to travel to many places in order to obtain various writs (orders), attend many hearings, and spend a lot of money before his case was decided.

[Source: *English Historical Documents*, vol. 2: 1042–1189, ed. David C. Douglas and George W. Greenaway, 2nd ed. (London and New York: Routledge, 1981), pp. 488–90 (notes modified).]

These are the expenses which I, Richard of Anstey, incurred in gaining possession of the land of my uncle. First of all I sent one of my men to Normandy to obtain the king's writ to put my adversaries on trial. This man spent half a mark on the journey. When my messenger had brought me the writ I took it to Salisbury that it might be sent back sealed with the queen's seal; in this journey I spent 2 silver marks.

On my return thence, hearing that Ralph Brito[2] was obliged to cross the Channel, I followed him as far as Southampton to speak with him and to ask him to convey the king's writ to the archbishop for me, because I knew that the suit ought to be transferred to the archbishop's court. In that journey I spent 22 shillings 7 pence, and lost a palfrey,[3] which I had bought for 15 shillings. Returning thence with the queen's writ, I went to Ongar and handed the writ to Richard of Lucé.[4] And when he had given me audience, he appointed a day, the

---

[1] A reference to the Cathars.

[2] Ralph Brito was one of Henry II's barons.

[3] I.e., a saddle horse.

[4] Richard of Lucé was the king's justiciar. At this time, the justiciar was the king's chief justice minister, but very soon, in the 1170s, he would take on greater powers, becoming a kind of substitute king when the king was not present.

eve of St. Andrew,[1] for my suit to be heard at Northampton. Before that day arrived, I sent Nicholas, my clerk, for Geoffrey of Troisgots and Alfreda, his sister, because she was my uncle's widow. Them he found at Burnham in Norfolk. This journey cost me 15 shillings and the loss of a packhorse, which I had bought for 9 shillings.

On my return I went with my friends and helpers to Northampton to plead my case, and on that journey I spent 54 shillings. There another day was appointed me at Southampton a fortnight later; on that journey I spent 57 shillings and lost a packhorse worth 12 shillings. After this came Ralph Brito from Normandy bringing me the king's writ transferring the suit to the archbishop's court. This writ I took to Archbishop Theobald, whom I found at Winchester, and on that journey I spent 25 shillings 4 pence. Then the archbishop appointed me the feast of St. Vincent, and the case was heard at Lambeth. There the case was adjourned until St. Valentine's day.[2] On this journey I spent 8 shillings 6 pence, and the case was heard at Maidstone.

Here the feast of Saints Perpetua and Felicitas[3] was appointed me. But before that day arrived I went to the bishop of Winchester to ask him to bear witness to the decree of nullity which had been previously decreed in a synod at London.[4] This journey cost me a silver mark. The bishop having agreed to testify, I went on the appointed day all prepared to plead my case at Lambeth. There I spent 37 shillings 6 pence, and the case was adjourned till the Monday following Laetare Jerusalem.[5] Before this I went for Master Ambrose, who was then with the abbot of St. Albans in Norfolk; on that journey I spent 9 shillings 4 pence. I sent also Samson, my chaplain, for Master Peter "de Mileto" at Buckingham. On this journey he lost his palfrey for which I recompensed him with a silver mark; he had spent there 7 shillings.

Having obtained the services of these clerks, I came with my counsel at the appointed day to London, spending on the journey 5 silver marks. Here the day Quasi modo geniti[6] was set for me, before which I sent my brother, John, overseas to the king's court, since it was told me that my adversaries had secured a writ from the king giving them leave not to plead until the king should return to England. For this cause I sent my brother for another writ, lest my suit should be held over on account of my adversaries' writ. In this journey my brother spent 3 silver marks. Meanwhile I myself went to Chichester to speak with Bishop Hilary and to get him to witness to the decree of nullity made in his presence by the bishop of Winchester in the synod at London. This I received in letters sent by him to the archbishop testifying to the decree. On that journey I spent 14 shillings 4 pence. So I came to London on the appointed day with my clerks, my witnesses and my counsel. There I remained four days, pleading my suit each day. This journey cost me 103 shillings.

Then the case was adjourned till Rogationtide.[7] And when I appeared at Canterbury on the appointed day, my adversaries declared they would not plead because of the summons to the king's army for the war of Toulouse. On that journey I spent 8 shillings and I returned thence without a day being fixed for further hearing....

[Finally after many further delays and fruitless journeys and two appeals to Rome, the plaintiff obtained a writ summoning the case before the king's court.]

We came then to the king at Woodstock, where we remained eight days; and at length by grace of the lord king and by the judgment of his court my uncle's land was adjudged to me. There I spent 7 pounds 10 shillings and 6 pence.

These are the presents which I gave to my counsel and to the clerks, who assisted me in the archbishop's court, namely 11 silver marks. In the court of the bishop of Winchester 14 silver marks, to Master Peter "de Mileto" 10 marks and a gold ring worth half a silver mark. To Master Robert "de Chimay" 1 mark. In the king's court I have spent in gifts, in gold and silver and in horses, 17½ marks. To Master Peter of Littlebury I gave 40 shillings. To the other counsel from among my friends, who had come regularly to the hearings of my suit, I gave in silver and in horses 12½ marks.

---

[1] November 29, 1158.

[2] February 14, 1159.

[3] March 7, 1159.

[4] This was the declaration of nullity of his uncle's second marriage.

[5] The fourth Sunday in Lent.

[6] The first Sunday after Easter.

[7] The Sunday and three days preceding Ascension Day, which is the 40th day after Easter.

6.5 The legislation of a Spanish king: *The Laws of Cuenca* (1189–1193). Original in Latin.

The town of Cuenca, originally founded by Muslims in al-Andalus, was conquered by King Alfonso VIII of Castile (r.1158–1214) in 1177. Soon thereafter he issued a set of laws (*fueros*) for the citizens. Unlike English laws, those of Cuenca were to be enforced by local—not royal—officials (*alcaldi; iudices*), though there were provisions for appealing the most serious cases to the king. The code makes clear that a few Muslims still lived in the town and that Jews and Christians regularly interacted there. Woman and children had numerous rights, and the laws paid particular attention to what today would be called "family law." What might explain this fact?

[Source: *The Code of Cuenca: Municipal Law on the Twelfth-Century Castilian Frontier*, trans. James F. Powers (Philadelphia: University of Pennsylvania Press, 2000), pp. 28–29, 66–69, 92, 160–65 (slightly modified, and notes making use of the Glossary on pp. 229–32).]

Prologue

… The memory of men is fragile and insufficient for a multitude of things, and for this reason one has proceeded with the sagacity to put the laws of legal statute and civil rights in writing. After meditative selection [these laws] sprouted from royal authority to calm the discord between citizens and inhabitants; thus some could crush villains by the greatest possible cunning, since they are protected by royal guarantee, and cannot subsequently be weakened by fraudulent subterfuge.

For this consideration, then, I, Alfonso, proclaimed king by the grace of God, the most powerful of the Hispanic kings, notice of whose immense greatness and concordant fame resonated far and wide, from the rising of the sun to the bounds of the earth, under whose domain the kings are happy to be subjected, under whose government the laws are pleased to be administered; I, the guide of those who take pride in the Hispanic kingdoms, codified the summation of the judicial institutions in behalf of safeguarding peace and the rights of justice between clergy and laity, between townsmen and peasants, among the needy and the poor; and I codified it, ordered it written with much care so that any question or discussion, as much in the petition as in the judicial action (as much for the cause as for the accusation), which occurs between the citizens and the inhabitants, removing all appeal, except those which later on excluded the laws, and having torn the veil of the sham, could determine under the judgment of the justice, once imputed and discerned, the cause of both parties to the tenor of the written laws and the use of the custom "in which rests the right and the norm of the language,"[1] the reason of each part having been expressed and versed, so let the law be defined under the supervision of the knighthood.

Thus, [this is] a king of such renowned authority, that from sea to sea the kings [who are] enemies of the name of Christ fear his name only, since they have experienced his power and have been crushed by him many times; [of such renowned authority that] Christian princes serve him as the first [lord], and from whom Don Conrado, illustrious descendant of the Roman Emperor, and Don Alfonso, king of León, are happy to have received the weapons of combat and his backing, a reminder of his goodness and of having kissed his hand.

After laying siege and after many tasks, tormented by numerous difficulties and distressed by the enemies within, nine months having passed, he made his entry into the city of Cuenca, preferring it to the others; since he chose Cuenca as Alphonsipolis, he preferred it for his residence, and he adopted its citizens as his favorite people in order to strengthen its prosperity, freedom, and distinction among the others he had liberated from the captivity of Babylon and from the yoke of the Pharaoh

---

[1] Horace, *Epistulae* 2.3.71–72.

with the weapons of his royal power, once he suppressed the filth of its idolatry.[1]

Therefore, so that so great a prerogative of dignity should be known, he conceded high rank to the inhabitants and settlers of Cuenca, as much to those already there as those to come; by this code of freedom, the tenor of which concerns matters of public affairs and its sentences, which are examined in justice with meditating decision and granted by royal agreement, he confirmed it forever with the seal of the royal effigy.

Happy is that marriage certainly when Law and Justice join in uniform alliance, so that when the Law instructs that one should be cleared, he is cleared by the Law, and that which it determines should be condemned, is condemned by Justice, which sufficiently favors definition by both. Thus Law is that which permits the honest and prohibits the opposite; Justice, on the other hand, is the virtue that concedes each one his rights, punishes the culprit, and acquits the innocent.

Disposing these things continually for the honor of Holy Mother Church and for the increase of the Catholic faith, which in the district of Cuenca remained overwhelmed in an extraordinary way, for God Living and True, to whom to serve is to rule and whose yoke is soft and his load light, they serve in freedom, and just as they obey the Commandments of a single God, they also obey the orders of a single king and prince.

Therefore, I, Alfonso, king by the grace of God, together with Leonor my wife the queen, and our serene son Fernando, whose birth distinguished the above city with serene and pleased look, grant to all the inhabitants of Cuenca and to their successors this summary of dignity and prerogative of freedom; and so that for posterity it could not be broken, I confirm it with the guarantee of our seal and with our royal protection....

Chapter X
The Right of Succession of Children and Parents

1. THE RIGHT OF SUCCESSION OF CHILDREN AND PARENTS

Any child should inherit the goods of his father and mother, movable goods as well as real estate. The father and mother [should inherit] the movable goods of the children. The father, however, should not have to inherit the real estate of his child which comes to the latter through inheritance. Regarding the other real estate which the parents acquire jointly, the one who survives, father or mother, should inherit this for lifetime use only, by right of inheritance through their child, if he lives at least nine days. After the death of the father or mother, the real estate returns to the estate.

For this reason I command that, although the surviving parent has to inherit this real estate for lifetime use, and the real estate has to revert to the estate, the survivor should provide bondsmen who will guard the real estate from harm. The real estate that belongs to the child through his estate should revert to that estate the day the survivor dies.

2. THE NEAREST RELATIVES OF A DEAD PERSON ARE HIS HEIRS

The relatives who are nearest [in blood] and also citizens should inherit the goods of their deceased relative. If someone comes forward as a closer relative than these others, this person should inherit the goods of the deceased but first should provide bondsmen who establish that this person should have been an inhabitant of Cuenca for at least ten years. Those who do not do this should not inherit.

3. THOSE WHO ENTER A MONASTIC ORDER

Whoever enters a monastic order should take with him only a fifth portion of his movable property, and the rest, joined with the entirety of his real estate, should remain for his heirs. It will be seen as unjust and inequitable that someone should disinherit his children by donating their movable property and real estate to the monks, because it is established in the code that nobody should disinherit their children.

4. CHILDREN ARE UNDER THE POWER OF THEIR PARENTS

Children should be under the power of their parents and are family members until they should contract marriage. And until that moment, everything the children acquire or obtain should belong entirely to their parents; the children holding nothing against their parents' will.

5. PARENTS RESPOND FOR THE CRIMES OF THEIR CHILDREN

Parents should respond for the crimes of their children, whether or not the latter should be sound in judgment.[2]

---

[1] Alfonso likens his capture of Cuenca from the Muslims to the liberation of the Jews from Babylon and Egypt.

[2] "Respond for" means to be legally responsible for.

If someone enters the home of another and commits any crime, whether or not they should be a hireling of the house, the owner of the house should not respond with a surety for them unless he defends them. If he defends them, he should respond for them or bring them to give juridical satisfaction. But if they do not return to the house of their *señor*, or the *señor* does not go forth in their defense, no one should respond for them but their parents.[1] Nevertheless, if a child commits a homicide, even though he should be in the pay of another, no one should respond for him except his parents, because they should pay the pecuniary penalties; however, the parents should not depart as enemies unless they are blamed for the homicide. Then, if they are accused and convicted of homicide, they are obligated also to depart from our city as enemies. If the child is bereft of one of his parents, the one who acts as his guardian should respond for him until the child is given the portion of goods that belongs to him. After the partition of goods, the guardian does not have to respond.

6. PARENTS DO NOT RESPOND FOR THE DEBTS OF THEIR CHILDREN

Parents should not respond for the loans or debts of their children.

7. THE DISTURBED CHILD

If a father or mother has a disturbed child and is concerned for paying the pecuniary penalties of the crimes that he might commit, he should hold the child captive or bound until he calms down or is treated, while he remains deranged, so that the child does not cause damage. The parents have to respond for any damage that he causes, even if they have renounced him in front of the council or have disinherited him. This precept is established so that none may say that their child is insane or disturbed and renounce him before the council and then, with concealment and deception, cause him to kill someone or start a fire or do any other harm.

8. SEPARATION OF THE WIFE AND THE HUSBAND

When husband and wife, for any reason and by common agreement, want to separate, only those things they have acquired together should be distributed equally and nothing else; they should also distribute equally the works that both have completed on their property. And after one of those who has been separated in life dies, the survivor should receive nothing from the other's goods, but rather the heirs of the dead person should be those to receive all his or her goods, and these should be divided among themselves.

9. THE PARTITION OF GOODS OF PARENTS AND CHILDREN

All partitions of goods that are done in the presence of three citizens and recorded should hold as firm, so that the partition or the names of the witnesses are written in the public record, because, if some or all of the witnesses have died, he who holds the document should swear with two citizens that this is authentic, and he should be believed, in case some of the heirs deny the partition. Likewise, the division and the partition are firm and sound that the parents, whether healthy or sick, had made for their heirs, being all present without exception and in agreement; because the partition done in another way by the father or the mother is not legal. The donation should also be accepted and sound that the father and mother confirm only by oath.

10. THE DOCUMENT OF PARTITION

The document of partition should have this formulation: "All should know absolutely, those present as well as those to come, that I, *N.*, desiring the end of all flesh, which one is born for, so that before a man should die he should pay the debts of nature, allot and concede to my heirs and successors that, by right of patrimony after my death, according to hereditary right, they should possess my things, all that I have acquired with my sweat and my service up to the present day, as much in movable property as in real estate, and in this manner: to *G.*, my firstborn son, the vineyard that is within the district of Cuenca, near the river, with the orchard that lies within it; I leave you also all the houses that I built or bought in the locale *N.*; to *R.*, my younger son, the field *N.* or the vineyard with the portion [of land] that belongs to it. Witnessed by those whose names appear below: *F.P.D.J.*

---

1   The *señor* was the male head of a family or household or, as in this case, an owner, employer, or master. Apparently at Cuenca many children did not live in the homes of their parents but rather were sent to other homes to work as maids, servants, or apprentices. The parents remained responsible for them if they committed a crime but not, as the next law makes clear, if they defaulted on a loan.

Era one thousand two hundred.[1] *N.*, being king. *N.*, being *iudex*. *N.*, being *merino*. *N.*, being *sagio*."[2]

11. ALSO REGARDING THE PARTITION

If the spouses have children and are not separated in life, and neither of the two has other children, when one of them dies, having settled all the common debts that they have contracted jointly, and having paid also the share of the dead for alms for their soul[3] and their shroud, their children or heirs should distribute all the goods of the dead among each other, both goods and real estate. If a child dies, the surviving parent should inherit his goods, as has already been said. But if the child has a descendant, the latter should succeed him [the child] and not the father or the mother....

Chapter XIII
No One Should Respond for Counseling

1. NO ONE SHOULD RESPOND FOR GIVING ADVICE

I command that no one should respond or pay any fine for giving advice. However, he should respond if he advises the selling of a Christian. I also command that each one should pay the same fine, even if he should go in assistance of another and the fight should be another's fight.

2. WHOEVER TAKES PART IN A GANG SHOULD PAY, EXCEPT THEIR WIVES

Whoever takes part in a gang in order to lend aid to someone should pay double the pecuniary fine for the crime that they have committed, even though he should be that one's son or his blood kin, except for his wife; if the wife takes part in the gang of her husband, or if the latter is in the gang of his wife, the couple do not have to

pay double [fines] for this, since it is a single fine for both.

3. HE WHO HOLDS ANOTHER'S WIFE

If someone holds another's wife, he should pay three hundred *solidi* and should be considered an enemy.[4]

4. HE WHO SELLS FOOD TO THE MUSLIMS

Whoever sells or gives weapons or food to the Muslims let him be hurled from the city cliffs, if it can be proved; but if not, he should clear himself with twelve citizens and should be believed; or he should swear alone and respond to the challenge by judicial combat,[5] the one which pleases the council more. We call food bread, cheese, and everything which one can eat, except for living livestock.

5. THE SERVANT WHO KILLS OR INJURES A CHRISTIAN

If someone's servant or Moor[6] hurts or kills a Christian, his master should pay the fine for the crime that he has committed or he should put the injurer in the hands of the plaintiff, the servant's master choosing that which pleases him more....

Chapter XXIX
Cases between Christians and Jews

1. CASES BETWEEN CHRISTIANS AND JEWS

If a Jew and a Christian litigate for something, two citizen *alcaldi*[7] should be designated, one of whom should be Christian and the other Jewish. If one of the litigants is not pleased by the judgment, he should appeal to four citizen *alcaldi*, two of whom should be Christian and two Jewish. These four should have final judgment. Whoever appeals the judgment of these four should know that

---

1 The date of the Era was 38 years ahead of the Year of Our Lord, so the date CE would be 1162. This chapter provides a form that must be filled out according to the facts and names of each case.

2 The *iudex* was the chief elected civil official of the town; the *merino* was the royal territorial administrator who received the king's rents from the town council; the *sagio* was the bailiff, town crier, and executioner. Naming these officials, along with the reigning king, was a way to authenticate the document and its date.

3 "Alms for their soul" refers to the distribution of money to the poor on behalf of the soul of the departed.

4 A *solidus* (pl. *solidi*) was a silver coin worth 1/20th of a silver pound.

5 "Judicial combat" was an ordeal by duel. It might be on foot or on horseback. Care was taken to choose combatants well matched in size, strength, and skill.

6 A "Moor" was a Muslim living in Spain; in this case he was the slave or servant of a Christian.

7 The *alcaldi* (sing. *alcaldus*) were elected officials who served as aldermen and judges in the parish; the word was derived from the Arabic *al-qadi*.

he will lose the case. These *alcaldi* should guard against judging anything else than what the Code of Cuenca prescribes.

2. WITNESSES BETWEEN A JEW AND A CHRISTIAN

The witnesses between a Christian and a Jew should be two citizens, one Christian and the other Jewish, and all the things denied by the testimony of these [two] should be confirmed and believed. Anyone who ought to testify should swear with double the sureties or on his feet, according to the Code of Cuenca. If it is the Christian who places his foot and is defeated in the case, the *iudex* should imprison him in the jail of the king until he pays.[1]

3. THE JEW WHO TESTIFIES THAT HIS DEBTOR WAS OUTSIDE JAIL

If the Jew testifies that the prisoner is outside jail, the *iudex* should put him in the power of the Jew until he pays. Moreover, if it is the Jew who places his foot and is defeated in the case, the *albedí* [Jewish *iudex*, chancery official] should imprison him in the jail of the king.

4. THE CHRISTIAN WHO TESTIFIES THAT HIS DEBTOR IS OUTSIDE JAIL

If it is the Christian who attests that the prisoner is outside jail, the *albedí* should place him in the prison of the Christians, from whence he should not leave until he pays.

5. THE TESTIMONY FOR DELIVERY OF SURETIES

Be it known concerning witnesses, whether a Christian or a Jew, [if] he delivers double the sureties and he does not redeem them within the term of nine days, he should lose them completely.

6. IF THE ALBEDÍ DOES NOT WANT TO DO JUSTICE

If the *albedí* does not do justice, he should pay ten *aurei*[2] to the *iudex* and, furthermore, the plaintiff should take as sureties with impunity what he can seize of the things of the Jews outside of the *alcacería* [district of shops Jews rented from the king]. The *iudex* should divide the above-mentioned ten *aurei* with the plaintiff.

7. THE IUDEX WHO DOES NOT WANT TO DO JUSTICE

If it is the *iudex* who does not do justice for a Jew, he should pay ten *aurei* to the *albedí* and, furthermore, the Jew should take as sureties all that he can seize of the things of the Christian....

16. THE PLACE AND TIME OF JUDGMENTS

The cases between Jews and Christians should be before the gate of the *alcacería* and not at the synagogue. The time of the meetings of the court should be from the completion of matins in the cathedral church until terce.[3] When they sound terce, they should conclude the judgments. He who does not present himself before the court should lose the case.

17. THE OATH OF THE JEW AND OF THE CHRISTIAN

For all claims, should they be Christian, should they be Jewish, up to a value of four *menkales*,[4] the Christian should swear without the cross and the Jew without the Torah. If the claim is worth four *menkales* or more, the Christian should swear on the cross and the Jew on the Torah. And if the Jew or the Christian does not want to swear, he should lose the case.

---

[1] The expressions "on his feet" and "places his foot" probably mean to undertake judicial combat. "Double the sureties" means double the payment—or goods equal to the payment—that was required to cover the penalty of the crime.

[2] The *aureus* (pl. *aurei*) was a gold coin.

[3] The timing of the judgments is here regulated by the canonical hours of the church: matins often began at sunrise; terce was the third hour, i.e. around 9 a.m.

[4] A *menkal* (pl. *menkales*) was a coin of copper or copper and silver mixed, valued at about ¼ of an *aureus*.

LOCAL LAWS AND ARRANGEMENTS

6.6 A manorial court: *Proceedings for the Abbey of Bec* (1246). Original in Latin.

The English royal courts were not only places where verdicts were handed down but also writing offices that carefully recorded cases and outcomes. In the thirteenth century, the proceedings of local manorial courts—*not* controlled by the king but rather by local lords—began to be recorded. The monastery of Bec, in Normandy, had numerous estates in England; on these manors its officials held court at various times during the year. The cases covered numerous petty offenses, whether against the lord of the manor or against royal law. The documents, as the excerpt below makes clear, consisted largely of lists of fines, for the proceedings were written up for lords (in this case the monastery of Bec) whose main interest lay in the income that the courts produced. What crimes were tried in manorial counts, and how much revenue did they produce?

[Source: *Select Pleas in Manorial and Other Seignorial Courts, Reigns of Henry III. and Edward I.*, ed. Frederic W. Maitland (London: Bernard Quaritch, 1889), pp. 7, 8, 9 (new notes and some modifications of original notes).]

Tooting [Surrey]. Sunday after Ascension Day.[1]

The court presented that the following had encroached on the lord's land, to wit, William Cobbler, Maud Robin's widow (fined 12 d.), John Shepherd (fined 12 d.), Walter Reeve (fined 2 s.), William of Moreville (fined 12 d.), Hamo of Hageldon (fined 12 d.), Mabel Spendlove's widow (fined 6 d.). Therefore they are in mercy.[2]

Godwin is in mercy for contemning to do what was bidden him on the lord's behalf. Fine, 12 d.

Roger Rede in mercy for detention of rent. Pledge, John of Streatham.[3] Fine, 6 d.

One acre which Sarah the widow held of the land of William Roce is seised into the lord's hand until she produces her warrantor.[4]

William of Streatham is in mercy for not producing what he was pledged to produce. Fine, 12 d.

Ruislip [Middlesex]. Tuesday after Ascension Day.

The court presents that Nicholas Brakespeare is not in a tithing and holds land. Therefore let him be distrained.[5]

Breakers of the assize:[6] Alice Salvage's widow (fined 12 d.), Agnotta the Shepherd's mistress, Roger Canon

---

[1] Tooting [Surrey] is the name of the manor. The court was held on the Sunday after Ascension, 1246.

[2] "In mercy" means that they are liable to a fine. A fine of 1 d. is one penny; a fine of 1 s. is one "solidus," or shilling; there were 12 pennies to a shilling.

[3] John of Streatham serves as "pledge," or guarantor, of Roger Rede's fine.

[4] "Seisin" is possession, and thus "seised into the lord's hand" means that the lord gains possession of the land; Sarah must produce a warrantor (someone to give assurances as to her right to hold the acre of land).

[5] "Not in a tithing": most freeholders (non-servile) men of a village were in a "tithing," that is, a group pledged to one another to keep the peace and to produce anyone who committed a crime. Nicholas Brakespeare is not in a tithing, so he must be dealt with in another way: by seizing his land and forcing him thereby to do something or accept some punishment.

[6] This probably refers to the assize of beer, which was a court that regulated the price of beer. Note how many women were involved in its brewing.

(fined 6 d.), the wife of Richard Chayham, the widow of Peter Beyondgrove, the wife of Ralph Coke (fined 6 d.), Ailwin (fined 6 d.), John Shepherd (fined 6 d.), Geoffrey Carpenter, Roise the Miller's wife (fined 6 d.), William White, John Carpenter, John Bradif.

Roger Hamo's son gives 20s. to have seisin of the land which was his father's and to have an inquest of twelve as to a certain croft which Gilbert Bisuthe holds.[1] Pledges, Gilbert Lamb, William John's son and Robert King.

Isabella Peter's widow is in mercy for a trespass which her son John had committed in the lord's wood. Fine, 18 d. Pledges, Gilbert Bisuthe and Richard Robin.

Richard Maleville is at his law[2] against the lord [to prove] that he did not take from the lord's servants goods taken in distress to the damage and dishonor of his lord [to the extent of] 20 s. Pledges, Gilbert Bisuthe and Richard Hubert.

Hugh Tree in mercy for his beasts caught in the lord's garden. Pledges, Walter Hill and William Slipper. Fine, 6 d.

[The] twelve jurors say that Hugh Cross has right in the bank and hedge about which there was a dispute between him and William White. Therefore let him hold in peace and let William be distrained for his many trespasses. (Afterwards he made fine for 12 d.) They say also that the hedge which is between the Widow Druet and William Slipper so far as the bank extends should be divided along the middle of the bank, so that the crest of the bank should be the boundary between them, for the crest was thrown up along the ancient boundary.

6.7 Doing business: *A Genoese societas* (1253). Original in Latin.

Medieval business arrangements called for numerous kinds of contracts, i.e., documents with legal force in court. The cities of the Mediterranean abounded in such documents, normally drawn up by notaries. One such arrangement was a *societas*, a partnership in which the partners normally pooled their money and labor and reaped equal profits or losses. All the members were liable for the others; there was no concept (yet) of limited liability. The *societas* contract recorded below was a bit unusual: two of the partners (Consolino and Friedrich) contributed their skill (in this case in metallurgy) but no money, while another, Orlando Paglia, gave money but no labor. The rest of the partners promised both money and work. The profits, too, were shared unequally.

[Source: *Medieval Trade in the Mediterranean World: Illustrative Documents*, ed. and trans. Robert S. Lopez and Irving W. Raymond (New York: Columbia University Press, 2001), pp. 194–95 (notes modified).]

Genoa, September 7, 1253

In the name of the Lord, amen. Orlando Paglia; Giovanni Puliti; Ranieri of Verona; Giacomo Migliorati; Consolino, son of the late Konrad, German; and Friedrich, German, acknowledge that they have jointly made among themselves a *societas* to last forever for the purpose of buying mines, furnaces, or veins for the production of silver in Sardinia or wherever God may guide them more [wisely]. In this *societas* said Orlando invested £100 Genoese; Giovanni Puliti, £50; Ranieri of Verona, £15; Giacomo Migliorati, £25; waiving the exception that the money has not been had or received in cash. According to [the conditions of] this *societas* all are to go to Sardinia or wherever God may guide them more [wisely] to do said work, except Orlando, who is not himself

---

1 "An inquest of twelve as to a certain croft": a croft is a piece of arable land; Roger Hamo's son has paid to have a jury of twelve men of the neighborhood inquire into Gilbert's rights in this croft.

2 "At his law": Richard proposes to clear himself with compurgators—men who will swear to his innocence.

going at present but may go whenever he likes and [may send] whatever messenger he wishes. And they are to share the expenses of said *societas* in food and drink and chartering of boats and renting of houses, both in sickness and in health, while engaged in said work; and they are to buy with [the capital of] said *societas* the equipment needed to do that work. And Consolino and Friedrich are to be in said *societas* with the abovementioned [investors] and to labor in good faith and without fraud, and to preserve and to protect said *societas*, and to give aid and counsel for the increase of said *societas*. They promise one another to make an accounting of the profit which God may grant to said *societas* every fourth month. And said Consolino and Friedrich are to have for their labor the sixth share of the profit which God may grant in that *societas*. And of the rest, [after deduction] of said sixth share, Orlando is to have a third share, Giovanni Puliti a third share, Ranieri and Giacomo another third share. And Consolino and Friedrich promised to the aforesaid not to forsake that *societas* in any way nor to leave

it unless for the purpose of going to Tuscany. And if they, or one of them, should leave for said cause, they promised to return to said *societas* within two or three months from the day they left. They all swore, placing their hands on the sacred and holy Gospels of God, to undertake, to complete, and to observe each and all [of the aforesaid conditions] and not to violate [them] in any [way] under penalty of £ 100 Genoese, the pact remaining as settled among them [as] mutually stipulated and solemnly promised and under pledge of their goods, [the penalty] being given by the one who does not observe to those who do observe [it]. And we may be sued, wherever any of us and any of our goods [may be], waiving the privilege of [choosing] the tribunal. Done in Genoa in the house where said Orlando lives. Witnesses: Giacomo of Parma, son of the late Marina, and Obertino of Reggio [Emilia]. 1253, tenth indiction, on the seventh day of September, between terce and nones.

Only one [instrument] was made.[1]

6.8 Women's work: *Guild Regulations of the Parisian Silk Fabric Makers* (13th c.). Original in French.

Craftspeople drew up their own laws to regulate themselves and guarantee the integrity and uniformity of their products. At Paris there were perhaps a dozen such trades in the time of King Philip Augustus (r.1180–1223), but the number had swelled to over a hundred by the time of Louis IX (r.1226–1270), as we know from the collection of regulations published in 1268 by Etienne de Boileau, Louis's appointee as provost of Paris from *c*.1261 to 1270. The regulations for the makers of silk fabrics in Boileau's book, given below, show that women as well as men were involved in important trades.

[Source: *Women's Lives in Medieval Europe: A Sourcebook*, ed. Emilie Amt (New York and London: Routledge, 1993), pp. 194–99 (notes added).]

The Craft of Silk Fabric

1. No journeywoman[2] maker of silk fabric may be a mistress of the craft until she has practiced it for a year and a day, after she has done her apprenticeship, because she

will be more competent to practice her craft and observe the regulations.

2. No mistress of this craft may take an apprentice for fewer than six years with a fee of four livres [pounds], or for eight years with forty sous, or for ten years with no

---

[1] This is an annotation of the notary, meaning that only one copy of the document was drafted for the parties.

[2] A journeywoman or journeyman was a day laborer; the job normally came after a long apprenticeship. Few laborers attained the status of mistress or master of the craft, who dominated the offices and policies of the guild.

fee; and she may have no more than two apprentices at the same time, and she may not take another until their apprenticeships are completed.

3. No mistress or journeywoman may work at night or on a feast day observed by the whole town.

4. No mistress of the craft may weave thread with silk, or foil with silk, because the work is false and bad; and it should be burned if it is found.[1]

5. No mistress or journeywoman of the craft may make a false hem or border, either of thread or of foil, nor may she do raised work of thread or foil. And if such work is found, it should be burned, because it is false and bad.

6. No mistress or journeywoman of the craft, after she has done her apprenticeship, may hire anyone who is not a mistress of the craft, but she may take work to do from whomever she likes.

7. It is ordered that all the mistresses of the said craft who send their work outside the town to be done must show it to those who are designated to watch over the craft, along with the work of their own house, to make sure that it is up to standard.

8. And anyone who infringes on any of the above regulations must pay eight Parisian sous, each time she is found at fault; of which the king will have five sous, and the craft guild twelve deniers, and the masters who oversee the craft two sous for their pains and for the work they do in overseeing the craft.

9. To safeguard this craft in the manner described above, there should be established three masters and three mistresses, who will swear by the Saints that they will make known to the provost of Paris[2] or to his representative all the infringements of the regulations of the said craft, to the best of their ability.

6.9 Men's work: *Guild Regulations of the Shearers of Arras* (1236). Original in French.

Wool, both raised domestically and imported from England, was the underpinning of the Flemish textile industry, the region's major export. Specialized labor was involved, all under the oversight of the drapers, who in turn were supervised by the merchants who sold the goods on the international market. First lowly spinners turned the wool into thread. Then the weavers created the cloth on great looms, often worked by two men. The dyers, prestigious owners of great vats, gave the cloth its color; alternatively, the thread itself was dyed before the weaving process. The fullers beat the cloth to shrink it and make it heavier. Finally the shearers cropped the nap of the cloth with great scissors to make it smooth. At Arras the regulations for the shearers were largely concerned with the fees that the workers had to pay, mainly to the Fraternity—i.e., the guild. What provisions in this document demonstrate the close alliance between the town government and the guild?

[Source: *A Source Book for Medieval Economic History*, ed. Roy C. Cave and Herbert H. Coulson (New York: Bruce Publishing Co., 1936), pp. 250–52 (notes added).]

Here is the Shearers' Charter, on which they were first founded.

This is the first ordinance of the shearers, who were founded in the name of the Fraternity of God and St. Julien,[3] with the agreement and consent of those who were at the time mayor and aldermen.[4]

1. Whoever would engage in the trade of a shearer shall be in the Confraternity of St. Julien, and shall

---

[1] Presumably, weaving thread or foil with the silk would contaminate its purity.

[2] The provost of Paris was the city's chief public magistrate.

[3] Guilds were religious and charitable as well as trade organizations.

[4] The mayor and aldermen were the chief magistrates of the town.

pay all the dues, and observe the decrees made by the brethren.

2. That is to say: first, that whoever is a master shearer shall pay 14 solidi to the Fraternity.[1] And there may not be more than one master shearer working in a house. And he shall be a master shearer all the year, and have arms for the need of the town.

3. And a journeyman shall pay 5 solidi to the Fraternity.

4. And whoever wishes to learn the trade shall be the son of a burgess[2] or he shall live in the town for a year and a day; and he shall serve three years to learn this trade.

5. And he shall give to his master 3 *muids* for his bed and board;[3] and he ought to bring the first *muid* to his master at the beginning of his apprenticeship, and another *muid* a year from that day, and a third *muid* at the beginning of the third year.

6. And no one may be a master of this trade of shearer if he has not lived a year and a day in the town, in order that it may be known whether or not he comes from a good place....

8. And if masters, or journeymen, or apprentices, stay in the town to do their work they owe 40 solidi, if they have done this without the permission of the aldermen of Arras.

9. And whoever does work on Saturday afternoon, or on the Eve of the Feast of Our Lady, or after Vespers on the Eve of the Feast of St. Julien, and completes the day by working, shall pay, if he be a master, 12 denarii, and if he be a journeyman, 6 denarii. And whoever works in the four days of Christmas, or in the eight days of Easter, or in the eight days of Pentecost, owes 5 solidi....

11. And an apprentice owes to the Fraternity for his apprenticeship 5 solidi.

12. And whoever puts the cloth of another in pledge shall pay 10 solidi to the Fraternity, and he shall not work at the trade for a year and a day.

13. And whoever does work in defiance of the mayor and aldermen shall pay 5 solidi.

14. And if a master flee outside the town with another's cloth and a journeyman aids him to flee, if he does not tell the mayor and aldermen, the master shall pay 20 solidi to the Fraternity and the journeyman 10 solidi: and they shall not work at the trade for a year and a day....

16. And those who are fed at the expense of the city shall be put to work first. And he who slights them for strangers owes 5 solidi: but if the stranger be put to work

he cannot be removed as long as the master wishes to keep him.... And when a master does not work hard he pays 5 solidi, and a journeyman 2 solidi....

18. And after the half year the mayor and aldermen shall fix such wages as he ought to have.

19. And whatever journeyman shall carry off from his master, or from his fellow man, or from a burgess of the town, anything for which complaint is made, shall pay 5 solidi.

20. And whoever maligns the mayor and aldermen, that is while on the business of the Fraternity, shall pay 5 solidi....

22. And no one who is not a shearer may be a master, in order that the work may be done in the best way, and no draper may cut cloth in his house, if it be not his own work, except he be a shearer, because drapers cannot be masters.

23. And if a draper or a merchant has work to do in his house, he may take such workmen as he wishes into his house, so long as the work be done in his house. And he who infringes this shall give 5 solidi to the Fraternity....

25. And each master ought to have his arms when he is summoned. And if he has not he should pay 20 solidi.

26–30. [Other army regulations.]

31. And whatever brother has finished cloth in his house and does not inform the mayor and aldermen, and it be found in his house, whatever he may say, shall forfeit 10 solidi to the Fraternity.

32. And if a master does not give a journeyman such wage as is his due, then he shall pay 5 solidi.

33. And he who overlooks the forfeits of this Fraternity, if he does not wish to pay them when the mayor and aldermen summon him either for the army or the district, then he owes 10 solidi, and he shall not work at the trade until he has paid. Every forfeit of 5 solidi, and the fines which the mayor and aldermen command, shall be written down. All the fines of the Fraternity ought to go for the purchase of arms and for the needs of the Fraternity.

34. And whatever brother of this Fraternity shall betray his confrère for others shall not work at the trade for a year and a day.

35. And whatever brother of this Fraternity perjures himself shall not work at the trade for forty days. And if he does so he shall pay 10 solidi if he be a master, but if he be a journeyman let him pay 5 solidi.

---

[1]   Solidi (sing. solidus) were silver coins.

[2]   I.e., a citizen of the town.

[3]   A *muid* was a unit of capacity, like a bushel.

36. And should a master of this Fraternity die and leave a male heir he may learn the trade anywhere where there is no apprentice.

37. And no apprentice shall cut to the selvage for half a year, and this is to obtain good work.[1] And no master or journeyman may cut by himself because no one can measure cloth well alone. And whoever infringes this rule shall pay 5 solidi to the Fraternity for each offense.

38. Any brother whatsoever who lays hands on, or does wrong to, the mayor and aldermen of this Fraternity, as long as they work for the city and the Fraternity, shall not work at his trade in the city for a year and a day.

And if he should do so, let him be banished from the town for a year and a day, saving the appeal to Monseigneur the King and his Castellan.[2]

39. And the brethren of this Fraternity, and the mayor and aldermen shall not forbid any brother to give law and do right and justice to all when it is demanded of them, or when some one claims from them. And he who infringes this shall not have the help of the aldermen at all.

BUREAUCRACY AT THE PAPAL CURIA

6.10 The growth of papal business: Innocent III, *Letters* (1200–1202). Original in Latin.

In the wake of the Gregorian Reform the papacy reorganized itself as a major court for all sorts of church matters—disputed elections, appeals from individual churches regarding their rights, decisions about canonical marriages, and many other issues. By the time of Innocent III (1198–1216), the pope was involved in many local church affairs. The three letters here illustrate this point for England. The first shows Innocent intervening in a case involving a priest who resigned his post; the second has him determining the fitness of a priest to continue his work; and the third shows him interceding in a property dispute. How do all these interests explain the rapid expansion of the papal bureaucracy?

[Source: *Selected Letters of Pope Innocent III concerning England* (1198–1216), ed. C.R. Cheney and W.H. Semple (London: Thomas Nelson and Sons, 1953), pp. 15, 23, 33–34 (notes modified).]

[Letter 1, February 5, 1200]

To the bishop, dean, and subdean of Lincoln.[3]

It has come to our hearing, on information from our beloved son Master Elias de Chieveley,[4] that having canonically obtained the church of Chieveley on the authority of the Apostolic See, and having had peaceful possession for some time, he was at length compelled, through his very great fear of the king, to promise on oath to resign it, and has in fact resigned it into the hands of the appropriate persons.[5] But because actions done under duress or through fear ought not to have binding force, by apostolic letter we command you that, if it be established to your satisfaction that Master Elias was forced to resign by such fear, as could and should affect

---

[1] The selvage is the woven edge of a fabric; apprentices were not to cut to the fabric's end until he (or possibly she) had some experience in shearing.

[2] The king of France at the time was St. Louis (Louis IX, r.1226–1270).

[3] Bishop Hugh I (St. Hugh of Avallon; r.1186–1200); the dean was Roger de Rolveston (1195–1223); the subdean was either Richard Kentensis or William de Bramfeld.

[4] Master Elias of Chieveley, Berkshire had obtained the church there by order of Pope Celestine III (1191–1198).

[5] I.e., to his ecclesiastical superiors. The king in question was John (r.1199–1216), who at the time was quarreling with the Church.

a man of courage, then notwithstanding the aforesaid oath (by which he was bound only to resign, but not precluded from seeking reinstatement) by ecclesiastical censure you will cause the aforesaid church to be restored to him without appeal.

No letter prejudicial to truth and justice etc. If you cannot all etc., then let two of you etc.[1]

The Lateran, the 5th of February.

[Letter 2, November 8, 1200]

To the bishop of Lincoln.[2]

Our beloved son A., a priest, appearing in our presence, by his own confession disclosed to us that, being so badly troubled by a certain physical ailment that desire for sleep and food seemed to have left him, with the idea of wakening some slight appetite for a meal he mounted a horse he had bred. The horse not being completely obedient to the reins, but prancing and leaping contrary to the rider's will, he pulled hard on the bridle and pricked with the spurs in order to curb its impetuosity. But the rein snapped, and the horse, as left to its own caprice, bolted at a gallop—when a woman, approaching from the side and carrying a baby, met it. The horse collided with her, threw its rider to a distance, and crushed the child. The priest himself, as a result of his sudden fall, was brought almost to the gates of death: ultimately he recovered, but has not since presumed to celebrate mass. As the foregoing account is uncorroborated, by apostolic letter we command you carefully to enquire into the truth and, if you find the occurrence to have happened as stated, not to debar the priest from celebrating the divine offices, since he will have committed homicide neither by will nor act, nor have deliberately attempted anything unlawful.

The Lateran, the 8th of November.

[Letter 3, March 6, 1202]

Innocent, bishop, servant of the servants of God, to his beloved sons the priors of St. Oswald and of Pontefract and Roger dean of Ledsham in the diocese of York, greeting and apostolic benediction.[3]

The petition of our beloved son William de Midelton has been read to us: it set forth that his father once pledged a piece of land at Ecclefechan to Ivo de Crossby of the diocese of York as security for a certain sum of money, and that, though the said Ivo in his lifetime and his son Richard after his death gained from that property the capital and more, nevertheless the said Richard, to the peril of his salvation, still holds it and refuses to return it. Therefore by apostolic letter we command you that, if the case is as stated, you should compel, without appeal, the said Richard to content himself with his capital, and to restore to the complainant the said land and any takings in excess of the capital sum, on threat of the penalty published in the Lateran Council against usurers.[4] If any witnesses cited have withdrawn through favor, hatred, or fear, you are to compel them, by ecclesiastical censure without appeal, to give evidence establishing the truth.

But if you cannot all take part in discharging this business, let two of you discharge it, notwithstanding.

The Lateran, the 6th of March, in the fifth year of our Pontificate.

---

[1] These are formulas so common as to allow abbreviation, rather like LOL today.

[2] There was no bishop, in fact; Hugh died in 1200 and no successor was appointed until 1203.

[3] St. Oswald in Yorkshire was a priory of Austin canons—that is, a community organized much like a monastery but made up of priests following the Rule of St. Augustine rather than of St. Benedict. The prior was Ralph (r.1199–1208). Pontefract, also in Yorkshire, was a Cluniac priory; its prior was Hugh (r.c.1184–c.1203). Roger of Ledsham, rural dean of Pontefract between 1191 and 1203, may be the third person addressed here.

[4] This was a reference to the decrees of the Third Lateran Council (1179).

6.11 Petitioning the papacy: *Register of Thomas of Hereford* (1281). Original in Latin.

This document is from the Episcopal Register of Thomas Cantilupe, bishop of Hereford (r.1275–1282). Episcopal registries, which came to be drawn up in the thirteenth century in England and elsewhere, were official record books, each put together by a scribe working for a bishop. They covered the gamut of episcopal activities, including visitations to monasteries (during which monks were interviewed and problems attended to), ordinations of priests, presentations of church benefices, excommunications, and, as here, appeals to the papal court. In this document, Bishop Thomas writes to his "proctors"—his agents—at the papal curia. All bishops depended largely on their manors to generate the income that they needed; when Thomas complains about the "poverty of the bishopric," he means that he can ill afford the costs of litigation. He has to go into debt to Italian bankers, whom he calls the "merchants of Pistoia." One case that Thomas is litigating has to do with "the cause against St. Asaph." This refers to his dispute with Anian II, bishop of St. Asaph, in Wales, who claimed the right to some of the same parishes that Thomas claimed. The pope referred the dispute to John Peckham, the archbishop of Canterbury (r.1279–1292), but Thomas, who was already disputing Peckham's jurisdiction over Hereford, appealed to the pope—at considerable cost.

[Source: *English Historical Documents*, vol. 3: 1189–1327, ed. Harry Rothwell (London: Routledge, 1975), pp. 763–65 (notes modified).]

To our proctors staying at the Roman court. To masters William Brun and John de Bitterley greeting. Although word has passed between us before and an account by letter followed afterwards upon the same matter, i.e. of "visiting"[1] every one of the cardinals, we think after deliberation that the burden of debt and the poverty of the bishopric do not permit this; yet, because we understand, know indeed, that affairs in the curia are not advanced at all unless there are visits general and particular, we send you on that account for the expediting of our affairs by letters of merchants of Pistoia one hundred pounds sterling to be received in sterling or *gros* of Tours. Which sum of money, though it seems little, can nevertheless be useful if carefully distributed, which in the judgment of some can be done in this way: viz [clearly], that sir Hugh, the English cardinal, should have thirty marks, sir Gerard, cardinal, our auditor,[2] ten pounds, and his household five marks. Sir Matthew Ruffus, cardinal, ten marks, sir Jordan, cardinal, ten marks, the vice-chancellor, fifteen pounds, the auditor of objections, ten marks, B. de Neapoli and another notary who is particularly outstanding and particularly intimate with the lord pope, twenty marks in equal portions; the chamberlain of the lord pope ten marks, the usher of the lord pope, forty shillings sterling. To others it seems that five marks can be deducted from the sum set aside for the vice-chancellor, so that he has ten marks only; from the two notaries and the chamberlain of the pope they can subtract seven and a half marks so that each of them has as much as the other. And so of the hundred pounds there will remain 33½ marks.[3]

To others it seems that it would be a good thing to bear in mind the pope, with whom the archbishop (from whom appeal is being made) is on familiar terms, to the extent of forty or fifty marks, first taking out of the list

---

[1] That is, "giving gifts."

[2] I.e., the judge delegated to hear the bishop's cause.

[3] The arithmetic is faulty, but could be corrected by assuming a copyist's error and reading fifteen marks (instead of pounds) for the vice-chancellor in the first scheme.

as many people as would together receive that amount of money. But to us it seems that the middle way is more profitable and honorable, though if necessity compels it, let the pope be considered in some way which will please him on whom it is recognized all favor depends. This however which we write about the pope we have no mind for, unless for lack of its being done our cause against St. Asaph and our other affairs were to be manifestly in danger. For which reason we should very much like you to present forty or fifty marks, or jewels to that amount, to the said lord rather by raising a new loan than that you should subtract any part of the aforementioned sum. For contracting which loan we are not sending you our signet because we do not believe that it is necessary for us to do this this time. The merchants of Pistoia, we believe, will, to oblige us, lend us on any sort of bond of ours that amount of money. But if it is not possible to provide for our needs through them or our other friends, then you may take out of the hundred pounds for the lord's use[1] as much as you consider expedient, distributing what is left of the said money amongst the others as shall seem expedient for advancing our cause and our other affairs. In the cause against St. Asaph let us hold in the main to the rule of the defendant, whose instinct is to drag out the cause as long as possible. In the aforementioned cause, however, in which we have an acceptance lately drawn up in legal form of the appeal from [the decision of] the lord archbishop of Canterbury, we do not wish to hunt for shameful and doubtful subterfuges with which to sway the mind of the judge or such things as might render us suspect in his eyes or by which danger might threaten us if we are sent back to the former judge: a thing which perhaps might be preferred by our adversary. We wish instead to avoid the manifold dangers while the cause is at the aforesaid court; so long as our expenses incurred in sending a modest mission to obtain a decision are first refunded to us, or at least claimed with sufficient force, before he from whose decision we are appealing defers to our appeal; on account of that, as in this method of distribution, with which as we have stated above we are in more agreement, there are 33½ marks left over for distribution, we very much wish our lord the Spanish cardinal (to whom we are writing) to have ten marks and sir Benedict, cardinal, and sir James, cardinal, or William, the French cardinal, whichever of these at the time of distribution is friendlier with the lord pope and in the pro-

motion of our affairs is able to exert more influence for us, to have ten marks, indeed eleven marks. What is left over after these we leave you to deal with jointly, for one or more other visits or for other necessary expenditure.

After the distribution, though, we should like our envoys to return to us with the utmost speed, with your letters recounting what has been done and the attitude of the recipients, along with other news worth mentioning.

Because we are (praised be the Most High) so restored spiritually and improved bodily that our body suffices these days for the labors, troubles and duties of our office, we propose to return home about the feast of St. Michael if the Lord allows, especially because the lord king has now written twice to us about this since Easter. And if you send back one of our envoys or someone else to us to tell us the exact state of our cause we shall be able to send back to you our pleasure in writing before our return by him or another from Fontaine, where we shall then be. Indeed we do not want you to retain even one of our envoys for too long, since messengers sufficiently reliable and faithful return from the curia every day, by whom you will be able to tell us what you have to say and we thank you for having reported the state of affairs at the curia to us by such hitherto.

We are indeed sending you the contents of the letters in which we write as you ask, and in the light of them you will be able to speak more circumspectly with them. Mr. Adam de Fileby, according to what we have heard, will arrive at the curia soon. In what frame of mind he is, though, towards us we do not know at all.[2] If in addition to the amounts distributed and necessary expenses four marks can be paid to Mr. E. de Warefelde as salary, then by all means let it be done; that too among other things you might tell us about. And because in addition to the ten marks which you have received from us and which you have expended on difficult business of ours, you have spent eight shillings sterling and three shillings and one penny of *gros* of Tours, as we understand from a certain schedule of yours sent to us, we very much want you to recompense yourselves from the money sent to you, if it can be done conveniently for us.

If you can distribute the said money to better advantage than is set out in any of the ways mentioned, then in the name of the Lord do as will be most useful to us, provided there is agreement about what is done. Farewell. Given at Brynum on 16 June, A.D. 1281.

---

[1] *Ad opus Domini*—in the context, this is probably the lord pope.

[2] Relations were strained.

6.12 Mocking the papal bureaucracy: *The Gospel According to the Marks of Silver* (*c.*1200). Original in Latin.

The sorts of experiences Thomas of Hereford had at the papal curia and recorded in his *Register*, above, p. 327, especially the tips and other expenses he had to pay, led some people to mock the papacy and to interpret its need for revenues as simple greed. *The Gospel according to the Marks of Silver* satirizes the curia in the cadences of the Gospel of St. Mark 1:1: "The beginning of the gospel of Jesus Christ, the Son of God."

[Source: *The Medieval Record: Sources of Medieval History*, ed. Alfred J. Andrea (Boston: Houghton Mifflin, 1997), p. 296.]

Here begins the Gospel according to the marks of silver. In that time, the pope said unto the Romans: "When the Son of Man comes to the seat of Our majesty,[1] first say unto him, 'Friend, wherefore art thou come?'[2] But if he should persevere in his knocking and give thee nothing,[3] cast him forth into the outer darkness."[4] And it came to pass that a certain poor cleric came to the lord pope's court and cried out, saying: "Have mercy even unto me, ye doorkeepers of the pope, because the hand of poverty has touched me.[5] For I am needy and poor, and I beg thee to relieve my calamitous misery."[6] They, however, upon hearing this were right indignant and said: "Friend, thy poverty go with thee to damnation.[7] Get thee behind me, Satan, because ye taste not of the things that savor of money.[8] Amen, Amen, I say unto thee, thou shalt not enter into the joy of thy Lord, until thou hast given the very last penny."[9] And the pauper went away and sold his cloak and tunic and everything that he owned, and he gave to the cardinals, and the doorkeepers, and the chamberlains.[10] But they said: "And this, what is it among so much?" And they cast him out before the gates,[11] and he going forth wept bitterly[12] and could not be consoled.

Thereafter there came to the court a certain rich, fat, well-fed,[13] and bloated cleric, who had committed murder while engaging in a riot.[14] He first gave to the doorkeeper, in the second place to the chamberlain, and in the third place to the cardinals.[15] And they took counsel among themselves as to who of them should have received the most.[16] But the lord pope, hearing that his cardinals and ministers had received so many gifts from the cleric, took ill well unto death.[17] Then the rich cleric sent unto him a sweet elixir of gold and silver, and straightway he was

---

[1] Matt. 25: 31.

[2] Matt. 26: 50.

[3] Luke 11: 5–13 and Matt. 7: 7–11.

[4] Matt. 25: 30.

[5] Matt. 15: 22.

[6] Job 19: 21.

[7] Acts 8: 20.

[8] Mark 8: 33.

[9] Matt. 5: 26.

[10] Matt. 13: 44–46.

[11] Matt. 22: 13.

[12] Matt. 26: 75.

[13] Deut. 32: 15.

[14] Mark 15: 7.

[15] Matt. 25: 14–15.

[16] Matt. 20: 10.

[17] Phil. 2: 27.

recovered.[1] Then the lord pope called unto himself his cardinals and ministers and said unto them: "Brothers, be watchful lest anyone seduce thee with empty words.[2]

For I give unto you an example that even as much as I take, ye also should take."[3]

....

CONFRONTATIONS

6.13 Henry II and Becket: *Constitutions of Clarendon* (1164). Original in Latin.

As part of his reform of the English legal system, Henry II (r.1154–1189) expected "criminous clerks"—that is, clerics who were suspected of commiting a crime—to come before his courts. "Clerks" included numerous members of the minor Church orders and thus a large proportion of the free male population. Archbishop Thomas Becket (r.1162–1170) wanted church courts to have jurisdiction over all clerical cases. Pressed by the pope as well as by numerous cardinals and bishops to give in to Henry, Becket reluctantly agreed in 1164. The king insisted on a public assent, and the *Constitutions of Clarendon* was the result. It cast the issue as a matter of tradition, claiming to record the "customs, liberties and privileges" that prevailed in the time of Henry I (r.1100–1135). The *Constitutions* did not end the dispute between Henry and Becket, however. Becket escaped to France, hurling excommunications from there against bishops and great laymen in England who, in his view, infringed on his rights. When Becket returned to England, Henry II famously (but perhaps apocryphally) let slip the words, "Will no one rid me of this turbulent priest?" Four knights in the royal entourage took to the road and murdered Becket in his cathedral at Canterbury (in 1170), turning him into an instant martyr. In the end most of the provisions of the *Constitutions* stood, regulating the relationship between royal courts and criminous clerks.

[Source: *English Historical Documents*, vol. 2: 1042–1189, ed. David C. Douglas and George W. Greenaway, 2nd ed. (London: Routledge, 1981), pp. 766–70 (notes modified).]

In the year 1164 from our Lord's Incarnation, being the fourth of the pontificate of Alexander,[4] and the tenth of Henry II, most illustrious king of the English, in the presence of the said king was made this record and declaration of a certain part of the customs, liberties and privileges of his ancestors, that is, of King Henry, his grandfather, and of other things which ought to be observed and maintained in the realm. And by reason of the dissensions and discords which had arisen between the clergy and the justices of the lord king and the barons of the realm concerning the customs and privileges of the realm, this declaration was made in the presence of the archbishops, bishops and clergy, and of the earls, barons and magnates of the realm. And these same customs were acknowledged by the archbishops and bishops, and the earls, barons, nobles and elders of the

---

[1] John 5: 9.

[2] Eph. 5: 6.

[3] John 13: 15.

[4] Alexander III (1159–1181).

realm. Thomas, archbishop of Canterbury; and Roger, archbishop of York; Gilbert, bishop of London; Henry, bishop of Winchester....[1]

Now of the acknowledged customs and privileges of the realm a certain part is contained in the present document, of which part these are the heads:

1. If a dispute shall arise between laymen, or between clerks and laymen, or between clerks, concerning advowson and presentation to churches, let it be treated and concluded in the court of the lord king.[2]

2. Churches within the fief of the lord king cannot be granted in perpetuity without his consent and concession.[3]

3. Clerks cited and accused of any matter shall, when summoned by the king's justice, come before the king's court to answer there concerning matters which shall seem to the king's court to be answerable there, and before the ecclesiastical court for what shall seem to be answerable there, but in such a way that the justice of the king shall send to the court of holy Church to see how the case is there tried. And if the clerk shall be convicted or shall confess, the Church ought no longer to protect him.[4]

4. It is not lawful for archbishops, bishops and beneficed clergy of the realm to depart from the kingdom without the lord king's leave. And if they do so depart, they shall, if the king so please, give security that neither in going, nor in tarrying, nor in returning will they contrive evil or injury against the king or the kingdom.[5]

5. Excommunicates ought not to give pledges of security for future good behavior nor take oaths, but only to give sufficient pledge of security to abide by the judgment of the Church in order to obtain absolution.

6. Laymen ought not to be accused save by accredited and lawful accusers and witnesses in the presence of the bishop, in such a way, however, that the archdeacon may not lose his right nor anything due to him thereby. And if the accused persons be such that no one either wishes or dares to prefer a charge against them, the sheriff, when requested by the bishop, shall cause twelve lawful men of the neighborhood or township to swear before the bishop that they will manifest the truth of the matter to the best of their knowledge.

7. No one who holds of the king in chief nor any of the officials of his demesne[6] shall be excommunicated, nor the lands of any of them placed under interdict, unless application shall first be made to the lord king, if he be in the realm, or to his chief justice, if he be abroad, that right may be done him; in such wise that matters pertaining to the royal court shall be concluded there, and matters pertaining to the ecclesiastical court shall be sent thither to be dealt with.

8. With regard to appeals, if they should arise, they should proceed from the archdeacon to the bishop, and from the bishop to the archbishop. And if the archbishop should fail to do justice, the case must finally be brought to the lord king, in order that by his command the dispute may be determined in the archbishop's court, in such a way that it proceed no further without the assent of the lord king.[7]

9. If a dispute shall arise between a clerk and a layman, or between a layman and a clerk, in respect of any holding which the clerk desires to treat as free alms, but the layman as lay fee, it shall be determined by the recognition of twelve lawful men through the deliberation,

---

[1] Here numerous bishops are named and said to have "agreed, and by word of mouth steadfastly promised on the word of truth to the lord king and his heirs, that these customs should be kept and observed in good faith and without evil intent." After that come the names of numerous "magnates and nobles of the realm."

[2] "Advowson and presentation" had to do with rights over churches. The Church claimed that suits arising out of such disputes had to do with spiritual matters, while the king regarded them as questions of property.

[3] I.e., the ownership of churches on royal estates was not to be transferred without the king's consent. The object of this clause was to preserve all the rights and services due the king. Becket raised no objection to this clause.

[4] I.e., a clerk accused of a grave offense, murder and the like, was to answer before the king's justice for the breach of the king's peace committed by the felony. He was then to be sent on the church court to answer there, as a clerk, to the homicide. If convicted, he would be "degraded," and the "Church ought no longer to protect him." He was then to be brought back to the king's court as a layman, to be sentenced to the penalties any other layman would suffer—that is, either death or mutilation. The provision that the "justice of the king shall send to the court of holy Church to see how the case is there tried" was meant to ensure that the offender would not escape.

[5] This clause was an attempt to prevent appeals to Rome.

[6] This clause protected the royal tenants-in-chief, i.e., those who held fiefs directly from the king.

[7] I.e., no appeals might proceed to Rome without the king's consent.

and in the presence of the king's chief justice, *whether* the holding pertains to free alms or to lay fee.[1] And if it be judged to pertain to free alms, the plea shall be heard in the ecclesiastical court; but if to lay fee, it shall be heard in the king's court, unless both of them shall claim from the same bishop or baron. But if each of them appeal concerning this fief to the same bishop or baron, the plea shall be heard in the latter's court, in such a way that he who was originally in possession shall not lose possession by reason of the recognition that has been made, until the matter has been settled by the plea.

10. If any one of a city or castle or borough or demesne manor of the lord king be cited by archdeacon or bishop for any offence for which he is obliged to make answer to them, and he refuse to give satisfaction at their citations, it is highly proper to place him under interdict;[2] but he ought not to be excommunicated until application has been made to the chief officer of the lord king in that town, in order that it may be adjudged proper for him to make satisfaction. But if the king's officer fails to act in this, he himself shall be at the mercy[3] of the lord king, and thereafter the bishop shall be allowed to coerce the accused by ecclesiastical justice.

11. Archbishops, bishops and all beneficed clergy of the realm, who hold of the king in chief, have their possessions from the lord king by barony and are answerable for them to the king's justices and officers; they observe and perform all royal rights and customs and, like other barons, ought to be present at the judgments of the king's court together with the barons,[4] until a case shall arise involving a judgment concerning mutilation or death.[5]

12. When an archbishopric or bishopric is vacant, or any abbey or priory of the king's demesne, it ought to be in the king's hand, and he shall receive from it all revenues and profits as part of his demesne. And when the time shall come to provide for the church, the lord king ought to summon the more important of the beneficed clergy of the church, and the election ought to take place in the lord king's chapel with the assent of the lord king and the advice of the clergy of the realm whom he shall summon for this purpose. And the clerk elected shall there do homage and fealty to the lord king as his liege lord for his life and limbs and his earthly honor, saving his order, before he is consecrated.[6]

13. If any of the magnates of the realm should forcibly prevent an archbishop or bishop or archdeacon from doing justice to himself or to his people, the lord king ought to bring him to justice. And if perchance anyone should forcibly dispossess the lord king of his right, the archbishops, bishops and archdeacons ought to bring him to justice, so that he may make satisfaction to the lord king.

14. The chattels of those who are under forfeiture to the king may not be retained by any church or cemetery against the king's justice, because they belong to the king, whether they be found within the churches or without.[7]

15. Pleas of debt due under pledge of faith, or even without pledge of faith, are to lie in the justice of the king.[8]

16. Sons of villeins ought not to be ordained without the consent of the lord on whose land they are known to have been born.[9]

---

[1] "Free alms" versus "lay fee" refer to the terms by which land was held. Land was held in "free alms" when it was held in exchange for prayers or other charitable activity; it was held in "lay fee" when it owed feudal obligations.

[2] "Interdict" refers to the ecclesiastical punishment of denying a person participation in most sacraments and burial in consecrated ground.

[3] "At the mercy of the lord king," i.e., liable to a royal fine.

[4] I.e., ecclesiastical tenants-in-chief of the crown were to hold their fiefs by ordinary feudal tenures and were bound by feudal laws and customs, including being present at court to give the king counsel.

[5] By canon law no churchman could be present at, or take part in, the "shedding of blood"; hence the ecclesiastical tenants-in-chief of the king were to leave the court when sentences of this nature were pronounced.

[6] King Henry I and his archbishop, Anselm, fought their own "Investiture Conflict" in the early twelfth century, and the outcome, which was a precedent for the Concordat of Worms, is here placed on record: the king had a role in the election of bishops—but did not appoint them outright—and the cleric, before consecration, did "homage and fealty" to the king for his "life and limbs and earthly honor"—that is, his temporal possessions.

[7] This clause asserted the king's right over the chattels—i.e., the movable property—left by those who had been condemned for treason or felony and had fled the country. Such possessions were often stored within ecclesiastical precincts, where they enjoyed the privilege of sanctuary. The king regarded this as an abuse of his rights.

[8] I.e., under the king's jurisdiction.

[9] A clause aimed at preventing the loss of villein (also spelled villan and villain) services to the lords.

This record of the aforesaid customs and privileges of the crown was drawn up by the archbishops, bishops, earls, barons, nobles and elders of the realm at Clarendon on the fourth day previous to the Purification of the Blessed Virgin Mary[1] in the presence of the lord Henry,[2] and of his father, the lord king. There are, moreover, many other great customs and privileges pertaining to holy mother-church and to the lord king and the barons of the realm which are not contained in this document. Let them be safe for holy Church and for our lord, the king and his heirs and the barons of the realm. And let them be inviolably observed for ever and ever.

6.14 Emperor and pope: *Diet of Besançon* (1157). Original in Latin.

In Germany, the election of Frederick I Barbarossa (r.1152–1190) brought peace after years of civil war. But the emperor's claim to overlordship in Italy—and in Rome—threatened the papacy's autonomy. The contest between ruler and pope in the empire was not about jurisdiction over criminous clerics, as it was in England; rather it was about how to understand the relationship between the institutions of empire and papacy. At Besançon the pope's emissaries reminded the emperor of the "dignity and honor" as well as the "emblem of the imperial crown" that the church at Rome had "conferred" on him—as if the symbol of empire had been the pope's to give. Adding insult to injury, the emissaries spoke of these gifts as "beneficia," a Latin word that meant both the neutral "benefits" and the potentially explosive "fiefs." Translated for the assembly by its more potent meaning, *beneficia* launched a diplomatic crisis. Ultimately the pope wrote a conciliatory letter to Frederick explaining that by *beneficia* he had meant only "good deeds," and the emergency passed. But the struggle between emperor and pope to define themselves with respect to each other continued.

[Source: *The Deeds of Frederick Barbarossa by Otto of Freising and his Continuator, Rahewin*, trans. Charles Christopher Mierow (New York: Columbia University Press, 1953), pp. 180–86 (slightly modified).]

8. ... In the middle of the month of October [1157] the emperor set out for Burgundy to hold a diet [meeting] at Besançon. Now Besançon is the metropolis of one of the three parts into which the renowned Charles the Great divided his empire for distribution among his three sons, all enjoying the royal title.[3] It is situated on the river Doubs. In this city practically all the chief men of that land had assembled, and also many ambassadors from foreign lands, namely, Romans, Apulians [i.e., from Apulia, in Italy], Tuscans, Venetians, Franks, English, and Spaniards, awaited the emperor's arrival. He was received with the most festive display and solemn acclaim. For the whole world recognized him as the most powerful and most merciful ruler, and undertook, with mingled love and fear, to honor him with new tokens of respect, to extol him with new praises.

But before our pen addresses itself to an account of the affairs of this province and its management, we must speak of the ambassadors of the Roman pontiff, Adrian [IV, 1154–1159]—why they came and how they departed—

---

[1] January 29, 1164.

[2] This was the son of Henry II, who died in 1183.

[3] After the death of Charlemagne (814) and his son Louis the Pious (840), the empire was divided among Louis's three sons. Besançon was in the portion that went to Lothar.

because the authority of this delegation was very great and their errand very serious. No one will complain at the prolixity of this account who considers carefully the importance of the matter and the length of time that this tempest has raged and still rages. The personnel of the embassy consisted of Roland, cardinal priest of the title of St. Mark and chancellor of the Holy Roman Church,[1] and Bernard, cardinal priest of the title of St. Clement, both distinguished for their wealth, their maturity of view, and their influence, and surpassing in prestige almost all others in the Roman Church.

Now the cause of their coming seemed to have an air of sincerity; but it was afterward clearly discerned that unrest and an occasion for mischief lay beneath the surface. One day, upon the prince's retiring from the uproar and tumult of the people, the aforesaid messengers were conducted into his presence in the more secluded retreat of a certain oratory and—as was fitting—were received with honor and kindness, claiming (as they did) to be the bearers of good tidings.

But the beginning of their speech appeared notable at the very outset. It is said to have been as follows: "Our most blessed father, Pope Adrian, salutes you, and the College of Cardinals of the Holy Roman Church, he as father, they as brethren." After a brief interval they produced the letter that they bore. Copies of this and other letters which passed back and forth in this time of confusion, I have taken pains to insert in this work that any reader who may wish to judge, attracted and summoned not by my words or assertions but by the actual writings of the parties themselves, may choose freely the side to which he desires to lend his favor. Now the content of the letter was as follows:

9. "Bishop Adrian, the servant of the servants of God, to his beloved son Frederick, the illustrious emperor of the Romans, greeting and apostolic benediction.

"We recollect having written, a few days since, to the Imperial Majesty, of that dreadful and accursed deed, an offense calling for atonement, committed in our time, and hitherto, we believe, never attempted in the German lands. In recalling it to Your Excellency, we cannot conceal our great amazement that even now you have permitted so pernicious a deed to go unpunished with

the severity it deserves. For how our venerable brother E[skil], archbishop of Lund, while returning from the apostolic see, was taken captive in those parts by certain godless and infamous men—a thing we cannot mention without great and heartfelt sorrow—and is still held in confinement;[2] how in taking him captive, as previously mentioned, those men of impiety, a seed of evildoers, children that are corrupters,[3] drew their swords and violently assaulted him and his companions, and how basely and shamefully they treated them, stripping them of all they had, Your Most Serene Highness knows, and the report of so great a crime has already spread abroad to the most distant and remote regions. To avenge this deed of exceptional violence, you, as a man to whom we believe good deeds are pleasing but evil works displeasing, ought with great determination to arise and bring down heavily upon the necks of the wicked the sword which was entrusted by divine providence to you 'for the punishment of evildoers and for the praise of them that do well,'[4] and should most severely punish the presumptuous. But you are reported so to have ignored and indeed been indifferent to this deed, that there is no reason why those men should be repentant at having incurred guilt, because they have long since perceived that they have secured immunity for the sacrilege which they have committed.

"Of the reason for this indifference and negligence we are absolutely ignorant, because no scruple of conscience accuses our heart of having in any way offended the glory of Your Serenity. Rather have we always loved, with sincere affection, and treated with an attitude of due kindness, your person as that of our most dear and specially beloved son and most Christian prince, who, we doubt not, is by the grace of God grounded on the rock of the apostolic confession.

"For you should recall, O most glorious son, before the eyes of your mind, how willingly and how gladly your mother, the Holy Roman Church, received you in another year, with what affection of heart she treated you, what great dignity and honor she bestowed upon you, and with how much pleasure she conferred the emblem of the imperial crown, zealous to cherish in her most kindly bosom the height of Your Sublimity, and doing nothing at all that she knew was in the least at variance with the royal will.

---

[1] Roland Bandinelli, later Pope Alexander III (1159–1181).

[2] Eskil (r.c.1100–1182) was archbishop of Lund (today Sweden but in Eskil's day part of Denmark). His efforts to free his church from the jurisdiction of the archbishop of Hamburg-Bremen may well have led to the "captivity" recorded here.

[3] See Isa. 1: 4.

[4] 1 Pet. 2: 14.

"Nor do we regret that we fulfilled in all respects the ardent desires of your heart; but if Your Excellency had received still greater benefits[1] at our hand (had that been possible), in consideration of the great increase and advantage that might through you accrue to the Church of God and to us, we would have rejoiced, not without reason.

"But now, because you seem to ignore and hide so heinous a crime, which is indeed known to have been committed as an affront to the Church universal and to your empire, we both suspect and fear that perhaps your thoughts were directed toward this indifference and neglect on this account: that at the suggestion of an evil man, sowing tares,[2] you have conceived against your most gracious mother the Holy Roman Church and against ourselves—God forbid!—some displeasure or grievance.

"On this account, therefore, and because of all the other matters of business which we know to impend, we have thought best to dispatch at this time from our side to Your Serenity two of the best and dearest of those whom we have about us, namely, our beloved sons, Bernard, cardinal priest of St. Clement's, and Roland, cardinal priest of St. Mark's and our chancellor, men very notable for piety and wisdom and honor. We very earnestly beseech Your Excellency that you receive them with as much respect as kindness, treat them with all honor, and that whatever they themselves set forth before Your Imperial Dignity on our behalf concerning this and concerning other matters to the honor of God and of the Holy Roman Church, and pertaining also to the glory and exaltation of the empire, you accept without any hesitation as though proceeding from our mouth. Give credence to their words, as if we were uttering them." [September 20, 1157.]

10. When this letter had been read and carefully set forth by Chancellor Rainald[3] in a faithful interpretation, the princes who were present were moved to great indignation, because the entire content of the letter appeared to have no little sharpness and to offer even at the very outset an occasion for future trouble. But what had particularly aroused them all was the fact that in the aforesaid letter it had been stated, among other things, that the fullness of dignity and honor had been bestowed upon the emperor by the Roman pontiff, that the emperor had received from his hand the imperial crown, and that he would not have regretted conferring even greater benefits (*beneficia*) upon him, in consideration of the great gain and advantage that might through him accrue to the Roman Church. And the hearers were led to accept the literal meaning of these words and to put credence in the aforesaid explanation because they knew that the assertion was rashly made by some Romans that hitherto our kings had possessed the imperial power over the City,[4] and the kingdom of Italy, by gift of the popes, and that they made such representations and handed them down to posterity not only orally but also in writing and in pictures. Hence it is written concerning Emperor Lothar, over a picture of this sort in the Lateran palace:

Coming before our gates, the king vows to safeguard the City,
Then, liegeman to the Pope, by him he is granted the crown.

Since such a picture and such an inscription, reported to him by those faithful to the empire, had greatly displeased the prince when he had been near the City in a previous year [1155], he is said to have received from Pope Adrian, after a friendly remonstrance, the assurance that both the inscription and the picture would be removed, lest so trifling a matter might afford the greatest men in the world an occasion for dispute and discord.

When all these matters were fully considered, and a great tumult and uproar arose from the princes of the realm at so insolent a message, it is said that one of the ambassadors, as though adding sword to flame,[5] inquired: "From whom then does he have the empire, if not from our lord the pope?" Because of this remark, anger reached such a pitch that one of them, namely, Otto, count palatine of Bavaria (it was said), threatened the ambassador with his sword. But Frederick, using his authority to quell the tumult, commanded that the ambassadors, being granted safe-conduct, be led to their quarters and that early in the morning they should set forth on their way; he ordered also that they were not to pause in the territories of the bishops and abbots, but to

---

[1] The word used was *beneficia*, which could mean "benefices" (i.e., fiefs) as well as benefits. The emperor and his attendants understood the first meaning, and they concluded that the pope claimed overlordship of the empire.

[2] Matt. 13: 25.

[3] Rainald of Dassel (*c.*1120–1167), archbishop of Cologne and imperial chancellor.

[4] Throughout this document, "the City" refers to Rome.

[5] See Horace, *Satires* 2.3.276.

return to the City by the direct road, turning neither to the right nor to the left. And so they returned without having accomplished their purpose, and what had been done by the emperor was published throughout the realm in the following letter [October 1157]:

11. "Whereas the Divine Sovereignty, from which is derived all power in heaven and on earth, has entrusted unto us, His anointed, the kingdom and the empire to rule over, and has ordained that the peace of the churches is to be maintained by the imperial arms, not without the greatest distress of heart are we compelled to complain to Your Benevolence that from the head of the Holy Church, on which Christ has set the imprint of his peace and love, there seem to be emanating causes of dissensions and evils, like a poison, by which, unless God avert it, we fear the body of the Church will be stained, its unity shattered, and a schism created between the temporal and spiritual realms.

"For when we were recently at the diet in Besançon and were dealing with the honor of the empire and the security of the Church with all due solicitude, apostolic legates arrived asserting that they bore to Our Majesty such tidings that the honor of the empire should receive no small increase. After we had honorably received them on the first day of their arrival, and on the second, as is customary, had seated ourself with our princes to hear their tidings, they, as though inspired by the Mammon of unrighteousness,[1] by lofty pride, by arrogant disdain, by execrable haughtiness, presented a message in the form of a letter from the pope, the content of which was to the effect that we ought always to remember the fact that the lord pope had bestowed upon us the imperial crown and would not even regret it if Our Excellency had received greater benefits (*beneficia*) from him.

"This was the message of fatherly kindness, which was to foster the unity of Church and empire, which was to bind them together in the bonds of peace, which was to bring the hearts of its hearers to harmony with both and obedience to both! Certain it is that at that impious message, devoid of all truth, not only did Our Imperial Majesty conceive a righteous indignation, but all the princes who were present were filled with so great fury and wrath that they would undoubtedly have condemned those two wicked priests to death, had not our presence averted this.

"Moreover, because many copies of this letter were found in their possession, and blank parchments with seals affixed that were still to be written on at their discretion, whereby—as has been their practice hitherto—they were endeavoring to scatter the venom of their iniquity throughout the churches of the Teutonic realm, to denude the altars, to carry off the vessels of the house of God,[2] to strip crosses of their coverings, we obliged them to return to the City by the way they had come, lest an opportunity be afforded them of proceeding further.

"And since, through election by the princes, the kingdom and the empire are ours from God alone, Who at the time of the passion of His Son Christ subjected the world to dominion by the two swords,[3] and since the apostle Peter taught the world this doctrine: 'Fear God, honor the king,'[4] whosoever says that we received the imperial crown as a benefice (*pro beneficio*) from the lord pope contradicts the divine ordinance and the doctrine of Peter and is guilty of a lie. But because we have hitherto striven to snatch from the hand of the Egyptians[5] the honor and freedom of the churches, so long oppressed by the yoke of undeserved slavery, and are intent on preserving to them all their rights and dignities, we ask Your University[6] to grieve at so great an insult to us and to the empire, hoping that your unwavering loyalty will not permit the honor of the empire, which has stood, glorious and undiminished, from the founding of the City and the establishment of the Christian religion even down to your days, to be disparaged by so unheard-of a novelty, such presumptuous arrogance, knowing that—all ambiguity aside—we would prefer to encounter the risk of death rather than to endure in our time the reproach of so great a disorder."

12. Having dealt thus with this matter, Frederick turned his attention to ordering the affairs of the empire in the kingdom of Burgundy.

---

[1] Luke 16: 9.

[2] Dan. 1: 2. The "Teutonic realm" is Germany.

[3] Luke 22: 38. Because Christ said of two swords, "It is enough," the passage was used as a justification for the equal power of the Church and the State.

[4] 1 Pet. 2: 17.

[5] See Ex. 18: 9; 1 Sam. 10: 18.

[6] I.e., the Pope as the Universal Pope.

6.15 King and nobles: *Magna Carta* (1215). Original in Latin.

After King John's sound defeat by the king of France at the Battle of Bouvines (1214), the barons of England, angry about losing their French possessions and chafing under the taxes and other indignities they had suffered at John's hands in his quest for revenues, rebelled. At Runnymede in 1215 they forced the king to give his assent to a charter that has come to be known as *Magna Carta*. In the version published below, the starred clauses indicate those that were not repeated when *Magna Carta* was reissued in 1225. What were the enduring provisions of this document, and whom did they benefit?

[Source: *English Historical Documents*, vol. 3: 1189–1327, ed. Harry Rothwell (London and New York: Routledge, 1975), pp. 316–24 (notes added).]

John, by the grace of God, king of England, lord of Ireland, duke of Normandy and Aquitaine, and count of Anjou, to the archbishops, bishops, abbots, earls, barons, justiciars, foresters, sheriffs, stewards, servants, and to all his bailiffs and faithful subjects, greeting. Know that we, out of reverence for God and for the salvation of our soul and those of all our ancestors and heirs, for the honor of God and the exaltation of holy church, and for the reform of our realm, on the advice of our venerable fathers, Stephen, archbishop of Canterbury, primate of all England and cardinal of the holy Roman church, Henry archbishop of Dublin, William of London, Peter of Winchester, Jocelyn of Bath and Glastonbury, Hugh of Lincoln,... [The names of numerous churchmen and barons follow.]

[1] In the first place have granted to God, and by this our present charter confirmed for us and our heirs for ever that the English church shall be free, and shall have its rights undiminished and its liberties unimpaired; and it is our will that it be thus observed; which is evident from the fact that, before the quarrel between us and our barons began, we willingly and spontaneously granted and by our charter confirmed the freedom of elections which is reckoned most important and very essential to the English church, and obtained confirmation of it from the lord pope Innocent III,[1] which we will observe and we wish our heirs to observe it in good faith for ever. We have

also granted to all free men of our kingdom, for ourselves and our heirs for ever, all the liberties written below, to be had and held by them and their heirs of us and our heirs.

[2] If any of our earls or barons or others holding of us in chief by knight service dies, and at his death his heir be of full age and owe relief[2] he shall have his inheritance on payment of the old relief, namely the heir or heirs of an earl £100 for a whole earl's barony, the heir or heirs of a baron £100 for a whole barony, the heir or heirs of a knight 100s, at most, for a whole knight's fee; and he who owes less shall give less according to the ancient usage of fiefs.

[3] If, however, the heir of any such be under age and a ward, he shall have his inheritance when he comes of age without paying relief and without making fine.

[4] The guardian of the land of such an heir who is under age shall take from the land of the heir no more than reasonable revenues, reasonable customary dues and reasonable services, and that without destruction and waste of men or goods;[3] and if we commit the wardship of the land of any such to a sheriff, or to any other who is answerable to us for its revenues, and he destroys or wastes what he has wardship of, we will take compensation from him and the land shall be committed to two lawful and discreet men of that fief, who shall be answerable for the revenues to us or to him to whom we have assigned them; and if we give or sell to anyone the

---

[1] Innocent III (1198–1216).

[2] "Relief" was the payment that the heir of a vassal made to the lord upon inheriting the fief.

[3] The king had previously sold wardships to men who cut down the trees and otherwise exploited the property, leaving little for the wards when they came into their inheritance.

wardship of any such land and he causes destruction or waste therein, he shall lose that wardship, and it shall be transferred to two lawful and discreet men of that fief, who shall similarly be answerable to us as is aforesaid.

[5] Moreover, so long as he has the wardship of the land, the guardian shall keep in repair the houses, parks, preserves, ponds, mills and other things pertaining to the land out of the revenues from it; and he shall restore to the heir when he comes of age his land fully stocked with ploughs and the means of husbandry according to what the season of husbandry requires and the revenues of the land can reasonably bear.

[6] Heirs shall be married without disparagement,[1] yet so that before the marriage is contracted those nearest in blood to the heir shall have notice.

[7] A widow shall have her marriage portion and inheritance forthwith and without difficulty after the death of her husband; nor shall she pay anything to have her dower or her marriage portion or the inheritance which she and her husband held on the day of her husband's death; and she may remain in her husband's house for forty days after his death, within which time her dower shall be assigned to her.[2]

[8] No widow shall be forced to marry so long as she wishes to live without a husband provided that she gives security not to marry without our consent if she holds of us or without the consent of her lord of whom she holds, if she holds of another.[3]

[9] Neither we nor our bailiffs will seize for any debt any land or rent, so long as the chattels of the debtor are sufficient to repay the debt....

*[10] If anyone who has borrowed from the Jews any sum, great or small, dies before it is repaid, the debt shall not bear interest as long as the heir is under age, of whomsoever he holds; and if the debt falls into our hands, we will not take anything except the principal mentioned in the bond.

*[11] And if anyone dies indebted to the Jews, his wife shall have her dower and pay nothing of that debt; and if the dead man leaves children who are under age, they shall be provided with necessaries befitting the holding of the deceased; and the debt shall be paid out of the residue, reserving, however, service due to lords of the land; debts owing to others than Jews shall be dealt with in like manner.[4]

*[12] No scutage or aid shall be imposed in our kingdom unless by common counsel of our kingdom, except for ransoming our person, for making our eldest son a knight, and for once marrying our eldest daughter; and for these only a reasonable aid shall be levied.[5] Be it done in like manner concerning aids from the city of London.

[13] And the city of London shall have all its ancient liberties and free customs as well by land as by water. Furthermore, we will and grant that all other cities, boroughs, towns, and ports shall have all their liberties and free customs.[6]

*[14] And to obtain the common counsel of the kingdom about the assessing of an aid (except in the three cases aforesaid) or of a scutage, we will cause to be summoned the archbishops, bishops, abbots, earls and greater barons, individually by our letters—and, in addition, we will cause to be summoned generally through our sheriffs and bailiffs all those holding of us in chief—for a fixed date, namely, after the expiry of at least forty days, and to a fixed place; and in all letters of such summons we will specify the reason for the summons. And when the summons has thus been made, the business shall proceed on the day appointed, according to the counsel of those present, though not all have come who were summoned.

*[15] We will not in future grant any one the right to take an aid from his free men, except for ransoming his person, for making his eldest son a knight and for once marrying his eldest daughter, and for these only a reasonable aid shall be levied.

---

1   The king had previously made money by forcing heirs to marry beneath them ("with disparagement"). In effect, he sold off diseased or disfigured widows and wards.

2   The dower was the gift the husband gave his new wife, which remained her property upon his death.

3   The king had previously been marrying widows to the highest bidder.

4   The Jews were the property of the king, who shared in their gains. Limiting the amounts that Jews might charge also affected the king.

5   Scutage was a money payment in lieu of military service, and it was much favored by the king, who could then hire warriors rather than make do with vassals who owed only 40 days' service. By denying the king the right to demand scutages without their consent (here and in clause 14) the barons were in effect denying the king's right to an effective army. Aids were customary payments from a vassal to his lord, but the king had been requiring these aids much more frequently, and for many more occasions, than was traditional.

6   For an example of such liberties see *Privileges for the Citizens of London* (above, p. 257).

[16] No one shall be compelled to do greater service for a knight's fee or for any other free holding than is due from it.

[17] Common pleas shall not follow our court, but shall be held in some fixed place.[1]

[18] Recognitions of *novel disseisin*, of *mort d'ancester*, and of *darrein presentment*, shall not be held elsewhere than in the counties to which they relate,[2] and in this manner—we, or, if we should be out of the realm, our chief justiciar,[3] will send two justices through each county four times a year, who, with four knights of each county chosen by the county, shall hold the said assizes in the county and on the day and in the place of meeting of the county court....

[20] A free man shall not be amerced [fined] for a trivial offence except in accordance with the degree of the offence, and for a grave offence he shall be amerced in accordance with its gravity, yet saving his way of living;[4] and a merchant in the same way, saving his stock-in-trade; and a villein shall be amerced in the same way, saving his means of livelihood—if they have fallen into our mercy:[5] and none of the aforesaid amercements shall be imposed except by the oath of good men of the neighborhood.

[21] Earls and barons shall not be amerced except by their peers, and only in accordance with the degree of the offence.

[22] No clerk shall be amerced in respect of his lay holding except after the manner of the others aforesaid and not according to the amount of his ecclesiastical benefice.

[23] No vill or individual shall be compelled to make bridges at river banks, except those who from of old are legally bound to do so.[6]

[24] No sheriff, constable, coroners, or others of our bailiffs, shall hold pleas of our crown.[7]

*[25] All counties, hundreds, wapentakes and trithings[8] shall be at the old rents without any additional payment, except our demesne manors....

*[27] If any free man dies without leaving a will, his chattels [movable goods] shall be distributed by his nearest kinsfolk and friends under the supervision of the church, saving to every one the debts which the deceased owed him.

[28] No constable or other bailiff of ours shall take anyone's corn [grain] or other chattels unless he pays on the spot in cash for them or can delay payment by arrangement with the seller.

[29] No constable shall compel any knight to give money instead of castle-guard if he is willing to do the guard himself or through another good man, if for some good reason he cannot do it himself; and if we lead or send him on military service, he shall be excused guard in proportion to the time that because of us he has been on service.

[30] No sheriff, or bailiff of ours, or anyone else shall take the horses or carts of any free man for transport work save with the agreement of that freeman.

[31] Neither we nor our bailiffs will take, for castles or other works of ours, timber which is not ours, except with the agreement of him whose timber it is.

[32] We will not hold for more than a year and a day the lands of those convicted of felony, and then the lands shall be handed over to the lords of the fiefs.

[33] Henceforth all fish-weirs [traps] shall be cleared completely from the Thames and the Medway and throughout all England, except along the sea coast.

[34] The writ called *Praecipe* shall not in future be

---

[1] For an example of the expenses involved in following the king's court around in order to pursue a suit, see *The Costs of Richard of Anstey's Lawsuit*, p. 313 above. In John's day the establishment of a permanent court at Westminster was in fact underway.

[2] *Novel disseisin, mort d'ancester*, and *darrein presentment* were the names of royal writs. By purchasing one of these, suitors could bring disputes involving property into the royal courts, where they would be heard locally by the king's justices, deciding on the basis of the sworn testimony of 12 jurors.

[3] The king's justiciar was by this time the king's representative in all matters.

[4] "Saving his way of living," that is, allowing him and his dependents enough to live on.

[5] "Fallen into our mercy," that is, liable to our—the king's—fines. Amercements are fines.

[6] The king claimed the right to compel the local population to repair bridges so that royal hunts could take place. John had ordered the repair of numerous bridges in order to impose heavy fines on those who did not comply.

[7] I.e., all criminal trials were to be held under the auspices of the king's justices.

[8] "Hundreds, wapentakes and trithings" were subdivisions of the county. The rents were collected by the sheriff, who gave a fixed portion to the royal treasury and kept the rest for himself.

issued to anyone in respect of any holding whereby a free man may lose his court.[1]

[35] Let there be one measure for wine throughout our kingdom, and one measure for ale, and one measure for corn, namely "the London quarter"; and one width for cloths whether dyed, russet or halberget, namely two ells within the selvedges. Let it be the same with weights as with measures.

[36] Nothing shall be given or taken in future for the writ of inquisition of life or limbs: instead it shall be granted free of charge and not refused.[2] ...

[39] No free man shall be arrested or imprisoned or disseised or outlawed or exiled or in any way victimized, neither will we attack him or send anyone to attack him, except by the lawful judgment of his peers or by the law of the land.[3]

[40] To no one will we sell, to no one will we refuse or delay right or justice.

[41] All merchants shall be able to go out of and come into England safely and securely and stay and travel throughout England, as well by land as by water, for buying and selling by the ancient and right customs free from all evil tolls, except in time of war and if they are of the land that is at war with us. And if such are found in our land at the beginning of a war, they shall be attached,[4] without injury to their persons or goods, until we, or our chief justiciar, know how merchants of our land are treated who were found in the land at war with us when war broke out; and if ours are safe there, the others shall be safe in our land....

*[47] All forests that have been made forest in our time shall be immediately dis-afforested; and so be it done with river banks that have been made preserves[5] by us in our time.

*[48] All evil customs connected with forests and warrens, foresters and warreners, sheriffs and their officials, river-banks and their wardens shall immediately be inquired into in each county by twelve sworn knights of the same county who are to be chosen by good men of the same county, and within forty days of the completion of the inquiry shall be utterly abolished by them so as never to be restored, provided that we, or our justiciar if we are not in England, know of it first....

*[51] As soon as peace is restored, we will remove from the kingdom all foreign knights, cross-bowmen, serjeants, and mercenaries, who have come with horses and arms to the detriment of the kingdom.

*[52] If anyone has been disseised [dispossessed] of or kept out of his lands, castles, franchises or his right by us without the legal judgment of his peers, we will immediately restore them to him: and if a dispute arises over this, then let it be decided by the judgment of the twenty-five barons who are mentioned below in the clause for securing the peace:[6] for all the things, however, which anyone has been disseised or kept out of without the lawful judgment of his peers by king Henry, our father, or by king Richard, our brother, which we have in our hand or are held by others, to whom we are bound to warrant them, we will have the usual period of respite of crusaders,[7] excepting those things about which a plea was started or an inquest made by our command before we took the cross; when however we return from our pilgrimage, or if by any chance we do not go on it, we will at once do full justice therein....

[54] No one shall be arrested or imprisoned upon the appeal of a woman for the death of anyone except her husband.[8] ...

*[56] If we have disseised or kept out Welshmen from lands or liberties or other things without the legal judg-

---

[1]   The royal writ *Praecipe* took a case out of local courts and put it under royal jurisdiction. The barons who demanded Magna Carta wanted to preserve their customary courts. Reading *Proceedings for the Abbey of Bec*, p. 320 above, may help to explain why.

[2]   Anyone accused of homicide and subject to trial by combat could claim that his accuser had brought charges "out of spite and hate" and buy a "writ of inquisition of life or limbs" that would require a local jury to determine whether trial by combat was lawful. This clause made the writ free.

[3]   This, the most famous clause of Magna Carta, was not a guarantee of trial by jury but was a privilege granted to all free men (a minority of the population, consisting of barons, knights [i.e. gentry] and some particularly substantial peasants who held free, rather than servile, land) that they be judged according to established procedures by members of their own class. To be "disseised" meant to be dispossessed of one's property.

[4]   I.e., seized.

[5]   The king had claimed the right to "afforest" whole districts, turning open land into forests, so that he might hunt there, and he had set apart river banks so that he might catch the birds flying there.

[6]   See clause 61.

[7]   The "respite for crusaders" was three years' immunity from all litigation and payment of debts.

[8]   A woman could choose her own champion in a trial by combat, and thus she was thought to have an unfair advantage in bringing a charge.

ment of their peers in England or in Wales, they shall be immediately restored to them; and if a dispute arises over this, then let it be decided in the March[1] by the judgment of their peers—for holdings in England according to the law of England, for holdings in Wales according to the law of Wales, and for holdings in the March according to the law of the March. Welshmen shall do the same to us and ours....

*[59] We will act toward Alexander, king of the Scots, concerning the return of his sisters and hostages and concerning his franchises and his right in the same manner in which we act towards our other barons of England, unless it ought to be otherwise by the charters which we have from William his father, formerly king of the Scots, and this shall be determined by the judgment of his peers in our court.

[60] All these aforesaid customs and liberties which we have granted to be observed in our kingdom as far as it pertains to us towards our men, all of our kingdom, clerks as well as laymen, shall observe as far as it pertains to them towards their men.

*[61] Since, moreover, for God and the betterment of our kingdom and for the better allaying of the discord that has arisen between us and our barons we have granted all these things aforesaid, wishing them to enjoy the use of them unimpaired and unshaken for ever, we give and grant them the under-written security, namely, that the barons shall choose any twenty-five barons of the kingdom they wish, who must with all their might observe, hold and cause to be observed, the peace and liberties which we have granted and confirmed to them by this present charter of ours, so that if we, or our justiciar, or our bailiffs or any one of our servants offend in any way against anyone or transgress any of the articles of the peace or the security and the offence be notified to four of the aforesaid twenty-five barons, those four barons shall come to us, or to our justiciar if we are out of the kingdom, and, laying the transgression before us, shall petition us to have that transgression corrected without delay. And if we do not correct the transgressions or if we are out of the kingdom, if our justiciar does not correct it, within forty days, reckoning from the time it was brought to our notice or to that of our justiciar if we were out of the kingdom, the aforesaid four barons shall refer that case to the rest of the twenty-five barons and those twenty-five barons together with the community of the whole land shall distrain and distress us in every way they can, namely, by seizing castles, lands, possessions,

and in such other ways as they can, saving our person and the persons of our queen and our children, until, in their opinion, amends have been made; and when amends have been made, they shall obey us as they did before. And let anyone in the land who wishes take an oath to obey the orders of the said twenty-five barons for the execution of all the aforesaid matters, and with them to distress us as much as he can, and we publicly and freely give anyone leave to take the oath who wishes to take it and we will never prohibit anyone from taking it. Indeed, all those in the land who are unwilling of themselves and of their own accord to take an oath to the twenty-five barons to help them to distrain and distress us, we will make them take the oath as aforesaid at our command. And if any of the twenty-five barons dies or leaves the country or is in any other way prevented from carrying out the things aforesaid, the rest of the aforesaid twenty-five barons shall choose as they think fit another one in his place, and he shall take the oath like the rest. In all matters the execution of which is committed to these twenty-five barons, if it should happen that these twenty-five are present yet disagree among themselves about anything, or if some of those summoned will not or cannot be present, that shall be held as fixed and established which the majority of those present ordained or commanded, exactly as if all the twenty-five had consented to it; and the said twenty-five shall swear that they will faithfully observe all the things aforesaid and will do all they can to get them observed. And we will procure nothing from anyone, either personally or through anyone else, whereby any of these concessions and liberties might be revoked or diminished; and if any such thing is procured, let it be void and null, and we will never use it either personally or through another.

*[62] And we have fully remitted and pardoned to everyone all the ill-will, indignation and rancor that have arisen between us and our men, clergy and laity, from the time of the quarrel. Furthermore, we have fully remitted to all, clergy and laity, and as far as pertains to us have completely forgiven, all trespasses occasioned by the same quarrel between Easter in the sixteenth year of our reign and the restoration of peace. And, besides, we have caused to be made for them letters testimonial patent of the lord Stephen archbishop of Canterbury, of the lord Henry archbishop of Dublin and of the aforementioned bishops and of master Pandulf about this security and the aforementioned concessions.

*[63] Wherefore we wish and firmly enjoin that the English church shall be free, and that the men in our

---

[1] The March was the border region between England and Wales.

kingdom shall have and hold all the aforesaid liberties, rights and concessions well and peacefully, freely and quietly, fully and completely, for themselves and their heirs from us and our heirs, in all matters and in all places for ever, as is aforesaid. An oath, moreover, has been taken, as well on our part as on the part of the barons, that all these things aforesaid shall be observed in good faith and without evil disposition. Witness the above-mentioned and many others. Given by our hand in the meadow which is called Runnymede between Windsor and Staines on the fifteenth day of June, in the seventeenth year of our reign.

CARING FOR THE BODY

6.16 The abbot of Cluny seeks medical help: *Letters between Peter the Venerable and Doctor Bartholomew* (*c.*1151). Original in Latin.

When Peter the Venerable, abbot of Cluny (see his *Miracles* above, p. 300) caught a cold, he sought medical advice from "Master Bartholomew." This was probably Bartholomew of Salerno (*fl. c.*1150–1180), the author of many important medical texts, including a widely read commentary on all the parts of the *Articella* (see above, p. 289). Peter the Venerable was not the only patient of Bartholomew, whose expertise was sought by "so many" (as Peter says) members of the French elites. Note how both patient and doctor invoke friendship as the foundation of their communications.

[Source: *Medieval Medicine: A Reader*, ed. Faith Wallis (Toronto: University of Toronto Press, 2010), pp. 406–9 (notes added from glossary). Translated by Faith Wallis.]

To Doctor Bartholomew

To our beloved Master Bartholomew, brother Peter, the humble abbot of Cluny, [sends] greetings and familiar affection.

Ever since I saw you at Cluny last year, I have held you ever in my heart and loved you most affectionately. For I cherished your great knowledge and loved even more that which is more worthy of love in any person, namely, your character, which is of the highest caliber. Hence because (as I said) I love you, I dare to ask you to love me as well. For this reason I bring certain matters to your notice as a friend, because I stand in need of your advice. For almost a year I have been repeatedly afflicted with the disease called catarrh [a head cold]; I have had it twice already, once in the summer and once in the winter or around that time. This year I came down with it at the end of summer and beginning of autumn. Prior to this, I had had [legal] cases and many meetings with the nobility of our territory. For this reason I was forced to postpone much longer than usual my customary bloodletting, which I normally have at the end of every second month.[1] And because the disease that I mentioned came upon me during that delay in bloodletting, I did not dare to go ahead with it the way I normally would, [... for bloodletting is dangerous....][2] I had learned from some people that bloodletting during catarrh would cause me

---

[1] The monks of Cluny practiced bloodletting as part of their monastic customs. Its procedures were minutely and carefully regulated.

[2] The passage is difficult to translate because some words are missing. But apparently Peter thinks (as he goes on to say) that a person will lose his voice if he has a bloodletting while suffering from a cold. As Peter says later in this letter, "My voice is necessary not only for reading, chanting, celebrating the heavenly liturgy... but particularly for preaching the word of God,... To put it plainly and concisely, the use of the voice is necessary to me as to any ruler of the Church of God."

to lose my voice entirely or to a very great extent, either permanently or for a long time. They added that if it were done, in some cases a close brush with death would not be out of the question. They also invoked the example of pack animals who, when they suffer from a similar disease and are bled by ignorant folk, can never or only rarely escape death. I listened to these things, and because I was afraid of what I heard, I postponed bloodletting for almost four months. But when the catarrh did not depart in the manner or at the time that was usual and I began to be dominated by a superabundance of blood or of phlegm (which I have more of than of any other humor), I feared that I would come down with some kind of fever.[1] But I did not wish to put off the bloodletting, choosing rather to lose the use of my voice for a time than to incur the loss of my health. So I underwent bloodletting; and because I had put it off longer than usual, it was done twice within three weeks and in very large quantity, and what my prophets predicted came to pass. The catarrh did not recede, nor was my voice able to return to its previous state for three months. Up to that time, [my] nature suffered under these things; and I felt those organs that are adjacent within the chest itself get worse because of I know not what humor, though I suspect it was phlegm, I brought up phlegm from my mouth in large quantities and often I was not able to relieve nature fully. The people whom I mentioned above say, as do the doctors, that [my] nature is suffering these things because in the aforementioned bloodletting, the heat of the blood was drawn off along with the blood itself, and so what was left behind was not able to expel the coldness of the already corrupted phlegm.[2] The bitter phlegm remained in the places where it was established, and spread through the veins or other vital channels to press down upon the chest, cause pain to the stomach, and block the normally free passage for the voice. But this judgment I leave to you. To counteract this symptom they advised me to use warm and moist things. Although I have obeyed them, they do not deny that the disease has grown greater because of the cold and moist quality. And so they are not satisfied with the consumption of warm and dry things (which is quite reasonable) in order that the medicine might purge the

disease not only in one quality but in both.[3] Nor have they been fully consistent in the opinion they have expressed to me; for they say that the pharynx, the trachea, and other terms which I do not know should be soothed with moist things, not irritated with dry things, at least as far as diet is concerned. As for the rest of the medicine, they said that vitriol can be beneficial, and hyssop, cumin, liquorice, figs—some or all of these with cooked wine, and given as a potion at bedtime. I tried it often, but all in vain. Again they swore that electuaries would be able to provide some remedy—the ones called *diadragantium*, *diabutyrum*, or preserved ginger.[4] I have not tried these to see whether they would help or hinder. There was much and varied discussion and debate about what to do next among those who then came to help the doctors. And although what they said sometimes seemed not completely reasonable to me, I yielded to them and for almost three months, as I said above, I have used the diet and medicine that they wanted. Up to this point, I see little or no improvement.

You remain, my dearest friend, my last resort; nor is there anyone else who can advise me, because as I have heard from so many about you and as I myself came to know directly from you in our intimate conversations last year, if I cannot have advice from you in these or similar matters, it would be futile for me to seek out another in our France. I would have preferred to tell you these things in person rather than to write them down to be read by your eyes, because although much can be conveyed to your understanding even when you are absent, it would perhaps be more effective if you were present. But because it would not be easy for me to journey to you or you to me, I ask in the meantime that whatever is permitted be done, at least as far as a friend can learn directly from the knowledge of his friend what friendship expects of him. And because it seemed inappropriate to summon you to me right now on this matter, I ask— indeed I call upon you as friend to friend—that you send to me quickly, for it is urgent, our countryman and well-beloved Bernard, your student, in whose reliability and good judgment your prudence confides (or so I hear), armed with your orders and with the medicines required against this plague, so that through him you may carry

---

[1] Phlegm was one of the four basic humors of the body postulated by Galenic medical theory. It was cold and wet.

[2] A corrupted humor was one that had been turned into a morbid substance by some qualitative excess, such as cold. Like rotting organic matter in the body, it had to be expelled. In this case the bloodletting, which should have done the job, was not effective.

[3] Consuming warm and dry things would be expected to help Peter purge (expel, either by vomiting or a bowel movement) the cold and wet corrupted humor.

[4] Electuaries were pastes licked from a spoon.

out effectively what I suppose cannot be done by you in person. Give him instructions as well as to whether I may or should undergo bloodletting in the usual way or put off bloodletting until I have taken the medicine you advise. I have already postponed it from the first of November to the Octave of Epiphany, when I write these things; nor would I give orders to repeat it without your advice. Hence, before postponement or reiteration produces anything worse, command which of the two it would be best to do. And lest you wonder that I am worried not only about recovering my health but also about recovering my voice, you should know that with my health preserved I am capable of remaining silent, by the grace of God, without much trouble, did my office not oblige me [to speak]. For what disadvantage would there be, as far as the salvation of the soul is concerned, if lacking tongue or voice I am not audible by men, but can be heard all the more by God? But because no small amount, indeed, a very large amount of my office consists in my tongue and voice, I cannot fulfill my office if the use of my voice is gone. My voice is necessary not only for reading, chanting, celebrating the heavenly liturgy—which I share with many under my authority—but particularly for preaching the word of God, since it is said to me by God through the prophet, "Cry out, spare not, lift up your voice like a trumpet."[1] How then can I cry without a voice? To put it plainly and concisely, the use of the voice is necessary to me as to any ruler of the Church of God, for either [rulers] are idle, and hence like "dumb dogs that cannot bark"[2] or if they are not lazy, they use the voice of John the Baptist: I am "a voice crying in the wilderness."[3]

Reply of Doctor Bartholomew

To his venerable lord Peter, by divine dispensation abbot of Cluny: his Bartholomew, such as he is, [sends greeting].

Having read the letter from your sublimity, I was grieved to learn that such a great man of the Church, and one so very necessary to her, was violently afflicted by bodily ailments. For I recall the experience of your humility and charity. When I came to Cluny last year, your affection received me, who deserved nothing from you, and even let me share your fraternal company, and in the end sent me home with gifts. Therefore desiring to be worthy of the affection that I have received from you, not by offering words but by performing deeds, I have dropped all other business to acquiesce to your petition. To this end I have not hesitated to send to your sublimity Bernard, our friend and associate—and if I may put it this way, the instrument of our operation—armed against those necessities which I have learned about from your letter. Indeed I myself, when it pleases your discretion and desire, will not refuse to come to you as to my father and lord. Meanwhile, let your discretion consider in advance that I have committed to the aforementioned Bernard oversight of my whole household, my assistants, and the sick [in my care]. For this reason, his absence will entail deprivation of many kinds for me, particularly if it takes more than a month for him to go and come back.

Concerning those things which pertain to your treatment, you may have this. In my view, bloodletting should be postponed until your voice begins to return to its full functioning, unless perhaps—and may this not be the case—necessity supervenes. For your nature is aggravated more by an excess of phlegm than an excess of blood, as I learned from clear indications when I stayed with you for few days last year. It is my opinion that cautery should be performed for your headache; do not be afraid that it will damage your sight.[4] Furthermore, your doctors were persuaded that you should use moist substances to soften the respiratory channels, and it seemed more beneficial to your discretion to use dry medications against the moist morbid matter. I reply that there is no contradiction here, though there might seem to be. For the same medication can be *actually* moist and *potentially* dry; to speak more plainly, the same thing will dry out and purge the morbid matter and at the same time moisten and soften. This is confirmed by authority: for example, according to the *Book of Degrees* [*ascribed to Constantine the African's On Grades*] myrrh is considered dry and hence dries out putrid humors, but nonetheless it is said to smooth the rough channels of the lungs and also the eyelids. It does this from its glutinous and gummy quality. Those medi-

---

[1] Isa. 58: 1.

[2] Isa. 16: 7.

[3] Isa. 40: 3; Matt. 3: 1; Mark 1: 3.

[4] Cautery involved applying a heated metal instrument to the affected part, either to sear the tissue or, as here, to divert the flow of humors through the body.

cations that dry by purging humor and also soften by moistening the trachea will be conducive to your health, by the grace of God. Furthermore, I have discussed with Bernard concerning baths and steam-baths, fumigations and fomentations about the chest,[1] and concerning pills that should be held under the tongue, pills for catarrh, a balsamic potion, gargles and the like. If he gives satisfaction to your reverence and goodness, please do not delay to send word back to us with all speed. If I learn from his account anything concerning your condition which ought to be done differently, I shall undertake diligent treatment.

Farewell, and may you find relief from the mercy of God and from the medications provided by us.

6.17 A doctor's bedside manner: *Advice from "Archimatthaeus"* (2nd half of 12th c.). Original in Latin.

What were the mutual expectations of doctor and patient? As medical knowledge in the West became professionalized, books of comportment helped guide the new relationship between the two sides of a medical consultation. Peter the Venerable and Bartholomew (see above, p. 342) tried to base their relationship on a model of friendship, but clearly doctors and patients were not exactly "friends." The book of good manners attributed to the physician Archimatthaeus (*fl.* 2nd half of twelfth century) and excerpted here was typical of advice manuals written for doctors throughout the Middle Ages. It includes two chief methods of diagnoses, observation of pulse and urine, as well as the main remedy prescribed by medieval doctors: change of diet.

[Source: Henry E. Sigerist, "Bedside Manners in the Middle Ages: The Treatise *De cautelis medicorum* Attributed to Arnold of Villanova," *Quarterly Bulletin, Northwestern University Medical School* 20 (1946): 141–43 (notes added). Translated by Henry E. Sigerist.]

Physician! When you shall be called to a sick man, in the name of God seek the assistance of the Angel who has attended the action of the mind and from inside shall attend departures of the body. You must know from the beginning how long the sick has been laboring, and in what way the illness has befallen him, and by inquiring about the symptoms, if it can be done, ascertain what the disease is. This is necessary because after having seen the feces and urine and the condition of the pulse you may not be able to diagnose the disease, but if you can announce the symptoms the patient will have confidence in you as if the author of his health and therefore one must devote greatest pains to knowing the symptoms.

Therefore, when you come to a house, inquire before you go to the sick whether he has confessed, and if he has not, he should confess immediately or promise you that he will confess immediately, and this must not be neglected because many illnesses originate on account of sin and are cured by the Supreme Physician after having been purified from squalor by the tears of contrition, according to what is said in the Gospel: "Go, and sin no more, lest something worse happens to you."[2]

---

[1] Fumigations involved burning a medicine to produce a smoke that was then inhaled or ingested. Fomentations were warm topical applications.

[2] John 5: 14.

Entering the sickroom, do not appear very haughty or over-zealous, and return, with the simple gesture, the greetings of those who rise to greet you. After they have seated themselves you finally sit down facing the sick; ask him how he feels and reach out for his arm, and all that we shall say is necessary so that through your entire behavior you obtain the favor of the people who are around the sick. And because the trip to the patient has sharpened your sensitivity, and the sick rejoices at your coming or because he has already become stingy and has various thoughts about the fee, therefore by your fault as well as his the pulse is affected, is different and impetuous from the motion of the spirits.[1] When it has quieted down on both parts, you shall examine the pulse in the left arm because although the right side would be satisfactory, yet it is easier to diagnose the motion of the heart in the left arm on account of its vicinity to the heart. Be careful that the patient does not lie on the right side because the compression would hinder the sense motion, nor should he stretch the fingers or make a fist. While you apply the fingers of your right hand you shall support with the left the patient's arm, because from greater sensibility you will distinguish the different and various motions more easily, and also because the patient's arm being so to say weak requires your support. If the arm is very full and fleshy you must press your fingers hard so as to get into the depth; if it is weak and lean you can feel the pulse sufficiently on the surface. You must examine the pulse to a hundred beats at the very least, so that you may form an opinion on the various kinds of pulses, and the patient's people should receive your words as the result of a long examination of the heart beat.

Finally you request to have the urine brought, and if the change in pulse indicates that the individual is sick; the kind of disease is still better indicated by the urine, but they will believe you to indicate and diagnose the disease not only from the urine but also from the pulse. While you look at the urine for a long time you pay attention to its color, substance and quantity and to its contents from the diversity of which you will diagnose the different kinds of diseases, as is taught in the Treatise on Urines, whereupon you promise health to the patient who is hanging on your lips. When you have left him, say a few words to the members of the household, say

that he is very sick, for if he recovers you will be praised more for your art; should he die his friends will testify that you had given him up.

Let me give you one more warning: do not look at a maid, or a daughter or a wife with an improper or covetous eye and do not let yourself be entangled in woman affairs—for there are medical operations that excite the helper's mind; otherwise your judgment is affected, you become harmful to the patient and people will expect less from you. And so, be pleasant in your speech, diligent and careful in your medical dealings, eager to help. And adhere to this without fallacy.

When you have been invited for dinner you should not throw yourself upon the party and at the table should not occupy the place of honor although it is customary to assign the place of honor to the priest and the physician. Then you should not disdain certain drinks, nor find fault with certain dishes, nor be disgusted perhaps because you are hardly accustomed to appease your hunger with millet bread in peasant fashion. If you act thus your mind will feel at ease. And while the attention is concentrated on the variety of dishes, inquire explicitly from some of the attendants about the patient or about his condition. If you do this the sick will have great confidence in you, because he sees that you cannot forget him in the midst of delicacies. When you leave the table and come to the sick, you must tell him that you have been served well, at which the patient greatly rejoices because he was very anxious to have you well served.

If it is the time and place to feed the sick you will feed him. It is necessary, however, that you set the time for the patient's meals, namely in intermittent fevers when the sick have a real remission; in continuous fevers when there happens to be a quiet moment because a decline of their fever does not occur before the crisis.[2] In intermittent fevers they must be fed before the attack and so early that when the attack comes the entire food [will] be digested, because otherwise nature will have to fight a war on two fronts and it will not be strong enough to digest what has been offered at the wrong moment nor will it be able to defeat the enemy disease. When the attack of fever has begun, wait until it has ceased and then wait for two more hours or for one at least, because the organs are exhausted from the preceding

---

[1] The spirits were the life forces that organized the body's principal functions, spreading through the body via its nerves, veins, and arteries.

[2] A crisis was the turning point in an illness. It determined whether the patient recovered or died. Intermittent fevers come and go, while continuous fevers never break.

battle and the attack of the enemy and do not want that a burden be imposed on them in the form of food, but after having so to say triumphed over the enemy they wish to have a rest.

You shall feed the sick according to the season of the year and according to the change of seasons and of the disease; and [the] quantity and quality of food must be varied according to the diseases, for you shall give the patient ampler food in intermittent than in continuous fever, more food in winter and spring, less in summer and autumn because they stand it very badly. The [patient's] age must be considered, and you will restore children more often than youths, because their consumption is greater on account of the liquidity of the humors and because they must grow, for it is according to nature to restore where there is a daily loss. Old people you will restore with less food because they have little heat and vigor; and also according to what they are accustomed to eat, because if they are accustomed to use an ampler and coarser diet you will not give them the same kind of food, but rather prescribe a liquid or moderate diet. You must fear constipation of the bowels or flux,[1] and if there is flux you must start out with coarser food such as quinces, sorb-apples, and medlars,[2] because they constipate through their thickness. If, however, there is constipation you will start out with lighter, liquid foods. Thus you will give prunes and the cooked juice of Damascene prunes because they quickly eject through their heaviness. If the condition of the bowels is between the two, you will begin with a lighter and more liquid diet because this is very useful to the sick and protects against greater harm. If the bowels have moved, give such a diet because it relieves the various organs. Thus you shall give first prunes cooked in water or pomegranates or almond milk that you shall prepare in the following way: almonds removed from the shells shall be put in hot water, whereupon they shall be ground thoroughly and a little cold water shall he added; the whole shall be stirred, strained through a clean linen cloth and given to drink. If however a little bread, that is the soft part of it, is cooked in the pot, that almond milk is better digested than if it is drunk

pure. After it has been prepared, a small amount must be poured off, and then one must remove by blowing or with a feather the oily substance that is on the surface because it is a hot matter. After this has been done, give several times chicken broth to drink or water in which the soft part of bread has been dissolved.

You shall also give barley flour and make it in the following way: first wash the barley in cold water, pour it over a stone and rub it so that it loses the skins, whereupon it must be rubbed and ground in a mortar or ground between millstones; then have the finer parts very well cooked and toward the end of the cooking add a little almond milk and present it to the sick. If, however, you wish to have ptisane,[3] cook the coarser parts of the barley in water and give him ptisane in a drink, or water in which bread has been soaked, cooked or not. And remember that while there is food in the stomach you shall not give diuretic water with syrup because such drinks force the food out of the stomach undigested or retard digestion.

Remember, furthermore, that in the beginning of the disease the physician endeavors to oppose it with digestive remedies, for he is the helper of nature and must aid it. Nature namely proceeds to making the crisis [in order] to triumph over the disease; she wishes to reduce the forces of the disease by changing the condition and quality of the matter and by dispersing it among the organs so that the parts [may] be separated from each other and she may reach her end and more easily than expected with complete results in one weak expulsion. In the same way, the physician in order to drive out the matter that must be driven out, must be prepared to treat the digested matters, according to the aphorism in the first book of Hippocrates. Consideration of the cause of the disease determines the choice of remedies that digest the humors; for if the patient suffers from cholera you will give him vinegar syrup; if he suffers from a cold humor you will give oxymel and everything else as I have said in another chapter.[4] Oh physician, thanks be given to God.

---

1 Diarrhea.

2 Sorb-apples and medlars are two apple-shaped fruits.

3 Barley water.

4 "Digest" here referred to the process by which the disease itself was "digested," restoring the body's normal humoral balance. Cholera referred to various acute gastrointestinal diseases. Oxymel was a medicinal mixture that included honey.

VERNACULAR LITERATURE

6.18 A troubadour love song: Bernart de Ventadorn, *When I see the lark* (*c.*1147-*c.*1170). Original in Old Occitan.

We know little with certainty about Bernart de Ventadorn, one of the most admired troubadours in his own time and ours. Among our few sources is a *vida*, or prose life, which says that he was the son of a baker in the castle of Ventadorn in the Limousin (the region around Limoges); that he fell in love with the lord's wife; and that, disappointed, he later loved none other than Eleanor of Aquitaine, daughter of the duke of Aquitaine, wife of the king of France, Louis VII, and then of the king of England, Henry II. Unfortunately the *vidas* are unreliable for their love stories. On the basis of the *vida* and other scraps of information, Bernart's activity is usually dated about 1147 to 1170. The only date that is certain, however, is 1172, when he was mentioned in a poem along with other troubadours, including one who is known to have died in that year. Bernart may actually have been the son of the viscount of Ventadorn, but the point is debated.

This song became a classic in the troubadour repertory. Even Dante imitated it in *Paradiso*, Canto 20, verses 73–75:

> Like a lark that soars in the air
> First singing, and then falls silent, happy
> In the last sweetness that gives it satisfaction...

[Source: William D. Paden, *An Introduction to Old Occitan* (New York: Modern Language Association, 1998), pp. 159–60. Translated and introduced by William D. Paden and Frances Freeman Paden.]

1
When I see the lark beat his wings
With joy in the rays of the sun
And forget himself and fall
In the warmth that fills his heart,
Oh, I feel so great an envy 5
Of one I see who's merry
I wonder that my heart
Does not melt with desire.

2
Oh, I thought I knew so much
About love, but how little I know! 10
I cannot stop loving her
Though I know she'll never love me.
She has stolen my heart and stolen herself
And me, myself, and all the world;
She stole herself and left me naught 15
But desire and a longing heart.

3
I despair of women.
I will never trust them again;
Just as I've always defended them,
I'll stop defending them now. 20
I see not a one of them gives me help
With the one who brings me to ruin,
So I fear and distrust them all,
For I know they all are the same.

4
Love is lost for certain, 25
And I never knew it at all;
If she who should have had the most
Has none, where shall I look?
Oh, it looks bad to whoever sees her,
That she lets this yearning wretch, 30
Who will get no good without her,
Die because she will not help.

5

I get no help with my lady
From God or mercy or right,
And it doesn't please her to love me,   35
So I'll not tell her my plight;
If she discards me and denies me,
She'll kill me, and dead, I'll answer;
If she abandons me, I will go away
A wretch in exile, I know not where.   40

6

I have not had power over my life
Or been myself since the time
She let me look into her eyes,
Into a mirror that gives delight.
Mirror, since I saw myself in you,   45
My sighs have caused my death;
I lost myself, as handsome Narcissus
Lost himself in the spring.[1]

7

My lady resembles a woman
In this, and for it I reproach her;   50
She does not want what she should,
And she does what she should not.
I have fallen into ill favor,
And behaved like the fool on the bridge;[2]
This happened to me, I don't know why,   55
Except that I climbed too high.

8

Tristan,[3] from me you'll hear no more,
For I go in despair, I know not where.
I'll stop my voice from singing
And hide from love and joy.   60

6.19 A trobairitz love song: La Comtessa de Dia, *I have been in heavy grief* (late 12th–early 13th c.). Original in Old Occitan.

La Comtessa ("the countess") de Dia (today Die) was a trobairitz, or woman troubadour, who sang in the late twelfth century or the early thirteenth. We know of about two dozen trobairitz, most of them by only one song apiece, but we have four by her. Although she must have hailed from Die, just north of Provence, she has not been identified with confidence. She may have been called Comtessa as the daughter of a count; we do not know if she ever married.

[Source: William D. Paden, *An Introduction to Old Occitan* (New York: Modern Language Association, 1998), pp. 58–59. Translated and introduced by William D. Paden and Frances Freeman Paden.]

1

I have been in heavy grief
For a knight that once was mine,
And I want it to be forever known
That I loved him too much.

I see now that I'm betrayed   5
For not giving him my love.
Bemused, I lie in bed awake;
Bemused, I dress and pass the day.

---

[1] Narcissus appears in Ovid's *Metamorphoses* 3, where he flees the nymph Echo, comes to a pond, loses himself in admiration of his reflection, and turns into a flower nodding over the water.

[2] According to a proverb, the fool does not dismount, but rides onto a narrow bridge, and so falls into the river.

[3] Tristan, the name of the lover of Isolde in contemporary romance, is here used as a poetic name for another troubadour who sang of love.

2

If only I could hold him
Naked in my arms one night!   10
He would feel ecstatic
Were I to be his pillow.
    Since I desire him more
Than Floris did Blanchefleur,[1]
I give him my heart and my love,   15
    My wit, my eyes, for as long as I live.

3

Splendid lover, charming and good,
When shall I hold you in my power?
If only I could lie with you one night
And give you a loving kiss!   20
    Know that I'd like
To hold you as my husband,
As long as you'd promise
To do what I desired.

6.20 A political song from the south of France: Bertran de Born, *Half a sirventés I'll sing* (1190). Original in Old Occitan.

Bertran de Born, one of the greatest political poets among the troubadours, was the lord of Autafort, today Hautefort ("High-Strong"), a castle in Aquitaine that survives today, although it has been much altered. In papers of French King Philip Augustus (r.1180–1223) Bertran's son was named last among the 70 wealthiest lords in France, and we have no reason to suppose the poet was less privileged. He was active as a poet from *c.*1180–1196, when he became a Cistercian monk. He may have died about 1215.

    In this *sirventés*, or political song, Bertran joyfully anticipates violent conflict between Richard Lionheart, king of England and duke of Aquitaine (r.1189–1199), and Alfonso VIII, king of Castile (r.1158–1214). War between them seemed to be imminent in June 1190. As a member of the landed aristocracy, Bertran regarded warfare as his natural occupation and a source of energizing value to society, regardless of any damages it might cause to unworthy usurers, burghers, and merchants.

[Source: William D. Paden, Tilde Sankovitch, and Patricia H. Stäblein, *The Poems of the Troubadour Bertran de Born* (Berkeley: University of California Press, 1986), pp. 399–401. Translated and introduced by William D. Paden and Frances Freeman Paden.]

1

Half a *sirventés* I'll sing about two kings:
Soon we shall see more knights
Following Alfonso, the king of Castile;
He is coming, I hear, and will want mercenaries.
But Richard will spend silver and gold   5
By bushels and barrels; he will be glad
To spend and give, and he'll spurn Alfonso's treaty—
He wants war more than a hawk wants quail!

2

If both kings are noble and brave,
Fields will soon be strewn with fragments   10
Of helmets and shields and saddles and swords,
And bodies split open, down to their breeches;
We shall see war-horses running wild,
And many a lance through chests and sides,
And joy and tears and grief and rejoicing.   15
The loss will be great, but the gain will be greater!

---

[1] In the French romance of *Floris and Blanchefleur* the young lovers are separated, reunited, and finally married. La Comtessa compares herself to the hero, not the heroine, as she does again with another romance in another song.

3
Trumpets, drums, standards and pennons
And ensigns and horses black and white
Soon we shall see, and the world will be good.
We'll take whatever the usurers have;   20
No driver of mules will travel in safety,
No burgher will go without fear,
Nor merchant coming from France.
He who happily takes will be rich!

4
But if the king comes, I trust in God   25
I'll be alive or cut to pieces;

5
If I am alive, it will be good luck,
And if I die it will be a release!

6.21 Fabliaux: *Browny, the Priest's Cow* and *The Priest Who Peeked* (13th c.). Original in Old French.

Originating in northern France and performed by jongleurs (who were also acrobats, musicians, dancers, and jugglers), fabliaux were popular entertainment for all classes, though today only about 150 are extant in manuscripts. Short, humorous poems, fabliaux were meant to make people laugh; they highlighted human foibles and poked fun at peasants, women, and—especially—priests. The priest in *The Priest Who Peeked* is one of the few clergymen who succeeds in his amorous intentions in a fabliau; the poet (Geren) wants to show how the husband is tricked. But in *Browny, the Priest's Cow* (which is by the most famous fablior of all, Jean Bodel [1165?–1210]), the priest (a different priest) gets his comeuppance for his greed. Although rough and bawdy, fabliaux were quite sophisticated poems, each written in rhyming couplets. For example, *Browny* begins:

> D'un vilain conte et de sa fame,
> c'un jor de feste Nostre Dame
> Aloient ourer à l'yglise,
> Li prestres, devant le servise,

Here *fame* rhymes with *Dame*, *l'yglise* with *servise*; and—as with all fabliaux—all of the lines contain exactly eight syllables. How do these poems pick up some themes of troubadour poetry while at the same time parodying courtly ideals?

[Source: *Cuckolds, Clerics, & Countrymen: Medieval French Fabliaux*, trans. John Du Val, ed. Raymond Eichmann (Fayetteville: University of Arkansas Press, 1982), pp. 31–32, 45–46.]

Browny, the Priest's Cow

Once, on blessed Mary's day,
A peasant took his wife to pray
And celebrate the mass in town.
Before the office, the priest came down
And turned to the people to deliver   5
His sermon: Blessed be the giver
Who gives for love of God in heaven.
God will return what has been given
Double to him whose heart is true.
"My wife!" the peasant said, "Did you   10

Hear what the parson up there said?
Whoever gives for God will get
The gift returned and multiplied?
What better use could we decide
For our cow, Berny, than to give her 15
To God through the priest? Besides, she never
Gave much milk." His wife said, "Good,
Since that's a fact, I think we should."
They rose at once and left together.
When they got home, the farmer tethered 20
His cow and led her from the shed
And took her back to town and said
To the priest, whose name was Constant, "Sir,
Here's my cow Berny. I'm giving her
To you because I love the Lord." 25
He handed him the tether cord
And swore that she was all he had.
"That's wise indeed," the parson said,
Who night and day kept careful watch
For any handout he could catch. 30
"Well done, my son. In peace depart.
If all my parish were as smart
And sensible as you, there'd be
Plenty of animals for me."
      The farmer left and made his journey 35
Home to his wife. The priest gave Berny
To one of his clerks to be secured
To *his* cow, Browny, till they were sure
She felt at home. The clerk pulled hard
And brought the cow to the backyard 40
And got the priest's fat cow and tied
Berny and Browny side by side,
Then turned around and left the cows.
The parson's cow preferred to browse,
And bent her head to keep on chewing, 45
But Berny balked: no, nothing doing.
She pulled the tether good and hard,
Dragging her out of the priest's yard,
Past houses and hemp fields, over bridges,
Through meadows and hedges, hills and ditches 50
Till home she came to her own backyard.
The parson's cow, who held back hard
The whole long way, came dragging after.
The farmer looked outside, and laughter
Filled his heart. He gave a cheer. 55
"Hey!" he shouted, "Look, my dear!
See how the good Lord multiplies.
Here's Berny back and Berny twice—
Only the second's brown, and bigger!

That's two for one the way I figure. 60
And now our barn's not big enough."
      My lords, this fabliau is proof
It's foolish not to give all you own.
The good things come from God alone.
They are not buried in the ground. 65
Nothing ventured, nothing found,
And nothing multiplied. That's how
God blessed the man who risked his cow:
Two for the peasant, none for the priest,
And those who have the most, get least. 70

The Priest Who Peeked

If you will kindly listen well
To my next tale, I'd like to tell
A short and courtly fabliau
As Guerin has it. Long ago
There lived a peasant who had wed 5
A maiden courteous, well bred,
Wise, beautiful, of goodly birth.
He cherished her for all his worth
And did his best to keep her pleased.
The lady loved the parish priest, 10
Who was her only heart's desire.
The priest himself was so afire
With love for her that he decided
To tell his love and not to hide it.
So off he started, running hard. 15
As he came running through their yard,
The peasant and his wife were sitting
Together at the table eating.
      The priest neither called their name nor knocked.
He tried the door. The door was locked 20
And bolted tight. He looked around
And up and down until he found
A hole to spy through and was able
To see the peasant at the table,
Eating and drinking as she served. 25
The priest indignantly observed
The way the peasant led his life,
Taking no pleasure of his wife.
And when he'd had enough of spying,
He pounded at the doorway, crying, 30
"Hey there, good people! You inside!
What are you doing?" The man replied,
"Faith, Sir, we're eating. Why not come
In here to join us and have some?"

—"Eating? What a lie! I'm looking   35
Straight through this hole at you. You're fucking."
—"Hush!" said the peasant, "Believe me,
We're eating, Sir, as you can see."
—"If you are," said the priest, "I'll eat my hat.
You're fucking, Sir. I can see that!   40
Don't try to talk me out of it.
Why not let me go in and sit?
You stand out here and do the spying,
And let me know if I've been lying
About the sight I'm looking at."   45

The peasant leapt from where he sat,
Unlocked the door and hurried out.
The priest came in, turned about,
Shut and latched and bolted the door.
However hard the peasant bore   50
The sight of it, the parson sped
To the peasant's wife. He caught her head,
Tripped her up and laid her down.
Up to her chest he pulled her gown
And did of all good deeds the one   55
That women everywhere want done.
He bumped and battered with such force
The peasant's wife had no recourse
But let him get what he was seeking.

And there the other man was, peeking   60
At the little hole, through which he spied
His lovely wife's exposed backside
And the priest, riding on top of her.
"May God Almighty help you, Sir,"
The peasant called, "Is this a joke?"   65
The parson turned his head and spoke:
"No, I'm not joking. What's the matter?
Don't you see: I have your platter.
I'm eating supper at your table."
"Goddammit, this is like a fable.   70
If I weren't hearing it from you,
I never would believe it true
That you aren't fucking with my wife."
"I'm not, Sir! Hush! As God's my life,
That's what I thought I saw you do."   75
The peasant said, "I guess that's true."
    That's how the peasant got confused,
Bewitched, befuddled, and confused,
By the priest and by his own weak brain
And didn't even feel the pain.   80
Because of the door, it still is said,
"Many a fool by God is fed."
Here ends the fabliau of the priest.

The End: Amen.

6.22 Romance: Chrétien de Troyes, *Lancelot* (*c*.1177–1181). Original in Old French.

Like the fabliaux, medieval romances were written in the vernacular. Those by Chrétien de Troyes, who wrote under the patronage of Marie of Champagne, more or less
mark the start of the genre. They were (and continue to be) celebrated for their art and
originality. Most of Chrétien's poems, including *Lancelot*, drew on stories, apparently
circulating orally, about King Arthur and his knights. They brought together (Chrétien
boasted of "conjoining") heroic and marvelous adventures in poems of around 7,000
lines. The first couplet suggests the flavor of the whole:

> Puis que ma dame de Chanpaigne
> Vialt que romans a feire anpraigne,

Every two lines, each of eight syllables, form similarly rhyming couplets that serve, in
aggregate, to both create and idealize norms of chivalric and courtly behavior. *Lancelot*
celebrates fearless warriors motivated by love, anger, and shame; it advertises the fine
manners of ladies and knights; it includes battles fought according to rules and regulated

by codes of honor. Unlike some romances, however, *Lancelot* treats the cult of love with gentle satire, as in a scene where the hero, Lancelot, adores his lady's hair as if it were a holy relic. And unlike the plots of most romances, the hero's lady, who is also King Arthur's wife, gladly commits adultery with her lover.

[Source: Chrétien de Troyes, *Lancelot: The Knight of the Cart*, trans. Burton Raffel (New Haven: Yale University Press, 1997), pp. 1–4, 7–13, 19–21, 25–30, 39–40, 47–48, 118–21, 132, 145–48 (notes added).]

Because my lady of Champagne[1]
Wants me to start a new
Romance, I'll gladly begin one,
For I'm completely her servant
In whatever she wants me to do,   5
And these are not flattering words.
Others, who like to wheedle
And coax, might start by saying
—And this, too, would not
Be flattery—that here was a princess   10
Who outshines every lady
Alive, as the winds of April
And May blow sweetest of all.
But I, by God, refuse
To spin sweet words about   15
My lady. Should I say: "This lady
Is worth her weight in queens,
One gem as good as silks
And onyx?" No, I won't,
But even if I don't, she is.   20
What I have to say is that this
Story has been better polished
By her work and wisdom than by mine.
As Chrétien begins this tale
Of Lancelot, the Knight   25
Of the Cart, he declares that the subject
And its meaning come from his lady.
She gave him the idea, and the story;
His words do the work of her matter.
     And he writes that once, on Ascension   30
Day, King Arthur held court
With all the splendor he loved,
Being so wealthy a king.
     And after dining, Arthur
Remained with his companions,   35
For the hall was full of barons,

And the queen[2] was there, and many
Other beautiful high-born
Ladies, exchanging elegant
Words in the finest French.   40
And Kay, who along with others
Had waited on table, ate
With his stewards. But as he sat down,
A singularly well-equipped knight[3]
Entered, armed to the teeth   45
And armored from head to foot.
Heavily armed as he was,
He walked straight to where
The king was seated among
His barons, but gave him no greeting,   50
Declaring: "Arthur, I hold
Many of your people captive—
Knights, ladies, girls—
But I didn't come here to tell you
I meant to let them go!   55
All I want you to know
Is that neither your wealth nor your strength
Is sufficient to get them back.
Understand me: you'll be sooner
Dead than able to do   60
A thing!" The king answered
That what he couldn't help
He could live with; but it did not make him
Happy. And then their visitor
Started to leave, but got   65
Only as far as the door
Before he turned, stopped,
And instead of descending the steps
Threw back this challenge: "King,
If you have a single knight   70
In this court of yours you can trust
To take your queen to the woods,

---

[1] Countess Marie de Champagne (1145–1198), oldest daughter of King Louis VII (r.1137–1180) and Eleanor of Aquitaine (1122–1204).

[2] Guinevere, Arthur's queen and, as we shall see, Lancelot's great love.

[3] Méléagant, as Chrétien reveals later.

Where I'll be going when I'm finished
Here, then I'll agree
To let him have those prisoners   75
I've got in my dungeons, provided
He can defeat me in battle,
It being understood
That possession of your queen is the prize
For victory." Many people   80
In the palace heard him; the court
Was astonished. The news was brought
To Kay, as he sat at his food,
And he rose at once, left
The table, and came to the king....   85

[Kay extracts the promise from Arthur and his queen
that any wish he makes will be granted. Kay then says:]

"I'll think myself a fortunate
Man, if you let me have it.
Your queen, who stands beside me,   175
Will be placed under my protection,
And we'll ride off to the woods
In search of the knight and his challenge."
The king was upset, but his word
Had been given, and he could not revoke it,   180
No matter how angry and sorrowful
It made him (which was easy to see).
The queen, too, was deeply
Displeased, and the whole palace
Denounced Kay's pride and presumption   185
In making such a demand.
And then the king took
The queen by the hand, and said,
"Lady, it can't be helped;
You must go with Kay." And the steward   190
Said, "Just trust her to me;
There's nothing to be afraid of.
You can count on me, my lord:
I'll bring her back safe
And sound!" Arthur gave him   195
Her hand, and Kay led her
Out, the entire palace
Following, frowning as they went.
The steward was fully armed,
Of course; his horse stood   200
In the courtyard, waiting, and beside it
The sort of palfrey fit
For a queen to ride, patient,
Calm, not pulling at the bit.
Slowly, the queen approached,   205

And, sighing sadly, mounted,
Then spoke in a voice so soft
No one was meant to hear her:
"Oh, my love, if only
You knew, you'd never let me   210
Take a step in this man's
Care!" It was barely a whisper,
But Count Guinables, who stood
Close by, heard what she'd said.
As they rode toward the woods, everyone   215
Watching, knights and ladies,
Were as sad as if she were being
Buried. They never expected
To see her again, in this life.
And so the steward, impelled   220
By his pride, took her to the woods.
For all their sorrow, none of them
Thought to follow along,
Until Sir Gawain quietly
Said to the king, his uncle,   225
"My lord, I'm quite astonished:
This strikes me as terribly wrong.
If you'll take my advice, as long
As there's time, and they're still in sight,
Let's ride along behind them,   230
You and I and whoever
Joins us, I simply can't keep
Myself from following after:
It makes no sense not to,
At least until we know   235
What happens to the queen, and how well
Kay can take care of her."
"We'll go, good nephew," said the king.
"Yours is a politic wisdom.
And now that you've spoken up,   240
Tell them to bring out our horses
And have them saddled and bridled,
So all we need do is mount."
As soon as the horses were ordered,
They were led out and readied. The king,   245
Of course, was the first to mount,
And then my lord Gawain,
And after him the others.
Everyone wanted to come,
But each in his own way,   250
Some of them armed to the teeth,
Some of them neither armored
Nor carrying weapons. But Gawain
Was fully armed, and had ordered
Two of his squires to bring   255

A pair of battle horses.
And then, as they neared the forest,
They saw Kay's horse, which they knew
At once, come jogging out,
Riderless, and observed that both   260
Its reins had been broken. And as
It approached they saw, too,
That the stirrup-leather was spotted
With blood, and the back of the saddle
Had been broken to bits. It was hardly   265
A pleasant sight; they nodded
And shrugged, knowing what had happened.
My lord Gawain galloped
Far ahead of the others,
Until he saw a knight[1]   270
Come riding slowly toward him
On a tired and heavy-footed
Horse, panting and drenched
With sweat. The knight greeted
My lord Gawain, and Gawain   275
Returned the greeting. And then,
Recognizing Gawain,
The knight stopped and said,
"My lord, I think you can see
What a sweat my horse is in;   280
He's no use at all, in this state.
I believe those horses over
There are yours: may I ask,
Please, that you do me the favor—
Which I'll gladly repay—of either   285
Letting me have, or lending me,
One, whichever you like?"
Said Gawain, "Take your pick:
The one you prefer is yours."
But the knight's need was so pressing   290
He made no attempt to choose
The better, or bigger, or faster,
But simply mounted the one
That happened to be closest, and galloped
Away at once. The horse   295
He left behind him fell dead,
So hard had he been ridden
That day, driven till he dropped.
Without losing a moment,
The knight dashed into   300
The forest, and Gawain followed
As fast as he could, until

He reached the foot of a hill.
Some distance further along
He found the horse the knight   305
Had taken, dead in the road,
And saw the signs of many
Mounted men, and broken
Shields and lances all around.
Clearly, there'd been a furious   310
Fight, involving a good many
Knights, and Gawain was upset
He'd had no part in the battle.
He didn't stop for long,
But rode rapidly ahead   315
Until, suddenly, he saw
The knight, alone and on foot,
In full armor, helmet
On his head, shield around his neck,
Sword at his side. And there   320
Was a cart—used, in those days,
As we use a pillory, now.
In any good-sized town
You'll find them by the thousand, but then
There was only one, and they used it   325
For every kind of criminal,
Exactly like the pillory
Today—murderers, thieves,
Those defeated in judicial
Combat, robbers who roamed   330
In the dark, and those who rode
The highways. Offenders were punished
By being set in the cart
And driven up and down
The town. Their reputations   335
Were lost, and the right to be present
At court; they lost all honor
And joy. Everyone knew
What the carts were for, and feared them;
They'd say, "If you see a cart   340
Coming your way, cross
Yourself, and pray to the Lord
On high, to keep you from evil."
The knight on foot, who had
No lance, came up behind   345
The cart and saw, seated
On the shaft, a dwarf, who like
A carter held a long whip
In his hands. And the knight said,

---

[1] This, as we later learn, is Lancelot.

"Dwarf, in the name of God,　　　　　　　　350
Tell me: have you seen my lady
The queen come by?" The dwarf
Low-born and disgusting, had no
Interest in telling the knight
Anything; "If you feel like taking　　　　　　355
A ride in this cart of mine,
You might find out, by tomorrow,
What's happened to the queen." The cart
Rolled slowly on, not stopping
For even a moment; and the knight　　　　　360
Followed along behind
For several steps, not climbing
Right up. But his hesitant shame
Was wrong. Reason, which warred
With Love, warned him to take care;　　　　365
It taught and advised him never
To attempt anything likely
To bring him shame or reproach.
Reason's rules come
From the mouth, not from the heart.　　　　370
But Love, speaking from deep
In the heart, hurriedly ordered him
Into the cart. He listened
To Love, and quickly jumped in,
Putting all sense of shame　　　　　　　　375
Aside, as Love had commanded....

[The knight (Lancelot) in the shameful cart and Sir
Gawain on horseback arrive at a castle and stay the night.
In the morning, the knight looks out a window and sees
a funeral procession. He notices:]

The bier, preceded by a noble
Knight, leading at his left
Hand a beautiful lady.
The knight at the window knew her
At once: this was the queen,　　　　　　　560
And his eyes followed her along
The path, watching with passionate
Care, thrilled at the sight,
For as long as he could, Then,
When he wasn't able to see her,　　　　　　565
His body went slack, he felt
He could let himself fall from the window,
And was halfway over the sill
When Gawain saw him and, from
Behind, pulled him back,　　　　　　　　570
Saying, "Be calm, my lord:
In the name of God, don't even

Think of committing such folly!
How wrong to despise your life!"
"He's right to despise it," said the lady [of the castle].　575
"Do you think there's anyone who hasn't
Heard what happened? Of course
He'd rather be dead, now
That he's ridden in the cart. For him,
Death would be better than life,　　　　　580
For all life holds is shame,
Contempt, and misery." Both knights
Asked for their armor and weapons,
And made themselves ready. And the lady
Displayed a noble politeness:　　　　　　585
Having jeered and mocked more
Than enough, now she gave
The knight, as a mark of affection
And respect, a horse and a spear.
And the knights left her like civilized　　　590
Men, well trained in courtesy,
Bowing and wishing her well,
Then riding away, following
After the procession they'd seen.
No one could exchange a word　　　　　　595
With either knight, they galloped
So fast. They rode hard
Down the road the queen had taken,
But couldn't catch the funeral
Party, which had hurried off.　　　　　　600
Leaving the fields, they crossed
A fence and found a well-kept
Road, which led them across
A forest. It was early morning
When they came to a crossroads and saw　　605
A girl, whom they both greeted,
Asking, with careful courtesy,
If by any chance she knew,
And was able to tell them, where
The queen had been taken. She answered　610
Soberly, saying, "Offer
Me enough and, yes,
I can certainly tell you. I can set you
On the right road, and name you
The land they've gone to and the knight　　615
Who's led them there. But you'll need
To be ready for immense hardships,
If you try to follow them! It takes
Pain and suffering to get there."
My lord Gawain replied,　　　　　　　620
"With God's good help, my lady,
I pledge myself and whatever

Strength I have to your service,
Whenever you need me, if only
You'll tell me the truth." The knight   625
Who'd ridden in the cart offered
More than all his strength,
Swearing, with all the force
And power that Love had given him,
That nothing would stand in his way   630
And, fearing nothing, he'd come
Whenever she called and do
Whatever she wanted done.
"You'll hear it all!" she cried,
And immediately began her tale: 635
      "On my faith, lords, a most powerful
Knight, Méléagant,
Son of the king of Gorre,
Has taken the queen to that land
No one visits and ever   640
Returns, forced to remain
In exile, serving that lord."
Then the knight of the cart demanded:
"Where can we find that land,
Lady? How do we get there?"   645
She answered, "I'll certainly tell you.
But understand: you'll meet
With many obstacles, and many
Dangers; it won't be easy,
Without the king's permission.   650
His name is Bademaguz...."

[The prescient lady is entirely correct. There are two
routes to the queen and each is equally dangerous. Lancelot and Gawain agree to split up. Lancelot gets to a river
crossing. A knight, accompanied by a lady, guards the
ford. He cries out, forbidding Lancelot to continue, but
Lancelot, lost in thoughts of love, hears nothing.]

The sentinel swore to make
Our knight pay: no shield would protect him,
Nor would the mail shirt he wore.
He spurred his horse to a gallop,   765
Then whipped it to its fastest pace,
And struck our knight so fiercely
That he stretched him out in the water
No one was allowed to cross.
His spear, too, fell   770
In the water, and the shield from around
His neck. But the water woke him:
Blinking, at best half-conscious,
Like someone just out of bed,

He jumped to his feet, astonished   775
To find himself where he was.
And then he saw the sentinel,
And shouted, "You! Why
Did you hit me? Explain yourself,
For I never knew you were there,   780
And I've done nothing to harm you."
"You did, by God," was the answer.
"Didn't you treat me like dirt
When I told you, three times over,
And as loud and clear as I could,   785
That you couldn't cross? You had
To hear me, at least the second
Time, or the third, but you rode
Right on, although I warned you
I'd strike if you entered that water."   790
But our knight immediately answered,
"As far as I'm concerned,
I never saw you and I never
Heard you! Maybe you did
Forbid me to cross. But I   795
Was lost in my thoughts. Believe me,
Just let me get my hands
On your bridle, and you'll regret it!"
"Oh, really?" the sentinel answered.
"And what will you do? Come over   800
Here and hang on my bridle,
If you're brave enough to try it.
All your boasting and threats
Aren't worth a fistful of ashes."
"There's nothing I'd like better,"   805
Our knight answered. "You'll see
Exactly what happens as soon as
I get my hands on you."
And then our knight waded
To the middle of the stream, and grasped   810
The sentinel's reins in his left
Hand, and seized his leg
With the right, pulling and twisting
So hard that the other cried out
In pain: he felt as if   815
His leg was about to be pulled
From his body, and begged our knight
To stop, saying, "Knight,
If you'd like to challenge me, man
To man, go get your horse,   820
And your shield, and your spear, and I'll gladly
Fight you." "By God, I won't
Let go," said our knight. "I'm afraid
You'll run away the minute

You're free." Deeply shamed, 825
The sentinel said, "Knight,
You can mount your horse in peace.
I promise I'll neither trick you
Nor run away. You've shamed me,
And now I'm angry." But our knight 830
Only replied, "Not
Till you've solemnly sworn you won't
Play tricks, or run, or ride
Toward me, or touch me, until
You see me mounted. I'd do you 835
A great favor, if I set you
Free, now that I've got you."
And so he swore, for he had to.
As soon as he had the sentinel's
Solemn word, our knight 840
Went to collect his shield
And spear, which had floated far
From the ford, carried by the swift
Current. Then he returned
And took possession of his horse. 845
And when he was back in the saddle
He hung the shield around
His neck, and set his spear
Against the saddle bow.
And then the knights ran 850
At one another as fast
As their horses could gallop. The sentinel
Struck the very first blow,
Striking so hard that his spear
Shattered. Then a blow from our knight 855
Drove him off his horse,
Deep down in the water.
And our knight leapt from his horse,
Sure he could drive in front of him
At least a hundred such enemies. 860
He drew his great steel sword
Just as the sentinel, leaping
Up, drew his, gleaming
Bright, and they fought once more,
Holding their shining shields 865
In front of them, protecting themselves,
For both sharp blades were busy,
Always moving, never
At rest. They beat at each other
Relentless, the fighting so furious 870
That our knight began to feel,
Deep in his heart, ashamed
To be at it so long, working
So hard to finish what he'd started,

And wondering if he'd ever succeed 875
In his mission, if a single knight
Could delay him. It seemed to him
That, just the day before,
If he'd met a hundred such knights
In a valley, he'd have beaten them all 880
By now; he was anxious, and worried,
Finding himself forced
To waste his time, and so many
Blows. He attacked the sentinel
So fiercely that he turned and ran, 885
Reluctantly giving up
Control of the ford. But our knight
Was not done: he chased the other
Down, and drove him to the ground
On all fours, swearing as he swung 890
His sword he'd soon regret
Tumbling a traveler in the stream
And interrupting his thoughts.
The girl who'd come with the sentinel
Heard these fearsome threats 895
And, much afraid, begged
Our knight not to kill him.
But the knight of the cart informed her
He couldn't show mercy to someone
Who'd made him suffer such shame. 900
So our knight came forward, sword
Raised, and the sentinel cried,
"For the sake of God, and for me,
Grant me the mercy I asked for!"
Our knight answered, "May God 905
Love me, I've never denied
Mercy to a man who did me
Wrong, if he asked in God's name.
I'll grant you mercy, this once,
For His sake. It's only right: 910
I can't refuse you, when you ask
Not in your own name, but His...."

[Lancelot continues on his way until he meets a beautiful girl, who invites him to stay the night at her castle, but only if he will sleep with her. Unwilling, but seeing no alternative, he agrees. But when it is time for them to bed together, he finds her attacked by a rapist and other heavily armed men. Then, to keep his word, he fights them off, and the girl takes him by the hand.]

Holding his hand, she led him
Back to the great hall.
He followed along, unhappy.

A bed stood ready in the middle 1200
Of the hall, beautifully made
With soft, flowing white sheets—
No flat straw mattress for them,
No rough and wrinkled blankets!
A coverlet of flowered 1205
Silk, double thickness,
Had been spread on top, and the girl,
Still wearing her chemise,
Lay on it. How hard it was
For him, taking off 1210
His shoes and undressing! He was sweating
Freely, but even suffering
As he was, he meant to honor
His pledge. Was he being forced?
Almost: he was forcing himself 1215
To sleep with the girl; his promise
Called him, and bent his will.
He lay on the bed, slowly,
Carefully, like her still wearing
His shirt, so cautious as he stretched 1220
Out on his back that no part
Of his body was touching hers.
Nor did he say a word—
As if he'd been a monk,
Forbidden to speak in his bed. 1225
He stared at the ceiling, seeing
Neither her nor anything
Else. He could not pretend
Goodwill. And why? His heart
Had been captured by another woman, 1230
And even a beautiful face
Cannot appeal to everyone.
The only heart our knight
Owned was no longer his
To command, having already 1235
Been given away; there was nothing
Left. Love, which rules
All hearts, allows them only
One home. "All hearts?" No:
All that Love finds worthy, 1240
Love's approval being worth
A great deal. And Love valued
Our knight higher than any,
Creating such pride in his heart
That I cannot blame him, and I will not, 1245
For renouncing what Love denied him
And striving for the love Love meant him
To have. The girl could see
Her company caused him discomfort;

He'd gladly have let her go, 1250
Clearly determined not
To touch her or seek her favor.
So she said, "With your permission,
My lord, I think I'll leave you,
And sleep in my own bed; 1255
You'll be more at your ease, alone.
I can't believe you find me
Delightful, or ever will."…

[In the morning Lancelot continues his journey along
with the girl of the castle. He comes across a comb with
a handful of the queen's hair caught in it. The girl of the
castle asks for the comb.]

He was willing
To hand it over, but first
He gently removed the queen's
Hair, not breaking a single
Strand. Once a man 1465
Has fallen in love with a woman
No one in all the world
Can lavish such wild adoration
Even on the objects she owns,
Touching them a hundred thousand 1470
Times, caressing with his eyes,
His lips, his forehead, his face.
And all of it brings him happiness,
Fills him with the richest delight;
He presses it into his breast, 1475
Slips it between his shirt
And his heart—worth more than a wagon-
Load of emeralds or diamonds,
Holy relics that free him
Of disease and infection: no powdered 1480
Pearls and ground-up horn
And snail shells for him! No prayers
To Saints Martin and James: his faith
In her hair is complete, he needs
No more. And their real power? 1485
You'd take me for a liar, and a fool,
If I told you the truth—if they offered him
Everything displayed at the Fair
Of Saint-Denis he wouldn't
Have exchanged the hairs he'd found 1490
For the whole bursting lot of it.
And if you're still hunting
The truth, let me tell you that gold
Refined a hundred times,
And then again, would have seemed 1495

To him, if you set that gold
Against a single strand
Of hair, darker than night
Compared to a summer's day....

[After many adventures, battles, and feats of strength and daring, Lancelot reaches the tower of courteous King Bademagu and his discourteous, wicked son Méléagant, who is holding the queen. Lancelot and Méléagant have a great battle, with the queen watching from a window. The battle rages, with Lancelot, badly wounded from a Sword Bridge that he had had to cross, weakening. Then he sees the queen.]

His powers and quickness had returned.
Love and his mortal hate—
Fiercer than any ever
Known—combined to make him
So fearsome that Méléagant   3735
Was suddenly afraid,
For never in all his life
Had an enemy seemed so strong,
Or pressed and hurt him so badly
As this knight was doing. He tried   3740
As hard as he could to keep him
At a distance, feinting, ducking,
Bobbing, badly hurt
Each time he was hit. Lancelot
Wasted no breath on threats,   3745
Kept driving him toward the tower
And the queen, over and over
Coming as close as he could,
Forcing Méléagant back,
Each rime, barely a foot   3750
Away from stepping out
Of her sight. So Lancelot led him
Up and down, this way
And that, always making him
Stop in front of his lady,   3755
The queen, who'd set his heart
On fire, just knowing she was
Watching—a fiercely roaring,
Burning-hot flame impelling him
Straight at Méléagant   3760
And pushing his helpless enemy
Forward and back like a cripple,
Tugging him along like a blind man
Or a beggar at the end of a rope.

The king saw his son   3765
Utterly overwhelmed
And was filled with pity and compassion:
He had to help, if he could.
But the queen, he knew, was the only
Possible source of assistance,   3770
So he turned to her and spoke:
"Lady, for as long as you've been
In my land you've had my love
And honor; I've served you well,
And always gladly, in every   3775
Way I could. Let me
Ask you, now, to repay me.
And the gift I ask you to give me
Could only be granted out
Of the purest love. I can see   3780
Quite well—there's not the slightest
Doubt—that my son has lost
This battle. And I speak to you, now,
Not on this score, but because
It's clear that Lancelot   3785
Could easily kill him, if he chose to.
I hope you want that no more
Than I do—not that my son
Has treated you well—he hasn't—
But simply because I beg you   3790
For your mercy. Let him live.
Let the final blow be withheld.
And thus you can tell me, if you choose,
How you value the honor
I've shown you." "Dear sir, if that's   3795
What you want, I want it, too.
I certainly hate and loathe
Your son, for the best of reasons,
But you indeed have served me
So well that it pleases me   3800
To please you by stopping the battle."
They had not whispered private
Words; both Lancelot
And Méléagant heard them.
Lovers are obedient men,   3805
Cheerfully willing to do
Whatever the beloved, who holds
Their entire heart, desires.
Lancelot had no choice,
For if ever anyone loved   3810
More truly than Pyramus[1]
It was him. Hearing her response,

---

[1] A famous lover celebrated by the Roman writer Ovid. Early in his career, Chrétien translated into French several works by Ovid.

As soon as the final word
Fell from her mouth, declaring,
"Dear sir, if you want the battle   3815
Stopped, I want that, too,"
Nothing in the world could have made him
Fight, or even move,
No matter if it cost his life....

[The queen will not speak to Lancelot (because, as it turns out, he had hesitated before entering the cart), but when she hears false rumors that he is dead, she repents.]

Accusing herself of sinful
Behavior, of wicked acts
Directed at the man whose heart
Had always been hers, and still
Would be hers, were he still alive,   4195
And knowing she'd been so cruel
Stole away her beauty.
The thought of such wickedness drained
And discolored her skin more
Than fasting or all-night vigils....   4200

[Eventually the two are reconciled. The queen invites him to come to see her at night at her window covered with iron bars.]

Lancelot greeted her with gentle
Warmth, which she returned,
Immense longing gripping   4595
Them both, each for the other.
No harsh or angry words
Passed between them: pressing
As close as they could, they were just
Able to clasp hand   4600
To hand. How it hurt them,
Unable to be together,
And how they cursed those iron
Bars! But Lancelot assured her,
Should she be willing, he'd come   4605
And join her: no iron bars
Could keep him out! The queen
Quickly replied, "Can't
You see? This iron's too thick
To bend, too strong to break.   4610
Please: don't even attempt it!
How could you possibly pull
Away a single one?"
"Ah, don't worry, my lady!
No iron can keep me out.   4615

Nothing can stop me from coming
To you, if you want me to come.
Just say the word, and consider it
As good as done. Your
Not wanting me in is the only   4620
Obstacle that could keep me out,
The only barrier I can't
Break down." "I want you in,"
Said the queen. "That's not the question.
But let me quickly return   4625
To bed, and lie there, and watch,
Because it won't be pleasant
Or at all amusing if my husband's
Steward, who's sleeping here,
Hears you at work, and wakes up.   4630
Besides, it's better for me
To be back in bed, not standing
Here for everyone to see."
"Go back to bed, lady,
But have no fear: this   4635
Is work I can do quietly.
These bars will come out quickly
And with hardly an effort, and no one
Will hear me or know what I've done."
    The queen hurried back   4640
To her bed, and the knight prepared
To pull the window apart.
Taking hold of the bars,
He bent them toward him until
They snapped away from their sockets.   4645
But the iron edge was so sharp
It cut through his little
Finger, down to the bone,
And sliced deep in the knuckle
Of the finger next to it. He had no   4650
Awareness of the blood running out,
Nor the wounds; he felt no pain,
His mind on other matters.
The window was high in the wall,
But Lancelot had no trouble   4655
Climbing quickly through.
Finding Sir Kay asleep,
He approached the queen's bed,
Bowing in adoration
Before the holiest relic   4660
He knew, and the queen reached out
Her arms and drew him down,
Holding him tight against
Her breast, making the knight
As welcome in her bed, and as happy,   4665

As she possibly could, impelled
By the power of Love, and her own
Heart. It was Love that moved her,
And she loved him truly, but he
Loved her a hundred thousand   4670
Times more, for if other hearts
Had escaped Love, his
Had not. His heart was so
Completely captured that the image
Of Love in all other hearts   4675
Was a pale one. And the knight had
What he wanted, for the queen willingly
Gave him all the pleasures
Of herself, held him in her arms
As he was holding her.   4680

It was so exceedingly sweet
And good—the kisses, the embraces—
That Lancelot knew a delight
So fine, so wondrous that no one
In the world had ever before   4685
Known anything like it, so help me
God! And that's all I'm allowed
To tell you; I can say no more.
These pleasures I'm forbidden to report
Were the most wonderful known   4690
The most delightful. That night,
And all night long, Lancelot
Experienced incredible joy.
But the dawn came, against
His will, and he had to leave.   4695

NEW DEVELOPMENTS IN RELIGIOUS SENSIBILITIES

6.23 Disciplining and purifying Christendom: *Decrees of Lateran IV* (1215). Original in Latin.

Called by Pope Innocent III (1198–1216), the Fourth Lateran Council was a turning point in the history of the Church. It codified many doctrines, policies, and practices that had hitherto been informal, local, or fuzzy. It meant to purify Christendom of the contaminating presence of heretics and Jews while determining the religious behavior and beliefs of those within the fold. In what ways did it continue the Church reform movement begun in the eleventh century? In what ways did it represent something new?

[Source: *Decrees of the Ecumenical Councils*, ed. Norman P. Tanner, vol. 1: *Nicaea I to Lateran V* (London and Washington, DC: Sheed & Ward and Georgetown University Press, 1990), pp. 230–31, 233–36, 245, 257–58, 265–67 (notes modified).]

Constitutions

1. ON THE CATHOLIC FAITH

We firmly believe and simply confess that there is only one true God, eternal and immeasurable, almighty, unchangeable, incomprehensible and ineffable, Father, Son and holy Spirit, three persons but one absolutely simple essence, substance or nature. The Father is from none, the Son from the Father alone, and the holy Spirit from both equally, eternally without beginning or end; the Father generating, the Son being born, and the holy Spirit proceeding; consubstantial and coequal, co-omnipotent and coeternal; one principle of all things, creator of all things invisible and visible, spiritual and corporeal; who by his almighty power at the beginning of time created from nothing both spiritual and corporeal creatures, that is to say angelic and earthly, and then created human beings composed as it were of both spirit and body in common. The devil and other demons were created by God naturally good, but they became evil by their own doing. Man, however, sinned at the prompting of the devil.

This holy Trinity, which is undivided according to its common essence but distinct according to the properties of its persons, gave the teaching of salvation to the human race through Moses and the holy prophets and his other servants, according to the most appropriate disposition of the times. Finally the only-begotten Son of God, Jesus Christ, who became incarnate by the action of the whole Trinity in common and was conceived from the ever virgin Mary through the cooperation of the holy Spirit, having become true man, composed of a rational soul and human flesh, one person in two natures, showed more clearly the way of life. Although he is immortal and unable to suffer according to his divinity, he was made capable of suffering and dying according to his humanity. Indeed, having suffered and died on the wood of the cross for the salvation of the human race, he descended to the underworld, rose from the dead and ascended into heaven. He descended in the soul, rose in the flesh, and ascended in both. He will come at the end of time to judge the living and the dead, to render to every person according to his works, both to the reprobate and to the elect. All of them will rise with their own bodies, which they now wear, so as to receive according to their desserts, whether these be good or bad; for the latter perpetual punishment with the devil, for the former eternal glory with Christ.

There is indeed one universal church of the faithful, outside of which nobody at all is saved, in which Jesus Christ is both priest and sacrifice. His body and blood are truly contained in the sacrament of the altar under the forms of bread and wine, the bread and wine having been changed in substance, by God's power, into his body and blood, so that in order to achieve this mystery of unity we receive from God what he received from us. Nobody can effect this sacrament except a priest who has been properly ordained according to the church's keys, which Jesus Christ himself gave to the apostles and their successors. But the sacrament of baptism is consecrated in water at the invocation of the undivided Trinity—namely Father, Son and holy Spirit—and brings salvation to both children and adults when it is correctly carried out by anyone in the form laid down by the church. If someone falls into sin after having received baptism, he or she can always be restored through true penitence. For not only virgins and the continent but also married persons find favor with God by right faith and good actions and deserve to attain to eternal blessedness....

3. ON HERETICS

We excommunicate and anathematize every heresy raising itself up against this holy, orthodox and catholic faith which we have expounded above. We condemn all heretics, whatever names they may go under. They have different faces indeed but their tails are tied together inasmuch as they are alike in their pride. Let those condemned be handed over to the secular authorities present, or to their bailiffs, for due punishment. Clerics are first to be degraded from their orders. The goods of the condemned are to be confiscated, if they are lay persons, and if clerics they are to be applied to the churches from which they received their stipends. Those who are only found suspect of heresy are to be struck with the sword of anathema, unless they prove their innocence by an appropriate purgation, having regard to the reasons for suspicion and the character of the person. Let such persons be avoided by all until they have made adequate satisfaction. If they persist in the excommunication for a year, they are to be condemned as heretics. Let secular authorities, whatever offices they may be discharging, be advised and urged and if necessary be compelled by ecclesiastical censure, if they wish to be reputed and held to be faithful, to take publicly an oath for the defense of the faith to the effect that they will seek, in so far as they can, to expel from the lands subject to their jurisdiction all heretics designated by the church in good faith. Thus whenever anyone is promoted to spiritual or temporal authority, he shall be obliged to confirm this article with an oath. If however a temporal lord, required and instructed by the church, neglects to cleanse his territory of this heretical filth, he shall be bound with the bond of excommunication by the metropolitan and other bishops of the province. If he refuses to give satisfaction within a year, this shall be reported to the supreme pontiff so that he may then declare his vassals absolved from their fealty to him and make the land available for occupation by Catholics so that these may, after they have expelled the heretics, possess it unopposed and preserve it in the purity of the faith—saving the right of the suzerain [ruler] provided that he makes no difficulty in the matter and puts no impediment in the way. The same law is to be observed no less as regards those who do not have a suzerain.

Catholics who take the cross and gird themselves up for the expulsion of heretics shall enjoy the same indulgence, and be strengthened by the same holy privilege, as is granted to those who go to the aid of the holy Land. Moreover, we determine to subject to excommunication believers who receive, defend or support heretics. We strictly ordain that if any such person, after he has been designated as excommunicated, refuses to render satisfaction within a year, then by the law itself he shall be branded as infamous and not be admitted to public offices or councils or to elect others to the same or to give testimony. He shall be intestable, that is he shall not have the freedom to make a will, nor shall he succeed to an inheritance. Moreover nobody shall be compelled to answer to him on any business whatever, but he may be compelled to answer to them. If he is a judge, sentences pronounced by him shall have no force and cases may not be brought before him; if an advocate, he may not be allowed to defend anyone; if a notary, documents drawn up by him shall be worthless and condemned along with their condemned author; and in similar matters we order the same to be observed. If however he is a cleric, let him be deposed from every office and benefice, so that the greater the fault the greater be the punishment. If any refuse to avoid such persons after they have been pointed out by the church, let them be punished with the sentence of excommunication until they make suitable satisfaction. Clerics should not, of course, give the sacraments of the church to such pestilent people nor give them a Christian burial nor accept alms or offerings from them; if they do, let them be deprived of their office and not restored to it without a special indult [privilege] of the apostolic see. Similarly with regulars,[1] let them be punished with losing their privileges in the diocese in which they presume to commit such excesses.

There are some who "holding to the form of religion but denying its power" (as the Apostle says),[2] claim for themselves the authority to preach, whereas the same Apostle says, "How shall they preach unless they are sent?"[3] Let therefore all those who have been forbidden or not sent to preach, and yet dare publicly or privately to usurp the office of preaching without having received the authority of the apostolic see or the catholic bishop of the place, be bound with the bond of excommunication and, unless they repent very quickly, be punished by another suitable penalty. We add further that each archbishop or bishop, either in person or through his archdeacon or through suitable honest persons, should visit twice or at least once in the year any parish of his in which heretics are said to live. There he should compel three or more men of good repute, or even if it seems expedient the whole neighborhood, to swear that if anyone knows of heretics there or of any persons who hold secret conventicles or who differ in their life and habits from the normal way of living of the faithful, then he will take care to point them out to the bishop. The bishop

himself should summon the accused to his presence, and they should be punished canonically [according to canon law] if they are unable to clear themselves of the charge or if after compurgation[4] they relapse into their former errors of faith. If however any of them with damnable obstinacy refuse to honor an oath and so will not take it, let them by this very fact be regarded as heretics. We therefore will and command and, in virtue of obedience, strictly command that bishops see carefully to the effective execution of these things throughout their dioceses, if they wish to avoid canonical penalties. If any bishop is negligent or remiss in cleansing his diocese of the ferment of heresy, then when this shows itself by unmistakable signs he shall be deposed from his office as bishop and there shall be put in his place a suitable person who both wishes and is able to overthrow the evil of heresy.

4. ON THE PRIDE OF GREEKS TOWARDS LATINS
Although we would wish to cherish and honor the Greeks who in our days are returning to the obedience of the apostolic see, by preserving their customs and rites as much as we can in the Lord, nevertheless we neither want nor ought to defer to them in matters which bring danger to souls and detract from the church's honor. For, after the Greek church together with certain associates and supporters withdrew from the obedience of the apostolic see, the Greeks began to detest the Latins so much that, among other wicked things which they committed out of contempt for them, when Latin priests celebrated on their altars they would not offer sacrifice on them until they had washed them, as if the altars had been defiled thereby. The Greeks even had the temerity to rebaptize those baptized by the Latins; and some, as we are told, still do not fear to do this. Wishing therefore to remove such a great scandal from God's church, we strictly order, on the advice of this sacred council, that henceforth they do not presume to do such things but rather conform themselves like obedient sons to the holy Roman church, their mother, so that there may be "one flock and one shepherd."[5] If anyone however does dare to do such a thing, let him be struck with the sword of excommunication and be deprived of every ecclesiastical office and benefice....

---

[1]   I.e., monks.

[2]   2 Tim 3: 5.

[3]   Rom. 10: 15.

[4]   A procedure whereby witnesses swear to the innocence of the accused.

[5]   John 10: 16.

21. ON CONFESSION BEING MADE, AND NOT REVEALED BY THE PRIEST, AND ON COMMUNICATING AT LEAST AT EASTER

All the faithful of either sex, after they have reached the age of discernment, should individually confess all their sins in a faithful manner to their own priest at least once a year, and let them take care to do what they can to perform the penance imposed on them. Let them reverently receive the sacrament of the Eucharist at least at Easter unless they think, for a good reason and on the advice of their own priest, that they should abstain from receiving it for a time. Otherwise they shall be barred from entering a church during their lifetime and they shall be denied a Christian burial at death. Let this salutary decree be frequently published in churches, so that nobody may find the pretense of an excuse in the blindness of ignorance. If any persons wish, for good reasons, to confess their sins to another priest let them first ask and obtain the permission of their own priest; for otherwise the other priest will not have the power to absolve or to bind them.[1] The priest shall be discerning and prudent, so that like a skilled doctor he may pour wine and oil[2] over the wounds of the injured one. Let him carefully inquire about the circumstances of both the sinner and the sin, so that he may prudently discern what sort of advice he ought to give and what remedy to apply, using various means to heal the sick person. Let him take the utmost care, however, not to betray the sinner at all by word or sign or in any other way. If the priest needs wise advice, let him seek it cautiously without any mention of the person concerned. For if anyone presumes to reveal a sin disclosed to him in confession, we decree that he is not only to be deposed from his priestly office but also to be confined to a strict monastery to do perpetual penance....

50. ON THE RESTRICTION OF PROHIBITIONS TO MATRIMONY

It should not be judged reprehensible if human decrees are sometimes changed according to changing circumstances, especially when urgent necessity or evident advantage demands it, since God himself changed in the New Testament some of the things which he had commanded in the Old Testament. Since the prohibitions against contracting marriage in the second and third degree of affinity, and against uniting the offspring of a second marriage with the kindred of the first husband, often lead to difficulty and sometimes endanger souls, we therefore, in order that when the prohibition ceases the effect may also cease, revoke with the approval of this sacred council the constitutions published on this subject[3] and we decree, by this present constitution, that henceforth contracting parties connected in these ways may freely be joined together. Moreover the prohibition against marriage shall not in future go beyond the fourth degree of consanguinity and of affinity, since the prohibition cannot now generally be observed to further degrees without grave harm. The number four agrees well with the prohibition concerning bodily union about which the Apostle says, that "the husband does not rule over his body, but the wife does; and the wife does not rule over her body, but the husband does";[4] for there are four humors in the body, which is composed of the four elements. Although the prohibition of marriage is now restricted to the fourth degree, we wish the prohibition to be perpetual, notwithstanding earlier decrees on this subject issued either by others or by us. If any persons dare to marry contrary to this prohibition, they shall not be protected by length of years, since the passage of time does not diminish sin but increases it, and the longer that faults hold the unfortunate soul in bondage the graver they are.

51. ON THE PUNISHMENT OF THOSE WHO CONTRACT CLANDESTINE MARRIAGES

Since the prohibition against marriage in the three remotest degrees has been revoked, we wish it to be strictly observed in the other degrees. Following in the footsteps of our predecessors, we altogether forbid clandestine marriages and we forbid any priest to presume to be present at such a marriage. Extending the special custom of certain regions to other regions generally, we decree that when marriages are to be contracted they shall be publicly announced in the churches by priests, with a suitable time being fixed beforehand within which whoever wishes and is able to may adduce a lawful impediment. The priests themselves shall also investigate whether there is any impediment. When there appears a credible reason why the marriage should not be contracted, the contract shall be expressly forbidden until there has been established from clear documents what

---

[1] The power to "bind and loose"—that is to impose penance and to absolve—is based on Matt. 16: 19 and 18: 18.

[2] See Luke 10: 34.

[3] The reference is to decisions of earlier councils.

[4] 1 Cor. 7: 4.

ought to be done in the matter. If any persons presume to enter into clandestine marriages of this kind, or forbidden marriages within a prohibited degree, even if done in ignorance, the offspring of the union shall be deemed illegitimate....

67. ON THE USURY OF JEWS

The more the Christian religion is restrained from usurious practices, so much the more does the perfidy of the Jews grow in these matters, so that within a short time they are exhausting the resources of Christians. Wishing therefore to see that Christians are not savagely oppressed by Jews in this matter, we ordain by this synodal decree that if Jews in future, on any pretext, extort oppressive and excessive interest from Christians, then they are to be removed from contact with Christians until they have made adequate satisfaction for the immoderate burden. Christians too, if need be, shall be compelled by ecclesiastical censure, without the possibility of an appeal, to abstain from commerce with them. We enjoin upon princes not to be hostile to Christians on this account, but rather to be zealous in restraining Jews from so great oppression. We decree, under the same penalty, that Jews shall be compelled to make satisfaction to churches for tithes and offerings due to the churches, which the churches were accustomed to receive from Christians for houses and other possessions, before they passed by whatever title to the Jews, so that the churches may thus be preserved from loss.

68. THAT JEWS SHOULD BE DISTINGUISHED FROM CHRISTIANS IN THEIR DRESS

A difference of dress distinguishes Jews or Saracens from Christians in some provinces, but in others a certain confusion has developed so that they are indistinguishable. Whence it sometimes happens that by mistake Christians join with Jewish or Saracen women, and Jews or Saracens with Christian women. In order that the offence of such a damnable mixing may not spread further, under the excuse of a mistake of this kind, we decree that such persons of either sex, in every Christian province and at all times, are to be distinguished in public from other people by the character of their dress—seeing moreover that this was enjoined upon them by Moses himself, as we

read.[1] They shall not appear in public at all on the days of lamentation and on passion Sunday; because some of them on such days, as we have heard, do not blush to parade in very ornate dress and are not afraid to mock Christians who are presenting a memorial of the most sacred passion and are displaying signs of grief. What we most strictly forbid, however, is that they dare in any way to break out in derision of the Redeemer. We order secular princes to restrain with condign [appropriate] punishment those who do so presume, lest they dare to blaspheme in any way him who was crucified for us, since we ought not to ignore insults against him who blotted out our wrongdoings.

69. THAT JEWS ARE NOT TO HOLD PUBLIC OFFICES

It would be too absurd for a blasphemer of Christ to exercise power over Christians. We therefore renew in this canon, on account of the boldness of the offenders, what the council of Toledo[2] providently decreed in this matter: we forbid Jews to be appointed to public offices, since under cover of them they are very hostile to Christians. If, however, anyone does commit such an office to them let him, after an admonition, be curbed by the provincial council, which we order to be held annually, by means of an appropriate sanction. Any official so appointed shall be denied commerce with Christians in business and in other matters until he has converted to the use of poor Christians, in accordance with the directions of the diocesan bishop, whatever he has obtained from Christians by reason of his office so acquired, and he shall surrender with shame the office which he irreverently assumed. We extend the same thing to pagans.

70. THAT CONVERTS TO THE FAITH AMONG THE JEWS MAY NOT RETAIN THEIR OLD RITE

Certain people who have come voluntarily to the waters of sacred baptism, as we learnt, do not wholly cast off the old person in order to put on the new more perfectly.[3] For, in keeping remnants of their former rite, they upset the decorum of the Christian religion by such a mixing. Since it is written, cursed is he who enters the land by two paths,[4] and a garment that is woven from linen and wool together should not be put on,[5] we therefore decree

---

[1] See Lev. 19: 19; Deut. 22: 5 and 22: 11.

[2] A reference to the Council of Toledo of 589, canon 14.

[3] See Col. 3: 9.

[4] See Ecclus. 2: 14 and 3: 28.

[5] See Deut. 22: 11.

that such people shall be wholly prevented by the prelates of churches from observing their old rite, so that those who freely offered themselves to the Christian religion may be kept to its observance by a salutary and necessary coercion. For it is a lesser evil not to know the Lord's way than to go back on it after having known it.

[71.] EXPEDITION FOR THE RECOVERY OF THE HOLY LAND

It is our ardent desire to liberate the holy Land from infidel hands. We therefore declare, with the approval of this sacred council and on the advice of prudent men who are fully aware of the circumstances of time and place, that crusaders are to make themselves ready so that all who have arranged to go by sea shall assemble in the kingdom of Sicily on June 1st after next: some as necessary and fitting at Brindisi and others at Messina and places neighboring it on either side, where we too have arranged to be in person at that time, God willing, so that with our advice and help the Christian army may be in good order to set out with divine and apostolic blessing. Those who

have decided to go by land should also take care to be ready by the same date. They shall notify us meanwhile so that we may grant them a suitable legate *a latere*[1] for advice and help. Priests and other clerics who will be in the Christian army, both those under authority and prelates, shall diligently devote themselves to prayer and exhortation, teaching the crusaders by word and example to have the fear and love of God always before their eyes, so that they say or do nothing that might offend the divine majesty. If they ever fall into sin, let them quickly rise up again through true penitence. Let them be humble in heart and in body, keeping to moderation both in food and in dress, avoiding altogether dissensions and rivalries, and putting aside entirely any bitterness or envy, so that thus armed with spiritual and material weapons they may the more fearlessly fight against the enemies of the faith, relying not on their own power but rather trusting in the strength of God. We grant to these clerics that they may receive the fruits of their benefices in full for three years, as if they were resident in the churches, and if necessary they may leave them in pledge for the same time.

6.24 Devotion through poverty: Peter Waldo in *The Chronicle of Laon* (1173–1178). Original in Latin.

Peter Waldo (d. *c.*1207), a wealthy merchant at Lyon, was inspired, like many people of his time, by the *Acts of the Apostles*. At some time in the 1170s, he rid himself of his material possessions and began to preach to his neighbors "to place your hopes in God and not in wealth." He and his followers (known at first as the Poor, or the Poor Men, but later on as the Waldensians) were initially embraced by the papacy but forbidden to preach. However, they continued to preach and were declared heretics in 1184. Their continued association with heresy may be seen in Jacques Fournier's *Episcopal Register*, p. 405 below. In the account printed here, written by an anonymous chronicler who was not entirely hostile to the movement, Peter is called Valdès, the original form of his name.

[Source: *The Birth of Popular Heresy*, ed. and trans. Robert I. Moore (New York: St. Martin's Press, 1975), pp. 111–13 (slightly modified).]

At about this time, in 1173, there was a citizen of Lyon named Valdès, who had made a great deal of money by the evil means of usury. One Sunday he lingered by a crowd that had gathered round a *jongleur*,[2] and was

much struck by his words. He took him home with him, and listened carefully to his story of how St. Alexis had died a holy death in his father's house. Next morning Valdès hastened to the schools of theology to seek advice

---

[1] "*A latere*" means "from the side [of the pope]." The pope is here saying that a papal legate is necessary.
[2] A *jongleur* was an entertainer.

about his soul. When he had been told of the many ways of coming to God he asked the master whether any of them was more sure and reliable than the rest. The master quoted to him the words of the Lord, "If thou wilt be perfect go sell what thou hast and give to the poor and thou shalt have treasure in heaven. And come follow me."[1]

Valdès returned to his wife and gave her the choice between having all his movable wealth or his property in land and water, woods, meadows, fields, houses, rents, vineyards, mills and ovens. She was very upset at having to do this and chose the property. From his movable wealth he returned what he had acquired wrongly, conferred a large portion on his two daughters, whom he placed in the order of Fontevrault[2] without his wife's knowledge, and gave a still larger amount to the poor. At this time a terrible famine was raging through Gaul and Germany. For three days a week, from Whitsun to St Peter-in-chains [May 27–August 1] Valdès generously distributed bread, soup and meat to anyone who came to him. On the Assumption of the Virgin [August 15] he scattered money among the poor in the streets saying, "You cannot serve two masters, God and Mammon."[3] The people around thought that he had gone out of his senses. Then he stood up on a piece of high ground and said, "Friends and fellow-citizens, I am not out of my mind, as you think. I have avenged myself on the enemies who enslaved me when I cared more for money than for God and served the creature more faithfully than the creator. I know that many of you disapprove of my having acted so publicly. I have done so both for my own sake and for yours: for my sake, because anybody who sees me with money in future will be able to say that I am crazy; for your sake, so that you may learn to place your hopes in God and not in wealth."

Next day as he was coming out of church Valdès begged a certain citizen, formerly a friend of his, for God's sake to give him something to eat. The man took him home, and said, "As long as I live I will provide you with the necessities of life." When his wife heard this story she was very upset, and rushed distraught to complain to the archbishop that Valdès had begged his bread from someone other than herself. This moved everybody who was with the archbishop to tears. The archbishop requested the citizen to bring his guest before him. The wife seized her husband by his tattered clothes, and said, "Is it not better, my man, for me to redeem my sins by giving you alms than a stranger?" After this, by the archbishop's command, he was not allowed to accept alms from anybody in the city except his wife.

1177 Valdès, the citizen of Lyon whom we have already mentioned, who had vowed to God that he would possess neither gold nor silver, and take no thought for the morrow, began to make converts to his opinions. Following his example they gave all they had to the poor and willingly devoted themselves to poverty. Gradually, both in public and in private, they began to inveigh against both their own sins and those of others.

1178 Pope Alexander III[4] held a council at the Lateran palace.... The council condemned heresy and all those who fostered and defended heretics. The pope embraced Valdès, and applauded the vows of voluntary poverty which he had taken, but forbade him and his companions to assume the office of preaching except at the request of the priests. They obeyed this instruction for a time, but later they disobeyed, and affronted many, bringing ruin on themselves.

---

[1] Matt. 19: 21.

[2] Fontevrault was a monastery founded by Robert of Arbrissel (c.1045–1116). It consisted of two houses, one for men and the other for women, both of which were presided over by the same female abbess.

[3] Matt. 6: 24; Luke 16: 13.

[4] Alexander III was pope from 1159 to 1181. In fact this council (Lateran III) was held in 1179.

6.25 Devotion through mysticism: Jacques de Vitry, *The Life of Mary of Oignies* (1213). Original in Latin.

Jacques de Vitry (d.1240) learned about Mary of Oignies while he was a regular canon (much like a monk but living according to the Rule of St. Augustine rather than Benedict) at Oignies, today in the north of France. Mary (1177–1213) led a nearby house of Beguines—a community in which women took no formal vows but nevertheless dedicated themselves to lives of piety. Jacques's support for the Beguines helped legitimize them: his biography made Mary into a kind of saint, while his direct appeal to the papacy in 1216 resulted in the Beguines' official recognition. Although they spent their days at simple tasks—caring for the sick, spinning, weaving—Beguines like Mary lived passionate lives, weeping cascades of tears as they contemplated the Lord. Comparing this account of a female saint with the early seventh-century lives of St. Radegund (above, pp. 38 and 44), how might you characterize the transformations that occurred in medieval conceptions of female piety?

[Source: *Medieval Women's Visionary Literature*, ed. Elizabeth Alvilda Petroff, trans. Margot King (New York: Oxford University Press, 1986), pp. 179–81 (a few notes added).]

BOOK I

CHAPTER 16

The beginning of her conversion to you, O Lord, the first fruits of her love, was your Cross and Passion. She heard you hearing and was afraid,[1] she considered your works and feared. One day when she was reflecting on the blessings you had sent and visited upon her and which you had graciously shown forth in the flesh to mankind, and while she was considering your torment upon the Cross, she found such grace of compunction and wept so abundantly that the tears which flowed so copiously from her eyes fell on the floor of the church and plainly showed where she had been walking. For a long time after this visitation, she could not look at an image of the Cross, nor could she speak of the Passion of Christ, nor hear other people speaking of it without falling into ecstasy by reason of her enfeebled heart. She therefore would sometimes moderate her sorrow and restrain the flood of her tears and, leaving behind His humanity, would raise her mind so that she might find some consolation in His unchangeableness. The more, however, she tried to restrain the vehemence of the flood, the more won-

drously did her ardor increase it. When she considered how great was He who had allowed Himself to be so humiliated for us her sorrow was redoubled and her soul renewed with sweet compunction and fresh tears.

CHAPTER 17

Once, just before Holy Thursday when the Passion of Christ was approaching, she began to offer herself up as a sacrifice to the Lord with an even greater flood of tears, sighs, and sobs. One of the priests of the church exhorted her with honey-tongued rebukes to pray in silence and to restrain her tears. Although she had always been bashful and would, with dovelike simplicity, make an effort to obey in all things, yet she knew that she could not restrain these tears. She therefore slipped quietly out of the church and hid herself in a secret place far from everyone, and she tearfully begged the Lord that he show this priest that it is not in man to restrain the impulse of tears when the waters flow with the vehemence of the blowing wind.[2]

On that very day while the priest was celebrating Mass, it happened that "the Lord opened and none shut"[3] and "He sent forth waters and they overturned the earth."[4]

---

[1] Hab. 3: 2.

[2] See Ps. 147: 18 and Exod. 14: 21.

[3] Isa. 22: 22.

[4] Job 12: 15.

His spirit was drowned with such a flood of tears that he almost suffocated. The harder he tried to restrain this force, the more drenched he became and the more soaked did the book and the altar become. What could he do, he who had been so lacking in foresight, he who had rebuked the handmaid of Christ? With shame and through personal experience he was taught what he previously had not learned through humility and compassion. Sobbing frequently and with disordered and broken speech, he barely avoided total collapse, which one of his acquaintances has testified. After Mass was finished, the handmaid of Christ returned to the church and told the priest everything that had happened, as if she herself had been present. "Now," she said, "you have learned through personal experience that man cannot restrain the impulse of the spirit 'when the south wind blows.'"[1]

CHAPTER 18

When a constant outburst of tears gushed forth from her eyes both day and night and ran down her cheeks and made the church floor all muddy, she would catch the tears in the linen cloth with which she covered her head. She went through many veils in this way since she had to change them frequently and put a dry one on in place of the wet one she had discarded.

In my love for her I suffered with her in her long fasts and frequent vigils and while she was enduring many such deluges of tears. I therefore asked her whether she felt any pain or discomfort as one is accustomed to experience in such a state of exhaustion. "These tears," she said, "are my refreshment. Night and day they are my bread. They do not impair my head but rather feed my mind. They do not torment me with pain but, on the contrary, they rejoice my soul with a kind of serenity. They do not empty the brain but fill the soul to satiety and soften it with a sweet anointing. They are not violently wrenched out but are freely given by the Lord."

CHAPTER 22

Having once tasted the spirit, she held as nothing all sensual delights until one day she remembered the time

when she had been gravely ill and had been forced, from necessity, to eat meat and drink a little wine for a short time. From the horror she felt at her previous carnal pleasure, she began to afflict herself and she found no rest in spirit until, by means of extraordinary bodily chastisements, she had made up for all the pleasures she had experienced in the past. In vehemence of spirit, almost as if she were inebriated, she began to loathe her body when she compared it to the sweetness of the Paschal Lamb[2] and, with a knife, in error cut out a large piece of her flesh which, from embarrassment, she buried in the earth. Inflamed as she was, however, by the intense fire of love, she did not feel the pain of her wound and, in ecstasy of mind, she saw one of the seraphim standing close by her. Much later when women were washing her corpse, they were amazed when they found the places of the wounds but those to whom she had made her confession knew what they were. Why do those who marvel at the worms which swarmed from the wounds of Simeon [Stylites] and are awe-struck at the fire with which Antony burnt his feet[3] not wonder at such strength in the frail sex of a woman who, wounded by charity and invigorated by the wounds of Christ, neglected the wounds of her own body?

CHAPTER 38

The prudent woman knew that after the sin of the first parents, the Lord enjoined penance through them to their sons, that is to say "you will earn your bread by the sweat of your brow."[4] This is the reason why she worked with her own hands as often as she could. In this way she mortified her body with penance, furnished the necessities of life to the poor, and acquired food and clothing for herself—that is, all the things she had given up for Christ. The Lord bestowed on her such strength in labor that she far exceeded her companions and was able to obtain for herself and for one companion the fruit of her hands and she gave heed to the words of the Apostle "Whoever will not work, will not eat."[5] She considered all exertion and labor sweet when she considered that the only begotten Son of the High King of heaven "who opens his hand and fills with blessing every living creature,"[6] was nourished by

---

[1] See Acts 28: 13.

[2] The Paschal Lamb, that is, the sacrificial lamb of the Jewish Passover, was understood to be a prefiguration of Christ.

[3] A reference to the temptations of Antony, as depicted in *The Life of St. Antony*, above, p. 27. Simeon Stylites was another saint whose ascetic practices—particularly his long endurance on a pillar—were well known.

[4] Gen. 3: 19.

[5] 2 Thess. 3: 10.

[6] Ps. 145: 16; Douay Ps. 144: 16.

Joseph's manual labor and by the work of the poor little Virgin. In quiet and silence she followed the injunction of the Apostle and by the labor of her hands she ate her bread, for her strength was in silence and hope. She so loved quiet and silence that she fled noisy crowds and once barely said a word from the Feast of the Holy Cross[1] until Easter. The Holy Spirit revealed to her that the Lord had accepted this silence and that especially because of it she had obtained from the Lord that she would fly up to heaven without going to Purgatory.[2]

BOOK II

CHAPTER 72

It frequently occurred that when the priest raised the Host, she saw between his hands the corporeal form of a beautiful boy and an army of the heavenly host descending with a great light. When the priest received the Host after the general confession, she saw in the spirit the Lord remain in the soul of the priest illuminating him with a wondrous brightness. If, on the other hand, he received it unworthily, she saw the Lord withdraw with displeasure and the soul of the wretched man would remain empty and dark. Even when she was not present in the church but remained in her cell, she prayed with her eyes covered with a white veil, as was her habit, and when Christ descended to the altar at the utterance of the sacred words, then, wondrously transformed, she felt His coming. If she was present at the reception of the sacrament of Extreme Unction by invalids,[3] she felt the presence of Christ when, with a multitude of saints, He tenderly strengthened the sick person, expelled demons, and purged the soul and, as it were, transfused Himself in light throughout the whole body of the invalid while the different limbs were being anointed.

CHAPTER 88

Sometimes it seemed to her that for three or more days she held Him close to her so that He nestled between her breasts like a baby, and she hid Him there lest He be seen by others. Sometimes she kissed him as though He were a little child and sometimes she held Him on her lap as if He were a gentle lamb. At other times the Holy Son of the Virgin manifested Himself in the form of a dove for the consolation of His daughter or He would walk around the church as if He were a ram with a bright star in the middle of his forehead and, as it seemed to her, He would visit His faithful ones.

6.26 The mendicant movement: St. Francis, *The Canticle to Brother Sun* (1225). Original in Umbrian dialect.

Saint Francis (1181/1182–1226) had an extraordinary impact on late medieval religious life. Born into a wealthy merchant family in Assisi, Francis, like Peter Waldo, had a conversion experience in his mid-twenties that led him to strip himself of all belongings and take up the lifestyle of a poor person—a mendicant—who preached and begged for his daily bread and lodging. His effect in the cities of Italy was electrifying: Francis gained numerous followers (called "friars" from the Latin term for brothers). Women too were drawn to his example. Francis, who wrote the poem printed here in his native dialect, loved simple language and poetry. In this *Canticle* he praised all of God's creation as part of his family. According to one of Francis's biographers, the verse beginning "Praised be You, my Lord, through those who give pardon for Your love," was written

---

[1] Celebrated on September 14.

[2] The doctrine of Purgatory, which was becoming increasingly important and precise in the thirteenth century, held that souls had to endure a period of purification in a place—Purgatory—for their venial (minor, forgivable) sins before they might enter heaven.

[3] Extreme Unction is the sacrament of anointing the sick and the dying.

in order to reconcile disputants at Assisi (it was successful!); while the verse "Praised be You, my Lord, through our Sister Bodily Death," was sung by Francis himself on his deathbed. How might you compare the sensibilities of Peter Waldo, Mary of Oignies, and Francis to arrive at a composite picture of the idea of "following Christ" at the turn of the thirteenth century?

[Source: *Francis and Clare: The Complete Works*, trans. Regis J. Armstrong and Ignatius C. Brady (New York: Paulist Press, 1982), pp. 38–39 (notes modified).]

1. Most High, all-powerful, good Lord,
   Yours are the praises, the glory, the honor, and all blessing.[1]
2. To You alone, Most High, do they belong,
   and no man is worthy to mention Your name.
3. Praised be You, my Lord, with all your creatures,
   especially Sir Brother Sun,
   Who is the day and through whom You give us light.
4. And he is beautiful and radiant with great splendor;
   and bears a likeness of You, Most High One.
5. Praised be You, my Lord, through Sister Moon and the stars,
   in heaven You formed them clear and precious and beautiful.
6. Praised be You, my Lord, through Brother Wind,
   and through the air, cloudy and serene, and every kind of weather
   through which You give sustenance to Your creatures.
7. Praised be You, my Lord, through Sister Water,
   which is very useful and humble and precious and chaste.

8. Praised be You, my Lord, through Brother Fire,
   through whom You light the night
   and he is beautiful and playful and robust and strong.
9. Praised be You, my Lord, through our Sister Mother Earth,
   who sustains and governs us,
   and who produces varied fruits with colored flowers and herbs.
10. Praised be You, my Lord, through those who give pardon for Your love
    and bear infirmity and tribulation.[2]
11. Blessed are those who endure in peace
    for by You, Most High, they shall be crowned.
12. Praised be You, my Lord, through our Sister Bodily Death,
    from whom no living man can escape.
13. Woe to those who die in mortal sin.
    Blessed are those whom death will find in Your most holy will,
    for the second death shall do them no harm.[3]
14. Praise and bless my Lord and give Him thanks
    and serve Him with great humility.

---

[1] See Rev. 4: 9, 11.
[2] Here Francis evokes Jesus, who bore "infirmity and tribulation."
[3] See Rev. 2: 11 and 20: 6.

6.27 Religious feeling turned violent: *Chronicle of Trier* (1231). Original in Latin.

Beginning in the twelfth century, the monks of the monastery of St. Matthias, just outside Trier, began keeping a *Gesta* or *Chronicle* of their city and its saints and religious institutions. For the year 1231 they recorded the burning of heretics "throughout the whole of Germany."

[Source: *Heresies of the High Middle Ages*, ed. and trans. Walter L. Wakefield and Austin P. Evans (New York: Columbia University Press, 1969), pp. 267–69 (notes modified).]

In the year of our Lord 1231 began a persecution of heretics throughout the whole of Germany, and over a period of three years many were burned. The guiding genius of this persecution was Master Conrad of Marburg;[1] his agents were a certain Conrad, surnamed Tors, and John, who had lost an eye and a hand. Both of these were said to have been converted heretics.[2] It is this Master Conrad who, renowned for active preaching, especially in behalf of the crusades, had built up a great following among the people; who interfered in the visitation of clergy and nuns and sought to constrain them to strict observance and continence;[3] and who, supported by apostolic authority and endowed with firmness of purpose, became so bold that he feared no one—not even a king or a bishop, who rated no higher with him than a poor layman. Throughout various cities the Preaching Friars [Dominicans] cooperated with him and with his afore-mentioned lieutenants; so great was the zeal of all that from no one, even though merely under suspicion, would any excuse or counterplea be accepted, no exception or testimony be admitted, no opportunity for defense be afforded, nor even a recess for deliberation be allowed. Forthwith, he must confess himself guilty and have his head shaved as a sign of penance, or deny his crime and be burned.

Furthermore, one who has thus been shaved must make known his associates, otherwise he again risks the penalty of death by burning. Whence it is thought that some innocents have been burned, for many, because of love of earthly existence or out of affection for their heirs, confessed themselves to have been what they were not and, constrained to make accusation, brought charges of which they were ignorant against those to whom they wished ill. Indeed, it was finally discovered that heretics instigated some of their number to permit themselves to be shaved in penance and thus to accuse Catholics and the innocent. Of such three were taken at Mainz; thereafter there was no one so pure of conscience as not to fear meeting a calamity of this sort. For no one dared, I will not say to intercede for the accused, but even to make the mildest observation in their behalf, for he would immediately be considered a defender of heretics. And, indeed, in accordance with the decision pronounced by the lord pope,[4] he [Conrad] proceeded against defenders and receivers of heretics exactly as against heretics themselves. Furthermore, if anyone had once abjured this impiety and was reported to have relapsed, he was apprehended and without any reconsideration was burned.

Nor was the diocese of Trier free from this infection. For in the city of Trier itself three groups of heretics were uncovered. There was burned a certain Leuchard, who was reputed to have been of a most saintly life, but who bewailed with dreadful laments the unjust banishment from heaven of Lucifer, whom she wished again restored to heaven. Nor was it surprising that such occurrences happened in other cities, since in Rome itself, according to a letter from the pope, not a few had been thus infected. There were a large number in this sect. Many

---

[1] Conrad of Marburg (d.1233) was a papal inquisitor in Germany.

[2] Conrad Tors was a Dominican; John a layman.

[3] I.e., self-control; discipline.

[4] Gregory IX (1227–1241).

of them were versed in the Holy Scriptures, which they had in German translation. Some, indeed, performed a second baptism; some did not believe in the sacrament of the Lord's body; some held that the body of the Lord could not be consecrated by evil priests; some said that the body of the Lord could be consecrated with salver and chalice in any place whatsoever, equally well by a man or a woman, whether ordained or not; some judged confirmation and extreme unction to be superfluous; some scorned the supreme pontiff, the clergy, and the monastic life; some denied the value of prayers of the Church for the souls of the dead; some took their own mothers in marriage, making amends for the consanguinity that existed by the payment of eighteen pence; some kissed a pallid man or even a cat, and performed still worse acts; some, believing all days to be the same, refused to keep holidays or fasts, and thus worked on feast days and ate meat on Good Friday. Let this suffice as a catalogue of their errors, not that we have listed them all but only noted the most outstanding.

At that time the archbishop of Trier convened a synod in which he publicly announced that the heretics in his diocese had a bishop, to whom they had given his own name, Theodoric, and that others did the same elsewhere after the bishops of other places; and he also announced that they shared in common a pope, whom they called Gregory after the bishop of the Church Universal, so that, should they be questioned about the faith, they could say that they had the same faith as did Pope Gregory and bishop so-and-so (giving the name of the bishop), naming our bishop and meaning theirs.

Three heretics were cited before this synod, of whom two were released and one burned.

TIMELINE FOR CHAPTER SIX

1125

*c.*1147– *c.*1170 BERNART DE VENTADORN, —
WHEN I SEE THE LARK

1150

—— *c.*1151 *LETTERS BETWEEN PETER AND BARTHOLOMEW*

1157 *DIET OF BESANÇON* ——

—— 1158–63 *ANSTEY'S LAWSUIT*

1164 *CONSTITUTIONS OF CLARENDON* ——

—— 1166 *ASSIZE OF CLARENDON*

1167–68 HELMOLD, *CHRONICLE OF THE SLAVS* ——

—— 1173–78 *CHRONICLE OF LAON*

*c.*1177–81 CHRÉTIEN DE TROYES, *LANCELOT* ——

1175

1190 BERTRAN DE BORN, *HALF A SIRVENTÉS I'LL SING* ——

—— 1189–93 *LAWS OF CUENCA*

LATE 12TH–EARLY 13TH C. COMTESSA DE DIA, ——
I HAVE BEEN IN HEAVY GRIEF

—— 2ND HALF OF 12TH C. *ADVICE FROM "ARCHIMATTHAEUS"*

1200

*c.*1200 *GOSPEL ACCORDING TO THE MARKS OF SILVER* ——

—— 1200–02 INNOCENT III, *LETTERS*

—— 13TH C. *BROWNY AND THE PRIEST WHO PEEKED*

1213 JACQUES DE VITRY, *LIFE OF MARY OF OIGNIES* ——

—— *c.*1215 CHONIATES, *O CITY OF BYZANTIUM*

1215 *DECREES OF LATERAN IV* ——

—— 1215 *MAGNA CARTA*

1225 ST. FRANCIS, *CANTICLE TO BROTHER SUN* ——

1225

—— 1231 *CHRONICLE OF TRIER*

1236 *SHEARERS' GUILD REGULATIONS* ——

—— 1246 *PROCEEDINGS FOR THE ABBEY OF BEC*

13TH C. *PARISIAN SILK GUILD REGULATIONS* ——

1250

1253 *A GENOESE SOCIETAS* ——

1275

—— 1281 *REGISTER OF THOMAS OF HEREFORD*

1300

To test your knowledge and gain deeper understanding of this chapter, please go to www.utphistorymatters.com for Study Questions.

VII

Discordant Harmonies (c.1250–c.1350)

EAST CENTRAL EUROPE IN FLUX

7.1 The Mongol Challenge: *The Secret History of the Mongols* (first half of the 13th c.). Original in Mongolian.

Although not, strictly speaking, "secret," the text known by that name was probably written for an exclusive group among the Mongols, perhaps limited to the royal family of the Khans itself. Celebrating the rise to power of Chinghis Khan (r.1206–1227)[1] and his son Ogodei (r.1229–1241), the *Secret History* begins with the origins of the Mongols and their warlike relations with other clans and tribes, such as the Tatars. It continues (in the excerpt below) with the clan leader Temujin's election as Khan and his new identity as Chinghis Khan. As the Mongols absorb the Tatars and other groups, according to the *Secret History*, they become the supreme military power of the region. In subsequent sections of the *Secret History*, Chinghis's hegemony widens as he takes over all of Central Asia; soon his son Ogodei moves into southern Russia, the Middle East, and Eastern Europe.

[Source: *The Secret History of the Mongols: The Origin of Chinghis Khan*, trans. Francis Woodman Cleaves, adapted by Paul Kahn (San Francisco: North Point Press, 1984), pp. 48–51, 71–74.]

Then they moved the whole camp
to the shores of Blue Lake in the Gurelgu Mountains.
Altan, Khuchar, and Sacha Beki conferred with each
  other there,
and then said to Temujin:
"We want you to be khan.
Temujin, if you'll be our khan
we'll search through the spoils

5

---

[1] In older books he is Ghengis Khan.

for the beautiful women and virgins,
for the great palace tents,
for the young virgins and loveliest women,   10
for the finest geldings and mares.
We'll gather all these and bring them to you.
When we go off to hunt for wild game
we'll go out first to drive them together for you to
    kill.
We'll drive the wild animals of the steppe together   15
so that their bellies are touching.
We'll drive the wild game of the mountains together
so that they stand leg to leg.
If we disobey your command during battle
take away our possessions, our children, and wives.   20
Leave us behind in the dust,
cutting off our heads where we stand and letting
    them fall to the ground.
If we disobey your counsel in peacetime
take away our tents and our goods, our wives, and
    our children.
Leave us behind when you move,   25
abandoned in the desert without a protector."
Having given their word,
having taken this oath,
they proclaimed Temujin khan of the Mongol
and gave him the name Chinghis Khan.   30

Once Chinghis had been elected
Ogele Cherbi, Bogorchu's young kinsman,
was named as his archer.
Soyiketu Cherbi promised him:
"I'll see to it   35
you'll never miss your morning drink,
you'll never miss your evening meal,"
and he became head cook.
Degei promised him:
"I'll see to it   40
that a lamb is brought in for the morning broth,
that another's brought in for the evening.
I'll herd the speckled sheep
and see that your carts are filled with their wool.
I'll herd the yellow sheep   45
and see that your flocks are filled with their number,"
and he became head shepherd.
Then his younger brother, Guchugur, promised:
"I'll see to it
that the lynch-pins are always tight on the wheels of
    your carts,   50
that the axletree doesn't break when the carts are on
    the road.

I'll be in charge of the tent carts."
Dodai Cherbi promised:
"I'll be in charge of the men and women who serve
    in your tents."
Then Chinghis appointed three men,   55
along with his brother Khasar,
to be his personal swordsmen, saying:
"Anyone who thinks they are stronger,
you'll strike off their heads.
Anyone who thinks they're more courageous,   60
you'll cut them in two.
My brother Belgutei will bring the geldings in from
    the pasture.
He will be in charge of the horses.
Mulkhalkhu will be in charge of the cattle.
Arkhai Khasar, Taghai, Sukegei, and Chakhurkhan,   65
these four warriors will be like my arrows,
like the arrows I shoot near and far."
Then Subetai the Brave promised him:
"I'll be like a rat and gather up others,
I'll be like a black crow and gather great flocks.   70
Like the felt blanket that covers a horse,
I'll gather up soldiers to cover you.
Like the felt blanket that guards a tent from the wind,
I'll assemble great armies to shelter your tent."
Then Chinghis Khan turned to Bogorchu and Jelme,
    and said: 75
"You two,
from the time when there was no one to fight beside
    me but my own shadow,
you were my shadow and gave my mind rest.
That will always be in my thoughts.
From the time when there was nothing to whip my
    horses with but their own tails,   80
you were their tails and gave my heart peace.
That will always be in my heart.
Since you were the first two who came to my side
you'll be chiefs over all the rest of the people."
Then Chinghis Khan spoke to the people, saying: 85
"If Heaven and Earth grant me their protection so
    that my powers increase,
then each of you elders of the clans
who've chosen to leave Anda Jamugha and follow me
will be happy with the choice that you've made.
I'll give you each your position and office."…   90

At the end of that winter
in the autumn of the Year of the Dog,
Chinghis Khan assembled his army at Seventy Felt
    Cloaks

to go to war with the four Tatar clans.
Before the battle began   95
Chinghis Khan spoke with his soldiers and set down
    these rules:
"If we overcome their soldiers
no one will stop to gather their spoils.
When they're beaten and the fighting is over
then there'll be time for that.   100
We'll divide their possessions equally among us.
If we're forced to retreat by their charge
every man will ride back to the place where we
    started our attack.
Any man who doesn't return to his place for a
    counterattack will be killed."
Chinghis Khan met the Tatar at Seventy Felt Cloaks   105
and made them retreat.
He surrounded them
and drove them back into their camp at Ulkhui
    Shilugeljid.
But as they destroyed the army of the four Tatar clans
Altan, Khuchar and Daritai ignored the orders
    Chinghis had set down   110
and they stopped with their men to gather the spoils.
When Chinghis Khan heard this, he said:
"They've broken their word,"
and he sent Jebe and Khubilai to punish them.
They took away from them everything they had
    gathered   115
and left them with nothing at all.
Having destroyed the Tatar army and taken their
    spoils,
a council was called to decide what to do with the
    captives.
Chinghis Khan presided over the great council
in a tent set away from the rest of the camp.   120
They said to each other:
"Since the old days
the Tatar have fought our fathers and grandfathers.
Now to get our revenge for all the defeats,
to get satisfaction for the deaths of our grandfathers
    and fathers,   125
we'll kill every Tatar man taller than the linch-pin
    on the wheel of a cart.
We'll kill them until they're destroyed as a tribe.
The rest we'll make into slaves and disperse them
    among us."
That being what they decided to do,
they filed out of the tent.   130
As they came out the door of the council tent
the Tatar chief, Yeke Cheren, asked Belgutei:

"What have you decided?"
Belgutei told him:
"We've decided to kill every man taller than the
    linch-pin on the wheel of a cart."   135
Hearing that, Yeke Cheren warned all the Tatar
    survivors
and they threw up a fort to fight us off.
We had to storm this fort
and many of our soldiers were killed.
Then after we'd finally forced the Tatar to surrender
    their fort   140
and were measuring them against the height of a
    linch-pin and executing them,
they saw there was no way to escape death.
They said to each other:
"Every man place a knife in his sleeve.
When the Mongol come to kill you,   145
take that man as your pillow."
And we lost many more of our soldiers.
When all of the Tatar men taller than the height of a
    linch-pin were dead,
Chinghis Khan made this decree:
"Because Belgutei revealed the decision we'd reached
    in the great council   150
many of our soldiers have died.
From now on Belgutei won't be allowed to take part
    in such councils.
He'll be in charge outside the council tent until it is
    over.
Let him judge the fights in the camp
and the men accused of lying and theft.   155
After the council is over and we've all drunk the holy
    wine
only then will Belgutei and Daritai be allowed to
    enter the tent."

From among all the Tatar women
Chinghis Khan took Yeke Cheren's daughter, Yesugen
    Khatun,
to be one of his wives.   160
After she'd become Chinghis Khan's wife she said to
    him:
"If the Khan loves me and wants to care for me,
if he thinks I'm good enough to be his wife,
then I have something to ask him.
I have an older sister named Yesui   165
who is a much better woman than I am
and would make you a much better wife.
But she was married to another man a short time ago
and now since your attack on our camp

who knows where she's gone?" 170

Hearing this, Chinghis Khan said to her:

"If your older sister is such a fine woman then I'll
    find her.

And when I do will you give her your place?"

And Yesugen Khatun answered him:

"If the Khan will search for Yesui, 175

just for the pleasure of seeing her again

I'd be happy to give her my place."

Chinghis ordered his soldiers to search for Yesugen's
    sister,

and they found her travelling through the woods
    with her husband.

When the soldiers approached them he ran away, 180

and our men brought Yesui Khatun back to our camp.

When Yesugen Khatun saw her elder sister again

she remembered her promise.

She stood up and gave her place to her sister,

then sat down below her in the line of the wives. 185

This older sister was a beautiful woman

just as Yesugen had said,

and Chinghis Khan loved her as well.

He married Yesui Khatun

and gave her a place in the line of his wives. 190

7.2 A Mongol reply to the pope: Guyuk Khan, *Letter to Pope Innocent IV* (1246). Original in Persian.

In the West the Mongols were often called Tatars or Tartars. In 1245, Pope Innocent IV (1243–1254) wrote two letters to "the emperor of the Tartars" to school him in the essentials of the Christian religion, informing him that the pope held "the keys of the kingdom of heaven," expressing amazement that the "emperor"—that is, the Great Khan (*khagan*)—would invade "many countries belonging both to Christians and to others," and asking him to do penance. The letters were delivered by two Franciscan friars, Lawrence of Portugal and John of Plano Carpini, who reached their destination just as Guyuk Khan (r.1246–1248), oldest son and successor of Ogodei, was being installed as Great Khan. Guyuk's reply, printed below, shows him as firm in his own beliefs and as certain of his self-righteousness as the pope was; his conquests, he said, were God-given: "How could anybody seize or kill by his own power contrary to the command of God?"

[Source: *The Mongol Mission: Narratives and Letters of the Franciscan Missionaries in Mongolia and China in the Thirteenth and Fourteenth Centuries*, ed. Christopher Dawson (New York: Sheed and Ward, 1955), pp. 85–86 (language modernized and some notes added).]

We, by the power of the eternal heaven,
Khan of the great Ulus[1]
Our command:—

    This is a version sent to the great Pope, that he may know and understand in the [Persian] tongue, what has been written. The petition of the assem-

bly held in the lands of the Emperor [for our support], has been heard from your emissaries.

If he reaches [you] with his own report, you who are the great Pope, together with all the Princes, come in person to serve us. At that time I shall make known all the commands of the *Yasa*.[2]

---

[1] Ulus is a large or small social group, here consisting of all the peoples under the supreme ruler as a community.

[2] The *Yasa* refers to the customs and laws of the Mongols.

You have also said that supplication and prayer have been offered by you, that I might find a good entry into baptism. This prayer of yours I have not understood. Other words which you have sent me: "I am surprised that you have seized all the lands of the Magyar and the Christians. Tell us what their fault is." These words of yours I have also not understood. The eternal God has slain and annihilated these lands and peoples because they have neither adhered to Chinghis Khan, nor to the Kha-gan,[1] both of whom have been sent to make known God's command, nor to the command of God. Like your words, they also were impudent; they were proud and they slew our messenger-emissaries. How could anybody seize or kill by his own power contrary to the command of God?

Though you also say that I should become a trembling Nestorian Christian, worship God, and be an ascetic, how do you know whom God absolves in truth, to whom He shows mercy? How do you know that such words as you speak are with God's sanction? From the rising of the sun to its setting, all the lands have been made subject to me. Who could do this contrary to the command of God?

Now you should say with a sincere heart: "I will submit and serve you." You yourself, at the head of all the Princes, come at once to serve and wait upon us! At that time I shall recognize your submission.

If you do not observe God's command, and if you ignore my command, I shall know you as my enemy. Likewise I shall make you understand. If you do otherwise, God knows what I know.

At the end of Jumada the second in the year 644.[2]

The Seal

We, by the power of the eternal Tengri,[3] universal Khan of the great Mongol Ulus—our command. If this reaches peoples who have made their submission, let them respect and stand in awe of it.

7.3 The Hungarian king bewails the Mongol invasions: Béla IV, *Letter to Pope Innocent IV* (*c.*1250). Original in Latin.

It was probably in 1250 that King Béla IV of Hungary (r.1235–1270) wrote a letter to Pope Innocent IV (1243–1254) on the situation in his country. The Mongols (or "Tartars") had already invaded Hungary in 1241–1242, and Béla greatly feared that they were preparing a second, definitive conquest of the West (which, however, never occurred). The letter described the difficulties that Hungary—and all of Europe—would face in case of this second assault. Above all, the king explained the general peril of his country, which was on the eastern frontier of Christendom: on one side, to be sure, were Christians, but on the other side were heretics and pagans. Traditionally understood as a complaint to the Pope and as a desperate demand for help from the great powers of Christendom, the letter may also be interpreted as Béla's attempt to use Hungary's frontier to create an ideology in the service of royal power. Hungary has always been situated on the eastern frontier of western Christendom; although strongly tied to the Christian side, it was bound to negotiate as well with its non-Christian neighbors when necessary.

[Source: Archivio Segreto Vaticano, AA Arm. I-XVIII-605; Augustin Theiner, *Vetera monumenta historica Hungariam sacram illustrantia*, vol.1: 1216–1352 (Rome, 1859), pp. 230–32. Translated and introduced by Piroska Nagy.]

---

[1] Khagan is the supreme ruler.

[2] I.e., 1246 CE.

[3] The Mongolian great god.

To the most holy father in Christ and Lord Innocent, by divine providence Supreme pontiff of the Holy Roman and Universal Church, Béla, king of Hungary by the same grace, with the respect both due and devoted. Most of the kingdom of Hungary has been reduced to a desert by the scourge of the Tartars, and it is surrounded like a sheepfold by different infidel peoples like the Ruthenians and the Brodniks[1] on the eastern side and the Bulgarians and Bosnian heretics against whom we have been fighting until now with our armies on the southern side. On the western and northern side there are Germans, from whom, because of our common faith, our kingdom should gain the fruit of some aid. However, it is not any fruit, but rather the thorns of war that our land is forced to endure as they snatch away the wealth of the country by unexpected plundering. For this reason— and especially because of the Tartars, whom the experience of war has taught us to fear in the same way as all the other nations that they have passed through have learned—after having asked for advice from the prelates and princes of our kingdom, we hasten to flee to the worthy vicar of Christ [the pope] and to his brethren, as to the sole and very last true protector of Christian faith in our ultimate need, so that what we all fear will not happen to us, or rather, through us, to you and to the rest of Christendom. Day after day news of the Tartars come to us: that they have unified their forces—and not only against us, with whom they are the most enraged, because we refuse to submit to them even after all that injury, while all the other nations that they put to the test became their tributaries, especially the regions which are at the east of our kingdom, such as Russia, the countries of the Cumans and the Brodniks, and Bulgaria, which in large part had once belonged to our dominion. It is rather against the whole of Christendom that their forces are unified, and, insofar as it is deemed certain by several trustworthy people, they have firmly decided to send their countless troops against the whole of Europe soon. Thus we are afraid that, if their people arrive, our subjects will be unable or even unwilling to withstand the cruelty of the Tartar ferocity in battle and, against our will, guided by fear, they will end up by submitting to their yoke, just as the above-mentioned neighbors have already done, unless by its careful consideration the far-sighted Apostolic see securely and powerfully fortifies our kingdom in order to comfort the peoples living in it.

Indeed we write this letter principally for two reasons: not to be accused of having shirked what is possible, and not to be considered negligent. As far as what is possible is concerned, we say that we can conclude after our experience that we did whatever was possible when we exposed ourselves and all we had to the heretofore unknown men and capabilities of the Tartars. As for negligence, we can by no means be accused of it. For, while the Tartars were still fighting against us in our country, we turned to the three principal courts of Christendom seeking help in this affair, namely yours, which is believed and held by Christians to be the highest and master of all the courts; [and we turned to the court] of the emperor,[2] to whom we even declared that we would be ready to submit ourselves if, during the time of the above-mentioned scourge he would have given us valid assistance and help; and we also turned for help to the court of the Franks.[3] But from all of them we received neither encouragement nor support, only words. In fact, we had recourse to all that was ours and, for the profit of Christendom, we humiliated our royal majesty and gave two of our daughters in marriage to two Ruthenian dukes and the third one to a Polish duke, aiming to learn through them and other friends of ours in the Eastern parts all the secret news about Tartars, so that this way we might face them and resist in a more suitable way their intentions and fraudulent schemes. We even received the Cumans into our kingdom, and—for shame!—today we defend our kingdom with pagans and put down the infidels of the Church with the help of pagans. Moreover, in order to defend the Christian faith, we have joined by marriage our first born son to a Cuman woman, in order to avoid the worst, and to have the possibility to create some occasion to bring them to the baptismal font—as we have already done more than once. So for all these and other reasons we very much hope that it is clear to the Sanctity of your Supreme pontiff, that in these oppressive times we have received no useful aid from any prince or people of the whole Christian Europe, with the exception of the knights Hospitaller in Jerusalem, whose brothers at our request have recently taken up arms against the pagans and the schismatics in defense of our kingdom and the Christian faith.[4] We have already placed part of them

---

[1] Steppe peoples with whom Hungary had to contend.

[2] Emperor Frederick II (r.1220–1250).

[3] The French king at this time was St. Louis (r.1226–1270).

[4] The Knights Hospitaller was a crusading order of warrior-monks. While originally formed to defend the Crusader States, it was also involved in numerous other military ventures.

in a very dangerous spot, namely in the neighborhood of the Cumans and the Bulgars beyond the Danube, in the area through which the Tartar army found its way to us at the time of the invasion of our kingdom. Regarding that region, we hope and intend that, if God helps our acts and those of the above-mentioned Hospitallers, the Apostolic See may find them sufficiently worthy to grant them its favor. Just as the Danube stretches to the sea of Constantinople, so we can succeed through them to propagate progeny of the Catholic faith, and thus they may bring useful aid to the Roman empire and also to the Holy Land. We have installed another part of them in the middle of our country, to defend the castles that we are constructing around the Danube, because our peoples are not accustomed to do this. For, after more than one discussion, our council decided that it would be more beneficial to us and to the whole of Europe to safeguard the Danube by fortifications: the Danube is the water of resistance.[1] It was here that Heraclius met Chosroes when he defended the Roman empire,[2] and it was here that we resisted—entirely unprepared, and thus badly injured—the Tartars for ten months, while our kingdom was still almost completely lacking fortifications and defenders. Because if—God forbid!—this territory were possessed by the Tartars, the door would be open for them to [invade] the other regions of the Catholic faith. This is in part because there is no sea to hamper their passage from here to other Christians, and in part it is because they can settle their families and animals—in which they abound—marvelously well here, better than elsewhere. Attila[3] may serve as an example of someone who, coming from the East to subdue the West, established the center of his authority in the middle of the kingdom of Hungary. On the other hand the emperors, who came fighting from the West in order to subdue the East, laid down their frontiers inside our country, however much they did for the organization of the army. May your pontifical Sanctity, pondering all this, find us worthy to procure a medicine before the wound rots. Indeed the multitude of wise people is very surprised that, in the present state of affairs, your Paternity permitted the departure of the king of France, such a noble member of the Church, from the frontiers of Europe.[4] The multitude is wondering and cannot cease to be amazed at the fact that your Apostolic Clemency offers substantial help to the empire of Constantinople and regions overseas, which, if they were lost—God forbid!—would not harm the inhabitants of Europe as much as if our kingdom alone passed into the possession of the Tartars. We take God and man as our witness that our necessity and the gravity of our situation are so great that, if the various dangers of the roads did not prevent us, we would send not only messengers, as we have done so far, but would personally come as a servant and fall down at your feet to proclaim before the face of the whole Church—so that we may be justified and excused—that, if your fatherly sanctity does not send us help and the need becomes overwhelming, against our will, we may reach an arrangement with the Tartars. So we humbly beseech you that the Holy Mother Church consider, if not ours, at least the merits of our predecessors, the holy kings who, full of devotion and reverence submitted themselves and their people, preaching to them the orthodox faith, and serving you with purity of faith and in obedience. That is why the Apostolic see promised to them and to their successors all grace and favor if any necessity threatened, at a moment when they did not even ask for it, as the course of things was prosperous for them. Alas, now this heavy constraint seems to be imminent. Thus open your fatherly heart, and in this time of persecution, extend your hand with the necessary support for the defense of the faith and for the public utility. Otherwise, if our petition—which is so necessary and so universally favorable for the faithful of the Roman Church—suffers a refusal (which we cannot believe) then we should be obliged by necessity, not like sons but like step-sons, excluded from the flock of the father, to beg for aid elsewhere. Dated in Patak the day of the bishop and confessor Saint Martin, III of the ides of November.

---

[1] "Water of resistance": i.e., the Danube is the watery frontier that will keep out the Tartars.

[2] A reference to the wars between Byzantine Emperor Heraclius (r.610–641) and the Persian King Chosroes II (r.590–628).

[3] The original contains the name Totila, as Béla confused Totila, king of the Ostrogoths (d.552), with Attila, leader of the Huns (d.453).

[4] St. Louis left for the Seventh Crusade in 1248.

7.4 Poland as a frontier society: *The Henryków Book* (*c*.1268). Original in Latin.

The Henryków Book was written by Peter, the third abbot of a Cistercian monastery founded in Henryków (Silesia) in the thirteenth century. The book contained a mix of history—much of it based on oral testimony—and legal documents; Peter intended it, he said, to protect his monastery against "the malice and iniquity of some." He meant claimants to the monastery's lands. Many of the people who threatened the monks' landholding were heirs of those who had previously donated or sold their land to the monastery. That explains why his book was organized around specific pieces of land, and why Peter mingled narratives about how the monastery got that land with documents that buttressed its claims. Historians can use Peter's account to analyze various tensions in Silesian society as well as the monastery's relationship to outside forces. Silesia (which at the time Peter was writing was a duchy of Poland) was a frontier region, lying between the old heartland of Poland (centered on Gniezno; see above, p. 214) and Germany. Peter noted the presence of German and Czech settlers in the region, but his focus was on the Piasts, the reigning ducal family in Poland. One branch of the Piasts held Silesia. For Peter there were two periods of history: the time of the good dukes (before 1241) and the time thereafter, which followed the invasion of Silesia by the "pagans"—by this term Peter meant the Mongols—and their defeat and slaying of Duke Henry II the Pious at the battle of Legnica (1241). This, according to Peter, ushered in a period of weak dukes—"boyish" or "juvenile" were the epithets Peter used for them—and led to the period of conflict and disorder in which he was writing. Compare the claims and behaviors of heirs in the instance of the Henryków monastery to those that appear in the charters of Cluny on p. 175. How did the Mongols, the dukes, the Northern Crusades, and the German settlers make Henryków's thirteenth-century Silesia different from Cluny's tenth- and eleventh-century Burgundy? To what extent can these differences be attributed simply to the passing of time? To what extent can they be explained by different local circumstances and Silesia's location on a frontier?

[Source: Piotr Górecki, *A Local Society in Transition:* The Henryków Book *and Related Documents* (Toronto: Pontifical Institute of Medieval Studies, 2007), pp. 104–8, 112–16 (notes modified). Translated by Piotr Górecki.]

HERE BEGINS THE TREATISE INTRODUCING THE FIRST BOOK ABOUT THE FOUNDATION OF THE CLOISTER OF SAINT MARY THE VIRGIN IN HENRYKÓW.

[1] Because the deeds of the mortals grow old and are dimmed by a fog of oblivion in the course of time and with the long succession of posterity, it has wisely been decreed to entrust them to the memory of succeeding generations by a record of letters. Therefore we, the First monks transferred from the holy and venerable community of the monastery of Lubiaz to plant the flower of divine service in Henryków, have decided to reveal to our successors by the present writing in what way—meaning from what persons and for what reason—this house has assumed the beginnings of its foundation.

And because through the succession of diverse times and persons the good deeds of the faithful are sometimes violated by the malice and iniquity of some among those who come after them, we have expressed in the present booklet, by a truthful narration, how—meaning from what persons and by what authority—the gifts of all the inheritances which this cloister has peacefully possessed since the beginnings [of the rule] the first Abbot Henry until the most recent times of the fourth Abbot Geoffrey,[1] have accrued to this church, and been confirmed in its eternal possession: so that the knights of Christ who slave for Almighty God in this place for a long time to come may be able to refute any claim leveled against them and answer the adversaries of their house with reasoned reflection, because, thanks to this book, they know the origins of each gift and the cause [of the monks' possession] of each inheritance....

ABOUT CIENKOWICE.

[45] We will say about Cienkowice how and why the cloister may possess part of it. In the days when the cloister of Henryków was being founded, there was a certain rather powerful knight by the name of Albert, and by the nickname of Lyka in Polish, who possessed [land] in Cieplowoda. This same Albert took as wife a daughter of a certain noble by the name of Dzierzko, and begat a daughter by her. When she was born, the wife herself died at once.[2] After her death, Albert granted to the cloister a part of his inheritance of Cieplowoda, in the amount of two plows,[3] to be possessed forever for the soul of his father, then dead, and for his own sins.

[46] *About the gift and the alms of Albert with Beard.* Albert made this gift in the year of the Lord 1229. That same year, Albert went to Prussia for the sins of his father and for his own sins.[4] But before he embarked on that journey, he ordained before the lord duke and the barons that if he should not return, the cloister of Henryków was to possess the entire territory of Cieplowoda; while if he did return, the cloister was to keep that part which he had granted earlier, in the amount of two plows. But because in those days men were simple, without the bile of malice, no privilege was requested from the duke about this deed at that time. Albert returned from Prussia healthy and whole, and later took a German wife by whom he begat sons and daughters. Yet, the cloister possessed from him

and from his sons the land which he had granted out of his Cieplowoda, peacefully and for many years.

[47] *What happened in the land after the pagans.* However, as soon as the pagans[5] entered this land, and did much in it that was worthy of lament, and after the celebrated Duke [Henry II] was killed, this land was dominated by knights, each of whom seized whatever pleased him from the duke's inheritances. Hence the said Albert procured for himself from the boyish Duke Boleslaw[6] two ducal inheritances adjoining his [estate], Cienkowice and Kubice, for a modest sum of money.

[48] *About the purchase.* In order, then, that [the sum of] this money, and the extent of the said inheritances, may be more fully known: this same Albert measured out in the said two villages thirty large hides, for which hides he gave the juvenile Duke Boleslaw thirty silver marks;[7] and, after eliminating the heirs of these villages, he joined these hides to his village of Cieplowoda. Hence the names of the said villages were completely obliterated, and changed to the name of Count Albert's village, Cieplowoda.

[49] *A further account of this.* While this and many similar evils, very harmful to the dukes, were taking place in the land, the said Albert began to settle his Cieplowoda, together with the aforesaid [two] villages, with Germans.[8] But because that portion [of Cieplowoda] which he had given to the cloister lay in the kind of place that prevented him from establishing a German village in one piece there unless he redeemed the cloister's arable fields for himself, he repeatedly asked lord Bodo, abbot of this cloister at that time, to resign to him the land which he had earlier given to the cloister for his sins, and to receive the same amount [of land] near the cloister's old boundaries, that is, in the corner of Cienkowice. Weary of his repeated insistence and prayers, at last the abbot finally—albeit reluctantly—consented to him, and made the exchange with him, receiving near the cloister's boundaries in Cienkowice as much [land] as he had held in Cieplowoda;

---

1 Abbots of Henryków during the years 1227–1234 and 1269–1273, respectively.

2 Presumably in childbirth.

3 "Two plows" indicates the area that two plows could till in a day.

4 Presumably as a crusader against the Baltic Prussians.

5 I.e., the Mongols.

6 Duke Boleslaw II the Bald (1220/1225–1278) was the oldest son of Henry II the Pious. He succeeded his father to the rule of the Duchy of Silesia in 1242, a year after the battle of Legnica.

7 A mark was a unit of account. In the Piast duchies it was equal to about 240 pence.

8 That is, he recruited new settlers from Germany and allotted land to them. In return, they paid him dues.

and he resigned to Count Albert what he was asking for. Hence the name of Cienkowice lives on today for the parcel which we have there.

[50] *Here ends the reason why the cloister possesses Cienkowice*. Here, brothers, the reason why you possess Cienkowice has been set out to you....

HERE BEGINS THE ACCOUNT OF THE GIFT OF SKALICE.

[65] Here begins a treatise on the reason why the cloister of Henryków possesses a third part of the inheritance of Skalice.

A preliminary treatise about this. In those days when the convent was first transferred to Henryków, there were certain uterine brothers, heirs of Skalice, of whom the older was called Nicholas, the younger Stephen. These two men were holding a third part of the whole inheritance of Skalice of that time. Nicholas was a priest, and was in those times the legitimate parish priest in the church of Old Henryków,[1] while his brother Stephen was a layman, then living in his inheritance of Skalice, but very modest in temporal things. Let it then be known that in those days Nicholas, the aforesaid parish priest of Henryków, used to receive tithes throughout the whole field of Henryków—that is to say, [from the area situated] against Skryboszów, and from the other part of the village up through [the stream called] the Morzyna—from the arable of Nicholas, at that time patron of this inheritance.[2] Hence his church in Henryków flourished with great revenues at the time. He received this tithe[3] from the cloister's plows[4] for a few years after the arrival of the convent at this place. So, after the arrival of the brothers at this place, he was quite happy, thinking that he was always going to receive the tithe from the clois-

ter's plows for himself. For which reason he said to his brother Stephen,

"I see that thanks to the arrival here of these brothers and my lords, my prebend[5] is increasing quite a bit. So I wish to assign the part of our inheritance which belongs to me to the cloister in eternal possession."

[66] *About the first gift of Skalice*. A few days after these things happened, this [parish priest] Nicholas, together with his brother Stephen, came up to the elder Duke [Henry I][6] in Niemcza, and before him granted to this cloister the two parts of their inheritance which belonged to them among their other brothers in Skalice, to be possessed forever, for their sins. And the third part Stephen then retained for himself, toward his needs.

[67] *In what year the gift of the same [donor] was made.* This gift was made before lord Duke Henry the elder in the year of the Lord 1233. But a privilege[7] about this was not requested from the lord duke at that time.

[68] *About the removal of the tithe of the village chapel.* After these things happened and a few days passed, lord Thomas of venerated memory—then bishop of the church of Wroclaw—entered this cloister with his retinue, and, upon noting that the brothers then dwelling here lived in the most acute poverty, asked lord Henry, abbot at that time, and the brothers about the cloister's revenues and external wealth. Upon hearing from the abbot and brothers that the cloister's plows were paying tithe [only] to the cloister's own chaplain, the lord bishop became very angry, summoned the same Nicholas chaplain[8] of Henryków to himself, and told him,

"You sit here by yourself and do nothing but sing with sparrows![9] So I want these brothers to receive tithe from this part of the village of Henryków for themselves, toward the aid of their bodies."

---

[1] It seems that Nicholas was already the priest of this parish church before it was given to the monastery of Henryków around the time of its foundation in 1222/1227.

[2] This is a reference *not* to Nicholas the parish priest but a different Nicholas who initiated the foundation of the monastery at Henryków.

[3] Tithes were revenues paid by the laity to their local church for its upkeep and services. They were theoretically equivalent to a tenth of the yearly income of a household, and they were required of all the faithful. Note that rather early in its history, the tithes of the parish church were given to Peter's monastery rather than the church itself.

[4] I.e., from land belonging to the monastery at Henryków.

[5] The "prebend" refers to the revenues attached to the church.

[6] Duke Henry I (r.1201–1238) was the father of Duke Henry II the Pious.

[7] That is, a written document recording the gift. Abbot Peter clearly appreciated the importance of written evidence, a relatively new development in Poland. As we see below, Duke Henry's successor was asked to draw up the privilege for the gift.

[8] This refers to Nicholas the parish priest.

[9] Evidently this referred to a thirteenth-century proverb for idleness.

Upon hearing these words, Chaplain Nicholas was distressed by a great sadness of mind, but did not answer anything right there. But later, after two years went by, he resigned the chapel of Henryków into the abbot's hands, and transferred himself to the Order of the [canons] regular in Kamieniec.[1] From that hour and time, the large revenue of the chapel in the village of Henryków was removed by the venerable lord Thomas, bishop of Wroclaw, and given to the cloister....

[69] *The first confirmation of Skalice.* When Duke Henry the elder died later [in 1238], and when his son Henry the younger ruled in his father's stead, and the said [priest] Nicholas was already confirmed in the aforesaid Order [of the canons regular in Kamieniec], his brother Stephen came up with a certain monk of Henryków by the name of Peter (sent by his father Abbot Bodo)[2] to the said lord duke in Olesnica, and there confessed before the duke and his barons that for their sins he, together with his brother, Priest Nicholas, earlier gave two parts of their inheritance to the cloister of Henryków before the elder duke, to be possessed forever. And the same Stephen added before the duke and barons, as if to repeat and renew the entire deed,

"Lord duke, I again make it known to your majesty in the audience of these nobles that my brother Nicholas and I granted before your father two parts of our inheritance, for the remedy of our souls, to be possessed forever by the cloister of Henryków. The third part I, Stephen, sold to this cloister for 27 silver marks. So because your father did not give a privilege about this, I—together with my fellow Peter, sent with me here by the lord abbot—ask and request that you deign to extend the privilege of your confirmation to the cloister of Henryków [in this matter]."

That hour, on the duke's order, a certain lord Conrad, chaplain of the court and parish priest in Löwenberg,[3] wrote a privilege about this deed, word for word, in the following way.

[70] *The privilege of confirmation.*

In the name of Our Lord Jesus Christ, amen. Inasmuch as over the course of time matters that have not been firmly committed to memory are easily lost to oblivion, we, Henry [II], by the grace of God duke of Silesia, Kraków, and [Great] Poland, wishing to provide a remedy against such defects, make it known in writing and offer full witness to present and future [persons] that, in the presence of the illustrious Duke Henry [I], our father of happy memory, certain brothers of Skalice, Nicholas and Stephen, granted out of the three parts of their inheritance which belonged to them among their other brothers, two parts to Saint Mary and to the brothers serving God there in Henryków, for the remedy of the souls of [their] father and mother, and for their own [souls], to be possessed [forever]; while after his brother took the habit and accepted [a monastic] observance, Stephen sold the third part to the house [of Henryków] for 27 silver marks, to be possessed by hereditary right. Provided that, by the direction and decree of our aforementioned father, and with our [own] agreement to this, neither he nor his successors shall henceforth have any power to redeem [Skalice].

In support of this matter, so that no one may ever by some bold deed dare to contradict this agreement, we ordered that the present page be strengthened with the protection of our seal. The witnesses of this matter are Count Stephen castellan of Niemcza, Count Boguslaw castellan of Ryczyn, Count Raclaw castellan of Wroclaw, Albert of Karczyn, Berthold the village bailiff of Pilawa, and very many others. Done in the year of the Incarnation of the lord 1239, on the fourth [day before the] calends of October [September 28].

[71] *How after the pagans Abbot Bodo dispatched John, Stephen's son, in various ways.* In those days when these two brothers, that is to say Nicholas and Stephen, confirmed the things written down above for the cloister of Henryków, Stephen had a single very small son, John by name. As soon as this John reached a responsible age, he often tried by Polish custom to revoke his uncle's and his father's deeds. But because he was always poor and modest in things, his malice achieved nothing of what he wanted.

[72] *That John resigned from the right to demand the father's inheritance.* Finally, lord Bodo, abbot of Henryków, seeking to avert future evil to this house, by giving

---

[1] This was a community of regular canons (that is, canons who lived according to a Rule, rather like monks). When Nicholas no longer received revenues from the tithes, he gave up his church.

[2] Bodo was the abbot of the monastery at Henryków who preceded Abbot Peter. It is just possible that the "monk Peter" mentioned here was in fact the young Abbot Peter. How likely is it that the monastery put pressure on Stephen to ask the new duke for a confirmation of his donation?

[3] A "chaplain for the court" was a priest in regular attendance on the duke or duchess or both. Here the cleric also functioned as a scribe.

John modest gifts brought it about that after the pagans this John came up to Duke Henry [III], who ruled in this land at that time, and before him and his nobles resigned from every right and every jurisdiction which he had, or may have had, in the said inheritance of his father, Skalice....

....

7.5 The Lithuanian duke flirts with Christianity: Duke Gediminas, *Letter to Pope John XXII* (1322) and *Letter to the Burghers of Lübeck, Rostock, Stralsund, Griefswald, Stettin, and Gotland* (May 26, 1323). Original in Latin.

Gediminas (*c.*1275–1341) was grand duke of the pagan duchy of Lithuania from 1315/1316 until his death in 1341. Often called the "founder of Lithuania's medieval power" and considered the most famous of Lithuania's medieval dukes, Gediminas is credited with consolidating Lithuania politically and expanding its land from the Baltic to the Black Sea. While the reign of Gediminas marks a period of great political and military achievements for Lithuania, it was also a time of unrelenting conflict with the Teutonic Knights.

Between 1322 and 1324, Gediminas addressed six letters to the Pope, the cities of Baltic Germany (the Hansa), and the mendicant orders of Saxony. The letters reflect three concerns: (1) indignation with the Teutonic Order, (2) the need to develop the Lithuanian economy, and (3) a provisional acceptance of Catholicism.[1] The following selection includes the grand duke's first letter to Pope John XXII (1316–1334)—the second of the Avignon popes—and a letter to member cities of the Hanseatic League. Why did Gediminas claim that he is ready to obey the Pope, as do "other Christian kings"? What were the various types of liberties and exemptions that Gediminas promises to new settlers? Why did he issue these invitations?

[Source: *Chartularium Lithuaniae res gestas magni ducis Gedeminne illustrans / Gedimino laiškai*, ed. Stephen C. Rowell (Vilnius: Leidykla Vaga, 2003), pp. 38–41, 58–62. Translated and introduced by Kristina Markman.]

Letter of Gediminas to Pope John XXII [1322]

To the most excellent father, lord John, the supreme pontiff of the Roman See, Gediminas, king of the Lithuanians and many Ruthenians,[2] etc.

For a long time, we[3] have heard that all the worshippers of the Christian faith ought to be subject to your authority and paternity, and that the Catholic faith itself is governed by the foresight of the Roman Church. It is henceforth that we declare to your reverence in the present letter, that our

---

[1]   The text of these letters survives in contemporary transcripts in the archives of Riga, Berlin, and the Vatican. The documents were reproduced from the originals at the request of Gediminas himself, who in the addendum to each letter instructed that it be copied for wider circulation.

[2]   *Ruthenia* is the Latin for the place name Rus'. In the 1240s, Lithuanian Grand Duke Mindaugas (*c.*1203–1263) conquered the region of Black Ruthenia (present-day western Belarus). From that time, Lithuanian dukes embarked upon a fervent campaign of expansion at the expense of the former principalities of Kievan Rus'. Gediminas's title—King of Lithuanians and many Ruthenians—reflects Lithuania's territorial acquisitions from the late thirteenth to early fourteenth centuries.

[3]   Note that Gediminas systematically used the "royal we" in place of "I."

predecessor, King Mindaugas, with his entire kingdom was converted to the faith of Christ,[1] but because of the atrocious injuries and innumerable treacheries of the master of the brothers of the Teutonic Order, they all withdrew from the faith, and as it were to our sorrow, until this very day, we remain in the error of our forefathers. For many times in order to make peace our predecessors sent their envoys to the archbishops of Riga[2] whom they [Teutonic Knights] brutally murdered, as is well known by [the case of] lord Ysarus,[3] who on behalf of lord Boniface[4] arranged a peace and truce with us and the brothers of the Teutonic Order and sent his letters to us, but, [when] the envoys were returning from lord Ysarus, [Teutonic Knights] killed some on the way, hung the others and forced them to drown themselves.

Likewise, our predecessor, King Vytenis,[5] sent a letter to the legate lord Francis and the lord Archbishop Frederick of Riga[6] asking that they send to him two brothers from the Franciscan Order, allotting them a place and already having built them a church. Knowing this, the Prussian brothers of the Teutonic house sent an army by a back route and set fire to said church. Moreover, they captured lord archbishops, bishops, and priests, as is well known from [the case of] lord John,[7] who died in the curia in the times of lord Boniface, and [from the case of] lord Archbishop Frederick, whom they treacherously drove out of the church. Likewise, [from the case of] one cleric, lord Berthold, whom they cruelly killed in the city of Riga, in his very own house.

Likewise, they lay waste to lands, as is clear in Semigallia[8]

and many others places. However, they say that they do this in order to defend Christians. Holy and revered Father, we do not fight Christians in order to destroy the Catholic faith, but in order to oppose injuries to our people, as do Christian princes and kings, which is well known because we have among us brothers from the Franciscan Order and the Dominican Order, to whom we have given full freedom to baptize, preach, and administer other sacred rites.

In fact, revered Father, we wrote you this so that you know why our forefathers regressed into the error of infidelity and disbelief. Now, however, holy and revered Father, we pray that you might take notice of our lamentable situation because we are ready, like other Christian kings, to obey you in everything and receive the Catholic faith, provided that we are restrained in nothing by said torturers, namely by said Master[9] and brethren.

Letter of Gediminas to the Burghers of Lübeck, Rostock, Stralsund, Griefswald, Stettin, and Gotland [May 26, 1323]

Gediminas, King of the Lithuanians and Ruthenians by the grace of God, Prince and Duke of Semigallia, to honorable men, prudent and honest counselors, magistrates and citizens of Lübeck, Rostock, Stralsund, Griefswald, Stettin,[10] and Gotland,[11] to merchants and artisans of all conditions, [sends] greetings and royal grace and favor.

Since all kingdoms, of which we hold one, are subject

---

[1] In 1253 Mindaugas was baptized and crowned King of Lithuania. After a short period of relative peace, civil war erupted in Lithuania and regional conflict with the Teutonic Order escalated. Mindaugas was assassinated in the fall of 1263. It is unknown whether he apostatized from Christianity as the letter states.

[2] The archbishopric of Riga in medieval Livonia was the most important Catholic archdiocese in the region. A constant power struggle ensued between the archbishop, the citizens of the city of Riga, and the Livonian Order.

[3] Archbishop of Riga 1300–1302.

[4] Boniface VIII (1294–1303) was elected pope on Christmas Eve, 1294.

[5] Vytenis, probably Gediminas's brother, was grand duke of Lithuania 1295–1316.

[6] Frederick von Pernstein, a Franciscan, was archbishop of Riga 1304–1341. In 1311, Pope Clement V sent Francis of Moliano to Riga to investigate charges of heresy brought against the Teutonic Order by Frederick. On the basis of Francis's findings, the Pope excommunicated the Livonian branch of the Teutonic Order for one year and imposed an interdict on the Order's lands in 1312.

[7] John III of Schwerin was archbishop of Riga 1294–1300. In 1297, the Teutonic Knights attacked the archbishop's castle, seized the archbishop, and held him prisoner for 33 days. In 1299, John traveled to Rome to plead his case in the papal curia, where he remained until his death in 1300, as noted in the letter.

[8] Semigallia or Zemgale (today in Latvia) was claimed by the Lithuanian dukes.

[9] Karl von Trier (1265–1324) was grandmaster of the Teutonic Order 1311–1324.

[10] Present-day city of Szczecin in West Pomerania, Poland.

[11] Gediminas addressed his invitation to the citizens of cities of the Hanseatic League. The migrations of such colonists into Lithuania would have meant an influx of skilled labor as well as secure contacts with the Hanseatic League.

to the heavenly king, Jesus Christ, just as form in matter[1] or as a slave in his master's house, although we appear the least of all kings, nevertheless, by the providence of God, we are the greatest in our own [realm], in which we retain [the right] to direct and to govern, to destroy and to save, to close and to open. For a little while now, you have crossed our borders without any inspection [on the way] to visit Novgorod and Pskov. All this we permitted for the sake of general good; now you have seen and heard from day to day all the harm [that befalls] your [people]. Our forefathers sent to you their envoys and letters, opened their land to you, [but] none of your people came, not even a dog from their parts rendered gratitude for our offers. May the things written above not frighten you. If [our forefathers] themselves promised one thing, with the blessing of God, we will double it. For that reason all the more, we have sent our letter to our Father, the most holy lord Pope, regarding a union with the church of God, and with indescribable impatience are awaiting the arrival of his legates, whose stay we guaranteed to oversee in writing. Therefore, consulting with your own, send to us from all your parts earnest envoys, true and worthy men of faith, above our signature and at the top of the present letter, confirmed by the royal seal, thereupon we promise to all of you, having given our pledge, that we will arrange such a peace between us, that even Christians have never experienced the like.

We will gather bishops, priests, devout members of the Franciscan and Dominican Orders, whose lives are praiseworthy and admirable; we do not wish such men to come who make monasteries into a refuge for thieves, sell alms to the detriment of their soul, and emerge from [their hideout] in thieving bands to harass and murder clerics; we advise every single ruler to beware of such monks himself.

In addition, above [that which was granted by] all our predecessors, we now grant according to royal decree in the present charter our land to be free, without any tolls, exaction of services and duties[2] to all merchants, knights, vassals, whom we will endow with incomes, to each according to his status. To artisans of all conditions, namely craftsmen, cobblers, carpenters, stonemasons, saltmakers,[3] millers, silversmiths, cross-bow makers, fishermen, or others of any condition, let them come with their children, wives, and livestock, let them come and go as they please, far-removed from all disturbances because, having given our pledge in these matters, we swore that they will remain safe and exempt from all wrongful attacks by my subjects.

To farmers who wish to come and reside in our kingdom, we offer and grant [the right] to cultivate up to ten years freely and without [paying] the *cens*,[4] and exemption from all royal dues for half that time; upon expiration of said period and also depending upon the fertility of their land, they will pay a tithe,[5] as in all other kingdoms or as they have been accustomed to give in their own; in such a way then, grain will be more abundant for us than the norm in all other kingdoms.

Let all people enjoy the civil law of the city of Riga,[6] unless by that time, in accordance with the sound counsel of men of distinction there will be found better. Consequently, so that we might make you more secure and certain, we have erected two churches for the Franciscan Order, one in our royal city called Vilnius[7] and another in Novgorodok,[8] and a third for the Dominican Order, so that anyone may worship God according to his rite.

Therefore, in order that our grant of privileges may remain impermeable and strong, we have ordered the present charter to be written and we reinforced it by affixing our seal; because knowing this—that we sent the same seal to our Lord and most holy Father and copied everything in our letter to him—[you can be assured] we will preserve this [grant] in its entirety. In this letter, we repudiate deniers of our seal just as if they were malicious

---

[1] Reference to the Aristotelian concept of the inseparability of matter and form.

[2] Here Gediminas refers to compulsory service owed to the lord, particularly military service, and the requisition of vehicles and horses for military purposes.

[3] Literally, Gediminas says, "those trained in the art of salt." The phrase may refer to miners, refiners, etc.

[4] The *cens* was an annual tax paid for the right to use and work land.

[5] The tithe was an annual compulsory tax in the amount of 10 per cent of all income, paid in currency or kind.

[6] Riga was granted Lübeck Law in 1201, though it did not become a member of the Hanseatic League until 1281. The law provided for self-government, making the city independent from royal oversight and dues. The offer of Lübeck law would have attracted many new colonists.

[7] This is the first known reference to Vilnius as a royal or capital city.

[8] Present-day Navahrudak, Belarus.

destroyers of the faith, heretics, liars, and men deprived of all honor. Through the duchy of the lord Boleslaw, Duke of Masovia,[1] everyone will be able to have secure entry to us, to our holdings.

Given in Vilnius, in the year of our Lord, 1323, on the feast of Corpus Christi. After the letter has been read in one city, we ask that under witness of devout and other worthy men of faith that it to be copied and sent without delay to another city so that our desire may be revealed to all. Farewell.

....

7.6 Pagan Lithuania in Christian Europe: Peter of Dusburg, *Chronicle of the Prussian Land* (*c*.1320–1326). Original in Latin.

Peter of Dusburg (d.*c*.1326) was a priest-brother of the Teutonic Order known for writing the *Chronicon terrae Prussiae* (*Chronicle of the Prussian Land*). Completed in 1326 and dedicated to Grandmaster Werner von Orseln, the chronicle is considered to be the most important surviving work of early Prussian historiography. At the time of its composition, the Order's military practices and harsh methods had come under pan-European criticism. The *Chronicle* provides not only detailed accounts of the Order's victories and heroic deeds, but also serves as an ideological affirmation of the Order's status and activities in the Baltic. The following selections are taken from the final chapters of the *Chronicle*, which deal exclusively with the Order's war against the Lithuanians. How does Peter portray the Lithuanians? In what ways are the accusations brought by Peter against the Lithuanians similar to those of Gediminas against the Teutonic Knights (see p. 388 above)?

[Source: Peter of Dusburg, *Chronicon Terrae Prussiae*, ed. Max Töppen in *Scriptores Rerum Prussicarum*, I, pp. 3–219, ed. Theodor Hirsch et al. (Frankfurt am Main: Minerva, 1861, rpt. 1965), pp. 186–194. Translated and introduced by Kristina Markman.]

341. *On the Devastation of the Diocese of Dorpat in the Land of Livonia.*

Meanwhile, when that army of the brothers was in said territories,[2] the Lithuanians with a great multitude of people entered the land of Livonia,[3] and besides other damages that they caused in the diocese of Dorpat[4] with fire and sword,[5] they killed more than five thousand Christians and led them away into eternal captivity....

---

1. Lord Boleslaw was Boleslaw II (*c*.1251–1313) and Duke of Masovia (today in east-central Poland) 1294–1313. Gediminas refers to the combined territory of his sons, Siemowit and Trojden, as the "duchy of the lord Boleslaw."

2. In the previous passage (not included), Peter described the Teutonic Order's raid into Lithuania.

3. Livonia was once the region associated with parts of present-day northwestern Latvia and southwestern Estonia. In the fourteenth century, the territory was subdivided between the largely autonomous branch of the Teutonic Order known as the Livonian Order, the archbishopric of Riga, and the bishoprics of Courland, Ösel-Wiek, and Dorpat.

4. The bishopric of Dorpat was a medieval catholic diocese, which existed from 1224 to 1558 and encompassed parts of present-day Estonia.

5. Peter's frequent reference to destruction caused by "fire and sword" has both biblical and literal connotations. E.g., "For the Lord shall judge by fire, and by his sword unto all flesh, and the slain of the Lord shall be many" (Isa. 66: 16); "There shall the fire devour thee: thou shalt perish by the sword" (Nah. 3: 15). Ancient and medieval warfare strategy included the destruction of the enemy's resources, e.g., fields, peasants, etc.

343. *On the Plunder of Reval, the Land of the Danish King.*

At the same time, David the castellan of Garth,[1] with an army of Lithuanians entered Reval, the land of the Danish king,[2] and besides other infinite damages which he inflicted upon said land with fire and sword, he captured and killed more than five thousand noble Christian men, women, girls, and others of both genders. He also killed many parish and monastic priests. He barbarically defiled and desecrated holy places, churches, sacred vestments and altar vessels, and anything else used for worship.

344. *On the Destruction of the City of Memel and Many Castles.*

In the same year [1323], on the third day after the feast of Pope St. Gregory,[3] Lithuanians from Samogitia[4] with their army took the city of Memel[5] and killed one priest-brother of the Teutonic Order. They also seized seventy people in that city, some of whom were killed, others taken away into eternal captivity. The city itself and three nearby newly converted castles, cogs[6] and other ships, and everything else that could be destroyed by fire, except only the castle inhabited by the brothers, they turned to ash....

346. *On the Destruction of the Duchy and City of Dobrzyń and the Death and Capture of Nine Thousand Christians.*

On the feast day of the Exaltation of the Holy Cross,[7] in the same year [1323], the Lithuanians, seeing that everything happens according to their will,[8] once again gathered a strong army and went to the duchy of the noble lady, Duchess [Anastasia] of Dobrzyń,[9] and did away with six thousand people of both genders, slaughtering some and miserably leading the others away into eternal servitude of the pagans. In addition, they killed seven parish priests and two brothers of the Order of Saint Benedict, along with six hundred clerics, both ordained and not ordained, who were found inside and outside the seminary. They also burnt ten parish churches, all the main villages, and the capital city of said duchy, called Dobrzyń, where they captured and killed two thousand Christians. Along with said damages, they also carried off so much plunder and such diverse things that since the Christian faithful are to remain in the eternal servitude of the pagans, the land of said duchy (deserving of mournful memory) will hardly ever be able to recover from said devastation; and certainly it ought to frighten and sadden that, due to the destruction of said duchy, easier access will be open for the infidels to the adjacent and neighboring lands of the Christians. Behold how much evil was brought upon the Christian faith and the faithful within the span of one and a half years; for almost twenty thousand Christians were killed by the pagans and led away into eternal captivity, and many cities and castles were completely destroyed....

---

1 A castellan was the custodian of a castle and surrounding territories, responsible for its keep and defense. As the castellan of Garth (present-day Grodno, Belarus), David (1283–1326) would have been one of the most important and trusted vassals of the grand duke of Lithuania. David is the most frequently mentioned Lithuanian in the *Chronicle*.

2 The Danish conquered Reval (present-day Tallinn, Estonia) in 1219.

3 March 15, 1323. The feast day of Pope Saint Gregory the Great is March 12.

4 Samogitia (Lithuanian: Žemaitija) is a region in northwestern Lithuania. The territory played a critical role in Lithuania's wars with the Teutonic Order as it geographically divided the land of the Order in Prussia from their holdings in Livonia. As a result, Samogitia remained one of the primary targets of Teutonic military campaigns.

5 Today Klaipėda, Lithuania.

6 A cog is a ship with a single mast and square-rigged sail, characteristic of the Baltic region.

7 September 14, 1323.

8 The tone is contemptuous. By drawing the reader's attention to the supposed arrogance of the Lithuanians, Peter rhetorically juxtaposes the pagans with the always humble and grateful Christian knights.

9 Dobrzyń was formerly a territory located in and around today's Dobrzyń nad Wisłą in Poland.

349. *On the Destruction of an Allod or the Estate of David of Garth.*

In the same year [1324], during Lent, three brothers and six hundred men[1] from Natangia[2] attacked the *allod*[3] or estate of David the castellan of Garth and burned it to the ground, and in addition to the dead, they led away thirty-eight men and one hundred horses along with a lot of other livestock....

356. *On the Legates of the Apostolic See and the Peace Made between the Pagans and Christians.*

In the same year [1324], the lord Pope John XXII, at the suggestion of brother Frederick from the Franciscan Order, the Archbishop of Riga[4] and [Riga's] fellow citizens, sent two legates to Livonia, namely Bartholomew, bishop of Electen,[5] and Bernard, abbot of the Benedictine monastery of St. Theofred[6] in the diocese of Aniciensis,[7] to baptize the king of the Lithuanians and Ruthenians.[8] On the eve [of the feast day] of the holy apostle and evangelist Matthew,[9] when they came to the city of Riga, they established a peace between said kings[10] and their subjects, on the one side, and the Christians on the other, and ordered them to strictly observe the authority of the Church, adding that whoever accidentally happens to become the violator of this peace, or do anything by word or deed, plan or action that could hinder this beneficial negotiation, or delay it in any way will receive the sentence of excommunication *ipso facto*, from which he cannot be absolved except by the Apostolic See,[11] before which he must present himself within three months to undergo there the penalty owed for his violation. After this, the legates sent loyal envoys to Gediminas, king of the Lithuanians, to offer him an arrangement, as commissioned to them by the Apostolic See, and to carefully find out if he, himself, along with the people of his kingdom would wish to receive the grace of baptism, and relinquishing idolatry humbly honor the name of our lord Jesus Christ.[12]

357. *On the Destruction of the Land of Masovia.*

Therefore, when the peace was confirmed and the brothers and other Christians in the lands of Livonia and Prussia and other neighboring areas truly believed that they ought not wage war, and they already arranged to forge their swords into plowshares and their spears into scythes, that wicked enemy of the faith and the faithful, like a deaf asp,[13] closed his ears to the salutary admonitions of the

---

[1] A typical invading army of the Teutonic Order consisted of a handful of Knight-Brothers (often no more than half a dozen) and hundreds of mercenaries, volunteers, lay knights, native recruits, and colonists who owed military service.

[2] Natangia (named after the Baltic tribe that once lived in the area) was formerly a region of Prussia covering present-day Kaliningrad Oblast in Russia. According to Peter, the Teutonic Knights subdued the last Natangian uprising in 1295. Since their territory was within the state of the Teutonic Order, Natangians owed military service to the Knights. They also served as mercenaries and volunteers in the army of the Teutonic Knights.

[3] An *allod* or *allodium* refers to hereditary land owned outright and exempt from feudal duties.

[4] Frederick von Pernstein, a Franciscan, was archbishop of Riga 1304–1341.

[5] The diocese of Electen (Alet, in France) was established in 1318. Bartholomew was its first bishop (r.1318–1333).

[6] Today the Abbey of Saint-Chaffre-du-Monastier (Chaffre is the French vulgarization of Théofrède).

[7] Today Le Puy-en-Velay, France.

[8] For the title, see above p. 388, n. 2.

[9] September 20, 1324. The feast day of Saint Matthew is September 21.

[10] Peter is referring to the legates' affirmation of the peace treaty concluded on October 2, 1323 between Gediminas, the Livonian Order, the viceroy of Reval, the archbishop, and the citizens of Riga. In August 1324, the Pope wrote to the grandmaster of the Teutonic Order in Prussia commanding him to uphold the treaty. The letter states that the Pope has sent legates to Riga, and anyone who stands in their way will be excommunicated.

[11] The papacy.

[12] A copy of the report made by the envoys of the papal legates survives.

[13] See Douay Ps. 57: 5: "Their madness is according to the likeness of a serpent: like the deaf asp that stoppeth her ears: / Which will not hear the voice of the charmers."

lord Pope, put forth to him by said envoys with great care, because when he had to think about his salvation and that of his people, namely how he could receive the sacrament of baptism with dignity and with due reverence, himself following in the footsteps of his predecessors, he turned all his efforts to the destruction of the faith and the faithful. In fact, [Gediminas] commanded that David, his castellan of Garth, with a strong army enter the land of Masovia and a city called Poltus[1] in the diocese of Ploczensis,[2] on the eleventh calends of December,[3] and devastate by fire and sword one hundred and thirty villages of said diocese of the Duke of Masovia and many estates of priests and nobles, and thirty parish churches and chapels along with many oratories dedicated to the glory of God. Impudently handling holy objects, sacred vestments and vessels, they killed priests, monastic and parish alike, and more than four thousand others of both genders, slaughtering some and leading away others into eternal captivity....

361. *On the Devastation of the Land of the Margraviate of Brandenburg and the Death and Capture of Six Thousand Christians.*

In the year of our Lord 1326, King Łokietek of Poland[4] asked Gediminas, king of the Lithuanians, whose daughter his son had just recently taken as a wife, to send him some soldiers from his people. [Gediminas], acquiescing to his request, sent him 1200 horsemen. At the behest of Łokietek, along with his men, with arms in hand, they invaded the land of Margraviate of Brandenburg[5] near the city of Frankfurt[6] and destroyed by fire and sword everything belonging to it, which included more than one hundred and forty villages, as many parish churches, three monastic houses and two pious convents of the Cistercian Order, and many other monastic and secular chapter houses, barbarically dragging monks and nuns from cloisters, ministers of the church and priests, carrying away sacred vessels, vestments, and other sacred objects. They killed the men but carried off women and many noble ladies along with virgins and children into captivity. Among these virgins was one noble woman, who on account of her eminence had no equal in beauty; a great dispute arose between the Lithuanians in regards to who was to have her, but so that it did not escalate into an altercation, a man approached her and cut her in half with his sword, saying: "She is divided into two parts. Let each take his equal share of her." And thus when that land lay waste and more than six thousand people had been killed or captured, they withdrew. A certain Pole, grieving about such a great massacre of Christians, followed this army, pretending to be a friend of the pagans, and when they had come to an opportune place and time, before the eyes of many, he killed David the castellan of Garth and leader of this war, who inflicted infinite evils, as mentioned above, against the faith and the faithful.

---

[1]   Today Pultusk, Poland.

[2]   Today the diocese of Plock in Poland.

[3]   November 21, 1324.

[4]   Wladyslaw I Łokietek or Wladyslaw the Elbow-High (1261–1333) became King of Poland in 1320 after twenty years of struggle to reunite the five duchies of Poland.

[5]   The Margraviate or March of Brandenburg was a principality of the Holy Roman Empire from 1157 to 1806. Armed conflict between Poland and Brandenburg arose over the land of Lubusz, located between them.

[6]   Today Frankfurt (Oder) in Brandenburg, Germany.

7.7 Bulgaria claims a saint: *The Short Life of St. Petka (Paraskeve) of Tarnov* (13th c.). Original in Old Church Slavonic.

After a successful revolt against Byzantine domination at the end of the twelfth century, Bulgaria established the Second Bulgarian Empire, with its ruler taking the title tsar (i.e., emperor). In the early thirteenth century, it went on the offensive against Byzantines (who by then had lost Constantinople to the crusaders and were divided into three successor states). Probably in 1231, after one such battle, Bulgarian Tsar Ivan Asen II (r.1218–1241) moved the relics of Saint Petka (in Greek Paraskeve) to his capital city of Tarnov (today Veliko Tarnovo), where she became the patron saint. Petka had been a tenth-century hermit in Kalikratia (in the Byzantine province of Thrace); in the twelfth century her local cult grew, and the patriarch of Constantinople commissioned a new *Life* for her. To this *The Short Life*, written in Old Church Slavonic for the needs of the Bulgarian church, added an account of the triumphant translation of Petka's relics to Tarnov. Why do you suppose a Bulgarian tsar would want to appropriate a nearby Byzantine saint?

[Source: Kiril Petkov, ed. and trans., *The Voices of Medieval Bulgaria, Seventh–Fifteenth Century: The Records of a Bygone Culture* (Leiden: Brill, 2008), pp. 274–76 (notes modified).]

On the same day [October 14][1] is the memory of the holy and blessed Paraskeve [Petka]. This holy and blessed Petka hailed from the village of Epivat, [in the district of] the city of Kalikratia. She was the daughter of faithful parents who were neither too wealthy nor too powerful, nor were they afflicted by poverty.

When she came of age, she took a firm decision to embrace the angelic life. She left her parents and friends and all those who lived in the world and followed Christ. Borne on the wings of virtue, she settled in the desert and remained there attached to silent life, which was, indeed, angelic, and tormented her body with fast and vigils. There she had no food and drink; tears and incessant prayers were her nourishment and sustenance. Spending all of her life in this way she enlightened herself with virtue in that place and lived a worthy life. Her reason and conscience were joined and bound together and were always aiming high. She did not wish to affiliate herself to anyone of this world but dwelled focused on the Lord and toiled along the steep and difficult road.

When she felt that her end was near, she left the desert and set off for Constantinople. She visited all the holy places and spent a short while there; then she went back to her native place, Kalikratia, and there she yielded up her blessed spirit in the hands of the living God and accepted the distinction of the heavenly crown.

It happened that in that time a certain sailor was afflicted by a deadly disease. He soon died and they buried him by a tower. His grave emitted such a foul odor that no one dared go down that road. A hermit dwelled in that place and he had to get down from the tower[2] and bury the corpse deeper to get rid of the stench. Other people heard about that and [wishing to help] took the body from the roadside [and began digging] to bury it right next to the body of the saint. When they saw her body—whole, perfectly preserved, and sound—they marveled. Then they thought that if that body had been holy, God would have revealed it through miracles, and so they went away, leaving the body there.

However, one of them, by the name of George, had a

---

[1] The *Short Life of Petka* is contained in a collection of short lives of saints that were used as daily readings in church. Evidently more than one of these was read on October 14.

[2] Apparently he lived on a column, in the manner of Symeon Stylites.

marvelous and terrifying dream: a certain queen sat on a throne and a multitude of officials were about her. At this sight he was seized by terror and fell down on his face. One of the bright men took him by the hand, lifted him up, and told him: "Man, don't you fear God? That body is holy! How could you bury that stinking and decaying corpse with the body of Petka, the servant of God?" [And the queen told him:] "Go right away and tell everyone to deliver me from that unbearable stench! If you do not do that, know that the divine fire will burn you and all of you will perish. Because I am human too, and my native land is Epivat."

That same night a woman by the name of Euthymia had the same vision. On the morning they told everyone about it. When they heard that, everyone took candles and gathered at the body of the saint. They dug out the body and laid it in a casket. Then they carried it to the church of the Holy Apostles where it pours out healing to this very day: the possessed get healed, the blind see the light, the lame get to walk, and the people afflicted by all kinds of disease get whole again.

The great Tsar Ivan Asen [II], son of the great and old Tsar Asen, heard about the miracles of the saint and strongly desired to transport the body of the saint to his land. Then the Franks ruled in Constantinople and paid tribute to Ivan Asen.[1] He, however, wanted neither silver nor precious stones, but set off with diligence and carried the saintly body to his glorious Tsarigrad[2] Tarnov. There he met it together with the patriarch, the entire clergy, and the people, and with candles, incense-burners, and every honor they laid her in the royal church.[3]

May through her prayers God welcome us in His Kingdom! Amen.

7.8 Bulgaria and Venice regularize commercial relations: *Oath and Treaty* (1347). Original in Italian.

In the fourteenth century, Venice was a mini-empire, holding islands and coastal regions in the Adriatic and Aegean Seas. It was beginning to expand within Italy as well. Bulgaria's Second Empire, buffeted by Mongol attacks in the mid-thirteenth century as well as encroachments on its territory by a growing Serbia, was on the wane, but it was still a useful ally for Venice as it jousted with the revived Byzantine empire (which had retaken Constantinople in 1261), opposed Hungarian expansion along the Dalmatian coast, and competed with Genoa for trade in the Black Sea area. Furthermore, Bulgarian markets offered cheap products—wheat (of excellent quality), barley, leather, honey, and beeswax (particularly prized)—while its elites (and even lesser folk) were eager to buy jewelry, fabrics, arms, glassware, soap, spices, and so on from Venetian traders. Nevertheless, commercial relations were tense; the Bulgarian tsar sometimes imposed "arbitrary taxes" on Venetian traders, a fact noted (and protested) by the Senate and doge at Venice. Out of these circumstances was born the *Oath and Treaty* of 1347.

[Source: Kiril Petkov, ed. and trans., *The Voices of Medieval Bulgaria, Seventh–Fifteenth Century: The Records of a Bygone Culture* (Leiden: Brill, 2008), pp. 235–36 (notes added).]

---

[1] The "Franks" were the Westerners, who had taken Constantinople in 1204. It is doubtful that they paid tribute to Ivan Asen II.

[2] Literally, this was an Old Church Slavonic translation of "City of the Caesar," which could mean Constantinople but here referred to Bulgaria's "imperial" city, Tarnov, today Veliko Tarnovo.

[3] The "patriarch" here refers to the archbishop of Bulgaria.

Oath and Treaty of the Lord Emperor of Zagora, Alexander.[1]

My tsardom gives this letter of safe conduct to my friends and brothers, the Venetian Franks,[2] and my tsardom swears in God the Father, in Virgin Mary, in the holy and life-giving cross, in the holy Paraskeva of Tarnov,[3] and in my soul, that all the Venetian merchants might come and go on their ships throughout my entire tsardom and be safe and sound.

They will pay customs of three percent. The son will not be punished for the father, nor the father for the son. If there is a shipwreck and the ship goes under, the people and their properties will be saved. For a load [in value] of one hundred *perperi* they will pay four *grosh*; for a volume of one hundred *modii*, three *grosh*. To weigh their wares on scales, one and a half *aspri*. The anchoring fee for a great ship [will be] two *perperi*; for a small ship, one *perper*.[4] If their merchandise does not sell in the land or on the water, let them go wherever they choose and pay nothing. Also, [the merchandise] cannot be sealed or held in the house of a Venetian without a court order.[5] Also, if a Venetian dies, no one is to touch his property but other Venetians. Also, they can buy and build a church and a *loggia* anywhere they please in the country without anyone putting obstacles to this decree.[6] If anyone goes against them, he will be a traitor of my tsardom.

This copy was sent by the Venetian Marco Leonardo, Consul of the Venetians in Varna,[7] in October 1352, accompanied by the letter of the same tsar [to the Doge Andrea Dandolo[8]] dated October 1352, as it is written, with a note by the said consul, namely: "I remind you that the *perper* of Varna weights sixteen carats and two thirds and costs six *grosh* and five *aspers*; the [Byzantine?] *perper* costs eight *aspers* and one *grosh*.

TRANSFORMATIONS IN THE CITIES

7.9 The *popolo* gains power: *The Ghibelline Annals of Piacenza* (1250). Original in Latin.

In the twelfth century, nobles dominated the towns of northern Italy, making their power concretely visible by building lofty town towers reminiscent of castles. In the thirteenth century, the nobles were nearly everywhere challenged by the *popolo*—a group composed mainly of artisans and shopkeepers but also often joined by interested or opportunistic nobles—who formed local armed bands, tried to oust the nobles, and demanded a role in communal government. In many cities the struggle between the commune and the *popolo* ended in a sort of stalemate, each group gaining its own officials and laws. Eventually, however, representatives of the *popolo* were integrated in some way alongside the head of the commune, the *podestà*. At Piacenza, an initial revolt of the *popolo* in the 1220s was

---

[1] I.e., Tsar Ivan Alexander (r.1331–1371).

[2] To the Bulgarians, all Westerners were "Franks."

[3] For the cult of Saint Paraskeva (Petka) see above, p. 395.

[4] *Grosh* and *aspri* were units of currency. A *perper* (pl: *perperi*) was also a unit of currency. *Modii* were units of measure. All these specifications regulated how much the Bulgarian customs officer could charge the Venetians.

[5] The provision of a court order protected the Venetians from what had been a frequent occurrence: the confiscation of their goods at the whim of the tsar or his officials.

[6] The right to build a *loggia* "anywhere" meant that the Venetians could build depots and offices not just along the Black Sea but wherever they pleased.

[7] An important Bulgarian port.

[8] Andrea Dandolo (r.1343–1354), the Venetian doge.

led by the nobleman Guglielmo Landi, but he was expelled in 1236. In 1250, according to the so-called *Ghibelline Annals of Piacenza* (from which the excerpt here is taken), the *popolo* rose up again during a period of grain shortage. Originally led by a man named Antolino Saviagata, the *popolo* later named Uberto de Iniquitate, from a noble family rival to the Landi family, to lead it. Soon factions within the *popolo* emerged, as different groups supported or opposed Uberto's policies.

[Source: *The Towns of Italy in the Later Middle Ages*, ed. and trans. Trevor Dean (Manchester and New York: Manchester University Press, 2000), pp. 158–60 (slightly modified).]

At the beginning of June, the Milanese army rode into the territory of Lodi with a great quantity of corn [grain] which they were sending to Parma, where there was a great shortage. They transported the corn as far as the Po [River] and then handed it over to the Piacentines…

In 1250 the common people of Piacenza saw that they were being badly treated regarding foodstuffs: first, because all the corn that had been sent from Milan, as well as other corn in Piacenza, was being taken to Parma, with farm laborers being forced to transport it without payment; second, because the Parmesans were touring Piacentine territory buying corn from the threshing floors and fields, which seemed very serious to the Piacentines. The Parmesans could do this in safety because Matteo da Correggio, a citizen of Parma, was podestà of Piacenza, and supported them as much as he could in having corn taken to Parma. Knowing about all this, on Friday July 27th early in the morning, Antolino Saviagata, at the instigation of the Scotti family, because he was their neighbor, and of others, gathered twenty or thirty leaders (consuls) of the popular societies of Piacenza in the church of San Pietro, with the purpose of going to the podestà and telling him to oppose this export of Piacentine corn to Parma. In the church they all swore to support each other if anything was said to them on account of this meeting. It was then maliciously reported to the podestà that Antolino Saviagata and others had gathered to cause damage and harm to the city of Piacenza. The podestà sent one of his judges… to the church; he arrested Antolino, but let the others leave. The podestà immediately held a general council and so maligned Antolino and his assembly that it was immediately decreed that no more than three people could assemble in the city, that the podestà had full power to inquire into Antolino's actions, and to put him to death if he deserved it. Some of those who had been at Antolino's gathering, fearing death, convened their own societies and told them they had done nothing wrong in the assembly; and

the societies decided to support their consuls within the law. Meanwhile, the podestà held Antolino in his home, not doing him any harm. The *populares*, inflamed by what had happened and by what was going on… took up arms and banners, rang their bells, gathered together and came to the podestà. The podestà, in fact, wanted to release Antolino on surety, more out of fear than love, but Antolino refused… His father was pressing him to let himself be bound over, and there were many magnates willing to stand surety for him, including Pietro Malvicini, Filippo Visdomini, Giacomo Visconti and Uberto de Iniquitate, but he refused them. The podestà, seeing the crowd coming towards him and hearing the bells ring, let Antolino go. Antolino was badly dressed, with shoes on his feet but nothing covering his legs. On his release, Antolino did not go home at once, but wishing to accomplish his desires, went well-supported to a certain well, where he found a great crowd of men armed for battle, and he addressed them, provoking and inducing them to do what he desired, reminding them of the great harms that had been done to the *popolo* over the past fifteen years, how they had been killed, condemned and expelled from one city to another, and that they would rather die than suffer any more… [The men of each of the six city districts] elected two consuls of the people…

On the following Saturday, all the consuls, with a great number of the *popolo*, came to the communal council. Antolino excused their presence, arguing and explaining that what had been done by the *popolo* was not done as an affront to the podestà, but to his honor and that of the Roman church, of the commune of Milan and their friends… The consuls of the *popolo* then assembled at Santa Maria del Tempio and resolved to issue statutes and to hold a council of the people. The statutes were passed, and on Sunday morning the council met in the church of San Pietro. There was such a press of people that they could not stay there, so they moved to the church of San Sisto. Among the first clauses [of the statutes]… was one about electing a rector of the *popolo*. Many men believed themselves to be leaders of the *popolo*, namely Fredenzio da Fontana, Filippo Visdomini, Uberto Zanardi, Guelfo Stricto… and when this clause was read out, great division arose among the *popolo*: some wanted one man, some another, and there was great clamor. Then [one man] said "Why do you not accept Uberto de Iniquitate, for he has already suffered many injuries and losses on your behalf?" And so he was elected by acclamation. Those who had betrayed the *popolo* and Guglielmo Landi—and there were many of them among both the consuls and the others present—complained loudly and wanted to leave the church to raise uproar, but some of those who had been unable to enter the church closed the doors so that they could not leave. They regarded lord Uberto as an excessively "imperial" man.[1] Once things had calmed down, however, they resumed their seats and took part in the election of consuls of the people: one or two from each society, according to its standing, with other men from each district of the city. Unanimously these elected Uberto de Iniquitate as podestà and rector of the *popolo* for one year. Envoys were sent to his home, and he came immediately and gladly took the oath of office, without consulting any of his relatives or friends. All of the *popolo* then accompanied him home with great rejoicing and honor. As he had been poorly dressed before, he later held a great meeting in the piazza San Pietro, dressed in scarlet with squirrel fur. This was attended by a huge crowd of men of the *popolo*, at the news of which many knights and commoners were scared to death because of the harm they had done him and the *popolo* in the past. And from that day on, he began to lead the *popolo*. After a short interval, he held another council in San Sisto, saying what some of his friends had said to him, that "a vassal of one year brings little profit and little loss," and so he was elected podestà of the *popolo* for five years, and after him his son Giannone. Men of the *popolo* who had relatives and friends among the Piacentine exiles began to tell them "Come, come back, brothers, exiles from Piacenza"; others though… strongly opposed this. However, such was the number of the former that the latter could do nothing: people today delight in upsetting things. And at last, Uberto de Iniquitate and his advisors were content to let the exiled *populares* return, but leaving the Landi… and other knights outside. Meanwhile, Antolino Saviagata… went to Milan as an envoy… on some business. There, either because he was offered money, or because he regretted what he had done, and fearing the return of the exiles whom he had persecuted and expelled, he sought to disobey and harm the *popolo*. Conspiring with others… he sought to return the city to its previous regime. When this was discovered by the podestà of the *popolo*, Antolino was captured and greatly tortured. But, because what he had done pleased Uberto de Iniquitate, who did not want the Landi and others to return, Uberto let him go unpunished, expelling him from the city. And thus faction arose among the *popolo*.

7.10 The Hanseatic League: *Decrees of the League* (1260–1264). Original in Latin.

The word "hansa" probably originally meant "armed convoy," but it came to be used of associations of merchants and especially of the merchants of the cities along the North and Baltic Seas. Lübeck served as a hinge between the two seas, and its decrees from 1260 to 1264, printed below, reveal that its legislation touched the other member cities as well. To what degree did the interests of the merchants override the interests of the various princes under whom the various cities were technically subject?

[Source: *A Source Book for Mediaeval History*, ed. Oliver J. Thatcher and Edgar Holmes McNeal (New York: Charles Scribner's, 1905), pp. 611–12 (slightly modified).]

---

[1] That is, he supported the imperial, rather than the papal, party.

We wish to inform you of the action taken in support of all merchants who are governed by the law of Lübeck.

(1) Each city shall, to the best of its ability, keep the sea clear of pirates so that merchants may freely carry on their business by sea. (2) Whoever is expelled from one city because of a crime shall not be received in another. (3) If a citizen is seized [by pirates, robbers, or bandits], he shall not be ransomed, but his swordbelt and knife shall be sent to him [as a threat to his captors]. (4) Any merchant ransoming him shall lose all his possessions in all the cities that have the law of Lübeck. (5) Whoever is proscribed[1] in one city for robbery or theft shall be proscribed in all. (6) If a lord besieges a city, no one shall aid him in any way to the detriment of the besieged city, unless the besieger is his lord. (7) If there is a war in the country, no city shall on that account injure a citizen from the other cities, either in his person or goods, but shall give him protection. (8) If any man marries a woman in one city, and another woman from some other city comes and proves that he is her lawful husband, he shall be beheaded. (9) If a citizen gives his daughter or niece in marriage to a man [from another city], and another man comes and says that she is his lawful wife, but cannot prove it, he shall be beheaded.

This law shall be binding for a year, and after that the cities shall inform each other by letter of what decisions they make.

7.11 Food scarcity at Constantinople: Athanasius I, Patriarch of Constantinople, *Letter* (1306–1307). Original in Greek.

While many western cities had secured a measure of self-government and economic independence by the thirteenth century, Constantinople remained tightly controlled by the Byzantine emperor himself. When grain became scarce in the capital at the beginning of the fourteenth century, the patriarch, Athanasius I (r.1289–1293 and 1303–1309) wrote to the emperor, Andronicus II Palaeologus (r.1282–1328), to solve the problem. He exhorted him with quotes from the Bible not to "yield to bribes" or to "drive the grain we yearn for out of the city." The issues were complex. The city was crowded with impoverished refugees from Anatolia, and middlemen who controlled the grain supplies kept prices high. Meanwhile, Catalans and Turks were raiding the Byzantine countryside and living off its grain, so the emperor ordered that no crops be grown near Constantinople. Compounding the problem, Venetian and Genoese merchants who brought grain to the city from the Black Sea region exported much of it to Italy, producing a "grain drain." Andronicus had probably taken bribes to allow them to do so. One way that the emperor eventually addressed the problem was by making peace with the ruler of Bulgaria and importing grain from there.

[Source: *The Correspondence of Athanasius I Patriarch of Constantinople: Letters to the Emperor Andronicus II, Members of the Imperial Family, and Officials*, ed. and trans. Alice-Mary Maffry Talbot (Washington, DC: Dumbarton Oaks, 1975), pp. 179, 181, 183.]

To the emperor concerning the famine which is afflicting the people

Formerly when I walked through the streets, one poor person would ask me for one thing, another for another, but now they complain as if with one voice about the

---

[1]   I.e., declared an outlaw.

grain, and almost everyone entreats me piteously that it not leave the capital, and bind me with oaths to put before any other request to your divine majesty a petition about the grain. I myself share their sorrow and suffering, and am persuaded of the plight of these people, and am able to estimate the distress which will befall my brethren and fellow poor, on account of the scarcity of food. And again as I estimate the suffering which such an evil will cause to the survivors of the threat to the Christians which has occurred on account of my sins, I entreat your divine majesty to heed and register in your mind my and their pleas for grain; and do not yield to bribes, either through the disease of greed or simply of friendship, preferring gold to God, Who ordered the bread to be distributed among the hungry,[1] but not that one should kill the people of God because of one's love of gold. "For what shall it profit them, if they shall gain the whole world" (which is impossible), "but will lose their soul?"[2] For it is impossible for someone to gain the whole world, but it is possible for everyone to lose his own soul, if he wishes. Very few people are unaware of the shame and blame which results from betraying a possible good for an evil which cannot be obtained anyhow. For they should keep in mind the words, "If wealth should flow in, set not your heart upon it,"[3] and "wealth unjustly collected shall be vomited up,"[4] and "they that will be rich fall into the temptation and snare of the devil,"[5] and "he who raises the price of grain is cursed by the people; but blessing be on the head of him that gives it."[6]

I make this request of your divine majesty: either let them be taught or rebuked, and do not have "faith in uncertain riches, but in the living God, who giveth us richly all things to enjoy."[7] Because it is terrible and worse than terrible for me and my brethren, my fellow poor and beggars, to fall at your feet and entreat you, a great and most pious king who is right-thinking and a lover of Christ, who is exceedingly merciful and is swayed by the sympathy and goodness of his own soul, and by the sorrow and affliction of his subjects, while a few gifts and bribes triumph over such good qualities, and drive the grain we yearn for out of the city as should not happen. In addition let the rich realize the incurable disease and affliction which is about to befall us needy people, and that "the spoils of the poor are in their houses,"[8] as, of their own accord, they close their ears so as not to hear about the man mocked by the Lord, because in his misplaced eagerness he "tore down his barns" in order to build "greater ones."[9] The cure for this disease will be found neither by ruler nor priest nor Levite, but only by your divine majesty together with a certain Samaritan [i.e., God] who did not pass by with loathing the man wounded by thieves.[10] For He gave your divine majesty the two pence, piety and empire, and cries out, "Inasmuch as ye have done it unto one of the least of these, ye have done it unto me."[11] And on His return He will give you the kingdom which He came to receive, even if the people of that time weren't willing to give to Him that which He had as God, and which He also has as man made God and ruler of heaven and earth; and He has decreed that He will arise again on account of the groans and misery of the poor; to Him be glory for ever and ever, Amen.

---

1   See Isa. 58: 7.
2   Mark 8: 36.
3   Ps. 62: 10; Douay Ps. 61: 11.
4   Job 20: 15.
5   1 Tim. 6: 9.
6   Prov. 11: 26.
7   1 Tim. 6: 17.
8   Isa. 3: 14.
9   Luke 12: 18.
10   For the priest and the Levite who did not help a robbery victim, and the Samaritan who did, see Luke 10: 31–32.
11   Matt. 25: 40.

7.12 Too big to fail? *A Great Bank Petitions the City Council of Siena* (1298). Original in Latin.

What happened when a medieval merchant defaulted? Although strict application of the law would have meant jailing the defaulter and selling off his property to pay off the debt, this rarely happened, at least in the Mediterranean region. Rather, the merchant left town while his friends obtained a safe-conduct for him for a period of time. Then the failing merchant returned home to negotiate with his creditors. Businesses that were jointly owned—such as *compagnie* and banks—were more problematic. Because "limited liability" did not yet exist, all the owners were liable for all company debts. In the case of banks, which gave out numerous loans, this meant that the default of even a small number of customers could lead to the bankruptcy of the whole. This was the problem that confronted the Bonsignore family, the owners of the *Magna Tabula*, the "Great Bank" of Siena in 1298, when it petitioned the city council (known as the Council of the Bell) to suspend joint liability and to give the partners extra time to pay back the bank's debts. Specifically, it asked that each partner be liable not for the entire debt of the bank but only for the percentage of debt corresponding to the capital he had invested in the company. The city council was unmoved. It turned down the request, and the Great Bank failed. Siena rapidly declined as a business center thereafter.

[Source: *Medieval Trade in the Mediterranean World: Illustrative Documents Translated with Introductions and Notes*, ed. and trans. Robert S. Lopez and Irving W. Raymond (New York: Columbia University Press, 2001), pp. 298–302 (notes modified).]

[Siena, August 9, 1298]

To you who are men of great discernment and wisdom, lords of the [Council] of Nine Governors and Defenders of the Commune and People of Siena, [the following] petition is submitted and set forth by the undersigned partners of the *societas* [partnership] known as "The *Societas* of the Sons of Bonsignore." Although self-praise is considered neither in good [taste] nor befitting, nevertheless the critical situation will be a reasonably sufficient excuse for the partners of said *societas*.

And so, although [the petitioners] trust that you know [the facts of the case], yet they recall to your minds that of all the *societates* of Tuscany, Lombardy, and indeed the whole world, this one has been held in greater honor than any other and in greater renown; that greater confidence has been placed in it by the lords popes of Rome, by cardinals, patriarchs, archbishops, bishops and other prelates of the Church, by kings, barons, counts, traders, and by other men of every condition; that it has also been an asset, indeed a very great asset, to the Commune of Siena at the Roman Curia, to the ambassadors of Siena [sent on missions] on this side of the mountains or beyond the mountains in the furtherance of the missions on which they were sent, and likewise in meeting the payment of moneys needed both for the conduct of said missions and for personal expenses.

And this is certain and well-known, that the *societas* has brought many honors and advantages to the Commune of Siena; that it has done honor to the merchants and citizens of Siena in the various parts of the world, and has given superior advice and perfect assistance to a great many in rescuing persons and goods; that, for the upholding and increase of the honor of the Commune of Siena, it bore many burdens in connection with customs duties, public loans, and the maintenance of horses, and indeed it bore a goodly share of said burdens; and, to conclude, it would be a heavy and difficult task to recount how great an advantage and how much honor has accrued to the Commune of Siena from the good standing of the *societas*. But since well-known facts need no proof, [the petitioners] rest content with the facts presented above, confident that your discerning minds know this well.

However, just as the status and government of this world forever remains [as it is], not because of the poor condition of [human] society but because of the sins of [men], and because they have not learned what is good from Him who is the Highest Good, [so likewise] the Enemy, [instigator] of discord, has sown among them discord of such nature, so deep, and continued for so long a time that any *societas* in this world would have been eventually destroyed and stripped of all its strength.[1] Yet, very great and almost incalculable though their loss may be, even now if said discord were removed and harmony were to follow, [the *societas*] would recover its strength and would surpass all other *societates* in power and with honor. And may He who can do all things bring this to pass.

But even if this cannot be, even now the *societas* is in a position to meet its obligations at the proper times and places and within the different time limits, as is its custom, to all its creditors and to those who are to receive anything from it. But because of their own discord and also at the urging and instigation of some citizens of Siena—who are acting ill and have no reason or cause for taking any action whatever—all their creditors are agitating and are demanding what the *societas* and its partners owe them; and they are making [these] demands upon certain partners and not upon all [as a body]. And this does not happen because of the poor condition of the *societas* but because of the envy and instigation of some persons, as has been stated above, and not because the *societas* has thus far refused to meet its obligations to anyone. Indeed from the day that discord arose and up to this day, the *societas* has met its obligations in regard to both capital and interest, as had been its custom before the days of discord, and it has already paid out 200,000 gold florins.

Yet, even if [the partners of] the *societas* were in full and good harmony, and all the creditors were to make a run on the *societas* at the same time and hour, the *societas* would fail to meet its obligations not because it is unable [to pay] but for the reason that whatever it is obligated to give it [first] must recover in different parts of the world from kings, counts, barons, and from other *societates* and individuals. And this was well-known to those who extended credit to said *societas*, since the said *societas* did not conceal that it received from [some] men but lent to all others, as every *societas* does. Therefore the demands should be considerate and moderate, so that even as the partners of the said *societas* cannot in one moment recover from all [who owe them], similarly they should not be forced in one moment to meet all their obligations so long as discord exists among them. But even if there were harmony and the [present] demands for payment were made not upon specifically indicated partners but upon the *societas* as a whole, the *societas* would still be unable to meet its obligations. Therefore the time has come for the city of Siena, which has gathered so many advantages and such great honor from the good standing of the said *societas*, to render [that service] to which it is obligated by nature.

The points that [the petitioners] ask and humbly supplicate to be done are as follows:

First: That those who are instigating the creditors of the *societas* to make such demands [for payment] be all equally ruled out. This can easily be done by a provision to be enacted by you and the General Council of the Bell, [to wit], that no one [partner] of the said *societas* may or should be compelled by the lord podestà, the captain, the consuls of the merchants,[2] by any ruler or official of the Commune of Siena to pay the debts of the said *societas* to a greater extent than that which falls to him in proportion to his capital. If such provision be enacted, those who are instigating the creditors to present demands, realizing that they cannot hurt those whom they have in mind, would refrain from further instigations; and the creditors would temper their less-than-honest demands and would make reasonable, honest, and ordinary demands, and at a proper time, because they know and will be in a position to know that the *societas* and the partners of the *societas* can fully meet their obligations to their creditors—provided, however, that their creditors stand by the partners, so that these may [in turn] collect [what is owing them]. For there

---

[1] Here the petitioners attempt to draw a comparison between the sad conditions of human society and those of the Bonsignore partnership. Both are in a position to thrive, but the devil endeavors to destroy them by instigating internal dissensions. There is a play on words between *societas* (human society in general) and *societas* (partnership).

[2] These were all communal officials, the first two always coming from outside Siena. The podestà had both military and judicial powers; he held office for one year. The captain referred to here was probably the executive officer for the *popolo*; he was supposed to balance the power of the podestà. The consuls of the merchants were officials of the merchants' guild at Siena, which had numerous privileges there.

is no *societas* in the world which would not fail if all its creditors made a run [on it]. And thus the said *societas* is not failing and could not fail because of inability [to pay], but because of the discord among its [partners] and because of those who are hoping for the destruction of the said *societas*, [a fate] that must not be tolerated in the slightest degree by you [gentlemen] and the Commune of Siena.

The second point that is petitioned for with humble supplication and prayer: That a suitable delay be granted to the partners of the said *societas* so that they may collect and thus meet their obligations in accordance with the demands of the creditors. And this is fully warranted by custom and by good business practice, and is furthermore sanctioned by imperial legislation.

The third point that is asked for, ever out of grace and with humble supplication: That it may please you to see to it that two ambassadors of the Commune of Siena go to the lord pope and speak in behalf of the said *societas*, and that he [the pope] use the influence of his holy office with the creditors of the said *societas* and especially with those creditors who reside at the Curia, to the end that, in presenting their demands, these creditors may not burden the partners of the *societas* except in the proportion that falls to each one; that the creditors may grant the partners a suitable delay, so that these may be in a position to collect from their creditors and so meet their obligations to the creditors [of the *societas*]; and that, in requiring that, the said lord pope bring to bear the weight of his holy office. And [you should] appoint an embassy in regard to the matters above-mentioned and anything else that you may deem necessary for the well being and reorganization of the said *societas*.

And you ought to be led to make provisions regarding said matters by [recollecting] the advantages which have accrued to the city from the good standing of the said *societas*, by your love for the citizens, so that....[1] For, if the provision should not be enacted, the indi-vidual partners who are being harassed for the total [debits of the *societas*] and who cannot bear [the burden], would be forced to leave [their posts], and the *societas* would not be able to collect what it has to recover in different parts of the world, and hence the city and the businessmen of the city would be oppressed by the reprisals which would be instituted against the Commune of Siena, and its merchants would no longer have free access to trade.

This petition is therefore just in each item. And it is better that said provision be enacted, so that those meet their obligations who are able and who ought to, as has been stated, rather than that so many citizens of this city—the partners of the said *societas*—should be scattered, and the *societas* be mined, and the merchants of the city of Siena incur restrictions and losses.

And note that the provision demands haste because, at the instigation of certain citizens of Siena, the creditors in the city of Rome have caused the seizure of the goods of said *societas* that were in the said city, and the factors [that is, the agents of the *societas*] have fled. Wherefore, lest the disgrace and such a great danger increase, [the partners] humbly petition you to help them aid justice and the advantage of the city. And [the partners] themselves offer to their creditors to assign trustworthy debtors [for the sums owing] to them,[2] if only the creditors be willing to wait so long as [the partners] collect and [in turn] meet their obligations.

The [arguments] presented above embody justice; they embody equity, honor for the city, the preservation of its citizens, and the liberty and security of its merchants; and they avert error and scandal.

May God, who can do all things, make His light to shine upon your hearts in these and all other matters that make or may make for the peace and good standing of the city and its territory; and may He preserve the city and its citizens and grant them beneficent peace....

[The petition was denied.]

---

[1] Some words have been dropped.

[2] This seems to mean that the partners shall earmark for each creditor any specific credit of the *societas* that may seem particularly easy to recover.

HERESIES AND PERSECUTIONS

7.13 Inquisition: Jacques Fournier, *Episcopal Register* (1318–1325). Original in Latin.

Jacques Fournier was Pope Benedict XII (1334–1342), the third pope at Avignon, and responsible for building the papal palace there. But before that, between 1317 and 1326, he was bishop of his native city of Pamiers, in southern France. Officials under his jurisdiction there took meticulous care to record and preserve the inquests into and confessions of 114 villagers suspected of heresy between 1318 and 1325. (Compare this use of an Episcopal register with that of the one drawn up for Thomas of Hereford, above, p. 327.) Most were accused of being dualists. (The church called them Cathars or Albigensians; the dissidents, however, typically called themselves "good men.") The original proceedings were in Old Occitan, the vernacular language of the region, but they were translated into Latin for the record. The result, as may be seen from the materials printed here regarding Guillaume Austatz—a wealthy peasant farmer and also the king's *baille*, or legal and fiscal authority—is a portrait of village life revealing friendships, enmities, gossip, and class tensions. Why might Guillaume's fellow villagers have testified against him? What leads you to think that Guillaume was innocent—or guilty?

[Source: *Medieval Popular Religion, 1000–1500: A Reader*, ed. John Shinners, 2nd ed. (Toronto: University of Toronto Press, 2006), pp. 485–504. Translated by John Shinners.]

Witnesses against Guillaume Austatz of Ornolac for the Crime of Heresy

In the year of the Lord 1320, May 11, Gaillarde, wife of Bernard Ros of Ornolac (sworn as a witness and questioned because the said Guillaume Austatz had spoken certain heretical words) said that about four years ago she was in her house at Ornolac, and Alazaïs, the wife of Pierre Mounié of the same place, was there with her. The said Guillaume arrived along with some other people whose names she says she does not recall. When they had gathered around the hearth in the house, they started talking about God and about the General Resurrection. Among other things, they said that God really needed to be great in power and strength since each human soul would return to its own body at the General Resurrection. Hearing this, Guillaume said, "And do you believe that God made as many human souls as there are men and women? Surely not! For when at death souls exit the human bodies they have been in, they steal into the bodies of children who have just been born; as they leave one body, they enter into another one." For, as he said, if

each human soul were to reclaim the very same body it had been in, since the world has lasted for many years, the whole world would be filled up with souls—so much so, as he said, that they couldn't be contained in the area between Toulouse and the Mérens Pass. For although souls are quite small, so many people have existed that their souls could not be contained within that space. When she heard these words, Alazaïs took the witness in her arms and held her closely. And when, after a while, Guillaume left the witness's house, Alazaïs said to her, "O godmother, these are evil words that Guillaume spoke," and the witness said that they were strong words.

Asked why she had concealed these words for such a long time, she said that she had not believed they were as serious as they are, but, goaded by her conscience, she had revealed them this year to the priest Bernard Petron, who was staying at Ornolac, so that he could counsel her what to do about them. And this priest, so she said, advised her to reveal the words to the lord bishop of Pamiers. So, led by her conscience, as she said, she reported these words to the bishop.

Asked if she had seen Guillaume take communion or

doing the other things which good and faithful Christians are accustomed to do, she responded that for the past twelve years she had lived in the village of Ornolac and she had never seen Guillaume take communion, not even when he was sick or on the feast days when people usually receive communion, though she had seen him going into the church. And she should know since, as she said, his mother-in-law is her sister. She said moreover that Guillaume, while he lived at Lordat where he was born, used to practice usury; but after he moved to Ornolac, he practiced no usury that she knew of.

Asked if she deposed the previous testimony out of hate, love, fear, or bad will, instructed, or suborned, she said no, but because it is the truth, as she said above.

In the same year on May 26, the said Gaillarde, wife of the said Bernard Ros, cited on the same day, appeared before the lord bishop in the episcopal see at Pamiers and was received by the lord bishop as a witness against Guillaume Austatz concerning some matters touching on the Catholic faith. Swearing an oath as a witness, she said and deposed that this year, around the feast of the nativity of St. John the Baptist [June 24], some money and some other things had been stolen from her which she had kept in a certain chest that had been broken into. The witness went to the said Guillaume (who was then and is now the *baille* [royal official] of Ornolac) and requested him to carry out his office, search for the thief, and to do what needed to be done for her to get her stolen things back. When he was unwilling to listen to her about her case, weeping and wailing she went to the church of Our Lady of Montgauzy to get a miracle from her to recover her money and property. In order to better get the miracle, she girded the candle on Blessed Mary's altar [probably by tying a string around it which she would later use to make a wick for another candle to be offered at the altar]. When she got back to Ornolac, she again asked Guillaume to investigate the theft, but he did not want to bother himself with it. The witness told him he should search for the money and things stolen from her just as he had searched for grain stolen from him that year. He told her that he had looked for the grain because he would have recognized it had he found it, but he wouldn't recognize her stolen money and property, as she said. And she said, "I put my trust in Blessed Mary of Montgauzy. I visited her and asked her to restore my stolen money and property; and I asked her to take revenge against those who stole from me if they don't

restore them." Then Guillaume told the witness in the presence of some other people whose names she does not recall (except for Julien de Ornolac from Ornolac), that Blessed Mary did not have the power to restore the witness's money and things. When she said that yes she did, and that what he had said was bad, and also that the Blessed Mary would avenge her, Guillaume said Blessed Mary did not kill people or commit murders....

The same year, July 25, the said Alazaïs, wife of Pierre Mounié, again appeared and offered testimony after she had been told to swear to tell the truth as a witness. She said that about two years ago she had lost her four sons one after the other and was terribly sad and depressed over this. One day when Guillaume had come back from his fields, he saw her standing in the doorway of her house looking quite depressed, and he asked her why she was so sad. She told him it was because she had so suddenly lost her four handsome boys. Guillaume told her not to be sad about this, for she would get her four dead sons back. And when she told Guillaume that she believed she would see her dead sons and get them back in paradise but not in this world, Guillaume told her that, on the contrary, she would get them back in this very world. For when she got pregnant the souls of her four dead sons would be reincarnated in the sons she conceived and carried in her womb; and in that way she would recover her dead sons in this world. Asked about those present, she said she did not recall that anyone was present except herself and Guillaume. Asked about the time and place, she answered as above.

Also she said that this year, on what day she did not recall, but after the [Waldensian] heretics Raymond de la Côte and the woman Agnes had been burned,[1] she and Guillaume were standing near the door of his house and Guillaume said that the bishop of Pamiers was a proud and harsh man. She said that a man who had great power could do much. And then Guillaume said that if Raymond and Agnes had been listened to and had had an audience, just as the bishop did, the bishop would be worthier of burning than Raymond and Agnes. And when the witness said that it was not theirs to judge this, Guillaume quickly went inside his house....

The year as above, July 27, Pierre de Bordas of Ornolac was sworn as a witness and asked to tell the truth plainly and fully about the above matters and others touching on the Catholic faith against Guillaume Austatz. He said that this year, after the heretic Raymond de la Côte was

---

[1] For the Waldensians in an earlier period, as depicted in the *Chronicle of Laon*, see above p. 368.

burned by the lord bishop of Pamiers and the inquisitor of Carcassone, when the news reached Ornolac, the witness; his wife, Alazaïs; Barchinona, the wife of the late Bernard de Bordas; and Guillaume Austatz were sitting at the table eating when Guillaume said that the heretic Raymond who had been burned was a good cleric, one of the better people in all Christendom. And it would have been better for [the region of] Sabarthès if the bishop of Pamiers had been burned instead of Raymond. Asked whether he heard Guillaume saying that this heretic was a good Christian and a holy man, and that, if he had been treated justly, he would not have been burned, he said that he does not recall. Asked if, when Guillaume said these words—that it would have been better for Sabarthès for the lord bishop to have been burned than the heretic—he agreed or disagreed with him or chastised him for these words, he responded that he said nothing to him, though it seemed to him that he had spoken badly, so he said....

The Confession of the Converted Heretic Guillaume Austatz

In the year of the Lord 1320, July 15, it came to the attention of the reverend father in Christ, Lord Jacques [Fournier], by God's grace bishop of Pamiers, that Guillaume Austatz of Ornolac in the diocese of Pamiers, had said and asserted before many people: that each human soul does not have its own body, but when it exits from one body, it steals into another body; and that even at the resurrection not every soul will resume its own body. He also said that each soul will not be rewarded or punished in the body it dwelled in, and that he personally did not trust that his soul would be saved or damned. He also said that, if each soul had its own body and was not reincarnated into another body, even though souls were very small, still the land of Sabarthès would be filled up from Toulouse all the way to the Mérens Pass—giving to understand through this that souls are corporeal. He also said that Raymond de la Côte, the heretic condemned this year by the lord bishop and the inquisitor of Carcassone, was a good Christian, and that what he taught was true. He also said that the church was not able to compel anyone to offer any specific thing at mass, but that it sufficed to offer a straw to the priest. Through these things it was apparent that he was a believer, favorer, and harborer of the Manichaean heretics and a member of their sect. The lord bishop informed himself about these matters and, wishing to question this man about them and other

things pertaining to the Catholic faith, about which he was vehemently suspect, he cited him by his letters to appear on this day. Guillaume, appearing before the lord bishop and Frère Gaillard de Pomiès (the lord inquisitor of Carcassone's deputy), was asked by the same simply and not under oath if he had said, taught, or believed the aforesaid heretical words. He responded no.

The same lord bishop, wishing to lead him back to faith and free him from danger, gave him some time (until early tomorrow evening) to think about the aforesaid; and because Guillaume said that his enemies made these denunciations, the lord bishop asked him who he thought his enemies were, and Guillaume answered that the priest and assistant priest of Ornolac were, and no one else.

The next day at early evening the said Guillaume appeared before the lord bishop in his episcopal chambers, assisted by Frère Gaillard de Pomiès, and made a physical oath that he would tell the truth plain and simple without any falsehoods intermixed about the aforesaid heretical articles and other matters pertaining to the Catholic faith, both insofar as they concerned him as the defendant and others, living or dead, as witnesses. After the articles contained in the preceding were explained to him again in the vernacular, he responded to the first article that he had never said nor did he believe that each human soul does not possess its own body.

To the second article he said he had not said or believed that the human soul, when it exits from its body, enters at that point or later into another body.

To the third article he said he believes that the human soul will rise and resume the flesh and bones it occupied in this life, and he never said or believed otherwise, so he said.

To the fourth article he said that at the General Judgment, a soul will be punished or rewarded in the body it occupied in this life, and he had never said or believed otherwise, so he said.

To the fifth article he said he had never said that if each human being who ever was, is, or will be had his own soul, then the land between Toulouse and the Mérens Pass would be filled up with the souls of the people of Sabarthès, past and present.

To the sixth article he said that he had never said that Raymond de la Côte was a good Christian.

To the seventh article he said that, repeating a statement he heard from a man from Chateauverdun (who was repeating a statement of the Romans), he had indeed said that the church could not compel anyone to make a specific offering, but that it sufficed to offer anything, no matter how small. But the man had not said that he believed this or was trying to discourage anyone from making agreeable or proper offerings. Asked the name of the man from Chateauverdun, he said that he did not know. Asked when he heard the man say these words, he said this year. Asked who else was present, he said he did not remember. Asked if he had seen heretics, believed in them, harbored them, or favored them, he said no.

Since the above information made it clear that the said Guillaume had neither told the truth about nor confessed the aforesaid heretical articles, the lord bishop arrested him and ordered him to be incarcerated immediately at Alemanns by his deputies, ordering him not to leave the castle without the lord bishop's permission.

The same year as above, August 11, Guillaume Austatz standing for judgment at the residence of the episcopal see of Pamiers before the lord bishop assisted by Frère Gaillard de Pomiès, said and confessed that three or four years ago—he did not really remember the time or day—he was in his house at Ornolac, and [either] Bartholomette, the wife of Arnaud d'Urs of Vicdessos, who was then staying at his house, or Alazaïs, wife of Pierre de Bordas, had lost a son whom she had discovered lying dead next to her in bed. But he did not remember, so he said, which of the two women had lost her son. And when this woman wept and wailed over the death of her son, and he saw and heard her, he said to the woman that she should not weep or wail because God would give that dead son's soul to the next child, boy or girl, that she conceived and bore, or else his soul will be in a good place in the next world. Asked what he understood it to mean when he said God would return the dead son's soul to whatever boy or girl the woman conceived or bore in the future, he said that he understood through these words that amends would be made to the woman with another child, and, so he said, though these words meant nothing, he said them anyway just as they came to his head. Asked if he had heard anyone saying that souls exiting human bodies reenter other human bodies, or if he had ever believed this or believed it still, he said he had never heard it from anyone, nor had he believed it, nor did he believe it now. Asked if he had ever said the same words or words to that effect to any person or persons except to Bartholomette or Alazaïs, he said he did not recall saying such words or words to that effect.

Also he said that around a year and a half ago he was in the village common of Ornolac and with him there, as he recalled, were Raymond de Ornolac, Pierre Doumenc, Pons Barrau, Guillaume de Aspira, Pierre de Gathlep, Bertrand de Ville, Raymond Benet the Younger, and some others he did not recall, so he said. Someone from among them, he did not remember who, started talking about the location of the souls of the dead, asking what place could hold as many souls as there were people who had died every day. Guillaume replied that they were received into paradise. And when those standing around asked him if paradise was so huge a place that it could hold every soul, he said that it was huge—so huge that if a house were made that occupied the whole area between Toulouse and Mérens, paradise would still be a bigger place and could hold many souls in it.

The same year as above, August 28, standing for judgment at the episcopal see of Pamiers before the lord bishop assisted by the said Frère Gaillard de Pomiès (the deputy of the lord inquisitor of Carcassone), Guillaume Austatz said and confessed that two and a half years ago or so, on the day that the said lord bishop first visited Sabarthès and the church of St. Martin of Ussat, the son of Alazaïs Mounié of Ornolac and also some other boy were burned by a fire that they had [accidentally] set in the house of Bernard Mounié. And when the said Alazaïs was crying over the loss of her son, Guillaume came over and visited Alazaïs at her house to console her about her son's death. While comforting her he said, "Godmother, don't weep and wail, for you can still get back the souls of your dead children." Alazaïs said that yes, she would get them back in paradise. He told her that in fact she would get them back in some son or daughter whom she would conceive and bear, for she was still young; and if she didn't get them back in a son or daughter, she would regain them in paradise.

The same year as above, August 29, standing for judgment at the aforesaid see before the said bishop assisted by the said Frère Gaillard de Pomiès, Guillaume Austatz said and confessed that eight years ago or so, as he recalled, his mother, Guillemette de Austatz, was cited for the crime of heresy by the lord inquisitor of Carcassone. When he heard this, he went on a market day to Lordat to be with his mother who had to go to Carcassone. And in his mother's house at Lordat they sat alone together by the fire and, as he said, he asked his mother if she thought she was guilty of heresy since she had been cited by the lord inquisitor. She said yes. And then he said to her, "How? Have you met heretics?" And she said yes: Pierre Authié and Prades Tavernier at Arnaud de Albiès's house in Lordat. And when he asked her why and how she had gone to that house to see these heretics, she said that late one evening she was standing at the door of her house, and Guillemette (the wife of the surgeon Arnaud Teisseire of Lordat and the daughter of the heretic Pierre Authié) arrived with Raymond Sabatié of Lordat. Then Raymond said to Guillaume's mother, "Come join Guillemette de Teisseire." She said "Gladly," so they went together (namely his mother, Guillemette, and Raymond) and went inside Albiès's house to a room where the heretics were. When they were at the door to the room, Raymond asked Guillaume's mother if she would like to see some holy men, and, quickly opening the door, they entered and found there the heretics Pierre Authié and Prades Tavernier, whom first Guillemette and next Raymond reverenced in a heretical fashion. When these two had greeted the heretics, they told Guillaume's mother she should adore them in the same way they had. Guillemette told her that this master [i.e., Pierre] was her [i.e., Guillemette's] father, and they taught her how she should adore them. And so his mother, after they had instructed her, reverenced the heretics. After this adoration, they stayed there with the heretics, and Pierre Authié preached to them. This heretic told them among other things that when children's souls exit after their death, they enter by stealth into the bodies of children who were generated and conceived after the death of the first children. This happens after the mother of the dead children conceives and bears other children....

On August 30, standing for judgment at the episcopal see of Pamiers before the lord bishop assisted by the said Frère Gaillard de Pomiès (the deputy of the lord inquisitor of Carcassone), Guillaume Austatz said and confessed that this year, after the heretic Raymond de la Côte was burned in the village of Alemanns, one Sunday the men of Ornolac (namely Pons Barrau, Guillaume de Aspira, Pierre Doumenc, Bernard de Ville, Guillaume Forsac, Raymond de Ornolac, all of them from Ornolac) were in the village common next to the elm tree there, and they were talking about the burning of the heretic. Guillaume arrived and said, "I'll tell you this for a fact: this fellow they burned was a good cleric—there was none better in these parts except the bishop of Pamiers. He constantly argued with the bishop and he disagreed with him, but he believed in God, Blessed Mary, and all the saints, and in the seven [sic] articles of faith, and he was a good Christian. And since he believed all these things, it was a great injustice to burn him." The men asked him why he was burned considering he was a good cleric and a good Christian, and he replied it was because he said the pope could not absolve sins and he denied purgatory—that is why he was burned.

Also he said that before he said these words in the village common of Ornolac, Raymond de Nan, who was staying with Pierre Mir, the canon of Foix, came to his house at Ornolac and told him, in the hearing of Pierre Bordas, Arnaud Pere, and Guillaume Garaud of Cha-

teauverdun, that a man had been burned at the village of Allemans by the bishop of Pamiers. People said he was a good cleric, and that he had disagreed with the bishop but believed in God, Blessed Mary, all the saints, and the seven articles of faith, and was a good Christian, and it was a great injustice to burn him. When Guillaume heard this, he suggested that "it would have been better for Sabarthès if the bishop of Pamiers had been burned instead of this man, for afterwards he wouldn't make us spend our money." By this he understood not that the bishop was a heretic, but that the bishop demanded a tithe on sheep called *carnelages* from the people of Sabarthès. This was why he said it would have been better for the lord bishop to be burned than the heretic. Asked if he then believed or still believes it would have been better for Sabarthès if the bishop had been burned instead of the heretic Raymond de la Côte, he said he believed it then when he spoke these words, and he held that opinion for fifteen days; but after fifteen days he did not believe it nor does he now. He was asked—when he believed it was better for Sabarthès to burn the lord bishop of Pamiers instead of the heretic since the bishop exacted the tithe of sheep from Sabarthès—whether he believed or still believes the bishop can justly demand the tithe. He said he thought the bishop could justly demand the tithe. He was asked, since he believed the bishop could justly demand the tithe, whether he believed the people of Sabarthès acted justly in refusing to pay the tithe. He said that although the bishop exacted the tithe according to law, the people of Sabarthès also justly refused to pay the tithe according to their customs. Asked why he believed it was better to burn the bishop than the heretic, since, when he said this, he thought the lord bishop justly demanded the tithe from the people of Sabarthès, he responded that he said this because of the expenses the lord bishop cost the people of Sabarthès....

He was asked if, when he said the heretic Raymond de la Côte was a good Christian and was unjustly burned, he knew that he had been condemned by the lord bishop and the inquisitor of Carcassone as a heretic and had been judged a heretic. He said he did indeed know that Raymond had been condemned as a heretic by the bishop and the inquisitor; still, it did not seem to him or to others with whom he spoke that he was a heretic since he believed in God, Blessed Mary, all the saints, and the seven articles of faith. This was why it seemed to him that Raymond was a good Christian and had been unjustly condemned. But later, when they considered that the lord bishop and the inquisitor would not have burdened themselves with so great a sin as killing a man unless it was just, it seemed to them that—although to some small degree they had unjustly condemned him—still, in some measure they had acted justly. He was asked whether, after he had heard it said—as he confessed—that Raymond had been condemned as a heretic since he did not believe the pope could absolve sins and he denied that purgatory existed, he then believed and still believes that Raymond had been justly condemned as a heretic for denying these two articles. He said that at the time he spoke these words, he did not believe that the heretic should have been condemned for not believing the two articles; but before then and after then he believed and still believes he was justly condemned as a heretic for denying the two articles. However, for fifteen days he remained convinced that he had been unjustly condemned for denying the articles. He was asked whether, at the time he believed Raymond had been unjustly condemned as a heretic for denying the two articles, he thought that to say the pope could not absolve sins and to deny that purgatory existed in the next world were heresies. He said that for those fifteen days he did not believe it was heresy to say the pope could not absolve sins and that purgatory did not exist. But before and after those fifteen days, he believed and still believes that to deny these two articles is heresy, and also that someone denying these articles should be justly condemned as a heretic.

The year as above, September 1, the said Guillaume Austatz appeared for judgment at the episcopal see before the lord bishop assisted by Frère Gaillard de Pomiès, the deputy of the lord inquisitor of Carcassone. He said and confessed that about five years ago he was at home, and Pierre Bordas and his wife Alazaïs and Barchinona Bordas were there. They started talking about the salvation of souls. He said that, if it were true what the priests say—namely that if someone wanted to be saved, it was necessary for him to confess all his sins, and, if he could, to restore or return everything he had taken from other people against their will—not ten out a hundred people will be saved. Better yet, not ten out of a thousand. For people do not confess their sins very well, either because they have forgotten them or because they are embarrassed to confess them; and they take lots of things from other people. So only a few out of many will be saved, if what the priests say is true. Asked if he then believed and still believes that when priests say these two things they are telling the truth, he said yes. Asked whether he believed he would be damned for eternity if he died and had not wanted to confess that he had knowingly committed simple fornication or loaned money at interest or had failed to return interest that he had received if he could, he said that he did.

Also, he had said he believed that if each soul had its own body, the world could scarcely hold these souls since, though they were very small, there were so many of them that they would fill up the world. From this it appeared that he believed souls were material. He was asked if he thought human souls were material and had physical parts: hands, feet, and other parts. He said that at the time he had said this, he believed human souls had the physical shape of a man or woman and parts resembling the human body. But now he believed human souls were spirits without parts resembling the human body.

He was asked whether he believed the saints dwelling in paradise could help people living in this world; he said yes. He was asked whether he had ever said otherwise. He said that this year around Pentecost, when Gaillarde Ros had lost five sous stolen from a chest, she complained to him that since he was the local *baille*, and since he had not immediately discovered who had committed the theft, she had asked Blessed Mary of Montgauzy to expose the thief. He said to Gaillarde, "And don't you think Blessed Mary would commit a greater sin if she revealed the person who stole the four [*sic*] sous from you? For wouldn't the thief be thrown into confusion and brought to justice [with the risk of capital punishment] by this than if Blessed Mary didn't return the four sous to you?" But he said this, so he said, as a joke, not really believing Blessed Mary would sin if she revealed the thief. He also did not think it would be a sin if she revealed the wrongdoer, or even if he were sentenced to death or killed by order of his superior.

He was asked if he had ever confessed the aforesaid heresies to a priest or in any other way. He said no, because he had not believed he had sinned by believing them and persisting in that belief. But now he realized that he had been gravely at fault for believing these errors, and he humbly begged absolution for the sentence of excommunication he incurred for believing them. He said he was prepared to perform any penance and suffer any penalty the lord bishop and the inquisitors enjoined on him for these things. But he was obliged that if he later recalls any other crime beyond that which he had confessed, or also if he remembers that someone else living or dead had committed this crime, as quickly as he can he will reveal this to the bishop, his successors, or the lord inquisitor of Carcassone. And the lord bishop, seeing his humility and contrition, absolved him in the church's due form from the sentence of excommunication he incurred for believing these heresies, provided that he fully confessed them and that he now and forevermore believes what the Roman Church preaches and teaches. But before granting him this absolution, he received from him an abjuration and oath as follows:

There Guillaume Austatz abjured all heresy, belief in, support of, defense of, harboring of, approval of the sect, life, or faith of, agreement with, and every other kind of participation with Manichaeans or Waldensians, etc... otherwise his absolution is not valid.

This was done in the presence of the said lord bishop, Frère Gaillard, Frère Arnaud de Caslar (both of the Order of Preachers at Pamiers),[1] and Master Guillaume Pierre Barthe, the lord bishop's notary, who recorded and wrote the preceding. And I, Rainaud, faithfully corrected all of it against the original copy.

The year as above, September 3, standing for judgment at the episcopal see of Pamiers before the lord bishop assisted by the said Frère Gaillard de Pomiès (deputy of the lord inquisitor of Carcassone), Guillaume Austatz heard the bishop read to him in the vernacular everything he confessed above. Asked whether everything he confessed against himself and against others in the above confession was true, he said yes. He said he wished and wishes to stand firm in this confession, seeking mercy that he be not judged upon the above matters; and he finished his business, and sought to be given a sentence and mercy for the above matters....

On the Sunday assigned to the said Guillaume Austatz, he appeared in the cemetery of St. John the Martyr and sentence was rendered to him by the lord bishop and the lord inquisitor in this manner: "May all know, etc...." Look for this sentence in the Sentence Book of the inquisition of heretical depravity, which sentence was issued against the said Guillaume Austatz on Sunday, March 2 in the said cemetery.

And I, the aforesaid Rainaud, faithfully corrected all of this against the original copy.

[We do not know whether Guillaume was punished or was allowed to return home.]

7.14 Procedures for isolating lepers: *Sarum Manual* (based on materials from *c.*1360s). Original in Latin.

Leprosy was a public disease: a disfigurement of the skin, easily seen by all. Today we identify leprosy with the illness caused by one bacillus, *mycobacterium leprae*, but in the Middle Ages people with many sorts of skin diseases were considered lepers. From at least the fourth century on, kissing lepers was an admirable attribute of many saints. For example, Fortunatus wrote of St. Radegund that "seizing some of the leprous women in her embrace, her heart full of love, she kissed their faces" (see above, p. 42). But lepers were also despised, and by the twelfth century their illness was understood to be the outward manifestation of a diseased and sinful soul. Leper hospitals were built, often just outside the walls of towns; they were provided with alms-boxes so that travelers entering the city might give a contribution to these most abject and marginal of human beings. Lepers were segregated: they were not allowed to live among or attend church with the healthy, and procedures for expelling lepers from their normal communities were written up. The one here comes from a fifteenth-century edition of the so-called *Sarum Manual*, a book of rites used initially in the diocese of Salisbury and then adopted throughout much of England. It was probably taken verbatim from the expulsion ritual used in some southern French dioceses in the 1360s, and it reflects the normal practice in Western Europe.

[Source: Rotha Mary Clay, *The Medieval Hospitals of England* (Frank Cass: London, 1909), Appendix A, pp. 273–76, revised by John Shinners, ed., *Medieval Popular Religion, 1000–1500: A Reader* (Toronto: University of Toronto Press, 1997), pp. 279–81.]

---

[1] The Order of Preachers refers to the Dominicans.

METHOD FOR CASTING OUT OR SEPARATING
THOSE WHO ARE SICK WITH LEPROSY FROM
THE HEALTHY.

First of all the sick man or leper clad in a cloak and in his usual dress, being in his house, ought to have notice of the coming of the priest who is on his way to the house to lead him to the church, and must in that guise wait for him. For the priest vested in surplice and stole, with the cross preceding him, makes his way to the sick man's house and addresses him with comforting words, pointing out and proving that if he blesses and praises God, and bears his sickness patiently, he may have a sure hope that though he be sick in body he may be whole in his soul, and may obtain the gift of everlasting health. And let him offer other words suitable to the occasion. When he has sprinkled him with holy water, let the priest lead the leper to the church, the cross leading the procession, the priest following, and then the leper. Within the church let a black cloth, if it is available, be set upon two trestles at some distance apart before the altar, and let the sick man take his place on bended knees beneath it between the trestles, after the manner of a dead man, although by the grace of God he yet lives in body and spirit, and in this posture let him devoutly hear mass. When this is finished, and he has been sprinkled with holy water, he must be led by the priest with the cross to the place where he will live. When they have arrived there, the priest shall counsel him with the words of holy scripture: "Remember thy last end, and thou shalt never sin"[1] Whence Augustine says, "He readily rejects all things, who ever bears in mind that he will die." Then the priest with a spade casts earth on both of his feet, saying "Be dead to the world, but live again with God." And he comforts him and strengthens his patience with the words of Isaiah spoken concerning our Lord Jesus Christ: "Truly he hath borne our infirmities and carried our sorrows, and we have thought him as it were a leper, and as one struck by God and afflicted."[2] Let him say also: "If in bodily weakness by means of suffering you become like Christ, you may

surely hope that you will rejoice in spirit with God. May the Most High grant this to you, numbering you among his faithful ones in the book of life. Amen."

It is to be noted that the priest must lead him to the church and from the church to his house as a dead man, chanting the Responsory *Libera me domine*.[3] Thus, the sick man should be covered with a black cloth. And the mass celebrated at his exclusion may be chosen either by the priest or by the sick man, but it is customary to say the following:

Introit: "They have surrounded me."[4] See Septuagesima Sunday. *Collect*: "Almighty and ever-eternal God, give everlasting salvation to those believing in you." *Epistle*: "Beloved, is any one of you sad?"[5] *Response*: "Have mercy on me." *Verse*: "For my bones are troubled."[6] Alleluia *Verse*: "He who heals." If during Lent, *Tract*: "Thou hast moved the earth."[7] *Gospel*: "Jesus entered Capharnaum."[8] *Offertory*: "Lord, hear me."[9] *Secret and Post-communion*: "Deliver Israel, O God, from all his tribulations."[10]

When leaving the church after mass the priest ought to stand at the door and sprinkle him with holy water. And he ought to commend him to the care of the people. Before mass the sick man ought to make his confession in the church but never again there. In leading him forth the priest again begins the Responsory *Libera me domine* with the other versicles. Then when he has come into the open fields he does as is aforesaid; and he ends by imposing prohibitions upon him in the following manner:

"I forbid you ever again to enter churches, or to go to a market, a mill, a bakehouse, or gatherings of people.

Also I forbid you ever to wash your hands or even any of your belongings in a spring or stream of water of any kind; and if you are thirsty you must drink water from your pot or some other vessel.

Also I forbid you ever henceforth to go out without your leper's dress, that you may be recognized by others; and you must not go outside your house unshod.

---

[1] Ecclus. 7: 40.

[2] Isa. 53: 4.

[3] "Free me, O Lord."

[4] Ps. 17: 11; Douay Ps. 16: 11. These quotations represent the initial verses of the various parts of the mass.

[5] James 5: 13.

[6] Ps. 6: 2; Douay Ps. 6: 3.

[7] Ps. 60: 2; Douay Ps. 59: 4.

[8] Luke 7: 1.

[9] Ps. 17: 1; Douay Ps. 16: 1.

[10] Ps. 25: 22; Douay Ps. 24: 22.

Also I forbid you, wherever you may be, to touch anything which you wish to buy other than with a rod or staff to show what you want.

Also I forbid you ever henceforth to enter taverns or other houses if you wish to buy wine; and have what they give you put into your cask.

Also I forbid you to have intercourse with any woman except your wife.

Also I command you when you are on a journey not to answer anyone who questions you until you have moved to the side of the road downwind from him so that he may not be harmed by you; and that you never go down a narrow lane lest you should meet someone.

Also I charge you that if you need to pass across some toll bridge over water or elsewhere you touch no posts or structures on the path where you cross until you have first put on your gloves.

Also I forbid you to touch infants or young folk, whoever they might be, or to give to them or to any others any of your possessions.

Also I forbid you henceforth to eat or drink in any company except that of lepers. And know that when you die you will be buried in your own house, unless you received permission beforehand to be buried in a church."

And note that before he enters his house, he ought to have a coat and shoes of fur, his own plain shoes, a clapper as his signal, a hood and a cloak, two pairs of sheets, a pot, a funnel, a belt, a small knife, and a bowl. His house ought to be small, with a cistern, a bed furnished with sheets, a pillow, a chest, a table and chair, a lamp, a shovel, a cup, and other necessities.

When all is complete the priest must point out to him the ten rules which he has made for him; and let him live on earth in peace with his neighbor. Next, in the presence of the people the priest must point out to him the Ten Commandments of God, that he may live in heaven with the blessed. And let the priest also point out to him that every day each faithful Christian is bound to say devoutly the Our Father, Hail Mary, and the Creed, and to protect himself with the sign of the cross, saying often *Benedicite*. The priest departs from him saying: "Worship God and give thanks to God. Have patience and the Lord will be with you. Amen."

7.15 Jews in England: *Statute of the Jewry* (1275) and *Petition of the "Commonalty" of the Jews* (shortly after 1275). Originals in Latin and French, respectively.

The endless need of King Henry III (r.1216–1272) for revenues hit the Jews of England hard. Numerous taxes, fines, and confiscations left many bankrupt. Some left the country. Meanwhile stories of Jewish ritual killings circulated, touching off mass executions. In 1231 the city of Leicester expelled its Jews, and between 1234 and 1243 numerous cities and even whole counties of England did likewise. When Edward I (r.1272–1307) came to the throne, he compounded the problem. Reacting to church canons against the "sin of usury," he issued the *Statute of the Jewry* in 1275, prohibiting Jews from charging interest and insisting that all current debts to Jews be settled quickly for less than was owed. In effect the *Statute* deprived the Jews of their livelihood. To compensate, it allowed Jews to become merchants, artisans, or farmers (though only for a short term). But, as the Jews pointed out in their *Petition of the "Commonalty,"* Jews could not be merchants or artisans, for they could not travel safely, and they would never be able to extend credit (since they were unlikely ever to be paid). Under such circumstances, they could not compete with Christians. In fact the *Statute* was an utter failure, and Edward ended by expelling all the Jews from England in 1290.

[Source: *English Historical Documents*, vol. 3: 1189–1327, ed. Harry Rothwell (London and New York: Routledge, 1975), pp. 411–13 (notes added).]

The Statute of the Jewry (1275)

Because the king has seen that many evils and instances of the disinheriting of good men of his land have happened as a result of the usuries which the Jews have made in the past, and that many sins have followed thereupon, the king, though he and his ancestors have always received great benefit from the Jewish people in the past, has nevertheless for the honor of God and the common benefit of the people, ordained and established that from now on no Jew shall lend anything at usury, either on land or rent or anything else, and that usuries shall not continue beyond the feast of St. Edward [October 13] last. Agreements made before that shall be kept, save that the usuries shall cease. All those who owe debts to Jews on pledges of movables are to clear them between now and Easter; if not the pledges shall be forfeited. And if any Jew shall lend at usury contrary to what the king has established the king will not concern himself either personally or through his officials to get him recovery of his loan, but will punish him at his discretion for the offence and will do justice to the Christian that he may recover his pledge.

And so that distresses for debts due to Jews shall not henceforth be so grievous, a half of the lands and chattels of Christians is to be kept for their sustenance,[1] and no distress for a debt owing to a Jew is to be made upon the heir of the debtor named in the Jew's deed or other person holding the land that was the debtor's before the debt is proved and acknowledged in court.

And if a sheriff or other bailiff has by the king's command to give a Jew, or a number of Jews, for a debt due to them seisin[2] of chattels or land to the value of the debt, the chattels are to be valued by the oaths of good men and be delivered to the Jew or Jews or to their agent to the amount of the debt, and if the chattels do not suffice, the lands shall be extended by the same oath before seisin is given to the Jew or Jews, to each one according to what is due to him, so that it may be known for certain that the debt is paid and the Christian may have his land again, saving always to the Christian half of his land and chattels for his sustenance as aforesaid, and the chief dwelling.

And if any movables be found hereafter in the seisin of a Jew and any one wishes to sue him, the Jew shall have his warranty if he is entitled to it, and if not, let him answer: so that in future he is not in this matter to be otherwise privileged than a Christian.

And that all Jews shall dwell in the king's own cities and boroughs, where the chirograph chests of the Jews are wont to be:[3] and that each Jew after he is seven years old shall wear a distinguishing mark on his outer garment, that is to say in the form of two Tables joined, of yellow felt of the length of six inches and of the breadth of three inches. And that each one after he is twelve years old shall yearly at Easter pay to the king, whose serf he is, a tax of three pence, and this be understood to hold as well for a woman as for a man.

And that no Jew have power to enfeoff[4] another, Jew or Christian, with houses, rents or tenements that he now has, or to alienate them in any other manner, or to acquit any Christian of his debt without special permission of the king, until the king shall have otherwise ordained thereon.

And as it is the will and sufferance of holy church that they may live and be preserved, the king takes them into his protection and grants them his peace; and wills that they may be safely preserved and defended by his sheriffs and his other bailiffs and faithful; and commands that none shall do them harm or damage or wrong in their bodies or in their goods movable or immovable and that they shall neither plead nor be impleaded in any court, nor be challenged or troubled in any court, save in the court of the king, whose bondmen they are. And that none shall owe obedience or service or rent save to the king or to his bailiffs in his name, unless it be for their dwellings which they now hold by paying rent, saving the right of holy church.

And the king grants them that they may live by lawful trade and by their labor and that they may have intercourse with Christians in order to carry on lawful trade by selling and buying. But that no Christian for this cause or any other shall dwell among them. And the king wills that they shall not by reason of their trading be put to scot and lot or tallaged,[5] with those of the cities and bor-

---

[1] As a legal term, "distress" means holding someone's property against the payment of a debt. Chattels are movable property, as opposed to land, which cannot be moved.

[2] I.e., legal possession.

[3] The "chirograph chests" were the boxes in which the records of debts were held. A chirograph was a document written in duplicate and cut such that the two parts would fit only with one another.

[4] I.e., to give a fief to.

[5] "Scot and lot" and tallage were taxes.

oughs where they live because they are liable for tallage to the king as his serfs and to no one other than the king.

Moreover the king grants them that they may buy houses and curtilages[1] in the cities and boroughs where they live, so that they hold them in chief of the king, saving to the lords of the fee[2] their services due and accustomed. And they may take and buy farms or land for the term of ten years or less, without taking homages or fealties[3] or such sort of obedience from Christians, and without having advowsons[4] of churches, that they may be able to gain their living in the world if they have not the means of trading or cannot labor. And this power of taking lands at farm shall be open to them only for fifteen years from this time forward.

Petition of the "Commonalty" of the Jews (shortly after 1275)

To our lord the king and to his council the commonalty of the Jews ask the favor of their assent and discretion on the things written below.

Because the new statutes will that the Jews should have seisin of half only of lands and rents pledged to them, leaving the other half of the lands and rents and the chief messuage[5] for the sustenance of the Christian who is the debtor of the Jew, this is their enquiry: if the debtor of the Jew dies without heir of his body and without wife and the lands and rents fall to a rich man or to someone who has enough of his own to live on without these lands and rents that are pledged to the Jew, in such circumstances shall the Jew have possession of the whole of the pledged property until the debt is paid, or not?

Besides this, our question is about a Christian who has borrowed money from Jews which is the king's money and this Christian has no lands, rents or chattels save a large house which he occupies worth 100 shillings or 10 marks a year and if it were sold would fetch 100 marks or £100, what seisin will the Jew have of his pledge for the recovery of the debt seeing that this Christian has nothing save this house.

Further, the commonalty of the Jews beseech our lord the king that the poor Jews, who have nothing whereby to live or trade, may have leave to sell their houses and their rents to other Jews richer than themselves: it would be worth as much to our lord the king for the one lot of Jews to have the rents and houses as the other, and he could not lose by it. That if they have not leave to sell their houses they will have to demolish them and sell the stone and timber to various people.

Furthermore, the commonalty of the Jews demonstrate that they would be compelled if they were to trade at all to buy dearer than a Christian and to sell dearer, for Christian merchants sell their merchandise on credit and if the Jew sold on credit he would never be paid a single penny. And Christian merchants can carry their merchandise far and near but if the Jew carried his beyond the...[6] he would be... and robbed. And they beseech our lord the king and his council that... such counsel in the Jewry that they can live in his time with his... as in the time of his ancestors since the Conquest.

---

[1] Yards or courtyards.

[2] "Fee" is equivalent to fief.

[3] Lords normally received homage and fealty from their vassals, but such relations were not permitted between Jews and Christians.

[4] The advowson was the right to an ecclesiastical benefice.

[5] Messuage is a house and the land and buildings attached to it.

[6] Here and elsewhere in this and the next sentence the writing is defaced and can no longer be read.

RULERS AND RULED

7.16 A charismatic ruler: Joinville, *The Life of St. Louis* (1272). Original in French.

Jean de Joinville (1225–1317) was a friend and confidant of King Louis IX (r.1226–1270), who would be canonized as St. Louis in 1297. Joinville met Louis on the Seventh Crusade in 1248 and remained in active service to the king thereafter. He began the first part of his *Life*, excerpted here, in 1272; he added a second part between 1298 and 1309. What did he admire most about the king? Did he have any criticisms? Compare his account of Louis's life with Jacques de Vitry's account of Mary of Oignies (above, p. 370). How did Joinville reconcile political power with sanctity?

[Source: Joinville and Villehardouin, *Chronicles of the Crusades*, trans. M.R.B. Shaw (New York: Penguin Books, 1963), pp. 163–79 (slightly modified).]

Part One

CHAPTER I: *THE SERVANT OF GOD*

In the name of God Almighty, I, Jean, Lord of Joinville, Seneschal[1] of Champagne, dictate the life of our good King, Saint Louis, in which I shall record what I saw and heard both in the course of the six years in which I was on pilgrimage in his company overseas, and after we returned to France. But before I speak to you of his great deeds and his outstanding valor, I will tell you what I myself observed of his good teaching and his saintly conduct, so that it may be set down in due order for the edification of those to whom this book is read.

This saintly man loved our Lord with all his heart, and in all his actions followed His example. This is apparent from the fact that as our Lord died for the love he bore His people, even so King Louis put his own life in danger, and that several times, for the very same reason. It was danger too that he might well have avoided, as I shall show you later.

The great love King Louis bore his people is shown by what he said, as he lay dangerously ill at Fontainebleau, to his eldest son, my Lord Louis. "My dear son," he said, "I earnestly beg you to make yourself loved by all your people. For I would rather have a Scot come from Scotland to govern the people of this kingdom well and justly than that you should govern them ill in the sight of all the world." This upright king, moreover, loved truth so well that, as I shall show you later, he would never consent to lie to the Saracens[2] with regard to any covenant he made with them.

He was so temperate in his appetite that I never heard him, on any day of my life, order a special dish for himself, as many men of wealth and standing do. On the contrary, he would always eat with good grace whatever his cooks had prepared to set before him. He was equally temperate in his speech. I never, on any single occasion, heard him speak evil of any man; nor did I ever hear him utter the name of the Devil—a name in very common use throughout the kingdom—which practice, so I believe, is not pleasing to God.

He used to add water to his wine, but did so reasonably, according as the strength of the wine allowed it. While we were in Cyprus he asked me why I did not mix my wine with water. I replied that this was on the advice of my doctors, who had told me that I had a strong head and a cold stomach, so that I could not get drunk. He answered that they had deceived me; for if I did not learn to mix my wine with water while I was still young, and wished to do so in my old age, gout and stomach troubles would take hold on me, and I should never be in good health. Moreover, if I went on drinking undiluted

---

[1] Technically a senechal was a royal officer. But Joinville inherited the title from his father, and in his case it was largely an honorific.

[2] The Saracens, i.e., the Muslims.

wine when I was old, I should get drunk every night, and it was too revolting a thing for any brave man to be in such a state.

The king once asked me if I wished to be honored in this world, and to enter paradise when I died. I told him I did. "If so," said he, "you should avoid deliberately saying or doing anything which, if it became generally known, you would be ashamed to acknowledge by saying 'I did this,' or 'I said that.'" He also told me not to contradict or call in question anything said in my presence—unless indeed silence would imply approval of something wrong, or damaging to myself, because harsh words often lead to quarrelling, which has ended in the death of countless numbers of men.

He often said that people ought to clothe and arm themselves in such a way that men of riper age would never say they had spent too much on dress, or young men say they had spent too little. I repeated this remark to our present king when speaking of the elaborately embroidered tabards that are in vogue today.[1] I told him that, during the whole of our voyage overseas, I had never seen such embroidered tabards, either on the king or on any one else. He said to me that he had several such garments, with his own arms embroidered on them, and they had cost him eight hundred *livres parisis*. I told him that he would have put his money to better use if he had given it to God, and had his clothes made of good plain taffeta bearing his arms, as his father had done.

King Louis once sent for me and said: "You have such a shrewd and subtle mind that I hardly dare speak to you of things concerning God. So I have summoned these two monks to come here, because I want to ask you a question." Then he said: "Tell me, seneschal, what is your idea of God?" "Your Majesty," I replied, "He is something so good that there cannot be anything better." "Indeed," said he, "you've given me a very good answer; for it's precisely the same as the definition given in this book I have here in my hand."

"Now I ask you," he continued, "which you would prefer: to be a leper or to have committed some mortal sin?" And I, who had never lied to him, replied that I would rather have committed thirty mortal sins than become a leper. The next day, when the monks were no longer

there, he called me to him, and making me sit at his feet said to me: "Why did you say that to me yesterday?" I told him I would still say it. "You spoke without thinking, and like a fool," he said. "You ought to know there is no leprosy so foul as being in a state of mortal sin; for the soul in that condition is like the Devil; therefore no leprosy can be so vile. Besides, when a man dies his body is healed of its leprosy; but if he dies after committing a mortal sin, he can never be sure that, during his lifetime, he has repented of it sufficiently for God to forgive him. In consequence, he must be greatly afraid lest that leprosy of sin should last as long as God dwells in paradise. So I beg you," he added, "as earnestly as I can, for the love of God, and for love of me, to train your heart to prefer any evil that can happen to the body, whether it be leprosy or any other disease, rather than let mortal sin take possession of your soul."

At another time King Louis asked me if I washed the feet of the poor on Maundy Thursday.[2] "Your Majesty," I exclaimed, "what a terrible idea! I will never wash the feet of such low fellows." "Really," said he, "that is a very wrong thing to say; for you should never scorn to do what our Lord Himself did as an example for us. So I beg you, first for the love of God and then for love of me, to accustom yourself to washing the feet of the poor."

This good king so loved all manner of people who believed in God and loved Him that he appointed Gilles le Brun, who was not a native of his realm, as High Constable of France, because he was held in such high repute for his faith in God and devotion to His service. For my part, I believe he well deserved that reputation. Another man, Master Robert de Sorbon,[3] who was famed for his goodness and his learning, was invited, on that account, to dine at the royal table.

It happened one day that this worthy priest was sitting beside me at dinner, and we were talking to each other rather quietly. The king reproved us and said: "Speak up, or your companions may think you are speaking ill of them. If at table you talk of things that may give us pleasure, say them aloud, or else be silent."

When the king was feeling in a mood for fun, he would fire questions at me, as for instance: "Seneschal, can you give me reasons why a wise and upright layman

---

[1] A tabard was a tunic worn over armor and embroidered with a coat of arms. "Our present king" was Louis's grandson Philip IV "The Fair," king of France (r.1285–1314).

[2] This is also known as Holy Thursday, the Thursday before Easter Sunday.

[3] Robert de Sorbon was Louis's chaplain and founder (in 1257) of the college of the Sorbonne, today the University of Paris. He had the title of Master because he was qualified, by his university training, to teach theology.

is better than a friar?" Thereupon a discussion would begin between Master Robert and myself. When we had disputed for some length of time the king would pronounce judgement. "Master Robert," he would say, "I would willingly be known as a wise and upright man, provided I were so in reality—and you can have all the rest. For wisdom and goodness are such fine qualities that even to name them leaves a pleasant taste in the mouth."

On the other hand, he always said that it was a wicked thing to take other people's property. "To 'restore,'" he would say, "is such a hard thing to do that even in speaking of it the word itself rasps one's throat because of the r's that are in it. These r's are, so to speak, like the rakes of the Devil, with which he would draw to himself all those who wish to 'restore' what they have taken from others. The Devil, moreover, does this very subtly; for he works on great usurers and great robbers in such a way that they give to God what they ought to *restore* to men."

On one occasion the king gave me a message to take to King Thibaut,[1] in which he warned his son-in-law to beware lest he should lay too heavy a burden on his soul by spending an excessive amount of money on the house he was building for the Predicants[2] of Provins. "Wise men," said the king, "deal with their possessions as executors ought to do. Now the first thing a good executor does is to settle all debts incurred by the deceased and restore any property belonging to others, and only then is he free to apply what money remains to charitable purposes."

One Pentecost the saintly king happened to be at Corbeil, where all the knights had assembled. He had come down after dinner into the court below the chapel, and was standing at the doorway talking to the Count of Brittany, the father of the present count—may God preserve him!—when Master Robert de Sorbon came to look for me, and taking hold of the hem of my mantle led me towards the king. So I said to Master Robert: "My good sir, what do you want with me?" He replied: "I wish to ask you whether, if the king were seated in this court and you went and sat down on his bench, at a higher place than he, you ought to be severely blamed for doing so?" I told him I ought to be. "Then," he said "you certainly deserve a reprimand for being more richly dressed than the king, since you are wearing a fur-trimmed mantle of fine green

cloth, and he wears no such thing." "Master Robert," I answered, "I am, if you'll allow me to say so, doing nothing worthy of blame in wearing green cloth and fur, for I inherited the right to such dress from my father and mother. But you, on the other hand, are much to blame, for though both your parents were commoners, you have abandoned their style of dress, and are now wearing finer woolen cloth than the king himself." Then I took hold of the skirt of his surcoat and of the surcoat worn by the king, and said to Master Robert: "See if I'm not speaking the truth." At this the king began to take Master Robert's part, and say all in his power to defend him.

A little later on the king beckoned to his son, the Prince Philip—the father of our present king—and to King Thibaut. Then, seating himself at the entrance to his oratory, he patted the ground and said to the two young men: "Sit down here, quite close to me, so that we won't be overheard." "But, my lord," they protested, "we should not dare to sit so close to you." Then the king said to me, "Seneschal, you sit here." I obeyed, and sat down so close to him that my clothes were touching his. He made the two others sit down next, and said to them: "You have acted very wrongly, seeing you are my sons, in not doing as I commanded the moment I told you. I beg you to see this does not happen again." They assured him it would not.

Then the king said to me that he had called us together to confess that he had wrongly defended Master Robert against me. "But," said he, "I saw he was so taken aback that he greatly needed my help. All the same you must not attach too great importance to anything I may have said in his defense. As the seneschal rightly says, you ought to dress well, and in a manner suited to your condition, so that your wives will love you all the more and your men have more respect for you. For, as a wise philosopher has said, our clothing and our armor ought to be of such a kind that men of mature experience will not say that we have spent too much on them, nor younger men say we have spent too little."

I will tell you here of one of the lessons King Louis taught me on our voyage back from the land overseas.[3] It so happened that our ship was driven on to the rocks off the island of Cyprus by a wind known as the *garbino*,

---

1 Thibaut (1201–1253) was count of Champagne and, starting in 1234, king of Navarre. He was a *trouvère*, that is, a troubadour who wrote in French rather than Old Occitan, the language of southern France.

2 Predicants was another word for the Dominicans.

3 Louis went overseas on two crusades. This refers to his first, the Seventh Crusade, which, like the next one, was a failure. Louis died in the course of his second crusade.

which is not one of the four great winds. At the shock our ship received the sailors were so frantic with despair that they rent their clothes and tore their beards. The king sprang out of bed barefoot—for it was night—and with nothing on but his tunic went and lay with arms outstretched to form a cross before the body of Our Lord on the altar, as one who expected nothing but death.

The day after this alarming event, the king called me aside to talk with him alone, and said to me: "Seneschal, God has just shown us a glimpse of His great power; for one of these little winds, so little indeed that it scarcely deserves a name, came near to drowning the King of France, his children, his wife, and his men. Now Saint Anselm says that such things are warnings from our Lord, as if God meant to say to us: 'See how easily I could have brought about your death if that had been My will.' 'Lord God,' says the saint, 'why do You thus threaten us? For when you do, it is not for Your own profit, nor for Your advantage—seeing that if You had caused us all to be lost You would be none the poorer, nor any the richer either if You had caused us to be saved. Therefore, the warning You send us is not for Your own benefit, but for ours, if we know how to profit by it.'

"Let us therefore," said the king, "take this warning God has sent us in such a way that if we feel there is anything in our hearts or our bodies that is displeasing to Him, we shall get rid of it without delay. If, on the other hand, we can think of anything that will please Him, we ought to see about doing it with equal speed. If we act thus our Lord will give us blessings in this world, and in the next greater bliss than we can tell. But if we do not act as we ought, He will deal with us as a good lord deals with his unfaithful servant. For if the latter will not amend his ways after he has been given warning, then his lord punishes him with death, or with penalties even harder to bear."

So I, Jean de Joinville, say: "Let the king who now reigns over us beware; for he has escaped from perils as great as those to which we were then exposed, or even greater. Therefore, let him turn from doing wrong, and in such a way that God will not smite him cruelly, either in himself or in his possessions."

In the conversations he had with me, this saintly king did every thing in his power to give me a firm belief in the principles of Christianity as given us by God. He used to say that we ought to have such an unshaken belief in all the articles of faith that neither fear of death nor of any harm that might happen to our bodies should make us willing to go against them in word or deed. "The Enemy,"[1] he would add, "works so subtly that when people are at the point of death he tries all he can to make them die with some doubt in their minds on certain points of our religion. For this cunning adversary is well aware that he cannot take away the merit of any good works a man has done; and he also knows that a man's soul is lost to him if he dies in the true faith.

"Therefore," the king would say. "it is our duty so to defend and guard ourselves against this snare as to say to the Enemy, when he sends us such a temptation: 'Go away! You shall not lure me from my steadfast belief in the articles of my faith. Even if you had all my limbs cut off, I would still live and die a true believer.' Whoever acts thus overcomes the Devil with the very same weapons with which this enemy of mankind had proposed to destroy him."

King Louis would also say that the Christian religion as defined in the creed was something in which we ought to believe implicitly, even though our belief in it might be founded on hearsay. On this point he asked me what was my father's name. I told him it was Simon. So he asked me how I knew it, and I replied that I thought I was certain of it, and believed it without question, because I had my mother's word for it. "Then," said he, "you ought to have a sure belief in all the articles of our faith on the word of the Apostles, which you hear sung of a Sunday in the Creed."

On one occasion the king repeated to me what Guillaume, Bishop of Paris, had told him about a certain eminent theologian who had come to see him. This man told the bishop that he wished to speak with him. "Speak as freely as you like, sir," said the bishop. However, when the theologian tried to speak to him he only burst into tears. So the bishop said: "Say what you have to say, sir; don't be disheartened; no one can be such a sinner that God can no longer forgive him." "Indeed, my lord," said the theologian, "I cannot control my tears. For I fear I must be an apostate, since I cannot compel my heart to believe in the sacrament of the altar, in the way that Holy Church teaches. Yet I know very well that this is a temptation of the Enemy."

"Pray tell me, sir," said the bishop, "do you feel any pleasure when the Enemy exposes you to this temptation?" "On the contrary, my lord," said the theologian, "it worries me as much as anything can." "Now," said

---

[1] "The Enemy" is the devil.

the bishop, "I will ask you whether you would accept any gold or silver if it were offered you on condition you allowed your mouth to utter anything derogatory to the sacrament of the altar, or the other sacraments of Holy Church?" "My lord," said the other, "I can assure you that nothing in the world would induce me to do so. I would rather have one of my limbs torn from my body than consent to say such a thing."

"I will now," said the bishop, "take a different approach. You know that the King of France is at war with the King of England; you also know that the castle nearest the boundary-line between their two domains is the castle of Rochelle in Poitou. So I will ask you a question: Suppose the king had set you to guard the castle of Rochelle, and had put me in charge of the castle of Montlhéri, which is in the very center of France, where the land is at peace, to which of us do you think the king would feel most indebted at the end of the war—to you who had guarded La Rochelle without loss, or to me who had remained in safety at Montlhéri?" "Why, in God's name, my lord," cried the theologian, "to me, who had guarded La Rochelle, and not lost it to the enemy."

"Sir," said the bishop, "my heart is like the castle of Montlhéri; for I have neither temptation nor doubts concerning the sacrament of the altar. For this reason I tell you that if God owes me any grace because my faith is secure and untroubled, He owes four times as much to you, who have kept your heart from defeat when beset by tribulations, and have moreover such good-will towards Him that neither worldly advantage, nor fear of any harm that might be done to your body, could tempt you to renounce Him. So I tell you to be comforted; for your state is more pleasing to Our Lord than mine." When the theologian heard this, he knelt before the bishop, at peace with himself, and well satisfied.

The king once told me how several men from among the Albigenses[1] had gone to the count of Montfort, who at the time was guarding their land for his Majesty, and asked him to come and look at the body of our Lord, which had become flesh and blood in the hands of the priest. The count had answered: "Go and see it for yourselves, you who do not believe it. As for me, I believe it firmly, in accordance with Holy Church's teaching on the sacrament of the altar. And do you know," he added, "what I shall gain for having, in this mortal life, believed what Holy Church teaches us? I shall have a crown in heaven, and a finer one than the angels, for they see God face to face and consequently cannot but believe."

King Louis also spoke to me of a great assembly of clergy and Jews which had taken place at the monastery of Cluny. There was a poor knight there at the time to whom the abbot had often given bread for the love of God. This knight asked the abbot if he could speak first, and his request was granted, though somewhat grudgingly. So he rose to his feet, and leaning on his crutch, asked to have the most important and most learned rabbi among the Jews brought before him. As soon as the Jew had come, the knight asked him a question. "May I know, sir," he said, "if you believe that the Virgin Mary, who bore our Lord in her body and cradled Him in her arms, was a virgin at the time of His birth, and is in truth the Mother of God?"

The Jew replied that he had no belief in any of those things. Thereupon the knight told the Jew that he had acted like a fool when—neither believing in the Virgin, nor loving her—he had set foot in that monastery which was her house. "And by heaven," exclaimed the knight, "I'll make you pay for it!" So he lifted his crutch and struck the Jew such a blow with it near the ear that he knocked him down. Then all the Jews took to flight, and carried their sorely wounded rabbi away with them. Thus the conference ended.

The abbot went up to the knight and told him he had acted most unwisely. The knight retorted that the abbot had been guilty of even greater folly in calling people together for such a conference, because there were many good Christians there who, before the discussion ended, would have gone away with doubts about their own religion through not fully understanding the Jews. "So I tell you," said the king, "that no one, unless he is an expert theologian, should venture to argue with these people. But a layman, whenever he hears the Christian religion abused, should not attempt to defend its tenets, except with his sword, and that he should thrust into the scoundrel's belly, and as far as it will enter."

CHAPTER 2: *THE SERVANT OF HIS PEOPLE*

In the midst of attending to the affairs of his realm King Louis so arranged his day that he had time to hear the Hours[2] sung by a full choir and a Requiem mass without

---

[1] The "Albigenses" (or Albigensians), like the Cathars and Manichaeans, was another name for those who called themselves "good men." For a document from the inquisition of an accused member of this group by the bishop of Pamiers, see above, p. 405.

[2] The Hours refers to the daily offices of prayer.

music. In addition, if it was convenient, he would hear low mass for the day, or high mass on Saints' days. Every day after dinner he rested on his bed, and when he had slept and was refreshed, he and one of his chaplains would say the Office for the Dead privately in his room. Later in the day he attended vespers, and compline at night.

A Franciscan friar once came to see him at the castle of Hyères, where we had disembarked on our return to France. In his sermon, intended for the king's instruction, he said that in his reading of the Bible and other books that speak of non-Christian princes he had never found, in the history of either heathen or Christian peoples, that a kingdom had been lost or had changed its ruler, except where justice had been ignored. "Therefore," said he, "let the king who is now returning to France[1] take good care to see that he administers justice well and promptly to his people, so that our Lord may allow him to rule his kingdom in peace to the end of his days." I have been told that the worthy man who taught the king this lesson lies buried at Marseille, where our Lord, for his sake, still performs many a fine miracle. He would never consent to remain with the king for more than a single day, however strongly his Majesty pressed him to stay. All the same, the king never forgot the good friar's teaching, but governed his kingdom well and faithfully according to God's law.

In dealing with each day's business, the king's usual plan was to send for Jean de Nesles, the good count of Soissons, and the rest of us, as soon as we had heard mass, and tell us to go and hear the pleadings at the gate of the city which is now called the Gate of Requests.

After he had returned from church the king would send for us, and sitting at the foot of his bed would make us all sit round him, and ask us if there were any cases that could not be settled except by his personal intervention. After we had told him which they were, he would send for the interested parties and ask them: "Why did you not accept what our people offer?" "Your Majesty," they would reply, "because they offer us too little." Then he would say: "You would do well to accept whatever they are willing to give you." Our saintly king would thus do his utmost to bring them round to a right and reasonable way of thinking.

In summer, after hearing mass, the king often went to the wood of Vincennes, where he would sit down with his back against an oak, and make us all sit round him. Those who had any suit to present could come to speak to him without hindrance from an usher or any other person. The king would address them directly, and ask: "Is there anyone here who has a case to be settled?" Those who had one would stand up. Then he would say: "Keep silent all of you, and you shall be heard in turn, one after the other." Then he would call Peter de Fontaines and Geoffry de Villette, and say to one or other of them: "Settle this case for me." If he saw anything needing correction in what was said by those who spoke on his behalf or on behalf of any other person, he would himself intervene to make the necessary adjustment.

I have sometimes seen him, in summer, go to administer justice to his people in the public gardens in Paris, dressed in a plain woolen tunic, a sleeveless overcoat of linsey-woolsey,[2] and a black taffeta cape round his shoulders, with his hair neatly combed, but no cap to cover it, and only a hat of white peacock's feathers on his head. He would have a carpet laid down so that we might sit round him, while all those who had any case to bring before him stood round about. Then he would pass judgment on each case, as I have told you he often used to do in the wood of Vincennes.

I saw the king on another occasion, at a time when all the French prelates had said they wished to speak with him, and he had gone to his palace to hear what they had to say. Bishop Guy of Auxerre, the son of William de Mello, was among those present, and he addressed the king on behalf of all the prelates. "Your Majesty," he said, "the Lords Spiritual of this realm here present, have directed me to tell you that the cause of Christianity, which it is your duty to guard and defend, is being ruined in your hands." On hearing these words the king crossed himself and said: "Pray tell me how that may be."

"Your Majesty," said the bishop, "it is because at the present time excommunications are so lightly regarded that people think nothing of dying without seeking absolution, and refuse to make their peace with the Church. The Lords Spiritual[3] require you therefore, for the love of God and because it is your duty, to command your provosts and your bailiffs[4] to seek out all those who allow

---

1   "France" refers to the Ile-de-France. Hyères was (and is) in Provence. Joinville is again referring to the king's return from the Seventh Crusade.

2   A coarse woven fabric made of wool and linen.

3   I.e., the bishops.

4   Provosts and bailiffs were royal officers.

themselves to remain under the ban of the Church[1] for a year and a day, and compel them, by seizure of their possessions, to get themselves absolved."

The king replied that he would willingly give such orders provided he himself could be shown without any doubt that the persons concerned were in the wrong. The bishop told him that the prelates would not on any account accept this condition, since they questioned his right to adjudicate in their affairs. The king replied that he would not do anything other than he had said; for it would be against God and contrary to right and justice if he compelled any man to seek absolution when the clergy were doing him wrong.

"As an example of this," he continued, "I will quote the case of the Count of Brittany, who for seven whole years, while under sentence of excommunication, pleaded his cause against the bishops of his province, and carried his case so far that in the end the Pope condemned all his adversaries. Now, if at the end of the first year I had forced the count to seek absolution, I should have sinned against God and against the man himself." So the prelates resigned themselves to accepting things as they were; and I have never heard tell that any further demand was made in relation to this matter.

In making peace with the King of England, King Louis acted against the advice of his council, who had said to him: "It seems to us that Your Majesty is needlessly throwing away the land you are giving to the King of England; for he has no right to it, since it was justly taken from his father." To this the king replied that he was well aware that the King of England had no right to the land, but there was a reason why he felt bound to give it to him. "You see," said he, "our wives are sisters and consequently our children are first cousins. That is why it is most important for us to be at peace with each other. Besides, I gain increased honor for myself through the peace I have made with the King of England, for he is now my vassal, which he has never been before."

The king's love for fair and open dealing may be gathered from his behavior in the case of a certain Renaud de Trit. This man had brought the king a charter stating that he had granted the county of Dammartin in Gouelle to the heirs of the late countess of Boulogne. However, the seal of the charter was broken, so that nothing remained of it except half the legs of the figure representing the king, and the stool on which his feet were resting. The king showed the seal to all of us who were members of his council, and asked us to help him come to a decision. We all unanimously expressed the opinion that he was not bound to put the charter into effect. Then he told Jean Sarrasin, his chamberlain, to hand him a charter he had asked him to get. As soon as this was in his hands the king said to us: "My lords, here is the seal I used before I went overseas, and you can clearly tell from looking at it that the impression on the broken seal corresponds exactly with that of the one that is whole. Therefore I could not, with a clear conscience, keep back this land." So the king sent for Renaud de Trit and said to him: "I restore your county to you."

7.17 The commons participate: *Summons of Representatives of Shires and Towns to Parliament* (1295). Original in Latin.

In 1264, the English rebel Simon de Montfort (1208–1265) called members of the commons in both town and country to a meeting of parliament. It became a precedent for subsequent assemblies. When King Edward I (r.1272–1307) issued summonses to a parliament of 1295, he sent out letters individually to the members of the higher clergy and his barons. At the same time, as the document here shows, he sent letters to the sheriffs of the realm to summon representatives of "the knights, citizens, and burgesses"—the commons.

[Source: *Translations and Reprints from the Original Sources of European History,* vol. 1, no. 6, *English Constitutional Documents*, ed. Edward Potts Cheyney (Philadelphia: Department of History of the University of Pennsylvania, 1902), p. 35.]

---

[1] "The ban of the church," was excommunication.

The king to the sheriff of Northamptonshire.

Since we intend to have a consultation and meeting with the earls, barons and other principal men of our kingdom with regard to providing remedies against the dangers which are in these days threatening the same kingdom, and on that account have commanded them to be with us on the Lord's day next after the feast of St. Martin,[1] in the approaching winter, at Westminster, to consider, ordain, and do as may be necessary for the avoidance of these dangers, we strictly require you to cause two knights from the aforesaid county, two citizens from each city in the same county, and two burgesses from each borough, of those who are especially discreet and capable of laboring, to be elected without delay, and to cause them to come to us at the aforesaid time and place.

Moreover, the said knights are to have full and sufficient power for themselves and for the community of the aforesaid county, and the said citizens and burgesses for themselves and the communities of the aforesaid cities and boroughs separately, then and there for doing what shall then be ordained according to the common counsel in the premises, so that the aforesaid business shall not remain unfinished in any way for defect of this power. And you shall have there the names of the knights, citizens and burgesses and this writ.

Witness the king at Canterbury, on the third day of October.

[Identical summonses were sent to the sheriffs of each county.]

7.18 The pope throws down the gauntlet: Boniface VIII, *Clericis laicos* (1296). Original in Latin.

Preparing for war against one another, kings Philip IV of France and Edward I of England taxed their clergy along with everyone else. But Pope Boniface VIII (1294–1303) vehemently objected, arguing in his bull *Clericis laicos* that laymen, even rulers, had "no control over the clergy," calling on clerics not to give in to royal demands, and threatening excommunication of all who ignored him. In response, Philip prohibited any gold or silver from leaving France, thus depriving the pope of a major revenue source. For his part, Edward declared the English clergy "outlaw"—that is, outside the protection of the law. Boniface backed down. Looking back at Gregory VII's *Letter to Hermann of Metz* on p. 260, how new would you consider Boniface's complaints about secular rulers and his notions of papal powers and rights?

[Source: *Translations and Reprints from the Original Sources of European History*, vol. 3, no. 6, *The Pre-Reformation Period*, ed. James Harvey Robinson (Philadelphia: Department of History of the University of Pennsylvania, 1907), pp. 23–25.]

Bishop Boniface, servant of the servants of God, in perpetual memory of this matter. Antiquity shows us that the laity has always been exceeding hostile to the clergy; and this the experience of the present time clearly demonstrates, since, not content with their limitations, the laity strive for forbidden things and give free reign to the pursuit of illicit gain.

They do not prudently observe that all control over the clergy, as well as over all ecclesiastical persons and their possessions, is denied them, but impose heavy burdens upon the prelates of the churches, upon the churches themselves, and upon ecclesiastical persons both regular and secular, exacting tallages[2] and other contributions from them. From such persons they require and extort

---

[1] I.e., the first Sunday after November 11.

[2] I.e., taxes.

the payment of a half, a tenth, a twentieth or some other quota of their property or income, and strive in many other ways to subject the churchmen to slavery and bring them under their control.

And (with grief do we declare it) certain prelates of the churches and ecclesiastical persons, fearing where they ought not to fear, and seeking a temporary peace, dreading to offend a temporal more than the eternal majesty, do, without having received the permission or sanction of the Apostolic See, acquiesce in such abuses, not so much from recklessness, as want of foresight. We, therefore, desiring to check these iniquitous practices, by the council of our brothers, do, of our apostolic authority, decree that whatever prelates and ecclesiastical persons, whether monastic or secular, whatever their order, condition or status, shall pay, or promise or agree to pay to laymen, any contributions or tallages, tenths, twentieths, or hundredths of their own, or their churches' revenues or possessions, or shall pay any sum, portion or part of their revenues or goods, or of their estimated or actual value, in the form of an aid, loan, subvention, subsidy or gift, or upon any other pretense or fiction whatsoever, without authority from this same Apostolic See,—likewise emperors, kings and princes, dukes, counts, barons, podestà, captains, officers, rectors, whatever their title, of cities, castles or other places wherever situated, or any other persons, whatever their rank, condition or status, who shall impose, exact or receive such payments, or who shall presume to lay hands upon, seize or occupy the possessions of churches or the goods of ecclesiastical persons deposited in the sacred edifices, or who shall order such to be seized or occupied, or shall receive such things as shall be seized or occupied,—likewise all who shall consciously lend aid, council or support in such undertakings, either publicly or privately,—shall, by the very act, incur the sentence of excommunication; corporations, moreover, which shall show themselves guilty in these matters, we place under the interdict.[1]

We strictly command all prelates and ecclesiastical persons above mentioned, in virtue of their obedience, and under penalty of deposition, that they shall not hereafter acquiesce in any such demands, without the express permission of the aforesaid Chair.[2] Nor shall they pay anything under pretext of any obligation, promise or declaration made in the past, or which may be made before this notice, prohibition or order shall be brought to their attention. Nor shall the above-mentioned laymen in any way receive any such payments. And if the former pay or the latter receive anything, they shall incur, by the act itself, the sentence of excommunication. No one, moreover, shall be freed from the above mentioned sentences of excommunication or of the interdict, except in the article of death, without the authority and special permission of the Apostolic See, since it is our intention to make no kind of compromise with such a horrible abuse of the secular power; and this notwithstanding any privileges, whatever their tenor, form or wording, conceded to emperors, kings or other persons above mentioned, for we will that such concessions as are in conflict with the preceding prohibitions shall avail no individual person or persons. Let no man at all, therefore, violate the page of this our decree, prohibition or order, or with rash assumption, contravene it. Whoever shall presume to attempt this, let him know that he shall incur the indignation of omnipotent God and of the blessed Peter and Paul, His apostles.

Given at Rome, at Saint Peter's, on the sixth day before the Kalends of March, in the second year of our Pontificate.

---

[1] The interdict deprived people in a particular area or district of the benefit of many of the sacraments.

[2] I.e., the Apostolic See.

7.19 The pope reacts again: Boniface VIII, *Unam sanctam* (1302). Original in Latin.

In 1301, King Philip IV of France arrested—on charges of treason—the bishop of Pamiers, Bernard Saisset (*c.*1232–*c.*1314), whom Boniface had named to the post without royal approval. Like Becket some 130 years before in England, Boniface demanded that the bishop be tried in a church court. In *Unam sanctam* he affirmed the superior power of the pope. Soon thereafter, he excommunicated Philip. How might you compare his claims for papal power in this bull with his assertions in *Clericis laicos*, above, p. 423?

[Source: *Translations and Reprints from the Original Sources of European History*, vol. 3, no. 6, *The Pre-Reformation Period*, ed. James Harvey Robinson (Philadelphia: Department of History of the University of Pennsylvania, 1907), pp. 20–23 (notes added).]

That there is one Holy Catholic and Apostolic Church we are impelled by our faith to believe and to hold—this we do firmly believe and openly confess—and outside of this there is neither salvation or remission of sins, as the bridegroom proclaims in Canticles, "My dove, my undefiled is but one; she is the only one of her mother; she is the choice one of her that bare her."[1] The Church represents one mystic body and of this body Christ is the head; of Christ, indeed, God is the head. In it is one Lord, and one faith, and one baptism. In the time of the flood, there was one ark of Noah, pre-figuring the one Church, finished in one cubit, having one Noah as steersman and commander. Outside of this, all things upon the face of the earth were, as we read, destroyed. This Church we venerate and this alone, the Lord saying through his prophets, "Deliver my soul, O God, from the sword; my darling from the power of the dog."[2] He prays thus for the soul, that is for Himself, as head, and also for the body which He calls one, namely, the Church on account of the unity of the bridegroom, of the faith, of the sacraments, and of the charity of the Church. It is that seamless coat of the Lord, which was not rent, but fell by lot.[3] Therefore, in this one and only Church, there is one body and one head,—not two heads as if it were a monster—namely, Christ and Christ's Vicar, Peter and Peter's successor, for the Lord said to Peter himself, "Feed my sheep:"[4] *my* sheep, he said, using a general term and not designating these or those sheep, so that we must believe that all the sheep were committed to him. If, then, the Greeks, or others, shall say that they were not entrusted to Peter and his successors, they must perforce admit that they are not of Christ's sheep, as the lord says in John, "there is one fold, and one shepherd."[5]

In this Church and in its power are two swords, to wit, a spiritual and a temporal, and this we are taught by the words of the Gospel, for when the Apostles said, "Behold, here are two swords"[6] (in the Church, namely, since the Apostles were speaking), the Lord did not reply that it was too many, but enough. And surely he who claims that the temporal sword is not in the power of Peter has but ill understood the word of our Lord when he said, "Put up thy sword in its scabbard."[7] Both, therefore, the spiritual and the material swords, are in the power of the Church, the latter indeed to be used for the Church, the former by the Church, the one by the priest, the other by the hand of kings and soldiers, but by the will and sufferance of the priest. It is fitting, moreover, that one sword should be under the other, and the temporal authority

---

1 See Song of Sol. 5: 2 and 6: 8.

2 Ps. 22: 20; Douay Ps. 21: 21.

3 See John 19: 23–24.

4 John 21: 15–17.

5 John 10: 16.

6 Luke 22: 38.

7 John 18: 11.

subject to the spiritual power. For when the Apostle said, "there is no power but of God and the powers that are of God are ordained," they would not be disposed in an orderly manner unless one sword were guided by the performance of the most exalted deeds. For, according to the Holy Dionysius,[1] the law of divinity is to lead the lowest through the intermediate to the highest. Therefore, according to the law of the universe, things are not reduced to order directly, and upon the same footing, but the lowest through the intermediate, and the inferior through the superior. It behooves us, therefore, the more freely to confess that the spiritual power excels in dignity and nobility any form whatsoever of earthly power, as spiritual interests exceed the temporal in importance. All this we see fairly from the giving of tithes, from the benediction and sanctification, from the recognition of this power and the control of these same things. For the truth bearing witness, it is for the spiritual power to establish the earthly power and judge it, if it be not good. Thus, in the case of the Church and the power of the Church, the prophecy of Jeremiah is fulfilled: "See, I have this day set thee over the nations and over the kingdoms"[2]—and so forth. Therefore, if the earthly power shall err, it shall be judged by the spiritual power; if the lesser spiritual power err, it shall be judged by the higher. But if the supreme power err, it can be judged by God alone and not by man, the apostles bearing witness saying, the spiritual man judges all things but he himself is judged by no one. Hence this power, although given to man and exercised by man, is not human, but rather a divine power, given by the divine lips to Peter, and founded on a rock for Him and his successors in Him [Christ] whom he confessed, the Lord saying to Peter himself, "Whatsoever thou shalt bind," etc.[3] Whoever, therefore, shall resist this power, ordained by God, resists the ordination of God, unless there should be two beginnings, as the Manichaean imagines. But this we judge to be false and heretical, since, by the testimony of Moses, not in the *beginnings*, but in the *beginning*, God created the heaven and the earth. We, moreover, proclaim, declare and pronounce that it is altogether necessary to salvation for every human being to be subject to the Roman Pontiff.

Given at the Lateran the twelfth day before the Kalends of December, in our eighth year, as a perpetual memorial of this matter.

7.20 The French king responds to Boniface: William of Plaisians, *Charges of Heresy against Boniface VIII* (1303). Original in Latin.

In the wake of *Unam sanctam*, William of Plaisians—a councilor to King Philip IV well trained in the law—claimed that Boniface was a heretic and drew up a bill of particulars that he presented at a great assembly of high churchmen and nobles at Paris. There was indeed some question about Boniface's election as pope, but mainly the charges below were invented—pure propaganda aimed at arousing public opinion. In that they were successful. Taking *Clericis laicos* and *Unam sanctam* into account, and considering how Guillaume Austatz defended himself against charges of heresy (above, p. 405), write what you think might be Boniface's replies to these charges.

[Source: *Philip the Fair and Boniface VIII: State vs. Papacy*, ed. Charles T. Wood, 2nd ed. (New York: Holt, Rinehart and Winston, 1967), pp. 64–65 (notes added).]

---

[1] Now known as Pseudo-Dionysius, a Syrian thinker (*fl. c.*500).

[2] Jer. 1: 10.

[3] A reference to Matt. 16: 18–19, where Jesus refers to Peter as the "rock" upon which he will build his church. The papacy was fond of quoting this as a foundational text.

I, William of Plaisians, say, advance, and affirm that Boniface, who now occupies the Holy See, will be found a perfect heretic, according to the heresies, prodigious facts, and perverse doctrines hereafter mentioned:

1. He does not believe in the immortality or incorruptibility of the rational soul, but believes that the rational soul is corrupted along with the body.

2. He does not believe in the life eternal,... and he has not been ashamed to assert that he would rather be a dog, ass, or any other brute than a Frenchman, which he would not say if he believed that a Frenchman had a soul....

4. He does not faithfully believe that, because of the words instituted by Christ, spoken by a faithful and ordained priest over a Host in the way set by the Church, it becomes the true body of Christ....

6. He is reported to claim that fornication is no more a sin than is rubbing one's hands together: and this he has said loudly and publicly.

7. He has often said that if nothing else could be done to humble the king and the French, he would ruin himself, the whole world, and the whole Church....

9. To perpetuate his most damnable memory he has had silver statues of himself erected in churches, in this way leading men into idolatry.

10. He has a private demon whose advice he follows in all things. Whence he has once said that if all the men in the world were on one side and he on the other, they could not deceive him, either in law or in deed, which is impossible unless he employs the demonic art. And all this is publicly known.

11. He is a soothsayer who consults diviners and oracles. And all this is publicly known.

12. He has publicly preached that the Roman pontiff cannot commit simony,[1] which is heretical to say....

14. Like a confirmed heretic, who claims the true faith as his alone, he has termed the French, notoriously a most Christian people, heretics....

15. He is a Sodomite and keeps concubines. And this is publicly and commonly known.

16. He has had many clerks killed in his presence, rejoicing in their deaths....

17. When he condemned a certain noble to prison, despite the latter's penitent pleas he forbade anyone to minister the sacrament of penance at the hour of death; from which it seems he believes that the sacrament of penance is not necessary for salvation.

18. He has compelled priests to violate the secrets of the confessional and, without the assent of those who confessed, has made their confessions public to their confusion and shame....

19. He fasts neither on fast days nor in Lent....

20. He has lowered and debased the status and rank of the cardinals, the black and white monks, and the Friars Minor and Preacher, often repeating that the world was being ruined by them, that they were false hypocrites, and that nothing good would happen to anyone who confessed to them....

21. Seeking to destroy the faith, he has long harbored an aversion against the king of France, in hatred of the faith, because in France there is and ever was the splendor of the faith, the grand support and example of Christendom....

23. It is notorious that the Holy Land has been lost as a result of his sins....

24. He is openly termed a simonist, indeed the font and source of simony, selling benefices to the highest bidder, imposing on the Church and bishops both serfdom and the *taille*,[2] so that he may enrich his family and friends with the patrimony of the Crucified and make them marquises, counts, and barons....

25. It is notorious that he has dissolved many legitimately consummated marriages against the precept of the Lord and to the hurt and scandal of many; and he raised to the cardinalate his married nephew, a man wholly unworthy and inexperienced, one who led and leads a notoriously dissolute life, while his wife was alive.... And all this is publicly known.[3]

26. It is notorious that he treated his predecessor Celestine inhumanely, a man of holy memory who led a holy life;[4] and that, because Celestine could not resign

---

[1] Simony was the purchasing of church offices; its name derived from Simon Magus, who in Acts 8: 18–24 offered money to Peter and John if they would give him the power to confer the Holy Spirit.

[2] *Taille* was a tax.

[3] Francesco Caetani, cardinal of Santa Maria in Cosmedin (r.1295–1317), was Boniface's nephew.

[4] Pope Celestine V (1294) had been a hermit and the founder of the Celestines. Almost as soon as he was elected pope, he wanted to abdicate, and his advisor, Benedetto Caetani, later Boniface VIII, encouraged him in this. Once out of office, Celestine was put into custody, for fear that he might become the focal point of a papal schism. But he appears to have died of natural causes.

and because, therefore, Boniface could not legitimately succeed to the Holy See, the latter threw him in prison and had him quickly and secretly killed. And all this is widely and publicly known by the whole world....

29. It is notorious that he seeks not the salvation of souls, but their perdition.

7.21 Assembly of the Estates General in Paris: *Grand Chronicles of France* (1314). Original in French.

The Estates General of France was roughly comparable to the English parliament, though it was not called so regularly, and it originated later. It was an assembly of the "estates" or "orders": the higher clergy, the nobles, and—sometimes—the non-noble laymen from the towns. The king called it together when he thought it would be in his interest: the first meeting was in 1302, when Philip the Fair and Boniface were in dispute. In fact, William of Plaisians's charges of heresy against Boniface VIII (see above, p. 426) were presented to one of the earliest such assemblies, held in Paris in 1303. That one did not include non-noble laity. But in 1314 the king called another meeting to get revenue, and this time he summoned the third estate as well. The meeting was described in the so-called *Grand Chronicles of France*, an ongoing, semi-official history written at Saint-Denis close to the time of the events it described.

[Source: *Medieval Representative Institutions: Their Origins and Nature*, ed. Thomas N. Bisson (Hinsdale, IL: The Dryden Press, 1973), p. 79 (slightly modified).]

In this year [1314], on the feast of St. Peter, August 1st, Philip the Fair, king of France, assembled numerous barons and bishops at Paris; and in addition he caused burghers of each city of the kingdom to be summoned. When they were assembled in the palace of Paris on the day aforesaid, Enguerran de Marigny, knight, chamberlain[1] to King Philip of France and governor of the whole kingdom, mounted a platform, at the king's order, with the king and the prelates and the barons who were sitting there on the said platform, where he was manifest to all, and preached to the people there before the platform as well as to the prelates aforesaid, making known the king's need and why he had caused them to come and convene.

[There follows Marigny's speech on the troubles with Flanders.]

Wherefore the said Enguerran on behalf of the king told the burghers of the communes assembled there that he wanted to know which of them would give him aid, or not, to mount an army against the Flemings in Flanders. And as Enguerran said this, his lord the king of France arose from his seat to see those who wanted to grant him aid. Then arose Stephen Barbete, burgher of Paris, and spoke for the said town, and represented the townsfolk, saying that they were all ready to give him aid, each as he was able, and even according to possibility, to go where he would lead them, at their own expense, against the said Flemings. And so the king thanked them. And after the said Stephen, all the burghers who had come there for the communes, responded that they would willingly give him aid, and the king thanked them.

---

[1] The chamberlain had access to the king's bedchamber and was thus among his most intimate courtiers.

MODES OF THOUGHT, FEELING, AND DEVOTION

7.22 Scholasticism: Thomas Aquinas, *Summa against the Gentiles* (1259–1264). Original in Latin.

Thomas Aquinas (*c.*1225–1274) was a Dominican, a university professor of theology, and perhaps the best known of the medieval scholastics—scholars who approached broad and significant topics systematically, using the tools of Aristotelian logic as their scaffolding. By his day, the entire corpus of Aristotle's works was available in Latin, and Thomas shows easy familiarity with all of it. He wrote the *Summa against the Gentiles* as a guide for missionaries working to convert the Muslims. For this reason, most of its arguments involved theological ideas that could be set forth through philosophy alone, without the aid of biblical revelation. Book 1 takes up the nature of God; Book 2 considers God's Creation and the nature of created creatures; Book 3 argues that the purpose of all creation, including human actions, institutions, and governments, is God; Book 4 takes up the topics that rely on revelation: the Trinity, the Incarnation, the sacraments, and so on. The excerpt below is from Book 3. Here Thomas discusses fornication and marriage. He begins, as always, with a proposition contrary to his own view: that "simple fornication is not a sin." He provides some arguments on its behalf, but in the main he refutes it. What developments in medieval logic do you see when considering the work of Avicenna, *Treatise on Logic*, above, p. 203; Abelard, *Glosses on Porphyry*, above, p. 288; and this work by Thomas? How does Thomas's view of the nature and obligations of sex and marriage accord with and differ from your own?

[Source: *Summa contra gentiles*, Book 3: *Providence*, Part II, trans. and ed. Vernon J. Bourke (Notre Dame, IN: University of Notre Dame Press, 1956), pp. 142–47, 150–52 (slightly modified).]

Chapter 122: The Reason Why Simple Fornication Is a Sin According to Divine Law, and That Matrimony Is Natural

[1] From the foregoing we can see the futility of the argument of certain people who say that simple fornication is not a sin. For they say: Suppose there is a woman who is not married, or under the control of any man, either her father or another man. Now, if a man performs the sexual act with her, and she is willing, he does not injure her, because she favors the action and she has control over her own body. Nor does he injure any other person, because she is understood to be under no other person's control. So, this does not seem to be a sin.

[2] Now, to say that he injures God would not seem to be an adequate answer. For we do not offend God except by doing something contrary to our own good, as has been said. But this does not appear contrary to man's good. Hence, on this basis, no injury seems to be done to God.

[3] Likewise, it also would seem an inadequate answer to say that some injury is done to one's neighbor by this action, inasmuch as he may be scandalized. Indeed, it is possible for him to be scandalized by something which is not in itself a sin. In this event, the act would be accidentally sinful. But our problem is not whether simple fornication is accidentally a sin, but whether it is so essentially.

[4] Hence, we must look for a solution in our earlier considerations. We have said that God exercises care over every person on the basis of what is good for him. Now, it is good for each person to attain his end, whereas it is bad for him to swerve away from his proper end. Now, this should be considered applicable to the parts, just as it is to the whole being; for instance, each and every part of man, and every one of his acts, should attain the proper end. Now, though the male semen is superfluous in regard to

the preservation of the individual, it is nevertheless necessary in regard to the propagation of the species. Other superfluous things, such as excrement, urine, sweat, and such things, are not at all necessary; hence, their emission contributes to man's good. Now, this is not what is sought in the case of semen, but, rather, to emit it for the purpose of generation, to which purpose the sexual act is directed. But man's generative process would be frustrated unless it were followed by proper nutrition, because the offspring would not survive if proper nutrition were withheld. Therefore, the emission of semen ought to be so ordered that it will result in both the production of the proper offspring and in the upbringing of this offspring.

[5] It is evident from this that every emission of semen in such a way that generation cannot follow, is contrary to the good for man. And if this be done deliberately, it must be a sin. Now, I am speaking of a way from which, *in itself*, generation could not result: such would be any emission of semen apart from the natural union of male and female. For which reason, sins of this type are called *contrary to nature*. But, if by accident generation cannot result from the emission of semen, then this is not a reason for it being against nature, or a sin; as for instance, if the woman happens to be sterile.

[6] Likewise, it must also be contrary to the good for man if the semen be emitted under conditions such that generation could result but the proper upbringing would be prevented. We should take into consideration the fact that, among some animals where the female is able to take care of the upbringing of offspring, male and female do not remain together for any time after the act of generation. This is obviously the case with dogs. But in the case of animals of which the female is not able to provide for the upbringing of offspring, the male and female do stay together after the act of generation as long as is necessary for the upbringing and instruction of the offspring. Examples are found among certain species of birds whose young are not able to seek out food for themselves immediately after hatching. In fact, since a bird does not nourish its young with milk, made available by nature as it were, as occurs in the case of quadrupeds, but the bird must look elsewhere for food for its young, and since besides this it must protect them by sitting on them, the female is not able to do this by herself. So, as a result of divine providence, there is naturally implanted in the male of these animals a tendency to remain with the female in order to bring up the young. Now, it is

abundantly evident that the female in the human species is not at all able to take care of the upbringing of offspring by herself, since the needs of human life demand many things which cannot be provided by one person alone. Therefore, it is appropriate to human nature that a man remain together with a woman after the generative act, and not leave her immediately to have such relations with another woman, as is the practice with fornicators.

[7] Nor, indeed, is the fact that a woman may be able by means of her own wealth to care for the child by herself an obstacle to this argument. For natural rectitude in human acts is not dependent on things accidentally possible in the case of one individual, but, rather, on those conditions which accompany the entire species.

[8] Again, we must consider that in the human species offspring require not only nourishment for the body, as in the case of other animals, but also education for the soul. For other animals naturally possess their own kinds of prudence whereby they are enabled to take care of themselves. But a man lives by reason, which he must develop by lengthy, temporal experience so that he may achieve prudence. Hence, children must be instructed by parents who are already experienced people. Nor are they able to receive such instruction as soon as they are born, but after a long time, and especially after they have reached the age of discretion. Moreover, a long time is needed for this instruction. Then, too, because of the impulsion of the passions, through which prudent judgment is vitiated,[1] they require not merely instruction but correction. Now, a woman alone is not adequate to this task; rather, this demands the work of a husband, in whom reason is more developed for giving instruction and strength is more available for giving punishment. Therefore, in the human species, it is not enough, as in the case of birds, to devote a small amount of time to bringing up offspring, for a long period of life is required. Hence, since among all animals it is necessary for male and female to remain together as long as the work of the father is needed by the offspring, it is natural to the human being for the man to establish a lasting association with a designated woman, over no short period of time. Now, we call this society *matrimony*. Therefore, matrimony is natural for man, and promiscuous performance of the sexual act, outside matrimony, is contrary to man's good. For this reason, it must be a sin.

[9] Nor, in fact, should it be deemed a slight sin for a man to arrange for the emission of semen apart from the

---

[1] Aristotle, *Nicomachean Ethics* 6.5 (1140b 19). "Vitiated" = impaired.

proper purpose of generating and bringing up children, on the argument that it is either a slight sin, or none at all, for a person to use a part of the body for a different use than that to which it is directed by nature (say, for instance, one chose to walk on his hands, or to use his feet for something usually done with the hands) because man's good is not much opposed by such inordinate use. However, the inordinate emission of semen is incompatible with the natural good; namely, the preservation of the species. Hence, after the sin of homicide whereby a human nature already in existence is destroyed, this type of sin appears to take next place, for by it the generation of human nature is precluded.

[10] Moreover, these views which have just been given have a solid basis in divine authority. That the emission of semen under conditions in which offspring cannot follow is illicit is quite clear. There is the text of Leviticus (18: 22–23): "thou shalt not lie with mankind as with womankind… and thou shalt not copulate with any beast." And in I Corinthians (6: 10): "Nor the effeminate, nor liers with mankind… shall possess the kingdom of God."

[11] Also, that fornication and every performance of the act of reproduction with a person other than one's wife are illicit is evident. For it is said: "There shall be no whore among the daughters of Israel, nor whoremonger among the sons of Israel" (Deut. 23: 17); and in Tobias (4: 13): "Take heed to keep thyself from all fornication, and beside thy wife never endure to know a crime"; and in I Corinthians (6: 18): "Fly fornication."

[12] By this conclusion we refute the error of those who say that there is no more sin in the emission of semen than in the emission of any other superfluous matter, and also of those who state that fornication is not a sin.…

Chapter 124: That Matrimony Should Be between One Man and One Woman

[1] It seems, too, that we should consider how it is inborn in the minds of all animals accustomed to sexual reproduction to allow no promiscuity; hence, fights occur among animals over the matter of sexual reproduction. And, in fact, among all animals there is one common reason, for every animal desires to enjoy freely the pleasure of the sexual act, as he also does the pleasure of food;

but this liberty is restricted by the fact that several males may have access to one female, or the converse. The same situation obtains in the freedom of enjoying food, for one animal is obstructed if the food which he desires to eat is taken over by another animal. And so, animals fight over food and sexual relations in the same way. But among men there is a special reason, for, as we said,[1] man naturally desires to know his offspring, and this knowledge would be completely destroyed if there were several males for one female. Therefore, that one female is for one male is a consequence of natural instinct.

[2] But a difference should be noted on this point. As far as the view that one woman should not have sexual relations with several men is concerned, both the aforementioned reasons apply. But, in regard to the conclusion that one man should not have relations with several females, the second argument does not work, since certainty as to offspring is not precluded if one male has relations with several women. But the first reason works against this practice, for, just as the freedom of associating with a woman at will is taken away from the husband, when the woman has another husband, so, too, the same freedom is taken away from a woman when her husband has several wives. Therefore, since certainty as to offspring is the principal good which is sought in matrimony, no law or human custom has permitted one woman to be a wife for several husbands. This was even deemed unfitting among the ancient Romans, of whom Maximus Valerius reports that they believed that the conjugal bond should not be broken even on account of sterility.[2]

[3] Again, in every species of animal in which the father has some concern for offspring, one male has only one female; this is the case with all birds that feed their young together, for one male would not be able to offer enough assistance to bring up the offspring of several females. But in the case of animals among whom there is no concern on the part of the males for their offspring, the male has promiscuous relations with several females and the female with plural males. This is so among dogs, chickens, and the like. But since, of all animals, the male in the human species has the greatest concern for offspring, it is obviously natural for man that one male should have but one wife, and conversely.

[4] Besides, friendship consists in an equality.[3] So, if it is not lawful for the wife to have several husbands, since

1 In Chapter 123, where Thomas argued that matrimony should endure for an entire lifetime.

2 Maximus Valerius, *Factorum et dictorum memorabilium* 2.1.4.

3 See Aristotle, *Nicomachean Ethics* 8.5 (1157b 36).

this is contrary to certainty as to offspring, it would not be lawful, on the other hand, for a man to have several wives, for the friendship of wife for husband would not be free, but somewhat servile. And this argument is corroborated by experience, for among husbands having plural wives the wives have a status like that of servants.

[5] Furthermore, strong friendship is not possible in regard to many people, as is evident from the Philosopher in *Ethics*, ch. 8.[1] Therefore, if a wife has but one husband, but the husband has several wives, the friendship will not be equal on both sides. So, the friendship will not be free, but servile in some way.

[6] Moreover, as we said,[2] matrimony among humans should be ordered so as to be in keeping with good moral customs. Now, it is contrary to good behavior for one man to have several wives, for the result of this is discord in domestic society, as is evident from experience. So, it is not fitting for one man to have several wives.

[7] Hence it is said: "They shall be two in one flesh" (Gen. 2: 24).

[8] By this, the custom of those having several wives is set aside, and also the opinion of Plato who maintained that wives should be common.[3] And in the Christian period he was followed by Nicolaus, one of the seven deacons.[4]

7.23 The vernacular comes into its own: Dante, *Inferno*, Canto V (Paolo and Francesca); *Paradiso*, Canto XXII (Meeting with St. Benedict) (1313–1321). Original in Italian.

Dante (1265–1321) used his native Tuscan to create a poetic language of great power. Born into a family that obtained noble status through mercantile activities (his father was a moneylender), his early aptitude for poetry was encouraged by his teachers. In his three-part poem *Divine Comedy*, Dante undertook a metaphorical journey to hell, purgatory, and heaven, meeting famous—and infamous—people along the way, and he used the experience to comment on all the issues of his day. The excerpts below, the first from the *Inferno* (Hell) and the second from *Paradiso* (Heaven), just begin to demonstrate the range of Dante's knowledge, interests, and imagination.

[Source: Dante Alighieri, *The Divine Comedy*, trans. and commentary by Charles S. Singleton, *Inferno* (Princeton, NJ: Princeton University Press, 1970), pp. 47, 49, 51, 53, 55, 57; *Paradiso* (Princeton, NJ: Princeton University Press, 1970), pp. 245, 247, 249, 251, 253 (notes added, adapted from the accompanying vols. of commentary by Singleton).]

Inferno Canto V

Thus I descended from the first circle into the second, which girds less space, and so much greater woe that it goads to wailing. There stands Minos, horrible and snarling: upon the entrance he examines their offenses, and judges and dispatches them according as he entwines.[5] I mean that when the ill-begotten soul comes before him,

---

[1] Aristotle, *Nicomachean Ethics* 8.6 (1158a 10).

[2] In Chapter 123.

[3] Plato, *Republic* 5.449D ff; *Timaeus* 18C.

[4] See St. Augustine, *De haeresibus* 5.

[5] The first circle of the nine circles of Hell is Limbo, but it is still a bit outside Hell proper. That begins where Minos—in legend a king of Crete and in Virgil's *Aeneid* a judge of men's lives in Hell—stands snarling. Since Hell is funnel-shaped, each successive circle in the descent is smaller in circumference than the one above it. While the spirits in Limbo sigh, those in the next circle wail in pain.

it confesses all; and that discerner of sins sees which shall be its place in Hell, then girds himself with his tail as many times as the grades he wills that it be sent down. Always before him stands a crowd of them; they go, each in his turn, to the judgment; they tell, and hear,[1] and then are hurled below.

"O you who come to the abode of pain," said Minos to me, when he saw me, pausing in the act of that great office, "beware how you enter and in whom you trust; let not the breadth of the entrance deceive you!" And my leader[2] [said] to him, "Why do you too cry out? Do not hinder his fated going: thus is it willed there where that can be done which is willed; and ask no more."

Now the doleful notes begin to reach me; now I am come where much wailing smites me. I came into a place mute of all light, which bellows like the sea in tempest when it is assailed by warring winds. The hellish hurricane, never resting, sweeps along the spirits with its rapine; whirling and smiting, it torments them. When they arrive before the ruin, there the shrieks, the moans, the lamentations; there they curse the divine power. I learned that to such torment are condemned the carnal sinners, who subject reason to desire.

And as their wings bear the starlings along in the cold season, in wide, dense flocks, so does that blast the sinful spirits; hither, thither, downward, upward, it drives them. No hope of less pain, not to say of rest, ever comforts them. And as the cranes go chanting their lays, making a long line of themselves in the air, so I saw shades come, uttering wails, borne by that strife; wherefore I said, "Master, who are these people that are so lashed by the black air?"

"The first of these of whom you wish to know," he said to me then, "was empress of many tongues. She was so given to lechery that she made lust licit in her law, to take away the blame she had incurred. She is Semiramis, of whom we read that she succeeded Ninus and had been his wife: she held the land the Sultan rules.[3] The next is she who slew herself for love and broke faith to the ashes of Sichaeus;[4] next is wanton Cleopatra.[5] See Helen, for whom so many years of ill revolved;[6] and see the great Achilles, who fought at the last with love.[7] See Paris, Tristan,"[8] and more than a thousand shades whom love had parted from our life he showed me, pointing them out and naming them.

When I heard my teacher name the ladies and the knights of old, pity overcame me and I was as one bewildered. "Poet," I began, "willingly would I speak with those two that go together and seem to be so light upon the wind."[9]

And he to me, "You shall see when they are nearer to us; and do you entreat them then by that love which leads them, and they will come."

As soon as the wind bends them to us, I raised my voice, "O wearied souls! come speak with us, if Another[10] forbid it not."

As doves called by desire, with wings raised and steady, come through the air, borne by their will to their sweet nest, so did these issue from the troop where Dido is, coming to us through the malignant air, such force had my compassionate cry.

"O living creature, gracious and benign, that go through the black air visiting us who stained the world with blood, if the King of the universe were friendly to us,

---

[1] The souls tell their sins and hear their judgment.

[2] Dante's "leader," "Master," and "teacher" is Virgil, whose portrayal of Aeneas's visit to the underworld is echoed by Dante in many of the images in the *Inferno*. Hence Virgil is also sometimes called "the poet."

[3] Semiramis is the Greek name of a queen of ancient Assyria. She was famous for her beauty and lust as well as for her prowess in war. Egypt, in Dante's time, was under the Sultan's rule. Apparently Dante confused Babylonia, a kingdom of the Assyrian empire, with Babylon (Old Cairo), a fortified city on the Nile.

[4] "She who slew herself for love" was Dido, Queen of Carthage, who, after mourning her husband Sichaeus, fell in love with Aeneas despite her vow to remain faithful to the memory of her husband. When Aeneas left Dido to found Rome, she stabbed herself.

[5] Cleopatra, queen of Egypt, was mistress of Julius Caesar and Mark Antony and was famous for her beauty and seductive ways.

[6] Helen was the beautiful wife of the king of Sparta. Her abduction by Paris led to the long Trojan War.

[7] In medieval romances, Achilles, the hero of the Trojan War, was in love with Polyxena and was lured to his death by a sham rendezvous with her.

[8] Tristan died for his love of Isolde.

[9] "So light upon the wind": Dante sees two spirits that are more violently tossed by the wind than the others. According to the principle of just punishment, the heightened violence of the wind signifies that their love was particularly passionate.

[10] The name of God is blasphemous in Hell. So Dante calls Him "Another."

we would pray Him for your peace, since you have pity on our perverse ill. Of that which it pleases you to hear and to speak, we will hear and speak with you, while the wind, as now, is silent for us.

"The city where I was born lies on that shore where the Po descends to be at peace with its followers.[1] Love, which is quickly kindled in a gentle heart, seized this one for the fair form that was taken from me—and the way of it afflicts me still. Love, which absolves no loved one from loving, seized me so strongly with delight in him,[2] that, as you see, it does not leave me even now. Love brought us to one death. Caina awaits him who quenched our life."[3]

These words were borne to us from them. And when I heard those afflicted souls I bowed my head and held it bowed until the poet said to me, "What are you thinking of?"

When I answered, I began, "Alas! How many sweet thoughts, what great desire, brought them to the woeful pass!"

Then I turned again to them, and I began, "Francesca, your torments make me weep for grief and pity; but tell me, in the time of the sweet sighs, by what and how did Love grant you to know the dubious desires?"

And she to me, "There is no greater sorrow than to recall, in wretchedness, the happy time; and this your teacher knows. But if you have such great desire to know the first root of our love, I will tell as one who weeps and tells. One day, for pastime, we read of Lancelot, how love constrained him; we were alone, suspecting nothing.[4] Several times that reading urged our eyes to meet and took the color from our faces, but one moment alone it was that overcame us. When we read how the longed-for smile was kissed by so great a lover, this one, who never

shall be parted from me, kissed my mouth all trembling. A Gallehault was the book and he who wrote it;[5] that day we read no farther in it." While the one spirit said this, the other wept, so that for pity I swooned, as if in death, and fell as a dead body falls.

Paradiso Canto XXII

Overwhelmed with amazement, I turned to my guide,[6] like a little child who always runs back to where it has most confidence; and she, like a mother who quickly comforts her pale and gasping son with her voice which is wont to reassure him, said to me, "Do you not know that you are in heaven, do you not know that heaven is all holy, and that whatever is done here comes of righteous zeal? How the song, and I by smiling, would have transmuted you, you can now conceive, since this cry has so much moved you;[7] wherein, had you understood their prayers, already would be known to you the vengeance which you shall see before you die. The sword of here on high cuts not in haste nor tardily, save to his deeming who in longing or in fear awaits it. But turn now to the others, for you shall see many illustrious spirits, if you direct your sight as I say."

As was her pleasure, I turned my eyes, and I saw a hundred little spheres which together were making themselves beautiful with their mutual rays. I was standing as one who within himself represses the prick of his desire, who does not make bold to ask, he so fears to exceed. And the greatest and most shining of those pearls came forward to satisfy my desire concerning itself.[8] Then within it I heard, "If you could see, as I do, the charity which

---

[1] The city is Ravenna and the speaker, who is not named until later, is Francesca, known as Francesca da Rimini (1255–1285). She was a real person, daughter of Guido da Polenta the elder, lord of Ravenna (d.1310) and the aunt of Guido Novello, Dante's host at Ravenna. She was married to Gianciotto Malatesta (d.1304). No contemporary chronicle or document mentions the love between Francesca and Paolo or their deaths, but the story is told by Boccaccio as well as by Dante.

[2] This is Paolo Malatesta (1246–1285), who is never named here. He was the brother of Gianciotto, Francesca's husband.

[3] Caina is a place in lower Hell.

[4] For Lancelot's love of Queen Guinevere, see above, p. 353.

[5] "A Gallehault was the book": In some versions of the Lancelot story, Gallehault brought Guinevere and Lancelot together for their first meeting and urged the two to kiss.

[6] After many experiences in Hell and Purgatory, Dante is now in Paradise, and his guide is no longer Virgil but Beatrice. At the most literal level, Beatrice was a Florentine woman whom Dante loved; she was the wife of Simone de' Bardi and died in 1290. But in Dante's poetry, Beatrice took on numerous spiritual meanings as well.

[7] "This cry": in Canto XXI, Dante heard a cry but did not understand its meaning.

[8] "The greatest and most shining of those pearls" is the spirit of St. Benedict, founder of Monte Cassino, author of *The Benedictine Rule* (see above, p. 17). For Dante he was the father of monasticism.

burns among us, you would have uttered your thoughts; but lest you, by waiting, be delayed in your lofty aim, I will make answer to the thought itself about which you are so circumspect.

"That mountain on whose slope Cassino lies was of old frequented on its summit by the folk deceived and perverse, and I am he who first bore up there His name who brought to earth that truth which so uplifts us; and such grace shone upon me that I drew away the surrounding towns from the impious worship that seduced the world. These other fires[1] were all contemplative men, kindled by that warmth which gives birth to holy flowers and fruits.

Here is Macarius, here is Romualdus, here are my brethren who stayed their feet within the cloisters and kept a steadfast heart."[2]

And I to him, "The affection you show in speaking with me, and the good semblance which I see and note in all your ardors, have expanded my confidence as the sun does the rose when it opens to its fullest bloom. Therefore I pray you—and do you, father, assure me if I am capable of receiving so great a grace, that I may behold you in your uncovered shape."

Whereon he, "Brother, your high desire shall be fulfilled up in the last sphere,[3] where are fulfilled all others and my own. There every desire is perfect, mature, and whole. In that alone is every part there where it always was, for it is not in space, nor has it poles; and our ladder reaches up to it, wherefore it steals itself from your sight. All the way thither the patriarch Jacob saw it stretch its upper part, when it appeared to him so laden with Angels.[4] But no one now lifts his foot from earth to ascend it, and my Rule remains for waste of paper. The walls, which used to be an abbey, have become dens, and the cowls are sacks full of foul meal. But heavy usury is not exacted so counter to God's pleasure as that fruit which makes the heart of monks so mad;[5] for whatsoever the Church has in keeping is all for the folk that ask it in God's name, not for kindred, or for other filthier thing.[6] The flesh of mortals is so soft[7] that on earth a good beginning does not last from the springing of the oak to the bearing of the acorn. Peter began his fellowship without gold or silver, and I mine with prayer and with fasting, and Francis his with humility; and if you look at the beginning of each, and then look again whither it has strayed, you will see the white changed to dark.[8] Nevertheless, Jordan driven back, and the sea fleeing when God willed, were sights more wondrous than the succor here."[9]

Thus he spoke to me, then drew back to his company, and the company closed together; then like a whirlwind all were gathered upward. My sweet lady,[10] with only a sign, thrust me up after them by that ladder, so did her power overcome my nature; nor ever here below,[11] where we mount and descend by nature's law, was motion so swift as might match my flight. So may I return, reader, to that devout triumph for the sake of which I often bewail my sins and beat my breast,[12] you would not have drawn out and put your finger into the fire so quickly as I saw the sign which follows the Bull, and was within it.[13]

---

[1] The spirits in Paradise are portrayed as radiant fires or flames.

[2] Macarius may refer to St. Macarius the Elder of Egypt (*c.*300–*c.*391) or St. Macarius the Younger of Alexandria (d.395). Both were disciples of St. Antony, for whose *Life* by Athanasius see above, p. 27. Romualdus was St. Romuald (d.1027), whose monastery at Camaldoli was strictly secluded from the world.

[3] This is the Empyrean, the summit of Heaven.

[4] In Gen. 28: 12, Jacob dreamed of a ladder reaching to heaven on which angels were ascending and descending. The ladder appears in *The Benedictine Rule* as the "steps of humility."

[5] In other words, even exorbitant usury, in which borrowers must pay high interest, is not so contrary to God's will as the Church taking money and making the monks avid for still more.

[6] Benedict wants the money to go to the poor, not to the families of churchmen or worse—to bastards and concubines.

[7] I.e., weak.

[8] Peter is St. Peter: in Acts 3: 6, he says he has no silver or gold. Francis is St. Francis of Assisi, the founder of the Franciscan Order.

[9] In other words, God rolled back the Jordan and parted the Red Sea, so do not despair.

[10] I.e., Beatrice.

[11] I.e., on earth.

[12] Dante hopes to return to Paradise.

[13] "The sign which follows the Bull," Taurus, is Gemini, the constellation under which Dante was born.

7.24 Medieval drama: *Directions for an Annunciation Play* (14th c.). Original in Latin.

Medieval drama grew out of church liturgy and the public hurly-burly of town life. By the thirteenth century many churches were acting out the events of the Annunciation (when the angel Gabriel announced to the Virgin Mary that she would "bring forth a son"). It was presented as an interlude during the mass, whether on the feast of the Annunciation itself (March 25) or during Advent (beginning the fourth Sunday before Christmas). The play employed a relatively small number of characters and some startling stagecraft. At Tournai (today in Belgium) an artificial dove—representing the Holy Spirit that impregnated Mary—descended from the cathedral vault; at Parma (in Italy) the actor portraying Gabriel himself swung down. In the version printed here, which was performed at Padua (also in Italy) in the fourteenth century, Gabriel handed the dove to Mary, who "put it under her cloak."

[Source: *Medieval Popular Religion, 1000–1500: A Reader*, ed. John Shinners (Peterborough, ON: Broadview Press, 1997), pp. 128–29 (notes added). Translated by John Shinners.]

On the day of the feast of the Annunciation, after dinner, let the great bell be rung at the usual time, and meanwhile let the clergy gather at the church; they should prepare themselves in the main sacristy,[1] some of them wearing their copes[2] and other required things. In this sacristy Mary, Elizabeth, Joseph, and Joachim[3] should stand ready with a deacon and a subdeacon holding silver books. At the appointed time they should leave the sacristy in procession and make their way to the place prepared for them. Leaving them there, the procession should continue to the baptistery where a boy should be waiting seated on a chair dressed as Gabriel. Let him be lifted up on the chair and carried from the baptistery into the church along the side aisle and taken up the steps next to the choir. The clergy should stand in the middle of the church arranged like a chorus. Meanwhile the subdeacon should begin the prophetic epistle: "The Lord spoke again to Achaz."[4] After the prophecy is finished, the deacon should start the Gospel: "The angel Gabriel was sent"[5] and proceed up to the words "And when the angel had come to her, he said." At that point, Gabriel, kneeling with two fingers of his right hand upraised,

should begin singing this antiphon in a loud voice: "Hail, Mary, full of grace, the Lord is with thee; blessed art thou among women." When this antiphon is finished, the deacon should continue reciting the Gospel up to the words "And the angel said to her." Then the Angel, again standing with his right hand completely open, should begin this antiphon: "Do not be afraid, Mary, for thou has found grace with God. Behold, thou shalt conceive in thy womb and shalt bring forth a son." When this antiphon is finished, the deacon should continue reciting up to the words "But Mary said to the angel." Then Mary should answer in a clear voice with this antiphon: "How shall this happen, angel of God, since I do not know man?" When this antiphon is finished, the deacon should continue reciting up to the words "And the angel answered and said to her"; and the Angel should again begin this verse: "Listen, Mary, virgin of Christ, the Holy Spirit shall come upon thee and the power of the Most High shall overshadow thee." But when he comes to the words "the Holy Spirit shall come upon thee," let him hold out a dove a little way from him. When this verse is finished, the deacon should continue reciting up to the

---

[1] The sacristy is the room in a church that houses the sacred vessels and vestments.

[2] A cope is a long church vestment, a sort of cloak.

[3] I.e., the actors portraying these characters in the drama. For the story of the Annunciation, see Luke 1: 26–38.

[4] Isa. 7: 10.

[5] Luke 1: 26.

words "But Mary said to the angel." When this is finished, Mary should stand up with her arms outstretched and begin saying in a loud voice, "Behold the handmaid of the Lord." Before the end of this antiphon, he should let go of the dove and Mary should take it and put it under her cloak. Antiphon: "Behold the handmaid of the Lord; be it done to me according to thy word."

When all this is ended, the deacon should continue on to the next verse, "Now in those days Mary arose and went with haste into the hill country" up to the words "And Elizabeth cried out with a loud voice, saying." Meanwhile, Mary should descend from her place and go over to where Elizabeth and Joachim are. Both of them should receive her according to the description in the Gospel. Having done this, Elizabeth should kneel, touch Mary's body with both hands, and begin this antiphon with a humble voice: "Blessed art thou among women and blessed is the fruit of thy womb!" When the anti-

phon is finished, Elizabeth should get up and, standing again, say this antiphon: "And how have I deserved that the mother of my Lord should come to me? For behold, the moment that the sound of thy greeting came to my ears, the babe in my womb leapt for joy. And blessed is she who has believed because the things promised her by the Lord shall be accomplished." When this is finished, the deacon should again continue up to "And Mary said." Then Mary should turn and face the people and in a loud voice sing at the eighth tone these three verses [i.e., the Magnificat]: "My soul magnifies the Lord, and my spirit rejoices in God my Savior; because he has regarded the lowliness of his handmaid; for, behold, henceforth all generations shall call me blessed." When this is finished, the organ should answer with one verse, and the choir with the next, and so on until the end. When this is all done, let everyone return to the sacristy.

7.25 The feast of Corpus Christi: *The Life of Juliana of Mont-Cornillon* (1261–1264). Original in Latin.

Many people, particularly women, were as devoted to the Eucharist as Juliana of Mont-Cornillon (1193–1258). Recall that when Mary of Oignies (above, p. 370) viewed the Host, she "saw between his hands the corporeal form of a beautiful boy." But Juliana, inspired by a vision, worked in addition to ensure that a special annual feast be declared for the Body of Christ (in Latin, "Corpus Christi"). Orphaned at the age of five, Juliana was raised at the house of Mont-Cornillon, a mixed institution for lepers as well as male and female religious founded by the citizens of near-by Liège. Eventually she became its prioress, was forced to leave for a time, was reinstated, and finally was forced out again. Her checkered career did not keep her from promoting Corpus Christi, and she was able to enlist the help of the canons of St. Martin of Liège, one of whom (though anonymous) very likely wrote the *Life* excerpted here. He wanted both to demonstrate Juliana's virtues and to give luster to her project. In this he may well have been successful: Jacques Pantaléon, a former archdeacon of Liège, established the feast of Corpus Christi in 1264, the last year of his pontificate as Urban IV. Taking into account the devotional life of St. Radegund (above, pp. 38 and 44), and Mary of Oignies (above, p. 370), what developments in female devotional practices can you trace? What evidence is there from the *Life of Juliana* that men, too, participated in the new Eucharistic devotion?

[Source: *The Life of Juliana of Mont-Cornillon*, trans. Barbara Newman (Toronto: Peregrina Publishing Co., [1988]), pp. 36–38, 80–84, 151.]

1.12. When she received the most holy Body of Christ, her only beloved and chosen—not only of a thousand but of all who dwell in heaven and earth[1]—then she was filled with such abundant dew of grace and devotion that her soul would melt like wax in the fire[2] and her spirit fail within her.[3] For then she would taste and see how good the Lord is[4] on receiving gifts of yet fuller grace. Indeed, in the feast of the sacred Body she experienced every delight and every savor of sweetness. For what the people of Israel received in a figure through the manna that rained down from heaven, Juliana received in reality when she partook of the living bread that came down from heaven, of which the manna was only a shadow.[5] Surely this bread tasted much sweeter and fresher, more delicious and more spiritual in Juliana's heart than the manna once did in the mouths of a carnal and stiff-necked people.

After receiving the Body of Christ our virgin liked to remain silent for at least a week. During that period she was upset by the approach of anyone whatsoever, except in the case of some great and urgent need or advantage. But you must not think that such an interval seemed long enough for her to celebrate the one she had received, for she would often tell the sisters who served her meals to give her no physical food at all for a month. Rather, they were not even to approach her, and they were to protect her from the approach of any visitors, whoever they might be. She felt certain there was such strength in the eating of that sacred bread that she did not doubt she could survive for so long, even physically, on the strength of such food. And she could easily have proved it, too, if the sisters who served her had not fallen short. But since Juliana was not given a period of rest and silence as long as she desired, she gave herself up yet again to the one she had received, the only one she loved. Utterly absorbed in spirit, the bride made way for her bridegroom. In overflowing intimate love and fervent fulfillment, she clung to him in a marvelous and ineffable union of spirit, and transformed by divine emotion, she could sense and savor nothing but God.

In short, to give you an idea of the singular privilege of grace that Christ bestowed on his handmaid when she received his Body and Blood, I need not conceal the fact that for many years before her death, whenever she received the Body of Christ (and she craved to do so often because of her boundless love), he revealed to her some new secret from his heavenly mysteries. But she concealed these secrets in such indiscreet humility (if it is right to say so) that she could justly appear to cry with the prophet, "My secret for myself! My secret for myself!"[6] Not only did she hide these secrets from strangers, but even to her closest and dearest friends she revealed them very rarely, except when she was drunk in the Spirit and could not be silent. From a tender age she was such a zealot for humility that, if anything she might say was likely to give her a reputation for saintliness, she would keep silent lest anyone think her better than she thought herself. Inwardly she despised herself, counting herself nothing in the privacy of her heart, and she did not want anyone else to prize her at a different value than she herself had decreed.

1.13. But behold! While the king was on his couch, his handmaid's nard [ointment] gave forth its fragrance.[7] From what follows, you can clearly understand how pleasing and acceptable a fragrance the sweet nard of Juliana's humility gave forth for Christ the King as he rested on his couch, that is, in the Father's bosom. He—the sublime Lord who looks upon the humble and beholds the proud from afar[8]—deigned to reveal his will to his handmaid above all mortals by means of a singular grace. To inaugurate a special feast in honor of the Sacrament of his most holy Body and Blood, a feast which Jesus Christ, the power of God and the wisdom of God, wished to be observed henceforth upon earth, he did not choose many of the noble and powerful of this world, of secular might or ecclesiastical rank. Rather, he who chose the weak of the world to confound the strong[9] wondrously chose the humble Juliana to accomplish this, having shown her a

---

[1] See Song of Sol. 5: 10.
[2] See Song of Sol. 5: 6.
[3] See Ps. 77: 3; Douay Ps. 76: 4.
[4] See Ps. 34: 8; Douay Ps. 33: 9.
[5] See John. 6: 48–51.
[6] Isa. 24: 16.
[7] See Song of Sol. 1: 11.
[8] Ps. 138: 6; Douay Ps. 137: 6.
[9] 1 Cor. 1: 24–27.

sign beforehand and divinely revealed its meaning. As for her, she prayed urgently to the Lord that such a lofty and difficult task might be imposed on someone else whose authority could achieve it more quickly. She received the reply that it should by all means begin with her, and even thereafter be promoted by humble people.

How this was revealed and accomplished, I will describe more fully at another time, if the Lord permits. But I have anticipated the subject here because in the preceding chapters I have mentioned the lifegiving Sacrament of Christ's Body and Blood, for which Christ's virgin had a marvelous affection, and also to inform readers more clearly that Christ wished to distinguish her with a special gift of his love....

2.6. From her youth, whenever Christ's virgin gave herself to prayer, she saw a great and marvelous sign. There appeared to her the full moon in its splendor, yet with a little breach in its spherical body. When she had seen this sign for a long time she was astonished, not knowing what it might mean. But she could not marvel enough over the fact that, whenever she was intent on prayer, the sign constantly impressed itself on her vision. After she had tried with all her might to make it go away, as she wished, and could not succeed, she began to trouble herself unduly in fear and trembling, thinking that she was being tempted. So she prayed and asked people she trusted to pray that the Lord would rescue her from a temptation she was suffering, as she said. But when she could not drive the importunate sign away by any effort, nor by any prayer of her own or other Christians, she finally began to wonder if perhaps, instead of trying so hard to drive it away, she should seek to discover some mystery in it.

Then Christ revealed to her that the moon was the present Church, while the breach in the moon symbolised the absence of a feast which he still desired his faithful upon earth to celebrate. This was his will for the increase of faith at the end of a senescent age, and also for the growth and grace of the elect: that once every year, the institution of the Sacrament of his Body and Blood should be recollected more solemnly and specifically than it was at the Lord's Supper, when the Church was gener-

ally preoccupied with the washing of feet and the remembrance of his Passion. On this feast of the memorial of the Sacrament, what was passed over lightly or negligently on ordinary days should be celebrated with greater attention. Christ revealed these things to his virgin, therefore, and commanded her that she herself should inaugurate this feast and be the first to tell the world it should be instituted. But Juliana, considering the sublimity of the matter and observing her own lowliness and frailty, was more astonished than words can tell. She replied that she could not do what she had been commanded. Yet every time she prayed, Christ admonished her to accept the task for which he had chosen her above all mortals. And she always answered, "Lord, release me, and give the task you have assigned me to great scholars shining with the light of knowledge, who would know how to promote such a great affair. For how could I do it? I am not worthy, Lord, to tell the world about something so noble and exalted. I could not understand it, nor could I fulfill it." But he responded that by all means, she should be the one to initiate this feast, and from then on it should be promoted by humble people. And once while she was praying, beseeching the Lord with all her heart to choose another for this task, she heard a voice saying, "I thank you, Father, Lord of heaven and earth, that you have hidden these things from the wise and understanding of this world, and revealed them to babes."[1] Even then she did not consent at once, but answered, "Rouse yourself, Lord, and raise up great scholars; and let me depart in peace, the least of your creatures."[2] And the voice came to her again, saying, "He has set in my mouth a new song, a song of praise to our God. I have not hidden your righteousness in my heart, I have told of your truth and your salvation: I have not hidden your mercy and your truth from the great congregation."[3]

2.7. Thus more than twenty years after this vision, when out of excessive humility Juliana had again prayed with unspeakable groaning[4] that Christ would give the task to someone else, but could not in the least obtain what she asked, she discerned that it was hard to kick against the goad of God's will[5] and submitted her will to his. For she had persisted in prayers and tears so long that she had no

---

[1]   Luke 10: 21.

[2]   Luke 2: 29.

[3]   Ps. 40: 3, 9; Douay Ps. 39: 4,11.

[4]   See Rom. 8: 26.

[5]   See Acts 9: 5.

more tears to weep, and her eyes shed pure blood instead. Let no one be scandalized that Christ's virgin appeared to consent so belatedly to the divine admonition, for the cause did not lie in negligence or in any lack of devotion toward the Sacrament, but only in the most profound humility. For she always maintained that she was most unworthy in the sight of the Lord to proclaim so great a feast to the world, excusing herself as well on account of her lack of experience and power. But the more she reckoned herself unworthy, the more Christ, who loves and teaches humility, reckoned her worthy.

Consenting at last to the admonition she had so often received, therefore, she began by telling the whole story to a venerable man, Dom John of Lausanne,[1] a canon of St. Martin of Liège, of blessed memory—a man she loved dearly because of his excellent holiness. Since he knew many great scholars and religious who came to him for his prayers, she asked him to set before them all she had told him, but without mentioning her name, in order to find out what great theologians might think of such a feast. See how a wise virgin behaves! She does nothing rashly, approaches nothing without counsel, but does everything in due time and with the utmost deliberation, discerning and wishing others to discern whether the spirits are from God.[2]

Let this be a lesson for men and women who are wise in their own eyes, believing in every spirit and thinking that whatever crosses their minds is a divine revelation. A sign is shown to Juliana, a mystery is revealed, a task is enjoined, or rather forced upon her, and all by him who can neither deceive nor be deceived. Even so, she submits everything to be reviewed by people who are learned in the divine law and possess the Spirit of God. But if the example of our virgin is not enough for them, let them hearken to Paul's behavior. Did he not decide to consult with others about his gospel, which he had received not from a human being but from Christ, lest somehow he should be running or had run in vain?[3] Where he is not secure, neither is Christ's handmaid. If anyone is, beware lest it be judged not security but rashness.

All these matters, then, were set before Dom Jacques of Troyes, then Archdeacon of Liège, a man extremely learned in the divine law and adorned with the merits of holiness, who, because he always showed himself faithful before the Lord in the little he received, was later found worthy to be set over much.[4] Afterward, in fact, he was made Bishop of Verdun, a post from which he was raised to Patriarch of Jerusalem. At last, as God wondrously advanced him, he was exalted to the papacy after Pope Alexander IV and took the name of Urban IV.[5] All these things were also set before Friar Hugh, then Prior Provincial of the Dominicans, who was later found worthy of promotion on his merits to Cardinal of the Roman Church;[6] and to the reverend father Dom Guiard, Bishop of Cambrai.[7] In those days these two men shone in the Church like the two great lights of heaven because of their life and learning. The matter was also related to the chancellor of Paris, an extremely erudite man,[8] and to the friars Gilles, John, and Gerard, lectors of the Dominicans in Liège,[9] along with many others who glistened like stars by virtue of their life and learning.

But when is the Holy Spirit ever divided against himself? When would he ever contradict himself? Certainly he did not say one thing by the mouth of his handmaid Juliana and another by the mouths of his faithful servants. No "yes and no" was found among them, but only "yes."[10] All these people, once they had carefully heard, understood, and considered the merits of this affair, pro-

---

[1] Dom is an honorific used before the names of churchmen.

[2] 1 John 4: 1.

[3] See Gal. 1: 12; 2: 2.

[4] See Matt. 25: 21.

[5] Jacques Pantaléon of Troyes, a shoemaker's son, was archdeacon of Liège in the 1240s, bishop of Verdun from 1253–1255, patriarch of Jerusalem from 1255–1261, and Pope Urban IV from 1261–1264. A few months before his death, he issued the bull *Transiturus* which established Corpus Christi as a feast for the universal Church.

[6] Hugh of St. Cher (d.1263), the famed theologian and exegete, was created cardinal presbyter of St. Sabina in 1244. In 1251–1252 he took an active role in promoting the feast of Corpus Christi in the diocese of Liège.

[7] Guido or Guiard held this office from 1238–1247; he visited Juliana in August 1242. A famous preacher, he was influential in the spread of Eucharistic piety.

[8] Philip the Chancellor (d.1236) was known for his elegant Latin hymns.

[9] A Dominican house of studies had been opened in Liège in 1234.

[10] See 2 Cor. 1: 19.

nounced with one mind that they could find no valid reason in divine law to preclude a special feast of the venerable Sacrament. It would be most fitting and right, it would increase both the honor of God and the growth and grace of the elect, if Mother Church were to celebrate every year a memorial of the institution of this Sacra- ment more specifically and solemnly than she had done before. When Christ's virgin learned of this unanimous opinion, she gave thanks to God that he had placed an answer in keeping with his will in the mouths of so many great dignitaries.

TIMELINE FOR CHAPTER SEVEN

13TH C. *SHORT LIFE OF ST. PETKA* ——— **1200**

——— 1ST HALF 13TH C. *SECRET HISTORY OF THE MONGOLS*

1225

——— 1246 GUYUK KHAN, *LETTER TO POPE INNOCENT IV*

*c.*1250 BÉLA IV, *LETTER TO POPE INNOCENT IV* ——— **1250**

1250 *GHIBELLINE ANNALS OF PIACENZA* ——— ——— 1259–64 THOMAS AQUINAS, *SUMMA AGAINST THE GENTILES*

1260–64 *DECREES OF HANSEATIC LEAGUE* ——— ——— 1261–64 *THE LIFE OF JULIANA OF MONT-CORNILLON*

*c.*1268 *HENRYKÓW BOOK* ———

——— 1272 JOINVILLE, *LIFE OF ST. LOUIS*

1275 *STATUTE OF THE JEWRY* ——— **1275**

SHORTLY AFTER 1275 *PETITION OF THE* ——— *"COMMONALTY" OF THE JEWS*

1295 *SUMMONS TO PARLIAMENT* ——— ——— 1296 BONIFACE VIII, *CLERICIS LAICOS*

1298 *BANK PETITION* (SIENA) ———

14TH C. *ANNUNCIATION PLAY* ——— **1300**

1302 BONIFACE VIII, *UNAM SANCTAM* ——— ——— 1303 WILLIAM OF PLAISIANS, *CHARGES OF HERESY*

1306–07 ATHANASIUS I, *LETTER ABOUT FAMINE* ——— ——— 1313–21 DANTE, *DIVINE COMEDY*

1314 *GRAND CHRONICLES OF FRANCE* ——— ——— 1318–25 JACQUES FOURNIER, *EPISCOPAL REGISTER*

*c.*1320–26 PETER OF DUSBURG, *CHRONICLE* ——— ——— 1322–23 *LETTERS OF GEDIMINAS*

1325

1347 *OATH AND TREATY* BETWEEN ——— BULGARIA AND VENICE **1350**

——— *c.*1360S *SARUM MANUAL*

1375

To test your knowledge and gain deeper understanding of this chapter, please go to www.utphistorymatters.com for Study Questions.

VIII

Catastrophe and Creativity (c.1350–c.1500)

8.1 A medical view: Nicephorus Gregoras, *Roman History* (1350s). Original in Greek.

Struck by the plague in 1347, the coastal cities of Byzantium were depopulated. Militarily weakened by civil war, Byzantium was now more vulnerable to the Turks, whose territories were inland. Nicephorus Gregoras (*c.*1293–1359/1361), a scholar, diplomat, theologian, and historian, wrote a highly objective report on the spread and medical effects of the plague in his *Roman*—that is "Byzantine"—*History*.

[Source: Christos S. Bartsocas, "Two Fourteenth Century Greek Descriptions of the 'Black Death,'" *Journal of the History of Medicine and Allied Sciences* 21 (1966): 395.]

During that time a serious and pestilential disease invaded humanity. Starting from Scythia and Maeotis and the mouth of the Tanais,[1] just as spring began, it lasted for that whole year, passing through and destroying, to be exact, only the continental coast, towns as well as country areas, ours and those that are adjacent to ours, up to Gadera and the columns of Hercules.[2]

During the second year it invaded the Aegean Islands. Then it affected the Rhodians, as well as the Cypriots and those colonizing the other islands. The calamity attacked men as well as women, rich and poor, old and young. To put matters simply, it did not spare those of any age or fortune. Several homes were emptied of all their inhabitants in one day or sometimes in two. No one could help anyone else, not even the neighbors, or the family, or blood relations.

The calamity did not destroy only men but also many animals living with and domesticated by men. I speak of dogs and horses and all the species of birds, even the rats that happened to live within the walls of the houses.

---

[1] The Don River.
[2] The Gibraltar Straits.

The prominent signs of this disease, signs indicating early death, were tumorous outgrowths at the roots of thighs and arms and simultaneously bleeding ulcerations, which, sometimes the same day, carried the infected rapidly out of this present life, sitting or walking. During that time, Andronicus, the youngest of the [emperor's] sons, died.

8.2 Processions at Damascus: Ibn Battuta, *Travels* (before 1368). Original in Arabic.

Pilgrim and adventurer Ibn Battuta (1304–1368) left his home in Tangiers in 1325 and had covered most of the Arab world by the end of his travels in 1354. He later dictated his observations about culture, geography, and custom. Interspersed with his descriptions were personal experiences, which he called "Anecdotes." The one recounted here recalled his trip to Damascus in July 1348, when he witnessed fasts, prayers, and processions meant to ward off the plague.

[Source: *The Travels of Ibn Battuta,* A.D. 1325–1354, trans. Hamilton A.R. Gibb, vol. 1 (Cambridge: Cambridge University Press, 1958), pp. 142–44 (notes omitted).]

Among the sanctuaries of Damascus which are celebrated for their blessed power is the Mosque of the Footprints (Masjid al-Aqdam), which lies two miles to the south of Damascus, alongside the main highway which leads to the illustrious Hijaz, Jerusalem, and Egypt. It is a large mosque, abundant in blessing, and possessing many endowments, and the people of Damascus hold it in great veneration. The footprints from which it derives its name are certain footprints impressed upon a rock there, which are said to be the print of the foot of Moses (on him be peace). Within this mosque there is a small chamber containing a stone with the following inscription upon it: "A certain saintly man used to see the Chosen [i.e., Muhammad] (God bless and give him peace) in his sleep, and he would say to him 'Here is the grave of my brother Moses (on him be peace).'" On the road in the vicinity of this mosque is a place called the Red Sandhill; and near Jerusalem and Jericho there is a place which is also called the Red Sandhill and which is revered by the Jews.

Anecdote. I witnessed at the time of the Great Plague at Damascus in the latter part of the month of Second Rabi' of the year 49 [July 1348] a remarkable instance of the veneration of the people of Damascus for this mosque. Arghun-Shah, king of the emirs and the Sultan's viceroy, ordered a crier to proclaim through Damascus that the people should fast for three days and that no one should cook in the bazaar during the daytime anything to be eaten (for most of the people there eat no food but what has been prepared in the bazaar). So the people fasted for three successive days, the last of which was a Thursday. At the end of this period the emirs, sharifs, qadis, doctors of the Law, and all other classes of the people in their several degrees, assembled in the Great Mosque, until it was filled to overflowing with them, and spent the Thursday night there in prayers and liturgies and supplications. Then, after performing the dawn prayer [on the Friday morning], they all went out together on foot carrying Qur'ans in their hands—the emirs too barefooted. The entire population of the city joined in the exodus, male and female, small and large; the Jews went out with their book of the Law and the Christians with their Gospel, their women and children with them; the whole concourse of them in tears and humble supplications, imploring the favor of God through His Books and His Prophets. They made their way to the Mosque of the Footprints and remained there in supplication and invocation until near midday, then returned to the city and held the Friday service. God Most High lightened their affliction; the number of deaths in a single day reached a maximum of two thousand, whereas the number rose in Cairo and Old Cairo to twenty-four thousand in a day.

8.3 Prayers at York: Archbishop William, *Letter to His Official at York* (July 1348). Original in Latin.

During the same month as the Damascus processions, the English archbishop of York William de la Zouche (r.1342–1352) wrote from his residence at Cawood, a few miles southwest of York, to arrange for special processions, prayers, and masses to be held in his diocese to ward off the plague, which had already hit France. What commonalities and what differences were there in York's Christian and Damascus's Islamic religious responses to the plague?

[Source: *The Black Death*, ed. and trans. Rosemary Horrox (Manchester: Manchester University Press, 1994), pp. 111–12.]

Since the life of man on earth is a war, no wonder if those fighting amidst the miseries of this world are unsettled by the mutability of events: now favorable, now contrary. For Almighty God sometimes allows those he loves to be troubled while their strength is perfected in weakness by an outpouring of spiritual grace. There can be no one who does not know, since it is now public knowledge, how great a mortality, pestilence, and infection of the air are now threatening various parts of the world, and especially England; and this is surely caused by the sins of men who, while enjoying good times, forget that such things are the gifts of the most high giver. Thus, since the inevitable human fate, pitiless death, which spares no one, now threatens us, unless the holy clemency of the Savior is shown to his people from on high, the only hope is to hurry back to him alone, whose mercy outweighs justice and who, most generous in forgiving, rejoices heartily in the conversion of sinners; humbly urging him with orisons and prayers that he, the kind and merciful Almighty God, should turn away his anger and remove the pestilence and drive away the infection from the people whom he redeemed with his precious blood.

Therefore we command, and order you to let it be known with all possible haste, that devout processions are to be held every Wednesday and Friday in our cathedral church, in other collegiate and conventual churches, and in every parish church in our city and diocese, with a solemn chanting of the litany, and that a special prayer be said in mass every day for allaying the plague and pestilence, and likewise prayers for the lord king and for the good estate of the church, the realm and the whole people of England, so that the Savior, harkening to the constant entreaties, will pardon and come to the rescue of the creation which God fashioned in his own image.

And we, trusting in the mercy of Almighty God and the merits and prayers of his mother, the glorious Virgin Mary, and of the blessed apostles Peter and Paul, and of the most holy confessor William and of all the saints, have released 40 days of the penance enjoined by the gracious God on all our parishioners and on others whose diocesans have approved and accepted this our indulgence, for sins for which they are penitent, contrite, and have made confession, if they pray devoutly for these things, celebrate masses, undertake processions or are present at them, or perform other offices of pious devotion.[1] And you are to ensure that these things are speedily put into effect in every archdeaconry within our diocese by the archdeacons or their officials. Farewell.

---

[1] The remission of penance was part of the theology of Purgatory. The archbishop here declares that certain pious acts carried out on earth were equivalent to 40 days of penance in Purgatory. Such a remission of days in Purgatory was called an indulgence.

8.4 Blaming the Jews: Heinrich von Diessenhoven, *On the Persecution of the Jews* (*c.*1350). Original in Latin.

In the thirteenth century, Jews were accused of having arcane and evil knowledge. In the fourteenth century this idea became lethal when the Black Death struck, as outcasts of every sort—lepers, beggars, and Jews—were accused of spreading poison. Soon the accusations focused on the Jews, who were killed (among other places) in parts of France, Germany, the Low Countries, and Italy. In the *Ecclesiastical History* of Heinrich von Diessenhoven (d.1376), a canon lawyer close to the Hapsburgs, the burning of Jews in Germany was God's way to confound His enemies. Taking into account earlier persecutions of Jews—R. Eliezer's poem (above, p. 267), the *Decrees of Lateran IV* (above, p. 363), the *Statute of the Jewry* (above p. 413)—consider how the plague added to and transformed their woes.

[Source: *The Black Death*, ed. and trans. Rosemary Horrox (Manchester: Manchester University Press, 1994), pp. 208–10 (some notes added).]

The persecution of the Jews began in November 1348, and the first outbreak in Germany was at Sölden, where all the Jews were burnt on the strength of a rumor that they had poisoned wells and rivers, as was afterwards confirmed by their own confessions and also by the confessions of Christians whom they had corrupted and who had been induced by the Jews to carry out the deed. And some of the Jews who were newly baptized said the same. Some of these remained in the faith but some others relapsed, and when these were placed upon the wheel[1] they confessed that they had themselves sprinkled poison or poisoned rivers. And thus no doubt remained of their deceitfulness which had now been revealed.

Within the revolution of one year, that is from All Saints [November 1] 1348 until Michaelmas [September 29] 1349 all the Jews between Cologne and Austria were burnt and killed for this crime, young men and maidens and the old along with the rest. And blessed be God who confounded the ungodly who were plotting the extinction of his church, not realizing that it is founded on a sure rock and who, in trying to overturn it, crushed themselves to death and were damned for ever.

But now let us follow the killings individually. First Jews were killed or burnt in Sölden in November, then in Zofingen they were seized and some put on the wheel,

then in Stuttgart they were all burnt. The same thing happened during November in Landsberg, a town in the diocese of Augsburg and in Beuron, Memmingen and Burgau in the same diocese. During December they were burnt and killed on the feast of St. Nicholas [December 6] in Lindau, on December 8 in Reutlingen, on December 13 in Haigerloch, and on December 20 in Horw they were burnt in a pit. And when the wood and straw had been consumed, some Jews, both young and old, still remained half alive. The stronger of them snatched up cudgels and stones and dashed out the brains of those trying to creep out of the fire, and thus compelled those who wanted to escape the fire to descend to hell. And the curse seemed to be fulfilled: "his blood be upon us and upon our children."[2]

On December 27 the Jews in Esslingen were burnt in their houses and in the synagogue. In Nagelten they were burnt. In the abovesaid town of Zofingen the city councillors, who were hunting for poison, found some in the house of a Jew called Trostli, and by experiment were satisfied that it was poison. As a result, two Jewish men and one woman were put on the wheel, but others were saved at the command of Duke Albrecht of Austria,[3] who ordered that they should be protected. But this made little difference, for in the course of the next year those he

---

[1] Breaking on the wheel was a form of torture.

[2] Matt. 27: 24: the people's response to Pilate's statement, "I am innocent of the blood of this just man [Christ]. Look you to it."

[3] Albert II (or Albrecht II), duke of Austria 1330–1358.

had under his protection were killed, and as many again in the diocese of Constance. But first those burnt in 1349 will be described in order.

Once started, the burning of the Jews went on increasing. When people discovered that the stories of poisoning were undoubtedly true they rose as one against the Jews. First, on January 2, 1349 the citizens of Ravensburg burnt the Jews in the castle, to which they had fled in search of protection from King Charles, whose servants were imprisoned by the citizens after the burning. On January 4th the people of Constance shut up the Jews in two of their own houses, and then burnt 330 of them in the fields at sunset on March 3rd. Some processed to the flames dancing, others singing and the rest weeping. They were burnt shut up in a house which had been specially built for the purpose. On January 12 in Buchen and on January 17 in Basel they were all burnt apart from their babies, who were taken from them by the citizens and baptized. They were burnt on January 21 in Messkirch and Waldkirch, on January 26 in Speyer, and on January 30 in Ulm, on February 11 in Überlingen, on February 14 in the city of Strasbourg (where it took six days to burn them because of the numbers involved), on February 16 in Mengen, on the 19th of the month in Sulgen, on the 21st in Schaff hausen and Zurich, on the 23rd in St. Gall and on March 3 in Constance, as described above, except for some who were kept back to be burnt on the third day after the Nativity of the Virgin [September 11].

They were killed and burnt in the town of Baden on March 18, and those in the castle below, who had been brought there from Rheinfelden for protection, were killed and then burnt. And on May 30 they were similarly wiped out in Radolfzell. In Mainz and Cologne they were burnt on August 23. On September 18, 330 Jews were burnt in the castle at Kyburg, where they had gathered from Winterthur and Diessenhoven and the other towns of their protector the Duke of Austria. But the imperial citizens did not want to go on supporting them any longer, and so they wrote to Duke Albrecht of Austria, who was protecting his Jewish subjects in the counties of Pfirt, Alsace and Kyburg, and told him that either he had them burnt by his own judges or they would burn them themselves. So the Duke ordered them to be burnt by his own judges, and they were finally burnt on September 18.

And thus, within one year, as I said, all the Jews between Cologne and Austria were burnt—and in Austria they await the same fate, for they are accursed of God. And I could believe that the end of the Hebrews had come, if the time prophesied by Elias and Enoch were now complete; but since it is not complete, it is necessary that some be reserved so that what has been written may be fulfilled: that the hearts of the sons shall be turned to their fathers, and of the fathers to the sons.[1] But in what parts of the world they may be reserved I do not know, although I think it more likely that the seed of Abraham will be reserved in lands across the sea than in these people. So let me make an end of the Jews here.[2]

---

[1] A reference to Mal. 4: 5–6: "Behold I will send you Elias the prophet, before the coming of the great and dreadful day of the lord. And he shall turn the heart of the fathers to the children and the hearts of the children to their fathers: lest I come and strike the earth with anathema." This text was taken to mean that after the coming of Antichrist the prophets Enoch and Elias would reconvert the apostates as a preliminary to the second coming of Christ and the Last Judgment. At the same time they would convert the Jews to Christianity. Heinrich's point is that because the second coming is not yet imminent, contemporary Jews could not be entirely wiped out or converted, because some had to survive to be converted by Enoch and Elias in the Last Days.

[2] The sentence is ambiguous and, given the anti-Jewish sentiments of the author, probably deliberately so. Its surface meaning is that he has come to the end of the two chapters devoted to the Jews and is now about to turn to other matters. But it could also be taken to mean that he hopes to see the extermination of the Jews in Europe, as there are likely to be enough elsewhere to meet the prophetic conditions laid down for Christ's second coming.

8.5 A legislative response: *Ordinances against the Spread of Plague at Pistoia* (1348). Original in Latin.

Many city governments responded to the plague by instituting new sanitation measures. They quickly recognized that the disease spread as infected people traveled from one place to another and as infected garments and corpses came into contact with the healthy. Although they had no germ theory, the idea that "bad air" and stench caused the plague led them to legislate particular slaughtering practices. At Pistoia the statutes promulgated in 1348 and printed below were revised less than a month later and then again a few weeks after that, illustrating how quickly the city responded to changing circumstances. How many statutes were concerned with travel in and out of Pistoia? How many with burial practices? How many with butchering? And how many—and why—with the consumption of luxury goods?

[Source: *The Black Death*, trans. Rosemary Horrox (Manchester: Manchester University Press, 1994), pp. 195–200 (some notes added).]

[2 May, 1348]

1. So that the sickness which is now threatening the region around Pistoia shall be prevented from taking hold of the citizens of Pistoia, no citizen or resident of Pistoia, wherever they are from or of what condition, status or standing they may be, shall dare or presume to go to Pisa or Lucca; and no one shall come to Pistoia from those places; penalty 500 pence. And no one from Pistoia shall receive or give hospitality to people who have come from those places; same penalty. And the guards who keep the gates of the city of Pistoia shall not permit anyone traveling to the city from Pisa or Lucca to enter; penalty 10 pence from each of the guards responsible for the gate through which such an entry has been made. But citizens of Pistoia now living within the city may go to Pisa and Lucca, and return again, if they first obtain permission from the common council—who will vote on the merits of the case presented to them. The licence is to be drawn up by the notary of the *anziani* and *gonfalonier* of the city.[1] And this ordinance is to be upheld and observed from the day of its ratification until October 1st, or longer if the council sees fit.

2. No one, whether from Pistoia or elsewhere, shall dare or presume to bring or fetch to Pistoia, whether in person or by an agent, any old linen or woollen cloths, for male or female clothing or for bedspreads; penalty 200 pence, and the cloth is to be burnt in the public piazza of Pistoia by the official who discovered it.[2] However it shall be lawful for citizens of Pistoia traveling within Pistoia and its territories to take linen and woollen cloths with them for their own use or wear, provided that they are in a pack or fardle [bundle] weighing 30 lb or less. And this ordinance is to be upheld and observed from the day of its ratification until 1 January. And if such cloth has already been brought into Pistoia, the bringer must take it away within three days of the ordinance's ratification; same penalty.

---

[1] Pistoia's government was dominated by the party of the *popolo*. Their chief administrators were twelve *anziani*, each elected for very short terms. The *popolo*'s chief military officers were the *capitano* and the *gonfalonier*. The other key figure in the city's government was the *podestà*, who held administrative, judicial, and military powers at the same time. Almost always a "foreigner" from another city, this official was supposed to be above family and party loyalties. All of these officers were expected to work together to enforce the sanitation ordinances of 1348.

[2] Later outbreaks of plague in Italian cities were often associated with the movement of cloth, and this requirement suggests that the connection may already have been noted. Contemporaries—who were not aware of the role played by fleas in the transmission of the disease—explained the connection as due to the trapping of corrupt air within the folds of fabric.

3. The bodies of the dead shall not be removed from the place of death until they have been enclosed in a wooden box, and the lid of planks nailed down[1] so that no stench can escape, and covered with no more than one pall, coverlet or cloth; penalty 50 pence to be paid by the heirs of the deceased or, if there are no heirs, by the nearest kinsmen in the male line. The goods of the deceased are to stand as surety for the payment of the penalty. Also the bodies are to be carried to burial in the same box; same penalty. So that the civic officials can keep a check on this, the rectors of the chapels in Pistoia must notify the *podestà* and *capitano* when a corpse is brought into their chapel, giving the dead man's name and the contrada [quarter] in which he was living when he died; same penalty. As soon as he has been notified, the *podestà* or *capitano* must send an official to the place, to find out whether this chapter of the ordinances is being observed, along with the other regulations governing funerals, and to punish those found guilty. And if the *podestà* or *capitano* is remiss in carrying out these orders he must be punished by those who appointed him; same penalty. But these regulations should not apply to the poor and destitute of the city, who are dealt with under another civic ordinance.

4. To avoid the foul stench which comes from dead bodies each grave shall be dug two and a half armslength deep, as this is reckoned in Pistoia;[2] penalty 10 pence from anyone digging or ordering the digging of a grave which infringes the statute.

5. No one, of whatever condition, status, or standing, shall dare or presume to bring a corpse into the city, whether coffined or not; penalty 25 pence. And the guards at the gates shall not allow such bodies to be brought into the city; same penalty, to be paid by every guard responsible for the gate through which the body was brought.

6. Any person attending a funeral shall not accompany the corpse or its kinsmen further than the door of the church where the burial is to take place, or go back to the house where the deceased lived, or to any other house on that occasion; penalty 10 pence. Nor is he to go the week's mind of the deceased; same penalty.[3]

7. When someone dies, no one shall dare or presume to give or send any gift to the house of the deceased, or to any other place on that occasion, either before or after the funeral, or to visit the house, or eat there on that occasion; penalty 25 pence. This shall not apply to the sons and daughters of the deceased, his blood brothers and sisters and their children, or to his grandchildren. The *podestà* and *capitano*, when notified by the rector as in chapter 3, must send an official to enquire whether anything has been done to the contrary and to punish those responsible.

8. To avoid waste and unnecessary expense, no one shall dare or presume to wear new clothes during the mourning period or for the next eight days; penalty 25 pence. This shall not apply to the wife of the deceased, who may if she wishes wear a new garment of any fabric without penalty.

9. No crier, summoner, or drummer of Pistoia shall dare or presume to invite or summon any citizen of Pistoia, whether publicly or privately, to come to a funeral or visit the corpse; nor shall anyone send the same summoner, trumpeter, crier, or drummer; penalty 10 pence from each crier, trumpeter, summoner, or drummer, and from the people by whom they have been employed.

10. So that the sound of bells does not trouble or frighten the sick, the keepers of the campanile of the cathedral church of Pistoia shall not allow any of the bells to be rung during funerals, and no one else shall dare or presume to ring any of the bells on such occasions; penalty 10 pence, to be paid by the keepers who allowed the bells to be rung and by the heirs of the dead man, or his kinsmen should he have no heirs. When a parishioner is buried in his parish church, or a member of a fraternity within the fraternity church, the church bells may be rung, but only on one occasion and not excessively; same penalty.

11. No one shall presume or dare to summon a gathering of people to escort a widow from the house of her dead husband, but only from the church to his burial place. But it shall be lawful for the widow's kinsmen to send up

---

[1] The bodies of ordinary people were generally buried in shrouds, although they might be carried to church in a coffin. This ordinance probably implies that they were to be buried in a coffin.

[2] A *bracchio* (armslength) in Pistoia measured between two and two and a half feet.

[3] This last sentence refers to a ban on attendance at the commemorative mass one week after a death.

to four women to escort the widow from her husband's house at other times. No one shall dare to attend such a gathering; penalty 25 pence, paid by those invited and by those who issued the invitation.

12. No one shall dare or presume to raise a lament or crying for anyone who has died outside Pistoia, or summon a gathering of people other than the kinsfolk and spouse of the deceased, or have bells rung, or use criers or any other means to invite people throughout the city to such a gathering; penalty 25 pence from each person involved.

However it is to be understood that none of this applies to the burial of knights, doctors of law, judges, and doctors of physic, whose bodies can be honored by their heirs at their burial in any way they please.

13. So that the living are not made ill by rotten and corrupt food, no butcher or retailer of meat shall dare or presume to hang up meat, or keep and sell meat hung up in their storehouse or over their counter; penalty 10 pence. And that the rulers of the craft of butchery must investigate these matters on every day when slaughtering occurs, and immediately denounce any offenders to the lords, *podestà* or *capitano*, or to one of their officials; same penalty from the rulers of the craft if they fail to carry out these things in person or by deputy. The *podestà* and *capitano* must each send someone to look into these matters, and punish those found guilty, along with the rulers of the craft if they have failed to denounce them. The word of any official who finds an infringement of the regulations shall be taken as sufficient evidence.

14. Butchers and retailers of meat shall not stable horses or allow any mud or dung in the shop or other place where they sell meat, or in or near their storehouse, or on the roadway outside; nor shall they slaughter animals in a stable, or keep flayed [skinned] carcasses in a stable or in any other place where there is dung; penalty 10 pence. An official of the *podestà* or *capitano* is to enquire closely into such matters, and his word is to be taken on any infringement of these ordinances.

15. No butcher or retailer of meat shall dare or presume to keep on the counter where he sells meat, meat from more than one ox, calf, or cow at once, although he can keep the meat of an ox or cow alongside that of a calf,

penalty 10 pence. The rulers of the craft must investigate the matter on every day on which animals are slaughtered and denounce any offenders to the *podestà* or *capitano* of the city; same penalty.

16. In May, June, July, and August butchers and retailers of meat shall slaughter meat on the days on which meat can be eaten, including Sundays and feast days, and sell it on the same day to those wishing to buy; the animals are to be vetted by the civic officials appointed for the purpose.[1]

17. No butcher or retailer shall dare or presume to kill any ox, cow or calf without first obtaining permission from officials of the *podestà* or *capitano*. As soon as the official's approval has been requested he shall go and see the animal, to decide whether it is healthy or not. When permission has been given the butcher himself must slaughter the animal properly in the official's presence; penalty 10 pence.

18. No butcher or any other retailer of meat shall kill any two- or three-year old boar or sow between March 1 and December 1; penalty 25 pence.

19. Butchers or retailers shall flay [skin] every two- or three-year old boar or sow killed between December 1 and March 1 before putting it on sale. If they wish to salt it down, that is permissible, but it must be flayed first; penalty 25 pence.

20. [Provisions for the election of officials to set the retail price of meat.]

21. For the better preservation of health, there should be a ban on all kinds of poultry, calves, foodstuffs, and on all kinds of fat being taken out of Pistoia by anybody; penalty 100 pence and the confiscation of the things being carried contrary to the ban. And whoever can capture such carriers and the things carried and take them to the gaol [jail] of the commune of Pistoia shall have half of the fine and of the value of the goods, after the fine has been paid and the goods sold to the highest bidder.

22. To avoid harm to men by stink and corruption, there shall in future be no tanning of skins within the city walls of Pistoia; penalty 25 pence.

---

[1] In other words, the importance of ensuring a supply of fresh meat meant that slaughtering could take place on days when it was usually banned.

23. [Provisions for enforcement including the proviso that anyone can denounce an offender before the *podestà* or *capitano*, and receive a quarter of the fine if the accusa- tion is upheld; the word of one man worthy of belief is to be sufficient evidence of guilt, or the statements of four men testifying to the common belief.]

THE OTTOMANS

8.6 A Turkish hero: Ashikpashazade, *Othman Comes to Power* (late 15th c.). Original in Turkish.

Writing in the late fifteenth century, the chronicler Ashikpashazade (d. after 1484) based his account of the founder of the Ottoman Turks (Othman) on earlier sources and on his sense of the sort of heroic past such a leader needed to have. He depicted Othman creating a new empire through a combination of fate, "feigned friendships," religious fervor, force, and cunning. How might you compare Ashikpashazade's heroic image of Othman with Joinville's picture of St. Louis on p. 416? How might you account for the differences?

[Source: *Die altosmanische Chronik des Asikpasazade*, ed. Friedrich Giese (Leipzig: Harrassowitz, 1929). Translated by Robert Dankoff.]

How Othman Ghazi became Sultan

Ertugrul Ghazi heard that Sultan 'Alaeddin[1] of the Seljuk dynasty had become King of Rum.[2] He said, "We have to determine the man's quality. We'll go to that country and perform the ghaza."[3] Ertugrul Ghazi had three sons, Othman, Gündüz, and Saruyati. Together they started out for Rum. While they were nomadizing in the province of Ghazi Hasan of Mosul, Ertugrul Ghazi sent his son Saruyati to 'Alaeddin, saying, "Provide us with a homeland and we will go and perform the ghaza." Sultan 'Alaeddin was extremely happy at their coming. The tek-fur[4] of Sultan Önü and of Karaja Hisar was submissive, so Sultan 'Alaeddin provided them with Söğüt as their homeland, which was between Karaja Hisar and Bilejik. In addition, he gave them the ranges of Mount Domanich and Ermeni Beli. They passed directly through Ankara and settled in that province.

Several years later, Ertugrul Ghazi died. They preferred Othman Ghazi to succeed him in Söğüt. As soon as Othman Ghazi succeeded his father, he began a policy of "feigned friendship" with the neighboring infidels. Meanwhile, he began hostilities with the emir of Germiyan[5] because the latter was constantly harassing the populace of the surrounding countryside. Othman Ghazi also began to mount hunting expeditions far and wide.

How Othman Ghazi began from Time to Time to Make Raids at Nighttime and in the Day

At Inegöl there was an infidel named Aya Nikola. When Othman went to the summer pasture or to the winter pasture, Aya Nikola used to harass the migration. Othman Ghazi complained of this to the tekfur of Bilejik, and said, "What we would like from you is to let us deposit our baggage with you when we go to the summer pasture." He agreed. So whenever Othman Ghazi went to

---

[1] Apparently 'Ala' al-Din Kay Qubad III, who ruled intermittently between 1284 and 1302.

[2] A reference to the Eastern Roman or Byzantine Empire, i.e., Anatolia.

[3] Ghaza means conducting raids on the infidels. The warrior who gains fame in the ghaza gains the title of Ghazi.

[4] Byzantine prince or governor. (The title "tekfur" is used for Christian emirs, or commanders.)

[5] Turkish emirate (*beglik*) of western Anatolia with its capital at Kütahya (ancient Cotiaeum).

the summer pasture, he loaded his baggage on oxen and sent them along with some women to be deposited in Bilejik castle. And when they returned from the summer pasture, they sent cheese and knotted rugs and flatweaves and lambs in the way of gifts. Then they took back their belongings and went on their way. These infidels trusted them completely; but the infidels of Inegöl were wary of Othman, and he of them.

One day, Othman Ghazi came through Ermeni Beli with seventy men in order to set fire to Inegöl at night. A spy informed the infidels, who set up an ambush. The spy's name was Araton. Othman Ghazi had a Balkan sailor in his service. He came and informed them that the ambush was situated where the pass of Ermeni Beli emerged into the valley. The ghazis put their trust in God and marched straight toward the ambush. They were all on foot. There were many infidels. A great battle took place. Othman's brother Saruyati's son, whose name was Bay Hoca, was martyred. This occurred near the village of Hamza Beg, where the pass of Ermeni Beli emerges. Also, there is a ruined caravansary next to his shrine. From there, they turned back and Othman went to the summer pasture.

How Othman Ghazi Had a Dream, to Whom He Told It, and What Its Interpretation Was

Othman Ghazi prayed, and for a moment he wept. He was overcome by drowsiness and he lay down and slept. Now in that vicinity there dwelt a certain holy sheikh named Edebali.[1] His many saintly qualities were evident, and he was believed by all the people. By name he was a dervish, but his dervishhood was concealed within;[2] he had an abundance of worldly goods and wealth, and he had torches and banners [signs of hospitality]. His guest-house was never empty, and Othman Ghazi also came sometimes and was the guest of this holy man.

As Othman Ghazi slept, he saw in his dream that a moon arose out of this holy man's breast and entered Othman Ghazi's breast. Then a tree sprouted out of Othman Ghazi's navel, and the shadow of the tree covered the entire world. In its shadow, there were mountains, with streams issuing from the foot of each mountain. And from these flowing streams some people drank, and some watered gardens, and some caused fountains to flow.

When he awoke, he came to the sheikh and told him the dream. The sheikh said, "Othman, my son! Sovereignty has been granted to you and your descendants. And my daughter Malhun is to be your wife." He immediately gave his daughter to Othman Ghazi and married them.

This sheikh, Edebali, who interpreted Othman Ghazi's dream and gave tidings of sovereignty for himself and his descendants, had a disciple with him whose name was Kumral Dede, son of Dervish Durdi. That dervish now spoke, "O Othman! Since sovereignty has been given to you, it is proper for you to give us some token of gratitude." Othman replied, "At whatever time I become king, I will give you a city." The dervish said, "This little village is sufficient for us: we have renounced the city." Othman Ghazi accepted this. The dervish said, "Give us a document to that effect." Othman Ghazi replied, "Do you think that I write documents, that you want a document from me? Here is my sword. It was left to me by my father and my grandfather. I will give it to you. And I will also give you a goblet. Let them remain together in your hands, and let them preserve this stamp. And if God accepts me for this service, my descendants will recognize this sign, and will accept your claim." Now that sword is still in the hands of Kumral Dede's descendants. And whenever any of Othman Ghazi's descendants saw that sword, they bestowed favors upon those dervishes and they renewed the sword's scabbard. Every one of the House of Othman who has become king has made a pilgrimage to that sword....

How Certain News Reached Sultan 'Alaeddin, and How the Infidels Were Treating the Muslims

Now news reached Sultan 'Alaeddin that the infidels had fought against Othman Ghazi with large forces and had martyred his brother Saruyati. The sultan said, "It is well-known that the tekfur of Karaja Hisar is our enemy; also that the emir of Germiyan does not like those strangers [i.e., the Ottomans]. The greater part of the infidels' activities is due to his heedlessness, I know that myself. Now let our own army gather immediately! Shall we let those infidels get away with such actions? Is the zeal of

---

[1] In this context, sheikh refers to a holy man or religious leader, in this case the head of a dervish order.

[2] A dervish was an ascetic belonging to one of several Islamic orders. Some performed whirling dances and vigorous chants as part of their devotions.

Islam no longer in us?" With this command, a great army gathered to attack Karaja Hisar.

Othman Ghazi also came and joined the battle on one side. After the fighting had gone on for a day or two, word arrived that the Tatar Bayinjar[1] had taken Eregli, laid waste the houses and the people, and set fire to the city. Sultan 'Alaeddin summoned Othman Ghazi and handed over to him all the equipment which he had brought to take to Karaja Hisar. He said, "Othman Ghazi, my son! Upon you are many tokens of good fortune. There is no one in the world who will withstand you and your descendants. With you are my prayers, the favor of God, the aspiration of the saints, and the miracles of the Prophet." With that, he returned to his province. Othman pressed the battle for several more days. In the end, he captured the fortress, took the tekfur, let the ghazis plunder the city, distributed the houses to the ghazis and to others, and made it a Muslim city. This victory occurred in 1288....

How the Infidels of Harman Kaya became Acquainted with Othman Ghazi and What They Did

Whenever Othman Ghazi, who was now emir of the Banner, mounted for a raid, Köse Mihal was always with him. Most of the servants of these ghazis were infidels from Harman Kaya. One day Othman Ghazi said to Mihal, "We want to ride against Darakchi Yenijesi. What do you say?" Mihal replied, "My Khan![2] Let us pass to Sorgun by way of Saru Kaya and Besh Tash so that we can cross the Sakarya River. Then the ghazis on the other side will join us. It will also be easy to strike at the province of Mudurni, which is a prosperous place. Also, Samsa Chavush is settled near that province. We can keep him informed of our movements, and he can let us know when the time is right."

Following this advice, they marched out and camped at the dervish lodge at Besh Tash. They inquired of the sheikh, "Does the river afford a crossing?" "By the grace of God, there is a crossing for the ghazis!" the sheikh replied. They let their horses graze, then mounted and came to the river bank, where they found Samsa Chavush ready and waiting. He conducted the ghazis straight to Sorgun. The infidels of that province were well acquainted with

Samsa Chavush. As soon as they saw him, and saw the army, they became submissive and obedient. The men and women came out to meet them. Among them was a rather distinguished infidel whom they summoned. He came and took a solemn oath with Othman Ghazi that they would accept whatever Samsa Chavush said....

How Köse Mihal Had a Wedding Party, Giving His Daughter to the Emir of Göl-flanoz

Köse Mihal made elaborate preparations, in order that the wedding party gain renown. When everything was ready, he sent people to summon the surrounding infidels and tekfurs. He also invited Othman Ghazi, and he informed the tekfurs, saying, "Come, get acquainted with this Turk so that you will be safe from his evil." They all came on the appointed day with elaborate gifts for the bride. Othman Ghazi arrived last. He brought good knotted carpets and flatweaves and herds of sheep. They were very pleased with Othman Ghazi's gifts. In short, the festivity went on for three days, and the tekfurs were astounded at Othman Ghazi's munificence. They found no opportunity to catch him up. As for Othman Ghazi, he showed great affection toward the tekfur of Bilejik. Previous to this, they had formed a friendship in absentia, as it were, since they had never met face to face; since Othman Ghazi used to deposit his goods in the Bilejik castle whenever he went to the summer pasture.

The Wedding Party of the Tekfur of Bilejik

Now the tekfur of Bilejik also planned to have a wedding party, for he was to marry the daughter of the tekfur of Yar Hisar. First he summoned Mihal and consulted with him, arranging the plot against Othman. They completed all the arrangements for the wedding. Then he sent out messengers to invite the surrounding tekfurs. Even before the messenger got to Othman Ghazi, the latter sent a herd of sheep to the tekfur of Bilejik, saying, "Let my brother feed these to the servants at the wedding; and when I arrive, I shall bring my gifts for the bride, God willing, although I really have no gifts that befit my brother." The reason he sent these even before the messenger arrived was that at Mihal's wedding party certain

---

[1] Leader of the Chingizid Mongol forces in Anatolia.

[2] Khan was the old Central Asian term for a ruler.

arrangements had already been made, and the tekfur had sent Mihal to Othman Ghazi with the invitation. And he had also sent a number of gold and silver utensils. But when Mihal came, he informed Othman Ghazi what the intention of the tekfurs was, and he warned him to be on his guard. He also delivered the invitation. Othman Ghazi gave him the proper rewards for serving as the messenger, and said, "Emir Mihal, go, extend many greetings from me to my brother. Tell him that now is the time for us to migrate to the summer pasture. Also that my wife and mother-in-law wish to become acquainted with my brother's mother. Also my brother knows well how things are between the emir of Germiyan and myself. He has always borne our burden until now. May he be so gracious as to bear it once again this year, and allow us to deposit in the castle the baggage belonging to my mother and myself."

Mihal went and delivered Othman Ghazi's message to the tekfur, who received it with great pleasure, then sent Mihal back to arrange the day on which Othman Ghazi was to arrive. In addition to all this, Othman, in his message, had said, "Our women are accustomed to the wide plateau. Bilejik is too narrow to hold the wedding party there." The tekfur agreed to this as well, and they held it at Chakir Pinar.

On the appointed day, Othman Ghazi loaded the oxen and sent them in the company of the women who always brought them. They entered the castle in the dark of evening. As soon as one or two trains of oxen had entered, out of the bales of felt poured men with naked swords, who cut down the gatekeepers. There were few men in the castle itself, since most of them had gone to the wedding celebration. The castle was taken.

Now let us see what Othman Ghazi was doing in the meantime. He had dressed a number of his head-risking ghazis in women's clothes, and he sent word to the following effect: "Let them be housed in a place apart so that our women will not be ashamed to see the tekfurs there." The tekfur was very pleased at this as well, thinking that the Turk's women as well as the men had fallen into his hands; so he housed them in a place apart. Othman Ghazi had also arranged with the oxen drivers to inform the tekfur that Othman himself would pay a visit at the time that they entered the castle. That very evening he did come, pretending that he did not wish his women to be left exposed. The tekfur received him cordially and put him up as a guest. But before the tekfur came to his own room, Othman Ghazi had mounted along with Mihal. The cry went up, "Hey! The Turk has escaped!" The tekfur also mounted, though he was rather tipsy, and pursued them as far as a nearby stream called Kadirayok, where he was caught. Othman Ghazi had the tekfur beheaded.

He continued riding and toward morning fell on Yar Hisar, captured its tekfur and the bride, and took most of the wedding guests captive. He then immediately sent Turgut Alp to Inegöl to prevent Aya Nikola from getting wind of events and escaping. Turgut Alp arrived in time and cordoned off Inegöl. Othman Ghazi brought all of the booty into Bilejik and saw to its disposition. Then they marched against Inegöl. As they approached, Othman Ghazi announced that the town would be open to plunder. When the ghazis heard the word "plunder," they raised a shout and poured into the castle. They cut up the tekfur, killed the men, and took the women captive, for this infidel had been the cause of many Muslims' being martyred.

To Whom They Gave the Bride Whom They Captured, She Being the Daughter of the Tekfur of Yar Hisar

Othman Ghazi gave her to his son Orkhan Ghazi. Her name was Lülüfer Khatun. At that time, Orkhan was still a young man. He also had another son ['Alaeddin] whom he used to place in charge of the migration.

Once they had conquered these four castles [Karaja Hisar, Bilejik, Yar Hisar, and Inegöl] they established justice in their realm. All the surrounding villages prospered, even more than in the time of the infidels, and people began to come here from other provinces when they heard how well the infidels here were faring.

In short, Othman Ghazi made a wedding party and gave Lülüfer Khatun to his son Orkhan Ghazi. This is the same Lülüfer Khatun who built a dervish lodge at the foot of the Bursa citadel near the Kapluja Gate. She is also the one who had the bridge constructed over the Lülüfer River, which is therefore known by her name. Murad Khan Ghazi and Süleyman Pasha were her sons, both by Orkhan Ghazi.[1] When she died, she was buried with Orkhan Ghazi in the Bursa citadel.

---

[1] Orkhan, the second Ottoman sultan, ruled c.1324–1360. His son Murad I ruled 1360–1389.

In What Manner Othman Ghazi Established the Friday Prayer, and How This Occurred in Every Town

When he took Karaja Hisar, the houses of the town were left empty, and quite a few people came from Germiyan and from other provinces asking Othman Ghazi for houses. Othman Ghazi gave them to them, and in a short time, the town was repopulated. He also gave them a number of churches which they made into mosques. They also set up a market.

Now these people decided that they wanted to perform the Friday congregational prayer, also that they wanted to have a qadi.[1] There was a holy man named Dursun Fakih who used to act as prayer-leader for those people. They explained their wish to him. He in turn came and spoke with Othman Ghazi's stepfather Edebali about it. While they were talking, Othman Ghazi came over and inquired into the matter. When he learned what they wanted, he said, "Do whatever seems correct to you." Dursun Fakih said, "My Khan! We must request permission from the sultan." Othman Ghazi replied, "I took this city by myself with my own sword. What does the sultan have to do with it that I should require his permission? God who bestowed the sultanate upon him also bestowed the office of khan on me by virtue of the ghaza. It is true that the sultan endowed me with this banner. But it is I who carried the banner into battle with the infidels! If he claims to be of the House of Seljuk, I claim to be the descendant of Gök Alp. And if he says that he came to this country before us, we say that my grandfather Süleyman Shah came before him."

This satisfied those people. They gave the offices of qadi and *khatib* [preacher] to Dursun Fakih. The Friday sermon was read first in Karaja Hisar. The festival sermon was read in Eskishehir, and they performed the festival prayer there. The first sermon given in the name of Othman took place in 689 [1290].

Othman Ghazi's Laws and Regulations

The qadi was established, the military commander was in place, the market was in operation, and the sermon was being read. These people wanted a law. A man came from Germiyan and said, "Sell me the tax concession on this market." "Go to the Khan," said the people. So he went to the Khan and repeated his request. "What is a tax?" said Othman Ghazi. The man replied, "For whatever comes into the market I shall take a small amount of money." "Do you have a debt outstanding against the people of this market, that you wish to take money from them?" "My Khan," he answered, "this is a custom. The rulers of all countries do this." "Did God command this, or have the emirs themselves instituted it?" "It is a custom, my Khan, which has come down to us from the beginning of time." At this Othman Ghazi became very angry: "Should a man's earnings belong to another? It is his own property. What have I put into it that I should tell him to give me money? Out with you, scoundrel! Do not speak to me thus, or it will be to your own harm."

Afterwards, the people came and said, "My Khan, it is customary to give a little something to the market guards." Othman Ghazi said, "Now, since you say so, let everyone who sells one load give two *akçes*.[2] But whoever sells nothing should give nothing. Anyone who breaks this law of mine, may God cause his ruin in this world and the next. Furthermore, upon whomever I bestow a land grant, let it not be taken from his hands without reason; and when he dies, let it be given to his son, however young he may be. And at the time of campaign, his servants should accompany him so that he will be fit to fight. Whoever holds to this law, may God be pleased with him; but if one of my descendants is caused to establish a law other than this law, may God not be pleased with him who established it and with him who causes it to be established."

---

[1]   Qadi: a judge of religious law.
[2]   A silver coin.

8.7 Diplomacy: *Peace Agreement between the Ottoman Sultan Mehmed II and the Signoria of Venice* (January 25, 1478). Original in Greek.

Mehmed II's sack of Constantinople was part of a larger plan to reconstitute the Roman Empire under his own rule. After 1453, Mehmed moved into the Balkans and the Aegean, coming up against the other major power in the region, Venice. Between 1463 and 1478, the Ottomans and Venetians waged war, although for much of that time Venice was looking for a way to make peace. This they finally arranged in 1478. Although all sides confirmed its provisions, the agreement has no signatures. Only the Venetian copy has survived, a scroll 23 inches long and 9½ inches wide, composed of pieces of Venetian paper pasted together. The top piece, with a scissors watermark, has Mehmed's gold *tugra*, or formal emblem, while the bottom piece has an eagle watermark and the text of the agreement. The first ten provisions repeat agreements previously made between the Ottomans and the Venetians. (They echo, as well, earlier agreements that the Venetians made with the Byzantines.) The remainder provides for Venice to surrender various territories and to pay the sultan large quantities of gold.

[Source: State Archives of Venice, ASV Documenti Turchi B1/2. Translated by Diana Gilliland Wright.]

I, the great lord and great emir, Sultan Mehmed-Bey,[1] son of the great and blessed lord Murad-Bey, do swear by the God of heaven and earth, and by our great prophet Mohammed, and by the seven *mushaf*[2] which we Moslems possess and confess, and by the 124 thousand prophets of God (more or less),[3] and by the faith which I believe and confess, and by my soul and by the soul of my father, and by the sword I wear:

Because my Lordship formerly had peace and friendship with the most illustrious and exalted Signoria of Venice, now again we desire to make a new peace and oath to confirm a true friendship and a new peace. For this purpose, the aforementioned illustrious Signoria

sent the learned and wise Sir Giovanni Dario,[4] secretary, as emissary to my Lordship so we might make the said peace with the following old and new provisions. For this my Lordship swears by the above-written oaths that just as there was formerly peace and friendship between us, namely, with their lords and men and allies, I now profess good faith and an open peace by land and sea, within and without the Straits,[5] with the villages, fortresses, islands, and lands that raise the banner of San Marco,[6] and those who wish to raise the flag in the future, and all those places that are in their obedience and supervision,[7] and to the commerce which they have as of today and are going to have in the coming years.

---

[1] Bey is a superior honorific in Turkish-related languages.

[2] The seven *mushaf* were the seven accepted versions of the Qur'an: this emphasized Mehmed's Sunni allegiance.

[3] The phrase "more or less" indicates that while they did not know the precise number of prophets, they did not wish to offend.

[4] Giovanni Dario, the special Venetian emissary who brought the peace agreement to completion, was given a knighthood by Mehmed for his services. Dario's house, which Venice gave him in appreciation, can be seen in Venice: though small, it is one of the most conspicuous on the Grand Canal.

[5] The Dardanelles, i.e., the strait that connects the Aegean Sea with the Sea of Marmara, the body of water that touches Constantinople's southern shore.

[6] The banner of San Marco is red with a gold Venetian lion and a book that reads, "Pace tibi, Marce, evangelista meus [Peace unto you, St. Mark, my Evangelist]." The patron saint of Venice, Mark's body is believed to be buried in San Marco.

[7] This clause of the agreement refers to various other minor lords in the Aegean who gave nominal homage to Venice.

[Confirmation of Previous Agreements.]

[1][1] First, no man of my lordship will dare to inflict injury on or opposition to the Signoria of Venice or its men: if this happens, my Lordship is obligated to punish them according to the cause: similarly, the most illustrious Signoria is obligated toward us.

[2] Further, from this day forward, if either land or other goods of the most illustrious Signoria and its men is taken by the men of my Lordship, it will be returned: similarly, they are obligated to my Lordship.

[3] Their men and their merchandise may come by land and by sea to every land of my Lordship, and all the merchandise and the galleys and the ships will be secure and at ease: they are similarly obligated toward us in their lands.

[4] Similarly, the Duke of Naxos and his brothers and their lords and men with their ships and other boats are in the peace.[2] They will not owe my Lordship any service, but the Venetians will hold them just as it all used to be.

[5] Further, all ships and galleys, that is merchantmen and the fleet of my Lordship, wherever they may encounter the Venetians, will have good relations and peace with them. Corsairs and klefts, wherever they are taken, will be punished.[3]

[6] If any Venetian incurs a debt or commits other wrong in the lands of my Lordship, the other Venetians will bear no responsibility: similarly, the Signoria of Venice [vows the same] to our men.

[7] If any Venetian slave flees and comes into Turkish hands and becomes a Moslem, they will give his master 1000 aspers;[4] if he is a Christian he will be sent back.[5]

[8] If any Venetian boat is wrecked on the land of my Lordship, all the men will be freed and all the merchandise returned to their agent: they are similarly obligated to our men.

[9] If any Venetian man dies in the lands of my Lordship, without a will or heir, his goods are to be given to the Venetian *bailo*; if no *bailo* is found, they will be given into Venetian hands. Venice will write what to do.[6]

[10] Further, the most illustrious Signoria will have the right and authority specifically to send a *bailo* to Constantinople, with his household, according to custom, who will be able to dispense justice and administer Venetian affairs, according to their custom. The governor[7] will be obligated to give him aid and cooperation. [New provisions and conditions for peace.]

[11] If the said *bailo* wants to secure his position during this time, he is obligated to give my Lordship every year a gift of 10,000 Venetian florins[8] from the commercial transactions.[9]

[12] Further, the most illustrious Signoria of Venice is obligated for every debt lying between us and for all debts whether common or private or of certain of their men, for all the past time before the war until today, to give to my Lordship 100,000 Venetian ducats within two years.[10] Further, my Lordship cannot look for past debts, either from the most illustrious Signoria of Venice or from its men.[11]

[13] Further, the most illustrious Signoria of Venice is obligated to hand over to my Lordship the fortress called Skodra[12] in Albania, except that it may remove the lord who is *rettor*, and the council, and all the other

---

[1] The numbers are not on the original document, but are found on the official Venetian Greek and Italian file copies.

[2] Duke of Naxos: this refers to Jacopo III Crispo, who ruled the Cycladic islands 1463–1480. One of his brothers, Giovanni III, ruled 1480–1494.

[3] Corsairs were pirates who were licensed by some official ruler, for example, a local Venetian or Ottoman governor. Klefts were bandits in Ottoman and Venetian territories in Greece.

[4] One thousand aspers was then equal to about 22 ducats, a reasonable, if modest, price for a slave.

[5] This matter of escaped slaves was a normal provision in treaties, frequently reiterated in correspondence.

[6] As will be seen in Section 10, Venice was represented in Constantinople by a *bailo* who governed the large Venetian trading community and who acted as Venetian consul *vis à vis* the Turks.

[7] The Ottoman governor of the city of Constantinople.

[8] "Gift": the Greek means "little baskets," a Byzantine term for an obligatory gift from peasants to their landholder. The Ottomans used florins interchangeably with ducats.

[9] Bayazid II, who succeeded his father Mehmed II in May 1481, reduced the annual 10,000 florins payment to 5,000.

[10] It took two years to pay half the money. The 100,000 was money owed by two Venetian entrepreneurs for leases on Turkish alum mines.

[11] The sultan here forgives the debts that were not specified in this agreement.

[12] The fortress of Skodra (Scutari, Skodar) had twice been under siege by Ottoman forces: the second had lasted since the previous May. Mehmed regarded the failure to take the fortress as a singular humiliation. It was handed over to him in March 1479 after the governor, Antonio de Leze, received a letter from Venice which began: "We don't doubt that you have already heard before this about the peace agreement."

men[1] who wish to depart, specifically, with their merchandise, if they have any. The Signoria will take the equipment and all other military materiel or whatever is found in the fortress at present without any opposition.

[14] Further, the most illustrious Signoria of Venice is specifically obligated to transfer to my Lordship the island of Lemnos, except that they will take the *rettor* and the Venetian citizens. The other men who want to go will take whatever they have to go wherever they want. Those who want to remain on the island will be pardoned for what they did up to this point.[2]

[15] Further, the most illustrious Signoria of Venice will hand over to my Lordship the present fortresses and lands which were taken in the war from my Lordship, that is, the lands in the Morea,[3] except that the men in their authority may go wherever they want with whatever they have. If any want to remain in the present territories and fortresses they will have complete pardons, specifically, for every act, if they did anything up to now.

[16] Further, my Lordship is obligated to hand over to them the occupied lands, that is, to the former borders of their fortresses which abut the lands of my Lordship on all sides.[4]

The above-written provisions are confirmed and ratified and sworn.

The present writing was done in the year 6987, the 12th indiction, the 25th of the month of January, in Constantinople.[5]

BYZANTIUM: DECLINE AND FALL

8.8 Before the fall: Patriarch Anthony, *Letter to the Russian Church* (1395). Original in Greek.

This impassioned letter to Grand Prince Vasily I of Moscow from Patriarch Anthony IV (r.1389–1390 and again 1391–1397) evokes the imperial ideal that once held sway at Byzantium. But it was by Anthony's time only a memory. At the end of the fourteenth century, the ruler of Moscow could boldly disparage the emperor, and the emperor, Manuel II Palaeologus (r.1391–1425), a weak vassal of the Ottoman sultan, could give no reply to their critiques. Byzantium had shrunk to include only a bit of Greece, a few islands, and the city of Constantinople, while the Turks were largely in control of vast regions that had once been Byzantine. Under these circumstances, the patriarch of Constantinople, not the emperor, was the only man with enough standing to reply to Vasily.

[Source: Deno John Geanakoplos, *Byzantium: Church, Society, and Civilization Seen through Contemporary Eyes* (Chicago: University of Chicago Press, 1984), pp. 143–44.]

---

[1] "All the other men" was understood to include the soldiers, and all other (male) residents, their families, movable possessions, and trade goods. The *rettor* was the governor.

[2] This is a blanket pardon for anyone who might have fought against Mehmed. Lemnos was captured by Mehmed in 1456, then taken, retaken, and ravaged by both sides for the next 20 years. Its strategic location at the approach to the Dardanelles made possession essential for the control of shipping.

[3] The Morea was the usual name for southern Greece.

[4] This became a major issue in settling Venetian-Ottoman boundaries in Greece and required a series of boundary commissions in which representatives and the oldest inhabitants from both sides worked out what should be the dividing line.

[5] The Ottomans used Byzantine dating. The year 6987 was 5509 (from the Creation in September to the Incarnation) 1478. As the Venetians counted their year from March 1, January was still 1478. While a number of Mehmed's letters and treaties use this dating, it is unclear whether this results from his secretaries following Byzantine precedents in dealing with the West, or whether it indicates his claim to rule the empire of the Romans. The peace agreement was not signed because in Ottoman tradition such documents, or ⁱahd-names, were considered to be issued unilaterally by the sultan.

The holy emperor has a great place in the church, for he is not like other rulers or governors of other regions. This is so because from the beginning the emperors established and confirmed the [true] faith in all the inhabited world. They convoked the ecumenical councils and confirmed and decreed the acceptance of the pronouncements of the divine and holy canons regarding the correct doctrines and the government of Christians. They struggled boldly against heresies, and imperial decrees together with councils established the metropolitan sees of the archpriests and the divisions of their provinces and the delineation of their districts. For this reason the emperors enjoy great honor and position in the Church, for even if, by God's permission, the nations [primarily the Ottoman Turks] have constricted the authority and domain of the emperor, still to this day the emperor possesses the same charge from the church and the same rank and the same prayers [from the church]. The *basileus* [emperor] is anointed with the great myrrh and is appointed *basileus* and *autokrator* of the Romans, and indeed of all Christians. Everywhere the name of the emperor is commemorated by all patriarchs and metropolitans and bishops wherever men are called Christians, [a thing] which no other ruler or governor ever received. Indeed he enjoys such great authority over all that even the Latins themselves, who are not in communion with our church, render him the same honor and submission which they did in the old days when they were united with us. So much more do Orthodox Christians owe such recognition to him....

Therefore, my son, you are wrong to affirm that we have the church without an emperor, for it is impossible for Christians to have a church and no empire. The *Basileia* [empire] and the church have a great unity and community—indeed they cannot be separated. Christians can repudiate only emperors who are heretics who attack the church, or who introduce doctrines irreconcilable with the teachings of the Apostles and the Fathers. But our very great and holy *autokrator*, by the grace of God, is most orthodox and faithful, a champion of the church, its defender and avenger, so that it is impossible for bishops not to mention his name in the liturgy. Of whom, then, do the Fathers, councils, and canons speak? Always and everywhere they speak loudly of the one rightful *basileus*, whose laws, decrees, and charters are in force throughout the world and who alone, only he, is mentioned in all places by Christians in the liturgy.

8.9 The fall bewailed: George Sphrantzes, *Chronicle* (before 1477). Original in Greek.

George Sphrantzes (1401–1477), born into a noble and pious family, was brought up at the imperial court in Byzantium and personally knew the last three emperors. For much of his adult life, until the fall of the Byzantine Empire, he served Constantine XI (r.1449–1453) as diplomat, ambassador, and spy. His *Chronicle*, which uses the vernacular Greek of the time rather than the classicizing Greek of most Byzantine historians, is an unusually personal and often eyewitness account. With the fall of Constantinople, Sphrantzes was briefly enslaved, as was his wife, whom he ransomed. He continued to work for the remnants of the imperial house until, in 1456, he and his wife retired to monasteries.

[Source: *The Fall of the Byzantine Empire: A Chronicle by George Sphrantzes*, 1401–1477, trans. Marios Philippides (Amherst: The University of Massachusetts Press, 1980), pp. 21, 57–66, 69–72, 141–42 (notes modified).]

I am George Sphrantzes the pitiful First Lord of the Imperial Wardrobe, presently known by my monastic name Gregory. I wrote the following account of the events that occurred during my wretched life.

It would have been fine for me not to have been born or to have perished in childhood. Since this did not happen, let it be known that I was born on Tuesday, August 30, 6909 [1401]. The revered and holy Lady Thomais, as my godmother, sponsored my baptism....

28.7 On October 31, 6957 [1447], our emperor Lord John passed away. He was fifty-six years, ten months, and eleven days old. On November 1, he was buried in the Monastery of the Pantocrator. He had been emperor for twenty-three years, three months, and ten days.

29.1 On November 13 of the same year, Lord Thomas arrived by ship in the City [i.e., Constantinople]; he had heard of the emperor's death only as he was passing through Callipolis.[1]

2. His arrival put an end to the intrigues of his brother Lord Demetrius, or rather to those of his agents to declare him emperor. Demetrius was not a despot and had not been born in the purple; he had an older brother still alive, a man who excelled in all good activities and was free from misfortune. Proper claim and justice prevailed by command of the holy empress, her sons the despots, and by the opinion and will of the nobility.

3. On December 6, I set out with an embassy to inform the sultan that the empress, the brothers, right of birth, and the love and wisdom of nearly the whole population of the City chose Lord Constantine emperor. The sultan approved the choice and sent me away with honor and gifts.

4. In the same days lords from the City were sent to the Morea: Alexius Philanthropenus Lascaris, who had been dispatched to the City by my master together with Lord Thomas the despot, on the despot's business with the emperor, and Manuel Palaeologus Iagrus. Lord Constantine the despot was crowned emperor at Mistra on January 6 [1448].[2]

5. On March 12 of the same year [1448], he came to the City on board a Catalan vessel and was received with joy by all.

6. In August of the same year, the honored despot Lord Thomas, who was born in the purple, departed for the Morea.

7. On September 1, 6958 [1449], Lord Demetrius the despot also left for the Morea. Before their departure, a reconciliation took place in the presence of their lady mother, their brother the emperor, and ourselves, the chosen nobles: they took oaths which they violated, and were rewarded with misfortunes, as I saw later. How they were disposed toward each other is not essential to my narration, as I was absent from the City and do not have accurate knowledge.

30.1. On October 14 of the same year [1449], I was dispatched to the *mepes*—that is king—of Georgia, King George, and to the emperor of Trebizond, Lord John Comnenus, with remarkable gifts and a great, impressive retinue consisting of young nobles, soldiers, celibate priests, singers, physicians, and musicians with their instruments.[3] The Georgians knew the names of our instruments but had not seen them before and wished to inspect and hear them. For this reason many came from the furthest parts of Georgia to hear them.

2. My mission in those places was to arrange a marriage for my emperor [Constantine IX Palaeologus], whichever of the two families seemed suitable to me. He required me to submit my unbiased report on the advantages and disadvantages of each for his final decision. I sent messengers and letters by messengers, and my lord answered me by others. But his messengers' boat was wrecked in the Amisus area[4] and before my lord and emperor discovered what had passed and sent others, I spent two years minus thirty days in those parts.

3. While I was there, on March 23 of the same year [1450], our memorable holy empress, who had taken the veil under the name Patience and had become a nun, passed away and was buried next to her late husband, our memorable emperor, in the Monastery of the Pantocrator.

4. In February 6959 [1451], Sultan Murad died. I had not learned of his death while I was in Georgia, but, when I reached Trebizond, the emperor Lord John Comnenus said to me: "Come, Mr. Ambassador, I have good news for you and you must congratulate me."

---

[1] Later, Callipolis became Gallipoli. "Lord Thomas" was one of the brothers of "Lord John"—Emperor John VIII Palaeologus (r.1425–1448). So were Lord Demetrius and Lord Constantine, mentioned below. Constantine became emperor (with the approval of Sultan Mehmed II). Demetrius and Thomas vied for control over the Morea (southern Greece); both were despots there until 1460, when they had to surrender it to the Turks.

[2] That the emperor of Constantinople was crowned at Mistra and not in the Church of Saint Sophia in Constantinople was thought by contemporary writers to be a serious break with tradition. Constantine is known to history as Constantine XI Palaeologus.

[3] The empire of Trebizond was one of the Greek successor states that emerged in the aftermath of the Fourth Crusade, when, in 1204, crusader armies conquered Constantinople.

[4] The Amisus area is the southern coast of the Black Sea.

I rose, bowed, and responded: "May God grant Your Holy Majesty a long reign, as you have always been kind to us in many ways. Even now you are about to grace us, once more, with good news. I regret I have nothing worthy of Your Majesty to compensate for this favor."

He related the sultan's death and said that Murad's son [i.e., Mehmed II] was now in power, had bestowed many honors on him, and had even decided to continue the friendship which that house had enjoyed with his father.

5. Overcome by grief, as if I had been told of the death of those dearest to me, I stood speechless. Finally, with considerable loss of spirit, I said: "Lord, this news brings no joy; on the contrary, it is a cause for grief." "How so, my friend?" he asked. And I responded: "The late sultan was an old man, had given up the conquest of our City, and had no desire of attempting anything like it again; he only wished for friendship and peace. This man, who just became sultan, is young and an enemy of the Christians since childhood; he threatens with proud spirit that he will put in operation certain plans against the Christians.

6. "Our City has been in financial stress and is in great need of funds since the days of the illness of the emperor, your son-in-law; my lord, the newly crowned emperor, wants a period of peace in order to straighten out the City's affairs. If God should grant that the young sultan be overcome by his youth and evil nature and march against our City, I know not what will happen. Indeed God would have granted a joyous occasion if this man, Murad's son, had died instead. It would have been truly good news, since Murad had no other son, and he would have become weaker from grief and died soon after. In the meantime that house would have become stronger and, at his death, increased into great honor."

The emperor responded: "You are one of the more prudent and most honored advisors of his house. You will know better about these matters. In any case, God has the power to bring about the best."

I said, "Indeed it is so, as you say." Our conversation was left at that.

31.1. After I heard this, and that the widow of the late sultan and daughter of the Serbian despot had returned to her parents with full honors, and as I was required to stay in Trebizond for many reasons, I sent by a boat leaving for the City some horses, two boys—whom the king of Georgia had taken as his booty in his expedition against Samahin and given to me as gifts—and some other things that had come into my possession as gifts or in other ways. I sat down and wrote a report to my lord the emperor concerning my mission in Georgia and my plans in Trebizond, as well as the reasons for my long stay.

2. Furthermore, I composed a second letter, the contents of which I will reveal presently, and gave one of the young nobles with me the letters. I sent him with the following instructions: "Present my first report to our lord the emperor when you pay your respects, and also give an oral, detailed version of our mission. Hand over my second letter on the following day."

3. The second letter ran as follows: "I was informed by the emperor of the sultan's death when I reached Trebizond. I also heard that the sultan's widow and cousin returned to her homeland and parents. So it seems to me better for many ends to propose marriage to her, should you agree to do it instead of my errand.

4. "I can discover only four arguments opposing this marriage: (1) Her family is inferior to yours; (2) the Church may object on the grounds of close kinship; (3) she has been married already; and (4) she is older and there is the factor that she may be in danger during childbirth, a common risk according to physicians.

5. "Against the first argument I suggest that it is not untoward, since she is not inferior to my lady, your memorable mother. Against the second, a marriage alliance with Trebizond will have to be pardoned by the Church if much money is donated to individual churches and to the poor. A pardon, on the other hand, will be more easily obtained if you marry in the Serbian House, in view of the fact that the Church, celibate priests, monks, nuns, and the poor are in the despot's debt and have respect for him.

6. "About the third argument I maintain that it is not against tradition; Lady Eudocia had been previously married to a Turkish chief of an insignificant and poor principality and had even given birth to his children before she married your grandfather. Your potential bride, by contrast, was the wife of a very powerful monarch, and she, it is generally believed, did not sleep with him. As for the fourth, it is up to God, and His will shall prevail.

7. "As the other advantages of this match have been demonstrated and her parents will gladly accept it, send one servant of your house, or a monk to test this proposal. Let there be no delay; do it."

8. When my messengers arrived in the City on May 28 [1451], the emperor was away, hunting wild boars. As soon as he was told of the return of the envoys from Georgia, he finished the hunt and came from the estate in high spirits. He rejoiced at the advice on the Serbian match, as my account will reveal later.

9. On the same night of May 28 I had a dream: it seemed to me that I was back in the City; as I made a

motion to prostrate myself and kiss the emperor's feet, he stopped me, raised me, and kissed my eyes. Then I woke up and told those sleeping by me: "I just had this dream. Remember the date."[1]

10. When my lord and emperor realized that I had not returned, but that the envoys were members of my retinue, he read my first report, became sad, appeared depressed, and accused me of tardiness. On the following day he read my second report and regained his cheer, as if I had returned. Immediately, he dispatched to Serbia Manuel Palaeologus, the nephew of Lady Cantacouzena, our protostrator's wife, to test this proposal of marriage.[2] Her parents listened to it with delight and were ready to settle the final details.

11. Then it was discovered that the sultan's widow had made a vow to God and decided that if He freed her from the house of her late husband she would not remarry for the rest of her life, but would remain in His service, as far as possible. Thus the proposed match failed.

12. In August of the same year [1451], our patriarch Lord Gregory [Mamas] fled the City and became an exile.[3]

32.1. On September 14, 6960 [1451], I arrived safely in the City on board the ship of Antonio Rizzo, the good man who later suffered martyrdom for his faith in Christ.[4] I had almost completed, or rather confirmed, a marriage with the House of Georgia, as I had come to the conclusion that a marriage with the House of Trebizond would be far less advantageous....

9. The document was prepared, signed, and sealed with gold. It specified that the daughter of the king would become the wife of the emperor and queen of Constantinople and that he would be her husband, according to the agreement reached by the king of Georgia and myself. We summoned the king's nobleman of the second rank, who had come with me in the City, and in his presence, my lord the emperor drew with his own hand three crosses in

red ink on the upper part of the document, thus providing the confirmation demanded by Georgian tradition. He handed the document to the envoy and, pointing at me, he said: "With God's help, this man, in charge of three ships, shall arrive next spring in order to bring her to me." The envoy bowed and departed.

33.1. In the beginning of the same year [September 1451], rumors began circulating that the sultan intended to occupy the straits around the district Asomatos in order to build a castle.[5] The emperor decided to send an envoy to the Morea to escort one of his brothers to the City, if he accepted and remained faithful to the terms of the agreement, so that if the need arose to review their policy toward the sultan, one of the two might travel to the rulers of the West.

2. Once this had been decided, the emperor one day issued the following orders to me: "First Lord of the Imperial Wardrobe, as I have decided, I command you to travel to the Morea and, however you manage it, see whichever of my two brothers is willing to come here. Then you are to sail on to Cyprus and visit my niece, the queen. I will prepare the necessary provisions so that, when you return from Cyprus, you will proceed to Georgia and bring your future empress."

3. I responded: "My affection and loyal service demand a response to your command. I fear that my wife, your servant and mother of your godchildren, will be angry and leave me either to become a nun or to remarry. Only the other day I came back from Georgia and my twenty-three-month mission. If I am to depart again now, she will have good reason to pursue either course."

The emperor laughed and said: "Tell her to agree that you undertake just these missions. I will make her an oath that I shall burden you no more in this way.

4. "Indeed, you know better what we have in mind and have both agreed together and plan to do. This is certain and needs no sworn statement: the embassies under you

---

[1] The significance of this dream undoubtedly had something to do with the date of May 28, as it was early in the morning of May 29, 1453 that Constantinople fell to Mehmed and the emperor perished in the assault.

[2] The protostrator held an important post at the imperial court.

[3] Gregory supported the provisions of the Council of Florence (1439), which declared the union of the Greek and Latin churches, recognized papal primacy, declared a form of the Creed congruent with the Catholic position, and recognized the existence of Purgatory. The whole package was extremely unpopular at Constantinople.

[4] Although Sphrantzes does not refer to Rizzo again, we know his fate. After the construction of the Turkish fortress Rumeli Hisari, all vessels sailing south were ordered to stop and allow inspection of their cargo. Antonio Rizzo ignored these instructions, and his vessel was sunk on November 26, 1452. Rizzo and his crew were captured and killed.

[5] Mehmed built the fortress of Rumeli Hisari on the European side of the Bosporus.

will be discontinued." By this agreement he meant that we should send word to Loucas Notaras, our grand duke, that he could not hold the position of chief intermediary.

The emperor went on: "Because of his status, it is impossible to take the position from him; he must give it up himself. Let him have the first place of honor in the court and the senates as well as some income from a different source. I must appoint two nobles, as my brother, the emperor, had done; not as intermediaries, but as officials who will be with me from early in the day until late in the night, while I perform my duties." All this came to pass.

5. Word was sent to our grand duke by Neophytus, the spiritual brother and celibate priest, the godfather of his children and mine, who resided at the Kharsianites Monastery. Notaras obeyed, whether willingly or unwillingly, I cannot tell. At any rate, he made it known that it had been his wish also to do so in the hope that his sons would be honored. So it was decided but did not come to pass, as our common misfortune overwhelmed all of us.

6. The emperor commanded that I fill one of the positions, and he was considering Nicolaus Goudeles for the other.[1] He added that if we were to find each other's company agreeable, a match could be arranged between my son and Goudeles' daughter. This appointment would bring the end of my missions as ambassador.

7. Then the emperor said: "I really wished to dispatch to the Morea some older official. But I want to issue instructions written by my own hand, which will include five options: it will list the first possible compromise; then a second, third, fourth, or, if necessary, a fifth. But I believe that if anyone is sent other than you, they will promise to him a village with a silver-sealed confirmation, or a hereditary estate, and he will immediately consent to grant to them the fifth alternative, which would be difficult for us.

8. "Concerning Cyprus, do you know the monk I met a few days ago? He brought me a message from my niece that she is in need of something; she would have told me in her own voice what she wanted; had it been possible, she would have sent her message through a loyal, trusted courtier, but she has none. As she does not have one and cannot make the trip, I must send a man whom I consider appropriate to hear her message.

9. "Who is more qualified? To reach a conclusion, there is no need for argument: it is you, since you have acted and made decisions for me, know me personally, and have been informed. How could anyone else complete this mission?"

I gave my answer to the emperor: "Admittedly it is as you say. My wife, your servant, agrees, since the circumstances demand it and because she will enjoy, as you promised me, a position, honors, and fame above the other noblewomen. As for the rest, I really have no advice for you." As it was time for lunch, I went home....

35.1. On March 26 of the same year 6960 [1452], the sultan occupied the straits with the intention of constructing his castle. I kept postponing my mission from day to day, because a land route was now out of the question and would be dangerous; I had to locate a suitable ship.

2. In June of the same year the war was finally brought to our area; the Turkish army charged, captured all inhabitants found outside the walls, and blockaded the City. When the erection of the castle had been completed, the sultan left on August 31 and attacked the fortifications of the City.

3. On September 3, 6961 [1452], he departed for Adrianople; for two days he had been apparently securing his castle and its position.

4. In autumn of the same year Turahan, with his sons and a huge army, invaded the Morea.[2] At that time the inhabitants of the Morea captured one of his sons.

5. On January 17 of the same year [1453], Lord Andreas Palaeologus was born, the successor and heir of the Palaeologan Dynasty.

6. On April 4 of the same year [1453], the sultan returned and laid siege to the City with all sorts of engines and stratagems by land and sea. He surrounded the entire 18 miles of the City with 400 small and large vessels from the sea and with 200,000 men on the land side. In spite of the great size of our City, our defenders amounted to 4,773 Greeks, as well as just about 200 foreigners.

7. I was in a position to know the exact figure of our strength for the following reason: the emperor ordered the tribunes to take a census of their communities and to record the exact number of men—laity and clergy—able to defend the walls, and what weapons each man had for defense. All tribunes completed this task and brought the lists of their communities to the emperor.

8. The emperor said to me: "This task is for you and no one else, as you are skilled in arithmetic and also know

---

[1] Goudeles was a powerful noble in Constantinople.

[2] Turahan was a Turkish general.

how to guard and keep secrets. Take these lists and compute, in the privacy of your home, the exact figure of available defenders, weapons, shields, spears, and arrows." I completed my task and presented the master list to my lord and emperor in the greatest possible sadness and depression. The true figure remained a secret known only to the emperor and to myself.

9. On Tuesday May 29 [1453], early in the day, the sultan took possession of our City; in this time of capture my late master and emperor, Lord Constantine, was killed. I was not at his side at that hour but had been inspecting another part of the City, according to his orders. Alas for me; I did not know what times Providence had in store for me!

10. My late emperor, the martyr, lived for forty-nine years, three months, and twenty days. His reign lasted four years, four months, and twenty-four days. He had been the eighth emperor of the Palaeologan Dynasty. The first was Michael, the second Andronicus, the third Michael, the fourth Andronicus, the fifth John, the sixth Manuel, the seventh John, and the eighth was Constantine. The Palaeologan Dynasty ruled over the City for 194 years, ten months, and four days.

11. I was taken prisoner and suffered the evils of wretched slavery. Finally I was ransomed on September 1, 6962 [1453], and departed for Mistra. My wife and children had passed into the possession of some elderly Turks, who did not treat them badly. Then they were sold to the sultan's Mir Ahor (i.e., Master of the Horse), who amassed a great fortune by selling many other beautiful noble ladies.

12. My children's beauty and proper upbringing could not be concealed; thus, the sultan found out and bought my children from his Master of the Horse for many thousand aspers. Thus their wretched mother was left all alone in the company of a single nurse; the rest of her attendants had been dispersed.

36.1. Perhaps one would like to know the emperor's preparations before the siege, while the sultan was gathering his forces, and the aid that we received from the Christians abroad.

2. No aid whatsoever was dispatched by other Christians. On the contrary, an official of the sultan was sent to the Serbian despot Lord George in order to ask him to be the intermediary for the treaty with the Hungarians. Even though a Christian scribe in the retinue of the envoy had been instructed by certain members of the Turkish Council to inform the despot that the sultan intended to march against Constantinople once the treaty was signed and to delay the conclusion of this treaty, the despot paid no attention to him; the wretch of a despot did not consider the fact that once the head has been removed the limbs perish also.

3. An important meeting of the senate was held in Venice. The doge Francesco Foscari was opposed to dispatching aid not because he was inept (indeed, our emperor Lord John and others who had met him and talked to him maintained that they had not seen a wiser man in Italy), but because of spite and malice; for spite generally overlooks advantage. The reason for his attitude was the following: Foscari had sent Alvise Diedo as his intermediary to Lord Constantine—who was then the despot of the Morea—to propose marriage between his daughter and Lord Constantine, promising a handsome dowry. Lord Constantine agreed to this betrothal, not so much because of the dowry, but because his territories would be joined to those of Venice. I advised him to agree more forcefully than others, and he took my advice.

4. Once Constantine had become emperor and come to the City, this marriage was out of the question. What nobleman or noblewoman would ever receive the daughter of a Venetian—even though he might be the glorious doge—as queen and lady for more than a short time? Who would accept his other sons-in-law as the emperor's fellow sons-in-law, and his sons as the brothers-in-law of the emperor? The doge insisted on the marriage and, after our final rejection, this man became our enemy. Thus during this meeting of the senate, even though the noblemen Alvise Loredano and Antonio Diedo argued and demonstrated that Venetian interests would be hurt if the City fell, they were unable to prevail.

5. In Rome what measures were taken by the Church to prevent our downfall? The cardinal of Russia happened to be in the City and I argued, as his intermediary to my late lord, the emperor, that he should be appointed patriarch in the hope that various advantages would come from him and the then pope, or, at least, that the name of the pope should be commemorated in our services.[1]

6. After many consultations and deliberations, my

---

[1] Isidore, formerly the metropolitan of Kiev and later the cardinal of all Russias, arrived in Constantinople on October 26, 1452, to enforce the decisions made at the Council of Florence. He was accompanied by a force of 200 archers. He remained in Constantinople during the siege, was taken captive during the sack, but managed to conceal his identity and escape to the West.

late master and emperor decided to abandon the first alternative altogether, since the appointed patriarch requires the obedience of all; otherwise riots and war ensue between him and those who are opposed to his appointment; especially at this time, when we were facing extreme war, what a misfortune to have a war inside the City as well! The emperor consented to have the pope's name commemorated in our services, by necessity, as we hoped to receive some aid. Whoever were willing would pronounce the commemoration in Saint Sophia; the rest would incur no blame and remain peaceful. These services took place on November 12.[1] Six months later we had received as much aid from Rome as had been sent to us by the sultan of Cairo.[2]

7. Although it was possible for the despot of Serbia to send money secretly from many places and, similarly, men, did anyone see a single penny? On the contrary, they provided huge financial aid and many men to the sultan who was besieging the City. Thus the Turks were able to boast in triumph that even Serbia was against us.[3]

8. Which of the Christians, the Trebizondian emperor, the lords of Walachia, or the Georgia king, contributed a single penny or a single soldier to our defense, openly or secretly?

8.10 After the fall: Archbishop Genady of Novgorod and Dmitry Gerasimov, *The Tale of the White Cowl* (end of the 15th c.). Original in Russian.

A cowl is a hood. Drawing on the belief that Constantine had given his empire to the papacy as well as predictions about the coming of the Kingdom of the Holy Spirit, Archbishop Genady of Novgorod and his co-writer, Dmitry Gerasimov, wrote of the fate of the White Cowl, symbol of Christ's Resurrection. First Emperor Constantine gave it to the pope. Then, as the papacy fell into heresy (from the point of view of the Greek Church), it was given to Philotheus, the patriarch of Constantinople. He, in turn, gave it to Vasily, archbishop of Novgorod, where it was to remain, crown of the "Third Rome." The idea was one of transmission, from "old" Rome (the Rome of Italy) to the "second" Rome (Constantinople) to the "final" Rome (Novgorod). Written thirty or forty years after the fall of Constantinople in 1453, the "prediction" of the triumph of Islam in the story was a foregone conclusion. But the pre-eminence of Novgorod in the story was only a pipe dream: already in 1478 Ivan III (r.1462–1505), ruler of Muscovy, had conquered the Republic of Novgorod and made Moscow the center of the Russian Church.

[Source: *Medieval Russia's Epics, Chronicles, and Tales*, ed. and trans. Serge A. Zenkovsky (New York: E.P. Dutton, 1963), pp. 268–74 (notes slightly modified).]

---

[1] On December 12, 1452, the union of the two Churches was solemnly celebrated in the Church of Saint Sophia. The Greek monks and most of the Greek inhabitants of Constantinople were opposed to the union. Consequently, on the eve of the fall, Constantinople was a divided city. Two political parties were formed: the unionists, headed by the Palaeologi and other Greeks, and the anti-unionists, headed by the grand duke Loucas Notaras, and by George Courtetsis Scholarius, who became the first patriarch under Mehmed's rule. It is no exaggeration to say that the situation in Constantinople was chaotic before—as during—the siege.

[2] In fact, Isidore's 200 archers were paid by the pope, and preparations in the West were under way to aid Constantinople. Venetian ships had been equipped by means of financial aid from the pope and had reached Chios when news of the fall reached them; consequently, they returned to Venice.

[3] The Serbian ruler was the vassal of the sultan.

At that time the Patriarch of Constantinople was Philotheus,[1] who was distinguished by his strict fasting and his virtuous ways. Once, he had a vision in the night of a youth from whom emanated light and who told him:

"Blessed teacher, in the olden times the Roman Emperor, Constantine, who, through the vision of the Holy Apostles Peter and Paul, was enlightened by God, decided to give Blessed Pope Sylvester the White Cowl to glorify the Holy Apostolic Church. Later, the unfaithful popes of the Latin heresies wanted to profane and destroy this cowl, but I appeared to the evil pope, and now this pope has sent this cowl to you. When the messengers arrive with it, you must accept it with all honors. Then send the White Cowl to the Russian land, to the city of Novgorod the Great with your written blessing. And there this cowl will be worn on the head of Vasily, Archbishop of Novgorod,[2] so that he may glorify the Holy Apostolic Cathedral of Holy Sophia and laud the Orthodox. There, in that land, the faith of Christ is truly glorified. And the popes, because of their shamelessness, will receive the vengeance of God." And having spoken these words, the youth became invisible.

The patriarch awoke filled with awe and joy and was unable to sleep throughout the remainder of the night. And he contemplated this vision. In the morning he ordered that the bells should sound the Matins, and when day came he summoned the Church council and revealed his vision. And all praised God, perceiving that a holy angel had appeared to the patriarch. Yet they did not fully understand the meaning of the message. When they were still in council and were filled with awe due to their great joy, there arrived a servant of the patriarch, and he announced to them that messengers had arrived from the Pope of Rome. The patriarch ordered that they be brought before him. The messengers came, bowed low to the patriarch, and gave him the message. The patriarch read the message and pondered it, praising God. He announced its contents to Emperor John who was reigning at that time and whose name was Cantacuzenus.[3] And then he went with the entire council to meet the bringers of the divine treasure which lay in an ark. He accepted it with all honors, broke the seal, and took from the ark the Holy White Cowl. He kissed it with reverence, and looked upon it with wonderment both for its creation and for the wonderful fragrance that emanated from it.

At that time the patriarch had diseased eyes and constant headaches, but when he placed the White Cowl upon his head, these afflictions immediately ceased to be. And he rejoiced with great joy and rendered glory to Christ, our Lord, to Constantine's blessed memory for his creating this wonderful cowl for Blessed Pope Sylvester. And he put the Holy Cowl on the golden salver [tray] that was also sent by the pope. He placed them in the great church in an honorable place until he could make a decision with the emperor's counseling.

After the White Cowl was sent from Rome, the evil pope, who was counseled by heretics, became angered against the Christian faith and was driven to a frenzy, extremely regretting his allowing the White Cowl to be sent to Constantinople. And he wrote an evil letter to the patriarch, in which he demanded the return of the White Cowl on the golden salver. The patriarch read this letter and, understanding the pope's evil and cunning design, sent him a letter in return that was based on Holy Scripture, and in it he called the pope both evil and godless, the apostate and precursor of the Antichrist. And the patriarch cursed the pope in the name of our Lord, Jesus Christ, the Holy Apostles, and the Church Fathers. And this letter came to the pope.

When the pope had read the letter and learned that the patriarch intended to send the White Cowl with great honor to the Russian land, to the city of Novgorod the Great, he uttered a roar. And his face changed and he fell ill, for he, the infidel, disliked the Russian land and could not even bear to hear of this land where the Christian faith was professed.

Patriarch Philotheus, having seen that the White Cowl was illumined with grace, began to ponder how he might keep it in Constantinople and wear it on his own head. He consulted with the emperor about the matter several times, and wanted to write to the other patriarchs and metropolitans to summon them to a council. After Matins one Sunday, the patriarch returned to his chambers and, after the usual prayers, lay down to rest. But he slept but lightly, and in this sleep he saw that two men, who were unknown to him, came through the door. And from them there emanated light. One of them was armed as a warrior and had an imperial crown upon his head. The other wore a bishop's vestments and was distinguished by his venerable white hair.

---

[1] Philotheus (r.1353–1354; 1364–1376) was patriarch of Constantinople.

[2] Vasily (r.1330–1352) was archbishop of Novgorod.

[3] John VI Cantacuzenus was emperor of Byzantium (r.1347–1354).

The latter spoke to the patriarch, saying: "Patriarch! Stop pondering your wearing of the White Cowl on your own head. If this were to be, our Lord, Jesus Christ, would have so predestined it from the founding of this city. And for a long time did divine enlightenment come from heaven, and then God's voice came to me and I learned that Rome had to betray God and embrace their Latin heresies. That is the reason I did not wish to wear this cowl upon my head, and thus I instructed other popes not to do so. And this imperial city of Constantinople will be taken by the sons of Hagar[1] because of its sins, and all holy shrines will be defiled and destroyed. Thus has it been predestined since the founding of this city.

"The ancient city of Rome will break away from the glory and faith of Christ because of its pride and ambition. In the new Rome, which will be the City of Constantinople, the Christian faith will also perish through the violence of the sons of Hagar. In the third Rome, which will be the land of Russia, the Grace of the Holy Spirit will be revealed. Know then, Philotheus, that all Christians will finally unite into one Russian nation because of its orthodoxy. Since ancient times and by the will of Constantine, Emperor of the Earth, the imperial crown of the imperial city is predestined to be given to the Russian tsar. But the White Cowl, by the will of the King of Heaven, Jesus Christ, will be given to the archbishop of Novgorod the Great. And this White Cowl is more honorable than the crown of the tsar, for it is an imperial crown of the archangelic spiritual order. Thus, you must send this Holy White Cowl to the Russian land, to the city of Novgorod the Great, as you were told to do in the vision of the angel. You should believe and trust in what I say: And when you send it to the Russian land, the Orthodox Faith will be glorified and the cowl will be safe from seizure by the infidel sons of Hagar and from the intended profanation by the Latin pope. And the grace, glory, and honor which were taken from Rome, as well as the Grace of the Holy Spirit, will be removed from the imperial city of Constantinople after its capture by the sons of Hagar. And all holy relics will be given to the Russian land in the predestined moment. And the Russian tsar will be elevated by God above other nations, and under his sway will be many heathen kings. And the power of the patriarch of this imperial ruling city will pass to the Russian land in the predestined hour. And that land will be called Radiant Russia, which, by the Grace of God, will be glorified with blessings. And its majesty will be strengthened by its orthodoxy, and it will become more honorable than the two Romes which preceded it."

And saying this, the man of the vision who was dressed in a bishop's vestment wished to leave, but the patriarch, seized by great awe, fell before the bishop and said: "Who are you, my lord? Your vision has seized me with great awe; my heart has been frightened by your words, and I tremble to my very bones."

The man in the bishop's vestments answered: "Don't you know who I am? I am Pope Sylvester, and I came to you because I was ordered by God to reveal to you the great mystery which will come to pass in the predestined time." Then, pointing to the other man in the vision, he added: "This is blessed Emperor Constantine of Rome to whom I gave rebirth in the holy font and whom I won over to the faith of our Lord, Jesus Christ. He was the first Christian emperor, my child in Christ, who created and gave me the White Cowl in place of the imperial crown." And saying this, he blessed the patriarch, and became invisible.

Waking up, the patriarch was seized with awe, remembering the words about the White Cowl and the conquest of Constantinople by the pagan sons of Hagar. And he wept for a long time. When the hour of the divine Mass arrived, the patriarch went to the church, fell before the icon of the Holy Mother of God, and remained lying there for some time. Then he arose, took the White Cowl with great reverence, kissed it piously, placed it upon his head, and then put it to his eyes and his heart. And his adoration for this cowl increased even more. And doing this, he wept. His clerics, who were around him and saw that he wept inconsolably, did not dare to inquire as to why he was weeping. Finally the patriarch ceased crying and told his clerics in detail of the vision of Pope Sylvester and Emperor Constantine. Having heard these words, the clerics wept sorrowfully, and exclaimed, "Thy will be done!"

The patriarch, mourning the forthcoming misfortunes of the city of Constantinople and fearing to trespass the divine will, told them that he must fulfill the will of the Lord and do with the White Cowl as he was commanded to do. After having deliberated with blessed Emperor John, he took the White Cowl and the golden salver, put them in the aforementioned ark, sealed it with his seal, and, as he was commanded by the holy angel and

---

[1] Both the Byzantines and the Russians called all nomads, whether they were Turks, Mongols, or Arabs, the sons of Hagar. "Hagar" refers to the handmaid of the biblical patriarch Abraham. Here it refers to the Ottomans.

Blessed Pope Sylvester, put in his epistle with his blessings, and in it he commanded Archbishop Vasily and all other bishops who would follow Vasily to wear the White Cowl upon their heads. He added many other honorable and marvelous gifts from his clergy for the bishopric of Novgorod the Great. And he also sent vestments with their embroidered crosses for the glorification of the Holy Apostolic Church. And all this was placed in another ark. And he gave these arks to a bishop named Eumeny, and sent him forth with both joy and sorrow.

In the bishopric of the city of Novgorod the Great was Archbishop Vasily who distinguished himself by his fasting and virtuous ways. Once, in the night, he prayed to God and then lay down to rest, but he slept but lightly, and had a dream in which he saw the angel of God. This angel of God, who had a handsome appearance and radiant face, appeared before him in the garb of a monk and with the White Cowl upon his head. With his finger he pointed to his head and in a low voice announced: "Vasily! This White Cowl which you see on my head is from Rome. In olden times the Christian Emperor Constantine created it in honor of Sylvester, Pope of Rome. He gave it to this pope to wear upon his head. But God Almighty did not permit the White Cowl to remain there because of their Latin heresies. Tomorrow morning you must go from the city with your clergymen and meet the bishop and messengers sent by the patriarch. And they will bring an ark, and in this ark you will find the White Cowl upon a golden salver. Accept it with all honors, for this White Cowl symbolizes the radiant Resurrection which came to pass on the third day. And from now on, you and all other archbishops of this city will wear it on your heads. And I have come to you to assure you before hand that all is as God wills it and to assuage any doubts you may have." And saying this, the angel became invisible.

Waking up, Archbishop Vasily was seized with awe and joy, pondering the meaning of the vision. The next morning he sent his clerics outside the city, to the crossroads, to see whether the messengers really would appear. In the vicinity of the city the servant of Archbishop Vasily met a Greek bishop who was unknown to him and who traveled to the city of Novgorod. They made a low obeisance [bow] and returned to the archbishop and told them all they had seen. The bishop then sent his messenger into the city to summon the clerics and the entire population.

And he ordered the tolling of the bells, and both he and his clerics donned their vestments.

The procession had not gone far from the Cathedral of Holy Sophia when they met the aforementioned bishop, sent by the patriarch and bearing the ark that had been sealed by the patriarch, and which contained the venerable gifts, came to Archbishop Vasily, made a low obeisance before him, and gave him the epistles of the patriarch. They blessed and greeted each other in Christ's name. Archbishop Vasily accepted the epistles of the patriarch and the arks bearing the venerable gifts. And he went with them to the Cathedral of Holy Sophia, the Wisdom of God. There he put them in the middle of the church in an honorable place and ordered that the patriarchal epistles be read aloud. When the Orthodox people, who were in the cathedral, heard these writings read aloud, they rendered glory to God and rejoiced with great joy. Archbishop Vasily opened one of the arks and removed the cover. And a wonderful fragrance and miraculous radiance spread through the church. Archbishop Vasily and all present were in wonderment, witnessing these happenings. And Bishop Eumeny, who was sent by the patriarch, wondered about these blessed deeds of God that he had witnessed. And they all rendered glory to God, and celebrated the service of thanksgiving.

Archbishop Vasily took the White Cowl from the ark and saw that it appeared exactly like the one he had seen on the angel's head in his vision. And he kissed it with reverence. At that same moment there came a sonorous voice from the icon of the Lord, which was in the cupola of the church, saying, "Holy, holy." And after a moment of silence there came the same voice, which thrice announced, "Ispola eti despota."[1] And when the archbishop and all those present heard these voices, they were seized with awe and joy. And they said, "The Lord have mercy upon us!" And the archbishop then ordered that all present in the church be silent, and he revealed to them his vision of the angel and his words concerning the White Cowl. And he told of his vision as it had happened and in detail, even as it was told to him by the angel in the night.

Giving thanks to God for sending this cowl, the archbishop went forth from the church, preceded by the deacons in holy vestments carrying tapers and singing hymns. And they proceeded with serenity and piety. And the people crowded round, jostling each other and jump-

---

[1] *Ispola eti despota* is Greek for "Many years to the lord," or, more loosely translated, "Long live the bishop." The Russians used this expression during the Church service, and it was always pronounced in Greek.

ing so that they might see the White Cowl on the archbishop's head. And all were in wonderment. Thus, in this way, thanks to the Grace of our Lord, Jesus Christ, and to the blessing of his Holiness Philotheus, Patriarch of Constantinople, the White Cowl became a symbol upon the heads of the archbishops of Novgorod. And Archbishop Vasily was overcome with great joy, and for seven days he feasted all priests, deacons, and clerics of the city of Novgorod the Great. And he also offered food and drink to the poor, to monks, and to prisoners. And he asked that the prisoners be released. During the divine service he placed the holy and venerable gifts of the patriarch in the Cathedral of Holy Sophia and with the blessings of all clerics. And the golden salver, on which the White

Cowl was placed, was also deposited in the Cathedral of Holy Sophia during the Mass.

The messengers of the patriarch who brought the Holy White Cowl were also shown great honor and they received many gifts. The archbishop sent gifts to the Emperor and Patriarch of Constantinople and sent the messengers forth with great honors. Thereafter, multitudes arrived from many cities and kingdoms to look upon, as if it were a miracle, the archbishop in the White Cowl. And they were in wonderment about it, and told of it in many lands. This Holy White Cowl was created by the first pious Christian Emperor, Constantine, for Blessed Pope Sylvester in the year 297 (5895). And this is the history of the Holy White Cowl up to this day.

WAR AND SOCIAL UNREST

8.11 Chivalric and non-chivalric models: Froissart, *Chronicles* (*c*.1400). Original in French.

Born in Valenciennes, just outside the kingdom of France, Jean Froissart (1337–*c*.1404) served the rulers of Hainaut, especially Philippa of Hainaut, wife of the English king Edward III (r.1327–1377). His most famous work was the *Chronicles*, a wide-ranging account of the first half of the Hundred Years' War. Late in life, he began to revise this work thoroughly, although he finished only a small section. Nevertheless, the result, parts of which are presented below, reflected his mature thinking on topics that Froissart had long written about: the glory of great feats of arms and the nature and purposes of chivalric warfare. What forms of violence did Froissart think knights were right to engage in? Were there limits to the violence that Froissart justified and celebrated? In what ways were Othman's ambitions and sense of chivalry in Ashikpashazade's *Othman Comes to Power* (above, p. 451) similar to and different from those of the Western knights who populate the pages of Froissart?

[Source: Froissart, *Chroniques. Début du premier livre. Edition du manuscrit de Rome Reg. lat. 869*, ed. George T. Diller (Geneva: Droz, 1972), pp. 303–7, 313–15, 633–39. Translated by Helen Nicholson.]

Chapter 78: Walter de Manny begins the War [1339]

As soon as Lord Walter de Manny discovered and realized that a formal declaration of war had been made against the king of France and that the bishop of Lincoln was on his way back [from delivering the king of England's declaration of war to the king of France], he gathered together 40 lances,[1] good companions from Hainaut and England, and left Brabant and rode by night and day until

---

[1] The best guess of the meaning of "one lance" is that it was made up of two men, one the combatant and the other his servant, and two horses.

he arrived in Hainaut. He and his people rode undercover and no one knew about them, except for themselves and a guide who led them where they wanted to go. Then they hid in the wood of Blaton. The noble knight had vowed in England in the hearing of ladies and lords that, "If war breaks out between my lord the king of England and Philip of Valois who calls himself king of France, I will be the first to arm himself and capture a castle or town in the kingdom of France." And he did not fail in this vow, for he came by night and hid in the wood of Wiers [in modern Belgium], very close to Mortagne [now in northern France]. When he had arrived there, he told his companions what he wanted to do and they agreed to his enterprise.

The town of Mortagne on the river Escaut—although it is very well protected—was in great danger of being captured that day, for Lord Walter de Manny and his band arrived at daybreak so close to the town that they hid in ambush in the hedges and bushes next to Mortagne. They had procured dresses and women's clothes, which they had acquired in a village on their road, and great flat baskets, in which women who are going to market put butter, eggs and cheeses. Four of their men dressed in the women's clothes and wrapped lovely white head-wraps of white cloth around their heads and they took the baskets, covered with white cloths, and made out that they were coming to market to sell their butter and cheese. They came to the gate at the hour of sunrise, and found it closed and the wicket gate half open, and a man who guarded it. He truly believed that these were women from a village close by who were coming to market, and he opened the wicket gate wide open so that they could enter with their baskets. When these men in women's clothing were inside, they seized hold of the porter and drew long knives which they were carrying under their gowns and said to him, "If you say one word, you're dead." The man was absolutely terrified and feared death, so he remained silent and still in their midst.

Here comes Lord Walter de Manny and his companions, who were following them at a distance; and they had left their horses in the hedges and bushes, quite close to Mortagne, under the guard of their servants. When they saw that their companions had control of the gate, they hurried as fast as they could and entered in by the wicket gate at their ease. Then they went towards the tower and the castle keep, and expected to find it badly guarded; but they did not, for it was shut up. Then they stopped short,

for they saw clearly that they had failed in their intentions and that it was worth nothing for them to hold the town without the castle. So they retraced their steps the way that they had come, and did not do any other damage to the town of Mortagne except that they set fire to two or three houses; and then they went out and mounted their horses and left without doing anything more. Many people from the town of Mortagne were still in their beds, and knew nothing about this adventure.

In order to accomplish his enterprise, Lord Walter de Manny and his companions rode and returned into Hainaut, and crossed the Escaut by a little bridge just below Condé. And that day they dined at the abbey of Vicoigne, and refreshed their horses there, and remained there until night. The country was not yet in a state of alarm. At sunset they mounted their horses and rode off, and passed through the Walers wood, and entered [the region of] Ostrevan. They had guides to lead them; and they came between Douai and Cambrai, passing the river of Sensee, which joins the Escaut at Bouchain. They rode until, at the hour of sunrise, they came to a castle, which is called Thun l'Evêque, sited on the river Escaut. They arrived at the very moment that the garrison of the castle were sending out the cattle to graze in the meadows that are close by, and the castellan[1] was still in his bed. So they entered in through the gate, for they found it standing open, and made themselves lords and masters of the gate, and kicked out all the men and women whom they found inside. The said Lord Walter de Manny kept the castle for himself, and put it in order and gave it to a brother of his, a knight, who is known as Lord Giles de Manny. For the rest of that year, the latter gave the people of Cambrai plenty of trouble. When the said Lord Walter de Manny had completed these enterprises, he returned to his lord the king of England, whom he found at Maligne. The king of England had arrived there and was holding a council there....

Chapter 79: The Sack of Southampton [Sept. 1338/1339]

Just as, when the king of England and the king of France issued their challenges to each other, the English began to plot how they could harm and bring damage, so too all that season the French, the king of France, and his council thought about nothing except how to make their prepa-

---

[1] The man in command of the castle's garrison.

rations by sea and land. Through the preparations that they saw and heard about they realized clearly enough that they would have war. They had established on the sea a number of Norman ships and a great crowd of Genoese and of mariners who are called "sea-going plunderers" [buccaneers]. Their leaders and commanders were Lord Charles Grimaldi, admiral of France, lord Hugh Quieret, [Nicholas] Behuchet and [Pietro] Barbavera; and they stationed themselves on the coast at Dieppe and Harfleur. As soon as the news of the king of England's challenge arrived at Paris, they were informed. Then these so-called plunderers left French waters and rode across the sea, and came, with the wind and the tide, to the harbor of Southampton [England], one Sunday when everybody was at mass. The town was taken so much by surprise that they had no opportunity to think about guarding their town and their harbor. All in all there were a good twenty thousand of these socalled plunderers, and for that day they were lords of Southampton. Those men, women and children who could escape fled to save themselves, and the raiders killed and captured many of them, and they carried off all the wool and cloth that they could find in the town. When the tide came back in, they got into their ships, but first they set fire to the town in more than 60 places, and then they left the harbor and embarked on the sea; and they went back towards Normandy, taking with them many prisoners, whom they later ransomed.

The news spread throughout England of how the Normans had been at Southampton and how they had captured it and robbed and pillaged everything. Then the English certainly felt that the war between France and England had really begun....

Chapter 81: *The Siege of Cambrai [1339]*

You know, as my history stated above, that the city of Cambrai [today in northern France] had gone into the presence of King Philip [VI of France] to complain that they had heard that the king of England, as representative of Louis of Bavaria, king of Germany and emperor of Rome, was coming in strength to lay siege to their town. They had begged the king, as people who wanted to support him in everything, to send them men-at-arms, because they felt that they did not have sufficient forces. The king gave his consent to this plea and sent to gar-

rison the city of Cambrai Lord Amé de Geneva, the Savoyard named "the Gaul of la Baume,"[1] Lord John [Guy] de Groullée, the lord of Vinai, Lord Louis de Chalon, Lord Tiebaut de Moruel, the lord [John] of Roye, the lord [John] of Fosseux, the lord of Biausaut, and a good 100 lances of good men-at-arms, knights and squires. He had all the castles of the Cambrai region equipped and resupplied with good men-at-arms so that no misfortune could take them by surprise. The lord [Enguerrand] of Coucy had sent around 40 lances of good comrades to Oisy in the Cambrai region, with [Robert] the lord of Clari at their head. The country was all prepared on the frontiers of Artois, Cambrai, and the Vermandois. As well as all this, King Philip issued a great summons throughout the whole of his kingdom and outside it, requesting his friends and commanding his subjects to come and fight the king of England, outside Cambrai or elsewhere. His intention was never to return to Paris until he had fought him; until then he would remain at Compiègne and send out his command.

When the king of England had lodged at Haspres for two days and many of his people had already crossed the sea and come to Naves, to Cagnoneles and the area around, he set out and approached Cambrai, halting at Iwuy in the Cambrai region. All the German lords crossed over in good order and came to set up siege before Cambrai. The second day after came the young count William of Hainaut and his uncle Lord John de Hainaut with a fine, large company of Hainauters. There were more than 500 lances, knights and squires, and they set up camp outside Cambrai. Six days later Duke John of Brabant arrived, with a good 900 helmets[2] in his company. Thus the English, German, Hainaut, and Teutonic men-at-arms surrounded the city of Cambrai.

Very soon after the duke of Brabant had joined the army outside Cambrai, the king of England begged and requested him to send a challenge to the king of France. The duke replied, saying that he would do so at once; but the king of France did not wish to do anything until such time as he saw that they were going to march on the kingdom of France. So the matter rested; but certainly the king of England intended never to withdraw until he had set fire to and burned the kingdom of France.

Those of the army had built a bridge across the River Escaut so that they could cross over to each other. Every day the English and the Germans raided across the

---

[1] Master of the French king's crossbowmen.

[2] A "helmet" in this context seems to mean a single armed warrior.

Cambrai region as far as Bapaumes. The whole country had been warned before Cambrai went under siege, and most of the people had carried their possessions into the fortresses and driven their animals before them a long way into Artois or the Vermandois, because whatever was found on the flat countryside was lost. So while the city of Cambrai was under siege there were several assaults and skirmishes, but the fine body of knights who were within the city took such great care of it that they took and received neither blame nor damage. Lord John de Hainaut, the lord of Valkenburg and some knights from Gueldre and Juliers left the siege one day and rode so far that they reached Oisy in the Cambrai region. Some of them dismounted at the barrier and there was a great skirmish, for the knights and the squires who were within the town on behalf of the lord of Coucy bore themselves valiantly and did not take any damage; and the Germans returned to the army without having achieved anything....

Chapter 186: Negotiations between Jacques d'Arteveld and Edward III [1340–1345]

At this time and at the same season Lord Godfrey de Harcourt, one of the greatest barons of Normandy, brother of the count of Harcourt and lord of Saint-Sauveur-le-Vicomte and of several towns in Normandy, incurred the great displeasure and hatred of the king of France. I am unable to explain the cause of this hatred to you, but it was so great that if the king of France could have laid hold of him in his anger he would have made him die a shameful death. The said Lord Godfrey had to hide, flee and leave the kingdom of France. He went to England to King Edward, offered him his service and placed himself under his command just as Lord Robert d'Artois had done formerly, and no one could ever make his peace with the king of France. The king of England received him and retained him at his side, and gave him sufficient means to maintain his position.

At this time that bourgeois of Ghent still reigned in the country of Flanders in great prosperity and power, Jacques d'Arteveld, who was a close ally of the king of England—so far as he could be, because he was always doubtful about the loyalty of the Flemings, whom he felt were unreliable. And he was right to be doubtful, as he came to such a miserable end, as I shall tell you. Above all he wished to disinherit the count of Flanders, Count Louis the Exile and his son Louis de Male; and he wished the king of England to inherit Flanders. This

man Jacques d'Arteveld used to say that Flanders would become a duchy and the prince of Wales would be duke.

On this account at this time, he had the king of England, his close comrade, come to Sluys; but when the king arrived, he did not disembark from his ship. The good towns of Flanders—that is to say the consuls—came to see him and make him welcome at Sluys and laid the whole country open to him and his people, at his command, and begged him to agree to come to Bruges and to Ghent, and said that everywhere he would be welcomed. The king, thanking them, replied very gently and said that at that moment he had not come to disembark on shore. That man Jacques d'Arteveld was present at all these discussions.

Soon afterwards, a conference was held on the king's ship, which was very large and beautiful, and was named the *Christofle*. All the consuls of the good towns of Flanders were present. Jacques d'Arteveld promised what was said above and demonstrated with various arguments, gilded with fine words, that it would be beneficial to accept the prince of Wales as their lord, and Flanders should be made into a duchy and the said duke and prince should stay in the country and govern the land and country of Flanders in all good customs, and maintain justice and reason for all people; and Jacques d'Arteveld begged the [consuls of the] good towns who were there to reply and give their opinion on this. At that they all exchanged glances and did not know what to say. In any case, they asked for permission to talk together, which was given to them. They all reached the same decision, and this was their reply: "Jacques, we have heard clearly what you said; and when we came here, we did not know that you were going to talk to us on this matter, and it came as news to us. And we cannot act on this by ourselves alone; it is necessary that all the land of Flanders agree; and when [representatives of the whole of the land are] assembled, it will be necessary to pick out and identify the rebels who do not wish to agree to this, and that they be publicly banished and lose what they now hold in the land of Flanders, without any hope of seeing it again or returning to it. In this way this inheritance can be secured, for, so far as we are concerned, we would very much like the prince of Wales as our lord, as has been proposed, saving and reserving the conditions aforesaid."

This reply greatly satisfied the king and his council, but the good towns of Flanders who had replied were asked when the king could expect their reply. They agreed on a month and a day; this was given to them. And they dined with the king in his own ship, and then departed and went back each to his place, some of them feeling abused and angered at this news they had heard, although they had replied to please the king and d'Arteveld. And it seemed to them a hard and strange thing to disinherit their lord, and if they did so they would be reputed to be infamous traitors for ever and ever. Nevertheless, d'Arteveld was so feared and dreaded in the land of Flanders that in fact none would have dared anger him or speak against his wishes. Jacques d'Arteveld remained with the king on his ships in Sluys after the rest had gone.

Chapter 187: Jacques d'Arteveld Is Assassinated at Ghent [1345]

As the news spread that Jacques d'Arteveld was aiming for the prince of Wales to be lord of Flanders and to make it a duchy, great murmuring arose throughout the county of Flanders. Some, who supported the king of England, said, "This would be a good thing." Others said the opposite, that it would be shameful, blameworthy and great treason to disinherit their lord. The good people were very distressed at this, more for the sake of the son, Count Louis de Male, than they were for the father, because he had been cruel, violent, harsh and terrible to them, for which reason they had driven him out of Flanders. But they kept Louis, the young son, and said that they would bring him up in their own way, and he would be more familiar with Flemish customs than his father had been.

At that time Duke John of Brabant had a young daughter to marry off, and as a wise, skilful and astute man he had in mind that a marriage between his daughter and the son of the count of Flanders would be very advantageous. The count of Flanders was in sufficient agreement, but he was not lord or master of his son, because the Flemings held and guarded him and were bringing him up under good guards and did not allow him to leave the town of Ghent. The duke of Brabant carefully considered what was going to happen, and how Jacques d'Arteveld was at that time so powerful in Flanders that everything was done by him and without him nothing was done; and he was informed of the news that the king of England was at Sluys and lay there at anchor, and that he and Jacques d'Arteveld on his behalf were procuring that the king's son, the prince of Wales, should be duke of Flanders. The said duke of Brabant feared that all these things would come about, for they could too easily happen, and he decided that he would put a monkey-wrench in the works.

As for what happened in the town of Ghent: while the king of England was still in his ship before Sluys, and waited for the reply from those of the land of Flanders, a very great dispute arose in the town of Ghent between the weavers of cloth and Jacques d'Arteveld, and all at the instigation and through the advancement of their dean,[1] whose name was Thomas Denis. The duke of Brabant is said to have been the cause of these events. One day more than 400 of these weavers, on the instructions of their dean, assembled in front of d'Arteveld's lodging, and surrounded it from the front and rear, and showed that they wanted to enter by force. When the servants of this d'Arteveld saw them coming like this they wondered what they wanted, for this was not the custom of those of Ghent, nor had other people come in this way to speak to their master nor wishing to force their way into the house. So they began to speak roughly to them and tried to drive them out by force, but they could not; they were beaten and insulted and wounded first.

Jacques d'Arteveld was shut up in his bedchamber, and had heard much of the words and the fighting. So he went to a window that overlooked a road where all these people were assembled and asked them, "Good people, what do you want? Why are you so upset?" They replied, "We want to talk to you. Come out." Then Jacques replied: "And if I come out there, what do you want to say?" "We want you to give us an account of the great riches that you have taken from Flanders as you liked over the last seven years, and tell us what you have done with the money and where you have put it." Then Jacques d'Arteveld saw clearly that the situation was becoming ugly. This was an unprecedented state of affairs, and its outcome was unpredictable. Hoping to appease the crowd with gentle words, he said: "Good people, all of you go back to your own lodgings, and within three days I will summon you and I will be able to render you such a good account of the money that you will be quite content." They replied with one voice: "We don't want to wait so long, but come out of your lodging and give us account."

Jacques d'Arteveld then realized that things were looking bad, and that his life was in danger. So he said: "My lords, my lords, stay there, I will come at once and speak to you." At these words they all stood quietly, and he came out of his room and went to his stable and his horses, intending to mount and leave by the back gate and go on his way, but he could not. For the lodging was so surrounded on all sides that immediately what he intended

---

[1] The president of the guild of weavers at Ghent.

to do was detected and noticed; and those who were guarding the door warned those who were at the front gate. Then a great tumult arose among them and they broke the doors by force and burst in, and came into the stable and found Jacques d'Arteveld who was getting ready to mount and go on his way. Immediately they attacked him and that man Thomas Denis, the dean of the weavers, gave him the first blow on the head with an axe, knocking him down. Jacques d'Arteveld had done him many good turns and had given him the position of dean of the weavers, and he was his comrade. Nevertheless all these things and affinities were forgotten and put to one side. There Jacques d'Arteveld, who held such high rank, honour and prosperity in Flanders, was miserably slain. No man or judge who would take or levy compensation for this deed was ever to be found in Ghent. Thus go the fortunes of this world; wise persons cannot nor ever should place too much trust in worldly prosperity.

8.12 National feeling: Jeanne d'Arc, *Letter to the English* (1429). Original in French.

Jeanne d'Arc (*c*.1412–1431), born to a peasant family in Lorraine, a region loyal to the French king during the Hundred Years' War, heard voices telling her to defeat the English. She went to the court of Charles, the dauphin, i.e., heir to the King of France, to persuade him of her mission against the English on his behalf. Dictated in March 1429, this *Letter to the English* was written while Jeanne was undergoing "tests" ordered by Charles to determine her orthodoxy and chastity. Female examiners attested to her virginity (this is why she called herself "the Maid"); while Jean Gerson (see below, p. 483), among other theologians, decided that her mission echoed those of biblical and classical heroines. In May 1429 the French army, accompanied by Jeanne riding under her own banner, defeated the English at Orléans. It was the psychological turning point of the Hundred Years' War. In July of the same year, Jeanne led Charles to Reims, where he was anointed king. But by the next year her fortunes had waned and, captured and sold to the English, she was tried in 1431 for witchcraft, heresy, and apostasy and, condemned for all, was burned at the stake. Her *Letter to the English*, copied by notaries working for the English side, was one of many letters she sent to recipients throughout Europe. It shows her radical identification of the divine plan with a particular king and kingdom. Comparing her ideas to those in crusading documents—especially Stephen of Blois's *Letter to His Wife* (above, p. 271), *The Conquest of Lisbon* (above, p. 278), and Helmold's *Chronicle of the Slavs* (above, p. 303)—how might you argue that Jeanne's nationalistic vision was inspired by crusading ideals? What other sources of inspiration do you see?

[Source: *Joan's Letter to the English*, trans. Nadia Margolis, in *Medieval Hagiography: An Anthology*, ed. Thomas Head (New York: Garland, 2000), pp. 821–22 (slightly modified).]

Jesus Mary,[1]

King of England and you, duke of Bedford,[2] who call yourself regent of the kingdom of France; you, William Pole, earl of Suffolk; John, Lord Talbot; and you, Thomas, lord of Scales—who call yourselves lieutenants of the said duke of Bedford: set things aright with the king of Heaven and render unto the Maid,[3] who has been sent here by God, the king of Heaven, the keys to all the good cities that you have pillaged and ravaged in France. The Maid has come on behalf of God to reclaim the blood royal. She is ready to make peace, if you are willing to settle with her by evacuating France and making restitution for whatever you have stolen. And all of you—archers, companions in arms, gentlemen, and others who are before the city of Orléans—go away, return to your country, by order of God. And if you do not do this, await news of the Maid, who will shortly pay you a visit, much to your disfavor, to inflict great damage upon you. King of England, if you do not do this, I am chief of the army[4] and am waiting to confront your men wherever they are in France; and I will make them leave, whether they wish to or not. And should they not obey, I will have them all killed. For I have

been sent here by God, king of Heaven, to chase you completely out of France, body for body,[5] if necessary. Should they wish to obey me, then I shall take mercy upon them. May you have no other thought than this, since you do not hold the kingdom of France by order of God, king of Heaven, son of Mary—but rather it is Charles who shall hold it as true heir. For God, king of Heaven, so wishes it, as revealed by the Maid unto Charles, who shall soon enter Paris in good company. If you do not believe this news sent on behalf of God via the Maid, then we shall strike you down, with such fury as has never been seen in France for a thousand years, wherever we might find you, if you do not comply with us. You may be sure that the king of Heaven will send more might to the Maid than you shall ever be able to muster against her and her good men, no matter how many times you attack; at the end of which we shall see on whose side God truly sits in Heaven. You, duke of Bedford, the Maid pleads and requests of you not to destroy yourself thus. If you comply with her, you may join her there where the French will achieve the greatest exploit ever for Christianity. Give us your answer whether you wish to make peace in the city of Orléans; and if you do not, much devastation will come to remind you.

8.13 Patriotism in Italy: Petro Gentili's *Speech to the Council and Citizens of Lucca* (1397). Original in Latin (introduction) and in Italian (speech).

In the fourteenth and fifteenth centuries, stronger northern Italian cities began to swallow their weaker neighbors, creating in the end a small number of city-states. Lucca, a commune that lived in the shadow of Pisa, came under Pisan rule from 1342 to 1369. The visit of Holy Roman Emperor Charles IV to Lucca in 1368 led eventually to its independence in exchange for a huge sum of money. The mid-1390s, however, saw Pisan

---

[1] Jeanne used this popular invocation on her military standard and several of her letters. The words were also inscribed upon the ring she always wore, a gift from her mother.

[2] When King Henry V died in 1422, his son—who immediately became King Henry VI (d.1471)—was only nine months old. Thus Duke John of Bedford (1389–1435) became regent. By the Treaty of Troyes (1420), and because he was also the principal architect of the Anglo-Burgundian alliance, Bedford ruled France as well as England. Controlling northern France including Paris and Rouen, he was thus Jeanne's most powerful adversary, both on the battlefield and at the Rouen trial.

[3] In her testimony on February 22, 1431, Jeanne said that she had originally said "Render to the king" here. Pro-English notaries may have changed her words to make her seem more vainglorious.

[4] In her testimony on February 22, Jeanne affirmed that she never called herself "chief of the army." Her original words may have been changed to make her look more delusional.

[5] In her testimony on February 22, Jeanne stated that she had never said this originally; it may have been added by her detractors to make her seem more bloodthirsty.

encroachment once again, and Lucca was obliged to raise money to hire forces to defend the city. Petro Gentili, the Luccan *gonfaloniere* (standard bearer), spoke before the commune's Council and leading citizens in favor of an *estimo*, an assessment of household resources that was the necessary preliminary to imposing a new tax on the city. His arguments prevailed. The image of the city as a "mother," with its citizens as her "children," was an emotional one not only at Lucca but in other Italian cities as well. It implied that the citizens were united by brotherly bonds. And, indeed, unlike most of the city-states of northern Italy, Lucca was free of serious factional strife until around the 1380s, when this changed. Already in 1392, one faction had effectively wiped out its chief rivals, and around 1400 its leader took over the commune, turning it into a signoria. How did Gentili's city patriotism compare with the patriotism of Jeanne d'Arc in France (above, p. 474)?

[Source: Katherine L. Jansen, Joanna Drell, and Frances Andrews, eds., *Medieval Italy: Texts in Translation* (Philadelphia: University of Pennsylvania Press, 2009), pp. 74–76 (notes slightly modified). Translated by Christine Meek.]

In the name of God amen, in the year of the Lord 1397, the fifth indiction, the eighth day of June. The Major and General Council of the People and Commune of Lucca summoned by the sound of the bell and the voice of the public crier, the trumpet first having been sounded, as is customary, on the mandate of the distinguished knight, lord Peter de' Bianchi of Bologna, the honorable *podestà* of the city of Lucca and its *contado*, force and district[1] and meeting in Lucca in the palace of the dwelling and residence of the lords *anziani*[2] and *gonfaloniere di giustizia* of the People and Commune of Lucca.[3] Present at the Council were the said lords in sufficient number and two thirds and more of the councilors of the said council and the prominent citizens named below. The said lords first decided in secret vote by balls and urn[4] that this Council should be summoned and held today and that the following matters should be proposed, voted and carried into effect. In the Council then, the due formalities having been observed, the honorable man Petro Gentili, *gonfaloniere di giustizia* of the People and Commune of Lucca, proposed that the council should consult and speak on the matter indicated below which had previously been

carefully considered by the said lords *anziani* and many wise citizens.

May the grace of the Holy Spirit be with us.

Honorable citizens and wise councillors. It is manifest to every man who has a true understanding and judgment of matters that liberty is among the dearest things that God placed on earth. And liberty can be recognized by its opposite, that is by servitude, and how harsh and bitter [it is] that there are many citizens alive who can and do render reliable testimony by proof and experience. Certainly it should truly be held that every good citizen would wish for death rather than to return to the hands of cruel and perfidious Pisans or any others. And who can doubt that those who govern Pisa have ever intended or continuously intend anything other than to think and plot how they can occupy our city and reduce it to servitude and place us and our liberty under their feet, that liberty which so many of our honorable citizens sought for so long and desire so much and finally obtained with the favor and grace of heaven, that is of God with the favor and grace of the Holy Church and of the Holy Empire and at inestimable cost and price

---

[1] Different sections of the surrounding rural area controlled by Lucca. The district was the area within a six-mile radius of Lucca, the *contado* was the largest part of Lucchese territory divided into vicariates, and the force was a small number of outlying villages most recently acquired.

[2] The *anziani* were nine in number, three from each of the three *terzieri* or wards into which Lucca was divided; they served for a two-month period alongside the *gonfaloniere*.

[3] The *gonfaloniere di giustizia*, or Standard Bearer of Justice, was the highest political office open to Lucchese citizens. He was chosen by a combination of election and lot to serve for a period of two months.

[4] Each councilor voted by placing in an urn a white ball for consent or a black ball for dissent.

to the citizens. And it is manifest that after we obtained our liberty we lived without harming any of our neighbors, always bearing many injuries with humility and patience, always seeking peace and asking for peace. But the insatiable appetite of our wicked neighbors by various tricks and deceits and by various ways and means has never wanted peace, but rather as you know has assaulted and attacked us and our lands and our men a thousand times with fire and sword with rapine, traps, and deceits, believing to achieve by warfare the end they seek, that is to put the yoke of servitude on our necks.[1] And there is no doubt that if we continued to show patience as we have long done he would have achieved his cruel, damnable, and poisonous intention. It is therefore necessary that we come to our own assistance valiantly and defend our liberty boldly with all our strength, and to avoid exposing our peasants and citizens to the danger of death or capture. This cannot be done without men at arms, cavalry and infantry, and they cannot be obtained or maintained without money. And the revenues of the commune are so reduced through adverse times and the cruel conditions of the world that they are not sufficient to cover the necessary expenditure. Wherefore, honorable citizens and councillors, Lucca your wretched mother, wishing to maintain herself in liberty for you, wishing to defend herself energetically against her venomous enemies, has recourse to you her dear and legitimate children [and] recommends herself to you and begs you tearfully not to allow her to perish, not to allow her to lose the name of her liberty. But that each one of you and her other children should and would support help and succor her, your dear sweet mother, each of you with what strength he can, and that you should stoutly aid, defend, and succor her in her needs, so that she be preserved in her happy liberty and you should not allow her to fall back under perfidious tyranny. Your Lucca asks no more from you than a very small part of what you can easily afford with fair distribution among the greatest, the middling, and the least, and it seems that this should be done in the following way; that is, it seems to be good, useful, and effective to make a general *estimo*, shared out equally so that each person pays his own share and no more. [He then goes on to propose three slightly different systems for making the *estimo*.]

8.14 The commons revolt: *Wat Tyler's Rebellion* (after 1381). Original in Anglo-French.

A pressing need for more revenue to fight the Hundred Years' War led the English Parliament to impose new poll taxes that hit the "commons" (*not* the House of Commons but rather peasants in the countryside and most people in the cities) very hard. Uncoordinated revolts in the countryside led eventually to coordinated ones, and two armies, one led by Wat Tyler, converged on London. Their chief demand was the end of serfdom. In the *Anonimal Chronicle of St. Mary's, York*, an anonymous author who often spelled Tyler "Teghler" or "Tighler" told the story in considerable detail, excerpted here. Although the rebels considered themselves loyal to the fourteen-year-old King Richard II (r.1377–1399), he and his counselors fled to the Tower of London. Later, when he met with the rebels at Mile End, Richard gave in to their demands, but the next day at Smithfield, the Mayor of London killed Tyler, and the insurrection largely fell apart. What does this account reveal about class prejudice and class mobility in fourteenth-century England?

[Source: Charles Oman, *The Great Revolt of* 1381 (New York: Greenwood Press, 1969), pp. 186–93, 196–99, 201–3, 205 (language slightly updated; notes added).]

---

1   Petro exaggerates; Pisa and Lucca had had peaceful relations for more than 20 years.

Because in the year 1380 the subsidies [taxes] were over lightly granted at the Parliament of Northampton and because it seemed to various Lords and to the commons that the said subsidies were not honestly levied, but commonly exacted from the poor and not from the rich, to the great profit and advantage of the tax-collectors and to the deception of the King and the commons, the Council of the King ordained certain commissions to make inquiry in every township how the tax had been levied. Among these commissions, one for Essex was sent to one Thomas Bampton,[1] seneschal of a certain lord, who was regarded in that country as a king or great magnate for the state that he kept. And before Whitsuntide[2] he held a court at Brentwood in Essex to make inquisition, and [he] showed the commission that had been sent him to raise the money which was in default and to inquire how the collectors had levied the aforesaid subsidy. He had summoned before him the townships of a neighboring hundred and wished to have from them new contributions, commanding the people of those townships to make diligent inquiry, and give their answers, and pay their due. Among these townships was Fobbing, whose people made answer that they would not pay a penny more because they already had a receipt from himself for the said subsidy. On which the said Thomas threatened them angrily, and he had with him two sergeants-at-arms of our lord the king. And for fear of his malice the folks of Fobbing took counsel with the folks of Corringham, and the folks of these two places made levies and assemblies and sent messages to the men of Stanford to bid them rise with them for their common profit. Then the people of these three townships came together to the number of a hundred or more, and with one assent went to the said Thomas Bampton, and roundly gave him answer that they would have no traffic with him nor give him a penny. On which the said Thomas commanded his sergeants-at-arms to arrest these folks, and put them in prison. But the commons made insurrection against him, and would not be arrested, and went about to kill the said Thomas and the said sergeants. On this Thomas fled towards London to the King's Council; but the commons took to the woods, for fear that they had of his malice, and

they hid there some time, till they were almost famished, and afterwards they went from place to place to stir up other people to rise against the lords and great folk of the country. And because of these occurrences Sir Robert Belknap, Chief Justice of the King's Bench, was sent into the county with a commission of Trailbaston,[3] and indictments against various persons were laid before him, and the folks of the countryside were in such fear that they were proposing to abandon their homes. Wherefore the commons rose against him, and came before him, and told him that he was a traitor to the King, and that it was of pure malice that he would put them in default by means of false inquests made before him. And they took him and made him swear on the Bible that never again would he hold such a session, nor act as a justice in such inquests. And they made him give them a list of the names of all the jurors, and they took all the jurors they could catch, and cut off their heads, and cast their houses to the ground. So the said Sir Robert took his way home without delay. And afterwards the said commons assembled together, before Whitsunday, to the number of some 50,000, and they went to the manors and townships of those who would not rise with them, and cast their houses to the ground or set fire to them. At this time they caught three clerks of Thomas Bampton, and cut off their heads, and carried the heads about with them for several days stuck on poles as an example to others. For it was their purpose to slay all lawyers, and all jurors, and all the servants of the King whom they could find. Meanwhile the great lords of that country and other people of substance fled towards London, or to other counties where they might be safe. Then the commons sent various letters to Kent and Suffolk and Norfolk that they should rise with them, and when they were assembled they went about in many bands doing great mischief in all the countryside.... And they made chief over them Wat Teghler of Maidstone, to maintain them and be their councillor.

And on the Monday next after Trinity Sunday[4] they came to Canterbury, before the hour of noon; and 4,000 of them entering into the Minster[5] at the time of High Mass, there made a reverence and cried with one voice to

---

1 Thomas Bampton was a tax collector, one of many who had not obtained the full amount expected and now returned to the townships for more money.
2 That is, before the week of Pentecost, which is the seventh Sunday after Easter.
3 This was a commission, begun under Edward I (d.1307), for justices to consider both criminal and quasi-criminal cases.
4 Trinity Sunday is the first Sunday after Pentecost.
5 A minster is a monastery church.

the monks to prepare to choose a monk for Archbishop of Canterbury, "for he who is Archbishop now is a traitor, and shall be decapitated for his iniquity." And so he was within five days after! And when they had done this, they went into the town to their fellows, and with one assent they summoned the Mayor, the bailiffs, and the commons of the said town, and examined them whether they would with good will swear to be faithful and loyal to King Richard and to the true commons of England or no. Then the mayor answered that they would do so willingly, and they made their oath to that effect. Then they [the rebels] asked them if they had any traitors among them, and the townsfolk said that there were three, and named their names. These three the commons dragged out of their houses and cut off their heads. And afterwards they took 500 men of the town with them to London, but left the rest to guard the town.

At this time the commons had as their councillor a chaplain of evil disposition named Sir John Ball, which Sir John advised them to get rid of all the lords, and of the archbishop and bishops, and abbots, and priors, and most of the monks and canons, saying that there should be no bishop in England save one archbishop only, and that he himself would be that prelate, and they would have no monks or canons in religious houses save two, and that their possessions should be distributed among the laity. For which sayings he was esteemed among the commons as a prophet, and labored with them day by day to strengthen them in their malice—and a fit reward he got, when he was hung, drawn, and quartered, and beheaded as a traitor. After this the said commons went to many places, and raised all the folk, some willingly and some unwillingly, till they were gathered together full 60,000. And in going towards London they met various men of law, and twelve knights of that country, and made them swear to support them, or otherwise they should have been beheaded. They wrought much damage in Kent, and notably to Thomas Haselden, a servant of the Duke of Lancaster, because of the hate that they bore to the said duke. They cast his manors to the ground and all his houses, and sold his beasts—his horses, his good cows, his sheep, and his pigs—and all his store of corn, at a cheap price. And they desired every day to have his head, and the head of Sir Thomas Orgrave, Clerk of Receipt and sub-Treasurer of England.

When the King heard of their doings, he sent his messengers to them, on Tuesday after Trinity Sunday, asking why they were behaving in this fashion and for what cause they were making insurrection in his land. And they sent back by his messengers the answer that they had risen to deliver him and to destroy traitors to him and his kingdom. The King sent again to them bidding them cease their doings, in reverence for him, till he could speak with them, and he would make, according to their will, reasonable amendment of all that was ill-done in the realm. And the commons, out of good feeling to him, sent back word by his messengers that they wished to see him and speak with him at Blackheath. And the King sent again the third time to say that he would come willingly the next day, at the hour of Prime,[1] to hear their purpose. At this time the King was at Windsor, but he removed with all the haste he could to London, and the Mayor and the good folks of London came to meet him, and conducted him in safety to the Tower of London. There all the Council assembled and all the lords of the land round about, that is to say, the Archbishop of Canterbury, Chancellor of England; the Bishop of London; and the Master of the Hospital of St. John's, Clerkenwell, who was then Treasurer of England; and the Earls of Buckingham[2] and Kent, Arundel, Warwick, Suffolk, Oxford, and Salisbury, and others to the number of 600.

And on the vigil of Corpus Christi Day,[3] the commons of Kent came to Blackheath, three leagues from London, to the number of 50,000, to wait for the King, and they displayed two banners of St. George and forty pennons.[4] And the commons of Essex came on the other side of the water to the number of 60,000 to aid them and to have their answer from the King. And on the Wednesday, the King being in the Tower of London, thinking to settle the business, had his barge got ready and took with him in his barge the Archbishop, and the Treasurer, and certain others of his Council, and four other barges for his train, and got him to Greenwich, which is three leagues from London. But there the Chancellor and the Treasurer said to the King that it would be too great folly to trust himself among the commons, for they were men without reason and had not the sense to behave properly. But the commons of Kent, since the King would not come to them because he was dissuaded by his Chancellor and

---

[1]   The first hour of the day, around 6 a.m.

[2]   An error. Buckingham was in Wales.

[3]   The feast of Corpus Christi is celebrated shortly after Pentecost; the vigil is the day before.

[4]   A pennon is a banner or streamer carried on a lance.

Treasurer, sent him a petition requiring that he should grant them the head of the Duke of Lancaster and the heads of fifteen other lords, of whom three were bishops, who were present with him in the Tower of London. And these were their names: Sir Simon Sudbury, Archbishop of Canterbury, Chancellor of England; Sir Robert Hales, Prior of the Hospital of St. John's, Treasurer of England; the Bishop of London; Sir John Fordham, Bishop-elect of Durham and Clerk of the Privy Seal; Sir Robert Belknap, Chief Justice of the King's Bench; Sir Ralph Ferrers; Sir Robert Plessington, Chief Baron of the Exchequer; John Legge, Sergeant-at-arms of the King; and Thomas Bampton aforesaid. This the King would not grant them, wherefore they sent to him again a yeoman,[1] praying that he would come and speak with them: and he said that he would gladly do so, but the said Chancellor and Treasurer gave him contrary counsel, bidding him tell them that if they would come to Windsor on the next Monday they should there have a suitable answer.

And the said commons had among themselves a watchword in English, "With whome haldes you?"; and the answer was, "With kinge Richarde and the true comons"; and those who could not or would not so answer were beheaded and put to death.

And at this time there came a knight with all the haste that he could, crying to the King to wait; and the King, startled at this, awaited his approach to hear what he would say. And the said knight came to the King telling him that he had heard from his servant, who had been in the hands of the rebels on that day, that if he came to them all the land should be lost, for they would never let him loose, but would take him with them all round England, and that they would make him grant them all their demands, and that their purpose was to slay all the lords and ladies of great renown, and all the archbishops, bishops, abbots and priors, monks and canons, parsons and vicars, by the advice and counsel of the aforesaid Sir John Ball.

Therefore the King returned towards London as fast as he could and came to the Tower at the hour of Tierce.[2] And at this time the yeoman who has been mentioned above hastened to Blackheath, crying to his fellows that the King was departed and that it would be good for

them to go on to London and carry out their purpose that same Wednesday. And before the hour of Vespers,[3] the commons of Kent came, to the number of 60,000, to Southwark, where was the Marshalsea.[4] And they broke and threw down all the houses in the Marshalsea and took out of prison all the prisoners who were imprisoned for debt or for felony. And they leveled to the ground a fine house belonging to John Imworth, then Marshal of the Marshalsea of the King's Bench and warden of the prisoners of the said place, and all the dwellings of the jurors and questmongers[5] belonging to the Marshalsea during that night. But at the same time, the commons of Essex came to Lambeth near London, a manor of the Archbishop of Canterbury, and entered into the buildings and destroyed many of the goods of the said Archbishop, and burnt all the books of register, and rules of remembrances belonging to the Chancellor, which they found there....

At this time the King was in a turret of the great Tower of London, and could see the manor of the Savoy and the Hospital of Clerkenwell, and the house of Simon Hosteler near Newgate, and John Butterwick's place, all on fire at once. And he called all his lords about him to his chamber, and asked counsel what they should do in such necessity. And none of them could or would give him any counsel, wherefore the young King said that he would send to the Mayor of the City to bid him order the sheriffs and aldermen to have it cried round their wards that every man between the age of fifteen and sixty, on pain of life and members, should go next morning (which was Friday) to Mile End, and meet him there at seven o'clock. He did this in order that all the commons who were encamped around the Tower might be induced to abandon the siege and come to Mile End to see him and hear him, so that those who were in the Tower could get off safely whither they would and save themselves. But it came to nothing, for some of them did not get the good fortune to be preserved. And on that Thursday, the said feast of Corpus Christi, the King, being in the Tower very sad and sorry, mounted up into a little turret towards St. Catherine's, where were lying a great number of the commons, and had proclamation made to them that they all should go peaceably to their homes, and he would pardon them all manner of their trespasses. But all cried

---

[1]   That is, one of their number; yeomen belonged to the class of farmers who owned their own plots of land.

[2]   The third hour of the day, around 9 a.m.

[3]   Vespers is at sunset.

[4]   The Marshalsea was a prison.

[5]   Questmongers were informers who then received a share of any fines they generated.

with one voice that they would not go before they had captured the traitors who lay in the Tower, nor until they had got charters to free them from all manner of serfdom, and had got certain other points which they wished to demand. And the King benevolently granted all and made a clerk write a bill in their presence in these terms: "Richard, King of England and France, gives great thanks to his good commons, for that they have so great a desire to see and to keep their king, and grants them pardon for all manner of trespasses and misprisions and felonies done up to this hour, and wills and commands that every one should now return to his own home, and wills and commands that each should put his grievances in writing and have them sent to him; and he will provide, with the aid of his loyal lords and his good council, such remedy as shall be profitable both to him and to them, and to all the kingdom." On this document he sealed his signet in presence of them all, and sent out the said bill by the hands of two of his knights to the folks before St. Catherine's. And he caused it to be read to them, and the knight who read it stood up on an old chair before the others so that all could hear. All this time the King was in the Tower in great distress of mind. And when the commons had heard the Bill, they said that this was nothing but trifles and mockery. Therefore they returned to London and had it cried around the City that all lawyers, and all the clerks of the Chancery and the Exchequer and every man who could write a brief or a letter should be beheaded, whenever they could be found. At this time they burnt several more houses in the City, and the King himself ascended to a high garret of the Tower and watched the fires. Then he came down again and sent for the lords to have their counsel, but they did not know how they should counsel him, and all were very discouraged.

And next day, Friday, the commons of the countryside and the commons of London assembled in fearful strength, to the number of 100,000 or more, besides some four score who remained on Tower Hill to watch those who were in the Tower. And some went to Mile End, on the Brentwood Road, to wait for the coming of the King, because of the proclamation that he had made. But some came to Tower Hill, and when the King knew that they

were there, he sent them orders by messenger to join their friends at Mile End, saying that he would come to them very soon. And at this hour of the morning he advised the Archbishop of Canterbury, and the others who were in the Tower, to go down to the Little Water-gate, and take a boat and save themselves. And the Archbishop did so, but a wicked woman raised a cry against him, and he had to turn back to the Tower, to his confusion.

And by seven o'clock the King came to Mile End, and with him his mother in a whirlecote,[1] and also the Earls of Buckingham,[2] Kent, Warwick, and Oxford, and Sir Thomas Percy, and Sir Robert Knolles, and the Mayor of London, and many knights and squires; and Sir Aubrey de Vere carried the sword of state. And when he was come the commons all knelt down to him, saying: "Welcome our Lord King Richard, if it pleases you, and we will not have any other king but you." And Wat Tighler, their leader and chief, asked in the name of the commons that he would allow them to take and deal with all the traitors against him and the law, and the King granted that they should have at their disposition all who were traitors, and could be proved to be traitors by process of law. The said Walter and the commons were carrying two banners and many pennons and pennoncels[3] while they made their petition to the King. And they required that for the future no man should be in serfdom, nor make any manner of homage or suit to any lord, but should give a rent of 4d.[4] an acre for his land. They asked also that no one should serve any man except by his own good will, and on terms of regular agreement.

And at this time the King made the commons draw themselves out in two lines, and proclaimed to them that he would confirm and grant it that they should be free, and generally should have their will, and that they might go through all the realm of England and catch all traitors and bring them to him in safety, and then he would deal with them as the law demanded.

Under color of this grant Wat Tighler and [some of] the commons took their way to the Tower to seize the Archbishop, while the rest remained at Mile End. During this time the Archbishop sang his mass devoutly in the Tower, and shrived[5] the Prior of the Hospitallers and

---

[1] A whirlecote was a wheeled carriage. But it is probably not true that the king's mother accompanied him, since all other accounts of the incident say that she remained in the Tower.

[2] Again an error: Buckingham was still in Wales.

[3] A pennoncel is a small pennon.

[4] I.e., four pennies.

[5] "To shrive" is to hear confession and give absolution to a penitent.

others, and then he heard two masses or three, and chanted the *Commendacione*, and the *Placebo*, and the *Dirige*, and the Seven Psalms, and a Litany, and when he was at the words "Omnes sancti orate pro nobis," the commons burst in, and dragged him out of the chapel of the Tower, and struck and hustled him rudely, as they did also the others who were with him, and dragged them to Tower Hill. There they cut off the heads of Master Simon Sudbury, Archbishop of Canterbury, and of Sir Robert Hales, Prior of the Hospital of St. John's, Treasurer of England, and of Sir William Appleton, a great lawyer and surgeon, and later chief physician to the king, and the Duke of Lancaster. And some time later they beheaded John Legge, the King's Sergeant-at-arms, and with him a certain juror. And at the same time the commons made proclamation that whoever could catch any Fleming or other alien of any nation, might cut off his head, and so they did after this. Then they took the heads of the Archbishop and of the others and put them on wooden poles and carried them before them in procession as far as the shrine of Westminster Abbey, in despite of them and of God and Holy Church; and vengeance descended on them no long time after....

Then the King caused a proclamation to be made that all the commons of the country who were still in London should come to Smithfield, to meet him there; and so they did.

And when the King and his train had arrived there they turned into the Eastern meadow in front of St. Bartholomew's, which is a house of canons: and the commons arrayed themselves on the west side in great battalions. At this moment the Mayor of London, William Walworth, came up, and the King bade him go to the commons and make their chieftain come to him. And when he was summoned by the Mayor, by the name of Wat Tighler of Maidstone, he came to the King with great confidence, mounted on a little horse, that the commons might see him.... Presently Wat Tighler, in the presence of the King, sent for a flagon of water to rinse his mouth because of the great heat that he was in, and when it was brought he rinsed his mouth in a very rude and disgusting fashion before the King's face. And then he made them bring him a jug of beer and drank a great draught, and then, in the presence of the King, climbed on his horse again. At this time a certain valet from Kent, who was among the King's retinue, asked that the said Walter, the chief of the commons, might be pointed out to him. And when he saw him, he said aloud that he knew him for the greatest thief and robber in all Kent. Watt heard these words and bade him come out to him, wagging his head at him in sign of malice; but the valet refused to approach, for fear

that he had of the mob. But at last the lords made him go out to him, to see what he [Wat] would do before the King. And when Watt saw him he ordered one of his followers, who was riding behind him carrying his banner displayed, to dismount and behead the said valet. But the valet answered that he had done nothing worthy of death, for what he had said was true, and he would not deny it, but he could not lawfully make debate in the presence of his liege lord, without leave, except in his own defense: but that he could do without reproof; for if he was struck he would strike back again. And for these words Watt tried to strike him with his dagger and would have slain him in the King's presence; but because he strove so to do, the Mayor of London, William Walworth, reasoned with the said Watt for his violent behavior and spite, done in the King's presence, and arrested him. And because he arrested him, the said Watt stabbed the Mayor with his dagger in the stomach in great wrath. But, as it pleased God, the Mayor was wearing armor and took no harm, but like a hardy and vigorous man drew his cutlass and struck back at the said Watt and gave him a deep cut on the neck and then a great cut on the head. And during this scuffle one of the King's household drew his sword and ran Watt two or three times through the body, mortally wounding him. And he spurred his horse, crying to the commons to avenge him, and the horse carried him some four score paces, and then he fell to the ground half dead. And when the commons saw him fall, and knew not how for certain it was, they began to bend their bows and to shoot, wherefore the King himself spurred his horse, and rode out to them, commanding them that they should all come to him to Clerkenwell Fields....

[Tyler was beheaded by the Mayor.]

And when the commons saw that their chieftain, Watt Tyler, was dead in such a manner, they fell to the ground there among the wheat, like beaten men, imploring the King for mercy for their misdeeds. And the King benevolently granted them mercy, and most of them took to flight. But the King ordained two knights to conduct the rest of them, namely the Kentishmen, through London and over London Bridge without doing them harm, so that each of them could go to his own home. Then the King ordered the Mayor to put a helmet on his head because of what was to happen, and the Mayor asked for what reason he was to do so, and the King told him that he was much obliged to him, and that for this he was to receive the order of knighthood. And the Mayor answered that he was not worthy or able to have or to spend a knight's estate, for he was but a merchant and had to live by traffic: but finally the King made him put on the helmet and took a sword in both his hands and dubbed him knight with great good will. The same day he made three other knights from among the citizens of London on that same spot, and these are their names—John Philpott, and Nicholas Bramber, and [blank in the MS.]:[1] and the King gave Sir William Walworth £100 in land, and each of the others £40 in land, for them and their heirs. And after this the King took his way to London to the Wardrobe to ease him of his great toils....

Afterwards the King sent out his messengers into various regions to capture the malefactors and put them to death. And many were taken and hanged at London, and they set up many gallows around the City of London and in other cities and boroughs of the south country. At last, as it pleased God, the King, seeing that too many of his liege subjects would be undone and too much blood spilt, took pity in his heart and granted them all pardon, on condition that they should never rise again, under pain of losing life or members, and that each of them should get his charter of pardon and pay the King as fee for his seal twenty shillings, to make him rich. And so finished this wicked war.

CRISES AND CHANGES IN THE CHURCH AND RELIGION

8.15 The conciliarist movement: Jean Gerson, *Sermon at the Council of Constance* (1415). Original in Latin.

Jean Gerson (1363–1429), chancellor of the University of Paris and a public intellectual of wide-ranging interests and influence, was called upon to address the Council of Constance (1414–1418) at a moment of crisis. Originally held under the auspices of John XXIII, the council seemed ready to depose him along with other popes, prompting John to flee in disguise in March 1415. His leaving—and calling on everyone else to follow him—threw the remaining prelates into a crisis of conscience: should they continue with the council without a papal sponsor? Gerson, a conservative who came to the conciliarist position only slowly, thought they could and must. His sermon, excerpted below, brought the logical vocabulary of scholasticism to bear on the legitimacy of a council. His speech was the turning point at Constance, leading the assembly to declare, about a month later in the decree known as *Haec sancta*, that "This holy synod... holds power directly from Christ; and... everyone of whatever estate or dignity he be, even papal, is obliged to obey it in those things which belong to the faith."[2] The Council deposed John and elected Martin V (1317–1331).

[Source: *Unity, Heresy and Reform, 1378–1460: The Conciliar Response to the Great Schism*, ed. C.M.D. Crowder (Kingston, ON: Limestone Press, 1986), pp. 76–82.]

... "Walk while ye have the light, lest darkness come upon you."[3] That light, most distinguished fathers, I repeat once more, that light is God, who is glorified in the council of the saints. As the psalmist says: "God is greatly to be feared in the assembly of the saints, and to be had in reverence of all them that are round about him."[4] We hold to this infallible promise of his: "Where two or three are gathered together in my name, there am

---

[1]   From a later passage, we know that the third person was John Standwyche.

[2]   *Haec sancta*, in *Unity, Heresy and Reform, 1378–1460: The Conciliar Response to the Great Schism*, ed. C.M.D. Crowder (Kingston, ON: Limestone Press, 1986), p. 83.

[3]   John 12: 35.

[4]   Ps. 89: 7; Douay Ps. 88: 8.

I in the midst of them."[1] The psalmist saw this when he sang: "I will praise the Lord with my whole heart in the assembly of the upright, and in the congregation."[2] And we see in this assembly of the upright the unfolding of the mighty work of God, the freely given and scarcely hoped for way of resignation.

So when God has done all things to please himself and that he may be glorified, whose delight is to be with the sons of men, how may he obtain greater glory than in a council of the upright? For his praise is in the Church of the saints. You, fathers and lords, true believers and pleasing to God, are required to behave so as to constitute a council of saints and upright men. God has placed you in the world as so many true lights. "You are the light of the world," he says.[3] If ever it is your role to purge and illuminate others and to make them perfect, now is it especially so, when this holy convention is met, when the assembly is brought together in one place, when the Church is assembled; as it is written in Maccabees how they prayed and sought God's mercy:[4] that with his aid it might be decided what needed to be done. The spirit immediately rejoices, raising its eyes to take in what is happening, seeing all those who have assembled on your behalf, that is, for your benefit, O Christian people. My spirit observes and rejoices with you, and breaks out into this song of the Church. The citizens of the Apostles and the servants of God are here today, bearing a torch and bringing light to their fatherland to give peace to the peoples and to set the Lord's people free. How will they free them? By urging and crying out: "Walk while ye have the light, lest darkness come upon you;" the darkness of divisions and schism, the darkness of so many errors and heresies, in a word, the horrible darkness of so many vices that pour out of the Church's wretched body on a limitless tide. Walk, therefore, while you have light, that these aspects of the darkness do not come upon you....

The first problem is to keep the sequence of what is to be said clear and short. Because nothing is long if put together in orderly fashion. In the meantime, having broached the theme, let us turn our attention to what has been said: that God is he "who is greatly to be feared in the assembly of saints, and to be had in reverence of all them that are round about him."[5] Let us fix our mind on that text from the psalmist for fear we stray too far afield. If I am not mistaken, we see there the fourfold cause of this holy synod, that is its efficient, formal, final and material cause.[6]

If anyone wants to know the efficient cause, that is clear enough: God, greatly to be feared. It is by his impulse, mercy, inspiration and influence that the Church is now brought together, just as the psalmist, lifted up by the spirit, prophesied in song: It is God that "gathers together the outcasts of Israel";[7] and gathered his elect from the four winds "from the east and from the west, from the north and from the south."[8] Only let us pray that he who has begun the work perfects it. O sacred assembly "lift up your eyes round about you and see"; "all these are gathered together, they have come to you."[9] May it happen to you as was spoken by the prophet Isaiah: "Then thou shalt see, and flow together, and thine heart shall fear, and be enlarged."[10] And if it is enlarged, surely, will not God fill it with his spirit?

Next, the formal cause is this very bringing together or association of the council of holy men formed and modeled in the Holy Spirit, the form and exemplar of our acts, who is the bond and connection linking separate members of the saints, making them one. The Church recognizes this when it asks in its own behalf that, gathered in the Holy Spirit, it may not be disturbed by the assault of any adversary.

If anyone goes further to ask for the final cause of this holy assembly, that, surely, is that God, greatly to be feared, should be glorified, as it is said in the words of the Apostle: "Do all to the glory of God."[11] This is the straight

---

1   Matt. 18: 20.

2   Ps. 111: 1; Douay Ps. 110: 1.

3   Matt. 5: 14.

4   See 1 Macc. 3: 44.

5   Ps. 89: 7; Douay Ps. 88: 8.

6   The idea of the four causes derives from Aristotle's logic.

7   Ps. 147: 2; Douay Ps. 146: 2.

8   Ps. 107: 3; Douay Ps. 106: 3.

9   Isa. 60: 5 and 49: 18.

10   Isa. 60: 5.

11   1 Cor. 10: 31.

and effective path to obtaining all that we wish, so long as we first seek his glory. He gave this to be understood, when he said: "Seek ye first the Kingdom of God and his righteousness, and all these things will be added unto you."[1]

Finally, all those who are round about God can be taken as the material cause, of itself unformed. For just as men by falling into schism, as a result, deform in some way or other God's creation, since, according to Plato and Aristotle, man is the end of all things, so it is necessary that all things are modified according to the requirements of their end. Thus, by the contrary argument, everything should be reformed by this council of holy men, the Lord beginning and shaping the work and bringing it to its final conclusion. For thus does the Church sing about Christ's precious blood: "The earth, sea, stars and heavens are washed in that flood."[2]...

[Thus] God, greatly to be feared, is glorified in this council of holy men, because he offers it sufficient and infallible authority as its efficient cause. That is the first foundation. Again for the second conclusion: God, greatly to be feared, guides and attracts all Christians in common to the unity of one true head, as the formative and model cause. That is the second foundation and the first basis of reform. Further, for the third conclusion: God, greatly to be feared, wills to be glorified thus in this council of holy men that all things may turn particularly to the honor and preservation of his law and faith, without which no one can please him. That is the third foundation and the second basis of reform. Last of all, the fourth conclusion: God, greatly to be feared, is prepared to grant through this council of holy men to all creation, and especially to mankind, a measure of the beauty, glory, order and dignity of reform, with suitable provision against those who continue, not in upright behavior but on the treadmill of vice. And that is the fourth conclusion on the last foundation, and the third basis of reform....

Twelve considerations are to be derived from the light of this teaching in the Creed and the Apostle,[3] like so many rays of the brilliant truth.

1 The unity of the Church consists in one head, Christ. It is bound fast together by the loving bond of the Holy Spirit by means of divine gifts, by qualities and attitudes, so to speak, which render the constitution of the mystical body harmonious, lively, and seemly, so as to undertake effectively the exercise of the spiritual aspects of life.

2 The unity of the Church consists in one secondary head, who is called supreme pontiff, vicar of Christ. And it is more creative, more various, more plentiful, and greater than the assembly of the synagogue was and than a civil assembly under one ruler, king, or emperor, is.

3 By the life-giving seed instilled into it by the Holy Spirit the Church has the power and capacity to be able to preserve itself in the integrity and unity of its parts, both essential or formal and material and changing.

4 The Church has in Christ a bridegroom who will not fail it. Thus, as the law stands, neither can Christ give the bride, his Church, a bill of divorce, nor the other way round.

5 The Church is not so bound by the bond of marriage to the vicar of her indefectible bridegroom that they are unable to agree on a dissolution of the tie and give a bill of divorce.

6 The Church, or a general council representing it, is so regulated by the direction of the Holy Spirit under authority from Christ that everyone of whatsoever rank, even papal, is obliged to hearken to and obey it. If anyone does not, he is to be reckoned a gentile and a publican. That is clear from the unchanging law of God set out in Matt. 18 [at v. 17]. A general council can be described in this way: a general council is an assembly called under lawful authority at any place, drawn from every hierarchical rank of the whole catholic Church, none of the faithful who requires to be heard being excluded, for the wholesome discussion and ordering of those things which affect the proper regulation of the same Church in faith and morals.

7 When the Church or general council lays anything down concerning the regulation of the Church, the pope is not superior to those laws, even positive laws. So he is not able, at his choice, to dissolve such legislation of the Church contrary to the manner and sense in which it was laid down and agreed.

---

[1] Matt. 6: 33.

[2] See Luke 21: 25.

[3] The part of the Apostles' Creed that Gerson quotes is, "I believe in the Holy Spirit, the giver of life." The apostle that he quotes is St. Paul in Eph. 4, where he speaks of the unity of the Church.

8 Although the Church and general council cannot take away the pope's plenitude of power, which has been granted by Christ supernaturally and of his mercy, it can, however, limit his use of it by known rules and laws for the edification of the Church. For it was on the Church's behalf that papal and other human authority was granted. And on this rests the sure foundation of the whole reform of the Church.

9 In many circumstances the Church or general council has been and is able to assemble without the explicit consent or mandate of a pope, even duly elected and alive. One instance among others is if a pope is accused and is summoned to hear, as a party to the dispute, the decision of the Church under the law of the Gospel, to which law he is subject, and he contumaciously[1] refuses to bring the Church together. Another case is where serious matters concerning the regulation of the Church fall to be decided by a general council and the pope contumaciously refuses to summon it. Another, if it has been laid down by a general council that it should be brought together from time to time. The other kind of situation is where there is reasonable doubt about the disputes of several claimants to the papacy.

10 If the Church or general council agrees on any way or lays down that one way is to be accepted by the pope to end schism, he is obliged to accept it. Thus he is obliged to resign, if that is the prevailing opinion, and when he goes further and offers resignation and anticipates the demand, more especially is he to be commended.

11 The Church or general council ought to be particularly dedicated to the prosecution of perfect unity, the eradication of errors, and the correction of the erring, without acceptance of persons.[2] Likewise to this: that the Church's hierarchical order of prelates and curates should be reformed from its seriously disturbed state to a likeness to God's heavenly hierarchy and in conformity to rules instituted in early times.

12 The Church has no more effective means to its own general reformation than to establish a continuous sequence of general councils, not forgetting the holding of provincial councils.

8.16 Taking part in the life of Christ: *The Book of Margery Kempe* (*c.*1430). Original in Middle English.

The Book of Margery Kempe was probably dictated to a scribe around 1430 by Margery Kempe, a well-to-do woman living in Bishop's Lynn (today King's Lynn) in Norfolk, England. Married to John Kempe, she had fourteen children. Just after her first child was born, she began to have conversations with Christ, and soon she was reporting visions, like the ones here, in which she took part in Christ's life and he in hers. (The translation here stays very close to the original words and rhythms.) Compare Margery's relationship with Christ with that of Mary of Oignies (above, p. 370). How might Margery's visions have been influenced by plays like the one for the Annunciation (see above, p. 436), which were very popular in fifteenth-century Norfolk?

[Source: Lynn Staley, ed. and trans., *The Book of Margery Kempe: A New Translation, Contexts, Criticism* (New York: W.W. Norton, 2001), pp. 15–16, 36–39 (some notes added).]

6. Another day this creature[3] gave herself to meditation, as she was bidden before, and she lay still, not knowing what she might best think. Then she said to our Lord Jesus Christ, "Jesus, what shall I think?" Our Lord Jesus answered to her mind, "Daughter, think on my mother, for she is the cause of all the grace that you have."

---

[1] I.e., with obstinate disobedience.

[2] "Acceptance of persons" means "partiality."

[3] Margery referred to herself as "this creature" or "the creature" throughout the *Book*.

And then anon she saw Saint Anne[1] great with child, and then she prayed Saint Anne if she could be her maiden and her servant. And anon our Lady[2] was born, and then she busied herself to take the child to herself and keep it until it was twelve years of age with good food and drink, with fair white clothes and white kerchiefs. And then she said to the blessed child, "Lady, you shall be the mother of God." The blessed child answered and said, "I would I were worthy to be the handmaiden of her who shall conceive the son of God." The creature said, "I pray you, Lady, if that grace fall on you, forsake not my service."

The blissful child passed away for a certain time, the creature being still in contemplation, and later came again and said, "Daughter, now am I become the mother of God."

And then the creature fell down on her knees with great reverence and great weeping and said, "I am not worthy, Lady, to do you service." "Yes, daughter," she said, "follow me, your service pleases me well."

Then she went forth with our Lady and with Joseph, bearing with her a vessel of sweetened and spiced wine. Then they went forth to Elizabeth, Saint John the Baptist's mother, and, when they met together, both of them worshipped each other, and so they dwelled together with great grace and gladness twelve weeks.[3]

And then Saint John was born, and our Lady took him up from the earth with all manner of reverence and gave him to his mother, saying of him that he would be a holy man, and blessed him. Afterward they took their leave of one another with compassionate tears. And then the creature fell down on her knees to Saint Elizabeth and asked her if she would pray for her to our Lady so that she might give her service and pleasure. "Daughter, it seems to me," said Elizabeth, "you do right well your duty."

And then went the creature forth with our Lady to Bethlehem and purchased her lodging every night with great reverence, and our Lady was received with a glad manner. Also she begged for our Lady fair white clothes and kerchiefs to swaddle her son when he was born, and, when Jesus was born, she prepared bedding for our Lady to lie in with her blessed son. And afterward she begged food for our Lady and her blessed child. Afterward she swaddled him with bitter tears of compassion, having mind of the sharp death that he should suffer for the love of sinful men, saying to him, "Lord, I shall fare fair with you; I shall not bind you sorely.[4] I pray you be not displeased with me."

7. And after, on the Twelfth Day,[5] when the three kings came with their gifts and worshipped our Lord Jesus Christ, being in his mother's lap, this creature, our Lady's handmaiden, beholding all the process by contemplation, wept wonder sore. And, when she saw that they would take their leave to go home again into their country, she might not suffer that they should go from the presence of our Lord; and, for wonder that they would go away, she cried wonder sore.

And soon after, came an angel and bade our Lady and Joseph go from the country of Bethlehem into Egypt. Then went this creature forth with our Lady, day by day purveying her lodging with great reverence, with many sweet thoughts and high meditations and also high contemplations, sometimes enduring in weeping two hours and often longer in the mind of our Lord's Passion, without ceasing, sometimes for her own sin, sometimes for the sins of the people, sometimes for the souls in purgatory, sometimes for those who are in poverty or in any trouble, for she desired to comfort them all. Sometimes she wept full plenteously and fill violently for desire of the bliss of heaven and because she was so long deferred therefrom. Then this creature coveted greatly to be delivered out of this wretched world. Our Lord Jesus Christ said to her mind that she should abide and languish in love. "For I have ordained you to kneel before the Trinity to pray for all the world, for many hundred thousand souls shall be saved by your prayers. And therefore, daughter, ask what you wish, and I shall grant you your asking." This creature said, "Lord, I ask mercy and preservation from everlasting damnation for me and for all the world; chastise us here however you wish and in purgatory, and keep us from damnation for your high mercy."…

21. During the time that this creature had revelations, our Lord said to her, "Daughter, you are with child."

She said again, "A,[6] Lord, how shall I then do for keeping of my child?"

---

[1] Saint Anne was the mother of the Virgin Mary.

[2] Our Lady is another term for the Virgin Mary.

[3] For the Gospel account of this visit, see Luke 1: 39–56.

[4] I.e., swaddle tightly.

[5] The Feast of the Epiphany, twelve days after Christmas, which celebrates the coming of the Wise Men.

[6] An interjection, like "Ah!" or "Oh!"

Our Lord said, "Daughter, dread you not, I shall ordain for a keeper."

"Lord, I am not worthy to hear you speak and thus to common with my husband.[1] Nevertheless, it is to me a great pain and great distress."

"Therefore is it no sin to you, daughter, for it is to you rather reward and merit, and you shall have never the less grace, for I will that you bring me forth more fruit."

Then said the creature, "Lord Jesus, this manner of living belongs to your holy maidens."

"Yes, daughter, believe right well that I love wives also, and specially those wives who would live chaste, if they might have their will, and do their business to please me as you do, for, though the state of maidenhood is more perfect and more holy than the state of widowhood, and the state of widowhood more perfect than the state of wedlock; yet daughter I love you as well as any maiden in the world. There may no man hinder me from loving whom I will and as much as I will; for love, daughter, quenches all sin. And therefore ask of me the gifts of love. There is no gift so holy as is the gift of love, nor nothing to be so much desired as love; for love may purchase what it can desire. And therefore, daughter, you may no better please God than continually to think on his love."

Then this creature asked our Lord Jesus how she should best love him.

And our Lord said, "Have mind of your wickedness and think on my goodness."

She said again, "I am the most unworthy creature that ever you showed grace unto on earth."

"A, daughter," said our Lord, "fear you not. I take no heed what a man has been, but I take heed what he will be. Daughter, you have despised yourself; therefore you shall never be despised by God. Have mind, daughter, what Mary Magdalene was, Mary the Egyptian, Saint Paul,[2] and many other saints who are now in heaven; for of unworthy I make worthy, and of sinful I make rightful. And so have I made you worthy to me, once loved and evermore loved with me. There is no saint in heaven whom you will speak with but he will come to you. Whom God loves, they love. When you please

God, you please his mother and all the saints in heaven. Daughter, I take witness of my mother, of all the angels in heaven, and of all the saints in heaven that I love you with all my heart, and I may not forego your love."

Our Lord said then to his blissful mother, "Blessed Mother, tell my daughter of the greatness of love I have unto her."

Then this creature lay still all in weeping and sobbing as though her heart should have burst for the sweetness of speech that our Lord spoke unto her soul. Quickly after the Queen of Mercy, God's mother, dallied[3] to the soul of this creature, saying, "My worthy daughter, I bring you sure tidings, witnessing my sweet son Jesus, with all angels and all saints in heaven who love you full highly. Daughter, I am your mother, your lady, and your mistress to teach you in all manner how you shall please God best."

She taught this creature and informed her so wonderfully that she was abashed to speak it or tell it to any— the matters were so high and so holy—save only to the anchorite who was her principal confessor; for he had the most knowledge of such things. And he charged this creature by virtue of obedience to tell him what ever she felt, and so she did.

22. As this creature lay in contemplation, sorely weeping in her spirit, she said to our Lord Jesus Christ, "A, Lord, maidens dance now merrily in heaven. Shall not I do so? For, because I am no maiden, lack of maidenhood is to me now great sorrow. It seems to me I wish I had been slain when I was taken from the font stone[4] so that I should never have displeased you, and then should you, blessed Lord, have had my maidenhead without end. A, dear God, I have not loved you all the days of my life, and that sorely rues me. I have run away from you, and you have run after me. I would fall into despair, and you would not allow me."

"A, daughter, how often have I told you that your sins are forgiven you and that we are joined together without end? You are to me a singular love, daughter, and therefore I promise you you shall have a singular grace in heaven, daughter, and I promise you I shall come to

---

[1] "Common with my husband," that is, have sexual intercourse with him.

[2] St. Paul began as Saul, one of the great persecutors of Christians. His dramatic conversion is described in Acts 9. "Mary Magdalene" was a follower of Jesus and among the first witnesses of the Resurrection. She is linked to passionate love of Jesus, to penitential grief, and to revelation. "Mary the Egyptian" was Mary of Egypt, a legendary fifth-century courtesan from Alexandria, who, upon conversion, left her life of luxury and sin for one of relentless penance and poverty.

[3] Spoke.

[4] I.e., at baptism.

your end at your dying with my blessed mother and my holy angels and twelve apostles, Saint Katherine, Saint Margaret, Saint Mary Magdalene, and many other saints who are in heaven, who give great worship to me for the grace that I give to you, God, your Lord Jesus.[1]

"You need dread no grievous pains in your dying, for you shall have your desire, that is to have more mind of my Passion than of your own pain. You shall not dread the devil of hell, for he has no power in you. He dreads you more than you do him. He is angry with you, for you torment him more with your weeping than does all the fire in hell; you win many souls from him with your weeping. And I have promised you that you should no other purgatory have than slander and speech from the world, for I have chastised you myself as I wished, by many great dreads and torments that you have had with evil spirits, both sleeping and waking for many years. And therefore I shall preserve you at your end through my mercy so that they shall no power have over you, neither in body nor in soul. It is great grace and miracle that you have your bodily wits for the vexation that you have had with them before. I have also, daughter, chastised you with the dread of my Godhead, and many times have I frightened you with great tempests of winds so that you thought vengeance would have fallen on you for sin. I have proved you by many tribulations, many great sorrows, and many grievous sicknesses in so much that you have been anointed for dead; and all through my grace have you escaped.

"Therefore dread you not, daughter, for with my own hands, which were nailed to the cross, I shall take your soul from your body with great mirth and melody, with sweet smells and good odors, and offer it to my Father in heaven. There you shall see him face to face, dwelling with him without end. Daughter, you shall be right welcome to my Father and to my mother and to all my saints in heaven, for you have given them drink full many times with tears of your eyes. All my holy saints shall enjoy your coming borne. You shall be fulfilled of all manner of love that you covet. Then shall you bless the time that you were wrought and the body that has you bought. He shall joy in you and you in him without end. Daughter, I promise you the same grace that I promised Saint Katherine, Saint Margaret, Saint Barbara,[2] and Saint Paul, in so much that what creature on earth, until the day of judgment, asks you any boon and believes that God loves you, he shall have his boon, or else a better thing. Therefore, those who believe that God loves you, they shall be blessed without end.

"The souls in purgatory shall joy in your coming home, for they know well that God loves you specially. And men on earth shall joy in God for you, for he shall work much grace for you and make all the world to know that God loves you. You have been despised for my love; and therefore you shall be worshipped for my love. Daughter, when you are in heaven, you shall be able to ask what you will, and shall grant you all your desire. I have told you before that you are a singular lover, and therefore you shall have a singular love in heaven, a singular reward, and a singular worship. And, forasmuch as you are a maiden in your soul, I shall take you by the one hand in heaven and my mother by the other hand, and so shall you dance in heaven with other holy maidens and virgins, for I may call you clearly bought and my own worthy darling. I shall say to you, my own blessed spouse, 'Welcome to me with all manner of joy and gladness, here to dwell with me and never to depart from me without end, but ever to dwell with me in joy and bliss, which no eye may see, nor ear hear, nor tongue tell, nor heart think; that I have ordained for you and for all my servants who desire to love me and please me as you do.'"

---

[1]   Saint Katherine of Alexandria was a legendary fourth-century virgin martyr. Saint Margaret's church at Lynn was where Margery worshipped.

[2]   Saint Barbara was a third-century virgin persecuted by her father for her conversion to Christianity.

8.17 The Hussite program: *The Four Articles of Prague* (1420). Original in Czech.

Inspired by the English priest and scholar John Wyclif to call for a reformed church, the Bohemian Jan Hus (1369/1371–1415) was burned at the stake by the Council of Constance. But in Bohemia his followers took up his cause, calling for a moral and less materialistic clergy and asking that even lay people be allowed full participation in both forms of the Eucharist—the bread *and* the wine. The Hussites were declared heretics, and the pope called a crusade against them. The first battles led the Hussites to articulate their views, which they summed up in four articles, frequently repeated in Hussite writings thereafter.

[Source: *The Crusade against Heretics in Bohemia, 1418–1437: Sources and Documents of the Hussite Crusades*, trans. and ed. Thomas A. Fudge (Aldershot: Ashgate, 2002), pp. 83–84.]

[First] ... throughout the Kingdom of Bohemia the word of God shall be freely preached and proclaimed by Christian priests.... [Second] the holy sacrament of the body and blood of the Lord, in both kinds of bread and wine, shall be freely given to all true Christians who are not prohibited on account of some deadly sin just as our Savior did in the beginning and so commanded it.... [Third] numerous priests and monks, supported by temporal law possess worldly goods in opposition to the commandments of Christ. This is to the detriment of their office and is also harmful to the lords of the secular estates. These priests shall be deprived of such power, which is unlawful, and in keeping with the Scriptures shall live lives of good repute in accordance with the pattern of Christ and the apostles.... [Fourth] all serious sins, particularly those committed publicly, along with other offences against the Law of God shall be prohibited and punished regardless of their estate,[1] by those who possess the power to do so. [This is to be done] so that the evil and slanderous rumors about this country might be removed for the common good of the people and the Kingdom of Bohemia....

If anyone wishes to accuse us verbally or in writing with anything evil, heretical, shameful or unclean, we would ask that such an individual not be believed. For such a one is speaking slander out of hatred and ill-will and is both malicious and a liar. We confess boldly before the Lord God and the entire world that with the help of God we have no other motive than to serve the Lord Jesus Christ with all of our hearts, power, strength and endurance and to be dedicated to the fulfillment of God's law and commandments which is appropriate for all good Christians. Any wicked enemy or anyone else who attempts to compel us away from this good we will withstand in keeping with the law and truth of God. On this position we shall defend the truth as well as ourselves against such violence through the use of secular weapons. Should something terrible happen through the zeal of one of our people, we assert that this is not our intention but we shall stand against all serious sins with God's help. And if someone comes to harm because of us it is because it was absolutely necessary or because that person is an enemy of God as well as of us. It is necessary to protect both ourselves and the law of God from such violence and cruelty. Beyond this, we declare with all solemnity that if it appears that we are incorrect in anything we are prepared to make amends and our hearts are open in all things to be instructed by enlightenment from the Holy Scriptures. Dated in the year of the Lord 1421.[2]

---

[1] I.e., regardless of social status.

[2] The date is 1420 by a modern calendar.

THE RENAISSANCE

8.18 Re-evaluating antiquity: Cincius Romanus, *Letter to His Most Learned Teacher Franciscus de Fiana* (1416). Original in Latin.

Serving Pope John XXIII at the Council of Constance (1414–1418), Cincius Romanus (or de Rusticis) (d.1445) and his humanist friends Poggius Bracciolini and Bartholomeus Montepolitianus took advantage of the turmoil at the Council to hunt for old manuscripts and reminisce about the glories of ancient Rome. Although employed by the Roman curia, Cincius and his friends preferred ancient pagan art over the churches and art of Christian Rome. And although they no doubt heard Gerson (p. 483 above) give his speech in modern Latin, they considered that language barbaric compared to the Latin of Cicero and other ancient Romans. Their new appreciation of antiquity—its monuments and its literature—were hallmarks of the Italian Renaissance mentality.

[Source: *Two Renaissance Book Hunters: The Letters of Poggius Bracciolini to Nicolaus de Niccolis*, trans. and ed. Phyllis Walter Goodhart Gordan (New York: Columbia University Press, 1974), pp. 187–90 (notes added).]

Let us break our silence occasionally, for it seems outrageous and contrary to the ties of friendship and against nature that those who are separated by a considerable distance, though they are bound by the strongest affection, should not take to writing letters back and forth, for simply thinking of an absent friend will not suffice when one is given the opportunity of writing to him. Since the chief pleasure in friendship derives from familiarity, people who receive letters, as symbols of their friends, find no small satisfaction in them. Therefore I urge you vigorously to be kind enough while you have the physical ability (for you have the mental ability all the time) to write me something. I promise to give my letters to be delivered to you to all the couriers leaving Constance for Rome. Take this letter as my assurance in the matter, like a hostage. But let us come to the point, which ought to make you very happy.

In Germany there are many monasteries with libraries full of Latin books. This aroused the hope in me that some of the works of Cicero, Varro, Livy, and other great

men of learning, which seem to have completely vanished, might come to light, if a careful search were instituted.[1] A few days ago, Poggius and Bartholomeus Montepolitianus and I, attracted by the fame of the library, went by agreement to the town of St. Gall. As soon as we went into the library, we found *Jason's Argonauticon*, written by C. Valerius Flaccus in verse that is both splendid and dignified and not far removed from poetic majesty.[2] Then we found some discussions in prose of a number of Cicero's orations which make clearly comprehensible many legal practices and many modern equivalents of ancient institutions. We also found one book, a small volume but remarkable in the greatness of its eloquence and wisdom: Lactantius, *On Men of Both Sorts*, which plainly contradicts the statements of those who claim that the state of mankind is lower than that of beasts and more hopeless.[3] Among other books we found Vitruvius, *On Architecture* and Priscian the grammarian's comments on some of the poems of Virgil.[4] There was also in that

---

[1] Cicero (106–43 BCE), Varro (116–27 BCE), and Livy (c.59 BCE–17 CE) were all classical Roman writers.

[2] C. Valerius Flaccus (*fl.* 1st c. CE) was another classical Roman writer.

[3] Lactantius (c.250–c.320 CE) was yet another Latin writer, but unlike the others mentioned here, he was a Christian.

[4] Vitruvius (*fl.* 1st c. CE) was a Roman architect. Priscian (*fl.* c.500 CE) wrote grammar books much in use during the Middle Ages. Virgil (70–19 BCE) was a great classical Latin poet.

library one book made of the bark of trees; some barks in the Latin language are called "libri," and from that, according to Jerome, books got their name.[1] Although this book was filled to overflowing with writings which were not exactly literature, still, because of its pure and holy antiquity I greeted it with the utmost devotion. In fact we have copies of all these books. But when we carefully inspected the nearby tower of the church of St. Gall in which countless books were kept like captives and the library neglected and infested with dust, worms, soot, and all the things associated with the destruction of books, we all burst into tears, thinking that this was the way in which the Latin language had lost its greatest glory and distinction. Truly, if this library could speak for itself, it would cry loudly: "You men who love the Latin tongue, let me not be utterly destroyed by this woeful neglect. Snatch me from this prison in whose gloom even the bright light of the books within cannot be seen." There were in that monastery an abbot and monks totally devoid of any knowledge of literature. What barbarous hostility to the Latin tongue! What damned dregs of humanity!

But why do I hate a tribe of barbarians for this kind of indifference to literature when the Romans, the parents of the Latin tongue, have inflicted a greater wound and heaped greater abuse on our native language, the prince over all the others? I call to mind innumerable libraries of Latin and Greek books in ruins in Rome which were carefully built by our ancestors, according to an inscription in Greek letters which was removed from the Porta Capena through one man's concern.[2] These libraries were destroyed partly through ignorance, partly through neglect, and partly so that the divine face of Veronica might be painted.[3] Anyway, I think that the perpetrators of this loathsome crime and those who did not stop them ought to suffer the severest punishment. Indeed if the laws say that he who has killed a man deserves capital punishment, what penalty and what suffering shall we require for those who deprive the public of culture, of the liberal arts, and actually of all nourishment of the human mind, without which men can hardly live at all or live like beasts? Two things used to stand out in Rome: the libraries and the monumental buildings which (and I shall omit the libraries) easily surpassed, in size and beauty, the pyramids of Egypt, the Basilica of Cyrus, and other wonders of the world which Herodotus mentions.[4] Every day you see citizens (if indeed a man should be called a citizen who is so degraded by abominable deeds) demolishing the Amphitheater or the Hippodrome or the Colosseum or statues or walls made with marvelous skill and marvelous stone and showing that old and almost divine power and dignity.[5] Truly I would prefer and would pay more for a small marble figure by Phidias or Praxiteles than for a living and breathing image of the man who turns the statues of those glorious men into dust or gravel.[6] But if anyone asks these men why they are led to destroy marble statues, they answer that they abominate the images of false gods. Oh voice of savages, who flee from one error to another! For it is not contrary to our religion if we contemplate a statue of Venus or of Hercules made with the greatest of skill and admire the almost divine art of the ancient sculptors.[7] But mistakes of this kind are to be blamed not only on those we have just mentioned but on the former governors of the city and on the popes, who have continually consented to this destructive behavior which lowers the dignity of mankind.

It happens too that many books of Holy Scripture and many sacred structures have been lost through the carelessness of those who represented Christ on earth. We consider them the more despicable because the cure for all evil is expected from them. But I believe they follow the dictum of some wretch who, when he doubted that he could acquire for himself the name of virtue, burned the temple of Diana at Ephesus.[8] So these priests of our religion, since they could not appreciate the excellence

---

[1] Jerome (*c*.347–419/420) was a Latin Church Father.

[2] The Porta Capena was one of the gates of ancient Rome.

[3] The "divine face of Veronica" is the image of Christ's face said to have been left on the cloth used to wipe his face (by Saint Veronica) as he carried his cross to Calvary.

[4] Herodotus (5th c. BCE) was a traveler and historian whose history of the Persian wars mentions (among many other things) the Egyptian and Persian monuments.

[5] The Amphitheater, Hippodrome, and Colosseum were huge stadiums built by the ancient Romans. Some of the ruins remain today.

[6] Phidias (*fl. c*.490-430 BCE) and Praxiteles (*fl.* 370–330 BCE) were famous ancient Athenian sculptors.

[7] Venus was a Roman goddess, Hercules a Greek and Roman god.

[8] Plutarch (*c*.46–after 119 CE), an ancient Greek biographer avidly read by humanists such as Cincius, reported that Eratostratus burned down the much-admired temple of Diana at Ephesus in 356 BCE in order to ensure eternal fame for himself.

and beauty of the City and could accomplish nothing, strove for this kind of ruin and destruction. Let us pursue such inhuman, such savage stupidity with curses. And you, my teacher, gifted as you are in both poetry and prose, write something against these destroyers of our illustrious monuments. If you do so, you will assure yourself henceforth immortal glory and them perpetual shame. Farewell.

8.19 A new theory of art: Leon Battista Alberti, *On Painting* (1435–1436). Original in Latin.

Trained in law and literature, Leon Battista Alberti (1404–1472) wrote dialogues, treatises, and poetry in both Latin and the vernacular. He was keenly interested in art and around 1435 composed *On Painting*. Dedicated to the most eminent architect of his day, Filippo Brunelleschi (1377–1446), the treatise celebrated Brunelleschi's nearly completed dome for the cathedral at Florence, an incredible engineering feat. (It was the largest dome ever built, and it used several new construction techniques.) Alberti himself eventually devoted himself to architectural projects, designing buildings at Rome, Rimini, Mantua, and Florence. How does his discussion of painting echo Cincius's enthusiasm for ancient writings?

[Source: Rocco Sinisgalli, ed. and trans., *Leon Battista Alberti: On Painting. A New Translation and Critical Edition* (Cambridge: Cambridge University Press, 2011), pp. 17–19, 74–78, 83–85 (notes modified).]

Prologue Addressed to Filippo Brunelleschi

I used to wonder and to regret at the same time that so many excellent and divine arts and sciences, which we see, through their works and copious historical accounts, during those very virtuous days of distant past, are thus now missing and almost entirely lost. Painters, sculptors, architects, musicians, geometrician, rhetoricians, augurs, and similar most noble and marvelous intellects today are found very rarely and [are] little to be praised. Hence I came to believe what many keep saying, that already Nature, mistress of things, by now aged and weary, no longer produced either giants or great minds like those which she produced very big and marvelous in her almost youthful and more glorious times. But as from the long exile, in which we the Alberti have grown old, I was returned to this fatherland of ours, very ornate above all others,[1] I recognized in many, but first in you,

Filippo, and in that our great friend Donato the sculptor, and in those others, who are so well praised for their intellect, Nencio, Luca, and Masaccio,[2] that they are not to be [thought] inferior to any who might have been in antiquity, however famous they could have possibly been in these arts. Thus I perceived that the possibility of acquiring distinction in whatever [the] endeavor lies in our industry and diligence no less than in the good disposition of Nature and of the times. I confess to you that for the ancients, of course, it was less difficult to reach a degree of excellence in those arts most difficult for us to master, because they had many models to learn from and to imitate. But, on the other hand, our fame should be greater if we, without teachers and [with] no example whatsoever, discover arts and sciences hitherto unheard of or never seen, Whoever would be stubborn or envious enough to deny praise to the architect Pippo, seeing such an enormous structure towering over the skies,

---

1. The Alberti family, originally from Florence, was exiled during the Ciompi rebellion (1378). The exile ended in 1428, and Alberti returned "to this fatherland of ours" in 1432.

2. Filippo was Filippo Brunelleschi (d.1446); Donato was Donatello (d.1446); Nencio was Lorenzo Ghiberti (d.1455); Luca was Luca Della Robbia (d.1482); Masaccio (d.1428). All were painters, sculptors, and/or architects in and around Florence.

and wide enough to cast its shadow all over the Tuscan people, made as it is without any beam or abundance of wooden supports, surely hard to believe as an artifice that it was done at this time when nothing of the kind was ever to have been seen in antiquity.[1] But praise of your virtues as well as of those of our Donato, together with those of others who are dear to me for their good behaviors, will be kept for another occasion. You just hold steady in your daily efforts to find things that bring perpetual fame and renown to your brilliant mind, and if occasionally you should find a moment of leisure, it would please me to have you look at this little work of mine "On Painting," which I composed, in your name, in the Tuscan language.[2] You will see three books: the first, entirely on mathematics, causes this pleasant and most noble art to spring from its roots in Nature. The second book places this art in the hands of the painter, articulated as it is in its parts and with a full explanation of it. The third shows how the painter should be and how he should acquire proper knowledge to master every aspect of the art of painting. Please, then, read my work with diligence, and if you think that anything in it has to be amended, do correct me. No writer was ever so learned as not to profit from learned friends. And I would like to be corrected by you first, so as not to be censured by detractors.

BOOK THREE:
The Painter

51. But to educate the painter to perfection, in order that he can obtain all the praises of which we have spoken, at the moment when several thoughts still remain that I think ought not to be completely neglected in these commentaries, let us report them in the briefest way possible.

52. It is the task of the painter to delimit and depict with lines and colors on a surface any assigned bodies to such a point that—given a certain distance and a certain position of the centric ray—painted things that you see appear, each [at the same time], prominent and very much like the assigned bodies.[3] The purpose of the painter is to obtain from a work praise, favor, and approval more than riches, a [feature] that he will certainly gain provided his painting will capture the eyes and hearts of the observers and, above all, will make [hearts] palpitate. We have said on what conditions these things can take place when we first spoke about composition and reception of light. But I wish that the painter, in order that he be able to obtain all these [conditions] in the best way, is firstly a man both honest and educated in the praiseworthy arts.[4] In fact, everyone knows how honesty—more so than admiration of every activity or art—is valid to gain the benevolence of the people. There are no doubts, then, that the benevolence of many contributes very much to procuring praise and, above all, riches [by] the artist, if it is true that the rich are sometimes moved by this benevolence more than by the skill of art, or rather offer earnings to him who firstly is modest and virtuous after they have dismissed another who may be, if you please, more skilled but perhaps dissolute. Things being so, the artist will have to be moderate in his morals, of great humanity and availability, in order to also obtain benevolence—[a] firm defense against poverty—and benefits, the best help to [the] perfection of art.

53. Furthermore, I wish that the painter be expert, as far as possible, in all liberal arts, but above all I desire in him the knowledge of geometry. I certainly agree with Pamphilus, a very ancient and very famous painter from whom the young nobles learned painting for the first time.[5] His opinion, in fact, was that no one by ignoring geometry would have been a good painter. Certainly, our rudiments, from which one extracts a whole, complete, and precise technique of painting, are easily assimilable by a geometrician. I also believe that for those who ignore this science neither rudiments nor some procedures of

---

[1] Pippo was a diminutive for Filippo (Brunelleschi). Here Alberti is praising the cathedral dome of Florence.

[2] The Tuscan language, i.e. the vernacular, an ancestor of modern Italian. The most recent scholarship argues that Alberti first wrote *On Painting* in Tuscan and then translated it, somewhat changed, into Latin.

[3] "The centric ray": Alberti subscribed to the theory that the eye emitted rays through which images were transmitted to the senses. The rays left the eye in a spreading bundle of straight lines. Some rays touched the extremities of objects. Others covered the whole surface. The centric ray went from the center of the eye right to the geometric center of the object. Alberti wanted the artist to reproduce with utter precision the way objects were perceived by the eye. But the ultimate point was to move the viewer to awe and praise.

[4] Echoing 1st c. CE Latin rhetorician Quintilian's *Institutio oratoria* 12.1.1.

[5] Echoing 1st c. CE Latin naturalist Pliny the Elder's *Naturalis historia* 35.76–77.

painting can be sufficiently comprehensible. I, therefore, claim that geometry absolutely must not be neglected by painters. It will not be useless if they will find pleasure very near to poets and orators; in fact, these certainly have many qualities in common with the painter. Indeed, those literary men, not little equipped with the knowledge of many things, will help to settle in the best way the composition of a *historia*,[1] a wholly praiseworthy undertaking that is first based on creativity. Or rather, this [undertaking] surely has such a force that even the creativity alone attracts without the painting. While one reads, one praises that famous description of Calumny that Lucian says [has been] depicted by Apelles.[2] Without doubt, I think it is not at all alien to the purpose to tell it, in order that painters remember that they must dedicate themselves to realize creations of this kind. There was in fact a man whose ears protruded in an overwhelming way; standing close to him there were two women: Ignorance and Superstition; somewhere else [there was] Calumny herself, who was approaching with the appearance of an attractive woman, but this [woman] in [her] face itself seemed callous beyond measure by cunning intention, while she held with the left hand a lighted torch and with the other hand dragged by the hair an adolescent in the act of turning [his] hands toward the sky. And her guide is a certain man, filled with pallor, disfigured, with frowning look, whom you would rightly compare to those whom a long fatigue will have exhausted in battle. They justly said that he was Envy. There are also two other female companions of Calumny in the act of arranging the ornaments of [their] mistress: Deceit and Fraud. Behind them, there is Penitence, covered in dark and very dirty robes in the act of lacerating herself. Very near, Truth follows, chaste and modest.[3] If this *historia* fascinates even the hearts just by narrating it, how mush beauty and seduction do you think has originated from the painting itself by the excellent painter?

54. And what [to say] of those three little young sisters to whom Hesiod gave the names of Aglaia, Euphrosine, and Thalia, who were depicted smiling, with hands intertwined among themselves, [and] adorned with loose and transparent clothes?[4] One wished that from them nobility of the heart was manifested, because one of the sisters gives, the other receives, and the third returns a kind gesture, levels that certainly must be present in every perfect, noble-minded heart. Do you perceive what great praise creations of this kind procure for the artist? For this reason, what I advise here is let the zealous painter become friendly and well disposed toward poets and orators and in general toward all others learned in letters. In fact, he will not only obtain the best suggestions from similar learned brains, but, really, he will enjoy also these creative ideas, which will bring him praise not of secondary importance in a painting. Phidias, an excellent painter, admitted to have learned from Homer particularly, how to paint the majesty of Jupiter.[5] In the same way, I think that we also will not only become more prolific but also more correct by reading our poets, provided that we will be more zealous in learning than in profit.

55. But the majority of times, more than learning, a thought upsets the scholars not less than the passionate [people]: the fact that they ignore the road of correct learning. Let us commence by saying, therefore, on what condition we should become experts in this art. Let the principle be that all levels of learning must be claimed from Nature herself. The process, indeed, of perfecting the art will be gained by means of diligence, study, and assiduousness. I would like, at least, that those who undertake the art of painting should follow what I see being done among teachers of writing. Those, in effect, first teach separately all characters of the alphabet. Thereafter they prepare to bring together the syllables and subsequently the expressions. Therefore, let our [painters] also follow this procedure in painting. At first, let them [learn] the edge of surfaces, [I would say] almost the elements of painting, then the connections of the same [surfaces]; from here on, let them learn by heart with precision the shapes of all members;[6] and all the differences that can

---

[1] A *historia* was a story told through visual means.

[2] A reference to 2nd c. CE Greek rhetorician Lucian, *De Calumnia*, 5.

[3] Later, *c.* 1494, Florentine painter Botticelli painted Calumny in accordance with Lucian's (and Alberti's) description.

[4] These were the Graces, named by 8th–7th c. BCE poet Hesiod in *Theogony*, 907. Alberti no doubt had in mind representations such as one at Pompeii.

[5] Phidias (d.430 BCE) was a Greek sculptor, painter, and architect. His work had been lost long before Alberti's day, but Alberti probably knew it from Roman copies, and he knew that Phidias had been praised in 1st c. CE Greek historian/geographer Strabo's *Geographia* 8.3.30.

[6] That is, parts of the body.

be found in the members. In fact, those [differences] are surely neither few nor insignificant. There will be those whose nose is hooked. There will be those who show flattened, curved, and wide nostrils; others who present flaccid cheeks; thin lips distinguish others; and above all the single members have, in their turn, something in particular that, when it will have been present in greater or lesser measure, then it renders the whole limb very different. Indeed, we see how the same members chubby in us as children and so to say rounded and smooth are, instead, with the arising of old age, harsher and rather bony. The scholar of painting, therefore, will take all these things from Nature herself, and he will meditate incessantly by himself on what condition each thing arises; and in this research he will persist continually with the eyes and with the mind. He will observe, in fact, the lap of a person who is sitting and the legs while they bend, inclining gently. He will notice the whole appearance and the conformation of the one who is in front of him. Finally, there will not be any part concerning which he ignores the aim and the symmetry, as the Greeks say. Well, among all components, let him not only prefer the resemblance of things but also, and above all, beauty itself. In a painting, in fact, beauty pleases beyond measure no more than is required. Demetrius, that famous ancient painter, did not reach the maximum level of praise, because he [was] more careful in expressing resemblance than beauty.[1] All approved parts, therefore, must be chosen from the most beautiful bodies. Consequently, not lastly, one needs to strive with zeal and energy in order to reach beauty, to master it, and, above all, to express it. Although this [feature] is the most difficult of all, because not all praises of beauty concentrate themselves in a single place, but certainly are disseminated and scattered, nevertheless one needs to extend every effort in looking for it and understanding it to perfection. In fact, he who will have learned to seize and take into consideration more difficult objects will overcome, at will, the minor ones. And there is nothing so difficult that you cannot continue till the end with study and perseverance.[2]

62. One must, therefore, adopt a moderate diligence in features,[3] and it is necessary to consult friends; or, better still, one also needs to receive all observers from every-

where during the execution of the work itself and [to] listen to them. This way, in fact, the painter's work will be pleasing to a great number of people. Therefore, one will not refuse [the] criticism and judgment of a great number of people, when it is still possible to meet with suggestions. They say that Apelles used to hide behind the picture both in order that the observers spoke more liberally and that he personally listened to them while they showed in a more sincere way faults of his work.[4] Therefore, I wish that our painters both listen more often freely and ask all people what they think, since this is an aid not only for definite objects but also to catch favor with respect to the painter. Truly, there is no one who does not consider [it] an honor for himself to express his own judgment on [the] works of others. One must not then fear in the least degree that the judgment of detractors and of the envious could take something away from the praises of a painter. In fact, [the] fame of the painter is obvious and very celebrated, and it has as a loquacious witness the well-painted work itself. Let him, therefore, listen to all, and let him at first value a thing on his own and correct it. Then, after having listened to all, let him follow [the advice of those] more expert.

63. These [are the notions] that I thought to report in the present commentaries on painting. If these are such as to offer an advantage and some usefulness to painters, I expect, above all, this prize for my toils: that they paint my face in their *historiae*, in such a way to proclaim, to posterity, that they are mindful of a benefit and grateful, or rather, that I have been a scholar of art.[5] On the contrary, if I did not satisfy their expectations at all, nevertheless let them not condemn the fact that we dared to undertake such a great subject. If, in fact, our talent has not been able to attain what is meritorious to attempt, they [the readers] should at least remember that in great events one is accustomed to consider praise the fact that you have desired that which was very difficult. Perhaps, there will be those who will amend our mistakes, and in this extraordinary and very valuable subject they will be able to help painters much more than we. I beg them again and again—Oh! If there will be some!—to engage with a happy and resolute mind this commitment, in which they, in person, both let themselves exercise talent and make this very noble art

---

[1] Echoing Quintilian, 12.10.9.

[2] Echoing 1st c. CE rhetorician Cicero, *De oratore* 2.16.69–70.

[3] Alberti has been talking about painters who are so worried about getting every detail right that they don't know when to stop.

[4] Apelles was a contemporary of Protogenes; the two artists both rivaled and admired one another. See Pliny 35.84.

[5] Alberti got his wish; he figures in the crowd scene that Masaccio painted in the "Saint Peter Enthroned" fresco in the Brancacci Chapel (Florence).

very refined. We, nevertheless, consider it a great satisfaction to have won this palm before [its] time, since we have been the first ones to write about this very fine art. Really, if we have not been able to take this truly most difficult undertaking to perfection in accordance with the readers' expectation, one needs to blame Nature for this more than us, which seems to have imposed this rule on things: that there exists no art that has not taken [its] origins from quite imperfect beginnings. In fact, they say that nothing is born [and is], at the same moment, also perfect.[1] Instead, they who will follow us—if there will be some more able than we with zeal and talent—these perhaps will make the art of painting perfect and complete.

The End

8.20 Defending women: Christine de Pisan, *The Book of the City of Ladies* (1404–1407). Original in French.

Born in Italy and educated in France, Christine de Pisan (*c*.1364–*c*.1429/1430) married at the age of 15 and was left a widow with two young children at age 25. Forced to support her family on her own, she turned to copying manuscripts and writing poetry and prose, both of which were commissioned by royal and other wealthy patrons. In *The Book of the City of Ladies* she defended the virtue, intelligence, and capabilities of women against the many men who disparaged the female sex. The book presents a dream or vision in which the author—with the help of three ladies (Reason, Rectitude, and Justice, all "daughters of God")—populates a new city with the best women from the past and present. Those worthy of the city are named in the course of question-and-answer dialogues between Christine and the three ladies. In the passage below, Christine asks Lady Reason about women's ability to govern. In the course of their discussion Queen Fredegund, wife of King Chilperic and the nemesis of Gregory of Tours (see above, p. 53), comes up. Compare Christine's and Gregory's opinions of Fredegund and speculate on why they might be so different.

[Source: Christine de Pizan, *The Book of the City of Ladies*, trans. Earl Jeffrey Richards, rev. ed. (New York: Persea Books, 1992), pp. 30–34.]

CHRISTINE ASKS REASON WHY WOMEN ARE NOT IN THE SEATS OF LEGAL COUNSEL; AND REASON'S RESPONSE.

"Most high and honored lady, your fair words [about a different matter] amply satisfy my thinking. But tell me still, if you please, why women do not plead law cases in the courts of justice, are unfamiliar with legal disputes, and do not hand down judgments? For these men say that it is because of some woman (who I don't know) who governed unwisely from the seat of justice."

"My daughter, everything told about this woman is frivolous and contrived out of deception. But whoever would ask the causes and reasons of all things would have to answer for too much in this question, even though Aristotle in the *Problemata* takes account of many things and even though his *Categoriae* contains the essences of so many natural actions.[2] Now, as to this particular question, dear friend, one could just as well ask why God did not ordain that men fulfill the offices of women, and women the offices of men. So I must answer this question by saying that just as a wise and well ordered lord organizes his domain so that one servant accomplishes one task and another servant another task, and that what the one does the other does not do, God has similarly ordained man and woman to serve Him in different offices and also to aid, comfort, and accompany one another, each in their ordained task, and to each sex has given a fitting and appropriate nature and inclination to fulfill their offices.

---

[1] Echoing Cicero, *Brutus* 18.71.

[2] The point is that even Aristotle's books on *Problems* and *Categories* cannot explain everything.

Inasmuch as the human species often errs in what it is supposed to do, God has given men strong and hardy bodies for coming and going as well as for speaking boldly. And for this reason, men with this nature learn the laws—and must do so—in order to keep the world under the rule of justice and, in case anyone does not wish to obey the statutes which have been established by reason of law, are required to make them obey with physical constraint and force of arms, a task which women could never accomplish. Nevertheless, though God has given women great understanding—there are many such women—because of the integrity to which women are inclined, it would not be at all appropriate for them to go and appear so brazenly in the courts like men, for there are enough men who do so. What would be accomplished by sending three men to lift a burden which two can carry easily?

But if anyone maintained that women do not possess enough understanding to learn the laws, the opposite is obvious from the proof afforded by experience, which is manifest and has been manifested in many women—just as I will soon tell—who have been very great philosophers and have mastered fields far more complicated, subtle, and lofty than written laws and man-made institutions. Moreover, in case anyone says that women do not have a natural sense for politics and government, I will give you examples of several great women rulers who have lived in past times. And so that you will better know my truth, I will remind you of some women of your own time who remained widows and whose skill governing—both past and present—in all their affairs following the deaths of their husbands provides obvious demonstration that a woman with a mind is fit for all tasks."

HERE SHE TELLS OF NICAULA, EMPRESS OF ETHIOPIA, AND AFTERWARDS ABOUT SEVERAL QUEENS AND PRINCESSES OF FRANCE.

"Please tell me where there was ever a king endowed with greater skill in politics, government, and sovereign justice, and even with such lofty and magnificent style as one can read about the most noble Empress Nicaula.[1] For though there had been many kings of great fame called pharaohs in the vast, wide, and varied lands which she governed, and from whom she was descended, during her rule this lady was the first to begin to live according to laws and coordinated policies, and she destroyed and abolished the crude customs found in the territories over which she was lord and reformed the rude manners of the savage Ethiopians. This lady accomplished even more praiseworthy deeds than reforming the rough manners

of others, according to the authors who speak of her. She remained the heiress of these pharaohs, and not just of a small land but of the kingdom of Arabia, Ethiopia, Egypt, and the island of Meroë (which is very long and wide and filled with all kinds of goods and is near to the Nile), which she governed with wonderful prudence. What more should I tell you about this lady? She was so wise and so capable a ruler that even the Holy Scriptures speak of her great virtue. She herself instituted laws of far-reaching justice for governing her people. She enjoyed great nobility and vast wealth—almost as much as all the men who have ever lived. She was profoundly learned in the Scriptures and all fields of knowledge, and she had so lofty a heart that she did not deign to marry, nor did she desire that any man be at her side."

HERE REASON SPEAKS OF A QUEEN OF FRANCE, NAMED FREDEGUND.

"I could tell you a great deal about ladies who governed wisely in ancient times, just as what I will presently tell you will deal with this question. In France there was once a queen, Fredegund, who was the wife of King Chilperic. Although she was cruel, contrary to the natural disposition of women, nevertheless, following her husband's death, with great skill this lady governed the kingdom of France which found itself at this time in very great unrest and danger, and she was left with nothing else besides Chilperic's heir, a small son named Clothar. There was great division among the barons regarding the government, and already a great civil war had broken out in the kingdom. Having assembled the barons in council, she addressed them, all the while holding her child in her arms: 'My lords, here is your king. Do not forget the loyalty which has always been present among the French, and do not scorn him because he is a child, for with God's help he will grow up, and when he comes of age he will recognize his good friends and reward them according to their deserts, unless you desire to disinherit him wrongfully and sinfully. As for me, I assure you that I will reward those who act well and loyally with such generosity that no other reward could be better.' Thus did this queen satisfy the barons, and through her wise government, she delivered her son from the hands of his enemies. She herself nourished him until he was grown, and he was invested by her with the crown and honor of the kingdom, which never would have happened if she had not been so prudent.

"Similarly, the same can be said of the most wise and in every instance virtuous and noble Queen Blanche [of Castile], mother of Saint Louis [King Louis IX] who gov-

---

[1] The "Queen of Sheba" of the Bible.

erned the kingdom of France while her son was a minor so nobly and so prudently that it was never better ruled by any man. Even when he was grown, she was still the head of his council because of her experience of wise government, nor was anything done without her, and she even followed her son to war."

FINDING A NEW WORLD

8.21 A new kind of map: Gabriel de Valseca, *Portolan Map* (1447).

Beginning *c.*1300, the coastline of the Mediterranean (and, by 1500, of Africa and other regions) was mapped on portolan charts with a precision hitherto unknown. Named after the Italian word *portolano* (from the Latin *portus*, meaning port), portolan charts were practical navigational guides. Whether fancy—with flags, town names, and even a compass rose—or simple, all used a spider's web of "rhumb lines." These were carefully constructed as a series of 32 equidistant spokes radiating from a point, each spoke indicating a wind direction. One color was used for the eight primary directions—north, northeast, east, and so on—while other colors indicated the half- and quarter-winds. Above all, sailors used these maps to skirt headlands, which otherwise would ground them, and to find estuaries, where they could obtain fresh water and access to inland routes. The portolan chart shown here, drawn by the Majorcan Gabriel de Valseca, follows the coastlines from the Strait of Gibraltar to the eastern end of the Mediterranean and across to the Black Sea, paying particular attention to the islands.

See Plate 15, p. 252, for a color reproduction of the *Portolan Map*.

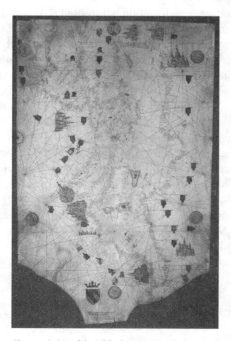

(By permission of the Bibliothèque nationale de France)

8.22 Taking Mexico: Hernán Cortés, *The Second Letter* (1520). Original in Spanish.

Hernán Cortés (1485–1547) confronted a "new world," but he interpreted it with the mental categories of the old. Determined to secure the rulers of Mexico as "vassals" of Emperor Charles V (r.1519–1558), he struck out on his own, without the authorization of his commanding officer, to stage his version of the *reconquista* of the new land. Setting up a community—complete with officials whose titles echoed those known in Spanish cities—Cortés sent representatives of his "municipality" to Spain to plead his cause to the emperor. His *Second Letter*, following on this visit, depicts him as a loyal upholder of the realm, working to secure vassals for His Majesty and to conquer and win souls on God's behalf. How might you argue that this letter is part of the crusading tradition?

[Source: Hernán Cortés, *Letters from Mexico*, trans. and ed. Anthony Pagden (New Haven, CT: Yale University Press, 2001), pp. 54–60.]

Most Powerful Lord, I traveled for three days through the country and the kingdom of Cempoal, where I was very well received and accommodated by all the natives. On the fourth day I entered a province which is called Sienchimalen,[1] in which there is a town which is very strong and built in a defensible position on the side of a very steep mountain. There is only one entrance, up steep steps which can only be climbed on foot and that with considerable difficulty. In the plain there are many villages and hamlets of five or three or two hundred inhabitants, so that there are in all as many as five or six thousand warriors; and this land is in the kingdom of Mutezuma [Montezuma]. Here they received me very well and generously provided the provisions I needed for the journey. They told me that they knew I was going to visit their lord Mutezuma, and that I should be confident he was my friend and had sent word that they were to give me every facility, for they served him by so doing. I responded to their great kindness by saying that Your Majesty had received news of him and had sent me to see him, and that I was going for no other purpose. Then I went over a pass which is at the frontier of this province, and we called it Nombre de Dios, because it was the first we had crossed in these lands: it is so rough and steep that there is none in Spain so difficult. But I did cross it, safely and without adverse incident. On the slopes below the pass there are other villages and a fortress called Ceyxnacan,[2] which also belongs to Mutezuma; here we were no less well received than at Sienchimalen; also, they told us, because Mutezuma wished it. And I replied as before.

From there I continued for three days through desert country which is uninhabitable because of its infertility and lack of water and because of the extreme cold. God knows how much my people suffered from thirst and hunger, and especially from a hail- and rainstorm that hit us there, which I thought would cause the deaths of many people from cold; and indeed several Indians from the island of Fernandina who had not enough to wear did die from it. After three days we crossed another pass not so steep as the first. At the top of it there was a small tower, almost like a wayside shrine, in which they kept a number of idols, and around the tower were more than a thousand cartloads of firewood, all very well stacked; for this reason we called it the Firewood Pass.[3] On the descent from this pass, between some very steep mountains, there is a valley thickly inhabited with people who seemed to be very poor. After going two leagues through this region without learning anything about it, I reached a flatter place where the chief of that valley appeared to live; for he had the largest and the best-constructed buildings we had seen in that land so far. They were all of dressed stone and very well built and very new, and

---

[1] Xicochimalco.

[2] Ixhuacan.

[3] Puerto de la Leña.

they had very large and beautiful halls in them and many rooms, also well built: this valley and town are called Caltanmí.[1] By the chief and the people I was very well received and lodged.

After I had spoken to him on behalf of Your Majesty and of the reason for my coming to these parts, I asked him if he was a vassal of Mutezuma or owed some other allegiance. And he showed surprise at my question, and asked who was not a vassal of Mutezuma, meaning that here he is king of the whole world. I replied by telling him of the great power of Your Majesty and of the many other princes, greater than Mutezuma, who were Your Highness's vassals and considered it no small favor to be so; Mutezuma also would become one; as would all the natives of these lands. I therefore asked him to become one, for if he did it would be greatly to his honor and advantage, but if, on the other hand, he refused to obey he would be punished. And to acknowledge that he had been received into Your Royal service, I begged him to give me some gold to send to Your Majesty. He replied that he had gold but would give me none unless Mutezuma commanded it, but that once this had been done he would surrender to me the gold and his own person and all that he had. So as not to offend him and for fear that some calamity might befall my endeavor and my journey, I dissembled as best I could and told him that very soon I would have Mutezuma order him to give the gold and all that he owned.

Here two other chieftains who held lands in that valley came to see me: one lived four leagues down the valley and the other two leagues up the valley, and they gave me several gold necklaces of little weight and value and seven or eight female slaves. After staying there four or five days, I left them all very pleased and went up the valley to the town of the other chief I spoke of, which is called Ystacmastitán.[2] His territory consists of some three or four leagues' extent of built-up land, lying in the valley floor beside a small river which runs through it. On a very high hill is this chief's house, with a better fortress than any to be found in the middle of Spain, and fortified with better walls and barbicans and earthworks. On top of this hill live some five or six thousand inhabitants with very good houses and somewhat richer than those living in the valley. Here likewise I was very well received, and this chief said that he was also a vassal of Mutezuma. I remained in this town three days, to allow my people to recover from the hardships they had suffered in the desert as well as to await the return of four native messengers from Cempoal who had come with me and whom I had sent from Catalmy to a very large province called Tascalteca,[3] which they told me was very close by, and so it seemed to be. They had also told me that the natives of this province were their friends and very hated enemies of Mutezuma, and they wished to be my allies for they were many and very strong. They shared a large frontier with Mutezuma and fought continual wars with him and would help me if Mutezuma wished to oppose me. But the whole time I was in that valley, which was eight days in all, the messengers did not return; so I asked those chieftains of Cempoal who traveled in my company why the messengers had not returned. They replied that the land must be far away and they could not return so quickly. When I saw how long they were in coming, and that the chieftains of Cempoal so assured me of the friendship and good faith of those of that province, I set out thither.

On leaving this valley I found a great barrier built of dry stone and as much as nine feet high, which ran right across the valley from one mountain range to the other. It was some twenty paces wide and all along the top was a battlement a foot and a half thick to provide an advantageous position for battle; it had only one entrance, some ten paces wide. At this entrance one wall doubled over the other, in the manner of a ravelin [a curved wall], within a space of forty paces, so that the entrance was not direct but had turns in it. When I asked the reason for this wall they replied that that was the frontier of the province of Tascalteca, whose inhabitants were Mutezuma's enemies and were always at war with him. The natives of the valley, because I was going to see Mutezuma their lord, begged me not to go through the territory of his enemies, for they might be hostile to me and do me some harm; they themselves would lead me to Mutezuma without leaving his territory, in which I would always be well received.

But those of Cempoal told me not to do this, but to go through Tascalteca, for what the others had said was only to prevent me from forming an alliance with that province. They said that all Mutezuma's people were wicked traitors and would lead me to a place whence I

---

[1] Most likely the modern Zautla.
[2] Ixtacamaxtitlan (Puebla).
[3] Tlaxcala.

could not escape. As I held those of Cempoal in greater esteem than the others, I took their advice, leading my men with as much caution as possible. And I, with some six horsemen, rode half a league ahead, not in anticipation of what later befell me, but to explore the land, so that if anything should happen I might have time to gather and instruct my men.

After proceeding four leagues, we reached the brow of a hill, and the two horsemen who went in front of me saw some Indians dressed in the feathers they wear in battle, and bearing swords and bucklers, who when they saw the horses began to run away. I arrived soon after and I called out to them to return and not to be afraid; as we approached them (there must have been about fifteen Indians) they banded together and began to throw spears and to call to others of their people who were in a valley. They fought so fiercely with us that they killed two horses and wounded three others and two horsemen. At this point the others appeared who must have been four or five thousand. Some eight horsemen were now with me, not counting the dead, and we fought them making several charges while we waited for the other soldiers whom I had sent a horseman to fetch; and in the fighting we did them some damage, in that we killed fifty or sixty of them and ourselves suffered no harm, although they fought with great courage and ferocity. But as we were all mounted we attacked in safety and retreated likewise.

When they saw our men approaching, they withdrew, for they were few, and left us the field. After they had gone, several messengers arrived, who said they came from the chieftains of that province and with them two of the messengers I had sent, who said that the lords of the province knew nothing of what those others had done; for they were of an independent community and had done it without his permission. They regretted what had happened and would pay me for the horses which had been killed; they wanted to be my friends, wished me good fortune and said I would be welcomed by them. I replied that I was grateful to them and that I held them as friends and would go where they said. That night I was forced to sleep in a river bed one league beyond where this happened, for it was late and the men were tired.

There I took all the precautions I could, with watchmen and scouts both on foot and on horseback. When it was light I departed, keeping my vanguard and baggage in close formation and my scouts in front. When, at sunrise, I arrived at a very small village I found the other two messengers weeping, saying that they had been tied up to be killed, but had escaped that night. Only a stone's throw from them there appeared a large number of Indians,

heavily armed, who with a great shout began to attack us with many javelins and arrows. I began to deliver the formal requerimiento [demand for peace] through the interpreters who were with me and before a notary, but the longer I spent in admonishing them and requesting peace, the more they pressed us and did us as much harm as they could. Seeing therefore that nothing was to be gained by the requerimiento or protestations we began to defend ourselves as best we could, and so drew us fighting into the midst of more than 100,000 warriors who surrounded us on all sides. We fought all day long until an hour before sunset, when they withdrew; with half a dozen guns and five or six harquebuses and forty crossbowmen and with the thirteen horsemen who remained, I had done them much harm without receiving any except from exhaustion and hunger. And it truly seemed that God was fighting for us, because from such a multitude, such fierce and able warriors and with so many kinds of weapons to harm us, we escaped so lightly.

That night I fortified a small tower on top of a hill, where they kept their idols. When it was day I left two hundred men and all the artillery behind and rode out to attack them with the horsemen, one hundred foot soldiers and four hundred Indians of those I brought from Cempoal, and three hundred from Yztaemestitan [sic]. Before they had time to rally, I burnt five or six small places of about a hundred inhabitants, and took prisoner about four hundred persons, both men and women; and returned to the camp having suffered no loss whatever. The following day at dawn, more than 149,000 men, who covered the entire ground, attacked the camp with such force that some of them broke in and fought the Spaniards hand to hand. We then went out and charged them, and so much did Our Lord help us that in four hours' fighting we had advanced so far that they could no longer harm us in the camp, although they still made some attacks. And so we fought until late, when they retired.

The following day I left before dawn by a different route, without being observed, with the horsemen, a hundred foot soldiers and my Indian allies. I burnt more than ten villages, in one of which there were more than three thousand houses, where the inhabitants fought with us, although there was no one there to help them. As we were carrying the banner of the Cross and were fighting for our Faith and in the service of Your Sacred Majesty in this Your Royal enterprise, God gave us such a victory that we killed many of them without ourselves receiving any hurt. Having gained our victory, we returned to camp a little after midday, for the enemy was gathering from all directions.

TIMELINE FOR CHAPTER EIGHT

1300

1348 ARCHBISHOP WILLIAM, ————— | ————— 1348 *PISTOIA ORDINANCES*
LETTER TO HIS OFFICIAL

*C.*1350 HEINRICH VON DIESSENHOVEN, ————— **1350**
PERSECUTION OF THE JEWS | ————— 1350S GREGORAS, *ROMAN HISTORY*

BEF. 1368 IBN BATTUTA, *TRAVELS* —————

————— AFT. 1381 *WAT TYLER'S REBELLION*

1395 ANTHONY, *LETTER TO RUSSIAN CHURCH* ————— | ————— 1397 PETRO GENTILI, *SPEECH*

*C.*1400 FROISSART, *CHRONICLES* ————— **1400**

1415 JEAN GERSON, *SERMON* ————— | ————— 1404–07 CHRISTINE DE PISAN, *CITY OF LADIES*

1420 *FOUR ARTICLES OF PRAGUE* ————— | ————— 1416 ROMANUS, *LETTER TO FRANCISCUS DE FIANA*

*C.*1430 *BOOK OF MARGERY KEMPE* ————— | ————— 1429 JEANNE D'ARC, *LETTER TO THE ENGLISH*

1447 GABRIEL DE VALSECA, *PORTOLAN MAP* ————— | ————— 1435–36 ALBERTI, *ON PAINTING*

1450

BEF. 1477 SPHRANTZES, *CHRONICLE* —————

1478 MEHMED'S AND VENICE'S *PEACE AGREEMENT* —————

————— LATE 15TH C. ASHIKPASHAZADE, *OTHMAN COMES TO POWER*

END OF 15TH C. *TALE OF THE WHITE COWL* ————— **1500**

————— 1520 HERNÁN CORTÉS, *SECOND LETTER*

1550

To test your knowledge and gain deeper understanding of this chapter, please go to www.utphistorymatters.com for Study Questions.

Sources

CHAPTER I

1.1 Toleration or favoritism? *Edict of Milan* (313). Excerpts from *Church and State through the Centuries: A Collection of Historic Documents with Commentaries*, trans. and ed. Sidney Z. Ehler and John B. Morrall. Copyright © 1954, The Newman Press. Used with permission of Paulist Press, Inc., New York/Mahwah, N.J. www.paulistpress.com.

1.2 Law: *The Theodosian Code* (438). Pharr, Clyde; *The Theodosian Code and Novels and the Sermondian Constitutions*. Copyright © 1952 in the name of the author, 1980 renewed in name of Roy Pharr, executor. Reprinted by permission of Princeton University Press.

1.4 Heretics: *A Donatist Sermon* (*c.*318). *Donatist Martyr Stories: The Church in Conflict in Roman North Africa*, trans. Maureen A. Tilley, Translated Texts for Historians, 24. Liverpool University Press, 1996. Reprinted by permission of Liverpool University Press.

1.5 Orthodoxy's declaration: *The Nicene Creed* (325). J.N.D. Kelly, *Early Christian Doctrines*, 2nd ed. Harper and Row, 1958. Courtesy of Continuum International Publishing Group.

1.6 Relating this world to the next: Augustine, *The City of God* (413–426). *Concerning the City of God against the Pagans by St Augustine*, translated by Henry Bettenson, introduced by John O'Meara (First published in Pelican Books 1972, Reprinted in Penguin Classics, 1984). Translation copyright © Henry Bettenson, 1972. Reproduced by permission of Penguin Books Ltd.

1.7 Monasticism: *The Benedictine Rule* (*c.*530–*c.*560). Reprinted by permission of the publisher from *The Rule of Saint Benedict*, edited and translated by Bruce L. Venarde, Dumbarton Oaks Medieval Library Volume 6, pp. 3, 7, 9, 17, 19, 21, 23, 29, 31, 33, 35, 37, 45, 47, 57, 59, 61, 79, 85, 87, 89, 97, 123, 125, 139, 141, 143, 161, 163, 177, 179, 187, 189, 191, 193, 229, Cambridge, Mass.: Harvard University Press, Copyright © 2011 by the President and Fellows of Harvard College.

1.9 The eremetical life: Athanasius, *Life of St. Antony of Egypt* (357). Athanasius of Alexandria, *Life of St. Antony of Egypt*, trans. David Brakke, in *Medieval Hagiography: An Anthology*, ed. Thomas Head. Garland, 2000. Courtesy of David Brakke.

1.11 St. Radegund as ascetic: Venantius Fortunatus, *The Life of St. Radegund* (before *c.*600). "Radegund, Queen of the Franks and Abbess of Poitiers (ca. 525–587)," in *Sainted Women of the Dark Ages*, JoAnn McNamara, John Halborg, E. Gordon Whatley, pp. 60–106. Copyright © 1992, Duke University Press. All rights reserved. Reprinted by permission of the publisher. www.dukeupress.edu

1.12 St. Radegund as relic collector: Baudonivia, *The Life of St. Radegund* (*c.*600). Venantius Fortunatus, *The Life of St. Radegund* (before *c.*600). "Radegund, Queen of the Franks and Abbess of Poitiers (ca. 525–587)," in *Sainted Women of the Dark Ages*, JoAnn McNamara, John Halborg, E. Gordon Whatley, pp. 60–106. Copyright © 1992, Duke University Press. All rights reserved. Reprinted by permission of the publisher. www.dukeupress.edu

1.13 Gothic Italy as Rome's heir: Cassiodorus, *Variae (State Papers)* (*c.*507–536). Cassiodorus: *Variae*, trans. S.J.B. Barnish. Copyright © 1992, Liverpool University Press. Reprinted by permission of Liverpool University Press.

1.14 Gothic Spain converts: *The Third Council of Toledo* (589). *Medieval Iberia: Readings from Christian, Muslim, and Jewish Sources,* 2nd ed., Olivia Remie Constable with Damian Zurro, trans. David Nirenberg, pp. 12–20. Copyright © University of Pennsylvania Press, 2011. Reprinted with permission of the University of Pennsylvania Press.

CHAPTER II

2.1 Byzantine village life and the education of a saint: *The Life of St. Theodore of Sykeon* (7th c.). Republished with permission of St. Valdimir's Seminary Press, from *Three Byzantine Saints: Contemporary Biographies translated from the Greek*, trans. Elizabeth Dawes and Norman H. Baynes. Copyright © 1977. Permission conveyed through Copyright Clearance Center, Inc.

2.3 The iconoclastic argument: *The Synod of 754*. Republished with permission of William B. Eerdmans Publishing Company, from *A Select Library of Nicene and Post-Nicene Fathers of the Christian Church*, 2nd series, ed. Philip Schaff and Henry Wace, Vol. 14: The Seven Ecumenical Councils. Copyright © 1971. Permission conveyed through Copyright Clearance Center, Inc.

2.4 Vilifying the iconoclasts: *The Chronicle of Theophanes Confessor* (before 818). *The Chronicle of Theophanes Confessor: Byzantine and Near Eastern History, AD 284–813*, ed. and trans. Cyril Mango and Roger Scott. Copyright © 1997. By permission of Oxford University Press.

2.5 Pre-Islamic Arabic poetry: Al-A'sha, *Bid Hurayra Farewell* (before 625). Michael A. Sells, "Bid Hurayra Farewell" from *Desert Tracings: Six Classic Arabian Odes by 'Alquama, Shanfara, Labid, 'Antara, Al-A'sha, and Dhu al-Rumma* © 1989 by Michael A. Sells. Reprinted by permission of Wesleyan University Press.

2.6 The sacred text: *Qur'an Suras* 1, 53:1–18, 81, 87, 96, 98 (*c.*610–622). Republished with permission of White Cloud Press, from *Approaching the Qur'an: The Early Revelations*, trans. Michael Sells. Copy-

right © 1999. Permission conveyed through Copyright Clearance Center, Inc.

2.7 Umayyad diplomacy: *The Treaty of Tudmir* (713). *Medieval Iberia: Readings from Christian, Muslim, and Jewish Sources*, ed. Olivia Remie Constable, trans. David Nirenberg, pp. 37–38. Copyright © University of Pennsylvania Press, 1997. Reprinted with permission of the University of Pennsylvania Press.

2.8 Taxation: *A Tax Demand in Egypt* (710). *Islam from the Prophet Muhammad to the Capture of Constantinople, Vol. 2: Religion and Society*, ed. and trans. Bernard Lewis (1987), p. 130. Copyright © 1974 by Bernard Lewis. By permission of Oxford University Press, USA.

2.9 Praising the caliph: Al-Akhtal, *The Tribe Has Departed* (*c.*692). Republished with permission of Indiana University Press, from *The Poetics of Islamic Legitimacy: Myth, Gender, and Ceremony in the Classical Arabic Ode*, Suzanne Pinckney Stetkevych. Copyright © 2002. Permission conveyed through Copyright Clearance Center, Inc.

2.10 A world explained by words: Isidore of Seville, *Etymologies* (*c.*615–*c.*630). *The Etymologies of Isidore of Seville*, ed. Stephen A. Barney, W.J. Lewis, J.A. Beach and Oliver Berghof. Copyright © 2006 Stephen A. Barney, W.J. Lewis, J.A. Beach and Oliver Berghof. Reprinted with the permission of Cambridge University Press.

2.13 Reforming the Continental church: *Letters to Boniface* (723–726). From *The Letters of Saint Boniface*, trans. Ephraim Emerton. Copyright © 1940 Columbia University Press. Reprinted with permission of the publisher.

2.14 Creating a Roman Christian identity for England: Bede, *The Ecclesiastical History of the English People* (731). Bede, *The Ecclesiastical History of the English People*, ed. Judith McClure and Roger Collins (1994), pp. 37–41, 55–59, 65–71, 152–59, 370–75, 397. By permission of Oxford University Press.

CHAPTER III

3.2 Byzantine guilds: *The Book of the Prefect* (912). A.E.R. Boak, "Notes and Documents: The Book of the Prefect," *Journal of Economic and Business History* 1 (1929): 600–02, 604–10.

3.3 The sale of a slave in Italy: *A Contract of Sale* (725). From *Medieval Trade in the Mediterranean World*, trans. and ed. Robert S. Lopez and Irving W. Raymond. Copyright © 2001 Columbia University Press. Reprinted with permission of the publisher.

3.4 An early view of the Prophet: Muhammad ibn Ishaq, *Life of Muhammad* (754–767). *The Life of Muhammad: A Translation of Ishaq's Sirat Rasul Allah*, trans. and ed. A. Guillaume. Oxford University Press, 1955, pp. 81–83, 104–07.

3.5 Hadith: Al-Bukhari, *On Fasting* (9th c.). *A Reader on Islam: Passages from Standard Arabic Writings Illustrative of the Beliefs and Practices of Muslims*, ed. Arthur Jeffery. Mouton & Co., 1962, pp. 88–90, 92–94, 98–101.

3.6 The "New Poetry": Abu Nuwas, *Turning the Tables* (*c*.800). Republished with permission of Oneworld, from *Abu Nuwas: A Genius of Poetry*, Philip Kennedy. Copyright © 2005. Permission conveyed through Copyright Clearance Center, Inc.

3.7 The minority—that is, Christian—view: *Chronicle of Albelda* (*c*.883). *Medieval Iberia: Readings from Christian, Muslim, and Jewish Sources*, ed. Olivia Remie Constable, trans. David Nirenberg, pp. 67, 70–74. Copyright © University of Pennsylvania Press, 1997. Reprinted with permission of the University of Pennsylvania Press.

3.8 An Islamic Andalusian voice: Ibn 'Abd Rabbihi, *I Have Never Seen* (before 940). *Poems of Arab Andalusia*, trans. Cola Franzen from the Spanish versions of Emilio Garcia Gómez. City Lights Books, 1989. Copyright © by Cola Franzen. Reprinted by permission of City Lights Books.

3.9 A Jewish poet in al-Andalus: Dunash ben Labrat, *There Came a Voice* (mid-10th c.). Reprinted from *Wine, Women, and Death: Medieval Hebrew Poems on the Good Life*, translated and edited by Raymond Scheindlin, by permission of the University of Nebraska Press. Copyright © 1986 by the Jewish Publication Society.

3.12 Modeling the state on Old Testament Israel: *The Admonitio Generalis* (789). *Christianity through the Thirteenth Century*, ed. Marshall W. Baldwin. Harper and Row, 1970.

3.13 Ideals of family and fidelity: Dhuoda, *Handbook for Her Son* (841–843). Reprinted from *Handbook for William: A Carolingian Woman's Counsel for Her Son* by Dhuoda, translated by Carol Neel, by permission of the University of Nebraska Press. Copyright © 1991 by the University of Nebraska Press.

3.14 The Slavic conversion: Constantine/Cyril, *Prologue to the Gospel* (863–867). Republished with permission of St. Vladimir's Seminary Press, from Roman Jakobson, "St. Constantine's Prologue to the Gospel," *St. Vladimir's Seminary Quarterly* 7. Copyright © 1963. Permission conveyed through Copyright Clearance Center, Inc.

3.16 The Bulgarians adopt Christianity: Pope Nicholas I, *Letter to Answer the Bulgarians' Questions* (866). Nicholas I, *Epistola 99*, in *Epistolae* 6, ed. Ernest Perels, Monumenta Germaniae Historica. Berlin, 1925. Translated by William L. North. Reprinted by permission of William L. North.

CHAPTER IV

4.1 Fragmentation in the Islamic world: Al-Tabari, *The Defeat of the Zanj Revolt* (*c*.915). Reprinted by permission from *The History of al-Tabari*, Vol. 37: *The 'Abbasid Recovery: The War Against the Zanj Ends A.D. 879–893/A.H. 266–279*, translated by Philip M. Fields, the State University of New York Press © 1987, State University of New York. All rights reserved.

4.2 The powerful in the Byzantine countryside: Romanus I Lecapenus, *Novel* (934). *The Land Legislation of the Macedonian Emperors*, trans. and ed. Eric McGeer. Pontifical Institute of Mediaeval Studies, 2000. Reprinted by permission of the Pontifical Institute of Mediaeval Studies.

4.4 Love and complaints in Angoulême: *Agreement between Count William of the Aquitanians and Hugh IV of Lusignan* (1028). Jane Martindale, "Conventum inter Guillelmum Aquitanorum comitem et Hugonem Chiliarchum," in *Status, Authority and Regional Power: Aquitaine and France, 9th to 12th Centuries*. Variorum, 1997. Translated by Thomas Greene and Barbara H. Rosenwein. Reprinted by permission of the translators.

4.5 The Peace of God at Bourges: Andrew of Fleury, *The Miracles of St. Benedict* (1040–1043). *The Peace of God: Social Violence and Religious Response in France around the Year 1000*, ed. Thomas Head and Richard Landes. Cornell University Press, 1992.

4.6 A castellan's revenues and properties in Catalonia: *Charter of Guillem Guifred* (1041–1075). Pierre Bonnassie, "The Banal Seigneury and the 'Reconditioning' of the Free Peasantry," in *Debating the Middle Ages: Issues and Readings*, ed. Lester

K. Little and Barbara H. Rosenwein. Basil Blackwell, 1988. Reproduced by permission of Wiley.

4.7 Military life: Constantine VII Porphyrogenitus, *Military Advice to His Son* (950–958). *Constantine Porphyrogenitus: Three Treatises on Imperial Military Expeditions*, ed. and trans. John F. Haldon. Österreichischen Akademie der Wissenschaften, 1997. Reproduced by permission of the publisher.

4.8 Imperial rule: Michael Psellus, *Portrait of Basil II* (c.1063). *Fourteen Byzantine Rulers: The Chronographia of Michael Psellus*, trans. Edgar R.A. Sewter. Penguin Books, 1966.

4.9 Education: Al-Qabisi, *A Treatise Detailing the Circumstances of Students and the Rules governing Teachers and Students* (before 1012). *Classical Foundations of Islamic Education Thought*, ed. Bradley J. Cook with Fathi H. Malkawi; trans. Michael Fishbein. Brigham Young University Press, 2010.

4.10 Political theory: Al-Farabi, *The Perfect State* (c.940–942). *Al-Farabi: The Perfect State*, ed. and trans. Richard Walzer (1985), pp. 231, 235, 239, 241, 253, 255, 257, 259. By permission of Oxford University Press.

4.11 Logic: Ibn Sina (Avicenna), *Treatise on Logic* (1020s or 1030s). *Avicenna's Treatise on Logic*, ed. and trans. Farhang Zabeeh, pp. 13–17, Martinus Nijhoff, 1971, with kind permission from Springer Science+Business Media B.V.

4.12 Hungary as heir of Rome: King Stephen, *Laws* (1000–1038). *The Laws of the Medieval Kingdom of Hungary, vol 1: 1000–1301*, trans. and ed. János M. Bak, György Bónis, and James Ross Sweeney. Charles Schlacks, Jr. Publisher, 1989. Reprinted by permission of the publisher.

4.13 Coming to terms with Catholic Poland: Thietmar of Merseburg, *Chronicle* (1013–1018). *Ottonian Germany: The Chronicon of Thietmar of Merseburg*, trans. David A. Warner. Manchester University Press, 2001.

4.15 Kievan Rus': *The Russian Primary Chronicle* (c.1113, incorporating earlier materials). *The Russian Primary Chronicle: Laurentian Text*, trans. and ed. Samuel Hazzard Cross and Olgerd P. Sherbowitz-Wetzor. Medieval Academy of America, 1953.

4.17 Literacy: King Alfred, *Prefaces* to Gregory the Great's *Pastoral Care* (c.890). *Alfred the Great: Asser's Life of King Alfred and Other Contemporary Sources* translated with an introduction by Simon Keynes and Michael Lapidge (Penguin Classics, 1983). This translation, introduction and notes copyright © Simon Keynes and Michael Lapidge, 1983. Reproduced by permission of Penguin Books Ltd.

4.18 Law: King Æthelred, *Law Code* (1008). *English Historical Documents*, Vol. 1: c. 300–1042, ed. Dorothy Whitelock, 2nd ed. Copyright © 1979, Routledge. Reproduced by permission of Taylor & Francis Books UK.

CHAPTER V

5.2 Ibn 'Abdun, *Regulations for the Market at Seville* (early 12th c.). *Islam: From the Prophet Muhammad to the Capture of Constantinople, vol. 2: Religion and Society*, ed. and trans. Bernard Lewis. Copyright © 1974 by Bernard Lewis. By permission of Oxford University Press, USA.

5.3 The role of royal patronage: Henry I, *Privileges for the Citizens of London* (1130–1133). *English Historical Documents*, Vol. 2: 1042–1189, ed. David C. Douglas and George W. Greenaway, 2nd ed. Copyright © 1981, Routledge. Reproduced by permission of Taylor & Francis Books UK.

5.4 The royal view: Henry IV, *Letter to Gregory VII* (1075). From *Imperial Lives and Letters*, ed. Robert L. Benson, trans. Theodor E. Mommsen and Karl F. Morrison. Copyright © 2000 Columbia University Press. Reprinted with permission of the publisher.

5.5 The papal view: Gregory VII, *Letter to Hermann of Metz* (1076). *The Register of Pope Gregory VII, 1073–1085* by H.E.J. Cowdrey (2002), pp. 208–11. By permission of Oxford University Press.

5.9 Martyrs in the Rhineland: Rabbi Eliezer b. Nathan ("Raban"), *O God, Insolent Men* (early to mid-12th c.). Abraham Habermann, *Sefer gezerot ashkenaz vetzarfat*. 1945, repr. 1971. Introduced and translated by Susan L. Einbinder.

5.11 The Muslim reaction: Ibn al-Athir, *The First Crusade* (13th c.). Republished with permission of the University of California Press, from *Arab Historians of the Crusades*, ed. and trans. (from Arabic) Francesco Gabrieli, trans. (from Italian) E.J. Costello. Copyright © 1969. Permission conveyed through Copyright Clearance Center, Inc.

5.12 The crusade in Spain and Portugal: *The Conquest of Lisbon* (1147–1148). From *De expugnatione Lyxbonensi: The Conquest of Lisbon*, trans. Charles

Wendell David. Copyright © 2001 Columbia University Press. Reprinted with permission of the publisher.

5.13 The pro-Norman position: William of Jumièges, *The Deeds of the Dukes of the Normans* (c.1070). *The Norman Conquest*, ed. and trans. R. Allen Brown. Edward Arnold, 1984. Reprinted by permission of Boydell & Brewer.

5.14 The native position: "Florence of Worcester," *Chronicle of Chronicles* (early 12th c.). *English Historical Documents*, Vol. 2: 1042–1189, ed. David C. Douglas and George W. Greenaway, 2nd ed. Copyright © 1981, Routledge. Reproduced by permission of Taylor & Francis Books UK.

5.16 Exploiting the Conquest: *Domesday Book* (1087). *Domesday Book: A Complete Translation*, ed. Ann Williams and G.H. Martin. Penguin, 2002. Copyright © Alecto Historical Editions. Reproduced by permission.

5.17 Logic: Abelard, *Glosses on Porphyry* (c.1100). *Basic Issues in Medieval Philosophy*, second edition, edited by Richard N. Bosley and Martin Tweedale. Broadview Press, 2006; page 353. Reprinted with the permission of Broadview Press.

5.20 The Cistercian view: St. Bernard, *Apologia* (1125). *The Cistercian World: Monastic Writings of the Twelfth Century* translated and edited with an introduction by Pauline Matarasso (Penguin Classics, 1993). Copyright © Pauline Matarasso, 1993. Reproduced by permission of Penguin Books Ltd.

CHAPTER VI

6.1 The Northern Crusades: Helmold, *The Chronicle of the Slavs* (1167–1168). From *The Chronicle of the Slavs*, by Helmold, Priest of Bosau, trans. Francis Joseph Tschan. Copyright © 1935 Columbia University Press. Reprinted with permission of the publisher.

6.2 The Fourth Crusade: Nicetas Choniates, *O City of Byzantium* (c.1215). Reprinted from *O City of Byzantium: Annals of Niketas Choniates* translated by Harry J. Magoulias. Copyright © 1984 Wayne State University Press, with the permission of Wayne State University Press.

6.3 English common law: *The Assize of Clarendon* (1166). *English Historical Documents*, Vol. 2:

1042–1189, ed. David C. Douglas and George W. Greenaway, 2nd ed. Copyright © 1981, Routledge. Reproduced by permission of Taylor & Francis Books UK.

6.4 English litigation on the ground: *The Costs of Richard of Anstey's Lawsuit* (1158–1163). *English Historical Documents*, Vol. 2: 1042–1189, ed. David C. Douglas and George W. Greenaway, 2nd ed. Copyright © 1981, Routledge. Reproduced by permission of Taylor & Francis Books UK.

6.5 The legislation of a Spanish king: *The Laws of Cuenca* (1189–1193). *The Code of Cuenca: Municipal Law on the Twelfth-Century Castilian Frontier*, trans. James F. Powers. University of Pennsylvania Press, 2000. Reprinted with permission of the University of Pennsylvania Press.

6.7 Doing business: *A Genoese societas* (1253). From *Medieval Trade in the Mediterranean World: Illustrative Documents*, trans. Robert S. Lopez and Irving W. Raymond. Copyright © 2001 Columbia University Press. Reprinted with permission of the publisher.

6.8 Women's work: *Guild Regulations of the Parisian Silk Fabric Makers* (13th c.). *Women's Lives in Medieval Europe: A Sourcebook*, ed. Emilie Amt. Copyright © 1993, Routledge. Reproduced by permission of Taylor & Francis Group LLC–Books.

6.9 Men's work: *Guild Regulations of the Shearers of Arras* (1236). *A Source Book for Medieval Economic History*, ed. Roy C. Cave and Herbert H. Coulson. Bruce Publishing Co., 1936.

6.10 The growth of papal business: Innocent III, *Letters* (1200–1202). *Selected Letters of Pope Innocent III Concerning England (1198–1216)*, ed. C.R. Cheney and W.H. Semple. Thomas Nelson and Sons, 1953.

6.11 Petitioning the papacy: *Register of Thomas of Hereford* (1281). *English Historical Documents*, Vol. 3: 1189–1327, ed. Harry Rothwell. Copyright © 1975, Routledge. Reproduced by permission of Taylor & Francis Books UK.

6.12 Mocking the papal bureaucracy: *The Gospel According to the Marks of Silver* (c.1200). From Alfred J. Andrea. *The Medieval Record*, 1e. © 1997 Wadsworth, a part of Cengage Learning Inc. Reproduced by permission. www.cengage.com/permissions.

6.13 Henry II and Becket: *Constitutions of Clarendon* (1164). *English Historical Documents*, Vol. 2: 1042–1189, ed. David C. Douglas and George W.

CHAPTER VII

CHAPTER VIII

Asikpasazade, ed. Friedrich Giese. Harrassowitz, 1929. Translated by Robert Dankoff. Reprinted by permission of Robert Dankoff.

8.7 Diplomacy: *Peace Agreement between the Ottoman Sultan Mehmed II and the Signoria of Venice* (January 25, 1478). State Archives of Venice, ASV Documenti Turchi B1/2. Translated by Diana Gilliland Wright. Reprinted by permission of Diana Wright.

8.8 Before the fall: Patriarch Anthony, *Letter to the Russian Church* (1395). Deno John Geanakoplos, *Byzantium: Church, Society, and Civilization Seen through Contemporary Eyes.* Copyright © 1984, University of Chicago Press. Reprinted by permission of the publisher.

8.9 The fall bewailed: George Sphrantzes, *Chronicle* (before 1477). Reprinted from T*he Fall of the Byzantine Empire: A Chronicle by George Sphrantzes, 1401–1477.* Copyright © 1980 by the University of Massachusetts Press and published by the University of Massachusetts Press.

8.10 After the fall: Archbishop Genady of Novgorod and Dmitry Gerasimov, *The Tale of the White Cowl* (end of the 15th c.). "Epiphanius the Wise: The Life, Acts, and Miracles of our Blessed ...", from *Medieval Russia's Epics, Chronicles, and Tales*, edited by Serge A. Zenkovsky, translated by Serge A. Zenkovsky, copyright © 1963, 1974 by Serge A. Zenkovsky; renewed © 1991 by Betty Jean Zenkovsky. Used by permission of Dutton, a division of Penguin Group (USA) Inc., and Betty Jean Zenkovsky.

8.11 Chivalric and non-chivalric models: Froissart, *Chronicles* (c.1400). Froissart, *Chroniques. Début du premier livre. Edition du manuscrit de Rome Reg. lat. 869*, ed. George T. Diller. Droz, 1972. Translated by Helen Nicholson. Reprinted by permission of Dr. Helen Nicholson.

8.12 National feeling: Jeanne d'Arc, *Letter to the English* (1429). "Joan's Letter to the English," trans. Nadia Margolis, in *Medieval Hagiography: An Anthology*, ed. Thomas Head. Garland, 2000. Courtesy of Nadia Margolis.

8.13 Patriotism in Italy: Petro Gentili's *Speech to the Council and Citizens of Lucca* (1397). Medieval Italy: Texts in Translation, ed. Katherine L. Jansen, Joanna Drell, and Frances Andrews, trans. Christine Meek. University of Pennsylvania Press, 2009. Reprinted with permission of the University of Pennsylvania Press.

8.14 The commons revolt: *Wat Tyler's Rebellion* (after 1381). Charles Oman, *The Great Revolt of 1381.* Greenwood Press, 1969. Copyright © ABC-CLIO Inc., 1906. Reproduced by permission.

8.15 The conciliarist movement: Jean Gerson, *Sermon at the Council of Constance* (1415). *Unity, Heresy and Reform, 1378–1460: The Conciliar Response to the Great Schism*, ed. C.M.D. Crowder. Edward Arnold, 1977. Reprinted by permission of Adele Crowder.

8.16 Taking part in the life of Christ: *The Book of Margery Kempe* (c.1430). From *The Book of Margery Kempe, A Norton Critical Edition* by Margery Kempe, translated by & edited by Lynn Staley. Copyright © 2001 by W.W. Norton & Company, Inc. Used by permission of W.W. Norton & Company, Inc.

8.17 The Hussite program: *The Four Articles of Prague* (1420). *The Crusade against Heretics in Bohemia, 1418–1437: Sources and Documents of the Hussite Crusades*, trans. and ed. Thomas A. Fudge. Ashgate, 2002. Reproduced by permission.

8.18 Re-evaluating antiquity: Cincius Romanus, *Letter to His Most Learned Teacher Franciscus de Fiana* (1416). From *Two Renaissance Book Hunters: The Letters of Poggius Bracciolini to Nicolaus de Niccolis*, ed. and trans. Phyllis Walter Goodhart Gordan. Copyright © 1974 Columbia University Press. Reprinted with permission of the publisher.

8.19 A new theory of art: Leon Battista Alberti, *On Painting* (1435–1436). *Leon Battista Alberti: On Painting. A New Translation and Critical Edition*, ed. and trans. Rocco Sinisgalli. Copyright © 2011 Rocco Sinisgalli. Reprinted with the permission of Cambridge University Press.

8.20 Defending women: Christine de Pisan, *The Book of the City of Ladies* (1404–1407). Part I: Sections 11–13 from *The Book of the City of Ladies*, by Christine de Pizan. Translated by Earl Jeffrey Richards. Copyright © 1982 by Persea Books, Inc.. Reprinted by permission of Persea Books, Inc., New York. All rights reserved.

8.22 Taking Mexico: Hernán Cortés, *The Second Letter* (1520). Hernán Cortés, *Letters from Mexico*, trans. and ed. Anthony Pagden. Yale University Press, 2001. Copyright © 1971 by Anthony Pagden. Revised edition copyright © 1986 by Yale University Press. Reprinted by permission of Yale University Press.

PLATES

1 Dome of the Rock (692). Dome of the Rock and Imam, Jerusalem and Dome of the Rock, View of Rock, Jerusalem. Copyright © Sonia Halliday Photographs.

2 Icon with Saint Demetrios (2nd half 10th c.). Icon with Saint Demetrios. Second half of the 10th century. Ivory, Overall: 7 ¾ x 4 ¾ x ⅜ in. (19.7 x 12.1 x 1 cm). The Cloisters Collection, 1970 (1970.324.3). The Metropolitan Museum of Art, New York, NY, USA. Image copyright © The Metropolitan Museum of Art. Image source: Art Resource, NY.

3 Reliquary Locket (10th–11th c.). Copyright © The Trustees of the British Museum.

4 Page from a Qur'an (993). KFQ 90, recto, The Nasser D. Khalili Collection of Islamic Art. Copyright © Nour Foundation. Courtesy of the Khalili Family Trust.

5 A Holy Vestment (late 10th–early 11th c.). Glockenkasel des Erzbischofs Willigis von Mainz, Inv.-Nr. 11/170.1-2, Photo No. D52112, Poto No. D31776. Reproduced by permission of the Bayerisches Nationalmuseum.

6 Tlemcen, Great Mosque (1236). Images reproduced by permission of Jonathan Bloom and Sheila Blair. Plan from Rachid Bourouiba, *L'art religieux musulman en Algerie*. S.N.E.D., 1973.

7 The Church as Reliquary: Sainte-Chapelle (1248). Sainte-Chapelle de Paris, nef de la chapelle haute, vers l'abside et la tribune des reliques. © Bernard Acloque / Centre des monuments nationaux.

8 Monstrance (*c.*1430). Monstranz, um 1430; Museum Schnutgen, G 97. Copyright © Rheinisches Bildarchiv Köln, rba_c012396.

9 Synagogue and Ark (1435). Ross.555.f.12v. Reproduced by permission of Biblioteca Apostolica Vaticana, with all rights reserved.

10 The Wienhausen Sepulcher (15th c.). The Tomb of the Holy Sepulchre and The Risen Christ, Kloster Wienhausen, reproduced by permission of Kloster Wienhausen/ Lüneburger Klosterarchive. The Tomb of the Holy Sepulchre (detail), Kloster Wienhausen, reproduced by permission of Elina Gertsman.

11 *Seal of Boris-Michael* (864–889). By kind permission of Dr. Ivan Jordanov.

12 *Boleslaw's Coin* (992–1000). Denar (typ GNEZDVN CIVITAS), MNK VII-P-798, from the collection of the National Museum in Krakow.

13 *The Jelling Monument* (960s). The Jelling Stone / Monument. Photographer unknown, Nationalmuseet, Denmark.

14 *The Bayeux Tapestry* (end of the 11th c.). Detail of the Bayeux Tapestry—11th Century. With special permission from the City of Bayeux.

15 Gabriel de Valseca, *Portolan Map* (1447). Registre C; 40333: Carte marine de la mer Méditerranée et de la mer Noire. Reproduced by permission of Bibliothèque nationale de France.

MAP

3.1 Major European Slave Exports (700–900). Michael McCormick, "Map 25.1: Main European Slave Exports: A.D. 700–900," *Origins of the European Economy: Communications and Commerce A.D. 300–900*. Cambridge University Press, 2001. Copyright © 2001 Michael McCormick. Reprinted with the permission of Cambridge University Press.

Index of Names, Places, and Readings